About this Book

Taming a language gone mad

To the uninitiated, a Jazz concert may sound cacophonous and undisciplined, when in fact it has its roots in structured classical music forms. And so it is with English, especially American English. Drawn from a multitude of sources, dragged across the Atlantic and further modified, it too seems to lack any sense of consistency. Though we have no formal system for codifying and regulating the language, there is a root system (accepted by scholars) onto which is grafted the never-ending changes (frequently decried by scholars) which characterize the language.

Written in an easy to understand, relaxed style, with handy references to assist the user, here is a (sometimes irreverent) handbook for anyone who seeks a better understanding of American English and how to use it most effectively.

WEBSTER'S GRAMMAR HANDBOOK

WEBSTER'S GRAMMAR HANDBOOK

PMC Publishing Company, Inc.

PMC Publishing Company, Inc.
118 East 28 Street
New York, New York 10016

Compiled and edited by J. Radcliffe

ISBN: 1-881275-16-7

TABLE OF CONTENTS

Part I - Background of American English

Part II - Escape from High School English

Part III - Basic Grammar — Putting It All Together

Part IV - Form/Style

Part V - Reference

Part I

Background of American English

Background of American English

Do you wonder why English spelling is so difficult? Why we don't just spell things the way they sound? Or say things the way they are spelled? Why different groups of letters all sound the same? Or why one group of letters gets pronounced in so many ways? How could anyone have come up with such a system?

Well, it wasn't done by just anyone, and certainly not by design. English was formed from a merging of primitive dialects which were then shaped and embellished by others. English didn't happen all at once in one place, but in isolated pockets of independent peoples who didn't have a common language even after they united to form a nation. And the changes continue . . . .

ENGLISH — A BRIEF HISTORY

If we want to understand today's English and its irregularities, we need to look at how it was formed and shaped over the past fifteen hundred years. We may then come to understand how futile were the attempts to regularize such things as spelling and pronunciation. We may even come to agree that English is far richer for never having had tight reins placed on it.

Exit Romans, enter Barbarians

Picture this. It's the middle of the fifth century. On an island called Britain, the native Celts have been ruled by the Romans for almost four hundred years. The Roman Empire runs into trouble and the troops are called home. As the Celts watch the Romans leave, they in turn are being watched by the Germanic peoples of northern Europe who see a fine land, ripe for settlement. As far as we know, the tribes which settle in Britain are not invading in force, but are part of a migration which lasts several generations. They gradually displace those Celts who survive their incursions. Apparently few Celts remain in the areas occupied by the tribes, for there is little trace of the Celtic tongue in the language that evolves. Ultimately pockets of Angles, Saxons,

Jutes, and Friscians are scattered throughout the whole of Britain except for Scotland and Wales, which remain in Celtic hands.

Consider the change which has taken place. The way of the Romans is to conquer, then inform the survivors that they are a part of the Roman Empire for which privilege they will be allowed to work their land and pay taxes to Rome. The Romans, proud of their own language and culture, are content to rule and remain largely indifferent to the customs and culture of the peoples they rule. The Celts, for their part, live a relatively civilized and orderly existence under the Romans. The Germanic tribes which fill the vacuum left by the departure of the Romans have no proud history and grand cause for which they fight; they simply want the land and view anyone occupying it as an inconvenience. There is no common language and the Germanic dialects, each altered by contact with others through trade or war, may be similar, but are not the same.

The Angles and Saxons

The new occupants of Britain have no central government and little contact with each other. Most tend to their own land and never leave the village where they are born, a way of life which persists for centuries. There is, however, change. Perhaps it begins with a tribal chieftain who wants to extend his holdings and sets out to plunder his neighbors. The victims of those incursions get together to protect themselves against the raider. They soon recognize that one has an abundance of something which the other can use and trade bonds are formed. Over the years, as alliances are formed and broken, villages take sides and change sides. Gradually power gravitates to centers which come to dominate large areas of the country and control shifts from the individual villages. Power itself shifts from one area to another and the language shifts with it. Dialects move from one part of the country to another, meet, blend, and change. There is no way to tell exactly when "English" emerges as a separate tongue distinct from the Germanic dialects which spawned it, just as there is no way to know why, with the Saxons dominating, the language comes to be called English after the more obscure Angles. Make no mistake about it, there is still no national language. Individual dialects command relatively small areas so that villagers from one area may understand villagers from another only with great difficulty or not at all.

Enter the Vikings . . .

Around the end of the eighth century, Viking raiders begin to probe the coast of England. These early raids are of little consequence (unless of course you live in one of the villages being sacked). In the middle of the ninth century, the Vikings attack in force and, after a series of battles, control of the northern part of England is ceded to them. The affect on the language is enormous. The Vikings seem to have no more proprietary interest in their language than the Germanic tribes which came before them. In some areas the inhabitants are speaking an English dialect, in others they are speaking a Scandinavian dialect and in others, a combination of both. Not only are words changinhg, but also structure. Differences between the northern and southern dialects become more pronounced.

And more Vikings . . .

While one group of Vikings flex their muscles in England, another group settle in the north of France. They abandon their roots almost entirely and adopt the local French customs and language. Known as Normans, they conquer England two hundred years later, in 1066. The language of the rulers of England is now a provincial French dialect; English is left for the peasants.

It is at this point that English gains a class distinction of sorts. Craftsmen and scholars are now coming from France bringing the language of their trades with them. French words are now used to describe the workings of the elite scholars, artists and craftsmen.

English, without official recognition, left to the Englanders, is changing dramatically. Regional differences are more pronounced with seemingly arbitrary differences in vocabulary, spelling, and grammar. Most important, the language is becoming a lot simpler. Lacking the guiding hand of scholars to point out the error of their ways, peasants are dropping the arbitrary genders and inflectional endings, in short, the unnecessary complications which have up until now plagued "correct" speech.

As the ruling Normans become increasingly isolated from the continent, they begin to think of themselves more as Englishmen than Frenchmen and English once more becomes the language of the land. Intermarriage plays a great part in the transition, for, as one scholar observes, "the children learn French from their fathers and English from their mothers." For many years, French will remain the official language, the language of the courts and parliament.

For even more years, informal communication will swing back and forth casually between the two languages, often in the same sentence, without affectation.

By the middle of the fifteenth century, thousands of French words have been adopted into English. In the year 1490, William Caxton prints the first book in English and recounts in the preface the story of a person traveling fifty miles who can not make himself understood when asking for food. It will be another century before that kind of situation is unusual.

By the time of Columbus' first voyage, English is the dominant language in England, but not until the time of Shakespeare and the voyage of the Pilgrims is it a language that can be understood by most Englishmen.

The English are not shy about coining new words (Shakespeare alone adds about 2000 words to the language) or borrowing from others. The practice continues as English goes abroad.

LET'S GO TO AMERICA

Words for a New World

When English travels to America, it begins to change almost as soon as it gets off the boat. Native American words, often shortened and modified, are borrowed to name unfamiliar wildlife and plants *(moose, hickory, squash, opossum, persimmon).* Settlers moving west feel that *meadow* doesn't describe the Great Plains and so *prairie* is borrowed from the French explorers. The furious snowstorms that blow down from the Rocky Mountains like a volley of shot are called by the word which means just that – *blizzard* – a usage that not only sticks, but finds its way back to England.

Words for a New Government

Politics plays a part in development of the language as well. The American legislative body is called *congress* and when an adjective is needed, *congressional* is coined, a word which makes scholars cringe because of the way in which it is formed. An Algonquin Indian word for *great man* is altered to make *mugwump, gerrymandering* is named for the Massachusetts governor who does it when he is in office, the Spanish word for freebooter has become *filibuster*, and although Whig and Tory come from England, the *Know-nothings* are a homegrown American product.

In the Congress of 1819-21, Felix Walker delivers a long, dull speech for his home county of Buncombe, North Carolina and a new word is coined. How ironic that *bunkum* and *bunk* are introduced by a member of Congress.

Words for a New Nation

The patriots of the American Revolution have mixed feelings about the language. Some think that a new language should be adopted to accentuate the split with England. Many who do not agree, fear that the influx of non-English speakers and the scattered pockets of settlers will not only alter the language but create a diversity of dialects which will undermine attempts to unify the nation. What is happening is that the language is being enriched by borrowing from the languages brought in by immigrants.

The Dutch settling in the Hudson River valley bring *boss, coleslaw* and *stoop.* The Germans in Pennsylvania give us *loafer, sauerkraut* and *noodle.* From the French in Louisiana comes *levee, portage* and *gopher.* The Spanish/Mexicans add *adobe, corral, hoosegow* and *vamoose.* Everyone brings something to the party and we all go home linguistically richer.

Culturally, the new nation is different from the old and shows it most in names for government offices and occupations, though there are other areas where terminology differs such as parts of an automobile and railway terms. The status of certain words or change in shades of meaning highlight cultural differences as well.

And more words for today

Changes in lifestyle, changes in awareness, changes in taste and changes in technology constantly bring new words into the language. Some of the words are new or newly borrowed, and many are just new to us.

Words like *sushi, sashimi, tofu, miso* and *nori* are reserved for aficionados of Japanese cooking until they became part of our pop culture and our language.

The word *ecology* is not new, but it doesn't become a part of everyday vocabulary until it becomes a political issue.

The computer has been around for over a generation, but then so has the word processor, work station, and photo copier none of which become a part of our vocabulary until they become an integral part of our lives. You may not know how a chip works or be able to define what it is, but you know what it is. You may not have an answering machine, camcorder or a VCR, but you know someone who does and all of those become part of our everyday vocabulary.

Popular culture coins new words or changes the meanings of old ones. Some of the words and meanings stick, some disappear almost as fast as they arrive.

There you have it – a brief summary of fifteen hundred years of linguistic evolution. We now have in America a collection of words that are generally understood throughout the land.

THE WORLD'S GREATEST VOCABULARY

Where has it gotten us?

The Oxford English Dictionary defines over 600,000 words! It has been estimated that scientific and technical terms amount to four or five times that number. Over three million words in total. Probably more when you consider that there are over a million names for insects alone. The weight of words is staggering.

Estimates vary widely as to how many words we know and how many we use. We may recognize as many as 50,000 words, although we would be hard pressed to define most of them. We often appreciate the context in which a word is used and understand without the ability to recite a precise definition. No problem, as long as we derive the meaning which is intended. Legal documents which spell out every facet of a subject in great detail and which should serve to clarify usually do quite the opposite, unless that is your area of expertise. If it isn't, and you truly want to understand what you're reading, you need a dictionary close at hand.

Of all those words we know, we probably use less than 3,000 on a regular basis. We might conclude from this that we not inclined to be adventurous in our speaking and writing; we fall into certain patterns and make little effort to change them.

Using even 3,000 words well can be formidable when you consider that the precise meaning of a word often changes over time and knowing the familiar definition may not be enough to adequately express a thought so that another person understands exactly what you mean.

And where are we going?

Anyone interested in the ways in which the language is changing need only read a newspaper or a news magazine. Even a staid old newspaper with its own style manual can not escape linguistic changes reflected in news stories, reviews or columnists' opinions.

As for those of us who use the language, hopefully we're going to make better use of the words which we know and gain the use of those with which we have only a passing acquaintance.

The way in which we use words has the same checkered past as the words themselves. The rules of grammar presented as inviolable are every bit as arbitrary as a word adopted from one source, modified by a prefix from another and a suffix from yet another. Structure is most important in forming a message that can be readily understood by another; nevertheless, there are rules devised only to suit a scholarly whim. It is well to know the difference.

Finally . . .

Enjoy! Don't let the language intimidate you. The more you learn, the more fun it becomes. You gain control, because you know that none of it was handed down on stone tablets. You realize that words were coined and massaged by people like us. (Perhaps a little smarter . . . perhaps not.)

Who knows but that you might introduce something new into the language. Changing a word a little or combining a couple of words to better suit your need strikes someone else who borrows and passes it on and then someone else borrows it and then . . . fifty years from now someone will agonize over its meaning and say "What fool . . .?"

If you want to know more . . .

For a very readable, informative and amusing tour through the history of the English language, the origin of words, etc. find a copy of ***The Mother Tongue: English & How It Got That Way,*** by Bill Bryson, published by William Morrow and Company.

Also recommended is an excellent book on the development of American English, ***Our Own Words,*** by Mary Helen Dohan, published by Penguin Books.

Part II

Escape from High School English

Escape from High School English

Writing and speaking in the classroom is extremely important, because we know that if it isn't done well it may be done again next semester. Unfortunately, that is often the only impression we retain except, perhaps, relief when it's over. Compulsory English courses are taught in a vacuum – basic grammar as though the language was created around a set of rules; great literature just because it's there with no explanation of why it is considered great.

The chances are slight that anyone will ever explain how the language was formed and, beyond disapproval of grammatically incorrect advertising slogans, how it continues to change and grow. No one mentions that you don't have to like Shakespeare to appreciate the color and power he brought to the language. Most important, little emphasis is placed on the primary function of language as a tool for communicating; work is judged on proper technique, not content.

It's time to escape. Time to view the rules of grammar as guidelines, helpful as long as they don't interfere with communication. Time to be more concerned with what we say than whether or not we say it properly. Time to express ourselves; to put our own mark on what we say and write.

THE IMPORTANCE OF COMMUNICATING WELL

Every time you speak or write, someone makes a judgment about you before even considering what is you have to say.

Most of us like ourselves the way we are and feel that others should accept us as we are; however, that's not realistic, for life is comprised of a series of brief encounters. Think about it. You may spend a lot of time with family members and a few close friends, while most of the people you know are little more than passing acquaintances. You make judgments about them based on brief encounters, just as they make judgments about you and who can tell what we're really like based on a brief encounter?

> You're absorbed in discussion with your colleagues. Someone you don't know approaches, listens for a bit, then attempts to join in. The way you interpret the first statement that person makes is dominated by your prejudices. An emphatic statement causes you to admire that person as decisive . . . or to resent the interruption of a know-it-all. A hesitant delivery checkered with pauses to search for words creates the image of someone who is diplomatic . . . or wishy-washy . . . or simply trying to ease into the group, though fearful of disapproval. Vocabulary and pronunciation further reinforce your first impression. The visual impression adds to the impact; whether overdressed or too casual, you see a snob, a sophisticate, an intellectual or an artist. A fool in a $600 suit is still a fool, but you perceive him differently because he is certainly no ordinary fool.

Now turn it around. You are the stranger approaching the group. How are you perceived? How do you *want* to be perceived?

You have just one chance

Fortunately, in the scenario described above there will probably be ample opportunity to correct (or confirm) the first impression. All too often, in your most important encounters, you will not be afforded that luxury. If you doubt this, consider how many times you have heard statements like these:

"We met last week and you created a terrible impression, but I'd like to get together again to see if we have anything in common."

"We received your letter of June 3, which was so garbled that we couldn't understand it and wonder if you would mind stopping by to explain further."

"We couldn't make any sense out of your report on the Briscoe situation, but several members did fall asleep and wonder if you would mind delivering it again next week."

When you first meet someone you think you would like to know better, you need to leave that person with the impression that you are worth knowing. A letter applying for a job has to convince the recipient that it is worthwhile to at least talk to you. On a job interview, you have to come across as the person who should be considered for the position. A letter to sell your idea or product must describe exactly what you are selling and why the buyer should give it more than passing consideration. A report, whether written or oral, should clearly define the subject (or problem), relate the pertinent facts and outline conclusions without confusing the reader.

One chance is often all you get to make the right impression: the impression that you could be a good friend, that you could fit into the workplace, that you are ready for a promotion. It is in your best interest to be certain that you make the best possible use of that one chance.

Improving communication does not mean changing the way you are; it means learning to express yourself so that others will receive a favorable first impression and give your thoughts and ideas a fair hearing. After that, it is up to you.

ELEMENTS OF EFFECTIVE COMMUNICATION

Effective communication requires a sender with a message and the ability to convey that message in such a way that the receiver reacts in precisely the way intended by the sender.

If you want to communicate effectively, consider the main elements in the above statement: the message, you (the sender), the receiver and your intent.

The message

Of course you know what it is you want to convey, but this is the place where you dot the i's and cross the t's. Be certain that what you say is in fact the message you want to deliver.

What are we dealing with here? your place in the cosmos, your reliability as an employee or your skills? your company's entire product line or a single product? the evil that men do or just one mistake, one time, on one order? an idea for world peace or just a way to get along with the guy in the next cubicle?

Be specific. Applying for a position, you need to determine whether you want to sell your experience, the perception of you as a member of a team or both. When you sell a product, decide whether to sell price, consistency, service or something else. When you sell a service, do you sell your company's reputation for service or your own? When you want to resolve a complaint, do you concentrate on the specific problem or the feeling that you aren't paying enough attention to the client? Do you press the company to solve a problem by focusing on cost, lost revenues or the importance of a particular customer? A report to your boss outlining a new procedure is not an invitation to write a history of the company (unless that's what he or she wants).

Be relevant. It may be difficult to remain focused, but it is certainly important if you want to get your message across without confusing your audience. Your perfect attendance record at lodge meetings is not going to carry as much weight as your skills when you apply for a job as an electrician and nobody but you cares that you meditate to Ravel's Bolero. On the other hand, having a clean sheet with the IRS and the local constabulary will be of importance when you apply for a job as treasurer. A report about a critical error in a shipment to a customer does not require a list of all errors made by the company since the beginning of time, but statistics about similar errors might be relevant if they relate to suggestions for avoiding a recurrence. Similarly, the customer doesn't want to hear about your superior product and your wonderful past record; however, there may be interest in how this happened and why you are sure it won't happen again.

You can broaden your message and still be relevant. If you are applying for a position which has been advertised, or responding to a request for information, you already have a good idea of what your audience wants; however, you may find it worthwhile to provide additional information. In a letter applying for a position you don't list your complete job history, but you may want to mention your experience and success in related areas. You won't be the first person hired for a job other than the one for which you applied. The response to a request for information about credit terms wouldn't be complete without mention of discounts for fast payment; information about a product should also include at least brief mention of similar products which you have available.

You, the messenger

You are the person with a message. You have appointed yourself the person to deliver the message. Can you do it? Are you sure you want to do it?

Of course you can do it, but don't be slow to to assess yourself and your abilities as an important part of the process. Remember, the goal is not the doing, it is the result, and you need to be sure that you can achieve the desired result.

Don't be shy about asking for help from someone who knows. People are always flattered to be asked, whether they show it or not. Have someone whose opinion you respect critique your letter or your notes for a speech. It can't hurt and it will probably help. Someone you know with the technical expertise which you need may bore the life out of you, but that person may also give you exactly the information you need to accomplish your purpose. And as a fringe benefit, you just might alter your perspective and make a new friend.

Don't oversell yourself, promising a lot more than you can deliver; if the truth isn't readily apparent, it will be, and probably sooner that you like. On the other hand, don't undersell yourself; make certain that the recipient knows exactly what it is that you *can* do, particularly if you have something to offer that others may not have.

Can you deliver in such a way that your audience will receive? You may be great at spouting technical jargon, but can you deliver an understandable message to an audience which lacks the technical background? Conversely, can you deliver a simple message with enough impact to register with a more knowledgeable audience. Can you deliver a sensitive message in such a way that emotion will not blur the message?

Approach the challenge with confidence. An old sales adage says that the most under-reported crime is underpricing. Now change that to read "undervaluing." Whether you are selling yourself or your product, have confidence in yor message and your ability to deliver that message. Know that when you clearly define the options, your audience cannot fail to understand that dealing with you is the only reasonable decision.

The receiver, your audience

Now that you know what you want to say and you know you can say it, you had better hope someone is listening. You may have an unknown audience or one which you know too well. How well you assess that audience determines whether or not you have wasted your time.

Consider the point of view of your audience, whether you are job hunting, selling a product, soothing a wounded ego or simply passing along information.

If you are trying to reach someone who does not know or care that you exist, you need to establish quickly that you have a product, a talent or something which is of value to that person, whereas a message to an old friend will probably open with a bit of familiar banter which confirms that you are still friends.

Are you trying to reach someone who is very busy (or should be)? Express your appreciation that he or she is taking time out of a busy schedule to respond to you.

Is this person familiar with your business? If not, you want to avoid technical terms which may be misunderstood.

Is a customer angry about a lost shipment or damaged merchandise? Don't begin by saying "It's no big deal." (Even if it is no big deal.) Present the facts, along with a solution, and let your customer decide.

Focus on the needs of your audience. People buying insurance don't care how much insurance you sold last year; they want to know how reliable you are when they have a claim. Tell busy people how you can save them time and frugal people how you can save them money.

Whether you are addressing a prospective employer, a prospective client or a group of co-workers, your message is of interest only to the extent that it can satisfy their needs. You have to make a judgment about what those needs are. If you guess wrong, you have to decide to take a different approach or recognize that you are addressing the wrong audience. A course in how to get rich in three easy lessons or one hard one is of no interest to someone who is already rich or doesn't care to be rich (or who is convinced you don't know what you're talking about).

Take advantage of feedback. When the boss mentions that he let someone go for being rude to a customer, don't tell the story about the argument you had with another customer. Sounds dumb to even mention it, but – it happens! Salesmen tell angry customers horror stories about problems or near misses. Job applicants talk about how they conned the boss at their last job. These are clearly people who are not listening and certainly not thinking.

Advertising agencies spend millions building profiles of prospective buyers for a product, then convince their clients to spend hundreds of millions more wooing that prospect; yet they often target the wrong market. You don't have millions, so do the best you can and you will probably be right as often as the professionals.

Your intent; the response you want

It's a bit glib to say you want a favorable response. Of course you do! But what is a favorable response? A pat on the head and a hearty "Well done"?

Here's where you put it all together. Is your intent to instruct? to inform? to persuade? to intimidate?

Whatever your goal, keep it in mind when you evaluate your message, the way you deliver that message and your audience.

If you are trying to convince a friend to take a college course to prepare for a promotion, decide whether your concern is about the course or the promotion. Can you think of other benefits of taking the course, whether or not the promotion becomes a reality? Are there ways to get the promotion without taking the course? Either way, set your sights and don't get side tracked.

Before telling someone how to do a job, focus on what you want to accomplish. Do you want that person to be able to immediately handle the task alone, or to simply grasp the concept of what needs to be done with you standing by ready to assist when necessary?

Do you need to convince your boss that you want a meeting to discuss a project? Then don't get so wrapped up in describing what you want to discuss at the meeting that minds are made up before the meeting takes place.

Are you sending out a memo which requires adherence to a procedure "or else"? If your intent is to be laughed at, this will do it. If compliance is your goal, be sure you have a specific punishment which fits the crime of non-compliance. (Incidentally, when you are being intimidating, it's not a bad idea to take a second look to be sure you are also being fair and rational; fifty lashes for wasting paper clips is not fair or rational.

Focus clearly on your purpose and stick with it, but do be sensible. Don't emulate the fellow who wouldn't take "yes" for an answer until the proper place in his presentation by which time his listener was so annoyed that he got a "no".

Be ready to shift gears when the response to your message doesn't meet your expectations. You can tell how well you are doing by the reaction to your message. When you don't get the anticipated response, be ready to do some fancy footwork. If your proposal is met with, "It can't be done," don't try to bully your way through the discussion. It's time to let the other person talk and if you listen well, there is an excellent chance you'll be given the answers you need to modify your presentation.

TOOLS FOR EFFECTIVE COMMUNICATION

Elsewhere in this book is a section called **Basic Grammar**, a compendium of the rules and notions which classify words as parts of speech as well as dictating sentence structure, punctuation, capitalization and such. An understanding of grammar is certainly an aid to communicating well, not so much for the rules themselves, but for the insight it can give into structuring our communication to be universally understood. This section might be described as an ante-grammar – a preface to the more formal structure of our communication.

Words, and the shades of meaning

Most of us use less than three thousand different words on a regular basis. However many words you use, they may not be adequate to properly express your thoughts all of the time. So how do you learn new words? You might try the old system of selecting a word from the dictionary and using it until you remember it. If it doesn't work, at least friends who recognize what you are doing will find it amusing.

To improve the way in which you express thoughts and ideas, look first at the words you use. Develop an awarenes of words used repeatedly and find replacements for them. Whenever appropriate, use replacements which are more colorful or descriptive. In all probability, the overused word does not always convey your message precisely, it just gets used out of habit; therefore, look for a word which will convey to your listener a more exact image, if possible.

Where are the new words? Well, it seems that we recognize more than ten times the number of words we use. Good place to start. Try to think of familiar words which are not normally a part of your vocabulary. Look them up, if you have to, to be sure of their meaning. Mental block? A good Thesaurus will give you synonyms for the word you are trying to replace and with any luck, at least a few will be familiar words that you don't ordinarily think to use. A peripheral benefit is that once you've jump started a few brain cells this way, more of them kick in and you begin to remember words you didn't think you knew. Spooky, huh?

Be selective about the words you use. Every grammarian has a pet peeve about words that are trite, in bad taste or used improperly. What you use is strictly up to you, but you should consider your audience. Years ago, Louis Armstrong described a concert he gave in England when George V was king. Despite a warning that it was a breach of etiquette to acknowledge the monarch's presence, Louis said that before playing one of the king's favorites, he looked up at the royal box, "And I said, 'This one's for you, Rex.' and I laid *You Rascal You* on him." He could do that; you can't, unless you play a great horn.

Colloquialisms can be effective, but not if they diminish your status in your listener's mind. Conversely, obscure words which do not fit you or your style can leave the impression that you are talking down to your audience.

Be alert to changes in the use of words. *Lady* and *gentleman* once indicated social status; today they are mostly used ironically or pejoratively. *Lady* in particular has fared badly in the last generation, from *my old lady* referring to a wife, then to a female companion, to banishment by those who want to shed the image of the frail dependent creature which the word *lady* suggests. You may not be beheaded for calling a king "Rex," but misuse of *lady* could point you in that direction. *Babe* or *girl* as an address for a woman past her majority might also satisfy any curiosity you have about drawing and quartering.

Avoid superfluous words. Fight the temptation to use two words meaning the same thing or almost the same thing when one will do the job or to indicate a comparison of something which represents an absolute such as *unique, perfect* or *full.*

In *actual fact,* the job was done well. *Actual* means existing in fact; a *fact* is anything actually existent.

again and again, over and over – Repetition can emphasize, but don't use it unless it does help.

all and sundry – *All* pretty much covers it.

They were *all united* in song. *United* makes the point unless, of course, they were singing *Happy Birthday* which is never sung in unison (or the same key).

He accepted *any and all* challenges. *All* covers it nicely; don't say more unless you really feel you need to make a point.

best of the best – May be acceptable for advertising copy hyping a professional wrestling match, but nothing else.

This is the *most deadly* (or *most lethal*) poison available. Watch out for this one, it can be deadly. *Deadly* and *lethal* both mean "liable or certain to cause death," and it's difficult to imagine being more dead as opposed to less dead except in colloquial expressions; however, there is a tendency to characterize a poison or illness as more liable to cause death or to cause death quicker. Hardly worth a great deal of discussion, except that there are other words which may cause similar difficulty. (See the next example.)

This is the *most square* board I have. The board is either square or not square. Presumably we are selecting from a number of boards which are not square and have chosen the board which is *most nearly square.* Same goes for **round**.

down in the ground, up in the sky – Trust me, we won't dig up in the ground if you promise not to fly down in the sky.

We *estimate* that *about* (or *approximately*) half the people voted. An estimate *is* an approximation.

She received a *great big* package. As opposed to a great small package, like a diamond, maybe?

huge giant – Perhaps a huge giant of a man needs to be differentiated from a small giant of a man, but it's doubtful.

They were *joined together* in marriage. Joined is enough; perhaps in a few years they will be joined apart.

little tiny – Like the giants, little tiny things probably need to be kept separate from big tiny things.

most unique – *Unique* is without equal, singular, one of a kind and cannot be compared to another.

one and the same – Can something be one and different?

She gave the *oral* report *verbally* to the entire committee. Beats having to write it all down orally; this one got printed, honest.

over and above – Perhaps over and under are one and different.

That's the *most perfect* dress I've seen. There may be many perfect things floating around out there, but they can't be compared; one is not more perfect than another.

planned in advance – Planning is a thing you do in advance; it's either planned or nothing was done in advance.

This is far from a complete list of potential sins; you have to go out and commit some of your own. The old saw says "Think before you speak." Better add, "Think about the words before you use them."

Use words that enhance your message, not detract from it.

Organizing words into coherent thoughts

A sentence is described as a group of words that expresses a complete thought. Much better to think of it as expressing a "coherent thought."

For information about the mechanics of sentence structure such as the parts which make up a sentence and types of sentences, see **Basic Grammar, Sentence Structure.** In this section we are primarily interested in the manner in which sentence structure colors your communication.

The English language affords us considerable flexibility to express our thoughts. We can make a series of concise statements which, taken together, form a complete picture . . .

> **They saw a truck. The truck was blue. It raced through the center of town. The truck was followed by a police car. The police car had its siren on.**

. . . we can wrap it all up together in a single package . . .

> **They saw the blue truck race through the center of town followed by a police car with its siren on.**

and we can make it confusing.

> **Racing through the center of town, they saw the police car following the blue truck with its siren on.**

Who's racing? and who has the siren? and we really don't talk or write like that, do we? DO WE? . . . Sometimes.

Sentence structure and repetition can set the tone of a communication:

> **Make sure the job gets done and while you're at it, get me a status report.**

> **Make sure the job gets done. Make sure it gets done now. And get me a status report.**

The first sentence above gets the message across with less sense of urgency and demand than the shorter sentences. The short statements are designed to punctuate the consciousness of the listener.

A longer sentence with a smooth flow which doesn't jolt the reader or listener presents the voice of reason, a logical presentation of information, as long as it doesn't become convoluted and confusing.

The longer sentence which recounts a series of events, elicits yet another image:

> **She ran down the hill, jumped the fence, and dashed across the field.**

> **The containers are sterilized, filled with liquid, capped, labeled and packed in boxes.**

An orderly, if somewhat breathless, account. A different approach might be two or more sentences with more descriptive information.

Use the style that gets the emotional response you want and make sure that the message is clear.

Punctuation, capitalization, and other demons

The only important rules of punctuation and capitalization are the ones which clarify your message.

A period, question mark or exclamation point at the end of a sentence tells the reader that your thought is completed. (Hopefully, to start up again before you begin the next sentence.)

The comma is an aid to understanding when used to separates items which might otherwise run together and create confusion. When you are in doubt about where to put a comma, say the sentence aloud. Place a comma where a pause is natural, where it is needed to separate a thought or a list of items. Be careful though that you don't get carried away and interfere with the flow of the thought. Use your best judgment, and you will usually be right.

Aside from the customary capitalization such as at the beginning of a sentence and a proper name, avoid the gratuitous use of capital letters except for a good reason. If the monthly meeting of the board of directors of your company is referred to in hushed tones, you may want to capitalize any reference to the Board Meeting in your correspondence. After all, these are not people you want to offend.

When in doubt as to whether a product is generic or proprietary, capitalize to be on the safe side; companies are protective of their trade names and erring on the side of caution is not likely to be criticized. Kleenex passed into our generic lexicon long ago, but any reference to the tissue had better be capitalized if you expect Kimberly-Clark to look favorably on any correspondence.

For more information about punctuation, capitalization and stuff like that, see **Basic Grammar.** In the meantime, use your own good judgment.

You don't need to know the parts of speech – but it helps

This is the toughest one to sell – it won't make you the life of the party, it won't even help you get invited to the party and it won't grow hair, but it is worthwhile to know something about the parts of speech.

Your ability to write and speak well doesn't depend on a thorough knowledge of the rules of grammar, but it helps to understand how words are used properly in order to avoid using them improperly. Make sure you know at least as much as your recipient about proper use of the language to avoid having him or her make any unfounded, nasty judgments about you based on the style of your presentation rather than its content.

ABOUT COMPUTERS AND WORD PROCESSORS

Just in case you've been asleep in a cave for the past ten years, it's time you knew—there aren't many typewriters around anymore. The word processor is replacing the typewriter and lest you think it's just more beaurocratic jargon like "maintenance engineer" for janitor, let's clarify the terms.

Overview of equipment and programs

The **word processor** is a computer dedicated to word processing functions such as translating key strokes to an internal memory, allowing editing of typed copy and printing the information stored. The word processor works much like a typewriter, except that entries from the keyboard appear on a small screen and are not transferred to paper until the operator activates a command to print. This allows the operator to review and edit the material before printing.

Word processors are generally unitized, that is, the keyboard, computer, screen and printer are all contained in a single piece of equipment about the size of a typewriter.

Capabilities of the machines vary widely. Some allow working with only one line at a time; others save a full page or more for subsequent editing. Some can only retain a document in memory while it is being processed; others accommodate an external storage device such as a floppy disk on which work can be saved for future editing. Some print in a single typewriter-style font, including bold and italics; others offer several fonts comprising different faces and sizes. All are programmed internally, that is, whatever the capabilities for editing and printing, they are part of the machine and cannot be changed. Some offer the operator assistance with vocabulary and spelling (see **Special help . . .**, below).

Generally, word processors are less expensive and take less space than a computer, but they have a more limited capability.

The **computer** referred to in this context is the micro-mini computer, desktop computer or personal computer, whichever term you prefer. They all apply to the same class of machine.

The personal computer is made up of several connecting elements comprising the CPU or central processing unit (which usually includes internal and external data storage capabilities), the keyboard, the monitor or screen and the printer.

The computer has the capability to perform a variety of tasks for which there are thousands of applications available. Because of this versatility, applications are not normally programmed into the system but are purchased separately according to the preference of the user.

Word processing applications for the computer cover a wide range in terms of cost and sophistication from simple typewriter emulation to desktop publishing with print quality type and graphics.

Correcting and editing

One of the main attractions of the word processor or the computer is the ability to edit work before printing thereby eliminating troublesome erasures. Those which have the capacity to save work for editing at a later date are most desirable because they allow corrections and updates for subsequent printing.

All but the simplest systems allow the copying of data from one document to another so that a standard paragraph can be typed once and used in other documents without retyping.

Many applications also have the capability to merge a file of names and addresses with a single document so that multiple copies of the document will be personalized for each recipient.

Special help with spelling, grammar and vocabulary

Most systems, particularly those which are computer-based, will check the document for correct spelling.

Some of the more sophisticated systems check for grammatical and other errors such as typing *as* for *is* or the improper use of words like *to, too* and *two.*

Some applications will hyphenate at the end of lines to avoid a ragged look.

Vocabulary options allow the user to call up synonyms and antonyms as possible substitutes for a word.

Caution! – don't get lazy. It's easy to take advantage of your application's capability and disregard the fact that it does not reflect your style. Be sure to check the computer's work carefully; you may not agree with the grammar or hyphenation system. Some of the programs are user sensitive and attempt to emulate your style by remembering when you override hyphenation or grammar suggestions; remember, however, that your style may change, and if you don't check up on the computer's work, it will never know.

Organizing and saving your files

When you first begin to save files, whether on a fixed disc in the computer or on external media such as floppies, you can't imagine ever having difficulty locating a document. Wrong. Bad thought! Bad thought! Wipe it out of your memory banks now!

Directories. The computer allows you to create directories (think of them as file folders) in which you can store your work. Some programs start you off with one data directory in which your work is stored to keep it separate from the program files. Based on the kind of work you are doing, decide how you want to organize your files. You may want to set up a directory for each client, for financial reports, sales reports, production reports, love letters, etc.

Files. These are the documents which you create. Some systems limit you to a combination of eight letters and numbers for the document name, some allow more. Decide how you want to organize the files within a directory so that you can easily retrieve them from a list in alpha-numeric order. You may want to include in the name a code for easy identification by type of document (letter, price bid, report) and when it was created. Establishing an orderly system which makes access and identification easy will be of immense help when you back up your work and when you need to reorganize. A system will allow you to manipulate groups of files instead of individual documents.

We make jokes about things "lost in the computer" until, like Walt Kelly's Pogo, "We has met the enemy and they is us."

There are books and applications with loads of information to keep you from tearing out your hair when you need help, so we won't go into any further detail beyond this brief warning – organize as though you are setting up a system to handle all of the data for a major corporation! The time you spend organizing at the beginning is nothing compared to the time and headache of trying to reorganize if your system proves inadequate in six months.

WORD PROCESSING TERMS

access To call up for revision or printing.

application Any task performed by the word processor or computer.

backup or **backup copy** An extra copy of programs or data made for protection against the loss of the original as a result of power failure, machine malfunction, etc.

batch printing The ability to line up multiple documents to print in sequence automatically, usually simultaneous with the creation or editing of other documents.

boilerplate Standardized copy which can be called up for insertion in documents as needed.

bold or **bold face** Type which is darker than the normal font; depending on the system, bold face may be a special font or it may be created by overtyping in the same font.

center The command which automatically centers a line of type between the margins or on a tab stop.

character Anything typed to print out plus the control characters which carry formatting instructions for the document. Normally, only the material which prints is visible on the screen, although most systems offer a view mode which allows viewing of the control characters.

copy May refer to the contents of a document; a duplicate of the document; the act of reproducing data under another name or to another disk (see **back up**); the act of reproducing a portion of a document elsewhere in the document or in another document (see also, **boilerplate, cut**)

control character See **character**.

continuous forms Forms which are attached in a continuous stream for feeding through a word processor or printer, perforated for separation after printing. Continuous forms may be plain bond, letterheads, invoices, checks, envelopes, etc.

CPU (central processing unit) The main part of the computer or word processing system which contains main memory and instructions to carry out system control functions.

create To start a new document with a distinctive name for identification.

CRT (Cathode Ray Tube) The viewing screen; also called *visual display* or *video display*.

cursor The on-screen indicator which shows where the next typed character will be entered.

cursor keys Special keys which move the cursor to a new position without changing anything else on the screen.

cut or **cut and paste** The ability to delete copy from a document and move it to another place in the document or to another document.

decimal alignment The ability to line up numbers in a column on a decimal point, usually a function of a tab setting.

default or **default settings** The settings, such as margins, which are built into the system as the standard format settings unless other settings are specified.

directory A division of the disk filing system which holds a group of files.

disk A device for storing data. A *fixed* or *hard* disk is usually housed within the computer or word processor. A *floppy* disk, also called a *diskette* is an external device which is inserted into a slot in the machine called a **disk drive.**

dot matrix printer A printer which uses dots to make up the image of letters and graphics. Quality of output varies from standard computer print to letter quality.

draft printer A dot-matrix printer which produces low-quality output suitable only for internal reports and files. (See also, **letter quality** and **near-letter quality.**)

edit keys Function keys or key combinations which perform editing functions such as *cut and paste; delete* character, word or line; *go to* next word, line or page; *format* type, etc.

enter key May be used to signify the end of a line similar to the carriage return on a typewriter. In those systems where the word processor or computer determines the line ending, the enter key is pressed at the end of a paragraph or to force a line break. Also used as a signal to execute some commands.

error message A brief on-screen message indicating that an operation cannot be performed as entered. Often accompanied by instructions for correcting.

field A part of a document or file record which is distinctly identified, usually by a name; for example, in a customer list, *last name* may be a field name and the *last name of the customer* in that record is the field.

file name The distinctive name or code assigned to a file to identify it for future use.

flush left The command which aligns text on the left hand side of the page.

flush right The command which aligns text on the right hand side of the page.

form feed The setting which tells the word processor and printer that continuous forms are being processed; that printing may proceed without delay between documents.

format Page layout specifications such as margins, tab settings, indents, line spacing, etc.

hard copy A printout on paper.

hardware The physical equipment such as the CPU, keyboard and printer.

header Text programmed to appear at the top of each page such as a title, page number or date.

highlight A feature which sets selected text apart by some means such as underlining or reversing, usually prior to formatting in some way.

hyphenation Use of the hyphen to divide a word between syllables at the end of a line of copy in order to make lines less ragged or connect the parts of a compound word.

justify The command which aligns text both left and right.

letter quality Refers to the quality of print produced by a good typewriter; the standard for judging the quality of print in business letters. (See also, **draft**

quality, near letter quality.)

line spacing The spacing between lines of printed copy, normally six lines to the inch. Some systems allow considerable control over the line spacing in a document.

merge The ability to combine elements from different files such as names and addresses from a data base file with a letter from a document file.

module One of the pieces of the hardware which make up a system, such as the printer, keyboard, etc.

monitor The screen on which work is viewed. See also, **CRT.**

NLQ, near-letter quality Dot matrix emulation of typewriter or letter quality print. (See also, **draft quality, letter quality**.)

paste A command to insert data which has been copied to a temporary file such as a clipboard. See also, **cut and paste**.

program Software. The set of instructions which enables the system to perform tasks such as word processing.

prompt A screen message which requires a response.

proportional spacing Typesetting in which the space provided for each letter is proportional to the size of the letter as compared to typewriter type which provides the same amount of space for each letter which results in distracting variations in the amount of white space between letters.

return See **enter**

scroll Moving the cursor up or down on the screen to move through the text of a document.

shared printer A system which allows more than one work station or terminal to share a printer.

software The programs and applications which enable the hardware to perform specific tasks .(See also, **hardware.**)

sort Data organized according to predetermined parameters. Document files, for example, might be sorted by name, by last save date, by size, etc.

word wrap A word processing program feature wherein text too long for a single line wraps to the next line.

work station Minimally, the keyboard and monitor connected to a remote printer and CPU or mainframe. Often has some computer capability and a disk drive.

Part III

Basic Grammar - Putting It All Together

Basic Grammar – Putting It All Together

Those of us convinced that English 101 was created only
as an instrument of torture don't have to
worry about it anymore. Right?

Thus far we've been dealing in the abstract – the transformation of English from tribal dialect to the language we speak today, the techniques of effective communication and finally, the use of some modern tools including word processors and computers.

Presumably, your purpose in reading this book is to communicate more effectively; therefore, we cannot escape a discussion of the of the basic elements which make up the language – the way in which random words are put together to form coherent thoughts. Surely you know something about grammar (probably more than you realize) or you wouldn't be able to communicate at all. Learning more, or putting a name to that which you know, will better equip you to critically assess your writing and speaking.

It may seem that categorizing words and analyzing sentences is strictly the work of scholars for some unknown purpose. In fact, it's a tool we can all use, not just to improve our communication but to make it more powerful; *it affects the way in which we view the things we say.* As we study the words that form our sentences and the sentences that form our thoughts and ideas, we begin to understand why something expressed in a certain way is crystal clear, while the same thing expressed in another way is vague, indistinct or even misleading. How it happens is not easily explained; it's magic. Like riding a bicycle. One minute you're faltering, concentrating on staying up to avoid making a fool of yourself in front of the entire neighborhood and the next minute you're riding, wondering what all the fuss was about.

Phrases
Phrases are discussed more completely in the section describing **Sentence Structure**. In this section, a phrase refers simply to the part of a sentence being discussed or a part of speech and the words associated with it.

PARTS OF SPEECH

In order to describe how words are used in the communication of ideas, all of the words in the language have been grouped into categories called parts of speech. Each category has its own set of guidelines for use of the words in the group. The eight parts of speech are as follows:

noun	**pronoun**	**verb**	**adjective**
adverb	**preposition**	**conjunction**	**interjection**

Not all words fit neatly into a single category; many are used in more than one way and are identified with the part of speech representing the particular way in which they are being used. Our interest is always in the way the word is being used in order to determine whether it is being used properly.

This is the sort of English up with which I will not put.
Winston Churchill

Proper grammar is elusive, not because it is so very difficult, but because the rules are frequently arbitrary and outdated. Perhaps it is, as someone said, "because the language is so alive and those who attempt to regulate its use are so dead." There is no doubt that guidelines make it easier to study and learn the language. It is, however, unfortunate that some guidelines have become rules which make no contribution to improving communication but often do an excellent job of confusing the communicator. The admonition not to end a sentence with a preposition, for example, was first put forth by a grammarian expressing his own preference. Eventually it became a rule which even Mr. Churchill laughed at. (Oops.) Among the frequently violated rules are some which seem reasonable, such as the use of *bigger* or *heavier* to compare two things and *biggest* or *heaviest* to compare more than two, but there is no way to misunderstand when the wrong word is used, so why the rule?

There seems to be general agreement about the parts of speech and their function, but disagreement about almost everything else. Little attempt will be made here to confront those disagreements except as passing considerations.

Nouns

A noun is usually described as "a person, place or thing". That's a bit misleading because we're inclined to think of *a thing* as an inanimate object. A bird isn't a person, nor a place, nor an inanimate object (unless it's dead).

A noun is a name. It is the name we give to what we're talking about.

Person is a noun and so are all the things we call a person (you know what I mean).

man woman child plumber doctor manager teacher runner

author clown lawyer baker butcher master servant chief

Creatures, animals and **plants** are nouns as are names of all living things.

dog bird bug tree vegetable bloodhound wren ant fox hen

oak spider crab gorilla pansy carrot rose godzilla cabbage

Place and all of the places we can name,

home office school field street club restaurant arena

as well as **objects.**

furniture tools air gold trash water teapot smoke

There are immaterial things such as **activities,**

running concert cooking speech reading sewing

and **concepts.**

honesty bravery theory day minute beauty

Function of the noun

The noun may function as a subject, as an object, as an adjective or as an adverb.

The *manager* is sending *you* the *financial report* by *messenger today*.

Subject – *manager*. The subject is the lead character in this little drama. Everything in this sentence concerns the manager: he or she is sending something, sending a report, sending to you, sending it by messenger, and sending it today. Agreed?

Direct object – *report*. The direct object clarifies what is being done by naming the recipient of the action. You are the recipient of the report, but the report is recipient of the action. Clear?

Indirect object – *you*. The indirect object describes to or for whom the action is taken. It always comes before the direct object in a sentence and takes the implied preposition *to* or *for*. Okay, so it sounds confusing; think of the sentence as saying, "The manager is sending (to) you. . ." or ". . .(for) you. . ."

If the sentence is changed to read, "The manager is sending the financial report to you. . .", the word *you* would become the object of the preposition *to*. If that's not confusing enough, read on.

Object of a preposition – *messenger*. A preposition is placed before a noun or pronoun to show its relationship with another word in the sentence. In this case the preposition is *by*, the prepositional phrase is *by messenger* and it tells how the report is being sent.

Hopefully you are not going to spend a lot of time differentiating between *indirect object* and *object of a preposition*. These two may never give you a problem, but knowing the difference can help if you are unsure of something you've written.

Enough of this, but (if you are interested) there's more in the section about **Prepositions**.

Adjective –*financial*. The noun *financial* is used as an adjective to modify (or clarify) *report* so that you know what type of report is being sent. For more, see the section about **Adjectives**.

Adverb – *today*. Here we have a noun used as an adverb, answering the question *when?* which modifies the verb *sending*. More about **Adverbs** in that section as well.

Common nouns

A common noun is one which we commonly use (wonder where the name came from?) to name a non-specific thing: *dog, cat, man, woman, piano.* The examples at the beginning of this section are all common nouns because each one is a name which does not designate a specific thing.

Modifiers do not change the classification of a common noun. The noun *cat* in the phrase *my cat, Callie* remains common (though she doesn't think so), even though the reference has been narrowed down to the cat which is mine. *Callie,* however, is the name of that particular cat and a proper noun.

Proper nouns

A proper noun is a specific name and begins with a capital letter. Don't capitalize a common noun used with a proper noun unless it is part of the name. Motors which you buy from a company named General, may be described as General motors, but if you address the automobile company, it's another matter. Products from the automobile company are General Motors cars (or whatever you choose to call them based on your experience).

Identification of a proper noun is not always clear. Many names used freely as generic (or common nouns) are brand names, such as Kleenex for tissues and Vaseline for salve. Use of brand names without capitalizing is a very sensitive issue among those who hold rights to the name. Some names have become so much a part of the language that no attempt is made to preserve the proprietary right to the name. If you know the difference, capitalize; if you are not sure, look it up.

The need for capitals is not always clear. Congratulating a friend on the invention of trashfood milk supplement is going to go much further if you don't insult him by implying that it isn't worthy of capitalization.

There is also the tendency to use substitute phrases as replacements for proper names such as *The Man Upstairs* for *God* or *Big Guy* for *boss.* In the first instance, the rules for capitalizing are clear in that any reference to a particular deity is capitalized. In the second, if the company tolerates this type of reference in informal correspondence, it is well to consider that *big guy* might be viewed as an unflattering reference to the boss's physique. When in doubt, capitalize.

Collective nouns

A collective noun is a noun which refers to a collection or group as a unit and does not have a word form to describe a single member.

collection group family company orchestra herd flock

board of directors or **board**

management (not to be confused with managers)

The collective noun is singular when referring to its members as a cohesive unit and plural when referring to their diversity. In each case it is important to maintain agreement between the noun, its pronouns, if any, and its verb.

The *board* is in agreement regarding the selection of a chairman. Singular, collective—the board as a unit is in agreement.

The *members of the board* are in agreement regarding the selection of a chairman. Plural, non-collective – changing *board* to *members of the board* alters reference to the board as a unit to that of several individuals.

The *board* have different opinions regarding the selection of a chairman. Plural, collective – the *different opinions* indicate that the board as a unit is not in agreement and we have the plurality of a disunited board.

The *board members* have different opinions on the selection of a chairman. Plural, non-collective again – changing *board* to *board members* we are again considering several individuals.

Note that diversity does not indicate animosity, but only difference; you can just as easily substitute *salad dressing* for *chairman* in the examples above.

Citing all of these examples may seem redundant, but it beats reciting a bunch of rules and leaving you to figure them out. By now you have probably also noticed the best way out of difficulty – change the wording of the sentence. That is the best solution when the correct form sounds awkward to you.

Also see **Plural nouns**, below, and the section describing **Relationships**.

Plural nouns

The plural of the noun shows that you are referring to more than one.

Most noun plurals are formed by adding *s* or *es* to the singular. There are, however, many exceptions including those which change spelling,

child, children **woman, women** **man, men**

goose, geese **mouse, mice** **die, dice**

foot, feet **ox, oxen** **tooth, teeth**

alumnus, alumni **medium, media** **datum, data**

addendum, addenda **crisis, crises**

those which do not change at all,

deer hose moose sheep species vermin

and those which give you a choice.

brother **brothers** or **brethren**

appendix **appendixes** or **appendices**

beau **beaus** or **beaux**

index **indexes** or **indices**

focus **focuses** or **foci**

The collective noun in its singular form as described above is singular when referring to the group as a single cohesive unit, plural when describing diversity. In addition, the noun itself may have a plural form.

a single **collection** of stamps or several stamp **collections**

a single **group** of people or several **groups** of people

a single **family** or several **families**

the **board of directors** of one company or the **boards of directors** of several companies, although, unless there is a need to be very specific, you are more likely to refer to **the boards** or **the directors** collectively.

The plural form of the collective noun is used in exactly the same fashion as any other plural.

The *boards* are in agreement regarding the selection of their chairman. Plural, because we are talking about several *boards,* which is the same as talking about several *things.* It does not matter whether they agree, disagree or play squat tag, each board is a *thing* and the subject is more than one of those *things* which is plural and ever more shall be so. (Whew!)

Possessive nouns

The possessive noun denotes possession or ownership. It also indicates relationship, though there is some disagreement about the use of a possessive noun when referring to an inanimate object. There are those who decry the use of phrases such as **the car's top** preferring, instead, **the top which is on the car** or **the top of the car.** It's entirely up to you, for the meaning is certainly clear and no reader of suspense stories is a stranger to **the wind's howling** or **the night's impenetrable darkness.**

To show possession, add apostrophe *s* to nouns which are singular and to plurals which do not end in *s*; add only the apostrophe to plurals which end in *s*.

The great challenge when using a possessive noun is to avoid confusing plural and possessive.

The *boy's* bicycle is black. Singular possessive – tells us that one boy possesses a black bicycle.

The *boys* bicycle every day. Plural only – tells us that bicycling is something done by more than one boy.

The *boys'* bicycles are all black. Plural possessive – tells us that more than one boy each possess a black bicycle.

The *boys'* bicycle is black. Still plural possessive – tells us that there is only one bicycle, but it is in the possession of more than one boy.

To test for possessive, restructure the phrase inserting the words *of* or *belonging to.*

The bicycle(s) *belonging to* the boy(s). As you can see, it works for all of the above sentences except the second.

The possessive form of collective nouns carries the same admonition to be careful not to confuse plurality with possession and, beyond that, requires only that you think about what you are trying to say.

The *group* display is effective. Singular only – *group* is a noun used as an adjective to describe the type of display.

The *group's* display is effective. Singular possessive – we are referring to the display belonging to one group.

The *group's* displays are effective. Singular possessive – this time we are referring to a single group which possesses more than one display.

The *groups'* displays are effective. Plural possessive – here we have more than one display each belonging to a different group.

Don't be discouraged; it's not as complicated as it seems. Correct usage merely requires a bit of thought and let's face it, that's one of the keys to effective communication – thinking about what you're saying.

Gender of nouns

Gender is the classification of words as **masculine, feminine** or none of the above, which is **neuter**. Neuter in the grammatical sense applies to words which do not make a distinction between masculine or feminine,

animal horse family parent bird bee

and those which have no sex.

rock building road car (even if you refer to it as *she*)

In English, gender is quite simple; probably no other language is as direct and rational. Old English arbitrarily assigned gender to nouns, which had to be used with the proper gender of article and adjective. If you have any doubts about how much our language is simplified by the loss of those gender nouns, browse through an English-Spanish, English-French, or English-German dictionary. The designation of a word as masculine, feminine or neuter frequently has no relation to the meaning of the word itself.

English words indicate gender in one of three ways: naming something by using one of a word pair which is different for male and female, prefacing a noun of indeterminate gender with one of those word pairs or by adding a gender-specific ending.

Some of the more familiar **word pairs** are:

male, female	**man, woman**	**he, she**
lad, lass	**brother, sister**	**him, her**
son, daughter	**father, mother**	**uncle, aunt**
nephew, niece	**sir, madam**	**husband, wife**
bull, cow	**ram, ewe**	**stallion, mare**
buck or **stag, doe**	**rooster, hen**	**drake, duck**
gander, goose	**waiter, waitress**	**groom, bride**
actor, actress	**lord, lady**	**king, queen**

The **gender-specific preface** is not nearly as common as in the past when it was usually a hyphenated word such as *she-lion* or *he-goat.* There are survivors, however, as in *girlfriend* and *boyfriend,* Today we are inclined to use an adjective to indicate gender such as *male secretary* or *female astronaut,* usually to describe an activity normally associated with the opposite sex. This usage is also on the decline as sex stereotypes disappear along with our wonderment that men and women do most things equally well.

Do not to confuse the gender-specific preface words with terms such as *man-hour* or *man-made* which use *man* to refer to the family of man, that is, people in general, rather than strictly male.

Gender-specific endings are few and the tendency is to avoid their use.

lion, lioness	**host, hostess**	**count, countess**
god, goddess	**baron, baroness**	**prince, princess**
usher, usherette	**fiancé, fiancée**	**executor, executrix**
aviator, aviatrix	**alumnus, alumna**	**bachelor, bachelorette**
hero, heroine	**comedian, comedienne**	

Okay, so what's the big deal? Why devote so much space to something described as "quite simple"?

Because I lied . . . a little. Because if you want to speak or write well you need only follow the rules, but if you want to communicate well you need to be aware of the time in which you live.

Our language has been shaped by a society which drew sharp distinctions between the strong male as hunter/provider and the weak female who stayed home to do simple things like cooking and having babies. As the role of men and women change, many take exception to the gender references and feel that they should also change. (Of course some are offended by the suggestion of change, some think it is downright silly and some don't think at all!)

The language is changing and will continue to change to reflect our society. *Chairman* is giving way to *chairperson* and *salesman* to *salesperson.* Some who feel *chairperson* is awkward, use simply *chair; salesperson* has evolved in some instances to *sales representative* though it can hardly be considered less awkward. There is resistance to the use of feminine endings, the feeling that *authoress* and *poetess* are condescending. Whatever your belief, you have a right to it, but be aware that insensitivity will detract from your message. More about this in the sections on **Pronouns, Adjectives** and **Style**.

***Gender* is a term used only in grammar – usually.** *Gender* is properly used in reference to the sexual orientation of words, especially nouns and pronouns. Describing a woman as one of *the female gender* is acknowledged in some dictionaries as a humorous reference or colloquialism or both. The fact that older dictionaries don't mention this usage at all would seem to indicate a change is taking place. Be guided accordingly.

Gerund

A gerund is a verb form ending in *-ing* that can be used as a noun. This won't come up often in conversation, but you might want to know the difference.

> **You should *run* for exercise.** *Run* is a verb, the action.
>
> **He is *running* for exercise.** *Running* is still a verb, a form of *run.*
>
> ***Running* is good exercise.** Aha! the **gerund**. *Running,* a verb form of *run,* is now the noun/name of what you are talking about.

Pronouns

A pronoun takes the place of a noun or nouns and, therefore, represents the name we give to what we're talking about. See **Noun**, above.

Function of the pronoun

The pronoun **substitutes** for a **specific noun**, an **implied noun** or an **unknown noun**. Don't throw up your hands yet. Examples are on the way.

The **specific noun,** called the **antecedent**, is one which has been voiced (or written) previously and can now be more easily expressed as a pronoun.

> **The father told *the father's daughter* that *the daughter* played better tennis than *the father* did.**
>
> Kind of clumsy? You bet! Now try substituting *his, she* and *he* in the sentence.
>
> **The father told *his* daughter that *she* played better tennis than *he* did.**

The **implied noun** is one which has not been voiced but which is understood.

> ***I* am speaking** (or **writing) and hope *you* are listening** (or **reading).** *I* refers to the speaker and *you* know who you are. Whichever end of the action you are on, presence is implied, the pronouns substituting for proper names.
>
> If the nouns are stated rather than implied, in this kind of sentence, it comes out **–I, John take you, Mary. . .** and vice-versa
>
> ***It* is really coming down.** *It* implies something unsaid which in this case is most likely rain or snow and you should know which if you are standing in it. Would be a lot bigger news if it was going up.

The **unknown noun** is usually, but not necessarily the subject of a question.

> ***Who* is coming down the path?**
>
> ***Which* airline lost our baggage this time?**
>
> ***What* day is this?**

You certainly can't specify the subject if you don't know its name. Before you are tempted to add *when, why* or *how* to this list, see the section on **adverbs**.

Personal pronouns

These guys are important because we use them so much and we often use them incorrectly. A personal pronoun can be very impersonal, but it always refers to a person except for the pronoun *it* which may refer to something else. **The personal pronoun shows to whom or what is referring by its form.** (Stay with me on this; there will be a quiz later.)

Remember (if you can), that the noun functions as a subject (nominative case from the Latin word for name) or an object (objective case). In any case (pardon the pun) the form of a noun remains the same regardless of how it is used. The personal pronoun, however changes form depending on its use.

The following list is for the **nominative case** (personal pronoun used as a subject).

First person refers to the speaker or speakers
singular ***I***, plural ***we***

***I* am going to the party.** *I* is the subject, the thing we're talking about.

***We* are going to the party, if you have money for gas.** *We* is the subject.

Second person refers to the person or persons spoken to
singular ***you***, plural ***you***

***You* are going to the party.** *You* is the subject.

Are all of *you* going without me? You is the subject. *All of you* indicates more than one person; *you* can be used alone, but the reference to more than one person is not as clear.

Third person refers to the person(s) or thing(s) spoken of
singular ***he, she*** or ***it,*** plural ***they***

***He* is going to the party.** *He* is the subject.

***She* is going with him.** Now *she* it is the subject.

***It* sounds like a great party.** *It* is the subject, standing in for *party.* The sentence could be reconstructed to say *The party sounds great.* or *The party, it sounds great.*

***They* are not taking me with them.** *They* is the subject.

The personal pronoun as an object (objective case) often gets us into trouble, because we use it in the wrong place.

The list which follows is for the **objective case**.

First person (speaker)
singular ***me,*** plural ***us***

Will you take *me* to the party? *Me* is the object of the verb *take.*

Please join *us* at the party. *Us* is the object of the verb *join.* (*You* is the implied subject as in *Will you join us at the party?*)

Second person (spoken to)
singular ***you,*** plural ***you***

We will be happy to join *you.* *You* is the object of the verb *join.*

We will be happy to join all of *you.* *You* is the object of the verb *join.* Here, again, *you* can be used alone (and probably would be) to imply a group.

Third person (spoken of)
singular ***him, her*** or ***it,*** plural ***them***

Let us join *him.* *Him* is the object of the verb *join.*

Let us join *her.* *Her* is the object of the verb *join.*

We will take *it* home with us. *It* is the object of the verb *take.*

Let's take *them* home too. *Them* is the object of the verb *take.*

The personal pronoun at the beginning of a sentence doesn't seem to give us any difficulty. Nor does the personal pronoun as an object.

So what's the problem? It's a thing called the **predicate pronoun**. When a pronoun refers back to a noun or pronoun which is the subject (nominative) it too must remain nominative.

It is *she* who called.

It is *her* who called?

Which is it?

Stop! Look the sentence over. The order of the sentence is getting us into trouble. *It* is standing in for *she;* you might consider *it* an anchor to hold down the beginning of the sentence (called an **expletive**) when the rest of the sentence is out of order. You can get out of trouble by analyzing the sentence as it is or you can correct the order as long as you are careful not to change the meaning.

It is *she.*

It is *her.*

It is she sounds the same to most people as *it is her*. Come on, admit it. When your favorite singer steps out on stage what do you say? "It's her!" But now try. . .

***She* is who called. *She* is the one who called.**

***Her* is who. . .** uh, oh.

She is (the one) who called compared to *her is (the one) who called* certainly makes it clear. So it is *she* who called. Your ears will lie to you if given a chance, especially if you've been hearing something wrong for most of your life.

Try changing the order of the words when in doubt . . . or adding words. Does *it is we* (or *they*) sound wrong to you? Flesh out the sentence.

It is *we* (who are the ones) who did something.

***We* did something.** It is *we,* for sure.

Again, before we move on: if correct grammar doesn't sound right to you, doesn't feel right to you or sounds affected, don't use it. Get rid of the awkward construction and express yourself in another way.

This seems like a good place to mention **who and whom.** Please don't cringe. It's easy.

Who is nominative (a subject), single and plural.

Whom is objective (an object), single and plural.

It is she who called.

Who refers to *she* which we already decided is nominative (see above). But *whom* did she call?

If this one gives you a problem, change the order of the words.

She called whom?

Still doesn't sound right? Substitute another word.

She called me?

Me is objective (see above) therefore you need the objective case of *who* which is *whom*. Again, if you don't like the way it sounds, when properly phrased, figure out another way to say it.

The **possessive case** of the personal pronoun also changes form depending on how it is being used. Often the possessive case is used as an adjective to modify a noun. To complicate matters, there are several possessives which have two forms (don't give up now), one of which is always used to modify a noun and one which is always used alone, as a pronoun. It's easiest to deal with if you always think of the possessive as a modifier.

A selection of simple sentences to illustrate the use of possessive person pronouns seems preferable to quoting a lot of rules. Hope you agree.

First person possessive (speaker)
singular —***my*** or ***mine***

***My* car has a dented fender.** *My* is used as an adjective to modify *car* by indicating ownership

The car with the dented fender is *mine*. *Mine* is a pronoun taking the place of *car* or more precisely, *my car*. The sentence could be rephrased as **The car with the dented fender is *my car*.** or ***My car* is the car with the dented fender.** Sorry to belabor that; just want to show how reconstructing the sentence can help clarify exactly what the word represents.

My* cars are here. The cars are *mine*.** Here you can see that changing the number of the noun which is being modified or replaced does not change the number or form of the possessive pronoun as long as the ownership is still in the hands of one person, me. Thus shall it ever be with modifiers; consider **the *brown* cow** versus **the *brown* cows** and **the cow is *brown versus **the cows are *brown*** (not *browns*, unless they belong to the Browns, but that's another story).

First person possessive (speaker)
plural –***our*** or ***ours***

***Our* car is a rust bucket.** *Our* modifies car, and is plural which indicates possession by more than one person.

This rust bucket is *ours*. *Ours* takes the place of *rust bucket*. ***Ours* is the rust bucket.**

***Our* cars are here. These cars are *ours*.** Again, no change in the modifier even though the number of the noun modified changes.

Second person (spoken to)
singular and plural are the same –***your*** or ***yours***

***Your* child isn't doing well in school.** *Your* modifies the noun *child*. The form is the same for the single or plural *you*, whether it is one spouse addressing another or a teacher addressing both parents.

The child with the glazed look is *yours*. (Yeah, sure.) *Yours* stands in for *your child* whether addressing one parent or both.

***Your* children are here. The children are *yours*.** Whether one child or many the personal pronoun is the same.

Third person (spoken of)
singular —***his, her*** or ***hers, its***

His* violin is on stage. The green case is *his. In the first sentence, *his* modifies *violin;* in the second, *green case* is replaced by the pronoun *his.* In both instances the pronoun takes the same form.

Her* banjo is in the car. The five-string banjo is *hers. In the first sentence, *her* modifies *banjo;* in the second, *five-string banjo* is replaced by the pronoun *hers.* In each case, the form is different. Why does *her* change form while *his* does not? Like so many of the anomalies in English, nobody knows.

***Its* stall is in the barn.** *Its* modifies stall. Examples of the use of *its* (a possessive form, remember) without a noun seem to be restricted to poetry or grammarians who are stretching a point to make a point and serve more to confuse than enlighten. If you should find an example you like, write it in here.

Third person (spoken of)
plural —***their*** or ***theirs***

***Their* zither is in the case.** *Their* modifies *zither.*

The zither in the case is *theirs.* *Theirs* replaces *zither.*

Their* zithers are in the case. The zithers in the case are *theirs. And finally, multiple zithers retain the same pronoun.

Whose is the possessive form of ***who.*** It is the same whether singular or plural, nominative or objective. Whose idea was it to make something so easy?

Whose car is this? This car is whose?

Whose cars are these? These cars are whose?

Attack of the like sounding words

There are words which sound like personal pronouns but have entirely different meanings. You are not likely to use *hours* for *ours, ewe* for *you* or *hymn* for *him.* In fact, we both know that you're not likely to make any of the mistakes mentioned in this book, but there are others who might and you should be aware of them.

To be sure that the words you write are saying what you mean, remember that the personal pronoun never takes an apostrophe to form the possessive, then redo the sentence using the complete words that make up any contractions you have used.

Its is the possessive form for *it*.
Its cage is clean. (No apostrophe, so it is possessive.)

It's is the contraction of *it is*.
_It's_ a clean cage. (*It is* a clean cage. It works!)

Their is the possessive form for *they*.
Their cage is clean.

They're is the contraction of *they are*.
They're in a clean cage.

Whose is the possessive form for *who* or *whom*.
Whose cage is this?

Who's is the contraction of *who is*.
Who's in this cage?

Your is the possessive form for *you*.
Your cage is ready.

You're is the contraction of *you are*.
You're in the wrong cage.

Got it? Now just keep your cage clean.

Indefinite pronouns

Indefinite pronouns are those which name things in a general way. Most indefinite pronouns express quantity, however imprecise.

Some of the commonly used indefinite pronouns:

all	**another**	**any**	**anybody**
anyone	**both**	**each**	**either**
everybody	**everyone**	**everything**	**few**
many	**most**	**neither**	**nobody**
none	**nothing**	**one**	**other**
several	**some**	**somebody**	**someone**
something	**somewhat**		

Certain pronoun phrases are also viewed as indefinite pronouns:

any one	**every one**	**each other**	**no one**
one another	**some one**		

If you are paying attention, you will have noticed that some words are on both of the above lists, first as a compound word, then as two separate words. Often the only difference is spelling; the words mean the same whichever form is used. Sometimes, a difference in structure can create a different shade of meaning and you may want to take advantage of it.

Someone will be held responsible. Refers to anyone, anywhere and perhaps more than one.

Some one of us (of you, of management) will be held responsible. Narrows the field and implies only one.

The phrases **one another** and **each other** deserve mention. *One another* refers to the action of more than two whereas *each other* refers to only two.

Love one another, like the song says, unless you are speaking of that special someone, in which case **you love each other.**

This is one of those preferences mentioned earlier in which there is no absolute right and wrong. Either way you say it will be understood, so if you disagree with the suggestion, love in the way which you find most comfortable.

As stated above, indefinite pronouns generally imply imprecise numbers, but you shouldn't be imprecise in the use of the terms.

Everybody wants to go. Nobody likes it. We have a tendency to voice the extreme even when its not exactly true.

Almost everyone wants to go. Few like it. Most do not like it. Using a modifier or a different word results in a statement that is still imprecise, but properly so, rather than a statement which is precisely incorrect.

Casual use of indefinite pronouns may be normal, accepted and even understood within your normal sphere of influence, but it can trivialize your message in some circles and reflect on your competence. Get in the habit of being as precise as you can all of the time and you will be precise when it is most important.

How many is a few? An insignificant amount, according to the dictionary. Some people claim that a few means three. It all depends on your frame of reference. If you have a million fruit flies and a few get away, a few could be a thousand. Twenty complaints about a product you sell could be described as few if you sold 20,000. It's all relative – just be sure that you and the receiver of your message are of like mind.

The **possessive form of the indefinite pronoun** is usually shown by adding apostrophe *s*, because, unlike the personal pronoun, there is no special form to show possession and the indefinite pronoun is usually used only in the singular (The word is singular even though its meaning implies plurality)

anybody's stuff	**anyone's stuff**	**everybody's stuff**
everyone's stuff	**nobody's stuff**	**one's stuff**
somebody's stuff	**someone's stuff**	

One exception is ***other*** which forms a plural by adding *s* and so takes an apostrophe after the *s* to show the plural possessive.

my *other* stuff – singular only

put it with the *others* – plural only

put it with the *others'* stuff – plural possessive

An oddity in English is the association of the adverb ***else*** with an indefinite pronoun.

anyone else **everyone else** **no one else**
someone else

When forming the possessive of the pronoun, *else* is treated as though it is part of the word and takes an apostrophe *s*.

anyone else's **everyone else's** **no one else's**
someone else's

Relative pronouns

The relative pronoun is a bridge which connects its antecedent (the noun to which it refers) to a new clause. It is particularly useful in avoiding clumsy construction when you have one clause imbedding in another.

A man *who* was a member of the group returned the next day. The pronoun *who* takes the place of man and forms a bridge between *man* and *member of the group*. It may be better understood if you consider the alternatives.

Two sentences – **The man was a member of the group. He returned the next day.**

A parenthetical phrase – **The man (he was part of the group) returned the next day.**

This violin, *which* she has been playing for years, is her most treasured possession. *Which* takes the place of *violin* and is the bridge between violin (Is that another pun? Shame.) and *she has been playing for years*. Again, consider the alternatives.

She has been playing this violin for years. It is her most treasured possession.

This violin (she has been playing it for years) is her most treasured possession.

Nothing wrong with the two sentences or the parenthetical phrase in the sentence, but there are times when you will want to vary the pace of your writing and this is one of the ways in which you can do it.

The relative pronouns ***who, whom*** or ***whose*** refer to a person, ***what*** or ***which*** refer to anything except a person and ***that*** refers to anything.

What requires some special consideration. It replaces *that which* and so should not be used where the antecedent is expressed.

> **This violin, *what* she has been...** don't sound good; nor do **This violin, *that which* she has been...** because the antecedent *violin* has been expressed and *what* or *that which* just don't fit. *Which* is correct – **This violin, *which* she has been...**
>
> **Do *what* you will to murder this language.** – a nasty sentiment, but grammatically correct.

That doesn't *require* special consideration, but does deserve it. For one thing, it finds a lot of work as a demonstrative pronoun (see below). For another, it exhibits a harsh, flat sound in contrast to *who* and *which,* and thus seems out of place in some situations where it is grammatically correct.

> **The lady, *whom* I have just met, ...** – is not likely to be described in the same tone as – **The scoundrel *that* stole my watch. ...**

Recognize that this is one of those personal preference things; consider your style, decide what sounds best to you and use it.

Other part-time relative pronouns are **but** and **such as**.

> **There, *but* for the grace of God, go I.**
>
> **My life, *such as* it is, is quite pleasant.**

Interrogative pronouns

> **An interrogative pronoun is one which introduces a question.**

Who or ***whom*** refers to a person.

> ***Who* chased the cat?**
>
> **To *whom* did you give the cat?**

Whose (possessive) generally refers to a person.

> ***Whose* cat is this?** *Whose* refers to a person — literally, ***What person owns* this cat?**

What and ***which*** refer to anything.

> ***What* is this?** Response depends on the nature of the creature or thing indicated; most likely a name or description.
>
> ***What* is she?** The question *Who is she?* is generally seeking a name and perhaps a common reference such as to whom the person in question is related or her position in the community. *What is she?* is more likely related to a conversation about occupation, religious preference, nationality, etc.
>
> ***Which* car is yours? *Which* of you chased the cat?**

Demonstrative pronouns

The demonstrative pronouns are ***this*** (*plural **these***) and ***that***(*plural **those***); *demonstrative* from the Latin, *to point out*, they literally or figuratively point out the proximity of the noun which they represent.

> ***This* is my coat and *that* is my hat.** *This* indicates a coat near at hand, whereas the hat is further away.
>
> ***These* people have shelter; what can be done about *those* who have none?** *These people* points to a specific group; *those*, with no antecedent, figuratively points to a group, out there, somewhere.

Had enough of pronouns? If not, browse through another text where you will probably find a class of pronouns not mentioned in this book, just as some described here are not on other lists. Weren't you warned that this is an inexact science and that there is no definitive text? That any book of grammar you choose will reflect in some way the predilections of the author or compiler? It means that you will have to think for yourself and make some judgments only you can make if you really want to use the language well.

Enough, already! Let's move on to **the action**.

Verbs – the action

Verbs are where the action is. A verb can initiate a thought expression in a one-word sentence.

> **Go! Come! Hurry! Drive! Dig! Smell! Eat! Smile! Enter! Drink! Ready! Aim! Fire!**

Function of the verb

The function of a verb is to indicate action or a state of being, usually with reference to time and condition of the action or state of being.

Don't panic! We can break that definition down to manageable chunks.

action – The verb tells you that *something is being done,* that some action is taking place. In all probability, you're familiar with this one. - **Joe *drives* the car. Sue *slaps* the smart-aleck writer.**

state of being – You might think of the verb as indicating a state of being when it's not describing an action. **Joe *is* nervous. Sue *appears* contented.** These are called *linking verbs* because they forge a link between the subject and a word describing the condition or state of being of the subject. For a more thorough discussion, see **Linking verbs,** below.

time and condition – The verb indicates *when the action takes place* (in the past, at present, in the future) and the *condition of the action,* (completed, in progress, not started) by its form. See **Forms of the verb,** below.

Forms of the verb

There is no way to ease into this gently, so let's just dive in and define all of those pesky forms, or at least the ones which seem important at the moment; we can elaborate on their idiosyncrasies later.

The infinitive – The infinitive might be considered the unadulterated form of a verb, one which is expressed without the limits of person or number imposed by attachment to a noun. The infinitive (think *infinity,* unlimited) covers an indefinite span of time and conditions.

It is better *to give* than to wash your socks.

See **Infinitives,** page 56.

Present tense – Also referred to as the ***present indicative*** (See **Mood,** below). The *present* form of a verb alludes to the time of the statement in which it appears.

She *speaks* as though she will never stop.

We might rephrase the sentence.

Whenever she *speaks,* it is as though she will never stop.

The reference is not to past or future, but to *that time when she speaks.*

Present participle – The present participle is a verb form which may also function as an adjective to describe a present action which is not completed.

The politician, *speaking* about his accomplishments, never seemed to take a breath.

The present participle form always ends in *-ing.*

Present progressive – The *present progressive* form differs little from the present participle. It describes a continuous action and is formed by joining a form of the verb *to be* to the present participle.

He *is speaking* as though he will never stop.

Present perfect – Also referred to as the ***present perfect tense.*** The *present perfect* defines an action which has just been completed. It is formed by using *have* or *has* with the *past participle* form of the verb.

He *has spoken* and is ready to take questions.

Past tense – Also called ***past indicative,*** the past tense indicates action, or a state of being that existed, in the past.

She spoke to the group last year.

Past participle – The past participle suggests an action which, though completed, is continuing.

Every place she went they heard her words *spoken* with pride.

Past progressive –The past progressive form differs little from the past participle. It describes a continuous action and is formed by joining a form of the verb *to be* to the present participle.

Every place she went, she *was speaking* with pride the words she wrote.

Past perfect –Also referred to as ***past perfect tense,*** the past perfect is formed by using *had* with the past participle of the verb. It indicates a past action which was completed prior to another event in the past.

He *had spoken* before the last meeting.

Future tense –The future tense makes a declaration about action to be taken or a condition anticipated in the future. The future tense is formed by using *shall* or *will* with the verb.

He *will speak* at the next meeting.

Future progressive – The future progressive describes a continuous action in the future and is formed by joining a form of the verb *to be* to the present participle.

They *shall be speaking* the words she wrote.

Future perfect – Also described as ***future perfect tense,*** the future perfect is formed by adding *shall have* or *will have* to the past participle of the verb to indicate an action whose completion is anticipated before another future event.

He *will have spoken* to the group twice after the next meeting.

The gerund –The gerund is a verb form, specifically the present participle, used as a noun. It is mentioned briefly in the section on **Nouns** and is of no more importance here than it was there.

Our obsession with cataloguing and relegating everything to nice neat slots has its merits, but sometimes it gets us into trouble. Especially when something doesn't fit into those nice neat slots and those doing the cataloguing can't agree where the misfit belongs. Thus far we've gone through a list of the more popular terms used to classify verbs which are, without doubt, the most difficult of the parts of speech to comprehend, probably because they are the most versatile. In any event this is the base on which we will build as we explore the use of verbs and other parts of speech in the rest of this section and sentence structure in the next.

The attempts to organize English have resulted in some loose fits for words, so don't be surprised by ambiguity, overlapping and downright disagreement from one text to another and even within a single text. The alternative is a static language which wouldn't be nearly as much fun.

Linking verbs

All verbs do not express action. A verb which expresses a state of being rather than the action of a noun is called a *linking verb* because its function is to connect the subject with another noun, a pronoun or an adjective which describes it. The most common *linking verbs* are the forms of **to be:**

be	**was**	**been**	**am**
is	**are**	**were**	**shall be**
will be	**shall have been**		**will have been**
had been	**may be**	**may have been**	
might be	**might have been**		**being**

Other *linking verbs* are:

appear	**become**	**feel**	**grow**
look	**hear**	**keep**	**prove**
seem	**smell**	**sound**	**stay**
taste	**turn**	**remain**	

Become and seem are almost always linking verbs. The other verbs in the list above may be either *linking* or *action* depending on how they are used.

The outside air *is* cold. The linking verb always requires the word or phrase which complements the noun. **The outside air is.** means nothing (unless you are a student of Zen – then it's like the sound of one hand clapping).

The flowers *smell* fragrant. *Smell* is used as a linking verb. In this example, if you leave off the complement, the sentence takes on an entirely different meaning.

Usually, the linking verb can be replaced by a form of *seem*, a good test if you want to determine the verb's function .

Auxiliary verbs

Until now, we've referred to verbs as a single word. That's only part of the story. The verb may, in fact, be a ***verb phrase*** made up of two or more words. In such cases, the last word in the *verb phrase*, the verb which indicates the action, is the ***principal verb*** and those which precede it are helpers or ***auxiliary verbs.***

The students *study* in the library.

The students *are studying* in the dorms.

The students *should have been studying* in the classroom.

The students *had better study* somewhere!

Some of the more common auxiliary verbs are:

am	**are**	**can**	**could**	**could be**
could have been		**did**	**do**	**does**
had	**had been**	**had better**	**had rather**	**has**
has been	**have**	**have been**	**is**	**may**
might	**must**	**must have**	**must have been**	
shall	**shall be**	**should**	**should have**	
should have been		**was**	**were**	**will**
will be	**would**	**would have**		

Infinitives – split and otherwise

The word *to* is a preposition; however, when it precedes a verb, it is considered to be part of an infinitive. The infinitive is, then, a *verb* preceded by the word *to.*

He has a desire *to write* well.

***To run* in the marathon is her goal.**

(Her goal *is to run* in the marathon.)

Sounds too simple, and it is. When auxiliaries such as **can, could, do, may, might, must, shall, should, will, would, had better** and **had rather** are used, the auxiliary phrase often replaces the word *to* in order to avoid awkward construction.

He felt that anyone with the ability *should write.*

(He felt that anyone with the ability *to write should do so.*)

Use of *to* is optional after some words such as:

bid	**dare**	**help**	**let**
make	**need**	**please**	**see**

Don't you dare (to) smoke in here!

Now for those nasty **split infinitives**. No big deal! There is a school of thought which dictates that modifiers should never be placed between *to* and its verb, thereby splitting the infinitive.

She has one wish, *to sing sweetly.*
versus
She has one wish, *to sweetly sing.*(split infinitive)

***To run swiftly* was his goal.**
versus
***To swiftly run* was his goal.** (split infinitive)

Test it out on any sentence of your choosing and you will likely find that the split infinitive doesn't distort meaning, but it is a bit awkward. *However,* there are times when the construction fits the mood of the message and *when that happens, use it!* NEXT!

Inflection

Inflection refers to the pattern of changes in words which properly express grammatical relationships such as case, number, gender, person, tense, etc. In verbs these are called **conjugation.** (See **Tense**, below.)

Tense

Tense? Indeed! Verbs always make us tense. But that's not what we need to discuss here.

As stated above, a verb indicates a time when the action takes place. The form of the verb which relates it to time is its **tense: past, present or future.** It is important to be familiar with these forms in order to convey a message that is not confusing.

The modified forms of the verb should be included in any listing of tense because they convey different shades of meaning.

present	**past**	**future**
present participle	**past participle**	
present progressive	**past progressive**	**future progressive**
present perfect	**past perfect**	**future perfect**

The general rule regarding tense is not to change within a sentence. The tense of a subordinate clause should agree with the tense of the main verb. Not as easy as it sounds, nor does it apply universally.

> **He *wants* to drive**, for example, in an indirect reference becomes **She *said* that he *wanted* to drive** changing *want* from the present tense to the past tense in order to force agreement with *said*, which is past tense. In this instance, you might view the rule as superfluous, because **She *said* that he *wants* to drive** loses nothing in translation. You would be right; however, there are times when the message will be unclear if there is not agreement in tense.

It is better to use the correct form so that you are sure that the communication will always be clear.

If the action expressed is continual, future or universal, the present tense may be retained in the subordinate clause.

She *said* that he always *wants* to drive.

She *said* that he will always *want* to drive.

She *said* that he still *wants* to drive.

The present tense may be retained in the subordinate clause for emphasis.

She *said* that he *is* driving.

If the clauses are independent, the tense need not agree.

If he *said* that, I *can't* stop him. Reiterating that which happened in the past is independent of the present action.

More of this in the sections on **Sentence structure** and **Relationships**. Just don't get tense about tense. (Isn't English fun?)

Regular verbs form the past tense and past participle by adding *-ed* to the verb. When the verb ends in a silent *e*, the *e* is not repeated; add only *-d*. Irregular verbs form the past tense and past participle in a variety of ways; there is no single rule governing their conjugation. The most commonly used irregular verbs are listed in the next section.

Rules for conjugating other forms of the verbs are contained in the section, **Forms of the verb**, above.

Irregular verbs

There is no way to identify and conjugate irregular verbs except to know which verbs are irregular or to look them up. You probably already know most from regular use and the list which begins on the next page will help.

In addition to the irregular verbs with their irregular conjugation, some of the regular verbs have alternative forms; those which are in general use have been included. The regular verbs on this list are easily recognized because they show two forms, one of which follows the rule for adding *-ed*.

This is not a complete list of the irregular verbs for English. Verbs and verb forms which are not in common use have been omitted as well as any in common use which we may have overlooked.

Principal parts of irregular verbs

Present	Past	Past Participle
arise	arose	arisen
awake	awoke	awoke
	awaked	awaked
be	was	been
bear	bore	borne
beat	beat	beat
		beaten
become	became	become
befall	befell	befallen
begin	began	begun
behold	beheld	beheld
bend	bent	bent
	bended	bended
bereave	bereft	bereft
	bereaved	bereaved
beseech	besought	besought
bet	bet	bet
	betted	betted
bid	bid	bid
	bade	bidden
bind	bound	bound
bite	bit	bitten
bleed	bled	bled
bless	blest	blest
	blessed	blessed
blow	blew	blown
break	broke	broken
breed	bred	bred
bring	brought	brought
build	built	built
burn	burnt	burnt
	burned	burned
burst	burst	burst
buy	bought	bought
can	could	

Principal parts of irregular verbs (continued)

Present	Past	Past Participle
cast	cast	cast
catch	caught	caught
choose	chose	chosen
cling	clung	clung
clothe	clad	clad
	clothed	clothed
come	came	come
cost	cost	cost
creep	crept	crept
cut	cut	cut
deal	dealt	dealt
dig	dug	dug
do	did	done
draw	drew	drawn
dream	dreamt	dreamt
	dreamed	dreamed
drink	drank	drunk
		drunken
drive	drove	driven
dwell	dwelt	dwelt
	dwelled	dwelled
eat	ate	eaten
fall	fell	fallen
feed	fed	fed
feel	felt	felt
fight	fought	fought
find	found	found
flee	fled	fled
fling	flung	flung
fly	flew	flown
forbear	forbore	forborne
forbid	forbade	forbidden
forget	forgot	forgotten
forsake	forsook	forsaken

Principal parts of irregular verbs (continued)

Present	Past	Past Participle
freeze	froze	frozen
get	got	gotten
		got
give	gave	given
go	went	gone
grind	ground	ground
grow	grew	grown
hang	hung	hung
	hanged	hanged
have	had	had
hear	heard	heard
hew	hewed	hewn
hide	hid	hidden
hit	hit	hit
hold	held	held
hurt	hurt	hurt
keep	kept	kept
kneel	knelt	knelt
	kneeled	kneeled
know	knew	known
lay	laid	laid
lead	led	led
leap	leapt	leapt
	leaped	leaped
leave	left	left
lend	lent	lent
let	let	let
lie	lay	lain
light	lit	lit
	lighted	lighted
lose	lost	lost
make	made	made
may	might	

Principal parts of irregular verbs (continued)

Present	Past	Past Participle
mean	meant	meant
meet	met	met
mow	mowed	mown
pay	paid	paid
plead	plead	plead
put	put	put
quit	quit quitted	quit quitted
read	read	read
rend	rent	rent
rid	rid	rid
ride	rode	ridden
ring	rang rung	rung
rise	rose	risen
run	ran	run
say	said	said
see	saw	seen
seek	sought	sought
sell	sold	sold
send	sent	sent
set	set	set
sew	sewed	sewn sewed
shake	shook	shaken
shall	should	
shave	shaved	shaven shaved
shed	shed	shed
shine	shone shined	shone shined
shoe	shod	shod
shoot	shot	shot
show	showed	shown, showed

Principal parts of irregular verbs (continued)

Present	Past	Past Participle
shred	shred shredded	shred shredded
shrink	shrank shrunk	shrunk shrunken
shut	shut	shut
sing	sang	sung
sink	sank sunk	sunk
sit	sat	sat
slay	slew	slain
slide	slid	slid slidden
sling	slung	slung
slit	slit	slit
sow	sowed	sown
speak	spoke	spoken
speed	sped	sped
spend	spent	spent
split	split	split
spread	spread	spread
spring	sprang sprung	sprung
stand	stood	stood
steal	stole	stolen
stick	stuck	stuck
sting	stung	stung
stink	stank stunk	stunk
strew	strewed	strewn strewed
stride	strode	stridden
strike	struck	stricken struck
strive	strove	striven
swear	swore	sworn
sweat	sweat sweated	sweat sweated

Principal parts of irregular verbs (continued)

Present	Past	Past Participle
sweep	swept	swept
swell	swelled	swollen swelled
swim	swam swum	swum
swing	swung	swung
take	took	taken
teach	taught	taught
tear	tore	torn
tell	told	told
think	thought	thought
throw	threw	thrown
thrust	thrust	thrust
tread	trod	trodden trod
wake	woke waked	waked
wear	wore	worn
wed	wed wedded	wed wedded
weep	wept	wept
wet	wet wetted	wet wetted
will	would	
win	won	won
wind	wound	wound
wring	wrung	wrung
write	wrote	written

Transitive and intransigent verbs

This is another one of those items that doesn't crop up often in polite conversation, but you may want to know about it just in case it comes up in the next section.

Verbs are classified as transitive or intransitive based on their relation to objects. **Transitive** describes a verb which requires an object to make the meaning of a sentence complete; an **intransitive** verb does not require an object. Many verbs may be used either way, depending on the sentence

The boy *reads* the *book* well. *Reads* in this sentence is transitive; *book* is the object and we need to know that to make this particular thought complete.

The girl *reads* well. *Reads* in this sentence is intransitive; the lack of an object makes it clear that this is a general comment about the girl's ability to read

Now, aren't you glad you know that?

Incidentally, *intransigent* means unable to compromise; rebellious – sounds like a lot of the verbs we've seen so far.

Mood, voice, person and number

So far we've looked at the ability of the verb to indicate time (**forms of the verb, tense**) and we've looked at some of the types of verbs (**linking verbs, auxiliary verbs, infinitives, regular verbs, irregular verbs**). Now we'll look at some of the other properties of verbs.

Mood is the manner in which the action or condition expressed by the verb is stated, whether actual (**indicative**), doubtful (**subjunctive**) or commanding (**imperative**). Yes, you might as well learn the names, because they could come up again.

Indicative –Think of *indicate,* to point out or direct attention to, a positive action. The indicative mood is a statement of fact or a question of fact.

This is my house, the only brick one on the block.

Where is your book? **I like to dance.**

Subjunctive – The word is from the Latin for subjoin, which is dumb. If you want to remember it coupled with what it describes, think of *submissive.* The subjunctive mood expresses a contingency, a supposition or desire. The statement is usually introduced by a conjunction of doubt, contingency, condition or possibility such as *if, though, unless* or *whether.*

If this *were* my house I'd have it painted.

I wish this *were* my book.

May I *have* this dance? (I wonder *if* I may have this dance?)

Imperative – The imperative mood expresses command, entreaty or exhortation. *Imperative* means obligatory which makes this one easy to remember.

Come with me to the house. **Read the book.**

Watch the dance and see how it flows.

Voice refers to the form of a *transitive verb* that indicates whether the subject is performing the action (**active**) or is being acted upon (**passive**).

Active – **She wrote the play.** The action *wrote* was performed by the subject *she.*

Passive – **The play was written by her.** The action *written* was performed on the subject *play.*

Person of the action described by a verb is the same as for the pronoun:

First person – the person or persons speaking.

Second person – the person or persons spoken to.

Third person – the person or persons spoken of.

This might be a good time to review persons as outlined in the section on **Pronouns.** You've probably forgotten it by now and we can wait. . . .

Number in grammar refers to the singular and plural forms of a word. The bad news is that verbs have singular and plural forms which must agree with the number of the noun or pronoun. The good news is that except for *to be,* the verb changes form *only* in the third person singular.

To be or not to be, that is maddening

To be is the weirdest verb we have. Naturally it's also the most useful and you can't ignore it. It has been written that the only way to learn the forms of *to be* is to memorize them. The writer obviously never hear of crib sheets. Here's yours with *to be* and the regular verb *call* together for comparison. Admittedly there is a great deal of redundancy because the forms don't change as much as you might imagine, but how can you know without seeing it? The verb forms are in **bold face** with helpers in *italics*.

	first person (speaking)	**second person** (spoken to)	**third person** (spoken of)
Present tense			
singular–**to be**	I **am**	you **are**	he, she, it **is**
singular–**call**	I **call**	you **call**	he, she, it **calls** (This is the only verb change which relates to number–third person singular.)
plural–**to be**	we **are**	you **are**	they **are**
plural–**call**	we **call**	you **call**	they **call**
Present perfect			
singular–**to be**	I *have* **been**	you *have* **been**	he, she, it *has* **been**
singular–**call**	I *have* **called**	you *have* **called**	he, she, it *has* **called**
	(Note that the rule was followed for forming the *present perfect* by using *have* with the *past participle* which in turn had been formed by adding *-ed* to the verb. To find the past participle of an irregular verb refer to the list of irregular verbs above.)		
plural–**to be**	we *have* **been**	you *have* **been**	they *have* **been**
plural–**call**	we *have* **called**	you *have* **called**	they *have* **called**

Past tense

singular–**to be**	I **was**	you **were**	he, she, it **was**
singular–**call**	I **called**	you **called**	he, she, it **called**
plural–**to be**	we **were**	you **were**	they **were**
plural–**call**	we **called**	you **called**	they **called**

Past perfect

singular–**to be**	I *had* **been**	you *had* **been**	he, she, it *had* **been**
singular–**call**	I *had* **called**	you *had* **called**	he, she, it *had* **called**

(The past perfect is formed by using had with the past participle.)

plural–**to be**	we *had* **been**	you *had* **been**	they *had* **been**
plural–**call**	we *had* **called**	you *had* **called**	they *had* **called**

Future tense

singular–**to be**	I *shall* **be**	you *will* **be**	he, she, it *will* **be**
singular–**call**	I *shall* **call**	you *will* **call**	he, she, it *will* **call**
plural–**to be**	we *shall* **be**	you *will* **be**	they *will* **be**
plural–**call**	we *shall* **call**	you *will* **call**	they *will* **call**

Future perfect

singular–**to be**	I *shall have* **been**	you *will have* **been**	he, she, it *will have* **been**
singular–**call**	I *shall have* **called**	you *will have* **called**	he, she, it *will have* **called**

(The future perfect is formed by adding *shall have* or *will have* to the past participle)

plural–**to be**	we *shall have* **been**	you *will have* **been**	they *will have* **been**
plural–**call**	we *shall have* **called**	you *will have* **called**	they *will have* **called**

Those nasty dangling participles

Better to split an infinitive than to dangle a participle. No joke. The split infinitive may sound awkward; the dangling participle can be downright confusing. The *participial phrase,* made up of the participle and its modifiers, is in turn modifying a noun. A *dangling participle* is one which was left hanging out there somewhere with no obvious attachment to the thing it is supposed to modify.

Walking through the woods, there were animals everywhere. Can't you just see it? Raccoons, bears and foxes strolling hand in hand in their Sunday best.

Walking through the woods, we could see there were animals everywhere. Sounds better. There are many ways to frame this sentence, none of which allow you to drop the *we* to which the participial phrase refers.

Sometimes the error is so subtle that it is hardly noticed.

Opening the door, the room seemed very large. Okay, so you realize that the room didn't open the door and you change the sentence. **Opening the door, *we* could see that the room seemed very large.**

Looking through the window, the room seemed very large. You could walk by this one all day without flinching. You might rationalize that you are dealing with a few unvoiced words and take the sentence to mean exactly what it does mean. ***We were* looking through the window, *and* the room seemed very large.** Sorry, but you can't (or rather, shouldn't) do it. It is only by chance that the meaning of the sentence does not appear to be confused by the dangling participle. Depending on the context, that is, what is said before and after this sentence, it's meaning may yet be in question.

Effective communication should clarify, not confuse and the dangling participle will almost always serve to confuse.

Odds and ends

Characteristic of a vital growing language, English is rife with idiosyncrasies which defy categorizing. Following are a few, though certainly not all, of the anomalies of the verb family.

Had ought is one of those phrases that should make you cringe. *Ought* means *should*, though it is more emphatic, implying a greater sense of obligation.

> **You *should* do something about that.** The statement engenders the feeling that you might do something if you feel like it.
>
> **You *ought to* do something about that.** Use of the word ought creates a stronger sense of obligation to do something.
>
> Use of the word *have* or *had* with *ought* is superfluous. Never mind that it is considered poor form, it doesn't add anything to the message; **You had ought to go** and **I have ought to do it** are old forms which have nothing to recommend them over **You ought to go** and **I ought to do it.**

Had rather and **had better** show up from time to time with mixed results.

I had rather is another old form which has been almost entirely displaced by *I would rather*. Both are correct, so you have only to think about what you are saying and decide which does the job best.

I had better and *you had better* are most frequently used to express the serious nature of the situation.

> **You should go** expresses what you might do if you are so inclined. **You ought to go** expresses a sense of greater obligation. **You had better go** implies that it is likely to get very unfriendly around here if you stay.

Shall and **will** are struggling to be freed from an outdated rule of grammar. To follow this you may want to refer to the crib sheet a few pages back. In the *future tense* you will note that *shall* has been used as an auxiliary in the first person, whereas *will* has been used for the second and third person. *Shall* in the first person expresses *anticipation of a future happening,* whereas *will* does the same in the second and third person. To express *demand or obligation*, the words are reversed; *will* is used for the first person and *shall* for the second and third person.

First person.

(Permissive, anticipation of a future happening.)
I shall wash the car tomorrow. Expresses an anticipated action.

(Directive, a demand or obligation.)
I will wash the car tomorrow. Expresses a determination to act.

Second person.

You will be pleased with the report. Anticipation.

You shall have the report in the morning. Determination.

Third person

She will start work in the morning. Anticipation.

She shall get all the help she needs. Determination.

Observe these distinctions if you want to use the traditional forms.

In contemporary usage, we are more likely to use *shall* and *will* interchangeably, with the emphasis on will as obligatory and shall as pemissive.

Should and **would**, the past tense for *shall* and *will*, may be found under the same dark cloud. *Should* is a synonym for *ought* and although it usually denotes *obligation*, it often indicates *anticipation*. *Would* is usually *permissive*, expressing *desire* or what *might* be expected. They are supposed to follow the same rules as *shall* and *will*, but contemporary usage often dictates quite the opposite.

You shall have the report in the morning expresses determination, but **You should have the report in the morning** may mean either *you have a right to expect the report in the morning*, or *if all goes well, I will have it for you in the morning*.

She shall get all the help she needs expresses determination, but **She should get all the help she needs** implies *I expect she will get all the help she needs, but I'm not really sure.*

Abbreviating *have* has caused a unique grammatical construction.
Expressions such as *would've, could've* and *might've* strike our ears as *would of, could of* and *might of* which then become committed to writing. Whether writing or speaking, *have* should not be abbreviated in this way. It is just plain sloppy, though of course you can've it your way if you want to.

For a list of words which are often confused, see pages 186-193

For a list of words with dual spellings, see pages 147-148

For a list of irregular verbs, see pages 61-66

For a list of commonly used superfluous words, see page 18

For a list the examples in this book by part of speech, see page 235

Adjectives

Adjectives add color and precision to our speech. Just as the verb gives life to the noun by indicating activity, the adjective gives life to the objects and ideas named by describing them. Adjectives are the words which give us the information to transfer the thing we are talking about from the universal pool of all similar things to a smaller group; perhaps even to a party of one.

Function

The function of an adjective is to clarify what we are talking about by enhancing and limiting the designation of a noun or pronoun.

Articles

The simplest of the adjectives are the articles **a, an,** and **the.** The article is a limiting adjective whose purpose is to point out and limit the noun.

The is the *definite* article and refers to one or more *specific* items.

the box – that box, there

the cars in the driveway – those cars, in that driveway

the house on the corner – that house, located on the corner

The may be used to point out something which is to be further described or something which needs no further description.

A and ***an*** are the indefinite articles and refer to an unspecified item in a group of items. *A* is used when the noun or modifier which follows it begins with a consonant sound. *An* is used when the noun or modifier is a vowel sound.

a box – any box

a car in the driveway – any car that is in the driveway

an artifact from the museum – any artifact from that museum

an outstanding citizen – any one of the outstanding citizens

Limiting adjectives

Limiting adjectives restrict the nouns which they describe by some reference to number or quantity. Limiting adjectives include the articles listed above, numbers, some of the indefinite pronouns which function as adjectives and adjectives which represent measure or frequency.

three blind mice	a **few** rules
daily newspaper	**double** trouble
both sides of the coin	**every** minute
some fun	**seventy-six** trombones

Numbers are nouns which can function as adjectives and include *cardinal numbers* and *ordinal numbers*. ***Cardinal numbers*** express a precise amount (one, two, three, four, etc.) ***Ordinal numbers*** express a relative position (first, second, third, fourth, etc.)

Following is a list of some of the most common limiting adjectives.

a	**an**	**all**	**any**	**both**
daily	**double**	**each**	**every**	**few**
half	**hourly**	**inch**	**many**	**mile**
monthly	**most**	**only**	**other**	**second**
several	**some**	**the**	**triple**	**weekly**

Pronouns as adjectives

It seems that at every turn we run into a part of speech masquerading as another part of speech. Sounds complicated, but it really isn't. It's just that it takes a lot of explaining. We've already seen that *indefinite pronouns* can function as adjectives. There are other pronouns which perform this function as well.

The **possessive form of a personal pronoun** may be used as an adjective.

Is *your* friend feeling ill? The pronoun *your* modifies *friend*.

This is *her* computer. The pronoun *her* modifies *computer*.

We like *our* new car. The pronoun *our* modifies *car*.

Demonstrative pronouns (*this, those, that* and *these*) may also function as adjectives. They retain the function of directing attention to or pointing out a noun while they modify the noun by limiting it.

***This* car is the one we bought.** *This* points out *car* **and** modifies, or limits it by singling it out from every other car.

I want to see *those* books. *Those* points out **and** modifies *books*.

Is *that* computer yours? *That* points out **and** modifies *computer*.

***These* grapes are sour.** *These* points out **and** modifies *grapes*.

Descriptive adjectives

The descriptive adjective is one which attributes a non-limiting quality or character to the noun or pronoun.

a *beautiful* child	**a *large* bird**
a *melodic* song	**a *black* sedan**
a *charming* play	**a *tense* scene**
an *exciting* event	**a *challenging* puzzle**

Comparisons

In addition to ascribing a quality to a noun, the adjective can show the extent to which the attribute applies to a this particular noun in relation to others. There are two degrees of comparison, the ***comparative degree*** and the ***superlative degree*** – three if you include the non-comparative form of the adjective, which is silly, because it makes no comparison.

The **comparative degree** is the form of the adjective used for comparing the relationship between two things.

Adjectives of a single syllable usually form the comparative by adding *-er* to the base to indicate a greater degree of the quality expressed.

His knife is *sharper* than mine.

(Of the two cars) the *smaller* is mine.

She keeps a *neater* desk than he does.

Adjectives of more than one syllable are usually preceded by *more* to show a comparison of quality.

This perfume is *more fragrant* (than the other one).

The *more beautiful* car is on the left. (Implying that there is only one car on the right.)

In similar fashion, *less* precedes the adjective to show a lesser degree of the quality.

Feeding a gorilla is *less difficult* than giving it a pedicure.

The **superlative degree** indicates the best of more than two.

Adjectives of a single syllable usually form the superlative by adding *-est* to the base.

His is the *sharpest* knife (of all the knives we have).

(Of all the cars) the *smallest* car is mine.

She keeps the *neatest* desk (in the office).

Adjectives of more than one syllable are usually preceded by most to show the highest degree of the quality compared.

This is the *most fragrant* perfume in the store.

She is the *most famous* writer (of all the writers) I know. (Here's an interesting turn of a phrase. *She* may be the *only* famous writer I know personally, but that's not what I want to say. The form of the sentence implies that I know at least two other writers who might be considered famous, but that may not true. My meaning is that *she is famous and I know her*, and, in spite of the misleading inference, the first sentence is probably the one I will use—but I digress. . .)

Similarly, *least* precedes the adjective to show the lowest degree of the quality compared.

The *least difficult* decision to make is to not mess with that gorilla at all.

We usually add *-er* or *-est* to the adjective of one syllable and use *more* or *most* to precede an adjective of two or more syllables to form comparatives. As you probably expect by now, there are a lot of exceptions. Some follow the basic rules of spelling such as dropping the silent *-e* , doubling consonants and changing a final *y* to *i* before adding *-er* or *-est*. A quick look ahead at the section on **Spelling** will help you to spot those.

Adjectives of more than one syllable which are accented on the last syllable may form comparatives by adding *-er* or *-est*. Most of these are awkward, however, and you will probably want to use *more* or *most*. Various other adjectives form comparisons in a manner which is contrary to the guidelines or which exhibits no definitive pattern.

The following examples and comments may be of some assistance.

Base	Comparative	Superlative	
bad	**worse**	**worst**	–follows no regular pattern
big	**bigger**	**biggest**	–adds *-er* or *-est;* double consonant spelling rule
clever	**cleverer** **more clever**	**cleverest** **most clever**	–either form is correct, but *cleverer* seems clumsier
cold	**colder**	**coldest**	–regular, adds *-er* or *-est*
difficult	**more difficult**	**most difficult**	–regular uses *more* or *most*
dry	**drier**	**driest**	–adds *-er* or *-est;* change *-y* to *i* spelling rule
famous	**more famous**	**most famous**	–regular, uses *more* or *most*
far	**farther**	**farthest**	–regular, adds *-er* or *-est*
	further	**furthest**	–no regular pattern
	(Note: *Farther* or *farthest* is used in the literal sense, to reference distance; *further* or *furthest* is used in the figurative sense, indicating time or degree.)		
good	**better**	**best**	–no regular pattern
heavy	**heavier**	**heaviest**	–adds *-er* or *-est;* change *-y* to *i* spelling rule
late	**later**	**latest**	–adds *-er* or *-est;* drop silent *-e* spelling rule
	latter	**last**	–no regular pattern
	(Note: *Later* or *latest* is used literally, of time; *latter* or *last* of relative position.)		

Base	Comparative	Superlative	(continued)
little	**less**	**least**	—no regular pattern
	(Note from the font of useless information: Less and least are adjectives as the comparative forms of little. When they are used to modify adjectives, they are adverbs. The same is true for more and most.)		
many	**more**	**most**	—no regular pattern
much	**more**	**most**	—no regular pattern
noble	**nobler**	**noblest**	—adds *-er* or *-est;* drop silent *-e* spelling rule
old	**elder**	**eldest**	—no regular pattern
	older	**oldest**	—regular, adds *-er* or *-est*
	(Note: Elder or eldest denote seniority with the implication of old age; older and oldest imply only the relationship of two or more ages.)		
out	**outer**	**outermost**	—see **Most**, below
polite	**politer**	**politest**	
	more polite	**most polite**	—either form is correct
pretty	**prettier**	**prettiest**	—adds *-er* or *-est;* change *-y* to *i* spelling rule
sad	**sadder**	**saddest**	—adds *-er* or *-est;* double consonant spelling rule
severe	**severer**	**severest**	—either form is correct, but
	more severe	**most severe**	*severer* seems awkward
soft	**softer**	**softest**	—regular, adds *-er* or *-est*
tender	**tenderer**	**tenderest**	—*tenderer* seems awkward; how about *more tender*?
wet	**wetter**	**wettest**	—adds *-er* or *-est;* double consonant spelling rule
willing	**more willing**	**most willing**	—regular uses *more* or *most*

Most acts erratically at times and forms the superlative by becoming a suffix to the adjective in words like *hindmost, innermost, outermost* and *uppermost*. Some of the superlatives such as *endmost, foremost* and *topmost* have no comparative degree.

Absolutes and almost absolutes

Not all things can be compared. **Numbers**, for example. If you have three apples, you can't have the most three apples of all those who have three apples. You can however, have the best three apples, but that is a comparison of quality, not quantity. A runner who comes in second can't be any more or less in second place even if there are three other runners who came in second. Second is an absolute position occupied by however many runners placed second. If the runner made a good showing in second place he might be described as having almost come in first.

The are numerous words which by definition do not allow comparison.

alone	**blind**	**dead**	**empty**
entire	**eternal**	**equal**	**final**
full	**last**	**lone**	**married**
mortal	**parallel**	**perfect**	**premanent**
perpetual	**perpendicular**	**round**	**single**
south	**square**	**straight**	**unique**
universal	**vertical**	**whole**	**wrong**

One figure may not be more *square* or *round* than another, two lines may not be more *perpendicular* or *parallel* than two other lines, one love cannot be more *perfect* than another and one person may not be more *dead* than another. They may, however, be *more nearly* square or round or perpendicular or parallel or perfect or dead. The above list is but a small sample of the qualities which cannot be compared. It is important to recognize these qualities in order to be precise in communicating exactly what is meant.

We voice many comparisons and approximations which do not fall into the good, better, best category. (Or good, gooder, goodest, depending on how well you've been following this section.) We speak of arriving *eightish* and staying for the *better part* of an hour, that we ate an *Italian type* meal served *family style.*

Adjectives allow us to form wonderful comparisons which make our expressions more colorful. Do yourself the honor of making proper comparisons so that your audience will listen and enjoy them as much as you do.

Proper adjectives

A proper adjective, which is a proper noun used to describe a characteristic or quality, is generally a product associated with a location or nationality. Note that the proper noun is usually capitalized and the common noun it modifies is not.

***Assam* tea**	***English* muffin**
***Swiss* watch**	***Turkish* towel**
***Irish* coffee**	***Scottish* tweed**
***British* ale**	***Venetian* blinds**
***Incan* artifacts**	***Norwegian* sardines**
***Belfast* linen**	***Mexican* pottery**

Many and few

Customarily, *many* signifies a large number with no special relationship to the total number.

There were *many* people at the fair.

Used with *the,* however, *many* implies a majority and usually refers to people.

The status quo will be changed by the force of the *many.*

In yet another switch, *many a* refers to a large number, but seems to single out individuals.

***Many* a fool has trod that path.** Expressed in this way, the statement has more impact than the simple sentence ***Many* fools have trod that path.**

Few also undergoes a subtle change in meaning when used with an article. Used alone, *few* refers to a small number of random people or things. With the article *a* or *the, few* becomes more selective.

Few are capable of leading. Of *any* total, there are a limited number who are capable.

A few are capable of leading. Of *this* total there are some, perhaps even identified, who are capable.

The people shall be governed by the few. The masses shall be led by a *select* few.

Predicate adjectives

Remember those *linking verbs* we mentioned earlier: all of the forms of *to be,* plus words like *appear, feel, look, seem,* etc.? If you will check your notes, you will find where we said that linking verbs serve to connect the subject with another noun, a pronoun or an adjective. Well, here's the adjective. It's singled out as the *predicate adjective* because it is in the *predicate* (take my word for it; you'll understand when we get to sentence structure), that is, it follows the *verb* although it modifies the *subject,* which appears *before the verb.* Got it?

Don't confuse the predicate adjective with an adjective in the predicate which modifies an object which is not the subject of the sentence.

The grass is *greener* in the well-kept yard. The predicate adjective *greener* modifies grass and is linked by is; the adjective *well-kept* modifies yard and is not a predicate adjective, literally, **The greener grass is in the well-kept yard.**

Nouns as adjectives

We've already seen that some nouns such as *proper nouns* and *numbers* function as adjectives. There are lots more. In fact, it's one of the ways in which we've made communication more precise; almost every article in common use is modified in some way by a noun.

bags – We have garbage bags, grocery bags, litter bags, paper bags, trash bags and doggy bags (which our doggy never sees).

disks – There are compact disks, computer disks, disk brakes, disk harrows and spinal disks (though it's usually spelled *discs*).

houses – We describe them as brick houses, clapboard houses, tree houses, chicken houses, dog houses, etc.

rings – We want a diamond ring, a gold ring, a brass ring or even a key ring, but not a bathtub ring.

shelf —The pantry shelf, the closet shelf and the book shelf are part of the house; the rock shelf and water shelf are left outside.

shoes – We have leather shoes, canvas shoes, deck shoes, golf shoes and tennis shoes. (It's tiring just to think about it.)

tape – We use plastic tape, paper tape and computer tape as well as magnetic tape which we use on a tape recorder or tape deck.

In many cases the modifying noun has been joined to the noun it modified to form a new noun.

bookcase	**book-end**	**bookplate**	**bookrack**
bookshop	**bottleneck**	**cameraman**	**carsick**
cheesecake	**cheesecloth**	**coattail**	**hatband**
hatbox	**hat-tree**	**lamplight**	**lamppost**
landscape	**piecework**	**seashore**	**shoehorn**
shoetree	**snakebite**	**snakeskin**	**snowball**
snowcap	**suitcase**	**teakettle**	**teammate**
teamwork	**teapot**	**teaspoon**	**textbook**

The only way to tell if you have a noun-turned-adjective modifying a noun or a single noun made from two nouns is to consult a dictionary.

No one knows exactly how or why these changes come about, mostly because they don't happen all at once. A particular style may be used by a writer, then by another, until finally it gets picked up in a textbook or dictionary. There is often no universal agreement: one dictionary may list both styles, while another lists only one and ignores or condemns the alternative.

To recognize how haphazard the business is, you only need to browse through a dictionary. Why is *teacup* one word and *coffee cup* is two? Why are *teapot, teakettle* and *teaspoon* one word, but *tea bag* and *tea caddy* are two? And if a *teaspoon* is used to measure and stir tea, what in the world would you use a *tablespoon* for?

Textbook and *schoolbook* are the only books named by a single word. All others are just *books* whose function needs to be further clarified, as an *address book*, a *phone book*, etc. We expect a *textbook* to be a *schoolbook*, a book of instruction, but most books contain text unless they are *blank books*. Also, a *book jacket* is as much a part of a book as the *bookplate* or *bookbinding,* so why is *book jacket* two words? We refer to a *bookstore* or *bookshop* as a special place, but a *grocery store* or *clothing store* or *auto shop* is a generic place until it gets a modifier to describe its function.

A person who does *piecework* works with *piece goods.* A *lamp shade* sits on the *lamppost* from which you get *lamplight.* If a *bookkeeper* does *bookwork,* shouldn't a *beekeeper* do *beework*? Often the compound word doesn't even relate to what it describes. *Pocketbook* does not seem an appropriate name for a purse which is not a book and isn't likely to fit in a pocket.

Gender orientation and other offensive adjectives

Time for a brief political message. Just as there are offensive nouns, there are adjectives which can make someone's blood boil. *Cute* is not offensive unless you describe a grown woman as a *cute girl.* Not so long ago, *handsome* was used to describe only women, then only men; now we use it regardless of sex. Describing a young man as a *good boy* may be a compliment, but an Afro-American adult won't be so delighted. (Don't confuse *good boy* with that champion of southern compliments, *good old boy.*) The more aware you are of what you are saying, the more you will change and improve not only your speech patterns, but your vocabulary as well.

Many find the very term *politically correct* offensive, and well they might. We can get so careful not to offend, that our message is lost. Don't let that happen, but then, don't be thoughtless either.

Adjectives and vocabulary

Earlier we mentioned all of those words that we recognize, but don't use. Adjectives are where we find the most room for improvement and where we find the most new words. English contains a number of adjectives which can be adapted to most situations. Those are the ones we get in the habit of using and working to death; words like *adorable, crazy, fine, lovely, swell, terrible.*

As we recognize the overworked words and replace them, communication not only becomes easier, but it acquires new vitality and depth.

Adverbs

Adverb means *to a verb,* indicating that it is a word added to a verb, presumably to modify its meaning. Adverbs serve to clarify our message by qualifying an action or description as it relates to time, place, manner or degree.

Function

The function of an adverb is to modify a verb, an adjective or another adverb.

Adjective or adverb?

Adverbs are most commonly formed by adding *-ly* to an adjective, though not all adverbs end in *-ly* nor are all words which end in *-ly* adverbs. There are a considerable number of adverbs which take the same form as an adjective.

Fundamentally, an adjective modifies a noun whereas an adverb modifies a verb or adjective (which is, in turn, modifying a noun). Considering that each may perform, to some degree, the function of the other, that is, an adjective may modify another adjective and an adverb may modify a noun or pronoun, one may wonder why we require two separate parts of speech. Why don't we have a single part of speech called a *modifier* which combines the qualities of the adjective and the adverb? Beats me.

It is only fair to point out that there is no general agreement that an adjective may modify another adjective or that an adverb may modify a noun. Some find it easier to ignore exceptions to the rules, to claim that they are not accepted practice or to perform some other linguistic sleight-of-hand which accounts for their presence.

This section is primarily for those who recognize that the suggestion of a universal *modifier* is heresy and have a need to know more about adverbs. Everyone else should be content to use modifiers without distinguishing between the parts of speech, consulting a dictionary whenever necessary to confirm proper usage.

As for distinguishing an adverb from an adjective, you can usually tell by the way the adverb is used. Does it modify a verb, an adjective or another verb? Does it answer the question where, when, how, or to what degree?

Forms of the adverb

Adding *-ly* to an adjective is the most common form of the adverb; however, the adverb created in this fashion may have a meaning which differs from the root adjective.

Adjective –		Adverb –	
	bad		**badly**
	beautiful		**beautifully**
	calm		**calmly**
	charming		**charmingly**
	clever		**cleverly**
	cold		**coldly**
	famous		**famously**
	foolish		**foolishly**
	good		**goodly**
	hard		**hardly**
	large		**largely**
	late		**lately**
	near		**nearly**
	nice		**nicely**
	polite		**politely**
	several		**severally**
	severe		**severely**
	strict		**strictly**
	tender		**tenderly**
	willing		**willingly**

There are many adverbs which do not end in *-ly*.

again	**here**	**how**	**now**
quite	**rather**	**seldom**	**since**
soon	**there**	**too**	**very**
when	**where**	**why**	

Some adverbs are also employed as adjectives. This can be most confusing, for there are adjectives such as *hard* which double as adverbs and, additionally, form an adverb by adding *-ly*. *Dead* may be adverb or adjective, and the adverbial form deadly may likewise be adverb or adjective.

above	**almost**	**courtly**	**daily**
dead	**deadly**	**easterly**	**far**
fast	**hard**	**hourly**	**late**
least	**less**	**little**	**lively**
manly	**much**	**near**	**oft**
often	**slow**	**southerly**	**stately**
then	**weekly**	**well**	**womanly**

Nouns as adverbs

Nouns as adverbs only sounds confusing. It is simply a noun doing what the adverb usually does, modifying a verb. A noun used in this manner retains the property of a noun to take an adjective.

They are going *camping*. *Camping* is a noun used as an adverb to tell *where they are going*.

They are leaving *Monday*. *Monday* is a noun used as an adverb to tell *when they are leaving*.

They are leaving next *Monday*. *Monday* retains the property of a noun which allows it to take an adjective; therefore, it has been modified by the adjective *next*.

We hiked seven *days* before turning back. *Days* is an adverb/noun which takes the adjective *seven*.

Adverbs of time and place

An adverb clarifies the action of a verb or the description of an adjective by indicating proximity. It gives us a reference point in relation to the action or description.

They are leaving *Monday* tells us *when* they are traveling.

They are traveling *home* tells us *where* they are traveling to.

The adverbs *home* and *Monday* in the above sentences tell us something about the action: *when* they are going and *where* they are going. Adverbs may relate a wide range of information relating to time or place, some quite specific, some rather vague.

They are leaving *now*. **They are leaving *eventually*.**

They are leaving *forever*. **They are leaving *here*.**

They travel *often*. **They are traveling *monthly*.**

They are traveling *backwards* around the world.

Adverbs of time and place answer questions like how soon? how often? before or after? for how long? where? in what direction?

Adverbs of manner and degree

Adverbs of manner and degree relate to the *properties* of the action or description; what is the *style* and how *complete* is the action or quality.

They left *quickly*. **They were dressed *nicely*.**

They departed *willingly*. **They treated us *badly*.**

They *seldom* spoke. **I *rather* like them.** **I *nearly* fainted.**

Adverbs of manner and degree answer questions like how? in what way? to what extent?

Interrogative adverbs

Certain adverbs begin a sentence which asks a question.

> ***When* did you first realize that adverbs were out to get you?**
>
> ***Where* do you think they came from?**
>
> ***Why* don't you just burn this book?**
>
> ***How* else do you plan to escape?**

You can often identify an adverb as a word which *answers* a question beginning with *when, where* or *how*?

Comparisons

Adverbs may show comparison in the same fashion as adjectives, by adding *-er* to the adverb or preceding the adverb by *more* for the comparative, and by using *-est* or *most* for the superlative. There are, moreover, irregular comparisons similar to those of the adjective.

Base	Comparative	Superlative
badly	**more badly**	**most badly**
courtly	**more courtly**	**most courtly**
deadly	**more deadly**	**most deadly**
fast	**faster**	**fastest**
foolishly	**more foolishly**	**most foolishly**
hard	**harder**	**hardest**
little	**less**	**least**
much	**more**	**most**
near	**nearer**	**nearest**
often	**more often**	**most often**
tenderly	**more tenderly**	**most tenderly**
well	**better**	**best**
willingly	**more willingly**	**most willingly**

There are adverbs which cannot be compared because they represent an absolute or an unknown.

again	**almost**	**before**	**ever**
here	**how**	**never**	**no**
now	**quite**	**since**	**then**
there	**too**	**very**	**when**
where	**why**	**yes**	

Stuff to watch out for

There are more than a few adverbs maligned by the authorities at any given time. They should be forgiven (the authorities, that is; you can't forgive an adverb) because there is no way to reprint books as fast as the language changes. Today's improper use is often tomorrow's clever phrase. In spite of that self-inflicted warning, let's take a look at some.

Badly is a word that is often used badly, especially when we say that we feel badly about something. *Badly* is an adverb which means *improperly, imperfectly,* or *unpleasantly.*

She plays the guitar *badly.*

He keeps our books *badly.*

They managed their affairs *badly.*

Substitute one of the synonyms for *badly* in these sentences and you will see that the word is used correctly. In short, you can *play, keep, manage, see, hear* or *run* badly, but you can't *feel* badly. Just drop in the synonyms and you will see that none fit. You might feel *imperfect* or *unpleasant,* but not *imperfectly* or *unpleasantly.* You may, however, feel *bad.*

The reason *badly* doesn't work is because you can't place an adverb after a linking verb. Remember, the linking verb has no other function except to link; therefore, you are attempting to modify the subject noun with an adverb and that is against the rules. The easiest way to be sure you are correct is to remember one of the synonyms for *badly* and try to substitute it. Or you might just try to learn some new synonyms for *bad* like *ill, sick, vile* or *evil.*

Good also seems to be a habitual offender. The reason is simple. Good is an adjective only and we often try to use it as an adverb in place of well.

She plays the guitar well.

He keeps our books well.

They manage their affairs well.

Nobody, no time, no how does nothin' *good,* but we can do anything *well.*

Real has a habit of dropping in to replace *really* at times. *Real* is an adjective that means *genuine. Really* is an adverb that means *actually* or is ***used without precise meaning for emphasis.*** **Really?**

She plays the guitar really well.

He keeps our books really well.

They manage their affairs really well. Really!

Almost turns into *most* when we get lazy. We know that *most* means the *greatest amount* and *almost* means *nearly*: nearly the best, nearly the worst, nearly *anything.* We get careless about pronouncing the *al-* and before long most becomes the word of choice.

She plays the guitar almost as well as her teacher. She knows most of the classics.

Won't belabor this with any more examples. You get the idea.

Prepositions

A preposition is one of those connectors that help tie thoughts together. The preposition itself is a word which indicates a relationship, generally one of position. The preposition and its object (normally a noun or pronoun) along with any modifiers of the object form the prepositional phrase. The prepositional phrase is a modifier, functioning in the manner of an adjective or an adverb, or the preposition with its object may be the subject of a sentence.

Function of the preposition

The function of a preposition is to show the relationship between words or groups of words in a sentence.

Commonly used prepositions

about	**above**	**across**	**after**
against	**along**	**among**	**around**
at	**before**	**behind**	**below**
beneath	**beside**	**between**	**beyond**
but	**by**	**concerning**	**considering**
down	**during**	**except**	**excepting**
for	**from**	**in**	**inside**
into	**like**	**near**	**of**
off	**on**	**out**	**outside**
over	**past**	**pending**	**per**
regarding	**save**	**saving**	**since**
through	**till**	**to**	**toward**
under	**until**	**unto**	**up**
upon	**with**	**within**	**without**

In addition, there are a number of phrases which function as compound prepositions.

according to	**along with**	**as to**
because of	**by means of**	**by reason of**
by way of	**contrary to**	**for the sake of**
in addition to	**in accordance with**	
in case of	**in care of**	**in front of**
in lieu of	**in regard to**	**in reference to**
in spite of	**instead of**	**on account of**
out of	**with reference to**	**with regard to**

Prepositional phrases

The prepositional phrase is the key to understanding prepositions. As described above, the prepositional phrase is comprised of the preposition and its object with any modifiers of the object.

***above* the mahogany desk** – *Desk* is the object of the preposition *above; the* and *mahogany* are adjectives which modify *desk.*

***behind* the old barn** – *Barn* is the object of the preposition *behind; the* and *old* are adjectives which modify *barn.*

***during* her speech** – *Speech* is the object of the preposition *during; her* is a pronoun/adjective which modifies *speech.*

***except* Sunday** – *Sunday* is the object of the preposition *except.*

***outside* these walls** – *Walls* is the object of the preposition *outside; these* is a pronoun/adjective which modifies *walls.*

***because of* you** – *You* is the object of the preposition *because of.*

***contrary to* popular opinion** – *Opinion* is the object of the preposition *contrary to; popular* is an adjective which modifies *opinion.*

***with reference to* your last order** – *Order* is the object of the preposition *with reference to; your* and *last* are adjectives which modify *order.*

Prepositional phrases in sentences

Used in a sentence, the prepositional phrase acts as an adverb or an adjective. The phrase itself is a relational modifier in that it describes something in relation to the noun, verb, adjective or adverb which it modifies.

The picture is *hanging* above the mahogany desk. – *Above the mahogany desk* is the prepositional phrase modifying the adjective *hanging.* (Functioning as an adverb, it answers the question, *where*?) If the sentence were changed to **The picture above the mahogany desk is mine**, the prepositional phrase would be acting as an adverb, modifying the verb *is.*

The children *are playing* behind the old barn. – *Behind the old barn* is the prepositional phrase modifying the verb *are playing.*

Dinner *was served* during her speech. – *During her speech* is the prepositional phrase modifying the verb *was served.*

We open *every* day except Sunday. – *Except Sunday* is the prepositional phrase modifying the adjective *every.*

Outside the wall *is* not safe. – *Outside the wall* is a prepositional phrase used as a noun, the subject of the verb *is.* Think of it this way – *outside the wall* names a place and that place cannot be named except by the entire phrase.

Because of you, I *will try* again. – *Because of you* is the prepositional phrase modifying the verb *will try.*

Words to watch

Inasmuch as the preposition describes a relationship, choosing the correct words for the prepositional phrase can be important to assure that you are conveying the correct message. Following is a sampling of the more common errors; some can convey a misleading message others are simply preferred form about which you have to make your own decisions.

About, around – Preferred usage dictates that only *about* can be used to mean *approximately.* **We expect to arrive home in *about* three hours.**
Around implies *encircling* or *circuitous;* however, some modern dictionaries do recognize *around* to mean *approximately* as a colloquialism and list *about* as a synonym. Take your pick.

Agree — *Agree to* is to give consent. **I *agree to* your plan.**
Agree with is to be of one mind, to concur. **I *agree with* you about the plan.**
We *agree to* a proposal and *agree with* a person.
Dictionaries don't cut any slack on this one. See **concur**, below.

Among, between — Preferred usage dictates that *between* be used when two are involved, *among* when there are more than two.
The two children split the candy *between* them.
The marbles were divided *among* five players.
Between, however, is often used for more than two. **It is a trade agreement *between* three nations.**

Behind, in back of — One of the definitions for *behind* is *at the back*, but if you want to indicate that one thing is *behind* another thing, use *behind*, not *in back of*, *in the back of* or *at the back of*.

Belong — *Belong to* is to be a part of a particular thing or group.
We *belong to* the club.
Castor and Pollux are two stars which *belong to* the constellation Gemini.
Belong with should be used to describe things merely placed together.
We *belong with* the members of the club.
Castor and Pollux *belong with* the stars in Gemini.
This distinction between *to* and *with* holds true for other prepositions as well which serve to express similar but slightly different meanings. (See **for, of, to and with**, below)

Beside, besides — *Beside* means at the side of or in proximity to; *besides* means in addition to or other than.
The large picture sat *beside* the small one. The pictures are side by side or at least, near each other.
There is another picture *besides* the two on the mantle. There is a third picture in addition to the two on the mantle.

Capacity — *Capacity of* calls for a specific quantity. **The tank has a *capacity of* twenty gallons.**
Capacity for indicates indeterminate potential. **He has a *capacity for* understanding.**
Capacity to indicates finite potential. **She has the *capacity to* win the race.**

Concur — *Concur in* indicates general agreement of the subjects. **We *concur in* our assessment of your plan.**

Concur on indicates agreement of the subjects in certain specifics. **We concur on several points (but disagree on others).**
Concur with is agreement between the subject(s) and another person. **I (we) concur with you on the merits of the plan.**
See **agree**, above.

Differ – To *differ from* is to be unlike. **The winters in New York differ from those in Florida.**
To *differ over* or *differ about* is to quarrel. **They differ over (about) the merits of the plan.**
To *differ with* is to merely disagree. **I must differ with your analysis of the findings.**

Different – It has oft been said that *different from* is the only correct form and that *different than* is incorrect. The British use it, why can't we?

Except – When you want to exclude something or someone, use *except*. **Take all of the furniture *except* the couch. Everyone passed the course except Charles.**
Traditionalists frown on the use of *outside of* for *except*, though modern dictionaries often acknowledge its use.
Accept means *to take when offered;* the use of *accept* or *accepting* is definitely wrong.

In, into – Which word you use depends on where you are. **They are running in the yard** tells us that they are running within the confines of the yard. **They are running into the yard** tells us that they are entering the yard from outside.

Inside, inside of, within – *Inside* refers to interior and should not be used to reference *time* or *distance*. Use *within* or *less than* to indicate approximations of time or distance. **We will be there *within* two hours. We ran out of gas *less than* five miles from home.**

More than, over – *More than* should be used to express quantity. **There are *more than* twenty students in the class.** Strictly speaking, *over* refers to relative position. Unstrictly speaking – ho hum.

Outside – Regardless of how you feel about using *outside of* to mean *except* (see **except**, above), you should not be comfortable using the phrase *outside of* when *outside* alone will do the job or especially when *outside* alone is more precise.
Outside the house alludes to all space that is not inside the

house, whereas **outside of the house** suggests the outer walls of the house.

Regard, regards – *Regards* is the plural form of *regard*. It is incorrect in the phrase *in regard to* or *with regard to*. To test it, substitute *relation* for *regard* in the phrases; then try *relations*.

Wait on – *Wait on* is often used incorrectly in place of *wait for*, which can be misleading. Wait on is to serve and wait for is to remain in readiness. **I will wait on my friends** implies that I will serve food, drinks, etc. **I will wait for my friends** indicates that I plan to be here when they are ready.

With – *With* usually means to be in the company of but may also denote opposition. It is well to be alert to statements which might have a dual meaning so as to clarify them. **Tom fought *with* John in court.** Did they oppose each other or together face a common adversary?

Things up with which I will not put

Prepositions perform a distinct function in the sentence. They should be used with forethought to help convey a message, not gratuitously to add clutter. In order to develop concise speech and writing patterns, avoid the use of prepositions which are unnecessary and add nothing to the clarity of the message.

Finally, there is that old business of ending a sentence with a preposition. In some situations it sounds awkward and should be avoided. In others, it's more awkward to avoid ending the sentence with the offending preposition. In most cases, the sentence can be reconstructed. Let's consider Mr. Churchill's statement.

This is the sort of English I will not put up with. Ends with a preposition; grammarians say it's wrong.

This is the sort of English up with which I will not put. Grammatically correct, but awkward; Mr. C. got a lot of laughs with this and so have many comedians.

I will not put up with this sort of English. All of the fun is taken out, but it does convey the message.

Conjunctions

Conjunction is the state of being joined together. Grammatically, a *conjunction* is the word or group of words which forges the link. Simple conjunctions which are most familiar are *if, and* , *or* and *but*. In addition to joining, the conjunction implies a relationship between the things joined and that is the characteristic which makes the choice of conjunction so very important. A poor choice can change the message which you are attempting to convey.

Function

The function of a conjunction is to form a bridge between two or more words or groups of words.

Coordinate and subordinate

The two main classes of conjunction are identified not by the conjunctions themselves, but by their function.

The **coordinate conjunction** is typified by the joining of two or more elements of equal standing within the sentence. The elements joined may be single words or groups of words.

apples *and* oranges **running *and* jumping**

blue *or* green **large *or* small** **to *and* fro**

the yellow airplane *and* the small car

the dogs of war, *and* the cat's meow

Peter, Paul *and* Mary played *and* sang at the concert.

Jack declined to go *because* his car was out of gas.

I like your idea, *but* we must act immediately.

However diverse these elements might seem, they have equal standing in that one is not dependent on the other within the context of the sentence. Note that the phrases in the compound sentences could stand alone as separate sentences indicating that they are not dependent on each other.

The **subordinate conjunction** is one that joins a subordinate clause to an independent clause. The subordinate clause is often a modifier and the subordinate conjunction may begin the sentence or join elements within it.

> ***When* my ship comes in, I'll be at the train station.**
>
> **History judges a politician not by the candidate's promises, *but* by the incumbent's deeds.**
>
> ***Except* for all the pain, exercise is fun!**
>
> **She reveled in her victory, *although* her opponent was stung by the defeat.**
>
> **This diet lets you eat all you want, *only* don't swallow.**

Apply the same test here as for the *coordinate conjunction* and you will see that you can divide the sentence into one phrase which can stand alone as a sentence and one which can not.

List of conjunctions

Most of the words in the following list have come up in discussion of other parts of speech. They are often used as conjunctions while maintaining the characteristics of another part of speech.

after	**also**	**although**	**and**
as	**because**	**before**	**both**
but	**either**	**except**	**for**
however	**if**	**lest**	**neither**
nevertheless	**nor**	**notwithstanding**	
only	**or**	**provided**	**save**
seeing	**since**	**so**	**still**
than	**that**	**then**	**therefore**
though	**unless**	**until**	**what**
when	**where**	**whereas**	**whereat**
whereby	**wherefore**	**wherein**	**whereof**
whereupon	**wherever**	**whether**	**while**
without	**yet**		

If you have a need to know how a word is being used in a specific instance, your only recourse is to carefully study the sentence and break it down. If you reach the wrong conclusion, take heart in knowing that practice will improve your performance and that in most instances two grammarians would likely disagree as well.

Correlative conjunctions

Remember the old admonition about *neither, nor?* that you must use *neither* with *nor* and *either* with *or?* Well, that is still true, and there are other conjunctions which are used in pairs as well. The admonition about using them together is not so stern, for many of the examples cited here do just as well with a different partner or even standing alone; however, both members of the team are often required for clarity.

as, as – I feel *as* confident about this *as* you do.

as, so – *As* the parent goes, *so* goes the child.

both, and – I am *both* surprised *and* pleased at the outcome

either, or – *Either* Judy *or* I will see that the food is ready.

if, then – *If* it rains, *then* we'll cancel the picnic.

neither, nor – *Neither* Judy *nor* I care to participate in the ceremony.

not only, but also – *Not only* is the food attractive, *but also* tasty.

now, then – *Now* we'll plan the trip, *then* we'll figure out how to pay for it.

though, yet – *Though* we live apart, *yet* we'll still be friends.

whether, or – *Whether* we like the idea *or* not, we have to go through with it.

Other connectives

There are other connectives which are not conjunctions, but which exhibit some conjunctive force in linking independent clauses or the dependent clause of which they are a part to an independent clause. These words are variously described as *coordinate* or *subordinate, independent or dependent, conjunctive adverbs or relative adverbs, linking* or *transitional.* For now, we'll view them as conjunctives for which we have no particular set of rules. Look them over and note any that are familiar, add a few of your own and we'll deal with their proper use in the section on **sentence structure.**

accordingly	**afterwards**	**again**
as a result	**at last**	**at the same time**
as well as	**besides**	**consequently**
conversely	**doubtless**	**eventually**
evidently	**finally**	**for example**
for instance	**for this reason**	**further**
furthermore	**hence**	**how**
in addition	**in any case**	**indeed**
in fact	**in like manner**	**in short**
likewise	**meanwhile**	**moreover**
namely	**nevertheless**	**next**
nonetheless	**now**	**on the contrary**
on the other hand	**otherwise**	**perhaps**
possibly	**that is**	**thus**
whenever	**whereby**	**wherein**
why	**wherefore**	

Interjections

Interjections lost much of their impact with the demise of the melodrama. Picture fair young maid, head thrown back, wrist touching forehead, uttering deathless lines like *Oh, woe is me!* , *Alas!*, and *Horrors!* Then the inevitable closing line as the moustached villain dressed in morning coat and top hat slinks out muttering *Curses! Foiled again!* Oh, well.

Probably the best reason for reading this section is to find something socially acceptable to say when hammer strikes finger.

The interjection changes the pace of the narrative and (hopefully) catches the readers attention.

Function

The function of an interjection is to express a sudden emotion or reaction.

Commonly used interjections

An interjection can be almost anything you choose. Words that emulate sounds, like **Biff! Bam! Boom!** Adjectives that are usually modifiers can be transformed to show high emotion, like **Beautiful! Excellent!**

ah!	**alas!**	**congratulations!**
good grief!	**great!**	**help!**
hey!	**hooray!**	**hurry!**
my goodness!	**never!**	**no!**
no way!	**oh!**	**ouch!**
outstanding!	**ugh!**	**what!?**
wow!		

Punctuation

Normally a strong interjection is punctuated by an exclamation point (!), or perhaps two or three. An exclamation that is part question might be punctuated by both an exclamation point and a question mark (!?). A mild exclamation may take only a comma. More in the section on **punctuation!**

Now that you know all about the parts of speech and how to use them correctly, put what you know into practice.

Begin by paying attention as you read through this book. You'll find lots of things you don't agree with. Newspapers are a great source of grammatical errors, because so much copy is written under such tight time constraints that the editors can be relied on to miss a lot!

Rest assured that once you develop the habit of paying attention and looking critically at what you read, it will become automatic and, at the same time, your vocabulary will miraculously begin to improve.

SENTENCE STRUCTURE

Wouldn't want to insult your intelligence by reminding you that a sentence is a group of words expressing a complete thought or that it begins with a capital letter and ends with a period, question mark or exclamation point. You'll just have to remember that from English 101. And if you've been reading e e cummings, you won't believe me anyway.

There is no embarrassment in telling you that effective communication depends on your ability to construct a sentence well. Simple sentences are just that—simple. As long as you pick the right words, there's not much chance of going wrong. Expressing more complex thoughts, however, requires a bit of organizational skill. You need to be sure that a sentence is laid out in such a way that it transmits exactly the message you intended. Only a word separates from pointing out a fat cow to the boss's wife to calling the boss's wife a fat cow.

Phrases and clauses

So far we've discussed the words that make up the language. Now let's put some of those words together.

A *phrase* is comprised of two or more related words which do not express a complete thought. You might think of it as a snatch of consciousness: a brief glimpse of reality such as a description of something, a bit of action or a place.

The phrase can be a **noun phrase** which is a noun or pronoun and its modifiers,

a man **the woman** **a small child**
the slim runner **a funny clown** **busy baker**
a black and white dog **a singing bird** **a big bug**
the tall tree **the fragrant red rose** **a deserted street**
a dimly lit Italian restaurant **antique furniture**

Noun phrases (continued)

sparkling water	**carpenter's tools**	**smelly trash**
crisp clean air	**bright gold**	**cracked old teapot**

the long black sleek shiny chauffeured limousine

a **verb phrase**, which is a verb with its modifiers,

are digging furiously	**were dancing gracefully**
smiled politely	**spoke loudly**
hurriedly entered	**aimed carelessly**
was eating sparingly	**is nervously tapping**

a **participial phrase**, a participle with its modifiers and complements,

slowly driving the car	**turning the page**
spoken with pride	**walking the dog**
called on the phone	**trembling with anticipation**
taking the time	**swelling with pride**

a **prepositional phrase**, which is a preposition with its object and modifiers,

toward the white house	**up the stairs**
in the back yard	**concerning the latest proposal**
like the blue sea	**over the garden wall**
under the bridge	**during the night**

or an **infinitive phrase**, an infinitive with its complements and modifiers.

to make a touchdown	**to work in the garden**
to begin the beguine	**to touch your toes**
to drive the red car	**to build a bookshelf**
to help a friend study	**to sing like an angel**

Basic Grammar - Putting It All Together

A *clause* is a group of related words which includes the thing talked about (noun, pronoun, or noun substitute) and the action or condition attributed to that thing (verb). A clause may be *independent* or *dependent*.

An **independent clause** expresses a complete thought which can stand alone as a sentence.

A **dependent clause**, also called a **subordinate clause** does not express a complete thought and therefore can not be a sentence by itself. It must be supported by an independent clause.

Think of an *independent* clause as the base of a sentence which expresses a complete thought. The *dependent* or *subordinate* clause serves to modify some portion of that expression and is *dependent on* or *subordinate to* the independent clause.

In the following examples, the dependent clause is underlined.

The board is in agreement regarding the selection of a chairman.

You should run for exercise while you watch your diet.

It sounds like a great band even if it is too loud.

She called yesterday to ask you to drive to the store.

Someone will be held responsible for the mistakes that were made.

Everywhere she went, she spoke with pride.

This violin, which she has been playing for years, is her most treasured possession.

Note that in the next to the last sentence, the dependent clause begins the sentence and in the last sentence, it is in the middle. There are no restrictions on placement of the dependent clause other than that its meaning should be clear. A cleverly turned phrase will pique a reader or listener's interest, but nothing is gained if the meaning is lost.

Essential parts – subject and predicate

The essential parts of a sentence are the subject and the predicate. The listener needs to know *what is the thing we are talking about* and *what do we have to say about that thing?*

The subject, the thing we are talking about

The subject may be the name of a single thing, or it may include the names of several. It may be simply the name, or it may include an elaborate description. Whatever its characteristics, however many or few words comprise it, the entire subject is called the **complete subject**. Following the section above on **phrases** there is a list of noun phrases, any of which qualifies as a complete subject.

The **simple subject** is the noun or pronoun by itself, without any modifiers. It is the simple subject to which the verb, or predicate, refers and which determines the form of the verb (see the section on **Relationships**).

Throughout the earlier sections on **nouns** and **pronouns**, there are numerous examples of both. Taken alone, without modifiers, any one of those nouns or pronouns is a *simple subject*.

The **compound subject** is made up of two or more nouns or noun clauses.

> ***Bob* and *Jill*. . .** ***The children* and *the adults*. . .**
>
> ***The fragrant red rose* and *the big black bug*. . .**
>
> ***Hunting* and *fishing*. . .** ***What you see* and *what you get*. . .**

Elements of the subject

The subject of a sentence is usually one or more nouns or pronouns modified by adjectives and adverbs which comprise the *noun phrase.* The subject may take other forms, however, such as a noun clause, a prepositional phrase, a gerund phrase or an infinitive phrase.

A **noun clause** is a dependent clause which takes the place of a noun and can be the subject of a sentence.

> ***What you see* and *what you get* are two different things.** A compound subject made up of two noun clauses. If the sentence were revised to ***What you see* is what you get** we have a subject *What you see* which is a noun clause and an object of the verb which is also a noun clause.

A **prepositional phrase** often indicates a place in relation to its object so that the subject is not the object itself, but the *somewhere else* described by the prepositional phrase. Clear?

> ***Under the car* is a pool of water.** *Under the car* defines the subject place which neither *under* nor *car* can describe by itself.

A **gerund phrase** is a verbal posing as a noun (you may recall) with its modifiers.

> ***Living well* is the best revenge.** *Living well* is a concept which is the subject for the verb *is.*

An **infinitive phrase** is made up of a verb, usually preceded by *to,* and its modifiers. The infinitive may function as a noun or a verb and can take an adverbial modifier.

> ***To understand completely* is most difficult.** *To understand* is the subject of the verb *is; completely* is an adverb which modifies understand.

The predicate, what we have to say about the subject

The predicate describes the action or condition attributed to the subject. The predicate may make one or a number of assertions about the subject. Like the subject, the attribute may be a single word (a verb) or an elaborate description (a verb with modifiers). The entire predicate, whether a single word or several, is the **complete predicate**. Following the section above on **phrases** there is a list of verb phrases, any of which qualifies as a complete predicate.

The **simple predicate** is the active or linking verb alone, without modifiers. It is the word which describes the action of the subject or links the subject to the expression which describes the condition of the subject.

Within the section on **verbs**, above, there are listed a number of action and linking verbs, any of which qualifies as a simple predicate.

The **compound predicate** is comprised of two or more verbs (simple predicates) joined by a conjunction.

smile and sing	**run and jump**
beg, steal or borrow	**aimed and fired**

ran part of the time and walked part of the time

Elements of the predicate

The predicate of a sentence is comprised of a verb which may take adverbial modifiers as well as direct and indirect objects with their adjectival and adverbial modifiers. (Try to say that five times fast.)

An **action verb** alone is the very minimum form of the predicate.

She *ran.* **He *swam.*** **They *drove.***

A **linking verb**, which does not express action, must have a noun, pronoun or adjective to complete its meaning.

In the following examples, the verb complements are underlined.

The weather here *is* very damp.[*linking verb – is*]

The spring flowers *have* a fragrant aroma.[*linking verb – have*]

This *must have been* a beautiful place.[*linking verb – must have been*]

Our visit *has been* most pleasant.[*linking verb – has been*]

The **direct object** names the recipient of the action.

In the following examples, the direct object is underlined.

> **The lead guitar just *lost* two <u>strings</u>.**[*verb – lost*]
>
> **We *sent* him a <u>message</u>.**[*verb – sent*]
>
> **She *read* the <u>book</u>.**[*verb – read*]

The **indirect object** describes to or for whom the action was taken.

In the following examples, the indirect object is underlined.

> **We *sent* <u>him</u> a message.**[*verb – sent*]
>
> **They *ate* <u>lobster</u> for lunch.**[*verb – ate*]

Sentence types

Here's another item that's tough to work into casual conversation, but, hey, you just might want to know about it – There are four basic styles of sentence depending on the manner in which a thought is expressed.

The **declarative sentence** makes a direct statement.

> **I just made a new batch of root beer.**

The **interrogative sentence** asks a question.

> **Would you like some?**

The **imperative sentence** gives a command or makes a request.

> **Help me carry the keg to the basement.**

The **exclamatory sentence** expresses sudden emotion.

> **Hey! Don't hog it all!**

Simple sentence

All of the examples given on the last two pages are simple sentences. A simple sentence is merely a single independent clause with no dependent clauses. Simple doesn't necessarily mean short, any more than compound or complex means long. A simple sentence can contain a number of phrases or very long phrases which make it seem complicated at first glance. The following example illustrates the point.

The lumber, paneling, siding, roofing shingles and hardware were loaded on the truck and taken to the building site. Six items (a compound subject) were *loaded and taken* (a compound predicate) equals one simple sentence.

Compound sentence

The compound sentence is made up of two or more independent clauses (or simple sentences) which have been combined into a single sentence. The compound sentence does not contain any subordinate clauses.

It's summertime. The living is easy. The fish are swimming. The cotton is high.
It's summertime, the living is easy, the fish are swimming and the cotton is high.

I thought thanksgiving was over. There are turkeys all around me.
I thought thanksgiving was over, and there are turkeys all around me.

Complex sentence

The complex sentence is a simple sentence with one or more dependent clauses.

In the follow examples, dependent clauses are underlined.

That was a beautiful beach we passed on the road.

When you arrive, please call me.

The girl who won the pie eating contest is my sister.

Before you go, kiss the cat good-bye.

Compound-complex sentence

A compound-complex sentence is a compound sentence which also has one or more dependent clauses.
In the following examples, the dependent clauses are underlined.

I thought thanksgiving was over, and the turkeys who rule the world are all around me.

Whenever it is convenient, you wash the car and I'll mow the lawn.

Compound-compound-complex sentence

Just kidding!

Incomplete sentence

Can we discuss this? Do you want to? Lets!

We speak in fragments. In words carefully molded to create a timeless impression like *okay!* *oh, yeah?* *forget it!* *why not?* *says you!* *cream and sugar,* *here!* *on the desk.*

But we don't write like that. Do we? Should we?

Communication is not merely words. If it were, everything written and spoken would be presented in a formal style according to a set of exacting rules. Instead, we change the order of our words and chop up our sentences in an endeavor to communicate our feelings and emotions, and to excite those same feelings in our listener. We want to impart a little of ourselves in our communication, which we often do when speaking. Writing is another matter. We have a chance to look things over, to decide whether or not they sound right, and to make changes. The results are frequently stiff and formal when that is not the impression we mean to convey. Whenever practicable, therefore, we should write the way we speak in order to give our writing a more personal touch and to keep it interesting.

Writing in the manner we speak requires that we regularly overlook or at least stretch the conventional rules. This section on **sentence structure** begins, *Wouldn't want to insult your intelligence. . . .*It could have said, *I wouldn't* or the editorial, *We wouldn't* or that great unknown entity, *Nobody would*. Whatever it *could* have been, the subject is superfluous to the point of the sentence. Some might concede that the subject is understood, while others would discard it as *not a sentence* and take off two points.

The reason for all of this preamble is not to advocate incomplete sentences, but to acknowledge that we may legitimately write sentences which seem incomplete from someone else's point of view, and we must always be alert to the danger of incomplete, *meaningless* or *misleading* sentences.

Whenever you attempt to communicate in a cryptic style, you run the risk of assuming too much. If a colleague enters your office with a cup of coffee in one hand and a sheaf of papers in the other while you are busy on the phone you might fire off a quick, "On the desk!" and turn away. What you don't realize until you turn quickly and spill it, is that the coffee, not the pile of papers, was left for you.

> **The door slammed and the calculator fell off the desk. He yelped in pain as it hit his foot.**

Not the error of incomplete sentences, but certainly one of assuming too much. What hit his foot, the door or the calculator? (Or is the reader being presumptuous by assuming that this is not explained earlier or later in the narrative?)

Let's take a look at a brief business communication:

> **Dear Ms. Rogers,**
>
> **I received a message that you called on the 25th at 4:30 PM.**
>
> **Your order for 25 widgets shipped today, the 26th.**
>
> **I do hope that this meets with your approval.**
>
> **I am sending this with my kindest personal regards.**
>
> **S. Kinsky**

Supposing, instead, that Mr. Kinsky dashed off a really brief note.

> **Ms. Rogers–**
>
> **Got your message. Order shipped. Hope you approve.**
>
> **Regards, S. Kinsky**

This sort of abbreviated informal communication is not uncommon, so it seems perfectly acceptable even though there is not a sentence in sight. However, Mr. Kinsky is not aware that there was another phone message and a letter, each containing different instructions and neither of which he received. Nor is he aware that his undated fax message didn't get through until the next day.

Let's try again.

> **Ms, Rogers–**
>
> **Received your phone message of the 25th at 4.30.**
>
> **Shipped your order for 25 widgets on the 26th.**
>
> **Hoping you approve.**
>
> **Best regards,**
>
> **S. Kinsky**

If you are uncomfortable writing incomplete sentences, by all means, avoid them. On the other hand, a so-called incomplete sentence often conveys a message which is more personal or dramatic. Just be sure it conveys the correct message, and don't overdo it.

RELATIONSHIPS

Relationships in grammar refer to the consistency of word forms used in a phrase, a clause and a sentence. Few things in a narrative stand out so much as a lack of agreement between the elements of a sentence.

Agreement of subject and verb

The verb should always agree with its subject in person and number. This means that if the subject is in the first person, the verb must be in the first person and if the subject is singular the verb must be singular.

Following is the conjugation of the verb **to be**, the most used and unfortunately, the most irregular of verbs; however, there is a pattern to its forms which makes them relatively easy to remember.

	Singular	Plural
Present tense		
First person —speaker	I **am**	We **are**
Second person —spoken to	You **are**	You **are**
Third person —spoken of	He, she, it **is**	They **are**
Past tense		
First person —speaker	I **was**	We **were**
Second person —spoken to	You **were**	You **were**
Third person —spoken of	He, she, it **was**	They **were**
Future tense		
First person —speaker	I **shall be**	We **shall be**
Second person —spoken to	You **will be**	You **will be**
Third person —spoken of	He, she, it **will be**	They **will be**

Note that ***are*** is the plural form for all three persons in the present tense and that ***were*** is the plural form for all three persons in the past tense; that ***be*** is the plural for all three persons in the future tense with the helper ***shall*** in the first person and ***will*** in the second and third. Note also that the singular forms are the same as the plurals with just four exceptions: ***am*** is the first person present singular, ***is*** is the third person present singular and ***was*** in the first and third person past singular.

Following is the conjugation of the verb **call** which is also set up to make its pattern easily discernible.

	Singular	Plural
Present tense		
First person —speaker	I **call**	We **call**
Second person —spoken to	You **call**	You **call**
Third person —spoken of	He, she, it **calls**	They **call**
Past tense		
First person —speaker	I **called**	We **called**
Second person —spoken to	You **called**	You **called**
Third person —spoken of	He, she, it **called**	They **called**
Future tense		
First person —speaker	I **shall call**	We **shall call**
Second person —spoken to	You **will call**	You **will call**
Third person —spoken of	He, she, it **will call**	They **will call**

Call is a regular verb and, as you can see, the conjugation is much simpler than it is for *to be.* All forms in the present tense are the same except for the third person singular. The past tense is one form, as is the future tense with the addition of the modifiers, *shall* and *will.*

Refer to the section on **verbs** for a more complete conjugation of the verbs *to be* and *call,* the rule for forming the past tense of regular verbs and a list of the principal parts of the most common irregular verbs.

It seems simple enough to follow the conjugation tables above, but more complicated expressions require some special considerations, particularly when the correct form doesn't sound right.

Verb with a compound subject

Usually the compound subject joins two or more elements and is therefore plural.

John and Robert *are* driving to Mexico.

When two or more elements are described as alternatives, that is, one or the other, the subject is singular.

Neither John nor Robert *is* driving.

Either John or Robert *is* driving.

Sometimes two elements which are joined refer to the same person or thing and are singular.

The wife and mother *is* also a distinguished lawyer.

Sometimes the elements joined form a unit and are a *dilemma.*

Meat and potatoes *is* the customary evening meal.

Meat and potatoes *are* the customary evening meal.

Potatoes and meat *is* the customary evening meal.

If you consider *meat and potatoes* as a single entity, the first sentence is correct. There is a school of thought, however, which says that when there are two or more items in the subject which disagree in number, the verb should agree with the nearest subject as in the second and third sentences above. It's up to you; pick the rule you like or the sentence which you think sounds best.

A word of caution – Make sure that it is clear to your audience whether you are referring to one person or two.

The president and chief operating officer *attends* all of the board meetings. Singular verb – implies that a single person fills both positions.

The president and chief operating officer *attend* all of the board meetings. Plural verb – presumes that we are talking about two different people or the writer selected the wrong verb form.

The president and chief operating officer both *attend* all of the board meetings. Meaning is clarified by the use of *both.*

Elements modified by a limiting adjective such as *each* or *every* are singular.

Each car and each truck *is* licensed separately.

Every doctor and every lawyer *is* not a crook.

An adverb such as *also, often, perhaps* or *usually* which precedes one of two singular elements joined by *and* modifies the verb in relation to that one element. The verb is therefore single, inasmuch as it relates to each element separately.

The car, and also the truck, *is* to be washed.

One egg, and often a spoonful of grits, *is* served for breakfast.

The politician, and perhaps his aide, *is* telling the truth.

John, and usually his wife, *attends* the conventions.

Naturally, if each element is plural the verb is plural.

Eggs, and often grits, *are* served for breakfast.

Modifying phrases

Modifying phrases which intervene between the subject and the verb never change the relationship between the two. Such phrases should be ignored when attempting to determine that the subject and verb are in agreement. Intervening phrases in the following sentences are shown in italics.

John and Robert, *after a quick trip home to pack,* are driving to Mexico.

The wife and mother, *holder of several degrees,* is also a distinguished lawyer.

Meat and potatoes, *plain but nourishing,* is the customary evening meal.

Each car and each truck, *regardless of the number of owners,* is licensed separately.

Every doctor and every lawyer, *regardless of what people say,* is not a crook.

When a plural isn't a plural

Up until now we've assumed that we can easily identity a noun as singular or plural with the possible exception of *meat and potatoes.* There are (naturally) other, similar combinations like *ham and eggs* or *nut and bolt,* which need to be considered in the context of the sentence.

A nut and bolt *is* required for assembly.

A nut and bolt *is*(?) on the workbench.

A nut and (a) bolt *are* on the workbench.

There are nouns like *scissors, trousers* and *pliers* which are plural and take a plural verb. Nobody knows why. However, if you say a *pair of scissors* or a *pair of trousers* or a *pair of pliers* which sounds like *more* than one they become singular. Nobody knows why that is, either.

The trousers *are* on the floor.

The pair of trousers *is* on the floor.

There are other nouns which are plural in form, but singular in meaning, such as news, politics, economics and mathematics.

The news *is* all good.

Politics *is* the name of the game.

Economics *is* far from an exact science.

Mathematics *is* the science of numbers.

Proper names of individuals and companies are usually singular even though they take a plural form.

Mr. Brothers *is* an excellent physician.

Chrysler Motors *is* fighting hard to compete.

Collective nouns take a singular verb when considering the noun as a cohesive group and a plural verb when considering its diversity. (See **Collective nouns.**)

Weights and measures and other stuff

Nouns which express quantity, weight or volume may be singular or plural depending on the context.

Five dollars *is* all I have left. Singular —*five dollars* is one unit.

Five dollar bills *are* all I have. Plural —*bill* is a unit; *five . . . bills* is more than one or plural.

Ten pounds *is* enough to fill the bag. Singular — *ten pounds* is a unit.

Half of the land *has* been ravaged. Singular —*the land* is a unit.

Half of the workers *have* left. Plural — *half of the workers* implies more than one person. (What do you say if you started with only two workers? Beats me!)

Some of the sandwiches *are* left. Plural — *some of the sandwiches* implies more than one sandwich.

Most of the punch *is* gone. Singular —*the punch* is a unit.

Pronoun with antecedent

Remember antecedents? That's the noun which is later represented by a pronoun. **The pronoun must agree with its antecedent in gender, person and number.**

Gender agreement

Gender agreement is uncomplicated in most situations.

Bob showed us *his* new car. Janet showed us *her* new car.

Janet and Bob showed us *their* new car.

Note that the plural makes no distinction by gender. If, however, the pronoun refers to only one of the nouns connected by *and*, the pronoun takes the gender of its antecedent.

Janet and Bob showed us *her* father's new car.

In the case of a limiting conjunction, such as *or* or *nor*, there are choices: offer both options, let the pronoun agree with the nearest antecedent, eliminate the pronoun or change the noun form.

No man or woman has ever given so freely of *his or her* time.

No man or woman has ever given so freely of *her* time.

No woman or man has ever given so freely of *his* time.

No man or woman has ever given so freely of time.

None have ever given so freely of their time.

The first three statements are decidedly awkward. The simplest solution to this problem, and most like it, is reconstruction. The fifth sentence will usually make the point. If it is necessary to mention *man or woman* elimination of the pronoun as in the fourth sentence loses nothing. Incidentally, if the object of the verb were tangible, such as a car, the indefinite article could be comfortably substituted for the pronoun.

No man or woman has ever given a car.

Agreement of person

Our motto is *Don't change persons in mid-stream.* A sentence should not start out in one person and end in another.

If anyone wants to join me, *you're* welcome to come along, doesn't cut it. **If anyone wants to join me, *he's* welcome to come along,** is correct, but it runs into that old gender problem. Why not just say, **Anyone who wants to join me is welcome to come along?**

When a pronoun follows two or more connected nouns and is referring to only one of them or neither of them, be sure that it is understood what the pronoun is referring to.

Neither Janet nor Joan are living in *her* new apartment. Say, what? Whose new apartment? Perhaps *her* relates to an earlier reference and if it doesn't, this sentence should be reconsidered.

PUNCTUATION

Punctuation is how you tell the reader when to take a breath.

Not far from the truth. Correct punctuation helps your reader comprehend your message. It also gives you some control of the pace of the narrative to further convey your feelings. And it you didn't tell some readers when to breath, they just might explode.

Uses of the period

The period is used to end a sentence, to end an abbreviation and to punctuate the elements in an outline.

End of a sentence

The period is used to indicate the end of a sentence not otherwise ended by a question mark, exclamation point or the period following an abbreviation.

It is also be used to indicate the end of an incomplete thought injected into a narrative.

> **As the car turned the corner, she let out a scream. *A high pitched, piercing shriek.* Then she fainted.**

Abbreviations

The period is used to indicate an abbreviation, although it is optional for some. See **Abbreviations**, in the reference section.

Outlines

In outlines, the period is used optionaJlly after letters or numbers designating sections and sub-sections.

The question mark

The question mark is used to indicate an interrogative and to mark textual data as questionable.

To mark the end of an interrogative

The question mark is used to mark the end of any sentence that asks a question (no kidding?), including a question in a quotation,

"Is it time to leave?" she asked.

or a declarative sentence formed as a question.

It's time to leave?

In imperative sentence which makes a request will take either a question mark or a period.

Will you please leave?

Will you please leave.

See also **Exclamation point**, below.

Within a sentence

The question mark is used optionally within a sentence to add emphasis to a multiple query.

Do you want to do this in three easy lessons, one hard one or not at all?

Do you want to do this in three easy lessons? one hard one? or not at all?

The question mark may be used in parenthesis within a sentence to show that there is some question about the information which precedes it.

I expect to arrive at noon (?) on Tuesday.

The exclamation point

The exclamation point is used to mark the end of an exclamatory sentence.

> **Watch out for that tree!** (George! George! George of the jungle.)
> **Will you please leave!**

The exclamation point is used after an interjection or after any word used as an interjection.

> **Hey!** **Excellent!** **Help!** **Beautiful!**

The exclamation point adds emphasis to imply a sense of urgency and to capture the reader's attention.

> **Look! Good grief! Get out of here!**

The interrobang

The interrobang is a combination of question mark and exclamation point to emphasize those statements which engender both wonderment and a strong emotional response: not quite a question, but certainly questionable.

> **She did what?!**
> **A recent study financed by the government reached the conclusion that people don't like to go to the dentist because they fear pain?!**

[Author's note: The interrobang was created by the author of a book by the same name. My copy was passed along and efforts to locate another have been to no avail. Any information about the book or the author would be appreciated and can be sent to the publisher of this book. JR.]

The uses of the comma

The comma is used to separate elements within a sentence, follow the opening of an informal letter, follow the closing of any letter, separate the elements in a date, separate the elements in an address, separate a persons name from his or her title and to section off large numbers.

Separating elements within a sentence

Here's one you are going to have to think about. Like mother said, it's for your own good. There are a number of rules which recount in great detail precisely how and when to use a comma. Most of them can be condensed into three simple rules.

Rule #1: Use a comma *only when it is necessary* to assure that the message will not be misunderstood.

Rule #2: Don't use a comma if it is *not necessary* and especially if it might obscure the meaning of a sentence.

Rule #3: Never forget Rule #2.

The comma should be used to **set off any phrase or clause which might otherwise be misread**. Here's the part where you have to concentrate. Avoid the temptation to drop in a bunch of commas just to break up a long sentence. Take a look at the sentence and try to recognize how it might be misread. Look for words and phrases which are incidental to the flow of the main body of the sentence and need to be set off by commas. Look at long sentences which have independent clauses which need separation. Find the natural breaks in the flow of a sentence; the places where a reader might pause to grasp a concept before moving on. Following are some tips to help you along.

Separate dependent clauses and phrases which are incidental to the main body of the sentence.

It's difficult to discuss politics, *even local politics,* without getting emotional.

After the party, *an elegant affair,* they went to the theater.

Separate independent clauses in a compound sentence, particularly if they are long and divergent.

The meeting lasted most of the afternoon, and they had to face the long drive home.

He learned his craft in the small theaters scattered throughout the country, but now he was playing Broadway.

Use a comma to separate a word which interrupts the flow of a sentence such as a mild interjection or a connective which modifies a clause even if it is at the beginning of a sentence. See **conjunctions** for a list of the modifiers.

The team fought hard to keep up the pace and, *consequently,* they won.

***Furthermore,* the movie was lousy.**

I can't believe you mean that, *Susan.*

Do not interrupt the flow of thought or split a clause by placing a comma between the subject and its verb or between the verb and its object. **The team fought hard, to keep up the pace and . . .** Wrong!

Do not use a comma to replace a conjunction. **The team fought hard to keep up the pace, consequently they won.** Wrong!

Do use a comma to follow the connective when a semicolon is used as the conjunction.

The team fought hard to keep up the pace; consequently, they won.

Do use your own good judgment! Read the sentence over after it has been punctuated. Don't hesitate to take out any commas that interrupt the flow unnecessarily and don't hesitate to add a comma if the sentence sounds like a runaway freight train.

Elements in a series

For the sake of clarity, words and clauses in a series need to be separated.

> **The dress comes in four colors: aqua, pink, orange or black.**
>
> **He set out to streamline the office, trim the budget, and increase the output.**
>
> **She competes in the 50 yard dash, hurdles and cross country run.**

The final comma before the conjunction is optional. Use if you need to for clarity or just because you like it. Other than for clarity, whichever form you adopt should be consistent throughout your document.

Independent modifiers

Independent modifiers are those modifiers which are not dependent on or directly associated with any other modifiers; two or more which modify the same member should be separated by a comma.

> **The *long, black* station wagon drove down the *dusty, winding, dirt* road.**

Quotations

Use a comma to separate a direct quotation from its source unless it is superseded by other punctuation.

> **She said, "I want to see the play."**
>
> **"I want to see the play," she said.**
>
> **"May I go to the play?" she asked.** Comma superseded by the question mark.

Opening and closing of a letter

Traditionally, the opening of an informal letter is followed by a comma,

Dear John, **Dear Susan,**

and the closing of any letter is followed by a comma.

Very truly yours, **Sincerely yours,**

Dates and addresses

The parts of dates and addresses are separated by commas.

January 27, 1993	**27 January, 1993**
Memorial Day, 1992	**the fourteenth of April, 1992**
2030 Belle Vue Way, #81	**118 East 28th Street, Suite #408**
Tallahassee, FL 32304	**New York, NY 10016**

Grammatical conventions aside, the Postal Service has instituted an incentive program for business which precludes all punctuation on address labels. Undoubtedly, financial considerations will dominate, so that before long it may be commonplace to eliminate punctuation from all addresses which doesn't seem to be in any way detrimental to aesthetics or function.

Names and titles

Titles after a name are normally separated by a comma, as are the elements of a name when they are reversed.

John M. Chavin, M.D.	**James Mahoney, Esq.**
Chavin, John M.	**Mahoney, James**

Numbers

Commas are used to separate the thousands in large numbers.

81,548 **7,071,639** **346,931**

The colon

The colon is used at the end of a clause to indicate that a word, a list, a phrase or another clause is to follow. It is used after the opening of a business letter and it is used after a division of time or literary reference to indicate that a subdivision follows.

The colon is used to end a clause introducing a list of items.

The parts of speech are as follows: Nouns, Pronouns, Verbs, Adjectives, Adverbs, Prepositions, Conjunctions and Interjections.

The colon is also used to highlight a clause to follow.

As you go through life, remember one thing: The most humiliating criticism is indifference.

Traditionally, the colon has followed the salutation in the opening of a business letter.

Dear Sir: **To whom it may concern:** **Dear Madam:**

Dear Sir or Madam, as the case may be: (My personal favorite)

Although some companies cling to this form, most prefer the personalized greeting followed by a comma. Now used primarily for occupant mailings, the demise of this very impersonal form has been hastened by the personalized computer letter.

The colon is used after a division of time, literature, etc. to indicate that a subdivision follows.

3:45 P.M. **15:45:17**

Isaiah 65:17 **Psalms 23:1**

Semicolon

The semicolon is used in place of a conjunction or in place of a comma.

In place of a conjunction

The semicolon is used to join two independent clauses with or without a modifying connective.

> **Sharon has a managerial position; she enjoys the rights and privileges which go with the responsibility.**

> **Sharon has a managerial position; therefore, she enjoys the rights and privileges which go with the responsibility.**

In place of a comma

There are situations which call for a comma where the use of a semicolon is preferred in the interest of clarity. Think of it as two-tier punctuation with the semicolon as the stronger element of the two.

A sentence containing a combination of incidental words, lists of words, clauses, or phrases which requires a comma before a conjunction might be clearer if a semicolon were used before the conjunction.

> **We carefully planned the trip, packed the car and were ready to set out for the campground; but our plans went awry when the car, an old Buick with failing brakes, refused to start.** A comma could be used before *but*; however, the semicolon is a stronger indicator in contrast to the commas, and further serves notice to your reader to take a well-earned breath. If the sentence were **We carefully planned the trip, packed the car and were ready to set out for the campground, but our plans went awry** and ended there, the comma is not a bad choice.

A list of phrases or clauses is best separated by semicolons, particularly if the clauses are punctuated by commas.

> **Among the things we packed for the trip was the small, green tent; two sleeping bags; a selection of fresh and freeze-dried foods; the lantern, with fuel for two nights; an assortment of pots, pans and eating utensils; and a change of clothes.**

As with the comma, don't overuse the semicolon and don't hesitate to use it when it clarifies your meaning.

The apostrophe

The apostrophe is used to show possession, to show plurals for symbols and to indicate missing letters in a contraction.

Showing possession

The apostrophe is used with *s* to show the possessive form of nouns which do not end in *s*.

one man's hat	**many men's hats**	**that woman's hat**
two women's hats	**this lawyer's case**	
the day's end	**the dog's bone**	**this theory's premise**

The apostrophe is used alone to show the possessive form of nouns which end in *s*.

the pliers' jaws   **the scissors' edge**   **Mr. Jones' car**

two authors' books   **those hens' eggs**

Singular nouns ending in *s*, such as *Jones* may also take an apostrophe *s* ending: it's the writer's choice.

The possessive of more than one taken together as a unit is shown by making the last member possessive.

Joan and Bob's house is on the outskirts of the city.

The restaurant and bar's Oriental decor is striking.

To indicate individual ownership, make each member possessive.

Joan's and Bob's houses are outside the city.

Plurals for symbols

The plural for individual letters, numbers and signs are indicated by apostrophe s.

Mind your p's and q's.

They are at 6's and 7's.

Can we use #'s to indicate pounds?

Contractions

The apostrophe is used to indicate the position of missing elements in contractions.

don't	**aren't**	**won't**	**haven't**
the summer of '42		**in November '86**	

About quotation marks

Quotation marks are used to set off direct quotations; titles of articles, poems, works of art and such; and special words or phrases such as slang, technical terms and nicknames.

Direct quotations

Only the exact words of the speaker or writer are enclosed in quotation marks.

She said, "I want to go, but only if we leave by dawn."

"There is nothing to fear, but fear itself."

Quotation marks are omitted for any quotation or portion thereof which is quoted indirectly.

She said that she wants to go, but "only if we leave by dawn."

She said that she wants to go, but only if we leave by dawn.

Either of the above two examples is correct, but only the second part of the sentence may be enclosed in quotation marks because they quote the speaker's exact words.

Punctuation within quotations

A *period* or a *comma* is always placed before the closing quotation mark.

John said, "The report is due this week."

"The report is due this week," said John.

The speaker is always separated from the quotation by a comma whether at the beginning of the sentence as in the first example above, or ringed by the quote as in the following example.

"The report is due next week," said Joan, "and it must be delivered on time."

Note that the quotation starts with a capital letter, but the second part of a split quotation does not, unless it is a new sentence.

"The report is due next week," said Joan. "It must be delivered on time."

The ***question mark*** or ***exclamation point*** is enclosed within the quotation marks when it applies only to the quote and outside the quotation marks when it applies to the entire sentence. Punctuation is not required within the quotation marks when punctuation is placed after the closing quotation mark.

"When do you need to leave?" he asked.

Who said, "I think, therefore I am"?

Any other punctuation in the sentence remains the same as it would be without a direct quotation.

Titles

Titles of short works such as magazine articles, essays, songs, poems, paintings and sculpture are set off by quotation marks. The rule of thumb is that anything long enough to appear in book form including plays, opera, collections of art, etc. are underlined or printed in italics. All other titles are set off by quotation marks.

Extraneous material in quotes

Quotation marks are used to direct attention to special words in a sentence such as slang, technical terms, colloquialisms, nicknames and material referred to elsewhere in the sentence.

Note that such highlighting may also be achieved by underlining, or printing in italics or bold face.

Single quotation marks

Single quotation marks are used in the same manner as double quotes to set off material already contained in double quotes – in effect, to set off a quotation within a quotation.

"I think she said, 'be ready by noon,'" Tom reported.

The hyphen

The hyphen is used to join the parts of certain compound words.

mother-in-law **pre-Columbian** **weak-headed**

It may also be used to create an expression comprised of several words which are to be taken as a unit.

cock-of-the-walk **holier-than-thou**

A hyphen is placed after the syllable of a word divided at the end of a line to indicate that the balance of the word follows on the next line.

The dash

A dash indicates a break in the flow of a sentence, usually to insert a parenthetical remark or for emphasis.

When I passed the house – the one at the end of the block – it was empty.

There's only one thing that can save us – Superchicken.

Parentheses and brackets

Parentheses are used to separate incidental information which would otherwise interrupt the flow of the sentence.

We set out on July 27 (Susan's birthday) to tour the area.

Parentheses are often used to separate confirming numbers in a sentence.

The admission price is eight dollars ($8.00) for advance reservations and ten dollars ($10.00) the day of the show.

Parentheses set off letters or numbers which are used in a sentence to enumerate items in a list.

> **Our goal is to see that you (a) understand the proper use of English and (b) use your knowledge to communicate effectively in the language.**

Parenthesis may be used to indicate lower level subdivisions in an outline. For example, the first, second, third, etc. levels might be, in order, I (Roman numerals), A, 1, a, (1), (a).

Incidentally, *parentheses* is plural; one (parenthes?) is a *parenthesis.*

Brackets are used to insert editorial commentary; that is, to indicate that the material inserted is not a part of the original material.

> **He said that they [the Jones family] have only lived in this area for six months.**

> **The letter mentioned, "there [sic] inability to cope."** The word *sic,* Latin for *thus,* is used in this context to show that the preceding word or phrase has been quoted verbatim and in the opinion of the one making the insertion is incorrect or at least questionable.

Indicating omissions - the ellipsis

The ellipsis (*plural* ellipses) is a series of three dots (or periods) used to indicate the omission of a word or words. When used at the end of a sentence, it is followed by the ending punctuation.

> **She said, "The report . . . is unacceptable."** The missing material is descriptive information which is not germane to the writer's point: that the report is unacceptable.

To improve readability - leaders

A line of periods, called leaders, is used to track the eye across the page of an index, a tabulated page or such.

Units sold this year 10,462

Defective units returned 9,248

CAPITALIZATION

The rules for capitalization are relatively clear and easy to follow; however, the writer often has options because there is no way to spell out every contingency, and even if it were possible, someone would disagree.

Words and phrases

The basic rule for capitalization specifies that proper nouns and adjectives are to be capitalized and that common nouns and adjectives are not capitalized. There are, however, many proper nouns which have become common, common nouns used with or as proper nouns, and titles of respect which are capitalized common nouns. Let's try to sort it out.

Names of individuals

The name of a person, whether real or fictional, is always capitalized.

John Jones　　Suzy Smith　　Mark Twain
Samuel Clemens　　Alfred E. Neumann

Titles

Titles or degrees which precede or follow a name are always capitalized.

Mr. John Jones **Rev. Suzy Smith** **Hon. Mark Twain**

Samuel Clemens, Esq. **Alfred E. Neumann, Ph.D.**

Ordinarily, a title such as reverend, president or doctor is capitalized only when used in conjunction with a proper name; however, titles of position or respect may be capitalized at the writer's discretion when the title clearly refers to a particular person.

Our President will be out of the office all week.

We're playing golf with the Doctor in the morning.

Organizations

The proper name of an organization is always capitalized.

Chamber of Commerce **Mothers Against Drunk Driving**

Florida State University **Justice Department**

Bank of America **Ford Motor Company**

A department within an organization is capitalized at the writer's discretion (or the company's edict).

Art Department or art department

Sales Department or sales department

Shipping Department or shipping department

Products

Names of products which are trade names are capitalized.

Coca Cola **Cadillac Seville** **Mountain Dew**

Many trade names such as Kleenex and Vaseline are commonly used generically; technically, however, they refer only to the product of the company which owns the rights to the name and should be capitalized.

Works of art

The words in the title of a work of art: painting, sculpture, music, play, etc. are capitalized except for articles, prepositions and conjunctions unless they are the first word in the title. *The* used before the title is not capitalized unless it is at the beginning of a sentence or part of the title.

Whistler's Mother **the Mona Lisa**

The Glorious Victory of the Sloop Santa Maria

Death of a Salesman **Swan Lake**

Publications and documents

The words in the title of a publication, an article, an essay, or a document are capitalized except for articles, prepositions and conjunctions unless they are the first word in the title. *The* used before the title is not capitalized unless it is at the beginning of a sentence or part of the title.

War and Peace **Poor Richard's Almanac**

The Sea and the Jungle

Zen Flesh, Zen Bones

the Declaration of Independence

My Life and Hard Times

Academics

School subjects are not capitalized unless they are a word which would be capitalized under another rule or are the name of a specific course.

economics	**Economics 101**
French	**Intermediate French**
programming	**Programming in COBOL**
computers	**Computer Basics**

Place names

The name of a building, monument, place or region is capitalized. The directions north, east, south and west are not usually capitalized, but may be when used to reference a specific region. *The* used before a name is not capitalized unless it is at the beginning of a sentence or part of the name.

Empire State Building **Hancock Building**
Sears Tower **Eiffel Tower**
Vietnam War Memorial **Great Wall of China**
Jefferson Memorial **Washington Monument**
Tiger Balm Gardens **the Gaza Strip**
Times Square **Little Italy**
Monroe Township **the Hoosier State**
the Wild West **the Eastern Seaboard**
the Orient **the East** (referring to the Orient)
Rocky Mountains **England and France**
French Riviera **Grand Canyon**
the South Pole **the Battery** (an area in New York City)

Events and Holidays

Special events, historic periods and holidays are capitalized.

the Winter Olympics **the World Series**
Bach Festival **Senior Prom**
Nicene Council **War of 1812**
Elizabethan Age **Roaring Twenties**
Christmas Day **New Year's Eve**
Labor Day **Thanksgiving**

Religious references

Most religious references are capitalized including names of religions, denominations, religious groups, deities and sacred works.

Christian	**Judaic**	**Islam**
Hindu	**Buddhist**	**Shinto**
Presbyterian	**Mormon**	**Methodist**
Lutheran	**Seventh Day Adventist**	
Holy Trinity Church	**Southern Baptist Convention**	
Temple Beth-El	**Missouri Synod**	**God**
Jehovah	**Jesus**	**Yahweh**
Holy Ghost	**Allah**	**Shiva**
Almighty	**Astarte**	**Zarathustra**
Holy Bible	**Koran**	**the Vedas**
Apostles Creed	**Sermon on the Mount**	

Names of rites and services are generally not capitalized.

worship service	**baptism**	**seder**
matins	**confession**	**bar mitzvah**

Pronouns referring to deities are capitalized at the writer's discretion.

In His service	**Jesus and his ministry**

Scientific and technical terms

The rules for terms of a scientific or technical nature are the same as for other terms: capitalize only proper nouns or adjectives. Doubtless many of the terms are unfamiliar, and the only recourse is a good dictionary.

Relationships

References to a relative are not capitalized unless they are used with a person's name or used in place of the person's name.

Cousin Edith **Uncle John**

Let me help you, Mother.

My sister is visiting this week.

Calendar

The names of the days and months are capitalized; whereas the seasons of the year are not unless they are personified.

Monday		**Tuesday**	**Wednesday**
January		**February**	**March**
winter	**spring**	**summer**	**fall**

Where is Winter, with his icy chill?

Compound and hyphenated names

Compound names which include a proper noun or adjective require that the proper name be capitalized, but not the common noun.

Darjeeling tea	**Irish linen**
Italian spaghetti	**French pastry**
Swiss chocolate	**Turkish bath**
Cincinnati chili	**New Orleans jazz**
Florida oranges	**Asian flu**

Hyphenated names are capitalized.

Schleswig-Holstein **Jacques-Louis David**

Proper nouns and adjectives with prefixes are capitalized, but the prefixes are not capitalized.

pro-American	**anti-French**
pre-Cambrian	**ex-President**

Capitalization in a sentence

The first word in a sentence is always capitalized, whether a complete sentence, a fragment or an interjection.

The pronoun *I* is always capitalized.

The first word in a direct quotation is capitalized if the quotation is itself a complete sentence.

He asked, "If you're so busy, how come you have so much time to tell me about it?"

When a complete sentence follows a colon, the first word of that sentence should be capitalized.

Please remember this: Fear of failure is worse than failure.

Capitalizing to show respect or for emphasis

Usually, reference to high office is capitalized to show respect.

the Queen	**the President**	**the Pope**

As indicated above, we may capitalize lesser titles when they clearly refer to a particular individual. We may also want to capitalize to show respect or emphasize the involvement of an unnamed individual, group or thing.

The Accountants reported that we are not over budget.

The Engineers report that we are on schedule.

There is nothing wrong with the Printing Press; it is the Paper that created the problem.

Just don't overdo it or the emphasis value will be lost.

NUMBERS

There is an abundance of rules for dealing with numbers in text and, as with most things, there is no universal agreement. The most important criterion is to protect the readability of your document and to be consistent.

Figures or spelled out

There is a guideline which says that a number should be spelled out if it is less than ten or divisible by ten.

one	**two**	**three**	**four**	**five**
six	**seven**	**eight**	**nine**	**ten**
twenty	**thirty**	**forty**	**fifty**	**sixty, etc.**

According to this rule, *one million, nine hundred forty-seven thousand, six hundred and eighty* should be written out, but it's doubtful that the creator of the rule had that in mind.

Another rule suggests that it is acceptable to write out any number of up to two words, which sounds reasonable.

All rules recommend consistency; that is, all of the numbers in a sentence *in series or related* should be either written as figures or spelled out. That is the best piece of advice contained in any rule.

Rules aside, common sense should prevail. The way in which numbers are expressed will depend largely on how many numbers there are, how large the numbers are and the type of document in which they are appearing.

Round numbers

Numbers which are approximations are usually written out to avoid confusing them with exact numbers.

> **There are about three thousand rules of grammar, but most people can agree on just two. Unfortunately they can't agree on which two.**

Approximations which would be too wordy if written out may be expressed in newspaper headline style; i.e., a number followed by the word *million, billion,* etc.

> **The population of New York City is approximately 7.1 million.**

Numbers in combination

Often a sentence will contain more than one number or set of numbers which relate to different items. Each number, or set of numbers should be assessed individually as to how they will be presented with consistency, not only in the one sentence, but in any related sentences in the narrative.

> **We have six runners for the 100-yard dash.**

> **Our inventory includes ten 25-watt bulbs, eight 50-watt bulbs and fourteen 100-watt bulbs.**

Numbers beginning a sentence

If it is at all avoidable, don't begin a sentence with a number. If, however, it is necessary, spell out the number at the start of the sentence regardless of how the rest of the numbers in that sentence are presented.

A FEW SPELLING RULES

Reading this section will not make you an expert speller. It will, however, help you to become a better speller. Modern English, including scientific and technical terms, comprises well over a million words. We may have a nodding acquaintance with as many as 50,000 of those words, but we use, on a regular basis, a few thousand at most and are plagued by the spelling of a few hundred. Learning about the construction of words alerts you to patterns which tell when spelling is most likely right, and allows concentration on those most likely wrong. Don't be put off by the meager examples in each section. They are there only to illustrate the point; be assured that there are always more words which follow a rule than there are exceptions.

As much as I hate to admit it, your old English teacher was right: If you don't know how to spell a word, look it up. Naturally, if you don't know the first letter of the word, you may have to look in more than one place. Sure, it's a pain, but if you are really interested in using the right word, consider one other thing your teacher probably forgot to tell you. Looking up the word can often prevent a misunderstanding. For example, it's good news if you *brake* your car, but not so good if you *break* it. Among those words often misspelled are a number of similar sounding words which mean quite different things such as *affect/effect, ascent/assent, adapt/adopt, altar/alter and accept/except.* See what I mean?

Dual spelling

Matters are further complicated by the words which have acceptable dual spellings. Common practice within our own sphere of influence (frequently requiring approval of instructor or supervisor) generally dictates which form we use. Many options such as *programme* are seldom used in America. The older forms of *-our* and *-re* as the last syllable of a word have generally been replace by *-or* and *-er* respectively. We tend to prefer *labor* to *labour, color* to *colour* and *center* to *centre,* but we use *theatre* as often as *theater*. Perhaps those in the theyatuh feel it smacks of culture. Common practice, however, does require consistency; whichever spelling you choose should be used all of the time.

acknowledgment acknowledgement

adviser advisor	**analog analogue**
caliber calibre	**catalog catalogue**
center centre	**encase incase**
enclose inclose	**encyclopedia encyclopaedia**
endorse indorse	**enquire inquire**
enrollment enrolment	**fledgling fledgeling**
gipsy gypsy	**gray grey**
judgment judgement	**maneuver manoeuvre**
medieval mediaeval	**naturalise naturalize**
orthopedic orthopaedic	**practice practise**
pretense pretence	**reflection reflexion**
smolder smoulder	**theater theatre**

Pronunciation

Looking up a word occasionally is the mark of a conscientious, careful writer; looking up the same word over and over again may imply something quite different. These few pages are a small effort to assist in the quest to be identified as something other than "quite different". Like most of us, you have millions of unused brain cells lying fallow; it is time to put them to work.

Careless pronunciation is a trap. Perhaps you want to describe something clever or inventive as *ingenious*, only you get careless and pick up *ingenuous*. *Ingenuous* means frank or sincere. Not bad, really, but not what you wanted to say.

Pronunciation is definitely an aid to proper spelling. It's usually much easier to spell a word correctly when you pronounce it properly, or to look it up when you are not quite sure.

Pronunciation can help in another way. When you look up a word, try pronouncing each syllable phonetically with a brief pause between syllables, taking care to pronounce each letter (even silent ones) and never varying the pronunciation of a particular letter. The result is a strange word which you wouldn't care to have another hear you say aloud, but one which will trigger your subconscious to tell you how to spell the word the next time you see it. Take *phonetically*, for example. Spelled the way it's normally pronounced, the results look like *fonetekly*, which could set the reader to looking for a German dictionary. Mentally sounded out one syllable at a time, however, it comes out *pho* (using a soft *f* or *p-ho* in our mental pronunciation to indicate *ph*), *net* (I can spell that), *i* (that, too), *cal* (and that), *ly* (and here's a bonus: pronouncing *cal* and *ly* separately insures that both *l*'s will get into the final spelling). You don't have to do this very many times before it becomes automatic and you stop looking up the same words over and over again.

The A-B-C's are not for children

Remember the cute rhyme in nursery school? See the colorful cards on the wall containing gaily decorated letters of the alphabet? You should have known what was to come when the colorful letters were replaced by stark black and white cards, capitals and lower case, with lines carefully drawn top, bottom and through the middle. You should have known that if you survived penmanship they would find another way to get you. And they are out there, singly and in groups.

We tend to concentrate on vowels because they give us the most problems. Just five vowels, *a, e, i, o, u* and one part-time vowel, *y*, are responsible for about twenty vowel sounds. Now any mathematician will tell you that it is no problem to create twenty distinct combinations out of five vowels. Unfortunately, this is English where any one of the sounds might come from several different spellings (*meat, meet, mete, deceit*) or any one spelling may engender a number of pronunciations (*rouge, rough, gouge, cough, thorough*).

Consonants are equally treacherous. The letter *s* masquerades part time as *z* (*suppose*), as *sh* (*sugar*), or quietly hides (*aisle, isle*). The *c* vacillates between being an *s* (*cede*) and a *k* (*care*) when it's not being an *sh* (*ocean*) or hiding behind a *k* (*acknowledge*). And the *k* - outrageous! Blatantly stands at the beginning of a word doing nothing (*knock, knee, know*). Almost as bad is the *p*, which normally well-behaved, when put with an *h*, thinks it's an *f* (*physician, phobia*). Association with *p* is not the only diversion of the *h*. Put it with a *g* and it can't decide whether to sound off like an *f* (*tough*) or be silent (*light*). Which brings us back to one of the same problems that exists with vowels, a single sound created by different spellings (*fool, photo, laugh*).

It's a wonder we can write this language at all. But these things have not been revealed to you to discourage you. By no means! They have been pointed out only to make you wary and to thirst for battle, so go forth and conquer - but be careful out there.

Tips about vowels

Unfortunately, there are no rules which can be applied consistently, however some of these may help when you think you know the spelling, but have a lingering doubt.

Silent -e

Many words having a long vowel sound in the last syllable take a silent *-e* at the end in contrast to similar words which have a short vowel sound.

bid	**bide**	**bit**	**bite**	**cap**	**cape**
hid	**hide**	**hop**	**hope**	**kit**	**kite**
mop	**mope**	**rid**	**ride**	**slop**	**slope**

Doubling vowels

Often the long *e* sound is achieved by doubling the vowel in contrast to the single *e* in a similar word.

bet	**beet**	**fed**	**feed**	**met**	**meet**
per	**peer**	**wed**	**weed**		

red **reed** – though we also have *read*, which may sound the same as either *red* or *reed*, depending on use

Unfortunately, there are numerous exceptions, most of which add *a* to the spelling instead of a second *e*.

bed	**bead**	**best**	**beast**	**men**	**mean**
net	**neat**	**pet**	**peat**	**set**	**seat**

In the case of the letter *o*, doubling often creates a short *u* sound.

cop	**coop**	**hop**	**hoop**	**hot**	**hoot**
lop	**loop**	**lot**	**loot**	**mod**	**mood**
rot	**root**	**tot**	**toot**		

A short vowel sound, in contrast to a long vowel sound in a similar word, often signals the presence of a double consonant.

baring	**barring**	**biter**	**bitter**	**caned**	**canned**
caper	**capper**	**coper**	**copper**	**cuter**	**cutter**
hoping	**hopping**	**later**	**latter**	**moping**	**mopping**
plater	**platter**	**taped**	**tapped**		

-ei- and -ie-

In at least one Chinese dialect the long sound of *i-e* properly inflected is a cry of distress. It is also appropriate for English spelling.

Let's begin with the rule you learned in school – "*i* before *e* except after *c*." That's easy enough . . . when it works. What your teacher forgot to tell you is that it works (almost always) *only* with the long *e* sound.

achieve	**believe**	**ceiling**	**chief**	**conceit**
conceive	**deceive**	**grief**	**niece**	**perceive**
piece	**receive**	**relieve**		

Words pronounced with a sound other than the long *e* don't follow the rule.

deign	**feign**	**feint**	**freight**	**heifer**
heir	**height**	**neigh**	**neighbor**	**reign**
reins	**seismic**	**their**	**veil**	**vein**
weigh	**weight**			

Some words with the long *e* sound are spelled contrary to the rule.

either	**financier**	**leisure**	**neither**	**seize**
specie	**weird**			

Prefixes

Normally a prefix added to a word changes its meaning without changing spelling. There are exceptions. (Who could have guessed?)

The good news is that the exceptions are modest and clear cut or of little concern to us here. Into the latter category fall words such as *inhabitable,* which means the same as *habitable.* The prefix *in-*, which means *not*, has been added without changing the spelling of the root word, but the meaning has not changed and both words are in common use. Compare that with *human* and *inhuman.* It's another "nobody knows why" situation.

The exceptions to the rule that spelling does not change all involve hyphens:

Hyphenate when joining *ex-*, *all-* or *self-* to a noun, such as *ex-president*, *all-inclusive,* or *self-proclaimed.*

Hyphenate when the prefix is used with a proper noun or adjective, such as *pro-American* or *un-American.*

Hyphenate to alleviate confusion such as creating a word which could be confused with another (*re-creation,* the act of creating again versus *recreation,* amusement) or to make the word easier to recognize (*re-emerge* rather than *reemerge*). You have some latitude with this one, but as in all things, be consistent.

There are about fifty prefixes in general use and nothing is to be gained by listing them all; however, it will be helpful to know the meaning of some which are often confused:

ante- means *before* as in *antedate*
anti- means *against* as in *antibody*

dis- means *separation* as in *disgrace*
dys- means *ill* or *bad* as in *dysfunction*

hyper- means *above* or *excessive* as in *hyperactive*
hypo- means *under* or *beneath* as in *hypodermic*

per- means *through* as in *pervade*
pre- means *before* as in *precede*
pro- means *forward* as in *proceed*

Suffixes

Dumping the silent *-e*

Usually, when a suffix beginning with a vowel (*-ed, -ing*) is added to a word with a final silent-*e,* the *-e* is dropped before the suffix is added.

bake	**baked**	**baker**	**baking**
brave	**braved**	**braver**	**braving**
home	**homed**	**homer**	**homing**
kite	**kited**	**kiter**	**kiting**
manage	**managed**	**manager**	**managing**
mope	**moped**	**moper**	**moping**
skate	**skated**	**skater**	**skating**

As you might expect, there are exceptions. After *c* or *g* the *-e* is retained before a suffix beginning with *a* or *o* (are you with me so far?) in order to preserve the soft sound of the *c* or *g.*

embrace embraceable	**notice noticeable**
outrage outrageous	**trace traceable**

Words with the suffix *-ment* keep the silent *-e* when it is preceded by a single consonant.

achieve achievement	**appease appeasement**
atone atonement	**induce inducement**
move movement	**place placement**

When the *-e* is preceded by two consonants it is usually dropped,

judge judgment	**acknowledge acknowledgment**

In England the *-e* is not dropped, and the form appears as an optional spelling in many American dictionaries. Just keep in mind that if you opt for the British spelling, do it that way all the time.

Finally, there are some common exceptions just to make sure that no one gets an A on the exam.

dye dyeing	**hoe hoeing**
involve involvement	**mile mileage**
singe singeing	**true truly**
whole wholly	

Doubling consonants

Following the silent *-e* rule, we drop the *-e* when adding endings like *-ed* and *-ing*. But how about their counterparts, the words with short vowel sounds which have no silent *-e*? How do we keep from confusing the two words? Simple. We double the consonant so that while *mope* becomes *moping*, *mop* becomes *mopping*. This usually works, but as you might have guessed, we don't get off that easily.

The above rule applies only to syllables that contain a single vowel so that *scoop* changes to *scooping* (*not scoopping*).

Words of more than one syllable require a further consideration, namely, which syllable is accented. Uh, oh!, we're back to pronunciation again. If the accent of *the word created* is on the last syllable before the suffix, follow the doubling consonant rule above.

confer con-fer´ring **defer de-fer´ring**

deter de-ter´ring **refer re-fer´ring**

If the accent of *the word created* is not on the last syllable, do *not* double the consonant.

confer con´fer-ence **credit cred´it-ing**

defer def´fer-ence **refer ref´er-ence**

***-er* versus *-or* ending**

The *-er* ending indicates the person, thing or action related to the root word and is the more common ending. Whenever in doubt, *-er* is the ending to use.

blow blower **cook cooker** **deal dealer**

eat eater **govern governer** **leap leaper**

learn learner **pay payer** **read reader**

speak speaker **teach teacher** **weep weeper**

Some words take only the *-or* ending.

actor **creditor** **elector**

elevator **governor** **visitor**

And a few words take either ending.

adviser **advisor** **embracer** **embracor**

operater **operator** **vender** **vendor**

-cede, -ceed, -sede endings

Only one word uses the *-sede* ending – **supersede.**

Three words use the *-ceed* ending.

exceed **proceed** **succeed**

All other words use the *-cede* ending.

concede **procede** **recede** **secede**

Memorize the four exceptions and you have one spelling lesson down pat!

Y as a vowel

We don't normally include *y* in our list of vowels, because it performs that function only part time. At the beginning of a word or syllable, it tends to function as a consonant; whereas, when it follows another consonant it functions as a vowel. If you wonder why anyone cares, read this sentence again, aloud, paying particular attention to the *y* sounds. In *you* and *paying*, it exhibits a hard sound, while in *why* and *anyone* it sounds like the *i* in *while*. Never mind that phonetic spelling could eliminate the *y*, we're concerned here with how to get along with it.

A final *y* preceded by a consonant changes to an *i* before all suffixes *except* those suffixes beginning with *i*.

fry	**fried**	**frying**
copy	**copier**	**copying**
rely	**relied**	**relying**
sixty	**sixtieth**	**sixtyish**
try	**tried**	**trying**

A final *y* preceded by a vowel generally doesn't change when a suffix is added,

boy	**boyish**	
play	**played**	**playing**
pray	**prayed**	**praying**
stay	**stayed**	**staying**
stray	**strayed**	**straying**

except sometimes. Go figure.

day daily	**gay gaily**	**lay laid**
pay paid	**say said**	

Hard c

As mentioned earlier the letter *c* often hides behind a *k*; this time you get to put it there. Words ending in a hard *c* add a *k* before suffixes beginning with the vowels *e* or *i*.

mimic	**mimicked**	**mimicker**	**mimicking**
panic	**panicked**	**panicking**	**panicky**
picnic	**picnicked**	**picnicker**	**picnicking**
traffic	**trafficked**	**trafficker**	**trafficking**

Suffixes beginning with *a* are added to the word ending with a hard *c* with no change in spelling.

angelic angelical	**critic critical**
mimic mimical	**pragmatic pragmatical**
specific specifically	**systematic systematically**
terrific terrifically	

Plurals

Forming a plural offers another challenge to the writer. Most plurals are formed by adding *s*.

author authors	**baker bakers**
butcher butchers	**chief chiefs**
clown clowns	**doctor doctors**
lawyer lawyers	**manager managers**
master masters	**plumber plumbers**
servant servants	**teacher teachers**

There are, however, enough exceptions to keep it interesting and to keep those who are concerned about being correct close to a dictionary.

Irregular nouns

The bad news is that one group of irregular nouns changes spelling in a random fashion.

addendum addenda	**alumnus alumni**
child children	**crisis crises**
criterion criteria	**datum data**
die dice	**foot feet**
goose geese	**man men**
medium media	**mouse mice**
ox oxen	**tooth teeth**
woman women	

Another group of nouns doesn't change at all.

deer	**fish**	**hose**	**gross**	**moose**
salmon	**series**	**sheep**	**species**	**vermin**

And yet another group allows you to make a choice.

appendix	**appendixes**	**appendices**
beau	**beaux**	**beaus**
brother	**brothers**	**brethren**
cactus	**cactuses**	**cacti**
criterion	**criterion**	**criteria**
focus	**focuses**	**foci**
formula	**formulas**	**formulae**
gymnasium	**gymnasiums**	**gymnasia**
hippopotamus	**hippopotamuses**	**hippopotami**
index	**indexes**	**indices**
medium	**mediums**	**media**
memorandum	**memorandums**	**memoranda**
radius	**radiuses**	**radii**

Must not forget those words which are always plural, even when referred to in the singular.

alms	**clothes**	**forceps**	**gallows**
nuptials	**pants**	**pliers**	**remains**
riches	**scissors**	**shears**	**suds**
tongs	**trousers**	**victuals**	

The good news is that most of these words are in common use and you will seldom encounter any which are unfamiliar.

Nouns ending in -f and -fe

Another erratic group are those nouns ending in *-f* and *-fe.* Some take an *s* to make the plural,

chef chefs	**chief chiefs**	**dwarf dwarfs**

whereas others change the *f* to *v* and add *s* or *es*,

calf calves	**half halves**	**knife knives**
shelf shelves	**thief thieves**	**wife wives**

and others leave it up to the writer to choose.

beef	**beefs**	**beeves**
hoof	**hoofs**	**hooves**
loaf	**loafs**	**loaves**
scarf	**scarfs**	**scarves**
wharf	**wharfs**	**wharves**

Nouns ending in *s, ss, z, sh, ch,* and *x*

Forming the "yet another group" group are nouns ending in *s, ss, z, sh, ch,* and *x*. If you can just remember that list of endings, you are home free - they (almost) all take *es*.

ax axes	**bush bushes**	**couch couches**
dress dresses	**loss losses**	**marsh marshes**
match matches	**punch punches**	**push pushes**
ranch ranches	**tax taxes**	**waltz waltzes**

And still there are exceptions: for example, the plural of **gross** is **gross**.

Nouns ending in -y

The letter *y* gets a little friendlier here. If a *-y* ending is preceded by a vowel simply add *s*.

boy boys	**day days**	**display displays**
play plays	**quay quays**	**tray trays**

If a *-y* ending is preceded by a consonant, change the *y* to *i* and add *es.*

beauty beauties **family families** **lady ladies**

memory memories **pansy pansies** **theory theories**

Compound nouns

These offer an interesting challenge. Really! Most compound nouns are made up of a subject and a modifier. In most cases, you have only to decide which is the subject or principal word and apply the rules for making it plural.

Easiest to deal with are the one word compounds..

bookcase bookcases	**bottleneck bottlenecks**
cameraman cameramen	**cheesecake cheesecakes**
coattail coattails	**congresswoman congresswomen**
fireman firemen	**hatbox hatboxes**
landscape landscapes	**shoetree shoetrees**
suitcase suitcases	**teammate teammates**
teapot teapots	**teaspoon teaspoons**

The last example brings us to an interesting consideration – **teaspoonful,** or *cupful* or *handful.* Is the plural *teaspoonfuls* or *teaspoonsful*? *Teaspoonfuls* is recognized as an acceptable plural because *teaspoonful* is a single entity: the quantity which can be held by a teaspoon. It is, however, awkward, and in spite of the argument that several *teaspoonsful* is equivalent, not to a measure, but to several teaspoons each full of something, it may be preferred. You have to decide.

Two word compound nouns are more fun. *Mother-in-law* becomes *mothers-in-law* because *mother* is the subject and *in-law* describes a relationship. The same principal applies to *editors-in-chief* and *ex-presidents.*

Notary public and *chairman of the board* offer a couple of unusual examples. The first is a *notary* who works in the public domain and a gathering of such men could be described as a group of *notaries public;* however, one might view the two words together as a title wherein each word carries equal weight in which case it would be a group of *notary publics. Attorney general* confronts us with the same logic so that either *attorneys general* or *attorney generals* is correct.

In the second example, a strong argument can be made that the gathered titans of industry are collectively *chairmen,* but of a like number of *boards* as each board has only one chairman. Thus we have a meeting of the *chairmen of the boards.* (Except for those boards which have co-chairmen). This is one of those places where there is no distinct right or wrong; we only hope that common sense will prevail and . . . you got it! . . . be consistent.

When there is no word in the compound that is clearly more important than the others, the plural is added at the end.

black-eyed Susan	**black-eyed Susans**
forget-me-not	**forget-me-nots**
jack-in the box	**jack-in-the-boxes**

In some cases, both parts of a compound should be plural.

manservant	**menservants**
woman lawyer	**women lawyers**

Minding your p's and q's

By this time you may be at 6's and 7's, but you should still be able to see where this rule is going with no if's, and's or but's. You have earned it; you deserve it: *an ironclad rule with no exceptions.*

The plural of a number, letter, word or symbol (+'s and *'s) is created by adding apostrophe *s*.

Nouns ending in -o

Nouns ending in *o* preceded by a consonant usually form the plural by adding *-es*.

hero	**heroes**	**potato**	**potatoes**	**tomato**	**tomatoes**

There are, of course, exceptions to the rule,

dynamo	**dynamos**	**photo**	**photos**	**piano**	**pianos**
silo	**silos**	**solo**	**solos**	**zero**	**zeros**

including some words which form the plural either way.

cargo	**cargos**	**cargoes**
motto	**mottos**	**mottoes**
tornado	**tornados**	**tornadoes**

Nouns ending in *o* preceded by a vowel take an *s* only.

cameo	**cameo**	**patio**	**patios**	**radio**	**radios**
trio	**trios**	**zoo**	**zoos**		

Proper nouns ending in *o* always take an *s* only.

Possessive plurals

Finally, another easy one. When you want to form the plural possessive, form the plural by the applicable rule (or exception) and if the word ends in an *s* add an apostrophe ('), otherwise add an apostrophe *s*.

ax	**axes**	**axes' handles**
brother	**brothers**	**brothers' share**
brother	**brethren**	**brethren's share**

child	children	children's toys
deer	deer	deer's grazing area
doctor	doctors	doctors' offices
man	men	men's room
mouse	mice	mice's holes
radius	radiuses	radiuses' lengths
radius	radii	redii's lengths
theory	theories	theories' premises
wife	wives	wives' tales
woman	women	women's lounge

And a serious note:

It may seem a waste of time to learn any rules of spelling when you consider all of the exceptions, but it's not. Most of the time when we need a little help it's simply a matter of being uncertain, and knowing the rules will often clear up that uncertainty. If it's a word we use often which is spelled contrary to the rules, we may look it up once and remember it for that very reason.

Hyphenation

Most grammarians have one bit of advice about hyphenation. Don't do it. As we deal with ever more sophisticated writing tools such as word processors and personal computers, we strive to turn out smarter looking documents which often require hyphenation.

Rather than get wrapped up in a lot of rules for hyphenation, follow just one: *use a dictionary and common sense.*

When a word is broken at the end of a line, make sure that enough of it is on the first line (at least three or four characters) to make a pronounceable syllable. If the eye can not track without the necessity of pausing or rereading, your message loses impact. Similarly, a stack of hyphens where words have been broken on line after line makes tracking difficult.

Part IV
Form and Style

Form and Style

In spite of the disapproval of my several English instructors, all overworked, underpaid and most assuredly under appreciated, who even now are spinning in their graves, in is necessary to impart my own immutable **First Law of Grammar**, to wit:

> **Whereas the primary mission of language is to communicate,**
> **and whereas nothing is writ in stone,**
> **Therefore, be it known that**
> **although generally accepted usage is preferred,**
> **When generally accepted usage interferes with clarity**
> **or is not up to the task at hand,**
> **Without hesitation or compunction, *Break the Rules.***

The importance of style cannot be overemphasized. Everything you do reflects a style, good or bad. Whether the communication is spoken or written, the style influences the recipient as much as the message itself.

GENERAL CONSIDERATIONS

Formal or casual?

The dictionary describes *formal* as **". . . in accordance with regular or established forms and methods, or with proper dignity."** Taken liberally, that definition should fit virtually everything we write. It doesn't mean we have to be stuffy, nor does it mean we can't show a little creativity; it simply means that we do have to work within the confines of that which is acceptable to those who judge what we've written.

Some of the suggestions in this section may sound casual; rest assured, they are not. *Casual* means ". . . occurring by chance . . . haphazard . . .careless." To be any of those things is far from our intent. We will, however, direct your attention to communication in a style that is relaxed and unselfconscious, a technique which does not occur by chance.

First, you must assess the style which prevails in your present situation. If all of the correspondence you see is staid and very formal, find out why. Is it tradition, laziness on the part of the writers, your supervisor's preference or company policy? Determine how much latitude you have to communicate in a more relaxed, informative style. You may want to test the waters by changing outdated phrases to better reflect the way you speak before attempting any radical changes in the tone of correspondence.

Consistency

The tone of your correspondence is influenced by your assessment of the recipient: a relaxed note to a coworker; a formal. deferential letter to an officer of the company. The way in which you view your relationship to clients will affect the way in which you address them in your letters. Try to develop a style which is comfortable to you and which lends itself to every situation. A letter to an important (and perhaps, stuffy) client or an officer of the company does not have to be framed in archaic prose to be respectful. Aim for a consistent style, best expressed as the way you speak or would like to speak. Be the same person in a letter or a report that you are when talking on the phone.

Be consistent, also, in tendering accurate information in a timely manner. A problem-solving letter, even if it has only preliminary information is worth far more on the heels of the problem than after someone has had several days to stew about it.

Leave Your Imprint

Develop a style which reflects you. If possible, let the reader know you sent the letter before he or she reaches the signature line. Writing in a conversational manner will do it if all of the other correspondence your recipient gets is couched in formal, archaic language.

You can also identify yourself by the greeting; the way in which you begin the letter; the letters you write because you care, not because you have to; the timeliness of your response; the way in which your relaxed style doesn't prevent you from getting to the point; the manner you have of summing up a problem, and the solution, concisely. All of these are discussed further in the section on **Business Letters.**

How to Offend the Recipient

Jab a sensitive nerve

Be relaxed, be friendly, but don't get too personal. The boss or client who refers jokingly to a spreading waistline or thinning hair is not extending an invitation to be ridiculed.

Jokes are fine, but be certain that they are in good taste. Whenever you are tempted to tell a story with racial, religious, sexual, etc. overtones or which may be offensive to the recipient, bite your tongue hard enough to make you yelp. Then you can change the subject, explaining that you bit your tongue.

Don't apologize

There is a conventional wisdom which holds that one should never open a letter with an apology. Poppycock! There are times when something goes wrong that a client or supervisor takes it personally and the first thing they want is an apology. There is, however, a right and wrong way.

A letter which begins by saying that you are sorry, but you don't know what happened and you hope it doesn't happen again is not going to be well received. An apology on a positive note, however, is another matter. Offering regrets that the incident occurred and that you are in the process of determining exactly what happened or are formulating a procedure to prevent recurrence is more likely to be well received. Continue by filling the recipient in on the status of your investigation or preliminary assessment of the situation. End with a promise to keep him or her informed and again offer regrets for any inconvenience you may have caused. Never mind that the client may have done something to create the problem; include that in your solution, not the finger pointing. He or she will get the message.

Any attempt to shift blame or avoid an apology to one who feels wronged will only feed the anger—don't do it unless that is your intent.

Mislead the recipient

You were told to do something, forgot it and a week later you're asked about it. Should you: (a) admit that you forgot; (b) suggest that your instructions may have been lost in the mail; (c) feign amnesia; or (d) claim you have a split personality and the message was given to your irresponsible half?

Misleading your recipient with vague or incorrect information is usually counter productive. It can cause a loss of confidence and at the very least engender a sense of frustration that *something* went wrong which neither of you can control.

Remember—it's not a life or death situation and the other person wants it to go away as much as you do. Owning up to a problem places the blame squarely on your shoulders. You get to be the recipient of someone else's frustration, but once vented, it's gone, and you can go on with your life. If you play your hand well, you may even wind up with a stronger relationship. Sure beats letting a problem fester while you squirm.

The Boss - the Final Arbiter

Any writing of consequence for most of us will be work or school related. The comments here are directed mainly to a work environment, but they apply equally well to school. The influence of the boss or a customer in the workplace is much the same as the instructor in school. For the student who thinks the pressure subsides when you got out into the real world – sorry about that. Nothing changes, except that hopefully you have the same boss for a lot longer than you have the same instructor.

Regardless of the influence, it affects your style. The degree to which you are subjected to influence, however, will vary tremendously from place to place. Though not very common, there are companies which have standards manuals for all written communication including channels of communication and a list of subjects which may (or may not) be communicated through those channels. Less structured, but certainly important, are the preferences of your immediate supervisor. He or she may have definite ideas about the configuration of written communication or may be pleased to avoid any involvement as long as you get the job done.

Guidelines for Effective Communication

Effective communication takes thought and planning

Develop a relaxed, comfortable style

Communicate in a timely manner

Be friendly without getting too personal

Apologize for errors, then offer a solution

Be direct and honest in what you have to say

DISTINCTIVE BUSINESS LETTERS

If the letter you are about to write is not important, don't write it. You're wasting your time, the time of the person who transcribes it and the time of the person who reads it.

Many otherwise interesting people seem to find it easiest to write stiff, artificial, uninteresting letters. Please don't misunderstand. The business letter's primary purpose is not to entertain, but it shouldn't put the reader to sleep, either.

The unstated message

The business letter carries more than the stated message; it carries a message about the writer and the way in which he or she conducts business. To get the most out of a letter, be sure that the *unstated message* is acceptable.

How do you regard the recipient? Do you think enough of the person to whom you are sending the letter to spell his or her name right? The business which relies on a word processor or computer has a distinct advantage – check the name carefully once, when it's put into the system, and it will come out correctly thereafter. Anyone who lacks this convenience is well advised to take a few seconds to be sure the name is correct every time. And don't rely entirely someone else who transcribed the letter; he or she may be very reliable, but the blame for any mistakes rests with you. The same is true for titles. Some people are very protective of theirs and you should be too. If there is any doubt about the spelling of a name or the wording of a title, taking a couple of minutes to call the person's office to confirm is good investment.

How do you regard the recipient's company? For most people, the company is an important part of their lives. They need to know that you respect their employer. Be sure the name is spelled correctly, and **put it in capital letters.**

How do you regard your message? Is it important enough to spell out clearly in a neat, well-fashioned letter? In this age of computers and word processors where erasures do not exist, the erasures in a letter prepared on a typewriter stand out more than at any time in the past and thus it is far more important to avoid them.

How competent are you? A sloppy letter, full of errors, written by someone who rambles and seems to have difficulty expressing himself or herself is not likely to engender confidence in the recipient.

Body of the letter

Grabber greetings

You have just a few seconds to make sure that the reader is alert to receive your message. An out-of-the-ordinary opening will do the trick. Dear So-and-so is fine, but why not change occasionally to show that it's not automatic?

> **Good morning, Ms. Jones.**
>
> **Good afternoon, Mr. Smith.**
>
> **Congratulations, Shirley.**

Or you can dive right in.

> **Just received your letter, Sam,**
> **and we're really pleased that you decided . . .**
>
> **How did you manage, Rosemary,**
> **to pull off the deal they said couldn't be done?**

The trick is to write the first sentence and then rework it, if necessary, to include the recipients name in the sentence.

Write the way you speak

The best way to give the reader a message which is distinctively you is to write the way you talk. Stiff, precise language in a letter is not wrong, it's just boring. If we want our letters to be remembered when others are forgotten, we need to be distinctive and writing in a conversational manner is one of the tools we have to make our communication memorable.

Obviously we can't include all of the pauses and hand gestures and facial expressions that are a part of face to face conversation, but we can adopt a conversational tone. Use short sentences and even phrases if they help make a point. Avoid overly long compound-complex sentences, if possible. Above all, avoid officious language which you are not likely to use when speaking.

as per your letter – legalese; use *according to your letter*

attached please find, enclosed please find – just say *attached is* or *enclosed is*

at the present time – most of us say *now*

contents noted – outdated

in compliance with your request – as you requested

in receipt of your letter, in response to your letter – of course you received the letter; why else would you be responding?

in the amount of – use *for $*______

please advise when – How about *inform me,* or *tell me* or *let me know when*?

please arrange to return – use *return* or *send*

pursuant to your instructions – use *per your instructions* or *as you requested*

we are desirous of receiving – *we would like* or *please send*

Be bright, be brief and be gone

An old adage for salesmen, it applies equally well to business letters: know what you want to talk about; say it concisely; stop and go away. There's always room for a personal comment when appropriate, but don't abuse it by rambling on needlessly. It does not make friends.

Types of business letters

Introductory letters

An introductory letter is any letter written to an unknown party to introduce the writer as a job applicant, a possible supplier of goods or services, etc. These are without doubt the toughest letters to write because you are writing to someone who not only doesn't know you, but doesn't have any reason to want to know you. And you usually don't know enough about the person to whom you are writing to customize the letter. You have only a slight chance the letter will even be read by the person to whom it is addressed. Most people who send out blind letters plan to send a lot of them in the hope of a few responses.

If you have some knowledge of the person you are trying to reach you may be able to tailor the letter in a way that improves your chance for response. The best way is to offer a service which the company needs and does not have available through current suppliers.

You can improve your chances with a clever opener, but not so clever that the letter gets tossed out with the occupant mailings. Once you've garnered attention with the opener, state your business briefly and ask for a response. Don't try to sell yourself or your entire line of products in that one shot; your goal is a response which will get you an appointment or a request for more information.

If you know something about the company, you might write a letter praising a product or a community project in which the company is involved. Well into the body of the letter, or even in a following letter, you mention that you would like to be associated with the company as an employee or a supplier.

In addition to asking for a response, some situations lend themselves to a follow-up call in which case you might indicate in the letter that you will call in a few days to arrange an appointment, answer any questions, etc.

Answering inquiries

It is extremely important that inquiries be answered as completely as possible, in a timely manner and scheduled for follow-up.

The response to an inquiry requires the same planning as any letter. The old *Dear-sir-thank-you-for-your-inquiry-here's-the-stuff-you-requested* letter doesn't cut it. The response needs to be personal, friendly and inviting further contact. Based on the type of inquiry, it may be prudent to include additional information. A follow-up call or letter is in order to be sure that the material received is satisfactory.

Orders

Orders keep the business going and repeat orders are the most inexpensive source of new business. Orders should be followed immediately with a friendly letter expressing thanks for the order, expressing confidence that the customer will be pleased and inviting a call if there are any questions or problems. In addition, it may be appropriate to convey additional information such as ship date, routing, etc. as well as a reminder of other products which may be of interest.

Follow-up

Use of the computer makes it easier than it has ever been to track our business activity. We can log in the dates when introductory letters were sent and to whom; when inquiries were answered; when orders were placed by product line and quantity. The allows for a very efficient follow-up system.

In addition to follow-up letters for inquiries and orders, we can schedule letters to go out when we think a client is getting low on product. The letter may be a friendly reminder that it is time to check inventory or it may simply be a request for assurance that the customer is happy with the product.

We can also inform clients any time we have a special buy on the particular product which they use or related products which they may use.

Good will letters

Good will letters are those you write because you care. Congratulations on a promotion or recognition of a personal achievement is just one more opportunity to keep in touch. Condolences on the loss of a loved one is a means to let the client know you care. Needless to say, these are brief business letters wherein no business is discussed.

Interoffice

Interoffice correspondence deserves the same care that outside correspondence receives. Interoffice may be more cryptic and in some cases more technical, but the admonition to write well should not be ignored. Whether writing to a superior or your peers, you face the same job of convincing them to agree with your requests.

Guidelines for Effective Business Letters

Rely on the appearance of the letter to create a favorable impression

Avoid conventional openings and hackneyed phrases

Write the way you speak

Be concise; say what you have to say, then stop

Use correspondence to develop and maintain a relationship

Don't underestimate the importance of interoffice communication

REPORTS

Probably the main difference between an academic and a business report is the manner in which the subject is selected – the student is usually required to select his own subject, whereas in the workplace there is a specific problem to be addressed. For this example, we'll use a hypothetical business problem.

Define the problem

Describing the problem properly is often the key to finding a solution.

The ABC Company

The ABC Company is a small company in the midwest which manufactures microwave ovens. Recently they have experienced a rash of complaints about damaged product manufactured exclusively for a large retailer. The rate is high – five to ten per cent in some cases – and in addition to the cost of returns, the Sales Department is concerned about a loss of customer confidence in the company's other products.

The problem

The problem seems simple enough – defective units are being shipped to a customer. But that description is too broad to help define a precise solution. The precise problem may involve inferior materials, poor workmanship, inadequate inspection, careless handling, etc. More information is needed to properly define the problem and outline remedial action.

Assemble the facts

Quality control – The Quality Control Department, which is responsible for inspecting the returned units, reports that the same part is broken on most of the units inspected. They also report that the parts are 100% inspected at the end of the assembly line.

Packing and shipping – The Shipping Department, which is also responsible for packing, reports that packing and shipping is the same as for other products which have had no damage reported.

Freight forwarder – The freight company confirms that the damaged units travel many of the same routes as, and often side by side with, units which have a history of no damage claims.

Purchasing – The Purchasing Department produces documentation to show that all materials purchased for the damaged units meet engineering specifications; however, they note that the packing material specifications call for a lighter material than that used for other products.

Suppliers – Supplier of the packing material confirms that a lighter material is used, but that it was tested and proved adequate for this lighter product.

Sales – After Engineering pointed the finger, Sales confirmed that the lighter material was specified to comply with the customer's request for a smaller over-all package size.

Customer – The customer confirms that the smaller package was requested in order to maximize the number of pieces they could pack in their warehouse units. Inspection of the customer's facility revealed that they re-piled the units on special pallets with all identification labels facing one way and stacked them higher than they were on the shipping pallet.

Engineering – Experimenting with the customer's warehouse packing, the Engineering Department determined that the packing is inadequate. The units are much heavier on one side, and so it is standard practice at the plant to alternate the packages when piling to distribute the weight. Turning the packages all one way puts too much stress on the lower packages. They also determined that the part which most often failed was a very tight fit which made it more susceptible to the extra pressure.

Redefine the problem

Based on the information compiled the problem might be defined as – **The stress placed on the package by the customer's warehousing methods which causes frequent failure of part X.**

Outline the options

Outlining the options means considering every possibility, regardless of how bizarre and establishing a cost for it.

Sometimes the outrageous leads to a simpler, though less obvious, solution. Remember the story of the man who went to his doctor and said, "Doc, it hurts when I do this," and the doctor said, "Don't do that." Your first option might be to stop making the unit. The cost of that decision is lost profits, possible loss of prestige and loss of position in the market place.

Among other options are strengthening the packaging, strengthening the part, redesign of the product, labeling both sides of the package coupled with educating the customer in the best way to re-stack, stacking at the plant on the customer's pallets so that re-stacking isn't necessary, etc.

In every case, consider the cost in dollars and the need for agreement of the parties involved in the change.

Suggest a solution

Usually, when the options are outlined, an obvious solution presents itself; however, the interest of all parties must be considered, so that it may be necessary to outline more than one choice.

Put it all together

What we have outlined is a problem solving technique, although most reports follow the same pattern. Any report which is not merely a statistical summary may imply an evaluation which requires research of fact and opinion regarding the subject.

In the summation, every report requires a heading which states the problem or objective, a brief summary of the pertinent facts, a list of the reasonable options and a detailed description of the recommended action including costs, penalties, potential problems, etc.

Key Elements in a Report

State the problem or purpose

Summarize the pertinent facts

Outline the options with their cost

Recommend a solution

PUBLIC SPEAKING

So you've been asked to give a speech. Or perhaps, like many of us, it came as an imperial command; the boss was asked to give a speech and doesn't want to do it, so he volunteered you. Either way, the subject matter was probably chosen for you, whether it's outlining the activities of your department for a group of fellow employees, telling the company story to a local civic group or describing a special process to a professional group.

The steps to planning and delivering a speech are not so difficult, but they do take a little time. Hopefully, you've been given enough notice to plan, research and run through the speech a few times before delivering it.

Relate the subject to the audience

Based on the length of the speech and the audience, you have to decide whether the subject matter should be technical or an overview, instructional or entertaining.

Research

Surely you are familiar with the subject or you wouldn't have been asked to speak, but you probably want to seek additional information. Scan through any books, reports, etc. you can find for facts to fill out what you already know and for new information. Don't worry about finding too much material; it's easier to cull out the excess than to try to stretch too little. The more you know, the more comfortable you will be with your subject.

In addition, interview anyone who knows anything about the subject. Transfer all of your notes to 3x5 cards referencing the source.

Anecdotes

One of the benefits of interviews is that they are a great source of anecdotes which can be used to liven up or change the pace of the speech. Make notes of anecdotes and withhold judgment about their use until you organize your presentation.

Plan the presentation

Flow

By now you should have a collection of note cards from your research. Supplement these with cards noting information and anecdotes drawn from your own experience.

If you have a general outline of the ground you plan to cover, sort the note cards under the various headings.

If you don't have an outline, use the notes to build one. Spread them out on a desk or table and put them in the order you feel they should be introduced. Identify any notes which might be a main heading or section of the presentation and isolate the cards which belong to that group. Create a heading for any group of notes which seem to fit in the same section and keep those together.

Review the outline to see that the information flows in a logical sequence. If not, make any necessary changes. A presentation which flows in an orderly fashion and is broken down into segments will not only be easier to for the listener to follow, but easier for you to deliver. In all likelihood, you will change the outline again before you're through, but this is a start.

Pacing

Review the outline again to critically assess the content of each section. Is there any way a section can be punched up with an anecdote or side comment? Do you want to consider the use of charts or graphs to better illustrate a point? Are there comparisons which you might use to make a point more dramatic?

All of this is part of the pacing. Standing in front of a room, reciting cold, hard facts while clinging to a podium until your knuckles are white is not only unnerving to the audience, it is likely to be unnerving to you. Anything you can do to change the pace in a natural manner is going to be more comfortable for everyone.

Length

There's no way to know exactly how long the speech will be until you have run through it a couple of times, but at this point you can probably make a good guess. Review the outline again and make some judgment about things which might be added or eliminated to correct the length.

Cue cards and props

Only you can determine what sort of notes you need on the podium. Some people are only comfortable with the speech written out in full, others use an outline, still others list only the main sections. One popular speaker years ago carried 3x5 cards in his left hand and referred to them occasionally when he spoke. They were blank! a prop to help him along.

A prop such as a chart or graph can help if it has written on it the key words you need as a guide; or it can be positioned on an easel in front of you with an outline on the back visible only to you.

Whatever method you choose, you may well change it as you practice the speech. Sometimes the information flows so well that a few key words is all you need. On the other hand, you may need the security of a typed copy of the full speech in front of you.

One word of caution – if there are any direct quotes in your speech, write them out on 3x5 cards, just in case. You may be able to talk about your company all day without a problem, but nothing could be more embarrassing than to forget the president's words or his name at a critical moment.

Practice, practice, practice

Avoid the temptation to write out the entire speech. You and your audience will both be more comfortable if you maintain a conversational style. Think of the speech in that way: as a conversation with a group of friends.

Dry run

Not until you run through the speech will you know exactly how long it is. And the first run-through is full of surprises.

This is when you discover that half of your outline contains one-liners: facts about the company which are stated in simple sentences and don't lend themselves to any embellishment. Your thirty minute speech could be barely fifteen minutes. Or when you realize that the process which is so familiar to you defies description in non-technical jargon.

To make matters worse, the material just doesn't seem to flow, and you have to revise the outline. Basically, this is when you work the hardest and sweat the most to pull it all together. But you do pull it all together.

Once the initial hurdles are past, run through the speech again to be sure that the material flows well and that the speech is about the right length.

Segment the presentation

Begin to view the speech as several small speeches. Divide it into segments according to your outline. Run through the segments individually until you are comfortable with them.

As you grow more comfortable with what you have to say, practice in front of a mirror so that you can see what your audience will see. Take a deep breath and look around the room before you begin. Speak slowly at first. Criticize your own performance and if you find it boring, try to be more animated without overdoing it. Change the volume, pitch and pace of your words when appropriate, just as you would in normal conversation. Above all, relax.

Final Notes

Prepare the notes that you will take with you: key words, outline or full text as well as copies of any direct quotations or statistics.

Now run through from beginning to end with only that material in front of you. You're ready!

Two more pieces of advice: Be sure you have a glass of water handy because even if you are not nervous, all that talking can give you a dry mouth. Don't open with a joke unless it's appropriate and a sure thing; starting out with a bomb can be devastating to you and your audience. Better to scatter some light humor through your presentation. Now, *that* can hold an audience.

Follow these rules and you will be so successful that the only thing you have to worry about is overconfidence which will keep you from working as hard on your next speech.

Guidelines for Effective Speaking

Know your subject well

Speak in terms your audience can understand

Vary the pace of the presentation with anecdotes or props

Keep final notes to a minimum

Practice until you are at ease telling your story

Keep a written copy of quotes or critical statistics

Relax, you're talking to friends

Part V
Reference

REFERENCE

CONFUSING WORDS

In spelling and in speaking, we are plagued by words which are, in some cases, so similar in spelling or meaning that we don't even suspect we are using a wrong word or that there is any difference between two words. Following is a list and explanation of the most common offenders.

accept, except *Accept* means to receive — *to accept a package;* to agree to — *to accept a decision;* to acknowledge — *to accept an invitation. Except* means to leave out — *No one is excepted from the restrictions* or *Take them all except the blue ones.*

adapt, adopt *Adapt* means to modify or make suitable — *to adapt to one's surroundings. Adopt* means to take as one's own — *to adopt an idea; to vote to adopt a resolution; to adopt a child.*

addition, edition *Addition* is the process of joining together or finding the sum of. *Edition* is the published form of a literary work — *de luxe edition* or *first edition;* total number of copies issued at one time — *an edition of 20,000.*

adopt See **adapt**

advice, advise *Advice* (soft *c* pronounced like an *s*) is a noun — *to give advice to a person. Advise* (hard *s* pronounce like a *z*) is a verb — *to advise a person.*

affect, effect *Affect* means to influence or act upon — *this won't affect you. Effect,* as a verb, means to bring about, to cause — *the treatments will effect a swift cure;* as a noun, means the result or outcome — *that is the effect of the treatment.*

aisle, isle *Aisle* is a passageway between seats in a church or theater. *Isle* is a small island.

alley, ally *Alley* is a narrow passageway between or behind buildings; a lane for bowling. *Ally* means to unite or enter into an alliance; an associate or helper.

all ready, already *All ready* (always two words) means that everyone is prepared — *We are all ready to go. Already* refers to a past time or by this time or by the time mentioned — *That has already been done.*

all right, alright *All right* is the correct spelling — *Everything is all right. Alright* is used mainly as an interjection in a narrative and is not considered acceptable for use in general correspondence — *"Alright, I'll go!"*

all together, altogether *All together* implies several acting in unison — *We must go all together,* or *All together now, sing! Altogether* represents a whole or the entirety — *This is altogether too much.*

allude, elude *Allude* means to make indirect or casual reference — *She alluded to his unkind remarks. Elude* means to avoid or escape — *The meaning of that word eludes me.*

ally See **alley**

already See **all ready**

altar, alter *Altar* is a raised table or platform which is the focal point of a place of worship. *Alter* means to change or modify.

altogether See **all together**

among, between *Among* is used to refer to more than two. *Between* usually refers to only two, but there are exceptions. See also **Prepositions, Words to watch.**

angel, angle *Angel* is a spiritual being. *Angle* is a geometric value formed by the joining of two lines.

appraise, apprise *Appraise* means to make an official evaluation — *He must appraise the property before we can set a price. Apprise* means to notify or inform — *Be sure to apprise her of our decision.*

ascent, assent *Ascent* means rising or climbing — *the ascent of the mountain* (by someone), *the ascent of the group up the mountain, the ascent of the plane into the heavens. Assent* means agreement or consent — *to assent to the course of action.*

bare, bear *Bare* means devoid of any covering. *Bear* means to support or hold up — *Can you bear the burden?*; a large mammal that lives in the woods.

baring, barring, bearing *Baring* means to uncover — *baring a secret. Barring* means apart from, excepting — *Barring traffic, we'll be there shortly. Bearing* means deportment, manner of carrying oneself — *a person of regal bearing;* endurance — *bearing up under pressure.*

between See **among**

born, borne, bourn *Born* means to be brought into being, as an offspring. *Borne* is the past participle of bear — *to have borne the load. Bourn* means that which limits, goal, end — *the bourn of one's life.*

breath, breathe *Breath* (pronounced with a short *e*) is a noun which means air inhaled or exhaled; a soft movement of air. *Breathe* (pronounced with a long *e*) is a verb which means to inhale or exhale; to whisper — *don't breathe a word to anyone.*

can, may *Can* expresses ability to do something — *You can* (are able to) *drive the car. May* expresses permission — *You may* (are allowed to) *drive the car.*

canvas, canvass *Canvas* describes a cloth used for sails, tents, etc.; a painting. *Canvass* is to go about soliciting orders, votes, etc.; a survey to determine preference.

capital, capitol *Capital* refers to something standing at the head or beginning: wealth used to make more wealth — *a capital investment*; the chief city of an area, usually the seat of government — *Atlanta is the capital of Georgia*; the first letter in a sentence — *a capital letter*; the member or section at the top of a column. *Capitol* refers to the building in which a legislature meets.

censor, censure *Censor*, as a noun, describes the official who examines material to be judged for rating, acceptability, etc. — *the censor has to see the material first*; as a verb, describes the act of deleting or suppressing material — *some of the best parts have been censored. Censure*, as a verb, is to express disapproval — *he was censured by his teammates for his conduct*; as a noun, is a formal reprimand expressing disapproval and which may include other discipline, punishment or forfeiture — *Censure was his only punishment.*

census, senses *Census* is an official count of the people of a country, area, etc. *Senses* (plural of *sense*) is a reference to awareness or rationality — *to come to your senses.*

cite, sight, site *Cite* means to quote or to call up as an authority or example — *to cite the words of Plato* or *to cite the instance when . . . . Sight* is the faculty of seeing — *my sight is fine*; a vision — *such a beautiful sight. Site* is a location — *the site of the battle.*

clothes, cloths *Clothes* are garments. *Cloths* is the plural of *cloth*, a piece of fabric.

complement, compliment A *complement* is that which fills up or completes — *The ship has her full complement of hands.* A *compliment* is praise — *I must compliment you on a delightful party.*

consul, council, counsel A *consul* is an officer residing in a foreign country to protect his country's interests. A *council* is an assemblage convened for consultation — *The Security Council is meeting today. Counsel* is guidance or advice — *She can counsel you on the proper steps to take;* a lawyer — *we sought the advice of counsel.*

corps, corpse A *corps* (pronounce like the core of an apple) is a military unit. A *corpse* is a dead body.

costume, custom *Costume* refers to apparel. *Custom* refers to common usage or practice.

credible, creditable *Credible* means worthy of being believed — *a credible story. Creditable* describes something worthy of praise — *The team made a creditable showing.*

custom See **costume**

dairy, diary A *dairy* is a place where milk products are processed and sold. A *diary* is a record of daily events.

decent, descent, dissent *Decent* means proper or respectable — *They are decent people. Descent* is the act of going downward — *We shall begin our descent shortly. Dissent,* as a verb, means to disagree — *I must dissent from your analysis;* as a noun, means a disagreement — *There is dissent among the people.*

desert, dessert *Desert* refers to a barren land; that which is deserved or merited — *his just deserts* ; to abandon. *Dessert* is something sweet served after a meal.

device, devise A *device* is a contrivance — *This device will allow you to save money heating your home. Devise* means to invent or contrive — *We have devised a plan for achieving our goals.*

diary See **dairy**

dissent See **decent**

dual, duel *Dual* denotes two. A *duel* refers to a struggle between two parties.

edition See **addition**

effect See **affect**

effective, effectual *Effective* means to produce a desired result — *The cost-cut-*

ting measures have been effective; in force, referring to a rule or law — *These new regulations are effective immediately. Effectual* means having the power to produce a desired result — *We can cut our costs by adopting effectual procedures.*

elicit, illicit *Elicit* is to draw out, as by inducement — *to elicit the truth. Illicit* describes a thing as unlawful or unauthorized.

elude See **allude**

eminent, imminent *Eminent* refers to one who is high in station, distinguished or prominent — *an eminent scientist. Imminent* describes something as about to happen, usually said of danger or evil — *The failure of the company is imminent.*

except See **accept**

formally, formerly *Formally* means in a formal manner — *to be greeted formally* or *to be formally attired. Formerly* refers to some time in the past — *Formerly, she was a lawyer.*

forth, fourth *Forth* indicates forward. *Fourth* refers to one of four equal parts; number four in succession.

gamble, gambol To *gamble* is to take a chance. *Gambol* is to play or frolic.

holly, holy, wholly *Holly* is a plant. *Holy* means to be hallowed or consecrated. *Wholly* means entirely.

hoping, hopping *Hoping* refers to desire. *Hopping* is moving about in short leaps.

illicit See **elicit**

imminent See **eminent**

instance, instants *Instance* refers to an occurrence as an illustration or example. *Instants* is the plural of *instant*, a particular point in time.

isle See **aisle**

lay, lie *Lay*, in the present tense, means to put or place — *Lay the book on the table*; as the past tense of lie, means to recline — *This morning, he was so tired, he had to lay* (not laid) *down. Lie* means to recline (present tense) — *Lie* (not lay) *down on the couch.*

learn, teach To *learn* is to acquire knowledge. To *teach* is to impart knowledge. The teacher teaches; the student learns.

lessen, lesson *Lessen* means to make less or decrease — *to lessen the work load. Lesson* is that which is learned or to be learned — *study tomorrow's lesson.*

loath, loathe *Loath* is an adjective which expresses reluctance —*He was loath to do the deed. Loathe* is a verb which expresses hatred or disgust —*I loathe the smell of the chemical plant.*

loose, lose *Loose* means not tight or not fastened —*a loose fit* or *on the loose. Lose* means to mislay or be deprived of —*to lose the book* or *to lose a privilege.*

may See **can**

medal, metal A *medal* is a small metal symbol, usually conferred for special achievement. *Metal* refers to a hard element or alloy.

morn, mourn *Morn* is a poetic term for morning. *Mourn* means to express sorrow or grief.

passed, past *Passed*, as a verb (past tense and past participle of pass), means to have gone by or left behind —*The car passed us on the road*; as an adjective, means to successfully complete an examination — *We passed the test. Past*, as an adjective, indicates that which is accomplished or ended — *our past achievements*; as a noun, refers to time gone by — *our sins of the past*; as a preposition, means beyond in time or place beyond —*The car went past us* or *it is past noon.*

peace, piece *Peace* is a state of tranquility; the absence of war. *Piece* is a portion or part of a greater whole.

persecute, prosecute *Persecute* is to harass or annoy consistently, especially because of race, religion or opinions. *Prosecute* is usually used in the legal sense and means to bring suit against.

personal, personnel *Personal* refers to an individual — *a personal matter* or *personal opinion. Personnel* refers to a group of people —*company personnel* or *the personnel department.*

piece See **peace**

plain, plane *Plain* means to be flat or smooth; to be unadorned; level, treeless land. A *plane* is a flat surface; a stage of development; an airplane; a tool for smoothing wood.

practicable, practical *Practicable* refers to that which is anticipated to be feasible or usable — *a practicable idea. Practical* pertains to actual use or experience —*a practical solution.*

precede, proceed *Precede* means to go before in order —*Dinner will precede the speeches. Proceed* means to go forward or to continue —*After a rest, we will proceed.*

precedence, precedents *Precedence* implies priority — *Education should take* *precedence over defense spending in the new budget. Precedents* is the plural of *precedent,* which describes previous or established procedure —*The case may be strengthened by citing precedents established in previous court rulings.*

presence, presents *Presence* is the state of being in attendance — *Your presence is requested at the meeting. Presents* are the gifts you give and receive.

principal, principle *Principal* means to be first in rank or importance — *She is to be the principal speaker. Principle* refers to a general truth or law — *the principle of a representative government*; moral standards collectively —*He is a man of principle.*

prosecute See **persecute**

quiet, quite *Quiet* refers to a state of calm or tranquility. *Quite* is an adverb which expresses absolute certainty, without reservation —*He is quite dead.*

rain, reign, rein *Rain* is a weather condition. To *reign* is to rule. *Rein* describes a strap to control an animal; the act of checking or halting —*get a rein on the outrageous spending.*

right, rite, write *Right* describes that which is accurate, correct, or true. A *rite* is a ceremony. To *write* is to compose or create; to commit to paper.

senses See **census**

serf, surf A *serf* is a peasant attached to the land. The *surf* is the swell of the sea breaking against land.

shone, shown *Shone* is the past tense and past participle of *shine. Shown* is the past participle of *show.*

sight See **cite**

site See **cite**

sole, soul *Sole* means only. *Soul* represents the vital as opposed to the physical characteristics of a person or thing; the moral or spiritual part of a person.

staid, stayed *Staid* describes a steady or sedate manner. *Stayed,* the past tense of *stay,* means stopped, remained or ceased.

stake, steak *Stake* is a pointed stick of wood. *Steak* is a piece of meat.

stationary, stationery *Stationary* refers to office supplies. *Stationery* means to be fixed in place.

stayed See **staid**

steak See **stake**

steal, steel *Steal* is to take without authority; to move stealthily. *Steel* is an alloy compound of iron; to make strong or unyielding – *to steel one's self against trouble.*

suite, sweet *Sweet* is a taste like sugar. A *suite* is a set of things which are intended to be used together –*a suite of offices* or a *bedroom suite* (furniture).

surf See **serf**

teach See **learn**

than, then *Than* is a conjunction which expresses comparison – *She is taller than you are. Then* usually denotes *at that time* – *We were young then*; or expresses relative time – *Wash the dishes, then take out the garbage;* as a conjunction, it means as a consequence –*I will do it then, since you won't.*

their, there, they're *Their* is the possessive of *they* –*their house. There* indicates a place away from the speaker –*It is over there. They're* is the contraction of *they are* –*they're going to do it.*

wander, wonder *Wander* is to roam about. *Wonder* is a feeling of surprise and curiosity.

weak, week *Weak* is to lack strength. *Week* is a period of seven days.

weather, whether *Weather* refers to the condition of the atmosphere; to pass through and survive, as a crisis. *Whether* introduces or implies an alternative –*whether (or not) you are going.*

wholly See **holly**

who's, whose *Who's* is the contraction of *who is* – *Who's going? Whose* is the possessive of *who* – *Whose sweater is this?*

write See **right**

your, you're *Your* is the possessive of *you* –*Is this your sweater? You're* is the contraction of *you are* –*You're going?*

ABBREVIATIONS

The abbreviation is a convenient form which should be used with discretion and a modicum of judgment.

In general, they are not used in the body of correspondence except for titles, certain literary or technical terms and acronyms.

Be sure that any abbreviations you use, particularly of a technical nature are familiar to your reader.

When in doubt about the use of an abbreviation, don't use it.

Personal names and titles

Given names are not abbreviated except in the accepted form of a company name

Geo. W. Smith & Sons, Inc.

or on the signature line of a letter, if that is the author's preference.

Titles before a name are usually abbreviated except that civil or military titles are spelled out when used with the last name only.

Mr. John J. Smith or **Mr. Smith**

Gen. Mark Clark or **General Clark**

Sen. Hubert H. Humphrey or **Senator Humphrey**

Titles, degrees, affiliations, etc. after a name are abbreviated after a full name and are not used after the last name only.

The title, etc. after a name is set off with a comma except for II, III, 2d or 3d denoting succession.

James A. Kingston, Jr. **James A. Kingston II**

The title esquire (Esq.) is not used with another title, before or after a name.

Organizations

Abbreviations in the name of an organization should follow the form used by the organization on its letterhead. The same is true of an acronym for the organizational name. When writing about an organization to a third party, be sure that any acronyms are familiar to the reader.

Commonly used abbreviations and acronyms are contained in the list of abbreviations on the following pages.

Place names

Abbreviations in street addresses may be written with or without periods.

City, state and zip codes should be separated by spaces without punctuation. The postal abbreviations for state names are included on the following pages.

Names of places, monuments, historic sites, etc. should be written out whenever possible to avoid confusion.

Measure and time

Despite the admonition to avoid abbreviations in text, it is not always practical to do so. The only recourse is to use good judgment to create a document which looks attractive, is easy to read and will be understood by the reader.

It can be awkward if the same terms need to be used a number of times when describing size or capacity. In such cases, abbreviations are preferred in the interest of brevity and clarity.

The days of the week and the months of the year are commonly abbreviated, however, spelling them out is preferred. The times of day, A.M. or P.M., are always abbreviated and may be lower case as well.

Commercial, scholarly and technical

Each endeavor has its own language with terms familiar only to those who take part. Just as care should be taken to avoid technical terms when addressing someone not familiar with the terms, far more care should be taken to avoid abbreviations which may be misunderstood.

A

a. about

AA Alcoholics Anonymous, author's alterations

AAA or **A.A.A.** Amateur Athletic Association, American Automobile Association, Automobile Association of America

AARP American Association of Retired Persons

A.A.U. Amateur Athletic Union

A.A.U.P. American Association of University Professors

A.A.U.W. American Association of University Women

A.B. Bachelor of Arts (Latin *Artium Baccalaureus*)

ABA American Bar Association, American Booksellers Association

abbr. or **abbrev.** abbreviation

abr. abridged, abridgment

abs. absent, absolute(ly) 3 abstract

a,/c or **A/C** account, account current

Ac *chem.* actinium

AC or **A.C.** or **a.c.** *electr.* alternating current

A.C. After Christ., Athletic Club

acad. academic, academy

acc. account, *gram.* accusative

accel. *music* accelerando, accelerate

acct. account, accountant

accus. *gram.* accusative

ack. acknowledge, acknowledgment

ACLU American Civil Liberties Union

ACS or **A.C.S.** American Chemical Society

A/cs Pay. accounts payable

A/cs Rec. accounts receivable

actg. acting

A.D. In the year of our Lord (Latin *anno domini*)

A.D.A. American Dental Association, Americans for Democratic Action

add. addenda, addendum., addition., address

ad fin. at, to, or toward the end (Latin *ad finem*)

adj. adjacent, adjective, adjunct

adm. administrative, administrator

Adm. Admiral

admin. administration, administrator

adv. in proportion (Latin *ad valorem*), *gram.* adverb, adverbial, advertisement

advt. advertisement

A.E.A. Actors' Equity Association

aeron. aeronautic, aeronautics

AFL or **A.F.L.** or **A.F. of L.** American Federation of Labor

AFL-CIO or **A.F.L.-C.I.O.** American Federation of Labor and the Congress of Industrial Organizations

Ag *chem.* Silver (Latin *argentum*)

A.G. Attorney General

agcy. agency

agr. agricultural, agriculture, agriculturist

AK Alaska

aka also known as

AKC or **A.K.C.** American Kennel Club

Al *chem.* aluminum

AL Alabama

Ald. or, as title, **Aldm.** alderman

alg. *math.* algebra

alt. alternate, alternating, alternative, alteration(s), altitude, *music* alto

alter. alteration

alum. aluminum

am. ammeter

Am *chem.* americium

Am. America, American

A.M. Master of Arts (Latin Artium Magister)

A.M. or **a.m.** *ante meridiem,* before noon.

AMA or **A.M.A.** American Management Association, American Medical Association

Amb. ambassador

Amer. America, American.

Am. Ind. American Indian.

amp. *electr.* amperage, ampere(s)

amp.-hr. *electr.* ampere-hour

amt. amount

anat. anatomical, anatomist, anatomy

and. *music* andante

Angl. Anglican, Anglicized

anim. animated, *music* animato

anon. anonymous

ans. answer, answered.

ant. antenna, antiquarian, antiquity, antonym

antilog. antilogarithm

antiq. antiquarian, antiquities

ap. apothecaries' (weight or measure)

approx. approximately

Apr. April

apt. (*pl.* **apts.**) apartment

Ar *chem.* argon

AR Arkansas

arch. archaic, archaism, architect, architectural, architecture.

archeol. archeology

archit. architecture

arg. silver (Latin *argentum*)

arith. arithmetic(al)

ARM adjustable-rate mortgage

Armen. Armenian

arr. arrange, arranged, arrangement(s), arrival, arrive, arrived

art. article

As *chem.* arsenic

ASA or **A.S.A.** American Standards Association

asb. asbestos

ASCAP or **A.S.C.A.P.** American Society of Composers, Authors and Publishers

A.S.P.C.A. American Society for the Prevention of Cruelty to Animals

assd. assigned

assn. association

assoc. associate, association

asst. assistant

astrol. astrologer, astrological, astrology

astron. astronomer, astronomical, astronomy

At *chem.* astatine

athl. athlete, athletic, athletics

atm. *physics* atmosphere, atmospheric

att. attention, attorney

atten. attention

attn. attention

attrib. attribute, attributive

atty. attorney

Atty. Gen. Attorney General

Au *chem.* gold (Latin *aurum*)

aud. audible, audit, auditor

Aug. August

auth. author, authority, authorized

auto. automatic, automotive

aux. or **auxil.** auxiliary

avdp. avoirdupois

ave. avenue

avg. average

avn. aviation

avoir. avoirdupois

AZ Arizona

az. azimuth

B

B *chem.* boron

Ba *chem.* barium

B.A. Bachelor of Arts (Latin *Baccalaureus Artium*)

bact. bacteriological, bacteriology.

bal. balance, balancing

bar. barometer, barometric

barit. *music* baritone

BASIC Beginner's All-purpose Symbolic Instruction Code

BBC or **B.B.C.** British Broadcasting Corporation

bbl. (*pl.* **bbls.**) barrel

B.C. Before Christ

BCD binary coded decimal

bd. (*pl.* **bds.**) board, bond

bd. ft. board feet.

bdl. bundle

Be *chem.* beryllium

bf or **b. f.** *printing* bold face

B/F brought forward

bg. (*pl.* **bgs.**) bag

Bi *chem.* bismuth

bibl. bibliographical

bibliog. bibliographer, bibliography

bicarb. sodium bicarbonate

b.i.d. *med.* twice a day (Latin *bis in die*)

biog. biographer, biographical, biography

biol. biological, biologist, biology

bk. (*pl.* **bks.**) bank, block., book

Bk *chem.* berkelium

bkt. basket(s), bracket

bl. bale(s), barrel(s), black, blue

b.l. or **B/L** bill of lading

bldg. building

blk. black, block, bulk

bls. bales., barrels

BLS Bureau of Labor Statistics

blvd. boulevard

b.o. back order

bor. borough.

bot. botanical, botanist, botany, bottle

br. branch, brother, bridge, brief

Br *chem.* bromine

Brit. Britain, British

bro. (*pl.* **bros.**) brother

B.S.A. Bibliographical Society of America, Boy Scouts of America

bsh. bushel

BTU, B.T.U. , b.t.u. or **btu** British thermal unit

bu. bushel(s)

bx. (*pl.* **bxs.**) box

C

C *chem.* carbon

c. about (Latin *circa*), centimeter(s), copyright, hundredweight, centigrade

C. Celsius

ca. about (Latin *circa*)

Ca *chem.* Calcium

CA California

CAB or **C.A.B.** Civil Aeronautics Board, Consumers Advisory Board

C.A.F. or **c.a.f.** cost and freight, cost, assurance and freight

cal. calendar, caliber, calorie(s)

canc. cancel, cancellation, canceled

cap. (*pl.* **caps.**) capacity, *printing* capitalize

CARE Cooperative for American Remittances Everywhere

cat. catalogue

cc. , **c.c.** or **cc** cubic centimeter(s), carbon copies

Cd *chem.* cadmium

Ce *chem.* Cerium

C.E. Chemical Engineer, Chief Engineer, Civil Engineer

CEA Council of Economic Advisers

cen. central, century

cent. centered, centigrade, centimeter(s)

cert. or **certif.** certificate

Cf *chem.* californium

cf. compare (Latin *confir*)

C.F. or **c.f.** cost and freight

C.F.I. or **c.f.i.** cost, freight, and insurance

c.f.m. or **cfm** cubic feet per minute

c.f.s. or **cfs** cubic feet per second

cg, cg. or **cgm.** centigram(s)

ch. or **Ch.** chapter

chem. chemical, chemist, chemistry

chg. (*pl.* **chgs.**) charge

chgd. charged

chm. or **chmn.** chairman

chron. or **chronol.** chronological, chronology

CIA Central Intelligence Agency

C.I.F. or **c.i.f.** cost, insurance, and freight

CIO or **C.I.O.** Congress of Industrial Organizations

circ. or **cir.** about (Latin *circa*), circular, circulation, circumference

cit. citation, cited, citizen

civ. civil., civilian

ck. (*pl.* **cks.**) cask, check

Cl *chem.* chlorine

clar. *music* clarinet

class. classic, classical, classification, classified, classify

clk. clerk, clock

C.L.U. Chartered Life Underwriter

Cm *chem.* curium

cm. or **cm** centimeter(s)

Co *chem.* cobalt

CO Colorado

c.o. or **c/o** care of

Co. or **co.** (*pl.* **cos.**)company

COBOL common business-oriented language

C.O.D. or **c.o.d.** cash on delivery, collect on delivery

C. of C. Chamber of Commerce

col. collected, collector, college, colonial, colony, color, colored, column

coll. colloquial, collect, collection, collector, college, collegiate

collat. collateral

colloq. colloquial, colloquialism, colloquially

com. commerce, commercial., common, commonly

Com. Commission, Commissioner, Committee

comb. combination, combining

coml. commercial

comm. commerce, commission, committee

comp. companion, comparative, compare, comparison, compilation, compiled, compiler, complete, composition, compositor, compound, compounded, comprising

cond. condition, *music* conducted, conductivity, conductor

conf. compare (Latin *confer*), conference

Cong. Congress, Congressional

conj. conjugation, conjunction conjunctive

cons. conserve, consigned, consignment, consolidated, consonant, construction

consol. consolidated

const. constant

constr. construction

cont. containing, contents, continue, continued, contract, contraction, contrary

contd. continued

contr. contract, contraction

contrib. contribution, contributor

CONUS Continental United States

co-op. or **coop.** cooperative

corol. or **coroll.** corollary

corp. corporation

corr. correct, corrected, correspondence, correspondent, corresponding

cp. compare

CPA or **C.P.A.** Certified Public Accountant

cr. created, credit, creditor

Cr *chem.* chromium

CR carriage return

crit. critic, criticism, criticize, critical

Cs *chem.* cesium

CST, C.S.T. or **c.s.t.** Central Standard Time

ct. cent(s), county, court, one hundred (Latin *centum*)

CT Connecticut

ctn. carton

ctr. center

cu. cubic

Cu *chem.* copper (Latin *cuprum*)

cu. cm. cubic centimeter(s)

cu. ft. cubic foot or feet

cu. in. cubic inch(es)

cur. currency, current

cu. yd. cubic yard(s)

cwt. hundredweight

cyl. cylinder, cylindrical

D

D *chem.* deuterium

d. or **D.** date, diameter, dose, *med.* give (Latin *da*)

D.A. District Attorney

dat. *gram.* dative

dau. daughter

db or **db.** decibel(s)

d. b. a. doing business as

dbl. double

DC District of Columbia

DC, D.C. or **d.c.** *electr.* direct current

dd. or **d/d** delivered

DE Delaware

deb. debenture

dec. deceased, decrease, decimeter

Dec. December

decd. deceased

decim. decimeter

decl. declension

def. defective, defendant, defense, deferred, defined, definition

deg. degree(s)

del. delegate, delete, deliver

Dem. Democrat, Democratic

demon. demonstrative

dep. departs, departure, depot, deputy

dept. department

der. derivation, derivative, derived

desc. descendant

det. detach, detachment, detail

devel. development

dia. diameter

Di *chem.* didymium

diag. diagram

dial. dialect, dialectal

diam. diameter

dict. dictionary

diff. difference, different

dim. dimension(s)

dim. or **dimin.** *music* diminuendo, diminutive

dipl. diplomat, diplomatic

dir. director

dist. distance, distant, district

dist. atty. or **Dist. Atty.** district attorney

distr. distribute, distribution, distributor

div. divided, dividend, division, divisor, divorce(d)

dlr. dealer

dlvy. delivery

doc. document

DOD Department of Defense

dom. domain, domestic, dominion

DOS disk operating system

doz. dozen(s)

Dr. Doctor, Drive

DST or **D.S.T.** or **d.s.t.** Daylight Saving Time

d.t. delirium tremens

dup. or **dupl.** duplicate

dwt. pennyweight

Dy *chem.* dysprosium

dyn. or **dynam.** dynamics

dz. dozen(s)

E

EBCDIC Extended Binary Coded Decimal Interchange Code

ECA Economic Cooperation Administration

ecol. ecological, ecology

econ. economic, economics, economy

ed. or **edit.** edited., edition., editor

EDP electronic dataprocessing

EDT or **E.D.T.** or **e.d.t.** Eastern Daylight Time

educ. education, educational

e.e. errors excepted

EEC European Economic Community

EEG *med.* electroencephalogram

EEOC Equal Employment Opportunity Commission

EFTS electronic funds transfer system

e.g. for example (Latin *exempli gratia*)

EIB or **E.I.B.** Export-Import Bank

EKG *med.* electrocardioigram

el. elevation

elec. electric, electrical, electrician

elem. element(s), elementary

elev. elevation

enc. enclosed, enclosure(s)

ency. encyclopedia

eng. or **engr.** engine, engineer, engineering, engraved, engraver, engaving

enl. enlarge(d), enlisted

env. envelope

eq. equal, equation, equator, equivalent

Er *chem.* erbium

erron. erroneous, erroneously

Es *chem.* einsteinium

ESOP employee stock option plan

esp. or **espec.** especially

ESP extrasensory perception

Esq. Esquire

est. established, estate, estimated, estuary

EST, E.S.T. or **e.s.t.** Eastern Standard Time

estab. established

ETA estimated time of arrival

et al. and others (Latin *et alii*)

Eu *chem.* europium

ex. examination, examined, example, except, excepted, exception, exchange

exam. examination, examined

exc. excellent, except, excepted, exception, exchange

exch. exchange., exchequer

excl. exclamation, exclusive

exec. executive, executor

exp. expense(s), expiration, expired, export, exported, exporter, express, experiment, experimental

ext. extension, external, externally, extinct, extra, extract

F

F *chem.* fluorine

F or **F.** fahrenheit

fac. facsimile, factor, factory

Fahr. Fahrenheit

fam. familiar, family

f.b. freight bill

FBI or **F.B.I.** Federal Bureau of Investigation

f.c. *printing* follow copy

FCC or **F.C.C.** Federal Communications Commission

FDA or **F.D.A.** Food and Drug Administration

FDIC or **F.D.I.C.** Federal Deposit Insurance Corporation

Fe *chem.* iron (Latin *ferrum*)

Feb. February

fed. federal, federated, federation

fem. feminine, female

ff *music* fortissimo

ff. folios, following

FHA Federal Housing Administration

FHLBB Federal Home Loan Bank Board

FICA Federal Insurance Contributions Act

fid. fidclity, fiduciary

FIFO first in, first out

fig. figurative(ly), figure(s)

FILO first in, last out

fl. floor, fluid, *music* flute

FL Florida

flex. flexible

fl. oz. fluid ounce(s)

Fm *chem.* fermium

FM or **F.M.** or **f.m.** frequency modulation

FMB Federal Maritime Board

FMCS Federal Mediation and Conciliation Service

F.O.B. or **f.o.b.** free on board

fol. folio, following

for. foreign, forest

FORTRAN formula translator

fpm or **f.p.m.** feet per minute

fps or **f.p.s.** feet per second

fr. fragment, from

Fr *chem.* francium

Fr. brother (Latin *Frater*), *Eccl.* Father., France, French

FRB Federal Reserve Bank, Federal Reserve Board

freq. frequency, frequent(ly)

Fri. Friday

frt. freight

FSLIC Federal Savings and Loan Insurance Corporation

ft. feet, foot, fort

FTC or **F.T.C.** Federal Trade Commission

furn. furnished, furniture

fwd. forward

G

g. or **g** gram(s)

Ga *chem.* gallium

GA Georgia

gals. gallons

GAO General Accounting Office

GATT General Agreement on Tariffs and Trade

Gd *chem.* gadolinium

gds. goods

Ge *chem.* germanium

gel. gelatinous

gen. gender, general, generally, generator, generic, genus

geog. geographer, geographic(al), geography

geol. geologist, geologic(al), geology

geom. geometric(al), geometry

ger. gerund

gloss. glossary

gm. gram(s)

G.M. general manager., Grand Master

GMT or **G.M.T.** or **G.m.t.** Greenwich mean time

GNP or **G.N.P.** gross national product

Gov. or **gov.** governor

Govt. or **govt.** government

G.P. general practitioner

GPM or **gpm** or **g.p.m.** gallons per minute

GPO or **G.P.O.** General Post Office, Government Printing Office

gr. grade, grain(s), gram(s), grammar, gross, group

gram. grammar, grammatical

gro. gross (unit of quantity)

gr. wt. grossweight

G.S.A. or **GSA** Girl Scouts of America, General Services Administration

gt. *bookbinding* gilt, great

guar. guaranteed

gym. gymnastics, gymnasium

H

H *chem.* hydrogen

hdbk. handbook

He *chem.* helium

Hf *chem.* hafnium

Hg *chem.* mercury (Latin *hydrargyrum*)

hgt. height

HI Hawaii

hist. historian, historical, history

HMO health maintenance organization

Ho *chem.* holmium

hon. honorably, honorary

Hon. Honorable

hor. horizon, horizontal

hort. horticulture, horticultural

hosp. hospital

HP or **hp, H.P.** or **h.p.** horsepower

ht. height

HUD Department of Housing and Urban Development

I

I *chem.* iodine

IA Iowa

ib. or **ibid.** in the same place (Latin *ibidem*)

IBT International Brotherhood of Teamsters

ICC or **I.C.C.** Interstate Commerce Commission

ICJ International Court of Justice

id. the same (Latin *idem*)

ID Idaho

I.D. or **i.d.** inside diameter

i.e. that is (Latin *id est*)

IL Illinois

illus. or **illustr.** illustrated, illustration, illustrator

IMF International Monetary Fund

imit. imitation

imp. imperative, imperfect, imperial, import, imported, importer., important

IN Indiana

in. inch(es)

In *chem.* indium

inc. inclosure, including, inclusive, income, incorporated, increase

incl. inclosure, including, inclusive

incog. incognito

incr. increased, increasing

ind. independent, index, indicated, indicative, indirect, industrial

indef. indefinite

indent. *printing* indention

indic. indicating, indicative, indicator

inf. below (Latin *infra*), inferior, infinitive, information

init. initial, in the beginning (Latin *initio*)

ins. inches, inspector, insular, insulated, insulation, insurance

insol. insoluble

insp. inspected, inspector

inst. instant, instantaneous, instrument(al)

Inst. Institute, Institution

instr. instruction, instrument(al)

int. intelligence, interest, interior, interjection, internal, international, interval, intransitive

inter. intermediate

interrog. interrogative

intr. intransitive

intro. introduction, introductory

inv. invented, invention, inventor, invoice

Io *chem.* ionium

i.q. the same as (Latin *idem quod*)

IQ or **I.Q.** intelligence quotient

Ir *chem.* iridium

irreg. irregular(ly)

IRS Internal Revenue Service

it. or **ital.** italic(s)

J

Jan. January

jct. or **jctn.** junction

jour. journal, journeyman

J.P. Justice of the Peace

Jr. or **jr.** junior

Jul. July

jun. junior

Jun. June

junc. junction

K

K *chem.* potassium

K or **k** kilo

KB or **Kb** kilobyte

kc. or **kc** kilocycle(s)

kg. or **kg** kilograms

km. or **km** kilometer(s)

Kr *chem.* krypton

KS Kansas

kv. or **kv** kilovolt(s)

kw. or **kw** kilowatt(s)

K.W.H., kwh, kilowatt hour(s)

KY Kentucky

L

l. or **l** liter

La *chem.* lanthanum

LA Louisiana

lab. laboratory

LAN local area network

lang. language

lat. latitude

LBO leveraged buyout

lb(s). pound(s) (Latin *libra, librae*)

l.c. in the place cited (Latin *lococitato*), *printing* lower case

L/C or **l/c** letter of credit

L.C.L. or **l.c.l.** less than carload lot

lect. lecture, lecturer

LED light-emitting diode

legis. legislation, legislature

lex. lexicon

l.f. or **lf.** *printing* lightface

lg. or **lge.** large

Li *chem.* lithium

lib. book (Latin *liber*), librarian, library

LILO last in, last out

LIFO last in, first out

lin. lineal., linear

ling. linguistics

liq. liquid., liquor

lit. liter, literal(ly), literary, literature

lith., litho. or **lithog.** lithograph, lithography

ll. lines

loc. cit. in the place cited (Latin *loco citato*)

long. longitude

Lr *chem.* lawrencium

ltd. or **Ltd.** limited

Lu *chem.* lutetium

M

m or **m.** meter(s)

Ma *chem.* masurium

MA Massachusetts

mach. machine, machinery, machinist

MADD Mothers Against Drunk Driving

mag. magazine, magnet, magnetism

manuf. manufacture(d), manufacturer, manufacturing

Mar. March

marg. margin, margina

mas. or **masc.** masculine

math. mathematical, mathematician, mathematics

max. maximum

mc or **m.c.** or **mc.** megacycle

M.C. Master of Ceremonies

Md *chem.* mendelevium

MD Maryland

M.D. Doctor of Medicine (Latin *MedicinaeDoctor*)

mdse. merchandise

ME Maine

ME, ME. or **M.E.** Middle English

meas. measure

mech. mechanical, mechanics, mechanism

med. medical,medicine, medium

mem. member, memoir, memorandum, memorial

memo. memorandum

mf or **mf.** *music* moderately loud (Ital. *mezzo forte*)

mfg. manufacturing

mfr. manufacture, manufacturer

mg., mg or **mgm** milligram(s)

Mg *chem.* magnesium

mgr. manager

MI Michigan

mi. mile(s)

min. mineralogical, mineralogy, minimum, minute(s)

misc. miscellaneous, miscellany

mk. mark(s)

mkt. market

ml. milliliter(s)

mm. or **mm** millimeter(s)

m.m. with the necessary changes (Latin *mutatis mutandis*)

Mn *chem.* manganese

MN Minnesota

mo. (*pl.* **mos.**) month(s)

Mo *chem.* molybdenum

MO Missouri

mod. moderate, *music* moderato, modern

Mon. Monday

m.p.h. or **mph** miles per hour

MS Mississippi

MS., MS, ms. or **ms** manuscript

msg. message

MSG monosodium glutamate

MSS. MSS, mss. or **mss** manuscripts

MST, M.S.T. or **m.s.t.** mountain standard time

Mt. or **mt.** (*pl.* **mts.**)mount, mountain

MT Montana

mtg. meeting

mtge. mortgage

mtn. mountain

mus. museum, music, musician

myth. or **mythol.** mythology

N

N *chem.* nitrogen

Na *chem.* sodium (Latin *natrium*)

NAACP or **N.A.A.C.P.** National Association for the Advancement of Colored People

NAM National Association of Manufacturers

NASA National Aeronautics and Space Administration

natl. national

NATO North Atlantic Treaty Organization

Nb *chem.* niobium

N.B. or **n.b.** note well (Latin *nota bene*)

NBS or **N.B.S.** National Bureau of Standards

NC North Carolina

NCAA or **N.C.A.A.** National Collegiate Athletic Association

Nd *chem.* neodymium

ND North Dakota

Ne *chem.* neon

NE Nebraska

NEA National Education Association

neg. negative

neut. neuter

N.G. or **n.g.** no good

NH New Hampshire

Ni *chem.* nickel

NJ New Jersey

NLRB or **N.L.R.B.** National Labor Relations Board

NM New Mexico

No *Chem.* nobelium

No. or **no.** north, northern, number

nom. nominative

Nos. or **nos.** numbers

NOW National Organization for Women

Nov. November

Np *Chem.* neptunium

N.P. Notary Public

nr. near

NRC National Research Council, Nuclear Regulatory Commission

N.S.F. or **N/S/F** not sufficient funds

N.S.P.C.A. National Society for the Prevention of Cruelty to Animals

Nt *chem.* niton

NTSB National Transportation Safety Board

nt. wt. net weight

num. numeral(s)

NV Nevada

NY New York

NYSE New York Stock Exchange

O

O *chem.* oxygen

OAS Organization of American States

obit. obituary

obj. object, objection, objective

obs. observation, obsolete

o.c. in the work cited (Latin *opere citato*)

OCR optical character recognition, optical character reading

Oct. October

O.D., OD or **o.d.** outside diameter, overdraft, overdrawn

OEEC or **O.E.E.C.** Organization for European Economic Cooperation

off. offered, office, officer, official

OH Ohio

OK Oklahoma

OMB Office of Management and Budget

op. cit. in the work cited (Latin *opere citato*)

OPEC Organization of Petroleum Exporting Countries

opp. opposed, opposite

ord. ordained, order, ordinal, ordinance, ordinary

OR Oregon

org. organic, organized

OSHA Occupational Safety and Health Administration

orig. original(ly)

Os *chem.* osmium

oz. (*pl.* **ozs.**) ounce

P

P *chem.* phosphorus

p.a. yearly (Latin *per annum*)

Pa *chem.* protactinium

PA Pennsylvania

PA press agent, public address system

P.A. or **P/A** power of attorney, purchasing agent

par. paragraph, parallel, parenthesis

part. participle, particular

pass. passage, passenger, passive

pat. patent(ed), pattern

patd. patented

Pat. Off. Patent Office

payt. payment

Pb *chem.* lead (Latin *plumbum*)

PBS Public Broadcasting Service

pc. (*pl.* **pcs.**) piece, price

P/C or **p/c** petty cash

PC personal computer

pct. percent

pd. paid

Pd *chem.* palladium

Pen. or **pen.** peninsula

per. period, person

perf. perfect, perforated

perm. permanent

pert. pertaining

Phar., phar., Pharm. or **pharm.** pharmaceutical, pharmacy

phil. philosopher, philosophical, philosophy

phon. phonetics

phot. photograph, photographic, photography

phr. phrase

PHS Public Health Service

phys. physical, physician, physicist, physics

pk. (*pl.* **pks.**) pack, park, peak, peck

pkg. package(s)

pkt. packet

pl. place, plural

plat. plateau

plu. plural

plur. plural, plurality

Pm *chem.* promethium

P.M. or **p.m.** afternoon (Latin *post meridiem*)

P.M. or **PM** Postmaster

Po *chem.* polonium

P.O. or **p.o.** postal order, post office

pop. popular, popularly, population

POP point of purchase

pos. positive, possessive

poss. possession, possessive, possible, possibly

pp. pages, *music* pianissimo

P.P. or **p.p.** parcel post, postpaid

p.p. parcel post, past participle

ppd. postpaid, prepaid

ppl. participial

p.p.m. or **ppm.** or **ppm** parts per million

ppr. or **p.pr.** present participle

P.P.S. or **p.p.s.** additional postscript (Latin *post postscriptum*)

pr. pair(s), paper, present, price, printing, pronoun

Pr *chem.* praseodymium

PR Puerto Rico, public relations

prec. preceding

pred. predicate

pref. preface, prefatory, preference, prefix

pres. present

Pres. President

pret. preterit

prim. primary, primitive

print. printing

prod. produce(d), product

Prof. or **prof.** professor

prog. progressive

prop. proper(ly), property, proposition, proprietor, proprietary

prov. province, provincial, provisional

prs. pairs

P.S. or **p.s.** postscript

p.s.f. or **psf** pounds per square foot

p.s.i. or **psi** pounds per square inch

PST, P.S.T. or **p.s.t.** Pacific Standard Time

psychol. psychological, psychologist, psychology

pt. part, pint(s), point(s)

Pt *chem.* platinum

PTA or **P.T.A.** Parent-Teacher Association

ptg. printing

pts. parts, pints, points

Pu *chem.* plutonium

pub. public, publication, published, publisher, publishing

pwt. pennyweight

Q

Q.E.D. Which was to be demonstrated (Latin *quod erat demonstrandum*)

qq.v. which see (Latin *quae vide*)

qt. quantity, quart(s)

ques. question

q.v. which see (Latin *quae vide*)

R

r. radius, rare, right-hand page (Latin *recto*)

Ra *chem.* radium

RAM random-access memory

Rb *chem.* rubidium

rcd. received

rd. road, rod(s), round

R.D. Rural Delivery

Re *chem.* rhenium

REA Rural Electrification Administration

rec. receipt, received, recipe, record, recorded, recorder, recording

recit. recitative

rec. sec. recording secretary

ref. reference, referred, refund

refl. reflection, reflective(ly), reflex, reflexive

reg. region, register(ed), regular(ly), Regulation

REIT real estate investment trust

rel. relating, relative(ly), released

rep. report, representative

repr. reprinted

req. required, request, requisition

res. research, residence, reserve, resides

resp. respective(ly), respondent

retd. retained, returned

rev. revenue, reverse(d), review(ed), revise(d), revision, revolution

RFD or **R.F.D.** Rural Free Delivery

r.h. relative humidity, right hand

Rh *chem.* rhodium

rhet. rhetoric(al)

RI Rhode Island

R.I.P. rest in peace(Latin *requiescat* or *requiescant in pace*)

RISC reduced instruction set computer

rm. (*pl.* **rms.**) ream, room

Rn *chem.* radon

RNA *biochem.* ribonucleic acid

rom. *printing* Roman (type)

ROM read-only memory

rpm or **r.p.m.** revolutions per minute

rps or **r.p.s.** revolutions per second

rpt. report

RR or **R.R.** railroad, rural route

R.S.V.P. or **r.s.v.p.** please reply (French *Répondez s'il vous plaît*)

rt. right

Ru *chem.* ruthenium

S

S *chem.* sulfur

Sa *chem.* samarium

Sat. Saturday, Saturn

SAT Scholastic Aptitude Test

sb. substantive

Sb *chem.* antimony (Latin *stibium*)

s.c. *printing* small capitals, supercalendered

Sc *chem.* scandium

SC South Carolina

s. caps *printing* small capitals

sci. science, scientific

SD South Dakota

Se *chem.* selenium

sec. according to (Latin *secundum*), secant, second(s), secondary, secretary, section(s), sector

SEC or **S.E.C.** Securities and Exchange Commission.

sect. section, sectional

secty. secretary

Sen. or **sen.** senate, senator, senior

sep. separate

Sep. or **Sept.** September

seq. sequel, sequence

ser. serial, series

sgd. signed

shpt. shipment

Si *chem.* silicon

sig. signature

sing. singular

Sm *chem.* samarium

Sn *chem.* tin (Latin *stannum*)

soc. social, society

sol. soluble, solution

sop. *music* soprano

sp. special, species, specific, specimen, spelling

sq. square

Sr *chem.* strontium

SRO or **S.R.O.** standing room only

st. street

sta. station, stationary

std. standard

ster. or **stg.** sterling

stge. storage

stk. stock

str. steamer, strait

sub. subscription, substitute, suburb, suburban

subj. subject, subjective(ly), subjunctive

subst. substantive, substitute

suf. or **suff.** suffix

Sun. Sunday

sup. above (Latin*supra*), superior, superlative, supplement, supplementary, supply

super. superintendent, superior

superl. superlative

supp. or **suppl.** supplement, supplementary

supr. supreme

supt. superintendent

sur. surcharge, surplus

surg. surgeon, surgery, surgical

surv. survey, surveying, surveyor, surviving

syl. or **syll.** syllable, syllabus

sym. symbol, symphony, symptom

syn. synonym

synop. synopsis

syst. system, systematic

T

t. teaspoon

T *chem.* tantalum

T. tablespoon

Ta *chem.* tantalum

tab. table(s), tabulate, tabulation

Tb *chem.* terbium

t.b. trial balance

tbs. or **tbsp.** tablespoon(s)

Tc *chem.* technetium

Te *chem.* tellurium

technol. technology

tel. telegram, telegraph, telegraphic, telephone

temp. temperature, temporary

ter. terrace, territorial, territory

term. terminal, termination, terminology

Th *chem.* thorium

Thur. Thursday

Ti *chem.* titanium

Tl *chem.* thallium

Tm *chem.* thulium

TN Tennessee

tng. training

top. topographical, topography

tp. township

tr. trace, train, transitive, translated, translation, translator, transpose

Tr *chem.* terbium

trans. transaction(s), transferred, *gram.* transitive, translated, translation, translator, transportation, transpose, transverse

transl. translated, translation

transp. transparent, transportation

treas. treasurer, treasury

trfd. transferred

tripl. triplicate

Tues. Tuesday

TVA or **T.V.A.** Tennessee Valley Authority

twp. township

TX Texas

typ. or **typog.** typographic(al), typography

U

U *chem.* uranium

UAW or **U.A.W.** United Automobile Workers

u.c. *music* soft pedal (Ital. *una corda,* one string), *printing* uppercase

UFO unidentified flying object

ult. ultimate(ly)

UN or **U.N.** United Nations

UNEF United Nations Emergency Force

UNESCO or **Unesco** The United Nations Educational, Scientific and Cultural Organization

UNICEF or **Unicef** United Nations Children's Fund

univ. universal(ly), university

unpub. unpublished

Ur *chem.* uranium

US or **U.S.** United States

USA or **U.S.A.** United States of America

U.S.C. & G.S. United States Coast and Geodetic Survey

USCG or **U.S.C.G.** United States Coast Guard

USDA United States Department of Agriculture

USIA or **U.S.I.A.** United States Information Agency

USPHS or **U.S.P.H.S.** United States Public Health Service

USPS United States Postal Service

USS or **U.S.S.** United States Ship (or Steamer or Steamship)

UT Utah

V

v. *gram.* verb, vocative, verse, version, versus, volt, voltage, volume

V *chem.* vanadium

VA Virginia

var. variant, variation, variety

VAT value added tax

v. aux. *gram.* auxiliary verb

vb. verb, verbal

Vd *chem.* vanadium

VDT video display terminal

ver. verse(s), version

VHF, vhf, V.H.F., or **v.h.f.** very high frequency

v.i. *gram.* intransitive verb

Vi *chem.* virginium

VI Virgin Islands

vil. village

VIP or **V.I.P.** very important person

VISTA Volunteers in Service to America

viz. namely (Latin *videlicet*)

vocab. vocabulary

vol. volume, volunteer

vols. volumes

vs. verse, versus

VSS versions

v.t. *gram.* transitive verb

VT Vermont

v.v. viceversa

W

W *chem.* tungsten (Latin *wolfram*)

WA Washington

W.b. , W/b, W.B. or **W/B** waybill

Wed. Wednesday

wf or **w.f.** *printing* wrong font

WHO World Health Organization

WI Wisconsin

wk. (*pl.* **wks.**) week, work

wkly. weekly

wt. weight

WV West Virginia

WY Wyoming

X

x-cp. , X.C. or **x.c.** Ex coupon

x-div. , X.D. or **x.d.** Ex dividend

Xe *chem.* xenon

x-ref. cross-reference

Y

Y *chem.* yttrium

Yb *chem.* ytterbium

yd. (*pl.* **yds.**) yard

yr. year, your

yrs. years, yours

Yt *chem.* yttrium

Z

Z. or **z.** zone

Zn *chem.* zinc

zool. zoological, zoologist, zoology

Zr *chem.* zirconium

FORMS OF ADDRESS

President of the United States

Address: Business: The President
The White House
Washington, D.C.

Social: The President and Mrs. ____ *(Last name)*
The White House
Washington, D.C.

Salutation: Formal: Mr. President:
Informal: Dear Mr. President:

Closing: Formal: Most respectfully yours,
Informal: Sincerely yours,

In conversation: Mr. President *or* Sir

Title of introduction: The President *or* Mr. ____ *(Last name)*

Vice President of the United States

Address:Business: The Vice President
United States Senate
Washington, D.C.

Social: The Vice President and Mrs. ____ (*Last name*)
Home address

Salutation:Formal: Mr. Vice President:
Informal: Dear Mr. Vice President:

Closing: Formal: Very truly yours,
Informal: Sincerely yours,

In conversation: Mr. Vice President *or* Sir

Title of introduction: The Vice President *or* Mr. ____ (*Last name*)

Chief Justice of the United States

Address:Business: The Chief Justice
The Supreme Court
Washington, D.C.

Social: The Chief Justice
or The Chief Justice and
Mrs. *or* Mr. ____ (*Last name*)
Home address

Salutation:Formal: Sir:
Informal: Dear Mr. *or* Ms. Chief Justice:

Closing: Formal: Very truly yours,
Informal: Sincerely yours,

In conversation: Mr. *or* Ms. Chief Justice; Sir *or* Madame

Title of introduction: The Chief Justice

Associate Justice of the Supreme Court

Address:Business: Mr. Justice *or* Madam Justice ____ (*Last name*)
The Supreme Court
Washington, D.C.

Social: Mr. Justice *or* Madam Justice ____ (*Full name*);
or Mr. Justice *or* Madam Justice and
Mrs. *or* Mr. ____ (*Last name*)
Home address

Salutation:Formal: Sir: *or* Madam:
Informal: Dear Mr. Justice:
or Madam Justice ____ (*Last name*):

Closing: Formal: Very sincerely yours,
Informal: Sincerely yours,

In conversation: Mr. Justice *or* Madam Justice;
Mr. Justice *or* Madam Justice ____ (*Last name*);
Sir *or* Madam

Title of introduction: Mr. Justice *or* Madam Justice ____ (*Last name*)

Cabinet Officer

Address:Business: The Honorable ____ (*Full name*)
Secretary of the Treasury,
Attorney General of the United States, etc.
Washington, D.C.

Social: The Honorable ____ (*Full name*);
or The Secretary of the Treasury
and Mrs. *or* Mr. ____ (*Last name*)
Home address

Salutation:Formal: Sir: *or* Dear Sir: *or* Madam:
Informal: Dear Mr. Secretary: *or* Dear Madam Secretary:

Closing: Formal: Very truly yours,
Informal: Sincerely yours,

In conversation: Mr. Secretary *or* Madam Secretary;
Mr. Attorney General;
Mr. *or* Ms. ____ (*Last name*)

Title of introduction: The Secretary of the Treasury,
Mr. ____ (*Last name*)
or The Secretary of the Treasury,
Ms. ____ (*Last name*)

Former President

Address:Business: The Honorable ____ (*Full name*)
Office address

Social: The Honorable ____ (*Full name*)
or The Honorable and Mrs. ____ (*Full name*)
Home address

Salutation:Formal: Sir:
Informal: Dear Mr. ____ (*Last name*):

Closing: Formal: Very truly yours,
Informal: Sincerely yours,

In conversation: Mr. ____ (*Last name*)*or* Sir

Title of introduction: The Honorable ____ (*Full name*)

United States Senator

Address:Business: The Honorable ____ (*Full name*)
United States Senate
Washington, D.C.

Social: The Honorable (*Full name*);
or The Honorable and Mrs. *or* Mr. ____(*Full name*)
Home address

Salutation:Formal: Sir: *or* Madam:
Informal: Dear Senator ____ (*Last name*):

Closing: Formal: Very truly yours,
Informal: Sincerely yours,

In conversation: Senator; *or* Senator ____ (*Last name*);
or Sir *or* Madam

Title of introduction: Senator ____ (*Last name*)

Speaker of the House of Representatives

Address:Business: The Honorable ____ (*Full name*)
The Speaker of the House of Representatives
Washington, D.C.

Social: The Speaker of the House of Representatives
and Mrs. *or* Mr. ____ (*Last name*)
Home address

Salutation:Formal: Sir: *or* Madam:
Informal: Dear Mr. *or* Madam Speaker:

Closing: Formal: Very truly yours,
Informal: Sincerely yours,

In conversation: Mr. *or* Madam Speaker; Sir *or* Madam

Title of introduction: The Speaker of the House of Representatives;
The Speaker, Mr. *or* Ms. ____ (*Last name*)

Member of the House of Representatives

Address: Business: The Honorable ____ (*Full name*)
United States House of Representatives
Washington, D.C.

Social: The Honorable ____ (*Full name*);
or The Honorable and Mrs. *or* Mr. ____ (*Full name*)
Home address

Salutation: Formal: Sir: *or* Madam:
Informal: Dear Mr. *or* Ms. ____ (*Last name*):

Closing: Formal: Very truly yours,
Informal: Sincerely yours,

In conversation: Mr. or Ms. ____ (*Last name*); Sir *or* Madam

Title of introduction: Representative ____ (*Last name*)

Ambassador of the United States

Address: Business: The Honorable ____ (*Full name*)
The Ambassador of the United States
American Embassy
(*City, Country*)

Social: The Honorable ____ (*Full name*);
or The Honorable and Mrs. *or* Mr. ____ (*Full name*)
Home address

Salutation: Formal: Sir: *or* Madam:
Informal: Dear Mr. *or* Madam Ambassador:

Closing: Formal: Very truly yours,
Informal: Sincerely yours,

In conversation: Mr. *or* Madam Ambassador; Sir *or* Madam

Title of introduction: The American Ambassador
or The Ambassador of the United States

Minister Plenipotentiary of the United States

Address:Business: The Honorable ___ (*Full name*)
The Minister of the United States
American Legation
(*City, Country*)

Social: The Honorable ____ (*Full name*);
or The Honorable and Mr. *or* Mrs. ____ (*Full name*)
Home address

Salutation:Formal: Sir: *or* Madam:
Informal: Dear Mr. *or* Madam Minister:

Closing: Formal: Very truly yours,
Informal: Sincerely yours,

In conversation: Mr. *or* Ms. ____ (*Last name*)

Title of introduction: Mr. *or* Ms. ____ (*Last name*), the American Minister

Consul of the United States

Address:Business: Mr. *or* Ms. ____ (*Full name*)
American Consul
(*City, Country*)

Social: Mr. and Mrs. (*Full name*)
Home address

Salutation:Formal: Sir: *or* Madam: *or* Dear Sir: *or* Madam:
Informal: Dear Mr. *or* Ms. ____ (*Last name*):

Closing: Formal: Very truly yours,
Informal: Sincerely yours,

In conversation: Mr. *or* Ms. ____ (*Last name*)

Title of introduction: Mr. *or* Ms. ____ (*Last name*)

Ambassador of a foreign country

Address:Business: The Honorable ____ (*Full name*)
The Minister of ____ (*Country*)
Washington, D.C.

Social: The Honorable and Mrs. *or* Mr. ____ (*Last name*)
Home address

Salutation:Formal: Sir: *or* Madam:
Informal: Dear Mr. *or* Madam Minister:

Closing: Formal: Very truly yours,
Informal: Sincerely yours,

In conversation: Mr. *or* Madam Minister; Sir *or* Madam

Title of introduction: The Minister of ____ (*Country*)

Governor of a State

Address:Business: The Honorable ____ (*Full name*)
Governor of (State)
(*Capital city, State*)

Social: The Honorable ____ (*Full name*);
or The Honorable and Mrs. *or* Mr. ____ (*Full name*)
Home address

Salutation:Formal: Sir: *or* Madam:
Informal: Dear Governor ____ (*Last name*):

Closing: Formal: Very truly yours,
Informal: Sincerely yours,

In conversation: Governor ____ (*Last name*) *or* Sir *or* Madam

Title of introduction: The Governor *or* The Governor of ____ (*State*)

State Senators and Representatives

Address in the same manner as U.S. Senators and Representatives

Mayor

Address:Business: Honorable ____ (*Full name*)
Mayor of ____ (*City*)
City Hall
(*City, State*)

Social: The Honorable ____ (*Full name*)
or The Honorable and Mrs. *or* Mr. ____ (*Full name*)
Home address

Salutation:Formal: Sir: *or* Madam:
Informal: Dear Mayor ____ (*Last name*):

Closing: Formal: Very truly yours,
Informal: Sincerely yours,

In conversation: Mr. Mayor *or* Madam Mayor

Title of introduction: Mayor ____ (*Last name*)

Protestant Bishop

Address:Business: The Right Reverend ____ (*Full name*)
Bishop of ____
(*City, State*)

Social: The Right Reverend and Mrs. ____ (*Full name*)
Home address

Salutation:Formal: Right Reverend Sir:
Informal: Dear Bishop Bowman:

Closing: Formal: Respectfully yours,
Informal: Sincerely yours,

In conversation: Bishop ____ (*Last name*)

Title of introduction: Bishop ____ (*Last name*)

Protestant Clergyman

Address:Business: The Reverend ____ (*Full name, followed by degree, if any*)
Church address

Social: The Reverend *or* Dr. and Mrs. *or* Mr. (*Full name*); *or* (*if husband and wife are both clergy*)
The Reverend Mr. and Mrs. ____ (*Last name*)
Home address

Salutation:Formal: Dear Sir *or* Madam:
Informal: Dear Mr. *or* Ms. *or* Dr. ____ (*Last name*):

Closing: Formal: Sincerely yours,
Informal: Sincerely yours,

In conversation: Mr. *or* Mrs. *or* Dr. ____ (*Last name*)

Title of introduction: Mr. *or* Mrs. *or* Dr. ____ (*Last name*)

Rabbi

Address:Business: Rabbi ____ (*Full name, followed by degree, if any*)
Synagogue address

Social: Rabbi *or* Dr. and Mrs. *or* Mr. ____ (*Full name*); *or* (if husband and wife are both rabbis)
The Rabbis Mr. and Mrs. ____ (*Last name*)
Home address

Salutation:Formal: Dear Sir *or* Madam:
Informal: Dear Rabbi *or* Doctor:

Closing: Formal: Sincerely yours,
Informal: Sincerely yours,

In conversation: Rabbi *or* Dr. ____ (*Last name*)

Title of introduction: Rabbi *or* Dr. ____ (*Last name*)

The Pope

Address: His Holiness Pope Paul VI
or His Holiness the Pope
Vatican City

Salutation: Your Holiness:

Closing: Your Holiness' most humble servant,

In conversation: Your Holiness

Title of introduction: *One is presented to:* His Holiness
or The Holy Father

Cardinal

Address: His Eminence (*First name*) Cardinal (*Last name*)
Archbishop of ____
(*City, State*)

Salutation:Formal: Your Eminence:
Informal: Dear Cardinal (*Last name*):

Closing: Your Eminence's humble servant,

In conversation: Your Eminence

Title of introduction: *One is presented to:*
His Eminence Cardinal ____ (*Last name*)

Roman Catholic Archbishop

Address: The Most Reverend ____ (*Full name*)
Archbishop of ____
(*City, State*)

Salutation:Formal: Your Excellency: *or* Most Reverend Sir:
Informal: Dear Archbishop (*Last name*):

Closing: Your Escellency's humble servant,

In conversation: Your Excellency

Title of introduction: *One is presented to:*
The Most Reverend ____ (*Last name*)
The Archbishop of ____

Roman Catholic Bishop

Address: The Most Reverend ____ (*Full name*)
Church address

Salutation: Formal: Your Excellency: *or* Most Reverend Sir:
Informal: Dear Bishop ____ (*Last name*):

Closing: Formal: Your obedient servant,
Informal: Sincerely yours,

In conversation: Your Excellency

Title of introduction: Bishop ____ (*Last name*)

Monsignor

Address: The Right Reverend Monsignor ____ (*Last name*)
Church address

Salutation: Formal: Right Reverend Monsignor:
Informal: Dear Monsignor Ryan:

Closing: Formal: I remain, Right Reverend Monsignor,
yours faithfully,
Informal: Faithfully yours,

In conversation: Monsignor ____ (*Last name*)

Title of introduction: Monsignor ____ (*Last name*)

Priest

Address: The Reverend ____ (*Full name, and the initials of his order*)
Church address

Salutation: Formal: Reverend Father:
Informal: Dear Father ____ (*Last name*):

Closing: Formal: I remain, Reverend Father,
yours faithfully,
Informal: Faithfully yours,

In conversation: Father *or* Father ____ (*Last name*)

Title of introduction: The Reverend Father ____ (*Last name*)

Member of a Religious Order

Address: Sister *or* Brother ____ (*Full name, and initials of the order)*
Home address

Salutation: Formal: Dear Sister: *or* Brother:
Informal: Dear Sister *or* Brother ____ (*First name*):

Closing: Formal: Respectfully yours,
Informal: Faithfully yours,

In conversation: Sister *or* Brother ____ (*First name*)
Title of introduction: Sister *or* Brother ____ (*First name*)

University Professor

Address: Business: Professor ____ (*Full name*)
Office address

Social: Professor *or* Dr. and Mrs. *or* Mr. ____ (*Full name*)
Home address

Salutation: Formal: Dear Professor *or* Dr. ____ (*Last name*):
Informal: Dear Mr. *or* Ms. ____ (*Last name*):

Closing: Formal: Very truly yours,
Informal: Sincerely yours,

In conversation: Professor *or* Dr. *or* Mr. *or* Ms. ____ (*Last name*)
Title of introduction: Professor *or* Dr. ____ (*Last name*)

Physician

Address: Business: ____ (*Full name*), M.D. *or* Dr. ____ (*Full name*)
Office address

Social: Dr. and Mrs. *or* Mr. ____ (*Full name*)
Home address

Salutation: Dear Dr. ____ (*Last name*):

Closing: Formal: Very truly yours,
Informal: Sincerely yours,

In conversation: Dr. ____ (*Last name*)
Title of Introduction: Dr. ____ (*Last name*)

Index

Index

Reference lists

On the theory that we learn by example, this book is sprinkled liberally with word lists and examples. Following is a list of the lists

WEBSTER'S SPELLING DICTIONARY

WEBSTER'S SPELLING DICTIONARY

PMC Publishing Company, Inc.

PMC Publishing Company, Inc.
118 East 28 Street
New York, New York 10016

ISBN: 1-881275-15-9

Ever wonder why English spelling is so difficult? Why we don't just spell things the way they sound? Why different groups of letters sound the same? Or why one group gets pronounced in so many ways? How could anyone have come up with such a system?

Well, it wasn't done by just anyone, and certainly not by design. Like most languages, English began as a merging of primitive dialects, shaped and embellished by the speech of those with whom it came in contact. However, it didn't evolve in one place at one time, but in somewhat isolated pockets of fiercely independent peoples.

ENGLISH - A BRIEF HISTORY

Picture this. It's the middle of the fifth century, on an island called Britain, occupied by Roman troops who rule the native Celts. The Roman Empire runs into trouble and the troops are called home. As the Celts watch the Romans leave, they in turn are being watched by the Germanic peoples of northern Europe who see a fine land, ripe for settlement. As far as we know, this is no sudden invasion, but rather a migration which takes place over a period of several generations. In the end, pockets of Angles, Saxons, Jutes, Friscians and others occupy the whole of Britain except for Scotland and Wales.

Consider the change which has taken place. The Romans invade, then inform the survivors that they are a part of the Roman Empire for which privilege they will be allowed to work their own land and pay taxes to Rome. The Romans, proud of their own language and culture, are content to rule and remain largely indifferent to the customs and culture of the peoples they rule. The Germanic tribes simply want the land and view anyone occupying it as an inconvenience. Unlike the Romans, there is no centralized authority and the Germanic dialects, though probably similar, are not the same, having been altered by contact with others through trade or war.

Germanic tribes are settling throughout the island. They interact in commerce and in war. Alliances for aggression and for protection are formed and broken. Dialects meet, blend, change and move from one part of the country to another. The Saxons emerge as the dominant group and so the language is called English after the more obscure Angles. Nobody knows why.

Enter the Vikings, attacking in such force that control of the northern part of England is ceded to them in the middle of the ninth century. They blend into the countryside and before long the addition of Scandinavian words further sharpens the differences between northern and southern dialects.

About the same time, another group of Vikings settle in the north of France adopting the local French provincial dialect. Called Normans, they invade England in 1066, changing the language of the aristocracy of England to a type of French; English is for the peasants.

English, left to the Englanders, changes dramatically. Regional differences become more pronounced, French words are adopted and adapted, but most important, it all becomes a lot simpler. Lacking the guidance of scholars to point out the error of their ways, peasants are dropping the arbitrary genders and inflectional endings, in short, the unnecessary complications to 'correct' speech.

As the Normans become increasingly isolated from the continent and assimilate in this land of England, they come to think of themselves more as Englishmen tha Frenchmen. By the time Columbus makes his first voyage, English is again th dominant language in England, but not until the time of Shakespeare and the voyag of the Pilgrims is it a language that can be understood by most Englishmen.

When the language travels to America, it undergoes further change, much of it describe the new environment and wildlife. Words like *moose, opossum* and *persim mon. Meadow* won't do for the Great Plains and *prairie* is borrowed from the Frenc Writers continue to borrow or create new words as they need them. Immigran from around the world add theirs.

There you have it; 1500 years of linguistic evolution. The frustration we feel over th vagaries of English spelling must have been felt ten times over by any wh attempted to standardize it. The effect of blending dialects, indiscriminate borrowin and arbitrary spelling is catastrophic.

Fortunately we now have in America a compendium of words that are mostly un derstood throughout the country. Unfortunately few can spell them, but the follow ing pages contain some information which may help.

A FEW SPELLING RULES

Reading this section will not make you an expert speller. It will, however, help yo to become a better speller. Modern English, including scientific and technical term comprises well over a million words. We may have a nodding acquaintance with many as 50,000 of those words, but we use, on a regular basis, a few thousand most and are plagued by the spelling of a few hundred. Learning about th construction of words alerts you to patterns which tell when spelling is most like right, and allows concentration on those most likely wrong. Don't be put off by th meager examples in each section. They are there only to illustrate the point; assured that there are always more words which follow a rule than there are exce tions.

As much as I hate to admit it, your old English teacher was right: If you don't kno how to spell a word, look it up. Naturally, if you don't know the first letter of th word, you may have to look in more than one place. Sure, it's a pain, but if you a really interested in using the right word, consider one other thing your teach probably forgot to tell you. Looking up the word can often prevent misunderstanding. For example, it's good news if you *brake* your car, but not so goo if you *break* it. Among those words often misspelled are a number of simil sounding words which mean quite different things such as *affect/effect, ascent/asse adapt/adopt, altar/alter and accept/except*. See what I mean?

Dual Spelling

Matters are further complicated by the words which have acceptable dual spellin such as *endorse/indorse, adviser/advisor, enrolment/enrollment,* or *vender/vend* Common practice within our own sphere of influence (frequently requiring approv of instructor or supervisor) generally dictates which form we use. Many options su as *programme* are seldom used in America. The older forms of *-our* and *-re* as the la syllable of a word have generally been replace by *-or* and *-er* respectively. We tend to prefer *labor* to *labour, color* to *colour* and *center* to *centre,* but we use *theatre* as often as *theater*. Perhaps those in the theyatuh feel it smacks of culture. Common practice, however, does require consistency; whichever spelling you choose should be used all of the time.

Pronunciation

Looking up a word occasionally is the mark of a conscientious, careful writer; looking up the same word over and over again may imply something quite different. These few pages are a small effort to assist in the quest to be identified as something other than "quite different". Like most of us, you have millions of unused brain cells lying fallow; it is time to put them to work.

Careless pronunciation is a trap. Perhaps you want to describe something clever or inventive as *ingenious,* only you get careless and pick up *ingenuous*. *Ingenuous* means frank or sincere. Not bad, really, but not what you wanted to say.

Pronunciation is definitely an aid to proper spelling. It's usually much easier to spell a word correctly when you pronounce it properly, or to look it up when you are not quite sure.

Pronunciation can help spelling in another way. When you look up a word, try pronouncing each syllable phonetically with a brief pause between syllables, taking care to pronounce each letter (even silent ones) and never varying the pronunciation of a particular letter. The result is a strange word which you wouldn't care to have another hear you say aloud, but one which will trigger your subconscious to tell you how to spell the word the next time you see it. Take *phonetically,* for example. Spelled the way it's normally pronounced, the results look like *fonetekly,* which could set the reader to looking for a German dictionary. Mentally sounded out one syllable at a time, however, it comes out *pho* (using a soft *f* or *p-ho* in our mental pronunciation to indicate *ph*), *net* (I can spell that), *i* (that, too), *cal* (and that), *ly* (and here's a bonus: pronouncing *cal* and *ly* separately insures that both *l*'s will get into the final spelling). You don't have to do this very many times before it becomes automatic and you stop looking up the same words over and over again.

The A-B-C's Are Not For Children

Remember the cute rhyme in nursery school? See the colorful cards on the wall containing gaily decorated letters of the alphabet? You should have known what was to come when the colorful letters were replaced by stark black and white cards, capitals and lower case, with lines carefully drawn top, bottom and through the middle. You should have known that if you survived penmanship they would find another way to get you. And they are out there, singly and in groups.

We tend to concentrate on vowels because they give us the most problems. Just five vowels, *a, e, i, o, u* and one part-time vowel, *y,* are responsible for about twenty vowel sounds. Now any mathematician will tell you that it is no problem to create twenty distinct combinations out of five vowels. Unfortunately, this is English where any one of the sounds might come from several different spellings (*meat, meet, mete, deceit*) or any one spelling may engender a number of pronunciations (*rouge, rough, gouge, cough, thorough*).

Consonants are equally treacherous. The letter *s* masquerades part time as (*suppose*), as *sh* (*sugar*), or quietly hides (*aisle, isle*). The *c* vacillates between being a (*cede*) and a *k* (*care*) when it's not being an *sh* (*ocean*) or hiding behind a (*acknowledge*). And the *k* - outrageous! Blatantly stands at the beginning of a wo doing nothing (*knock, knee, know*). Almost as bad is the *p*, which normally we behaved, when put with an *h*, thinks it's an *f* (*physician, phobia*). Association with *p* not the only diversion of the *h*. Put it with a *g* and it can't decide whether to sou off like an *f* (*tough*) or be silent (*light*). Which brings us back to one of the sa problems that exists with vowels, a single sound created by different spellings (*fo photo, laugh*).

It's a wonder we can write this language at all. But these things have not been vealed to you to discourage you. By no means! They have been pointed out only make you wary and to thirst for battle, so go forth and conquer - but be careful c there.

Tips on Vowels

Silent -e

Like most of the rules this works only part of the time. Usually words havi a long vowel sound in the last syllable require a silent *-e* at the end (*ca mope, slope, kite, cure*). There are, however, many exceptions such as *meet* a *feet* (long *e* marked by doubling), *achieve* and *piece* (silent *i* and silent *e*) or *ch* and *thief* (silent *i*, see **-ei- and -ie-**, below).

-ei- and -ie-

In at least one Chinese dialect the long sound of *i-e* properly inflected is a of distress. It is also appropriate for English spelling.

Let's begin with the rule you learned in school - "*i* before *e* except after That's easy enough . . . when it works. What your teacher forgot to tell you that it works (almost always) only with the long *e* sound. Words like *gr piece, conceit and perceive* follow the rule.

Spellings pronounced with a sound other than the long *e* don't follow the r (*weigh, veil, freight, their*).

Some words with the long *e* sound like *either, leisure, neither, seize, specie* a *weird* don't follow any rule.

Prefixes

Normally a prefix added to a word changes its meaning without changing spelli There are exceptions. (Who could have guessed?) The good news is that the exce tions are modest and clear cut or of no real concern to us here. Into the latter ca gory fall words such as *inhabitable*, which means the same as *habitable*. The prefix *i* which means *not*, has been added without changing the spelling of the root wo but the meaning has not changed and both words are in common usage. Compa that with *human/inhuman*. It's another "nobody knows why" situation.

The exceptions which are of concern to us here all involve hyphens:

Hyphenate when joining *ex-*, *all-* or *self-* to a noun, such as *ex-president*, *all-inclusive*, or *self-proclaimed*.

Hyphenate when the prefix is used with a proper noun or adjective, such as *pro-American* or *un-American*.

Hyphenate to alleviate confusion such as creating a word which could be confused with another (*re-creation*, the act of creating again versus *recreation*, amusement) or to make the word easier to recognize (*re-emerge* rather than *reemerge*). You have some latitude with this one, but as in all things, be consistent.

There are about fifty prefixes in general use and nothing is to be gained by listing them all; however, it can be helpful to know the meaning of some which are similar:

ante- means *before* as in *antedate*,
  whereas *anti-* means *against* as in *antibody*
dis- means *separation* as in *disgrace*,
  whereas *dys-* means *ill* or *bad* as in *dysfunction*
hyper- means *above* or *excessive* as in *hyperactive*,
  whereas *hypo-* means *under* or *beneath* as in *hypodermic*
per- means *through* as in *pervade*,
  whereas *pre-* means *before* as in *precede*
  and *pro-* means *forward* as in *proceed*

Suffixes

Dumping the Silent -e

Usually, when a suffix begins with a vowel (*-ed*, *-ing*), the final *-e* is dropped and the suffix is added (*mope*, *moping*; *kite*, *kited*). As usual there are exceptions. After *c* or *g* the *-e* is retained before a suffix beginning with *a* or *o* (are you with me so far?) in order to preserve the soft sound of the *c* or *g* (*notice*, *noticeable*; *outrage*, *outrageous*).

Words with the suffix *-ment* keep the silent *-e* (*place*, *placement*) unless the *-e* is preceded by two consonants in which case it is dropped (*judge*, *judgment*; *acknowledge*, *acknowledgment*). In England the *-e* is not dropped which makes it an optional spelling in many American dictionaries. Just keep in mind that if you opt for the English spelling, keep it that way all the time.

Finally there are some common exceptions just to make sure that no one gets an A on the exam (*true*, *truly*; *hoe*, *hoeing*; *singe*, *singeing*; *dye*, *dyeing*; *whole*, *wholly*; *mile*, *mileage*).

Doubling Consonants

Following the silent *-e* rule, we drop the *-e* when adding endings like *-ed* and *-ing*. But how about their counterparts, the words with short vowel sounds which have no silent *-e*? How do we keep from confusing the two words? Simple. We double the consonant so that while *mope* becomes *moping*, *mop* becomes *mopping*. This usually works, but as you might have guessed, we don't get off that easily.

For one thing, the above rule applies only to syllables that contain a sin vowel so that *scoop* changes to *scooping* (not *scoopping*).

Words of more than one syllable require a further consideration, name which syllable is accented. Uh, oh!, we're back to pronunciation again. If accent of the word created is on the last syllable, follow the doubling con nant rule above (*defer, defer´ring; refer, refer´ring*). If the accent of the wo created is not on the last syllable, do not double the consonant (*cre cred´iting; refer, ref´erence*).

-er versus -or ending

The *-er* ending indicates the person, thing or action related to the root wo (*maker, speaker, driver*) and is the more common ending; when in doubt, use Some words take only the *-or* ending (*actor, creditor, elevator, visitor*), and a f words take either.

-cede, -ceed, -sede endings

The most common of these three endings is *-cede* (*precede, secede*) and, glo be!, the exceptions are few (*supersede, exceed, proceed and succeed*). Memor those four words and you will have one spelling lesson down pat.

Y as a Vowel

We don't normally include *y* in our list of vowels, because it performs t function only part time. At the beginning of a word or syllable, it tends function as a consonant; whereas, when it follows another consonant functions as a vowel. If you wonder why anyone cares, read this sente aloud, paying particular attention to the *y* sounds. In *you* and *paying*, exhibits a hard sound, while in *why* and *anyone* it sounds like the *i* in *wh* Never mind that phonetic spelling could eliminate the *y*, we're concern here with how to get along with it.

A final *y* preceded by a consonant (*fry, copy, sixty*) changes to an *i* before suffixes (*fried, copier, sixtieth*) except those suffixes beginning with i (*fryi copying, sixtyish*).

A final *y* preceded by a vowel (*pray, boy*) generally doesn't change whe suffix is added (*pray, prayed, praying; boy, boyish*) except sometimes (*day, da lay, laying, laid*). Go figure.

Hard c

As mentioned earlier the letter *c* often hides behind a *k*; this time you ge put it there. Words ending in a hard *c* add a *k* before suffixes beginning w a vowel (*panic, panicky, panicking; mimic, mimicked, mimicker*).

Plurals

Forming a plural offers another challenge to the writer. Most plurals are formed adding *s*, but there are plenty of exceptions as you will see.

Irregular Nouns

The bad news is that one group of irregular nounds changes spelling in a random fashion (*child, children; woman, women; man, men; goose, geese; mouse, mice*) while another doesn't change at all (*sheep, deer, fish*). The good news is that these are mostly words in common use and you should seldom encounter unfamiliar ones.

Nouns Ending in -f and -fe

Another tricky group is comprised of nouns ending in *-f* and *-fe;* some take an *s* to make the plural (*chief, chiefs; dwarf, dwarfs*), whereas others change the *f* to *v* and add *s* or *es* (*calf, calves; knife, knives*).

Yet Another Group

Forming the "yet another group" are nouns ending in *s, ss, z, sh, ch,* and *x*. If you can just remember that list of endings, you are home free - they all add *es.*

Nouns Ending in -y

The letter *y* gets a little friendlier here. If the *-y* ending is preceded by a vowel simply add *s;* if it is preceded by a consonant, change the *y* to *i* and add *es.*

Compound words

These offer an interesting challenge. Really! Most compound words are made up of a subject and a modifier. You only have to decide which is which and then apply the rules for making the subject plural.

Easiest are the one word compounds such as *fireman, firemen* or *congresswoman, congresswomen.*

Two word compound nouns are more fun. *Mother-in-law* becomes *mothers-in-law* because *mother* is the subject and *in-law* describes a relationship. The same principal applies to *editors in chief* and *ex-presidents.*

Notary public and *chairman of the board* offer a couple of unusual examples. The first is a *notary* who works in the public domain and a gathering of such men could be described as a group of *notaries public;* however, one might view the two words together as a title wherein each word carries equal weight in which case it would be a group of *notary publics.* In the second example, a strong argument can be made that the gathered titans of industry are collectively *chairmen,* but of a like number of *boards* as each board has only one chairman. Thus we have a meeting of the *chairmen of the boards.* (Except for boards which have co-chairmen). This is one of those places where there is no distinct right or wrong; we only hope that common sense will prevail and . . . you got it! . . . be consistent.

Minding Your p's and q's

By this time you may be at 6's and 7's, but you should still be able to see where this rule is going with no if's, and's or but's. You have earned it; you deserve it: an ironclad rule with no exceptions. THE PLURAL OF A NU BER, LETTER, WORD OR SYMBOL (+'s and -'s) IS CREATED BY ADDIN 's.

Nouns Ending in -o

Nouns ending in *o* and preceded by a consonant usually form the plural adding *-es* (*hero, heroes; potato, potatoes*); however, there are a number exceptions (*photo, photos; piano, pianos; solo, solo; silo, silos*)

Nouns ending in *o* preceded by a vowel take an *s* only (*radio, radios; zoo, zo trio, trios*)

Proper nouns ending in *o* always take an *s* only.

Possessive Plurals

Finally, another easy one. When you want to form the plural possessi form the plural by the applicable rule (or exception) and if the word ends an *s* add an apostrophe ('), otherwise add an apostrophe *s* (*'s*).

Hyphenation

Most grammarians have one bit of advice about hyphenation. Don't do As we deal with ever more sophisticated writing tools such as word processors a personal computers, we strive to turn out smarter looking documents which oft require hyphenation. Rather than get wrapped up in a lot of rules, follow just o "Use common sense." When a word is broken at the end of a line, make sure th enough of it is on the first line (at least three or four characters) so that the eye c track it without the necessity of pausing or rereading. Otherwise your message los impact. Similarly, a stack of hyphens where words have been broken on line aft line makes tracking difficult. Most syllables follow pronunciation, but not all. Th dictionary has eliminated the non-breaking syllables except when they are accente You'll recognize them in words like *a'ble*; you certainly wouldn't improve the look your document by leaving *a-* on one line and carrying *ble* to the next.

And finally

Enjoy! Don't let the language intimidate you. The more you learn, the more fun it b comes. You feel in control, because you know that none of it was handed down stone tablets. You realize that words were coined and massaged by people like u (Perhaps a little smarter . . . perhaps not.) Who knows but that you might introdu something new into the language. Changing a word a little or combining a couple words to better suit your need strikes someone else who borrows and passes it and then someone else borrows it and then . . . fifty years from now someone w agonize over its spelling and say "What fool . . .?"

A

aard´vark
Aa´ron
ab-a-ca´
aback
ab´a-cus
abaft
ab-a-lo´ne
aban´don
aban´doned
aban´don-er
aban´don-ment
abase
abased
abas´ed-ly
abase´ment
abash
abash´ment
aba´sia
abas´ing
abat´able
abate
abate´ment
ab´a-tis
aba´tor
ab´ba-cy
ab-ba´tial
ab´bey
ab-bre´vi-ate
ab-bre´vi-at-ed
ab-bre´vi-at-ing
ab-bre-vi-a´tion
ab´di-ca-ble
ab´di-cate
ab´di-cat-ing
ab-di-ca´tion
ab´di-ca-tor
ab´do-men
ab-dom´i-nal
ab-du´cent
ab-duct´
ab-duc´tion
ab-duc´tor
abeam
abe-ce-dar´i-an
abed
ab-en-ter´ic
Ab´er-deen
ab-er´rance
ab-er´ran-cy
ab-er´rant
ab-er-ra´tion
abet
abet´ted
abet´ting
abet´tor
abey´ance
abey´ant
ab-hor´
ab-horred´
ab-hor´rence
ab-hor´rent
ab-hor´ring
abid´ance
abide
abid´ing
ab´i-e-tate
abil´i-ties
abil´i-ty
ab-ject´, ab´ject
ab-jure´
ab-jur´ing
ab-late´
ab-la´tion
ab´la-tive
ablaze´
a´ble
a´ble—bod´ied
abloom
ab-lu´tion
ab-lu´tion-ary
a´bly
ab´ne-gate
ab-ne-ga´tion
ab´ne-ga-tive
ab-nor´mal
ab-nor-mal´i-ties
ab-nor-mal´i-ty
ab-nor´mal-ly
ab-nor´mi-ty
aboard
abode
abol´ish
ab-o-li´tion
ab-o-li´tion-ism
ab-o-li´tion-ist
ab-o-ma´sum
A´—bomb
abom´i-na-ble
abom´i-na-bly
abom´i-nate
abom´i-nat-ed
abom-i-na´tion
ab-o-rig´i-nal
ab-o-rig´i-ne
abort
abor´ti-cide
abor´ti-fa´cient
abor´tion
abor´tion-ist
abort´ive
abound
abound´ing
about
about—face´
above
above´board
ab-ra-ca-dab´ra
abrad´ant
abrade
abrad´ed
abrad´ing
A´bra-ham
abran´chi-an
abran´chi-ate
abra-si-om´e-ter
abra´sion
abra´sive
ab-re-ac´tion
abreast
abridge
abridge´a-ble
abridg´ing
abridg´ment
abroad
ab´ro-ga-ble
ab´ro-gate
ab´ro-gat-ed
ab´ro-gat-ing
ab-ro-ga´tion
ab´ro-ga-tive
ab´ro-ga-tor
ab-rupt´
ab-rup´tion
ab-rupt´ly
ab-rupt´ness

Ab´sa-lom
ab´scess
ab´scessed
ab-scond´
ab-scond´ed
ab´sence
ab´sent
ab-sen-tee´
ab-sen-tee´ism
ab´sent-ly
ab´sent-mind-ed
ab´sinthe
ab-sin´thi-an
ab´so-lute
ab´so-lute´ly
ab-so-lu´tion
ab´so-lut-ism
ab´so-lut-ist
ab-so-lu-tis´tic
ab´so-lu-tive
ab-sol´u-to-ry
ab-solv´a-ble
ab-solve´
ab-solved´
ab-sol´vent
ab-solv´er
ab-solv´ing
ab-sorb´
ab-sorb-a-bil´i-ty
ab-sorbed´
ab-sorb´ed-ly
ab-sor-be-fa´cient
ab-sorb´ent
ab-sorb´ing
ab-sorp´tion
ab-sorp´tive
ab-stain´
ab-stained´
ab-stain´er
ab-ste´mi-ous
ab-ste´mi-ous-ly
ab-sten´tion
ab-sten´tious
ab-ster´gent
ab-ster´sion
ab´sti-nence
ab´sti-nent
ab´stract
ab-stract´ed
ab-stract´ed-ly
ab-strac´tion
ab-strac´tive
ab´stract-ly
ab-stric´tion
ab-struse´
ab-struse´ly
ab-surd´
ab-surd´i-ty
ab-surd´ly
abu´lia
abu´lic
abun´dance
abun´dant
abun´dant-ly
abuse
abused
abus´er
abus´ing
abu´sive
abu´sive-ly
abu´sive-ness
abut
abu´ti-lon
abut´ment
abut´tal
abut´ted
abut´ter
Aby´dos
abysm´
abys´mal
abys´mal-ly
abyss
abyss´al
Ab-ys-sin´ia
aca´cia
ac´a-deme
ac-a-dem´ic
ac-a-dem´i-cal
ac-a-dem´i-cal-ly
ac-a-de-mi´cian
acad´e-my
Aca´dia
ac´a-leph
ac-a-na´ceous
ac-an-tha´ceous
acan-tho-ceph´a-lan
acan´thoid
acan´thous
acan´thus
acap-pel´la
acap´su-lar
ac-a-ri´a-sis
ac´a-roid
acar´pel-ous
acar´pous
acat-a-lec´tic
acau´dal
acau´date
acau-les´cent
acau´line
ac-cede´
ac-ced´ence
ac-ce-le-ran´do
ac-cel´er-ate
ac-cel-er-a´tion
ac-cel´er-a-tive
ac-cel´er-a-tor
ac-cel´er-a-to-ry
ac´cent
ac-cen-tu-al´i-ty
ac-cen´tu-ate
ac-cen-tu-a´tion
ac-cept´
ac-cept-a-bil´i-ty
ac-cept´a-ble
ac-cept´ance
ac-cep-ta´tion
ac-cept´ed
ac-cept´er
ac-cep´tor
ac´cess
ac-ces´sa-ri-ly
ac-ces´sa-ry
ac-ces-si-bil´i-ty
ae-ces´si-ble
ac-ces´sion
ac-ces-so´ri-al
ac-ces´so-ri-ly
ac-ces´so-ry
ac-ciac-ca-tu´ra
ac´ci-dence
ac´ci-dent
ac-ci-den´tal
ac-ci-den´tal-ly
ac-cip´i-tral
ac-cip´i-trine
ac-claim´

ac-claim´ing
ac-cla-ma´tion
ac-clam´a-to-ry
ac-cli´mat-a-ble
ac-cli´mate
ac-cli´mat-ed
ac-cli-ma´tion
ac-cli-ma-ti-za´tion
ac-cli´ma-tize
ae-cliv´i-ty
ac-cli´vous
ac-co-lade´
ac´co-lade
ac-com´mo-date
ac-com´mo-dat-ing
ac-com-mo-da´tion
ac-com´mo-da-tive
ac-com´pa-nied
ac-com´pa-nies
ac-com´pa-ni-ment
ac-com´pa-nist
ac-com´pa-ny
ac-com´plice
ac-com´plish
ac-com´plished
ac-com´plish-ment
ac-compt´
ac-cord´
ac-cord´a-ble
ac-cord´ance
ac-cord´ant
ac-cord´ed
ac-cord´ing
ac-cord´ing-ly
ac-cor´di-on
ac-cor´di-on-ist
ac-cost´
ac-couche-ment´
ac-cou-cheur´
ac-count´
ac-count-a-bil´i-ty
ac-count´a-ble
ac-count´an-cy
ac-count´ant
ac-count´ing
ac-cou´ter
ac-cou´ter-ment
ac-cred´it
ac-cres´cence
ac-cre´tion
ac-cre´tive
ac-cru´al
ac-crue´
ac-crue´ment
ac-cru´ing
ac-cum´ben-cy
ac-cum´bent
ac-cu´mu-late
ac-cu´mu-lat-ing
ac-cu´mu-la´tion
ac-cu´mu-la-tive
ac-cu´mu-la-tor
ac´cu-ra-cy
ac´cu-rate
ac´cu-rate-ly
ac´cu-rate-ness
ac-curs´ed
ac-cus´al
ac-cu-sa´tion
ac-cu´sa-tive
ac-cus´a-to-ry
ac-cuse´
ac-cused´
ac-cus´er
ac-cus´ing
ac-cus´ing-ly
ac-cus´tom
ac-cus´tomed
ac-e-naph´thy-lene
aceph´a-lous
ac´er-ate
acer´bi-ty
ac´er-ose
ac´er-ous
acer´vate
aces´cent
ac-e-tab´u-lum
ac-et-al´de-hyde
acet´a-mide
ac-et-an´i-lid
ac´e-tate
ace´tic
ace´ti-fy
ac´e-tone
ace´tous
ace´tum
ace´tyl
ace´tyl-ac´e-tone
acet-y-la´tion
acet´y-lene
ac-e-tyl´ic
ace´tyl-sal-i-cyl´ic
ached
ache´ni-al
Ach´er-on
achiev´able
achieve
achieved´
achieve´ment
achiev´ing
Achil´les
ach´ing-ly
ach-ro-mat´ic
ach-ro-mat´i-cal-ly
achro´ma-tism
achro´ma-tize
achro´ma-tous
acic´u-lar
ac´id
acid´ic
acid-i-fi-ca´tion
acid´i-fied
acid´i-fy
ac-i-dim´e-ter
acid-i-met´ric
acid´i-ty
ac´id-proof
acid´u-late
acid-u-la´tion
acid´u-lous
ac´i-er-ate
acin´i-form
ac-knowl´edge
ac-knowl´edge-a-ble
ac-knowl´edg-ing
ac-knowl´edg-ment
aclin´ic
ac´me
ac´ne
ac´o-lyte
acon´dy-lous
ac´o-nite
ac-o-ni´tum
acon´ti-um
a'corn
acot-y-le´don
acous´tic

acous´ti-cal
acous´ti-cal-ly
ac-ous-ti´cian
acous´tics
ac-quaint´
ac-quaint´ance
ac-quaint´ance-ship
ac-quaint´ed
ac-qui-esce´
ac-qui-es´cence
ac-qui-es´cent
ac-qui-esc´ing
ac-quire´
ac-quire´ment
ac-quir´er
ac-quir´ing
ac-qui-si´tion
ac-quis´i-tive
ac-quit´
ac-quit´tal
ac-quit´tance
ac-quit´ted
ac-quit´ting
a´cre
a´cre-age
ac´rid
ac´ri-dine
acrid´i-ty
ac´rid-ly
ac-ri-mo´ni-ous
ac´ri-mo-ny
ac´ro-bat
ac-ro-bat´ic
ac-ro-bat´ics
ac´ro-gen
acrog´e-nous
acro´le-in
ac´ro-lith
ac-ro-me-gal´ic
ac-ro-meg´a-ly
acro´mi-on
acron´i-cal
ac´ro-nym
acroph´o-ny
acrop´o-lis
across
acros´tic
acrot´ic
ac´ro-tism

ac´ry-late
acryl´ic
ac-ry-lo-ni´trile
ac´ti-nal
act´ing
ac-tin´ia
ac-tin´ic
ac´ti-nism
ac-tin´i-um
ac´ti-noid
ac-ti-nol´o-gy
ac-ti-no-my´cin
ac-ti-no-my-co´sis
ac´tion
ac´tion-able
Ac´ti-um
ac´ti-vate
ac-ti-va´tion
ac´ti-va-tor
ac´tive
ac´tive-ly
ac´tiv-ist
ac-tiv´i-ties
ac-tiv´i-ty
ac´tor
ac´tress
ac´tu-al
ac-tu-al´i-ty
ac´tu-al-ly
ac-tu-ar´i-al
ac´tu-ar-ies
ac´tu-ary
ac´tu-ate
ac´tu-at-ing
ac-tu-a´tion
ac´tu-a-tor
ac´u-ate
acu´i-ty
acu´le-ate
acu´men
acu´mi-nate
acu-mi-na´tion
ac´u-punc-ture
acute
acute´ly
acute´ness
acy´clic
ac´yl-ate
ad´age

ada´gio
Ad´am
ad´a-mant
ad-a-man´tine
Ad´ams
adapt
adapt-a-bil´i-ty
adapt´able
ad-ap-ta´tion
adapt´er
adapt´ive
adap´tor
ad-ax´i-al
add´a-ble
add´ed
ad-den´da
ad-den´dum
ad´der
add´i-ble
ad´dict
ad-dict´ed
ad-dic´tion
Ad´dis Ab´a-ba
Ad´di-son
ad-dit´a-ment
ad-di´tion
ad-di´tion-al
ad-di´tion-al-ly
ad´di-tive
ad´dle
ad´dled
ad-dress´
ad-dress-ee´
ad-dress´er
ad-dress´ing
Ad-dres´so-graph
ad-dres´sor
ad-duce´
ad-du´cent
ad-duc´i-ble
ad-duc´ing
ad-duct´
ad-duc´tion
ad-duc´tor
Ad´e-la
Ad´e-laide
Ad´el-bert
A´den
ade´nia

aden´i-form
ad-e-ni´tis
ad-e-no-fi-bro´ma
ad´e-noid
ad´e-noi´dal
ad-e-no´ma
adept
adept´ly
adept´ness
ad´e-qua-cy
ad´e-quate
ad´e-quate-ly
ad-here´
ad-her´ence
ad-her´ent
ad-he-res´cent
ad-her´ing
ad-he´sion
ad-he´sive
ad-he´sive-ly
ad-hib´it
ad-hi-bi´tion
ad-i-a-bat´ic
ad-i-an´tum
ad-i-aph´o-rous
adi-a-ther´man-cy
adieu
ad in-fi-ni´tum
ad in´ter-im
adios
adip´ic
ad-i-poc´er-ous
ad´i-pose
ad-i-pos´i-ty
Ad-i-ron´dack
ad-ja´cen-cy
ad-ja´cent
ad-ja´cent-ly
ad-jec-ti´val
ad´jec-tive
ad-join´
ad-joined´
ad-join´ing
ad-journ´
ad-journed´
ad-journ´ment
ad-judge´
ad-judg´ing
ad-ju´di-cate
ad-ju´di-cat-ing
ad-ju-di-ca´tion
ad-ju´di-ca-tive
ad-ju´di-ca-tor
ad´junct
ad-junc´tive
ad-ju-ra´tion
ad-jur´a-to-ry
ad-jure´
ad-ju´ror
ad-just´
ad-just´a-ble
ad-just´er
ad-just´ment
ad-jus´tor
ad´ju-tant
ad´ju-tant gen´er-al
ad´ju-vant
ad—lib´
ad lib´i-tum
ad-mi-nic´u-lar
ad-min´is-ter
ad-min´is-trate
ad-min-is-tra´tion
ad-min´is-tra-tive
ad-min´is-tra-tor
ad-min´is-tra-trix
ad´mi-ra-ble
ad´mi-ra-bly
ad´mi-ral
ad´mi-ral-ty
ad-mi-ra´tion
ad-mire´
ad-mired´
ad-mir´er
ad-mir´ing
ad-mir´ing-ly
ad-mis-si-bil´i-ty
ad-mis´si-ble
ad-mis´sion
ad-mis´sive
ad-mit´
ad-mit´tance
ad-mit´ted
ad-mit´ted-ly
ad-mit´ting
ad-mix´ture
ad-mon´ish
ad-mon´ish-ment
ad-mo-ni´tion
ad-mon´i-to-ry
ado
ado´be
ad-o-les´cence
ad-o-les´cent
adopt'
adopt´a-ble
adopt´er
adop´tion
adop´tive
ador´a-ble
ador´a-bly
ad-o-ra´tion
adored´
ador´er
ador´ing
adorn
adorned
adorn´ing
adorn´ment
adown´
ad-re´nal
adrift
adroit
adroit´ly
ad-sci-ti´tious
ad-sorb´
ad-sorb´ent
ad-sorp´tion
ad-sorp´tive
ad-u-lar´ia
ad´u-late
ad-u-la´tion
ad´u-la-to-ry
adult
adul´ter-ant
adul´ter-ate
adul-ter-a´tion
adul´ter-a-tor
adul´ter-er
adul´ter-ess
adul´ter-ous
adul´tery
adult´hood
adult´i-cide
ad-um´bral
ad-um´brant
ad´um-brate

ad va-lo´rem
ad-vance´
ad-vanced´
ad-vance´ment
ad-vanc´ing
ad-van´tage
ad-van-ta´geous
ad-van-ta´geous-ly
ad-ve´nience
ad´vent
ad-ven-ti´tious
ad-ven´tive
ad-ven´ture
ad-ven´tur-er
ad-ven´ture-some
ad-ven´tur-ess
ad-ven´tur-ous
ad´verb
ad-verb´i-al
ad´ver-sar-ies
ad´ver-sary
ad´verse
ad´verse-ly
ad-ver´si-ty
ad-vert´
ad-vert´ence
ad-vert´ent
ad-vert´ent-ly
ad´ver-tise
ad-ver-tise´ment
ad´ver-tis-er
ad´ver-tis-ing
ad-vice´
ad-vis-a-bil´i-ty
ad-vis´a-ble
ad-vise´
ad-vised´
ad-vis´ed-ly
ad-vise´ment
ad-vis´er
ad-vis´ing
ad-vi´sor
ad-vis´o-ry
ad´vo-ca-cy
ad´vo-cate
ad´vo-ca-tor
ad-voc´a-to-ry
Ae-ge´an
ae´gis
Ae-ne´as
Ae-ne´id
ae´ne-ous
Ae´o-lus
ae´on
aer´ate
aer-a´tion
aer´a-tor
aer´i-al
aer´i-al-ist
ae´rie
aer-if´er-ous
aer-i-fi-ca´tion
aer-o´bic
aero-do-net´ics
aero-dy-nam´ic
aero-dy-nam´ics
aer-og´ra-phy
aer-ol´o-gy
aer-om´e-ter
aer´o-mo-tor
aer´o-naut
aero-nau´ti-cal
aero-nau´ti-cal-ly
aero-nau´tics
aer´o-plane
aer´o-scope
aero-scop´ic
aer-os´co-py
ae´rose
aer´o-sol
aero-ther-a-peu´tics
ae-ru´gi-nous
a´ery
Aes-cu-la´pi-an
Ae´sop
aes´thete
aes-thet´ic
aes-thet´i-cal-ly
Aet´na
afar
af-fa-bil´i-ty
af´fa-ble
af´fa-bly
af-fair´
af-fect´
af-fec-ta´tion
af-fect´ed
af-fect´i-ble
af-fec´tion
af-fec´tion-ate
af-fec´tion-ate-ly
af-fec´tive
af´fer-ent
af-fi´ance
af-fi´anced
af-fi´ant
af-fi-da´vit
af-fil´i-ate
af-fil-i-a´tion
af-fin´i-ties
af-fin´i-ty
af-firm´
af-firm´a-bly
af-firm´ance
af-fir-ma´tion
af-firm´a-tive
af-firm´a-tive-ly
af-firm´a-to-ry
affix
af-fla´tus
af-flict´
af-flic´tion
af-flict´ive
af´flu-ence
af´flu-ent
af´flu-ent-ly
af-ford´
af-for-es-ta´tion
af-fray´
af´fri-cate
af-fric´a-tive
af-fright´
af-front´
af-front´ive
af-fu´sion
Af´ghan
Af-ghan´i-stan
afield´
afire
aflame
afloat
aflut´ter
afoot
afore´men-tioned
afore´said
afore´thought
a-fore´time

a for-ti-o´ri
afoul
afraid
afresh
Af´ri-ca
Af´ri-can
Af-ri-kan´der
af´ter
af´ter-birth
af´ter-burn-er
af´ter-care
af´ter-deck
af´ter-ef-fect
af´ter-glow
af´ter-life
af´ter-math
af-ter-noon´
af´ter-taste
af´ter-thought
af´ter-ward
af´ter-wards
again
against
Ag-a-mem´non
agape
a´gar
Ag´as-siz
ag´ate
ag´ate-ware
aga´ve
aged, ag´ed
age´less
a´gen-cies
a´gen-cy
agen´da
a´gent
ag-glom´er-ate
ag-glom-er-a´tion
ag-glu´ti-nant
ag-glu´ti-nate
ag-glu-ti-na´tion
ag-glu´ti-na-tive
ag-gran´dize
ag-gran´dize-ment
ag´gra-vate
ag´gra-vat-ed
ag´gra-vat-ing
ag-gra-va´tion
ag´gra-va-tor
ag´gre-gate
ag´gre-gate-ly
ag´gre-gat-ing
ag-gre-ga´tion
ag´gre-ga-tive
ag´gre-ga-to-ry
ag-gres´sion
ag-gres´sive
ag-gres´sive-ness
ag-gres´sor
ag-griev´ance
ag-grieve´
ag-grieved´
aghast´
ag´ile
ag´ile-ly
ag´ile-ness
agil´i-ty
ag´ing
ag´i-tate
ag´i-tat-ed
ag´i-tat-ed-ly
ag´i-tat-ing
ag-i-ta´tion
ag´i-ta-tive
ag´i-ta-tor
agleam´
ag´let
aglow
ag´mi-nat-ed
ag-na´tion
ag-no´men
ag-nom´i-nal
ag-no´sia
ag-nos´tic
ag-nos´ti-cal
ag-nos´ti-cal-ly
ago
agog
agon´ic
ag-o-nis´tic
ag´o-nize
ag´o-niz-ing
ag´o-ny
ag´o-ra
ag-o-ra-pho´bia
agraph´ia
agrar´i-an
agree
agree-a-bil´i-ty
agree´a-ble
agree´a-bly
agreed´
agree´ing
agree´ment
agres´tic
Agric´o-la
ag-ri-cul´tur-al
ag-ri-cul´tur-al-ist
ag´ri-cul-ture
ag-ri-cul´tur-ist
ag´ri-mo-ny
Agrip´pa
agrol-o-gy
ag-ro-nom´ic
ag-ro-nom´ics
agron´o-mist
agron´o-my
ag-ros-tol´o-gy
aground
ag-ryp-not´ic
a´gue
a´gue-weed
a´gu-ish
A´hab
ahead
ahoy
Ai´da
aide´—de—camp
ai-grette´
ai-guille´
al-lan´thus
ai´le-ron
ail´ment
aim´less
Ai´nu
air base
air´borne
air brake
air´brush
air coach
air´—con-di´tion
air´—con-di´tioned
air´—cool
air´craft
air´drome
air´drop
Aire´dale

air ex-press´
air´field
air´foil
air force
air´freight
air hole
air´i-ly
air´i-ness
air´ing
air´less
air lift
air line
air´mail
air´man
air´—mind´ed
air-om´e-ter
air´plane
air pock´et
air´port
air pres´sure
air´proof
air pump
air raid
air ri´fle
air´ship
air´sickness
air space
air´speed
air´strip
air´tight
air´way
air well
air´wor-thy
air´y
aisle
Aix—la—Cha-pelle´
Ajac´cio
ajar
akin
Ak´ron
Al-a-bam´a
Al-a-bam´i-an
al-a-bam´ine
al´a-bas-ter
a la carte
alack
alac´ri-ty
Alad´din
a la king
Al-a-me´da
Al´a-mo
a la mode
al´a-nine
al´a-nyl
a´lar
alarm´
alarm´ing
alarm´ing-ly
alarm´ist
alar´um
a´la-ry
alas
Alas´ka
Alas´kan
Al-ba´nia
Al´ba-ny
al´ba-tross
al-be´it
Al´bert
al-bi´no
al-bi´nos
al´bo-lite
al´bum
al-bu´men
al-bu´min
al-bu´mi-nize
al-bu-mi-noi´dal
al-bu-mi-no´sis
al-bu´mi-nous
al-bu-min-u´ria
al-bu-min-u´ric
Al´bu-quer-que
al-bur´num
Al-cae´us
al-cal´de
al´ca-mine
Al´ca-traz
al-ca´zar
Al-ces´tis
al-chem´ic
al-chem´i-cal-ly
al´che-mist
al´che-my
Al-ci-bi´a-des
Al´ci-des
al´co-hol
al-co-hol´ic
al-co-hol-ic´i-ty
al´co-hol-ism
Al´cott
al´cove
al´der
al´der-man
al-der-man´ic
Al´der-ney
Al´drich
alert
alert´ly
alert´ness
Ales-san´dria
Aleut
Aleu´tian
Al-ex-an´der
Al-ex-an-dret´ta
Al-ex-an´dria
al-fal´fa
al-fres´co
al´ga
al´gae
al´ge-bra
al-ge-bra´ic
al-ge-bra´i-cal
al-ge-bra´i-cal-ly
Al-ge´ria
Al-giers´
al-go-lag´nia
al-gol´o-gy
al-gom´e-ter
al-go-met´ri-cal
Al-gon´quin
al´go-rithm
Al-ham´bra
a´li-as
A´li Ba´ba
al´i-bi
al´i-bi-ing
al-i-bil´i-ty
al´i-dade
al´ien
al´ien-a-ble
al´ien-ate
al´ien-at-ing
al´ien-a´tion
al´ien-ist
alif´er-ous
alight
align

align´ment
alike
al´i-ment
al-i-men´tal-ly
al-i-men´ta-ry
al-i-men-ta´tion
al´i-mo-ny
aline
aline´ment
al´i-ped
al´i-quant
al´i-quot
Al´i-son
alive
ali-vin´cu-lar
aliz´a-rin
al´ka-li
al-ka-lim´e-ter
al-ka-lim´e-try
al´ka-line
al-ka-lin´i-ty
al-ka-li-za´tion
al´ka-lize
al´ka-loid
al´ka-loid-al
al´ka-net
al´ke-nyl
al´kyl
al´kyl-ate
al´kyl-ene
al´kyl-ize
Al´lah
all—Amer´i-can
Al´lan
al-lan-to´ic
al-lan-toi´dal
all´—around´
al-lay´
al-lay´ing
al-le-ga´tion
al-lege´
al-lege´a-ble
al-leged´
al-leg´ed-ly
Al-le-ghe´nies
Al-le-ghe´ny
al-le´giance
al-leg´ing
al-le-gor´ic
al-le-gor´i-cal
al´le-go-ries
al´le-go-rist
al´le-go-rize
al´lego-ry
al-le´gro
al-le-lu´ia
Al´len-town
al´ler-gen
al-ler´gic
al´ler-gy
al-le´vi-ate
al-le´vi-at-ing
al-le-vi-a´tion
al-le´vi-a-tive
al´ley
al´leys
al´ley-way
al-li-a´ceous
al-li´ance
al-lied´
al-lies´
al´li-ga-tor
all´—im-por´tant
al-lit´er-ate
al-lit-er-a´tion
al-lit´er-a-tive
al´lo-ca-ble
al´lo-cate
al´lo-cat-ing
al-lo-ca´tion
al-log´a-mous
al-log´a-my
al-lot´
al-lot´ment
al-lo-troph´ic
al-lo-trop´ic
al-lot´ro-py
al-lot´ted
al-lot´ting
al-low´
al-low´a-ble
al-low´ance
al-lowed´
al-low´ed-ly
al´loy
all right
all´-spice
al-lude´
al-lure
al-lured´
al-lure´ment
al-lur´ing
al-lu´sion
al-lu´sive
al-lu´sive-ly
al-lu´sive-ness
al-lu´vi-al
al-lu´vi-on
al-lu´vi-um
al´ly
al-ly´ing
al´lyl
al´lyl-amine´
al-lyl´ic
Al´ma
al´ma-gest
al´ma ma´ter
al´ma-nac
al-might´y
al´mond
al´mo-ner
al´most
alms´house
al´ni-co
alo´di-um
al´oe
al´oes
al´oes-ol
al-o-et´ic
aloft´
al´o-gism
alo´ha
al´o-in
alone
along
along-side´
Alon´so, Alon´zo
aloof
aloof´ness
al-o-pe´cia
aloud
al-pac´a
al´pha
al´pha-bet
al-pha-bet´ic
al-pha-bet´i-cal
al´pha-bet-ize

al´pha-nu-mer´ic
Al´phe-us
Al-phon´so
Al´pine
al-read´y
al-right´
Al´sace
Al´sace—Lor-raine´
Al-sa´tian
al´sike
al´tar
al´ter
al-ter-a-bil´i-ty
al´ter-a-ble
al-ter-a´tion
al´ter-cate
al-ter-ca´tion
al´ter e´go
al-ter´nant
al´ter-nate
al´ter-nat-ed
al´ter-nate-ly
al´ter-nat-ing
al-ter-na´tion
al-ter´na-tive
al´ter-na-tor
al-the´a
al-though´
al-tim´e-ter
al-tis´o-nant
al´ti-tude
al-ti-tu´di-nal
al-ti-tu-di-nar´i-an
al´to
al´-to-geth-er
Al´ton
Al-too´na
al´tru-ism
al´tru-ist
al-tru-is´ti-cal-ly
al´u-del
al´um
alu´mi-na
alu-mi-nif´er-ous
al-u-min´i-um
alu´mi-nize
alu´mi-nous
alu´mi-num
alum´na
alum´nae
alum´ni
alum´nus
al´u-nite
al´ways
alys´sum
a´mah
amal´gam
amal´ga-mate
amal-ga-ma´tion
amal´ga-ma-tor
Aman´da
Am-a-ril´lo
am-a-ryl´lis
amass
amass´-a-ble
amass´ment
am´a-teur
am´a-teur-ish
am´a-teur-ism
Ama´ti
am´a-tol
am´a-to-ry
am-au-ro´sis
amaze
amazed
amaz´ed-ly
amaze´ment
amaz´ing
amaz´ing-ly
Am´a-zon
Am-a-zo´ni-an
am´a-zon-ite
am-bas´sa-dor
am-bas-sa-do´ri-al
am-bas´sa-dress
am´ber
am´bi-ent
am-bi-gu´i-ty
am-big´u-ous
am-bi´tion
am-bi´tious
am-biv´a-lence
am-biv´a-lent
am´ble
am´bled
am´bling
am´bling-ly
am-blys´to-ma
Am´brose
am-bro´sia
am-bro´si-al
am´bry
am´bu-lance
am´bu-late
am´bu-la-to-ry
amb-ur´bi-al
am´bus-cade
am-bus-cad´er
am´bush
am´bushed
am´bush-er
am´bush-ment
ame´ba
Ame´lia
ame´lio-ra-ble
ame´lio-rate
ame-lio-ra´tion
ame´lio-ra-tive
ame´lio-ra-tor
a´men´
ame-na-bil´i-ty
ame´na-ble
amend
amend´a-ble
amend´ed
amend´ment
amends
amen´i-ties
amen´i-ty
Amer´i-ca
Amer´i-can
Amer-i-can´a
Amer´i-can-ism
Amer-l-can-i-za´tion
Amer´i-can-ize
am´e-thyst
am-e-trom´e-ter
am-e-tro´pia
Am´herst
ami-a-bil´i-ty
a´mi-a-ble
a´mi-a-bly
am-i-ca-bil´i-ty
am´i-ca-ble
am´i-ca-bly
am´ice
amid

am´ide
amid´ic
ami´do
ami´do-gen
amid´ships
amidst
Am´i-ens
ami´go
amine
ami´no
ami´no acid
ami-no-ben-zo´ic
Am´ish, A´mish
amiss
ami-to´sis
ami-tot´ic
am´i-ty
am´me-line
am´me-ter
am-mi-a´ceous
Am´mon
am-mo´nia
am-mo´ni-ac
am-mo´ni-ate
am-mon´ic
am´mo-nite
Am´mon-ite
am-mo´ni-um
am-mu-ni´tion
am-ne´sia
am´nes-ty
am-ni-ot´ic
amoe´ba
am-oe-bae´an
among
amongst
amor´al
amo-ral´i-ty
amor´al-ly
am´o-rous
amor´phism
amor´phous
am-or-ti-za´tion
am´or-tize
am´or-tiz-ing
A´mos
amount
amour
A´moy

am´per-age
am´pere
am´per-sand
am-phi-ar-thro´sis
Am-phib´ia
am-phib´i-an
am-phib´i-ous
am-phic´ty-on
am-phi-dip´loi-dy
am´phi-gen
am-phig´e-nous
am-phi-gor´ic
am´phi-go-ry
am-phip´o-da
am´phi-the-a-ter
am-phi-the´ci-um
Am´phi-tri-te
am´pho-ra
am´ple
am´ple-ness
am-pli-fi-ca´tion
am´pli-fied
am´pli-fi-er
am´pli-fy
am´pli-fy-ing
am´pli-tude
am´ply
am´poule
am-pul´la
am´pu-tate
am´pu-tat-ed
am´pu-tat-ing
am-pu-ta´tion
am´pu-tee´
am-ri´ta
Am-rit´sar
Am´ster-dam
amuck
am´u-let
A´mund-sen
amus´a-ble
amuse
amused´
amus´ed-ly
amuse´ment
amu´sia
amus´ing
amus´ive
A´my

anach´ro-nism
anach-ro-nis´tic
anach´ro-nous-ly
an-a-clas´tic
an-a-con´da
Anac´re-on
an-aer-o´bia
an-aer-o´bic
an-aes-the´sia
an-a-glyph´ic
anag´ly-phy
an-a-glyp´tics
an-a-gog´i-cal
an´a-gram
an-a-gram-mat´ic
a´nal
an-al-ge´sia
an-al-ge´sic
an´a-log
an-a-log´i-cal_
an-a-log´i-cal-ly
anal´o-gies
anal´o-gist
anal´o-gous
an´a-logue
anal´o-gy
anal´y-ses
anal´y-sis
an´a-lyst
an-a-lyt´ic
an-a-lyt´i-cal
an-a-lyt´i-cal-ly
an´a-lyze
an´a-lyz-ing
an-am-ne´sis
an-a-mor´pho-sis
an-an´drous
An-a-ni´as
an-a-paes´tic
anaph´o-ra
an-aph-ro-dis´i-ac
an-a-phy-lax´is
an´a-plas-ty
an-ap-tot´ic
an´arch
an-ar´chic
an-ar´chi-cal
an´ar-chism
an´ar-chist

an-ar-chis´tic
an´ar-chy
An-a-to´lia
an-a-tom´i-cal
anat´o-mist
anat´o-mize
anat´o-my
anat´ro-pous
an´ces-tor
an-ces´tral
an´ces-tress
anlces-try
An-chi´ses
an´chor
an´chor-age
an´cient
an´cient-ly
an´cil-lary
an´con
An-co´na
an-co´ne-al
an-cy-lo-sto-mi´a-sis
An-da-lu´sia
An´da-man
an-dan´te
An-de´an
An´der-sen
An´der-son
An´des
an´de-site
and´i-ron
An-dor´ra
An´do-ver
An-dre´
An´drew
An´drews
An´dro-clus
an-droe´ci-um
an´dro-gen
an-drog´y-nous
An-drom´a-che
An-drom´e-da
An´dros
an´dro-sin
an´ec-dot-al
an´ec-dote
an-ec-dot´ic
an-ec-dot´i-cal
an´ec-dot-ist
ane´mia
ane´mic
an-e-mo-log´i-cal
an-e-mom´e-ter
anem´o-ne
an-e-moph´i-lous
an-e-mo´sis
anent
an´er-oid
an-es-the´sia
an-es-the-si-ol´o-gist
an-es-thet´ic
anes´the-tist
anes´the-tize
aneu´ria
an´eu-rysm
anew
an-frac-tu-os´i-ty
an´ga-ry
an´gel
An´ge-la
an-gel´ic
an-gel´i-ca
an-gel´i-cal
an-gel´i-cal-ly
An´gell
An´ge-lo
An´ge-lus
an´ger
An´ge-vin
an-gi´na
an-gi´na pec´to-ris
an´gi-o-cyst
an-gi-o´ma
an-gi-om´a-tous
an-gi-op´-a-thy
an´gi-o-sperm
an-gi-o-sper´mous
an-gi-os´to-my
Ang´kor
an´gle
an´gler
an-gle-worm
An´gli-can
an´gli-cism
an-gli-ci-za´tion
an´gli-cize
an´gling
An´glo—Amer´i-can
An´glo-phile
An´glo—Sax´on
An-go´la
Am-go´ra
an´gri-ly
an´gri-ness
an´gry
ang´strom
An-guil´la
an´guish
an´guished
an´gu-lar
an-gu-lar´i-ty
An´gus
an-hi-dro´sis
An´hwei´
an´ile
an´i-lide
an´i-line
anil´i-ty
an´i-mate
an´i-mat-ed
an´i-mat-ing
an-i-ma´tion
an´i-mism
an-i-mos´i-ty
an´ion
an´ise
an´i-seed
An-jou´
an´kle
an´klet
an-ky-lo´sis
an-ky-los´to-ma
an´nal
an´nal-ist
an-nal-is´tic
an´nals
An´nam
An-nap´o-lis
Ann Ar´bor
an-neal´
an-nealed´
an´ne-lid
An-nette´
an-nex´
an-nex´a-ble
an-nex-a´tion
an-ni´hi-la-ble

an-ni´hi-late
an-ni-hi-la´tion
an-ni´hi-la-tor
An´nis-ton
an-ni-ver´sa-ries
an-ni-ver´sa-ry
An´no Dom´i-ni
an´no-tate
an-no-ta´tion
an´no-ta-tor
an-nounce´
an-nounce´ment
an-nounc´er
an-nounc´ing
an-noy´
an-noy´ance
an-noyed´
an´nu-al
an-nu´i-tant
an-nu´i-ty
an-nul´
an´nu-lar
an-nu-lar´i-ty
an´nu-let
an-nulled´
an-nul´ling
an-nul´ment
an-nun´ci-ate
an-nun-ci-a´tion
an-nun´ci-a-tor
an´ode
an´o-dyne
anoint
anoint´ed
anoint´er
anoint´ment
anom´a-lism
anom-a-lis´tic
anom´a-lous
anom´a-lous-ly
an´o-nym
an-o-nym´i-ty
anon´y-mous
anon´y-mous-ly
Anoph´e-les
an-oth´er
An´schluss
an´ser-ine
an´swer
an´swer-a-ble
ant-ac´id
An-tae´us
an-tag´o-nism
an-tag´o-nist
an-tag-o-nis´tic
an-tag´o-nize
Ant-arc´tic
Ant-arc´ti-ca
An-tar´es
an´te
ant´eat-er
an´te-bel´lum
an-te-ced´ent
an´te-cham-ber
an´te-date
an-te-di-lu´vi-an
an´te-lope
an´te me-rid´i-em
an-ten´na
an-te-pen´di-um
an-te-pe´nult
an-te-pe-nul´ti-mate
an-te´ri-or
an´te-room
ant-he´li-on
ant-hel-min´tic
an´them
an-the´mi-on
an´ther
an´ther-al
an-ther-id´i-um
an-the´sis
an-tho-cy´a-nin
an-tho´di-um
an-thog´e-nous
an-tho-log´i-cal
an-thol´o-gist
an-thol´o-gize
an-thol´o-gy
An´tho-ny
an´tho-taxy
an´thra-cene
an´thra-ces
an´thra-cite
an-thra-qui-none´
an-thra-qui-no´nyl
an´thrax
an-thro-po-gen´e-sis
an-thro-pog´e-ny
an-thro-pog´ra-phy
an´thro-poid
an-thro-po-log´i-cal
an-thro-pol´o-gist
an-thro-pol´o-gy
an-thro-pom´e-ter
an-thro-po-met´ric
an-thro-pom´e-try
an-thro-po-morph´ic
an´ti-air´craft
an-ti-bi-ot´ic
an´ti-bod-ies
an´ti-body
an-ti-cat´a-lyst
an-ti-cath´ode
an´ti-chlor
An´ti-christ
an-tic´i-pant
an-tic´i-pate
an-tic´i-pat-ed
an-tic´i-pat-ing
an-tic-i-pa´tion
an-tic´i-pa-tive
an-tic´i-pa-to-ry
an-ti-cler´i-cal
an-ti-cli´max
an-ti-cli-no´ri-um
an-ti-cy´clone
an-ti-cy-clon´ic
an´ti-dot-al
an´ti-dote
an-ti-drom´ic
An-tie´tam
an´ti-freeze
An-ti´gua
an-ti-he´lix
an-ti-his´ta-mine
An-til´les
an-ti-log´a-rithm
an-til´o-gism
an-til´o-gy
an-ti-mis´sile
An´ti-och
An-ti´o-chus
an-ti-pas´to
an-ti-pa-thet´ic
an-ti-pa-thet´i-cal
an-tip´a-thy

an-ti-phlo-gis´tic
an´ti-phon
an-tiph´o-nal
an-tiph´o-nary
an-tiph´ra-sis
an-tip´o-dal
an´ti-pode
an-tip-o-de´an
an-tip´o-des
an-ti-quar´i-an
an´ti-quary
an´ti-quate
an´ti-quat-ed
an´ti-quat-ing
an-tique´
an-tiq´ui-ty
an-ti—Sem´i-tism
an-ti-sep´sis
an-ti-sep´tic
an-ti-se´rum
an-ti-slav´ery
an-ti-so´cial
an-tith´e-sis
an-ti-thet´ic
an-ti-tox´in
an-ti-tra´gus
an-ti-trust´
an-ti-typ´ic
an-ti-typ´i-cal
ant´ler
ant´lered
An-toi-nette´
An-to´nia
An-to´nio
An´to-ny
an´to-nym
ant´proof
An´trim
Ant´werp
an-u´rous
an´vil
anx-i´e-ty
anx´ious
anx´ious-ly
an´y
an´y-body
an´y-how
an´y-one
an´y-place
an´y-thing
an´y-way
an´y-where
aor´ta
aor´tic
apace
Apach´e
Ap-a-lach-i-co´la
apart
apart´heid
apart´ment
ap-a-tet´ic
ap-a-thet´ic
ap-a-thet´i-cal-ly
ap´a-thy
ape´like
ape´ri-ent
ape-ri-od´ic
aper-i-tif´
ap´er-ture
a´pex
aph´a-nite
aph-a-nit´ic
apha´sia
apha´si-ac
apha´sic
a´phid
A´phis
aphlo-gis´tic
apho´nia
aphon´ic
aph´o-rism
aph-o-ris´tic
apho´tic
aphra´sia
aph-ro-dis´i-ac
Aph-ro-di´te
a´pi-an
api-ar´i-an
a´pi-ary
ap´i-cal
ap´i-ces
apiece
ap´ish
ap´ish-ly
apiv´o-rous
ap-la-nat´ic
aplen´ty
aplomb
ap´nea
apoc´a-lypse
apoc-a-lyp´tic
Apoc´ry-pha
apoc´ry-phal
Ap´o-des
apod´o-sis
Apol´lo
apol-o-get´ic
ap-o-lo´gia
apol´o-gies
apol´o-gize
apol´o-gy
ap-o-neu-ro´sis
ap-o-phyl´lite
ap-o-plec´tic
ap-o-plec´ti-cal
ap´o-plexy
ap-o-si-o-pe´sis
apos´ta-sy
apos´tate
apos´ta-tize
apos-te-ri-o´ri
apos´tle
apos´tle-ship
apos´to-late
ap-os-tol´ic
ap-os-tol´i-cal
ap-os-tol´i-cism
apos-to-lic´i-ty
apos´tro-phe
ap-os-troph´ic
apos´tro-phize
apoth´e-car-ies
apoth´e-cary
Ap-pa-la´chi-an
ap-pall´
ap-palled´
ap-pall´ing
ap´pa-nage
ap-pa-rat´us
ap-par´el
ap-par´eled
ap-par´ent
ap-pa-ri´tion
ap-peal´
ap-peal´a-ble
ap-pealed´
ap-peal´er

ap-peal´ing
ap-pear´
ap-pear´ance
ap-peared´
ap-pear´ing
ap-peas´a-ble
ap-pease´
ap-pease´ment
ap-peas´er
ap-peas´ing
ap-peas´ing-ly
ap-pel´lant
ap-pel´late
ap-pel-la´tion
ap-pel´la-tive
ap-pend´
ap-pend´age
ap-pend´aged
ap-pend´an-cy
ap-pend´ant
ap-pen-dec´to-my
ap-pend´ed
ap-pen´di-cal
ap-pen-di-ci´tis
ap-pen-dic´u-lar
ap-pen´dix
ap-per-ceive´
ap-per-cep´tion
ap-per-cep´tive
ap´pe-tite
ap´pe-tiz-er
ap´pe-tiz-ing
Ap´pi-an
ap-plaud´er
ap-plaud´ing
ap-plause´
ap´ple
ap´ple-sauce
Ap´ple-ton
ap-pli´ance
ap-pli-ca-bil´i-ty
ap´pli-ca-ble
ap´pli-cant
ap-pli-ca´tion
ap´pli-ca-tive
ap-plied´
ap-pli´er
ap-pli-que´
ap-ply´

ap-ply´ing
ap-point´
ap-point´a-ble
ap-point´ed
ap-poin-tee´
ap-point´er
ap-point´ing
ap-point´ment
Ap-po-mat´tox
ap-por´tion
ap-por´tioned
ap-por´tion-er
ap-por´tion-ment
ap´po-site
ap-po-si´tion
ap-pos´i-tive
ap-prais´a-ble
ap-prais´al
ap-praise´
ap-praised´
ap-praise´ment
ap-prais´er
ap-prais´ing
ap-prais´ing-ly
ap-pre´cia-ble
ap-pre´ci-ate
ap-pre´ci-at-ed
ap-pre´ci-at-ing
ap-pre-ci-a´tion
ap-pre´cia-tive-ly
ap-pre´cia-to-ry
ap-pre-hend´
ap-pre-hend´ed
ap-pre-hend´ing
ap-pre-hen-si-bil´i-ty
ap-pre-hen´si-ble
ap-pre-hen´sion
ap-pre-hen´sive
ap-pren´tice
ap-pren´ticed
ap-pren´tice-ship
ap-prise´
ap-prised´
ap-pris´ing
ap-proach´
ap-proach-a-bil´i-ty
ap-pro-ba´tion
ap´pro-ba-tive
ap´pro-ba-tive-ness

ap-pro´pri-ate
ap-pro´pri-at-ed
ap-pro´pri-at-ly
ap-pro´pri-ate-ness
ap-pro´pri-at-ing
ap-pro-pri-a´tion
ap-prov´a-ble
ap-prov´al
ap-prove´
ap-proved
ap-prov´ing
ap-prov´ing-ly
ap-prox´i-mate
ap-prox´i-mat-ed
ap-prox´i-mate-ly
ap-prox´i-mat´ing
ap-prox-i-ma´tion
ap-pur´te-nance
ap-pur´te-nant
a´pri-cot
A´pril
a´pron
apse
ap´sis
Ap´tera
ap´ter-al
ap-te´ri-um
ap´ter-ous
ap´ti-tude
apt´ly
apt´ness
Apu´lia
aq´ua
aq´ua-lung
aq-ua-ma-rine´
aq´ua-plane
aq´ua-relle
aquar´i-um
Aquar´i-us
aquat´ic
aq´ue-duct
a´que-ous
Aq´ui-la
aq´ui-line
Aqui´nas
Aq´ui-taine
Aq-ui-ta´nia
Ar´ab
ar-a-besque´

Ara´bia
Ar´a-bic
Ar´ab-ist
Arach´ne
arach´noid
Ar´a-gon
Ar´al
Arap´a-ho
Ar´a-rat
ar´ba-lest
ar´bi-ter
ar´bi-tra-ble
ar´bi-trage
ar´bi-trag-er
ar´bi-tral
ar-bit´ra-ment
ar´bi-trar-i-ly
ar´bi-trary
ar´bi-trate
ar´bi-trat-ed
ar´bi-trat-ing
ar-bi-tra´tion
ar´bi-tra-tive
ar´bi-tra-tor
ar´bi-tress
ar´bor
ar-bo´re-al
ar-bo-res´cent
ar-bo-re´tum
ar´bo-rize
ar´bor-ous
ar´bor-vi´tae
ar-bu´tus
ar-cade´
Ar-ca´dia
Ar-ca´di-an
ar-chae-ol´o-gy
ar-cha´ic
ar-cha´i-cal-ly
ar´cha-ist
ar-cha-is´tic
art-cha-ism
arch´an´gel
arch´bish´op
arch-bish´op-ric
arch´dea´con
arch´di´o-cese
arch´du´cal
arch´duch´ess
arch´duch´y
arch´duke´
Ar-che´an
arched
arch´en´e-my
arch´er
arch´ery
arch´fiend´
Ar´chi-bald
Ar-chi-me´de-an
ar-chi-pel´a-go
ar´chi-tect
ar-chi-tec´tur-al
ar´chi-tec-ture
ar´chi-trave
ar-chi´val
ar´chive
ar´chi-vist
arch´way
arc´ing
Arc´tic
Arc´tic Cir´cle
ar´dent
ar´dent-ly
ar´dor
ar´du-ous
ar´du-ous-ly
ar´ea
ar´e-al
ar´ea-way
are´o-la
Ar-e-op´a-gus
A´res
Ar-gen-ti´na
Ar´gen-tine
ar´gil
Ar´give
Ar´go-lis
Ar´go-naut
Ar-gonne´
Ar´gos
ar´go-sy
ar´gue
ar´gu-ment
ar-gu-men-ta´tion
ar-gu-men´ta-tive
Ar´gus
Ar´gyle
Ar´gyll
a´ria
ar´id
arid´i-ty
Ar´i-el
A´ri-es
aright
arise
aris´en
aris´ing
Ar-is´ti-des
ar-is-toc´ra-cy
aris´to-crat
aris-to-crat´ic
Ar-is-toph´a-nes
Ar´is-tot-le
aris´to-type
arith´me-tic
ar-ith-met´i-cal
arith-me-ti´cian
Ar-i-zo´na
Ar´kan-sas
Ar´ling-ton
ar-ma´da
ar-ma-dil´lo
Ar-ma-ged´don
ar´ma-ment
ar´ma-ture
arm´chair
Ar-me´nia
Ar-me´ni-an
Ar-men-tieres´
arm´ful
arm´hole
ar´mies
ar´mi-stice
arm´let
ar´mor
ar´mored
ar´mor-er
ar´mo-ry
arm´pit
Arm´strong
ar´my
ar´ni-ca
Ar´nold
aro´ma
ar-o-mat´ic
arose
around

arous´al
arouse
arous´ing
ar-peg´gio
ar-raign´
ar-raign´ment
ar-range´
ar-range´ment
ar-rang´er
ar-rang´ing
ar´ras
ar-ray´
ar-rear´
ar-rest´
ar-rest´ed
ar-rest´er
ar-res´tive
ar-res´tor
ar-rive´
ar-riv´ing
ar´ro-gance
ar´ro-gan-cy
ar´ro-gant
ar´ro-gate
ar´ro-gat-ing
ar-ro-ga´tion
ar´row
ar´row-head
ar´row-root
ar-roy´o
ar´se-nal
ar´se-nate
ar´se-nic
ar´son
ar´son-ist
Ar´te-mis
ar-te´ri-al
ar´ter-ies
ar-te-ri-o-scle-ro´sis
ar´tery
ar-te´sian
art´ful
art´ful-ly
ar-thrit´ic
ar-thri´tis
ar´thro-pod
Ar-throp´o-da
ar-throp´o-dal
Ar´thur
Ar-thu´ri-an
ar´ti-choke
ar´ti-cle
ar-tic´u-lar
ar-tic´u-late
ar-tic´u-lat-ed
art´i-er
ar´ti-fact
ar´ti-fice
ar-tif´i-cer
ar-ti-fi´cial
ar-ti-fi-ci-al´i-ty
ar-ti-fi´cial-ly
ar-til´ler-ist
ar-til´lery
ar-til´lery-man
ar´ti-san
art´ist
ar-tiste´
ar-tis´tic
ar-tis´ti-cal
ar-tis´ti-cal-ly
ar´tist-ry
art´less
art´y
Ar´un-del
Ar´yan
as-bes´tos
As´bury
as-cend´
as-cend´an-cy
as-cend´ant
as-cend´ing
as-cen´sion
as-cent´
as-certain´
as-cer-tain´a-ble
as-cer-tain´ment
as-cet´ic
as-cet´i-cism
As´cham
ascor´bic
as-co-spor´ic
As´cot
as-cribe´
as-crib´ing
as-crip´tion
asep´sis
asep´tic
asex´u-al
asex-u-al´i-ty
As´gard
ashamed
asham´ed-ly
ash´en
Ashe´ville
ashore
ash´y
A´sia
A´sia Mi´nor
aside
as´i-nine
askance´
askew´
aslant´
asleep´
as-par´a-gus
as´pect
as´pen
as-per´i-ty
as-perse´
as-per´sion
as-per-so´ri-um
as´phalt
as´pho-del
as-phyx´ia
as-phyx´i-ate
as-phyx´i-at-ing
as-phyx-i-a´tion
as´pic
as-pi-dis´tra
as´pi-rant
as´pi-rate
as-pi-ra´tion
as´pi-ra-tor
as-pir´a-to-ry
as-pire´
as´pi-rin
as-pir´ing
as-pir´ing-ly
As-ple´ni-um
as-sail´
as-sail´a-ble
as-sail´ant
As-sam´
as-sas´sin
as-sas´si-nate
as-sas-si-na´tion

as-sas´si-na-tor
as-sault´
as´say
as-sem´bla-ble
as-sem´blage
as-sem´ble
as-sem´bling
as-sem´bly
as-sem´bly-man
as-sent´
as-sent´er
as-sert´
as-sert´er
as-ser´tion
as-ser´tive
as-ser´tor
as-ser´to-ry
as-sess´
as-sess´a-ble
as-sess´ment
ar´ses´sor
as´set
as-sev´er-ate
as-sev-er-a´tion
as-si-du´i-ty
as-sid´u-ous
as-sign´
as-sign-a-bil´i-ty
as-sign´a-ble
as-sig-na´tion
as-sign-ee´
as-sign´ment
as-sim´i-late
as-sim´i-lat-ing
as-sim-i-la´tion
as-sim´i-la-tive
as-sim´i-la-tor
as-sim´i-la-to-ry
as-sist´
as-sist´ance
as-sist´ant
as-sist´ed
as-sist´er
as-sist´ing
as-sis´tor
as-so´cia-ble
as-so´ci-ate
as-so´ci-at-ing
as-so-ci-a´tion

as-so´cia-tive
as-sort´
as-sort´ed
as-sort´ment
as-suage´
as-suage´ment
as-suag´ing
as-sua´sive
as-sum´a-ble
as-sum´a-bly
as-sume´
as-sum´ed-ly
as-sum´er
as-sum´ing
as-sump´tion
as-sur´ance
as-sure´
as-sured´
as-sur´ed-ly
as-sur´ed-ness
as-sur´ing
as-sur´gent
As-syr´ia
as´ter
as´ter-isk
astern
as´ter-oid
as´ter-oi´dal
asth´ma
asth-mat´ic
asth-mat´i-cal
astig´ma-tism
astir´
as-ton´ish
as-ton´ished
as-ton´ish-ing
as-ton´ish-ment
As´tor
As-to´ria
as-tound´
as-tound´ed
as-tound´ing
astrad´dle
as´tral
astray´
astride´
as-trin´gen-cy
as-trin´gent
as´tro-labe

as-trol´o-ger
as-tro-log´i-cal
as-trol´o-gy
as-trom´e-try
as´tro-naut
as-tron´o-mer
as-tro-nom´ic
as-tro-nom´i-cal
as-tro-nom´i-cal-ly
as-tron´o-my
as-tro-phys´i-cal
as-tro-phys´i-cist
as-tro-phys´ics
as-tute´
as-tute´ly
as-tute´ness
asun´der
asy´lum
asym-met´ric
asym-met´ri-cal
asym-met´ri-cal-ly
asym´me-try
as´ymp-tote
asyn-ap´sis
asyn´chro-nism
as-yn-det´i-cal-ly
asyn´de-ton
asys´to-le
at´a-bal
At-a-lan´ta
at´a-vic
at´a-vism
at´a-vist
at-a-vis´ti-cal-ly
atax´ia
atax´ic
Atch´i-son
ate-lier´
a´the-ism
a´the-ist
athe-is´tic
athe-is´ti-cal
athe-is´ti-cal-ly
Athe´na
Ath´ens
athirst´
ath´lete
ath-let´ic
ath-let´ics

th´os
threp´sia
thwart´
tilt´
t-lan´tic
t´las
t´mo-sphere
t-mo-spher´ic
t-mo-spher´i-cal
t-mo-spher´i-cal-ly
t´oll
t´om
tom´ic
tom´i-cal
t-o-mic´i-ty
t´om-ize
t´om-iz-eraton´al
to-nal´i-ty
tone
tone´ment
ton´ing
top
´tri-um
tro´cious
tro´cious-ly
troc´i-ty
t´ro-phied
t´ro-phy
trop´ic
t´ro-pine
t´ro-pos
t-tach´
t-tach´a-ble
t-ta-che´
t-tached´
t-tach´ment
t-tack´
t-tacked´
t-tack´er
t-tain´
t-tain-a-bil´i-ty
t-tain´a-ble
t-tain´a-ble-ness
t-tain´der
t-tain´er
t-tain´ment
t-taint´
t´tar
t-tempt´

at-tempt´a-ble
at-tempt´er
at-tend´
at-tend´ance
at-tend´ant
at-ten´tion
at-ten´tive
at-ten´tive-ly
at-ten´u-ate
at-ten-u-a´tion
at-test´
at-tes-ta´tion
at´tic
At´ti-ca
At´ti-la
at-tire´
at-tir´ing
at´ti-tude
at-ti-tu´di-nize
at-tor´ney
at-tor´ney gen´er-al
at-tract´
at-tract-a-bil´i-ty
at-tract´a-ble
at-tract´a-ble-ness
at-trac´tion
at-tract´ive
at-tract´ive-ly
at-trac´tor
at´tri-bute
at-tri-bu´tion
at-trib´u-tive
at-tri´tion
at-tune´
at-tun´ing
atyp´i-cal
au´burn
auc´tion
auc-tion-eer´
au-da´cious
au-dac´i-ty
au´di-ble
au´di-bly
au´di-ence
au´dio
au´dit
au-di´tion
au´di-tor
au-di-to´ri-um

au´di-to-ry
Au´du-bon
au´ger
aug-ment´
au gra´tin
Augs-burg
au´gur
au´gu-ry
Au´gust
Au-gus´ta
Au´gus-tine, Au-gus´tine
Au-gus´tus
auk
auld lang syne
au´ra
au´ral
au´re-ate
Au-re´lia
au´re-ole
Au-re-o-my´cin
au re-voir´
au´ri-cle
au´ri-cled
au-ric´u-lar
au-rif´er-ous
au-ro´ra
au-ro´ra bo-re-al´is
aus´cul-tate
aus-cul-ta´tion
aus´pice
aus-pi´cious
aus-pi´cious-ly
aus-tere´
aus-ter´i-ty
Aus´ter-litz
Aus´tin
Aus-tra-la´sia
Aus-tra´lia
Aus´tria
au-then´tic
au-then´ti-cal-ly
au-then´ti-cate
au-then-ti-ca´tion
au-then-tic´i-ty
au´thor
au-thor-i-tar´i-an
au-thor´i-ta-tive
au-thor´i-ty

au-tho-ri-za´tion
au´tho-rize
au´tho-rized
au´tho-riz-ing
au´thor-ship
au´tism
au´to
au-to-bi-og´ra-pher
au-to-bi-o-graph´ic
au-to-bi-o-graph´i-cal
au-to-bi-og´ra-phy
au-toc´ra-cy
au´to-crat
au-to-crat´ic
au-to-crat´i-cal-ly
au´to—da—fé´
au-to-gen´ic
au´to-graph
au-tog´ra-pher
au-to-graph´ic
au-tog´ra-phy
au-to-ki-net´ic
au´to-mat
au-to-mat´ic
au-to-mat´i-cal
au-to-mat´i-cal-ly
au-to-ma´tion
au-tom´a-tism
au-tom´a-ton
au-to-mo-bile´
au-to-mo-bil´ist
au-to-mo´tive
au-ton´o-mous
au-ton´o-my
au´top-sy
au-to-sug-ges´tion
au´tumn
au-tum´nal
Au-vergne´
aux-il´ia-ry
avail
avail-a-bil´i-ty
avail´a-ble
availed´
av´a-lanche
Av´a-lon
avant´—garde´
av´a-rice
av-a-ri´cious

av-a-ri´cious-ly
av´a-tar
a´ve
A´ve Ma-ri´a
avenge
avenged
aveng´er
aveng´ing
Av´en-tine
av´e-nue
aver
av´er-age
averred´
aver´ring
averse
aver´sion
avert
avert´ed
a´vi-ary
a´vi-ate
avi-a´tion
a´vi-a-tor
avi-a´trix
av´id
avid´i-ty
av´id-ly
Avi-gnon´
A´vis
av-o-ca´do
av-o-ca´dos
av-o-ca´tion
avoid
avoid´a-ble
avoid´ance
avoid´ed
av-oir-du-pois´
A´von
avouch
avow
avow´al
avowed
avun´cu-lar
a´wait´
awake
awaked
awak´en
awak´en-ing
award
award´ed

aware
aware´ness
awash
away
awe
awea´ry
aweigh
awe´some
awe´stricken
awe´struck
aw´ful
aw´ful-ly
awhile
awk´ward
awk´ward-ly
awk´ward-ness
awl
aw´ning
awoke
awry
ax
ax´es
ax´il-lary
ax´i-om
ax-i-o-mat´ic
ax-i-o-mat´i-cal
ax-i-o-mat´i-cal-ly
ax´is
ax´le
ax-om´e-ter
aye
Ayr´shire
aza´lea
az-i-mi´no
az´i-muth
Azores
Az´tec
az´ure

B

Ba´al
bab´bitt
bab´ble
bab´bler
bab´bling
Ba´bel
ba´bied
ba´bies

ba-boon´
ba´by
ba´by-hood
ba´by-ing
ba´by-ish
Bab´y-lon
Bab-y-lo´nia
Bab-y-lo´ni-an
bac-ca-lau´re-ate
bac´ca-rat
bac´cha-nal
bac-cha-na´lian
bac-chant´
bac-chant´e
Bac´chus
bach´e-lor
bach´e-lor-hood
bac´il-lary
ba-cil´li
ba-cil´lus
bac-i-tra´cin
back´ache
back´bite
back´bit-ing
back´bone
back´break-ing
back door
back´drop
back´er
back´field
back´fire
back´gam-mon
back´ground
back´hand
back´hand-ed
back´ing
back´lash
back´log
back´side
back´slide
back´slid-ing
back´stage´
back´stairs
back´stop
back´stroke
back´talk
back´track
back´ward
back´ward-ness
back´wash
back´wat-er
back-woods´
back-woods´man
back-yard´
ba´con
bac-te´ria
bac-te´ri-al
bac-te´ri-cide
bac´ter-id
bac-te-ri-o-log´i-cal
bac-te-ri-ol´o-gist
bac-te-ri-ol´o-gy
bac-te´rio-phage
bac-te´ri-um
badge
badg´er
bad-i-nage´
bad´ly
bad´min-ton
Bae´de-ker
baf´fle
baf´fler
baf´fling
bag´a-telle´
bag´gage
bag´gage-man
bag´gage room
bag´gy
Bagh´dad
ba´gnio
bag´pipe
bag´piper
ba-guette´
Ba-ha´i
Ba-ha´ma
Ba-hi´a
Bah-rain´
bai´liff
bai´li-wick
bail´ment
bails´man
bait
Ba´ke-lite
bak´er
bak´ery
bak´ing
Ba´laam
bal´ance
bal´anc-er
bal´anc-ing
Bal-bo´a
bal-brig´gan
bal´co-nies
bal´co-ny
bal´der-dash
bald´ness
bal´dric
Bald´win
baled
ba-leen´
bale´ful
Bal´four
Ba´li
balk
Bal´kan
balk´i-er
balk´ing
balk´y
bal´lad
bal-lade´
bal´lad-ry
bal´last
ball bear´ing
bal-le-ri´na
bal´let
bal-lis´tic
bal-lis-ti´cian
bal-lis´tics
bal´lo-net´
bal-loon´
bal-loon´ist
bal´lot
bal´lot box
ball´play-er
ball´room
bal´ly-hoo
balm
balm´i-ly
balm´i-ness
Bal-mor´al
balm´y
ba-lo´ney
bal´sa
bal´sam
Bal´tic
Bal´ti-more
Bal-zac´

bam-bi´no
bam-boo´
bam-boo´zle
bam-boo´zler
ban
ba´nal
ba-nal´i-ty
ba-nan´a
Ban´croft
ban´dage
ban´dag-ing
ban-dan´na
ban´dit
ban´dit-ry
ban-dit´ti
band´mas-ter
ban´do-leer´
bands´man
band´stand
band´wag-on
ban´dy
ban´dy-ing
ban´dy—leg-ged
bane´ful
Bang´kok
Ban-gla-desh´
ban´gle
Ban´gor
ban´ish
ban´ish-ment
ban´is-ter
ban´jo
bank´ ac-count
bank´book
bank´ draft
bank´er
bank´ing
bank´note
bank´rupt
bank´rupt-cy
banned
ban´ner
ban´quet
ban´quet-er
Ban´quo
ban´shee
ban´tam
ban´tam-weight
ban´ter
ban´ter-ing-ly
Ban´tu
ban´yan
ban-zai´
ba´o-bab
bap´tism
bap´tis´mal
Bap´tist
bap´tis-tery
bap-tize´
bap-tized´
bap-tiz´ing
Bar-ab´bas
Bar-ba´dos
Bar´ba-ra
bar-bar´i-an
bar-bar´ic
bar´ba-rism
bar-bar´i-ty
bar´ba-rize
Bar-ba-ros´sa
bar´ba-rous
Bar´ba-ry
bar´be-cue
barbed
barbed wire
bar´ber
bar´ber-ry
bar´ber-shop
bar´bi-tal
bar-bi´tu-rate
bar-bi-tu´ric
Bar´bi-zon
bar´ca-role
Bar-ce-lo´na
bare
bare´back
bared
bare´faced
bare´foot
bare´—hand-ed
bare´head-ed
bare´ly
bar´gain
bar´gain-er
barge
barge ca-nal´
barge´mas-ter
bar´i-tone
bar´i-um
bar´keep-er
bar´ken-tine
bark´er
bark´ing
bar´ley
bar´ley-corn
bar´maid
bar´man
Bar´na-bas
bar´na-cle
barn´dance
barn´storm-er
barn´storm-ing
Bar´num
barn´yard
bar´o-graph
ba-rom´e-ter
bar-o-met´ric
bar-o-met´ro-graph
bar´on
bar´on-age
bar´on-ess
bar-on-et´
bar-on-et´age
bar´on-et-cy
bar´ony
ba-roque´
bar´racks
bar-ra-cu´da
bar-rage´
barred
bar´rel
bar´ren
bar´ren-ness
bar-rette´
bar´ri-cade
bar´ri-cad´ing
bar´ri-er
bar´ring
bar´ris-ter
bar´room
bar´row
bar´tender
bar´ter
Bar-thol´o-mew
Ba-ruch´
ba´sal
ba´sal-ly

ba-salt´
base
base´ball
base´board
base´ hit
Ba´sel
base´less
base´ line
base´ly
base´ment
bash´ful
bash´ful-ness
ba´sic
ba´si-cal-ly
bas´il
ba-sil´i-ca
ba-sil´i-can
bas´i-lisk
ba´sin
ba´sis
bask
bas´ket
bas´ket-ball
bas´ket-ry
bas´ket-work
Basque
Bas´ra
bas´—re-lief´
bass
bas´set
bas-si-net´
bas´so
bas-soon´
bass´wood
bas´tard
bas´tardy
baste
bas-tille´
bast´ing
Ba-ta´via
bate
bat´fish
bath
bathe
bath´er
bath´ing
bath´robe
bath´room
Bath-she´ba
bath´y-sphere
ba-tik´
ba-tiste´
ba-ton´
Bat´on Rouge
bat-tal´ion
bat´ten
bat´ter
bat´ter-ies
bat´ter-ing
bat´tery
bat´tle
bat´tle cruis´er
bat´tle cry
bat´tle-field
bat´tle-ground
bat´ty
Ba-tum´
bau´ble
baux´ite
Ba-var´ia
bawd´y
bawl
Ba-yeux´
bay´o-net
Ba-yonne´
bay´ou
Bay´reuth
ba-zaar´
ba-zoo´ka
beach
beach´comb-er
beach´head
bea´con
bead´ed
bead´ing
bead´y
bea´gle
beaked
beak´er
beamed
beam´ing
bear
bear´able
beard´ed
beard´less
bear´er
bear´ing
bear´ish
bé-ar-naise´
bear´skin
beast´ly
beat´en
beat´er
be-at´i-fied
be-at´i-fy
beat´ing
be-at´i-tude
beau
Beau´fort
beau geste
Beau-mar-chais´
Beau´mont
Beau´re-gard
beau´te-ous
beau´ties
beau´ti-fi-ca´tion
beau´ti-fied
beau´ti-fi-er
beau´ti-ful
beau´ti-ful-ly
beau´ti-fy
beau´ti-fy-ing
beau´ty
beaux
beaux arts
bea´ver
be-calm´
be-cause´
Beck´et
beck´on
beck´on-ing
be-cloud´
be-come´
be-com´ing
be-daub´
be-daze´
be-daz´zle
be-daz´zling
bed´bug
bed´clothes
be-deck´
be-dev´il
be-dev´il-ment
be-dew´
bed´fast
bed´fel-low
Bed´ford

bed´jack-et
bed´lam
Bed´ou-in
bed´pan
bed´post
be-drag´gle
bed´rid-den
bed´rock
bed´room
bed´sheet
bed´side
bed´sore
bed´spread
bed´spring
bed´stead
bed´time
beech
beef
beef´eat-er
beef´steak
beef-y
bee´hive
bee´line
Beel´ze-bub
beer
Beer-she´ba
beer´y
bees´wax
beet
Bee´tho-ven
bee´tle
bee´tle-browed
be-fall´
be-fall´en
be-fell´
be-fit´
be-fit´ting
be-fog´
be-fogged´
be-fog´ging
be-fore´
be-fore´hand
be-foul´
be-friend´
be-fud´dle
be-get´
beg´gar
beg´gar-ly
beg´ging
be-gin´
be-gin´ner
be-gin´ning
be-gone´
be-go´nia
be-grime´
be-grudge´
be-grudg´ing
be-grudg´ing-ly
be-guile´
be-guil´er
be-guil´ing-ly
be-half´
be-have´
be-haved´
be-hav´ing
be-hav´ior
be-hav´ior-ism
be-hav-ior-is´tic
be-head´
be-held´
be-he´moth
be-hest´
be-hind´
be-hind´hand
be-hold´
be-hold´en
be-hold´er
be-hold´ing
be-hoove´
beige
be´ing
Bei´rut
be-la´bor
be-lat´ed
be-lay´
be-lea´guer
be-lea´guered
Bel´fast
Bel´fort
bel´fry
Bel´gian
Bel´gium
be-lie
belief´
be-li´er
be-liev´a-ble
be-lieve´
be-lieved´
be-liev´er
be-liev´ing
be-lit´tle
be-lit´tling
Be-lize´
bel-la-don´na
bell´boy
Bel-leau´
belles let´tres
bell´hop
bel´li-cose
bel-lig´er-ence
bel-lig´er-en-cy
bel-lig´er-ent
bel´low
bell´weth-er
bel´ly
bel´ly-band
Bel´mont
be-long´
be-longed´
be-long´ings
be-loved´, be-lov´ed
be-low´
Bel-shaz´zar
belt´ed
be-mire´
be-mir´ing
be-moan´
be-muse´
be-mused´
be-mus´ing
Be-na´res
bend´ed
bend´er
bend´ing
be-neath´
be-ne-di´ci-te
ben´e-dict
Ben-e-dic´tine
ben-e-dic´tion
ben-e-dic´to-ry
ben´e-fac-tion
ben´e-fac-tor
ben´e-fac-tress
be-nef´ic
ben´e-fice
ben´e-ficed
be-nef´i-cence

be-nef'i-cent
ben-e-fi'cial
ben-e-fi'cial-ly
ben-e-fi'cia-ries
ben-e-fi'cia-ry
ben'e-fit
ben'e-fit-ed
ben'e-fit-ing
Be'nes
be-nev'o-lence
be-nev'o-lent
Ben'gal
be-night'ed
be-nign'
be-nig'nant
be-nig'nant-ly
be-nig--ni-ty
be-nign'ly
ben'i-son
Ben'ja-min
Bent'ley
be-numb'
Ben'ze-drine
ben'zene
ben'zine
ben'zo-ate
ben'zol
Be'o-wulf
be-queath'
be-quest'
be-rate'
be-rat'ed
be-rat'ing
Ber'ber
be-reave'
be-reaved'
be-reave'ment
be-reav'ing
be-reft'
Ber'es-ford
be-ret'
ber'ga-mot
Ber'gen
Ber'-ge-rac'
beri-ber'i
Ber'ing
Berke'ley
Berk'ley
Berk'shires

Ber-lin'
Ber-mu'da
Bern'hardt
ber'ries
ber'ry
ber-serk'
ber-serk'er
berth
Ber'tha
ber'yl
be-ryl'li-um
be-seech'
be-seeched'
be-seech'ing
be-set'
be-set'ting
be-side'
be-sides'
be-siege'
be-sieg'er
be-sieg'ing-ly
be-smear'
be-smirch'
be'som
be-sot'
be-sot'ted
be-spat'ter
be-speak'
be-spoke'
Bes-sa-ra'bia
Bes'se-mer
bes'tial
bes-ti-al'i-ty
bes'tial-ly
be-stir'
be-stow'
be-stow'al
be-strew'
be-stride'
be-strode'
be'ta
be-take'
be'tel
Be'tel-geuse
Beth'a-ny
Beth'el
Be-thes'da
Beth'le-hem
Beth-sa'i-da

be-tide'
be-to'ken
be-tray'
be-tray'al
be-tray'er
be-troth'
be-troth'al
be-throthed'
bet'ter
bet'ter-ment
be-tween'
be-twixt'
bev'el
bev'eled
bev'el-ing
bev'er-age
bev'ies
bev'y
be-wail'
be-ware'
be-wil'der
be-wil'dered
be-wil'dered-ly
be-wil'der-ing
be-wil'der-ing-ly
be-wil'der-ment
be-witch'
be-witch'ing
be-witch'ment
be-yond'
be-zique'
Bhu-tan'
bi-an'nu-al
bi-an'nu-al-ly
bi'as
bi'ased
bi'as-ing
bi-ax'i-al
Bi'ble
Bib'li-cal
Bib'li-cal-ly
bib'li-o-graph
bib-li-og'ra-pher
bib'li-o-graph'ic
bib-li-og'ra-phy
bib-li-o-ma'nia
bib'li-o-phile
bib-li-oph-i-lis'tic
bib'li-o-pol'ic

bib´u-lous
bi-cam´er-al
bi-car´bon-ate
bi-cen-ten´a-ry
bi-cen-ten´ni-al
bi´ceps
bi-chlo´ride
bick´er
bick´er-ing
bi-con´vex
bi-cus´pid
bi-cus´pi-date
bi´cy-cle
bi´cy-cler
bi´cy-clist
bid´da-ble
Bid´de-ford
bid´den
bid´der
bid´ding
bid´dy
bide
Bid´e-ford
bid´ing
bi-en´ni-al
bi-en´ni-al-ly
bier
bi-fa´cial
bi-far´i-ous-ly
bi´fid
bi´fo-cal
bi´fur-cate
bi´fur-cat-ed
bi-fur-ca´tion
big´a-mist
big´a-mous
big´a-mous-ly
big´a-my
big´ger
big´heart-ed
big´horn
big´ot
big´ot-ed
big´ot-ry
bi-ki´ni
bi-la´bi-al
bil´an-der
bi-lat´er-al
bi-lat´er-al-ly
Bil-ba´o
bil´ber-ry
bil´i-ary
bi-lin´gual
bil´ious
bill´board
bil´let
bil´let—doux
bill´fish
bill´fold
bil´liards
Bil´lings
bil´lion
bil´lion-aire
bil´low
bil´lowy
bi-met´al-list
bi-month´ly
bi´na-ry
bin-au´ral
Bing´ham-ton
bin´go
bin´na-cle
bin-oc´u-lar
bi-no´mi-al
bio-chem´i-cal
bi´o-chem´ist
bio-chem´is-try
bio-de-grad´a-ble
bio-de-grade´
bio-ecol´o-gy
bio-gen´e-sis
bi´o-graph
bi-og´ra-pher
bio-graph´ic
bio-graph´i-cal
bi-og´ra-phy
bio-log´ic
bio-log´i-cal
bi-ol´o-gist
bi-ol´o-gy
bi-om´e-try
bi-on´ic
bio-nom´ics
bi´op-sy
bi´o-sphere
bio-tox´in
bi-par´ti-san
bi-par´tite
bi-par-ti´tion
bi´ped
bi´plane
bi-po´lar
bi-quar´ter-ly
birch´bark
birch´en
bird´call
bird´lime
bird´man
bird's´—eye
bi-ret´ta
Bir´ming-ham
birth
birth´day
birth´mark
birth´place
birth´stone
Bis´cay
bis´cuit
bi´sect´
bi-sec´tion
bi´sec´tor
bish´op
bish´op-ric
bis´muth
bi´son
bisque
bis´ter
bi-sul´fide
bitch
bite
bit´er
bit´ing
bit´ten
bit´ter
bit´ter-ly
bit´tern
bit´ter-ness
bit´ter-root
bit´ters
bit´ter-sweet
bi-tu´men
bi-tu´mi-nous
bi-va´lent
bi´valve
bi-val´vu-lar
biv´ouac
biv´ouacked

biv´ouack-ing
bi-week´ly
bizarre´
bi-zarre´ness
Bizet
blab
blab´ber
black´ball
black´ber-ry
black´bird
black´board
black´cap
black´en
black´ened
black´en-er
black´—eyed
Black´feet
Black´foot
black´guard
black´head
Black Hills
black´ing
black´jack
black´list
black´ly
black´mail
black´out
black sheep
black´smith
black´thorn
blad´der
blade
blade´less
blame´wor-thy
blam´ing
blanch
blanch´er
blanch´ing
blanc-mange´
bland
blan´dish
blan´dish-ment
bland´ly
bland´ness
blank´book
blan´ket
blank´ly
blank´ness
blare

blar´ney
bla-sé´
blas´pheme
blas´phem-er
blas´phem-ing
blas´phe-mous
blas´phe-my
blast´ed
blas´tu-la
bla´tant
bla´tant-ly
blath´er-skite
blaze
blazed
blaz´er
blaz´ing
bleach´er
bleak
bleak´ly
blear´i-ness
blear´y
bleat´ing
bleed´ing
blem´ish
blem´ish-er
blend´er
blend´ing
Blen´heim
bless
blessed, bless´ed
bless´ed-ly
bless´ed-ness
bless´ing
blind´er
blind´fold
blind´ing
blind´ly
blind´ness
blink´er
blink´ing
bliss´ful
bliss´ful-ly
blis´ter
blis´tery
blithe
blithe´ly
blithe´some
blitz´krieg
bliz´zard

block
block-ade´
block-ad´ed
block-ad´ing
block´buster
block´head
block´house
blond´ness
blood bank
blood´cur-dling
blood´hound
blood´i-ness
blood´less
blood´let-ting
blood pres´sure
blood´shed
blood´shot
blood´stain
blood´stained
blood´stone
blood´suck-er
blood´thirst-i-ly
blood´thirsty
blood´ vessel
blood´y
bloom´ers
bloom´ing
bloom´ing-ly
blos´som
blotch
blotch´y
blot´ted
blot´ter
blow´er
blow´fly
blow´gun
blow´hole
blow´i-ness
blown
blow´out
blow´pipe
blow´torch
blow´up
blub´ber
blub´bery
bludg´eon
blue
Blue´beard
blue´bell

blue´berry
blue´bird
blue´bon-net
blue book
blue´coat
blue´—eyed
blue´fish
blue´grass
blue´jacket
blue´ jay
blue laws
blue moon
blue´print
blue´stock-ing
blue´stone
blu´et
bluff´er
bluff´ing
blu´ing
blun´der
blun´der-buss
blun´der-er
blun´der-ing
blur
blurred
blur´ring
blushed
blush´ing
blus´ter
blus´ter-ing
blus´ter-ous
blus´tery
bo´a
boar
board´er
board´walk
boast´er
boast´ful
boast´ing-ly
boat´build-er
boat club
boat´hook
boat´house
boat´ing
boat´man
boat´swain
bobbed
bob´bin
bob´bing

bob´cat
bob´o-link
bob´sled
bob´tail
bob´white´
Boc-cac´cio
bod´ice
bod´i-ly
bod´kin
bod´y
bod´y-guard
bo´gey
bog´gish
bog´gle
bog´gy
Bo-go-ta´
bo´gus
bo´gy
Bo-he´mia
boil´er
boil´ing
Boi´se
bois´ter-ous
bois´ter-ous-ly
bold´face
bold´ly
bold´ness
Bo-li´var
Bo-liv´ia
boll
boll´ wee´vil
bo´lo
Bo-lo´gna
Bol´she-vik
Bol´she-vism
bol´ster
bolt´er
bomb
bom-bard´
bom´bar-dier´
bom-bard´ment
bom´bast
bom-bas´tic
bom-bas´ti-cal
Bombay´
bomb bay
bomb´er
bomb´proof
bomb´shell

bomb´sight
bo´na fide
bo-nan´za
Bo´na-parte
Bo-na-ven-tu´ra
bon´bon
bond´age
bond´ed
bond´man
bonds´man
bond´wom-an
bone´dry
bone´less
bon´er
bon´fire
Bon´i-face
bon jour
bon´net
bon vi-vant´
bon vo-yage´
boo´dle
book
book a´gent
book´bind-er
book´bind-ery
book´case
book club
book col-lec´tor
book´dealer
book´end
book´ie
book´ish
book´keep-er
book´keep-ing
book´let
book´mak-er
book´mark
book´plate
book´rack
book re-view´
book´sell-er
book´shelf
book´shop
book´store
book´worm
boo´mer-ang
boon´dog-gle
boor´ish
boost´er

boot´black
boot´ed
boo´tee´
booth
boot´leg
boot´leg-ger
boot´leg-ging
boot´less
boot tree
boo´ty
booze
booz´er
booz´y
bo´rax
Bor-deaux´
bor´der
bor´dered
bor´der-land
bor´der-line
bore
bore´dom
Bor´gia
bo´ric
bor´ing
born
borne
Bor´neo
bo´ron
bor´ough
bor´row
bor´row-er
borsch
bos´om
boss´ism
boss´y
Bos´ton
bo´sun
Bos´well
bo-tan´i-cal
bot´a-nist
bot´a-nize
bot´a-ny
botch
botch´y
both´er
both´er-some
Bo-tswa´na
Bot-ti-cel´li
bot´tle

bot´tle-neck
bot´tle—nosed
bot´tler
bot´tle wash´er
bot´tling
bot´tom
bot´tom-land
bot´tom-less
bot´u-lism
bou-clé´
bou-doir´
bou-gain-vil´lea
bough
bought
bouil´la-baisse´
bouil´lon
boul´der
bou´le-vard
Bou-logne´
bounce
bounc´er
bounc´ing
bound
bound´a-ries
bound´a-ry
bound´ed
bound´less
boun´te-ous
boun´ti-ful
boun´ty
bou-quet´
bour´-bon
bour´geois
bour´geoise
bour´geoi-sie´
bourne
bourse
bou´ton-niere´
bo´vine
bow´el
bow´er
bow´ery
bow´ie
bow´knot
bowl
bow´leg
bow´leg-ged
bowl´er
bow´line

bowl´ing
bow´man
bow´string
box´car
box´er
box´ing
box kite
box´wood
boy
boy´cott
boy´cott-er
boy´hood
boy´ish
boy´ish-ness
Boyle
boy´sen-ber-ry
brace´let
brac´er
brach´i-al
brac´ing
brack´en
brack´et
brack´ish
brag´gart
bragged
brag´ger
brag´ging
Brah´ma
Brah´min
Brahms
Braille
brain cell
brain´i-er
brain´less
brain´wash-ing
brain´work
brain´y
braise
braised
brais´ing
brake
brake´man
bram´ble
bram´bly
Bran´deis
Bran´den-burg
bran´died
brand´—new
bran´dy

Bran´dy-wine
bran´ni-gan
Bra-sí´lia
brass´ie
bras-siere´
brass´y
bra-va´do
brave´heart-ed
brave´ly
brav´ery
brav´est
bra´vo
bra-vu´ra
brawl
brawl´er
brawn
brawn´i-er
brawn´i-est
brawn´i-ness
brawn´y
bra´zen
bra´zier
Bra-zil´
bra-zil´wood
braz´ing
breach
bread
bread´pan
breadth
bread´win-ner
break
break´able
break´age
break´down
break´er
break´fast
break´neck
break´through
break´up
break´wa-ter
breast
breast´bone
breast´plate
breath
breathe
breath´er
breath´ing
breath´less
breath´less-ly
breath´taking
bred
breech
breech´es
breed
breed´er
breed´ing
breeze
breeze´way
breez´y
Bre´men
Bren´ner
breth´ren
Bret´on
bre-vet´
bre-vet´ted
bre´via-ry
brev´i-ty
brew´er
brew´ery
brew´ing
bri´ar
bribed
brib´er
brib´ery
bric´—a—brac
brick´lay-er
brick´work
brick´yard
brid´al
bride´groom
brides´maid
bridge´head
Bridge´port
Bridge´wa-ter
bridge´work
bri´dle
bri´dling
brief´ing
brief´ly
bri´er
brig´a-dier
brig´an-dine
brig´an-tine
bright´—eyed
bright´ly
bright´ness
Brigh´ton
bril´liance
bril´lian-cy
bril´liant
brim´stone
bring
bring´er
bring´ing
brink
bri´o-lette
bri-quet´
bri-quette´
bris´ket
brisk´ly
brisk´ness
bris´tle
bris´tling
Bris´tol
Brit´ain
Bri-tan´nia
Brit´ish
Brit´on
Brit´ta-ny
brit´tle
broach
broad
broad´brim
broad´cast
broad´cloth
broad´en
broad´loom
broad´ly
broad´—mind-ed
broad´—mind-ed-ness
broad´side
broad´tail
Broad´way
bro-cade´
bro-cad´ed
broc´co-li
bro-chette´
brochure´
Brock´ton
bro´gan
brogue
broi´dery
broil
broil´er
bro´kage
broke
bro´ken

bro´ken-heart-ed
bro´ker
bro´ker-age
bro´mide
bro´mine
bro´mo-form
bro-mom´e-try
bron´chi-al
bron-chi´tis
bron´chus
bron´co
Bron´te
bron´to-saur
bronze
bronz´ing
brooch
brood´er
brood´ing
brook´let
Brook´line
Brook´lyn
broom´stick
broth
broth´el
broth´er
broth´er-hood
broth´er—in—law
broth´er-ly
brougham
brow´beat
brow´beat-ing
brown´ie
brown´out
brown´stone
browse
brows´ing
bruise
bruised
bruis´er
bruis´ing
bru-net´
Bruns´wick
brunt
brusque´ly
Brus´sels
bru´tal
bru-tal´i-ty
bru´tal-ize
bru´tal-ly
brute
brut´ish
Bru´tus
bub´ble
bub´bling
bub´bling-ly
bub´bly
bu-bon´ic
buc´ca-neer
Bu-chan´an
Bu´cha-rest
buck´a-roo
buck´board
buck´et
buck´et-ful
buck´eye
Buck´ing-ham
buck´le
buck´ler
buck´ling
buck´saw
buck´shot
buck´skin
buck´thorn
buck´tooth
buck´wheat
bu-col´ic
Bu´da-pest
Bud´dha
Bud´dhism
Bud´dhist
bud´dy
budge
bud´get
bud´get-ary
bud´get-ed
bud´ge-teer
bud´get-er
bud´get-ing
Bue´na Vis´ta
Bue´nos Ai´res
buf´fa-lo
buf´fa-loes
buff´er
buf´fet
buf-foon´
buf-foon´ery
bug´a-boo
bug´bear
bug´gy
bu´gle
bu´gler
bu´gling
build´er
build´ing
build´up
built´—in
bul-ba´ceous
bul´bar
bul´bous
Bul-gar´ia
bulge
bulg´er
bulg´ing
bulk´head
bulk´i-er
bulk´i-ness
bulk´y
bull´dog
bull´doze
bull´doz-er
bull´doz-ing
bul´let
bul´le-tin
bul´let-proof
bull´fight
bull´fight-er
bull´finch
bull´frog
bull´head
bull´head-ed
bul´lied
bul´lion
bull´ish
bul´lock
bull´pen
Bull Run
bull's´—eye
bull´whip
bul´ly
bul´ly-ing
bul´ly-rag
bul´rush
bul´wark
bum´ble-bee
bum´bling
bum´boat
bump´er

bump´i-er
bump´kin
bump´tious
bump´y
bunch
bunch´i-er
bunch´y
bun´co
bun´der
bun´dle
bun´dling
bun´ga-low
bung´hole
bun´gle
bun´gled
bun´gler
bun´gling
bun´gling-ly
bun´ion
bun´ker
bunk´house
bun´ko
bun´ny
Bun´sen
bunt´er
bunt´ing
Bun´yan
buoy
buoy´age
buoy´an-cy
buoy´ant
Bur´bank
bur´den
bur´den-some
bu´reau
bu-reauc´ra-cy
bu´reau-crat
bu-reau-crat´ic
bu-rette´
bur´geon
bur´gess
bur´glar
bur´gla-ries
bur-glar´i-ous
bur´glar-ize
bur´glar-proof
bur´gla-ry
Bur-goyne´
Bur´gun-dy
bur´i-al
bur´ied
bur´ies
bur´lap
Bur´leigh
bur´lesque´
bur´lesqued´
bur-lesqu´er
bur´ley
bur´li-ness
Bur´ling-ton
bur´ly
Bur´ma
burned
burn´er
bur-net´
Bur´ney
burn´ing
burn´ish
bur-noose´
burn´sides
burnt
bur´ro
Bur´roughs
bur´row
bur´row-er
bur´sa
bur´sar
bur-sar´i-al
bur´sa-ry
bur-si´tis
burst
burst´ing
Bur´ton
Bu-run´di
bur´y
bur´y-ing
bur´y-ing ground
bus´es
bush´el
bush´i-er
Bush´man
bush´mas-ter
bush´rang-er
bush´whack-er
bush´y
bus´ied
bus´i-er
bus´i-est
bus´i-ly
bus´i-ness
bus´i-ness-like
bus´i-ness-man
bus´kin
bus´ses
bus´tard
bus´tle
bus´tled
bus´tler
bus´tling
bus´tling-ly
bus´y
bus´y-body
bus´y-ness
bu´tane
butch´er
butch´ery
but´ler
butte
but´ter
but´ter-cup
but´ter-fat
but´ter-fin-ger
but´ter-fish
but´ter-fly
but´ter-milk
but´ter-nut
but´ter-scotch
but´tery
but´tocks
but´ton
but´ton-hole
but´ton-wood
but´tress
bu-tyr´ic
bux´om
bux´om-ness
buy´er
buy´ing
buz´zard
buzz´er
buzz saw
by´gone
by´law
by´—line
by´pass
by´path
by´play

by´—prod-uct
Byrd
by´road
By´ron
bys´sus
by´stand-er
by´way
by´word
Byz´an-tine
By-zan´tium

C

ca-bal´
cab´a-la
cab-a-lis´tic
cab-a-lis´ti-cal
ca-bal-le´ro
ca-ban´a
cab-a-ret´
cab´bage
cab´by
ca´ber
ca-ber-net´
cab´in
cab´in boy
cab´i-net
cab´i-net-mak-er
cab´i-net-work
ca´ble
ca´ble-gram
ca´bling
cab´man
cab´o-chon
ca-boose´
Cab´ot
cab´ri-ole
cab-ri-o-let´
cab´stand
ca-ca´o
cach´a-lot
cache
cached
ca-chet´
ca-cique´
cack´le
cack´ling
ca-coph´o-ny
cac´ti
cac´tus
ca-dav´er
ca-dav´er-ous
cad´die
cad´dis
cad´dish
cad´dy
ca´dence
ca´den-cy
ca-den´za
ca-det´
Cad´il-lac
Ca-diz´
Cad´me-an
cad´mi-um
Cad´mus
cad´re
ca-du´ce-us
Cae´sar
Cae-sar´e-an
cae-su´ra
ca-fe´
caf-e-te´ria
caf´feine
caf´tan
Ca-ga-yan´
cage´ling
ca´gey
ca´gi-er
cai´man
cairn
Cai´ro
cais´son
cai´tiff
Ca´ius
ca-jole´
ca-jol´ery
Ca´jun
cake´box
cake mix´er
cake pan
cake´walk
cal´a-boose
Ca-la´bria
Ca-lais´
cal´a-mine
cal´a-mite
ca-lam´i-tous
ca-lam´i-ty
cal-cif´er-ous
cal-ci-fi-ca´tion
cal´ci-fy
cal-cim´e-ter
cal´ci-mine
cal-ci-na´tion
cal´cine
cal´cin-er
cal´cite
cal´ci-um
cal´cu-la-ble
cal´cu-late
cal´cu-lat-ing
cal-cu-la´tion
cal´cu-la-tive
cal´cu-la-tor
cal´cu-lus
Cal-cut´ta
Cal-de-ron´
cal´dron
Ca´leb
Cal-e-do´nia
cal´en-dar
cal´en-der
Cal´ends
ca-len´du-la
cal´en-ture
calf
calf´skin
Cal´ga-ry
Cal-houn´
Cal´i-ban
cal´i-ber
cal´i-brate
cal-i-bra´tion
cal´i-bra-tor
cal´i-co
Cal-i-for´nia
Ca-lig´u-la
cal´i-per
ca´liph
cal-is-then´ics
calk
calk´ing
call´able
Cal-la´o
call´er
Cal´les
cal-lig´ra-pher

cal-li-graph´ic
cal-lig´ra-phy
call´ing
cal-li´o-pe
Cal-lis´to
cal-los´i-ty
cal´lous
cal´low
cal´lus
cal´lus-es
calm
calm´ly
calm´ness
ca-lor´ic
cal-o-ric´i-ty
cal´o-rie
cal´o-ries
cal-o-rif´ic
cal-o-rim´e-ter
cal´o-rize
ca-lotte´
cal´u-met
ca-lum´ni-ate
ca-lum-ni-a´tion
ca-lum´ni-a-tor
cal´um-nies
ca-lum´ni-ous
ca-lum´ni-ous-ly
cal´um-ny
Cal´va-ry
calve
Cal´vert
calves
Cal´vin
Cal´vin-ism
cal-vi´ti-es
calx
Cal´y-don
ca-lyp´so
ca-lyp´tra
ca´lyx
ca-ma-ra´de-rie
cam-a-ril´la
cam´ber
cam´bi-um
Cam-bo´dia
Cam´bria
Cam´bri-an
cam´bric
Cam´bridge
Cam´den
cam´el
ca-mel´lia
Cam´e-lot
Cam´em-bert
cam´eo
cam´era-man
Cam´er-oon
Ca-mil´la
Ca-mille´
ca-mion´
cam´i-sole
cam´o-mile
Ca-mor´ra
cam´ou-flage
Cam-pa´gna
cam-paign´
cam-paign´er
cam-pa-ni´le
Camp´bell
camp´er
camp´fire
camp´ground
cam´phor
cam-phor´ic
cam´pus
Ca´naan
Can´a-da
ca-nal´
ca-nal´boat
ca-nal-i-za´tion
ca-nal´ize
ca´na-pé
ca-nard´
ca-nar´ies
ca-nar´y
ca-nas´ta
Can´ber-ra
can´can
can´cel
can´celed
can´cel-er
can´cel-ing
can-cel-la´tion
can´cer
can´cer-ous
can-de-la´bra
can-de-la´brum
can-des´cence
can-des´cent
can´did
can´di-da-cy
can´di-date
can´did-ly
can´did-ness
can´died
can´dies
can´dle
can´dle-light
Can´dle-mas
can´dle-nut
can´dle-pow-er
can´dor
can´dy
Can´field
ca´nine
Ca´nis
can´is-ter
can´ker
can´ker-ous
canned
can´ner
can´nery
Cannes
can´ni-bal
can´ni-bal-ism
can-ni-bal-is´tic
can´ni-bal-ize
can´ni-ly
can´ni-ness
can´ning
can´non
can´non-ade´
can´non-ball
can´non-eer
can´not
can´nu-la
can´ny
ca-noe´
ca-noe´ing
ca-noe´ist
ca-noes´
can´on
ca´ñon
can´on-ness
ca-non´i-cal
can-on-i-za´tion

can´on-ize
can´on-ry
can´ o´pen-er
can´o-pies
can´o-py
can´ta-loupe
can-tan´ker-ous
can-ta´ta
can-teen´
can´ter
Can´ter-bury
can´ti-le-ver
can´to
Can´ton
Can´ton-ese´
can´tor
Ca-nuck´
Ca-nute´
can´vas
can´vas-back
can´vass
can´vass-er
can´yon
ca-pa-bil´i-ties
ca-pa-bil´i-ty
ca´pa-ble
ca´pa-bly
ca-pa´cious
ca-pac´i-tance
ca-pac´i-ty
Ca-pel´la
ca´per
Ca-per´na-um
Ca-pet´
cap´ful
ca´pi-as
cap-il-la´ceous
cap-il-lar´i-ty
cap´il-lary
cap´i-ta
cap´i-tal
cap´i-tal-ism
cap´i-tal-ist
cap-i-tal-is´tic
cap-i-tal-i-za´tion
cap´i-tal-ize
cap´i-tan´
cap´i-tate
cap-i-ta´tion
cap´i-tol
ca-pit´u-lar
ca-pit´u-late
ca´pon
ca-pote´
Cap-pa-do´cia
Ca-pri´
ca-pric´cio
ca-price´
ca-pri´cious
Cap´ri-corn
cap´ri-ole
cap´size
cap´siz-ing
cap´su-lar
cap´sule
cap´tain
cap´tain-cy
cap´tion
cap´tious
cap´ti-vate
cap´ti-vat-ing
cap-ti-va´tion
cap´ti-va-tor
cap´tive
cap-tiv´i-ty
cap´tor
cap´ture
cap´tur-ing
cap´u-chin
Cap´u-let
Car´a-cal´la
Ca-ra´cas
car´a-cole
car´a-cul
ca-rafe´
car´a-mel
car´a-pace
car´at
car´a-van
car-a-van´sa-ry
car´a-vel
car´a-way
car´bide
car´bine
car´bi-nol
car-bo-hy´drate
car-bol´ic
car´bo-lize
car´bon
car-bo-na´ceous
car´bon-ate
car-bon-a´tion
car´bon di-ox´ide
car-bon´ic
car-bon-if´er-ous
car´bon-ize
car-bo-run´dum
car´boy
car´bun-cle
car´bu-ret-or
car´ca-jou
car´cass
car-cin´o-gen
car-ci-no´ma
car´da-mom
card´board
Car´de-nas
car´di-ac
Car´diff
car´di-gan
car´di-nal
card´ing
car´dio-gram
car-di-og´ra-phy
Car-do´zo
card´play-er
card´room
card ta´ble
ca-reen´
ca-reer´
care´free
care´ful
care´ful-ly
care´ful-ness
care´less
care´less-ly
care´less-ness
ca-ress´
ca-ress´ive
ca-ress´ive-ly
car´et
care´tak-er
Ca-rew´
care´worn
car´fare
car´go
car´goes

Car´ib
car´i-bou
car´i-ca-ture
car´i-ca-tur-ist
car´ies
car´il-lon
car´il-lon-neur´
car-i-o´ca
car´i-ous
Car-lisle´
car´load
Car-lot´ta
Car-lyle´
car´man
Car´mel
car´mine
car´nage
car´nal
car-nal´i-ty
car´nall-ite
car´nal-ly
car-na´tion
Car´ne-gie
car-ne´lian
car´ni-val
car´ni-vore
car-niv´o-rous
car´ol
car´ol-er
Car-o-li´na
car´om
ca-rot´id
ca-rous´al
ca-rouse´
ca-rous´ing
car´pal
Car-pa´thi-an
car´pen-ter
car´pen-try
car´pet
car´pet-bag
car´pet-bag´ger
car´pet-ing
car´riage
car´ri-er
car´ri-on
car´rot
car´roty
car-rou-sel´

car´ried
car´ry
car´ry-all
car´ry—o´ver
cart´age
Car-ta-ge´na
carte blanche
car-tel´
cart´er
Car´ter
Car´thage
Car-thu´sian
Car-tier´
car´ti-lage
car-ti-lag´i-nous
car-tog´ra-pher
car-to-graph´ic
car-tog´ra-phy
car´ton
car-toon´
car-toon´ist
car´tridge
cart´wheel
Ca-ru´so
carv´er
carv´ing
car-y-at´id
car-y-at´id-al
car-y-op´sis
ca-sa´ba
Ca-sa-blan´ca
Cas-a-no´va
cas-cade´
case´ hard´en
ca-sein´
case´mate
case´ment
cash´book
cash´ew
cash-ier´
cash´mere
cas´ing
ca-si´no
cask
cas´ket
Cas´per
Cas-san´dra
Cas´sius
cas´sock

cas´so-wary
cast
cas-ta-net´
cast´a-way
caste
cast´er
cas´ti-gate
cas-ti-ga´tion
Cas-tile´
cast´ing
cast iron
cas´tle
cas´tor
cas´trate
cas-tra´tion
ca´su-al
ca´su-al-ly
ca´su-al-ness
ca´su-al-ty
ca´su-ist
ca´su-is´tic
ca-su-is´ti-cal-ly
ca´su-is-try
cat´a-clysm
cat-a-clys´mic
cat´a-comb
cat´a-falque
cat´a-lep-sy
cat-a-lep´tic
Cat-a-li´na
cat´a-log
cat´a-log-er
cat´a-log-ing
ca-tal´pa
ca-tal´y-sis
cat´a-lyst
cat-a-lyt´ic
cat´a-lyze
cat´a-lyz-er
cat-a-ma-ran´
cat´a-mount
cat´a-pult
cat´a-ract
ca-tarrh´
ca-tas´tro-phe
cat-a-stroph´ic
cata-ton´ic
Ca-taw´ba
cat´bird

cat´boat
cat´call
catch´all
catch´er
catch´i-er
catch´word
catch´y
cat-e-che´sis
cat´e-chism
cat-e-chis´mal
cat´e-chist
cat-e-chi-za´tion
cat´e-chize
cat-e-chu´men
cat-e-chu´men-al
cat-e-gor´i-cal
cat-e-gor´i-cal-ly
cat´e-go-rize
cat´e-go-ry
ca´ter
ca´ter-er
cat´er-pil-lar
cat´fish
cat´gut
ca-thar´sis
ca-thar´tic
Ca-thay´
ca-the´dral
Cath´er
Cath´er-ine
cath´e-ter
cath´ode
Cath´o-lic
Ca-thol´i-cism
cath-o-lic´i-ty
ca-thol´i-cize
cat´kin
cat´like
cat´nap
cat´nip
Ca´to
cat—o´—nine´—tails
cat's´—eye
Cats´kill
cat's´—paw
cat´sup
cat´tail
cat´tle
cat´tle-man

cat´ty
cat´walk
Cau-ca´sian
cau´cus
cau´dal
cau´dle
caught
cau´li-flow-er
caus´al
cau-sa´tion
caus´a-tive
cause´less
caus´er
cause´way
caus´ing
caus´tic
caus´ti-cal-ly
cau-ter-i-za´tion
cau´ter-ize
cau´tery
cau´tion
cau´tion-ary
cau´tious
cau´tious-ly
cav´al-cade´
cav´a-lier´
cav´al-ry
cav´al-ry-man
Cav´en-dish
cav´ern
cav´ern-ous
cav´i-ar
cav´il
cav´i-ties
cav´i-ty
cavort´
ca-vort´ing
cay´enne´
cay´man
cay´use
cease
ceased
cease´less
cease´less-ly
ceas´ing
ce´dar
cede
ced´ed
ce-dil´la

ced´ing
ceil
ceil´ing
Cel´a-nese
cel´e-brant
cel´e-brate
cel´e-brat-ed
cel-e-bra´tion
cel´e-bra-tor
ce-leb´ri-ty
ce-ler´i-ty
cel´ery
ce-les´tial
cel´i-ba-cy
cel´i-bate
cel´lar
cel´lar-age
cel´list
cel´lo
cel´lo-phane
cel´lu-lar
cel´lule
cel´lu-loid
cel´lu-lose
Cel´si-us
Celt´ic
ce-ment´
cem´e-ter-ies
cem´e-tery
cen´o-bite
cen´o-taph
Ce-no-zo´ic
cen´ser
cen´sor
cen-so´ri-al
cen´sor-ship
cen´sur-a-ble
cen´sure
cen´sured
cen´sur-ing
cen´sus
cen´tare
cen´taur
cen-ta´vo
cen-te-nar´i-an
cen-ten´a-ry
cen-ten´ni-al
cen´ter
cen´ter-board

cen´ter-piece
cen´ti-grade
cen´ti-gram
cen´ti-li-ter
cen´ti-me-ter
cen´ti-pede
cen´tral
cen-tral-i-za´tion
cen´tral-ize
cen-trif´u-gal
cen´tri-fuge
cen-trip´e-tal
cen´trum
cen-tu´ri-al
cen-tu´ri-on
cen´tu-ry
Ce´phe-id
ce-ram´ic
ce-ram´ics
ce-ram´ist
Cer´ber-us
ce´re-al
cer-e-bel´lar
cer-e-bel´lum
cere´bral
cere´brum
cer-e-mo´ni-al
cer´e-mo-nies
cer-e-mo´ni-ous
cer´e-mo-ny
Ce´res
ce´ric
ce-rise´
ce´rite
cer´tain
cer´tain-ly
cer´tain-ties
cer´tain-ty
cer´ti-fi-a-ble
cer-tif´i-cate
cer-ti-fi-ca´tion
cer´ti-fied
cer´ti-fies
cer´ti-fy
cer´ti-fy-ing
cer´ti-tude
ce-ru´le-an
ce-ru´men
Cer-van´tes
cer´ve-lat
cer´vi-cal
cer´vix
ce-sar´e-an
ces-sa´tion
ces´sion
cess´pit
cess´pool
ce´tyl
Cey-lon´
Ce-zanne´
Cha´blis
Cha´co
chafed
cha´fer
chaf´fer
chaf´ing
chaf´ing dish
Cha´gres
cha-grin´
cha-grined´
chain gang
chain re-ac´tion
chain´—smoke
chain stitch
chain store
chain´work
chair´man
chair´man-ship
chaise longue
Chal´ce-don
Chal-de´a
cha´let
chal´ice
chalk´i-ness
chalk´y
chal´lenge
chal´lenge-a-ble
chal´leng-er
chal´leng-ing
cham´ber
cham´bered
cham´ber-maid
cha-me´leon
cham´ois
cham-pagne´
cham-pi´gnon
cham´pi-on
cham´pi-on-ship
Cham-plain´
Champs Ely-sées
chance´ful
chan´cel
chan´cel-lery
chan´cel-lor
chan´cel-lor-ship
Chan´cel-lors-ville
chan´cery
chanc´y
chan´de-lier´
chan´dler
chan´dlery
change´able
changed
change´ful
change´less
chang´er
chang´ing
chan´nel
chan´neled
chan´nel-ing
Chan´ning
chant´er
chan´ti-cleer
cha´os
cha-ot´ic
cha-peau´
cha-peaux´
chap´el
chap´er-on
chap´i-ter
chap´lain
chap´let
Chap´lin
chap´ter
char´ac-ter
char-ac-ter-is´tic
char-ac-ter-is´ti-cal-ly
char-ac-ter-i-za´tion
char´ac-ter-ize
char´ac-tery
charade´
char´coal
charge´able
char´gé d'af-faires´
charged
charg´er
charg´ing

char´i-ot
char´i-o-teer´
cha-ris´ma
char´is-mat´ic
char´i-ta-ble
char-i-ties
char´i-ty
char´la-tan
Char´le-magne
Charles´ton
Charles´town
Char´ley
Char´lotte
Char´lottes-ville
Char´lotte-town
charm´er
charm´ing
charm´ing-ly
char´nel
chart´er
chartreuse´
chart room
char´wom-an
char´y
Cha-ryb´di-an
Cha-ryb´dis
chased
chas´er
chas´ing
chasm
chas´mal
chasm´y
chasse´pot
chas-seur´
chas´sis
chaste
chas´ten
chas-tise´
chas-tise´ment
chas-tis´er
chas´ti-ty
cha-teau´
cha-teaux´
Cha-teau-bri-and´
Cha-teau—Thier-ry´
cha´te-laine
Chat´ham
Chat-ta-hoo´chee
Chat-ta-noo´ga
chat´tel
chat´ter
chat´ter-box
chat´ter-er
Chat´ter-ton
chat´ti-ly
chat´ting
chat´ty
Chau´cer
chauf´fer
chauf´feur
chau´vin-ism
chau´vin-ist
cheap´en
cheap´ened
cheap´ly
cheap´ness
cheat´er
check´book
cheek´er
check´er-board
check´ered
check´ers
check girl
check´mate
check´—out
check´rein
check´room
check´up
ched´dar
cheek´bone
cheek´y
cheer´er
cheer´ful
cheer´ful-ly
cheer´ful-ness
cheer´i-ly
cheer´less
cheer´y
cheese´cake
cheese´cloth
cheese knife
cheese´par-ing
chees´i-ness
chees´y
chee´tah
chef
chef d'oeu´vre
Che´khov
Chel´sea
Chel´ten-ham
chem´i-cal
che-mise´
chem´ist
chem´is-try
chemo-ther´a-py
che-nille´
che´quer
Cher´bourg
cher´ish
Cher´o-kee
che-root´
cher´ries
cher´ry
cher´ub
che-ru´bic
cher´u-bim
Ches´a-peake
Chesh´ire
chess´board
chess´man
Ches´ter
Ches´ter-field
Ches´ter-ton
chest´nut
chest´y
che-va-lier´
Chev´i-ot
Chev´ro-let´
chev´ron
chew´ing
Chey-enne´
Cheyne
Chiang´ Kai-shek´
Chi-an´ti
Chi-ca-go
chi-cane´
chi-ca´nery
chick´a-dee
Chick-a-hom´i-ny
Chick-a-mau´ga
Chick´a-saw
chick´en
chick´en-heart´ed
chicken pox
chick´pea
chick´weed
chi´cle

chic´o-ry
chide
chid´ing
chief´ly
chief´tain
chif-fon´
chif´fo-robe
chig´ger
chi´gnon
Chi-hua´hua
child´bear-ing
child´bed
child´birth
child´hood
child´ish
child´ish-ly
child´ish-ness
child´less
child´like
chil´dren
Chil´e
chil´i
chill´i-ness
chill´ing
Chil-lon´
chill´y
chimed
chim´er
chim´ing
chim´ney
chim´ney-piece
chim´ney pot
chim´ney sweep
chim´pan-zee
Chi´na
chi´na-ber-ry
Chi´na-man
Chi´na-town
chi´na-ware
chin-chil´la
Chi-nese´
Chin-kiang
chinned
chin´ning
chi-nook´
chintz
Chi´os
chip´munk
chipped
Chip´pen-dale
chip´per
Chip´pe-wa
chip´ping
chi-rog´ra-pher
chi´ro-graph´ic
chi-rog´ra-phy
chi´ro-man-cy
chi-rop´o-dist
chi-rop´o-dy
chi´ro-prac´tic
chi´ro-prac´tor
chis´el
chis´eled
chis´el-er
chis´el-ing
chit´chat
chi-val´ric
chiv´al-rous
chiv´al-ry
chlor-am´ide
chlor-am´ine
chlo´rate
chlor´dane
chlo´ric
chlo´ride
chlo´ri-dize
chlo´ri-nate
chlo-rin-a´tion
chlo´rine
chlo´rite
chlo´ro-form
chlo´ro-my-ce´tin
chlo´ro-phyll
chock´—full´
choc´o-late
Choc´taw
choice´ly
choic´est
choir
choked
choke´damp
chok´er
chok´ing
chol´er
chol´era
chol´er-ic
choose
choos´ing
chop´house
Cho´pin
chop´per
chop´ping
chop´py
chop´stick
chop su´ey
cho´ral
chord
chord´al
chore
cho-re´a
chore´man
cho-re-og´ra-pher
cho-re-og´ra-phy
cho´ric
cho´ri-on
cho´ris-ter
cho-rog´ra-phy
cho´roid
chor´tle
chor´tling
cho´rus
chose
cho´sen
chow´der
chrism
Chris´ta-bel
chris´ten
chris´ten-dom
chris´ten-ing
Chris´tian
chris-ti-an´ia
Chris-tian´i-ty
chris´tian-ize
Christ´like
Christ´ly
Christ´mas
Christ´mas-tide
Chris´to-pher
chro´ma
chro´mate
chro-mat´ic
chro-mat´i-cal-ly
chro´ma-tin
chro´ma-tism
chro-mat´o-gram
chro-ma-tog´ra-phy
chro-mat´o-scope

chrome
chro´mic
chro´mite
chro´mi-um
chro´mo-gen
chro-mom´e-ter
chro´mo-some
chro´mo-sphere
chron´ic
chron´i-cal-ly
chron´i-cle
chron´i-cler
chron´i-cling
chron´o-graph
chro-nog´ra-pher
chron-o-log´ic
chron-o-log´i-cal
chro-nol´o-gist
chro-nol´o-gy
chro-nom´e-ter
chron-o-met´ric
chrys´a-lis
chry-san´the-mum
chrys´o-lite
chub´by
chuck´le
chuck´led
chuck´le-head
chuck´ling
chuff´y
chuk´ker
chum´mi-ly
chum´my
Chung-king
chunk´y
church´go-er
Church´ill
church´ly
church´man
church´ward-en
church´yard
churl´ish
churl´ish-ly
churl´ish-ness
churn´er
chute
chut´ney
ci-bo´ri-um
ci-ca´da
cic´a-tri-ces
cic-a-tri´cial
cic´a-trix
cic´a-trize
Cic´e-ro
cic-e-ro´ne
ci´der
ci-gar´
cig-a-rette´, cig-a-ret´
ci-gar´—shaped
cil´ia
cil´i-ary
cil´i-ate
Ci-li´cia
cin-cho´na
Cin-cin-nat´i
cinc´ture
cin´der
Cin-der-el´la
cin´e-ma
cin-e-mat´o-graph
cin-e-ma-tog´ra-pher
cin-e-ma-tog´ra-phy
cin´er-a-tor
cin´na-bar
cin´na-mon
cinque´foil
ci´on
ci´pher
cir´ca
Cir-cas´sian
Cir´ce
cir´cle
cir´cled
cir´clet
cir´cling
cir´cuit
cir-cu´i-tous
cir´cu-lar
cir-cu-lar-i-za´tion
cir´cu-lar-ize
cir´cu-late
cir-cu-la´tion
cir´cu-la-tive
cir´cu-la-tor
cir´cu-la-to-ry
cir´cum-am´bi-ent
cir´cum-cise
cir´cum-ci´sion
cir-cum´fer-ence
cir-cum-fer-en´tial
cir´cum-flex
cir-cum´flu-ent
cir-cum-lo-cu´tion
cir-cum-loc´u-to-ry
cir-cum-nav´i-gate
cir-cum-nav-i-ga´tion
cir-cum-nu-ta´tion
cir´cum-po´lar
cir´cum-scis´sile
cir´cum-scribe
cir-cum-scrip-tion
cir´cum-spect
cir-cum-spec´tion
cir´cum-stance
cir´cum-stanced
cir´cum-stan´tial
cir´cum-stan´tial-ly
cir-cum-stan´ti-ate
cir´cum-vent
cir-cum-ven´tion
cir-cum-vo-lu´tion
cirque
cir-rho´sis
cir-rhot´ic
Cis-ter´cian
cis´tern
cit´a-del
ci-ta´tion
ci´ta-to-ry
cite
cith´a-ra
cit´ies
cit´i-fy
cit´ing
cit´i-zen
cit´i-zen-ry
cit´i-zen-ship
cit´ral
cit´rate
cit´re-ous
cit´ric
cit´rin
cit´ron
cit-ro-nel´la
cit´rous
cit´rus
cit´y

cit´y—state
civ´et
civ´ic
civ´ics
civ´il
ci-vil´ian
ci-vil´i-ty
civ-i-li-za´tion
civ´i-lize
civ´i-lized
civ´i-liz-ing
civ´il-ly
civ´il serv´ice
clab´ber
claim´ant
claim´er
clair-voy´ance
clair-voy´ant
cla´mant
clam´bake
clam´ber
clam´mi-ness
clam´my
clam´or
clam´or-ous
clam´shell
clan-des´tine
clang´or
clang´or-ous
clan´nish
clans´man
clap´board
clapped
clap´per
clap´ping
clap´trap
claque
Clar´ence
Clar´en-don
clar´et
clar-i-fi-ca´tion
clar´i-fied
clar´i-fy
clar´i-fy-ing
clar´i-net´
clar´i-on
clar´i-ty
clas´sic
clas´si-cal
clas´si-cal-ly
clas´si-cism
clas´si-cist
clas´si-fi-a-ble
clas-si-fi-ca´tion
clas´si-fi-ca-to-ry
clas´si-fied
clas´si-fy
clas´si-fy-ing
clas´sis
class´mate
class´room
clas´tic
clat´ter
clat´tered
Clau´di-us
claus´al
clause
claus-tro-pho´bia
clav´i-chord
clav´i-cle
cla-vic´u-lar
cla-vier´
claw´like
clay´ey
clay´more
clean—cut
clean´er
clean´li-ness
clean´ly
clean´ness
cleanse
cleansed
cleans´er
cleans´ing
clean´up
clear´ance
clear´—cut
clear´—eyed
clear´head-ed
clear´ing
clear´ing-house
clear´ly
clear´ness
clear´—sight-ed
cleav´age
cleaved
cleav´er
cleav´ing
clem´a-tis
Cle-men-ceau´
clem´en-cy
Clem´ens
clem´ent
Clem´en-tine
Cle-o-pat´ra
cler´gy
cler´gy-man
cler´ic
cler´i-cal
Cler´mont
Cleve´land
clev´er
clev´er-ly
clev´er-ness
clev´is
clew
cli-che´
click
click´er
cli´ent
cli´en-tele´
Clif´ford
Clif´ton
cli-mac´ter-ic
cli-mac´tic
cli´mate
cli-mat´ic
cli´max
climbed
climb´er
climb´ing
clinch´er
cling´ing
cling´stone
cling´y
clin´ic
clin´i-cal
clink´er
Clin´ton
clipped
clip´per
clip´ping
clique
clit´o-ris
clo-a´ca
cloak´room
clob´ber

cloche
clock´mak-er
clock tow´er
clock´wise
clock´work
clod´hopper
clois´ter
clois´tral
closed
close´—fist-ed
close´—fit-ting
close´—hauled
close´—lipped
close´y
close´mouthed
close´ness
clos´est
clos´et
close´—up
clo´sure
cloth
clothe
clothes
clothes´line
cloth´ier
cloth´ing
cloth´yard
clo´ture
cloud´burst
cloud´i-ness
cloud´y
clo´ven
clo´ver
Clo´vis
clown´ish
cloy´Ing
cloy´ing-ly
club´ba-ble
clubbed
club´bing
club´foot
club´house
club´man
club´room
club´wom-an
clum´si-er
clum´si-ly
clum´si-ness
clum´sy
Clu´ny
clus´ter
clut´ter
Clydes´dale
coach´man
co-ad´ju-tant
co-ad-ju´tor
co-ad´u-nate
co-ag´u-la-ble
co-ag´u-late
co-ag-u-la´tion
co-ag´u-la-tive
co-ag´u-la-tor
coal barge
coal bin
coal box
coal car
coal cel´lar
coal chute
coal deal´er
co-a-lesce´
co-a-les´cence
co-a-les´cent
co-a-lesc´ing
coal´field
coal gas
coal hod
co-a-li´tion
coal mine
coal scut´tle
coal shov´el
coal tar
coal yard
coarse
coarse´ly
coarse´ness
coast´al
coast´er
coast guard
coast´line
coast´wise
coat´ing
coat of arms
coat of mail
coat´room
coat´tail
co´au´thor
coax
co-ax´i-al
coax´ing
coax´ing-ly
co´balt
cob´ble
cob´bler
cob´ble-stone
co´bra
Co´burg
cob´web
cocaine
coc´cus
coc-cyg´e-al
coc´cyx
coch´lea
cock-ade´
cock´a-too
cock´crow
cock´er
cock´er-el
cock´eyed
cock´le
cock´le-shell
Cock´ney
Cock´ney-ism
cock´pit
cock´sure
cock´tail
cock´y
co´co
co´coa
co´co-nut
co-coon´
cod´dle
cod´ed
co-de-fend´ant
co´deine
cod´fish
codg´er
cod´i-cil
cod-i-fi-ca´tion
cod´i-fied
cod´i-fy
cod´ling
co´—ed´
co-ed-u-ca´tion
co-ed-u-ca´tion-al
co´ef-fi´cient
co-e´qual
co-erce´

co-erc´i-ble
co-erc´ing
co-er´cion
co-er´cive
co-ex-ist´
co-ex-is´tence
co-ex-is´tent
co-ex-ten´sive
cof´fee
cof´fee-house
cof´fee-pot
cof´fer
cof´fin
co´gen-cy
co´gent
cog´i-ta-ble
cog´i-tate
cog´i-tat-ing
cog-i-ta´tion
cog´i-ta-tive
co´gnac
cog-ni´tion
cog´ni-za-ble
cog´ni-zance
cog´ni-zant
cog´wheel
co-hab´It
co-hab´i-tant
co´heir
co-here´
co-her´ence
co-her´ent
co-her´er
co-he´sion
co-he´sive
co-he´sive-ness
co´hort
coif-feur´
coif-fure´
coin
coin´age
co-in-cide´
co-in´ci-dence
co-in´ci-dent
co-in-ci-den´tal
co-in-cid´ing
coin´er
co-in-sure´
co´i-tus

coked
cok´ing
col´an-der
Col´bert
Col´by
Col´ches-ter
Col´chis
cold´—blood-ed
cold cream
cold´heart-ed
cold´ly
cold´ness
cold´proof
cole´slaw
Col´gate
col´ic
col´icky
col-i-se´um
co-li´tis
col-lab´o-rate
col-lab´o-rat-ing
col-lab-o-ra´tion
col-lab´o-ra-tor
col-lage´
col-lapse´
col-lapsed´
col-laps´i-ble
col-laps´ing
col´lar
col´lar-band
col´lar-bone
col´lar but-ton
col-late´
col-lat´er-al
col-lat´ing
col-la´tion
col-la´tor
col´league
col-lect´
col-lect´ed
col-lect´i-ble
col-lec´tion
col-lec´tive
col-lec´tive-ly
col-lec´tiv-ist
col-lec´tor
col´leen
col´lege
col´leg-er

col-le´gi-al
col-le´gian
col-le´giate
col-lide´
col-lid´ing
col´lie
col´lier
co´liery
col´li-gate
col´li-ma-tor
col-li´sion
col´lo-cate
col-lo-ca´tion
col´loid
col-loi´dal
col-lo-qui-al
col-lo´qui-al-ism
col-lo´qui-al-ly
col´lo-quy
col-lude´
col-lud´ing
col-lu´sion
col-lu´sive
col-lu´sive-ly
co-logne´
Co-lom´bia
Co-lom´bo
co´lon
co-lon´
col´o-nel
co-lo´ni-al
co-lon´ic
col´o-nies
col´o-nist
col-o-ni-za´tion
col´o-nize
col-on-nade´
col´o-ny
col´o-phon
col´o-pho-ny
col´or
Col-o-rad´o
col-or-a´tion
col-or-a-tu´ra
col´or—blind
col´or-cast
col´ored
col´or-ful
col´or-ing

col´or-ist
col´or-less
co-los´sal
Col-os-se´um
Co-los´si-an
co-los´sus
colt´ish
Co-lum´bia
col´um-bine
Co-lum´bus
col´umn
co-lum´nar
col´um-nist
co´ma
Co-man´che
co´ma-tose
co´ma-tose-ly
com´bat
com-bat´ant
com-bat´ing
com-bat´ive
comb´er
com-bi-na´tion
com´bi-na-tive
com-bine´
com-bin´ing
com-bus´ti-ble
com-bus´tion
co-me´di-an
co-me´di-enne
com´e-dies
com´e-dy
come´li-ness
come-ly
com´er
com´et
com´fit
com´fort
com´fort-able
com´fort-ably
com´fort-er
com´fort-less
com´ic
com´i-cal
com´ing
com´i-ty
com´ma
com-mand´
com´man-dant
com´man-deer´
com-mand´er
com-mand´ing
com-mand´ment
com-man´do
com-man´dos
com-mea´sure
com-mem´o-rate
com-mem´o-rat-ing
com-mem-o-ra´tion
com-mem´o-ra-tive
com-mence´
com-mence´ment
com-menc´ing
com-mend´
com-mend´able
com-men-da´tion
com-men´da-to-ry
com-men-su-ra-bil´i-ty
com-men´su-rate
com-men´su-rate-ly
com-men-su-ra´tion
com´ment
com´men-tary
com´men-ta-tor
com´merce
com-mer´cial
com-mer´cial-ism
com-mer´cial-ize
com-mer´cial-ized
com-mer´cial-ly
com-min´gle
com-min´gling
com-mis´er-a-ble
com-mis´er-ate
com-mis-er-a´tion
com´mis-sar
com-mis-sar´i-at
com´mis-sary
com-mis´sion
com-mis´sion-aire´
com-mis´sioned
com-mis´sion-er
com-mit´
com-mit´ment
com-mit´tal
com-mit´ted
com-mit´tee
com-mit´tee-man
com-mit´ting
com-mode´
com-mo´di-ous
com-mod´i-ties
com-mod´i-ty
com´mo-dore
com´mon
com´mon-al-ty
com´mon-er
com´mon-ly
com´mon-place
com´mon sense
com´mon-wealth
com-mo´tion
com-mu´nal
com-mune´
com-mu´ni-ca-ble
com-mu´ni-cant
com-mu´ni-cate
com-mu´ni-cat-ing
com-mu´ni-ca´tion
com-mu´ni-ca-tive
com-mu´ni-ca-tor
com-mu´nion
com-mu´ni-qué
com´mu-nism
com´mu-nist
com´mu-nis´tic
com-mu´ni-ties
com-mu´ni-ty
com-mut´able
com´mu-tate
com-mu-ta´tion
com´mu-ta-tor
com-mute´
com-mut´er
com-mut´ing
Co´mo
Com´o-ros
co´mose
com´pact
com´pa-nies
com-pan´ion
com-pan´ion-able
com-pan´ion-ship
com-pan´ion-way
com´pa-ny
com´pa-ra-ble

com-par´a-tive
com-par´a-tive-ly
com-par´a-tor
com-pare´
com-par´ing
com-par´i-son
com-part´ment
com´pass
com´pass-es
com-pas´sion
com-pas´sion-ate
com-pat-i-bil´i-ty
com-pat´i-ble
com-pa´tri-ot
com´peer
com-pel´
com-pelled´
com-pel-ling
com-pen´di-ous
com-pen´di-um
com-pen´sa-ble
com´pen-sate
com´pen-sat-ing
com-pen-sa´tion
com´pen-sa-tive
com´pen-sa-tor
com-pen´sa-to-ry
com-pete´
com´pe-tence
com´pe-tent
com-pet´ing
com-pe-ti´tion
com-pet´i-tive
com-pet´i-tive-ly
com-pet´i-tor
com-pi-la´tion
com-pile´
com-pil´er
com-pil´ing
com-pla´cence
com-pla´cen-cy
com-pla´cent
com-pla´cent-ly
complain´
com-plain´ant
com-plaint´
com-plai´sance
com-plai´sant
com´ple-ment
com-ple-men´tal
com-ple-men´ta-ry
com-plete
com-plete´ly
com-plete´ness
com-ple´tion
com´plex
com-plex´ion
com-plex´ioned
com-plex´i-ty
com-pli´a-ble
com-pli´ance
com-pli´ant
com´pli-cate
com´pli-cat-ed
com-pli-ca´tion
com-plic´i-ty
com-plied´
com´pli-ment
com-pli-men´ta-ry
com-ply´
com-ply´ing
com-po´nent
com-port´
com-port´ment
com-pose´
com-posed´
com-pos´ed-ly
com-pos´er
com-pos´ite
com-po-si´tion
com-pos´i-tor
com´post
com-po´sure
com´pote
com´pound
com-pre-hend´
com-pre-hend´ible
com-pre-hen´si-ble
com-pre-hen´sion
com-pre-hen´sive
com´press
com-pressed´
com-press´ible
com-press´ing
com-pres´sion
com-pres´sive
com-pres´sor
com-prise´
com-pris´ing
com´pro-mise
comp-tom´e-ter
comp-trol´ler
com-pul´sion
com-pul´sive
com-pul´so-ry
com-punc´tion
com-put´able
com-pu-ta´tion
com-pute´
com-put´er
com-put´ing
com-put´ist
com´rade
com´rade-ship
con´cave
con-ceal´
con-ceal´ment
con-cede´
con-ced´ed
con-ced´er
con-ced´ing
con-ceit´
con-ceit´ed
con-ceit´ed-ly
con-ceiv-abil´i-ty
con-ceiv´able
con-ceiv´ably
con-ceive´
con-ceiv´ing
con´cen-trate
con´cen-trating
con-cen-tra´tion
con´cen-tra-tor
con-cen´tric
con-cen´tri-cal
con-cen-tric´i-ty
con´cept
con-cep´ta-cle
con-cep´tion
con-cep´tual
con-cern´
con-cerned´
con-cern´ing
con-cern´ment
con´cert
con-cert´ed
con-cer-ti´na

con-cer´to
con-ces´sion
con-ces´sion-aire´
con-ces´sion-ary
conch
con-cierge´
con-cil´i-a-ble
con-cil´i-ate
con-cil´i-at-ing
con-cil-i-a´tion
con-cil´i-a-tor
con-cil´ia-to-ry
con-cise´
con-cise´ly
con-cise´ness
con-ci´sion
con´clave
con-clude´
con-clud´ing
con-clu´sion
con-clu´sive
con-clu´sive-ly
con-coct´
con-coct´er
con-coc´tion
con-com´i-tant
con´cord
con-cor´dance
con-cor´dant
con´course
con´crete, con-crete´
con-crete´ly
con-cre´tion
con´cu-bine
con-cur´
con-curred´
con-cur´rence
con-cur´rent
con-cur´ring
con-cus´sion
con-demn´
con-dem-na´tion
con-dem´na-to-ry
con-demned´
con-demn´er
con-demn´ing
con-den´sate
con-den-sa´tion
con-dense´
con-dens´er
con-dens´ing
con-de-scend´
con-de-scend´ence
con-de-scend´ing
con-de-scend´ing-ly
con-de-scen´sion
con-dign´
con´di-ment
con-di´tion
con-di´tion-al
con-di´tion-al-ly
con-di-tioned
con-dole´
con-do´lence
con-dol´ing
con-do-min´i-um
con-don´ance
con-do-na´tion
con-done´
con´dor
con-duce´
con-du´cive
con´duct
con-duct´ance
con-duct´ed
con-duc´tion
con-duc´tive
con-duc´tor
con´duit
cone´—shaped
con-fec´tion
con-fec´tion-ary
con-fec´tion-er
con-fec´tion-ery
con-fed´er-a-cy
con-fed´er-ate
con-fed-er-a´tion
con-fer´
con´fer-ee´
con´fer-ence
con-ferred´
con-fer´ring
con-fess´
con-fessed´
con-fess´ed-ly
con-fes´sion
con-fes´sion-al
con-fes´sor
con-fet´ti
con´fi-dant
con´fi-dante
con-fide´
con-fid´ed
con´fi-dence
con´fi-dent
con-fi-den´tial
con-fi-den´tial-ly
con´fi-dent-ly
con-fid´ing
con-fig-u-ra´tion
con-fine´
con-fine´ment
con-fin´er
con-fin´ing
con-firm´
con-firm´able
con-fir-ma´tion
con-fir´ma-to-ry
con-firmed´
con-fis´ca-ble
con´fis-cate
con´fis-cat-ing
con-fis-ca´tion
con-fis´ca-to-ry
con-fla-gra´tion
con´flict
con-flic´tion
con-flic´tive
con´flu-ence
con´flu´ent
con´flux
con-form´
con-form´ance
con-for-ma´tion
con-form´ist
con-form´i-ty
con-found´
con-found´ed-ly
con-fra-ter´ni-ty
con-front´
con-fron-ta´tion
Con-fu´cius
con-fuse´
con-fused´
con-fus´ed-ly
con-fus´ing
con-fu´sion

con-fu-ta´tion
con-fu´ta-tive
con-fute´
con-geal´
con-geal´ment
con-ge-la´tion
con-ge´nial
con-ge-nial´i-ty
con-gen´i-tal
con´ger
con-gest´
con-gest´ed
con-ges´tion
con-glom´er-ate
con-glom-er-a´tion
con-glu-ti-na´tion
Con´go
con-grat´u-lant
con-grat´u-late
con-grat´u-lat-ing
con-grat-u-la´tion
con-grat´u-la-tor
con-grat´u-la-to-ry
con´gre-gate
con-gre-ga´tion
con-gre-ga´tion-al
Con-gre-ga´tion-al-ist
con´gress
con-gres´sio-nal
con´gress-man
con´gress-wom-an
con-gru´ence
con-gru´en-cy
con-gru´ent
con-gru´i-ty
con´gru-ous
con´ic
con´i-cal
con´i-fer
con-jec´tur-al
con-jec´tur-al-ly
con-jec´ture
con-join´
con-joint´
con´ju-gal
con´ju-gal-ly
con´ju-gate
con-ju-ga´tion
con´ju-ga-tor

con-junc´tion
con-junc´tive
con-junc-ti-vi´tis
con-junc´ture
con-ju-ra´tion
con´jure, con-jure´
con´jur-er
con´ju-ror
con-nect´
con-nect´ed
con-nect´ed-ly
con-nect´er
Con-nect´i-cut
con-nec´tion
con-nec´tive
con-nec-tiv´i-ty
con-nec´tor
conn´ing
conn´ing tower
con-niv´ance
con-nive´
con´nois-seur´
con-no-ta´tion
con´no-ta-tive
con´no-ta-tive-ly
con-note´
con-not´ing
con´quer
con´quered
con´quer-ing
con´quer-or
con´quest
con-quis´ta-dor
con-san´guine
con-san-guin´eous
con-san-guin´i-ty
con´science
con´science-less
con´science—
strick´en
con-sci-en´tious
con-sci-en´tious-ly
con´scious
con´scious-ly
con´scious-ness
con´script
con-scrip´tion
con´se-crate
con´se-crat-ing

con-se-cra´tion
con-sec´u-tive
con-sec´u-tive-ly
con-sen´su-al
con-sen´sus
con-sent´
con-sent´er
con´se-quence
con´se-quent
con-se-quen´tial
con´se-quent-ly
con-serv´an-cy
con-ser-va´tion
con-serv´a-tism
con-serv´a-tive
con´ser-va-tor
con-serv´a-to-ry
con-serve´
con-serv´ing
con-sid´er
con-sid´er-a-ble
con-sid´er-a-bly
con-sid´er-ate
con-sid´er-ate-ly
con-sid-er-a´tion
con-sid´ered
con-sid´er-ing
con-sign´
con-sig-na´tion
con´sign-ee´
con-sign´ment
con-sign´or
con-sist´
con-sist´ence
con-sist´en-cy
con-sist´ent
con-sist´ent-ly
con´sis-to´ri-al
con-sis´to-ry
con-so-la´tion
con-sol´a-to-ry
con-sole´
con-sol´i-date
con-sol´i-dat-ing
con-sol-i-da´tion
con-sol´ing
con-sol´ing-ly
con´som-mé´
con´so-nance

con´so-nant
con´so-nan´tal
con´so-nant-ly
con-sort´
con-sor´ti-um
con-spic´u-ous
con-spic´u-ous-ly
con-spir´a-cy
con-spir´a-tor
con-spir´a-to´ri-al
con-spire´
con-spir´ing
con´sta-ble
con-stab´u-lary
Con´stance
con´stan-cy
con´stant
Con´stan-tine
Con´stan-ti-no´ple
con´stant-ly
con´stel-late
con-stel-la´tion
con´ster-nate
con-ster-na´tion
con´sti-pate
con´sti-pat-ed
con-sti-pa´tion
con-stit´u-en-cy
con-stit´u-ent
con´sti-tute
con-sti-tu´tion
con-sti-tu´tion-al
con-sti-tu-tion-al´i-ty
con-sti-tu´-tion-al-ly
con´sti-tu-tive
con-strain´
con-strained´
con-straint´
con-strict´
con-stric´tion
con-stric´tive
con-stric´tor
con-strin´gent
con-struct´
con-struc´tion
con-struc´tive
con-struc´tive-ly
con-struc´tor
con-strue´
con-strued´
con-stru´ing
con´sul
con´sul-ar
con´sul-ate
con-sult´
con-sul´tant
con-sul-ta´tion
con-sum´able
con-sume´
con-sumed´
con-sum´er
con-sum´ing
con-sum´mate
con-sum-ma´tion
con-sump´tion
con-sump´tive
con´tact
con´tac-tor
con-ta´gion
con-ta´gious
con-tain´
con-tain´er
con-tain´ing
con-tain´ment
con-tam´i-nant
con-tam´i-nate
con-tam´i-nat-ed
con-tam´i-nat-ing
con-tam-i-na´tion
con-tem´pla-ble
con´tem-plate
con´tem-plat-ing
con-tem-pla´tion
con-tem´pla-tive
con-tem-po-ra´ne-ous
con-tem´po-rary
con-tem´po-rize
con-tempt´
con-tempt´ible
con-tempt´ibly
con-temp´tu-ous
con-temp´tu-ous-ly
con-tend´
con-tend´er
con-tent´
con-tent´ed
con-tent´ed-ly
con-ten´tion
con-ten´tious
con-ten´tious-ly
con-tent´ment
con´tents
con-ter´mi-nous
con´test
con-test´able
con-tes´tant
con´text
con-ti-gu´i-ty
con-tig´u-ous
con-tig´u-ous-ly
con´ti-nence
con´ti-nent
con-ti-nen´tal
con-tin´gen-cy
con-tin´gent
con-tin´u-al
con-tin´u-al-ly
con-tin´u-ance
con-tin-u-a´tion
con-tin´u-a-tive
con-tin´ue
con-tin´u-ing
con-ti-nu´i-ty
con-tin´u-ous
con-tin´u-ous-ly
con-tin´u-um
con-tort´
con-tor´tion
con-tor´tive
con´tour
con´tra-band
con´tra-cep´tion
con´tra-cep´tive
con´tract
con-tract´ed
con-tract´ile
con-trac´tion
con´trac-tor
con-trac´tu-al
con-tra-dict´
con-tra-dic´tion
con-tra-dic´to-ri-ly
con-tra-dic´to-ry
con-tra-dis-tinc´tion
con-tral´to
con-trap´tion
con-tra-pun´tal

con-tra-ri´e-ty
con´trar-i-ness
con´trary
contrast´
con-tra-vene´
con-tra-ven´tion
con-trib´ute
con-trib´ut-ing
con-tri-bu´tion
con-trib´u-tor
con-trib´u-to-ry
con-trite´
con-trite´ly
con-tri´tion
con-triv´ance
con-trive´
con-triv´er
con-triv´ing
con-trol´
con-trol´la-ble
con-trol-led´
con-trol´ler
con-trol´ling
con-tro-ver´sial
con´tro-ver-sy
con´tro-vert
con-tuse´
con-tu´sion
co-nun´drum
con-va-lesce´
con-va-les´cence
con-va-les´cent
con-va-lesc´ing
con-vect´
con-vec´tion
con-vec´tor
con-vene´
con-ve´nience
con-ve´nient
con-ve´nient-ly
con-ven´ing
con´vent
con-ven´tion
con-ven´tion-al
con-ven´tion-al´i-ty
con-ven´tu-al
con-verge´
con-ver´gence
con-ver´gent
con-verg´ing
con-vers´able
con-ver´sant
con-ver-sa´tion
con-ver-sa´tion-al
con-ver-sa´tion-al-ist
con-verse´
con-verse´ly
con-vers´ing
con-ver´sion
con-ver´sive
con´vert
con-vert´er
con-vert´ible
con-ver´tor
con´vex
con-vex´i-ty
con-vey´
con-vey´ance
con-vey´ing
con´vict
con-vic´tion
con-vince´
con-vinc´ing
con-vinc´ing-ly
con-viv´i-al
con-viv-i-al´i-ty
con-vo-ca´tion
con-voke´
con-vok´ing
con´vo-lute
con-vo-lu´tion
con´voy
con´voyed
con-vulse´
con-vul´sion
con-vul´sive
con-vul´sive-ly
coo´ing
cook´book
cook´er
cook´ery
cook´ie
cook´stove
cool´er
Coo´lidge
coo´lie
cool´ly
cool´ness
coop´er
coop´er-age
co-op´er-ate
co-op-er-a´tion
co-op´er-a-tive
co-op´er-a-tor
co—opt´
co-or´di-nate
co-or-di-na´tion
co-or´di-na-tor
coot´ie
Co-pen-ha´gen
Co-per´ni-can
cop´i-er
cop´ies
co´pi´lot
cop´ing
co´pi-ous
co´pi-ous-ly
co´pi-ous-ness
cop´per
cop´per-head
cop´per-plate
cop´pice
co´pra
copse
Cop´tic
cop´u-la
cop´u-late
cop-u-la´tion
cop´u-la-tive
cop´y
cop´y-book
cop´y-ing
cop´y-ist
cop´y-right
co-quet´
co´quet-ry
co-quette´
co-quet´ting
co-quett´ish
co-qui´na
cor´a-cite
cor´al
cor´bel
cord
cord´age
cor´date
cord´ed

Cor-de´lia
cor´dial
cor-dial´i-ty
cor´dial-ly
cor-dil-le´ra
cord´ite
Cór´do-ba
cor´don
cor´do-van
cor´du-roy
cord´wood
core
co-re-la´tion
cor´er
co-re-spon´dent
co-ri-an´der
Cor´inth
Co-rin´thi-an
cork´screw
corn bread
corn´cob
cor´nea
cor´ne-al
Cor-ne´lia
cor´ner
cor´ner-stone
cor-net´
cor-net´ist
corn´flower
cor´nice
Cor´nish
corn´stalk
corn´starch
cor-nu-co´pia
Corn´wall
Corn-wal´lis
co-rol´la
cor´ol-lary
co-ro´na
Cor-o-na´do
cor´o-nary
cor-o-na´tion
cor´o-ner
cor´o-net´
cor´po-ral
cor-po-ral´i-ty
cor´po-rate
cor-po-ra´tion
cor-po´re-al
cor-po-re´i-ty
corps
corpse
cor´pu-lence
cor´pu-lent
cor´pus
Cor´pus Chris´ti
cor´pus-cle
cor-pus´cu-lar
cor-ral´
cor-rect´
cor-rec´tion
cor-rec´tion-al
cor-rec´tive
cor-rect´ly
Cor-reg´i-dor
cor´re-late
cor-re-la´tion
cor-rel´a-tive
cor-re-spond´
cor-re-spon´dence
cor-re-spon´dent
cor-re-spond´ing
cor-re-spon´sive
cor´ri-dor
cor´ri-gi-ble
cor-rob´o-rate
cor-rob-o-ra´tion
cor-rob´o-ra-tive
cor-rob´o-ra-tor
cor-rob´o-ra-to-ry
cor-rode´
cor-rod´i-ble
cor-rod´ing
cor-ro´sion
cor-ro´sive
cor´ru-gate
cor´ru-gat-ed
cor-ru-ga´tion
cor-rupt´
cor-rupt´er
cor-rup´tion
cor-rup´tive
cor-sage´
cor´sair
corse´let
cor-se-let´
cor´set
Cor´si-ca
cor´tege
cor´tex
cor´ti-cal
cor-ti-cos´ter-one
cor´ti-sone
co-sig´na-to-ry
cos-met´ic
cos´mic
cos´mi-cal-ly
cos-mog´ra-pher
cos-mog´ra-phy
cos-mo-log´-i-cal
cos-mol´o-gy
cos´mo-naut
cos-mo-pol´i-tan
cos´mos
Cos´sack
cos´tal
Cos´ta Ri´ca
cos´ter
cost´li-ness
cost´ly
cos´tume
cos´tum-er
co´te-rie
co-til´lion
cot´tage
cot´tag-er
cot´ter
cot´ton
cot´ton-seed
cot´ton-tail
cot´ton-wood
cou´gar
cou´lee
coun´cil
coun´cil-man
coun´sel
coun´sel-or
coun´te-nance
coun´ter
coun´ter-act´
coun´ter-at-tack
coun´ter-bal-ance
coun´ter-check
coun´ter-claim
coun´ter-clock´wise
coun´ter-es-pi-o-nage
coun´ter-feit

coun´ter-feit-er
coun´ter-foil
coun´ter-ir´ri-tant
coun´ter-mand
coun´ter-march
coun´ter-mine
coun´ter-pane
coun´ter-part
coun´ter-plot
coun´ter-point
coun´ter-poise
coun´ter-rev-o-lu´tion
coun´ter-sign
coun´ter-sink
coun´ter-weight
count´ess
coun´ties
count´less
coun´tries
coun´tri-fied
coun´try
coun´try-man
coun´try-side
coun´try-wom-an
coun´ty
coup´ d´etat´
cou-pé´
coupe
cou´ple
cou´pler
cou´plet
cou´pling
cou´pon
cour´age
cou-ra´geous
cou´ri-er
course
cours-er
cour´te-ous
cour´te-sy
court´house
cour´tier
court´li-ness
court´ly
court´—mar-tial
court´room
court´ship
court´yard
cous´in
cou-ture´
cou-tu´rier
cov´e-nant
cov´e-nan-ter
cov´e-nan-tor
Cov´en-try
cov´er
cov´er-age
cov´ered
cov´er-let
cov´ert
cov´er-ture
cov´et
cov´e-tous
cov´e-tous-ness
cov´ey
cow´ard
cow´ard-ice
cow´bell
cow´boy
cow´er
cow´hide
cow´lick
cowl´ing
co´—work´er
cow´pox
cow´rie
cox´comb
cox´swain
coy´ness
coy´ote
coz´en
coz´en-age
co´zi-est
co´zi-ly
co´zy
crab ap´ple
crab´bed
crab´bing
crab´by
crab´grass
crack´down
crack´er
crack´ing
crack´le
crack´ling
crack´—up
Cra´cow
cra´dle
cra´dling
craft´i-ly
craft´i-ness
crafts´man
crafts´man-ship
craft´y
crag´gi-ness
crag´gy
cram
crammed
cram´ming
cramped
cran´ber-ry
craned
cra´ni-al
cran´ing
cra-ni-ol´o-gy
cra´ni-um
crank´case
crank´i-ness
crank´y
Cran´mer
cran´nied
cran´ny
crashed
crass´ly
Cras´sus
cra´ter
crat´ing
cra-vat´
cra´ven
crav´ing
craw´fish
crawl´ing
crawl´y
cray´fish
cray´on
crazed
cra´zi-ly
cra´zi-ness
craz´ing
cra´zy
creak
creak´y
cream´er
cream´ery
cream´y
creased
creas´ing

cre-ate´
cre-at´ing
cre-a´tion
cre-a´tive
cre-a´tive-ly
cre-a´tor
crea´ture
cre´dence
cre-den´tial
cred-i-bil´i-ty
cred´i-ble
cred´it
cred´it-able
cred´i-tor
cre´do
cre´dos
cred´u-lous
creek
creep´er
creep´ing
creep´y
cre´mate
cre-ma´tion
cre´ma-to-ry
Cre´ole
cre´o-sol
cre´o-sote
crepe
cre-scen´do
cres´cent
cres´set
Cres´si-da
crest´ed
crest´fall-en
cre-ta´ceous
Cre´tan
cre´tin-isin
cre´tonne
cre-vasse´
crev´ice
crew´el
crib´bage
crib´bing
crib´work
crick´et
crick´et-er
cried
cri´er
Cril´lon

Cri-me´a
crim´i-nal
crim-i-nal´i-ty
crim-i-no-log´i-cal
crim-i-nol´o-gist
crim-i-nol´o-gy
crim´son
cringe
cringed
cring´ing
crin´gle
cri´nite
crin´kly
crin´o-line
crip´ple
crip´pled
crip´pling
cri´ses
cri´sis
crisp´ing
crisp´ly
crisp´ness
crisp´y
criss´cross
Cris-to´bal
cri-te´ri-on
crit´ic
crit´i-cal
crit´i-cism
crit´i-cize
crit´i-ciz-ing
cri-tique´
croak´er
Croat
Cro-a´tia
cro-chet´
cro-cheted´
cro-chet´er
cro-chet´ing
crock´ery
Crock´ett
croc´o-dile
cro´cus
Croe´sus
Croix de guerre
crom´lech
Crom´well
cro´ny
crook´ed

crooked
croon´er
crop´per
cro-quet´
cro-quette´
cross´bar
cross´bill
cross´bones
cross´bow
cross´bred
cross´breed
cross´—coun´try
cross´cut
cross—ex-am-i-
na´tion
cross´—ex-am´ine
cross´—eyed
cross´—grained
cross´ing
cross´—leg-ged
cross´let
cross´ly
cross´over
cross´piece
cross´—pol´li-nate
cross´—pol-li-na´tion
cross´—ref´er-ence
cross´road
cross sec´tion
cross´—stitch
cross´walk
cross´ways
cross´wise
cross´word
crotch´et
crotch´ety
crou´pi-er
crou´ton
crow´bar
crowd´ed
crow´foot
crow´ing
crowned
cru´cial
cru´ci-ble
cru´ci-fer
cru-cif´er-ous
cru´ci-fied
cru´ci-fix

cru-ci-fix´ion
cru´ci-fy
crude´ly
cru´di-ty
cru´el
cru´el-ly
cru´el-ty
cru´et
cruised
cruis´er
cruis´ing
crul´ler
crum´ble
crum´bling
crum´bly
crum´pet
crum´ple
crum´pling
crunch´ing
cru-sade´
cru-sad´er
cru-sad´ing
Cru´soe
crus-ta´cean
crust´ed
crust´y
crux
cru-zei´ro
cry
cry´ing
cry´o-gen
cry-o-gen´ics
crypt-anal´y-sis
cryp´tic
cryp´to-gam
cryp´to-gram
cryp-tog´ra-pher
cryp-tog´ra-phy
crys´tal
crys´tal-line
crys-tal-lin´i-ty
crys´tal-lite
crys-tal-li-za´tion
crys´tal-lize
Cu´ba
cub´by-hole
cubed
cu´bic
cu´bi-cal

cu´bi-cal-ly
cu´bi-cle
cub´ism
cu´bit
cu´bi-tal
cuck´old
cuck´oo
cu´cum-ber
cud´dle
cud´dled
cud´dling
cud´gel
cud´gel-er
cui-sine´
cuisse
cul´—de—sac
cul´i-nary
cull´ing
cul´mi-nate
cul-mi-na´tion
cu-lotte´
cul-pa-bil´i-ty
cul´pa-ble
cul´prit
cul´ti-va-ble
cul´ti-vate
cul´ti-vat-ed
cul-ti-va´tion
cul´ti-va-tor
cul´tur-al
cul´ture
cul´tured
cul´vert
cum´ber
Cum´ber-land
cum´ber-some
cum lau´de
cum´mer-bund
cu´mu-late
cu-mu-la´tion
cu´mu-la-tive
cu´mu-lus
cun´ning
cup´bear-er
cup´board
cup´cake
cu-pel´
cup´ful
Cu´pid

cu-pid´i-ty
cup´like
cu´po-la
cup´ping
cur-abil´i-ty
cur´able
Cu´ra-cao´
cu-ra´re
cu´rate
cu´ra-tive
cu-ra´tor
curb´ing
curb´stone
cur´dle
cur´dling
cure
cure´—all
cure´less
cur´few
cu´ria
Cu-rie´
cur´ing
cu´rio
cu-ri-os´i-ty
cu´ri-ous
cur´lew
cur´li-cue
curl´i-ness
curl´ing
curl´y
cur´rant
cur´ren-cy
cur´rent
cur´ri-cle
cur-ric´u-lar
cur-ric´u-lum
cur´ried
cur´ri-er
cur´ry
cur´ry-ing
cursed
curs´ing
cur´so-ry
cur-tail´
cur-tail´ment
cur´tain
cur´tal
curt´ly
curt´sy

cur-va´ceous
cur´va-ture
curved
curv´ing
cush´ion
cus´pi-dal
cus´pi-dor
cus´tard
Cus´ter
cus-to´di-al
cus-to´di-an
cus´to-dy
cus´tom
cus´tom-ar´i-ly
cus´tom-ary
cus´tom-er
cus´tom-house
cus´tom—made
cut´away
cut glass
cu´ti-cle
cut´lass
cut´ler
cut´lery
cut´let
cut´off
cut´out
cut´ter
cut´ting
cut´tle
cut´tle-fish
cut´wa-ter
cut´worm
cy´a-nide
cy-a-no´sis
cy-ber-net´ics
Cyc´la-des
cy´cle
cy´clic
cy´cli-cal
cy´cling
cy´clist
cy´clone
cy-clo-pe´dia
Cy´clops
cy´clo-tron
cyg´net
cyl´in-der
cy-lin´dri-cal
cy´ma-rose
cy-ma´ti-um
cym´bal
cyn´ic
cyn´i-cal
cyn´i-cism
cy´no-sure
cy´press
cyp´ri-noid
Cyp´ri-ot
Cy´prus
Cy´ra-no
Cyr´il
Cy´rus
cyst
cys´tic
cy-tol´o-gy
cy´to-plasm
czar
czar´e-vitch
cza-rev´na
cza-ri´na
czar´ism
Czech
Czech´o-slo´vak
Czech´o-slo-va´kia

D

dab´bing
dab´ble
dab´bling
Dac´ca
dachs´hund
Da´cron
dac´tyl
dac-tyl´ic
dac-ty-li´tis
dad´dy
daf´fo-dil
dag´ger
da-guerre´o-type
dahl´ia
dai´lies
dai´ly
dain´ties
dain´ti-ly
dain´ti-ness
dain´ty
dair´ies
dair´y
dair´y-ing
dair´y-man
da´is
dai´sies
dai´sy
Da-kar´
Da-ko´ta
Dal´las
dal´li-ance
dal´lied
dal´ly
dal´ly-ing
Dal-ma´tian
dam
dam´age
dam´ag-ing-ly
dam´a-scene
Da-mas´cus
dam´ask
dammed
dam´ming
damn
dam´na-ble
dam-na´tion
damned
damn´ing
damn´ing-ly
Dam´o-cles
Da´mon
damp´en
damp´en-er
damp´er
damp´ing
dam´sel
Da´na
danced
danc´er
danc´ing
dan´de-li-on
dan´der
dan´dle
dan´druff
dan´dy
dan´ger
dan´ger-ous
dan´ger-ous-ly
dan´gle

dan´gled
dan´gler
dan´gling
Dan´iel
Dan´ish
dank´ness
dan-seuse´
Dan´te
Dan´ube
Dan´ville
Dan´zig
dap´per
dap´ple
Dar-da-nelles´
dare´dev-il
Dar-i-en´
dar´ing
Dar-jee´ling
dark´en
dark horse
dark´ly
dark´ness
dark´room
dar´ling
Darm´stadt
Dart´mouth
Dar´win
dash´board
dashed
dash´er
dash´ing
das´tard
das´tard-ly
da´ta
dat´ed
date´less
dat´ing
da´tum
daub´er
daub´ery
daugh´ter
daugh´ter—in—law
daunt´less
daunt´less-ly
dau´phin
dav´en-port
Da´vid
Da´vis
da´vit
daw´dle
daw´dler
daw´dling
Daw´son
day´break
day´dream
day let´ter
day´light
day´star
day´time
Day´ton
Day-to´na
dazed
daz´ed-ly
daz´ing
daz´zle
daz´zling
daz´zling-ly
dea´con
dead´en
dead´eye
dead´fall
dead´li-er
dead´line
dead´li-ness
dead´lock
dead´ly
dead´wood
deaf´en
def´en-ing
deaf´en-ing-ly
deaf´—mute
deaf´ness
deal´er
deal´ing
dealt
Dear´born
dear´ie
dear´ly
dear´ness
dearth
death´blow
death´like
death´ly
death rate
death's´—head
death´watch
de-ba´cle
de-bar´
de-bar-ka´tion
de-bar´ment
de-bar´ring
de-base´
de-based´
de-base´ment
de-bas´ing
de-bat´able
de-bate´
de-bat´er
de-bat´ing
de-bauch´
de-bauch´ee
de-bauch´er
de-bauch´ery
de-ben´ture
de-bil´i-tate
de-bil´i-tat-ed
de-bil-i-ta´tion
de-bil´i-ty
deb´it
deb´o-nair´
Deb´o-rah
dé-bou-ché´
debt´or
de-bunk´
de´but
deb´u-tante
dec´ade
dec´a-dence
dec´a-dent
dec´a-logue
de-camp´
de-camp´ment
de-cant´
de-cant´er
de-cap´i-tate
de-cap-i-ta´tion
dec´a-pod
De-cap´o-lis
de-cath´lon
De-ca´tur
de-cay´
de-cayed´
de-cay´ing
de-cease´
de-ceased´
de-ce´dent
de-ceit´

de-ceit´ful
de-ceit´ful-ness
de-ceive´
de-ceiv´er
de-ceiv´ing-ly
de-cel´er-ate
de-cel-er-a´tion
De-cem´ber
de´cen-cy
de´cent
de-cen´ter
de´cent-ly
de-cen-tral-i-za´tion
de-cen´tral-ize
de-cep´tion
de-cep´tive
dec´i-bel
de-cide´
de-cid´ed-ly
dec´i-mal
dec´i-mate
dec-i-ma´tion
dec´i-me-ter
de-ci´pher
de-ci´pher-able
de-ci´sion
de-ci´sive
de-ci´sive-ly
de-claim´
dec-la-ma´tion
dec-la-ra´tion
de-clar´a-tive
de-clar´a-to-ry
de-clare´
de-clas´si-fy
de-clin´able
dec-li-na´tion
de-clin´a-to-ry
de-cline´
de-clined´
de-clin´ing
de-cliv´i-ty
de-cli´vous
de-code´
de-cod´ing
dé-col-le-tage´
dé-col-le-té´
de-col´or-ize
de-com-pose´

de-com-po-si´tion
de-con-tam´i-nate
de-con-tam-i-na´tion
de-cor´
dec´o-rate
dec-o-ra´tion
dec´o-ra-tive
dec´o-ra-tor
dec´o-rous
de-co´rum
de-coy´
de-coyed´
de-coy´ing
de´crease´
de-cree´
de-creed´
de-cree´ing
dec´re-ment
de´crem-e-ter
de-crep´it
de-crep´i-tate
de-crep´i-tude
de´cre-scen´do
de-cres´cent
de-cry´
ded´i-cate
ded-i-ca´tion
ded´i-ca-to-ry
de-duce´
de-duced´
de-duc´i-ble
de-duc´ing
de-duct´
de-duct´ible
de-duc´tion
de-duc´tive
deep´en
deep´—root-ed
deep´—seat-ed
deer´skin
de-face´
de-faced´
de-fac´ing
de fac´to
def-a-ma´tion
de-fam´a-to-ry
de-fame´
de-fault´
de-fault´er

de-fea´si-ble
de-feat´
de-feat´ed
de-feat´ist
def´e-cate
def-e-ca´tion
de´fect
de-fect´ed
de-fec´tion
de-fec´tive
de-fend´
de-fend´ant
de-fend´er
de-fense´
de-fense´less
de-fen-si-bil´i-ty
de-fen´si-ble
de-fen´sive
de-fer´
def´er-ence
def´er-ent
def-er-en´tial
de-fer´ra-ble
de-ferred´
de-fer´ring
de-fi´ance
de-fi´ant
de-fi´ant-ly
de-fi´cien-cy
de-fi´cient
def´i-cit
de-fied´
de-file´
de-file´ment
de-fil´ing
de-fin´able
de-fine´
de-fin´ing
def´i-nite
def´i-nite-ly
def-i-ni´tion
de-fin´i-tive
de-flate´
de-fla´tion
de-fla´tion-ary
de-flect´
de-flec´tion
de-flec´tive
de-flec´tor

De-foe´
de-fo´li-ate
de-for´est
de-form´
de-form-abil´i-ty
de-form´able
de-for-ma´tion
de-for´ma-tive
de-formed´
de-for´mi-ty
de-fraud´
de-frau-da´tion
de-fraud´ed
de-fray´
de-frayed´
de-fray´ing
de-frost´
de-frost´er
deft´ly
deft´ness
de-funct´
de-fy´
de-fy´ing
De-gas´
de-gen´er-a-cy
de-gen´er-ate
de-gen-er-a´tion
de-gen´er-a-tive
deg-ra-da´tion
de-grade´
de-grad´ed
de-grad´ing
de-gree´
de-hu-mid´i-fi-er
de-hy´drate
de-hy-dra´tion
de-ic´er
deic´tic
de-i-fi-ca´tion
de´i-fied
deign
de´ist
de´i-ties
de´i-ty
de-ject´ed
de-ject´ed-ly
de-jec´tion
de ju´re
Del´a-ware
de-lay´
de-layed´
de-lay´ing
de´le
de-lec´ta-ble
de-lec-ta´tion
del´e-ga-cy
del´e-gate
del-e-ga´tion
de´le-ing
de-lete´
de-let´ed
de-le´tion
Del´hi
De´lia
de-lib´er-ate
de-lib-er-a´tion
de-lib´er-a-tive
del´i-ca-cies
del´i-ca-cy
del´i-cate
del´i-cate-ly
del-i-ca-tes´sen
de-li´cious
de-light´
de-light´ed
de-light´ful
De-li´lah
de-lin´e-ate
de-lin-e-a´tion
de-lin´e-a-tor
de-lin´quen-cy
de-lin´quent
de-lir´i-ous
de-lir´i-um
de-liv´er
de-liv´er-able
de-liv´er-ance
de-liv´er-er
de-liv´er-ies
de-liv´ery
Del´phi
del´phi-nine
del´ta
del´toid
de-lude´
de-lud´ed
de-lud´ing
del´uge
del´uged
de-lu´sion
de-lu´sive
de-lu´so-ry
de-luxe´
delve
delved
delv´ing
de-mag´net-ize
dem´a-gog´ic
dem´a-gogue
dem´a-gogu-ery
dem´a-gogy
de-mand´
de-mand´ed
de-mean´
de-mean´or
de-ment´ed
de-men´tia
de-mer´it
De-me´tri-us
dem´i-god
dem´i-john
de-mil-i-ta-ri-za´tion
de-mil´i-ta-rize
de-mise´
dem´i-tasse
de-mo-bi-li-za´tion
de-mo´bi-lize
de-moc´ra-cy
dem´o-crat
dem´o-crat´ic
de-moc´ra-tize
de-mog´ra-pher
de´mo-graph´ic
de-mog´ra-phy
de-mol´ish
dem-o-li´tion
de´mon
de-mon-e-ti-za´tion
de-mon´e-tize
de-mo´ni-ac
de´mo-ni´a-cal
de-mon´ic
de´mon-ism
de-mon-ol´a-try
de-mon-ol´o-gy
de-mon´stra-ble
de-mon´stra-bly

dem´on-strate
dem´on-strat-ing
dem-on-stra´tion
de-mon´stra-tive
dem´on-stra-tor
de-mor-al-iza´tion
de-mor´al-ize
de-mor´al-iz-ing
De-mos´the-nes
de-mote´
de-mot´ed
de-mo´tion
de-mur´
de-mure´
de-mur´rage
de-mur´ral
de-murred´
de-mur´rer
de-mur´ring
de-na´tion-a-lize
de-nat´u-ral-ize
de-na´tur-ant
de-na´tured
den-e-ga´tion
de-ni´al
de-nied´
de-ni´er
de-nies´
den´i-grate
den´im
den´i-zen
Den´mark
Den´nis
de-nom´i-nate
de-nom-i-na´tion
de-nom-i-na´tion-al
de-nom-i-na´tion-al-ism
de-nom´i-na-tive
de-nom´i-na-tor
de-no-ta´tion
de-note´
de-not´ing
de-noue-ment´
de-nounce´
de-nounced´
de-nounce´ment
de-nounc´ing
dense
dense´ly
den´si-ty
den´tal
den-ta-tion
den´ti-cle
den´ti-frice
den´til
den´tin
den´tist
den´tis-try
den-ti´tion
den´ture
de-nude´
de-nun´ci-ate
de-nun-ci-a´tion
de-nun´ci-a-to-ry
Den´ver
de-ny´
de-ny´ing
de-o´dor-ant
de-o´dor-ize
de-o´dor-iz-er
de-on-tol´o-gy
de-part´
de-part´ed
de-part´ment
de-part-men´tal
de-par´ture
de-pend´
de-pend-abil´i-ty
de-pend´able
de-pen´dence
de-pen´den-cy
de-pen´dent
de-pict´
de-pic´tion
dep´i-late
de-pil´a-to-ry
de-plete´
de-plet´ed
de-ple´tion
de-plor´able
dep-lo-ra´tion
de-plore´
de-plored´
de-plor´ing
de-ploy´
de-ploy´ment
de-po´lar-ize
de-pop´u-late
de-pop-u-la´tion
de-port´
de-por-ta´tion
de-port´ed
de-port-ee´
de-port´ment
de-pos´al
de-pose´
de-posed´
de-pos´ing
de-pos´it
de-pos´i-tary
de-pos´it-ed
dep-o-si´tion
de-pos´i-tor
de-pos´i-to-ry
de´pot
dep-ra-va´tion
de-prave´
de-praved´
de-prav´i-ty
dep´re-cate
dep´re-cat-ing
dep-re-ca´tion
dep´re-ca-to-ry
de-pre´cia-ble
de-pre´ci-ate
de-pre-ci-a´tion
dep´re-date
dep-re-da´tion
dep´re-da-tor
dep´re-da-to-ry
de-press´
de-pres´sant
de-pressed´
de-press´ible
de-press´ing
de-pres´sion
de-pres´sor
de-priv´al
dep-ri-va´tion
de-prive´
de-prived´
de-priv´ing
depth
dep-u-ta´tion
de-pute´
dep´u-ties

dep´u-tize
dep´u-ty
de-rail´
de-rail´ment
de-range´
de-range´ment
de-rang´ing
der´by
der´e-lict
der-e-lic´tion
de-ride´
de-rid´ing
de-ri´sion
de-ri´sive
de-ri´sive-ly
de-ri´so-ry
der-i-va´tion
de-riv´a-tive
de-rive´
de-rived´
de-riv´ing
der´ma-toid
der-ma-tol´o-gist
der-ma-tol´o-gy
der´mis
der-nier´
de-rog´a-to-ry
der´rick
der´rin-ger
der´vish
des´cant
Des-cartes´
de-scend´
de-scend´ant
de-scend´ed
de-scend´er
de-scend´ible
de-scent´
de-scrib´able
de-scribe´
de-scribed´
de-scrip´tion
de-scrip´tive
des-cry´
des-cry´ing
Des-de-mo´na
des´e-crate
des-e-cra´tion
des´e-cra-tor

de-seg´re-gate
de-seg-re-ga´tion
de-sen´si-tize
des´ert´
de-sert´er
de-ser´tion
de-serve´
de-served´
de-serv´ed-ly
de-serv´ing
des´ic-cate
des-ic-ca´tion
des´ic-ca-tor
de-sid-er-a´ta
de-sid-er-a´tum
de-sign´
de-sign´able
des´ig-nate
des-ig-na´tion
des´ig-na-tive
des´ig-na-tor
de-sign´ed-ly
des´ig-nee´
de-sign´er
de-sign´ing
de-sir-abil´i-ty
de-sir´able
de-sire´
de-sir´ous
de-sist´
de-sis´tance
Des Moines
des´o-late
des-o-la´tion
De So´to
de-spair´
de-spaired´
de-spair´ing
des-per-a´do
des-per-a´does
des´per-ate
des´per-ate-ly
des-per-a´tion
de-spic´a-ble
de-spis´able
de-spise´
de-spised´
de-spis´ing
de-spite´

de-spite´ful
de-spoil´
de-spoil´er
de-spoil´ing
de-spo-li-a´tion
de-spond´
de-spon´dence
de-spon´den-cy
de-spon´dent
des´pot
des-pot´ic
des-pot´i-cal
des´po-tism
des-sert´
des-ti-na´tion
des´tine
des´ti-nies
des´ti-ny
des´ti-tute
des-ti-tu´tion
de-stroy´
de-stroyed´
de-stroy´er
de-struc´ti-ble
de-struc´tion
de-struc´tive
de-struc´tive-ness
de-tach´
de-tach´able
de-tached´
de-tach´ment
de-tail´
de-tain´
de-tect´
de-tect´able
de-tec´ta-phone
de-tec´tion
de-tec´tive
de-tec´tor
de-ten´tion
de-ten´tive
de-ter´
de-ter´gent
de-te´ri-o-rate
de-te-ri-o-ra´tion
de-te´ri-o-ra-tive
de-ter´min-able
de-ter´mi-nant
de-ter´mi-nate

de-ter-mi-na´tion
de-ter´mine
de-ter´mined
de-ter´mined-ly
de-ter´mi-nism
de-ter´mi-nist
deterred´
de-ter´rent
de-ter´ring
de-ter´sive
de-test´
de-test´able
de-tes-ta´tion
de-throne´
det´o-na-ble
det´o-nate
det-o-na´tion
det´o-na-tor
de´tour
de-tract´
de-trac´tion
de-trac´tor
de-trac´to-ry
det´ri-ment
det-ri-men´tal
De-troit´
deuc´ed
Deutsch´land
de´va
De Va-le´ra
de-val´u-ate
de-val-u-a´tion
dev´as-tate
dev´as-tat-ed
dev´as-tat-ing
dev-as-ta´tion
de-vel´op
de-vel´oped
de-vel´op-er
de-vel´op-ing
de-vel´op-ment
de-vel´op-men´tal
de´vi
de´vi-ate
de-vi-a´tion
de-vice´
dev´il
dev´il-fish
dev´il-ish
dev´il-ment
dev´il-ry
dev´il-try
de´vi-ous
de´vi-ous-ly
de-vis´able
de-vise´
dev´i-sor´
de-vi-tal-iza´tion
de-vi´tal-ize
de-vo´cal-ize
de-void´
de-voir´
dev-o-lu´tion
de-volve´
de-volve´ment
de-volv´ing
Dev´on
Dev´on-shire
de-vote´
de-vot´ed
de-vot´ed-ly
dev´o-tee´
de-vo´tion
de-vo´tion-al
de-vour´
de-vout´
de-vout´ly
dew´ber-ry
dew´drop
Dew´ey
dew´i-ness
De Witt´
dew´lap
dew´point
dew´y
dex´ter
dex-ter´i-ty
dex´ter-ous
dex´ter-ous-ly
dex´trose
dex´trous
di-a-be´tes
di´a-bet´ic
di-a-bol´ic
di-a-bol´i-cal
di-ab´o-lism
di´a-caus´tic
di-a-crit´ic
di-a-crit´i-cal
di´a-dem
di´ag-nose
di-ag-no´sis
di-ag-nos´tic
di-ag-nos-ti´cian
di-ag´o-nal
di-ag´o-nal-ly
di´a-gram
di´a-gram-mat´ic
di´a-gram-mat´i-cal
di´al
di´a-lect
di´a-lec´tal
di´a-lec´tal-ly
di-a-lec´tic
di-a-lec´ti-cal
di-a-lec´ti-cism
di´aled
di´al-ing
di´a-log
di´a-logue
di-al´y-sis
di´a-lyt´ic
di-a-lyt´-i-cal-ly
dia-mag-net´ic
di-am´e-ter
di-am´e-tral
di-a-met´ric
di-a-met´ri-cal
di´a-mond
Di-an´a
di-a-net´ic
di´a-no-et´ic
di´a-per
di-aph´a-nous
di´a-phragm
di´a-phrag-mat´ic
di-aph´y-sis
di´a-ries
di´a-rist
di-ar-rhe´a
di´a-ry
Di´as
di´a-stat´ic
di´a-stol´ic
di´a-sto-mat´ic
di´a-ther-my
di-ath´e-sis

di´a-thet´ic
di´a-tom
di-atom´ic
di-at´om-ite
di´a-ton´ic
di´a-tribe
Di-az´
dib´ble
di-chro-mat´ic
dick-cis´sel
Dick´ens
Dick-en´si-an
dick´er
dick´ey
Dick´in-son
Dic´ta-phone
dic´tate
dic´tat-ing
dic-ta´tion
dic´ta-tor
dic-ta-to´ri-al
dic-ta´tor-ship
dic´tion
dic´tio-nar-ies
dic´tio-nary
Dic´to-graph
dic´tum
did´dle
die cut´ter
died
Di-e´go
die´mak-er
Dieppe
di´et
di´e-tary
di´et-er
di-e-tet´ic
di-e-ti´tian
dif´fer
dif´fered
dif´fer-ence
dif´fer-ent
dif-fer-en´tia-ble
dif-fer-en´tial
dif-fer-en´ti-ate
dif-fer-en-ti-a´tion
dif´fi-cult
dif´fi-cul-ties
dif´fi-cul-ty
dif´fi-dence
dif´fi-dent
dif-fract´
dif-frac´tion
dif-fuse´
dif-fus´ible
dif-fu´sion
dif-fu´sive
dig´a-my
di-gas´tric
di´gest
di-gest-ibil´i-ty
di-gest´ible
di-ges´tion
di-ges´tive
dig´ger
dig´ging
dig´it
dig´i-tal
dig-i-tal´is
dig´i-ta-lize
dig´ni-fied
dig´ni-fied-ly
dig´ni-fy
dig´ni-fy-ing
dig´ni-tar-ies
dig´ni-tary
dig´ni-ties
dig´ni-ty
di-gress´
di-gres´sion
di-lap´i-date
di-lap´i-dat-ed
di-lap-i-da´tion
dil-a-ta´tion
di-late´
di-lat´ing
di-la´tion
dil´a-to-ry
di-lem´ma
dil-et-tante´
dil-et-tant´ism
dil´i-gence
dil´i-gent
dil´u-ent
di-lute´
di-lut´ing
di-lu´tion
di-men´sion
dim´er-ous
dim´e-ter
di-min´ish
di-min-u-en´do
dim-i-nu´tion
di-min´u-tive
dim´ly
dimmed
dim´ming
dim´ness
dim´ple
dim´pling
di-nar´
dined
din´er
di-nette´
dingh´y
din´gi-ness
din´gle
din´gy
din´ing
din´ing room
din´ner
din´ner-time
din´ner-ware
di-noc´er-as
di´no-saur
di-oc´e-san
di´o-cese
Di-o-cle´tian
Di-og´e-nes
di-ox´ide
diph-the´ria
diph´thong
di-plo´ma
di-plo´ma-cy
dip´lo-mat
dip-lo-mat´ic
dip-lo-mat´i-cal-ly
dipped
dip´per
dip-so-ma´nia
di-rect´
di-rec´tion
di-rect´ly
di-rect´ness
di-rec´tor
di-rec´tor-ate
di-rec´to-ry

dirge
dir´i-gi-ble
dirt´i-er
dirt´i-ly
dirt´i-ness
dirt-y
dis-abil´i-ty
dis-a´ble
dis-a´bled
dis-a´bling
dis-ad-van´tage
dis-ad-van-ta´geous
dis-af-fect´ed
dis-af-fec´tion
dis-af-firm´ance
dis-af-fir-ma´tion
dis-agree´
dis-agree´able
dis-agree´ment
dis-al-low´
dis-al-low´ance
dis-ap-pear´
dis-ap-pear´ance
dis-ap-peared´
dis-ap-point´
dis-ap-point´ed
dis-ap-point´ment
dis-ap-prov´al
dis´ap-prove´
dis´ap-prov´ing
dis´ap-prov´ing-ly
dis-arm´
dis-ar´ma-ment
dis-ar-range´
dis-ar-range´ment
dis-ar-ray´
di-sas´ter
di-sas´trous
di-sas´trous-ly
dis-avow´
dis-avow´al
dis-band´
dis-bar´
dis-bar´ment
dis-bar´ring
dis-be-lief´
dis-be-lieve´
dis-be-liev´er
dis-bur´den

dis-burse´
dis-burse´ment
dis-burs´ing
disc
dis´card
dis-cern´
dis-cern´ible
dis-cern´ibly
dis-cern´ing
dis-cern´ment
dis´charge
dis-ci´ple
dis´ci-plin´able
dis-ci-pli-nar´i-an
dis´ci-pli-nary
dis´ci-pline
dis´ci-plin-er
dis-claim´
dis-claim´er
dis-cla-ma´tion
dis-close´
dis-clo´sure
dis-col´or
dis-col-or-a´tion
dis-com´fort
dis-com´fort-able
dis´con-cert´
dis-con-nect´
dis-con-nect´ed
dis-con-nec´tion
dis-con´so-late
dis-con´so-late-ly
dis-con-tent´
dis-con-tent´ed
dis-con-tin´u-ance
dis-con-tin-u-a´tion
dis-con-tin´ue
dis-con-ti-nu´i-ty
dis-con-tin´u-ous
dis´cord
dis-cor´dance
dis-cor´dant
dis´count
dis-coun´te-nance
dis-cour´age
dis-cour´age-ment
dis-cour´ag-er
dis-cour´ag-ing
dis´course

dis-cour´te-ous
dis-cov´er
dis-cov´er-er
dis-cov´er-ies
dis-cov´ert
dis-cov´ery
dis-cred´it
dis-cred´it-able
dis-creet´
dis-creet´ly
dis-crep´an-cy
dis-crete´
dis-cre´tion
dis-cre´tion-ary
dis-crim´i-nate
dis-crim´i-nat-ing
dis-crim-i-na´tion
dis-crim´i-na-to-ry
dis´cus
dis-cuss´
dis-cussed´
dis-cuss´ible
dis-cus´sion
dis-dain´
dis-dain´ful
dis-dain´ful-ly
dis-ease´
dis-eased´
dis-eas´es
dis-em-bark´
dis-em-bar-ka´tion
dis-em-bar´rass
dis-em-bod´i-ment
dis-em-bod´y
dis-em-bogue´
dis-em-bow´el
dis-en-a´ble
dis-en-chant´
dis-en-chant´ment
dis-en-cum´ber
dis-en-gage´
dis-en-tan´gle
dis-es-tab´lish
dis-es-tab´lish-ment
dis-fa´vor
dis-fig´ure
disfig´ur-ing
dis-gorge´
dis-grace´

dis-grace´ful
dis-grun´tle
dis-grun´tled
dis-guise´
dis-guis´ed-ly
dis-gust´
dis-gust´ed
dis-gust´ed-ly
dis-gust´ing
dis-gust´ing-ly
dis-ha-bille´
dis-har-mo´ni-ous
dis-har´mo-ny
dis-heart´en
di-shev´el
di-shev´eled
dis-hon´est
dis-hon´es-ty
dis-hon´or
dis-hon´or-able
dish´wash-er
dis-il-lu´sion
dis-il-lu´sion-ment
dis-in-cli-na´tion
dis-in-clined´
dis-in-fect´
dis-in-fec´tant
dis-in-fec´tion
dis-in-gen´u-ous
dis-in-her´it
dis-in´te-grate
dis-in-te-gra´tion
dis-in-ter´
dis-in´ter-est-ed
dis-in´ter-est-ed-ness
dis-join´
dis-joint´
dis-joint´ed
dis-junct´
dis-junc´tion
dis-junc´tive
disk
dis-like´
dis´lo-cate
dis-lo-ca´tion
dis-lodge´
dis-loy´al
dis-loy´al-ty
dis´mal

dis´mal-ly
dis-man´tle
dis-man´tling
dis-mast´
dis-may´
dis-mem´ber
dis-mem´ber-ment
dis-miss´
dis-mis´sal
dis-mis´sion
dis-mount´
dis-obe´di-ence
dis-obe´di-ent
dis-obey´
dis-obeyed´
dis-or´der
dis-or´dered
dis-or´der-li-ness
dis-or´der-ly
dis-or-ga-ni-za´tion
dis-or´ga-nize
dis-own´
dis-par´age
dis-par´age-ment
dis-par´ag-ing-ly
dis-par´ate
dis-par´i-ty
dis-pas´sion-ate
dis-patch´
dis-patch´er
dis-pel´
dispelled´
dis-pel´ling
dis-pens´abil´i-ty
dis-pens´able
dis-pen´sa-ry
dis-pen-sa´tion
dis-pense´
dis-pens´er
dis-per´sal
dis-per´sant
dis-perse´
dis-pers´ible
dis-per´sion
di-spir´it
di-spir´it-ed
dis-place´
dis-placed´
dis-place´ment

dis-play´
dis-please´
dis-pleas´ing
dis-plea´sure
dis-pos´able
dis-pos´al
dis-pose´
dis-pos´er
dis-po-si´tion
dis-pos-sess´
dis-pro-por´tion
dis-pro-por´tion-al
dsi-pro-por´tion-ate
dis-prove´
dis-put´able
dis-pu´tant
dis-pu-ta´tion
dis-pu-ta´tious
dis-pu´ta-tive
dis-pute´
dis-qual-i-fi-ca´tion
dis-qual´i-fied
dis-qual´i-fy
dis-qui´et
Dis-rae´li
dis-re-gard´
dis-re-pair´
dis-rep´u-ta-ble
dis-rep´u-ta-bly
dis-re-pute´
dis-re-spect´
dis-re-spect´able
dis-re-spect´ful
dis-robe´
dis-rupt´
dis-rup´tion
dis-sat-is-fac´tion
dis-sat´is-fied
dis-sat´is-fy
dis-sect´
dis-sect´ed
dis-sec´tion
dis-sec´tor
dis-sem´blance
dis-sem´ble
dis-sem´bler
dis-sem´i-nate
dis-sem-i-na´tion
dis-sem´i-na-tor

dis-sen´sion
dis-sent´
dis-sent´er
dis´ser-tate
dis-ser-ta´tion
dis´ser-ta-tive
dis-serv´ice
dis-sev´er
dis´si-dence
dis´si-dent
dis-sil´ien-cy
dis-sil´ient
dis-sim´i-lar
dis-sim-i-lar´i-ty
dis-sim-i-la´tion
dis-sim´u-late
dis-sim-u-la´tion
dis´si-pate
dis´si-pat-ed
dis-si-pa´tion
dis´si-pa-tor
dis-so´ci-ate
dis-so´ci-a´tion
dis-sol-u-bil´i-ty
dis-sol´u-ble
dis´so-lute
dis-so-lu´tion
dis-solv´able
dis-solve´
dis-sol´vent
dis-solv´ing
dis´so-nance
dis´so-nan-cy
dis´so-nant
dis-suade´
dis-sua´sive
dis-sua´sive-ly
dis´taff
dis-tain´
dis´tal
dis´tance
dis´tant
dis´tant-ly
dis-taste´
dis-taste´ful
dis-tem´per
dis-ten´tion
dis-till´
dis-till´able
dis´til-late
dis-til-la´tion
dis-till´er
dis-till´ery
dis-till´ing
dis-tinct´
dis-tinc´tion
dis-tinc´tive
dis-tinct´ly
dis-tinct´ness
dis-tin´guish
dis-tin´guish-able
dis-tin´guish-ably
dis-tin´guished
dis-tort´
dis-tort´ed
dis-tor´tion
dis-tor´tive
dis-tract´
dis-tract´ible
dis-trac´tion
dis-trac´tive
dis-traught´
dis-tress´
dis-tress´ful
dis-tress´ing
dis-trib´u-tary
dis-trib´ute
dis-tri-bu´tion
dis-trib´u-tive
dis-trib´u-tor
dis´trict
dis-trust´
dis-trust´ful
dis-turb´
dis-tur´bance
dis-turb´er
dis-un´ion
dis-unite´
dis-use´
dith´er
dit´to
dit´ty
di-uret´ic
di-ur´nal
di´va
di-van´
div´er
di-verge´
di-ver´gence
di-ver´gen-cy
di-ver´gent
di-ver´gent-ly
di´vers
di-verse´
di-verse´ly
di-ver-si-fi-ca´tion
di-ver´si-fied
di-ver´si-fy
di-ver´sion
di-ver´si-ty
di-vert´
di-ver-tic´u-lum
di-ver´tise-ment
Di´ves
di-vest´
di-vide´
di-vid´ed
div´i-dend
di-vid´er
di-vid´u-al
div-i-na´tion
di-vin´a-to-ry
di-vine´
di-vine´ly
di-vin´er
div´ing
di-vin´i-ty
di-vis-i-bil´i-ty
di-vis´i-ble
di-vi´sion
di-vi´sion-al
di-vi´sive
di-vi´sor
di-vorce´
di-vor´cee´
di-vorce´ment
div´ot
di-vul´gate
di-vulge´
di-vulge´ment
di-vulg´ing
Dix´ie
Dix´on
diz´zi-ly
diz´zi-ness
diz´zy
dob´bin

Do´ber-man pin´scher
doc´ile
doc´ile-ly
dock´et
dock fore´man
dock´hand
dock´man
dock´mas-ter
dock rent
dock´side
dock´yard
doc´tor
doc´tor-al
doc´tor-ate
doc´tri-naire´
doc´tri-nal
doc´trine
doc´u-ment
doc´u-men´ta-ry
doc-u-men-ta´tion
dod´der
do-dec´a-gon
dodg´er
dodg´ing
do´er
doe´skin
does´n't
dog´bite
dog´cart
dog´catch-er
dog col´lar
dog days
doge
dog´—eared
dog´fight
dog´fish
dog´ged
dog´ged-ly
dog´ger-el
dog´gery
dog´ging
dog´gy
dog´house
do´gie
dog´ma
dog-mat´ic
dog-mat´i-cal
dog-mat´i-cal-ly
dog´ma-tism
dog´ma-tist
dog´ma-tize
dog rose
dog´wood
doi´lies
doi´ly
do´ing
dol´ce
dol´drum
dole´ful
dole´ful-ly
dol´lar
dol´ly
dol´man
dol´men
do´lo-mite
Do-lo´res
dol´phin
do-main´
Domes´day
do-mes´tic
do-mes´ti-cate
do-mes-ti-ca´tion
do-mes-tic´i-ty
dom´i-cal
dom´i-cile
dom´i-nance
dom´i-nant
dom´i-nate
dom-i-na´tion
dom´i-neer´
dom´i-neer´ing
Dom´i-nic
Do-min´i-can
do-min´ion
Dom´i-nique
dom´i-no
dom´i-noes
Don´ald
do-nate´
Don-a-tel´lo
do-nat´ing
do-na´tion
Don´a-tism
do-nee´
Don´e-gal
Don Ju´an
don´key
don´na
Donne
do´nor
Don Qui-xo´te
don't
doo´dle
doo´dling
dooms´day
door´bell
door´keep-er
door´knob
door´man
door´nail
door´plate
door´post
door´sill
door´step
door´stone
door´way
door´yard
doped
dop´ing
Dor´ches-ter
Dor´ic
dor´man-cy
dor´mant
dor´mer
dor´mi-ent
dor´mi-to-ries
dor´mi-to-ry
Dor´o-thy
dor´sal
Dor´set-shire
Dort´mund
do´ry
dos´age
dosed
do-sim´e-try
dos´ing
dos´ser
dos´sier
dot´age
dot´ed
dot´ing
dot´ish
dot´ted
dot´ty
dou´ble
dou´ble—bar´reled
dou´ble cross

dou´ble en-ten´dre
dou´ble-head´er
dou´ble—quick´
dou´blet
dou´bling
dou-bloon´
dou´bly
doubt
doubt´able
doubt´ful
doubt´ful-ly
doubt´less
douche
douch´ing
dough´boy
Dough´er-ty
dough´nut
dough´ty
dough´y
Doug´las
doused
dous´ing
Do´ver
dove´tail
dow´a-ger
dowd´y
dow´el
dow´er
down´cast
down´fall
down´heart-ed
down´hill´
down´pour
down´right
down´stairs´
down´stream
down´throw
down´town´
down´trod´den
down´ward
down´y
dow´ries
dow´ry
dows´er
dox´y
doz´en
doz´ing
drab´ness
drach´ma
Dra´co
draft
draft-ee´
draft´i-ly
drafts´man
draft´y
dragged
drag´ging
drag´gle
drag´net
drag´on
drag´on-et´
drag´on-fly
dra-goon´
drag´rope
drain´age
drain´er
drain´pipe
drain pump
drain valve
dra´ma
dra-mat´ic
dra-mat´i-cal-ly
dram´a-tist
dram-a-ti-za´tion
dram´a-tize
dram´shop
drap´er
drap´ery
drap´ing
dras´tic
dras´ti-cal-ly
draught
draught´y
draw´back
draw´bar
draw´bridge
draw-ee´
draw´er
draw´ing
drawl´ing
dray´age
Dray´ton
dread´ful
dread´ful-ly
dread´nought
dream´er
dream´i-ly
dream´i-ness
dream´ing
dream´land
dream´less
dreamt
dream´y
drear´i-ly
drear´i-ness
drear´y
dredg´er
dredg´ing
Drei´ser
Dres´den
dress´er
dress´ing
dress´ing gown
dress´ing room
dress´mak-er
dress´mak-ing
dress´y
Drey´fus
drib´ble
drib´bled
dri´er
drift´age
drift´er
drift´ing
drift´wood
drift´y
drilled
drill´er
drill´ing
drill´mas-ter
dri´ly
drink´able
drink´er
Drink´water
dripped
drip´ping
driv´el
driv´en
driv´er
drive´way
driv´ing
driz´zle
driz´zly
drom´e-dary
droop´ing
droop´y
drop´let

dropped
drop´per
drop´ping
drop´sy
drought
dro´ver
drowned
drows´i-ly
drows´i-ness
drows´y
drub´bing
drudge
drudg´ery
drudg´ing
drug clerk
drugged
drug´ging
drug´gist
drug´store
drummed
drum´mer
drum´ming
Drum´mond
drum´stick
drunk´ard
drunk´en
drunk´en-ness
Dry´den
dry-dock
dry´er
dry´goods
dry´ing
dry´ly
dry´ness
du´al
du´al-ism
du-al´i-ty
du´al-ly
dub´bing
du´bi-ous
du´bi-ous-ly
du´bi-ta-ble
Dub´lin
Du-buque´
du´cal
duc´at
duch´ess
duck´bill
duck´ling
duck´weed
duck´y
duct´less
dud´geon
due bill
du´el
du´el-ist
du-et´
duf´fel
duf´fer
dug´out
duke´dom
dul´lard
dull´ness
dul´ly
Du-luth´
du´ly
Du´ma
Du-mas´
Du Mau-rier´
dumb´bell
dumb´wait-er
dum´dum
dum´found
dum-my
dump´i-ness
dump´ling
dump´y
Dun´bar
Dun´can
dunce
Dun-dee´
dun-ga-ree´
Dun´ge-ness´
dun´geon
dunk´er
Dun´kirk
dun´nage
dun´ning
du´o
du´o-dec´i-mal
du-o-dec´i-mo
du´o-de´nal
du´o-den´ary
du-o-de´num
dup´able
duped
dup´ery
dup´ing
du´plex
du-plex´i-ty
du´pli-cate
du-pli-ca´tion
du´pli-ca-tive
du´pli-ca-tor
du-plic´i-ty
Du-quesne´
du-ra-bil´i-ty
du´ra-ble
du´rance
du-ra´tion
du-ress´
Dur´ham
dur´ing
dusk´i-ness
dusk´y
Dus´sel-dorf
dust bowl
dust´cloth
dust cov´er
dust´er
dust´pan
dust´proof
dust´y
Dutch´man
du´te-ous
du´te-ous-ly
du´ti-able
du´ties
du´ti-ful
du´ty
Dvo´rak
dwarf´ish
dwell´er
dwell´ing
dwell´ing place
dwelt
dwin´dle
dwin´dling
dyed
dye´ing
dy´ing
dyke
dy-nam´ic
dy-nam´i-cal
dy-nam´ics
dy´na-mism
dy´na-mite

elate
elat´ed
el´a-ter
elat´er-id
elat´er-in
el-a-te´ri-um
ela´tion
El´ba
el´bow
el´bow-room
el´der
el´der-ber-ry
el´der-ly
el´dest
El Do-ra´do
El´ea-nor
El-e-a´zar
elect
elec´tion
elec´tion-eer´
elec´tive
elec´tor
elec´tor-al
elee´tor-ate
Elec´tra
elec´tric
elec´tri-cal
elec´tri-cal-ly
elec-tri´cian
elec-tric´i-ty
elec-tri-fi-ca´tion
elec´tri-fied
elec´tri-fy
elec´tro
elec-tro-anal´y-sis
elec-tro-car´dio-gram
elec-tro-car´dio-graph
elec-tro-chem´i-cal
elec-tro-chem´is-try
elec´tro-cute
elec-tro-cu´tion
elec´trode
elec-tro-dy-nam´ics
elec-tro-graph´ic
elec-trog´ra-phy
elec-trol´y-sis
elec´tro-lyte
elec-tro-lyt´ic
elec-tro-lyt´i-cal
elec´tro-lyze
elec´tro-mag-net
elec´tro-mag-net´ic
elec-tro-mag´net-ism
elec-trom´e-ter
elec´tro-met´ric
elec´tro-mo-tive
elec´tron
elec-tron´ic
elec-tro-os-mo´sis
elec-troph´o-rus
elec´tro-plate
elec´tros
elec´tro-scope
elec-tro-scop´ic
elec-tro-stat´ic
elec-tro-ther´a-py
elec-tro-ton´ic
elec-trot´o-nus
elec´tro-type
elec´tro-typ-er
elec´trum
elec´tu-ary
el-ee-mos´y-nary
el´e-gance
el´e-gan-cy
el´e-gant
el´e-gant-ly
el´e-gi´ac
el´e-gist
el´e-gize
el´-e-gy
el´e-ment
el-e-men´tal
el-e-men-tar´i-ly
el-e-men´ta-ry
el´e-phant
el-e-phan-ti´a-sis
el´e-phan´tine
El-eu-sin´i-an
Eleu´sis
el´e-vate
el´e-vat-ed
el-e-va´tion
el´e-va-tor
elev´en
elev´enth
elf´in
elf´ish
El´gin
E´li
Eli´as
elic´it
elic-i-ta´tion
elic´i-tor
elide´
elid´ible
elid´ing
el-i-gi-bil´i-ty
el´i-gi-ble
Eli´hu
elim´i-nant
elim´i-nate
elim-i-na´tion
elim´i-na-tor
El´i-ot
Eli´sha
elite
elix´ir
Eliz´a-beth
Eliz-a-be´than
Elk´hart
El´li-ot
el-lipse´
el-lips´es
el-lip´sis
el-lip´soid
el-lip´soi´dal
el-lip´-tic
el-lip´ti-cal
el-lip-tic´i-ty
El-mi´ra
el-o-cu´tion
el-o-cu´tion-ary
el-o-cu´tion-ist
El-o-him´
El-o-his´tic
eloign´er
elon´gate
elon-ga´tion
elope´
elope´ment
elop´er
elop´ing
el´o-quence
el´o-quent
el´o-quent-ly
El Pas´o

El Sal´va-dor
else´where
elu´ci-date
elu-ci-da´tion
elu´ci-da-tive
elude´
elud´ible
elud´ing
elu´sion
elu´sive
elu´so-ry
El´vis
el´vish
El´wood
Ely-see´
ema´ci-ate
ema-ci-a´tion
em´a-nate
em-a-na´tion
em´a-na-tive
eman´ci-pate
eman-ci-pa´tion
eman´ci-pa-tor
emas´cu-late
emas-cu-la´tion
em-balm´
em-balm´er
em-balm´ment
em-bank´
em-bank´ment
em-bar-ca-de´ro
em-bar´go
em-bar´goed
em-bar´goes
em-bark´
em-bar-ka´tion
em´bar-ras´
em-bar´rass
em-bar´rassed
em-bar´rass-es
em-bar´rass-ing
em-bar´rass-ing-ly
em-bar´rass-ment
em´bas-sies
em´bas-sy
em-bat´tle
em-bed´
em-bed´ded
em-bel´lish
em-bel´lish-ment
em´ber
em-bez´zle
em-bez´zled
em-bez´zle-ment
em-bez´zler
em-bit´ter
em-bla´zon
em-bla´zon-ment
em-bla´zon-ry
em´blem
em´blem-at´ic
em-blem-at´i-cal
em-blem-at´i-cal-ly
em-blem´a-tize
em´ble-ment
em-bod´i-ment
em-bod´y
em-bold´en
em-bol´ic
em´bo-lism
em-bo-lis´mic
em´bo-lus
em-bos´om
em-boss´
em-bossed´
em-boss´er
em-boss´ing
em-bow´el
em-bow´er
em-brace´
em-brac´er
em-brac´ery
em-brac´ing
em-broi´der
em-broi´der-er
em-broi´dery
em-broil´
em-broil´ment
em-brown´
em´bryo
em-bry-og´e-ny
em-bry-ol´o-gy
em´bry-o-nal
em-bry-on´ic
em´bry-os
emend
em´er-ald
emerge
emer´gence
emer´gen-cies
emer´gen-cy
emer´gent
emerg´ing
emer´i-tus
emer´sion
Em´er-son
em´ery
em´i-grate
em´i-grat-ing
em-i-gra´tion
emi-gre´
E´mil
Emile
Em´i-ly
em´i-nence
em´i-nen-cy
em´i-nent
em´i-nent-ly
emir
emir´ate
em´is-sar-ies
em´is-sary
emis´sion
emis´sive
emit
emit´ted
emit´ter
emit´ting
Em-man´u-el
emol´lient
emol´u-ment
emote
emot´er
emot´ing
emo´tion
emo´tion-al
emo´tion-al-ism
emo´tion-al-ly
emo´tive
em-pan´el
em-pan´el-ing
em-path´ic
em´pa-thy
em´per-or
em´pery
em´pha-ses
em´pha-sis

em´pha-size
em´pha-siz-ing
em-phat´ic
em-phat´i-cal-ly
em-phy-se´ma
em´pire
em-pir´i-cal
em-pir´i-cism
em-pir´i-cist
em-place´ment
em-ploy´
em-ploy-ee´
em-ploy´er
em-ploy´ment
em-po´ri-um
em-pow´er
em´press
em-prise´
emp´tied
emp´ti-er
emp´ties
emp´ti-ness
emp´ty
emp´ty—hand-ed
emp´ty—head-ed
emp´ty-heart-ed
emp´ty-ing
e´mu
em´u-late
em-u-la´tion
em´u-la-tive
em´u-la-tive-ly
em´u-la-tor
em´u-la-to-ry
em´u-lous
em´u-lous-ly
emul-si-fi-ca´tion
emul´si-fied
emul´si-fi-er
emul´si-fy
emul´sion
emul´sive
en-a´ble
en-a´bling
en-act´
en-ac´tive
en-act´ment
en-am´el
en-am´eled
en-am´el-er
en-am´el-ware
en-am´or
en-am´ored
en-camp´
en-camp´ment
en-cap´su-late
en-car´nal-ize
en-case´
en-cas´ing
en-caus´tic
en´ce-phal´ic
en-ceph´a-lit´ic
en-ceph-a-li´tis
en-ceph´a-lo-gram
en-ceph-a-lo-graph´ic
en-ceph-a-log´ra-phy
en-ceph´a-loid
en-ceph´a-lon
en-ceph-a-lop´a-thy
en-chain´
en-chant´
en-chant´er
en-chant´ing
en-chant´ment
en-chant´ress
en-chase´
en-chi-la´da
en-cir´cle
en-cir´cle-ment
en-cir´cling
en´clave
en-clit´ic
en-close´
en-clos´er
en-clos´ing
en-clo´sure
en-coi´gnure
en-co´mi-ast
en-com´pass
en´core
en-coun´ter
en-cour´age
en-cour´age-ment
en-cour´ag-ing
en-crat´ic
en-croach´
en-croach´ment
en-crust´
en-crus-ta´tion
en-cum´ber
en-cum´brance
en-cyc´lic
en-cyc´li-cal
en-cy-clo-pe´dia
en-cy-clo-pe´dic
en-cy-clo-pe´dism
en-cy-clo-pe´dist
en-cyst´
en-cys-ta´tion
en-cyst´ment
en-dear´
en-dear´ing
en-dear´ment
en-deav´or
en-deav´ored
en-de´mi-al
en-dem´ic
en-dem´i-cal-ly
en-de-mic´i-ty
en-de-mi-ol´o-gy
en´de-mism
En´di-cott
end´ing
en´dive
end´less
end´less-ly
end´long
end man
end´most
en-do-car´di-um
en´do-carp
en´do-cri´nal
en´do-crine
en´do-crin-o-log´ic
en-do-cri-nol´o-gy
en´do-crin´o-path´ic
en-do-cri-nop´a-thy
en-doc´ri-nous
en´do-der´mal
en´do-gam´ic
en-do-ge-net´ic
en-do-ge-nic´i-ty
en-dog´e-nous
en-dog´e-nous--ly
en-do-me-tri´tis
en-do-me´tri-um
en´do-mor´phic

en´do-plasm
en´do-plas´ma
en´do-plas´mic
en-dors´able
en-dorse´
en-dors´ee´
en-dorse´ment
en-dors´er
en-dors´ing
en´do-sperm
en-dow´
en-dow´ment
en´drin
en-due´
en-dur´able
en-dur´ance
en-dure´
en-dur´ing
end´ways
end´wise
en´e-ma
en´e-mies
en´e-my
en-er-gei´a
en-er-get´ic
en-er-get´i-cal
en-er-get´i-cal-ly
en´er-gies
en´er-gism
en´er-gize
en´er-giz-er
en´er-gy
en´er-vate
en-er-va´tion
en´er-va-tor
en-face´
en-fant´
en-fee´ble
en-fee´bling
en-fold´
en-force´
en-force´able
en-forc´ed-ly
en-force´ment
en-forc´er
en-forc´ing
en-fran´chise
en-fran´chise-ment
en-gage´
en-gaged´
en-gage´ment
en-gag´ing
en-gen´der
en´gine
en-gi-neer´
en-gi-neer´ing
en´gine room
en´gine-ry
En´gland
En´glish
En´glish-man
En´glish-wom-an
en-graft´
en-grave´
en-grav´er
en-grav´ing
en-gross´
en-gross´ing
en-gross´ment
en-gulf´
en-hance´
en-hance´ment
en-hanc´ing
en-har-mon´ic
enig´ma
enig-mat´ic
enig-mat´i-cal
enig-mat´i-cal-ly
enig´ma-tize
En-i-we´tok
en-join´
en-join´der
en-joy´
en-joy´able
en-joy´ably
en-joy´ment
en-kin´dle
en-lace´
en-large´
en-large-ment
en-light´en
en-light´en-ment
en-list´
en-list-ee´
en-list´ment
en-liv´en
en-mesh´
en´mi-ties
en´mi-ty
en-no´ble
en-no´bling
en-nui´
enor´mi-ty
enor´mous
enor´mous-ly
E´nos
enough´
en-phy-tot´ic
en-quire´
en´quiry
en-rage´
en rap-port´
en-rapt´
en-rap´ture
en-rav´ish
en-rich´
en-rich´ment
en-robe´
en-roll´
en-rolled´
en-roll´ing
en-roll´ment
en route
en-sam´ple
en-sconce´
en-sem´ble
en-shrine´
en-shroud´
en´sign
en-slave´
en-slave´ment
en-slav´er
en-slav´ing
en-snare´
en-sue´
en-su´ing
en-sure´
en-tail´
en-tail´ment
en-tan´gle
en-tan´gle-ment
en-tan´gler
en-tan´gling
en´ta-sis
En-teb´be
en´ter
en-ter-al´gia

en-ter´ic
en-ter-i´tis
en´ter-on
en´ter-prise
en´ter-pris-ing
en´ter-pris-ing-ly
en-ter-tain´
en-ter-tain´er
en-ter-tain´ing
en-ter-tain´ment
en-thet´ic
en-thrall´
en-thrall´ing
en-thrall´ing-ly
en-throne´
en-thuse´
en-thu´si-asm
en-thu´si-ast
en-thu-si-as´tic
en-thu-si-as´ti-cal-ly
en-tice´
en-tice´ment
en-tic´ing
en-tire´
en-tire´ly
en-tire´ty
en´ti-ties
en-ti´tle
en´ti-ty
en-tomb´
en-tomb´ment
en-to-mol´o-gist
en-to-mol´o-gy
en´tou-rage´
en´trails
en-train´
en´trance
en´trance-way
en-tranc´ing
en-tranc´ing-ly
en´trant
en-trap´
en-trap´ment
en-trap´ping
en´tre
en-treat´
en-treat´ies
en-treat´ing
en-treat´ing-ly
en-treat´y
en´trée
en-trench´
en-trench´ment
en´tre-nous
en´tre-pre-neur´
en-tre-pre-neur´i-al
en´tries
en-trust´
en´try
en´try-way
en-twine´
enu´mer-ate
enu-mer-a´tion
enu´mer-a-tive
enun´ci-ate
enun-ci-a´tion
enun´cia-tive
enun´ci-a-tor
en-vel´op
en´ve-lope
en-vel´oped
en-vel´op-ing
en-vel´op-ment
en´vi-able
en´vi-ably
en´vied
en´vies
en´vi-ous
en´vi-ous-ly
en-vi´ron
en-vi´ron-ment
en-vi´ron-men´tal
en-vi´rons
en-vis´age
en-vi´sion
en´voy
en´vy
en´vy-ing
en´vy-ing-ly
en-wrap´
en´zyme
e´on
ep´au-let
é´pée
é´pée-ist
ephed´rine
ephem´era
ephem´er-al
ephem´er-id
ephem´er-is
ephem´er-on
eph´od
eph´or
E´phra-im
Eph´ra-ta
ep´i-bol´ic
ep´ic
ep´i-cal
ep´i-cal-ly
ep´i-can´thic
ep´i-can´thus
ep´i-carp
ep´i-cede
ep´i-cene
ep´i-cen´ter
ep´i-cen´trum
ep´i-crit´ic
ep´i-cure
Ep´i-cu-re´an
ep´i-cur-ism
Ep´i-cu-rus
ep´i-dem´ic
ep-i-dem´i-cal
ep-i-de-mic´i-ty
ep-i-de-mi-o-log´i-cal
ep-i-de-mi-ol´o-gy
ep´i-der´mal
ep-i-du´ral
ep´i-gas´tric
ep-i-gas´tri-um
ep´i-ge´al
ep-i-glot´tis
ep´i-gone
ep´i-gram
ep´i-gram-mat´ic
ep´i-gram-mat´i-cal
ep-i-gram´ma-tist
ep´i-graph
epig´ra-pher
ep´i-graph´ic
epig´ra-phy
ep-i-la´tion
ep´i-la-tor
ep´i-lep-sy
ep´i-lep´tic
ep´i-logue
ep´i-mer

ep-i-mer-i-za´tion
ep´i-mer-ize
ep´i-nas-ty
ep-i-neph´rine
ep-i-neu´ri-um
ep´i-nine
Epiph´a-ny
epis´co-pa-cy
epis´co-pal
Epis´co-pa´lian
epis´co-pal-ism
epis´co-pate
ep´i-sode
ep-i-sod´ic
ep-i-sod´i-cal
ep-i-sod´i-cal-ly
epis´tle
ep´i-stome
ep´i-taph
epit´a-sis
ep-i-tha-la´mi-on
ep-l-tha-la´mi-um
ep-i-the´li-al
ep-i-the-li-o´ma
ep´i-the-li-om´a-tous
ep-i-the´li-um
ep´i-them
epith´e-sis
ep´i-thet
epit´o-me
ep´i-tom´i-cal
epit-o-mize
epit´ro-phy
e plu´ri-bus u´num
ep´och
ep´och-al
ep´ode
ep´o-nym
ep´o-nym´ic
ep´os
ep-ox´y
ep´si-lon
Ep´som
eq-ua-bil´i-ty
eq´ua-ble
e´qual
e´qualed
e´qual-ing
equal´i-ty

e´qual-i-za´tion
e´qual-ize
e´qual-iz-er
e´qual-ly
equa-nim´i-ty
equate´
equa´tion
equat´ive
equa´tor
equa-to´ri-al
eq´uer-ry
eques´tri-an
eques´tri-enne´
e´qui-an´gu-lar
equi-an-gu-lar´i-ty
e´qui-dis´tant
e´qui-lat´er-al
equil´i-brant
equil´i-brate
equil-i-bra´tion
equi-lib´rist
equi-lib´ri-stat
equi-lib´ri-um
eq´ui-lin
e´quine
e´qui-noc´tial
e´qui-nox
equip´
eq´ui-page
equip´ment
eq´ui-poise
equi-pol´lence
equipol´lent
equi-pon´der-ate
e´qui-po-ten´tial
equipped´
equip´ping
eq´ui-ta-ble
eq´ui-tes
eq´ui-ties
eq´ui-ty
equiv´a-lence
equiv´a-len-cy
equiv´a-lent
equiv´o-cal
equiv´o-cate
equiv´o-ca´tion
e´ra
era-di-a´tion

erad´i-ca-ble
erad´i-cate
erad-i-ca´tion
erad´i-ca-tive
erad´i-ca-tor
eras´able
erase´
erased
eras´er
eras´ing
Eras´mus
era´sure
Er´a-to
Er-a-tos´the-nes
er´bi-um
erect
erec´tile
erec-til´i-ty
erec´tion
erect´ly
erec´tor
erect´ness
er´e-mite
er-e-mit´i-cal
er´ga-tive
er´go
er´gone
er´got
er-got´ic
er´go-tism
er´go-tize
Er´ic
E´rie
erig´er-on
Er´in
erin´e-um
er´in-ite
er´i-nose
er´mine
erode´
erod´ible
erog´e-nous
Er´os
ero´sion
ero´sive
erot´ic
erot´i-cism
err-abil´i-ty
er´rand

er´rant
er´rant-ry
er-ra´ta
er-rat´ic
er-rat´i-cal-ly
er-ra´tum
erred
er´rhine
err´ing
err´ing-ly
er-ro´ne-ous
er-ro´ne-ous-ly
er´ror
er´ror—proof
er´satz
erst´while´
eruct´
eruc´tate
eruc-ta´tion
er´u-dite
er-u-di´tion
erupt´
erup´tion
erup´tive
er-y-sip´e-las
er-y-the´ma
er´y-thrine
eryth´ro-blast
eryth´ro-scope
er´y-throse
eryth´ro-sin
er-y-thro´sis
eryth´ru-lose
es´ca-drille
es´ca-lade
es´ca-la-tor
es-cal´lop
es-cal´loped
es-cam´bio
es-cap´able
es´ca-pade
es-cape´
es-caped´
es´cap-ee´
es-cape´ment
es-cap´ing
es-ca´pism
es-cap´ist
es´ca-role
es-carp´ment
es´char
es´cha-rot´ic
es-cheat´
es-chew´
es-chew´al
es´cort´
es´cri-toire
es´crow
es-cu´do
es´cu-lent
es´cu-lin
es-cutch´eon
Es´ki-mo
esoph´a-ge´al
esoph´a-go-scope
esoph´a-gus
es´o-ter´ic
es-o-ter´i-cal-ly
es-pe´cial
es-pe´cial-ly
Es-pe-ran´to
es´pi-o-nage
es´pla-nade
es-pous´al
es-pouse´
es-pous´er
es-pous´ing
es-prit´
es-py´
es´quire
es´say
es´say-ist
es´sence
es-sen´tial
es-sen-ti-al´i-ty
es-sen´tial-ly
Es´sex
es-tab´lish
es-tab´lished
es-tab´lish-ment
es-tate´
es-teem´
es´ter
es-ter´i-fy
es´ter-ize
Es´ther
es-thet´ic
es-thet´ics
Es-tho´nia
es´ti-ma-ble
es´ti-mate
es-ti-ma´tion
es´ti-ma-tor
es´ti-va-tor
Es-to´nia
es-top´
es-trange´
es-trange´ment
es-trang´ing
es-tray´
es´tro-gen
es´tro-gen´ic
es´trous
es´tu-a-rine
es´tu-ary
et cet´era
etch´ing
eter´nal
eter´nal-ly
eter´ni-ty
ete´sian
E´than
eth´ane
eth´a-nol
Eth´el
eth´ene
e´ther
ethe´re-al
ethe-re-al´i-ty
ethe´re-al-ize
ethe´re-ous
ether´i-fy
ether-iza´tion
e´ther-ize
eth´ic
eth´i-cal
eth´ics
eth-i-on´ic
Ethi-o´pia
eth´moid
eth-moi´dal
eth´nic
eth´ni-cal
eth´ni-cal-ly
eth-nic´i-ty
eth´no-cen´tric
eth-no-graph´ic

eth-no-graph´i-cal
eth-nol´o-gist
eth-nol´o-gy
eth´yl
eth´yl-ate
eth´yl-ene
eth´yl-e´nic
ethyl´ic
ethyl´i-dene
ethy´nyl
e´ti-o-late
e´ti-o-log´i-cal
et´i-quette
Etrus´can
e´tude
et-y-mo-log´i-cal
et-y-mol´o-gist
et-y-mol´o-gy
eu´ca-lypt
eu´ca-lyp´tic
eu-ca-lyp´tole
eu-ca-lyp´tus
eu´cha-ris
Eu´cha-rist
Eu-cha-ris´tic
Eu´clid
Eu-clid´e-an
Eu-do´ra
Eu´gene
eu-gen´ic
eu´ge-nol
eu-he´mer-ism
eu-lo´gia
eu´lo-gies
eu´lo-gist
eu´lo-gis´tic
eu-lo-gis´ti-cal
eu´lo-gize
eu´lo-gy
Eu´nice
eu-on´y-mous
eu-on´y-my
eu-pep´tic
eu´phe-mism
eu´phe-mis´tic
eu´phe-mize
eu-phon´ic
eu-pho´ni-ous
eu-pho´ni-um

eu´pho-ny
eu-phor´bia
eu-pho´ria
eu-phor´ic
Eu-phra´tes
Eur-a´sian
Eu-re´ka
Eu-rip´i-des
Eu´rope
Eu-ro-pe´an
eu-ryth´mics
Eu-sta´chian
eu-then´ics
evac´u-ate
evac-u-a´tion
evac´u-ee´
evade´
evad´ing
eval´u-ate
eval-u-a´tion
ev-a-nes´cence
ev´a-nes´cent
evan´gel
e´van-gel´ic
e´van-gel´i-cal
Evan´ge-line
evan´ge-lism
evan´ge-list
evan´ge-lis´tic
evan´ge-lize
Ev´ans-ton
Ev´ans-ville
evap´o-ra-ble
evap´o-rate
evap´o-rat-ing
evap-o-ra´tion
evap´o-ra-tive
evap´o-ra-tor
eva´sion
eva´sive
evec´tion
e´ven
e´ven-fall
e´ven-hand-ed
e´ven-ing
e´ven-ly
e´ven-ness
e´ven-song
event´

event´ful
e´ven-tide
even´tu-al
even´tu-al´i-ty
even´tu-al-ly
even´tu-ate
ev´er
Ev´er-est
Ev´er-ett
Ev´er-glades
ev´er-green
ev-er-last´ing
ev-er-last´ing-ly
ev-er-more´
ever´sion
evert´
ever´tor
ev´ery
ev´ery-body
ev´ery-day
ev´ery-one
ev´ery-thing
ev´ery-where
evict´
evic´tion
evic´tor
ev´i-dence
ev´i-denc-ing
ev´i-dent
ev´i-den´tial
ev´i-dent-ly
e´vil
e´vil-do-er
e´vil-ly
e´vil—mind-ed
e´vil-ness
evince´
evinc´ible
evinc´ing
evis´cer-ate
evis-cer-a´tion
evis´cer-a-tor
ev´i-ta-ble
ev´o-ca-ble
evo-ca´tion
evoc´a-tive
e´vo-ca-tor
evoc´a-to-ry
evoke´

evok´ing
ev´o-lute
ev-o-lu´tion
ev-o-lu´tion-ary
ev-o-lu´tion-ist
evolve´
evolve´ment
evolv´ing
evul´sion
ewe
ew´er
ex-ac´er-bate
ex-ac´er-bat-ing
ex-ac-er-ba´tion
ex-act´
ex-act´able
ex-act´ing
ex-ac´tion
ex-ac´ti-tude
ex-act´ly
ex-act´ness
ex-ag´ger-ate
ex-ag´ger-at-ed
ex-ag-ger-a´tion
ex-ag´ger-a-tive
ex-ag´ger-a-tor
ex-alt´
ex-al-ta´tion
ex-alt´ed
ex-alt´er
ex-am´
ex-am´in-able
ex-am-i-na´tion
ex-am´ine
ex-am´in-er
ex-am´ple
ex-an´i-mate
ex-an-the´ma
ex-as´per-ate
ex-as´per-at-ing
ex-as´per-at-ing-ly
ex-as-per-a´tion
Ex-cal´i-bur
ex´ca-vate
ex-ca-va´tion
ex´ca-va-tor
ex-ceed´
ex-ceed´ing
ex-ceed´ing-ly
ex-cel´
ex-celled´
ex´cel-lence
ex´cel-len-cy
ex´cel-lent
ex´cel-lent-ly
ex-cel´ling
ex-cel´si-or
ex-cept´
ex-cept´able
ex-cept´ing
ex-cep´tion
ex-cep´tion-able
ex-cep´tion-al
ex-cep´tion-al-ly
ex´cerpt
ex-cerpt´er
ex-cerpt´ible
ex-cess´
ex-ces´sive
ex-ces´sive-ly
ex-change´
ex-change´able
ex-chang´ing
ex´che-quer
ex-cip´i-ent
ex´cis-able
ex´cise
ex-ci´sion
ex-cit-abil´i-ty
ex-cit´able
ex-cit´ant
ex-ci-ta´tion
ex-cit´a-tive
ex-cite´
ex-cit´ed-ly
ex-cite´ment
ex-cit´er
ex-cit´ing
ex-ci´tor
ex-claim´
ex-cla-ma´tion
ex-clam´a-to-ry
ex-clud´able
ex-clude´
ex-clud´ing
ex-clu´sion
ex-clu´sive
ex-clu´sive-ly
ex-clu´sive-ness
ex-cog´i-tate
ex-com-mu´ni-cate
ex-com-mu-ni-ca´tion
ex-co´ri-ate
ex-co-ri-a´tion
ex´cre-ment
ex-cres´cence
ex-cres´cen-cy
ex-cres´cent
ex-cre´ta
ex-crete´
ex-cre´tion
ex´cre-to-ry
ex-cru´ci-ate
ex-cru´ci-at-ing
ex-cru-ci-a´tion
ex-cul-pa´tion
ex-cul´pa-to-ry
ex-cur´rent
ex-cur´sion
ex-cur´sion-ist
ex-cur´sive
ex-cus´able
ex-cu´sa-to-ry
ex-cuse´
ex-cus´ing
ex´e-crate
ex-e-cra´tion
ex´e-cut-able
ex-ec´u-tant
ex´e-cute
ex-e-cu´tion
ex-e-cu´tion-er
ex-ec´u-tive
ex-ec´u-tor
ex-ec´u-to´ri-al
ex-ec´u-to-ry
ex-ec´u-trix
ex-em´plar
ex-em´pla-ry
ex-em´pli-fy
ex-empt´
ex-empt´ible
ex-emp´tion
ex-emp´tive
ex´er-cis-able
ex´er-cise
ex´er-cis-er

ex-ert´
ex-er´tion
ex-ert´ive
Ex´e-ter
ex-fo-li-a´tion
ex´hal´ant
ex-ha-la´tion
ex´hale
ex-haust´
ex-haust´ed
ex-haust´er
ex-haust´ible
ex-haus´tion
ex-haus´tive
ex-liaus´tive-ly
ex-haust´less
ex-hib´it
ex-hi-bi´tion
ex-hi-bi´tion-er
ex-hi-bi´tion-ism
ex-hi-bi´tion-ist
ex-hib´i-tive
ex-hib´i-tor
ex-hib´i-to-ry
ex-hil´a-rant
ex-hil´a-rate
ex-hil-a-ra´tion
ex-hil´a-ra-tive
ex-hil´a-ra-to-ry
ex-hort´
ex-hor-ta´tion
ex-hort´a-to-ry
ex-hu-ma´tion
ex-hume´
ex´i-gen-cies
ex´i-gen-cy
ex´i-gent
ex´ile
ex-il´ic
ex-ist´
ex-is´tence
ex-is´tent
ex-is-ten´tial
ex-is-ten´tial-ism
ex-is-ten´tial-ist
ex´it
ex-o-don´tist
ex´o-dus
ex´o-gam´ic
ex-og´e-nous
ex-og´a-my
ex-on´er-ate
ex-on-er-a´tion
exo-pep´ti-dase
ex-oph´a-gy
ex-oph-thal´mic
ex-or´bi-tance
ex-or´bi-tant
ex-or-ci-sa´tion
ex´or-cise
ex´or-cis-er
ex´or-cism
ex´or-cist
exo-skel´e-tal
exo-skel´e-ton
ex-os-to´sis
ex´o-ter´ic
ex´o-ther´mic
ex-ot´ic
ex-ot´i-cal-ly
ex-ot´i-cism
ex-pand´
ex-pand´able
ex-pand´er
ex-panse´
ex-pan-si-bil´i-ty
ex-pan´si-ble
ex-pan´sion
ex-pan´sive
ex par´te
ex-pa´ti-ate
ex-pa-ti-a´tion
ex-pa´tri-ate
ex-pa-tri-a´tion
ex-pect´
ex-pect´able
ex-pect´an-cy
ex-pect´ant
ex-pect´ant-ly
ex-pec-ta´tion
ex-pect´a-tive
ex-pec´to-rant
ex-pec´to-rate
ex-pec-to-ra´tion
ex-pec´to-ra-tor
ex-pe´di-en-cy
ex-pe´di-ent
ex-pe´di-ent-ly
ex´pe-dite
ex´pe-dit-er
ex´pe-dit-ing
ex-pe-di´tion
ex-pe-di´tion-ary
ex-pe-di´tious
ex-pe-di´tious-ly
ex-pel´
ex-pel´la-ble
ex-pel´lant
ex-pelled´
ex-pel-lee´
ex-pel´ling
ex-pend´
ex-pend´able
ex-pend´i-ture
ex-pense´
ex-pen´sive
ex-pen´sive-ly
ex-pe´ri-ence
ex-pe´ri-enced
ex-pe´ri-enc-ing
ex-pe´ri-en´tial
ex-per´i-ment
ex-per´i-men´tal
ex-per´i-men´tal-ly
ex-per-i-men-ta´tion
ex-per´i-ment-er
ex-pert´
ex-per-tise´
ex´pert-ly
ex´pert-ness
ex´pi-ate
ex-pi-a´tion
ex´pi-a-tor
ex´pi-a-to-ry
ex-pi-ra´tion
ex-pir´ato-ry
ex-pire´
ex-pired´
ex-pir´ing
ex-pi´ry
ex-plain´
ex-plain´able
ex-pla-na´tion
ex-plan´a-tive
ex-plan´a-to-ry
ex´ple-tive
ex-plic´a-ble

ex´pli-cate
ex-pli-ca´tion
ex-plic´a-tive
ex´pli-ca-tor
ex-plic´a-to-ry
ex-plic´it
ex-plic´it-ly
ex-plode´
ex-plod´er
ex-plod´ing
ex-ploit´
ex-ploit´able
ex-ploi-ta´tion
ex-ploit´ative
ex-ploit´er
ex-plo-ra´tion
ex-plor´ative
ex-plor´a-to-ry
ex-plore´
ex-plor´er
ex-plor´ing
ex-plo´sion
ex-plo´sive
ex-plo´sive-ly
ex-po´nent
ex-po-nen´tial
ex-po-nen´tial-ly
ex-po´ni-ble
ex´port
ex-port´able
ex-por-ta´tion
ex-port´er
ex-pose´
ex-po-sé´
ex-posed´
ex-pos´er
ex-pos´ing
ex-po-si´tion
ex-pos´i-tive
ex-pos´i-tor
ex-pos´i-to-ry
ex post fac´to
ex-pos´tu-late
ex-pos-tu-la´tion
ex-pos´tu-la-to-ry
ex-po´sure
ex-pound´
ex-pound´er
ex-press´
ex-press´age
ex-press´er
ex-press´ible
ex-press´ing
ex-pres´sion
ex-pres´sion-ism
ey´pres´sion-less
ex-pres´sive
ex-pres´sive-ly
ex-press´ly
ex-press´man
ex-pres´sor
ex-press´way
ex-pro´pri-ate
ex-pro-pri-a´tion
ex-pro´pri-a-tor
ex-pul´sion
ex-pul´sive
ex-punge´
ex´pur-gate
ex-pur-ga´tion
ex´pur-ga´tor
ex-pur´ga-to-ry
ex-quis´ite
ex-quis´ite-ly
ex-sert´
ex-sert´ed
ex-ser´tile
ex-ser´tion
ex´sic-cate
ex-sic-ca´tion
ex-stip´u-late
ex´tant
ex-tem´po-ral
ex-tem´po-rary
ex tem´po-re
ex-tem-po-ri-za´tion
ex-tem´po-rize
ex-tem´po-riz-er
ex-tend´
ex-tend´ed
ex-tend´er
ex-tend´ible
ex-ten-si-bil´i-ty
ex-ten´si-ble
ex-ten´sion
ex-ten´si-ty
ex-ten´sive
ex-ten´sive-ly
ex-ten´sor
ex-tent´
ex-ten´u-ate
ex-ten´u-at-ing
ex-ten-u-a´tion
ex-ten´u-a-tor
ex-ten´u-a-to-ry
ex-te´ri-or
ex-te´ri-or-ize
ex-ter´mi-nate
ex-ter-mi-na´tion
ex-ter´mi-na-tive
ex-ter´mi-na-tor
ex-ter´mi-na-to-ry
ex-ter´nal
ex-ter-nal´i-ty
ex-ter´nal-ize
ex-ter´nal-ly
ex´ter-o-cep´tive
ex´ter-o-cep´tor
ex-tinct´
ex-tinc´tion
ex-tinc´tive
ex-tin´guish
ex-tin´guish-able
ex-tin´guish-er
ex-tol´
ex-tolled´
ex-tol´ling
ex-tor´sion
ex-tort´
ex-tort´ed
ex-tor´tion
ex-tor´tion-ate
ex-tor´tion-er
ex-tor´tion-ist
ex-tort´ive
ex´tra
ex´tract
ex-tract´able
ex-trac´tion
ex-trac´tive
ex-trac´tor
ex´tra-cur-ric´u-lar
ex´tra-dit-able
ex´tra-dite
ex´tra-dit-ing
ex-tra-di´tion
ex´tra-ju-di´cial

ex-tral´i-ty
ex´tra-mar´i-tal
ex´tra-mu´ral
ex-tra´ne-ous
ex-traor´di-nar´i-ly
ex-traor´di-nary
ex-trap´o-late
ex´tra-sen´so-ry
ex-tra-ter-ri-to´ri-al
ex-trav´a-gance
ex-trav´a-gant
ex-trav-a-gan´za
ex-trav-a-sa´tion
ex-treme´
ex-treme´ly
ex-tre´mism
ex-trem´ist
ex-trem´i-ty
ex-tric´a-ble
ex´tri-cate
ex-tri-ca´tion
ex-trin´sic
ex-trin´si-cal-ly
ex-tro-ver´sion
ex´tro-vert
ex´tro-vert-ish
ex-tro-ver´tive
ex-trude´
ex-trud´er
ex-trud´ing
ex-tru´si-ble
ex-tru´sion
ex-tru´sive
ex-tu´ber-ance
ex-u´ber-ance
ex-u´ber-ant
ex-u´ber-ate
ex´u-date
ex-u-da´tion
ex-ude´
ex-ult´
ex-ult´ance
ex-ult´ant
ex-ul-ta´tion
ex-ult´ing-ly
ex´urb
ex-ur´ban-ite
eye´ball
eye´bright
eye´brow
eye´cup
eyed
eye´glass
eye´hole
eye´ing
eye´lash
eye´let
eye´lid
eye´piece
eye´shade
eye´sight
eye´sore
eye´spot
eye´strain
eye´strings
eye´tooth
eye´wash
eye´wa-ter
eye´wink
eye´wit-ness
Eze´ki-el
Ez´ra

F

Fa´bi-an
fa´ble
fa´bled
fab´ric
fab´ri-cant
fab´ri-cate
fab-ri-ca´tion
fab´ri-ca-tor
fab´u-list
fab´u-lous
fab´u-lous-ly
fa-çade´
face´able
faced
fac´er
fac´et
fac´et-ed
fa-ce´tious
fa´cial
fa´ci-end
fa´cient
fa´ci-es
fac´ile
fac´ile-ness
fa-cil´i-tate
fa-cil´i-ties
fa-cil´i-ty
fac´ing
fac-sim´i-le
Fac´tice
fac-tic´i-ty
fac´tion
fac´tion-al
fac´tious
fac´tious-ly
fac-ti´tious
fac-ti´tious-ly
fac´ti-tive
fac´tor
fac´tor-age
fac-to´ri-al
fac´to-ries
fac-tor-i-za´tion
fac´tor-ize
fac´to-ry
fac´tu-al
fac´tu-al-ly
fac´ul-ties
fac´ul-ty
fad
fad´dist
fade
fade´—out
fad´er
fa-e´na
Fa-en´za
fa´er-ie
fa´ery
Fa´gin
fag´ot
fag´ot-ing
Fahr´en-heit
fail´ing
fail´ing-ly
faille
fail´ure
fai´ne-ance
fai´ne-an-cy
fai´ne-ant
faint
faint´ed
faint´heart-ed

faint´ish
faint´ly
faint´ness
fair´ies
fair´lead
fair´ly
fair´—mind-ed
fair´ness
fair´sized
fair´—spo-ken
fair´way
fair´y
fair´y-hood
fair´y-land
fair´y-like
fair´y tale
fait ac-com-pli´
faith´ful
faith´ful-ly
faith´ful-ness
faith´less
fak´er
fa-kir´
fal´con
fal´con-er
fal´con-et´
fal´con-ry
fal´de-ral
Falk´land
fal´la-cies
fal-la´cious
fal-la´cious-ly
fal´la-cy
fall´en
fal-li-bil´i-ty
fal´li-ble
fall´ing
Fal-lo´pi-an
fall´out
fal´low
false´heart-ed
false´hood
false´ly
false´ness
fal-set´to
fal-set´tos
false´work
fal-si-fi-ca´tion
fal´si-fied
fal´si-fi-er
fal´si-fy
fal´si-fy-ing
fal´si-ty
Fal´staff
fal´ter
fal´ter-ing
famed
fa-mil´ial
fa-mil´iar
fa-mil-iar´i-ty
fa-mil-iar-iza´tion
fa-mil´iar-ize
fa-mil´iar-ly
fam´i-lies
fam´i-ly
fam´ine
fam´ish
fa´mous
fa´mous-ly
fa-nat´ic
fa-nat´i-cal
fa-nat´i-cism
fan´cied
fan´ci-er
fan´cies
fan´ci-ful
fan´ci-ful-ly
fan´cy
fan´cy—free
fan´cy-ing
fan´cy-work
fan-dan´go
Fan´euil
fan´fare
fanged
fanned
fan´ning
Fan´ny
fan´on
fan´tail
fan-ta´sia
fan´ta-size
fan-tas´tic
fan-tas´ti-cal
fan-tas´ti-cal-ly
fan´ta-sy
fan´tod
fan´wise
far´away
farce
far´cial
far´ci-cal
far-ci-cal´i-ty
far´cy
far´del
fare-well´
far´—famed
far´fetched
far´—flung
Far´go
fa-ri´na
farm´er
farm´house
farm´ing
farm´stead
farm´yard
far´—off
Fa-rouk´
Far´ra-gut
far´—reach-ing
far´row
far´see-ing
far´sight-ed
far´ther
far´ther-most
far´thest
far´thing
fas-cic´u-lar
fas-cic´u-late
fas´ci-nate
fas´ci-nat-ed
fas´ci-nat-ing
fas´ci-nat-ing-ly
fas-ci-na´tion
fas´ci-na-tor
fas-cine´
fas´cism
Fas´cist
fash´ion
fasb´ion-able
fash´ion-ably
fast-ten
fas´ten-er
fas´ten-ing
fas-tid´i-ous
fas-tid´i-ous-ness
fas-tig´i-ate

fas-tig´i-at-ed
fas-tig´i-um
fast´ing
fast´ness
fa´tal
fa´tal-ism
fa´tal-ist
fa-tal-is´tic
fa-tal-is´ti-cal-ly
fa-tal´i-ty
fa´tal-ly
fat´ed
fate´ful
fa´ther
fa´ther-hood
fa´ther—in—law
fa´ther-land
fa´ther-less
fa´ther-like
fa´ther-li-ness
fa´ther-ly
fath´om
fath´om-able
Fa-thom´e-ter
fath´om-less
fat´i-ga-ble
fa-tigue´
fa-tigued´
fa-tigu´ing
fa-tigu´ing-ly
Fat´i-ma
fat´ling
fat´ness
fat´ten
fat´ten-er
fat´ter
fat´tish
fat´ty
fa-tu´i-ty
fau´cal
fau´cal-ize
fau´ces
fau´cet
fau´cial
fault´find-ing
fault´i-er
fault´i-ly
fault´i-ness
fault´less
fault´y
faun
fau´na
fau´nal
fau´vism
faux pas
fa´vism
fa´vor
fa´vor-able
fa´vor-ably
fa´vored
fa´vor-er
fa´vor-ite
fa´vor-it-ism
fa´vus
fawn
faze
fe´al-ty
fear´ful
fear´ful-ly
fear´less
fear´less-ly
fear´less-ness
fear´some
fea´sance
fea-si-bil´i-ty
fea´si-ble
feath´er
feath´er-bed-ding
feath´er-brain
feath´ered
feath´er-edge
feath´er-head
feath´er-ing
feath´er-less
feath´er-weight
feath´ery
fea´ture
fea´tured
fea´ture-less
feb-ri-fa´cient
fe-brif´er-ous
fe-brif´ic
fe-brif´u-gal
feb´ri-fuge
feb´rile
fe-bril´i-ty
Feb´ru-ary
fe´cal
fe´ces
feck´less
fec´u-la
fec´u-lence
fec´u-lent
fe´cund
fed´er-a-cy
fed´er-al
fed´er-al-ese
fed´er-al-ism
fed´er-al-ist
fed-er-al-is´tic
fed-er-al-iza´tion
fed´er-al-ize
fed´er-ate
fed-er-a´tion
fed´er-a-tive
fe-do´ra
fee´ble
fee´ble-heart-ed
fee´ble-mind-ed
fee´ble-ness
fee´bly
feed´er
feed´ing
feed pipe
feed´stuff
feed valve
feel´er
feel´ing
feel´ing-ly
feign
feigned
feign´er
feint
feld´spar
feld´spath-ic
fe-lic´i-tate
fe-lic-i-ta´tion
fe-lic´i-tous
fe-lic´i-ty
fe´lid
fe´line
fe-lin´i-ty
fell´er
fell´ness
fel´low
fel´low-ship
fel´on

fe-lo´ni-ous
fe-lo´ni-ous-ly
fel´o-ny
felt´er
felt´ing
fe´male
fe-mal´i-ty
fem´i-na-cy
fem-i-nal´i-ty
fem-i-ne´i-ty
fem´i-nine
fem-i-nin´i-ty
fem´i-nism
fem´i-nist
fe-min´i-ty
fem´i-nize
femme fa-tale´
fem´o-ral
fe´mur
fence
fenced
fence´less
fenc´er
fen´ci-ble
fenc´ing
fend´er
fen-es-tel´la
fe-nes´tra
fen´es-trat-ed
fen-es-tra´tion
fen´nel
fe-ra´cious
fe-rac´i-ty
fe´ral
Fer´ber
fer´—de—lance´
Fer´di-nand
fer´e-to-ry
fer´i-ty
fer-ment´
fer-ment´able
fer-men-ta´tion
fer-ment´a-tive
fer-ment´er
fer-men´tive
Fer-nan´dez
fe-ro´cious
fe-ro´cious-ness
fe-roc´i-ty
Fer-ra´ra
fer´ret
fer´ret-er
fer´ri-age
fer´ric
fer´ried
fer´ries
fer-rif´er-ous
fer-ri-na´trite
Fer´ris wheel
fer´ro-cene
fer-ro-mag-net´ic
fer-ro-mag´net-ism
fer-rom´e-ter
fer´rous
fer´rule
fer´ry
fer´ry-boat
fer´ry-ing
fer´ry-man
fer´tile
fer-til´i-ty
fer´til-iz-able
fer-til-iza´tion
fer´til-ize
fer´til-iz-er
fer´u-la
fer´ule
fer´ven-cy
fer´vent
fer´vent-ly
fer´vid
fer´vor
fes´cue
fes´tal
fes´ter
fes´ti-val
fes´tive
fes-tiv´i-ty
fes-toon´
fe´tal
fe-ta´tion
fetch´ing
fete
fe´tial
fe´ti-ci´dal
fe´ti-cide
fet´id
fe-tid´i-ty
fe-tip´a-rous
fet´ish
fet´ish-ism
fet´lock
fe´tor
fet´ter
fet´tle
fe´tus
feud
feu´dal
feu´dal-ism
feu-dal-iza´tion
feu´dal-ize
feu´dal-ly
feu´da-to-ry
feud´ist
fe´ver
fe´vered
fe´ver-ish
fe´ver-ish-ly
fe´ver-ous
few´ness
fi-an-cé´
fi-an-cée´
fi-as´co
fi´at
fib´bing
fi´ber
fi´ber-board
Fi´ber-glas
fi´ber-ize
fi´bril
fi´bril-lary
fib-ril-la´tion
fi´bril-lous
fi´brin
fi´broid
fi´bro-in
fi-bro´ma
fi-bro´sis
fi-bro-si´tis
fi´brous
fib´u-la
fib´u-lar
fick´le
fick´le-ness
fic´tile
fic´tion
fic´tion-al

fic-ti´tious
fic-ti´tious-ly
fid´dle
fid´dler
fid´dle-sticks
fid´dling
fi-del´i-ty
fid´get
fid´gety
fi-du´cial
fi-du´cial-ly
fi-du´ci-ary
field day
field´er
field glass
Field´ing
field mar´shal
field´piece
field´work-er
fiend
fiend´ish
fierce
fierce´ly
fierce´ness
fierc´er
fi´eri-ness
fi´ery
fi-es´ta
fif-teen´
fif-teenth´
fif´ti-eth
fif´ty
fight´er
fight´ing
fig´ment
fig´ur-al
fig´u-rant
fig´u-rate
fig´u-rate-ly
fig-u-ra´tion
fig´u-ra-tive
fig´u-ra-tive-ly
fig´ure
fig´ured
fig´ure-head
figu-rine´
fil´a-ment
fil-a-men´ta-ry
fil´a-men´tous

fi´lar
fi-lar´ia
fi-lar´i-al
fil-a-ri´a-sis
fil´a-ture
fil´bert
filch´er
fil´er
fi-let´
fi-let´ mi-gnon´
fil´i-al
fil-i-a´tion
fil´i-bus-ter
fil´i-ci´dal
fil´i-cide
fil´i-gree
fil´ing
Fil-i-pi´no
fill´er
fil´let
fill´ing
fil´lip
fil´ly
film´i-er
film´y
fil´ter
fil-ter-abil´i-ty
fil´ter-able
fil´ter-er
filth´i-er
filth´i-ly
filth´i-ness
filth-y
fil-tra-bil´i-ty
fil´tra-ble
fil´trate
fil-tra´tion
fin´able
fi-na´gle
fi-na´gling
fi´nal
fi-nal´e
fi´nal-ist
fi-nal´i-ty
fi´nal-ly
fi-nance´
fi-nan´cial
fi-nan´cial-ly
fin-an-cier´

fi-nanc´ing
fin´back
find´er
find´ing
fine´ly
fine´ness
fin´er
fin´ery
fine´spun´
fi-nesse´
fin´ger
fin´ger-nail
fin´ger-print
fin´ger-tip
fin´i-al
fin´i-cal
fin´ick-ing
fin´icky
fin´is
fin´ish
fin´ished
fin´ish-er
fi´nite
Fin´land
Finn´ish
fin´ny
fiord
fire ant
fire´arm
fire´ball
fire´box
fire´brand
fire´brick
fire´bug
fire´crack-er
fire´dog
fire´—eat-er
fire en´gine
fire´fly
fire´less
fire´light
fire´man
fire´place
fire´plug
fire´pow-er
fire´proof
fire´—re-sist´ant
fire´side
fire´stone

fire tow´er
fire´trap
fire wall
fire´wa-ter
fire´wood
fire´works
fir-ing
fir´kin
fir´ma-ment
fir-ma-men´tal
fir-man´
firm´er
firm´ly
firm´ness
fir´ry
first aid
first´born
first´hand
first´ling
first´ly
first´—rate
first wa´ter
fis´cal
fis´cal-ly
fish´er
fish´er-man
fish´ery
fish´hook
fish´i-ly
fish´i-ness
fish´ing
fish´line
fish´mon-ger
fish´tail
fish´wife
fish´worm
fish´y
fis´sile
fis´sion
fis´sion-able
fis´sure
fis´sur-ing
fist´ic
fist´i-cuff
fis´tu-la
fis´tu-lous
fitch´et
fit´ful
fit´ful-ly
fit´ly
fit´ness
fit´ted
fit´ter
fit´ting
fit´ting-ly
Fitz-ger´ald
Fitz-pat´rick
five´fold
fiv´er
fix´able
fix´ate
fix-a´tion
fix´a-tive
fixed
fix´ed-ly
fix´ed-ness
fix´ing
fix´ture
fizz´er
fiz´zle
fiz´zling
fjord
flab´ber-gast
flab´bi-er
flab´bi-ness
flab´by
flac´cid
flac´cid-ly
flac´on
flag´el-lant
flag´el-late
flag-el-la´tion
flag´el-la-tor
fla-gel´lum
flagged
flag´ging
flag´man
flag´on
flag´pole
fla´grance
fla´gran-cy
fla´grant
fla´grant-ly
flag´ship
flag´staff
flag´stone
flail
flair
flaked
flak´i-er
flak´ing
flak´y
flam´beau
flam-boy´ance
flam-boy´an-cy
flam-boy´ant
flamed
fla´men
fla-men´co
flame´proof
flam´ing
fla-min´go
fla-min´gos
flam´ma-ble
flam´y
Flan´ders
flange
flank´er
flan´nel
flap´er-on
flap´jack
flapped
flap´per
flap´ping
flare
flare´—up
flar´ing
flash´board
flash´i-ly
flash´i-ness
flash´ing
flash´light
flash´y
flat´boat
flat´—bot´tomed
flat´foot
flat´head
flat´iron
flat´ness
flat´ten
flat´ter
flat´ter-er
flat´ter-ing
flat´tery
flat´top
flat´ware
flat´worm

flaunt
flaunt´er
flaunt´ing
flau´tist
Fla´via
fla´vin
fla´vone
fla´vor
fla´vor-ing
flaw´less
flax´en
flax´seed
flax´y
flay´er
flea´bite
flec´tion
flec´tion-al
fledged
fledg´ing
fledg´ling
fleece
fleec´i-er
fleec´i-ness
fleec´y
flee´ing
fle´er
fleet´ing
fleet´ly
fleet´ness
Flem´ing
Flem´ish
flesh´—col-ored
flesh´i-ness
flesh´less
flesh´ly
flesh´pot
flesh´y
fletch´er
fletch´er-ize
fleur—de—lis´
flew
flex-i-bil´i-ty
flex´i-bi-lize
flex´ible
flex´ion
flex-om´e-ter
flex´or
flex-u-os´i-ty
flex´u-ous
flex´ur-al
flex´ure
flib´ber-ti-gib-bet
flick´er
flick´er-ing-ly
flick´ery
fli´er
flight
flight´i-ness
flight´less
flight´y
flim´si-ly
flim´si-ness
flim´sy
flinched
flinch´ing
fling´ing
flint´lock
flint´y
flip´pan-cy
flip´pant
flipped
flip´per
flip´ping
flir-ta´tion
flir-ta´tious
flirt´er
flirt´ing-ly
flit´ter
flit´ting
fliv´ver
float´able
float´er
float´ing
floc´cu-lence
floc´cu-lent
flocked
flock´y
flogged
flog´ging
flood´gate
flood´light
flood´proof
floor´ing
floor´walk-er
flopped
flop´pier
flop´ping
flop´py
flo´ral
Flor´ence
Flor´en-tine
flo-res´cence
flo-res´cent
flo´ret
flo´ri-at-ed
flo-ri-cul´tur-al
flo´ri-cul-ture
flor´id
Flor´i-da
flo-rid´i-ty
flor´id-ly
flor´id-ness
flor´u-lent
floss´y
flo´tage
flo-ta´tion
flo-til´la
flot´sam
flounce
flounced
flounc´ing
floun´der
floun´dered
floun´der-ing
flour´ish
flour´ished
flour´ish-ing
flout´ed
flout´ing
flow´er
flow´ered
flow´er-et
flow´er-i-ly
flow´er-ing
flow´er-pot
flow´ery
flown
fluc´tu-ant
fluc´tu-ate
fluc´tu-at-ed
fluc´tu-at-ing
fluc-tu-a´tion
flu´en-cy
flu´ent
fluff´i-er
fluff´i-ly
fluff´i-ness

fluff'y
flu'id
flu-id'ic
flu-id'i-ty
fluk'y
flun'ky
fluo-chlo'ride
flu-or-ap'a-tite
flu'o-rene
flu'o-re-nyl
flu-o-resce'
flu-o-res'ce-in
flu-o-res'cence
flu-o-res'cent
flu-o-resc'ing
flu-or'ic
flu'o-ri-date
flu-o-ri-da'tion
flu'o-ride
flu'o-ri-dize
flu'o-ri-nate
flu'o-rine
flu'o-rite
flu-o-ro-ace'tic
flu'o-ro-graph'ic
flu-o-rog'ra-phy
flu-o-ro'sis
flu'or-spar
flur'ried
flur'ries
flur'ry
flur'ry-ing
Flush'ing
flus'ter
flus-ter-a'tion
flus-tra'tion
flut'ed
flut'er
flut'ing
flut'ist
flut'ter
flut'tered
flut'ter-ing
flut'tery
flu'vi-al
flu'vi-a-tile
flu-vi-ol'o-gy
flux'ible
fly'away
fly'catcher
fly'er
fly'ing
fly'ing fish
fly'leaf
fly'speck
fly'trap
fly'weight
fly'wheel
foamed
foam'i-er
foam'ing
Foam'ite
foam'y
fo'cal
fo-cal-iza'tion
fo'cal-ize
fo'cused
fo'cus-er
fo'cus-ing
fod'der
fog'gi-er
fog'gi-ly
fog'gy
fog'horn
fo'gy
foiled
foil'ing
foist'ed
fold'ed
fold'er
fold'ing
fo'li-age
fo'li-ate
fo'li-at-ed
fo-li-a'tion
fo'lic
fo'lio
fo'li-o-late
folk'lore
folksy
folk'way
fol'li-cle
fol-lic'u-lar
fol-lic'u-lin
fol-lic-u-li'tis
fol'low
fol'lowed
fol'low-er
fol'low-ing
fol'low—through
fol'low—up
fol'ly
fo-ment'
fo-men-ta'tion
fo-ment'er
fon'dant
fon'dle
fon'dled
fon'dler
fon'dling
fond'ly
fond'ness
fon-du'
fon-due'
Fon-taine-bleau'
food'stuff
fool'ery
fool'har-di-ness
fool'har-dy
fool'ing
fool'ish
fool'ish-ly
fool'ish-ness
fool'proof
fools'cap
foot'age
foot'ball
foot'bath
foot'board
foot'bridge
foot'ed
foot'fall
foot'hill
foot'hold
foot'ing
foot'less
foot'light
foo'tling
foot'loose
foot'man
foot'mark
foot'note
foot'pad
foot'path
foot'print
foot'room
foot' rule

foot´sore
foot´step
foot´stool
foot´walk
foot´wear
foot´work
foot´worn
for´age
for´aged
for´ag-er
for´ag-ing
for-as-much
for´ay
for-bade´
for-bear´
for-bear´ance
for-bid´
for-bid´dance
for-bid´den
for-bid´der
for-bid´ding
for-bore´
forced
force´ful
force´meat
for´ceps
forc´er
forc´ible
forc´ibly
forc´ing
ford´able
for-do´
fore´arm
fore´bear
fore-bode´
fore-bod´ing
fore´cast
fore´cast-er
fore´cas-tle
fore-close´
fore-clo´sure
fore-doom´
fore´fa-ther
fore´fin-ger
fore´foot
fore´front
fore´go-ing
fore´gone´
fore´ground
fore´hand
fore´hand-ed
fore´head
for´eign
for´eign-er
fore-judge´
fore´know´
fore´knowl-edge
fore´la-dy
fore´land
fore´leg
fore´lock
fore´man
fore´mast
fore´most
fore´name
fore´noon
fo-ren´sic
fo-ren´si-cal
fo-ren´si-cal-ly
fore-or-dain´
fore-or´di-nate
fore-or-di-na´tion
fore´part
fore´paw
fore´quar-ter
fore-run´
fore´run-ner
fore´sail
fore-saw´
fore-see´
fore-see´able
fore-see´ing
fore-seen´
fore-shad´ow
fore-short´en
fore´sight
fore´skin
fore-stall´
fore´stay
for´est-ed
for´est-er
for´est-ry
fore´taste
fore-tell´
fore-tell´er
fore-tell´ing
fore´thought
fore-told´
for-ev´er
for-ev-er-more´
fore-warn´
fore´wom-an
fore´word
for´feit
for´feit-er
for´feit-ure
for´fi-cate
for-gath´er
for-gave´
forge
forge´able
forg´er
for´gery
for-get´
for-get´ful
for-get´ful-ness
for´ge-tive
for-get´—me—not
for-get´ta-ble
for-get´ting
forg´ing
for-give´
for-giv´en
for-give´ness
for-giv´ing
for-go´
for-go´ing
for-gone´
for-got´
for-got´ten
fo´rint
forked
fork´ed-ly
for-lorn´
for-lorn´ly
for´mal
for´mal-ism
for´mal-ist
for-mal-is´tic
for-mal´i-ty
for´mal-ize
for´mal-iz-er
for´mal-iz-ing
for´mal-ly
form-am´ide
form-am´i-dine
for´mat

for´mate
for-ma´tion
form´a-tive
form´a-zan
for´mer
for´mer-ly
for´mic
For-mi´ca
for´mi-cary
for´mi-cate
for´mi-cide
for-mi-da-bil´i-ty
for´mi-da-ble
form´less
For-mo´sa
for´mu-la
for´mu-la-ri´zable
for´mu-lar-iza´tion
for´mu-lar-ize
for´mu-late
for-mu-la´tion
for´mu-la-tor
for-nent´
for´ni-cate
for-ni-ca´tion
for´ni-ca-tor
for´nix
for-sake´
for-sak´en
For´se-ti
for-sook´
for-sooth´
for-swear´
for-sworn´
for-syth´ia
fort
for´ta-lice
forte
forth
forth´com-ing
forth´right
forth-with´
for´ti-eth
for-ti-fi-ca´tion
for´ti-fied
for´ti-fi-er
for´ti-fy
for-tis´si-mo
for´ti-tude
fort´night
fort´night-ly
for´tress
for-tu´i-tism
for-tu´i-tous
for-tu´i-ty
For-tu´na
for´tu-nate
for´tu-nate-ly
For-tu-na´tus
for´tune
for´ty
fo´rum
for´ward
for´ward-er
for´ward-ly
for´ward-ness
fos´sa
fos´sick
fos´sil
fos-sil-if´er-ous
fos-sil-i-za´tion
fos´sil-ize
fos-so´ri-al
fos´ter
foul
fou-lard´
foul´ly
foul´ness
foun-da´tion
found´er
found´ling
found´ries
found´ry
foun´tain
foun´tain-head
foun´tain pen
four´fold
four´—foot-ed
Fou´ri-er
four´—post-er
four´ score
four´some
four´square
four-teen´
four-teenth´
fourth
fowl
Fow´ler
fowl´er
fox´glove
fox´hole
fox´hound
fox´i-ness
fox´tail
fox ter´ri-er
fox´—trot
fox´y
foy´er
fra´cas
frac´tion
frac´tion-al
frac´tion-ary
frac´tion-ate
frac-tion-a´tion
frac´tious
frac-tog´ra-phy
frac´tur-al
frac´ture
frag´ile
fra-gil´i-ty
frag´ment
frag-men´tal
frag´men-tary
frag-men-ta´tion
frag´ment-ed
frag´ment-ize
fra´grance
fra´gran-cy
fra´grant
frail
frail´ties
fram-be´sia
framed
fram´er
frame´—up
frame´work
fram´ing
franc
fran-çais´
Fran´ces
fran´chise
Fran´cis
fran´co-lin
Fran-co´nia
Fran´co-phile
Fran-co-pho´bia
fran-gi-bil´i-ty

fran´gi-ble
fran-gi-pan´i
frank
Frank´en-stein
Frank´fort
frank´furt-er
fran´kin-cense
Frank´ish
Frank´lin
frank´lin-ite
frank´ly
frank´ness
fran´tic
fran´ti-cal-ly
frap-pé´
fra´ter
fra-ter´nal
fra-ter´ni-ty
frat-er-ni-za´tion
frat´er-nize
frat´ri-ci-dal
frat´ri-cide
frau
fraud´u-lence
fraud´u-len-cy
fraud´u-lent
fraud´u-lent-ly
fräu´lein
Fraun´ho-fer
frayed
fraz´zle
fraz´zling
freak´ish
freck´le
freck´led
Fred-er-i´ca
Fred´er-ick
Fred´er-icks-burg
free´board
free´boot-er
free´born
freed´man
free´dom
free´hand
free´hold
free´ly
free´man
free´martin
Free´mason

fre´er
fre´est
free´stone
free´think-er
free´way
free-wheel´ing
free´will
freez´er
freez´ing
freight´age
freight´er
frem´i-tus
Fre´mont
fre´nal
French´man
Fre-neau´
fre-net´ic
fre´num
fren´zied
fren´zy
Fre´on
fre´quen-cy
fre´quent
fre-quen-ta´tion
fre´quent-ly
fres´co
fres´co-er
fres´coes
fresh´en
fresh´et
fresh´ly
fresh´man
fresh´ness
fresh´wa´ter
Fres´no
fret´ful
fret´ful-ly
fret´saw
fret´ted
fret´ty
fret´work
Freud´i-an
fri´ar
fri´ary
Fri´bourg
fric-as-see´
fric´tion
fric´tion-al
Fri´day

fried´cake
friend´less
friend´li-er
friend´li-ly
friend´li-ness
friend´ly
friend´ship
frieze
frig´ate
fright
fright´en
fright´ened
fright´en-ing
fright´ful
fright´ful-ly
fright´ful-ness
frig´id
fri-gid´i-ty
frill´ing
frill´y
fringed
fring´ing
fring´y
Fris´co
Fri´sian
fris´ket
frisk´i-er
frisk´i-ly
frisk´y
frit´il-lary
frit´ter
friv´ol
fri-vol´i-ty
friv´o-lous
frizz´ing
friz´zle
friz´zling
friz´zly
frock
frog´bit
frog´man
frol´ic
frol´icked
frol´ick-ing
frol´ic-some
front´age
fron´tal
fron-ta´lis
fron-tier´

fron-tiers´man
fron´tis-piece
front´less
front´let
front—page
frost´bite
frost´bit-ten
frost´i-ness
frost´ing
frost´proof
frost´y
froth´i-er
froth´i-ly
froth´y
fro´ward
frowned
frown´ing
frow´zi-er
frow´zi-ness
frow´zy
froze
fro´zen
fruc´tose
fru´gal
fru-gal´i-ty
fru´gal-ly
fru´gal-ness
fruit´age
fruit´er
fruit´er-er
fruit´ful
fruit´ful-ness
fruit´i-ness
fru-i´tion
fruit´less
fruit-y
frump´y
frus´trate
frus´trat-ed
frus´trat-er
frus´trat-ing
frus-tra´tion
fru´ti-cose
fry´er
fuch´sia
fu´cu-lose
fu´cus
fud´dle
fud´dling
fudge
fu´el
fu´el-er
fu-ga´cious
fu-ga´cious-ly
fu-gac´i-ty
fu´gi-tive
fu´gle
fu´gle-man
fugue
Füh´rer
Fu-ji-ya´ma
ful-fill´
ful-fill´ing
ful-fill´ment
ful´gu-rant
ful-gu-ra´tion
ful´gu-rite
ful´gu-rous
fu-lig´i-nous
full´back
full´—blown´
full´—dress´
Ful´ler
fuller
full´—fledged´
full´ness
ful´ly
ful´mar
ful´mi-nate
ful´mi-nat-ing
ful-mi-na´tion
ful´mi-na-tor
ful´mi-na-to-ry
ful-min´ic
ful´mi-nous
ful-min-u´ric
ful´some
ful´some-ness
Ful´ton
fu-mar´ic
fu´ma-role
fu´ma-to-ry
fum´ble
fum´bler
fum´bling
fumed
fu´mi-gate
fu´mi-gat-ing
fu-mi-ga´tion
fu´mi-ga-tor
fum´ing
fum´y
func´tion
func´tion-al
func´tion-ary
func´tion-ate
fun-da-men´tal
fun-da-men´tal-isin
fun-da-men´tal-ist
fun-da-men´tal-ly
fu´ner-al
fu´ner-ary
fu-ne´re-al
fu-nest´
fun´gal
fun´gi
fun-gi-bil´i-ty
fun´gi-ble
fun´gi-ci-dal
fun´gi-cide
fun-gif´er-ous
fun-giv´o-rous
fun´goid
fun-gos´i-ty
fun´gous
fun´gus
full´gus—proof
fu´ni-cle
fu-nic´u-lar
fun´nel
fun´neled
fun´nel-ing
fun´ni-er
fun´ni-ly
fun´ny
fur
fur´bish
fur´bish-er
fur´cal
fur´cu-lum
fu´ri-bund
fu´ri-ous
fu´ri-ous-ly
fur´long
fur´lough
fur´nace
fur´nish

fur´nish-er
fur´nish-ings
fur´ni-ture
fu´ror
fu´rore
furred
fur´ri-er
fur´ri-ness
fur´ring
fur´row
fur´ry
fur´ther
fur´ther-ance
fur´ther-more
fur´ther-most
fur´thest
fur´tive
fur´tive-ly
fu´run-cle
fu-run-cu-lo´sis
fu´ry
fu´ryl
furze
fu´sain
fus´cous
fuse
fused
fu-see´
fu´sel
fu´se-lage
fu-si-bil´i-ty
fu´si-ble
fu´sil
fu´si-lier
fu´sil-lade
fus´ing
fu´sion
fuss´i-ly
fuss´y
fus´tic
fus´ti-er
fus´ti-ly
fus´ty
fu´tile
fu´tile-ly
fu-til´i-ty
fut´ur-al
fu´ture
fu´tur-ism
fu´tur-ist
fu-tu´ri-ty
fuze
fuzz´i-ness
fuzz´y

G

gab´ar-dine
ga´ba-rit´
gab´bing
gab´ble
gab´bro
gab´by
ga-belle´
gab´er-dine
ga´bi-on
ga´ble
ga´bled
ga´bling
Ga-bon´
Ga´bri-el
ga´by
gad´about
gad´ding
gad´fly
gad´get
gad´ge-teer´
gad´get-ry
ga´did
ga´doid
Gael´ic
gaff´er
gage
gag´er
gagged
gag´ging
gai´ety
gai´ly
gai´ner
gain´ful
gain´said
gain´say
Gains´bor-ough
gait
gait´ed
gait´er
Ga´ius
ga´la
ga-lac´tic
Gal´a-had
gal´an-tine
ga-lan´ty
Ga-la´pa-gos
Gal-a-te´a
Ga-la´tia
Ga-la´tian
ga´lax
ga-lax´i-al
gal´axy
ga´lea
ga´le-ate
ga-le´gine
ga-le´i-form
Ga´len
ga-le´na
ga-le´nic
ga-len´i-cal
Ga-li´cia
Gal´i-lee
gal´in-gale
gal´lant
gal´lant-ly
gal´lant-ries
gal´lant-ry
gal´lery
gal´ley
gal´leys
gal´liard
Gal´lic
gall´ing
gal´li-ot
gal´li-um
gal´li-vant
gal´lon
gal-loon´
gal´lop
gal´loped
gal´lop-er
gal´lop-ing
Gal´lo-way
gal´lows
gall´stone
gal´op
ga-lore´
ga-losh´
ga-losh´es
Gals´wor-thy

gal-van´ic
gal´va-nism
gal-va-ni-za´tion
gal´va-nize
gall-va-niz-ing
gal-va-nom´e-ter
gal´va-no-met´ric
gal-va-nom´e-try
gal-van´o-scope
gal-va-not´ro-pism
Gal´ves-ton
Gal´way
gam-ba´do
gam´be-son
Gam´bia
gam´bier
gam´bit
gam´ble
gam´bler
gam´bling
gam´bol
gam´boled
gam´bol-ing
gam´brel
game´cock
game´keep-er
game´ness
game´some
game´ster
ga-met´ic
ga-met´i-cal-ly
gam´e-toid
gam´ic
gam´i-ly
gam´in
gam´i-ness
gam´ing
gam´ma
gam´mer
gam´mon
gam´ut
gam´y
gan´der
Gan´dhi
gan´dy danc-er
Gan´ges
gan´gly
gang´plank
gan´grene
gan´gre-nous
gang´ster
gang´way
gan´net
gant´let
gan-try
gaol
gaped
gap´er
gap´ing
gapped
gap´ping
ga-rage´
Ga-rand´
gar´bage
gar´ble
gar´bled
gar´bling
gar-çon´
gar´den
gar´den-er
gar-de´nia
Gar´di-ner
gar´di-nol
Gard´ner
Gar´eth
Gar´field
gar´fish
Gar-gan´tua
gar-gan´tu-an
gar´gle
gar´gled
gar´gling
gar´goyle
Gar-i-bal´di
gar´ish
gar´land
gar´lic
gar´licky
gar´ment
gar´ner
gar´net
gar´ni-er-ite
gar´nish
gar´nish-ee´
gar-nish-ee´ing
gar´nish-er
gar´nish-ment
gar´ni-ture
gar´ret
Gar´rick
gar´ri-son
gar-rote´
gar-rot´ed
gar-rot´ing
gar-ru´li-ty
gar´ru-lous
gar´ru-lous-ly
gar´ter
Gar´y
gas´con-ade´
gas´e-ous
gashed
gas´house
gas´i-fi-able
gas-i-fi-ca´tion
gas´i-fy
gas´ket
gas´light
gas mask
gas-o-line´
gas-om´e-ter
gas´o-met´ric
gas´ser
gas´sing
gas sta´tion
gas´sy
gas´tight
gas-trec´to-my
gas´tric
gas-tri´tis
gas-tro-en-ter-i´tis
gas-tro-in-tes´ti-nal
gas-trol´o-ger
gas-tro-nom´ic
gas-tro-nom´i-cal
gas-tron´o-my
gas´tro-pod
gas´tru-la
gas´works
gate
gate´post
gate´way
gath´er
gath´ered
gath´er-ing
gat´ing
Gat´ling

gauche
gauche´ly
gau´cho
gau´chos
gaud´ery
gaud´i-er
gaud´i-ly
gaud´i-ness
gaud´y
gauge
gauged
gaug´er
gaug´ing
Gau-guin´
gau´lei-ter
Gaull´ist
gaunt´let
gaunt´ly
gauss
Gau-tier´
gauze
gauz´i-ness
gauz´y
ga-vage´
gav´el
gav´el-er
ga´vi-al
ga-votte´
Ga-wain´
gawk´i-ly
gawk´i-ness
gawk´y
gay´ness
Ga´za
ga-ze´bo
gazed
ga-zelle´
gaz´er
ga-zette´
gaz´et-teer´
gaz´ing
gear´ing
gear´shift
gear´ wheel
gee´zer
Gei´ger
gei´sha
gel
gel´a-tin
gel´a-tin-ase
ge-lat´i-nate
ge-lat-i-ni-za´tion
ge-lat´i-nize
ge-lat´i-niz-er
ge-lat´i-no-chlo´ride
ge-lat´i-nous
ge-la´tion
geld´ed
geld´ing
gel´id
ge-lid´i-ty
gel´ig-nite
gelled
gel´ling
gel´ose
gel-se´mic
gel-se´mi-um
Ge-ma´ra
gem´i-nate
gem-i-na´tion
gem´i-na-tive
Gem´i-ni
gem´ma
gem´mate
gem-ma´tion
gemmed
ge-mot´
gen´darme
gen´der
gene-a-log´i-cal
gene-a-log´i-cal-ly
gene-al´o-gist
gene-al´o-gy
gen-ecol´o-gy
gen´era
gen´er-al
gen-er-a-lis´si-mo
gen-er-al´i-ty
gen-er-al-iza´tion
gen´er-al-ize
gen´er-al-ly
gen´er-al-ship
gen´er-ate
gen´er-at-ing
gen-er-a´tion
gen´er-a-tive
gen´er-a-tor
gen´er-a´trix
ge-ner´ic
ge-ner´i-cal
ge-ner´i-cal-ly
gen-er-os´i-ty
gen´er-ous
gen´er-ous-ly
gen´e-sis
ge-net´
ge-net´ic
ge-net´i-cal
ge-net´i-cist
ge-net´ics
Ge-ne´va
Gen´e-vese´
Gen´e-vieve
Gen´ghis Khan
ge´nial
ge-ni-al´i-ty
ge´nial-ly
gen´ic
ge-nic´u-late
ge´nie
gen´in
gen´i-tal
gen´i-ti´val
gen´i-tive
gen´i-ture
ge´nius
Gen´oa
gen´o-ci´dal
gen´o-cide
Gen´o-ese´
ge´nome
ge´no-type
ge´no-typ´ic
gen´re
gen-teel´
gen-teel´ly
genth´ite
gen´tian
gen´tian-in
gen´tile
gen-til´i-ty
gen-tis´ic
gen´ti-sin
gen´tle
gen´tle-man
gen´tle-ness
gen´tle-wom-an

gen´tlest
gent´ly
gen´trice
gen´try
gen´u-flect
gen-u-flec´tion
gen´u-flec´to-ry
gen´u-ine
gen´u-ine-ly
gen´u-ine-ness
ge´nus
ge´o-des´ic
ge-od´e-sy
ge´o-det´ic
ge´o-det´i-cal
ge-od´ic
Ge-o-dim´e-ter
Geoff´rey
ge-og´e-nous
ge´og-nos´tic
ge-og´ra-pher
ge-o-graph´ic
ge-o-graph´i-cal
ge-o-graph´i-cal-ly
ge-og´ra-phy
ge-o-log´ic
ge-o-log´i-cal
ge-ol´o-gist
ge-ol´o-gy
ge-o-mag-net´ic
ge-o-mag´net-ism
ge-om´e-ter
ge-o-met´ric
ge-o-met´ri-cal
ge-om-e-tri´cian
ge-om´e-triz-er
ge-om´e-try
ge-o-phys´i-cal
ge-o-phys´i-cist
ge´o-phys´ics
ge-o-po-lit´i-cal
ge-o-pol-i-ti´cian
ge-o-pol´i-tics
George´town
Geor´gia
ge-o-tech-nol´o-gy
ge-ot-ri-cho´sis
ge´o-trop´ic
Ge-raint´

Ger´ald
Ger´al-dine
ge-ran´ic
ge-ra´ni-ol
ge-ra´ni-um
ge-ra´nyl
Ge-rard´
ge-rat´ic
ge´rent
Ger´hard
ger-i-a-tri´cian
ger-i-at´rics
Ger´man
ger-man´der
ger-mane´
Ger-man´ic
ger´ma-nite
ger-ma´ni-um
Ger´ma-ny
ger´mi-ci´dal
ger´mi-cide
ger´mi-nal
ger´mi-nant
ger´mi-nate
ger-mi-na´tion
ger´mi-na-tor
germ´proof
Ge-ron´i-mo
ger´ry-man-der
Ger´trude
ger´und
ge-run´di-al
ger´un-di´val
ge-run´dive
Ge´ry-on
ges´so
ge-sta´po
ges´tate
ges´tat-ing
ges-ta´tion
ges´tic
ges-tic´u-late
ges-tic-u-la´tion
ges-tic´u-la-tive
ges-tic´u-la-to-ry
ges´ture
ges´tur-ing
get´away
get´ta-ble

get´ting
Get´tys-burg
get´up
gey´ser
Gha´na
ghar´ry
ghast´li-ness
ghast´ly
gha´zi
gher´kin
ghet´to
ghost
ghost´like
ghost´li-ness
ghost´ly
ghost´write
ghost´writ-ten
ghoul´ish
gi´ant
giaour
gib´ber
gib´ber-ish
gib´bet
gib´bon
Gib´bons
gibe
gib´ing
gib´let
Gi-bral´tar
Gib´son
gid´di-ly
gid´di-ness
gid´dy
Gid´e-on
gift´ed
gi-gan-te´an
gi-gan-tesque´
gi-gan´tic
gi-gan´tism
gig´gle
gig´gling
gig´o-lo
gig´ot
Gil´bert
gild
gil´der
gild´ing
gilled
gil´ly-flow-er

gilt
gilt´—edged
gim´bal
gim´baled
gim´let
gim´mal
gim´mick
gin´ger
gin´ger-bread
gin´ger-li-ness
gin´ger-ly
gin´ger-snap
gin´gery
ging´ham
gin-gi´val
gin-gi-vi´tis
gink´go
gin´seng
Gio-van´ni
gi-raffe´
Gi-rard´
gir´a-sol
gird´er
gird´ing
gir´dle
gir´dler
gir´dling
girl´hood
girl´ish
girl´ish-ly
girth
gist
gi-tal´in
gi-tox-i-gen´in
git´tern
give´away
giv´en
giv´er
giv´ing
giz´zard
gla-bel´la
gla´brate
gla´brous
gla-cé´
gla´cial
gla´cial-ist
gia´cial-ly
gla´ci-ate
gla-ci-a´tion
gla´cier
gla-ci-ol´o-gy
gla´cis
glad´den
glad´i-ate
glad´i-a-tor
glad´i-a-to´ri-al
gia-di-o´lus
glad´ly
glad´ness
glad´some
Glad´stone
Glad´ys
glair
glam´o-rous
glam´our
glance
glanc´ing
glan´ders
glan´du-lar
glan´du-lous
glare
glar´ing
glar´y
Glas´gow
glass´es
glass´ful
glass´i-ly
glass´ine´
glass´i-ness
glass´ware
glass´y
Glas-we´gian
glau-co´ma
glau-co´ma-tous
glau´co-nite
glau´cous
glazed
glaz´er
gla´zier
glaz´ing
gleam
gleam´ing
gleam´y
glean´er
glean´ing
glebe
glee´ful
glee´man
Glen-gar´ry
glen´oid
gli´al
glib´best
glib´ly
glide
glid´er
glid´ing
glim´mer
glim´mer-ing
glim´mer-ing-ly
glimpse
glimps´ing
glis´ten
glis´ter
glit´ter
glit´ter-ing
glit´ter´y
gloam´ing
gloat´ing
glob´al
gio-bal´i-ty
glob´al-ly
glo´boid
glo´bose
glob´u-lar
glob-u-lar´i-ty
glob´ule
glob´u-lin
glom´er-ate
glom-er-a´tion
glo-mer´u-lar
glom´er-ule
gloom´i-ly
gloom´i-ness
gloom´ing
gloom´y
glo´ria
glo-ri-fi-ca´tion
glo´ri-fied
glo´ri-fi-er
glo´ri-fy
glo´ri-fy-ing
glo´ri-ole
glo´ri-ous
glo´ri-ous-ly
glo´ry
glos´sal
glos-sar´i-al

glos´sa-rist
glos´sa-ry
gloss´er
glos´si-ly
glos´si-ness
gloss´me-ter
gloss´y
Glouces´ter
Glouces´ter-shire
gloved
glov´er
glov´ing
glow´er
glow´er-ing
glow´er-ing-ly
glow´ing
glow´worm
glu-car´ic
glu´ci-num
glu´ci-tol
glu´ci-tyl
glu´co-nate
glu´con´ic
glu-co-pro´tein
glu-co´sa-mine
glu´cose
glu-co´si-dase
glu´co-side
glu-cu-ron´ic
glu-cu´ro-nide
glue
glued
glu´ey
glu´i-ness
glu´ing
glum´ly
glum´ness
glut´acon´ic
glu´ta-mate
glu-tam´ic
glu´ta-mine
glu´ten
glu´te-nin
glu´ti-nous
glu´ti-nous-ly
glut´ted
glut´ton
glut´ton-ous
glut´tony
gly-ce´mia
gly-ce´mic
glyc´er-ate
gly-cer´ic
glyc´er-ide
glyc´er-in
glyc´er-ol
glyc´er-yl
gly-cid´ic
glyc´i-dol
gly´cine
gly´co-gen
gly-co-gen´ic
gly-co-gen-ol´y-sis
gly-co-gen-o-lyt´ic
gly´col
gly-col´y-sis
gly-co-lyt´ic
gly-co-pro´tein
gly´cyl
glyph´ic
glyp´tic
gnarl
gnarled
gnarl´y
gnash
gnat
gnat´like
gnaw
gnawed
gnaw´ing
gneiss
gneiss´oid
gnome
gno´mic
gnom´ish
gno´sis
gnos´tic
gnos´ti-cism
gnu
Go´a
goad´ed
goal´keep-er
goa-tee´
goat´herd
goat´skin
goat´suck-er
gob´bet
gob´ble
gob´bler
gob´bling
Go´bi
gob´let
gob´lin
go´by
god´child
god´daugh-ter
god´dess
god´fa-ther
god´—fear-ing
god´—giv-en
god´head
Go-di´va
god´less
god´less-ness
god´like
god´li-ness
god´ly
god´moth-er
god´par-ent
god´send
god´ship
god´son
God´speed´
God´win
Goeb´bels
go´er
Goe´thals
Goe´the
go-et´ic
gog´gle
gog´gling
gog´let
Goi-del´ic
go´ing
goi´ter
goi´tro-gen´ic
goi-tro-ge-nic´i-ty
Gol-con´da
gold´beat-er
gold´brick
gold´en
gold´en—haired
gold´en-rod
gold´—filled
gold´finch
gold´fish
gold´i-locks

gold´smith
gold stick
golf´er
Gol´gi
gol´iard
Go-li´ath
gom´bo
gom´er-al
Go-mor´rah
go´nad
go-na´di-al
gon´do-la
gon-do-lier´
Gon´er-il
gon´fa-lon
gon-fa-lon-ier´
gon´fa-non
go-nid´i-al
go-nid´i-um
go-ni-om´e-ter
go-ni-o-met´ric
go-ni-om´e-try
go´ni-on
go´ni-um
gon´of
gon-or-rhe´a
gon-or-rhe´al
goo´ber
good—by´
good—for—noth´ing
good´—heart-ed
good hu´mor
good—hu´mored
good´ies
good´ish
good´li-ness
good´ly
good´man
good´ness
good night
good´wife
good will
good´y
Good´year
goof´y
goo´gly
goo´gol
goose
goose´ber-ry
goose´flesh
goose´foot
goose´herd
goose´neck
goose´—step
go´pher
Gor´di-an
Gor´don
gored
gorge
gor´geous
gor´geous-ly
gorg´er
gor´ger-in
gor´get
gorg´ing
Gor´gon
gor´gon-ize
Gor-gon-zo´la
gor´hen
go-ril´la
gor´ing
gor´lic
gor´y
gos´ling
gos´pel
gos´pel-er
gos´sa-mer
gos´san
gos´sip
gos´sip-ing
gos´sip-red
gos´sipy
gos-soon´
gos-syp´i-trin
Goth´am
Goth´ic
got´ten
goug´ing
gou´lash
gourd
gour´mand
gour´mand-ism
gour´man-diz-er
gour´met
gout
gout´y
gov´ern
gov´ern-able
gov´ern-ance
gov´er-nante
gov´er-ness
gov´ern-ment
gov-ern-men´tal
gov´er-nor
gov´er-nor—gen´er-al
gov´er-nor-ship
gow´an
gowned
grab´bing
grab´ble
Grac´chi
grace´ful
grace´ful-ly
grace´ful-ness
grace´less
grac´ile
grac´ing
gra´cious
gra´cious-ly
grack´le
gra´date
gra-da´tion
gra-da´tion-al
grad´a-to-ry
grad´ed
grad´er
gra´di-ent
gra´dine
grad´ing
grad´u-al
grad´u-al-ism
grad´u-al-ist
grad´u-al-ly
grad´u-ate
grad´u-at-ing
grad-u-a´tion
grad´u-a-tor
graf-fi´to
graft´age
graft´er
graft´ing
gra´ham
Grain´ger
grain´ing
grain´y
gral-la-to´ri-al
gram

gram´a
gra-mer´cy
gram´ine
gra-min´e-ous
gram´mar
gram-mar´i-an
gram´mar school
gram-mat´i-cal
gram´pus
Gra-na´da
gran-a-dil´la
gra´na-ry
gran´dam
grand´aunt
grand-child
grand´chil-dren
grand-daugh-ter
gran´deur
grand´fa-ther
gran-dil´o-quence
gran-dil´o-quent
gran´di-ose
gran-di-os´i-ty
gran-di-o´so
grand´moth-er
grand´par-ent
Grand Rap´ids
grand´son
grand´stand
grang´er
gran´ger-ize
gran´ite
gran´ite-ware
gra-nit´ic
gran´it-ite
gran´ny
grant-ee´
grant´er
Gran´tha
grant´or
grants´ite
gran´u-lar
gran-u-lar´i-ty
gran´u-late
gran´u-lat-ed
gran´u-lat-er
gran´u-lat-ing
gran-u-la´tion
gran´u-la-tor
gran´ule
grape´fruit
grape juice
grap´ery
grape´shot
grape´skin
grape´vine
graph´ic
graph´i-cal
graph´i-cal-ly
graph´ite
gra-phit´ic
graph´i-tize
grap´nel
grap´ple
grap´pling
grap´y
grasped
grasp´er
grasp´ing
grasp´ing-ly
grass´hop-per
grass´land
grass´y
grate
grate´ful
grate´ful-ly
grat´er
Gra´tian
grat-i-fi-ca´tion
grat´i-fied
grat´i-fi-er
grat´i-fy
grat´i-fy-ing
grat´in
grat´ing
gra´tis
grat´i-tude
gra-tu´i-ties
gra-tu´i-tous
gra-tu´i-ty
grat´u-late
grat-u-la´tion
grat´u-la-to-ry
grave´dig-ger
grav´el
grav´eled
grav´el-ly
grave´ly
grav´en
grave´ness
Gra´ven-stein
grav´er
grave´stone
grave´yard
grav´i-cep´tor
grav´id
gra-vid´i-ty
grav-i-met´ric
gra-vim´e-try
grav´i-sphere
grav´i-tate
grav´i-tat-er
grav´i-tat-ing
grav-i-ta´tion
grav-i-ta´tion-al
grav´i-ta-tive
grav-i-tom´e-ter
grav´i-ton
grav´i-ty
gra-vure´
gra´vy
gray
gray´beard
gray´ish
gray´ling
gray´ness
graze
graz´er
gra´zier
graz´ing
grease´wood
greas´i-ly
greas´i-ness
greas´y
great
Great Brit´ain
great´coat
great gross
great´heart-ed
great´ly
great´ness
greave
Gre´cian
greed´i-ly
greed´i-ness
greed´y
Gree´ley

green´back
green´bri-er
green´ery
green´—eyed
green´horn
green´house
green´ing
green´ish
Green´land
green´ling
green´ness
green´room
green´sward
Green´wich
green´wood
greet´ing
greg´a-rine
gre-gar´i-ous
gre-gar´i-ous-ness
Gre-go´ri-an
Greg´o-ry
grem´lin
Gre-na´da
gre-nade´
gren´a-dier
gren´a-dine´
Gre-no´ble
Gresh´am
Gre´ta
Gret´chen
Gret´na
grey
grey´hound
grib´ble
grid´dle
grid´dle cake
grid´iron
grief
grief´strick-en
griev´ance
grieve
griev´ing
griev´ing-ly
griev´ous
griev´ous-ly
grif´fin
grif´fon
grift´er
grill
gril´lage
grille
grill´room
grim´ace
gri-mal´kin
grime
grim´i-er
grim´ly
grim´mer
grim´ness
grim´y
grin
grin-de´lia
grind´er
grind´ery
grind´ing
grind´stone
grin´go
grin´gos
grinned
grin´ning
grip
gripe
griph´ite
grip´ing
grippe
grip´ping
Gri-sel´da
gri-sette´
gris´kin
gris´li-er
gris´li-ness
gris´ly
gris´tle
gris´tly
grist´mill
grit´ting
grit´ty
griz´zle
griz´zled
griz´zly
groaned
groan´ing-ly
gro´cer
gro´cer-ies
gro´cery
grog´gery
grog´gi-ness
grog´gy
grog´ram
grog´shop
groin
grom´met
grooms´man
groove
groov´ing
grope
gro´per
grop´ing
gros´beak
gross´ly
gross´ness
gro-tesque´
gro-tesque´ly
gro-tes´que-rie´
grot´to
grouch´i-ness
grouch´y
ground crew
ground´er
ground floor
ground´hog
ground´less
ground´ling
ground plan
ground´work
grou´per
grouse
grous´er
grout´er
grov´el
grov´eled
grov´el-er
grov´el-ing
grow´er
grow´ing
growl´er
grown´—up
growth
grubbed
grub´bi-er
grub´bing
grub´by
grub´stake
grudge
grudg´ing
grudg´ing-ly
gru´el

gru´el-ing
grue´some
gruff´ly
grum´ble
grum´bler
grum´bling
gru´mose
grump´i-ness
grump´y
Grun´dy
grun´ion
grunt´er
grunt´ing
Gru-yère´
gry´phon
gua-ca-mo´le
Gua-dal-ca-nal´
Gua´de-loupe´
Guam
gua´na-mine
gua´nase
gua´ni-dine
gua-nif´er-ous
gua´nine
gua´no
guar´an-tee´
guar-an-tee´ing
guar´an-ties
guar´an-tor
guar´an-ty
guard´ed
guard´ed-ly
guard´house
guard´i-an
guard´i-an-ship
guard´room
guards´man
Gua-te-ma´la
gua´va
gu´ber-na-to´ri-al
gud´geon
Gud´run
Guelph
gue-non´
guer´don
Guern´sey
guer-ril´la
guess´ing
guess´work

guest
guest´ room
guf-faw´
Gui-an´a
guid´able
guid´ance
guide´book
guide´post
guid´ing
Gui´do
gui´don
guild
guil´der
guild´hall
guile´ful
guile´less
Guil´ford
guil´le-mot
guil´lo-tine
guilt
guilt´i-ly
guilt´i-ness
guilt´less
guilt´y
guin´ea
Guin´ea
Guin´e-vere
guise
gui-tar´
gul´let
gull-ibil´i-ty
gull´ible
gul´lies
Gul´li-ver
gul´ly
gu´lose
gu-los´i-ty
gulped
gum´bo
gum´drop
gum´ma
gummed
gum´mi-ness
gum-mo´sis
gum´mous
gum´my
gump´tion
gum´shoe
gun´boat

gun´fire
gun´flint
Gun´ite
gun´lock
gun´man
gun´met-al
gun´nel
gun´ner
gun´nery
gun´ning
gun´ny
gun´pow-der
gun´run-ner
gun´shot
gun´smith
gun´stock
Gun´ther
gun´wale
gup´py
gur-gi-ta´tion
gur´gle
gur´glet
gur´gling
gu-ru´
gush´er
gush´ing
gush´y
gus´set
gus-ta´tion
gus´ta-to-ry
Gus-ta´vus
gust´i-ly
gust-to
gust´y
Gu´ten-berg
gut´ta
gut´ted
gut´ter
gut´ter-snipe
gut´ting
gut´tur-al
gut-tur-al´i-ty
Guy-an´a
guy´ing
guz´zle
guz´zling
gym-na´si-arch
gym-na´si-ast
gym-na´si-um

gym´nast
gym-nas´tic
gym-nas´tics
gym-nos´o-phist
gym´no-sperm
gym´no-sper´mous
gym-no-stom´a-tous
gy-ne´co-crat
gy-ne-co-log´i-cal
gy-ne-col´o-gist
gy-ne-col´o-gy
gyn-i-at´rics
gyn´ics
gypped
gyp´ping
gyp´sum
gyp´sy
gy´rate
gy-ra´tion
gy´rat-ing
gy´ra-tor
gy´ra-to-ry
gyr´fal-con
gy´ro-com-pass
gy-rom´e-ter
gy´ro-plane
gy´ro-scope
gy-ro-scop´ic
gy-ro-sta´bi-liz-er
gy-ro-stat´ics
gy´rus

H

ha´be-as
ha´be-as cor´pus
hab´er-dash-er
hab´er-dash-ery
hab´it
hab-it-abil´i-ty
hab´it-able
hab´i-tant
hab´i-tat
hab-i-ta´tion
ha-bit´u-al
ha-bit´u-al-ly
ha-bit´u-ate
ha-bit-u-a´tion
hab´i-tude
ha-bit´ué
ha-ci-en´da
hack´le
hack´ler
hack´ly
hack´man
hack´ney
hack´neyed
hack´saw
had´dock
Ha´des
Ha´dri-an
ha´fiz
Ha-ga´nah
Ha´gar
Ha´gen
hag´fish
hag-ga´da
hag´gard
hag´gis
hag´gle
hag´gling
Hague
Hai´fa
Hai´le Se-las´sie
hail´stone
hail´storm
hair´breadth
hair´brush
hair´cloth
hair´cut
hair´dress-er
hair´i-ness
hair´like
hair´line
hair oil
hair´pin
hair´split-ter
hair´split-ting
hair´spring
hair ton´ic
hair´y
Hai´ti
Ha-la´kah
ha-la´tion
hal´a-zone
hal´berd
hal´cy-on
half
half´back
half´—baked´
half´—breed
half´heart-ed
half hour
half´—mast´
half´—moon´
half note
half´pence
half´pen-ny
half step
half ti´tle
half´tone
half´—truth´
half´way
half´—wit´ted
hal´i-but
hal´ide
hal´i-dom
Hal´i-fax
hal´ite
hal-i-to´sis
hal´i-tus
hal´lan
hal-lel´
hal-le-lu´jah
Hal´ley
hal´ling
hall´mark
hal-loo´
hal´low
hal´lowed
hal´lowed-ness
Hal´low-een´
hal-lu´ci-nate
hal-lu-ci-na´tion
hal-lu´ci-na-to-ry
hal-lu-ci-no´sis
hal´lux
hall´way
ha´lo
hal´o-gen
hal´o-gen-ate
hal-o-hy´drin
ha-lom´e-ter
hal´o-phyte
ha-lot´ri-chite
hal´ter
hal´tere

halt´ing
halt´ing-ly
halve
halves
halv´ing
hal´yard
Ham-ble-to´ni-an
Ham´burg
ham´burg-er
Ham´e-lin
Ham´il-ton
Ham´ite
ham´let
Ham´mar-skjöld
ham´mer
ham´mer-head
ham´mer-less
ham´mock
Ham´mond
Hamp´den
ham´per
Hamp´shire
Hamp´ton
ham´ster
ham´string
ham´strung
Ham´tramck
han´a-per
Han´cock
hand´bag
hand´ball
hand´bill
hand´book
hand´cart
hand´cuff
hand´ed
Han´del
hand´ful
hand´hold
hand´i-cap
hand´i-capped
hand´i-cap-ping
hand´i-craft
hand´i-crafts-man
hand´i-ly
hand´i-ness
hand´i-work
hand´ker-chief
han´dle
han´dle-bar
han´dler
hand´less
han´dling
hand´made´
hand´maid
hand´maid-en
hand´picked´
hand´rail
hand´saw
hand´shake
hand´some
hand´some-ly
hand´som-est
hand´spike
hand´spring
hand´work
hand´worked´
hand´writ-ing
hand´y
hand´y-man
han´gar
hang´dog
hang´er
hang´ing
hang´man
hang´nail
hang´out
hang´over
han´ker
han´ker-ing
Han´kow´
Han´na
Han´nah
Han´ni-bal
Ha-noi´
Han´o-ver
Han´sard
han´sel
han´som
Ha´nuk-kah
hap´haz´ard
hap´less
hap´ly
hap´pen
hap´pen-ing
hap´pi-ly
hap´pi-ness
hap´py
Haps´burg
hap´to-glo´bin
har´a—kir´i
ha-rangue´
ha-rangued´
ha-rangu´er
ha-rangu´ing
ha-rass´
ha-rassed´
ha-rass´ing
ha-rass´ment
har´bin-ger
har´bor
har´bor-age
hard´en
hard´en-er
hard´—eyed
hard´—faced
hard´—fist-ed
hard´hand-ed
hard´head
hard´head-ed
hard´—heart-ed
har´di-hood
har´di-ly
har´di-ness
Har´ding
hard´—look-ing
hard´ly
hard´ness
hard´ship
hard´tack
hard´top
hard´ware
hard´wood
har´dy
hare´bell
hare´lip
ha´rem
Har´lem
har´le-quin
har-le-quin-ade´
Har´ley
har´lot
harm´ful
harm´ful-ly
harm´less
harm´less-ly
harm´less-ness

har-mo´ni-al
har-mon´ic
har-mon´i-ca
har-mon´ics
har-mo´ni-ous
har´mo-nist
har-mo-ni-za´tion
har´mo-nize
har´mo-niz-ing
har´mo-ny
har´ness
Har´old
harp´er
harp´ing
harp´ist
har-poon´
harp´si-chord
har´py
har´que-bus
har´ri-dan
har´ri-er
Har´ri-et
Har´ris-burg
Har´ri-son
har´row
har´ry
harsh´ly
harsh´ness
har´te-beest
Hart´ford
Hart´ley
har´um—scar´um
Har´vard
har´vest
har´vester
Har´vey
ha´sen-pfef-fer
hash´ish
has´sle
has´sled
has´sock
has´tate
has´ten
hast´i-ly
hast´i-ness
hast´ing
Has´tings
hast´y
hat´band
hat´box
hat´brush
hatch´er
hatch´ery
hatch´et
hatch´ing
hatch´ment
hatch´way
hate´ful
hate´ful-ly
hat´er
hat´ing
hat´ rack
ha´tred
hat´stand
hat´ter
Hat´ter-as
haugh´ti-ly
haugh´ti-ness
haugh´ty
haul´age
haul´er
haunch
haunt´ed
haut´boy
Ha-va´na
have´lock
ha´ven
have´—not
Ha´ver-hill
hav´er-sack
hav´er-sine
hav´oc
hav´ocked
hav´ock-ing
Ha-wai´i
hawk´er
Haw´kins
haw´ser
haw´thorn
Haw´thorne
hay´cock
hay fe´ver
hay´field
hay´loft
hay´mak-er
Hay´mar-ket
hay´mow
hay´rack
hay´stack
hay´ward
hay´wire
haz´ard
haz´ard-ous
ha´zel
ha´zel-nut
ha´zi-ly
ha´zi-ness
haz´ing
ha´zy
head´ache
head´band
head´dress
head´ed
head´er
head´first´
head´gear
head´i-ness
head´ing
head´land
head´less
head´light
head´line
head´long
head´man
head´mas-ter
head´piece
head´quar-ters
head´room
head´ship
heads´man
head´spring
head´stone
head´strong
head´wait´er
head´wa-ters
head´way
head´work
head´y
heal´er
heal´ing
health´ful
health´ful-ness
health´i-er
health´i-est
health´i-ly
health´i-ness
health´y

heaped
heard
hear´er
hear´ing
heark´en
hear´say
hearse
heart´ache
heart´beat
heart´break
heart´break-ing
heart´bro-ken
heart´burn
heart´ed
heart´en
heart´felt
hearth
hearth´stone
heart´i-ly
heart´i-ness
heart´land
heart´less
heart´rend-ing
hearts´ease
heart´sick
heart´string
heart´y
heat´ed
heat´ed-ly
heat´er
heath
hea´then
heath´er
heath´y
heaved
heav´en
heav´en-ly
heav´en-ward
heav´er
heav´i-er
heav´i-ly
heav´i-ness
heave-ing
heav´y
heav´y—du´ty
heav´y—eyed
heav´y—fist-ed
heav´y—foot-ed
heav´y—hand-ed
heavy´heart-ed
heav´y-set
heav´y-weight
He-bra´ic
He´bra-ism
He´bra-ist
He´brew
Heb´ri-des
He´bron
hec´a-tomb
heck´le
heck´ler
heck´ling
hec´tare
hec´tic
hec´ti-cal-ly
hec´to-graph
hec´to-graph´ic
hec´to-li-ter
hec´to-me-ter
hec´tor
Hec´u-ba
hed´er-in
hedge´hog
hedg´er
hedge´row
hedg´ing
he´dral
heed´ful
heed´less
heed´less-ness
heel´er
heft´i-er
heft´i-est
heft´y
He´gel
He-ge´li-an
He-ge´li-an-ism
heg´e-mon´ic
he-gem´o-ny
He-gi´ra
Hei´del-berg
heif´er
Hei´fetz
height
height´en
Heim´dall
Hei´ne
hei´nous
hei´nous-ly
heir
heir´ess
heir´loom
Hei´sen-berg
Hel´e-na
he-li´a-cal
he-li-an´thus
hel´i-cal
hel´i-ces
he-lic´i-ty
hel´i-coi´dal
hel´i-con
hel´i-cop-ter
he´lio-cen´tric
he´lio-graph
he-li-og´ra-phy
he-li-om´e-ter
He´li-os
he´lio-scope
he´lio-trope
he-li-ot´ro-pism
he´lio-ty-pog´ra-phy
hel´i-port
he´li-um
he´lix
Hel´las
hell´—bent
hell´cat
Hel´len
Hel´lene
Hel-len´ic
Hel´le-nism
He´le-nis´tic
Hel´les-pont
hell´fire
hell´gram-mite
hel´lion
hell´ish
hel´lo´
hel´met
hel´met-ed
hel´minth
hel-min´thic
helms´man
He-lo-ise´
hel´ot
help´er
help´ful

help´less
help´less-ly
help´less-ness
help´mate
help´meet
Hel´sin-ki
hel´ter—skel´ter
Hel-ve´tia
Hel-vet´ic
Hel-ve´tii
hel´vite
he´vol´ic
he-ma-fi´brite
he-mag-glu´ti-nin
he´mal
he-mal-bu´men
he´ma-tal
he-ma-te´in
he-mat´ic
hem´a-tite
hem´a-tit´ic
he´ma-toid
hem´a-to-lite
he-ma-tol´o-gy
he-ma-to´ma
he-ma-tom´e-ter
hem´a-to-por´phy-rin
hem´a-tose
he-ma-to´sis
he´mic
Hem´ing-way
hem´i-sphere
hem´i-spher´ic
hem´i-spher´i-cal
hem´i-spher´i-cal-ly
hem´i-sphe´roid
hem´i-stich
hem´i-stich´al
hem´lock
he´mo-glo-bin
he-mo-glo-bi-nom´e-ter
he´moid
he´mo-lymph
he-mol´y-sin
he-mol´y-sis
he´mo-lyt´ic
he-mom´e-ter
he-mo-phil´ia
he-mo-phil´i-ac
he-mop´ty-sis
hem´or-rhage
hem´or-rhag´ic
hem´or-rhoid
hem´or-rhoi´dal
hem´or-rhoids
he-mo-sid´er-in
he-mo-sid-er-o´sis
he-mo-stat´ic
hemp´en
hemp´seed
hem´stitch
hence´forth´
hence-for´ward
hench´man
hen´coop
Hen´der-son
hen´na
hen´nery
hen´peck
he´par
hep-a-ti´tis
hep-a-ti-za´tion
He-phaes´tus
hep-ta-dec´yl
hep´ta-gon
hep-tag´o-nal
hep-tam´e-ter
hep´tar-chy
He´ra
Her-a-cle´a
Her´a-cles
Her-a-cli´tus
her´ald
he-ral´dic
her´ald-ry
herb´age
herb´al
Her-bar´ti-an
Her´bert
her´bi-ci´dal
her´bi-cide
Her´cu-les
Her´der
herd´er
herds´man
here´abouts
here-af´ter
here´by
he-red-i-ta-bil´i-ty
he-red´i-ta-ble
her-e-dit´a-ment
he-red-i-tar´i-ly
he-red´i-tary
he-red´i-ty
Her´e-ford
here´in´
here´in-af´ter
here-in-be-fore´
here-of´
her´e-sy
her´e-tic
he-ret´i-cal
here´to-fore´
here´upon´
here-with´
her´i-ot
her´i-ta-ble
her´i-tage
her´i-tance
her´i-tor
Her´man
Her´mes
her-met´ic
her-met´i-cal
her-met´i-cal-ly
her´mit
her´mit-age
her´nia
her-ni-ar´in
he´ro
Her´od
He-ro´di-as
he´roes
he-ro´ic
he-ro´i-cal
her´o-in
her´o-ine
her´o-ism
her´on
He´ron
her´pes
her´ring
her´ring-bone
Her´schel
her-self´
Hert´ford

Hert´ford-shire
hes´i-tan-cy
hes´i-tant
hes´i-tant-ly
hes´i-tate
hes´i-tat-er
hes´i-tat-ing
hes´i-tat-ing-ly
hes-i-ta´tion
hes´i-ta-tive
Hes´per-is
Hes´per-us
Hes´se
Hes´sian
het´er-o-dox
het´er-o-doxy
het´ero-dyne
het´er-oe´cious
het-er-og´a-mous
het-er-o-ge-ne´i-ty
het-er-o-ge´neous
het-er-og´e-nous
het-er-og´e-ny
het-er-og´o-ny
het-er-og´ra-phy
het-ero-ki-ne´sis
het-er-ol´o-gy
het-er-ol´y-sis
het´er-om´er-ous
het-er-on´o-mous
het-er-on´y-mous
het-ero-ou´sia
het´er-o-pol´y
het-er-os´co-py
het-ero-zy-go´sis
het-ero-zy´gote
het-ero-zy´gous
heu-ris´tic
hew´ing
hex´a-chlo´ro-eth´ane
hex-a-dec´ane
hex-a-em´er-on
hex´a-gon
hex-ag´o-nal
hey´day
Hez-e-ki´ah
hi-a´tus
Hi-a-wa´tha
hi-ber-nac´u-lum
hi-ber´nal
hi´ber-nate
hi´ber-nat-ing
hi-ber-na´tion
hi´ber-na-tor
Hi-ber´nia
Hi-ber´nian
hi-bis´cus
hic´cough
hic´cup
hick´o-ry
hi-dal´go
hid´den
hide´bound
hid´e-ous
hid´e-ous-ly
hid´e-ous-ness
hid´ing
hi-dro´sis
hi-drot´ic
hi´er-arch
hi´er-ar´chal
hi´er-ar´chi-cal
hi´er-ar-chy
hi´er-at´ic
hi´er-o-crat´i-cal
hi´er-o-dule
hi´er-o-glyph´ic
hi´er-o-glyph´i-cal
hi´er-o-glyph´i-cal-ly
hi´—fi
high´ball
high´born
high´boy
high´bred
high´brow
high chair
high-fa-lu´tin
high fi-del´i-ty
high´—flown´
high´—fre´quen-cy
high´—grade
high´—hand-ed
high´—hat´
high´land
High´land-er
high´lev´el
high´light
high´ly
high´—mind-ed
high´ness
high´road
high school
high seas
high´—spir´it-ed
high´—strung´
high´—ten´sion
high´—test´
high´way
high´way-man
hi´jack
hi´jack-er
hik´er
hik´ing
hi-lar´i-ous
hi-lar´i-ty
Hil´a-ry
Hil´de-brand
hill´bill´y
hill´i-ness
hill´ock
hill´ocked
hill´side
hill´top
hill´y
hi´lum
Him´a-lay´a
hi-mat´i-on
him-self´
Hin´den-burg
hin´der
hind´most
hind´quar-ter
hin´drance
hind´sight
Hin´du
Hin´du-stan´
hinge
hing´ing
hint´er
hin´ter-land
hint´ing-ly
hip´bone
hip´po-cras
Hfp-poc´ra-tes
Hip´po-crat´ic
hip´po-drome
Hip-pol´y-tus

hip-po-pot´a-mus
Hi´ram
hire´ling
hir´ing
Hi-ro-hi´to
Hir´o-shi´ma
hir´sute
His-pa´nia
His-pan´ic
His-pa-nio´la
hiss´ing
his´ta-mine
his´to-log´i-cal
his-tol´o-gy
his-tol´y-sis
his-to´ri-an
his-tor´ic
his-tor´i-cal
his-tor´i-cal-ly
his-to-ric´i-ty
his´to-ries
his-to-ri-og´ra-pher
his´to-ry
his-tri-on´ic
his-tri-on´i-cal
his-tri-on´ics
hitch´hike
hitch´hik-er
hith´er
hith´er-to´
Hit´ler
hit´ting
hoard
hoard´ing
hoar´frost
hoar´i-ness
hoarse
hoarse-ly
hoarse-ness
hoar´y
hoax
hoax´er
hob´ble
hob´bler
hob´bling
hob´by
hob´by-horse
hob´gob-lin
hob´nail
hob´nob
hob´nob-bing
ho´bo
ho´boes
Ho´bo-ken
hock´ey
ho´cus
ho´cus—po´cus
hodge´podge
Hodg´kin's
hod´o-graph
Hoff´mann
Ho´garth
hog´back
hog´ging
hog´gish
hogs´head
hog´tie
Ho´hen-stau-fen
Ho´hen-zol-lern
hoi pol-loi´
hoist´ed
hoist´er
ho´kum
Hol´bein
hold´back
hold´er
hold´fast
hold´ing
hold´over
hold´up
hol´i-day
ho´li-ness
ho´lism
Hol´land
hol´lan-daise´
Hol´land-er
hol´low
hol´low-ness
hol´ly
hol´ly-hock
Hol´ly-wood
hol´o-caust
hol´o-graph
hol´o-graph´ic
Hol´stein
hol´ster
ho´ly
Hol´yoke
hom´age
hom´ag-er
hom´bre
Hom´burg
home´bred´
home brew
home´land
home´less
home´like
home´li-ness
home´ly
home´made´
home´mak-er
ho´meo-path
ho´meo-path´ic
home´own-er
hom´er
Ho´mer
Ho-mer´ic
home´sick
home´sick-ness
home´spun
home´stead
home´stead-er
home town
home´ward
home´work
hom´ey
hom´i-ci-dal
hom´i-cide
hom´i-ly
hom´i-ny
Ho´mo
ho-mog´a-my
ho-mo-ge-ne´i-ty
ho-mo-ge´neous
ho-mog-e-ni-za´tion
ho-mog´e-nize
ho-mog´e-niz-er
ho-mog´e-niz-ing
ho-mog´e-nous
ho-mog´e-ny
ho-mog´o-ny
hom´o-graph
ho´mo-log
ho-mo-log´i-cal
ho-mol´o-gize
ho-mol´o-gous
ho´mo-logue

ho-mol´o-gy
ho-mol´y-sis
ho-mon´y-mous
hom´o-phone
ho-moph´o-nous
ho-moph´o-ny
ho-mop´ter-ous
Ho´mo sap´i-ens
ho-mo-sex´u-al
ho-mo-sex-u-al´i-ty
ho´mo-spor´ous
ho-mo-tax´is
ho´mo-thet´ic
Hon-du´ran
Hon-du´ras
honed
hon´est
hon´est-ly
hon´es-ty
hon´ey
hon´ey-bee
hon´ey-comb
hon´ey-dew
hon´eyed
hon´ey-moon
hon´ey-suck-le
hon´ing
Hon´i-ton
honk´y—tonk
Hon´o-lu´lu
hon´or
hon´or-able
hon´or-ably
hon-o-rar´i-um
hon´or-ary
Ho-no´ria
hon-or-if´ic
hood´ed
hood´lum
hoo´doo
hood´wink
hoof´beat
hoofed
hoof´print
hoo´kah
hook´er
hook´up
hook´worm
hook´y
hoo´li-gan
hoo-ray´
hoose´gow
Hoo´sier
Hoo´ver
hope´ful
hope´ful-ly
hope´ful-ness
hope´less
hope´less-ly
Ho´pi
Hop´kins
hop´lite
hop´per
hop´scotch
ho´ra
Hor´ace
Ho´rae
ho´ra-ry
Ho-ra´tian
Ho-ra´tio
Ho-ra´tius
horde
ho-ri´zon
hor´i-zon´tal
hor´i-zon´tal-ly
hor´mone
hor-mon´ic
horn´beam
horn´bill
horn´book
hor´net
horn´less
horn´pipe
horn´swog-gle
horn´y
hor´o-loge
ho-rol´o-ger
hor´o-log´ic
ho-rol´o-gist
ho-rol´o-gy
hor´o-scope
ho-ros´co-py
hor-ren´dous
hor´ri-ble
hor´ri-bly
hor´rid
hor-rif´ic
hor´ri-fied
hor´ri-fy
hor´ror
hor´ror—struck
hors d´oeuvre
horse
horse´back
horse´flesh
horse´fly
horse´hair
horse´hide
horse´laugh
horse´less
horse´man
horse´man-ship
horse op´era
horse pis´tol
horse´play
horse´pow-er
horse´rad-ish
horse sense
horse´shoe
horse´sho-er
horse´tail
horse´whip
horse´wom-an
hors´ey
hor´ta-to-ry
Hor´tense
hor-ti-cul´tur-al
hor´ti-cul-ture
hor´ti-cul´tur-ist
Ho´rus
ho-san´na
Ho-se´a
ho´sier
ho´siery
hos´pice
hos-pit´a-ble
hos-pit´a-bly
hos´pi-tal
hos´pi-tal-er
hos-pi-tal´i-ty
hos-pi-tal-iza´tion
hos´pi-tal-ize
hos-pi´ti-um
hos´po-dar
hos´tage
host´al
hos´tel

hos´tel-ry
host´ess
hos´tile
hos-til´i-ty
hos´tler
hot´bed
hot´box
hot dog
ho-tel´
hot´foot
hot´head
hot´head-ed
hot´house
hot´ly
hot´ness
hot´spur
hot´—tem´pered
Hou-di´ni
Hou´dry
hound
hour´glass
hou´ri
hour´ly
house´boat
house´break-ing
house´bro-ken
house´coat
house flag
house´fly
house´ful
house´hold
house´hold-er
house´keep-er
house´keep-ing
house´less
house´line
house´maid
house or´gan
house´room
house´top
house´warm-ing
house´wife
house´wife-ry
house´work
hous´ing
Hous´ton
hov´el
hov´er
hov´er-ing
How´ard
how-be´it
how´dah
how-ev´er
how´it-zer
howl´er
how´lite
how-so-ev´er
Hub´bard
hub´bub
Hu´bert
huck´le-ber-ry
huck´ster
hud´dle
hud´dling
Hud´son
huff´i-ly
huff´i-ness
huff´ish
huff´y
huge´ly
hugged
hug´ging
Hu´gue-not
hu´la
hu´la—hu´la
hulk´ing
hul´la-ba-loo
hu´man
hu-mane´
hu-mane´ly
hu´man-isin
hu´man-ist
hu-man-is´tic
hu-man-i-tar´i-an
hu-man-i-tar´i-an-ism
hu-man´i-ty
hu´man-ize
hu´man-kind
hu´man-ly
Hum´ber
Hum´bert
hum´ble
hum´ble-ness
hum´bling
hum´bly
Hum´boldt
hum´bug
hum´drum
hu´mer-al
hu´mer-us
hu´mic
hu´mid
hu-mid´i-fied
hu-mid´i-fy
hu-mid´i-ty
hu´mi-dor
hu-mi-fi-ca´tion
hu-mil´i-ate
hu-mil´i-at-ing
hu-mil-i-a´tion
hu-mil´i-ty
hu´mi-ture
hummed
hum´ming
hum´ming-bird
hum´mock
hu´mor
hu´mor-esque´
hu´mor-ist
hu´mor-ous
hu´mor-ous-ly
hu´mous
hump´back
hump´backed
Hum´phrey
hump´y
hu´mus
hunch´back
hunch´backed
hun´dred
hun´dred-fold
hun´dredth
hun´dred-weight
Hun´ga-ry
hun´ger
hun´ger-ing
hun´gri-er
hun´gri-ly
hun´gri-ness
hun´gry
hun´ker
hunt´er
hunt´ing
Hun´ting-don
Hun´ting-ton
hunt´ress
hunts´man

hur´dle
hur´dler
hur´dy—gur´dy
hurl´er
hur´ly—bur´ly
Hu´ron
hur-rah´
hur´ri-cane
hur´ried
hur´ried-ly
hur´ry
hur´ry—scur´ry
hurt´er
hurt´ful
hurt´ing
hur´tle
hur´tling
hus´band
hus´band-man
hus´band-ry
hush pup´py
husk´er
husk´i-ly
husk´i-ness
husk´ing
husk´y
hus-sar´
hus´sy
hus´ting
hus´tle
hus´tler
hus´tling
Hutch´ins
Hutch´in-son
Hux´ley
hy´a-cinth
hy´a-cin´thine
Hy-a-cin´thus
Hy´a-des
hy´a-line
hy-a-lin-iza´tion
hy-al´o-gen
hy-al´o-phane
hy-a-lu´ro-nate
hy´brid
hy-brid-iza´tion
hy´brid-ize
Hy´der-a-bad.
hy´dra

hy-drac´id
hy-drac´ry-late
hy-dra-cryl´ic
Hy´dra—Mat´ic
hy´dra-mine
hy-dran´gea
hy´drant
hy-dras´ti-nine
hy´drate
hy-dra´tion
hy´dra-tor
hy-drau´lic
hy´dra-zide
hy-draz´i-dine
hy´dra-zine
hy-dra-zo´ic
hy´dra-zone
hy´dride
hy-dri-od´ic
hy-dri´o-dide
hy-dro-acous´tic
hy´dro-car´bon
hy´dro-cele
hy-dro-ceph´a-lous
hy-dro-ceph´a-lus
hy-dro-chlo´ric
hy-dro-chlo´ride
hy-dro-cin-nam´ic
hy-dro-cor´ti-sone
hy-dro-cy-an´ic
hy-dro-dy-nam´ics
hy-dro-elec´tric
hy-dro-flu-or´ic
hy-dro-flu´or-ide
hy´dro-foil
hy-dro-form´ate
hy´dro-gen
hy´dro-gen-ate
hy-drog´e-nous
hy-drog´no-sy
hy-drog´ra-pher
hy´dro-graph´ic
hy-drog´ra-phy
hy´droid
hy´dro-lase
hy-drol´o-gy
hy-drol´y-sate
hy-drol´y-sis
hy´dro-lyt´ic

hy´dro-lyze
hy-dro-me-chan´i-cal
hy-drom´e-ter
hy´dro-met´ric
hy-drom´e-try
hy-dro´ni-um
hy-drop´a-thy
hy´dro-phane
hy-dro-pho´bia
hy-dro-pho´bic
hy´dro-phone
hy´dro-phyte
hy-drop´ic
hy´dro-plane
hy´dro-pon´ics
hy´dro-qui-none´
hy´dro-scope
hy-dro-scop´ic
hy´dro-some
hy´dro-sphere
hy´dro-stat
hy-dro-stat´ics
hy´dro-sul´fide
hy-dro-ther´a-py
hy´drous
hy-drox´ide
hy-drox-im´i-no
hy-drox´y-am´i-no
hy-drox´yl
hy-drox´y´amine´
hy-drox´yl-ate
hy-drox´y-my´cin
hy-drox´y-zine
hy-e´na
hy-e-tog´ra-phy
hy-e-tol´o-gy
hy-e-tom´e-ter
hy´ge-ist
hy´giene
hy´gi-en´ic
hy-gi-en´i-cal-ly
hy´gien´ist
hy-grom´e-ter
hy´gro-met´ric
hy-grom´e-try
hy-gro-my´cin
hy´gro-scope
hy´gro-scop´ic
hy´men

hymn
hym´nal
hym´no-dy
hym-nol´o-gy
hy´oid
hyp-al-ge´sia
hy´per-ac´id
hy-per-acid´i-ty
hy-per´bo-la
hy-per´bo-le
hy´per-bol´ic
hy´per-bol´i-cal
hy´per-bol´i-cal-ly
hy-per´bo-lize
hy-per´bo-loi´dal
hy´per-crit´i-cal
hy-per-du´lia
hy-per-e´mia
hy´per-gol
hy-per-go-lic´i-ty
hy-per´i-cin
hy´per-in
Hy-pe´ri-on
hy´per-on
hy-per-o´pia
hy´per-os-to´sis
hy-per-phys´i-cal
hy-per-pi-e´sia
hy-per-pla´sia
hy-per-pne´a
hy-per-sen´si-tive
hy-per-son´ic
hy´per-sthene
hy-per-ten´sion
hy-per-ten´sive
hy-per-thy´roid
hy-per´tro-phic
hy-per´tro-phy
hy´phen
hy´phen-ate
hy-phen-a´tion
hyp´noid
hyp-nol´o-gy
hyp-no´sis
hyp-not´ic
hyp-not´i-cal-ly
hyp´no-tism
hyp´no-tist
hyp´no-tize
hyp´no-tiz-ing
hy´po-caust
hy-po-chon´dria
hy-po-chon´dri-ac
hy´po-chon-dri´a-cal
hy-poc´ri-sy
hyp´o-crite
hyp-o-crit´i-cal
hyp-o-crit´i-cal-ly
hy´po-der´mal
hy´po-der´mic
hy-po-der´mi-cal-ly
hy-po-der´mis
hy´po-eu-tec´tic
hy-pog´a-my
hy-po-gas´tric
hyp´o-gene
hy-po-gen´ic
hy-pog´e-nous
hy-poph´y-sis
hy-po-pla´sia
hy-pos´ta-sis
hy´po-style
hy-po-sul´fite
hy-pot´e-nuse
hy-poth´ec
hy-poth´e-cary
hy-poth´e-cate
hy-poth-e-ca´tion
hy-poth´e-ca-tor
hy-poth´e-ses
hy-poth´e-sis
hy-poth´e-size
hy-po-thet´i-cal
hy-po-thet´i-cal-ly
hy-pox-e´mia
hy-pox´ia
hyp-sog´ra-phy
hyp-som´e-ter
hyp-som´e-try
hy´son
hys´sop
hys-taz´a-rin
hys-ter-ec´to-my
hys-ter-e´sis
hys-ter-et´ic
hys-te´ria
hys-ter´ic
hys-ter´i-cal
hys-ter´i-cal-ly
hys-ter´ics
hys-ter-or´rha-phy
hys-ter-os´co-py
hys-ter-ot´o-my
hy´ther-graph

I

i´amb
iam´bic
iam´bus
iat´ri-cal
Ibe´ria
Ibe´ri-an
i´bex
i´bis
Ib´sen
ice´ bag
ice´berg
ice´boat
ice´box
ice´cap
ice cream
iced
Ice´land
ice´man
Ich´a-bod
ich-thy-o-log´i-cal
ich-thy-ol´o-gist
ich-thy-ol´o-gy
ich-thy-oph´a-gous
ich-thy-oph´a-gy
ich´thyo-saur
ich-thy-o´sis
ich´thy-ot´ic
ic´i-cle
ic´i-ly
ic´i-ness
ic´ing
i´con
icon´ic
icon´o-clasm
icon´o-clast
icon´o-clas´tic
ico-nom´e-ter
icon´o-scope
ic-ter´ic
ic´ter-us

ic´tus
ic´y
I´da-ho
ide´a
ide´al
ide´al-ism
ide´al-ist
ide´al-is´tic
ide´al-iza´tion
ide´al-ize
ide´al-ly
i´de-ate
ide-a´tion
i´dem
iden´tic
iden´ti-cal
iden´ti-fi-a-ble
iden-ti-fi-ca´tion
iden´ti-fied
iden´ti-fies
iden´ti-fy
iden´ti-ty
ide-oc´ra-cy
i´deo-graph
ide-og´ra-phy
ideo-log´i-cal
ide-ol´o-gist
ide-ol´o-gy
Ides
id-i-oc´ra-cy
id´i-o-cy
id´io-gram
id´i-o-lect
id´i-om
id´i-o-mat´ic
id-i-om´e-ter
id´i-o-path´ic
id-i-op´a-thy
id-i-o-syn´cra-sy
id´i-ot
id-i-ot´ic
id-i-ot´i-cal
id-i-ot´i-cal-ly
id´i-ot-ism
id´i-tol
i´dle
i´dled
i´dle-ness
i´dler
i´dling
i´dly
i´dol
idol´a-ter
idol´a-trize
idol´a-trous
idol´a-try
i´dol-ism
idol-i-za´tion
i´dol-ize
ido´ne-ous
i´dyll
idyl´lic
i´dyll-ist
ig´loo
Ig-na´tian
Ig-na´ti-us
ig´ne-ous
ig-nite´
ig-nit´er
ig-nit´ing
ig-ni´tion
ig´ni-tron
ig-no-bil´i-ty
ig-no´ble
ig-no-min´i-ous
ig-no-min´i-ous-ly
ig´nomi-ny
ig-no-ra´mus
ig´no-rance
ig´no-rant
ig´no-rant-ly
ig-nore´
Ig-o-rot´
igua´na
igua´no-don
i´lex
il´i-ac
Il´i-ad
il´i-um
ilk
ill´—ad-vised´
il-lapse´
il-la´tion
il´la-tive
ill´—bred
il-le´gal
il-le-gal´i-ty
il-leg-i-bil´i-ty
il-leg´i-ble
il-le-git´i-ma-cy
il-le-git´i-mate
ill´—fat´ed
ill´—fa´vored
ill´—fit´ting
ill´—got´ten
ill´hu´mored
il-lib´er-al
il-lic´it
il-lim´it-able
il-lin´i-um
Il´li-nois´
il´lite
il-lit´er-a-cy
il-lit´er-ate
ill´—man´nered
ill´—na´tured
ill´ness
i´log´i-cal
ill´—o´mened
ill´—starred´
ill´—tem´pered
ill´—timed´
il-lu´mi-nant
il-lu´mi-nate
il-lu-mi-na´tion
il-lu´mi-nat-ing
il-lu-mi-na´tion
il-lu´mi-na-tive
il-lu´mi-na-tor
il-lu´mine
il-lu´min-er
il-lu´min-ing
il-lu-mi-nom´e-ter
ill´—us´age
ill´—use´
il-lu´sion
il-lu´sive
il-lu´so-ri-ly
il-lu´so-ry
il´lus-trate
il´lus-trat-ing
il-lus-tra´tion
il-lus´tra-tive
il´lus-tra-tor
il-lus´tri-ous
il-lu´vi-al
il-lu´vi-ate

il-lu-vi-a´tion
Il-lyr´ia
im´age
im´ag-ery
imag´in-able
imag´i-nal
imag´i-nary
imag´i-na´tion
imag´i-na-tive
imag´ine
imag´in-ing
im´ag-ism
im´ag-ist
im´ag-is´tic
im-bal´ance
im´be-cile
tm-be-cil´i-ty
im-bed´
im-bibe´
im-bib´er
im-bi-bi´tion
im´bri-cate
im´bri-cat-ed
im-bri-ca´tion
im-bro´glio
imbrue´
im-bru´ing
im-bue´
im-bu´ing
im´i-do
imid´o-gen
im-i-ta-bil´i-ty
im´i-ta-ble
im´i-tate
im-i-ta´tion
im´i-ta-tive
im´i-ta-tor
im-mac´u-la-cy
im-mac´u-late
im´ma-nence
im´ma-nent
Im-man´u-el
im-mar´gin-ate
im-ma-te´ri-al
im-ma-te-ri-al´i-ty
im-ma-ture´
lm-ma-tur´i-ty
im-mea´sur-able
im-mea´sur-ably
im-me´di-a-cy
im-me´di-ate
im-me´di-ate-ly
im-med´i-ca-ble
Im´mel-mann
im-mem´o-ra-ble
im-me-mo´ri-al
im-mense´
im-mense´ly
im-men´si-ty
im-men´su-ra-ble
im-merge´
im-merse´
im-mersed´
im-mers´ible
im-mers´ing
im-mer´sion
im´mi-grant
im´mi-grate
im-mi-gra´tion
im´mi-nence
im´mi-nent
im-mit´i-ga-ble
im-mo´bile
im-mo-bil´i-ty
im-mo-bi-li-za´tion
im-mo´bi-lize
im-mod´er-a-cy
im-mod´er-ate
im-mod-er-a´tion
im-mod´est
im´mo-late
im-mo-la´tion
im-mor´al
im-mo-ral´i-ty
im-mor´al-ly
im-mor´tal
im-mor-tal´i-ty
im-mor-tal-iza´tion
im-mor´tal-ize
im-mo´tile
im-mov-a-bil´i-ty
im-mov´able
im-mov´ably
im-mune´
im-mu´ni-ty
im-mu-ni-za´tion
im´mu-nize
im-mu-nol´o-gy
im-mure´
im-mur´ing
im-mu-ta-bil´i-ty
im-mu´ta-ble
im´pact
im-pair´
im-pair´ment
im-pale´
im-pal´ing
im-pal´pa-ble
im-pan´el
im-pan´eled
im-par´i-ty
im-park´
im-par´lance
im-part´
im-par-ta´tion
im-par´tial
im-par-tial´i-ty
im-par´tial-ly
im-part´ible
im-pass-abil´i-ty
im-pass´able
im´passe
im-pas-si-bil´i-ty
im-pas´si-ble
im-pas´sion
im-pas´sion-ate
im-pas´sioned
im-pas-sive
im-pas´sive-ly
im-pas-siv´i-ty
im´pa-ter´nate
im-pa´tience
im-pa´tient
im-pa´tient-ly
im-pav´id
im-peach´
im-peach-abil´i-ty
im-peach´able
iin-peach´ment
im-pearl´
im-pec-ca-bil´i-ty
im-pec´ca-ble
im-ped´ance
im-pede´
im-ped´ible
im-pe´di-ent
im-ped´i-ment

im-ped-i-men´ta
im-ped-i-men´tal
im-ped-i-men´ta-ry
im-ped´ing
im-ped´i-tive
im-pe-dom´e-ter
im-pe´dor
im-pel´
im-pelled´
im-pel´lent
im-pel´ler
im-pel´ling
im-pend´
im-pend´ent
im-pend´ing
im-pen-e-tra-bil´i-ty
im-pen´e-tra-ble
im-pen´i-tence
im-pen´i-tent
im-pen´nate
im-per´a-tive
im-per´a-tive-ly
im´pe-ra´tor
im-per-a-to´ri-al
im-per-cep´ti-ble
im-per-cep´ti-bly
im-per´fect
im-per-fec´tion
im-per´fect-ly
im-per´fect-ness
im-per´fo-rate
im-per´fo-rat-ed
im-per-fo-ra´tion
im-pe´ri-al
im-pe´ri-al-ism
im-pe´ri-al-ist
im-pe´ri-al-is´tic
im-pe´ri-al-ly
im-per´il
im-per´iled
im-per´il-ing
im-pe´ri-ous
im-pe´ri-ous-ly
im-per´ish-able
im-pe´ri-um
im-per´ma-nence
im-per´ma-nent
im-per-me-abil-i-ty
im-per´me-able
im-per-scrip´ti-ble
im-per´son-al
im-per´son-al-ly
im-per´son-ate
im-per-son-a´tion
im-per´son-a-tor
im-per-sua´si-ble
im-per´ti-nence
im-per´ti-nen-cy
im-per´ti-nent
im-per-turb-abil´i-ty
im-per-turb´able
im-per-tur-ba´tion
im-per´vi-ous
im-pe-ti´go
im´pe-trate
im-pet-u-os´i-ty
im-pet´u-ous
im-pet´u-ous-ly
im´pe-tus
im-pi´e-ty
im-pinge´
im-pinge´ment
im-ping´er
im-ping´ing
imp´ish
im-placa-bil´i-ty
im-plac´a-ble
im-plant´
im-plan-ta´tion
im-plas-tic´i-ty
im-plau´si-ble
im´ple-ment
im-ple-men´tal
im´pli-cate
im-pli-ca´tion
im´plica-tive
im-plic´it
im-plic´it-ly
im-plied´
im-pli´ed-ly
im-plor´a-to-ry
im-plore´
im-plor´ing
im-plor´ing-ly
im-plo´sion
im-plo´sive
im-ply´
im-po-lite´
im-pol´i-tic
im-pon´der-able
im-port´
im-port´able
im-por´tance
im-por´tant
im-por´tant-ly
im-por-ta´tion
im-port´er
im-por´tu-na-cy
im-por´tu-nate
im´por-tune´
im´por-tun´ing
im-por-tu´ni-ty
im-pose´
im-pos´ing
im-po-si´tion
im-pos-si-bil´i-ty
im-pos´si-ble
im´post
im-pos´tor
im-pos´ture
im´po-tence
im´po-ten-cy
im´po-tent
im-pound´
im-pov´er-ish
im-pov´er-ish-ment
im-pow´er
im-prac-ti-ca-bil´i-ty
im-prac´ti-ca-ble
im-prac´ti-call
im-prac-ti-cal´i-ty
im´pre-cate
im-pre-ca´tion
im´pre-ca-tor
im´preca-to-ry
im-pre-cise´
im-preg-na-bil´i-ty
im-preg´na-ble
im-preg´nate
im-preg-na´tion
im-preg´na-tor
im´pre-sar´i-al
im-pre-sar´io
im-pre-scrip´ti-ble
im-press´
im-press´able
im-press´ibil´i-ty

im-press´ible
im-pres´sion
im-pres´sion-able
im-pres´sion-ism
im-pres-sion-is´tic
im-pres´sive
im-pres´sive-ly
im-press´ment
im-pri-ma´tur
im´print
im-pris´on
im-pris´on-ment
im-prob-a-bil´i-ty
im-prob´a-ble
im-pro´bi-ty
im-promp´tu
im-prop´er
im-prop´er-ly
im-pro´pri-ate
im-pro-pri´e-ty
im-prov´able
im-prove´
im-prove´ment
im-prov´er
im-prov´i-dence
im-prov´i-dent
im-prov´ing
im-provi-sa´tion
im-prov´i-sa-tor
im´pro-vise
im´pro-vis-ing
im-pru´dence
im-pru´dent
im-pru´dent-ly
im´pu-dence
im´pu-dent
im-pu-dic´i-ty
im-pugn´
im-pugn´able
im-pugna´tion
im-pugn´er
im-pu´is-sant
im´pulse
im-pul´sion
im-pul´sive
im-pul´sive-ly
im-pu´ni-ty
im-pure´
im-pu´ri-ty
im-put´able
im-pu-ta´tion
im-pu´ta-tive
im-pute´
im-put´ing
in-abil´i-ty
in ab-sen´tia
in-ac-ces-si-bil´i-ty
in-ac-ces´si-ble
in-ac´cu-ra-cy
in-ac´cu-rate
in-ac´tion
in-ac´ti-vate
in-ac-ti-va´tion
in-ac´tive
in-ac-tiv´i-ty
in-ad´e-qua-cy
in-ad´e-quate
in-ad-mis´si-ble
in-ad-ver´tence
in-ad-ver´tent
in-ad-ver´tent-ly
in-ad-vis´able
in-a´lien-able
in-al´ter-able
in-ane´
in-an´i-mate
in-an´i-ty
in-ap-peas´able
in-ap´pe-tence
in-ap´pli-ca-ble
in-ap´po-site
in-ap-pre´cia-ble
in-ap-pre´cia-tive
in-ap-proach´able
in-ap-pro´pri-ate
in-apt´
in-ap´ti-tude
in-ar-tic´u-late
in-ar-ti-fi´cial
in-ar-tis´tic
in-as-much´
in-at-ten´tion
in-at-ten´tive
in-au´di-ble
in-au´gu-ral
in-au´gu-rate
in-au´gu-rat-ing
in-au-gu-ra´tion
in-aus-pi´cious
in-aus-pi´cious-ly
in´board
in´born
in´bred
in´breed-ing
in´built
In´ca
in-cal´cu-la-ble
in-cal´cu-la-bly
in-ca-les´cent
in-can-desce´
in-can-des´cence
in-can-des´cent
in-can-ta´tion
in-ca-pa-bil´i-ty
in-ca´pa-ble
in-ca-pa´cious
in-ca-pac´i-tate
in-ca-pac-i-ta´tion
in-ca-pac´i-ty
in-car´cer-ate
in-car-cer-a´tion
in-car´di-nate
in-car´na-dine
in-car´nate
in-car-na´tion
in-case´
in-cau´tious
in-cen´di-a-rism
in-cen´di-ary
in´cense
in-cens´ing
in-cen´tive
in-cep´tion
in-cep´tive
in-cep´tor
in-cer´ti-tude
in-ces´san-cy
in-ces´sant
in-ces´sant-ly
in´cest
in-ces´tu-ous
in-cho´ate
in-cho´ate-ly
in-cho´a-tive
inch´worm
in´ci-dence
in-ci-dent

in-ci-den´tal
in-ci-den´tal-ly
in-cin´er-ate
in-cin-er-a´tion
in-cin´er-a-tor
in-cip´i-ence
in-cip´i-ent
in-cise´
in-ci´sion
in-ci´sive
in-ci´sor
in-cit´ant
in-ci-ta´tion
in-cite´
in-cite´ment
in-cit´er
in-cit´ing
in-ci´to-ry
in-ci-vil´i-ty
in-civ´ism
in-clem´en-cy
in-clem´ent
in-clin´able
in-cli-na´tion
in-cli´na-to-ry
in-cline´
in-clined´
in-clin´ing
in-cli-nom´e-ter
in-close´
in-clud´able
in-clude´
in-clud´ed
in-clud´ing
in-clu´sion
in-clu´sive
in-co-erc´i-ble
in-cog-ni´to
in-co-her´ence
in-co-her´ent
in-com-bus´ti-ble
in´come
in´com-ing
in-com-men´su-ra-ble
in-com-men´su-rate
in-com-mode´
in-com-mo´di-ous
in-com-mu´ni-ca-ble
in-com-mu-ni-ca´do
in-com´pa-ra-ble
in-com-pat-i-bil´i-ty
in-com-pat´i-ble
in-com´pe-tence
in-com´pe-ten-cy
in-com´pe-tent
in-com-plete´
in-com-plete´ly
in-com-pli´ant
in-com-pre-hen´si-ble
in-com-pre-hen´sion
in-com-press´i-ble
in-com-put´able
in-con-ceiv´able
in-con-ceiv´ably
in-con-clu´sive
in-con-cus´si-ble
in-con-dens´able
in-con-gru´i-ty
in-con´gru-ous
in-con-sec´u-tive
in-con´se-quence
in-con´se-quent
in-con-se-quen´tial
in-con-sid´er-a-ble
in-con-sid´er-ate
in-con-sid-er-a´tion
in-con-sist´en-cy
in-con-sist´ent
in-con-sol´a-ble
in-con´so-nance
in-con´so-nant
in-con-spic´u-ous
in-con´stan-cy
in-con´stant
in-con-test-abil´i-ty
in-con-test´able
in-con´ti-nence
in-con´ti-nent
in-con-tro-vert´i-ble
in-con-ve´nience
in-con-ve´nien-cy
in-con-ve´nient
in-con-vert´i-ble
in-con-vin´ci-ble
in-cor´po-ra-ble
in-cor´po-rate
in-cor´po-rat-ed
in-cor-po-ra´tion
in-cor´po-ra-tive
in-cor´po-ra-tor
in-cor-po´re-al
in-cor-po-re´i-ty
in-cor-rect´
in-cor-ri-gi-bil´i-ty
in-cor´ri-gi-ble
in´cor-rupt´
in-cor-rupt-i-bil´i-ty
in-cor-rupt´i-ble
in-creas´able
in-crease´
in-creas´er
in-creas´ing
in-cred-i-bil´i-ty
in-cred´i-ble
in-cred´i-bly
in-cre-du´li-ty
in-cred´u-lous
in-cred´u-lous-ly
in´cre-ment
in´cre-men´tal
in-cre´to-ry
in-crim´i-nate
in-crim-i-na´tion
in-crim´i-na-to-ry
in-crust´
in-crus-ta´tion
in´cu-bate
in-cu-ba´tion
in´cu-ba-tor
in´cu-bous
in´cu-bus
in-cul´cate
in-cul-ca´tion
in-cul´ca-tor
in-cul´pate
in-cul-pa´tion
in-cul´pa-to-ry
in-cum´ben-cy
in-cum´bent
in-cum´ber
in-cum´brance
in-cu-nab´u-la
in-cu-nab´u-lum
in-cur´
in-cur´a-ble
in-cu´ri-ous
in-cur´ra-ble

in-curred´
in-cur´rence
in-cur´ring
in-cur´sion
in-cur-sive
in´cur-vate
in´cur-va´tion
in-debt´ed
in-debt´ed-ness
in-de´cen-cy
in-de´cent
in-de-ci´pher-able
in-de-ci´sion
in-de-ci´sive
in-de-clin´able
in´de-com-pos´able
in-dec´or-ous
in-de-co´rum
in-deed´
in-de-fat-i-ga-bil´i-ty
in-de-fat´i-ga-ble
in´de-fea´si-ble
in-de-fen´si-ble
in-de-fin´a-ble
in-def´i-nite
in-def´i-nite-ly
in-de-lib´er-ate
in-del-i-bil´i-ty
in-del´i-ble
in-del´i-ca-cy
in-del´i-cate
in-dem-ni-fi-ca´tion
in-dem´ni-fied
in-dem´ni-fies
in-dem´ni-fy
in-dem´ni-tor
in-dem´ni-ty
in-dent´
in-den-ta´tion
in-dent´ed
in-dent´er
in-den´tion
in-den´ture
in-de-pen´dence
in-de-pen´den-cy
in-de-pen´dent
in-de-pen´dent-ly
in-de-scrib´able
in-de-struc-ti-bil´i-ty
in-de-struc´ti-ble
in-de-ter´min-able
in-de-ter´mi-nate
in-de-ter-mi-na´tion
in´dex
in´dex-er
in´dex-es
In´dia
In´di-an
In-di-an´a
In-di-an-ap´o-lis
in´di-cate
in-di-ca´tion
in-dic´a-tive
in´di-ca-tor
in-dic´a-to-ry
in´di-ces
in-di´cia
in-dic´o-lite
in-dict´
in-dict´able
in-dict´er
in-dic´tion
in-dict´ment
in-dict´or
In´dies
in-dif´fer-ence
in-dif´fer-ent
in-dif´fer-ent-ly
in´di-gen
in´di-gence
in-dig´e-nous
in´di-gent
in-di-gest´ible
in-di-ges´tion
in-dig´nant
in-dig´nant-ly
in-dig-na´tion
in-dig´ni-ty
in´di-go
in-dig´o-lite
In´di-go-sol
in-dig´o-tin
in-di-rect´
in-di-rec´tion
in-di-rect´ly
in-di-rect´ness
in-dis-cern´ible
in-dis-creet´
in´dis-crete´
in-dis-cre´tion
in-dis-crim´i-nate
in-dis-crim´i-nate-ly
in-dis-crim-i-na´tion
in-dis-pens´able
in-dis-pose´
in-dis-posed´
in-dis-po-si´tion
in-dis-put´able
in-dis-sol´u-ble
in-dis-tinct´
in-dis-tinc´tive
in-dis-tinct´ly
in-dis-tinct´ness
in-dis-tin´guish-able
in-dite´ment
in-di-vert´ible
in-di-vid´u-al
in-di-vid´u-al-ism
in-di-vid´u-al-ist
in-di-vid-u-al-is´tic
in-di-vid-u-al´i-ty
in-di-vid´u-al-ize
in-di-vid´u-al-ly
in-di-vis-i-bil´i-ty
in-di-vis´i-ble
In´do—Chi´na
in-doc´ile
in-doc´tri-nate
in-doc-tri-na´tion
in-doc´tri-na-tor
in´do-lence
in´do-lent
in´do-line
in-dom´i-ta-ble
In´do-ne´sia
in´door
in´doors´
in-dorse´
in-dors´ee´
in-dorse´ment
in-dors´er
in-dox´yl
in´drawn
in-du´bi-ta-ble
in-duce´
in-duce´ment
in-duc´er

in-duc´ible
in-duc´ing
in-duct´
in-duc´tance
in-duct-ee´
in-duc´tile
in-duc-til´i-ty
in-duc´tion
in-duc´tive
in-duc-tiv´i-ty
in-duc-tom´e-ter
in-duc´tor
in-duc-to´ri-um
in-due´
indulge´
in-dul´gence
in-dul´gent
in-dul´gent-ly
in-dulg´er
in-dulg´ing
in´du-line
in-du´pli-cate
in´du-rate
in-du-ra´tion
in´du-ra-tive
In´dus
in-du´si-um
in-dus´tri-al
in-dus´tri-al-ism
in-dus´tri-al-ist
in-dus-tri-al-iza´tion
in-dus´tri-al-ize
in´dus-tries
in-dus´tri-ous
in-dus´tri-ous-ly
in´dus-try
in´dwell-ing
in-e´bri-ant
in-e´bri-ate
in-ebri-a´tion
in-ebri´ety
in-ed-i-bil´i-ty
in-ed´i-ble
in-ef-fa-bil´i-ty
in-ef´fa-ble
in-ef-face´able
in-ef-fec´tive
in-ef-fec´tive-ly
in-ef-fec´tu-al
in-ef-fec-tu-al´i-ty
in-ef-fi-ca´cious
in-ef´fi-ca-cy
in-ef-fi´cien-cy
in-ef-fi´cient
in-elas´tic
in-elas-tic´i-ty
in-el´e-gance
in-el´e-gant
in-el-i-gi-bil´i-ty
in-el´i-gi-ble
in-el´o-quent
in-eluc´ta-ble
in-elud´ible
in-ept´
in-ep´ti-tude
in-equal´i-ty
in-eq´ui-ta-ble
in-eq´ui-ty
in-erad´i-ca-ble
in-eras´able
in-err´able
in-er´rant
in-ert´
in-ert´ance
in-er´tia
in-er´tial
in-es-cap´a-ble
in-es-sen´tial
in-es´ti-ma-ble
in-ev-i-ta-bil´i-ty
in-ev´i-ta-ble
in-ev´i-ta-ble-ness
in-ev´i-ta-bly
in-ex-act´
in-ex-ac´ti-tude
in-ex-cus´able
in-ex-haust-i-bil´i-ty
in-ex-haust´ible
in-ex-is´tence
in-ex-is´tent
in-ex-o-ra-bil´i-ty
in-ex´o-ra-ble
in-ex´o-ra-bly
in-ex-pe´di-en-cy
in-ex-pe´di-ent
in-ex-pen´sive
in-ex-pe´ri-ence
in-ex-pe´ri-enced
in-ex´pert
in-ex´pi-a-ble
in-ex-plain´able
in-ex-plica-bil´i-ty
in-ex-plic´a-ble
in-ex-plic´it
in-ex-press´i-ble
in-ex-pres´sive
in-ex-pug´na-ble
in-ex-punng´-ible
in-ex-ten´si-ble
in-ex-tin´guish-able
in-ex´tir-pa-ble
in ex-tre´mis
in-ex-trica-bil´i-ty
in-ex-tric´a-ble
in-ex-tric´a-bly
in-fal-li-bil´i-ty
in-fal´li-ble
in´fa-mous
in´fa-my
in´fan-cy
in´fant
in-fan´ti-cide
in´fan-tile
in´fan-ti-lism
in´fan-tine
in´fan-try
in´fan-try-man
in´farct
in-farc´tion
in-fat´u-ate
in-fat´u-at-ed
in-fat-u-a´tion
in-fect´
in-fect´ant
in-fect´ible
in-fec´tion
in-fec´tious
in-fec´tive
in-fec´tor
in-fe-lic´i-tous
in-fe-lic´i-ty
in-fer´
in-fer´able
in´fer-ence
in-fer-en´tial
in-fe´ri-or
in-fe-ri-or´i-ty

in-fer´nal
in-fer´no
in-ferred´
in-fer´ring
in-fer´tile
in-fer-til´i-ty
in-fest´
in-fes´tant
in-fes-ta´tion
in-fest´er
in-feu-da´tion
in´fi-del
in-fi-del´i-ty
in´field
in-fil´trate
in-fil-tra´tion
in´fil-tra-tive
in-fil´tra-tor
in´fi-nite
in´fi-nite-ly
in-fin-i-tes´i-mal
in-fin´i-ti´val
in-fin´i-tive
in-fin´i-ty
in-firm´
in-fir´ma-ry
in-fir´mi-ty
in-flame´
in-flam´ing
in-flam-ma-bil´i-ty
in-flam´ma-ble
in-flam-ma´tion
in-flam´ma-to-ry
in-flat´able
in-flate´
in-flat´ed
in-flat´er
in-flat´ing
in-fla´tion
in-fla´tion-ary
in-fla´tion-ist
in-fla´tor
in-flect´
in-flect´ible
in-flec-tion
in-flec´tor
in-flex-i-bil´i-ty
in-flex´i-ble
in-flict´
in-flict´er
in-flic´tion
in-flo-res´cence
in-flo-res´cent
in´flow
in´fluence
in´flu-enc-er
in´flu-en´tial
in-flu-en´za
in´flux
in-fold´
in-form´
in-for´mal
in-for-mal´i-ty
in-for´ma-lize
in-for´mal-ly
in-for´mant
in-for-ma´tion
in-form´a-tive
in-form´er
in-fract´ible
in-frac´tion
in-fran´gi-ble
in´fra-red´
in-fra-son´ics
in´fra-sound
in´fra-struc-ture
in-fre´quen-cy
in-fre´quent
in-fre´quent-ly
in-fringe´
in-fringe´ment
in-fring´er
in-fring´ing
in-fu´ri-ate
in-fu´ri-at-ing
in-fu-ri-a´tion
in-fuse´
in-fu´si-ble
in-fu´sion
in-fu-so´ri-al
in-gen´er-ate
in-ge´nious
in-ge´nious-ly
in´ge-nue
in-ge-nu´i-ty
in-gen´u-ous
In´ger-soll
in-gest´
in-ges´tant
in-ges´tion
in´gle
in-glo´ri-ous
in´got
in-grained´
in´grate
in-gra´ti-ate
in-gra´ti-at-ing
in-gra-ti-a´tion
in-gra´tia-to-ry
in-grat´i-tude
in-gra-ves´cence
in´gra-ves´cent
in-grav´i-date
in-gre´di-ent
In´gres
in´gress
in-gres´sion
in´grown
in´growth
in´gui-nal
in-gur´gi-tate
in-hab´it
in-hab-it-abil´i-ty
in-hab´i-tant
in-hab-i-ta´tion
in-hab´it-er
in-hal´ant
in-ha-la´tion
in´ha-la-tor
in-hale´
in-hal´er
in-hal´ing
in-har-mon´ic
in-har-mo´ni-ous
in-here´
in-her´ence
in-her´ent
in-her´it
in-her´it-able
in-her´i-tance
in-her´i-tor
in-her´i-tress
in-he´sion
in-hib´it
in-hib´it-er
in-hi-bi´tion
in-hib´i-tor

in-hib´i-to-ry
in-hos-pit´a-ble
in-hos-pi-tal´i-ty
in-hu´man
in-hu-mane´
in-hu-man´i-ty
in-hu-ma´tion
in-im´i-cal
in-im´i-cal-ly
in-im´i-ta-ble
in-iq´ui-tous
in-iq´ui-ty
ini´tial
ini´tial-ly
ini´ti-ate
ini-ti-a´tion
ini´tia-tive
ini´tia-to-ry
in-ject´
in-jec´tion
in-jec´tor
in-ju-di´cious
in-junc´tion
in-junc´tive
in´jure
in´ju-ries
in´jur-ing
in-ju´ri-ous
in´ju-ry
in-jus´tice
ink bottle
ink´horn
ink´i-er
in´kle
in´kling
ink´stain
ink´stand
ink´well
ink´y
in´laid
in´land
in´—law
in´lay
in´let
in´ly
in´mate
in me-mo´ri-am
in´most
in-nas´ci-ble
in´nate´
in-nate´ly
in´nel-ite
in´ner
in´ner-most
in-ner´vate
in-ner-va´tion
in´ning
inn´keep-er
in´no-cence
in´no-cent
in´no-cent-ly
in-noc´u-ous
in-nom´i-nate
in´no-vate
in-no-va´tion
in´no-va-tor
in´no-va-to-ry
in-nox´ious
in-nu-en´do
in-nu-en´does
in-nu´mer-a-ble
in-nu-tri´tion
in-oc´u-la-ble
in-oc´u-late
in-oc´u-lat-ing
in-oc-u-la´tion
in-oc´u-la-tor
in-of-fen´sive
in-op´er-a-ble
in-op´er-a-tive
in-op-por-tune´
in-op-por-tune´ness
in-or´di-na-cy
in-or´di-nate
in-or´di-nate-ly
in-or-gan´ic
in-or-gan´i-cal-ly
in-os´cu-late
ino´si-tol
in´put
in´quest
in-qui´e-tude
in´qui-line
in-quire´
in-quir´er
in´quir-ies
in-quir´ing
in-quir´ing-ly
in´quiry
in-qui-si´tion
in-quis´i-tive
in-quis´i-tive-ly
in-quis´i-tive-ness
in-quis´i-tor
in´road
in-sane´
in-san´i-tary
in-san´i-ty
in-sa-tia-bil´i-ty
in-sa´tia-ble
in-sa´tiate
in-scrib´able
in-scribe´
in-scrib´er
in-scrib´ing
in-scrip´tion
in-scru´ta-ble
in´sect
in-sec-ti-ci´dal
in-sec´ti-cide
in´sec-ti´val
in-se-cure´
in-se-cur´i-ty
in-sem´i-nate
in-sem-i-na´tion
in-sen´sate
in-sen-si-bil´i-ty
in-sen´si-ble
in-sen´si-tive
in-sen´tient
in-sep´a-ra-ble
insert´
in-ser´tion
in-ser´tive
in´ses-so´ri-al
in´set
in-shore´
in-side´
in-sid´er
in-sid´i-ous
in-sid´i-ous-ly
in´sight
in-sig´ne
in-sig´nia
in-sig-nif´i-cance
in-sig-nif´i-cant
in-sin-cere´

in-sin-cere´ly
in-sin-cer´i-ty
in-sin´u-ate
in-sin-u-a´tion
in-sin´u-a-tor
in-sip´id
in-si-pid´i-ty
in-sip´i-ence
in-sist´
in-sis´tence
in-sis´tent
in-sis´tent-ly
in-sist´er
in-so-bri´e-ty
in´so-late
in-so-la´tion
in´sole
in´so-lence
in´so-lent
in-sol-u-bil´i-ty
in-sol´u-ble
in-solv´able
in-sol´ven-cy
in-sol´vent
in-som´nia
in´so-much´
in-spect´
in-spec´tion
in-spec´tor
in-spec´to-scope
in-spir´able
in-spi-ra´tion
in-spi-ra´tion-al
in-spir´a-tive
in-spir´a-to-ry
in-spire´
in-spir´er
in-spir´ing
in-spir´it
in-spis´sate
in-spis´sa-tor
in-sta-bil´i-ty
in-sta´ble
in-stall´
in-stal-la´tton
in-stalled´
in-stall´ing
in-stall´ment
in´stance
in´stan-cy
in´stant
in-stan-ta´neous
in-stan-ta´neous-ly
in-stan´ter
in´stant-ly
in´star
in-stau-ra´tion
in-stead´
in´step
in´sti-gate
in´sti-gat-ing
in-sti-ga´tion
in´sti-ga-tor
in-still´
in-stilled´
in-still´ing
in´stinct
in-stinc´tive
in-stinc´tive-ly
in´sti-tute
in-sti-tu´tion
in-sti-tu´tion-al
in´sti-tu-tor
in-struct´
in-struct´ed
in-struct´ible
in-struc´tion
in-struc´tion-al
in-struc´tive
in-struc´tor
in´stru-ment
in-stru-men´tal
in-stru-men-tal´i-ty
in-stru-men-ta´tion
in-sub-or´di-nate
in-sub-or-di-na´tion
in-sub-stan´tial
in-suf´fer-able
in-suf-fi´cien-cy
in-suf-fi´cient
in´suf-fla-tor
in´su-lar
in-su-lar´i-ty
in´su-late
in´su-la´tion
in´su-la-tor
in´su-lin
in´sult
in-sul-ta´tion
in-su´per-able
in-sup-port´able
in-sup-press´ible
in-sur´able
in-sur´ance
in-sure´
in-sured´
in-sur´er
in-sur´gence
in-sur´gen-cy
in-sur´gent
in-sur´ing
in-sur-mount´able
in-sur-rec´tion
in-sus-cep´ti-ble
in-tact´
in´take
in-tan-gi-bil´i-ty
in-tan´gi-ble
in-tar´sia
in´te-ger
in´te-gra-ble
in´te-gral
in´te-grate
in-te-gra´tion
in´te-gra-tive
in´te-gra-tor
in-teg´ri-ty
in´tel-lect
in-tel-lec´tu-al
in-tel-lec´tu-al-ism
in-tel-lec´tu-al-ly
in-tel´li-gence
in-tel´li-genc-er
in-tel´li-gent
in-tel-li-gen´tial
in-tel´li-gent-ly
in-tel-li-gi-bil´i-ty
in-tel´li-gi-ble
in-tem´er-ate
in-tem´per-ance
in-tem´per-ate
in-tend´
in-tend´ance
in-tend´an-cy
in-tend´ant
in-tense´
in-tense´ly

in-ten-si-fi-ca´tion
in-ten´si-fied
in-ten´si-fies
in-ten´si-fy
in-ten´sion
in-ten´si-ty
in-ten´sive
in-ten´sive-ly
in-tent´
in-ten´tion
in-ten´tion-al
in-ten´tion-al-ly
in-tent´ly
in-tent´ness
in-ter´
in-ter-act´
in-ter-ac´tion
in-ter´ca-late
in-ter-ca-la´tion
in-ter-cede´
in-ter-ced´ing
in-ter-cel´lu-lar
in´ter-cept
in-ter-cep´tion
in-ter-cep´tor
in-ter-ces´sion
in-ter-ces´sor
in-ter-ces´so-ry
in´ter-change
in-ter-change´able
in-ter-clav´i-cle
in-ter-col-le´giate
in-ter-co-lo´ni-al
in´ter-com
in-ter-com-mu´ni-cate
in-ter-com-mu-ni-ca´tion
in-ter-cos´tal
in´ter-course
in-ter-den´tal
in-ter-de-pen´dence
in-ter-de-pen´dent
in-ter-dict´
in-ter-dic´tion
in-ter-dic´tor
in´ter-est
in´ter-est-ed
in´ter-est-ing
in-ter-fere´
in-ter-fer´ence
in-ter-fe-ren´tial
in-ter-fer´ing
in-ter-fer-om´e-ter
in-ter-fer-om´e-try
in-ter-fer´on
in-ter-fuse´
in-ter-fu´sion
in-ter-gla´cial
in´ter-grade
in´ter-im
in-te´ri-or
in-ter-ject´
in-ter-jec´tion
in-ter-jec´tor
in-ter-jec´tur-al
in-ter-knit´
in-ter-lace´
in-ter-lam´i-nate
in-ter-lay´
in-ter-leave´
in-ter-lin´e-al
in-ter-lin´e-ar
In-ter-lin´gua
in´ter-lin-ing
in´ter-lock
in-ter-lo-cu´tion
in-ter-loc´u-tor
in-ter-loc´u-to-ry
in´ter-lop-er
in´ter-lude
in-ter-lu´nar
in´ter-mar´riage
in´ter-mar´ry
in-ter-med´dle
in-ter-med´dler
in-ter-me´di-ary
in-ter-me´di-ate
in-ter´ment
in-ter-mez´zo
in-ter´mi-na-ble
in-ter´mi-na-bly
in-ter-min´gle
in-ter-min´gling
in-ter-mis´sion
in´ter-mit´
in-ter-mit´tent
in-ter-mit´tent-ly
in-ter-mix´
in-ter-mix´ture
in-tern´
in-ter´nal
in-ter´nal-ly
in-ter-na´tion-al
in-ter-na´tion-al-ism
in-ter-na´tion-al-ist
in-ter-na´tion-al-ize
in-ter-na´tion-al-ly
in-ter-nec´ine
in-terned´
in-ter´nist
in´tern-ship
in´ter-o-cep´tive
in-ter-pel´late
in-ter-pel-la´tion
in-ter-pen´e-trate
in-ter-plan´e-tary
in´ter-play
in-ter-pose´
in-ter-pos´ing
in-ter-po-si´tion
in-ter´pret
in-ter´pret-able
in-ter-pre-ta´tion
in-ter´pre-ta-tive
in-ter´pret-er
in-ter´pre-tive
in-ter-ra´cial
in-ter-ra´di-al
in-terred´
in-ter-reg´num
in-ter-re-late´
in-ter-re-lat´ed
in-ter-re-la´tion
in-ter-re-la´tion-ship
in-ter´ring
in-ter´ro-gate
in-ter-ro-ga´tion
in-ter-rog´a-tive
in-ter´ro-ga-tor
in-ter-rog´a-to-ry
in-ter-rupt´
in-ter-rupt´ed
in-ter-rupt´er
in-ter-rupt´ible
in-ter-rupt´ing
in-ter-rup´tion

in-ter-sect´
in-ter-sec´tion
in´ter-space
in-ter-sperse´
in-ter-sper´sion
in´ter-state´
in-ter-stel´lar
in-ter´stice
in-ter´stic-es
in-ter-sti´tial
in´ter-twine
in´ter-twist
In´ter-type
in´ter-val
in-ter-vene´
in-ter-ven´er
in-ter-ve´nor
in-ter-ven´tion
in-ter-ven´tion-ist
in´ter-view
in´ter-view-er
in´ter-weave
in-ter-wo´ven
in-tes´tate
in-tes´ti-nal
in-tes´tine
in´ti-ma
in´ti-ma-cy
in´ti-mate
in´ti-mate-ly
in´ti-mat-er
in-ti-ma´tion
in-tim´i-date
in-tim-i-da´tion
in-tim´i-da-tor
in-tol´er-able
in-tol´er-ably
in-tol´er-ance
in-tol´er-ant
in-tone´
in-ton´ing
in-tox´i-cant
in-tox´i-cate
in-tox´i-cat-ing
in-tox-i-ca´tion
in-tox-im´e-ter
in-tra-cel´lu-lar
in-trac-ta-bil´i-ty
in-trac´ta-ble

in´tra-dos
in-tra-mo-lec´u-lar
in-tra-mu´ral
in-tran´si-gent
in-tran´si-tive
in-tra-state´
in-tra-tel-lu´ric
in-tra-ve´nous
in-treat´
in-trep´id
in-tre-pid´i-ty
in´tri-ca-cy
in´tri-cate
in´tri-gant´
in-trigue´
in-trigued´
in-trigu´er
in-trigu´ing
in-trigu´ing-ly
in-trin´sic
in-trin´si-cal
in-trin´si-cal-ly
in-tro-duce´
in-tro-duc´tion
in-tro-duc´to-ry
in-tro-jec´tion
in´tro-mit´tent
in´tro-spect´
in-tro-spec´tion
in-tro-spec´tive
in-tro-ver´si-ble
in-tro-ver´sion
in´tro-vert
in-trude´
in-trud´er
in-tru´sion
in-tru´sive
in-trust´
in-tu-i´tion
in-tu´i-tive
in-tu-mes´cence
in-tus-sus-cep´tion
in´un-date
in-un-da´tion
in´un-da-tor
in-un´da-to-ry
in-ure´
in-ur´ing
in-util´i-ty

in-vade´
in-vad´er
in-vad´ing
in-vag´i-nate
in-vag-i-na´tion
in-val´id
in-val´i-date
in-val-i-da´tion
in´va-lid-ism
in-va-lid´i-ty
in-val´u-able
in-var´i-able
in-var´i-ably
in-var´i-ant
in-va´sion
in-vec´tive
in-veigh´
in-vei´gle
in-vei´gling
in-vent´
in-vent´able
in-ven´tion
in-ven´tive
in-ven´tor
in-ven-to´ri-al
in´ven-to-ries
in´ven-to-ry
in-ve-rac´i-ty
In´ver-ness
in-verse´
in-ver´sion
in-vert´
in-vert´ase
in-ver´te-brate
in-vert´er
in-vert´ible
in-ver´tor
in-vest´
in-ves´ti-gate
in-ves-ti-ga´tion
in-ves´ti-ga-tor
in-ves´ti-ture
in-vest´ment
in-ves´tor
in-vet´er-ate
in-vig´i-late
in-vig´o-rate
in-vig´o-rat-ing
in-vig-o-ra´tion

in-vin-ci-bil´i-ty
in-vin´ci-ble
in-vi-o-la-bil´i-ty
in-vi´o-la-ble
in-vi´o-la-cy
in-vi´o-late
in-vis-i-bil´i-ty
in-vis´i-ble
in-vi-ta´tion
in-vi´ta-to-ry
in-vite´
in-vit´er
in-vit´ing
in-vit´ing-ly
in´vo-cate
in-vo-ca´tion
in-voc´a-tive
in´vo-ca-tor
in-voc´a-to-ry
in´voice
in´voic-ing
invoke´
in-vok´ing
in-vol-un-tar´i-ly
in-vol´un-tary
in´vo-lute
in´vo-lut-ed
in-vo-lu´tion
in-volve´
in-volve´ment
in-volv´ing
in-vul-ner-a-bil´i-ty
in-vul´ner-a-ble
in-vul-tu-a´tion
in´ward
in´ward-ly
in´weave´
in´wo-ven
in´wrought
i´o-date
iod´ic
i´o-dide
i´o-di-nate
i´o-dine
io´do-form
io-do-hy´drin
io-dom´e-try
io-do´ni-um
io-do-phthal´e-in
io-do-pyr´a-cet
io-dox´y-ben-zene´
iod´y-rite
i´on
Io´nia
Io´ni-an
Ion´ic
io´ni-um
ion-iza´tion
i´on-ize
io-nom´e-ter
ion´o-sphere
ion´o-spher´ic
io´ta
io´ta-cism
I´o-wa
ip´e-cac
ip-o-me´a
ip´so fac´to
Ips´wich
I´ra
ira´de
Iran´
Iraq´
iras-ci-bil´i-ty
iras´ci-ble
irate´
ire´ful
ire´ful-ly
Ire´land
Irene´
iren´ic
Iri-an´
iri-da´ceous
iri-dec´to-my
ir-i-des´cence
ir-i-des´cent
irid´ic
irid´i-um
iri-di-za´tion
i´ris
iris-a´tion
I´rish
I´rish-man
I´rish-wom-an
iri´tis
irk´some
Ir´ma
i´ron
i´ron-bound
i´ron-clad
i´ron gray´
iron´ic
iron´i-cal
iron´i-cal-ly
i´ron-ing
i´ron-mas-ter
i´ron-mon-ger
i´ron-side
I´ron-sides
i´ron-stone
i´ron-ware
i´ron-wood
i´ron-work
i´ro-ny
Ir´o-quois
ir-ra´di-ate
ir-ra-di-a´tion
ir-rad´i-ca-ble
ir-ra´tio-nal
Ir-ra-wad´dy
ir-re-claim´able
ir-rec´on-cil-able
ir-re-cov´er-able
ir-re-deem´able
ir-re-den´ta
ir-re-den´tist
ir-re-duc-ibil´i-ty
ir-re-duc´ible
ir-re-frag´a-ble
ir-re-fran´gi-ble
ir-re-fut-abil´i-ty
ir-re-fut´able
ir-reg´u-lar
ir-reg-u-lar´i-ty
ir-reg´u-lar-ly
ir-rel´e-vance
ir-rel´e-vant
ir-re-li´gion
ir-re-li´gious
ir-re´me-able
ir-re-me´di-able
ir-re-mov´able
ir-rep´a-ra-ble
ir-re-place´able
ir-re-press´ible
ir-re-proach´able
ir-re-sist´ible

ir-re-sist´ibly
ir-re-sol´u-ble
ir-res´o-lute
ir-res´o-lute-ly
ir-res-o-lu´tion
ir-re-solv´able
ir-re-spec´tive
ir-re-spon-si-bil´i-ty
ir-re-spon´si-ble
ir-re-triev´able
ir-rev´er-ence
ir-rev´er-ent
ir-re-vers-ibil´i-ty
ir-re-vers´ible
ir-rev-o-ca-bil´i-ty
ir-rev´o-ca-ble
ir-rev´o-ca-bly
ir´ri-ga-ble
ir´ri-gate
ir-ri-ga´tion
ir´ri-ga-tor
ir-rig´u-ous
ir-ri´sion
ir-ri-ta-bil´i-ty
ir´ri-ta-ble
ir´ri-ta-bly
ir´ri-tan-cy
ir´ri-tant
ir´ri-tate
ir´ri-tat-ing
ir´ri-ta´tion
ir-rup´tion
ir-rup´tive
Ir´ving
I´saac
Is´a-bel
is-acous´tic
Is-a-do´ra
Isa´iah
i´sa-tin
i´sa-tin´ic
Is-car´i-ot
is-che´mia
is´chi-al
is´chi-at´ic
is´chi-um
Ish´ma-el
Ish´tar
i´sin-glass
I´sis
Is-lam´
Is-lam´ic
is´land
is´land-er
is´let
i´so-bar
i´so-bath
iso-bath´y-therm
i´so-chro-mat´ic
isoch´ro-nal
i´so-chrone
isoch´ro-nism
isoch´ro-nous
iso-cla´site
iso-cli´nal
Isoc´ra-tes
iso-gon´ic
i´so-la-ble
i´so-lat-able
i´so-late
iso-la´tion
iso-la´tion-ist
Isolde´
iso-leu´cine
isol´o-gous
iso-mag-net´ic
i´so-mer
iso-mer´ic
isom´er-ism
isom´er-ize
iso-met´ric
iso-met´ri-cal´ly
iso-me-tro´pia
iso-mor´phic
iso-mor´phism
iso-ni´a-zid
ison´o-my
iso-oc´tane
iso-phthal´ic
iso-pi-es´tic
i´so-pod
iso-pol´i-ty
i´so-prene
iso-pre´noid
iso-pro´pa-nol
i´so-pro´pyl
isos´ce-les
iso-stat´ic
i´so-ther´al
i´so-there
i´so-therm
iso-ther´mal
i´so-ton´ic
iso-to-nic´i-ty
i´so-tope
i´so-top´ic
i´so-to-py
i´so-tron
iso-trop´ic
isot´ro-pous
isot´ro-py
i´so-zyme
Is´ra-el
Is´ra-el-ite
is´su-able
is´su-ance
is´sue
is´su-ing
Is´tan-bul´
isth´mi-an
isth´mus
is´tle
Is´tri-an
it´a-con´ic
Ital´ian
ital´ic
ital´i-cize
ital´i-ciz-ing
ital´ics
It´a-ly
itch´i-ness
itch´y
i´tem
i´tem-iza´tion
i´tem-ize
it´er-ance
it´er-ate
it-er-a´tion
it´er-a-tive
Ith´a-ca
itin´er-an-cy
itin´er-ant
itin´er-ary
itin´er-ate
its
it-self´
I´van

i´vied
i´vo-ry
i´vy
Iz-mir´

J

jabbed
jab´ber
jab´bing
ja-bot´
jac-a-ran´da
ja´cinth
jack´al
jack´a-napes
jack´ass
jack´boot
jack´daw
jack´et
jack´knife
jack´—o'—lan-tern
jack plane
jack´pot
jack´rab-bit
Jack´son
Jack´son-ville
jack´straw
Ja´cob
jac´o-net
Jac´quard
Jac´que-line
jacque´mi-not
Jac-que-rie´
jac-ta´tion
jac-ti-ta´tion
jac´u-late
jad´ed
jade´ite
Jaf´fa
ja´ger
jag´ged
jag´gery
jag´uar
jai alai´
jail´bird
jail´break
jail´er
Jai-pur´
jal´ap
jal´a-pin
ja-lop´y
jal´ou-sie
Ja-mai´ca
jam-ba-lay´a
jam´bo-ree´
James´town
jam´ming
Jan´et
jan´gle
jan´gling
Jan´ice
jan´i-tor
Jan´sen
Jan´u-ary
Ja´nus
Ja-pan´
Jap´a-nese´
Ja´pheth
ja-ra´be
jar´di-niere´
Ja´red
jar´gon
jar´gon-ize
jar-goon´
jaro-vi-za´tion
jar´rah
jarred
jas´mine
Ja´son
jas´per
jaun´dice
jaun´ti-ly
jaun´ty
Jav´a
Jav´a-nese´
jav´e-lin
jaw´bone
jay´walk-er
jeal´ous
jeal´ous-ly
jeal´ou-sy
Jean-nette´
jeer´ing-ly
Jef´fer-son
Jef-fer-so´ni-an
Jef´frey
Je-ho´vah
je-ju´nal
je-june´
Jek´yll
jell
jel´lied
jel´li-fy
jel´ly
jel´ly-fish
Je-mi´mah
Jen´kins
Jen´ner
Jen´nie
Jen´ni-fer
jen´ny
jeop´ard
jeop´ar-dize
jeop´ar-diz-ing
jeop´ar-dy
Jer-e-mi´ah
Jer´i-cho
jerk´i-ly
jer´kin
jer´ky
Je-rome´
Jer´ry
jer´sey
Je-ru´sa-lem
Jes´se
Jes´sie
jest´er
jest´ing-ly
Jes´u-it
Je´sus
jet´lin-er
jet´sam
jet´ties
jet´ting
jet´ti-son
jet´ty
jew´el
jew´eled
jew´el-er
jew´el-ry
jew´fish
Jew´ish
Jew's harp
Jez´e-bel
jib´bing
jib´boom
jif´fy

jig´ger
jig´gle
jig´gling
jig´saw
jilt´ed
jim´mied
jim´my
jin´gle
jin´gling
jin´go
jin´goes
jit´ney
jit´ter-bug
jit´ters
jit´tery
Jo´ab
Job
job´ber
job´bery
job´bing
job´hold-er
job´less
jock´ey
jock´eys
joc´u-lar
joc-u-lar´i-ty
joc´und
jo-cun´di-ty
jodh´pur
Jo´el
jog´ging
jog´gle
jog´gling
Jo´hann
Jo-han´nes
Jo-han´nes-burg
Jo-han´nine
Jo-hans´son
john´ny-cake
John´son
John-so´ni-an
John´ston
Johns´town
join´der
join´er
join´ery
joint´ed
joint´er
joint´ly
joint´ress
joist
joked
jok´er
joke´ster
jok´ing
jok´ing-ly
Jo-li-et´
jol-li-fi-ca´tion
jol´li-fy
jol´li-ly
jol´li-ty
jol´ly
jol´ly-boat
Jo´nah
Jon´a-than
jon´quil
Jop´lin
Jop´pa
Jor´dan
Jo-se´
Jo´seph
jo´se-phine
Jo-se´phus
Josh´ua
Jo-si´ah
jos´tle
jos´tled
jos´tling
jot´ted
jot´ting
jounce
jounc´ing
jour´nal
jour´nal-ism
jour´nal-ist
jour-nal-is´tic
jour-nal-is´ti-cal-ly
jour´nal-ize
jour´ney
jour´neyed
jour´ney-man
jour´neys
joust
joust´er
jo´vial
jo-vial´i-ty
jo´vial-ly
Jo´vi-an
joy´ance
joy´ful
joy´ful-ly
joy´ous
joy´ous-ly
joy´ous-ness
joy´ride
Jua´rez
ju´ba
ju´bi-lance
ju´bi-lant
ju´bi-late
Ju-bi-la´te
ju-bi-la´tion
ju´bi-lee
Ju´dah
Ju-da´ic
Ju´da-ism
Ju´das
Ju-de´a
Ju-de´an
Judg´es
judge´ship
judg´ing
judg´ment
ju´di-ca-tive
ju´di-ca-to-ry
ju´di-ca-ture
ju-di´cial
ju-di´ciary
ju-di´cious
ju-di´cious-ly
Ju´dith
ju´do
Ju´dy
ju´gal
jug´ger-naut
jug´gle
jug´gler
jug´glery
jug´gling
ju´glone
Ju-go-slav´ia
jug´u-lar
jug´u-late
juic´i-ly
juic´i-ness
juic´y
ju-jit´su

ju´jube
juke´box
ju´lep
Ju´lia
Ju´lian
Ju-li-an´a
ju-lienne´
Ju´liet
Ju´lius
Ju-ly´
jum´ble
jum´bled
jum´bling
jum´bo
jump´er
jump´ing
jump´y
junc´tion
junc´tur-al
junc´ture
Ju´neau
Jung´frau
jun´gle
jun´gly
jun´ior
ju-nior´i-ty
ju´ni-per
Ju´nius
Jun´ker
junk´er
jun´ket
jun´ke-teer´
junk´man
Ju´no
jun´ta
jun´to
Ju´pi-ter
Ju´ra
ju´ral
ju´rane
Ju-ras´sic
ju´rat
ju-rel´
ju-rid´i-cal
ju´ries
ju-ris-dic´tion
ju-ris-pru´dence
ju´rist
ju-ris´tic
ju´ror
ju´ry
ju´ry-man
jus´tice
jus-ti´cia-ble
jus-ti´ci-ar
jus´ti-fi-able
jus-ti-fi-ca´tion
jus-tif´i-ca-to-ry
jus´ti-fied
jus´ti-fi-er
jus´ti-fy
Jus´tin
just´ly
just´ness
Jut´land
jut´ting
Ju´ve-nal
ju-ve-nes´cent
ju´ve-nile
jux´ta-pose
jux-ta-po-si´tion

K

ka-bu´ki
Ka-bul´
ka-chi´na
Kaf´fir
kai´nos-ite
kai´ser
ka´ka
Kal-a-ma-zoo´
ka-lei´do-scope
ka-lei´do-scop´ic
Kal´i-spel´
Kal´muck
ka´long
ka´ma-la
Kam-chat´ka
ka-mi-ka´ze
Kam-pa´la
kan´ga-roo´
Kan´san
Kan´sas
kan-tar´
ka´olin
ka-olin´ic
ka´olin-ite
ka´pok
kap´pa
Ka-ra´chi
kar´at
Ka-ren´
kar´ma
Kar´nak
kar-rool
kar´yo-some
Kash´mir
ka-tab´a-sis
kat´a-bat´ic
Ka-tan´ga
Kath´a-rine
ka´ty-did
kau´ri
ka´va
kay´ak
Ka-zan´
Kear´ney
Kear´ny
ked´dah
keel´haul
keel´son
keen´ly
keen´ness
keep´er
keep´ing
keep´sake
Kel´ler
Kel´logg
Kel´ly
ke´loid
kel´pie
Kel´vin
Ken´il-worth
Ken´ne-bec
Ken´ne-dy
ken´nel
Ken´sing-ton
Kent´ish
Ken-tuck´y
Ke´nya
Ken´yon
Ke´o-kuk
Kep´ler
ker´a-toid
Ker´a-tol
ker-a-tol´y-sis

ker-a-to´sis
ker´a-tot´ic
ker´chief
ker´chiefed
Ke-ren´sky
kerf
ker´mes
ker´mes-ite
ker´mis
kerned
ker´nel
ker´neled
ker´o-gen
ker´o-sene
Ker´ry
ker´sey
kes´trel
ke´ta-zine
ke´tene
ke´ti-mine
ke-to-gen´e-sis
ke-to-gen´ic
ke´tone
ke-ton´ic
ket´tle
ket´tle-drum
kev´el
key´board
keyed
key´hole
key´note
key´stone
khad´dar
khak´i
Khar´toum´
Khmer
Khy´ber
kib´itz
kib´itz-er
ki´bosh
kick´back
kick´off
kick´shaw
kid´ded
kid´ding
kid´nap
kid´naped
kid´nap-er
kid´nap-ing
kid´napped
kid´nap-per
kid´nap-ping
kid´ney
Kil-i-man-ja´ro
Kil-ken´ny
Kil-lar´ney
kill´er
kill´ing
kill´joy
kiln
ki´lo
kil´o-cy-cle
kil´o-gram
kil´o-li-ter
ki-lom´e-ter
kilo-met´ric
kil´o-ton
kil´o-watt
kil´o-watt—hour
Kil-pat´rick
kilt´ed
kil´ter
Kim´ber-ley
ki-mo´no
ki-mo´nos
kin´der-gar-ten
kin´der-gart-ner
kind´heart-ed
kin´dle
kind´less
kind´li-ness
kin´dling
kind´ly
kind´ness
kin´dred
kin-e-mat´ics
kin-e-mat´o-graph
kin´e-scope
ki-ne´sics
kin-e-sim´e-ter
ki-ne-si-ol´o-gy
kin-es-the´sia
kin-es-the´sis
kin´es-thet´ic
ki-net´ic
ki-ne´to-graph
ki-ne´to-graph´ic
ki-ne´to-phone
Ki-ne´to-scope
kin´folk
king´bird
king´dom
king´fish
king´fish-er
king´less
king´let
king´li-ness
king´ly
king´pin
king´ship
Kings´ley
Kings´ton
kin´ka-jou
kin´kled
kink´y
kin´ship
kins´man
kins´wom-an
ki´osk
Kip´ling
Ki´o-wa
kip´per
kir´tle
kis´met
kiss´able
kitch´en
kitch´en-ette´
kitch´en-maid
kitch´en-ware
kit´ten
kit´ten-ish
kit´ti-wake
kit´ty
ki´va
Ki-wa´nis
ki´wi
Klam´ath
Klee´nex
klep-to-ma´nia
klep-to-ma´ni-ac
Kling´sor
Klon´dike
knack´er
knag´gy
knap´sack
knav´ery
knav´ish

knead
knee´cap
kneed
knee´—deep´
knee´—high´
kneel´ing
knick´er-bock-er
knick´ers
knick´knack
knife
knight´hood
knight´li-ness
knight´ly
knit
knit´ter
knit´ting
knives
knobbed
knob´by
knob´ker-rie
knock´about
knock´down
knock´er
knock´out
knoll
knot´hole
knot´ted
knot´ter
knot´ting
knot´ty
know´able
know´—how
know´ing
know´ing-ly
knowl´edge
knowl´edge-able
Knox´ville
knuck´le
knuck´led
knuck´ling
knurl´y
ko-a´la
Ko´dak
Ko´di-ak
ko´la
ko-lin´sky
kol-khoz´
koo´doo
ko´peck
Ko-ran´
Ko-re´a
ko´ru-na
ko´sher
kow´tow
kra´ken
Kreis´ler
Krem´lin
kreu´zer
krim´mer
Krish´na
kro´na
kro´ne
kryp´ton
Ku´blai Khan
ku´du
kud´zu
Ku´fic
ku-lak´
kum´quat
Kur´di-stan´
ku´ru
ku-rus´
Ku-wait´
ky´ack
ky´a-nize
ky´mo-graph
ky-mog´ra-phy
kyn-uren´ine
ky-pho´sis
ky-phot´ic

L

lab´a-rum
la´bel
la´beled
la´bel-er
la´bel-ing
la´bile
la-bil´i-ty
la´bi-lize
la´bio-den´tal
la´bi-um
la´bor
lab´o-ra-to-ry
la´bored
la´bor-er
la-bo´ri-ous
la-bo´ri-ous-ly
la´bor-ite
Lab´ra-dor
lab´ra-dor-ite
la´bret
la´broid
la´brum
La Bru-yère´
la-bur´num
lab´y-rinth
lab-y-rin´thi-an
lab-y-rin´thine
lac´co-lith
lac´er-ate
lac´er-at-ing
lac-er-a´tion
lac-er-til´i-an
lace´work
lach´es
lach´ry-mal
lach´ry-ma-to-ry
lach´ry-mose
lac´ing
lack-a-dai´si-cal
Lack-a-wan´na
lack´ey
lack´ing
lack´lus-ter
La-co´nia
la-con´ic
la-con´i-cal-ly
lac´o-nism
lac´quer
lac´ri-mal
lac´ri-ma-to-ry
la-crosse´
lac´ta-ry
lac´tase
lac´tate
lac´te-al
lac´te-ous
lac-tes´cence
lac-tes´cent
lac´tic
lac-tif´er-ous
lac´to-fla´vin
lac-tom´e-ter
lac-to-pro´tein
lac´tose

la-cu´na
lac´u-nary
la-cu´nu-lose
la-cus´trine
lac´y
lad´der
lad´die
lad´en
lad´en-ing
la´dies
lad´ing
la´dle
la´dle-ful
la´dy
la´dy-bird
la´dy-bug
la´dy-fin-ger
la´dy—kill-er
la´dy-like
la´dy-ship
la´dy's maid
la´dy's slip-per
La-fay-ette´
lag´an
la´ger
lag´gard
lag´ging
la-goon´
la-goon´al
La´gos
lais´sez—faire
lai´tance
la´i-ty
lake´side
lal-la´tion
la´ma
la´ma-ism
la´ma-sery
lam-baste´
lamb´da
lamb´doid
lam´ben-cy
lam´bent
lam´bert
Lam´beth
lamb´kin
lam´bre-quin
lamb´skin
la-mé´
la-mel´lar
lam´e´late
la-mel´lose
lame´ly
lame´ness
la-ment´
lam´en-ta-ble
lam´en-ta-bly
lam-en-ta´tion
la-ment´ed
lam´i-na
lam´i-na-graph
lam-i-nag´ra-phy
lam´i-nal
lam´i-nar
lam´i-nate
lam-i-na´tion
lam´i-na-tor
lam-i-ni´tis
lam´pad
lamp´black
lam´pi-on
lamp´light
lam-poon´
lamp´post
lam´prey
lamp´stand
la´nate
Lan´ca-shire
Lan´cas-ter
Lan´ce-lot
lan´ce-o-lar
lan´ce-o-late
lanc´er
lan´cet
lan´cet-ed
lance´wood
lan´ci-nate
lanc´ing
lan´dau
lan´dau-let´
land´ed
land´fall
land´grave
land´hold-er
land´ing
land´ing craft
land´ing field
land´ing gear
land´ing strip
land´la-dy
land´less
land´locked
land´lop-er
land´lord
land´lub-ber
land´mark
Lan´dor
land´own-er
land´—poor
land´scape
land´slide
land´slip
lands´man
Land´sturm
land´ward
Lang´shan
lang´spiel
lan´guage
lan´guid
lan´guid-ly
lan´guish
lan´guished
lan´guish-ing
lan´guor
lan´guor-ous
la´ni-ary
La-nier´
lank´i-er
lank´y
lan´o-lin
la´nose
Lan´sing
Lan´ston
lan-ta´na
lan´tern
lan´tha-nide
lan´yard
La-oc´o-on
Laos
lap´dog
la-pel´
lap´i-dary
lap-i-da´tion
la-pid´i-fy
la-pil´lus
lap´in
La-place´

Lap´land
lap´pet
lap´ping
lapsed
laps´ing
lap´wing
Lar´a-mie
lar´ce-nist
lar´ce-nous
lar´ce-ny
lar´der
large´ly
large´ness
larg´er
lar-gess´
larg´est
lar´go
lar´i-at
lar´ine
lark´spur
lar´rup
lar´va
lar´vae
lar´val
lar´vi-cid-al
lar´vi-cide
lar-vic´o-lous
lar-viv´o-rous
la-ryn´ges
lar´yn-git´ic
lar-yn-gi´tis
la-ryn´go-log´i-cal
lar-yn-gol´o-gist
lar-yn-gol´o-gy
la-ryn´go-scope
lar-yn-gos´co-py
la-ryn´go-spasm
lar´ynx
La Salle
la´ser
lash´ing
las´sie
las´si-tude
las´so
las´so-er
last´ing
last´ly
latch´et
latch´key
latch´string
la-teen´
late´ly
la´ten-cy
late´ness
la´tent
la´tent-ly
lat´er
lat´er-al
lat´er-al-ly
lat´er-ite
lat´er-i´tious
lat-er-i-za´tion
lat´est
la´tex
lath
lathe
lath´er
lath´er-ing
lath´ing
lath´work
lat´i-ces
lat-i-cif´er-ous
Lat´i-mer
Lat´in
Lat´in-ist
La-tin´i-ty
lat´ish
la´tite
lat´i-tude
lat-i-tu´di-nal
lat-i-tu-di-nar´i-an
lat-i-tu´di-nous
La´tium
La-to´na
la-tri´a
la-trine´
la´tron
lat´ter
lat´tice
lat´tice-work
lat´tic-ing
Lat´via
laud-abil´i-ty
laud´able
lau-dan´i-dine
lau´da-nine
lau-dan´o-sine
lau´da-num
lau-da´tion
laud´a-tive
lau´da-to-ry
Lau´der
Laud´ian
laugh´able
laugh´ing
laugh´ing-stock
laugh´ter
launched
launch´er
laun´der
laun´dress
laun´dries
Laun´dro-mat
laun´dry
laun´dry-man
Lau´ra
lau´rate
lau´re-ate
lau´rel
lau´reled
Lau´rence
Lau-ren´tian
Lau´ren-tide
lau´ric
Lau´ri-er
lau´ryl
Lau-sanne´
lau´ter
la´va
la-vage´
lav´a-liere´
la-va´tion
lav´a-to-ry
lav´en-der
la´ver
lav´ing
lav´ish
law´—abid´ing
law´break-er
law´ful
law´giv-er
law´less
law´less-ness
law´mak-er
law´mak-ing
Law´rence
law´suit

law´yer
lax-a´tion
lax´a-tive
lax´i-ty
lay´er
lay-ette´
lay´man
lay´off
lay´out
laz´ar
laz´a-ret´
laz-a-ret´to
Laz´a-rus
la´zi-er
la´zi-ly
la´zi-ness
la´zy
leach
lead´en
lead´er
lead´er-ship
lead´ing
leads´man
lead´y
leaf´age
leaf´less
leaf´let
leaf´y
league
lea´guer
leak´age
leak´proof
leak´y
lean
lean´ing
lean´ness
leap´frog
leap´ing
leap year
learned
learn´er
learn´ing
leased
lease´hold
leas´ing
leath´er
leath´er-ine´
leath´ern
Leath´er-neck
leath´er-work
leath´ery
leav´en
Leav´en-worth
leav´ing
Leb´a-nese´
Leb´a-non
lech´er-ous
lech´ery
lec´i-thin
lec´i-thin-ase
lec´tern
lec´tion
lec´tor
lec´ture
lec´tured
lec´tur-er
lec´tur-ing
ledg´er
lee´board
leech
leer´ing
leer´ing-ly
leer´y
lee´ward
lee´way
left—hand´ed
left´ist
left´over
leg´a-cies
leg´a-cy
le´gal
le´gal-is´tic
le-gal´i-ty
le-gal-iza´tion
le´gal-ize
le´gal-ly
leg´ate
leg´a-tee´
le-ga´tion
le-ga´to
leg´end
leg´end-ary
le-ger´i-ty
leg´ged
leg´gings
Leg´horn
leg-i-bil´i-ty
leg´i-ble
le´gion
le´gion-ary
le´gion-naire´
leg´is-late
leg-is-la´tion
leg´is-la-tive
leg´is-la-tor
leg-is-la-to´ri-al
leg´is-la-ture
le-git´i-ma-cy
le-git´i-mate
le-git´i-ma-tize
le-git´i-mist
le-git´i-mize
le-git´i-miz-ing
leg´man
leg´ume
le-gu´min
le-gu´mi-nous
Le´high
Leices´ter
Leip´zig
leis´ter
lei´sure
lei´sure-ly
lem´an
lem´ma
lem´ming
lem´on
lem´on-ade´
le´mur
Le´na
lend´er
lend´ing
length
length´en
length´i-er
length´wise
length´y
le´nience
le´nien-cy
le´nient
le´nient-ly
Len´in
Len´in-grad
Len´in-ism
len´i-tive
len´i-ty
Len´ox

len-ta-men´te
len-tan´do
Lent´en
len´ti-cel
len-tic´u-lar
len-tig´i-nous
len-ti´go
len´til
Leon´ard
le´o-nine
le´o-nite
leop´ard
Le´o-pold
le´o-tard
Le-pan´to
lep´er
lep´re-chaun
lep-rol´o-gy
lep-ro-sar´i-um
le-pro´sis
lep´ro-sy
lep-rot´ic
lep´rous
lep´ton
lep´tus
Ler-nae´an
Les´bi-an
Les´bos
le´sion
Le-so´tho
les-see´
less´en
less´er
les´son
les´sor
let´down
le´thal
le-thal´i-ty
le-thar´gic
le-thar´gi-cal-ly
leth´ar-gize
leth´ar-gy
Le-ti´tia
let´ter
let´ter box
let´ter car´ri-er
let´rered
let´ter-head
let´ter-ing
let´ter—per´fect
Lett´ish
let´tre de ca-chet´
let´tuce
let´up
leu´cine
leu´cite
leu-co´ma
leu´co-maine
leu´co-noid
leu-cop´te-rin
leu-cot´o-my
leu-cov´o-rin
leu-ke´mia
leu-ke´mic
leu´ker-gy
leu´ko-cyte
leu´ko-cyt´ic
leu´ko-cy-to´sis
leu-ko-pe´nia
leu-ko-poi-e´sis
leu´ko-poi-et´ic
leu-kor-rhe´a
leu-ko´sis
lev´an
Le-vant´
Le-vant´er
Lev´an-tine
le-va´tor
lev´ee
lev´el
lev´eled
lev´el-er
lev´el-ing
lev´el-ly
lev´er
lev´er-age
lev´er-et
Le´vi
lev´i-able
le-vi´a-than
lev´i-gate
lev´i-ga-tor
lev´i-rate
lev´i-rat´ic
lev´i-tate
lev´i-tat-ing
lev-i-ta´tion
Le´vite
le-vit´i-cal
Le-vit´i-cus
lev´i-ty
le´vo-gy´rate
le´vo-ro-ta´tion
le-vo-ro´ta-to-ry
lev´u-lose
lev´y
lev´y-ing
lewd´ness
Lew´is
Lew´i-sohn
lew´is-ite
lew´is-son
Lew´is-ton
Lew´is-town
lex´i-cal
lex-i-cog´ra-pher
lex´i-co-graph´ic
lex-i-co-graph´i-cal
lex-i-cog´ra-phy
lex´i-con
lex-ig´ra-phy
Lex´ing-ton
Ley´den
li-a-bil´i-ty
li´able
li´ai-son
li-a´na
li´ar
li-ba´tion
li´bel
li´bel-ant
li´beled
li´bel-ee´
li´bel-er
li´bel-ing
li´bel-lee´
li´bel-ous
lib´er-al
lib´er-al-ism
lib´er-al-is´tic
lib-er-al´i-ty
lib-er-al-iza´tion
lib´er-al-ize
lib´er-al-ly
lib´er-ate
lib-er-a´tion
lib´er-a-tor

Li-be´ria
lib-er-tar´i-an
li-ber´ti-cide
lib´er-tine
lib´er-ty
li-bid´i-nal
li-bid´i-nous
li-bi´do
Li´bra
li-brar´i-an
li´brary
li-bra´tion
li´bra-to-ry
li-bret´tist
li-bret´to
li-bret´tos
li´bri-form
Lib´ya
li´cens-able
li´cense
li´censed
li´cens-ee´
li´cens-er
li´cens-ing
li´censor
li-cen´ti-ate
li-cen´tious
li-cen´tious-ness
li´chen
li´chen-in
lic´it
lic´o-rice
lic´tor
lid´o-caine
Lieb´frau-milch
Liech´ten-stein
Lie´der-kranz
liege
lien
lien´or
li´en-tery
lieu-ten´an-cy
lieu-ten´ant
life
life belt
life´blood
life´boat
life buoy
life´guard
life´less
life´like
life´line
life´long
life net
life raft
life´sav-er
life´sav-ing
life´time
lift´er
lig´a-ment
lig´and
li´gate
li-ga´tion
lig´a-ture
li´geance
light´ed
light´en
light´ened
light´en-ing
light´er
light´er-age
light´—fin-gered
light´heart-ed
light´house
light´ing
light´ness
light´ning
light´proof
light´ship
light´tight
light´weight
light´—year
lig´ne-ous
lig-nes´cent
lig´ni-fy
lig´nite
lig´u-late
lig´ure
lik´able
like´li-hood
like´ly
lik´en
like-ness
like´wise
lik´ing
li´lac
Lil´i-an
Lil´ien-thal
lil´ies
Lil´ith
Lille
Lil´li-put
lil´y
Li´ma
lim´ber
lim´bo
Lim´burg-er
lim´bus
lime´ade
lime´kiln
lime´light
lim´er-ick
lime´stone
lime´wa-ter
li´min-al
lim´it
lim´i-tary
lim-i-ta´tion
lim´it-ed
lim´it-less
lim´ner
lim-nol´o-gy
lim´ou-sine
lim´pet
lim´pid
lim-pid´i-ty
lim´pid-ly
limp´ly
lim´y
lin´able
lin´age
lin-a-mar´in
linch´pin
Lin´coln
lin´dane
Lind´bergh
lin´den
lin´eage
lin´eal
lin´ea-ment
lin´ear
lin-ear´i-ty
lin´eate
lin-ea´tion
line´man
lin´en
lin´er

line´up
lin´ger
lin-ge-rie´
lin´go
lin´gua
lin´gual
lin´guist
lin-guis´tic
lin-guis´ti-cal-ly
lin-guis-ti´cian
lin-guis´tics
lin´guis-try
lin´gu-late
ling´y
lin´i-ment
li´nin
lin´ing
link´age
link´ing
lin´net
Li´no-type
lin´seed
lin´sey
lin´sey—wool´sey
lin´tel
lint´er
li´on
Li´o-nel
li´on-ess
li´on-heart-ed
li-on-iza´tion
li´on-ize
li´on-like
lip´ide
li-po´ic
lip´oid
lip-oi-do´sis
li-pol´y-sis
lip´o-lyt´ic
li-po´ma
li-po-ma-to´sis
lip-o-pro´tein
lip´stick
li´quate
li-qua´tion
liq´ue-fa´cient
liq-ue-fac´tion
liq´ue-fied
liq´ue-fy
liq´ue-fy-ing
li-ques´cence
li-ques´cent
li-queur´
liq´uid
liq´uid-am´bar
liq´ui-date
liq´ui-da´tion
liq´ui-da-tor
li-quid´i-ty
liq´ui-dus
li´quor
li´ra
Li´sa
Lis´bon
lis´e-ran
lisp´er
lisp´ing
lisp´ing-ly
lis´some
lis´ten
lis´ten-er
Lis´ter
list´er
Lis-te´ria
Lis´ter-ize
list´less
list´less-ness
lit´a-ny
li´tchi´
li´ter
lit´er-a-cy
lit´er-al
lit´er-al-ly
lit´er-ary
lit´er-ate
lit-e-ra´ti
lit-e-ra´tim
lit´er-a-tor
lit´er-a-ture
lith´arge
lithe´some
lith´ia
lith´i-um
lith´o-cho´lic
lith´o-graph
li-thog´ra-pher
lith´o-graph´ic
li-thog´ra-phy
lith´oid
lith´o-log´ic
li-thol´o-gy
lith´o-mor´phic
lith´o-pone
lith´o-sol
lith´o-sphere
Lith´u-a´nia
lit´i-ga-ble
lit´i-gant
lit´i-gate
lit-i-ga´tion
lit´i-ga-tor
li-ti´gious
li-ti´gious-ly
lit´mus
li´to-tes
lit´ter
lit´tle
lit´to-ral
li-tur´gi-cal
li-tur´gi-cal-ly
lit´ur-gist
lit´ur-gy
liv´able
live´li-hood
live´li-ness
live´long
live´ly
liv´en
liv´er
liv´er-ied
Liv´er-pool
liv´er-wort
liv´er-wurst
liv´ery
liv´ery-man
live´stock
liv´id
li-vid´i-ty
liv´ing
liv´ing room
Liv´ing-ston
Li-vo´ni-an
li´vre
Liv´y
lix-iv´i-ate
liz´ard
lla´ma

lla´no
Llew-el´lyn
load´er
loaf
loaf´er
loam´y
loath
loathe
loath´er
loath´ing
loath´some
loaves
lo´bar
lo´bate
lo-ba´tion
lobbed
lob´bied
lob´bing
lob´by
lob´by-ing
lob´by-ist
lo-bec´to-my
lo-bot´o-my
lob´ster
lob´u-lar
lob´ule
lob´u-lose
lo´cal
lo-cale´
lo-cal´i-ty
lo-cal-iza´tion
lo´cal-ize
lo´cal-iz-er
lo´cal-ly
lo´cant
Lo-car´no
lo´cate
lo-cat´er
lo-cat´ing
lo-ca´tion
loc´a-tive
lo´ca-tor
lo-chet´ic
Loch´in-var
lock´age
lock´er
lock´et
lock´jaw
lock´out
lock´smith
lock´step
lock´stitch
lock´up
lo´co
lo-co-mo´tion
lo-co-mo´tive
lo-co-mo´tor
loc´u-lar
loc´u-late
lo´cust
lo-cu´tion
lode´star
lode´stone
lodg´er
lodg´ing
lodg´ment
loft´i-ly
loft´i-ness
loft´y
lo´gan-ber-ry
lo´ga-nin
log´a-rithm
log´a-rith´mic
log-a-rith´mi-cal
log-a-rith´mi-cal´ly
log´book
log´ger-head
log´gia
log´ging
lo´gia
log´ic
log´i-cal
log´i-cal-ly
lo-gi´cian
lo´gi-on
lo-gis´tic
lo-gis-ti´cian
lo-gis´tics
log´o-gram
log´o-gram-mat´ic
lo-gog´ra-phy
lo-gom´a-chy
log´o-pe´dic
log-or-rhe´a
Lo´gos
log´o-type
log´wood
Lo´hen-grin
loin´cloth
Lo´is
loi´ter
loi´ter-er
Lol´lard
loll´ing
lol´li-pop
Lom´bard
Lom´bar-dy
lo´ment
Lo´mond
Lon´don
Lon´don-der-ry
Lon´don-er
lone´li-ness
lone´ly
lone´some
long´boat
long—dis´tance
longe´ing
long´er
lon´ge-ron
long´est
lon-gev´i-ty
lon-ge´vous
Long´fel-low
long´—haired
long´hand
long´head-ed
long´horn
long´ing
lon´gi-tude
long´—lived´
long´—range´
long´shore-man
long´—suf´fer-ing
long´—term
long´—wind-ed
look´er
look´ing
look´ing glass
look´out
loo´ny
loop´hole
loop´y
loose´—leaf
loose´ly
loos´en
loot´er

Lo´pez
lop´per
lop´sid-ed
lo-qua´cious
lo-quac´i-ty
lo´ran
lord´li-ness
lord´ship
Lor´e-lei
Lo-ren´zo
Lo-ret´ta
lor´i-cate
lo´ris
Lorraine´
lor´ries
lor´ry
lo´ry
los´able
Los An´ge-les
los´er
los´ing
Los´sen
loss´er
Lo-thar´io
lo´tion
lot´tery
lot´to
lo´tus
loud´ness
loud´speak-er
Lou´is
Lou-i´sa
Lou-ise´
Lou-i-si-an´a
Lou´is-ville
lounged
loung´er
loung´ing
louse
lous´i-ness
lous´y
lout´ish
lou´ver
Lou´vre
lov´able
lov´age
love´bird
love´less
love´li-er
love´li-ness
love´lorn
love´ly
lov´er
love´sick
low´boy
low´bred
low´brow
low´—cut´
low´down
Low´ell
low´er
low´er case
low´er-ing
low´—grade´
low´land
low´li-ness
low´ly
low´—pres-sure
low´—rate´
low´—spir-it-ed
lox
loy´al
loy´al-ist
loy´al-ly
loy´al-ty
Loy-o´la
loz´enge
Lu-an´da
lub´ber
Lub´bock
Lu´beck
lu´bri-cant
lu´bri-cate
lu-bri-ca´tion
lu´bri-ca-tor
lu-bri´cious
lu-bric´i-ty
lu´bri-cous
lu´cen-cy
lu´cent
Lu-cerne´
Lu´cia
lu´cid
lu-cid´i-ty
lu´cid-ness
lu´ci-fer
lu-cif´er-ase
lu-cif´er-in
lu-cif´er-ous
Lu-cin´da
Lu´cite
Lu´cius
luck´i-er
luck´i-est
luck´i-ly
luck´less
luck´y
lu´cra-tive
lu´cre
Lu-cre´tia
Lu-cre´tius
lu´cu-brate
lu-cu-bra´tion
lu´cu-bra-tor
lu´cu-lent
Lu-cul´lan
Lu´cy
lu´di-crous
lu´di-crous-ness
lu-di-fi-ca´tion
Lud´low
Lud´wig
lu´es
lug´gage
lug´ger
lug´ging
lug´worm
luke´warm
lull´a-by
lum-ba´go
lum´bar
lum´ber
lum´ber-jack
lum´ber-man
lum´ber-yard
lum´bri-coid
lu-mi-naire´
lu´mi-nary
lu-mi-nesce´
lu-mi-nes´cence
lu-mi-nom´e-ter
lu´mi-nous
lum´mox
lump´i-er
lump´i-ly
lump´ish
lump´y

lu´na
lu´na-cy
lu´nar
lu´nate
lu´na-tic
lu-na´tion
lunch´eon
lunch´eon-ette´
lunch´room
lunged´
lung´er
lung´ing
lu-pet´i-dine
lu´pine
lu´pin-ine
lu´pu-lin
lu´pu-lone
lu´pus
lurch
lurched
lurch´ing
lured
lu´rid
lu´rid-ly
lur´ing
lurk´er
lurk´ing
lus´cious
lush´ly
Lu-si-ta´nia
lus´ter
lus´ter-ware
lust´ful
lust´i-er
lust´i-ly
lus´tral
lus´trate
lus-tra´tion
lus´tring
lus´trous
lus´trum
lust´y
lu´ta-nist
lu´te-in
lu´te-in-ize
lu´te-o-lin
lu´te-ous
lu-te´tium
Lu´ther
Lu´ther-an
lu´ti-din´ic
lut´ist
lux´ate
lux-a´tion
Lux´em-bourg
lux-u´ri-ance
lux-u´ri-ant
lux-u´ri-ate
lux-u´ri-at-ing
lux´u-ries
lux-u´ri-ous
lux´u-ry
Lu-zon´
ly´can-thrope
ly´can-throp´ic
ly-can´thro-py
ly-cée´
ly-ce´um
Ly-cur´gus
lydd´ite
Lyd´ia
Lyd´i-an
ly´ing
Lyl´y
lymph
lymph-ad-e-ni´tis
lymph-ad-e-nop´a-thy
lym-phan´gi-al
lym-phat´ic
lym´pho-cyte
lymph´oid
lym-pho-ma-to´sis
lym´pho-sar-co´ma
lynch
lynch´ing
lynx
ly´on-naise
Ly´ons
ly´rate
lyr´ic
lyr´i-cal
ly´ri-form
ly-ser´gic
Lys´i-as
ly-sim´e-ter
ly´sin
ly´sine
ly´so-gen´ic
Ly´sol
ly´so-some
lyt´ic

M

ma-ca´bre
ma-ca´co
mac-ad´am
mac-ad-am-iza´tion
mac-ad´am-ize
Ma-ca´o
mac-a-ro´ni
mac´a-roon´
ma-cas´sar
ma-caw´
Mac-beth´
Mac-Dow´ell
ma´cé-doine´
Mac´e-don
Mac-e-do´nia
mac´er-al´
mac´er-ate
mac-er-a´tion
mac´er-a-tor
ma-chet´e
Ma-chia-vel´li
mach-i-na´tion
mach´i-na-tor
ma-chine´
ma-chine´ gun
ma-chin´ery
ma-chine´ shop
ma-chine´ tool
ma-chin´ist
ma-chree´
Mac-ken´zie
mack´er-el
Mack´i-nac
mack´i-naw
mack´in-tosh
Mac-Mil´lan
Ma´con
mac´ra-me´
mac´ro-cosm
mac´ro-cos´mic
mac´ro-cy´clic
mac-ro-cy-to´sis
mac-rog´ra-phy

mac´ro-mol´e-cule
ma´cron
mac´ro-phys´ics
mac-rop´sia
mac´u-la
mac-u-la´tion
mac´u-la-ture
mac´ule
Mad´a-gas´car
mad´am
ma-dame´
Ma-da-ria´ga
mad´cap
mad´den
mad´den-ing
mad´der
mad´dest
Ma-dei´ra
Mad´e-line
ma-de-moi-selle´
mad´house
Mad´i-son
mad´ly
mad´man
mad´ness
Ma-don´na
ma-dras´
mad´re-pore
Ma-drid´
mad´ri-gal
mael´strom
mae´stro
Maf´e-king
maf´fick
Ma´fia
maf´ic
mag´a-zine´
Mag´da-len
Mag´de-burg
Ma-gel´lan
Mag´el-lan´ic
ma-gen´ta
Mag-gio´re
mag´got
ma´gi
mag´ic
mag´i-cal
mag´i-cal-ly
ma-gi´cian
Ma´gi-not´
ma-gis´ter
mag-is-te´ri-al
mag´is-tery
mag´is-tra-cy
mag´is-trate
mag´is-tra-ture
mag´ma
Mag´na Car´ta
mag´na cum lau´de
Mag´na-flux
mag-na-nim´i-ty
mag-nan´i-mous
mag´nate
mag-ne´sia
mag-ne´sium
mag´net
mag-net´ic
mag-net´i-cal-ly
mag´net-ism
mag´net-ite
mag´net-iz-able
mag-net-iza´tion
mag´net-ize
mag-ne´to
mag´ne-to-graph
mag-ne-tom´e-ter
mag-ne-to-met´ric
mag-ne-tom´e-try
mag-ne´to-mo´tive
mag´ne-ton
mag-ne´tos
mag´ne-tron
Mag-nif´i-cat
mag-ni-fi-ca´tion
mag-nif´i-cence
mag-nif´i-cent
mag-nif´i-co
mag´ni-fied
mag´ni-fi-er
mag´ni-fy
mag´ni-fy-ing
mag´ni-tude
mag-no´lia
mag´num
mag´pie
Mag´yar
Ma-ha´bha´ra-ta
Ma-han´
ma-ha-ra´ja
ma-ha-ra´ni
ma-hat´ma
Mah´—Jongg´
ma-hog´a-ny
Ma-hom´et
ma-hout´
Mah-rat´ta
maid´en
maid´en-hair
maid´en-head
maid´en-ly
maid´ser-vant
mail´able
mail´bag
mail´box
mail´er
mail-lot´
mail´man
Mai-mon´i-des
Maine
Main´er
main´land
main´ly
main´mast
main´sail
main´spring
main´stay
main-tain´
main´te-nance
maî´tre d'hô-tel´
maize
ma-jes´tic
ma-jes´ti-cal
ma-jes´ti-cal-ly
maj´es-ty
ma-jol´i-ca
ma´jor
Ma-jor´ca
ma-ior-do´mo
ma´jor gen´er-al
ma-jor´i-ties
ma-jor´i-ty
Ma-kas´sar
make´—be-lieve
make´fast
mak´er
make´shift
make´up

make´weight
mak´ing
Mal´a-bar
Ma-lac´ca
Mal´a-chi
mal´a-chite
mal´ad-just´ed
mal´ad-just´ment
mal´ad-min´is-ter
mal-ad-min-is-tra´tion
mal´a-droit´
mal´a-dy
Mal´a-ga
mala-gue´na
mal-aise´
ma-lar´ia
ma-lar´i-al
Ma-la´wi
Ma-lay´
Ma-lay´a
Ma-lay´an
Ma-lay´sia
Mal´colm
mal´con-tent
Mal´dives
mal-e-dic´tion
mal´e-fac´tion
mal´e-fac´tor
ma-lef´ic
ma-lef´i-cence
ma-lef´i-cent
ma-le´ic
ma-lev´o-lence
ma-lev´o-lent
mal-fea´sance
mal´for-ma´tion
mal´formed´
Ma´li
mal´ic
mal´ice
ma-li´cious
ma-li´cious-ly
ma-lif´er-ous
ma-lign´
ma-lig´nan-cy
ma-lig´nant
ma-lig´ni-ty
Ma-lines´
ma-lin´ger
ma-lin´ger-er
mal´lard
mal´lea-ble
mal´let
mal´low
mal-nu-tri´tion
mal´odor
mal-o´dor-ous
mal-o´dor-ous-ly
mal´prac-tice
Mal´ta
Mal-tese´
Mal´thus
malt´ose
mal´treat´
mal´treat´ment
malt´y
mal-va´ceous
mam´ba
mam´bo
mam´ma
mam´mal
mam-ma´li-an
mam-ma-lif´er-ous
mam-mal´o-gy
mam´ma-ry
mam-mif´er-ous
mam´mil-lary
mam´mil-late
mam´mon
mam´moth
man´a-cle
man´a-cling
man´age
man´age-abil´i-ty
man´age-able
man´age-ment
man´ag-er
man´a-ge´ri-al
man´ag-ing
Ma-na´gua
man´akin
ma-ña´na
Ma-nas´sas
Ma-nas´seh
man—at—arms
man´a-tee
Man´ches-ter
Man´chu´
Man´chu-kuo´
Man-chu´ria
Man´da-lay´
man´da-rin
man´date
man-da´tor
man´da-to-ry
man´del-ate
man-del´ic
Man´de-ville
man´do-lin´
man´do-lin´ist
man´drake
man´drel
man´drill
man´—eat-er
ma-nege´
ma´nes
Ma-net´
ma-neu´ver
ma-neu´ver-abil´i-ty
ma-neu´ver-er
man´ful
man´ful-ly
man´ga-nate
man´ga-nese
man-gan´ic
man-ga-nif´er-ous
man´ga-nite
man´ga-nous
man´ger
man´gi-er
nian´gi-ly
man´gi-ness
man´gle
man´gler
man´gling
man´go
man´goes
man´go-nel
man´grove
man´gy
man´han-dle
Man-hat´tan
man´hole
man´hood
man´—hour´
ma´nia

ma´ni-ac
ma-ni´a-cal
man´ic
man´ic—de-pres´sive
Man-i-che´an
man-i-co´ba
man´i-cure
man´i-cur-ist
man´i-fest
man-i-fes´tant
man-i-fes-ta´tion
man´i-fest-ly
man-i-fes´to
man-i-fes´tos
man´i-fold
man´i-fold-er
man´i-kin
Ma-nil´a
ma-nil´la
man´i-ple
ma-nip´u-late
ma-nip-u-la´tion
ma-nip´u-la-tive
ma-nip´u-la-tor
ma-nip´u-la-to-ry
Man-i-to´ba
man´i-tou
man´kind´
man´like
man´li-ness
man´ly
man´na
man´ne-quin
man´ner
man´ner-ism
man´ner-less
man´ner-ly
man´ni-kin
man´nose
man´nu-ron´ic
man—of—war
ma-nom´e-ter
man´o-met´ric
ma-nom´e-try
man´or
man´o-stat
man´pow-er
man´rope
man´sard
man´ser-vant
man´sion
man´slaugh-ter
man´slay-er
man´stop-per
man´sue-tude
man´ta
man-teau´
man´tel
man´tel-et
man´tel-piece
man´tel-shelf
man-til´la
man´tis
man´tle
man´tling
man´u-al
man´u-al-ly
man´u-duc´tive
Man´u-el
man-u-fac´to-ry
man-u-fac´ture
man-u-fac´tur-er
man-u-fac´tur-ing
man-u-mis´sion
ma-nure´
ma´nus
man´u-script
Manx
man-y
man-za-ni´ta
Mao´ri
ma´ple
ma-quette´
mar´a-bout
ma-ra-ca
Mar´a-cai´bo
mar-a-schi´no
Ma-ra´tha
mar´a-thon
ma-raud´
ma-raud´er
ma-raud´ing
mar´ble
mar´bled
Mar´ble-head
mar´ble-ize
mar´bling
marc
mar´ca-site
mar-cel´
march´er
mar´chio-ness
Mar´cia
Mar-co´ni
Mar´co Po´lo
Mar´di Gras
Ma-ren´go
mare´s nest
mare´s tail
mar´ga-rate
Mar´ga-ret
mar´ga-rine
mar´ga-rite
mar-ga-ro´san-ite
Mar´gery
mar´gin
mar´gin-al
mar-gi-na´lia
mar´gin-ate
Mar´got
mar´grave
mar´gue-rite´
Ma-ri´a
ma-ri-a´chi
Mar´i-an
Mar-i-co´pa
Ma-rie´
Mar-i-et´ta
mar´i-gold
mar-i-hua´na
mar-i-jua´na
ma-rim´ba
ma-ri´na
mar´i-nade´
mar´i-nate
mar´i-nat-ing
mar-i-na´tion
ma-rine´
mar´i-ner
Ma-ri´nist
ma-rin´ist
Mar´i-on
mar´i-o-nette´
mar´i-tal
mar´i-tal-ly
mar´i-time
Mar´i-us

mar´jo-ram
Mar´jo-ry
mark´ed-ly
mark´er
mar´ket
mar-ket-abil´i-ty
mar´ket-able
mar´ket-er
mar´ket-ing
mar´ket-place
Mark´ham
marks´man
marks´man-ship
Marl´bor-ough
mar´lin
mar´line
marl´ite
mar-lit´ic
Mar´lowe
mar´ma-lade
Mar´mi-on
mar-mo´re-al
mar´mo-set
mar´mot
ma-roon´
marque
mar-quee´
Mar-que´san
mar´quess
mar´quess-ate
mar´que-te-rie
mar´que-try
Mar-quette´
mar´quis
mar-quise´
mar´qui-sette´
mar´riage
mar´riage-able
mar´ried
mar-ron´ gla-cé´
mar´row
mar´row-bone
mar´ry
Mar-seil-laise´
Mar-seilles´
mar´shal
mar´shal-cy
mar´shaled
mar´shal-er

Mar´shall
marsh gas
marsh´i-ness
marsh´mal-low
marsh-y
mar-su´pi-al
Mar-tel´
Mar-tel´lo
mar´ten
mar´tens-ite
Mar´tha
mar´tial
mar´tial-ly
Mar´tian
mar´tin
Mar-ti-neau´
mar´ti-net´
mar´tin-gale
mar-ti´ni
Mar´ti-nique´
Mar´tin-mas
mar´tyr
mar´tyr-dom
mar´tyr-ize
mar´vel
mar´veled
mar´vel-ing
mar´vel-ous
mar´vel-ous-ly
Marx´ian
Marx´ism
Mar´y
Mar´y-land
mar´zi-pan
Ma-sa-ryk´
mas-car´a
mas´cle
mas´cot
mas´cu-line
mas-cu-lin´i-ty
ma´ser
mash´er
mash´ie
mask´er
mas´och-ism
mas´och-ist
mas´och-is´tic
ma´son
ma-son´ic

Ma´son-ite
ma´son-ry
Mas´o-rete
Mas´o-ret´ic
masqu´er
mas´quer-ade´
Mas´sa-chu´setts
mas´sa-cre
mas´sa-cred
mas´sa-crer
mas´sa-cring
mas-sage´
mas-sag´er
mas-sag´ing
mas´sa-sau´ga
mas-sé´
mas-se´ter
mas-seur´
mas-seuse´
mass´i-ness
mas´sive
mass meet-ing
mas´so-ther´a-py
mass´y
mas´ta-ba
mast´er
mas´ter—at—arms
mas´ter-dom
mas´ter-ful
mas´ter-ful-ly
mas´ter-ly
mas´ter-piece
mas´ter-ship
mas´ter-work
mas´tery
mast´head
mas´tic
mas´ti-cate
mas-ti-ca´tion
mas´ti-ca-tor
mas´ti-ca-to-ry
mas´tiff
mas-tit´ic
mas-ti´tis
mas´to-don
mas´toid
mas-toi´dal
mas-toid-i´tis
mat´a-dor

match´able
match´board
match´less
match´lock
match´mak-er
match´mak-ing
match´wood
ma´té
mate´lot
ma´ter
ma-te´ri-al
ma-te´ri-al-ism
ma-te´ri-al-ist
ma-te´ri-al-is´tic
ma-te´ri-al-is´ti-cal-ly
ma-te´ri-al-ism
ma-te´ri-al´i-ty
ma-te-ri-al-iza´tion
ma-te´ri-al-ly
ma-te-ri-el´
ma-ter´nal
ma-ter´nal-ly
ma-ter´ni-ty
math-e-mat´i-cal
math-e-mat´i-cal-ly
math-e-ma-ti´cian
math-e-mat´ics
ma-thet´ic
Ma-til´da
mat´in
mat´in-al
mat´i-nee´
mat´ing
ma´tri-arch
ma´tri-ar´chal
ma´tri-arch-ate
ma´tri-ar-chy
ma´tri-ces
ma´tri-ci´dal
ma´tri-cide
ma-tric´u-late
ma-tric-u-la´tion
ma-tri-lin´eal
mat´ri-mo´ni-al
mat´ri-mo-ny
ma´trix
ma´tron
ma´tron-age
ma´tron-ize
ma´tron-li-ness
ma´tron-ly
mat´ted
mat´ter
Mat´ter-horn
mat´ter—of—fact´
Mat´thew
Mat-thi´as
mat´ting
mat´tock
mat´tress
mat´u-rate
mat-u-ra´tion
ma-ture´
ma-ture´ly
ma-ture´ness
ma-tur´i-ty
ma-tu´ti-nal
mat´zoth
Maugham
maul´er
maund´er
Maun´dy
Mau-pas-sant´
Mau-re-ta´nia
Mau-rice´
Mau-ri-ta´nia
Mau-ri´ti-us
Mau-rois´
Mau´ser
mau-so-le´um
mauve
mau´vine
mav´er-ick
ma´vis
mawk´ish
max-il´la
max´il-lary
max-il´lo—pal´a-tal
max´im
max´i-mal
max´i-mal-ist
Max-i-mil´ian
max´im-ite
max´i-mize
max´i-miz-er
max´i-mum
Max´well
Ma´ya
may´be
May Day
may´fish
May´flow-er
may´hap
may´hem
Mayo
may´on-naise
may´or
may´or-al-ty
may´pole
May´time
maz´a-rine´
maze
ma´zer
maz´i-ly
ma-zur´ka
ma-zut´
maz´y
maz´zard
McCar´thy
McClel´lan
McCor´mick
McKin´ley
me´a cul´pa
mead´ow
mead´owy
mea´ger
mea´ger-ly
meal´i-ness
meal´time
meal´worm
meal´y
meal´y-mouthed
mean
me-an´der
me-an´drous
mean´ing
mean´ing-ful
mean´ing-less
mean´ly
mean´ness
meant
mean´time
mean´while
mea´sles
mea´sly
mea-sur-abil´i-ty
mea´sur-able

mea´sure
mea´sured
mea´sure-ment
meat´y
Mec´ca
me-chan´ic
me-chan´i-cal
me-chan´i-cal-ly
mech-a-ni´cian
me-chan´ics
mech´a-nism
mech´a-nis´tic
mech-a-ni-za´tion
mech´a-nize
Mech´lin
Meck´len-burg
me-con´ic
med´al
med´aled
med´al-ist
me-dal´lic
me-dal´lion
med´dle
med´dler
med´dle-some
Me-de´a
me´dia
me´di-al
me´di-an
me-di-as-ti-ni´tis
me-di-as-ti´num
me´di-ate
me´di-ate-ly
me-di-a´tion
me´di-a-tive
me´di-a-tize
me´di-a-tor
me´di-a-to´ri-al
me´di-a-to-ry
med´ic
med´i-ca-ble
med´i-cal
med´i-cal-ly
me-dic´a-ment
med´i-cate
med-i-ca´tion
med´i-ca-tive
Med´i-ce´an
Med´i-ci
me-dic´i-na-ble
me-dic´i-nal
med´i-cine
med´i-cine bag
med´i-cine man
med´i-co
medie´val
medie´val-ist
Me-di´na
me´di-o´cre
medi-oc´ri-ty
med´i-tate
med-i-ta´tion
med´i-ta-tive
med´i-tat-or
Med´i-ter-ra´ne-an
me´di-um
me´di-um-is´tic
med´lar
med´ley
me-du´sa
meek´ly
meek´ness
meer´schaum
meet´ing
meet´ing-house
meet´ly
meg´a-cy-cle
meg´a-ga-mete´
meg´a-lith´ic
meg´a-lo-saur
meg´a-phone
meg´a-pod
meg´a-ton
mei´o-nite
mei-o´sis
mei-ot´ic
mei´ster
mel´a-mine
me´an-cho´lia
me´an-cho´li-ac
mel´an-chol´ic
mel´an-choly
Me-lanch´thon
Mel-a-ne´sia
me-lange´
me-lan´ger
me-lan´ic
mel´a-nin
mel´a-nism
mel´a-no
mel´a-noid
mel-a-no´ma
mel-a-no-stib´i-an
me-lan´ter-ite
mel-an-tha´ceous
Mel´bourne
Mel´chi-or
Mel-chiz´e-dek
meld´er
Mel-e-a´ger
me´lee
me-le´na
me-lez´i-tose
me-li-a´ceous
mel-i-bi´ose
mel´ic
Mel´i-cent
mel´i-lite
mel´i-lot
me´lio-rate
me-lio-ra´tion
me´lio-ra-tive
me´lio-rism
me´lio-rist
me-lior´i-ty
mel´is-mat´ic
Me-lis´sa
mel´i-tose
mel-lif´er-ous
mel-lif´lu-ence
mel-lif´lu-ent
mel´low
mel´low-ness
me-lo´de-on
me-lo´dia
me-lod´ic
me-lod´i-cal-ly
me-lo´di-on
me-lo´di-ous
me-lo´di-ous-ly
mel´o-dist
mel´o-dize
mel´o-dra-ma
mel´o-dra-mat´ic
mel´o-dram´a-tist
mel´o-dy
mel´oid

melo-ma´nia
mel´on
mel´o-nite
Mel´rose
melt-abil´i-ty
melt´able
melt´er
mel´ton
Mel´ville
mem´ber
mem´ber-ship
mem-bra-na´ceous
mem´bra-nate
mem´brane
mem´bra-nous
me-men´to
me-men´tos
Mem´non
mem´oir
mem-o-ra-bil´ia
mem-o-ra-bil´i-ty
mem´o-ra-ble
mem-o-ran´da
mem-o-ran´dum
me-mo´ri-al
me-mo´ri-al-ist
me-mo´ri-al-ize
me-mo´ri-al-iz-ing
me-mo´ri-am
mem´o-ries
mem-o-ri-za´tion
mem´o-rize
mem´o-riz-er
mem´o-riz-ing
mem´o-ry
Mem´phis
men´ace
men´ac-ing
men´ac-ing-ly
mé-nage´
me-nag´er-ie
me-naph´thone
Menc´ken
men-da´cious
men-da´cious-ly
men-dac´i-ty
Men´del
men-de-le´vi-um
Men´dels-sohn
mend´er
men´di-can-cy
men´di-cant
men-dic´i-ty
Men-e-la´us
men´folk
men-ha´den
men´hir
me´nial
Mé´ni-ère´
me-nin´ge-al
me-nin´ges
me-nin-gi-o´ma
men´in-git´ic
men-in-gi´tis
me-nin´go-cele
me-nin-go-coc´cus
Men´no-nite
Me-nom´i-nee
men-o-pau´sal
men´o-pause
Me-no´rah
men-or-rha´gia
men´ses
men´stru-al
men´stru-ate
men-stru-a´tion
men´stru-um
men-su-ra-bil´i-ty
men´su-ra-ble
men´su-ral
men-su-ra´tion
men´su-ra-tive
men´tal
men-tal´i-ty
men´tal-ly
men´thane
men´tha-nol
men´the-none
men´thol
men´tho-lat-ed
men´thyl
men´ti-cide
men´tion
men´tion-able
men´tion-er
men´tor
men´u
me-pro´ba-mate
mer´can-tile
mer´can-til-ism
mer-cap´tan
mer-cap´to
mer-cap-tom´er-in
mer´cap-tu´ric
Mer-ca´tor
mer´ce-nary
mer´cer
mer´cer-ize.
mer´cer-iz-ing
mer´cery
mer´chan-dise
mer´chan-dis-er
mer´chan-dis-ing
mer´chant
mer´chant-able
mer´chant-man
Mer´cia
mer´cies
mer´ci-ful
mer´ci-ful-ly
mer´ci-ful-ness
mer´ci-less
mer´cu-rate
mer-cu´ri-al
mer-cu´ri-al-ism
mer-cu-ri-al´i-ty
mer-cu´ric
mer-cu´ro-chrome
mer-cu´rous
mer´cu-ry
mer´cy
Mer´e-dith
mere´ly
me-re-ol´o-gy
mer´est
mer-e-tri´cious
mer-gan´ser
merge
mer´gence
Mer´gen-tha-ler
merg´er
Mer´i-den
me-rid´i-an
me-ringue´
me-ri´no
me-ri´nos
mer´ion

mer´ism
mer´i-stem
mer´i-ste-mat´ic
mer´it
mer´it-ed
mer-i-to´ri-ous
mer´lin
mer´maid
mer´man
mer-o-he´dral
mer´ri-ly
Mer´ri-mac
mer´ri-ment
mer´ri-ness
mer´ry
mer´ry—an´drew
mer´ry—go—round
mer´ry-mak-er
mer´ry-mak-ing
me´sa
mes´al-liance´
mes´ar-te-ri´tis
mes-cal´
mes´ca-line
mes-dames´
mesh´work
mesh´y
me´si-al
mes´ic
mes´i-dine
mes´i-tyl
me-sit´y-lene
mes´mer´ic
mes´mer-ism
mes-mer-iza´tion
mes´mer-ize
mes´mer-iz-ing
mes´nal-ty
mes´o-blast
meso-car´dia
mes´o-carp
mes´o-derm
mes´o-der´mal
mes´o-lite
mes´o-mer´ic
me-som´er-ism
mes´on
mes´o-neph´ric
mes´o-neph´ros
Mes-o-po-ta´mia
mes´o-sphere
mes´o-the´li-um
mes´o-tron
Mes´o-zo´ic
mes-quite´
mes´sage
mes´sa-line´
mes´sen-ger
Mes-si´ah
Mes´si-an´ic
mes-sieurs´
mess´i-ness
mess´mate
mess´y
mes-ti´zo
mes-ti´zos
me-tab´a-sis
meta-bi´o-sis
meta-bi-ot´ic
met´a-bol´ic
me-tab´o-lism
me-tab´o-lite
me-tab´o-liz-able
me-tab´o-lize
met´a-bo´rate
met´a-car´pus
met´age
met´a-ge-net´ic
me-tag´ra-phy
met´al
met-al´de-hyde
met´al-ing
met´al-ist
me-tal´lic
met-al-lif´er-ous
met´al-line
met´al-lize
me-tal´lo-graph´ic
met-al-log´ra-phy
met´al-loid
met´al-lur´gic
met´al-lur´gi-cal
met´al-lur-leist
met´al-lur-gy
met´al-ware
met´al-work
met´al-work-ing
met´a-mer
met´a-mer´ic
me-tam´er-ism
me-tam´er-ized
meta-mor´phic
meta-mor´phism
meta-mor´phose
meta-mor´pho-ses
meta-mor´pho-sis
met´a-phor
met-a-phor´i-cal
met´a-phrase
meta-phys´i-cal
meta-phy-si´cian
met´a-phys´ics
met´a-pro´tein
met´a-sta-ble
me-tas´ta-sis
met´a-stat´ic
met´a-tar´sal
meta-tar´sus
me-tath´e-sis
meta-thet´ic
meta-tho´rax
Meta-zo´a
met-en-ceph´a-lon
me´te-or
me-te-or´ic
me´te-or-ite
me-te-or-it´ics
me-te-or´o-graph
me-te-o-rog´ra-phy
me´te-or-oid
me-te-oro-log´i-cal
me-te-o-rol´o-gist
me-te-o-rol´o-gy
me-te-or-om´e-ter
me´te-or-o-scope
me-te-or-os´co-py
me´ter
meth-ac´ry-late
meth-acryl´ic
meth´a-done
meth-al´lyl
meth´ane
meth´a-nol
meth´a-no´lic
meth-a-nol´y-sis
meth-a-nom´e-ter
meth-an´the-line

me-theg´lin
me-the´na-mine
meth´ene
meth´ide
meth´ion´ic
me-thi´o-nine
me´thi-um
meth´od
me-thod´i-cal
me-thod´i-cal-ly
Meth´od-ism
meth´od-ize
meth-od-ol´o-gy
me-tho´ni-um
Me-thu´se-lah
meth´yl
me-thyl´ic
me-thyl´i-dyne
meth´yl-naph´tha-
lene
meth´yl-ol-ure´a
me-tic-u-los´i-ty
me-tic´u-lous
mé-tier´
me-ton´y-my
met´ope
met´o-pon
met´ric
met´ri-cal
me-tri´cian
met´ri-fy
me-tri´tis
me-trol´o-gist
me-trol´o-gy
met´ro-nome
met´ro-nom´ic
met´ro-pole
me-trop´o-lis
met´ro-pol´i-tan
met´tle
met´tled
met´tle-some
Mex´i-can
Mex´i-co
mez´za-nine´
mez´zo
mez´zo—so-pra´no
mez´zo-tint
mho´me-ter

Mi-am´i
mi-as´ma
mi´ca
Mi´cah
mi-cel´lar
mi-celle´
Mi´chael
Mich´ael-mas
Mi-chel-an´ge-lo
Mi-chele´
Mich´i-gan
mi´cro-anal´y-sis
mi´cro-an-a-lyt´ic
mi´crobe
mi-cro´bi-al
mi-cro´bic
mi-cro´bi-cide
mi´cro-bio-log´i-cal
mi´cro-bi-ol´o-gist
mi´cro-bi-ol´o-gy
mi´cro-blade
mi´cro-card
mi´cro-ceph´a-ly
mi´cro-chem´is-try
mi´cro-cir´cuit
mi´cro-copy
mi´cro-cosm
mi´cro-cos´mic
mi´cro-fiche
mi´cro-film
mi´cro-gram
mi´cro-graph
mi´cro-graph´ic
mi-crog´ra-phy
mi´cro-groove
mi´cro-ma-chin´ing
mi-cro-me-rit´ics
mi-crom´e-ter
mi-cro-met´ri-cal
mi-rom´e-try
mi´cro-mod´ule
mi´cron
mi´cron-ize
mi-cro-or´ga-nism
ml´cro-phone
ml´cro-phon´ic
ml´cro-proc´es-sor
mi´cro-pro´gram
mi-cro-py-rom´e-ter

mi´cro-scope
mi´cro-scop´ic
mi-cros´co-py
mi´cro-seism
mi´cro-some
mi´cro-spore
mi´cro-tome
mi´cro-wave
mic´tu-rate
mic-tu-ri´tion
mid´af´ter-noon´
Mi´das
mid´brain
mid´day´
mid´den
mid´dle
mid´dle—aged´
mid´dle-man
mid´dle—of—the—
road´
mid´dle weight
mid´dy
midg´et
mi-di´
Mid´i-an
mid´iron
mid´land
mid´most
mid´night
mid´rib
mid´riff
mid´ship-man
mid´ships
mid´stream´
mid´sum´mer
mid´way
mid-week´ly
mid´west´
mid´west´ern
Mid-west´ern-er
mid´wife
mid´wife-ry
mid´win´ter
mid´year´
mien
might
might´i-er
might´i-ly
might´i-ness

might´y
mi-gnon´
mi´gnon-ette´
mi´graine
mi´grant
mi´grate
mi´grat-ing
mi-gra´tion
mi´gra-to-ry
mi-ka´do
mi-la´dy
Mi-lan´
milch
mil´dew
mil´dew-proof
mil´dewy
mild´ly
mild´ness
Mil´dred
mile´age
mile´post
mile´stone
mil-i-a´ria
mil´i-ary
mi-lieu´
mil´i-tan-cy
mil´i-tant
mil´i-tant-ly
mil-i-tar´ily
mil´i-ta-rism
mil´i-ta-rist
mil´i-ta-ris´tic
mil-i-ta-ri-za´tion
mil´i-ta-rize
mil´i-ta-riz-ing
mil´i-tary
mil´i-tate
mil´i-tat-ing
mi-li´tia
mi-li´tia-man
mil´i-um
milk bar
milk´er
milk´—fed
milk´i-ness
milk´ leg
milk´—liv-ered
milk´man
milk run
milk shake
milk´weed
milk´y
Mi´lay´
mill´board
mill´dam
mil-le-nar´i-an
mil´le-nary
mil-len´ni-al
mil-len´ni-um
mil´le-pede
mill´er
mil-les´i-mal
mil´let
mil´li-am´me-ter
mil´li-am´pere
mil´liard
mil´li-ary
mil´li-gram
Mil´li-kan
mil´li-me-ter
mil´li-mi´cron
mil´li-ner
mil´li-nery
mill´ing
mil´lion
mi´lion-aire´
mil´lionth
mil´li-pede
mill´pond
mill´race
mill´stone
mill´stream
mill wheel
Milne
mi´lo
mi-lord´
Milque´toast
Mil-ton´ic
Mil-wau´kee
mim´e-o-graph
mim´er
mi-me´sis
mi-met´ic
mim´e-tite
mim´ic
mim´icked
mim´ick-er
mim´ick-ing
mim´ic-ry
mim´ing
mi-mo´sa
mi-mo´sine
min´able
min´a-to-ri-ly
min´a-to-ry
mince´meat
mince´ pie´
minc´er
minc´ing
Min-da-nao´
Min´del
mind´er
mind´ful
mind´less
mind read´ing
min´er
min-er-ag´ra-phy
min´er-al
min´er-al-ize
min´er-al-iz-er
min´er-al-og´i-cal
min-er-al´o-gist
min-er-al´o-gy
Mi-ner´va
min-e-stro´ne
min´gle
min´gling
min´i-a-ture
min´i-a-tur-ist
min´i-kin
min´im
min´i-mal
min-i-mi-za´tion
min´i-mize
min´i-miz-er
min´i-mum
min´ing
min´ion
min´is-ter
min´is-te´ri-al
min-is-te´ri-um
min´is-trant
min-is-tra´tion
min´is-tries
min´is-try
min´i-track
min´i-um

min´i-ver
Min-ne-ap´o-lis
min´ne-sing-er
Min-ne-so´ta
min´now
Mi-no´an
mi-nom´e-ter
mi´nor
Mi-nor´ca
mi-nor´i-ty
Mi´nos
Min´o-taur
min´ster
min´strel
min´strel-sy
mint´age
mint´er
min´u-end
min-u-et´
Min´u-it
mi´nus
mi-nus´cu-lar
min´us-cule
min´ute
min´ute hand
mi-nute´ly
min´ute-man
mi-nute´ness
mi-nu´tia
mi-nu´ti-ae
Mi´o-cene
mi-o´sis
mi-ot´ic
mir´a-belle´
mi-rab´i-lite
mir´a-cle
mi-rac´u-lous
mi-rac´u-lous-ly
mir´a-dor
mi-rage´
Mi-ran´da
mired
Mir´i-am
mir´ing
mir´ror
mirth´ful
mirth´less
mis-ad-ven´ture
mis-al-li´ance
mis´an-thrope
mis´an-throp´ic
mis´an-throp´i-cal-ly
mis-an´thro-pist
mis-an´thro-py
mis-ap-pli-ca´tion
mis´ap-plied´
mis´ap-ply´
mis´ap-pre-hend´
mis-ap-pre-hen´sion
mis-ap-pro´pri-ate
mis-ap-pro-pri-a´tion
mis-ar-range´ment
mis-be-com´ing
mis-be-got´ten
mis-be-have´
mis-be-hav´ing
mis-be-hav´ior
mis-be-lief´
mis-be-lieve´
mis-be-liev´er
mis-cal´cu-late
mis-cal-cu-la´tion
mis-call´
mis-car´riage
mis-car´ried
mis-car´ry
mis-car´ry-ing
mis´cege-na´tion
mis-cel-la-ne´i-ty
mis-cel-la´neous
mis´cel-la-ny
mis-chance´
mis´chief
mis´chief—mak-er
mis´chie-vous
mis´chie-vous-ly
mis-con-ceive´
mis-con-cep´tion
mis-con´duct
mis-con-struc´tion
mis´con-strue´
mis´cre-ance
mis´cre-an-cy
mis´cre-ant
mis´cre-ate´
mis-cre-a´tion
mis-cue´
mis-deal´
mis-deed´
mis-de-mean´ant
mis´de-mean´or
mis-di-rect´
mis-di-rec´tion
mis-do´er
mis-do´ing
mi´ser
mis´er-a-ble
mis´er-a-bly
mi´ser-ly
mis´ery
mis-fea´sance
mis-fire´
mis´fit´
mis-for´tune
mis-gave´
mis-give´
mis-giv´ing
mis-gov´ern
mis-gov´ern-ment
mis-guid´ance
mis-guide´
mis-guid´ed
mis-han´dle
mis-han´dling
mis´hap
mis´hear´
mis´in-form´
mis´in-for-ma´tion
mis-in-ter´pret
mis´in-ter-pre-ta´tion
mis-judge´
mis-judg´ment
mis-laid´
mis-lay´
mis-lay´ing
mis-lead´
mis-lead´ing
mis-led´
mis-like´
mis-man´age
mis-man´age-ment
mis-match´
mis-mate´
mis-mat´ing
mis-name´
mis-no´mer
mi-sog´a-mist

mi-sog´a-my
mi-sog´y-nist
mi-sog´y-ny
mi-sol´o-gy
miso-ne´ism
mis-place´
mis-place´ment
mis´print
mis-pri´sion
mis´pro-nounce´
mis-pro-nounc´ing
mis-pro-nun-ci-a´tion
mis-quo-ta´tion
mis´quote´
mis´quot´ing
mis´read´
mis´rep-re-sent´
mis-rep-re-sen-ta´tion
mis-rule´
mis-rul´ing
mis´sal
mis-shape´
mis-shap´en
mis´sile
mis´sile-ry
miss´ing
mis´sion
mis´sion-ar-ies
mis´sion-ary
Mis-sis-sip´pi
mis´sive
Mis-sou´ri
mis-speak´
mis-spell´
mis-spelled´
mis-spell´ing
mis-spelt´
mis-spent´
mis-state´
mis-state´ment
mis-step´
mis-tak´able
mis-take´
mis-tak´en
mis-tak´en-ly
mis-tak´ing
mis´ter
mist´i-ness
mis´tle-toe

mis-took´
mis´tral
mis-treat´
mis-treat´ment
mis´tress
mis-tri´al
mis-trust´
mis-trust´ful
mist´y
mis-un-der-stand´
mis-un-der-stand´ing
mis-un-der-stood´
mis-us´age
mis-use´
mis-us´ing
Mitch´ell
mi´ter
mit´i-gate
mit´i-gat-ing
mit-i-ga´tion
mit´i-ga-tive
mit´i-ga-tor
mit´i-ga-to-ry
mi-to´sis
mi-tot´ic
mi´tral
mi´trate
mit´ten
mix´er
mix´ture
mix´—up
Miz´pah
miz´zen
miz´zen-mast
mo´a
Mo´ab-ite
moan´ing
mobbed
mob´bing
mo´bile
mo-bil´i-ty
mo-bi-li-za´tion
mo´bi-lize
moc´ca-sin
mo´cha
mo-chi´la
mock´er
mock´ery
mock´ing

mock´ing-bird
mock´ing-ly
mod´al
mod´al-ism
mo-dal´i-ty
mod´el
mod´eled
mod´el-ing
mod´er-ate
mod´er-ate-ly
mod´er-at-ing
mod-er-a´tion
mod´er-a-tor
mod´ern
mod´ern-ism
mod´ern-ist
mod´ern-is´tic
mo-der´ni-ty
mod-ern-iza´tion
mod´ern-ize
mod´ern-iz-ing
mod´ern-ly
mod´ern-ness
mod´est
mod´est-ly
mod´es-ty
mod´i-cum
mod´i-fi´able
mod-i-fi-ca´tion
mod´i-fi-ca-to-ry
mod´i-fied
mod´i-fi-er
mod´i-fy
mod´i-fy-ing
mod´ish
mo-diste´
mod-u-la-bil´i-ty
mod´u-lar
mod´u-late
mod-u-la´tion
mod´u-la-tor
mod´u-la-to-ry
mod´ule
mo´dus ope-ran´di
mo´dus vi-ven´di
mo´gul
mo´hair
Mo-ham´med
Mo-ham´med-an

Mo-ha´ve
Mo´hawk
Mo-hi´can
mo´hole
moi´e-ty
moil´ing
moi´ra
moi-ré´
moist´en
moist´en-er
moist´ly
moist´ness
mois´ture
mois´ture-proof
mo´lar
mo-lar´i-ty
mo´la-ry
mo-las´ses
mold
mold´able
mold´board
mold´er
mold´i-ness
mold´ing
mold´y
mo-lec´u-lar
mol´e-cule
mole´hill
mole´skin
mo-lest´
mo-les-ta´tion
mo-lest´er
Mo-li´na
mol-les´cent
mol-li-fi-ca´tion
mol´li-fied
mol´li-fy
mol´li-fy-ing
mol´li-sol
mol´lusk
Mol´ly
mol´ly-cod-dle
Mo-lo-kai´
Mo´lo-tov
mol´ten
molt´er
Mo-luc´ca
mo-lyb´date
mo-lyb´de-nite
mo-lyb´de-num
mo-lyb´dic
mo´ment
mo´men-tar´i-ly
mo´men-tary
mo´ment-ly
mo-men´tous
mo-men´tum
Mon´a-can
mon´a-chal
mon´a-chism
Mo´na-co
mo´nad
mo-nad´ic
mo-nad-is´tic
mo-nad´nock
mon´arch
mo-nar´chal
mo-nar´chi-al
mo-nar´chi-an-ism
mo-nar´chic
mo-nar´chi-cal
mon´ar-chism
mon´ar-chist
mon´ar-chy
mon´as-te´ri-al
mon´as-tery
mo-nas´tic
mo-nas´ti-cism
mon´atom´ic
mon-ax´i-al
mon´a-zite
Mon´day
Mo-net´
mon-e-tar´i-ly
mon´e-tary
mon´e-tite
mon-e-ti-za´tion
mon´e-tize
mon´ey
mon´ey-bags
mon´eyed
mon´ey-mak-er
mon´ey-mak-ing
mon´ey or-der
mon´eys
mon´ey-wort
mon´ger
Mon´gol
Mon-go´lia
Mon´gol-oid
mon´goose
mon´grel
Mon´i-ca
mon´i-ker
mo-ni´tion
mon´i-tor
mon´i-to´ri-al
mon´key
mon´key-ish
mon´keys
mon´key-shine
monk´hood
monk´ish
monks´hood
Mon´mouth
mon´o-ac´id
mon´o-acid´ic
mon´o-am´ide
mon´o-amine´
mon´o-ba´sic
mon´o-chord
mon´o-chro-mat´ic
mono-chro´ma-tor
mon´o-chrome
mon´o-chro´mous
mo-noch´ro-nous
mon´o-cle
mo-noc´u-lar
mo-nod´ic
mo-nod´i-cal-ly
mon´o-dra´ma
mon´o-dy
mo-noe´cious
mon´o-gam´ic
mo-nog´a-mist
mo-nog´a-mous
mo-nog´a-my
mon´o-ge-net´ic
mon´o-gen´ic
mo-nog´e-nism
mo-nog´e-ny
mo-nog´o-ny
mon´o-gram
mon´o-gram-mat´ic
mon´o-grammed
mon´o-graph
mo-nog´ra-pher

mon´o-graph´ic
mo-nog´y-ny
mo-nol´a-try
mon´o-lith
mon´o-lith´ic
mon´o-log
mo-nol´o-gist
mon´o-logue
mon´o-ma´nia
mon´o-ma´ni-ac
mon´o-ma-ni´a-cal
mon´o-mer
mo-nom´er-ous
mon´o-me-tal´lic
mon´o-met´al-lism
mo-nom´e-ter
mo-no´mi-al
Mo-non-ga-he´la
mon´o-nu-cle-o´sis
mon´o-plane
mo-nop´o-list
mo-nop´o-lis´tic
mo-nop-o-li-za´tion
mo-nop´o-lize
mo-nop´o-ly
mo-nop´so-ny
mon´o-rail
mon´o-spor´ous
mon´o-stome
mon´o-strophe
mon´o-syl-lab´ic
mon´o-syl´la-ble
mon´o-the-ism
mon´o-the-ist
mon´o-the-is´tic
mon´o-tone
mo-not´o-nous
mo-not´o-ny
mon´o-treme
mo-not´ri-chous
mo-not´ro-py
Mon´o-type
mon´o-typ´ic
mon´o-va´lent
mon-ox´ide
Mon-roe´ Doc´trine
Mon-ro´via
mon-sei-gneur´
mon-sieur´
mon-si´gnor
mon-soon´
mon´ster
mon´strance
mon-stros´i-ty
mon´strous
mon-tage´
Mon-taigne´
Mon-tan´a
Mon´te Car´lo
Mon´te-ne´grin
Mon´te-ne´gro
Mon´te-rey
Mon´ter-rey´
Mon´tes-quieu´
Mon´tes-so´ri
Mon-te-vi-de´o
Mon-te-zu´ma
Mont-gol-fier´
Mont-gom´ery
month´ly
Mon-ti-cel´lo
mon-tic´u-late
mon´ti-cule
Mont-mar´tre
Mont-pe´lier
Mon´tre-al´
mon´u-ment
mon-u-men´tal
mood´i-ly
mood´i-ness
mood´y
mooed
moo´ing
moon´beam
moon´eye
moon´fish
moon´less
moon´light
moon´lit
moon´rise
moon´shine
moon´shin-er
moon´stone
moon´struck
moor´age
moor´hen
moor´ing
Moor´ish
moor´land
moped
mop´ing
mop´pet
mop´ping
mo-quette´
mor´al
mo-rale´
mor´al-ism
mor´al-ist
mor´al-is´tic
mo-ral´i-ty
mor-al-iza´tion
mor´al-ize
mor´al-ly
mo-rass´
mor-a-to´ri-um
mor´a-tory
Mo-ra´vi-an
mo-ra´vite
mo-ray´
mor´bid
mor-bid´i-ty
mor´bid-ly
mor-bose´
mor-da´cious
mor-dac´i-ty
mor´dan-cy
mor´dant
Mor´de-cai
mor´dent
mo-reen´
more-o-ver
mo´res
Mor´gan
mor´ga-nat´ic
Mor´gan-ton
Mor´gan-town
Mor´gen-thau
morgue
mor´i-bund
mor-i-bun´di-ty
mo-rin´done
mo´rin-ite
mo´ri-on
Mor´ley
Mor´mon
Mor´mon-ism
Mor´mon-ite

morn´ing
morn´ing glo´ry
morn´ing star
Mo´ro
Mo-roc´can
Mo-roc´co
mo´ron
mo-ron´ic
mo-rose´
mo-rose´ly
mo-rose´ness
mo-ros´i-ty
mor´pheme
mor-phe´mics
Mor´pheus
mor´phine
mor-phog´ra-phy
mor´pho-line
mor´pho-log´ic
mor-pho-log´i-cal
mor-phol´o-gist
mor-phol´o-gy
mor-phom´e-try
mor´ris
mor´row
mor´sal
mor´sel
mor´tal
mor-tal´i-ty
mor´tal-ly
mor´tar
mor´tar-board
mort´gage
mort´ga-gee´
mort´gag-ing
mort´ga-gor´
mor-ti´cian
mor-ti-fi-ca´tion
mor´ti-fied
mor´ti-fy
mor´ti-fy-ing
Mor´ti-mer
mor´tise
mor´tis-er
mor´tis-ing
Mor´ton
mor´tu-ary
mor´u-la
mo-sa´ic
mo-sa´i-cism
Mos´cow
Mo-selle´
Mo´ses
Mos´lem
mosque
mos-qui´to
mos-qui´toes
moss´back
moss´—grown
moss´i-er
moss´i-ness
moss´y
most´ly
mo-tel´
mo-tet´
moth´—eat-en
moth´er
moth´er-hood
moth´er—in—law
moth´er-land
moth´er-less
moth´er-li-ness
moth´er-ly
moth´proof
mo-tif´
mo´tile
mo-til´i-ty
mo-tion
mo´tion-less
mo´ti-vate
mo´ti-vat-ing
mo-ti-va´tion
mo-tive
mo´tive-less
mo-tiv´i-ty
mot´ley
mo´tor
mo´tor-bus
mo´tor-cade
mo´tor-car
mo´tor-cy-cle
mo´tor-cy-clist
mo´tor-ist
mo-tor-iza´tion
mo´tor-ize
mo´tor-man
mot´tle
mot´tled
mot´tling
mot´to
mot´toes
mouf´lon
mou-lage´
mou-lin´
mount´able
moun´tain
moun´tain-eer´
moun´tain-ous
moun´te-bank
mount´ed
mount´er
mount´ing
Mount Ver´non
mourn´er
mourn´ful
mourn´ing
mous´er
mouse´tail
mouse´trap
mousse-line´
Mous-sorg´sky
mous´tache
mous´y
mouth´ful
mouth´piece
mou´ton
mov-a-bil´i-ty
mov´able
move´ment
mov´er
mov´ie
mov´ies
mov´ing
mowed
mow´er
mow´ing
mown
Mo-zam-bique´
Mo´zart
mu-ced´i-nous
mu´cic
mu´cid
mu-cif´er-ous
mu´ci-lage
mu´ci-lag´i-nous
muck´rake
muck´y

mu´coid
mu´cous
mu´cus
mud´dle
mud´dled
mud´dy
mud´fish
mud´guard
mu-ez´zin
muf´fin
muf´fin-eer´
muf´fle
muf´fler
muf´fling
muf´ti
mug´ger
mug´gi-ness
mug´ging
mug´gy
mug´wump
Mu-ham´mad
mu-lat´to
mu-lat´toes
mul´ber-ry
mulch´er
mulct
mul´ish
mul´lah
mull´er
mul´let
mul´li-gan
mul-li-ga-taw´ny
mul´lion
mul-ti-cel´lu-lar
mul´ti-col´ored
mul´ti-di-men´sion-al
mul´ti-di-rec´tion-al
mul´ti-dis´ci-pli-nary
mul´ti—eth´nic
mul´ti-fam´i-ly
mul´ti-far´i-ous
mul´ti-fid
mul´ti-form
mul´ti-fu´el
mul´ti-lat´er-al
mul´ti-lay-er
mul-ti-lev´el
mul´ti-lin´gual
mul´ti-me´dia
mul-ti-mil´lion-aire´
mul´ti-na´tion-al
mul´ti-pack
mul´ti-ped
mul´ti-ple
mul´ti-plex
mul´ti-pli-able
mul´ti-plic´a-ble
mul-ti-pli-cand´
mul-ti-pli-ca´tion
mul´ti-pli-ca´tive
mul-ti-plic´i-ty
mul´ti-plied
mul´ti-pli-er
mul´ti-ply
mul´ti-ply-ing
mul´ti-tude
mul-ti-tu´di-nous
mul´ti-va´lent
mum´ble
mum´bling
mum´mer
mum´mery
mum´mi-fy
mum´my
Mun´chau-sen
mun´dane´
mun´go
Mu´nich
mu-nic´i-pal
mu-nic-i-pal´i-ty
mu-nic´i-pal-ize
mu-nif´i-cence
mu-ni´tion
mu´ral
mu-rar´i-um
mur´der
mur´der-er
mur´der-ess
mur´der-ous
mu´ri-at´ic
Mu-ril´lo
mu´rine
mu´ri-um
murk´i-er
murk´i-ly
murk´y
mur´mur
mur´mur-ing
mur´mur-ous
Mur´phy
mur´rain
mu-sa´ceous
mus´ca-dine
mus´ca-rine
mus´cat
mus´ca-tel´
mus´cle
mus´cle—bound
Mus´co-vite
Mus´co-vy
mus´cu-lar
mus-cu-lar´i-ty
mus´cu-la-ture
mused
mu-se-og´ra-phy
mu-se-ol´o-gy
mus´er
mu-sette´
mu-se´um
mush´room
mush´y
mu´sic
mu´si-cal
mu´si-cale´
mu´si-cal-ly
mu-si´cian
mu-si-col´o-gy
mus´ing
musk deer
Mus-ke´gon
mus´ket
mus-ke-teer´
mus´ket-ry
musk´mel-on
Mus-ko´gee
musk´—ox
musk´—ox-en
musk´rat
musk´y
mus´lin
mus´sel
Mus-so-li´ni
muss´y
mus´tache
mus´tang
mus´tard
mus´te-line

mus´ter
must´i-ness
must´y
mu-ta-bil´i-ty
mu´ta-ble
mu´ta-gen´ic
mu´tant
mu´tase
mu´tate
mu´tat-ing
mu-ta´tion
mu´ta-tive
mut´ed
mute´ly
mute´ness
mu´ti-late
mu-ti-la´tion
mu´ti-la-tor
mu´ti-neer´
mut´ing
mu´ti-nied
mu´ti-nous
mu´tiny
mu´ti-ny-ing
mut´ism
mu´ton
mut´ter
mut´ter-ing
mut´ton
mut´ton-head
mu´tu-al
mu´tu-al-ism
mu-tu-al´i-ty
mu´tu-al-iza´tion
mu´tu-al-ly
mu´tu-el
mu´tule
mu-zhik´
muz´zle
muz´zle—load-er
muz´zling
my-al´gia
my-ce´li-oid
my-ce´li-um
My-ce´nae
my-ce-to´ma
my-col´o-gist
my-col´o-gy
my-co-my´cin
my-co´sis
my´e-lo-cyte
my´e-loid
my-e-lo-ma-to´sis
my´e-lom´a-tous
my-e-lop´a-thy
my-e-lo´sis
my´na
my-o-car-di´tis
my-o´ma
my-op´a-thy
my-o´pia
my-op´ic
my´o-sin
my-o-si´tis
my-os´mine
my-ot´o-my
myr´i-ad
myr´i-am-e-ter
myr´i-a-pod
myr´i-cyl
myr-in-gi´tis
my-ris´tate
my-ris´tic
My´ron
myrrh
myrrh´ic
myr´tle
my-self´
mys´ter-ies
mys-te´ri-ous
mys-te´ri-ous-ly
mys´tery
mys´tic
mys´ti-cal
mys´ti-cism
mys´ti-fi-ca´tion
mys´ti-fied
mys´ti-fy
mys´ti-fy-ing
mys´ti-fy-ing-ly
mys-tique´
myth´ic
myth´i-cal
myth´i-cal-ly
myth´i-cist
myth´i-cize
my-thog´ra-pher
myth-o-log´i-cal
my-thol´o-gist
my-thol´o-gy
myth-o-ma´nia
myx-ede´ma
myx´o-bac-te´ri-al
myx-o-ma-to´sis

N

nab´bing
na´bob
na´cre
na´cre-ous
na´crite
na´dir
na-ga´na
Na´ga-sa´ki
nag´ging
Na-go´ya
nah´co-lite
Na´hum
na´iad
nail´er
nail´wort
nain´sook
Nai-ro´bi
na-ive´
na-ive-té´
na´ked
na´ked-ness
nam´by—pam´by
name´able
name´less
name´ly
nam´er
name´sake
nam´ing
Na-mur´
Na-nai´mo
Nan´cy
nan-keen´
Nan´king´
na´no-gram
na´noid
Nan´sen
Nantes
Nan-tuck´et
na-ol´o-gy
Na-o´mi

na´palm
nape
na-phaz´o-line
naph´tha
naph´tha-lene
naph´tha-len´ic
naph-thal´ic
naph´thene
naph´the-nic
naph´thi-o-nate
naph´thi-on´ic
naph´thyl
naph´thy-lene
Na´pi-er
nap´kin
Na´ples
Na-po´leon
nap´per
nap´ping
nar´ce-ine
nar´cis-sism
nar´cis-sist
nar-cis´sus
nar´co-lep-sy
nar-co-lep´tic
nar-co´ma
nar-co´sis
nar-cot´ic
nar´co-tism
nar´co-tize
nard
nar´es
nar´gi-leh
nar-in-gen´in
na-rin´gin
nar´is
Nar-ra-gan´sett
nar´rate
nar-ra´tion
nar´ra-tive
nar´ra-tor
nar´row
nar´row—gage´
nar´row-ly
nar´row—mind´ed
nar´row-ness
Nar-va´ez
na´sal
na-sa´lis

na-sal´i-ty
na´sal-ize
na´sal-ly
Nash´ville
na´si-on
na´so-scope
Nas´sau
nas´tic
nas´ti-ly
nas´ti-ness
nas´ty
na´tal
Na-tal´
na´tant
na-ta´tion
na-ta-to´ri-al
na-ta-to´ri-um
na´ta-to-ry
Natch´ez
Na´than
Na-than´iel
na´tion
na´tion-al
na´tion-al-ism
na´tion-al-ist
na´tion-al-is´tic
na-tion-al´i-ty
na-tion-al-iza´tion
na´tion-al-ize
na´tion-al-ly
na´tion-wide´
na´tive
na´tive—born´
na´tive-ly
na´tive-ness
na´tiv-ism
na´tiv-is´tic
na-tiv´i-ty
na´tri-um
na´tro-lite
na´tron
nat´ti-ly
nat´ty
nat´u-ral
nat´u-ral-ism
nat´u-ral-ist
nat´u-ral-is´tic
nat-u-ral-iza´tion
nat´u-ral-ize

nat´u-ral-ly
nat´u-ral-ness
na´ture
na´tur-o-path
na-tur-op´a-thy
naught
naugh´ti-ly
naugh´ti-ness
naugh´ty
nau´pli-us
Na-u´ru
nau´sea
nau´se-ate
nau´se-at-ed
nau´seous
nau´ti-cal
nau´ti-cal-ly
nau´ti-lus
Nav´a-ho, Nav´a-jo
na´val
Na-varre´
na´vel
na-vic´u-lar
na´vies
nav-i-ga-bil´i-ty
nav´i-ga-ble
nav´i-gate
nav-i-ga´tion
nav´i-ga-tor
na´vy
na´vy yard
Naz´a-rene
Naz´a-reth
Na´zi
na´zi-ism
na´zism
Ne-an´der-thal
Ne-a-pol´i-tan
neap tide
near´by´
Ne-arc´tic
near´est
near´ly
near´ness
near´sight-ed
neat´ly
neat´ness
Ne´bo
Ne-bras´ka

neb´ris
Neb-u-chad-nez´zar
neb´u-la
neb´u-lae
neb´u-lar
ne-bu´li-um
neb-u-los´i-ty
neb´u-lous
nec´es-sar´i-ly
nec´es-sary
ne-ces´si-tar´i-an
ne-ces´si-tate
ne-ces´si-ties
ne-ces´si-tous
ne-ces´si-tous-ly
ne-ces´si-ty
Neck´er
neck´er-chief
neck´ing
neck´lace
neck´line
neck´piece
neck´tie
neck´wear
nec´ro-bi-o´sis
nec´ro-log´i-cal
ne-crol´o-gist
ne-crol´o-gy
nec´ro-man-cer
nec´ro-man-cy
ne´crop-sy
ne-cro´sis
ne-crot´ic
nec´ro-tize
ne-crot´o-my
nec´tar
nec-tar´e-ous
nec´tar-ine´
nec´ta-ry
need´ful
need´i-er
need´i-est
need´i-ness
nee´dle
nee´dle-fish
nee´dle-ful
nee´dle-like
nee´dle-point
nee´dler
need´less
need´less-ly
need´less-ness
nee´dle-wom-an
nee´dle-work
need´y
ne'er´—do—well
ne-far´i-ous
ne-gate´
ne-ga´tion
neg´a-tive
neg´a-tive-ly
neg´a-tiv-ism
neg´a-tiv-is´tic
neg-a-tiv´i-ty
neg´a-to-ry
neg´a-tron
ne-glect
ne-glect´er
ne-glect´ful
neg-li-gee´
neg´li-gence
neg´li-gent
neg´li-gent-ly
neg-li-gi-bil´i-ty
neg´li-gi-ble
ne-go-tia-bil´i-ty
ne-go´tia-ble
ne-go´ti-ate
ne-go´ti-at-ing
ne-go-ti-a´tion
ne-go´ti-a-tor
Ne´gro
ne´gus
Ne-he-mi´ah
Neh´ru
neigh
neigh´bor
neigh´bor-hood
neigh´bor-ing
neigh´bor-li-ness
neigh´bor-ly
nei´ther
Nel´son
Nem´bu-tal
ne-mes´ic
nem´e-sis
nem´o-ral
Ne´o-Ant-er´gan
ne´o-blast
Ne´o-cene
ne´o-clas´si-cal
neo-dym´i-um
ne-og´a-my
Ne´o-lith´ic
ne´o-log´i-cal
ne-ol´o-gism
ne-ol´o-gist
ne-ol´o-gy
ne´o-my´cin
ne´on
ne´o-phyte
ne-o-pla´sia
ne´o-plasm
ne´o-prene
Neo-sy-neph´rine
ne´o-ter´ic
ne-ot´er-ism
ne-ot´o-cite
Ne-pal´
Nep´a-lese´
ne-pen´the
ne-pen´the-an
neph´e-line
neph´e-lin-ite
neph´e-lite
neph´ew
ne-phol´o-gy
neph´o-scope
neph´ric
neph´rite
ne-phrit´ic
ne-phri´tis
ne-phrol´o-gy
nep´o-tism
Nep´tune
Ne´re-id
ne-rit´ic
Ne´ro
ner´o-li
ne-rol´i-dol
Ne-ro´ni-an
ner-ter-ol´o-gy
ner´vate
ner-va´tion
nerve´less
ner´vine
nerv´ing

ner-vos´i-ty
ner´vous
ner´vous-ly
ner´vous-ness
nerv´y
nest´er
nes´tle
nes´tling
Nes´tor
neth´er
Neth´er-lands
neth´er-most
net´ting
net´tle
net´tled
net´work
neu´ral
neu-ral´gia
neu-ral´gic
neu´rine
neu-rit´ic
neu-ri´tis
neu´ro-gen´ic
neu-rog´lia
neu-rog´ra-phy
neu´roid
neu-ro-log´i-cal
neu-rol´o-gist
neu-rol´o-gy
neu-rol´y-sis
neu-ro´ma
neu´ron
neu´ro-nal
neu-ron´ic
neu´ro-path´ic
neu-rop´a-thy
neu-rop´ter-ous
neu-ro´ses
neu-ro´sis
neu-rot´ic
neu-rot´i-cism
neu-rot´o-my
neu´ro-trop´ic
neu-rot´ro-pism
neu´ter
neu´tral
neu´tral-ism
neu-tral´i-ty
neu-tral-i-za´tion
neu´tral-ize
neu´tral-iz-er
neu´tral-ly
neu-tri´no
neu´tron
Ne-vad´a
nev´er
nev´er-more´
nev´er-the-less´
ne´vus
New´ark
new´born
New´burgh
New´cas-tle
new´com-er
new´el
new´fan´gled
New´found-land
New Guin´ea
New Hamp´shire
New Ha´ven
New Jer´sey
new´ly
New´man
New´market
New Mex´i-co
new´ness
New Or´leans
New´port
news´boy
news´cast
news´cast-er
news´ deal-er
news´let-ter
news´man
news´pa-per
news´pa-per-man
news´print
news´reel
news´room
news´stand
news´y
New´ton
New Zea´land
nex´us
ni´a-cin
ni-a-cin´a-mide
Ni-ag´a-ra
nib´ble
nib´bling
nib´lick
Nic´a-ra´gua
nice´ly
Ni´cene
nice´ness
nic´est
ni´ce-ty
niche
Nich´o-las
nick´el
nick-el-if´er-ous
nick´el-ine´
nick-el-o´de-on
nick´el—plate
nick´el-type
nick´er
nick´name
nic-o-tin´amide
nic-o-tin´ate
nic´o-tine
nic´o-tin´ic
nic´o-tin-ism
nic-o-ti´no-yl
nic´o-tin-u´ric
nic´ti-tate
nic-ti-ta´tion
ni´dor
ni´dus
Nie´buhr
niece
Nietz-sche
nif´ty
Ni´ger
Ni-ge´ria
ni´ger-ite
nig´gard
nig´gard-ly
night´cap
night´club
night´fall
night´gown
night´hawk
night´in-gale
night´long
night´ly
night´mare
night´shirt
night´time

ni-gres´cence
ni-gres´cent
ni´grous
ni´hi-lism
ni´hi-list
ni´hi-lis´tic
ni-hil´i-ty
Ni´ke
nim´ble
nim´ble-ness
nim´bly
nim´bo-stra´tus
nim´bus
ni-mi´e-ty
Nim´rod
nin´com-poop
nine´fold
nine´pins
nine´teen´
nine´teenth´
nine´ti-eth
nine´ty
Nin´e-veh
nin´ny
ninth
ninth´ly
Ni´o-be
ni-o´bic
ni-o´bi-um
ni´pa
nip´e-cot´ic
nip´per
nip´ping
nip´ple
Nip´pon
nip´py
Ni-sei´
Nis´sen
ni´sus
ni´ter
nit´id
ni-tid´i-ty
ni-tra-mine´
ni´trate
ni´tra-tor
ni´tric
ni´tride
ni´trid-ize
ni-tri-fi-ca´tion
ni´tri-fy
ni´trile
ni´trite
ni-tro-an´i-line
ni´tro-gen
ni´tro-gen-ate
ni-tro´gen-ize
ni-trog´en-ous
ni-tro-glyc´er-in
ni-tro´lic
ni-trom´e-ter
ni-tro´ni-um
ni-tros-amine´
ni´tro-sate
ni-tro´so
ni´trous
nit´wit
Nix´on
No´ah
No-bel´
no-bel´i-um
no-bil´i-ary
no-bil´i-ty
no´ble
no´ble-man
no´ble-ness
no´ble-wom-an
no´bly
no´body
no-car-di-o´sis
no´cent
noc-ti-lu´ca
noc-tiv´a-gant
noc´to-vi-sion
noc-tur´nal
noc´turne
noc´u-ous
nod´al
no-dal´i-ty
nod´ding
nod´dle
nod´dy
nod´i-cal
nod´u-lar
nod´ule
No-el´
nog´gin
no´how
noise´less
noise´less-ly
nois´i-ly
nois´i-ness
nois´ing
noi´some
nois´y
No-ko´mis
no´lo con-ten´de-re
no´mad
no-mad´ic
no-mad´i-cal
no´mad-ism
nom´arch
nom´archy
nom de plume
no´men-cla-tor
no´men-cla-ture
nom´ic
nom´i-nal
nom´i-nal-ly
nom´i-nal-ism
nom´i-nal-ist
nom´i-nal-ize
nom´i-nate
nom´i-nat-ed
nom-i-na´tion
nom´i-na-tive
nom´i-na-tor
nom´i-nee´
no-moc´ra-cy
nom´o-gram
nom´o-graph´ic
no-mog´ra-phy
no-mol´o-gy
nom-o-thet´ic
non-ac-cept´ance
non-a-co´sane
non-a-dec´ane
non´age
nona-ge-nar´i-an
non-ag-gres´sion
non´a-gon
non-ap-pear´ance
non´cha-lance´
non´cha-lant´
non´cha-lant-ly
non-com-bat´ant
non-com-mis´sioned
non-com-mit´tal

non com´pos men´tis
non-con-duc´tor
non-con-form´ist
non-con-form´i-ty
non-co-op-er-a´tion
non´de-script
no´nene
non-en´ti-ty
non-es-sen´tial
none´such
non-ex-is´tence
non-ex-is´tent
non-fea´sance
non´fic´tion
non-ful-fill´ment
non-in-ter-ven´tion
non-join´der
non-me-tal´lic
non-ni-trog´e-nous
non´pa-reil´
non´parous
non-par-tic´i-pat-ing
non-par´ti-san
non´pay´ment
non´plus´
non-plussed´
non-plus´sing
non-pro-duc´tive
non-prof´it
non pro-se´qui-tur
non-res´i-dence
non-res´i-dent
non-sec-tar´i-an
non´sense
non-sen´si-cal
non se´qui-tur
non´skid´
non´stop´
non´suit´
non´sup-port´
non-un´ion
noo´dle
no-ol´o-gy
noon´day
noon´tide
noon´time
no´pal
no´pi-nene
No´ra
Nor´dic
Nor´folk
no´ria
nor´mal
nor´mal-cy
nor-mal´i-ty
nor´mal-ize
nor´mal-iz-er
nor´mal-ly
Nor´man
Nor´man-dy
nor´ma-tive
Nor´ris
Norse´man
North Amer´i-ca
North-amp´ton
North Car-o-li´na
North Da-ko´ta
north´east´
north-east´er
north-east´er-ly
north-east´ern
north-east´ward
north´er
north´er-ly
north´ern
north´ern-er
north´ern-most
north´land
North-um´ber-land
North-um´bri-an
north´ward
north´ward-ly
north´west´
north´west´er-ly
north-west´ern
Nor´way
Nor´wich
nose bag
nose´band
nose´bleed
nose´—dive
nose´gay
no´se-lite
nose´piece
nos´ing
no-sog´ra-phy
nos-o-log´i-cal
no-sol´o-gist
no-sol´o-gy
nos-tal´gia
nos-tal´gic
nos-tol´o-gy
nos´tril
nos´trum
nos´y
no´ta-ble
no´ta-ble-ness
no´ta-bly
no´tam
no-tar´i-al
no´ta-ries
no´ta-rize
no´ta-ry
no´ta-ry pub´lic
no-ta´tion
notched
notch´er
note´book
not´ed
note´less
note´pa-per
note´wor-thi-ly
note´wor-thi-ness
note´wor-thy
noth´ing
noth´ing-ness
no´tice
no´tice-able
no´tice-ably
no´tic-ing
no´ti-fi-ca´tion
no´ti-fied
no´ti-fi-er
no´ti-fy
no´ti-fy-ing
not´ing
no´tion
no´tion-al
No-to-gae´an
no-to-ri´e-ty
no-to´ri-ous
no-to´ri-ous-ly
no-to-un´gu-late
Not´ting-ham
not-with-stand´ing
nou´gat
nour´ish

nour´ish-ing
nour´ish-ment
nou-veau´ riche
No´va Sco´tia
no-va´tion
nov´el
nov´e´ette´
nov´el-ist
nov-el-is´tic
nov´el-ize
no-vel´la
nov´el-ties
nov´el-ty
No-vem´ber
no-ve´na
nov´ice
no-vi´tiate
No´vo-cain
now´a-days
no´way
no´ways
no´where
no´wise
nox´ious
noz´zle
nu´ance
nub´bin
nu´chal
nu´ci-form
nu´cle-ar
nu´cle-ate
nu-cle-a´tion
nu´cle-a-tor
nu´clei
nu-cle´ic
nu´cle-us
nu´clide
nu-clid´ic
nude´ness
nudged
nudg´er
nudg´ing
nud´ism
nud´ist
nu´di-ty
nu´ga-to-ry
nug´get
nui´sance
nul-li-fi-ca´tion

nul´li-fied
nul´li-fi-er
nul´li-fy
nul´li-fy-ing
nul´li-ty
num´ber
num´bered
num´ber-er
num´ber-less
numb´fish
numb´ing
num´bles
numb´ly
numb´ness
nu´men
nu-mer-a-ble
nu´mer-al
nu´mer-ary
nu´mer-ate
nu-mer-a´tion
nu´mer-a-tive
nu´mer-a-tor
nu-mer´i-cal
nu-mer´i-cal-ly
nu-mer-ol´o-gy
nu´mer-ous
nu´mi-nous
nu-mis-mat´ics
nu-mis´ma-tist
num´skull
nun´ci-a-ture
nun´cio
nun´cu-pa-tive
nun´like
nun´nery
nup´tial
nup-ti-al´i-ty
Nur´em-berg
nurse´maid
nurse-er
nur´sery
nur´sery-man
nurs´ing
nurs´ling
nur´tur-al
nur´ture
nur´tur-ing
nut´crack-er
nut´hatch

nut´meg
nu´tria
nu´tri-ent
nu´tri-lite
nu´tri-ment
nu-tri´tion
nu-tri´tion-al
nu-tri´tion-ist
nu-tri´tious
nu´tri-tive
nut´shell
nut´ter
nut´ti-er
nut´ti-ness
nut´ting
nut´ty
nuz´zle
Ny-an´za
ny´lon
nymph
nym´pha
nym-phae-a´ceous
nymph´al
nymph´a-lid
nym-pho-ma´nia

O

Oa´hu
oak´en
Oak´land
oa´kum
oar´fish
oar´lock
oars´man
oars´man-ship
oa´ses
oa´sis
oat´cake
oat´en
oat´meal
O´be-ah
obe´di-ence
obe´di-ent
obe´di-ent-ly
obei´sance
obei´sant
obe´li-al
ob´e-lisk

ob´e-lus
Ober-am´mer-gau
O´ber-lin
O´ber-on
obese´
obe´si-ty
obey´
obey´ing
ob-fus´cate
ob-fus-ca´tion
ob-fus´ca-tor
ob-fus´ca-to-ry
obit´u-ar-ies
obit´u-ary
ob´ject
ob-jec-tee´
ob-jec-ti-fi-ca´tion
ob-jec´ti-fy
ob-ject´ing
ob-jec´tion
ob-jec´tion-able
ob-jec´tive
ob-jec´tive-ly
ob-jec´tive-ness
ob-jec´tiv-ism
ob-jec-tiv´i-ty
ob-jec´tor
ob´jet d'art
ob-ju-ra´tion
ob´jur-gate
ob-jur-ga´tion
ob´jur-ga-tor
ob´last
ob´late
ob-la´tion
ob´la-to-ry
ob´li-gate
ob´li-gat-ing
ob-li-ga´tion
ob´li-ga-tor
oblig´a-to-ry
oblige´
ob´li-gee´
oblig´er
oblig´ing
oblig´ing-ly
ob´li-gor´
oblique´
oblique´ly
oblique´ness
ob-liq´ui-tous
ob-liq´ui-ty
ob-lit´er-ate
ob-lit-er-a´tion
ob-lit´er-a-tive
ob-lit´er-a-tor
ob-li-ves´cence
ob-liv´i-on
ob-liv´i-ous
ob´long
ob´long´at-ed
ob´lo-quy
ob-mu-tes´cence
ob-nox´ious
ob-nu-bi-la´tion
o´boe
o´bo-ist
ob´o-lus
ob-scene´
ob-scene´ly
ob-scen´i-ty
ob-scu´rant
ob-scu´ran-tism
ob-scu-ra´tion
ob-scure´
ob-scure´ly
ob-scure´ness
ob-scur´ing
ob-scu´ri-ty
ob-se-cra´tion
ob´se-quies
ob-se´qui-ous
ob-se´qui-ous-ness
ob-seq´ui-ty
ob´se-quy
ob-serv´able
ob-serv´ance
ob-serv´ant
ob-ser-va´tion
ob-serv´a-tive
ob-serv´a-to-ry
ob-serve´
ob-serv´er
ob-serv´ing
ob-sess´
ob-ses´sion
ob-ses´sive
ob-ses´sor
ob-sid´i-an
ob-so-les´cence
ob-so-les´cent
ob´so-lete´
ob´so-lete´ness
ob´sta-cle
ob-stet´ri-cal
ob-ste-tri´cian
ob-stet´rics
ob´sti-na-cy
ob´sti-nance
ob´sti-nate
ob´sti-nate-ly
ob-strep´er-ous
ob-struct´
ob-struct´er
ob-struc´tion
ob-struc´tion-ism
ob-struc´tion-ist
ob-struc´tive
ob-struc´tor
ob-tain´
ob-tain´able
ob-tain´ment
ob-test´
ob-tes-ta´tion
ob-trude´
ob-trud´er
ob-trud´ing
ob-tru´sion
ob-tru´sive
ob-tru´sive-ly
ob-tund´
ob-tund´ent
ob´tu-rate
ob-tu-ra´tion
ob´tu-ra-tor
ob-tuse´
ob-tu´si-ty
ob-verse´
ob-verse´ly
ob-ver´sion
ob´ver-tend
ob´vi-ate
ob´vi-at-ing
ob-vi-a´tion
ob´vi-a-tor
ob´vi-ous
ob´vi-ous-ly

ob´vi-ous-ness
ob´vo-lute
oc-a-ri´na
oc-ca´sion
oc-ca´sion-al
oc-ca´sion-al-ism
oc-ca´sion-al-ly
oc´ci-den´tal
oc-ci-den´ta´ize
oc-clude´
oc-clud´ent
oc-clud´ing
oc-clu´sal
oc-clu´sion
oc-clu´sive
oc-cult´
oc-cul-ta´tion
oc-cult´ism
oc-cult´ist
oc´cupan-cy
oc´cu-pant
oc-cu-pa´tion
oc-cu-pa´tion-al
oc´cu-pa-tive
oc´cu-pied
oc´cu-pi-er
oc´cu-py
oc´cu-py-ing
oc-cur´
oc-curred´
oc-cur´rence
oc-cur´rent
oc-cur´ring
o´cean
ocea-nar´i-um
Oce-an´ia
oce-an´ic
ocean-og´ra-pher
ocean-o-graph´ic
ocean-og´ra-phy
ocel´late
o´ce-lot
o´cher
o´cher-ous
o'clock´
oc´ta-gon
oc-tag´o-nal
oc-ta-he´dral
oc-ta-he´dron
oc´tal
oc´ta-mer
oc-tam´er-ous
oc-tam´e-ter
oc´tane
oc-tan´gu-lar
oc-ta-no´ate
oc´ta-nol
oc´ta-no´yl
oc´tant
oc-tan´tal
oc-ta´val
oc´ta-va´lent
oc´tave
Oc-ta´vi-us
oc-ta´vo
oc-ta´vos
oc-ten´ni-al
oc-tet´
Oc-to´ber
oc-to-ge-nar´i-an
oc-tog´e-nary
oc-to´ic
oc´to-nary
Oc-top´o-da
oc´to-pus
oc´to-roon´
oc´u-lar
oc´u-list
odd´i-ty
odd´ly
odd´ment
odd´ness
Odes´sa
od´ic
odif´er-ous
O´din
odi-om´e-ter
o´di-ous
od´ist
o´di-um
o´do-graph
odom´e-ter
odon-tal´gia
odon-ti´tis
odon´to-gen´ic
odon-tol´o-gy
odon-tom´e-ter
o´dor
o´dor-ant
odor-if´er-ous
o´dor-ize
o´dor-less
odor-om´e-ter
o´dor-ous
Odys´seus
Od´ys-sey
oed´i-pal
Oed´i-pus
of´fal
off´beat
off´cast
off´—cen´ter
off´—col´or
of-fend´
of-fend´er
of-fend´ing
of-fense´
of-fen´sive
of-fen´sive-ness
of´fer
of´fer-ing
of-fer-to´ri-al
of´fer-to-ry
off´hand´ed
of´fice
of´fice-hold-er
of´fi-cer
of-fi´cial
of-fi´cial-dom
of-fi´cial-ese´
of-fi´cial-ly
of-fi´ci-ant
of-fi´ci-ary
of-fi´ci-ate
of-fi-ci-a´tion
of-fi´ci-a-tor
of-fic´i-nal
of-fi´cious
of-fi´cious-ly
off´ing
off´ish
off´set
off-set´ting
off´shoot
off-shore´
off´side´
off´spring

off´stage´
of´ten
of´ten-times
Og´den
o´gee´
o´give
o´gle
O´gle-thorpe
o´gling
o´gre
o´gre-ish
o´gress
Ohi´o
ohm
ohm´age
ohm´ic
ohm´me-ter
oil cake
oil´cloth
oil´er
oil field
oil´i-ness
oil´man
oil paint´ing
oil´skin
oil slick
oil´stone
oil well
oil´y
oint´ment
Ojib´way, Ojib´wa
oka´pi
okay´
o´ken-ite
O´ki-na´wa
Okla-ho´ma
ok´o-nite
o´kra
O´laf
old´en
old—fash´ioned
old´ish
old´ness
old´ster
old´—time´
old—tim´er
old´—world´
o´le-a´ceous
ole-ag´i-nous
ole-an´der
ole-an´drin
o´le-ate
olec´ra-non
o´le-fin
o´le-fin´ic
ole´ic
o´le-in
o´leo
o´le-o-graph
o-le-og´ra-phy
o´le-o-mar´ga-rine
ole-om´e-ter
ole-o-res´in
ole´o-yl
ol-fac´tion
ol-fac´tive
ol-fac-tom´e-ter
ol-fac´to-ry
ol´i-garch
ol´i-gar´chic
ol´i-gar-chy
ol-i-ge´mia
ol-i-gop´o-ly
ol-i-gop´so-ny
ol´i-va´ceous
ol´i-vary
ol´ive
oliv´en-ite
Ol´i-ver
ol-i-ves´cent
Ol´i-vet
Oliv´ia
ol´i-vine
ol´la
olym´pi-ad
Olym´pi-an
Olym´pic
Olym´pus
O´ma-ha
Oman´
O´mar Khay-yam´
omeg´a
om´e-let
o´men
omen-ol´o-gy
omen´tum
o´mer
om´i-cron
om´i-nous
om´i-nous-ly
omis´si-ble
omis´sion
omis´sive
omit´
omit´ted
omit´ting
om´ni-bus
om´ni-far´i-ous
om-nif´ic
om-nif´i-cence
om-nif´i-cent
om-nim´e-ter
om-nip´o-tence
om-nip´o-tent
om-ni-pres´ence
om-ni-pres´ent
om´ni-range
om-ni´science
om-ni´scient
om-niv´o-rous
omo-pho´ri-on
on´a-ger
o´nan-ism
o´nan-ist
once—o´ver
on-com´e-ter
on´com-ing
on-cot´o-my
on´do-graph
on-dom´e-ter
on´du-le´
one´—armed´
one´—celled´
one´—eyed
one´—horse´
Onei´da
onei´ric
one´—leg´ged
one´ness
one´—piece´
on´er-ous
one-self´
one´—sid´ed
one´—step
one´time
one´—track´
one´—way´

one´—world´er
on´ion
on´ion-skin
on´look-er
on´ly
On-on-da´ga
on´rush
on´set
on´shore´
on´slaught
On-tar´io
on´to
on-tog´e-ny
on´to-log´i-cal
on-tol´o-gist
on-tol´o-gy
o´nus
on´ward
on´yx
o´o-lite
oo-lit´ic
ool´o-gy
oo´long
oom´e-ter
oozed
ooz´ing
ooz´y
opa-cim´e-ter
opac´i-ty
o´pal
opal-esce´
opal-es´cence
opal-es´cent
o´pal-ine
o´pal-oid
opaque´
opaque´ly
opaqu´er
opaqu´ing
o´pen
o´pen—air´
o´pen—door´
o´pen-er
o´pen—eyed´
o´pen—faced
o´pen-hand´ed
o´pen-heart-ed
o´pen—hearth
open house´
o´pen-ing
o´pen-ly
o´pen—mind´ed
o´pen-mouthed´
o´pen-ness
o´pen-work
op´era
op´er-a-ble
op´era glass
op´er-and´
op´er-at-able
op´er-ate
op-er-at´ic
op-er-at´i-cal-ly
op-er-a´tion
op-er-a´tion-al
op´er-a-tive
op´er-a-tor
oper´cu-lar
oper´cu-lum
op-er-et´ta
op´er-on
op´er-ose
Ophe´lia
oph´i-cleide
ophid´i-an
ophi-ol´a-try
ophi-ol´o-gy
O´phir
ophit´ic
oph-thal´mia
oph-thal´mic
oph-thal-mi´tis
oph-thal´mo-log´ic
oph-thal-mo-log´i-cal
oph-thal-mol´o-gist
oph-thal-mol´o-gy
oph-thal-mom´e-ter
oph-thal´mo-met´ric
oph-thal´mo-scope
oph-thal-mos´co-py
opine
opin´ion
opin´ion-at-ed
opin´ion-a-tive
o´pi-um
opos´sum
op´pi-dan
op-pi-la´tion
op-po´nent
op´por-tune´
op´por-tune´ly
op-por-tune´ness
op-por-tun´ism
op-por-tun´ist
op-por-tun-is´tic
op-por-tu´ni-ty
op-pos-abil´i-ty
op-pos´able
op-pose´
op-pos´ing
op´po-site
op-po-si´tion
op-press´
op-press´ible
op-pres´sion
op-pres´sive
op-pres´sor
op-pro´bri-ate
op-pro´bri-ous
op´so-nin
op´ta-tive
op´tic
op´ti-cal
op-ti´cian
op´tics
op´ti-mal
op´ti-mal-ize
op´ti-me
op-tim´e-ter
op´ti-mism
op´ti-mist
op´ti-mis´tic
op-ti-mis´ti-cal-ly
op´ti-mum
op´tion
op´tion-al
op-tom´e-ter
op´to-met´ric
op-tom´e-trist
op-tom´e-try
op´u-lence
op´u-len-cy
op´u-lent
o´pus
or´a-cle
orac´u-lar
orac-u-lar´i-ty

o´ral
o´ral-ly
Oran´
or´ange
or´ange-ade´
or´ange-wood
orang´utan
orate´
ora´tion
or´a-tor
or-a-tor´i-cal
or-a-tor´i-cal-ly
or-a-to´rio
or´a-to-ry
or-bic´u-lar
or´bit
or´bit-al
or´bit-ed
or´bit-er
or´bit-ing
or´chard
or´chard-ist
or´ches-tra
or-ches´tral
or´ches-trate
or-ches-tra´tion
or´chid
or-dain´
or´deal
or´der
or´dered
or´der-li-ness
or´der-ly
or´di-nal
or´di-nance
or-di-nar´i-ly
or´di-nary
or´di-nate
or-di-na´tion
ord´nance
or´dure
orec´tic
oreg´a-no
Or´e-gon
Ores´tes
or´gan
or´gan-dy
or-gan´ic
or-gan´i-cal-ly
or-gan´i-cism
or-gan´i-cist
or´ga-nism
or´gan-ist
or´ga-niz´able
or-ga-ni-za´tion
or´ga-nize
or´ga-niz-er
or´ga-niz-ing
or´gasm
or-gas´tic
or´gi-ast
or´gi-as´tic
or´gies
or´gone
or´gu-lous
or´gy
o´ri-el
o´ri-ent
ori-en´tal
Ori-en´tal-ism
Ori-en´tal-ist
o´ri-en-tate
ori-en-ta´tion
o´ri-en-ta´tor
or´i-fice
or´i-fi´cial
or´i-gin
orig´i-nal
orig-i-nal´i-ty
orig´i-nal-ly
orig´i-nate
orig´i-nat-ing
orig-i-na´tion
orig´i-na-tive
orig´i-na-tor
O´ri-no´co
o´ri-ole
Ori´on
Or-lan´do
Or´leans
Or´lon
or´mo-lu
or´na-ment
or´na-men´tal
or-na-men-ta´tion
or´nate´
or-nate´ness
or´nery
or-nith´ic
or´ni-thine
or-nith´o-log´i-cal
or-ni-thol´o-gist
or-ni-thol´o-gy
or´ni-thop-ter
or-ni-tho´sis
or-ni-thot´o-my
or´nith-u´ric
or´o-graph´ic
orog´ra-phy
o´ro-ide
orol´o-gy
orom´e-ter
or´o-met´ric
o´ro-tund
oro-tun´di-ty
or´phan
or´phan-age
or´phan-hood
Or´phe-um
Or´pheus
or´phic
or´phism
or´phrey
or´pi-ment
or´pine
or´rery
or´ris
or´ris-root
Or´sat
or´thi-con
or-tho-don´tia
or´tho-don´tic
or´tho-don´tist
or´tho-dox
or´tho-doxy
or´tho-ep´ic
or´tho-ep´i-cal-ly
or-tho´epist
or-tho´epy
or´tho-for´mic
or-tho-gen´e-sis
or-thog´na-thous
or-thog´o-nal
or-thog´ra-pher
or-tho-graph´ic
or-thog´ra-phy
or-thom´e-try

or´tho-pe´dic
or´tho-pe´dist
or-thop´nea
or-thop´ter-al
or-thop´tics
or´tho-scop´ic
or-tho´sis
or-thos´ti-chy
or-thot´ro-pism
or´tho-typ´ic
or´to-lan
o´ryx
O´sage´
Osa´ka
o´sa-zone
Os´car
Os-ce-o´la
os´cil-late
os-cil-la´tion
os´cil-la-tor
os´cil-la-to-ry
os-cil´lo-graph
os-cil-lom´e-ter
os-cil´lo-scope
os´cu-lar
os´cu-late
os-cu-la´tion
os´cu-la-to-ry
Osh´kosh
Osi´ris
Os´lo
os-mi-rid´i-um
os´mi-um
os-mo´sis
os-mot´ic
os-phre´sis
os´prey
Os´sa
os´se-ous
os´si-cle
os-sic´u-lar
os-si-cu-lec´to-my
os-si-fi-ca´tion
os-sif´i-ca-to-ry
os´si-fied
os´si-fy
os´si-fy-ing
Os´si-ning
os´su-ary

os´te-al
os-te-ec´to-my
os´te-it´ic
os-te-i´tis
os-tend´
os-ten´si-ble
os-ten´si-bly
os-ten´sive
os-ten´sive-ly
os-ten-ta´tion
os-ten-ta´tious
os-ten-ta´tious-ly
os-te-o-chon-dro´sis
os-te-oc´la-sis
os-te-ol´o-gist
os-te-ol´o-gy
os-te-ol´y-sis
os-te-o´ma
os´te-o´ma-tous
os-te-om´e-try
os´teo-my-e-li´tis
os´te-o-path
os´te-o-path´ic
os-te-op´a-thy
os´te-o-plas-ty
os-te-ot´o-my
os´ti-ary
os´ti-ole
os-to´sis
os´tra-cism
os´tra-cize
os´tra-ciz-ing
os´trich
Os´wald
Os-we´go
otal´gia
Othel´lo
oth´er
oth´er-wise
o´ti-ose
oti-os´i-ty
oti´tis
oti´tis me´dia
o´to-log´ic
otol´o-gy
otos´co-py
oto´sis
Otran´to
ot-ta´va

Ot´ta-wa
ot´ter
Ot´to
ot´to-man
ought
Oui´da
Oui´ja
ounce
ou´ri-cu-ry´
our-self´
our-selves´
oust´er
out-bal´ance
out-bid´
out´board
out´bound´
out´break
out´build
out´build-ing
out´burst
out´cast
out´class´
out´come
out´crop
out´crop-ping
out´cry
out´curve
out´did
out´dis´tance
out-do´
out-done´
out´door´
out-doors´
out´er
out´er-most
out´face´
out´field
out´field-er
out´fit
out´fit-ter
out´flank
out´flow
out-gen´er-al
out´go
out´go´ing
out´grew´
out´grow´
out´growth
out´house

out-ing
out´land
out´land-er
out-land´ish
out´last´
out´law
out´law-ry
out´lay
out´let
out´line
out-live´
out´look
out´ly-ing
out-ma-neu´ver
out´mod´ed
out-num´ber
out—of—date
out—of—doors
out—of—the—way
out´pa-tient
out´play´
out´point´
out´post
out´pour
out´pour-ing
out´put
out´rage
out-ra´geous
out-ra´geous-ly
out´rag-er
out´ran´
ou-trance´
out´rank´
ou-tré´
out´reach
out´rid-er
out´rig-ger
out´right
out´root´
out´run´
out´run-ner
out-sell´
out´set
out´shine
out´shone
out-side´
out-sid´er
out´sit´
out´size
out´skirts
out-smart´
out´soar´
out´speak´
out´spo´ken
out´spread´
out-stand´
out-stand´ing
out´stay´
out´stretch´
out-stretched´
out´strip´
out-stripped´
out´ward
out´ward-ly
out-wear´
out-weigh´
out´wit´
out´wit´ted
out´work´
out-worn´
o´val
oval´i-form
oval´i-ty
ovar´i-an
ovari-ec´to-my
ovar´i-ole
ovar-i-ot´o-my
ova-ri´tis
o´va-ry
o´vate
ova´tion
ov´en
ov´en-bird
ov´en-ware
o´ver
o´ver-act´
o´ver-ac-tiv´i-ty
o´ver-all
o´ver-arm´
over-awe´
over-bal´ance
o´ver-bear´
over-bear´ing
o´ver-bid´
o´ver-blown´
o´ver-board
o´ver-bold´
o´ver-bore
o´ver-borne´
o´ver-build´
o´ver-bur´den
over-came´
over-cap´i-tal-ize
o´ver-cast
over-charge´
over-cloud´
o´ver-coat
over-come´
o´ver-crowd´
over-did´
over-do´
over-done´
o´ver-dose
o´ver-draft
over-draw´
over-drawn´
over-dress´
o´ver-drive´
o´ver-due´
o´ver-eat
over-es´ti-mate
over-fed´
o´ver-feed´
o´ver-flow
over-grown´
o´ver-growth
o´ver-hand
o´ver-hang´
o´ver-haul´
o´ver-head
over-hear´
o´ver-hung
o´ver-joy´
o´ver-joyed
o´ver-laid
o´ver-land
o´ver-land-er
o´ver-lap´
over-lap´ping
o´ver-lay
o´ver-load´
o´ver-look´
o´ver-lord
o´ver-ly
o´ver-match´
o´ver-much´
over-night´

o´ver-pass
over-pay´
over-play´
over-pop-u-la´tion
over-pow´er
over-pro-duc´tion
over-ran´
over-rate´
over-reach´
over-ride´
over-rule´
over-run´
over-seas´
over-see´
o´ver-seer
o´ver-set´
over-shad´ow
o´ver-shoot´
over-shot´
o´ver-sight´
o´ver-size´
over-sleep´
over-slept´
over-state´
over-stay´
over-step´
over-stock´
o´ver-stuffed
o´ver-sup-ply´
overt´
over-take´
over-tak´en
over-tax´
over-threw´
over-throw´
over-thrown´
o´ver-time
o´ver-tired´
overt´ly
o´ver-tone
over-took´
o´ver-ture
over-turn´
o´ver-wear
o´ver-wea´ry
over-ween´ing
o´ver-weight
over-whelm´
over-whelm´ing
over-whelm´ing-ly
over-work´
over-worked´
o´ver-wrought´
Ov´id
o´vi-duct
o´vi-form
ovig´er-ous
ovi-na´tion
o´vine
o´void
o´vo-vi-vip´a-rous
o´vu-lar
o´vu-late
ovu-la´tion
o´vu-la-to-ry
o´vule
o´vum
Ow´en
Ow´ens-boro
ow´ing
owl´et
owl´ish
own´er
own´er-ship
ox´bow
ox´cart
ox´en
Ox´ford
ox´heart
ox´i-dant
ox´i-dase
ox´i-da´tion
ox´i-da-tive
ox´ide
ox´i-diz-able
ox-i-di-za´tion
ox´i-dize
ox´i-diz-er
ox-id´u-lat-ed
ox-im´e-ter
ox´i-met´ric
ox´in-dole
ox´tail
ox´tongue
oxy-acan´thine
oxy-acet´y-lene
ox´y-bi´o-tin
ox´y-gen
ox´y-gen-ate
ox-y-gen-a´tion
ox´y-gen´ic
ox´y-gen-ize
oxy-sul´fide
oxy-tet-ra-cy´cline
oys´ter
oys´ter bed
oys´ter-man
Oz´a-lid
O´zark
o´zone
o´zon-ide
o´zon-if´er-ous
o´zon-iz-er
ozo´no-sphere

P

pab´u-lum
paced
pace´mak-er
pac´er
pach´y-derm
pachy-san´dra
pach´y-tene
pac´i-fi-able
pa-cif´ic
pa-cif´i-cal-ly
pa-cif´i-cate
pac-i-fi-ca´tion
pac´i-fi-ca-tor
pa-cif´i-ca-to-ry
pac´i-fied
pac´i-fi-er
pac´i-fism
pac´i-fist
pac´i-fis´tic
pac´i-fy
pac´i-fy-ing
pac´ing
pack´age
pack´ag-er
pack´ag-ing
Pack´ard
pack´er
pack´et
pack´ing
pack´ing-house

pack´man
pack rat
pack´sack
pack´sad-dle
pack´thread
pac´tion
pad´ding
pad´dle
pad´dle-fish
pad´dler
pad´dle wheel
pad´dling
pad´dock
pad´dy
pad´lock
pa´dre
pa-dro´ne
Pad´ua
Pa-du´cah
pae´an
pae´on
pa´gan
pa´gan-ism
pa´gan-ize
pag´eant
pag´eant-ry
paged
pag´er
Pag´et
pag´i-nal
pag´i-nate
pag-i-na´tion
pag´ing
pa-go´da
pa-gu´ri-an
pail´ful
pain´ful
pain´ful´ly
pain´less
pain´less-ly
pains´tak-ing
pains´tak-ing-ly
paint box
paint´brush
paint´er
paint´ing
paint´work
pai-sa´no
Pais´ley

pa-ja´ma
Pak´i-stan
pal´ace
pa-la´ceous
pal´a-din
pal-at-abil´i-ty
pal´at-able
pal´a-tal
pal´ate
pa-la´tial
pa-lat´i-nate
pal´a-tine
pal-a-ti´tis
pa-lav´er
pa´lea
pale´face
pale´ness
pa´leo-graph´ic
pa-le-og´ra-phy
Pa´leo-lith´ic
pa-le-ol´o-gy
pa-le-on-tol´o-gist
pa-le-on-tol´o-gy
Pa´leo-zo´ic
Pa-ler´mo
Pal´es-tine
pal´ette
pal´frey
pal´in-drome
pal´ing
pal-in-gen´e-sis
pal-i-sade´
Pal-la´di-an
pal-la´di-um
pall´bear-er
pal´let
pal´let-ize
pal-lette´
pal´li-ate
pal´li-at-ing
pal-li-a´tion
pal´lia-tive
pal´li-a-tor
pal´lia-to-ry
pal´lid
pal´li-um
pall´—mall´
pal´lor
palmar´i-an

pal´mate
palma´tion
palm´er
pal´met´to
palm´ist
palm´is-try
pal´mi-tate
pal´mi-tin
palm leaf
palm´y
pal-o-mi´no
Pa´los
pal-pa-bil´i-ty
pal´pa-ble
pal´pa-bly
pal´pate
pal-pa´tion
pal´pebral
pal´pi-tant
pal´pi-tate
pal´pi-tat-ing
pa´pi-ta´tion
pal´sy
pal´ter
pal´tri-ness
pal´try
pal-y-nol´o-gy
Pam´e-la
pam´pa
pam´per
pamph´let
pam´phlet-ize
pan-a-ce´a
pa-nache´
Pan´a-ma
Pan—Amer´i-can
pan´a-ry
pan-a-tel´a
pan´cake
pan-chro-mat´ic
pan´cre-as
pan´cre-at´ic
pan´cre-a-tin
pan-cre-a-ti´tis
pan´da
pan-dem´ic
pan-de-mo´ni-um
pan´der
Pan-do´ra

pan-dow´dy
pan´du-rate
pan´el
pan´el-board
pan´eled
pan´el-ing
pan´el-ist
pan´han-dle
pan´han-dling.
pan´ic
pan´icked
pan´ick-ing
pan´icky
pan´i-cle
pan´ic—strick-en
pan´nier
pan´ning
pan´o-ply
pan-o-ram´a
pan´o-ram´ic
pan-soph´ic
pan´so-phism
pan´sies
pan´sy
pan-ta-loon´
pan-te-the´ine
pan´the-ism
pan´the-ist
pan´the-is´tic
pan´the-lism
pan´the-on
pan´the-on´ic
pan´ther
pant´ing
pan´to-graph
pan-tog´ra-pher
pan-tol´o-gy
pan-tom´e-ter
pan´to-mime
pan´to-mim´ic
pan´to-mimist
pan´to-then´ic
pan´tries
pan´try
pan´zer
pa´pa-cy
pa-pa´in
pa´pal
pa-paw´
pa-pay´a
pa´per
pa´per-back
pa´per-board
pa´per boy
pa´per chase
pa´per cut-ter
pa´per-hang-er
pa´per knife
pa´per-like
pa´per—thin´
pa´per-weight
pa´per work
pa´pery
pa-pier—mâ-ché´
pa-pil´la
pap´il-lary
pap-il-lo´ma
pap-il-lo´ma-to´sis
pap´il-lom´a-tous
pap´il-lose
pap-il-los´i-ty
pa-poose´
pa-pri´ka
Pap´ua
papy´rus
par´a-ble
pa-rab´o-la
par´a-bol´ic
par´a-bol´i-cal
pa-rab´o-lize
pa-rab´o-loid
pa-rab´o-loi´dal
par´a-chute
par´a-chut-ist
Par´a-clete
pa-rade´
pa-rad´er
pa-rad´ing
par´a-digm
par´a-di-sa´ic
par´a-dise
par´a-di-si´a-cal
par´a-dox
par´a-dox´i-cal
par´af-fin
par´af-fin´ic
para-gen´e-sis
par´a-gon
pa-rag´o-nite
par´a-graph
par´a-graph-er
par´a-graph´i-cal-ly
Par´a-guay
par´a-keet
par´al-lax
par´al-lel
par´al-leled
par´al-lel-ing
par´al-lel-ism
par-al-lel´o-gram
par-al-lel-om´e-ter
pa-ral´o-gism
pa-ral´o-gize
pa-ral´y-sis
par´a-lyt´ic
par-a-ly-za´tion
par´a-lyze
par´a-lyzed
par´a-lyz-ing
Par-a-mar´i-bo
par-a-me´cium
pa-ram´e-ter
par´a-mount
par´amour
par-a-noi´a
par´a-noi´ac
par´a-noid
par´ant-he´li-on
par´a-pet
par´a-pet-ed
par´aph
par´a-pha´sia
par-a-pher-na´lia
par´a-phrase
par´a-phras-er
par´a-phras-ing
pa-raph´ra-sis
par´a-phrast
par´a-phras´tic
pa-raph´y-sis
para-ple´gia
par´a-ple´gic
pa-rap´sis
par´a-se-le´ne
par´a-site
par-a-sit-e´mia
par´a-sit´ic

par´a-sit´i-cal
par-a-sit´i-ci´dal
par-a-sit´i-cide
par´a-sit-ism
par´a-si-tize
par-a-sito´sis
par´a-sol
para-syn´the-sis
para-tax´is
para-thi´on
par´a-thy´roid
par´a-troop-er
pa-rat´ro-phy
par´a-vane
par´boil
par´cel
par´celed
par´cel-ing
par´cel post
par´ce-nary
parch´ment
par´don
par´don-able
par´don-er
pared
par´ent
par´ent-age
pa-ren´tal
par-en´ter-al
pa-ren´the-ses
pa-ren´the-sis
pa-ren´the-size
par´en-thet´ic
par´en-thet´i-cal
par´en-thet´i-cal-ly
par´ent-hood
pa-ret´ic
par ex-cel-lence´
par-fait´
par-he´lion
pa-ri´ah
Par´i-an
pa-ri´e-tal
pari-mu´tu-el
par´i-nar´ic
par´ing
Par´is
par´ish
pa-rish´io-ner
par´i-son
par´i-ty
par´ka
park´er
Par´kin-son
park´way
par´lance
par´lay
par´ley
par´lia-ment
par-lia-men-tar´i-an
par´lia-men´ta-ry
par´lor
par´lor car
par´lous
Par´ma
Par´me-san
Par-nas´sus
Par-nell´
pa-ro´chial
par´o-died
par´o-dist
par´o-dis´tic
par´o-dy
par´o-dy-ing
pa-role´
pa-roled´
pa-rol-ee´
pa-rol´ing
par´o-nym
pa-ron´y-mous
pa-ro´tic
pa-rot´id
par´ous
par´ox-ysm
par´ox-ys´mal
par-quet´
par´que-try
par´ri-ci´dal
par´ri-cide
par´ried
par´rot
par´ry
par´ry-ing
parse
pars´ley
pars´nip
par´son
par´son-age
par-tage´
par-take´
par-tak´en
par-tak´er
part´ed
part´er
par´the-no-gen´e-sis
par´the-no-ge-net´ic
Par´the-non
par´tial
par-tial´i-ty
par´tial-ly
par-ti-bil´i-ty
par-tic´i-pant
par-tic´i-pate
par-tic-i-pa´tion
par-tic´i-pa-tor
par-ti-cip´i-al
par´ti-ci-ple
par´ti—col-ored
par-tic´u-lar
par-tic-u-lar´i-ty
par-tic´u-lar-ize
par-tic´u-lar-ly
par-tic´u-late
par´ties
part´ing
par´ti-san
par´ti-san-ship
par-ti´tion
par-ti´tion-er
par-ti´tion-ing
par´ti-tive
part´ly
part´ner
part´ner-ship
par-took´
par´tridge
part´—time´
par´ty
par´ve-nu
par´vo-line
Pas´a-de´na
pas´chal
pa-sha
pass´able
pass´ably
pas´sage
pas´sage-way

Pas-sa´ic
pass´book
pas-sé´
passe-men´terie
pas´sen-ger
pass´er
pass´er-by
pas´si-ble
pas´sim
pas-sim´e-ter
pass´ing
pas´sion
pas´sion-ate
pas´sion-ate-ly
pas´sion-less
pas´sive
pas´sive-ly
pas´sive-ness
pas´siv-ism
pas´siv-ist
pas-siv´i-ty
pass´key
Pass´over
pass´port
pass´word
paste´board
past´ed
pas-tel´
past´er
pas´tern
Pas-teur´
pas-teur-iza´tion
pas´teur-ize
pas-tille´
pas´time
past´i-ness
past´ing
pas´tor
pas´tor-age
pas´to-ral
pas-to-rale´
pas´to-ral-ism
pas´to-ral-ist
pas´to-ral-ize
pas´tor-ate
pas-to´ri-um
pas´torship
pas-tra´mi
pas´tries
pas´try
pas´try-cook
pas´tur-able
pas´tur-age
pas´ty
pa-ta´gi-um
Pat-a-go´nia
Pa-taps´co
patch´er
patch´ery
patch´i-ness
patch´work
patch´y
pâ-té´ de foie gras´
pa-tel´la
pat´ent
pat-ent-abil´i-ty
pat´ent-able
pat´en-tee´
pat´ent-ly
pat´en-tor
pa´ter
pa-ter´nal
pa-ter´nal-ism
pa-ter´nal-is´tic
pa-ter´nal-ly
pa-ter´ni-ty
Pat´er-son
pa-thet´ic
pa-thet´i-cal-ly
path´find-er
path´less
path-o-ge-nic´i-ty
pa-thog´e-ny
path´o-log´i-cal
pa-thol´o-gist
pa-thol´o-gy
pa-thom´e-ter
pa´thos
pa-tho´sis
path´way
pat´i-ble
pa´tience
pa´tient
pa´tient-ly
pat´i-na
pat-i-na´tion
pat´io
pa´tois
pa´tri-arch
pa´tri-ar´chal
pa´tri-arch-ate
pa´tri-archy
Pa-tri´cia
pa-tri´cian
pa-tri´ci-ate
pat´ri-cid´al
pat´ri-cide
Pat´rick
pat´ri-mo´ni-al
pat´ri-mo-ny
pa´tri-ot
pa´tri-ot´ic
pa´tri-ot´i-cal-ly
pa´tri-ot-ism
pat´ri-pas´si-an
pa-trol´
pa-trolled´
pa-trol´ler
pa-trol´ling
pa-trol´man
pa´tron
pa´tron-age
pa´tron-ess
pat´ro-nite
pa´tron-ize
pa´tron-iz-ing
pat-ro-nym´ic
pat-ro-nym´i-cal-ly
pat´ter
pat´tern
pat´terned
pat´tern-mak-er
Pat´ter-son
pat´ting
pat´ty
pat´u-lous
pau´ci-ty
Pau´li
Pau-li´na
Pau-line´
Paul´ist
paunch´i-ness
paunch´y
pau´per
pau´per-ism
pau´per-ize
paus´al

paus´ing
pave´ment
pav´er
pa-vil´ion
pav´ing
Pav´lov
pawn´bro-ker
pawn´brok-ing
Paw-nee´
pawn-ee´
pawn´er
pawn´shop
Paw-tuck´et
pay´able
pay´day
pay-ee´
pay´er
pay´ing
pay´mas-ter
pay´ment
pay-o´la
pay´roll
Pea´body
peace´able
peace´ably
peace´ful
peace´ful-ly
peace´ful-ness
peace´mak-er
peace of´fer-ing
peace pipe
peace´time
peach´blos´som
peach´blow
peach´y
pea´cock
pea´hen
pea jack´et
peaked
pea´nut
pearl ash
pearl´er
pearl´i-ness
pearl´ite
pearl´y
pear´—shaped
Pear´son
Pea´ry
peas´ant
peas´ant-ry
peat´y
pea´vey
peb´ble
peb´bled
peb´bling
peb´bly
pe-can´
pec´ca-ble
pec-ca-dil´lo
pec-ca-dil´loes
peck´er
peck´ing
pec´tase
pec´tate
pec´ten
pec´tic
pec´tin
pec´tin-ase
pec´ti-nate
pec-tin´ic
pec´to-ral
pec´tous
pec´tus
pec´u-late
pec´u-lat-ing
pec-u-la´tion
pec´u-la-tor
pe-cu´liar
pe-cu-liar´i-ty
pe-cu´liar-ly
pe-cu´li-um
pe-cu´niar´i-ly
pe-cu´niary
ped´a-gog´ic
ped´a-gog´i-cal
ped´a-gogue
ped´a-gogy
ped´al
ped´aled
pe-dal´fer
ped´al-ine
ped´ant
pe-dan´tic
pe-dan´ti-cal-ly
pe-dan´ti-cism
ped´ant-ry
ped´ate
ped´dle
ped´dler
ped´dlery
ped´dling
ped´er-ast
ped´er-as-ty
Pe´der-sen
ped´es-tal
pe-des´tri-an
pe-des´tri-an-ism
pe´di-at´ric
pe-di-a-tri´cian
pe-di-at´rics
ped´i-cel
ped´i-cle
pe-dic´u-lar
pe-dic-u-lo´sis
pe-dic´u-lous
ped´i-cure
ped´i-form
ped´i-gree
ped´i-ment
ped´i-men´tal
ped-i-men-ta´tion
ped´o-cal
pe-dol´o-gy
pe-dom´e-ter
Pe´dro
peel´er
peel´ing
peep´er
peep´hole
peer´age
peer´ess
peer´less
pee´vish
pee´vish-ness
Peg´a-sus
peg´ging
Pei´ping´
pei-ram´e-ter
pej´o-ra-tive
Pe´kin-ese´
Pe´king´
pe´koe
pel´age
Pe-la´gian
Pel´ham
pel´i-can
Pe´li-on

pel-la´gra
pel-la´grous
pel´let
pel´let-er
pel´let-ize
pel´li-cle
pel-lic´u-lar
pell´—mell´
pelt´er
pel´try
pel´vic
pel´vis
pe´nal
pe-nal-iza´tion
pe´nal-ize
pe´nal-iz-ing
pen´al-ties
pen´al-ty
pen´ance
pe-na´tes
pench´ant
pen´cil
pen´ciled
pen´cil-ing
pen´cil-ler
pen´dant
pen-de-loque´
pen´dency
pen´dent
pen-den´tive
pend´ing
pen-drag´on
pen´du-lous
pen´du-lum
Pe-nel´o-pe
pe´ne-plain´
pe-ne-pla-na´tion
pen-e-tra-bil´i-ty
pen´e-tra-ble
pen-e-tra´lia
pen-e-tram´e-ter
pen´e-trance
pen´e-trate
pen´e-trat-ing
pen-e-tra´tion
pen´e-tra-tive
pen´e-tra-tor
pen-e-trom´e-ter
pen´guin
pen´hold-er
pen-i-cil´lin
pen-i-cil´lin-ase
pen-i-cil-li-o´sis
pen-i-cil´li-um
pe-nin´su-la
pe-nin´su-lar
pe´nis
pen´i-tence
pen´i-tent
pen´i-ten´tial
pen-i-ten´tia-ry
pen´i-tent-ly
pen´knife
pen´man
pen´man-ship
pen name
pen´nant
pen´nate
pen´nies
pen´ni-less
pen´ning
pen´ni-nite
pen´non
Penn-syl-va´nia
pen´ny
pen´ny-roy´al
pen´ny-weight
pen´ny—wise´
pen´ny-worth
Pe-nob´scot
pe´no-log´i-cal
pe-nol´o-gist
pe-nol´o-gy
pen point
Pen-sa-co´la
pen´sion
pen´sion-ary
pen´sion-er
pen´sive
pen´sive-ly
pen´stock
pen´ta-cle
pen´ta-gon
pen-tag´o-nal
pen-tag´o-nal-ly
pen´ta-he´dral
pen-ta-hy´drite
pen´ta-mer
pen-tam´er-al
pen-tam´er-ous
pen-tam´e-ter
Pen´ta-teuch
pen-tath´lon
Pen´te-cost
pent´house
pen´to-bar´bi-tal
Pen´to-thal
pent´—up´
pe-nu´che
pe´nult
pe-nul´ti-mate
pe-num´bra
pe-nu´ri-ous
pen´ury
pen´writ-ten
Pen-zance´
pe´on
pe´on-age
pe´o-nies
pe´o-ny
peo´ple
peo´pling
Pe-o´ria
pep´per
pep´per-box
pep´per-corn
pep´per-mint
pep´pery
pep´py
pep´sin
pep´sin-if´er-ous
pep´tic
pep´ti-dase
pep´to-nate
pep´tone
pep-to-niz-a´tion
pep´to-nize
per´ad-ven´ture
per-am´bu-late
per-am´bu-lat-ing
per-am-bu-la´tion
per-am´bu-la-tor
per-am´bu-la-to-ry
per an´num
per-bo´rate
Per´bu´nan
per-cale´

per´ca-line
per cap´i-ta
per-ceiv´able
per-ceiv´ably
per-ceive´
per-ceiv´er
per-cent´
per-cent´age
per-cent´ile
per´cept
per-cep-ti-bil´i-ty
per-cep´ti-ble
per-cep´ti-bly
per-cep´tion
per-cep´tive
per-cep´tu-al
per-chance´
perch´er
per´co-late
per-co-la´tion
per´co-la-tor
per cu´ri-am
per-cuss´
per-cus´sion
per-cus´sive
Per´cy
per di´em
per-di´tion
per´e-grine
pe-rei´ra
pe-rei´rine
pe-remp´tive
pe-remp´to-ri-ly
pe-remp´to-ri-ness
pe-remp´to-ry
pe-ren´nial
per´fect
per-fect´er
per-fect´ibil´i-ty
per-fect´ible
per-fec´tion
per-fec´tion-ism
per-fec´tive
per´fect-ly
per-fec´to
per-fec´tor
per-fec´tos
per-fer´vid
per-fid´i-ous
per-fid´i-ous-ly
per-fid´i-ous-ness
per´fi-dy
per´fo-rate
per´fo-rat-ed
per-fo-ra´tion
per´fo-ra-tive
per´fo-ra-tor
per-force´
per-form´
per-form´able
per-form´ance
per-form´er
per´fume
per-fum´er
per-fum´ery
per-func´to-ri-ly
per-func´to-ry
per-fu´sion
per-fu´sive
per´go-la
per-haps´
pe´ri
per´i-clase
Per´i-cles
per´i-gee
per´i-he´lion
per´il
per´iled
per´il-ing
per´il-ous
per´il-ous-ly
pe-rim´e-ter
per´i-met´ric
per´i-met´ri-cal
pe-rim´e-try
pe´ri-od
pe´ri-od´ic
pe-ri-od´i-cal
pe-ri-od´i-cal-ly
pe-ri-o-dic´i-ty
peri-pa-tet´ic
peri-pe-tei´a
pe-rip´e-ty
pe-riph´er-al
pe-riph´er-al-ly
pe-riph´ery
per´i-phrase
pe-riph´ra-sis
per´i-phras´tic
per´i-scope
per´i-scop´ic
per´ish
per´ish-able
pe-ris´sad
peri-to-ni´tis
peri-vis´cer-al
per´i-win-kle
per´jure
per´jur-er
per´jur-ing
per-ju´ri-ous
per´jury
perk´i-ness
Per´kins
perk´y
per´ma-nence
per´ma-nen-cy
per´ma-nent
per´ma-nent-ly
per-man´ga-nate
per-me-abil´i-ty
per´me-able
per´meame-ter
per´me-ance
per´me-ant
per´me-ate
per-me-a´tion
per´me-ative
Per´mi-an
per-mis-si-bil´i-ty
per-mis´si-ble
per-mis´sion
per-mis´sive
per-mit´
per-mit´ted
per´mit-tee´
per-mit´ting
per-mit-tiv´i-ty
per-mut´able
per-mu-ta´tion
per´mu-ta-tor
per-mute´
per-ni´cious
per-nick´e-ty
per-ni-o´sis
Pe-ron´
per´o-ne´al

per´orate´
per-ora´tion
pe-ro´sis
per-ox´i-dase
per-ox´ide
per-ox´y-di-sul´fate
per-pen-dic´u-lar
per´pe-trate
per-pe-tra´tion
per´pe-tra-tor
per-pet´u-al
per-pet´u-al-ly
per-pet´u-ate
per-pet-u-a´tion
per-pet´u-a-tor
per-pe-tu´ity
per-plex´
per-plexed´
per-plexed´ness
per-plex´ing
per-plex´i-ty
per´qui-site
per´ron
per´ry
per´se-cute
per-se-cu´tion
per´se-cu-tor
per´se-cu-to-ry
per-se-ver´ance
per-sev´er-a-tive
per´se-vere´
per´se-ver´ing
Per´shing
Per´sia
per´si-flage
per-sim´mon
per-sist´
per-sist´ence
per-sist´en-cy
per-sist´ent
per-sist´ent-ly
per-sist´er
per-snick´e-ty
per´son
per-so´na
per´son-able
per´son-age
per´son-al
per-son-al´i-ty
per´son-al-ize
per´son-al-ly
per´son-al-ty
per-so´na non gra´ta
per´son-ate
per-son-a´tion
per-son-i-fi-ca´tion
per-son´i-fi-er
per-son´i-fy
per-son´i-fy-ing
per´son-nel´
per-spec´tive
per-spi-ca´cious
per-spi-cac´i-ty
per-spi-cu´ity
per-spic´u-ous
per-spir´able
per-spi-ra´tion
per-spi´ra-tive
per-spir´a-to-ry
per-spire´
per-spir´ing
per-suad´able
per-suade´
per-suad´er
per-suad´ing
per-sua´si-ble
per-sua´sion
per-sua´sive
per-sua´sive-ly
per-tain´
per´ti-na´cious
per´ti-na´cious-ly
per-ti-nac´i-ty
per´ti-nence
per´ti-nen-cy
per´ti-nent
pert´ly
per-turb´
per-turb´able
per-tur-ba´tion
per-turb´ed-ly
per-turb´er
per-tus´sal
per-tus´sis
Pe-ru´
pe-ruke´
pe-rus´able
pe-rus´al
pe-ruse´
pe-rus´er
pe-rus´ing
per-vade´
per-vad´ing
per-va´sion
per-va´sive
per-va´sive-ly
per-verse´
per-verse´ly
per-verse´ness
per-ver´sion
per-ver´sity
per-ver´sive
per-vert´
per-vert´ed
per-vert´er
per-vert´i-ble
per-vi-ca´cious
per-vi-cac´i-ty
per´vi-ous
per´y-lene
pe-se´ta
Pe-sha´war
pes´ky
pe´so
pes´sa-ry
pes´si-mism
pes´si-mist
pes-si-mis´tic
pes-si-mis´ti-cal-ly
pes´ter
pes´tered
pest´house
pes´ti-ci´dal
pes-tif´er-ous
pes´ti-lence
pes´ti-lent
pes´ti-len´tial
pes´tle
pes-tol´o-gy
pet´al
pet´aled
pet´al-ism
pet´al-ite
pet´a-lo-dy
pet´al-ous
pet´cock
Pe´ter

pe´tered
Pe´ters-burg
pe-tit´
pe-tite´
pe-ti´tion
pe-ti´tion-ary
pe-ti´tion-er
pe-tits´ fours
Pe´trarch
pe´trel
pe-tres´cent
Pe´tri
pet-ri-fac´tion
pet´ri-fac´tive
pet-ri-fi-ca´tion
pet´ri-fied
pet´ri-fy
pe´tro-chem´i-cal
Pet´ro-grad
pet´rol
pet´ro-lage
pet-ro-la´tum
pet´ro-lene
pe-tro´leum
pe-trol´ic
pet´ro-lif´er-ous
pet´ro-lize
pet´ro-log´ic
pet-ro-log´i-cal
pet-ro-log´i-cal-ly
pe-trol´o-gist
pe-trol´o-gy
pe-tro´sal
pet´rous
pe-trox´o-lin
pet´ti-coat
pet´ti-fog
pet´ti-fog´ger
pet´ti-fog-gery
pet´ti-ly
pet´ti-ness
pet´tish
pet´tish-ness
pet´ty
pet´u-lance
pet´u-lan-cy
pet´u-lant
pe-tu´nia
pe´wit
pew´ter
pew´ter-er
pfef´fer-nuss
pfen´nig
pha-com´e-ter
pha´e-ton
pha´lanx
phal´a-rope
phal´lic
phal´lus
phan-er-os´co-py
phan´tasm
phan-tas-ma-go´ria
phan-tas-ma-gor´ic
phan-tas´ma-gor´i-cal
phan-tas´mal
phan´tom
phan´to-scope
phar´aoh
Phar´i-sa´ic
Phar´i-sa-ism
Phar´i-see
phar´ma-ceu´ti-cal
phar-ma-ceu´tics
phar-ma-ceu´tist
phar´ma-cist
phar-ma-cog´no-sy
phar-mac´o-lite
phar´ma-co-log´i-cal
phar-ma-col´o-gist
phar-ma-col´o-gy
phar-ma-co-pe´ia
phar-ma-co-poe´ia
phar´ma-cy
Pha´ros
pha-ryn´ge-al
phar-yn-gi´tis
pha-ryn´go-log´i-cal
phar-yn-gol´o-gy
pha-ryn´go-scope
phar-yn-gos´co-py
phar-yn-got´o-my
phar´ynx
phase
phase´me-ter
pha-se´o-lin
phas´er
pha´sic
pha´si-tron
pha´sor
pheas´ant
phen´a-cite
phe´no-bar´bi-tal
phe´no-cop´y
phe´nol
phe-no´lic
phe-nol´o-gist
phe-nol´o-gy
phe´nol-phthal´ein
phe-nom´e-na
phe-nom´e-nal
phe-nom´e-nal-ism
phe-nom´e-no-log´i-cal
phe-nom-e-nol´o-gy
phe-nom´e-non
phe´no-plast
phe´no-type
phen-ox´ide
phe-nox´y-ace´tic
phen´yl
phi´al
Phi Be´ta Kap´pa
Phil-a-del´phia
phi-lan´der
phi-lan´der-er
phil´an-throp´ic
phi-lan´thro-pist
phi-lan´thro-py
phil´a-tel´ic
phi-lat´e-list
phi-lat´e-ly
phil´har-mon´ic
phil´hel-len´ic
phil´i-a-ter
Phil´ip
Phi-lip´pi-ans
Phil´ippine
Phil´is-tine
Phi´lo
phil-o-den´dron
phil´o-graph
phi-log´y-ny
phil´o-log´i-cal
phi-lol´o-gist
phi-lol´o-gy
phil´o-mel
phil-o-pe´na

phil´o-pro-gen´i-tive
phi-los´o-pher
phil´o-soph´ic
phil´o-soph´i-cal
phil´o-soph´i-cal-ly
phi-los´o-phism
phi-los´o-phize
phi-los´o-phiz-er
phi-los´o-phy
phil´ter
phle-bit´ic
phle-bi´tis
phleb´o-graph´ic
phle-bog´ra-phy
phle-bot´o-my
phlegm
phleg-mat´ic
pho´bia
pho´bic
phoe´be
Phoe´bus
Phoe-ni´cia
Phoe´nix
phon-au´to-graph
pho´ne-mat´ic
pho-net´ic
pho-net´i-cal-ly
pho-ne-ti´cian
pho-net´i-cize
pho´ne-tism
pho´ne-tist
Phone´vi-sion
phon´ic
pho´no-gen´ic
pho´no-gram
pho´no-graph
pho-no-graph´ic
pho-nog´ra-phy
pho´no-lite
pho´no-log´i-cal
pho-nol´o-gist
pho-nol´o-gize
pho-nol´o-gy
pho-nom´e-ter
pho-nom´e-try
pho´no-phore
pho-noph´o-rous
pho´no-typy
pho´ny
pho-re´sis
phor´e-sy
pho-ret´ic
pho-rom´e-ter
pho-rom´e-try
phos´phate
phos´phat´ic
phos´pha-tize
phos´phide
phos´phi-nate
phos´phine
phos´phite
phos´pho-nate
phos´phor
phos´pho-rate
phos-pho´re-al
phos´pho-resce´
phos-pho-res´cence
phos´pho-res´cent
phos´phor´ic
phos´pho-rism
phos-phor´o-gen
phos´pho-ro-gen´ic
phos-pho-rol´y-sis
phos´pho-rous
phos´pho-rus
phos´pho-ryl-ase
pho´tics
pho´to
pho-to-chem´is-try
pho´to-chro-my
pho´to-elec´tric
pho´to-en-grav´ing
pho´to-flash
pho´to-gene
pho´to-gen´ic
pho-to-gram´me-try
pho´to-graph
pho-tog´ra-pher
pho´to-graph´ic
pho-tog´ra-phy
pho´to-gra-vure´
pho´to-ki-ne´sis
pho´to-lith´o-graph
pho´to-li-thog´ra-phy
pho-tol´y-sis
pho´to-lyt´ic
pho-tom´e-ter
pho´to-met´ric
pho-tom´e-try
pho´ton
pho´to-nas´tic
pho-top´a-thy
pho-to-pho-re´sis
pho´to-play
phot-op-tom´e-ter
pho´to-re-cep´tor
pho´to-sen´si-tive
pho´to-stat
pho´to-stat-ed
pho-to-syn´the-sis
pho-tot´o-nus
pho´to-tran-sis´tor
pho´to-troph´ic
pho-to-trop´ic
pho-tot´ro-pism
pho´to-typy
Pho-tron´ic
phras´able
phras´al
phrase
phra´se-o-gram
phra-se-og´ra-phy
phra-se-ol´o-gy
phrase-er
phras´ing
phre-net´ic
phren´ic
phren-i-cot´o-my
phre-ni´tis
phren-o-log´i-cal
phre-nol´o-gist
phre-nol´o-gy
phren´o-sin
Phryg´i-an
phyl´lo-por´phy-rin
phy´lo-ge-net´ic
phy-log´e-ny
phy´lum
phys-i-at´rics
phys´ic
phys´i-cal
phys´i-cal-ly
phy-si´cian
phys´i-cist
phys´icked
phys´ick-ing
phys´ics

phys-i-og´no-my
phys-i-og´ra-pher
phys´io-graph´ic
phys-i-og´ra-phy
phys-i-ol´a-ter
phys´i-o-log´i-cal
phys-i-ol´o-gist
phys-i-ol´o-gy
phys-i-om´e-try
phys-i-os´o-phy
phys´io-ther´a-py
phy-sique´
pi´a-nis´si-mo
pi-an´ist
pi-a-niste´
pi´a-nis´tic
pi-an´o
pi-an´o-forte
pi-an´os
pi-as-sa´va
pi-as´ter
pi-az´za
pi´ca
pic´a-dor
Pic´ar-dy
pic´a-resque´
pic´a-roon´
Pi-cas´so
pic-a-yune´
Pic´ca-dil´ly
pic´ca-lil´li
pic´co-lo
pic´co-lo-ist
pic´e-in
pi´cene
pic´e-ous
pick´a-back
pick´a-nin-ny
pick´ax
pick´er
pick´er-el
pick´et
pick´et-er
pick´et-ing
Pick´ett
pick´ing
pick´le
pick´led
pick´ling
pick´lock
pick´pock-et
pick´up
Pick´wick
pic´nic
pic´nicked
pic´nick-er
pic´nick-ing
pic´to-graph
pic´to-graph´ic
pic-to-graph´i-cal-ly
pic-tog´ra-phy
pic-to´ri-al
pic´tur-able
pic´ture
pic-tur-esque´
pic´tur-esque´ness
pic´tur-ing
pid´dle
pid´dler
pid´dling
pid´gin
pie´bald
pieced
pièce de ré´sis-tance´
piece goods
piece´meal
piec´er
piece rate
piece´work
pie chart
piec´ing
pie´crust
Pied´mont
pie´man
pie´plant
pierced
pierc´er
pierc´ing
pier´head
Pi-e´ri-an
pi-er´i-dine
Pier´rot
pi´etism
pi-etis´tic
pi´e-ty
pif´fle
pi´geon
pi´geon-eer´
pi´geon-hole
pi´geon—toed
pi´geon-wing
pig´fish
pig´gery
pig-gish
pig´head-ed
pig iron
pig´ment
pig´men-tary
pig-men-ta´tion
pi´gnon
pig´nut
pig´pen
pig´skin
pig´stick-ing
pig´sty
pig´tail
pig´weed
pike´man
pike perch
pik´er
pike´staff
pi-laf´
pi-las´ter
Pi´late
pil´chard
pi´le-ate
pi´le-at-ed
pi-le´o-lus
pi´le-ous
pil´er
pil´fer
pil´fer-age
pil´grim
pil´grim-age
pi-lif´er-ous
pil´ing
pil´lage
pil´lag-er
pil´lar
pil´lared
pill´box
pil´lion
pil´lo-ried
pil´lor-ize
pil´lo-ry
pil´low
pil´low-case

pil´low-slip
pil´lowy
pi´lot
pi´lot-age
pi´lot-house
Pil´sner
pil´u-lar
pi-men´to
pi-mien´to
pim´per-nel
pim´ple
pim´pled
pim´ply
pi´na
pi-na´ceous
pin´a-coid
pin´a-coi´dal
pin´a-col
pi-nac´o-late
pi-nac´o-lone
pin´a-fore
pi´nane
pi-nas´ter
pin´ball
pince´—nez´
pin´cers
pinch´beck
pinch´er
pinch´—hit
pin´cushion
Pin´dar
Pin-dar´ic
pin´e-al
pine´ap-ple
Pi-ne´ro
pin´ery
pi-ne´tum
pi´ney
pin´feath-er
pin´fold
Ping´—Pong
pin´head
pin´hole
pin´ion
pink´er
pink´eye
pink´ish
pink´root
pin´ky
pin mon-ey
pin´na
pin´nace
pin´na-cle
pin´mate
pin´ning
pi-no-cam´phe-ol
pi´noch-le
pin´point
pin´tle
pin´to
pin´up
pin´weed
pin´wheel
pin´worm
pin´y
pi´nyl
pi´o-neer´
pi´o-neered´
pi-os´i-ty
pi´ous
pi´ous-ly
pip´age
pipe dream
pipe´ful
pipe´line
pipe or´gan
pip´er
piper´a-zine
pi-per´ic
pi-per´i-dine
pip´er-ine
pipe´stem
pipe´stone
pip´ing
pip´kin
pip´pin
pi´quan-cy
pi´quant
pi-qué´
pique
piqued
pi-quet´
piqu´ing
pi´ra-cy
Pi-rae´us
pi-ra´nha
pi´rate
pi-rat´i-cal
pi´rogue
pir´ou-ette´
pir´ou-ett´ed
pir´ou-ett´ing
Pi´sa
Pis´ces
pis´mire
pis-tach´io
pis´til
pis´til-late
pis´tol
pis´ton
pitch´blende
pitch´er
pitch´fork
pitch´ing
pitch´stone
pitch´y
pit´e-ous
pit´e-ous-ly
pit´fall
pith´i-ly
pith´i-ness
pith´y
pit´i-able
pit´ied
pit´i-er
pit´ies
pit´i-ful
pit´i-ful-ly
pit´i-less
pit´man
pit saw
pit´tance
pit´ted
pit´ter—pat´ter
pit´ting
Pitts´burg
Pitts´burgh
pi-tu´i-tary
pi-tu´i-tous
pit´y
pit´y-ing
Pi´us
pi-val´ic
piv´ot
piv´ot-al
piv´ot-er
pix´ie

pix´i-lat-ed
pix´y
Pi-zar´ro
piz-ze-ri´a
piz´zi-ca´to
placa-bil´i-ty
plac´a-ble
plac´ard
pla´cate
pla´cat-er
pla´cat-ing
pla-ca´tion
pla´ca-tive
pla´ca-to-ry
place´able
pla-ce´bo
place´—kick
place´ment
pla-cen´ta
plac´en-tary
pla-cen´tate
plac-en-ta´tion
plac-en-ti´tis
plac´er
pla´cet
plac´id
pla-cid´i-ty
plac´id-ly
plac´ing
plack´et
plac´oid
pla´gia-rism
pla´gia-rist
pla´gia-ris´tic
pla´gia-rize
pla´gia-riz-ing
pla´gia-ry
plague
plagu´ed
plagu´ing
pla´guy
plaid
plain´—laid´
plain´ly
plain´ness
plains´man
plain´tiff
plain´tive
plain´tive-ly
plait
plait´er
pla´nar
pla-nar´ia
pla-nar´i-an
pla-nar´i-ty
pla-na´tion
plan´chet
plan-chette´
plan´er
plan´et
plan-e-tar´i-um
plan´e-tary
plan-e-tes´i-mal
plan´et-oid
plan´et-oi´dal
plan-et-o-log´ic
plan´et-ol´o-gy
plan´gen-cy
plan´gent
plank´ing
plank´—sheer
plank´ton
planned
plan´ner
plan´ning
plan´o-graph
pla-nog´ra-phy
pla-nom´e-ter
plan´o-sol
plan´tain
plan-ta´tion
plant´er
plan´ti-grade
plant´ing
plant louse
pla´num
plaque
pla-quette´
plash´y
plas´ma
plas´mic
plas-min´o-gen
plas-mo-di´a-sis
plas-mo´di-um
plas´ter
plas´tered
plas´ter-er
plas´ter-ing
plas´ter-work
plas´tic
plas´ti-ca-tor
plas-ti-cim´e-ter
plas-tic´i-ty
plas´ti-cize
plas´ti-ciz-er
pla-teau´
plat´ed
plate´ful
plate glass
plat´en
plat´er
plat´form
pla-ti´na
plat´ing
plat´i-nize
plat´i-num
plat´i-tude
plat-i-tu´di-nize
plat´i-tu´di-nous
Pla´to
pla-ton´ic
pla-toon´
plat´ter
plat´y-pus
plau´dit
plau-si-bil´i-ty
plau´si-ble
plau´sive
play´able
play´back
play´bill
play´boy
play´er
play´fel-low
play´ful
play´ful-ly
play´ful-ness
play´go-er
play´ground
play´house
play´ing card
play´mate
play´—off
play´room
play´script
play´thing
play´time

play´wright
plaz´a
plea
plead´able
plead´er
plead´ing
plead´ing-ly
pleas´ance
pleas´ant
pleas´ant-ly
pleas´ant-ness
pleas´ant-ry
pleas´ing
plea´sur-able
plea´sure
pleat
pleat´ed
pleat´er
plebe
ple-be´ian
pleb´i-scite
pledged
pledg-ee´
pledg´er
pled´get
pledg´ing
pled´gor
ple´nar-ty
ple´na-ry
plen´i-po-ten´tia-ry
plen´i-tude
plen´te-ous
plen´ti-ful
plen´ti-ful-ly
plen´ty
pleth´o-ra
pleth´o-ric
pleu´ra
pleu´ral
pleu´ri-sy
pleu-rit´ic
Plex´i-glas
plex-im´e-ter
plex´us
pli-a-bil´i-ty
pli´a-ble
pli´an-cy
pli´ant
pli´cate
pli-ca´tion
plied
pli´ers
plight
plinth
plod´ded
plod´der
plod´ding
plot´less
plot´ter
plot´ting
plov´er
plow
plow´boy
plow´er
plow´—hand
plow´ing
plow´man
plow´share
pluck´er
pluck´i-er
pluck´y
plug´board
plug´ging
plug´—ug-ly
plum
plu´mage
plu´mate
plumb
plum-ba´gin
plum-ba´go
plum´bate
plumb bob
plumb´er
plum´bif´er-ous
plumb´ing
plum´bite
plumb line
plum´bous
plum´ing
plum´met
plump´er
plump´ness
plu´mule
plum´y
plun´der
plun´der-er
plun´der-ous
plung´er
plung´ing
plu-per´fect
plu´ral
plu´ral-ism
plu-ral´i-ty
plu´ral-ize
plu´ral-ly
plu´ri-va´lent
plush´y
Plu´tarch
plu´tar-chy
Plu´to
plu-toc´ra-cy
plu´to-crat
plu´to-crat´ic
plu-to´ni-an
plu-ton´ic
plu´to-nism
plu-to´ni-um
plu´vi-al
plu´vi-ous
ply´ing
Plym´outh
ply´wood
pneu-drau´lic
pneu-mat´ic
pneu-mat´i-cal-ly
pneu-ma-tic´i-ty
pneu-ma-tol´o-gy
pneu-ma-tol´y-sis
pneu-ma-tom´e-ter
pneu-ma-to´sis
pneu-mec´to-my
pneu-mo-coc´cus
pneu-mol´o-gy
pneu-mo´nia
pneu-mon´ic
pneu-mo-ni´tis
poach´er
Po-ca-hon´tas
pock´et
pock´et-book
pock´et-ful
pock´et-knife
pock´mark
pod´ding
po´de-sta´
podg´i-ness
podg´y

po-di´a-trist
po-di´a-try
po´di-um
po´do-lite
po´em
po´e-sy
po´et
po´et-as-ter
po´et-ess
po-et´ic
po-et´i-cal
po-et´i-cal-ly
po-et´ics
po´et-ize
po´et-ry
po-grom´
poi´gnan-cy
poi´gnant
poin-ci-an´a
poin-set´tia
point´—blank´
point´—de-vice´
point´ed
point´ed-ly
point´er
poin´til-lism
point´less
Poi-ret´
poised
pois´er
pois´ing
poi´son
poi´son-er
poi´son i´vy
poi´son-ous
Poi-tiers´
pok´er
pok´ing
pok´y
Po´land
po´lar
po-lar-im´e-ter
po-lar´i-met´ric
Po-lar´is
po-lar´i-scope
po-lar´i-ty
po-lar-iza´tion
po´lar-ize
po´lar-iz-er
po´lar-iz-ing
po-lar´o-graph´ic
po-lar-og´ra-phy
Po´lar-oid
po´lar-on
pol´der
pole´ax
pole´cat
po-lem´i-cal
po-lem´i-cal-ly
po-lem´i-cist
pol´e-mize
po-len´ta
pol´er
pole´star
pole´—vault
po´li-a-nite
po-lice´
po-lice´man
pol´i-cies
po-lic´ing
pol´i-clin´ic
pol´i-cy
pol´i-cy-hold-er
Po´lio
po´lio-my-e-li´tis
po-li-o´sis
pol´ish
Pol´ish
pol´ish-er
pol´it-bu-ro
po-lite´
po-lite´ly
po-lite´ness
pol´i-tic
po-lit´i-cal
po-lit´i-cal-ly
pol-i-ti´cian
po-lit´i-cize
pol´i-tic-ly
pol´i-tics
pol´i-ty
Po-litz´er
pol´ka
pol´ka—dot
pol´kaed
pol´lack
pol´lard
pol´len
pol´len-ize
pol´len-iz-er
poll´er
pol´li-nate
pol´li-nat-ing
po´li-na´tion
pol´li-nif´er-ous
pol-lin´i-um
pol-li-no´sis
pol´li-wog
poll´ster
poll tax
pol-lu´cite
pol-lu´tant
pol-lute´
pol-lut´er
pol-lut´ing
pol-lu´tion
Pol´lux
po´lo
po´lo-ist
pol´o-naise´
pol´y-acryl´ic
pol´y-am´ide
pol´y-an´drous
pol´y-an-dry
poly-an´thus
poly-ar´gy-rite
poly-ba´sic
poly-ba´site
pol´y-chro-ism
poly-chro-mat´ic
pol´y-chrome
pol´y-chro-my
pol´y-clin´ic
pol´y-crase
poly-cy-the´mia
po-lyd´y-mite
pol´y-ene
pol´y-es-ter
poly-eth´yl-ene
po-lyg´a-la
pol´y-gam´ic
po-lyg´a-mist
po-lyg´a-mous
po-lyg´a-my
po-lyg´e-ny
pol´y-glot
pol´y-gon

po-lyg´o-nal
pol´y-graph
pol´y-graph´ic
po-lyg´ra-phy
po-lyg´y-ny
pol´y-he´dral
pol´y-he´dron
pol´y-hi-dro´sis
pol´y-i´so-bu´tyl-ene
pol´y-i´so-top´ic
pol´y-kar´y-on
pol´y-math
po-lym´a-thy
pol´y-mer
pol´y-mer´ic
po-lym´er-ism
po-lym-er-i-za´tion
po-lym´er-ize
po-lym´er-iz-er
po-lym´er-ous
pol´y-me-ter
pol´ym-nite
pol´y-mor´phic
pol´y-mor´phism
pol´y-mor´phous
Pol´y-ne´sia
Pol´y-ne´sian
pol´y-no´mi-al
poly-nu-cle-o´sis
pol´yp
pol-yp-ec´to-my
poly-pep´tide
poly-pha´gia
po-lyph´a-gous
pol´y-phase
Pol´y-phe´mus
pol´y-ploid
pol´y-ploi-dy
pol´yp-tych
pol´y-se´mous
poly-sty´rene
pol´y-syl-lab´ic
pol´y-syl´la-ble
pol´y-tech´nic
pol´y-tech´ni-cal
pol´y-the-ism
pol´y-the-ist
pol´y-the-is´tic
poly-ton´al-ism

pol´y-to-nal´i-ty
pol´y-trop´ic
poly-u´re-thane
poly-va´lent
poly-vi´nyl
pom´ace
po-ma´ceous
po-made´
po-ma´tum
pome´gran-ate
Pom-er-a´nia
pom´mel
pom´meled
pom´pa-dour
pom´pa-no
Pom-peii´
Pom´pey
pom´—pom
pom´pon
pom-pos´i-ty
pomp´ous
Pon´ce
Pon´ce de Le-ón´
pon´cho
pon´chos
pond´age
pon´der
pon´der-abil´i-ty
pon´der-able
pon-der-o´sa
pon-der-os´i-ty
pon´der-ous
po´nies
pon´tage
Pon´ti-ac
pon´tiff
pon-tif´i-cal
pon-tif´i-cate
pon-tif´i-ca-tor
pon´tine
Pon´tius
pon-toon´
po´ny
poo´dle
pool´room
poor farm
poor´house
poor´ly
poor´ness

pop´corn
pope´dom
pop´e-line´
pop´ery
pop´gun
pop´in-jay
pop´ish
pop´lar
pop´lin
pop-lit´e-al
Po-po-ca-te´petl
pop´over
pop´per
pop´pies
pop´ping
pop´py
pop´py-cock
pop´u-lace
pop´u-lar
pop-u-lar´i-ty
pop-u-lar-iza´tion
pop´u-lar-ize
pop´u-lar-ly
pop´u-late
pop-u-la´tion
pop´u-list
pop´u-lous
pop´u-lous-ness
por´ce-lain
por´cine
por´cu-pine
pore
por´gy
po-rif´er-ous
pork´er
pork´y
por-nog´ra-pher
por-no-graph´ic
por-nog´ra-phy
po-rom´e-ter
po´ro-scope
po-ros´co-py
po´rose
po-ros´i-ty
po-rot´ic
po´rous
por´phin
por´phy-rit´ic
por´phyr-ox´ine

por´poise
por´ridge
por-ta-bil´i-ty
por´ta-ble
por´tage
por´tal
Port—au—Prince
por-tend´
por´tent
por-ten´tous
por´ter
por´ter-age
por´ter-house
port-fo´lio
port´hole
Por´tia
por´ti-co
por´ti-coes
por´tion
Port´land
port´li-er
port´li-ness
port´ly
por´trait
por´trai-ture
por-tray´
por-tray´al
por´tress
Ports´mouth
Por´tu-gal
Por´tu-guese´
por-tu-lac´a
posed
Po-sei´don
pos´er
pos´ing
pos´it
po-si´tion
po-si´tion-er
pos´i-ti´val
pos´i-tive
pos´i-tive-ly
pos´i-tiv-ism
pos´i-tiv-is´tic
pos-i-tri´no
pos´i-tron
pos-i-tro´ni-um
po-sol´o-gy
pos´se
pos-sess´
pos-sessed´
pos-sess´es
pos-ses´sion
pos-ses´sive
pos-ses´sive-ly
pos-ses´sive-ness
pos-ses´sor
pos-ses´so-ry
pos´set
pos-si-bil´i-ty
pos´si-ble
pos´si-bly
pos´sum
post´age
post´al
post-ax´i-al
post´boy
post´card
post´date´
post´er
pos-te´ri-or
pos-ter´i-ty
pos´tern
post-gla´cial
post-grad´u-ate
post´haste´
post´hu-mous
post´hu-mous-ly
post-hyp-not´ic
post´man
post´mark
post´mas-ter
post-me-rid´i-an
post-mil-len´ni-al
post´mis-tress
post´—mor´tem
post of fire
post-or´bit-al
post´paid´
post-pone´
post-pone´ment
post-pran´di-al
post´script
pos´tu-lant
pos´tu-late
pos´tu-lat-ing
pos-tu-la´tion
pos´tu-la-tor
pos´tur-al
pos´ture
pos´tur-ing
post´war´
pos´y
po-ta-bil´i-ty
po´ta-ble
po-tage´
po-tam´ic
pot´ash
po-tas´si-um
po-ta´tion
po-ta´to
po-ta´toes
Pot-a-wat´o-mi
pot´bel-lied
pot´bel-ly
pot´boil-er
pot´boy
Po-tem´kin
po´ten-cy
po´tent
po´ten-tate
po-ten´tial
po-ten-ti-al´i-ty
po-ten´tial-ly
po´tent-ly
poth´er
pot´hole
pot´hook
pot´house
po-tion
pot´luck´
Po-to´mac
pot´pie
pot´pour-ri´
Pots´dam
pot´shot
pot´tage
pot´ted
pot´ter
pot´ter-ies
pot´tery
pot´tle
Pough-keep´sie
poul´ter-er
poul´tice
poul´try
pounc´er

pounc´ing
pound´age
pound´al
pound cake
pound´er
pound´—fool´ish
pour
poured
pour´er
pour´ing
pout´er
pout´ing
pout´ing-ly
pout´y
pov´er-ty
pov´er-ty—strick´en
pow´der
pow´dered
pow´dery
pow´er
pow´ered
pow´er-ful
pow´er-ful-ly
pow´er-house
pow´er-less
Pow´ha-tan´
pow´wow
prac-ti-ca-bil´i-ty
prac´ti-ca-ble
prac´ti-cal
prac-ti-cal´i-ty
prac´ti-cal-ly
prac´ti-cal-ness
prac´tice
prac´ticed
prac´tic-er
prac´tic-ing
prac-ti´tion-er
prae´ci-pe
prae´di-al
prae-mu-ni´re
prae´tor
prag-mat´ic
prag-mat´i-cal-ly
prag´ma-tism
prag´ma-tist
Prague
prai´rie
prais´er
praise´wor-thy
prais´ing
pra´line
pranced
pranc´er
pranc´ing
prank´ish
prank´ster
prase
prat´er
prat´ing
pra-tique´
prat´tle
prat´tler
prax-e-ol´o-gy
Prax-it´e-les
prayed
prayer
prayer book
prayer´ful
preached
preach´er
preach´ing
preach´ment
preach´y
pre´am-ble
pre´ar-range´
pre-ar-range´ment
pre-ax´i-al
pre-car´i-ous
pre-car´i-ous-ness
prec´a-to-ry
pre-cau´tion
pre-cau´tion-ary
pre-cau´tious
pre-ced´able
pre-cede´
prec´e-dence
prec´e-den-cy
prec´e-dent
prec-e-den´tial
pre-ced´ing
pre-cen´tor
pre´cept
pre-cep´tive
pre-cep´tor
pre-cep-to´ri-al
pre-cep´to-ry
pre-cep´tress
pre-ces´sion
pre-ces´sion-al
pre´cinct
pre-ci-os´i-ty
pre´cious
prec´i-pice
pre-cip´i-tance
pre-cip´i-tan-cy
pre-cip´i-tant
pre-cip´i-tate
pre-cip´i-tate-ly
pre-cip´i-tate-ness
pre-cip-i-ta´tion
pre-cip´i-ta-tive
pre-cip´i-ta-tor
pre-cip´i-tin
pre-cip-i-tin´o-gen
pre-cip´i-tous
pre-cip´i-tous-ly
pré-cis´
pre-cise´
pre-cise´ly
pre-cise´ness
pre-ci´sian
pre-ci´sion
pre-ci´sive
pre-clin´i-cal
pre-clude´
pre-clud´ing
pre-clu´sion
pre-clu´sive
pre-co´cious
pre-coc´i-ty
pre´con-ceive´
pre-con-ceiv´ing
pre-con-cep´tion
pre-con-cert´
pre-con-cert´ed
prec´o-nize
pre-cor´di-um
pre-cur´sive
pre-cur´sor
pre-cur´so-ry
pre-da´cious
pre-dac´i-ty
pre-da´tion
pred´a-tor
pred´a-to´ri-ly
pred´a-to-ry

pre-de-cease´
pred´e-ces-sor
pre-den´ta-ry
pre´des-ti-nar´i-an
pre-des´ti-nate
pre-des-ti-na´tion
pre-des´tine
pre-de-ter´mi-nate
pre-de-ter-mi-na´tion
pre-de-ter´mine
pre-de-ter´min-ing
pred-i-ca-bil´i-ty
pred´i-ca-ble
pre-dic´a-ment
pred´i-cant
pred´i-cate
pred´i-cat-ing
pred-i-ca´tion
pred´i-ca-tive
pred´i-ca-to-ry
pre-dict´
pre-dict´able
pre-dic´tion
pre-dic´tive
pre-dic´tor
pre´di-gest´
pred´i-lec´tion
pre´dis-pose´
pre-dis-pos´ing
pre-dis-po-si´tion
pred-nis´o-lone
pre-dom´i-nance
pre-dom´i-nant
pre-dom´i-nate
pre-dom-i-na´tion
pre-em´i-nence
pre-em´i-nent
pre-em´i-nent-ly
pre-empt´
pre-emp´tion
pre-emp´tive
pre-emp´tor
pre-emp´to-ry
preened
pre´ex-ist´
pre-ex-is´tent
pre-fab´ri-cate
pre-fab´ri-ca-tor
pref´ace

pref´ac-ing
pref´a-to´ri-ly
pref´a-to-ry
pre´fect
pre-fec-to´ri-al
pre´fec-ture
pre-fer´
pref´er-a-bil´i-ty
pref´er-a-ble
pref´er-a-bly
pref´er-ence
pref´er-en´tial
pre-fer´ment
pre-ferred´
pre-fer´ring
pre-fig-u-ra´tion
pre-fig´u-ra-tive
pre-fig´ure
pre´fix
pre-for-ma´tion
pre-fron´tal
preg-na-bil´i-ty
preg´na-ble
preg´nan-cy
preg´nant
pre-hen´si-ble
pre-hen´sile
pre-hen-sil´i-ty
pre-hen´sion
pre-his-tor´ic
pre´his-tor´i-cal-ly
pre´judge´
pre-judg´ment
prej´u-dice
prej´u-di´cial
pre´—ju-di´cial
prel´ate
pre-lim´i-nary
prel´ude
pre-lu´di-al
pre´ma-ture´
pre´ma-ture´ly
pre-ma-tur´i-ty
pre-med´i-cal
pre-med´i-tate
pre-med-i-ta´tion
pre-med´i-ta-tive
pre-med´i-ta-tor
pre-mier´

pre-miere´
pre-mier´ship
pre´mil-le-nar´i-an
pre-mil-len´i-al-ism
prem´ise
pre´mi-um
pre´mo´lar
pre-mon´ish
pre-mo-ni´tion
pre-mon´i-to-ry
pre-na´tal
pren´tice
pre-oc´cu-pan-cy
pre-oc-cu-pa´tion
pre-oc´cu-pied
pre-oc´cu-py
pre-or-dain´
pre-or-di-na´tion
pre-paid´
prep-a-ra´tion
pre-par´a-tive
pre-par´a-to-ry
pre-pare´
pre-pared´
pre-par´ed-ness
pre-par´er
pre-pay´
pre-pay´ment
pre-pon´der-ance
pre-pon´der-ant
pre-pon´der-ate
pre-pon´der-at-ing
pre-pose´
prep-o-si´tion
prep-o-si´tion-al
pre-pos-sess´
pre-pos-sess´ing
pre-pos-ses´sion
pre-pos´ter-ous
pre-pos´ter-ous-ly
pre-po´ten-cy
pre-po´tent
pre´puce
pre-req´ui-site
pre-rog´a-tive
pres´age
pres´age-ful
pres´by-ter
pres-byt´er-ate

pres-by-te´ri-al
Pres-by-te´ri-an
pre´school´
pre´science
pre-scind´
pre-scis´sion
Pres´cott
pre-scribe´
pre-scrib´er
pre-scrib´ing
pre´script
pre-scrip´ti-ble
pre-scrip´tion
pre-scrip´tive
pres´ence
pres´ent
pre-sent´able
pre-sen-ta´tion
pre-sen´ta-tive
pres´ent—day´
pres´en-tee´
pre-sent´er
pre-sen´ti-ment
pres´en-tist
pres´ent-ly
pre-sent´ment
pre-serv´able
pres-er-va´tion
pre-serv´a-tive
pre-serve´
pre-serv´er
pre-side´
pres´i-den-cy
pres´i-dent
pres´i-dent—elect´
pres´i-den´tial
pre-sid´er
pre-sid´i-al
pre-sid´ing
pre-sid´io
pre-sid´i-um
press agent
press´board
press´er
press´—gang
press´ing
press´man
press´mark
pres´sor

press´room
pres´sure
pres´sur-ize
press´work
pres-ti-dig-i-ta´tion
pres-ti-dig´i-ta-tor
pres-tige´
pres-tig´i-ous
pres´to
Pres´ton
Pres´tone
pre-sum´able
pre-sum´ably
pre-sume´
pre-sumed´
pre-sum´er
pre-sump´tion
pre-sump´tive
pre-sump´tu-ous
pre-sup-pose´
pre-sup-po-si´tion
pre-tend´
pre-tend´ed
pre-tend´er
pre-tense´
pre-ten´sion
pre-ten´tious
pre-ten´tious-ness
pret´er-ist
pret´er-it
pre-ter´i-tal
pret-er-i´tion
pre-ter´i-tive
pre-ter-mit´
pre´ter-nat´u-ral
pre´text
Pre-to´ria
pret´ti-fied
pret´ti-fy
pret´ti-ly
pret´ti-ness
pret´ty
pre-typ´i-fy
pret´zel
pre-vail´
pre-vail´ing
prev´a-lence
prev´a-lent
pre-var´i-cate

pre-var-i-ca´tion
pre-var´i-ca-tor
pré-ve-nance´
pre-ven´ience
pre-ven´ient
pre-vent´
pre-vent´able
pre-vent´ative
pre-vent´er
pre-ven´tion
pre-ven´tive
pre´view
pre´vi-ous
pre´vi-ous-ly
pre-vi´sion
pre-war´
prey
Pri´am
pri´a-pism
Pri-a´pus
Prib´i-lov
price´less
pric´er
pric´ing
prick´er
prick´ing
prick´le
prick´ling
prick´ly
pride´ful
prid´ing
priest´craft
priest´ess
priest´hood
Priest´ley
priest´ly
pri´ma-cy
pri´ma don´na
pri´ma fa´cie
pri´mage
pri´mal
pri´ma-quine
pri-mar´i-ly
pri´mary
pri´mate
pri-ma´tial
pri-ma-tol´o-gy
pri´ma-ve´ral
prime´ly

prime´ness
prim´er
pri-me´val
prim´ing
prim´i-tive
prim´i-tiv-ism
prim´ness
pri-mo-gen´i-tary
pri-mo-gen´i-tor
pri´mo-gen´i-ture
pri-mor´di-al
prim´rose
prim´u-line
pri´mus
prince´dom
prince´li-ness
prince-ly
prin´ceps
prin´cess
Prince´ton
prin´ci-pal
prin-ci-pal´i-ty
prin´ci-pal-ly
prin´ci-pal-ship
prin´ci-pate
prin´ci-ple
print´able
print´er
print´ery
print´ing
print´less
pri´on
pri´or
pri´or-ate
pri´or-ess
pri-or´i-ty
pri´or-ship
pri´o-ry
Pris-cil´la
prism
pris-mat´ic
pri-som´e-ter
pris´on
pris´on-er
pris´sy
pris´tine
pri´va-cy
pri´vate
pri´va-teer´
pri´va-teers´man
pri´vate-ly
pri´vate-ness
pri-va´tion
priv´a-tive
pri´vat-ize
priv´et
priv´i-lege
priv´i-leged
priv´i-ly
priv´i-ty
priv´y
priz´able
prize´fight
prize ring
priz´ing
prob´a-bi-lism
prob-a-bil´i-ty
prob´a-ble
prob´a-bly
pro´bate
pro´bat-ing
pro-ba´tion
pro-ba´tion-al
pro-ba´tion-ary
pro-ba´tion-er
pro´ba-tive
pro´ba-to-ry
prob´ing
pro´bi-ty
prob´lem
prob´lem-at´ic
prob´lem-at´i-cal
prob´lem-at´i-cal-ly
prob´o-la
pro-bos´cis
pro-bos´cis-es
pro´caine
pro´ca-the´dral
pro-ce´dur-al
pro-ce´dure
pro-ceed´
pro-ceed´ing
pro-ce-phal´ic
proc´ess
proc´ess-ing
pro-ces´sion
pro-ces´sion-al
pro-ces´sion-ary
proc´es-sor
pro-claim´
proc-la-ma´tion
pro-clam´a-to-ry
pro-clit´ic
pro-cliv´i-ty
pro-cli´vous
pro-con´sul
pro-con´sul-ate
pro-cras´ti-nate
pro-cras-ti-na´tion
pro-cras´ti-na-tor
pro´cre-ant
pro´cre-ate
pro-cre-a´tion
pro´cre-ative
pro´cre-a-tor
pro-crus´te-an
proc-ti´tis
proc-tol´o-gy
proc´tor
proc-to´ri-al
proc´tor-ship
proc´to-scop´ic
proc-tos´co-py
pro-cum´bent
pro-cur´able
proc´u-ra-cy
proc-u-ra´tion
proc´u-ra-tor
proc´u-ra-to-ry
pro-cure´
pro-cured´
pro-cure´ment
pro-cur´er
pro-cur´ess
pro-cur´ing
prod´ding
prod´i-gal
pro-dig-i-o´sin
pro-di´gious
prod´i-gy
pro-duce´
pro-duc´er
pro-duc´ible
pro-duc´ing
prod´uct
pro-duct-ibil´i-ty
pro-duc´tion

pro-duc´tive
pro-duc´tive-ness
pro-duc-tiv´i-ty
pro´em
prof-a-na´tion
pro-fan´a-to-ry
pro-fane´
pro-fane´ly
pro-fan´er
pro-fan´ing
pro-fan´i-ty
pro´fert
pro-fess´
pro-fess´ant
pro-fessed´
pro-fess´ed-ly
pro-fes´sion
pro-fes´sion-al
pro-fes´sion-al-ism
pro-fes´sion-al-ly
pro-fes´sor
pro´fes-so´ri-al
pro-fes-so´ri-at
pro-fes´sor-ship
prof´fer
prof´fered
pro-fi´cien-cy
pro-fi´cient
pro´file
prof´it
prof´it-able
prof´it-ably
prof´i-teer´
prof´it-er
prof´it-less
prof´li-ga-cy
prof´li-gate
prof´lu-ence
prof´lu-ent
pro-found´
pro-found´ly
pro-fun´di-ty
pro-fuse´
pro-fuse´ly
pro-fu´sion
pro-fu´sive
pro-gen´i-tor
pro-gen´i-to´ri-al
pro-gen´i-ture

prog´e-ny
pro-ges´ter-one
prog´na-thous
prog-no´sis
prog-nos´tic
prog-nos´ti-cate
prog-nos-ti-ca´tion
prog-nos´ti-ca-tor
pro´gram
pro´gramed
pro-gram-mat´ic
pro´gram-mer
pro´gram-ming
prog´ress
pro-gres´sion
pro-gres´sion-al
pro-gres´sion-ist
prog´ress-ist
pro-gres´sive
pro-gres´sive-ly
pro-gres´siv-ism
pro-hib´it
pro-hib´it-er
pro-hi-bi´tion
pro-hi-bi´tion-ist
pro-hib´i-tive
pro-hib´i-to-ry
proj´ect
pro-ject´ed
pro-jec´tile
pro-jec´tion
pro-jec´tive
pro-jec´tor
pro-lapse´
pro-late´
pro-la´tive
pro´le-tar´i-an
pro-le-tar´i-an-ism
pro-le-tar´i-at
pro-lif´er-ate
pro-lif´er-a-tive
pro-lif´er-ous
pro-lif´ic
pro-lif´i-ca-cy
pro-lif´i-cal-ly
pro-lif-i-ca´tion
pro-li-fic´i-ty
pro-lig´er-ous
pro´line

pro-lix´
pro-lix´i-ty
pro-loc´u-tor
pro´log
pro´log-ize
pro´rogue
pro-long´
pro-lon´gate
pro-lon-ga´tion
pro-longed´
pro-lu´sion
pro-lu´so-ry
pro´ma-zine
prom´e-nade´
prom´e-nad´er
prom´i-nence
prom´i-nent
prom´i-nent-ly
prom-is-cu´i-ty
pro-mis´cu-ous
prom´ise
prom´is-ee´
prom´is-er
prom´is-ing
prom´i-sor
prom´is-so-ry
prom´on-to-ry
pro-mote´
pro-mot´er
pro-mot´ing
pro-mo´tion
pro-mo´tion-al
pro-mo´tive
prompt
prompt´er
promp´ti-tude
prompt´ly
prompt´ness
prom´ul-gate
promul-ga´tion
prom´ul-ga-tor
pro´nate
prone´ness
prong´horn
pro-nom´i-nal
pro-no´tus
pro´noun
pro-nounce´
pro-nounce´able

pro-nounced´
pro-nounce´ment
pro-nounc´ing
pro-nun-cia-men´to
pro-nun-ci-a´tion
proof´er
proof´read
proof´read-er
prop´a-ga-ble
prop-a-gan´da
prop-a-gan´dist
prop-a-gan´dize
prop´a-gate
prop-a-ga´tion
prop´a-ga-tive
prop´a-ga-tor
pro-pam´i-dine
pro´pane
pro´pa-nol
pro-par´gyl
pro-pel´
pro-pel´lant
pro-pelled´
pro-pel´lent
pro-pel´ler
pro-pel´ling
pro-pense´
pro-pen´si-ty
pro´pe-nyl
prop´er
pro´per-din
prop´er-ly
prop´er-tied
prop´er-ties
prop´er-ty
proph´e-cies
proph´e-cy
proph´e-sied
proph´e-si-er
proph´e-sy
proph´et
proph´et-ess
pro-phet´ic
pro-phet´i-cal
pro´phy-lac´tic
pro-phy-lax´is
pro´pi-o-late
pro-pi-ol´ic
pro´pi-o-nate
pro-pi-on´ic
pro´pi-o-nyl
pro-pi-on´y-late
pro-pi´ti-ate
pro-pi-ti-a´tion
pro-pi´ti-a-tor
pro-pi´ti-a-to-ry
pro-pi´tious
pro-po´de-um
pro-po´nent
pro-por´tion
pro-por´tion-able
pro-por´tion-al
pro-por´tion-ate
pro-por´tion-ate-ly
pro-por´tioned
pro-pos´al
pro-pose´
pro-pos´er
pro-pos´ing
prop-o-si´tion
prop-o-si´tion-al
pro-pound´
pro-pound´er
pro-pri´e-tary
pro-pri´e-tor
pro-pri´e-tor-ship
pro-pri´e-to-ry
pro-pri´e-tress
pro-pri´e-ty
pro-pul´sion
pro-pul´sive
pro-pul´so-ry
pro´pyl-ene
pro-pyl´ic
prop´y-lite
pro-ra´ta
pro-rat´able
pro-rate´
pro-rat´er
pro-ra´tion
pro-ro-ga´tion
pro-rogue´
pro-sa´ic
pro-sa´i-cal-ly
pro-sce´ni-um
pro-sciut´to
pro-scribe´
pro-scrip´tion
pro-scrip´tive
pro-scrip´tive-ly
prose
pros´e-cute
pros-e-cu´tion
pros´e-cu-tor
pros´e-cu-to-ry
pros-e-cu´trix
pros´e-lyte
pros´e-lyt-ism
pros´e-lyt-ize
pros´e-lyt-iz-er
pros´er
pros´i-er
pro´sit
pro-slav´ery
pros´o-pite
pros-o-pla´sia
pros´pect
pro-spec´tive
pro-spec´tive-ly
pros´pec-tor
pro-spec´tus
pros´per
pros-per´i-ty
pros´per-ous
pros´per-ous-ly
pros´tate
pros-tat´ic
pros-ta-ti´tis
pros-ter-na´tion
pros-then´ic
pros´the-sis
pros-thet´ic
pros´the-tist
pros-tho-don´tics
pros´ti-tute
pros-ti-tu´tion
pros´trate
pros´trat-ing
pros-tra´tion
pros´tra-tor
pros´y
pro´ta-gon
pro-tag´o-nist
prot´amine´
pro´te-ase
pro-tect´
pro-tect´ant

pro-tect´ing
pro-tect´ing-ly
pro-tec´tion
pro-tec´tion-ism
pro-tec´tion-ist
pro-tec´tive
pro-tec´tive-ly
pro-tec´tor
pro-tec´tor-ate
pro-tec´to-ry
pro-tec´tress
pro´té-gé´
pro´té-gée´
pro´te-ide
pro´tein
pro-tem´po-re
pro-te-ol´y-sin
pro-te-ol´y-sis
pro´teo-lyt´ic
Prot´ero-zo´ic
pro´test
Prot´es-tant
Prot´es-tant-ism
prot´es-ta´tion
pro-test´er
pro-test´ing
Pro´teus
proth´e-sis
pro-thon´o-tary
pro-tho´rax
pro-throm´bin
pro´tide
pro´to-blast
pro´to-clas´tic
pro´to-col
pro´to-gen
pro-tog´y-ny
pro´ton
pro´ton-ate
pro´to-plasm
pro´to-plas´mal
pro´to-plas´mic
pro´to-plast
pro´to-stele
pro´to-trop´ic
pro-tot´ro-py
pro´to-typ´al
pro´to-type
pro´to-typ´i-cal
prot-ox´ide
pro-to-zo´a
pro´to-zo´al
pro´to-zo´an
pro-tract´
pro-tract´ed
pro-tract´i-ble
pro-trac´tile
pro-trac´tion
pro-trac´tive
pro-trac´tor
pro-trude´
pro-tru´si-ble
pro-tru´sion
pro-tru´sive
pro-tru´sive-ly
pro-tu´ber-ance
pro-tu´ber-ant
pro-tu´ber-ate
proud´ly
proust´ite
prov´able
proved
prov´en
prov´e-nance
Pro-ven-cal´
Prov´ence
prov´en-der
pro-ve´nience
prov´er
prov´erb
pro-ver´bi-al
pro-vide´
pro-vid´ed
prov´i-dence
prov´i-dent
prov´i-den´tial
pro-vid´er
pro-vid´ing
prov´ince
Prov´ince-town
pro-vin´cial
pro-vin´cial-ism
pro-vin-ci-al´i-ty
pro-vin´cial-ly
prov´ing
pro-vi´sion
pro-vi´sion-al
pro-vi´sion-al-ly
pro-vi´sion-ary
pro-vi´sion-er
pro-vi´so
pro´vi-so-ri-ly
pro-vi´so-ry
pro-vi´sos
prov-o-ca´tion
pro-voc´a-tive
pro-voc´a-to-ry
pro-voke´
pro-vok´ing
pro-vo-lo´ne
pro´vost
prov´ost-al
pro´vost mar´shal
prow´ess
prowl´er
prox´ies
prox´i-mal
prox´i-mate
prox´i-mate-ly
prox-im´i-ty
prox´i-mo
prox´y
prude
pru´dence
pru´dent
pru-den´tial
prud´ery
Prud´hoe
prud´ish
pru-nel´la
prun´er
pru´ne-tin
prun´ing
pru-ri´tus
Prus´sia
prus´si-ate
pried
pry´ing
psalm
psalm´ist
psal´tery
pseud´an-dry
pseud-ar-thro´sis
pseu´do
pseu´do-aquat´ic
pseu´do-carp
pseu´do-cu´mi-dine

pseu´do-nym
pseu-don´y-mous
pseu´do-pod
pseu´do-po´di-um
pseu-dos´co-py
pseu-dos´to-ma
psil-an´thro-py
psi-lo-mel´ane
psi-lo´sis
psi-lot´ic
psit´ta-cine
psit-ta-co´sis
psit´ta-cot´ic
pso´as
pso-phom´e-ter
pso-ri´a-sis
pso´ri-at´ic
pso-ro´sis
psy´cha-gog´ic
psy´cha-gogy
psych´as-the´nia
psy´che
psy-che-om´e-try
psy-chi-at´ric
psy-chi´a-trist
psy-chi´a-try
psy´chic
psy´chi-cal
psy´chi-cal-ly
psy-cho-anal´y-sis
psy-cho-an´a-lyst
psy´cho-an-a-lyt´ic
psy-cho-an-a-lyt´i-cal
psy-cho-an´a-lyze
psy´cho-gen´ic
psy-cho-ge-nic´i-ty
psy-chog-no´sis
psy´cho-graph´ic
psy-chog´ra-phy
psy´cho-lep-sy
psy-cho-lep´tyc
psy´cho-log´i-cal
psy-cho-log´i-cal-ly
psy-chol´o-gist
psy-chol´o-gize
psy-chol´o-gy
psy-chom´a-chy
psy-chom´e-ter
psy´cho-met´ric
psy-chom-e-tri´cian
psy-chom´e-try
psy-cho-neu-ro´sis
psy-cho-neu-rot´ic
psy-cho-nom´ics
psy´cho-path
psy´cho-path´ic
psy-chop´a-thist
psy-chop´a-thy
psy-cho´sis
psy-cho-so-mat´ic
psy-cho-ther´a-py
psy-chot´ic
psy´cho-trine
psy-chrom´e-ter
psy-chrom´e-try
psyl´li-um
pter´o-dac´tyl
pte-ro´ic
pter´o-pod
pter´o-yl
pte-ryg´i-um
pter´y-goid
pti-san´
Ptol´e-ma´ic
Ptol´e-my
pto-maine´
pto´sis
pty´a-lin
pty´a-lism
pu´ber-ty
pu-ber´u-lent
pu-ber´u-lon´ic
pu-bes´cence
pu-bes´cent
pu´bic
pu-bi-ot´o-my
pub´lic
pub´li-can
pub-li-ca´tion
pub´lic house
pub´li-cist
pub-lic´i-ty
pub´li-cize
pub´lic-ly
pub´lic—spir´it-ed
pub´lish
pub´lish-able
pub´lish-er
Pub´li-us
Puc-ci´ni
puck´er
puck´ered
puck´ery
puck´ish
pud´ding
pud´dle
pud´dler
pud´dling
pudg´i-ness
pudg´y
pueb´lo
pueb´los
pu´er-ile
pu-er-il´i-ty
pu-er´per-al
pu-er-pe´ri-um
Puer´to Ri´co
puff´er
puf´fin
puff´i-ness
puff´y
Pu´get
pu´gi-lism
pu´gi-list
pu´gi-lis´tic
pug-na´cious
pug-na´cious-ly
pug-nac´i-ty
pug nose
pug´—nosed
Pu-las´ki
pul´chri-tude
pul-chri-tu´di-nous
pu´le-gone
pu´li-cide
pul´ing
Pul´itz-er
pull´er
pul´let
pul´ley
pull´ing
Pull´man
pull´over
pul´lu-late
pul-lu-la´tion
pul-mom´e-ter
pul´mo-nary

pul-mon´ic
Pul´mo-tor
pulp´er
pulp´i-ness
pul´pit
pul´pi-teer´
pulp´ous
pulp´wood
pulp´y
pul´sate
pul´sa-tile
pul-sa´tion
pul´sa-tive
pul-sa´tor
pul´sa-to-ry
pulsed
puls´er
pul-sim´e-ter
puls´ing
pul-som´e-ter
pul´ver-iz-able
pu´ver-i-za´tion
pul´ver-ize
pul´ver-iz-er
pu´ver´u-lent
pu´ma
pu´mi-cate
pum´ice
pum´mel
pump´age
pump´er
pum´per-nick-el
pump´kin
punch´er
pun-chi-nel´lo
punc´tate
punc´tat-ed
punc-ta´tion
punc´ti-form
punc-til´io
punc-til´i-ous
punc´tu-al
punc-tu-al´i-ty
punc´tu-al-ly
punc´tu-ate
punc-tu-a´tion
punc´tu-a-tor
punc´tur-able
punc´ture
punc´tured
punc´tur-ing
pun´dit
pun´gen-cy
pun´gent
Pu´nic
pu-nic´ic
pu´ni-ness
pun´ish
pun´ish-able
pun´ish-er
pun´ish-ment
pu´ni-tive
Pun´jab
punned
pun´ning
pun´ster
punt´er
pun´ty
pu´ny
pu´pa
pu´pal
pu´pil
pu-pil-lar´i-ty
pu´pil-lary
pu´pil-late
pu-pil-lom´e-ter
Pu-pin´
pup´pet
pup´pe-teer´
pup´pet-ry
pup´py
Pur´cell
pur´chas-able
pur´chase
pur´chased
pur´chas-er
pur´chas-ing
Pur-due´
pu-ree´
pure´ly
pure´ness
pur-ga´tion
pur´gative
pur´ga-to´ri-al
pur-ga-to´ri-an
pur´ga-to-ry
purge
purg´er
purg´ing
pu-ri-fi-ca´tion
pu-rif´i-ca-to-ry
pu´ri-fi-er
pu´ri-fy
Pu´rim
pu´rine
pur´ism
pur´ist
pu-ris´tic
pu´ri-tan
pu-ri-tan´i-cal
pu´ri-tan-ism
pu´ri-ty
pur´lin
pur-loin´
pu´ro-my´cin
pur´ple
pur-port´
pur´pose
pur´pose-ful
pur´pose-ful-ly
pur´pose-less
pur´pose-ly
pur´pos-ive
purr´ing
purse—proud
purs´er
purs´ing
pur-su´al
pur-su´ance
pur-su´ant
pur-su´ant-ly
pur-sue´
pur-sued´
pur-su´er
pur-su´ing
pur-suit´
pur´sy
pur´te-nance
pu´ru-lence
pu´ru-lent
pur-vey´
pur-vey´ance
pur-vey´or
pur´view
push´ball
push but´ton
push´cart

push´er
push´ing
push´over
push´pin
push´—pull´
pu´sil-lan´i-mous
puss´y
puss´y-foot
puss´y wil´low
pus´tu-lant
pus´tu-lar
pus´tu-late
pus-tu-la´tion
pus´tule
pus´tu-lous
pu-ta´men
pu´ta-tive
pu´tre-fied
pu´tre-fy
pu´tre-fy-ing
pu-tres´cence
pu´trid
pu-trid´i-ty
put-tee´
putt´er
put´ty
puz´zle
puz´zle-ment
puz´zler
puz´zling
Pyg-ma´lion
pyg´my
py´lon
py-lo-rec´to-my
py-lor´ic
py-lo´ro-plas-ty
py-lo´rus
py-or-rhe´a
pyr´a-cene
pyr´a-mid
py-ram´i-dal
pyr´a-mid-er
pyr´a-mid´i-cal
Pyr´a-mus
pyre
py´rene
Pyr´e-nees
pyre-tol´o-gy
Py´rex
py-rex´ia
py-rex´in
pyr´i-bole
py-rid´ic
pyr´i-dine
pyr-i-din´i-um
pyr-i-dox´ine
py´rite
py-rit´es
py-rit´ic
py´ro-graph´ic
py-rog´ra-phy
py´ro-lig´ne-ous
py-rol´o-gy
py-ro-lu´site
py-rol´y-sis
py´ro-lyze
py-ro-ma´nia
py-ro-ma´ni-ac
py-rom´e-ter
py´rone
py-ro´sis
py´ro-sphere
py´ro-tech´nic
py-ro-tech´ni-cal
py-rox´ene
py-rox´e-nite
py-rox´y-lin
pyr´rhic
Pyr´rhus
Py-thag´o-ras
Pyth´i-an
Pyth´i-as
py´thon
py-thon´ic

Q

Qa´tar
quack´ery
quad´ra-ges´i-mal
quad´ran-gle
quad-ran´gu-lar
quad´rant
qua-dran´tal
quad´rate
qua-drat´ic
quad´ra-ture
qua-dra´tus
qua-dren´ni-al
qua-dren´ni-al-ly
qua-dren´ni-um
quad´ric
quad´ri-lat´er-al
quad´ri-lin´gual
qua-drille´
qua-dril´lion
quad-ri-ple´gic
quad´ri-va´lent
qua-driv´i-um
qua-droon´
qua-drum´vi-rate
quad´ru-ped
quad´ru-pe-dal
quad-ru´ple
quad-rup´let
quad´ru-plex
qua-dru´pli-cate
quad-ru´pling
quaff
quaffed
quag´mire
qua´hog
quaint´ly
quaked
Quake-er
quak´ing
qual-i-fi-ca´tion
qual´i-fied
qual´i-fy
qual´i-fy-ing
qua-lim´e-ter
qual´i-ta-tive
qual´i-ta-tive-ly
qual´i-ty
qualm
qualm´ish
quan´da-ry
quan´tile
quan´ti-ta-tive
quan´ti-ta-tive-ly
quan´ti-ty
quan´tum
quar´an-tine
quar´an-tin-er
quar´rel
quar´reled
quar´rel-ing

quar´rel-some
quar´ry
quar´tan
quar´ter
quar´ter-back
quar´ter-deck
quar´tered
quar´ter-ing
quar´ter-ly
quar´ter-mas-ter
quar´tern
quar-tet´
quar´tile
quar´to
quar´tos
quarts
quartz
quartz-if´er-ous
quartz´ite
quartz-it´ic
quartz´ose
qua´si
quat´er-nary
qua´train
qua´tre
qua´ver
qua´vered
qua´ver-ing
quay
quea´si-ly
quea´si-ness
quea´sy
Que-bec´
queen´li-ness
queen´ly
Queens´ber-ry
Queens´land
queer´ly
quelled
quell´er
Que-moy´
quenched
quench´er
quench´less
Quen´tin
quer´ce-tin
que´ried
que´rist
quer´u-lous
que´ry
que´ry-ing
ques´tion
ques´tion-able
ques´tion-er
ques´tion-ing
ques´tion-ing-ly
ques´tion mark
ques´tion-naire´
quet-zal´
queue
queu´er
queu´ing
quib´ble
quib´bled
quib´bler
quib´bling
quick´en
quick´en-ing
quick´—fire´
quick´lime
quick´ly
quick´ness
quick´sand
quick´set
quick´—set´ting
quick´sil-ver
quick´step
quick´—tem´pered
quick´—wit´ted
qui-es´cence
qui-es´cent
qui´et
qui´et-ism
qui´et-ly
qui´et-ness
qui´e-tude
qui-e´tus
quilt´ed
quilt´ing
quin´a-crine
quin´a-mine
qui´na-ry
quin-az´o-line
quin-cun´cial
Quin´cy
qui-nel´la
quin´i-dine
qui-nie´la
qui´nine
Quin-qua-ges´i-ma
quin-quen´ni-al
quin´sy
quin´tal
quin´tant
quin-ter´ni-on
quin-tes´sence
quin´tes-sen´tial
quin-tet´
quin´tic
quint-tile
quin-tu´ple
quin-tup´let
quin-tu´pling
quipped
quip´ping
quip´ster
quire
Quir´i-nal
quir´i-tar´i-an
Quis´ling
quit´claim
quit´rent
quit´tance
quit´ted
quit´ter
quit´ting
quit´tor
quiv´er
quiv´ered
quiv´er-ing
qui vive
quix-ot´ic
quix-ot´i-cal-ly
quix´o-tism
quiz
quizzed
quiz´zi-cal
quiz´zing
quoin
quoit
quon´dam
Quon´set
quo´rum
quo´ta
quot-abil´i-ty
quot´able
quo-ta´tion

quote
quot´ed
quot´er
quo-tid´i-an
quo´tient
quot´ing

R

rab´at
Ra-bat´
ra-ba´to
rab´bet
rab´bet-ed
rab´bi
rab´bin-ate
rab-bin´ic
rab-bin´i-cal
rab´bit
rab´bit-ry
rab´ble
rab´bler
Rab´e-lais´
rab´id
ra-bid´i-ty
ra´bies
rac-coon´
race´course
race´horse
rac´e-mate
ra-ceme´
rac´er
race´track
race´way
Ra´chel
ra-chel´
Rach-man´i-noff
ra´cial
ra´cial-ism
ra´cial-ly
ra-ci-a´tion
rac´i-ly
Ra-cine´
rac´ing
rac´ism
rac´ist
rack´er
rack´et
rack´e-teer´
rack´ety
rack rail
ra´con
rac´on-teur
rac´y
ra´dar
ra´dar-scope
Rad´cliffe
ra´di-ac
ra´di-al
ra´di-an
ra´di-ance
ra´di-an-cy
ra´di-ant
ra´di-ant-ly
ra´di-ate
ra-di-a´tion
ra´di-a-tive
ra´di-a-tor
rad´i-cal
rad´i-cal-ism
rad´i-cal-ly
rad´i-cand
rad´i-cate
rad-i-ca´tion
rad´i-cle
ra´dii
ra´dio
ra´dio-ac´tive
ra´dio-ac-tiv´i-ty
ra´dio—fre´quen-cy
ra´dio-gram
ra´dio-graph
ra-di-og´ra-pher
ra´dio-graph´ic
ra-di-og´ra-phy
ra´dio-i´so-tope
ra´dio-lar´i-an
ra-di-o-log´i-cal
ra-di-ol´o-gist
ra-di-ol´o-gy
ra-di-ol´y-sis
ra-di-om´e-ter
ra-dio-met´ric
ra´di-on´ic
ra´dio-nu´clide
ra´dio-phone
ra´di-os
ra-di-os´co-py
ra´dio-sonde
ra´dio-tel´e-gram
ra´dio-tel´e-graph
ra-dio-tel´e-phone
ra´dio-te-leph´o-ny
ra´dio-ther´a-py
ra´dio-tho´ri-um
rad´ish
ra´di-um
ra´di-us
ra´dix
ra´dome
ra´don
rad´u-la
raf´fia
raff´ish
raff´ish-ly
raf´fle
raf´fled
raf´fling
raf´ter
rafts´man
rag´a-muf-fin
rag´ged
rag´ged-ness
rag´ing
rag´lan
rag´man
ra-gout´
rag´pick-er
rag´time
rair´weed
raid´er
rail´er
rail´head
rail´ing
rail´lery
rail´road
rail´road-ing
rail´way
rain´band
rain´bow
rain cloud
rain´coat
rain´drop
rain´fall
rain gage
rain´i-er
Rai-nier´

rain´less
rain´mak-er
rain pipe
rain´proof
rain´storm
rain´tight
rain´wa´ter
rain´y
rais´er
rai´sin
rais´ing
rai-son´
ra´ja, ra´jah
Raj´put
raked
rake´hell
rake´—off
rak´er
rak´ing
rak´ish
Ra´leigh
ral´lied
ral´ly
ral´ston-ite
Ram´a-dan
Ra´man
ram´ble
ram´bler
ram´bling
ram-bunc´tious
Ram´e-ses
ram-i-fi-ca´tion
ram´i-fied
ram´i-fy
ram´i-fy-ing
ram´jet
rammed
ram´ming
Ra-mo´na
ram´page
ram-pa´geous
ram´pag-er
ram´pag-ing
ram´pant
ram´part
ram´pi-on
ram´rod
ram´shack-le
ram´u-lose
ranch´er
ran-che´ro
ranch´man
ran´cho
ran´cid
ran-cid´i-ty
ran´cor
ran´corous
Ran´dolph
ran´dom
ran´dom-ize
ranged
rang´er
rang-ette´
rang´ing
Ran-goon´
rang´y
ra-ni´
ra´nine
rank´er
ran´kle
ran´kled
ran´kling
rank´ness
ran´sack
ran´som
ran´som-er
rant´er
rant´ing
ra-pa´cious
ra-pa´cious-ness
Raph´a-el
rap´id
rap´id—fire
ra-pid´i-ty
rap´id-ly
ra´pier
rap´ine
rap´ist
rap-pa-ree´
rapped
rap´ping
rap-port´
rap-proche-ment´
rap-scal´lion
rapt´ly
rap-to´ri-al
rap´ture
rap´tur-ous
rare´bit
rar´e-fac´tion
rar´e-fied
rar´e-fy
rare´ly
rare´ness
rar´i-ty
ras´cal
ras-cal´i-ty
ras´cal-ly
rash´er
rash´ly
rash´ness
rasp´ber-ry
rasp´er
rasp´ing
Ras-pu´tin
ras´ter
ra´sure
ratch´et
ra´tel
rate´pay-er
rat´er
rath´er
raths´kel-ler
rat-i-fi-ca´tion
rat´i-fied
rat´i-fy
rat´i-fy-ing
rat´ing
ra´tion
ra´tio-nal
ra´tio-nale´
ra´tio-nal-ism
ra´tio-nal-ist
ra-tio-nal-is´tic
ra-tio-nal´i-ty
ra-tio-nal-iza´tion
ra´tio-nal-ize
ra´tio-nal-ly
rat´ite
rat´line
ra-toon´
rat´proof
rat-tan´
rat´tle
rat´tler
rat´tle-snake
rat´tle-trap

rau´cous
rau´vite
rav´age
rav´ag-er
rav´ag-ing
rav´el
Ra-vel´
rav´eled
rave´lin
rav´el-ing
ra´ven
rav´en-ing
Ra-ven´na
rav´en-ous
rav´in
ra-vine´
rav´ing
rav-i-o´li
rav´ish
rav´ish-er
rav´ish-ing
rav´ish-ment
raw´boned´
raw´hide
ra´win-sonde
Ray´mond
ray´on
ra´zon
ra´zor
ra´zor-back
raz´zle—daz-zle
re-act´
re-ac´tance
re-ac´tion
re-ac´tion-ary
re-ac´tive
re-ac´tor
read-abil´i-ty
read´able
re-ad-dress´
read´er
read´i-ly
read´i-ness
read´ing
Read´ing
read´ing room
re-ad-just´
re-ad-just´ment
read´y
read´y—made
re-af-firm´
re-a´gent
re´al
re-al´gar
re´al-ism
re´al-ist
re´al-is´tic
re-al-is´ti-cal-ly
re-al´i-ty
re-al-iza´tion
re´al-ize
re´al-ly
realm
re´al-tor
re´al-ty
ream´er
re-an´i-mate
reap´er
re-ap-pear´
re-ap-pear´ance
re-ap-point´
rear ad´mi-ral
rear guard
re-arm´
re-ar´ma-ment
re-ar-range´
re-ar-range´ment
re-ar-rang´ing
rear´ward
re-as-cend´
rea´son
rea´son-able
rea´son-able-ness
rea´son-ably
rea´son-er
rea´son-ing
re-as-sem´ble
re-as-sert´
re-as-sume´
re-as-sur´ance
re´as-sure´
re´as-sur´ing
reav´er
re-awak´en
re´bate
re´bat-er
re´bec
Re-bec´ca
reb´el
re-belled´
re-bel´ling
re-bel´lion
re-bel´lious
re-bel´lious-ly
re´birth´
re´born´
re-bound´
re-buff´
re-build´
re-built´
re-buke´
re-buk´ing
re´bus
re-but´
re-but´ta-ble
re-but´tal
re-but´ted
re-but´ting
re-cal´ci-trance
re-cal´ci-trant
re-ca-les´cence
re´ca-les´cent
re-call´
re-cant´
re-can-ta´tion
re´cap´
re-ca-pit´u-late
re-ca-pit´u-la´tion
re-ca-pit´u-la-to-ry
re´capped´
re´cap´ping
re-cap´ture
re-cast´
re-cede´
re-ced´ed
re-ced´ence
re-ced´er
re-ced´ing
re-ceipt´
re-ceipt´or
re-ceiv´able
re-ceive´
re-ceiv´er
re-ceiv´er-ship
re-ceiv´ing
re´cen-cy
re-cen´sion

re´cent
re´cent-ly
re-cep´ta-cle
re-cep´ti-ble
re-cep´tion
re-cep´tion-ist
re-cep´tive
re-cep-tiv´i-ty
re-cep´tor
re´cess
re´cess´er
re-ces´sion
re-ces´sion-al
re-ces´sive
re-charge´
rec´i-pe
re-cip´i-ence
re-cip´i-ent
re-cip´ro-ca-ble
re-cip´ro-cal
re-cip´ro-cal-ly
re-cip´ro-cate
re-cip-ro-ca´tion
rec-i-proc´i-ty
re-ci´sion
re-cit´al
rec-i-ta´tion
rec´i-ta-tive´
re-cite´
re-cit´er
re-cit´ing
reck´less
reck´less-ly
reck´less-ness
reck´on
reck´on-ing
re-claim
re-claim´able
rec-la-ma´tion
re-clin´able
rec-li-na´tion
re-cline´
re-clin´er
re-clin´ing
rec´luse
re-clu´sive
rec-og-ni´tion
rec´og-niz-able
re-cog´ni-zance
rec´og-nize
re-cog´ni-zee´
rec´og-niz-er
re-cog´ni-zor´
re-coil´
re—coil´
rec-ol-lect´
re—col-lect´
rec-ol-lec´tion
re-com-bi-na´tion
re´com-bine´
re-com-mence´
rec-om-mend´
rec-om-men-da´tion
rec-om-mend´a-to-ry
re-com-mit´
re-com-mit´tal
re-com-mit´ment
rec´om-pense
rec´om-pens-er
rec´om-pens-ing
re-con´cen-trate
rec´on-cil-able
rec´on-cile
rec´on-cile-ment
rec´on-cil-er
rec-on-cil-i-a´tion
rec´on-cil´ia-to-ry
rec´on-dite
re-con-di´tion
re-con´nais-sance
recon-noi´ter
re-con´quer
re-con´se-crate
re-con-sid´er
re-con-sid´er-a´tion
re-con´sti-tute
re-con-struct´
re-con-struc´tion
re-cord´
re-cord´able
rec-or-da´tion
re-cord´er
re-count´
re-coup´
re´course
re-cov´er
re-cov´er-able
re-cov´ery
rec´re-ant
rec´re-ate
re—cre-ate´
rec-re-a´tion
re—cre-a´tive
rec´re-a-tive
rec´re-ment
rec-re-men´tal
rec´re-men-ti´tious
re-crim´i-nate
re-crim´i-nat-ing
re-crim-i-na´tion
re-crim´i-na-to-ry
re-cru-des´cence
re-cru-des´cent
re-cruit´
re-cruit´er
re-cruit´ment
rec´tal
rec´tan-gle
rec-tan´gu-lar
rec´ti-fi-able
rec-ti-fi-ca´tion
rec´ti-fied
rec´ti-fi-er
rec´ti-fy
rec´ti-tude
rec´tor
rec´tor-ate
rec´tor-ship
rec´to-ry
rec´tum
rec´tus
re-cum´ben-cy
re-cum´bent
re-cu´per-ate
re-cu-per-a´tion
re-cu´per-a-tive
re-cur´
re-curred´
re-cur´rence
re-cur´rent
re-cur´ring
re-cur´sive
re-cur´vate
re-dact´
re-dac´tion
re-dac´tor
re-dan´

red´bird
red´—blood´ed
red´breast
red´bud
red´cap
red´coat
red´den
red´dish
re-dec´o-rate
re-deem´
re-deem´able
re-deem´er
re-demp´ti-ble
re-demp´tion
re-demp´tive
re-demp´tor
re-demp´to-ry
re-de-ploy´
re-de-ploy´ment
red´—faced
red´—hand´ed
red´head
red´head-ed
red her´ring
red´—hot´
re-di-rect´
re-dis´count
re-dis-cov´er
re-dis-cov´ery
re-dis-trib´ute
re-dis-tri-bu´tion
re-dis´trict
red lead
red´—lead´
red´—let´ter
red´ness
red´o-lence
re-dou´ble
re-dou´bling
re-doubt´
re-doubt´able
re-dound´
re-draw´
re-dress´
re-dress´able
re-dress´er
red´skin
red tape
re-duce´
re-duc´er
re-duc´ible
re-duc´ing
re-duc´tase
re-duc´tion
re-duc´tive
re-duc´tone
re-dun´dan-cy
re-dun´dant
re-du´pli-cate
re-du-pli-ca´tion
red´wing
red´wood
re-ech´o
reed´y
reef´er
re-elect´
re-elec´tion
reel´er
re-em-bark´
re-en-act´
re-en-force´
re-en-force´ment
re-en-gage´
re´en-list´
re-en´ter
re-en´trant
re-en´try
re-es-tab´lish
re-es-tab´lish-ment
re-ex-am-i-na´tion
re-ex-am´ine
re-fas´ten
re-fec´tion
re-fec´to-ry
re-fer´
ref´er-able
ref´er-ee´
ref´er-ence
ref-er-en´dum
refer´ent
ref´er-en´tial
re-ferred´
re-fer´ring
re-fill
re-fill´able
re-fine´
re-fined´
re-fine-ment
re-fin´er
re-fin´ery
re-fin´ing
re-fit´
re-flect´
re-flec´tance
re-flect´ible
re-flec´tion
re-flec´tive
re-flec-tom´e-ter
re-flec-tom´e-try
re-flec´tor
re-flec´tor-ize
re´flex
re-flex´ive
re-flex-iv´i-ty
ref´lu-ent
re´flux
re-for´est
re-for-est-a´tion
re-form´
re-form´able
ref-or-ma´tion
re-for´ma-tive
re-for´ma-to-ry
re-form´er
re-fract´
re-frac´tion
re-frac´tive
re-frac-tom´e-ter
re-frac´to-met´ric
re-frac-tom´e-try
re-frac´tor
re-frac´to-ri-ness
re-frac´to-ry
re-frain´
re-fran´gi-ble
ref-re-na´tion
re-fresh´
re-fresh´ing
re-fresh´ment
re-frig´er-ant
re-frig´er-ate
re-frig´er-at-ing
re-frig-er-a´tion
re-frig´er-a-tor
re-frin´gent
re-fu´el
ref´uge

ref´u-gee
re-ful´gence
re-ful´gent
re´fund
re-fur´bish
re-fur´nish
re-fus´al
re-fyse´
re—fuse´
re-fus´ing
re-fut´able
re-fut´ably
re-fut´al
ref-u-ta´tion
re-fute´
re-fut´er
re-fut´ing
re-gain´
re´gal
re-gale´
re-ga´lia
re-gal´ing
re-gal´i-ty
re´gal-ly
re-gard´
re-gard´ing
re-gard´less
re-gat´ta
re´ge-late
re´ge-la´tion
re´gen-cy
re-gen´er-a-cy
re-gen´er-ate
re-gen-er-a´tion
re-gen´er-a-tive
re-gen´er-a-tor
re´gent
re-gime´
reg´i-men
reg´i-ment
reg´i-men´tal
reg-i-men´ta-ry
reg-i-men-ta´tion
Re-gi´na
Reg´i-nald
re´gion
re´gion-al
reg´is-ter
reg´is-tered
reg´is-tra-ble
reg´is-trar
reg´is-trate
reg-is-tra´tion
reg´is-try
reg´let
reg´nant
Re-gnault´
reg´o-sol
re-gress´
re-gres´sion
re-gres´sive
re-gres´sor
re-gret´
re-gret´ful
re-gret´ful-ly
re-gret´ta-ble
re-gret´ta-bly
re-gret´ted
re-gret´ting
reg´u-lar
reg-u-lar´i-ty
reg´u-lar-ize
reg´u-lar-ly
reg´u-lat-able
reg´u-late
reg-u-la´tion
reg´u-la-tive
reg´u-la-tor
reg´u-la-to-ry
reg´u-lus
re-gur´gi-tate
re-gur-gi-ta´tion
re-ha-bil´i-tate
re-ha-bi´i-ta´tion
re-ha-bil´i-ta-tive
re´hash´
re-hears´al
re-hearse´
re-hears´er
re-hears´ing
re-heat´
Re´ho-both
Reichs´tag
re´ify
reign
re-im-burs´able
re-im-burse´
re-im-burse´ment
re-im-port´
re-im-por-ta´tion
rein
re-in-car´nate
re-in-car-na´tion
rein´deer
Rei´necke
re-in-force´
re-in-forced´
re-in-force´ment
re-in-sert´
re-in-stall´
re-in-stal-la´tion
re-in-state´
re-in-state´ment
re-in-sure´
re-in-te-gra´tion
re-in-vest´
re-in-vig´o-rate
re-is´sue
re-it´er-ate
re-it-er-a´tion
re-it´er-a-tive
re-ject´
re-ject´able
re-ject´er
re-jee´tion
re-jec´tor
re-joice´
re-joic´ing
re-join´
re-join´der
re-ju´ve-nate
re-ju-ve-na´tion
re-ju´ve-na-tor
re-kin´dle
re-lapse´
re-lapsed´
re-laps´er
re-laps´ing
re-late´
re-lat´ed
re-lat´er
re-lat´ing
re-la´tion
re-la´tion-ship
rel´a-tive
rel´a-tive-ly
rel´a-tiv-ism

rel´a-tiv´i-ty
re-la´tor
re-lax´
re-lax-a´tion
re-lax´ed-ly
re-lax-om´e-ter
re´lay
re´layed
re-lease´
re-leased´
re-leas´er
re-leas´ing
rel´e-ga-ble
rel´e-gate
rel´e-gat-ed
rel-e-ga´tion
re-lent´
re-lent´ing
re-lent´ing-ly
re-lent´less
rel´e-vance
rel´e-van-cy
rel´e-vant
re-li-abil´i-ty
re-li´able
re-li´ably
re-li´ance
re-li´ant
rel´ic
rel´ict
re-lied´
re-lief´
re-lief´er
re-liev´able
re-lieve´
re-lieved´
re-liev´er
re-liev´ing
re-li´gion
re-li-gi-os´i-ty
re-li´gious
re-li´gious-ly
re-lin´quish
rel´i-quary
rel´ish
rel´ish-able
rel´ish-ing
re-load´
re´lo-cate´

re-lu´cence
re-luc´tance
re-luc´tant
re-luc´tant-ly
rel-uc-tiv´i-ty
re-lume´
re-lu´mine
re-ly´
re-ly´ing
re-made´
re-main´
re-main´der
re-main´ing
re-mand´
re-mand´ment
rem´a-nence
rem´a-nent
re-mark´
re-mark´able
re-mark´ably
Re-marque´
re-marque´
re-mar´riage
re-mar´ry
Rem´brandt
re-me´di-able
re-me´di-al
rem´e-died
rem´e-dies
rem´e-di-less
rem´e-dy
re-mem´ber
re-mem´brance
re-mind´
re-mind´er
Rem´ing-ton
rem-i-nisce´
rem-i-nis´cence
rem-i-nis´cent
rem-i-nis´cent-ly
rem-i-nis´cer
rem-i-nis´cing
re-miss´
re-miss-ibil´i-ty
re-miss´ible
re-mis´sion
re-mis´sive
re-miss´ness
re-mit´

re-mit´tance
re-mit´ted
re-mit´tee´
re-mit´tent
re-mit´ter
re-mit´ting
rem´nant
re-mod´el
re-mod´eled
re-mon-e-ti-za´tion
re-mon´e-tize
re-mon´strance
re-mon´strant
re-mon´strate
re-mon-stra´tion
re-mon´stra-tive
re-mon´stra-tor
rem´on-toir´
re-morse´
re-morse´ful
re-morse´less
re-mote´
re-mote´ly
re-mote´ness
re-mot´est
re-mount´
re-mov-abil´i-ty
re-mov´able
re-mov´al
re-move´
re-moved´
re-mov´er
re-mov´ing
re-mu´ner-a-ble
re-mu´ner-ate
re-mu-ner-a´tion
re-mu´ner-a-tive
Re´mus
ren´ais-sance´
Ren´ais-sant´
re-name´
Re-nan´
re-nas´cence
re-nas´cent
ren-coun´ter
ren´der
ren´der-able
ren´dez-vous
rend´ible

rend´ing
ren-di´tion
Re-né´
ren´e-gade
re-nege´
re-neg´er
re-neg´ing
re-new´
re-new´able
re-new´al
re-newed´
re-new´ed-ly
ren´net
ren´nin
Re´no
Re-noir´
re-nom´i-nate
re-nom-i-na´tion
re-nounce´
re-nounce´ment
re-nounc´ing
ren´o-vate
ren´o-vat-ing
ren-o-va´tion
ren´o-va-tor
re-nown´
re-nowned´
rent´able
rent´al
rent´er
rent´ing
re-nun-ci-a´tion
re-nun´ci-a-to-ry
re-oc´cu-py
re-o´pen
re-or-ga-ni-za´tion
re-or´ga-nize
re-paid´
re-paint´
re-pair´
re-pair´able
re-pair´er
re-pair´man
rep´a-ra-ble
rep-a-ra´tion
re-par´a-tive
re-par´a-to-ry
rep´ar-tee´
re-par-ti´tion
re-past´
re-pa´tri-ate
re-patri-a´tion
re-pay´
re-pay´ing
re-pay´ment
re-peal´
re-peal´able
re-peal´er
re-peat´
re-peat´able
re-peat´ed
re-peat´ed-ly
re-peat´er
re-pel´
re-pelled´
re-pel´len-cy
re-pel´lent
re-pel´ling
re-pent´
re-pent´ance
re-pent´ant
re-peo´ple
reper-cus´sion
reper-cus´sive
rep´er-toire
rep´er-to-ry
rep´e-tend
rep-e-ti´tion
rep´e-ti´tious
rep-e-ti´tious-ly
re-pet´i-tive
re-pine´
re-place´
re-place´able
re-place´ment
re-plac´ing
re-plant´
re-plen´ish
re-plen´ish-er
re-plen´ish-ment
re-plete´
re-ple´tion
re-ple´tive
re-plev´in
rep´li-ca
rep´li-cate
rep-li-ca´tion
re-plied´
re-ply´
re-ply´ing
re-port´
re-port´er
re-pose´
re-pose´ful
re-pos´ing
re´po-si´tion
re-pos´i-to-ry
re´pos-sess´
re-pos-ses´sion
re-pous-sé´
Rep´plier
rep-re-hend´
rep-re-hen-si-bil´i-ty
rep-re-hen´si-ble
rep-re-hen´sion
rep-re-hen´sive
rep-re-sent´
rep-re-sent´a-ble
rep-re-sen-ta´tion
rep-re-sent´a-tive
rep-re-sent´er
re-press´
re-press´er
re-press´ible
re-pres´sion
re-pres´sive
re-pres´sor
re-prieve´
rep´ri-mand
re-print´
re-pri´sal
re-prise´
re-proach´
re-proach´ful
re-proach´ful-ly
re-proach´ing
rep´ro-ba-cy
rep´ro-bate
rep-ro-ba´tion
re´pro-duce´
re´pro-duc´er
re´pro-duc´ible
re´pro-duc´ing
re-pro-duc´tion
re-pro-duc´tive
re-pro-duc-tiv´i-ty
re-proof´

re-prove´
re-prov´ing
re-prov´ing-ly
rep´tile
rep-til´ian
re-pub´lic
re-pub´li-can
re-pub´li-can-ism
re-pub-li-ca´tion
re-pub´lish
re-pu´di-ate
re-pu-di-a´tion
re-pu´di-a-tor
re-pug´nance
re-pug´nan-cy
re-pug´nant
re-pulse´
re-puls´ing
re-pul´sion
re-pul´sive
re-pur´chase
rep´u-ta-ble
rep´u-ta-bly
rep-u-ta´tion
re-pute´
re-put´ed
re-put´ing
re-quest´
re-quest´er
req´ui-em
re-qui-es´cat
re-quire´
re-quire´ment
re-quir´er
re-quir´ing
req´ui-site
req-ui-si´tion
re-quit´al
re-quite´
re-quit´ed
re-quit´ing
re-read´
rer´e-dos
re-sal´able
re´sale
re-scind´
re-scind´able
re-scind´ment
re-scis´si-ble

re-scis´sion
re´script
re-scrip´tive
res´cu-able
res´cue
rea´cued
res´cu-er
res´cu-ing
re´search´
re-search´er
re-seat´
re-sect´able
re-sec´tion
re-sell´
re-sem´blance
re-sem´ble
re-sem´bler
re-sem´bling
res´ene
re-sent´
re-sent´ful
re-sent´ful-ly
re-sent´ment
res-er-va´tion
re-serve´
re-served
re-serv´ed-ly
re-serv´ist
res´er-voir
re-set´
re-set´ting
re-set´tle-ment
re-ship´
re-side´
res´i-dence
res´i-den-cy
res´i-dent
res´i-den´tial
res-i-den´ti-ary
re-sid´ing
re-sid´u-al
re-sid´u-ary
res´i-due
re-sid´u-um
re-sign´
res-ig-na´tion
re-signed´
re-sign´ed-ly
re-sil´ience

re-sil´ien-cy
re-sil´ient
re-sil´ient-ly
re-sil-i-om´e-ter
res´in
res´in-a´ceous
res´in-ate
res´in-ous
resist´
re-sist´ance
re-sist´ant
re-sist´er
re-sist-ibil´i-ty
re-sist´ible
re-sis-tiv´i-ty
re-sist´less
re-sis´tor
re-sold´
re-sol´u-ble
res´o-lute
res´o-lute-ly
res-o-lu´tion
res-o-lu´tion-er
re-sol´u-tive
re-solv´able
re-solve´
re-solved´
re-solv´ed-ly
re-solv´ent
re-solv´er
re-solv´ing
res´o-nance
res´o-nant
res´o-nate
res´o-na-tor
res-or´cin-ol
res´or-cyl´ic
re-sorp´tive
re-sort´
re-sound´
re-sound´ed
re-sound´ing
re-sound´ing-ly
re´source
re-source´ful
re-source´ful-ly
re-source´ful-ness
re-spect´
re-spect-abil´i-ty

re-spect´able
re-spect´ably
re-spect´er
re-spect´ful
re-spect´ful-ly
re-spect´ing
re-spec´tive
re-spec´tive-ly
res´pi-ra-ble
res-pi-ra´tion
res´pi-ra-tor
res´pi-ra-to-ry
re-spire´
re-spir´ing
res´pite
re-splen´dence
re-splen´den-cy
re-splen´dent
re-spond´
re-spon´dence
re-spon´den-cy
re-spon´dent
re-spond´er
re-sponse´
re-spons´er
re-spon-si-bil´i-ty
re-spon´si-ble
re-spon´si-bly
re-spon´sive
re-spon´sive-ly
re-spon´sive-ness
re-spon´sor
re-spon´so-ry
re´state´
res´tau-rant
res´tau-ra-teur´
rest´ful
res´ti-form
res-ti-tu´tion
res´tive
rest´less
rest´less-ly
rest´less-ness
re´stock´
res-to-ra´tion
re-stor´ative
re-store´
re-stor´er
re-stor´ing
re-strain´
re-strained´
re-straint´
re-strict´
re-strict´ed
re-stric´tion
re-stric´tive
re-sult´
re-sult´ant
re-sume´
ré´su-mé´
re-sum´ing
re-sump´tion
re-sump´tive
re-sur´gence
re-sur´gent
res´ur-rect´
res´ur-rec´tion
res´ur-rec´tor
re-sus´ci-ta-ble
re-sus´ci-tate
re-sus-ci-ta´tion
re-sus´ci-ta-tor
re´tail
re´tail-er
re-tain´
re-tain´er
re-tain´ing
re-take´
re-tal´i-ate
re-tal-i-a´tion
re-tal´i-a-tive
re-tal´ia-to-ry
re-tard´
re-tard´ant
re-tar-da´tion
re-tard´a-to-ry
re-tard´ed
retch
re-tell´
re-tent´
re-ten´tion
re-ten´tive
re-ten-tiv´i-ty
re-ten´tor
ret´i-cence
ret´i-cent
ret´i-cle
re-tic´u-lar
re-tic´u-late
re-tic-u-la´tion
ret´i-cule
re-tic´u-lin
re-tic´u-li´tis
ret´i-na
ret´i-nal
re-tin´a-lite
ret´i-nene
ret-i-ni´tis
ret´i-nol
ret´i-nue
re-tir´al
re-tire´
re-tired´
re-tir´ee´
re-tire´ment
re-tir´ing
re-told´
re-tort´
re-tort´er
re-tor´tion
re-touch´
re-trace´
re-trace´able
re-trac´ing
re-tract´
re-tract´able
re-trac-til´i-ty
re-trac´tion
re-trac´tive
re-trac´tor
re´tral
re´tread´
re-treat´
re-trench´
re-trench´ment
ret-ri-bu´tion
re-trib´u-tive
re-trib´u-to-ry
re-triev´able
re-triev´al
re-trieve´
re-triev´er
re-triev´ing
ret´ro-ac´tive
ret-ro-ces´sion
ret´ro-gra´da-to-ry
ret´ro-grade

ret´ro-gress
ret-ro-gres´sion
ret´ro-gres´sive
ret´ro-spect
ret-ro-spec´tion
ret´ro-spec´tive
ret´ro-vert´ed
re-turn´
re-turn´able
re-turn´ee´
Reu´ben
re-un´ion
re-unite´
re-unit´ing
re-val´u-ate
re-val-u-a´tion
re-vamp´
re-veal´
rev´eil-le
rev´el
rev-e-la´tion
rev´e-la-tor
re-vel´a-to-ry
rev´eled
rev´el-er
rev´el-ing
rev´el-ry
rev´e-nant
re-venge´
re-venge´ful
re-venge´ful-ness
re-veng´er
re-veng´ing
rev´e-nue
re-ver´able
re-ver´ber-ant
re-ver´ber-ate
re-ver-ber-a´tion
re-ver´ber-a-tor
re-vere´
rev´er-ence
rev´er-end
rev´er-ent
rev´er-en´tial
rev´er-ent-ly
rev´er-ie
re-ver´ing
re-ver´sal
re-verse´
re-vers´er
re-vers-ibil´i-ty
re-vers´ible
re-vers´ing
re-ver´sion
re-ver´sion-ary
re-vert´
re-vert´er
re-vert´ible
re-view´
re-view´able
re-view´er
re-vile´
re-vile´ment
re-vil´er
re-vil´ing
re-vise´
re-vised´
re-vis´er
re-vi´sion
re-vis´it
re-vis-i-ta´tion
re-vi´so-ry
re-vi´tal-ize
re-viv´al
re-viv´al-ist
re-vive´
re-viv´i-fy
re-viv´ing
rev-i-vis´cence
rev-i-vis´cent
re-vi´vor
rev-o-ca-bil´i-ty
rev´o-ca-ble
rev-o-ca´tion
rev´o-ca-to-ry
re-vok´able
re-voke´
re-vok´er
re-vok´ing
re-volt´
re-volt´er
re-volt´ing
re-volt´ing-ly
rev´o-lu-ble
rev-o-lu´tion
rev´o-lu´tion-ary
rev-o-lu´tion-ist
rev-o-lu´tion-ize
re-volv´able
re-volve´
re-volv´er
re-volv´ing
re-vue´
re-vul´sion
re-vul´sive
re-ward´
re-ward´able
re´write´
Rey´kja-vik
Rey´nard´
Reyn´olds
rhap-sod´ic
rhap-sod´i-cal
rhap´so-dist
rhap´so-dize
rhap´so-diz-ing
rhap´so-dy
rhe´a
rhe´a-dine
rhe-mat´ic
Rhenish
rhe´ni-um
rhe-om´e-ter
rhe´o-stat
rhe´o-stat´ic
rhe´tor
rhet´o-ric
rhe-tor´i-cal
rhet-o-ri´cian
rheum
rheu-mat´ic
rheu´ma-tism
rheu´ma-toid
rhine´stone
rhi-noc´er-os
rhi´zome
Rhode Is´land
Rho-de´sia
Rho´di-an
rho´dic
rho´di-um
rho´di-zon´ic
rho-do-chro´site
rho-do-den´dron
rho-do´ra
rhom´bic
rhom´bo-clase

rhom´bus
Rhon´da
rhu´barb
rhyme
rhyme´ster
rhym´ing
rhythm
rhyth´mic
rhyth´mi-cal
rhyth´mi-cal-ly
Ri-al´to
rib´ald
rib´al-dry
ribbed
rib´bing
rib´bon
rib´boned
ri-bo-fla´vin
ri´bo-nu-cle´ic
Ri-car´do
rice field
ric´er
Rich´ard
Riche´lieu´
rich´es
rich´ly
Rich´mond
rich´ness
Rich´ter
rick´ets
rick-ett´si-al
rick´ety
rick´sha
ric´o-chet
ric´o-cheted
rid´able
rid´dance
rid´den
rid´der
rid´ding
rid´dle
rid´dled
ride´able
ri´dent
rid´er
rid´er-less
ridge
ridge´pole
ridg´ing
ridg´y
rid´i-cule
ri-dic´u-lous
ri-dic´u-lous-ly
rid´ing
rif´fle
rif´fling
riff´raff
ri´fle
ri´fle-man
ri´fle pit
ri´fling
rig-a-to´ni
rigged
rig´ger
rig´ging
right
right´—an´gled
righ´teous
righ´teous-ness
right´er
right´ful
right´ful-ly
right´—hand-ed
right´ist
right´ly
right´—mind-ed
right´ness
right´—of—way
rig´id
ri-gid´i-ty
rig´id-ly
rig´or mor´tis
rig´ma-role
rig´or
rig´or-ous
rig´or-ous-ly
Ri´ley
rime
rim´less
rimmed
rim´ming
rin´der-pest
ring´bolt
ring´bone
ring´dove
ringed
ring´er
ring´ing
ring´lead-er
ring´let
ring´mas-ter
ring´side
ring´ster
ring´worm
rins´able
rinsed
rins´er
rins´ing
Ri´o de Ja-nei´ro
Ri´o Grande
ri´ot
ri´ot-er
ri´ot-ous
ri´ot-ous-ly
ri-par´i-an
rip´en
ripe´ness
rip´ping
rip´ple
rip´pled
rip´pling
rip´rap
rip´saw
ris´en
ris´er
ris-i-bil´i-ty
ris´i-ble
ris´ing
risk´i-ness
risk´y
ris-qué´
ris-sole´
rite
rit´u-al
rit´u-al-is´tic
ri´val
ri´valed
ri´valing
ri´val-ry
riv´er
Ri-ve´ra
riv´er-ain
riv´er-bank
riv´er-side
riv´et
riv´et-er
riv´et-ing

Riv-i-er´a
riv´u-let
Ri-yadh´
ri-yal´
road´bed
road´house
road´side
road´stead
road´ster
road´way
roam´er
Ro´a-noke
roast´ed
roast´er
robbed
rob´ber
rob´bery
rob´bing
Rob´ert
Robes´pierre
rob´in
rob´ing
Rob´in-son Cru´soe
ro´ble
ro´bot
ro-bust´
ro-bus´tious
ro-bust´ness
Ro-cham-beau´
Ro-chelle´
Roch´es-ter
rock´bound
Rock´e-fel-ler
rock´er
rock´et
rock´e-teer´
rock´et-er
rock´et-ry
Rock´ford
Rock´ies
rock´ing
rock´ing chair
rock-oon´
rock´—ribbed´
rock salt
rock´work
rock´y
ro´dent
ro´deo
Rod´er-ick
Ro-din´
roe´buck
roent´gen
roent´gen-o-graph
roent-gen-og´ra-phy
Rog´er
ro-gnon´
rogue
rogu´ery
rogu´ish
rogu´ish-ness
rois´ter
rois´ter-er
rois´ter-ous
Ro´land
roll´back
roll call
rolled
roll´er
roll´er skate
rol´lick-ing
rol´lick-some
roll´ing
roll´ing mill
roll´ing pin
roll top
Röl´vaag
ro´ly—po´ly
Ro-ma´gna
ro-maine´
Ro´man
ro-man´
ro-mance´
ro-manc´er
ro-manc´ing
Ro´man-esque´
Ro-man´ic
Ro´man-ism
Ro´man-ist
ro-ma´ni-um
Ro´man-ize
Ro´ma-nov
ro-man´tic
ro-man´ti-cal-ly
ro-man´ti-cism
ro-man´ti-cist
Ro´meo
Rom´ish
romp´er
romp´ish
Rom´u-lus
roof´er
roof gar´den
roof´ing
roof´less
roof´tree
rook´ery
rook´ie
room´er
room-ette´
room´ful
room´mate
room´y
Roo´se-velt
roost´er
root´ed
root´er
root´less
root´let
root´stock
roped
rop´er
rope´walk-er
rop´ing
Roque´fort
Ror´schach
ro-sa´lia
Ros´a-lind
Ros´a-mond
Ro-sa´rio
ro´sa-ry
Ros´coe
ro´se-ate
rose´bud
rose´bush
rose cold
rose´—col-ored
rose fe-ver
rose´mary
ro-se´o-la
Ro-set´ta
ro-sette´
rose wa´ter
rose´wood
Rosh Ha-sha´nah
ro´sier
ros´i-ly

ros´in
ros´in-ate
ros´i-ness
Ros-set´ti
Ros-si´ni
ros´ter
ros´trum
ros´y
Ro-tar´i-an
ro´ta-ry
ro´tat-able
ro´tate
ro-ta´tion
ro´ta-tive
ro´ta-tor
ro´ta-to-ry
rote
ro´te-noid
ro´te-none
Roth´schild
ro-tis´ser-ie
ro´to-graph
ro´to-gra-vure´
ro´tor
rot´ten
rot´ten-ness
Rot´ter-dam
rot´ting
ro-tund´
ro-tun´da
ro-tun´di-ty
ro-tund´ly
roué´
Rou´en´
rouged
rough´age
rough´cast
rough´dry
rough´en
rough´er
rough´hew
rough´house
rough´ly
rough´neck
rough´ness
rough´rid-er
rough´shod
rou-lade´
rou-lette´

Rou-ma´nian
round´about
round´er
Round´head
round´house
round´ish
round´ly
round´ness
round´—shoul-dered
round´up
round´worm
roused
rous´ing
rous´ing-ly
Rous-seau´
roust´about
route
rout´ed
rout´er
rou-tine´
rout´ing
rov´er
rov´ing
row´an
row´boat
row´dies
row´di-ness
row´dy
row´dy-ish
row´dy-ism
Row-e´na
row´er
row´lock
roy´al
roy´al-ist
roy´al-ly
roy´al-ty
Ru-bai-yat´
rubbed
rub´ber
rub´ber-ize
rub´bing
rub´bish
rub´ble
rub´down
Ru´bens
ru-be´o-la
Ru´bi-con
ru´bi-cund

ru-bi-cun´di-ty
ru-bid´i-um
ru-big´i-nous
Ru´bin-stein
ru´ble
ru´brene
ru´bric
ru´by
ruck´us
rud´der
rud´di-ness
rud´dy
rude´ly
rude´ness
rud´est
ru´di-ment
ru´di-men´ta-ry
Ru´dolf
Ru´dolph
rue´ful
rue´ful-ly
ruffed
ruf´fi-an
ruf´fle
ruf´fled
ruf´fler
ruf´fling
Ru´fus
Rug´by
rug´ged
Ruhr
ru´in
ru´in-ate
ru-in-a´tion
ru´ined
ru´in-ing
ru´in-ous
rul´able
ruled
rul´er
rul´ing
Ru-ma´nia
rum´ba
rum´ble
rum´bler
rum´bling
ru´mi-nant
ru´mi-nate
ru-mi-na´tion

rum´mage
rum´mag-er
rum´mag-ing
rum´my
ru´mor
rump´er
rum´ple
rum´pled
rum´pling
rum´pus
run´about
run´a-gate
run´around
run´away
run´down
run´ner
run´ner—up´
run´ning
runt´y
run´way
ru-pee´
Ru´pert
rup´tur-able
rup´ture
rup´tured
rup´tur-ing
ru´ral
ru´ral-ly
rush´ing
rush´light
rush´y
Rus´kin
Rus´sell
rus´set
Rus´sia
Rus´sian
rus´tic
rus´ti-cate
rus-ti-ca´tion
rus´ti-ca-tor
rus-tic´i-ty
rust´i-ly
rust´i-ness
rus´tle
rus´tler
rust-tling
rust´proof
rust´y
ru´ta-ba´ga
Ru-the´ni-an
ru-then´ic
ru-the´ni-ous
ru-the´ni-um
Ruth´er-ford
ruth´less
ruth´less-ly
ruth´less-ness
Rut´land
rut´ted
rut´ty
Rwan´da
Ryu´kyu

S

Sab´a-oth
Sab´a-ti´ni
Sab´bath
sab-bat´i-cal
sa´ber
sa´ble
sabot´
sab´o-tage
sab´o-teur´
sa´bra
sac
sac´cha-rate
sac-char´ic
sac´cha-ride
sac´cha-rin
sac´cha-rin-ate
sac´cha-rine
sac-cha-rin´ic
sac´cu-lat-ed
sa-chet´
sack
sack´cloth
sack´ful
sack´ing
sac´ra-ment
sac´ra-men´tal
sac-ra-men´ta-ry
Sac´ra-men´to
sa´cred
sac´ri-fice
sac´ri-fi´cial
sac´ri-fic-ing
sac´ri-lege
sac´ri-le´gious
sac´ro-il´i-ac
sac´ro-sanct
sac´ro-sanc´ti-ty
sac´ro-sci-at´ic
sac´rum
sad´den
sad´der
sad´dle
sad´dle-bag
sad´dle-bow
sad´dler
sad´dlery
Sad´du-cee
sa´dism
sa´dist
sa-dis´tic
sa-dis´ti-cal-ly
sad´ly
sad´ness
sa-fa´ri
safe—con´duct
safe´guard
safe´keep-ing
safe´ly
saf´est
safe´ty
safe´ty match
safe´ty pin
safe´ty valve
saf´flor-ite
saf´fron
sa´ga
sa-ga´cious
sa-gac´i-ty
sag´a-more
sage´brush
sage´ly
sagged
sag´ging
Sag´i-naw
sag´it-tal
Sag-it-tar´i-us
sag´it-tate
Sag-ue-nay´
Sa-ha´ra
sa´hib
Sai-gon´
sail´boat

sail´cloth
sailed
sail´fish
sail´or
saint´ed
saint´hood
saint´li-ness
saint´ly
Sai-pan´
sa´ke
Sa-kha-lin´
sa-laam´
sal-abil´i-ty
sal´able
sa-la´cious
sa-la´cious-ly
sa-lac´i-ty
sal´ad
Sal-a-man´ca
sal´a-man-der
sa-la´mi
sal´a-ried
sal´a-ry
Sa´lem
Sa-ler´no
sales´girl
sales´man
sales´man-ship
sales´per-son
sales´room
sales´wom-an
sa´lience
sa´lient
sal´i-fy
sa-lim´e-ter
sa-li´na
sal-i-na´tion
sa´line
sa-lin´i-ty
Salis-bury
sa-li´va
sal´i-vary
sal´i-vate
sal-i-va´tion
sal´lied
sal´low
sal´ly
sal´ly-ing
sal´ly port
salm´on
Sal-mo-nel´la
Sa-lo´me
sa-lon´
Sa-lon´i-ka
sa-loon´
sa-loon´keep-er
sal´si-fy
sal-ta´tion
salt´cel-lar
salt´ed
salt´ery
salt´i-er
sal´tire
salt marsh
salt´ness
salt-pe´ter
salt´y
sa-lu´bri-ous
sa-lu´bri-ty
Sa-lu´ki
sal-u-tar´i-ly
sal´u-tary
sal-u-ta´tion
sa-lu-ta-to´ri-an
sa-lu´ta-to-ry
sa-lute´
sa-lut´ing
sal´va-ble
Sal´va-dor
sal´vage
sal´vage-able
sal´vag-er
sal-va´tion
salved
sal´ver
sal´via
salv´ing
sal´vo
sal´vor
Salz´burg
Sa-mar´ia
sa-mar´i-um
Sam´ar-kand
sam´ba
sam-bu-ni´grin
same´ness
Sa-mo´a
Sa´mos
sam´o-var
sam´pan
sam´ple
sam´pler
sam´pling
Sam´son
Sam´u-el
sa´mu-rai
San An-to´nio
san-a-to´ri-um
San´cho
sanc-ti-fi-ca´tion
sanc´ti-fied
sanc´ti-fy
sanc´ti-fy-ing
sanc´ti-mo´ni-ous
sanc´ti-mo-ny
sanc´tion
sanc´tion-er
sanc´ti-ty
sanc´tu-ary
sanc´tum
san´dal
san´daled
san´dal-wood
sand´bag
sand´bank
sand´blast
sand´box
sand´er
sand´glass
sand´hog
San Di-e´go
sand´i-er
sand´i-ness
sand´man
San Do-min´go
sand´pa-per
sand´pip-er
sand´stone
sand´storm
San-dus´ky
sand´wich
sand´y
san-er
sane´ly
san´for-ize
San Fran-cis´co
sang-froid´

san´gui-nar´i-ly
san-guin´a-rine
san´gui-nary
san´guine
san-guin´e-ous
san-guin´o-lent
San-he´drin
san´i-dine
sa´ni-ous
san-i-tar´i-an
san´i-tar´i-ly
san´i-tar´ium
san´i-tary
san-i-ta´tion
san´i-tiz-er
san´i-ty
San Joa-quin´
San Ma-ri´no
San Sal´va-dor
San Se-bas´tian
San´skrit
San´ta Bar´ba-ra
San´ta Claus
San´ta Fe
San´ta Ma-ri´a
San-ta-ya´na
San´ti-a´go
San´to Do-min´go
São To-mé´ and Prín´ci-pe
sap´id
sa-pid´i-ty
sap´i-ence
sap´i-ent
sap´i-en´tial
sap´less
sap´ling
sa-pon-i-fi-ca´tion
sa-pon´i-fy
sap´per
sap´phire
sap´ping
sap´py
sap´suck-er
sap´wood
sar´a-band
Sar´a-cen
Sar-a-cen´ic
Sar´a-gos´sa
Sar´ah
Sa´ra-je-vo
Sa-ran´
Sar-a-to´ga
Sa-ra´tov
Sa-ra´wak
sar´casm
sar-cas´tic
sar-cas´ti-cal-ly
sar-co´ma
sar-co´ma-toid
sar-co-ma-to´sis
sar-com´a-tous
sar-coph´a-gi
sar-coph´a-gus
sar-cop´side
sar-dine´
Sar-din´ia
sar-don´ic
sar-don´i-cal-ly
sar-don´yx
sar-gas´so
sa´ri
sa-rong´
sar-sa-pa-ril´la
sar-to´ri-al
sar-to´ri-us
sa-shay´
Sas-katch´e-wan
sas´sa-fras
Sa´tan
sa-tan´ic
sa-tan´i-cal
sa-tan´i-cal-ly
satch´el
sat´ed
sa-teen´
sat´el-lite
sat´el-lit-ed
sat´el-lit-oid
sat-el-lit-o´sis
sat´el-loid
sa-tia-bil´i-ty
sa´tia-ble
sa´ti-ate
sa-ti-a´tion
sa-ti´e-ty
sat´in
sat´in-et´
sat´iny
sat´ire
sa-tir´ic
sa-tir´i-cal
sat´i-rist
sat´i-rize
sat´i-riz-ing
sat-is-fac´tion
sat´is-fac´to-ri-ly
sat´is-fac´to-ry
sat´is-fied
sat´is-fy
sat-u-ra-bil´i-ty
sat´u-ra-ble
sat´u-rate
sat´u-rat-ed
sat´u-rat-er
sat´u-rat-ing
sat-u-ra´tion
sat´u-ra-tor
Sat´ur-day
Sat´urn
sat-ur-na´lia
Sat-ur-na´lian
Sa-tur´ni-an
sat´ur-nine
sat-ur-nin´i-ty
sa´tyr
sa-tyr´ic
sauce´pan
sau´cer
sau´ci-ly
sau´ci-ness
sau´cy
Sau´di
sau´er-bra-ten
sau´er-kraut
Sault Sainte Ma-rie´
sau´na
saun´ter
saun´ter-ing
sau´sage
sau-té´
sau-téd´
sau-téed´
sau-té´ing
sau-terne´
sav´able
sav´age

sav´age-ly
sav´age-ry
sa-van´na
Sa-van´nah
sa-vant´
sa-vate´
saved
sav´er
sav´in
sav´ing
sav´ior
sa´voir faire´
sa´vor
sa´vor-ous
sa´vory
Sa-voy´
sav´vy
saw´buck
saw´dust
saw´horse
saw´mill
saw´yer
Sax´on
Sax´o-ny
sax´o-phone
sax´o-phon-ist
say´ing
scab
scab´bard
scabbed
scab´bing
scab´bler
scab´by
sca´bies
scaf´fold
scaf´fold-ing
sca´lar
scal´a-wag
scald´ed
scald´er
scaled
sca-lene´
scal´er
scal´ing
scal´lion
scal´lop
scal´loped
scal´pel
scalp´er

scal´y
scam´per
scan´dal
scan-da´iza´tion
scan´dal-ize
scan´dal-monger
scan´dal-ous
scan´dia
Scan-di-na´via
scanned
scan´ner
scan´ning
scan´sion
scant´i-ly
scant´i-ness
scant´ly
scant´y
scape´goat
scape´grace
scap´u-la
scap´u-lar
scar´ab
scarce
scarce´ly
scar´city
scare´crow
scared
scarf´er
scar-i-fi-ca´tion
scar´i-fi-ca-tor
scar´i-fied
scar´i-fy
scar´i-ly
scar´ing
scar´let
scarred
scar´ring
scary
scathe
scathed
scathe´less
scath´ing
scat-o-log´ic
scat-o-log´i-cal
sca-tol´o-gy
scat´ter
scat´ter-brain
scat´tered
scav´eng-er

scav´eng-ing
sce-nar´io
sce-nar´ist
sce´nery
sce´nic
scent
scent´ed
scent´er
scent´less
scep´ter
scep´tic
scep´ti-cal
scep´ti-cism
sche´di-asm
sched´ule
sched´uled
sched´ul-ing
Sche-her-a-zade´
sche´ma
sche-mat´ic
sche´ma-tism
sche´ma-tist
scheme
schem´er
schem´ing
Sche-nec´ta-dy
scher´zo
Schia-pa-rel´li
schism
schis-mat´ic
schist
schist´oid
schist´ose
schis´to-some
schiz´oid
schiz-o-phre´nia
schiz´o-phren´ic
schle-miel´
schnap´per
Schnau´zer
Schnitz´ler
schol´ar
schol´ar-ly
schol´ar-ship
scho-las´tic
scho-las´ti-cal
scho-las´ti-cal-ly
scho-las´ti-cism
school bell

school board
school´book
school´boy
school bus
school´child
school´girl
school´house
school´ing
school´man
school´mas-ter
school´mate
school´mis-tress
school´room
school´teach-er
school´work
school´yard
schoo´ner
Scho´pen-hauer
Schu´bert
Schu´mann
Schuy´ler
Schuyl´kill
Schweit´zer
Schwei´zer
sci-at´ic
sci-at´i-ca
sci´ence
sci-en´tial
sci-en-tif´ic
sci-en-tif´i-cal-ly
sci´en-tist
scim´i-tar
scin-til´la
scin´til-late
scin´til-lat-ing
scin-til-la´tion
scin´til-la-tor
scin-til-lom´e-ter
sci-o-graph´ic
sci´on
scis´sors
sclar´e-ol
scle-ri´a-sis
scle-ri´tis
scle-rot´ic
scle-ro-ti´tis
scle´rous
scoff´er
scold´er
scold´ing
scold´ing-ly
sconce
scone
scoop´er
scoop´ful
scoot´er
scope
scorch´ing
scored
scor´ing
scorn´er
scorn´ful
scorn´ful-ly
Scor´pio
scor´pi-on
Scotch´—I´rish
Scotch´man
scot´—free´
Scot´land
Scots´man
Scot´tish
scoun´drel
scourge
scourg´er
scourg´ing
scout´ing
scout´mas-ter
scowl´er
scowi´ing-ly
scrab´ble
scrab´bler
scrab´bling
scrag´gly
scrag´gy
scram´ble
scram´bling
Scran´ton
scrap´book
scraped
scrap´er
scrap´ing
scrapped
scrap´ping
scrap´ple
scrap´py
scratch
scratch´er
scratch´i-ness
scratch´proof
scratch´y
scrawl´er
scrawl´y
scrawn´i-ness
scrawn´y
scream´er
scream´ing
screech
screech´y
screen
screen´er
screw´driv-er
scrib´ble
scrib´bler
scrib´bling
scribe
scrib´er
scrim´mage
scrim´mag-er
scrimp´i-ly
scrimp´y
scrip
script
scrip-to´ri-um
scrip´tur-al
scrip´ture
scriv´en-er
scroll
scroll´work
scro´tum
scrounge
scroung´ing
scrub
scrub´bing
scrub´by
scrump´tious
scru´ple
scru-pu-los´i-ty
scru´pu-lous
scru´pu-lous-ly
scru´ti-nize
scru´ti-ny
scud´ded
scuf´fle
scuf´fling
scull
scul´lery
sculp´tor

sculp´tur-al
sculp´ture
scum´bled
scum´my
scur-ril´i-ty
scur´ri-lous
scur´ried
scur´ry
scur´ry-ing
scur´vi-ly
scur´vy
scut´ter
scut´tle
scut´tle-butt
scut´tling
Scyl´la
scythe
scyth´ing
Sea´bee
sea´board
sea´coast
sea´drome
sea´far-er
sea´far-ing
sea fight
sea´food
sea´fowl
sea´girt
sea´go-ing
sea´—green
sea gull
sea horse
seal´able
seal´ant
sea legs
seal´er
seal´ery
sea lev´el
seal-ine´
seal´ing wax
sea li´on
sea lord
seal ring
seal´skin
Sea´ly-ham
sea´man
sea´manship
sea´men
seam´i-ness
seam´less
seam´stress
seam´y
sé´ance
sea´plane
sea´port
search´able
search´er
search´ing
search´light
search war´rant
sea rov´er
sea ser´pent
sea´shore
sea´sick
sea´sick-ness
sea´side
sea´son
sea´son-able
sea´son-al
sea´son-ing
seat´ed
seat´er
seat´ing
Se-at´tle
sea ur´chin
sea´wall
sea´ward
sea´way
sea´weed
sea´wor-thy
seb´a-cate
se-ba´ceous
Se-bas´tian
se-cede´
se-ced´ed
se-ced´er
se-ced´ing
se-ces´sion
se-ces´sion-ist
se-clude´
se-clud´ed
se-clud´ed-ly
se-clud´ing
se-clu´sion
se-clu´sive
Sec´o-nal
sec´ond
sec´ond-ar´i-ly
sec´ond-ary
sec´ond—class
sec´ond-er
sec´ond-hand´
sec´ond-ly
sec´ond—rate´
se´cre-cy
se´cret
sec´re-tar´i-al
sec-re-tar´i-at
sec´re-tary
se-crete´
se-cret´ed
se-cre´tin
se-cre´tion
se´cre-tive
se´cret-ly
se-cre´to-ry
sect
sec-tar´i-an
sec-tar´i-an-ism
sec´ta-ry
sec´tion
sec´tion-al
sec´tion-al-ism
sec´tion-al-ly
sec´tion-al-ize
sec´tor
sec´tor-al
sec-to´ri-al
sec´u-lar
sec´u-lar-ism
sec´u-lar-ist
sec-u-lar´i-ty
sec-u-lar-iza´tion
sec´u-lar-ize
se-cure´
se-cure´ly
se-cur´ity
se-dan´
se-date´
se-date´ly
se-date´ness
sed´a-tive
sed´en-tar´i-ly
sed´en-tary
sedge
sedg´y
sed´i-ment

sed´i-men-tar´i-ly
sed´i-men´ta-ry
sed-i-men-ta´tion
se-di´tion
se-di´tion-ary
se-di´tious
se-duce´
se-duce´ment
se-duc´er
se-duc´i-ble
se-duc´ing
se-duc´tion
se-duc´tive
se-du´li-ty
sed´u-lous
seed´er
seed´ing
seed´less
seed´ling
seeds´man
seed´time
seed´y
see´ing
seek´er
seem´ing
seem´ing-ly
seem´ly
seep´age
seer´suck-er
see´saw
seethe
seethed
seeth´ing
seg´ment
seg-men´tal
seg-men´tal-ly
seg´men-tary
seg-men-ta´tion
seg´re-ga-ble
seg´re-gate
seg-re-ga´tion
seg-re-ga´tion-ist
sei´gneur´
seine
seis´mic
seis-mic´i-ty
seis´mism
seis´mo-graph
seis-mog´ra-pher
seis´mo-graph´ic
seis-mog´ra-phy
seis-mo-log´ic
seis-mo-log´i-cal
seis-mol´o-gist
seis-mol´o-gy
seis-mom´e-ter
seis´mo-met´ric
seiz´able
seize
seiz´er
seiz´ing
sei´zor
sei´zure
sel´dom
se-lect´
se-lect´ance
se-lect´ee´
se-lec´tion
se-lec´tive
se-lec-tiv´i-ty
se-lect´man
se-lec´tor
sel´e-nate
se-le´ni-um
self—as-sur´ance
self—cen´tered
self—com-mand´
self—con´fi-dence
self—con´fi-dent
self—con´scious
self—con´scious-ness
self—con-tained´
self—con-tra-dic´tion
self—con-trol´
self—de-fense´
self—de-ni´al
self—de-ter-mi-na´tion
self—dis´ci-pline
self—es-teem´
self—ev´i-dent
self—gov´ern-ment
self—help´
self—im-por´tance
self—im-por´tant
self—im-posed´
self´ish
self´ish-ly
self´ish-ness
self´less
self—made´
self—pit´y
self—pos-sessed´
self—pos-ses´sion
self—pres-er-va´tion
self—pro-tec´tion
self—re-gard´
self—re-li´ance
self—re-li´ant
self—re-spect´
self—re-spect´ing
self—sac´ri-fice
self´same
self—sat´is-fied
self—seek´ing
self´—start-er
self—suf-fi´cien-cy
self—suf-fi´cient
self—sup-port´ing
self—willed´
sell´er
sell´ing
selt´zer
sel´vage
selves
se-man´tic
se-man´ti-cist
se-man´tics
sem´a-phore
sem´a-phor´ic
sem´a-phor-ist
se-masi-ol´o-gy
sem´blance
se-mei-ol´o-gy
se´mei-ot´ic
se´men
se-mes´ter
se-mes´tral
sem´i-an´nu-al
sem´i-ar´id
sem´i-cir-cle
sem´i-cir´cu-lar
sem´i-co-lon
sem´i-con´scious
sem´i-de-tached´
sem´i-dine
sem´i-fi-nal

sem´i-lu´nar
sem´i-month´ly
sem´i-nal
sem´i-nar
sem´i-nary
sem´i-na´tion
Sem´i-nole
sem´i-pre´cious
Sem´ite
Se-mit´ic
Sem´i-tism
sem-o-li´na
se´na-ry
sen´ate
sen´a-tor
sen-a-to´ri-al
send´er
send´ing
send´—off
Sen´e-ca
se-ne´cic
sen´e-ga
Sen´e-gal
se´nile
se-nil´i-ty
sen´ior
se-nior´i-ty
sen´na
Sen-nach´er-ib
se-nor´
se-no´ra
se-no-ri´ta
sen-sa´tion
sen-sa´tion-al
sen-sa´tion-al-ism
sensed
sense´less
sen-si-bil´i-ty
sen´si-ble
sen´si-bly
sen´sile
sens´ing
sen´si-tive
sen´si-tive-ness
sen-si-tiv´i-ty
sen-si-tiza´tion
sen´si-tize
sen´si-tiz-er
sen-si-tom´e-ter

sen-so´ri-al
sen-so´ri-um
sen´so-ry
sen´su-al
sen´su-al-ist
sen-su-al-is´tic
sen-su-al´i-ty
sen´su-ous
sen´su-ous-ly
sen´tence
sen-ten´tial
sen-ten´tious
sen´tience
sen´tient
sen´ti-ment
sen-ti-men´tal
sen-ti-men´tal-ism
sen-ti-men´tal-ist
sen-ti-men-tal´i-ty
sen-ti-men´tal-ize
sen-ti-men´tal-ly
sen´ti-nel
sen´ti-neled
sen´try
se´pal
se´paled
sep-a-ra-bil´i-ty
sep´a-ra-ble
sep´a-rate
sep´a-ra-tee´
sep´a-rate-ly
sep-a-ra´tion
sep´a-rat-ist
sep´a-ra-tor
se´pia
Sep-tem´ber
sep-ten´ary
sep-ten´ni-al
sep-tet´
sep´tic
sep-ti-ce´mia
sep-tic´i-ty
sep-tif´ra-gal
sep-til´lion
sep´ti-mal
sep´tu´age-nar´i-an
Sep-tu´a-gint
sep´tum
sep´tu-ple

sep-tup´let
sep-tu´pli-cate
sep´ul-cher
se-qua´cious
se-quac´i-ty
se´quel
se-que´la
se´quence
se´quent
se-quen´tial
se-quen´tial-ly
se-ques´ter
se-ques´tered
seques´trate
seques-tra´tion
se´quin
se´quined
se-quoi´a
se-ra´glio
ser´al
se-ra´pe
ser´aph
se-raph´ic
ser´a-phim
Ser´bia
Ser-bo´ni-an
ser´e-nade´
ser´e-nad´er
ser´e-nad´ing
ser-en-dip´i-ty
se-rene´
se-rene´ly
se-ren´i-ty
serf´dom
serge
ser´geant
ser´geant at arms
se´ri-al
se´ri-al-ly
se-ri-a´tim
se-ri´ceous
ser´i-cin
se´ries
ser´if
se´ri-ous
se´ri-ous-ly
se´ri-ous-ness
ser´mon
ser-mon´ic

ser´mon-ize
se´ro-log´ic
se´ro-log´i-cal
se-rol´o-gist
se-rol´o-gy
se-ro-si´tis
se-ros´i-ty
se´rous
ser´pent
ser´pen-tine
ser´pen-tin-ite
ser-pi´go
ser´rate
ser´rat-ed
ser-ra´tion
ser´ried
ser´ru-late
ser´ry
se´rum
ser´vant
served
serv´er
serv´ice
serv´ice-able
ser´vile
ser-vil´i-ty
serv´ing
ser´vi-tor
ser´vi-tude
ser´vo-mech´a-nism
ser´vo-mo´tor
ses´a-me
ses´qui-cen-ten´ni-al
ses´sion
se-ta´ceous
set´back
se´ti-ger
se´ton
set-tee´
set´ter
set´ting
set´tle
set´tle-ment
set´tler
set´tling
set´—to
set´up
sev´en
sev´en-fold

sev´en-teen´
sev´en-teenth´
sev´enth
sev´en-ti-eth
sev´en-ty
sev´en-ty—six´
sev´er
sev´er-able
sev´er-al
sev´er-al-ly
sev´er-ance
se-vere´
sev´ered
se-vere´ly
se-ver´i-ty
Se-ville´
sew
sew´age
Sew´ard
sew´er
sew´er-age
sew´ing
sex-a-ge-nar´i-an
sex-ag´e-nary
sex´tant
sex-tet´
sex-tette´
sex´ton
sex-tu´ple
sex-tup´let
sex-tu´pli-cate
sex´u-al
sex-u-al´i-ty
shab´bi-ness
shab´by
shack´le
shack´led
shack´ling
shade
shad´ed
shad´er
shad´i-er
shad´ing
shad´ow
shad´owy
shad´y
shag´bark
shagged
shag´ging

shag´gy
shah
shake
shake´down
shak´en
shak´er
Shake´speare
Shake-spear´ean
shak´i-ly
shak´ing
shak´y
shale
shal-lot´
shal´low
sham
sha´man
sha´man-ism
sham´ble
sham´bles
shame
shamed
shame´faced
shame´ful
shame´ful-ly
shame´less
shame´less-ly
sham´ing
shammed
sham´mer
sham´ming
sham-poo´
sham-pooed´
sham´rock
Shang´hai´
Shan´gri—La´
shank´er
Shan´non
shan-tung´
shan´ty
shaped
shape´less
shape´li-ness
shape´ly
shap´er
shap´ing
shar´able
share´crop-per
share´hold-er
shar´er

sha-rif´
shar´ing
shark´skin
Shar´on
sharp´en
sharp´en-er
sharp´en-ing
sharp´er
sharp´ly
sharp´ness
sharp´shoot-er
sharp´—sight-ed
Shas´ta
shat´ter
shat´tered
shaved
shave´ling
shave´tail
shav´en
shav´er
shav´ing
shawl
Shaw-nee´
sheaf
shear
shear´er
shear´ing
sheath
sheathe
sheathed
sheath´er
sheath´ing
sheath knife
sheaves
She´ba
shed´ding
sheen
sheep
sheep´cote
sheep dog
sheep´fold
sheep´herd-er
sheep´ish
sheep´skin
sheep´walk
sheer
sheer´ness
sheet´age
sheet an´chor
sheet´ing
sheet iron
Shef´field
sheik
shek´el
shelf
shel-lac´
shel-lacked´
she´lack´ing
shell´er
shell´fish
shell´proof
shell shock
shel´ter
shel´tered
shel´ter-ing
shelve
shelves
shelv´ing
Shen-an-do´ah
she-nan´i-gan
shep´herd
shep´herd-ess
Sher´a-ton
sher´bet
Sher´i-dan
sher´iff
Sher´lock
Sher´man
sher´ry
Sher´wood
Shet´land
shib´bo-leth
shield
shield´er
shift´er
shift´i-er
shift´i-ly
shift´ing
shift´less
shift´less-ness
shift´y
shi´le´lagh
shil´ling
Shi´loh
shim´mer
shim´mery
shim´ming
shim´my
shin´bone
shin´dig
shine
shin´er
shin´gle
shin´gled
shin´i-er
shin´ing
shin´ny
shin´plas-ter
shin´y
ship´board
ship´build-er
ship´build-ing
ship´load
ship´mas-ter
ship´mate
ship´ment
ship´own-er
shipped
ship´per
ship´ping
ship´ping room
ship´shape
ship´worm
ship´wreck
ship´wright
ship´yard
shirk
shirk´er
shirr
shirred
shirr´ing
shirt´ing
shirt´sleeve
shirt´waist
shiv´er
shiv´ered
shiv´ery
shoal
shoat
shock´er
shock´ing
shock´proof
shod´di-ness
shod´dy
shoe
shoe box
shoe brush

shoe´horn
shoe´ing
shoe´lace
shoe´mak-er
shoe pol´ish
shoe store
shoe´string
sho´gun
shoot´er
shoot´ing
shoot´ing star
shop´keep-er
shop´lift
shop´lift-er
shopped
shop´per
shop´ping
shop´talk
shop´walk-er
shop´worn
shore´line
shore´ward
shor´ing
shorn
short´age
short´cake
short cir´cuit
short´com-ing
short´en
short´en-ing
short´hand
short´hand´ed
short´horn
short´—lived´
short´ly
short´ness
short´sight-ed
short´stop
short—term´
short´wave´
short´—wind´ed
Sho-sho´ne
shot´gun
should
shoul´der
shoul´der blade
shoul´dered
shout´ed
shoved
shov´el
shov´eled
shov´el-er
shov´el-ful
shov´el-ing
shov´er
shov´ing
show´boat
show´case
show´down
showed
show´er
show´er bath
show´ery
show´i-ly
show´ing
show´man
show´man-ship
shown
show´room
show´y
shrap´nel
shred´ded
shred´ding
Shreve´port
shrewd
shrewd´ly
shrewd´ness
shrew´ish
Shrews´bury
shriek
shrieked
shriek´ing
shrill´ness
shril´ly
shrimp
shrined
shrin´er
shrink´able
shrink´age
shrink´er
shriv´el
shriv´eled
shriv´el-ing
shriv´en
shriv´ing
Shrop´shire
shroud´ed
Shrove´tide
shrub´bery
shrub´bi-ness
shrub´by
shrugged
shrug´ging
shrunk´en
shuck´ing
shud´der
shuf´fle
shuf´fle-board
shuf´fled
shunned
shun´ning
shunt´ing
shut´down
shut´—in
shut´off
shut´out
shut´ter
shut´ting
shut´tle
shut´tle-cock
Shy´lock
shy´ly
shy´ness
shy´ster
Si-am´
Si´a-mese´
Si-be´lius
Si-be´ria
sib´i-lance
sib´i-lant
sib´i-la-to-ry
sib´ling
Sic´i-ly
sick´en
sick´en-ing
sick´en-ing-ly
sick´ish
sick´le
sick´led
sick´li-er
sick´li-ness
sick´ly
sick´ness
sick´room
side arm
side´board
side´burns

sid´ed
side´long
side´sad-dle
side step
side´swipe
side´track
side´walk
side´ways
sid´ing
si´dle
si´dled
si´dling
siege
Sieg´fried
sieg´ing
Si-en´a
si-en´na
si-er´o-zem
si-er´ra
Si-er´ra Le-one´
Si-er´ra Ma´dre´
si-es´ta
sieve
siev´er
sift´er
sigh´ing
sight´ed
sight´er
sight´less
sight´ly
sight´see-ing
sight´seer
sig´ma
sig´ma-tism
sig´moid
sig-moid-ec´to-my
sig-moid-os´to-my
sig´nal
sig´naled
sig´nal-ing
sig´nal-ize
sig´nal-ly
sig´na-ry
sig´na-to-ry
sig´na-ture
sign´board
sig´net
sig-nif´i-cance
sig-nif´i-cant
sig-nif´i-cant-ly
sig-ni-fi-ca´tion
sig-nif´i-ca-tive
sig´ni-fied
sig´ni-fy
sig´ni-fy-ing
sign´post
si´lage
si´lence
si´lenc-er
si´lenc-ing
si´lent
si´lent-ly
Si-le´sia
Si-le´sian
sil-hou-ette´
sil-hou-et´ted
sil´i-ca
sil´i-cate
sil-i-ca-ti-za´tion
sil´i-ca-tor
sil´i-con
sil´i-cone
sil-i-co´sis
sil-i-cot´ic
silk´en
silk´i-er
silk´i-ness
silk—stock´ing
silk´weed
silk´worm
silk´y
sil´li-ness
sil´ly
si´lo
si´los
si-lox´ane
si´ta´tion
sil´va
sil´van
sil´ver
sil´ver gray
sil´ver—plat´ed
sil´ver-smith
sil´ver-ware
sil´ver-work
sil´very
Sim´e-on
sim´i-an
sim´i-lar
sim-i-lar´i-ty
sim´i-lar-ly
sim´i-le
si-mil´i-tude
sim´mer
si´mo-nize
si´mon—pure´
sim-pat´i-co
sim´per
sim´pered
sim´per-er
sim´per-ing
sim´ple
sim´ple-heart-ed
sim´pler
sim´plest
sim´ple-ton
sim´plex
sim-plic´i-ty
sim-pli-fi-ca´tion
sim´pli-fied
sim´pli-fy
sim´pli-fy-ing
sim´ply
sim´u-lant
sim´u-late
sim´u-lat-ing
sim-u-la´tion
sim´u-la-tive
sim´u-la-tor
si´mul-cast
si´mul-ta´neous
si´mu´ta´neous-ly
Si´nai
Sin´bad
sin-cere´
sin-cere´ly
sin-cer´est
sin-cer´i-ty
sine
sin´e-cure
sin´e-cur-ist
sin´ew
sin´ewy
sin´ful
Sing´a-pore
singe
singed

singe´ing
sing´er
sing´ing
sin´gle
sin´gle—hand´ed
sin´gle—mind´ed
sin´gle-ness
sin´gle-stick
sin´glet
sin´gle-ton
sin´gle-tree
sin´gling
sin´gly
sing´song
sin´gu-lar
sin-gu-lar´i-ty
sin´gu-lar-ly
sin´is-ter
sin´is-tral
sink´age
sink´er
sink´hole
sink´ing
sink´ing fund
sin´less
sinned
sin´ner
sin´ning
sin-u-os´i-ty
sin´u-ous
si´nus
si-nus-i´tis
si´nus-oi´dal
Sioux
Sioux Cit´y
si´phon
si´phon-age
si-pid´i-ty
sipped
sip´ping
sired
si´ren
sir´ing
sir´loin
si-roc´co
sir´up
sis´sy
sis´ter
sis´ter-hood
sis´ter—in—law
sis´ter-ly
Sis´tine
site
Sit´ka
sit´ter
sit´ting
sit´ting room
sit´u-ate
sit´u-at-ed
sit-u-a´tion
six´fold
six´—foot´
six´pence
six´—shoot-er
six´teen´
six´teenth´
sixth
six´ti-eth
six´ty
siz´able
siz´able-ness
siz´ar
sized
siz´ing
siz´zle
siz´zled
siz´zling
siz´zling-ly
skald
skat´ed
skat´er
skat´ing
skeet´er
skein
skel´e-tal
skel´e-ton
skel´e-ton-ize
skep´tic
skep´ti-cal
skep´ti-cism
sketch
sketch´book
sketched
sketch´i-est
sketch´i-ly
sketch´y
skew´er
ski
skid´ded
skid´ding
skied
skies
ski´ing
skilled
skil´let
skill´ful
skill´ful-ly
skill´ful-ness
skimmed
skim´mer
skim´ming
skimp´i-est
skimp´i-ly
skimp´ing
skimp´y
skin´—deep´
skin´flint
skinned
skin´ner
skin´ni-est
skin´ni-ness
skin´ning
skin´ny
skin´tight´
skip´per
skip´ping
skir´mish
skir´mish-er
skirt´er
skirt´ing
skit´ter
skit´tish
skit´tles
skiv´er
sku´dug´gery
skulk
skulk´er
skulk´ing
skull
skull´cap
skunk
sky´—blue´
sky´lark
sky´light
sky´line
sky´rock-et
sky´scrap-er

sky´ward
sky´writ-ing
slack´en
slack´ened
slack´er
slack´ness
slag´gy
slain
slake
slaked
slak´er
slak´ing
slam´—bang´
slammed
slam´ming
slan´der
slan´der-er
slan´der-ous
slang´i-ly
slang´y
slant´ing
slant´wise
slapped
slap´ping
slap´stick
slash´ing
slate
slat´ed
slath´er
slat´ing
slat´ted
slat´tern
slat´ting
slaugh´ter
slaugh´ter-house
slav´er
slav´ery
Slav´ic
slav´ish
slay´er
slay´ing
slea´zi-er
slea´zy
sled´ding
sledge
sledge´ham-mer
sleek´ly
sleep´er
sleep´i-ly
sleep´i-ness
sleep´ing
sleep´ing car
sleep´less
sleep´walk-er
sleep´walk-ing
sleep´y
sleet´i-ness
sleet´y
sleeve´less
sleigh
sleigh´ing
sleight
slen´der
slen´der-ize
slen´der-ness
slept
sleuth
slew
sliced
slic´er
slic´ing
slick´en-side
slick´er
slick´ness
slide
slide rule
slid´ing
sli´er
slight
slight´ing
slight´ly
slime
slim´i-er
slim´i-ness
slim´ness
slim´y
sling´er
sling´shot
slink´ing
slipped
slip´per
slip´pered
slip´per-i-ness
slip´pery
slip´ping
slip´shod
slith´er
slith´ery
slit´ting
sliv´er
sli´ver
slob´ber
slob´ber-ing
sloe
sloe´berry
sloe gin
slo´gan
slog´ging
sloop
slope
sloped
slop´ing
slopped
slop´pi-ly
slop´ping
slop´py
slosh´y
sloth´ful
slot´ted
slouch
slouch´i-ly
slouch´ing
slouch´y
slough
Slo´vak
Slo-vak´ia
slov´en
slov´en-li-ness
slov´en-ly
slow´ly
slow´ness
sludge
sludg´er
sludg´y
slug´gard
slug´gish
sluice
sluice´way
sluic´ing
slum´ber
slum´ber-ous
slum´ming
slurred
slur´ring
slush
slush´i-ness
slush´y

slut´tish
sly´ly
sly´ness
smack´ing
small´ish
small´ness
small´pox
small´—time´
smart´en
smart´ly
smart´ness
smashed
smash´up
smat´ter
smat´ter-ing
smeared
smell´er
smell´ing
smell´y
smelt
smelt´er
smiled
smil´ing
smil´ing-ly
smirch
smirk´ing
smite
smith-er-eens´
Smith-so´ni-an
smith´y
smit´ten
smock´ing
smoke´house
smoke´less
smok´er
smoke´stack
smok´i-er
smok´ing
smok´y
smol´der
smol´dered
smol´der-ing
smooth
smooth´bore
smooth´en
smooth´ly
smooth´ness
smor´gas-bord
smoth´er
smoth´ered
smudge
smudg´er
smudg´i-ly
smudg´ing
smudg´y
smug´gle
smug´gler
smug´ly
smut´ti-ness
smut´ty
Smyr´na
snaf´fle
sna´fu´
snagged
snag´ging
snake´root
snak´i-ly
snak´y
snap´drag-on
snap´per
snap´pi-ly
snap´pish
snap´py
snap´shot
snared
snare drum
snar´ing
snarled
snarl´ing
snarl´ing-ly
snarl´ish
snatch´er
snatch´y
sneaked
sneak´er
sneak´i-ly
sneak´i-ness
sneak´ing
sneak´y
sneer´ing
sneeze
sneezed
sneez´er
sneez´ing
snick´er
snick´er-ing
sniff´er
sniff´ing
snif´fle
snif´ter
snip´er
snip´ing
snipped
snip´pet
snip´pi-er
snip´ping
snip´py
sniv´el
sniv´el-er
sniv´el-ing
snob´bery
snob´bish
snook´er
snoop´er
snoop´ery
snored
snor´er
snor´ing
snor´kel
snort´er
snort´ing
snout
snow´ball
snow´bank
snow´bird
snow´—blind
snow´bound
snow´drift
snow´drop
snow´fall
snow´flake
snow´i-er
snow line
snow´plow
snow´shed
snow´shoe
snow´storm
snow—white
snow´y
snubbed
snub´ber
snub´bing
snub´by
snub´—nosed
snuff´box
snuff´er
snuf´fle

snuf´fled
snug´gle
snug´gled
snug´gling
snug´gly
snug´ly
snug´ness
soak´age
soak´ing
soap´box
soap´er
soap´i-er
soap´i-ness
soap op´era
soap´stone
soap´suds
soap´y
soar
soar´ing
sob´bing
so´ber
so´ber-ly
so´ber—mind-ed
so-bri´e-ty
so´bri-quet
so—called
soc´cer
so-cia-bil´i-ty
so´cia-ble
so´cial
so´cial-ism
so´cial-ist
so-cial-is´tic
so´cial-ite
so-ci-al´i-ty
so-cial-iza´tion
so´cial-ize
so´cial-ly
so-ci´a-try
so-ci´e-tal
so-ci´e-ty
so-ci-oc´ra-cy
so´ci-o-log´ic
so´ci-o-log´i-cal
so´ci-o-log´i-cal-ly
so-ci-ol´o-gist
so-ci-ol´o-gy
sock´et
Soc´ra-tes
so´da
so´da-lite
so-dal´i-ty
so´da wa´ter
sod´den
sod´ding
so´di-um
Sod´om
sod´omy
so´fa
so´far
So´fi´a
soft—boiled
soft´en
soft´en-er
soft´en-ing
soft´heart-ed
soft´ly
soft´ness
soft´—shell
soft´—soap
soft´y
sog´gi-ly
sog´gi-ness
sog´gy
soil´age
soiled
soi-rée´
Sois-sons´
so´journ
so´journ-er
sol´ace
sol´aced
sol´ac-er
sol´ac-ing
so´lar
so´lar-ism
so-lar´i-um
so-lar-iza´tion
so-las´o-nine
sol´der
sol´dered
sol´dier
sol´dier-ly
sol´diery
sol´e-cism
sol´e-cist
sol´e-cis´tic
sole´ly
sol´emn
so-lem´ni-ty
sol-em-ni-za´tion
sol´em-nize
sol´emn-ly
so´le-noid
so-lic´it
so-lic-i-ta´tion
so-lic´i-tor
so-lic´i-tous
so-lic´i-tude
so-lic´i-tu´di-nous
sol´id
sol´i-dar´ic
sol´i-da-ris´tic
so´i-dar´i-ty
so-lid-i-fi-ca´tion
so-lid´i-fied
so-lid´i-fy
so-lid´i-ty
sol´id-ly
sol´id-ness
so-lil´o-quist
so-lil´o-quize
so-lil´o-quy
sol´i-taire
sol´i-tar-i-ly
sol´i-tary
sol´i-tude
sol´lar
so´lo
so´lo-ist
Sol´o-mon
So´lon
sol´stice
sol-u-bil´i-ty
sol´u-bi-liz-er
sol´u-ble
sol´ute
so-lu´tion
sol´u-tizer
solv-abil´i-ty
solv´able
solved
sol´ven-cy
sol´vent
solv´ing
So-ma´li
So-ma´lia

so-mat´ic
so-mat´i-cal-ly
so-ma-ti-za´tion
so´ma-to-gen´ic
so-ma-tol´o-gy
som´ber
som´ber-ness
som-bre´ro
som-bre´ros
some´body
some´day
some´how
some´one
som´er-sault
Som´er-set
Som´er-ville
some´thing
some´time
some´times
some´what
some´where
som-nam´bu-late
som-nam´bu-la-tor
som-nam´bu-lism
som-nam´bu-list
som-nam´bu-lis´tic
som´no-lence
som´no-lent
som´no-lent-ly
so´nar
so-na´ta
son-a-ti´na
song´bird
song´ster
song´stress
son´ic
son—in—law
son´net
son´ne-teer´
son´ny
so-nom´e-ter
So-no´ra
son-o-res´cent
son´o-rif´er-ous
so-nor´i-ty
sono´rous
sono´rous-ly
soon´er
soon´est
sooth
soothe
soothed
sooth´er
sooth´ing
sooth´ing-ly
sooth´say-er
soot´i-ness
soot´y
So-phi´a
soph´ism
soph´ist
soph´is-ter
so-phis´tic
so-phis´ti-cate
so-phis´ti-cat-ed
so-phis-ti-ca´tion
soph´is-try
Soph´o-cles
soph´o-more
soph´o-mor´ic
sop´o-rif´ic
sop´ping
sop´py
so-pra´no
Sor-bonne´
sor´cer-er
sor´cer-ess
sor´cery
sor´did
sor´did-ly
sore´ly
sore´ness
sor´ghum
so-ror´i-ty
sor´rel
sor´ri-ness
sor´row
sor´row-ful
sor´row-ful-ly
sor´ry
sort´able
sor´ter
sor´tie
sor´ti-lege
sot´tish
sot´to vo´ce
souf-flé´
sought
soul´ful
soul´ful-ly
soul´less
soun´der
sound´ing
sound´less
sound´ly
sound´ness
sound´proof
soup´i-er
soup´y
source
sour´ly
sour´ness
South-amp´ton
South Car-o-li´na
South Da-ko´ta
south´east´
south-east´er-ly
south-east´ern
south´er-ly
south´ern
south´ern-er
south´ern-most
south´land
south´ward
South´wark
south´west´
south-west´er-ly
south-west´ern
sou-ve-nir´
sov´er-eign
sov´er-eign-ty
so´vi-et
soy
soy´a
soy´bean
Space´ Age
space´craft
spaced
space´man
space´men
space´ship
space´walk
spac´ing
spa´cious
spa´cious-ness
spack´le
spack´led

spack´ling
spade
spad´ed
spad´er
spade´ful
spade´work
spad´ing
spa-ghet´ti
span´gle
span´gled
span´gly
Span´iard
span´iel
Span´ish
spank´er
spank´ing
spanned
span´ner
span´ning
spared
spare´ness
spare´rib
spar´ing
spar´ing-ly
spar´kle
spar´kler
spark´let
spar´kling
spar´kling-ly
sparred
spar´ring
spar´row
sparse´ly
spar´si-ty
Spar´ta
Spar´tan
Spar´tan-burg
spasm
spas-mod´ic
spas-mod´i-cal-ly
spas-mol´y-sis
spas-mo-lyt´ic
spas´tic
spas´ti-cal-ly
spas-tic´i-ty
spa´tial
spa-ti-al´i-ty
spa´tial-ly
spa-ti-og´ra-phy
spat´ter
spat´ting
spat´u-la
spawned
spawn´er
speak´able
speak´easy
speak´er
speak´ing
spear´fish
spear´head
spear´man
spear´mint
spe´cial
spe´cial-ist
spe-ci-al´i-ty
spe-cial-iza´tion
spe´cial-ize
spe´cial-ly
spe´cial-ty
spe´cie
spe´cies
spec´i-fi-able
spe-cif´ic
spe-cif´i-cal-ly
spec-i-fi-ca´tion
spec-i-fic´i-ty
spec´i-fied
spec´i-fi-er
spec´i-fy
spee´i-fy-ing
spec´i-men
spe-ci-os´i-ty
spe´cious
speck´le
speck´led
speck´ling
spec´ta-cle
spec´ta-cled
spec-tac´u-lar
spec-tac-u-lar´i-ty
spec-tac´u-lar-ly
spec´ta-tor
spec´ta-to´ri-al
spec´ter
spec´tral
spec-trog´ra-phy
spec´tro-scope
spec´tro-scop´ic
spec´tro-scop´i-cal
spec-tros´co-pist
spec-tros´co-py
spec´trum
spec´u-late
spec´u-lat-ing
spec-u-la´tion
spec´u-la-tive
spec´u-la-tor
sped
speech
speech´i-fy
speech´less
speed´boat
speed´er
speed´i-ly
speed´ing
speed lim´it
speed-om´e-ter
speed´ster
speed´way
speed´well
speed´y
spe´le-ol´o-gist
spe´le-ol´o-gy
spell´bind-er
spell´bound
spell´er
spell´ing
spe-lunk´er
spend´er
spend´ing
spend´thrift
spent
sper-ma-ce´ti
sper-mat´ic
sper´ma-tin
sper-ma-ti-za´tion
sper´ma-to-zo´ic
sper´ma-to-zo´id
sper-ma-to-zo´on
spher´al
sphere
spher´i-cal
spheri-cal´i-ty
sphe-ric´i-ty
sphe´roid
sphe-roi´dal
sphe-roi´dal-ly

spheroid-ic´i-ty
sphinc´ter
sphinc-ter-ot´o-my
sphin-gom´e-ter
sphinx
spice´bush
spiced
spic´i-ly
spic´i-ness
spic´ing
spic´u-la
spic´u-lar
spic´ule
spic´y
spi´der
spi´der web
spi´dery
spiel´er
spig´ot
spiked
spike´let
spike´nard
spik´i-ness
spik´ing
spik´y
spill´age
spilled
spill´er
spill´ing
spill´way
spin´ach
spi´nal
spin´dle
spin´dler
spin´dling
spin´dly
spin´drift
spine´less
spin´et
spin´na-ker
spin´ner
spin´ning
spin´ning wheel
spi´nose
spi-nos´i-ty
spi´nous
Spi-no´za
spin´ster
spin´ster-hood
spi´nule
spi´nu-les´cent
spin´y
spir´a-cle
spi-rac´u-lar
spi´ral
spi-ral´e
spi´raled
spi´ral-ing
spi´ral-ly
spi´rant
spir´it
spir´it-ed
spir´it-ism
spir´it-is´tic
spir´it-less
spir´i-tu-al
spir´i-tu-al-ism
spir´i-tu-al-ist
spir´i-tu-al-is´tic
spir-i-tu-al´i-ty
spir´i-tu-al-ize
spir´i-tu-al-ly
spir´i-tu-el´
spir-i-tu-os´i-ty
spir´i-tu-ous
spi´ro-graph
spi´roid
spir´y
spite
spit´ed
spite´ful
spit´fire
spit´ing
spit´ting
spit´tle
spit-toon´
splash´ing
splash´y
splat´ter
spleen´ish
splen´dent
splen´did
splen´did-ly
splen-dif´er-ous
splen´dor
splen´dor-ous
sple´nic
sple-ni´tis
sple´ni-um
spliced
splic´er
splic´ing
splin´ter
splin´tered
split´—lev´el
split´ting
splotch´y
splurge
splurged
splut´ter
spoil´age
spoiled
spoil´er
spoil´ing
spoils´man
Spo-kane´
spo´ken
spokes´man
sponge
sponged
spong´er
spong´i-ness
spong´ing
spong´y
spon´sor
spon-so´ri-al
spon´sor-ship
spon-ta-ne´i-ty
spon-ta´ne-ous
spook´ish
spook´y
spoon´er-ism
spoon´ful
spo-rad´ic
spo-rad´i-cal-ly
spo-ran´gia
spo-ran´gi-um
spore
sport´i-er
sport´i-est
sport´i-ly
sport´i-ness
sport´ing
spor´tive
sports´cast-er
sports´man
sports´man-like

sports´man-ly
sports´man-ship
sports´men
sports´wear
sports´wom-an
sports´women
sports´writ-er
sport´y
spot
spot´less
spot´less-ly
spot´less-ness
spot´light
spot´ted
spot´ter
spot´ti-er
spot´ti-est
spot´ti-ly
spot´ting
spot´ty
spous´al
spouse
spout´er
sprained
sprawl´er
sprawl´ing
sprayed
spray´er
spread´er
spread´ing
sprig´gy
spright´li-ness
spright´ly
spring´board
spring´bok
spring´er
Spring´field
spring´i-ness
spring´ing
spring´time
spring´y
sprin´kle
sprin´kler
sprin´kling
sprint´er
sprite
sprit´sail
sprock´et
sprout
spruce
spruced
spruce´ly
spruc´ing
spry´ly
spu´mous
spum´y
spunk´i-ness
spunk´y
spurge
spu´ri-ous
spu´ri-ous-ly
spurn´ing
spurred
spur´ring
spurt´ed
spur´tive
sput´nik
sput´ter
sput´ter-ing
spu´tum
spy´glass
spy´ing
squab´ble
squab´bled
squab´bling
squad
squad´ron
squa´lene
squal´id
squa-lid´i-ty
squall
squall´er
squall´y
squal´or
squan´der
squan´dered
squan´der-ing
square
squared
square dance
square´ly
squar´er
square root
squar´ing
squash
squash´i-ness
squash´ing
squash´y
squat´ted
squat´ter
squat´ting
squat´ty
squaw
squawk
squawked
squawk´er
squeak
squeak´i-ly
squeak´ing
squeak´y
squeal´er
squeal´ing
squea´mish
squea´gee
squeezed
squeez´er
squeez´ing
squelched
squid
squil´la
squint´ed
squint´er
squint´ing
squire
squir´ing
squirm´y
squir´rel
squirt
squirt´ed
squirt´ing
stabbed
stab´bing
sta´bile
stab-i-lim´e-ter
sta-bil´i-ty
sta-bi-li-za´tion
sta´bil-i-za´tor
sta´bi-lize
sta´bi-liz-er
sta´ble
sta´bled
sta´ble-mate
sta´bling
stac-ca´to
stach´y-drine
stacked
stack´er

stac´te
sta´di-um
staffed
staff´er
Staf´ford
stage´coach
stage´craft
staged
stage´hand
stag´er
stag´ger
stag´ger-ing
stag´hound
stag´ing
stag-mom´e-ter
stag´nan-cy
stag´nant
stag´nate
stag´nat-ing
stag-na´tion
stag´y
staid
stain´er
stain´ing
stain´less
stair´case
stair´way
staked
stak´ing
stalac´tite
stal´ac-tit´ic
sta´lag
stalag´mite
stal´ag-mit´ic
stale´mate
stale´ness
stal´er
Sta´lin
Sta´lin-grad
stalk´er
stalk´ing
stal´lion
stal´wart
sta´men
Stam´ford
stam´i-na
stam´mer
stam´mer-er
stam´mer-ing
stamped
stam-pede´
stamp´er
stance
stanch
stan´chion
stan´dard
stan´dard—bear-er
stan´dard-iza´tion
stan´dard-ize
stand´by
stand´ee´
stand´ing
Stan´dish
stand´ish
stand´off
stand´pipe
stand´point
stand´still
Stan´ford
sta´nine
Stan´ton
stan´za
sta´pes
staph-y-lo-coc´cus
staph-y-lot´o-my
sta´ple
sta´pled
sta´pler
sta´pling
star´board
starch´er
starch´i-ness
starch´y
stared
star´er
star´fish
star´gaz-er
star´ing
stark´ly
star´less
star´let
star´light
star´like
star´ling
star´lit
star´lite
starred
star´ring
star´ry
star´ry—eyed
star´—shaped
star shell
star´—span´gled
start´er
star´tle
star´tling
star-va´tion
starve
starved
starv´er
starv´ing
sta´sis
state´craft
stat´ed
state´hood
state´house
state´li-ness
state´ly
state´ment
Stat´en Is´land
stat´er
state´room
states´man
states´man-ship
state´wide
stat´ic
stat´i-cal-ly
stat´i-ce
sta´tion
sta´tion-ary
sta´tio-ner
sta´tio-nery
sta´tion-mas-ter
stat´ism
stat´ist
sta-tis´tic
sta-tis´ti-cal
sta-tis´ti-cal-ly
stat-is-ti´cian
sta-tis´tics
sta´tor
stat´u-ary
stat´ue
stat´u-esque´
stat´u-ette´
stat´ure
sta´tus

stat´ut-able
stat´ute
stat´u-to-ry
staunch
staunch´ly
stay´ing
stead´fast
stead´i-ly
stead´i-ness
stead´y
steal
steal´age
stealth
stealth´i-ly
stealth´i-ness
stealth´y
steam´boat
steam boil´er
steam en´gine
steam´er
steam´fit-ter
steam´roll-er
steam´ship
steam shov´el
steam ta´ble
steam´tight
steam´y
steel
steel´works
steel´y
steep´en
steep´er
stee´ple
stee´ple-chase
stee´ple-jack
steep´ly
steep´ness
steer´age
stego-sau´rus
stel´lar
Stel´lite
stel´lu-lar
stem´less
stemmed
stem´ming
sten´cil
sten´ciled
sten´cil-ing
ste-nog´ra-pher
sten´o-graph´ic
sten´o-graph´i-cal-ly
ste-nog´ra-phy
sten´o-type
sten´o-typ-ist
sten-to´ri-an
step´child
step´daugh-ter
step´fa-ther
step—in
step´lad-der
step´moth-er
steppe
step´per
step´ping
step´ping—stone
step´son
stere-og-no´sis
ste´reo-graph
stere-og´ra-pher
ste´reo-graph´ic
stere-om´e-ter
stereo-met´ric
stere-om´e-try
ste´reo-phon´ic
stere-oph´o-ny
stere-op´sis
stere-op´ti-con
ste´re-op´tics
ste´reo-scope
ste´reo-scop´ic
stere-os´co-pist
stere-os´co-py
stere-ot´o-my
stere-ot´ro-pism
ste´reo-type
ste´reo-typ-er
ste´reo-typ-ing
ste´reo-typy
ster´ic
ster´i-cal-ly
ster´ile
ste-ril´i-ty
ster-i-liza´tion
ster´i-lize
ster´i-liz-er
ster´let
ster´ling
stern´ly
stern´ness
ster´num
ster´oid
ste-roi´dal
steth´o-scope
steth´o-scop´ic
ste-thos´co-py
stet´ted
Steu´ben
Steu´ben-ville
ste´ve-dore
Ste´vens
Ste´ven-son
stew´ard
stew´ard-ess
stew´ard-ship
Stew´art
stew´pan
stick´er
stick´ful
stick´i-er
stick´i-ness
stick´ing
stick´le
stick´le-back
stick´y
stiff´en
stiff´en-er
stiff´en-ing
stiff´ly
stiff—necked
stiff´ness
sti´fle
sti´fling
stig´ma
stig-mat´ic
stig-mat´i-cal
stig´ma-tism
stig´ma-tist
stig-ma-ti-za´tion
stig´ma-tize
sti-let´to
still´born
still´—hunt
still´ness
stilt´ed
stim´u-lant
stim´u-late
stim-u-la´tion

stim´u-la-tive
stim´u-la-tor
stim´u-li
stim´u-lus
sting´er
stin´gi-er
stin´gi-ness
sting´ing
stin´gy
stink´er
stink´ing
stink´weed
stint´ing
sti´pend
stip´ple
stip´pled
stip´pling
stip´u-late
stip´u-lat-ing
stip-u-la´tion
stip´u-la-tor
stip´u-la-to-ry
stir
stirred
stir´ring
stir´rup
stitch´er
stitch´ing
stoc-ca´do
stock-ade´
stock´bro-ker
stock dove
stock´hold-er
Stock´holm
stock´ing
stock´job-ber
stock´man
stock mar´ket
stock´pile
Stock´ton
stock´y
stock´yard
stodg´i-ness
stodg´y
sto´gie
sto´ic
sto´i-cal
sto´i-cism
stoked
stok´er
stok´ing
sto´len
stol´id
sto-lid´i-ty
stol´id-ly
sto´ma
stom´ach
stom´ach-ache
stom´ach-er
sto-mach´ic
stom´a-ta
stone´bass
stone´boat
stone crush´er
stone´cut-ter
stoned
Stone´henge
stone´ma-son
stone proof
stone´wall
stone´ware
stone´work
ston´i-ly
ston´i-ness
ston´ing
ston´y
stop´gap
stop´page
stopped
stop´per
stop´ping
stop´watch
stor´age
sto´rax
stored
store´house
store´keep-er
store´room
sto´ried
stor´ing
stork
storm´i-ly
storm´i-ness
storm´proof
storm´y
sto´ry
sto´ry-tell-er
stout´ness
stove´pipe
sto´ver
stow´age
stow´away
stra-bis´mal
stra-bis´mus
strad´dle
strad´dler
strad´dling
Stradi-var´i-us
strafed
straf´ing
strag´gle
strag´gler
strag´gling
strag´gly
straight
straight´away
straight´edge
straight´en
straight´en-er
straight´for´ward
strained
strain´er
strait
strait´en
strait´ened
strait´jacket
strait´laced
strand´er
strange´ly
strange´ness
stran´ger
stran´gle
stran´gler
stran´gling
stran´gu-late
stran-gu-la´tion
strapped
strap´ping
stra´ta
strat´a-gem
stra-te´gic
stra-te´gi-cal
strat´e-gist
strat´e-gy
Strat´ford
stra-tic´u-late
strat-i-fi-ca´tion

strat´i-fied
strat´i-fy
strat´i-fy-ing
strat´i-graph´ic
stra-tig´ra-phy
strat´o-cu´mu-lus
strat´o-sphere
strat´o-spher´ic
stra´tum
stra´tus
straw´ber-ry
straw´board
stray´er
stray´ing
streak´i-ness
streak´y
stream
stream´er
stream´let
stream´line
stream´lined
street
street´car
strength
strength´en
strength´en-ing
strength´less
stren´u-ous
strep´ta-mine
strep´to-coc´cic
strep-to-coc-co´sis
strep-to-coc´cus
strep-to-my´cin
stressed
stretch´er
strewed
strewn
stri´at´ed
stri-a´tion
strick´en
strick´le
strict´ly
strict´ness
stric´ture
stri´dent
strid´er
strid´ing
strid´u-late
strid-u-la´tion
strid´u-la-to-ry
strid´u-lous
strife
strik´er
strik´ing
stringed
strin´gen-cy
strin´gent
string´er
string´i-ness
string´ing
string´piece
string´y
striped
strip´er
strip´ing
strip´ling
stripped
strip´ping
strive
striv´en
striv´ing
stro´bo-scop´ic
stro´bo-tron
stro´ga-noff
stroked
strok´er
strok´ing
stroll´er
strong´—arm
strong´box
strong´hold
strong´ly
strong´point
strong room
strop´ping
struc´tur-al
struc´tur-al-ly
struc´ture
stru´del
strug´gle
strug´gled
strug´gling
strum´ming
strum´pet
strut´ted
strut´ting
strych´nine
strych´nin-ism
stubbed
stub´ber
stub´bi-ness
stub´bing
stub´ble
stub´bly
stub´born
stub´born-ness
stub´by
stuc´co
stuc´co-er
stuc´co-work
stuck´—up
stud´ded
stud´ding
Stu´de-bak-er
stu´dent
stud´ied
stud´ied-ly
stu´dio
stu´dious
stud´y
stud´y-ing
stuff
stuffed
stuff´i-ly
stuff´i-ness
stuff´ing
stuff´y
stul-ti-fi-ca´tion
stul´ti-fied
stul´ti-fy
stul´ti-fy-ing
stum´ble
stum´bling
stum´bling block
stump´age
stump´y
stunned
stun´ning
stunt´ed
stu´pe-fied
stu´pe-fi-er
stu´pe-fy
stu´pe-fy-ing
stu-pen´dous
stu´pid
stu-pid´i-ty
stu´pid-ly

stu´por
stu´por-ous
stur´died
stur´di-ly
stur´di-ness
stur´dy
stur´geon
stut´ter
stut´tered
stut´ter-ing
Stutt´gart
Stuy´ve-sant
styled
sty´let
styl´ing
styl´ish
styl´ist
sty-lis´tic
sty´lite
styl-i-za´tion
styl´ize
sty´mie
sty´mied
sty´mie-ing
styp´tic
sty´rene
suave
suave´ly
suav´i-ty
sub-al´tern
sub-atom´ic
sub-ce-les´tial
sub´cel-lar
sub´cla´vi-an
sub´com-mit-tee
sub-con´scious
sub´con-trac-tor
sub´cu-ta´ne-ous
sub´di-vide
sub´di-vid-ing
sub´di-vi-sion
sub-due´
sub-du´ing
sub´ject
sub-jec´tion
sub-jec´tive
sub-jec´tiv-ism
sub-jec-tiv´i-ty
sub´join´

sub´ju-gate
sub´ju-gat-ing
sub-ju-ga´tion
sub´ju-ga-tor
sub-junc´tive
sub´lease´
sub´les´see´
sub´les´sor
sub´let´
sub´let´ting
sub´li-mate
sub´li-mat-ing
sub-li-ma´tion
sub-lime´
sub-lime´ly
sub-lim´in-al
sub-lim´i-ty
sub´ma-rine
sub-merge´
sub-merged´
sub-mer´gence
sub-mer´gible
sub-mer´sal
sub-merse´
sub-mersed´
sub-mers´ible
sub-mers´ing
sub-mer´sion
sub-mis´sion
sub-mis´sive
sub-mit´
sub-mit´ted
sub-mit´ting
sub-nor´mal
sub-nor-mal´i-ty
sub-or´di-nate
sub-or´di-nate-ly
sub-or-di-na´tion
sub-or´di-na-tive
sub-orn´
sub-or-na´tion
sub-pe´naed
sub-poe´na
sub-poe´naed
sub-poe´na-ing
sub´ro-gate
sub-ro-ga´tion
sub ro´sa
sub-scribe´

sub-scrib´er
sub-scrib´ing
sub-scrip´tion
sub-scrip´tive
sub´se-quence
sub´se-quent
sub´se-quen´tial
sub-ser´vi-ence
sub-ser´vi-ent
sub-serv´ing
sub-side´
sub-sid´ence
sub-sid´i-ary
sub-sid´ing
sub-si-di-za´tion
sub´si-dize
sub´si-dy
sub-sist´
sub-sist´ence
sub-sist´ent
sub-son´ic
sub´stance
sub-stan´tial
sub-stan-ti-al´i-ty
sub-stan´tial-ly
sub-stan´ti-ate
sub-stan-ti-a´tion
sub´stan-tive
sub´sta-tion
sub-stit´u-ent
sub´sti-tut-able
sub´sti-tute
sub´sti-tut-ed
sub´sti-tut-ing
sub-sti-tu´tion
sub´sti-tu-tive
sub´stratum
sub´struc´ture
sub-sump´tive
sub-tend´
sub´ter-fuge
sub-ter-ra´nean
sub-ter-ra´ne-ous
sub´tle
sub´tle-ty
sub´tly
sub-tract´
sub-tract´er
sub-trac´tion

sub-trac´tive
sub-trop´i-cal
sub´urb
sub-ur´ban
sub-ur´ban-ite
sub-ven´tion
sub-ver´sion
sub-ver´sion-ary
sub-ver´sive
sub-vert´
sub-vert´er
sub-vert´ible
sub´way
suc-ceed´
suc-cess´
suc-cess´ful
suc-cess´ful-ly
suc-ces´sion
suc-ces´sive
suc-ces´sor
suc-cinct´
suc-cinct´ly
suc-cin´ic
suc´cor
suc´co-ry
suc´co-tash
suc´cu-lent
suc-cumb´
suck´er
suck´le
suck´ler
suck´ling
Su´cre
su´crose
suc´tion
Su-dan´
sud´den
sud´den-ly
suds-y
sue
sued
suede
su´et
su´ety
Su´ez´
suf´fer
suf´fer-able
suf´fer-ance
suf´fer-er
suf´fer-ing
suf-fice´
suf-ficed´
suf-fic´er
suf-fi´cien-cy
suf-fi´cient
suf-fic´ing
suf´fix
suf´fo-cate
suf´fo-cat-ing
suf-fo-ca´tion
suf´fo-ca-tive
Suf´folk
suf´fra-gan
suf´frage
suf´frag-ette´
suf-frag-ett´ism
suf´frag-ist
suf-fus´able
suf-fuse´
suf-fus´ing
suf-fu´sion
suf-fu´sive
sug´ar
sug´ar beet
sug´ar-boat
sug´ar bush
sug´ar cane
sug´ared
sug´ar-i-ness
sug´ar-loaf
sug´ar ma´ple
sug´ar-plum
sug´ary
sug-gest´
sug-gest-ibil´i-ty
sug-gest´ible
sug-ges´tion
sug-ges´tive
su´i-ci´dal
su´i-ci´dal-ly
su´i-cide
su´ing
suit-abil´i-ty
suit´able
suit´ably
suit´case
suite
suit´ing
suit´or
su-ki-ya´ki
sul´fa
sul-fa-cet´a-mide
sul´fa-di´a-zine
sul-fa-gua´ni-dine
sul-fa-mer´a-zine
sul´fa-meth´y´thi´a-zole
sul´fam´ic
sulf-am´ide
sul-fam´o-yl
sul-fa-nil´a-mide
sul´fa-nil´ic
sul´fate
sul´fa-tize
sul´fide
sulf-ox´ide
sul´fur
sul´fu-rate
sul-fu´re-ous
sul´fu-ret-ed
sul-fu´ric
sul´fu-rize
sul´fu-rous
sul´fur-yl
sulk´i-ly
sulk´i-ness
sulk´y
sul´len
sul´len-ly
sul´len-ness
sul´lied
Sul´li-van
sul´ly
sul´tan
su´tan´a
sul´tan-ate
sul-tan´ic
sul´tri-er
sul´tri-ness
sul´try
su´mac
Su-ma´tra
Su-mer´i-an
sum´ma cum lau´de
sum-mar´i-ly
sum-ma-ri-za´tion
sum´ma-rize

sum´ma-ry
sum-ma´tion
sum´mer
sum´mer-house
sum´mer-time
sum´mery
sum´ming
sum´mit
sum´mit-ry
sum´mon
sum´moned
sum´mon-er
sum´mon-ing
sum´monsed
sump´ter
sump´tu-ary
sump-tu-os´i-ty
sump´tu-ous
sun´beam
sun´bon-nct
sun´burn
sun´burned
sun´burst
sun´dae
Sun´day
sun´der
sun´der-ance
sun´dew
sun´di-al
sun´down
sun´down-er
sun´dries
sun´dry
sun´fast
sun´fish
sun´flow-er
sun´glass-es
sunk´en
sun´lamp
sun´less
sun´light
sun´lit
sun´ni-er
sun´ning
sun´ny
sun´rise
sun´set
sun´shine
sun´shiny
sun´spot
sun´stroke
sun´struck
sun´up
su´per
su-per-a-bil´i-ty
su´per-a-ble
su-per-abun´dance
su-per-abun´dant
su-per-an´nu-ate
su-per-an´nu-at-ed
su-per-an-nu-a´tion
su-perb´
su-perb´ly
su´per-car-go
su-per-cil´i-ary
su-per-cil´i-ous
su-per-co-lum´nar
su-per-er´o-gate
su-per-er-o-ga´tion
su´per-erog´a-to-ry
su´per-fe-ta´tion
su-per-fi´cial
su-per-fi-ci-al´i-ty
su-per-fi´cial-ly
su-per-fi´cies
su´per-fine
su-per-flu´i-ty
su-per´flu-ous
su´per-heat´ed
su´per-hu´man
su´per-im-pose´
su´per-im-po-si´tion
su-per-in-duce´
su´per-in-tend´
su-per-in-tend´en-cy
su-per-in-tend´ent
su-pe´ri-or
su-pe-ri-or´i-ty
su-per´la-tive
su´per-man
su´per-mar-ket
su-per´nal
su´per-na´tant
su-per-nat´u-ral
su´per-nat´u-ral-is´tic
su´per-nu´mer-ary
su´per-pose
su-per-po-si´tion
su´per-pow-er
su´per-sat´u-rate
su-per-sat-u-ra´tion
su-per-scrip´tion
su-per-sede´
su´per-sed´ing
su-per-sen´si-ble
su-per-sen´si-tive
su-per-sen´so-ry
su-per-son´ic
su´per-star
su-per-sti´tion
su-per-sti´tious
su´per-struc´ture
su´per-tank-er
su´per-vene´
su-per-ve´nience
su´per-ven´ing
su-per-ven´tion
su´per-vise
su´per-vis-ing
su-per-vi´sion
su´per-vi-sor
su´per-vi´so-ry
su´per-volt-age
su´per-weap-on
su´per-wom-an
su-pine´
sup´per
sup´per-time
sup-plant´
sup-plan-ta´tion
sup-plant´er
sup´ple
sup´ple-ment
sup´ple-men´tal
sup´ple-men-tar´i-ly
sup´ple-men´tary
sup-ple-men-ta´tion
sup´ple-ness
sup-ple´tive
sup´pli-ance
sup´pli-ant
sup´pli-cant
sup´pli-cate
sup´pli-cat-ing
sup-pli-ca´tion
sup´pli-ca-to-ry
sup-plied´

sup-pli´er
sup-ply´
sup-ply´ing
sup-port´
sup-port-abil´i-ty
sup-port´able
sup-port´er
sup-port´ing
sup-port´ive
sup-pos´able
sup-pos´al
sup-pose´
sup-posed´
sup-pos´ing
sup-po-si´tion
sup´po-si´tion-al-ly
sup-pos´i-ti´tious
sup-pos´i-to-ry
sup-press´
sup-press´ible
sup-pres´sion
sup-pres´sor
sup´pu-rate
sup´pu-rat-ing
sup-pu-ra´tion
sup´pu-ra-tive
sup´pu-ta´tion
su´pra
su´pra-re´nal
su-prem´a-cy
su-preme´
su´ra
su´ral
sur´base
sur-cease´
sur´charge
sur´cin-gle
sur´coat
sure´fire´
sure´foot-ed
sure´ly
sure´ness
sur´er
sur´est
sure´ty
sur´face
sur´faced
sur´fac-er
sur´fac-ing
sur-fac´tant
sur´feit
surf´y
surge
sur´geon
sur´gery
sur´gi-cal
surg´ing
su´ri-cate
Su´ri-nam
sur´li-ly
sur´li-ness
sur´ly
sur-mis´able
sur-mise´
sur-mis´ing
sur-mount´
sur-mount´able
sur-mount´ed
sur´name
sur-pass´
sur-pass´ing
sur´plice
sur´plus
sur´plus-age
sur-pris´able
sur-pris´al
sur-prise´
sur-prised´
sur-pris´ed-ly
sur-pris´ing
sur-re´al-ism
sur-re´al-ist
sur-re´al-is´tic
sur-ren´der
sur-rep-ti´tious
sur´rey
sur´ro-gate
sur´ro-gat-ed
sur´ro-gat-ing
sur-round´
sur-round´ed
sur-round´ing
sur´tax
sur-tout´
sur-veil´lance
sur-veil´lant
sur-vey´
sur-vey´ing
sur-vey´or
sur-viv´al
sur-vive´
sur-vi´vor
sur-vi´vor-ship
sus-cep-ti-bil´i-ty
sus-cep´ti-ble
sus´pect
sus-pend´
sus-pend´ed
sus-pend´er
sus-pend´ible
sus-pense´
sus-pen´si-ble
sus-pen´sion
sus-pen´so-ry
sus-pi´cion
sus-pi´cious
Sus´que-han´na
Sus´sex
sus-tain´
sus-tained´
sus-tain´ing
sus-tain´ment
sus´te-nance
sus´ten-tac´u-lar
sus´ten-ta´tion
sus´ten-ta-tive
sut-tee´
su´ture
su´tur-ing
su´ze-rain
su´ze-rain-ty
svelte
swabbed
swab´bing
swab´ble
Swa´bia
swad´dle
swad´dled
swad´dling
swag´ger
swal´low
swal´low-tail
swa´mi
swamp
swamp´er
swamp´land
swamp´y

swank´i-ness
swank´y
swan´like
swan´nery
swans´down
swarmed
swarm´er
swarm´ing
swarth´i-ly
swarth´i-ness
swarth´y
swash´buck-ler
swas´ti-ka
swatch
swath
swathe
sway´backed
sway´ing
Swa´zi-land
swear´ing
sweat´er
sweat´i-ly
sweat´i-ness
sweat´shop
sweat´y
Swe´den
swee´ny
sweep´er
sweep´ing
sweep´stakes
sweet´bread
sweet´bri-er
sweet corn
sweet´en
sweet´ened
sweet´en-ing
sweet flag
sweet´heart
sweet´ish
sweet´ly
sweet´meats
sweet´ness
sweet pea
sweet´shop
swelled
swell´ing
swel´ter
swel´ter-ing
swerve
swerved
swerv´ing
swift´er
swift´ly
swift´ness
swim´mer
swim´mer-et´
swim´ming
swim´ming-ly
swin´dle
swin´dler
swin´dling
swing´ing
swin´ish
swiped
swip´ing
swirl´ing
switch
switch´back
switch´board
switch´er
switch´man
Switz´er-land
swiv´el
swiv´eled
swiv´el-ing
swol´len
swoon
swoon´ing
swoop
sword
sword´fish
sword grass
sword knot
sword´play
swords´man
swords´man-ship
sworn
syc´a-more
sych´no-car´pous
sy-co´ni-um
syc´o-phan-cy
syc´o-phant
sy-co´sis
Syd´ney
syl-lab´ic
syl-lab´i-cate
syl-lab´i-cat-ing
syl-lab-i-ca´tion
syl-lab-i-fi-ca´tion
syl-lab´i-fied
syl-lab´i-fy
syl-lab´i-fy-ing
syl´la-bize
syl´la-ble
syl´la-bus
syl-lep´sis
syl´lo-gism
syl-lo-gis´ti-cal
syl´van
sym-bi´o-sis
sym´bi-ot´ic
sym´bol
sym-bol´ic
sym-bol´i-cal
sym´bol-ism
sym´bol-is´tic
sym-bol iza´tion
sym´bol-ize
sym-bol´o-gy
sym-met´ri-cal
sym´me-trize
sym´me-try
sym´pa-thet´ic
sym´pa-thize
sym´pa-thiz-er
sym´pa-thiz-ing
sym´pa-tho-lyt´ic
sym´pa-thy
sym-phon´ic
sym-pho´ni-ous
sym´pho-nize
sym´pho-ny
sym-po´di-um
sym-po´si-ac
sym-po´si-um
symp´tom
symp-to-mat´ic
symp-to-mat´i-cal-ly
symp´tom-a-tize
symp-tom-a-tol´o-gy
syn´a-gogue
syn´apse
syn´ar-thro´sis
syn-chon-drot´o-my
syn´chro-nism
syn´chro-nis´tic
syn-chro-ni-za´tion

syn´chro-nize
syn´chro-niz-er
syn´chro-niz-ing
syn-chron´o-graph
syn´chro-nous
syn´chro-ny
syn´chro-scope
syn´chro-tron
syn´cline
syn´co-pate
syn´co-pat-ed
syn´co-pat-ing
syn-co-pa´tion
syn´co-pa-tor
syn´co-pe
syn-cop´ic
syn´di-cal-ism
syn´di-cate
syn´di-cat-ing
syn-di-ca´tion
syn´di-ca-tor
syn´drome
syn-er´e-sis
syn-er´gic
syn´er-gism
syn-er-gis´ti-cal
syn-i-ze´sis
syn´od
syn´od-al
syn-od´i-cal
syn-od´i-cal-ly
syn-oe´cious
syn´o-nym
syn´o-nym´ic
syn-o-nym´i-ty
syn-on´y-mous
syn-on´y-my
syn-op´sis
syn-op´tic
syn-tac´ti-cal
syn´tax
syn-tec´tic
syn´the-sis
syn´the-sist
syn´the-size
syn´the-siz-er
syn´the-siz-ing
syn-thet´ic
syn-thet´i-cal
syn-thet´i-cal-ly
syn´the-tize
syn´thol
syph´i-lis
syph´i-lit´ic
sy´phon
Syr´a-cuse
Syr´ia
sy-ringe´
sy-rin´ge-al
sy-rin´gic
sy-rin´gin
syr-in-gi´tis
syr´up
sys´tem
sys´tem-at´ic
sys´tem-at´i-cal-ly
sys´tem-a-ti-za´tion
sys´tem-a-tize
sys-tem´ic
sys-tem-iza´tion
sys´tem-ize
sys´to-le
sys-tol´ic

T

tabbed
tab´bing
tab´by
tab´er-na-cle
tab´er-nac´u-lar
Tab´i-tha
ta´ble
tab´leau
tab´leaux
ta´ble-cloth
ta´ble d'hôte´
ta´ble-land
ta´ble-spoon
ta´ble-spoon-ful
tab´let
ta´ble-ware
ta´bling
tab´loid
ta-boo´
ta´bor
tab´u-lar
tab´u-late
tab´u-lat-ing
tab-u-la´tion
tab´u-la-tor
ta-chom´e-ter
tach´o-met´ric
ta-chom´e-try
tac´it
tac´it-ly
tac´i-turn
tac-i-tur´ni-ty
tack´le
tack´ler
tack´ling
tack´y
Ta-co´ma
tact´ful
tact´ful-ly
tac´ti-cal
tac´ti-cal-ly
tac-ti´cian
tac-tic´i-ty
tac´tics
tac´tile
tac-til´i-ty
tact´less
tac-tom´e-ter
tac´tu-al
tad´pole
taf´fe-ta
taf´fy
Ta-ga´log
tagged
tag´ging
Ta-hi´ti
Ta´hoe
tail´board
tail´er
tail´less
tail´light
tai´lor
tai´lored
tai´lor-ing
tai´lor—made´
tail´piece
tail´race
tail´spin
taint
Tai´pei´
Tai´wan´

take´down
tak´en
take´off
tak´er
tak´ing
talc
tal´cum
tale´bear-er
tal´ent
tal´ent-ed
ta´les
tales´man
tal´i-on
tal´is-man
talk´a-thon
talk´a-tive
talk´er
Tal´la-has´see
tal´lied
tal´low
tal´ly
Tal´mud
Tal-mud´ic
Tal´mud-ist
tal´on
ta-lon´ic
Ta´los
tam´able
ta-ma´le
tam´a-rack
tam´a-rind
tam´a-risk
tam´bour
tam´bou-rine´
tame´able
tamed
tame´ness
tam´er
tam´ing
Tam´ma-ny
tam´—o´—shan-ter
Tam´pa
tamp´er
Tam-pi´co
tam´pon
tan´a-ger
Tan´a-gra
Ta-nan´a-rive
tan´bark
tan´dem
Tan´gan-yi´ka
tan´ge-lo
tan´ge-los
tan´gent
tan-gen´tial
tan-ger-e´tin
tan´ger-ine´
tan-gi-bil´i-ty
tan´gi-ble
Tan-gier´
tan´gle
tan´gled
tan´gling
tan´go
tan´goed
tang´y
tank´age
tan´kard
tank´er
tanned
tan´ner
tan´nery
tan´nic
tan´nin
tan´ning
tan-tal´ic
tan´ta-lite
tan´ta-lize
tan´ta-liz-er
tan´ta-lum
tant´amount
tan´trum
Tan-za-ni´a
Tao´ism
taped
tape´line
tape mea´sure
ta´per
ta´per-ing
tap´es-try
ta-pe´tum
tape´worm
tap-i-o´ca
ta´pir
tap-is´
tapped
tap´ping
tap´room
tap´root
tap´ster
tar-an-tel´la
ta-ran´tu-la
tar´di-ly
tar´di-ness
tar´dy
tar´get
tar´ge-teer´
tar´iff
Tar´king-ton
tar´nish
tar´nish-able
ta´ro
tar-pau´lin
tar´pon
tar´ra-gon
tarred
tar´ried
tar´ring
tar´ry
tar´ry-ing
tar´sal
tar´sus
tar´tan
tar´tar
Tar-tar´ian
tar-tar´ic
Tar´ta-ry
task´mas-ter
Tas-ma´nia
tas´ma-nite
tas´sel
tas´seled
tas´sel-ing
taste´ful
taste´less
tast´er
tast´i-ness
tast´ing
tast´y
Ta´tar
tat´ter
tat´tered
tat´tle
tat´tler
tat´tle-tale
tat-too´
tat-too´er

taught
taunt
taunt´er
taunt´ing
taunt´ing-ly
Taun´ton
taupe
Tau´rus
tav´ern
taw´dri-ness
taw´dry
tawn´i-er
tawn´y
tax-abil´i-ty
tax´able
tax-a´tion
tax´—ex-empt´
tax´i-cab
tax´i-der´mic
tax´i-der-mist
tax´i-der-my
tax´ied
tax´i-me-ter
tax´ing
tax´o-nom´ic
tax-on´o-my
tax´pay-er
Tchai-kov´sky
teach´able
teach´er
teach´ing
tea´cup
tea´house
tea´ket-tle
teal
team´mate
team´ster
team´work
tea par´ty
tea´pot
tear´ful
tear gas
tear´ing
tear´less
tea´room
tear sheet
teased
teas´er
teas´ing

tea´spoon
tea´spoon-ful
tea´time
tech-ne´ti-um
tech´ni-cal
tech-ni-cal´i-ty
tech-ni´cian
Tech´ni-col-or
tech´nics
tech-nique´
tech-noc´ra-cy
tech´no-crat
tech-nog´ra-phy
tech-no-log´i-cal
tech-nol´o-gy
Te-cum´seh
te´di-ous
te´di-um
teen´—ag´er
tee´ter
teethed
teeth´ing
tee´to-tal-er
Tef´lon
teg-men´tal
teg´mi-nal
teg´u-men
teg´u-ment
teg´u-men´tary
Te-he-ran´
Teh-ran´
Te-huan´te-pec
Tel-Au´to-graph
Tel´ Aviv´
tel´e-cast
tel´e-gram
tel´e-graph
te-leg´ra-pher
tel´e-graph´ic
te-leg´ra-phy
tele-ki-ne´sis
tel´e-me-ter
tel´e-met´ric
te-lem´e-try
tel´e-mo-tor
tel´e-path´ic
te-lep´a-thy
tel´e-phone
tel´e-phon´ic

te-leph´o-ny
tel´e-pho´to
tel´e-pho-tog´ra-phy
Tel´e-Promp´Ter
tel´e-scope
tel´e-scop´ic
tel´e-scop´i-cal-ly
te-les´co-py
tel´e-sis
Tel´e-type
tel´e-typ-ist
tel´e-vise
tel´e-vi-sion
tel´e-vi-sor
tell´er
tell´tale
tel-lu´ri-an
tel-lu´ric
tel´lu-ride
tel-lu´ri-um
tem´per
tem´pera
tem´per-a-ment
tem´per-a-men´tal
tem´per-ance
tem´per-ate
tem´per-a-ture
tem´pered
tem´per-er
tem´pest
tem-pes´tu-ous
tem´plar
tem´plate
tem´ple
tem´plet
tem´po
tem´po-ral
tem-po-ral´i-ty
tem´po-rar´i-ly
tem´po-rary
tem´po-rize
tem´po-riz-er
tempt
tempt´able
temp-ta´tion
tempt´er
tempt´ing
tempt´ress
tem´pus fu´git

ten-a-bil´i-ty
ten´a-ble
te-na´cious
te-nac´i-ty
te-nac´u-lum
ten´an-cy
ten´ant
ten´ant-able
ten´ant-ry
tend´ance
tend´en-cy
tend´er
ten´der-foot
ten´der-heart-ed
ten´der-iz-er
ten´der-loin
ten´der-ness
ten-di-ni´tis
ten´di-nous
ten´don
ten´dril
Ten´e-brae
Te-ne-ri´fe
ten´et
ten´fold
Ten´ite
Ten´nes-see´
ten´nis
Ten´ny-son
ten´on
ten´or
ten´pen-ny
ten´pins
ten´si-ble
ten´sile
ten´sion
ten´son
ten´sor
ten-so´ri-al
ten´—strike
ten´ta-cle
ten-tac´u-lar
tent´age
ten´ta-tive
tent´ed
tent´er
ten´ter-hook
te-nu´i-ty
ten´u-ous

ten´ure
te´pee
tep´id
te-pid´i-ty
te-qui´la
ter´a-con´ic
ter´a-cryl´ic
Ter´ence
ter´gite
ter´gum
term´er
ter´mi-na-ble
ter´mi-nal
ter´mi-nate
ter-mi-na´tion
ter´mi-na-tor
ter´mi-ni
ter-mi-nol´o-gy
ter´mi-nus
ter´mite
ter´mor
Terp-sich´o-re
terp´si-cho-re´an
ter´race
ter´ra—cot´ta
ter´ra fir´ma
ter-rain´
Ter-ra-my´cin
ter´ra-pin
terr-a´que-ous
ter-rar´i-um
ter-raz´zo
Ter´re Haute
ter-rene´
ter-res´tri-al
ter´ri-ble
ter´ri-bly
ter´ri-er
ter-rif´ic
ter-rif´i-cal-ly
ter´ri-fied
ter´ri-fy
ter´ri-to´ri-al
ter´ri-to-ry
ter´ror
ter´ror-ism
ter´ror-ist
ter´ror-ize
ter´ry-cloth

terse
terse´ly
terse´ness
ter´tiary
Ter-tul´lian
tes´sel-late
tes´sel-lat-ed
tes-sel-la´tion
tes´ta
test´able
tes´ta-cy
tes´ta-ment
tes´tate
tes´ta-tor
tes-ta´trix
test´er
tes´ti-cle
tes-tic´u-lar
tes-ti-fi-ca´tion
tes´ti-fy
tes-ti-mo´ni-al
tes´ti-mo-ny
tes´ti-ness
tes´tis
tes-tos´ter-one
test tube
tes-tu´di-nal
tes-tu-di-nar´i-ous
tes´ty
tet´a-nus
tet´a-ny
te-tar´to-he´dral
te´tar-toi´dal
tête—à—tête
teth´er
teth´ered
tet-ra-cy´cline
tet´ra-eth´yl
tet´ra-gon
te-tram´er-ous
te-tram´e-ter
tet´ra-mine
tet´ra-zine
tet-ra-zo´li-um
te-traz´o-lyl
tet´ra-zone
tet´ri-tol
te-tron´ic
tet´rose

te-trox´ide
tet´ryl
Teu´ton
Tex´an
Tex-ar-kan´a
Tex´as
text´book
tex´tile
tex´tu-al
tex´tu-ary
tex´tur-al
tex´ture
Thack´er-ay
Thai´land
tha-lam´ic
thal´a-mus
tha-las´sic
Tha´les
tha-lid´o-mide
thal-lif´er-ous
thal´line
thal´li-um
thal´lo-phyte
thal´lus
Thames
thank´ful
thank´ful-ness
thank´less
thanks´giv´ing
thatch´er
thau´ma-site
the´ar-chy
the´a-ter
the-at´ri-cal
The´ban
Thebes
thegn
the´ism
the´ist
the-is´tic
the-mat´ic
them-selves´
thence´forth
thence´for´ward
then´o-yl
the-oc´ra-cy
the´o-crat´ic
The-oc´ri-tus
the-od´i-cy
the-od´o-lite
the-od´o-lit´ic
The´o-dore
The´o-do´sia
the´o-gon´ic
the-og´o-ny
the-o-lo´gian
the´o-log´i-cal
the-ol´o-gize
the-ol´o-gy
the-om´a-chy
the´o-mor´phic
the´o-pa-thet´ic
the´o-path´ic
the-op´a-thy
the-oph´a-ny
the´o-rem
the´o-re-mat´ic
the´o-ret´i-cal
the-o-re-ti´cian
the´o-rist
the-o-ri-za´tion
the´o-rize
the´o-ry
the´o-soph´ic
the-os´o-phist
the-os´o-phy
ther´a-peu´tic
ther´a-peu´ti-cal-ly
ther´a-pist
ther´a-py
there´abouts
there´af´ter
there´by´
there´fore´
there-in´
there-of´
there-on´
The-re´sa
there´upon´
there´with´
ther´mal
ther´mi-cal-ly
Ther´mi-dor
therm´i´on
therm´ion´ic
therm´is´tor
ther´mite
ther´mo-chro-mism
ther´mo-cou-ple
ther´mo-du´ric
ther´mo-dy-nam´ic
ther´mo-elec´tric
ther-mog´ra-pher
ther´mo-graph´ic
ther-mol´y-sis
ther´mo-lyt´ic
ther-mom´e-ter
ther´mo-met´ric
ther´mo-met´ri-cal-ly
ther-mom´e-try
ther´mo-nu´cle-ar
ther-moph´i-ly
ther´mo-pile
Ther´mos
ther´mo-scop´ic
ther´mo-stat
ther´mo-stat´ic
ther´mo-ther´a-py
ther-mot´ro-pism
the-sau´rus
the´ses
the´sis
Thes´pi-an
Thes´sa-lo´ni-an
Thes´sa-ly
the´tin
the-ur´gic
the´ur-gy
the-ve´tin
thi-am´ide
thi-am´i-nase
thi-am´ine
thia-naph´thene
thi-an´threne
thi´a-zole
thi-az´o-line
thi´a-zol-sul´fone
thick´en
thick´en-ing
thick´et
thick´ness
thick´set´
thick´—skinned´
thief
thiev´ery
thieves
thiev´ing

thiev´ish
thigh´bone
thim´ble
thim´ble-ful
thi-mer´o-sal
think´er
think´ing
thin´ner
thin´ness
thin´—skinned´
thi´o-fla´vine
third
third´ly
thirst
thirst´i-ly
thirst´i-ness
thirst´y
thir´teen´
thir´ti-eth
thir´ty
this´tle
this´tle-down
thith´er
thi-u-ro´ni-um
thix-ot´ro-py
Thom´as
thong
tho-rac´ic
tho-rac´i-co-lum´bar
tho-ra´co-scope
tho-ra-cos´to-my
tho´rax
Tho-reau´
thor´ic
tho-rif´er-ous
tho´rite
tho´ri-um
thorn´y
tho´ron
thor´ough
thor´ough-bred
thor´ough-fare
thor´ough-go-ing
thor´ough-ly
thor´ough-ness
though
thought´ful
thought´ful-ly
thought´ful-ness
thought´less
thought´less-ness
thou´sand
thou´sand-fold
thou´sandth
thrall´dom
thrash´er
thra-son´i-cal
thread´bare
thread´er
thread´worm
thread´y
threat´en
threat´en-ing
three´fold
three´pence
three´score
three´some
thre´i-tol
thre´node
thre-nod´ic
thren´o-dist
thren´o-dy
thre´o-nine
thresh´er
thresh´old
threw
thrift´i-er
thrift´i-ly
thrift´i-ness
thrift´less
thrift´y
thrill´er
thrill´ing
thrips
thrive
thriv´ing
throat
throat´i-ness
throat´y
throb´bing
throe
throm´bin
throm´bo-an´gi-i´tis
throm-bo-cy-to´sis
throm-bo-plas´tin
throm-bo´sis
throm-bot´ic
throm´bus
throng
throt´tle
throt´tled
through
through-out´
throw
thrush
thrust´er
thrust´ing
thud´ding
thu´le
thu´li-um
thumb´nail
thumb´screw
thump´er
thun´der
thun´der-bird
thun´der-bolt
thun´der-cloud
thun´der-er
thun´der-head
thun´der-ous
thun´der-ous-ly
thun´der-show-er
thun´der-storm
thun´der-struck
Thurs´day
thwart
thyme
thy´mic
thy´mine
thy´mol
thy´mus
thy´roid
thy-roi´dal
thy-roid-ec´to-my
thy-roid-i´tis
thy´ro-nine
thy-rot´ro-phin
thy-rox´ine
thyr´soid
thyr´sus
thy´sa-nu´ran
thy´sa-nu´rous
ti-ar´a
Ti´ber
Ti-bet´
tib´ia
tib´i-al

tick´er
tick´et
tick´et-er
tick´i-ci´dal
tick´i-cide
tick´ing
tick´le
tick´ler
tick´lish
Ti-con-der-o´ga
tid´al
tid´bit
tid´dly-winks
tide´wa-ter
ti´di-ly
ti´di-ness
ti´ding
ti´dy
tie´—in
tie´mann-ite
Tien´tsin´
tier
Tier´ra del Fue´go
tie´—up
tif´fa-ny
tif´fin
ti´ger
ti´ger-ish
ti´ger lily
tight´en
tight´en-er
tight´en-ing
tight´rope
tight´wad
ti´gress
Ti´gris
til´de
Til´den
tiled
til´ing
till´able
till´age
till´er
tilt´er
tim´ber
tim´bered
tim´ber-man
tim´ber wolf
tim´ber-work
tim´bre
tim´brel
tim´brelled
Tim´buk-tu´
time´—hon´ored
time´keep-er
time´li-er
time´li-ness
time´ly
time´piece
tim´er
time´ta-ble
tim´id
ti-mid´i-ty
tim´ing
tim´o-rous
tim´o-thy
tim´pa-ni
tim´pa-nist
tinc´ture
tin´der
tin´foil
tinge´ing
tin´gle
tin´gled
tin´gling
ti´ni-er
tin´ker
tin´kle
tin´kling
tin´ner
tin´ni-er
tin´ny
tin´sel
tin´seled
tin´smith
tint´er
tin-tin-nab-u-la´tion
tin-tin-nab´u-lous
tint-om´e-ter
tin´type
tin´ware
ti´ny
tip´off
Tip-pe-ca-noe´
tip´per
Tip-pe-rar´y
tip´pet
tip´ping
tip´ple
tip´si-ly
tip´staff
tip´ster
tip´sy
tip´toe
tip´—top
ti-rade´
Ti-ra´ne
tired´ly
tire´less
tire´some
tir´ing
Tish-chen´ko
tis´sue
ti´tan
ti´ta-nate
ti-ta´nia
ti-tan´ic
ti-ta-nif´er-ous
ti´ta-nite
ti-ta´ni-um
ti-tan´ous
ti´ter
tith´able
tithe
tith´er
tith´ing
Ti´tian
ti´tian-esque´
Ti´ti-ca´ca
tit´il-late
tit´i-vate
ti´tle
ti´tled
tit´mouse
Ti´to-ism
ti´trate
ti-tra´tion
tit´ter
tit-u-ba´tion
tit´u-lar
tit´u-lary
toad´stool
toad´y
toast´er
toast´mas-ter
to-bac´co
to-bac´co-nist

to-bac´cos
To-ba´go
to-bog´gan
to-bog´gan-er
to-col´o-gy
to-coph´er-ol
toc´sin
to-day´
tod´dle
tod´dler
tod´dy
tof´fee
to´ga
to´gaed
to´gat-ed
to-geth´er
to-geth´er-ness
tog´ging
tog´gle
tog´gler
To´go
toil´er
toi´let
toi´let-ry
toi-lette´
toil´some
toil´worn
To´kay´
to´ken
To´kyo
To-le´do
tol´er-a-ble
tol´er-a-bly
tol´er-ance
tol´er-ant
tol´er-ate
tol-er-a´tion
toll´booth
toll´gate
Tol´stoy
to´lu
tol´u-ate
tol´u-ene
tol´yl-ene
tom´a-hawk
to-ma´to
to-ma´toes
tom´boy
tomb´stone

tom´cat
tom-fool´ery
to-mog´ra-phy
to-mor´row
tom´—tom
ton´al
to-nal´i-ty
tone´less
ton´er
to-net´ics
Ton´ga
tongue
tongue´less
tongu´er
tongue´—tied
tongu´ing
ton´ic
to-nic´i-ty
to-night
to´nite
ton´nage
ton-neau´
ton´o-log´i-cal
to-nom´e-ter
ton´o-met´ric
to-nom´e-try
ton´sil
ton-sil-lec´to-my
ton-sil-li´tis
ton-sil-lot´o-my
ton-so´ri-al
ton´sure
ton´tine
tool´box
tool crib
tool´er
tool´hold-er
tool´ing
tool kit
tool´room
tooth´ache
tooth´brush
tooth´less
tooth´paste
tooth´pick
tooth pow-der
tooth´some
to´paz
to´paz-ine

top´coat
to-pec´to-my
to-pee´
To-pe´ka
top´er
top´flight´
top-gal´lant
top hat
top´—heavy
to´pi-ary
top´ic
top´i-cal
top´knot
top´mast
top´most
top´—notch´
top´o-deme
to-pog´ra-pher
topo-graph´i-cal
topo-graph´i-cal-ly
to-pog´ra-phy
top´o-log´i-cal
top´per
top´ping
top´ple
top´pling
top´sail
top´side
top´soil
top´sy—tur´vy
toque
To´rah
torch´bear-er
torch´light
torch´wood
to´re-ador
to-reu´tic
to´ric
to´rii
to-rin´gin
tor-ment´
tor-men´tor
tor-na´do
tor-na´does
to´roid
to-roi´dal
To-ron´to
tor-pe´do
tor-pe´do boat

tor-pe´does
tor´pid
tor-pid´i-ty
tor´por
tor´por-if´ic
torque
torque´me-ter
Tor´rens
tor´rent
tor-ren´tial
tor´rid
tor-si-om´e-ter
tor´sion
tor´so
tort
tor´te
tor-ti´lla
tor´tious
tor´toise
tor´toise-shell
tor-tu-os´i-ty
tor´tu-ous
tor´tu-ous-ly
tor´ture
tor´tur-er
tor´tur-ing-ly
tor´tur-ous
toss´ing
toss´—up
tot´able
to´tal
to´taled
to´tal-ing
to-tal´i-tar´i-an
to-tal-i-tar´i-an-ism
to-tal´i-ty
to´tal-i-za-tor
to´tal-ize
to´tal-iz-er
to´tal-ly
to´tem
to´tem-ism
tot´ing
tot´ter
tou´can
touch´down
tou-ché´
touch-i-ly
touch´i-ness
touch´ing
touch´stone
touch´y
tough
tough´en
tough´ness
Tou-lon´
Tou-louse´
tou-pee´
tour´ism
tour´ist
tour´ma-line
tour´na-ment
tour´ney
tour´ni-quet
tou´sle
tou´sled
tout´er
tow´age
to´ward
tow´boat
tow´el
tow´eled
tow´el-ing
tow´er
tow´ered
tow´er-ing
tow´head
tow´line
town´ house
towns´folk
town´ship
towns´man
towns´peo-ple
tow´path
tow´rope
tox-e´mia
tox-e´mic
tox´ic
tox-ic´i-ty
tox´i-co-log´i-cal
tox-i-col´o-gist
tox-i-col´o-gy
tox-i-co´sis
tox-if´er-ous
tox´i-ge-nic´i-ty
tox´in
tox´i-pho´bia
tox-oph´i-lite
tra-bec´u-la
trace´able
trac´er
trac´ery
tra´chea
tra´che-al
tra-che´idal
tra-che-i´tis
tra-che-ot´o-my
tra-cho´ma
tra-chom´a-tous
tra-chyt´ic
trac´ing
track´age
track´er
track´less
track´man
track´walk-er
trac-ta-bil´i-ty
trac´ta-ble
trac´tion
trac´tive
trac´tor
trade´—in
trade´—last
trade´mark
trade name
trad´er
trade school
trades´man
trade un´ion
trade wind
trad´ing
tra-di´tion
tra-di´tion-al
tra-di´tion-ary
trad´i-tive
trad´i-tor
tra-duce´
tra-duc´er
tra-duc´ible
Tra-fal´gar
traf´fic
traf´fic-able
traf´ficked
traf´fick-er
traf´fick-ing
tra-ge´di-an
tra-ge´di-enne´

trag´e-dy
trag´ic
trag´i-cal
trag´i-cal-ly
trag´i-com´e-dy
trail´er
train´ee´
train´er
train´ing
train´load
train´man
trait
trai´tor
trai´tor-ous
trai´tress
traj´ect
tra-jec´tile
tra-jec´to-ry
tram´mel
tram´meled
tram´mel-ing
tramp´er
tram´ple
tram´pling
tram´po-line´
tram´way
tran´quil
tran´quil-ize
tran´quil-iz-er
tran-quil´li-ty
trans-act´
trans-ac´tion
trans´at-lan´tic
trans-ceiv´er
tran-scend´
tran-scen´den-cy
tran-scen´dent
tran´scen-den´tal
tran-scen-den´tal-ism
trans-con-ti-nen´tal
tran-scribe´
tran-scrib´er
tran´script
tran-scrip´tion
trans-duc´er
trans-duc´tor
tran-sect´
tran´sept
trans´e-unt
trans´fer
trans-fer´able
trans´fer-ase
trans´fer-ee´
trans-fer´ence
trans´fer-en´tial
trans-ferred´
trans-fer´rer
trans-fer´ring
trans-fig-u-ra´tion
trans-fig´ure
trans-fix´
trans-fix´ion
trans-form´
trans-for-ma´tion
trans-for-ma´tion-al
trans-form´a-tive
trans-form´er
trans-fus´able
trans-fuse´
trans-fu´sion
trans-gress´
trans-gres´sion
trans-gres´sor
trans-hu´mance
tran´sien-cy
tran´sient
tran-sil´ience
tran-sil´ient
tran-sis´tor
tran-sis´tor-ize
tran´sit
tran´sit-er
tran-si´tion
tran-si´tion-al
tran´si-tive
tran´si-to-ry
trans-late´
trans-la´tion
trans-la´tor
trans-lit´er-ate
trans-lit´er-a-tor
trans-lu´cence
trans-lu´cen-cy
trans-lu´cent
trans-mi´grate
trana-mi-gra´tion
trano-mi´gra-to-ry
trans-mis´si-ble
trans-mis´sion
trans-mit´
trans-mit´ta-ble
trans-mit´tal
trans-mit´ter
trans-mut-abil´i-ty
trans-mut´able
trans-mu-ta´tion
trans-mute´
trans-oce-an´ic
tran´som
trano-pa-cif´ic
trans-par´en-cy
trans-par´ent
tran-spir´able
tran-spi-ra´tion
tran-spir´a-to-ry
tran-spire´
tran-spi-rom´e-ter
trans-plant´
trans-plan-ta´tion
tran-spon´der
trans-port´
trans-por-ta´tion
trans-pose´
trans-po-si´tion
trans-sex´u-al
trans-sex´u-al-ism
trans-ship´
trans-ship´ping
trans-ver´sal
trans-verse´
trans-vert´er
trans-vert´ible
trans-ves´tism
trans-ves´tite
trap´door
tra-peze´
tra-pe´zi-form
tra-pe´zi-um
trap´e-zoid
trap´e-zoi´dal
trap´per
trap´pings
Trap´pist
trap´shoot-ing
trash´y
trau´ma
trau-mat´ic

trau´ma-tism
trau´ma-tize
travail´
trav´el
trav´eled
trav´el-er
trav´el-ing
trav´el-og
trav´el-ogue
tra-vers´able
tra-vers´al
trav´erse
trav´er-tine
trav´ois
trawl´er
treach´er-ous
treach´ery
trea´cle
tread´ing
trea´dle
tread´mill
trea´son
trea´son-able
trea´son-ous
trea´sure
trea´sur-er
trea´sure trove
trea´sury
treat
treat´er
trea´ties
trea´tise
treat´ment
trea´ty
tre´ble
tre´bled
tree fern
tree frog
tree´ing
tree´less
tree´nail
tree toad
tree´top
tre´foil
trek´king
trel´lis
trel´lised
trel´lis-work
trem´ble
trem´bling
trem´bling-ly
tre-men´dous
tre-men´dous-ly
trem´or
trem´u-lous
trench
tren´chan-cy
tren´chant
tren´cher
Tren´ton
tre-pan´
trep-a-na´tion
tre-pan´ning
tre-phine´
trep-i-da´tion
tre-pid´i-ty
tres´pass
tres´pass-er
tres´tle
tres´tle-man
tri´ad
tri´al
tri´an-gle
tri-an´gu-lar
tri-an´gu-late
tri-an-gu-la´tion
trib´al
tribe
tribes´man
trib-u-la´tion
tribu´nal
trib´u-nate
trib´une
trib´u-ni´cial
trib´u-tary
trib´ute
tri´ceps
trich-i-no´sis
tri-chlo´ride
tri-cho´sis
tri-chot´o-my
trick´ery
trick´i-ly
trick´i-ness
trick´le
trick´ster
trick´y
tri´col-or
tri´cot
tri-crot´ic
tri´cro-tism
tri-cus´pid
tri´cy-cle
tri-cy´clic
tri´dent
tri´er
Trier
Tri-este´
tri´fle
tri´fler
tri´fling
tri-fo´cal
tri-fo´li-ate
tri-fo´li-o-late
trig´ger
tri´gon
trig´o-nal
tri-go-ni´tis
trig-o-nom´e-ter
trig-o-no-met´ric
trig-o-nom´e-try
tri-lat´er-al
tril´lion
tril´li-um
tri´lo-bite
tri-log´ic
tril´o-gy
tri´mer-ide
trim´er-ous
tri-mes´ic
trim´e-ter
trim´mer
trim´ming
tri´na-ry
Trin´i-dad
Trin´i-ty
trin´ket
tri-no´mi-al
tri´o
Tri´o-nal
tri-par´ti-ble
tri-par´tite
tri´par-ti´tion
tri´pe-dal
trip´—ham-mer
tri´ple
tri-ple´gia

trip´let
trip´lex
trip´li-cate
trip-li-ca´tion
tri-plic´i-ty
tri´pod
trip´o-dal
tri-pod´ic
Trip´o-li
trip´ping-ly
tri´reme
tri-sect´
tri-sec´tion
tri-se´mic
tri-so´mic
tris´ti-chous
Tris´tram
tri-syl-lab´ic
tri-syl´la-ble
trite´ness
trit´i-um
tri´ton
tri´umph
tri-um´phal
tri-um´phant
tri´umph-ing
tri-um´vir
tri-um´vir-al
tri-um´vi-rate
tri´une
tri-va´lence
tri-va´lent
triv´et
triv´ia
triv´i-al
triv-i-al´i-ty
triv´i-um
tro´car
tro-cha´ic
tro-chan´ter
tro´che
troch-e-am´e-ter
tro´chee
troch´i-lus
troch´le-ar
tro-choi´dal
tro-chom´e-ter
trod´den
trog´lo-dyte
Troi´lus
Tro´jan
troll´er
trol´ley
trol´lop
Trol´lope
trom-bi-di´a-sis
trom-bone´
trom-bon´ist
tro-mom´e-ter
tro-nom´e-ter
troop
troop´er
troop´ship
tro-pae´o-lin
tro´pane
trope
troph´ic
tro´phied
tro´phy
trop´ic
trop´ic acid
trop´i-cal
tro´pism
tro-pol´o-gy
trop´o-lone
tro-pom´e-ter
trop´o-phyte
tro´po-sphere
trop-tom´e-ter
Trot´sky
trot´ter
trot´ting
trou´ba-dour
trou´ble
trou´bled
trou´bler
trou´ble-some
trou´blous
trough
trounce
troupe
troup´er
troup´i-al
trou´sers
trous´seau
trou-vère´
tro´ver
trow´el
trow´eled
tru´an-cy
tru´ant
Truck´ee
truck´er
truck´le
truck´ling
truck´man
truc´u-lence
truc´u-lent
trudge
trud´gen
trudg´ing
tru´est
truf´fle
tru´ism
tru-is´tic
tru´ly
trum´pery
trum´pet
trum´pet-er
trun´cate
trun´cat-ed
trun-ca´tion
trun´cheon
trun´dle
trunk´ful
trunk line
trun´nion
truss´ing
trust´ee´
trust-ee´ship
trust´ful
trust´i-ly
trust´ing
trust´wor-thi-ness
trust´wor-thy
trust´y
truth´ful
truth´ful-ness
try´ing
try´out
try´sail
try square
tryst
tryst´er
tsar
tset´se
tu´ba

tub´al
tub´ba-ble
tu´ber
tu´ber-cle
tu-ber´cu-lar
tu-ber´cu-lin
tu-ber-cu-lo´sis
tu-ber´cu-lous
tube´rose
tu´ber-ous
tub´ing
tu´bu-lar
tu-bu-la´tion
tu´bule
tuck´er
Tuc-son´
Tu´dor
Tues´day
tu´fa
tuft´ed
tuft´er
tug´boat
tug´—of—war´
tu-i´tion
tu-la-re´mia
tu´lip
tu´lip-wood
Tul´sa
tum´ble
tum´ble-down
tum´bler
tum´ble-weed
tum´bling
tum´brel
tu´mid
tu´mor
tu´mult
tu-mul´tu-ous
tu´mu-lus
tu´na
tun´able
tun´dra
tune´ful
tune´less
tung´sten
tung´stic
tu´nic
tu´nicked
tun´ing
tun´ing fork
Tu´nis
Tu-ni´sia
tun´nel
tun´neled
tun´nel-er
tun´ny
tu´pe-lo
tur´ban
tur´baned
tur´bid
tur-bid´i-ty
tur´bi-nal
tur´bi-nate
tur´bine
tur´bo-charg-er
tur´bo-jet
tur´bo-prop
tur´bot
tur´bu-la-tor
tur´bu-lence
tur´bu-lent
tu-reen´
turf´man
tur´gen-cy
Tur-ge´nev
tur´gent-ly
tur-ges´cence
tur-ges´cent
tur´gid
tur-gid´i-ty
tur´gor
Tur-got´
Tu´rin
Tur´ke-stan´
tur´key
tur´keys
Turk´ish
tur´mer-ic
tur´moil
turn´buck-le
Turn´bull
turn´coat
turn´down
Tur´ner
turn´er
tur´nip
turn´key
turn´out
turn´over
turn´pike
turn´spit
turn´stile
turn´ta-ble
tur´pen-tine
tur´pi-tude
tur´quoise
tur´ret
tur´ri-lite
tur´tle
tur´tle-dove
Tus´ca-loo´sa
Tus´can
Tus´ca-ny
Tus-ke´gee
tusk´er
tus´sle
tu´te-lage
tu´te-lar
tu´te-lary
tu´tor
tu´tored
tu-to´ri-al
tu-to´ri-al-ly
tut´ti—frut´ti
Tu-tu-i´lan
tux-e´do
tu-yere´
twad´dle
twan´gle
twang´y
tweet´er
tweez´ers
twelfth
twen´ti-eth
twen´ty
twid´dle
twi´light
twing´ing
twi´—night
twin´ing
twin´kle
twin´kling
twin´ning
twist´er
twitch
twitch´er
Twitch´ell

twit´ter
twit´ting
two´fold
two´pence
two´some
two´—step
tycoon´
ty´ing
Ty´ler
tym-pan´ic
tym´pa-nist
tym-pa-ni´tes
tym´pa-nit´ic
tym´pa-num
tym´pa-ny
Tyn´dall
typ´able
type´cast
type´found-er
type met´al
type´script
type´set-ter
type wash
type´write
type´writ-er
type´writ-ing
type´writ-ten
typh-li´tis
typh-lol´o-gy
ty´phoid
ty-phoi´dal
ty-phoi´din
ty-phon´ic
ty-phoon´
ty´phous
ty´phus
typ´i-cal
typ-i-fi-ca´tion
typ´i-fy
typ´ist
ty-pog´ra-pher
ty-po-graph´ic
ty-po-graph´i-cal
ty-pog´ra-phy
ty-ran´ni-cal
ty-ran´ni-cide
tyr´an-nize
tyr´an-nous
tyr´an-nous-ly
tyr´an-ny
ty´rant
ty´ro
Tyrol´
Tyro´le-an
Tyr´o-lese´
Ty-rone´
ty´ro-sine
tyro-sin-o´sis

U

Uban´gi
ubi´e-ty
ubiq´ui-tar´i-an
ubiq´ui-tary
ubiq´ui-tous
ubi´qui-ty
ud´der
udom´e-ter
u´do-me´tric
Ugan´da
ug´li-fy
ug´li-ness
ug´ly
ukase´
Ukraine´
Ukrain´ian
uku-le´le
u´la-ma´
ul´cer
ul´cer-ate
ul-cer-a´tion
ul´cer-a-tive
ul´cer-ous
ul´na
ul´nar
ul-nar´e
ul´ster
ul-te´ri-or
ul´ti-ma
ul´ti-ma-cy
ul´ti-mate
ul-ti-ma´tum
ul´ti-mo
ul´tra
ul´tra-ism
ul´tra-ma-rine´
ul-tra-mon´tan-ism
ul´tra-mun´dane´
ul-tra-son´ic
ul-tra-vi´o-let
ul´tra vi´res
ul´tra-vi´rus
ul´u-lant
ul´u-late
ul´u-la´tion
Ulys´ses
um´ber
um-bil´i-cal
um-bil´i-cus
um´bra
um´brage
um´bra´geous
um-brel´la
Um´bri-an
um´pir-age
um´pire
un-abat´ed
un-a´ble
un-abridged´
un-ac-cept´able
un-ac-com´pa-nied
un-ac-count´able
un-ac-cus´tomed
un-ac-quaint´ed
un-adorned´
un-adul´ter-at-ed
un-af-fect´ed
un-afraid´
un-aid´ed
un-al´loyed
un-al´ter-able
un-al´tered
un-am-bi´tious
un—Amer´i-can
un-a´mi-able
un-aneled´
una-nim´i-ty
unan´i-mous
un-an-nounced´
un-an´swer-able
un-ap-proach´able
un-ar´gued
un-armed´
u´na-ry
un-ashamed´
un-asked´

un-as-sail´able
un-as-sist´ed
un-as-sum´ing
un-at-tached´
un-at-tain´able
un-at-tend´ed
un-at-trac´tive
un-au´tho-rized
un-avail´ing
un-avoid´able
un-aware´
un-bal´anced
un-bear´able
un-beat´en
un-be-com´ing
un-be-lief´
un-be-liev´able
un-be-liev´er
un-be-liev´ing
un-bend´
un-bend´ing
un-ben´e-ficed
un-bent´
un-bi´ased
un-bid´den
un-bind´
un-blam´able
un-bleached´
un-blem´ished
un-blink´ing
un-blush´ing
un-bolt´ed
un-born´
un-bos´om
un-bound´
un-bound´ed
un-break´able
un-bri´dled
un-bro´ken
un-buck´le
un-bur´den
un-but´ton
un-called—for
un-can´ny
un-ceas´ing
un-cer-e-mo´ni-ous
un-cer´tain
un-cer´tain-ty
un-chained´
un-chal´lenged
un-change´able
un-changed´
un-char´i-ta-ble
un-chart´ed
un-chaste´
un-checked´
un-chris´tian
un´cial
un-cir´cum-cised
un-civ´il
un-civ´il-ized
un-clad´
un-clasped´
un´cle
un-clean´
un-cloud´ed
un-com´fort-able
un-com´mon
un-com-mu´ni-ca-tive
un-com-plain´ing
un-com´pro-mis-ing
un-con-cern´
un-con-cerned´
un-con-di´tion-al
un-con´quer-able
un-con´quered
un-con´scio-na-ble
un-con´scious
un-con´scious-ness
un-con-sti-tu´tion-al
un-con-trol´la-ble
un-con-trolled´
un-con-ven´tion-al
un-cor-rupt´ed
un-count´ed
un-cou´ple
un-couth´
un-cov´er
un-cov´ered
un-crowned´
unc´tion
unc´tu-ous
un-cul´ti-vat-ed
un-cul´tured
un-cured´
un-daunt´ed
un-de-cid´ed
un-dec´yl-ene
un´dec´y-len´ic
un-de-feat´ed
un-de-filed´
un-de-fined´
un-dem-o-crat´ic
un-de-mon´stra-ble
un-de-mon´stra-tive
un-de-ni´able
un´der
un´der-brush
un´der-clothes
un´der-cloth´ing
un´der-cov´er
un´der-cur-rent
un´der-cut
un´der-dog
un-der-es´ti-mate
un´der-foot´
un´der-glaze
un´der-go´
un´der-gone´
un-der-grad´u-ate
un´der-ground
un´der-growth
un´der-hand-ed
un´der-line
un´der-ling
un´der-ly-ing
un´der-mine´
un´der-neath´
un-der-nour´ished
un´der-paid´
un´der-pass
un-der-priv´i-leged
un´der-rate´
un´der-score
un´der-sec´re-tary
un´der-sell´
un´der-shirt
un´der-side
un´der-signed
un´der-sized
un´der-slung
un´der-stand´
un-der-stand´able
un-der-stand´ing
un´der-state-ment
un´der-stood´
un´der-study

un´der-take
un´der-tak-er
un´der-tak´ing
un´der-tone
un´der-took´
un´der-tow
un-der-val-u-a´tion
un´der-wa´ter
un´der-wear
un´der-weight
un´der-went´
un´der-world
un´der-write
un´der-writ-er
un´der-writ´ten
un-de-served´
un-de-sir´able
un-de-vel´oped
un-dis´ci-plined
un-dis-cov´ered
un-dis-mayed´
un-dis-put´ed
un-dis-turbed´
un-di-ver´si-fied
un-di-vid´ed
un-do´
un-do´ing
un-done´
un-doubt´ed-ly
un-dreamed´
un-dress´
un-due´
un´du-lant
un´du-late
un´du-lat-ed
un-du-la´tion
un´du-la-to-ry
un-du´ly
un-dy´ing
un-earned´
un-earth´
un-earth´ly
un-eas´i-ly
un-eas´i-ness
un-eas'y
un-ed´u-cat-ed
un-em-ployed´
un´em-ploy´ment
un-end´ing
un-en-dur´able
un-e´qual
un-e´qualed
un-equiv´o-cal
un-err´ing
un-e´ven
un-e´ven-ness
un-event´ful
un-ex-am´pled
un-ex-cep´tion-al
un-ex-pect´ed
un-ex-plained´
un-ex-plored´
un-ex´pur-gat-ed
un-fail´ing
un-fair´
un-faith´ful
un-fa-mil´iar
un-fas´ten
un-fath´om-able
un-fa´vor-able
un-feel´ing
un-feigned´
un-feign´ed-ly
un-fet´tered
un-fil´ial
un-fin´ished
un-fit´
un-fit´ted
un-fit´ting
un-flag´ging
un-fledged´
un-flinch´ing
un-fold´
un-fore-seen´
un-for-get´ta-ble
un-for-giv´able
un-for´tu-nate
un-found´ed
un-fre´quent-ed
un-friend´ly
un´ful-filled´
un-furl´
un-fur´nished
un-gain´ly
un-gen´er-ous
un-god´ly
un-gov´ern-able
un-gra´cious
un-grate´ful
un-ground´ed
un´gual
un-guard´ed
un´guent
un´guen-tary
un-guen´tous
un´gu-la
un´gu-lar
un´gu-late
un-hal´lowed
un-ham´pered
un-hap´pi-ly
un-hap´pi-ness
un-hap´py
un-harmed´
un-har´ness
un-health´y
un-heard´
un-heed´ed
un-heed´ing
un-hes´i-tat-ing-ly
un-hinge´
un-ho´ly
un-hon´ored
un-horse´
un-hur´ried
un-hurt´
u´ni-bi´va´lent
u´ni-cel´lu-lar
u´ni-corn
un-iden´ti-fied
u´ni-fi-able
uni-fi-ca´tion
unif´ic
u´ni-fied
uni-fo´li-o-late
u´ni-form
u´ni-form-i-tar´i-an
uni-form´i-ty
u´ni-fy
u´ni-fy-ing
uni-ju´gate
uni-lat´er-al
un-imag´i-na-tive
un-im-paired´
un-im-peach´able
un-im-por´tance
un-im-por´tant

un-im-proved´
un-in-cor´po-rat-ed
un-in-flam´ma-ble
un-in-formed´
un-in-hab´it-ed
un-in-i´ti-at-ed
un-in´jured
un-in-tel´li-gi-ble
un-in-ten´tion-al
un-in´ter-est-ed
un-in-ter-rupt´ed
un-in-vit´ed
un´ion
un´ion-ism
un´ion-ist
un´ion-ize
unip´a-rous
uni-pla´nar
unip´o-tent
unique´
unique´ly
u´ni-son
unis´o-nance
unis´o-nous
u´nit
unit´able
Uni-tar´i-an
u´ni-tary
unite´
unit´ed
unit´ing
u´ni-tive
u´nit-ize
u´ni-ty
u´ni-va´lence
u´ni-va´lent
u´ni-valve
u´ni-ver´sal
uni-ver-sal´i-ty
u´ni-verse
uni-ver´si-ty
univ´o-cal
un-just´
un-jus´ti-fi-able
un-kempt´
un-kind´
un-kind´li-ness
un-kind´ness
un-known´

un-lace´
un-law´ful
un-learned´
un-leash´
un-leav´ened
un-less´
un-let´tered
un-like´
un-like´li-hood
un-like´ly
un-lim´ber
un-lim´it-ed
un-liq´ui-dat-ed
un-list´ed
un-load´
un-lock´
un-loose´
un-luck´y
un-man´age-able
un-man´ly
un-man´ner-ly
un-mar´ried
un-masked´
un-mea´sur-able
un-mel´lowed
un-mend´able
un-men´tion-able
un-mer´chant-able
un-mer´ci-ful
un-mis-tak´able
un-mit´i-gat-ed
un-mixed´
un-mor´al
un-mort´gaged
un-moved´
un-nat´u-ral
un-nec-es-sar´i-ly
un-nec´es-sary
un-nerve´
un-no´ticed
un-ob-served´
un-ob-tru´sive
un-oc´cu-pied
un-of-fi´cial
un-o´pened
un-or´ga-nized
un-orig´i-nal
un-or´tho-dox
un-os´ten-ta´tious

un-pack´
un-paid´
un-pal´at-able
un-par´al-leled
un-par´don-able
un-par-lia-men´ta-ry
un-per´fo-rat-ed
un-per-turbed´
un-pleas´ant
un-pleas´ant-ness
un-pol´ished
un-pop´u-lar
un-pop-u-lar´i-ty
un-prac´ti-cal
un-prec´e-dent-ed
un-pre-dict´able
un-prej´u-diced
un-pre-med´i-tat-ed
un-pre-pared´
un-pre-ten´tious
un-prin´ci-pled
un-print´able
un-proc´essed
un-pro-duc´tive
un-pro-fes´sion-al
un-prof´it-able
un-pro-pi´tious
un-pro-tect´ed
un-pro-voked´
un-pub´lished
un-pun´ished
un-qual´i-fied
un-quench´able
un-ques´tion-able
un-ques´tioned
un-qui´et
un-quote´
un-rav´el
un-read´y
un´re´al
un-re-al´i-ty
un-rea´son-able
un-rec´og-niz-able
un-re-con-struct´ed
un-reel´
un-re-flec´tive
un-re-gen´er-ate
un-re-lent´ing
un-re-li´able

un-re-li´gious
un-re-mit´ting
un-re-mu´ner-at-ed
un-re-mu´ner-a-tive
un-rep-re-sent´a-tive
un-re-quit´able
un-re-quit´ed
un-re-served´
un-rest´
un-re-strained´
un-re-strict´ed
un-rid´dle
un-righ´teous
un-ripe´
un-ri´valed
un-roll´
un-ruf´fled
un-ru´ly
un-safe´
un-sal´able
un-san´i-tary
un-sat-is-fac´to-ry
un-sat´is-fied
un-sat´u-rat-ed
un-sa´vory
un-scathed´
un-schol´ar-ly
un-sci-en-tif´ic
un-scram´ble
un-scru´pu-lous
un-search´able
un-sea´son-able
un-seat´
un-seem´ly
un-seen´
un-self´ish
un-self´ish-ness
un-set´tled
un-shak´able
un-shak´en
un-shav´en
un-sheathe´
un-shod´
un-sight´ly
un-signed´
un-skilled´
un-skill´ful
un-snarl´
un-so´cia-ble
un-sol´der
un-so-lic´it-ed
un-so-lic´i-tous
un-so-phis´ti-cat-ed
un´sound´
un-spar´ing
un-speak´able
un-spe´cial-ized
un-spec´u-la-tive
un-spoiled´
un-spot´ted
un-sta´ble
un-stained´
un-stead´i-ly
un-stead´y
un-strung´
un-stud´ied
un-sub-stan´tial
un-suc-cess´ful
un-suit´able
un-suit´ed
un-sul´lied
un-sup-port´ed
un-sur-passed´
un-sus-pect´ed
un-sym-pa-thet´ic
un-taint´ed
un-tam´able
un-tamed´
un-tan´gle
un-tar´nished
un-taught´
un-ten´able
Un´ter-mey-er
un-think´able
un-think´ing
un-ti´dy
un-tie´
un-til´
un-time´ly
un-tir´ing
un-ti´tled
un-told´
un-touch´able
un-touched´
un-to´ward
un-trained´
un-tram´meled
un´trans-lat´able
un-tra-vers´able
un-tried´
un-trou´bled
un-true´
un-truth´ful
un-tu´tored
un-used´
un-u´su-al
un-u´su-al-ness
un-ut´ter-able
un-var´nished
un-var´y-ing
un-veil´
un-ven´ti-lat-ed
un-ver´i-fied
un-vir´tu-ous-ly
un-vit´ri-fied
un-want´ed
un-war´i-ly
un-war´rant-able
un-war´rant-ed
un-war´y
un-washed´
un-wa´ver-ing
un-wea´ried
un-wel´come
un-whole´some
un-wield´y
un-will´ing
un-will´ing-ness
un-wise´
un-wit´ting
un-wont´ed
un-work´able
un-world´ly
un-wor´thi-ness
un-wor´thy
un-wo´ven
un-wrap´
un-writ´ten
un-yield´ing
up´braid´
up´bring-ing
up´—coun´try
up´date
up´end´
up´grade´
up-heav´al
up-held´

up-hill´
up-hold´
up-hol´ster
up-hol´ster-er
up-hol´stery
up´keep
up´land
up´lift
upon´
up´per
up´per-cut
up´per-most
up´right
up´right-ness
up´ris-ing
up´roar
up´roar´i-ous
up-roar´i-ous-ly
up´root
up´set
up-set´
up´shot
up´si-lon
up´stage
up´stairs´
up-stand´ing
up´start
up´state´
up´stat-er
up´stream´
up´stroke
up´thrust
up´—to—date´
up´turn
up´ward
U´ral
ural´i-tize
Ura´nia
Ura´nian
uran´ic
u´ra-nin
u´ra-nin-ite
ura´ni-um
U´ra-nus
ur´ban
ur´bane´
ur-ban´i-ty
ur´chin
ure´a
ure-am´e-ter
ure´mia
ure´mic
ure-om´e-ter
ure´ter
ure´ter-al
u´re-thane
ure´thra
ure-thri´tis
uret´ic
ure´yl-ene
ur´gen-cy
ur´gent
ur´gent-ly
urg´ing
u´ri-nal
uri-nal´y-sis
u´ri-nary
u´ri-nate
uri-na´tion
u´rine
u´ri-nol´o-gy
u´ro-fla´vin
u´ro-gen´i-tal
urog´ra-phy
u´ro-leu´cic
uro-li-thi´a-sis
uro-li-thol´o-gy
u´ro-log´ic
urol´o-gist
urol´o-gy
uro-poi-e´sis
u´ro-poi´et´ic
uros´co-py
ur´si-gram
ur´sine
Ur´su-la
Ur´su-line
ur-ti-ca´ceous
ur-ti-car´ia
ur-ti-ca´tion
U´ru-guay
us-abil´i-ty
us´able
us´age
us´ance
use´ful
use´ful-ness
use´less
use´less-ness
us´er
ush´er
u´su-al
u´su-al-ly
u´su-rer
usu´ri-ous
usurp´
usur-pa´tion
usurp´er
u´su-ry
U´tah
uten´sil
u´ter-ine
u´ter-us
U´ti-ca
util-i-tar´i-an
util-i-tar´i-an-ism
util´i-ty
u´ti-li-za´tion
u´ti-lize
u´ti-liz-er
ut´most
Uto´pia
uto´pi-an
u´tri-cle
utric´u-lar
utric´u-li-form
ut´ter
ut´ter-ance
ut´ter-most
uva´rov-ite
u´vea
uve-i´tis
uvi-ton´ic
u´vu-la
u´vu-lar
uvu-li´tis
ux´o´ri-al
ux-or´i-cide

V

va´can-cy
va´cant
va´cate
va´cat-ing
va-ca´tion
va-ca´tion-ist

vac´ci-nal
vac´ci-nate
vac-ci-na´tion
vac´ci-na-tor
vac-cine´
vac´il-late
vac´il-lat-ing
vac-il-la´tion
vac´il-la-to-ry
vac´u-ist
va-cu´i-ty
vac-u-o-la´tion
vac-u-om´e-ter
vac´u-ous
vac´u-ous-ly
vac´u-um
vag´a-bond
vag´a-bond-age
va-gar´i-ous
va´gary
va-gil´i-ty
va-gi´na
vagi´nal
vag´i-nate
vag-i-nec´to-my
vag-i-ni´tis
va-got´o-my
va´gran-cy
va´grant
vague
vague´ly
va´guish
va´gus
vain-glo´ri-ous
vain´glo-ry
vain´ness
val´ance
val-e-dic´tion
val-e-dic-to´ri-an
val´e-dic´to-ry
va´lence
Va-len´cia
val´en-tine
Va-le´ra
val´et
Val-hal´la
val´iant
val´id
val´i-date
val-i-da´tion
va-lid´i-ty
val´ine
va-lise´
val´ley
val´leys
val´or
va´o-ri-za´tion
val´o-rize
val´or-ous
val´or-ous-ly
Val´pa-rai´so
val´u-able
val´u-ably
val-u-a´tion
val´ue
val´ued
val´ue-less
val´u-ing
val´val
val´vate
valve
val´vu-lar
val´vu-late
vam´pire
vam´pir-ism
va-na´di-um
Van Bu´ren
Van-cou´ver
van´dal
van´dal-ism
van-dyke´
Va-nes´sa
van´guard
va-nil´la
va-nil´lic
vanil´lin
van´ish
van´i-ty
van´quish
van´quish-er
van´tage
vap´id
va-pid´i-ty
vap´id-ly
va-pog´ra-phy
va´por
va-por-es´cence
va´por-if´ic
va-por-im´e-ter
va´por-iz-able
va-por-iza´tion
va´por-ize
va´por-iz-er
va´por-ous
va-que´ro
var-i-a-bil´i-ty
var´i-a-ble
var´i-ance
var´i-ant
var´i-at-ed
var-i-a´tion
var-i-cel´la
var´i-col-ored
var´i-cose
var-i-co´sis
var-i-cos´i-ty
var´ied
var´ie-gate
var´ie-gat-ed
var-ie-ga´tion
va-ri´e-tal
va-ri´e-ty
var´i-form
va-ri´o-la
var´i-o-late
var-i-o-la´tion
var´i-o-lite
var´i-o-lit´ic
var´i-o-loid
va-ri´o-lous
var-i-om´e-ter
var-i-o´rum
var´i-ous
var´i-ous-ly
var´i-type
var´let
var´nish
var´nish-er
var´si-ty
var´us
var´y
vas´cu-lar
vas-cu-lar´i-ty
vas-ec´to-my
Vas´e-line
vas´sal
vas´sal-age

Vas´sar
vas´ti-tude
vast´ly
vast´ness
vat´ic
Vat´i-can
va-tic´i-nal
va-tic-i-na´tion
va-tic´i-na-tor
vaude´ville
vault´ing
vaunt´ing
vav´a-sor
vec´tion
vec´tor
vec-to´ri-al
veer´ing-ly
vee´ry
veg´e-ta-ble
veg´e-tal
veg-e-tar´i-an
veg-e-tar´i-an-ism
veg´e-tate
veg-e-ta´tion
veg´e-ta´tion-al
veg´e-ta-tive
veg´e-tism
veg´e-tive
ve´he-mence
ve´he-ment
ve´he-ment-ly
ve´hi-cle
ve-hic´u-lar
veil´ing
veined
vein´ing
ve-la´men
ve´lar
ve-lar´i-um
Ve-las´quez
veldt
ve´li-ca´tion
vel´lum
ve-loc´i-pede
ve-loc´i-ty
ve-lom´e-ter
ve-lour´
ve´lum
ve-lu´men
vel´vet
vel´vet-een´
vel´vety
ve´nal
ve-nal´i-ty
ve-nat´ic
ve-na´tion
ven´dace
ven´dage
vend´er
ven-det´ta
ven-det´tist
vend´ible
ven-di´tion
ven´dor
ve-neer´
ve-neer´er
ven´er-able
ven´er-ate
ven-er-a´tion
ven´er-a-tor
ve-ne´re-al
ve-ne-re-ol´o-gy
Ve-ne´tian
Ven-e-zu-e´la
ven´geance
venge´ful
ve´nial
Ven´ice
ven´i-son
ven´om
ven´om-ous
ve-nos´i-ty
ve´nous
ve´nous-ly
vent´er
ven´ti-late
ven-ti-la´tion
ven´ti-la-tor
ven´tral
ven´tri-cle
ven-tric´u-lar
ven´tri-lo´qui-al
ven-tril´o-quism
ven-tril´o-quist
ven-tril´o-quis´tic
ven-tril´o-quy
ven´ture
ven´tur-er
ven´ture-some
ven-tu´ri
ven´tur-ing
ven´tur-ous
Ve´nus
ve-ra´cious
ve-ra´cious-ly
ve-rac´i-ty
Ve´ra-cruz
ve-ran´da
ver´a-scope
ver´bal
ver-bal´i-ty
ver-bal-iza´tion
ver´bal-ize
ver´bal-iz-er
ver´bal-ly
ver-ba´tim
ver´bi-age
verb´ify
ver-bose´
ver-bos´i-ty
ver-bo´ten
ver´dan-cy
ver´dant
ver´der-er
Ver´di
ver´dict
ver´di-gris
ver´din
ver´di-ter
Ver-dun´
ver´dure
ver´dur-ous
ver´dur-ous-ness
ver´e-cund
verge
verg´er
Ver´gil
verg´ing
ver´i-fi-able
ver-i-fi-ca´tion
ver´i-fied
ver´i-fy
ver´i-ly
ve´rism
ver´i-ta-ble
ver´i-tas
ver´i-ty

ver´meil
ver-mi-cel´li
ver´mi-cide
ver-mic´u-lar
ver-mic-u-la´tion
ver-mic´u-lite
ver´mi-form
ver´mif´u-gal
ver´mi-fuge
ver-mil´ion
ver´min
ver-mi-na´tion
ver-mi-no´sis
ver´min-ous
ver´min-ous-ly
Vermont´
ver-mouth´
ver-nac´u-lar
ver-nac´u-lar-ism
ver´nal
ver-na´i-za´tion
ver´nal-ize
ver´nal-ly
ver-na´tion
Ver´ner
ver´ni-er
Ver´non
Ve-ro´na
ve-ron´i-ca
Ver-sailles´
ver´sa-tile
ver´sa-tile-ly
ver-sa-til´i-ty
versed
ver-si-fi-ca´tion
ver´si-fied
ver´si-fi-er
ver´si-fy
ver´sion
ver´sus
ver´te-bra
ver´te-brae
ver´te-bral
ver´te-brate
ver´tex
ver´ti-cal
ver´ti-cal-ly
ver´ti-ces
ver´ticil´late
ver-tic´i-ty
ver´ti-go
verve
ver´y
ves´i-cant
ves´i-cate
ves´i-cle
ve-sic´u-lar
Ves-pa´sian
ves´per
ves´per-al
Ves-puc´ci
ves´sel
Ves´ta
ves´tal
vest´ed
vest-ee´
ves´ti-ary
ves-tib´u-lar
ves´ti-bule
ves´tige
ves-tig´ial
ves-tig´ial-ly
vest´ment
ves´try
ves´try-man
ves´tur-al
ves´ture
Ve-su´vi-us
vetch
vet´er-an
vet-er-i-nar´i-an
vet´er-i-nary
ve´to
ve´toed
ve´to-er
ve´toes
ve´to-ing
vex-a´tion
vex-a´tious
vex´ed-ly
vex´il-lary
vi´a
vi-a-bil´i-ty
vi´able
vi´a-duct
vi´al
vi-a´tor
vi´bran-cy
vi´brant
vi´brate
vi´brat-ing
vi-bra´tion
vi-bra´tion-al
vi-bra´to
vi´bra-tor
vi´bra-to-ry
vib´rio
vib´ri-on´ic
vib-ri-o´sis
vic´ar
vic´ar-age
vic´ar—gen´er-al
vi-car´i-al
vi-car´i-ate
vi-car´i-ous
vi-car´i-ous-ly
vice ad´mi-ral
vice—chan´cel-lor
vice—con´sul
vice—pres´i-den-cy
vice—pres´i-dent
vice´roy
vice´roy-al-ty
vi´ce ver´sa
Vi´chy
vi-chys-soise´
Vi´ci
vi-cin´i-ty
vi´cious
vi´cious-ness
vic´tim
vic´tim-ize
vic´tor
Vic-to´ria
vic-to´ri-ous
vic´to-ry
Vic-tro´la
vict´ual
vict´ualed
vict´ual-er
vi-cu´na
vid´eo
Vi-en´na
Vi´en-nese´
Viet´nam´
view´point
vig´il

vig´i-lance
vig´i-lant
vig-i-lan´te
vig-i-lan´tism
vi-gnette´
vi-gnet´ter
vig´or
vig´or-ous
vi´king
vile´ly
vile´ness
vil-i-fi-ca´tion
vil´i-fi-er
vil´i-fy
vil´i-fy-ing
vil´i-pend
vil´la
vil´lage
vil´lag-er
vil´lain
vil´lain-ous
vil´lainy
vil-la-nel´la
vil-la-nelle´
vil-lat´ic
vil´lein
vil´li
vil´li-form
vil-los´i-ty
vil´lus
Vil´na
vi´na
vin-ai-grette´
Vin-cennes´
Vin´cent
vin-ci-bil´i-ty
vin´ci-ble
vin´di-ca-ble
vin´di-cate
vin-di-ca´tion
vin´di-ca-tive
vin´di-ca-tor
vin´di-ca-to-ry
vin-dic´tive
vin-dic´tive-ly
vin´e-gar
vin´e-gary
vin´ery
vine´yard
vi´nic
vin-i-fi-ca´tion
vi´nous
vin´tage
vin´tag-er
vint´ner
vin´y
vi´nyl
vi´nyl-a´tion
vi´nyl-ene
Vi´nyl-ite
Vin´yon
vi´ol
vi-o´la
vi´ol-able
vi´o-la´ceous
vi´o-late
vi-o-la´tion
vi´o-la-tor
vi´o-lence
vi´o-lent
vi´o-let
vi-o-lin´
vi-o-lin´ist
vi-o-lon-cel´list
vi´per
vi´per-ous
vi-ra´go
vi´ral
vir´eo
vi-res´cence
vi-res´cent
Vir´gil
vir´gin
vir´gin-al
Vir-gin´ia
vir-gin´i-ty
vir-gin´i-um
vir´i-al
vi´ri-ci´dal
vir´i-des´cent
vi-rid´i-ty
vir´ile
vir´il-ism
vi-ril´i-ty
vi-rol´o-gy
vi-ro´sis
vir-tu´
vir´tu-al
vir-tu-al´i-ty
vir´tue
vir-tu-os´i-ty
vir-tu-o´so
vir´tu-ous
vir´u-lence
vir´u-lent
vi´rus
vi´sa
vis´age
vis´aged
vis´—à—vis´
vis´cera
vis´cer-al
vis´cid
vis-cid´i-ty
vis´cin
Vis´co-liz-er
vis-com´e-ter
vis´co-scope
vis´cose
vis-co-sim´e-ter
vis-cos´i-ty
vis´count
vis´count-ess
vis´cous
Vish´nu
vis-i-bil´i-ty
vis´i-ble
Vis´i-goth
vi´sion
vi´sion-ary
vi´sioned
vis´it
vis´i-tant
vis-i-ta´tion
vis´i-tor
vi´sor
vis´ta
Vis´tu-la
vi´su-al
vis-u-al´i-ty
vi-su-al-iza´tion
vi´su-al-ize
vi´su-al-iz-er
vi´su-al-ly
vi-ta´ceous
vi´tal
vi-tal´i-ty

vi-tal-iza´tion
vi´tal-ize
vi´ta-min
vi´ta-scope
vi´ti-ate
vi´ti-at-ed
vi-ti-a´tion
vi´ti-a-tor
vit´i-cul-ture
vit´i-cul´tur-ist
vit´rain
vit´re-ous
vi-tres´cence
vi-tres´cent
vi-tres´ci-ble
vit´ri-fi-able
vit-ri-fi-ca´tion
vit´ri-form
vit´ri-fy
vit´ri-ol
vit´ri-o-lat-ed
vit´ri-ol´ic
vit-ri-os´i-ty
vit´u-line
vi-tu´per-ate
vi-tu-per-a´tion
vi-tu´per-a-tive
vi´va
vi-va´cious
vi-va´cious-ly
vi-vac´i-ty
vi´van-dier´
vi-vant´
vi-var´i-um
vi´va vo´ce
Viv´i-an
viv´id
vi-vid´i-ty
viv´id-ly
viv´id-ness
viv-i-fi-ca´tion
viv´i-fied
viv´i-fy
vivi-par´i-ty
vi-vip´a-rous
vi-vip´a-rous-ly
viv´i-sect
viv´i-sec´tion
vix´en
vix´en-ish
viz´ard
vi-zier´
vizs´la
Vlad´i-vos-tok´
vo´ca-ble
vo-cab´u-lary
vo´cal
vo´cal-ist
vo-cal-iza´tion
vo´cal-ize
vo´cal-iz-er
vo-ca´tion
vo-ca´tion-al
voc´a-tive
voc´a-tive-ly
vo-cif´er-ant
vo-cif´er-ate
vo-cif-er-a´tion
vo-cif´er-ous
vo-cif´er-ous-ly
vo-cod´er
vod´ka
vogue
voice´less
voic´ing
void´able
voile
vo´lant
vo´lar
vol´a-tile
vo´a-til´i-ty
vo´a-til-iza´tion
vol´a-til-ize
vol-can´ic
vol-ca´no
vol-ca´noes
vol´ca-nol´o-gy
vo-lem´i-tol
Vol´ga
vol-i-ta´tion
vo-li´tion
vol´i-tive
vol´ley
vol´ley-ball
vol´plane
vol´plan-ist
Vol´stead-ism
Vol´ta
volt´age
vol-ta´ic
Vol-taire´
vol-tam´e-ter
vol´ta-met´ric
volt´—am´me-ter
volt´me-ter
vo´u-bil´i-ty
vol´u-ble
vol´ume
vol-u-me-nom´e-ter
vo-lu´me-ter
vol´u-met´ric
vo-lu-mi-nos´i-ty
vo-lu´mi-nous
vol´un-tar´i-ly
vol´un-ta-rism
vol´un-tary
vol´un-tary-isin
vol´un-teer´
vol´un-teered
vo-lup´tu-ary
vo-lup´tu-ous
vo-lup´tu-ous-ly
vo-lup´tu-ous-ness
vo-lu´tion
vol´vu-lus
vom´it
vom´it-er
voo´doo
voo´doo-ism
vo-ra´cious
vo-rac´i-ty
vo-ra´go
vor´tex
vor´ti-cal-ly
vor-ti-cel´la
vor´ti-ces
vor-tic´i-ty
Vosges
vot´able
vo´ta-ress
vo´ta-rist
vo´ta-ry
vot´er
vot´ing
vo´tive
vouch´er
vouch-safe´

vow´el
vox po´pu-li
voy´age
voy´ag-er
voy´a-geur´
Vul´can
vul´can-ite
vul-can-iza´tion
vul´can-ize
vul´can-iz-er
vul´gar
vul-gar´i-an
vul´gar-ism
vu´gar´i-ty
vul´gar-iza´tion
vul´gar-ize
vul´gar-ly
vul-ner-a-bil´i-ty
vul´ner-a-ble
vul´ner-ary
vul´pine
vul´ture
vul´tur-ous
vul´va
vul´var
vul-vi´tis
vy´ing

W

Wa´bash
wab´ble
wack´y
wad´ding
wad´dle
wad´dled
wad´dling
wad´er
wad´ing
wa´fer
waf´fle
waft´age
waft´er
wag´er
wag´es
wage´work-er
wag´gish
wag´gle
wag´gling
wag´ing
Wag´ner
Wag´ner-ism
wag´on
wag´on-er
wag´on-ette´
wag´on-load
wag´tail
wa-hi´ne
waif
Wai-ki-ki´
wail´ing
wain´scot
wain´wright
waist´band
waist´coat
waist´line
wait´er
wait´ing room
wait´ress
waive
waiv´er
wake´ful
wake´ful-ness
wak´en
wak´en-er
wak´en-ing
Wa-la´chi-an
Wal´den
Wal´den´si-an
Wal´do
Wal´dorf
walk´away
walk´er
walk´ie—talk´ie
walk´ing
walk´out
wal´la-by
Wal´lace
Wal-la´chia
wall´board
Wal´len-stein
Wal´ler
wal´let
wall´eyed
wall´flow-er
Wal-loon´
wal´lop
wal´lop-er
wal´lop-ing
wal´low
wall´paper
wal´nut
Wal´pole
wal´rus
Wal´ter
Wal´tham
Wal´ton
waltz
waltz´er
wam´pum
wan´der
wan´der-er
wan´der-ing
wan´der-lust
wan´gle
wan´gled
wan´gling
wan´ing
wan´ly
wan´ness
want´ing
wan´ton
wan´ton-ly
wan´ton-ness
wap´en-take
wap´i-ti
war´ble
war´bler
war´bling
war cry
war´den
war´denship
ward´er
war´der-ship
ward´robe
ward´room
ward´ship
ware´house
ware´room
war´fare
war´fa-rin
war´i-ly
war´i-ness
war´like
war´lock
warm´er
warm´heart-ed

war´monger
warmth
warn´er
warn´ing
warp
warp´age
war´path
warp´ing
war´ra-gal
war´rant
war´rant-ee´
war´rant-er
war´ran-tor´
war´ran-ty
war´ren
war´rior
War´saw
war´ship
war´time
wart´y
War´wick
war´y
wash´able
wash´ba-sin
wash´board
wash´bowl
wash´cloth
washed—out
wash´er
wash´er-wom-an
wash´ing
Wash´ing-ton
wash´out
wash´room
wash´stand
wash´tub
wasp´ish
was´sail
was´sail-er
Was´ser-mann
wast´age
waste´bas-ket
waste´ful
waste´land
waste´pa-per
wast´er
wast´ing
was´trel
watch´case
watch´dog
watch´er
watch´ful
watch´ful-ness
watch´mak-er
watch´man
watch´tow-er
watch´word
wa´ter
wa´ter bug
Wa´ter-bury
wa´ter clock
wa´ter-col-or
wa´ter-course
wa´ter-cress
wa´ter-fall
wa´ter-fowl
wa´ter-front
wa´ter gap
wa´ter gas
wa´ter-glass
wa´ter lev-el
wa´ter lily
wa´ter-line
wa´ter-log
wa´ter-logged
Wa´ter-loo´
wa´ter main
wa´ter-man
wa´ter-mark
wa´ter-mel-on
wa´ter me-ter
wa´ter mill
wa´ter pipe
wa´ter po-lo
wa´ter-pow-er
wa´ter-proof
wa´ter rat
wa´ter-shed
wa´ter-side
wa´ter snake
wa´ter-spout
wa´ter ta-ble
wa´ter-tight
wa´ter tow-er
wa´ter wag-on
wa´ter-way
wa´ter-wheel
wa´ter-works
wa´tery
watt´age
Wat-teau´
wat´tle
watt´me-ter
Wau-ke´gan
Wau´sau
wave´length
wave´let
wave´me-ter
wav´er
wa´ver
wa´ver-er
wa´ver-ing
wa´ver-ing-ly
Wa´ver-ley
wav´i-est
wav´ing
wav´y
wax´en
wax´i-est
wax´i-ness
wax´ing
wax pa-per
wax´works
wax´y
way´bill
way´far-er
way´far-ing
way´laid
way´lay
way´side
way´ward
way´worn
wayz´goose
weak
weak´en
weak´ened
weak´fish
weak´ling
weak´—mind-ed
weak´ness
wealth
wealth´i-er
wealth´y
wean´er
weap´on
weap´on-eer´
wear´able

wear´er
wea´ri-ful
wea´ri-less
wea´ri-ly
wea´ri-ness
wear´ing
wea´ri-some
wea´ri-some-ly
wea´ry
wea´sand
wea´sel
wea´seled
weath´er
weath´er—beat-en
weath´er-board
weath´er-cock
weath´ered
weath´er-ing
weath´er-man
weath´er-proof
weath´er—strip
weath´er vane
weave
weav´er
weav´er-bird
weav´ing
webbed
web´bing
We´ber
web´—foot-ed
Web´ster
wed´ded
wed´ding
wedge—shaped
wedg´ing
Wedg´wood
wed´lock
Wednes´day
weed´er
weed´y
week
week´day
week´end
week´ly
weep´er
weep´ing
wee´vil
weigh
weight
weight´i-ness
weight´y
weir
weird
weird´ly
weird´ness
wel´come
weld´er
wel´fare
wel´kin
well—bal´anced
well—be-haved´
well´—be´ing
well´born
well´bred´
Wel´ling-ton
well´—known´
well´—nigh´
wells´ite
well´spring
well´—to—do´
well´—
trained´welsh´er
Welsh´man
wel´ter
wel´ter-weight
wend´ing
were´wolf
Wes´ley
Wes´sex
West Ches´ter
west´er
west´er-ly
west´ern
west´ern-er
West In´dies
West´ing-house
West´min-ster
West´more-land
West-pha´lia
West Vir-gin´ia
west´ward
wet´back
weth´er
wet´ness
wet´ting
Wey´mouth
whack´ing
whale´back
whale´boat
whale´bone
whal´er
whal´ery
whal´ing
wharf
wharf´age
wharf´in-ger
Whar´ton
wharves
what-ev´er
what´not
what-so-ev-er
wheat´en
whee´dle
whee´dled
wheel´bar-row
wheel´base
wheeled
wheel´er
wheel´horse
wheel´house
Wheel´ing
wheel´wright
wheeze
wheez´i-ly
wheez´i-ness
wheez´ing-ly
wheez´y
whelp
when´as´
whence
when-ev´er
when´so-ev´er
where´abouts
where´as´
where´at´
where´by´
where´fore´
where´in´
where´of´
where´so-ev´er
where´upon´
wher-ev´er
where´with´
where´with-al
wher´ry
wher´ry-man
wheth´er

whet´stone
whet´ting
whey
which-ev´er
which´so-ev´er
whif´fen-poof
whif´fet
whif´fle
whif´fle-tree
while
whi´lom
whim´per
whim´pered
whim´per-ing
whim´si-cal
whim-si-cal´i-ty
whim´sy
whined
whin´ing
whin´ing-ly
whin´nied
whin´ny
whip´cord
whip hand
whip´lash
whip´per-snap-per
whip´pet
whip´ping
whip´poor-will
whip´saw
whip´stitch
whirl´er
whirl´i-gig
whirl´pool
whirl´wind
whirl´y-bird
whir´ring
whisk´er
whisk´ered
whis´key
whis´kies
whis´ky
whis´per
whis´pered
whis´per-ing
whist
whis´tle
whis´tler
Whis-tle´ri-an
whis´tling
white´bait
white´cap
white´—col´lar
white´fish
White´hall
white´—hot´
white lead
white´ly
whit´en
white´ness
whit´en-ing
white´wall
white´wash
white wa´ter
white´wood
whith´er
whit´ing
whit´ish
whit´low
Whit´man
Whit´ti-er
whit´tle
whit´tled
whit´tling
whiz´zer
who-dun´it
who-ev´er
whole´heart-ed
whole´sale
whole´sal-er
whole´some
whole wheat
whol´ly
whom-so-ev´er
whoop
whoop´ee
whoop´ing
whoop´ing cough
whop´per
whop´ping
whore
whorl
who-so-ev´er
Wich´i-ta
wick´ed
wick´ed-ly
wick´ed-ness
wick´er
wick´ered
wick´er-work
wick´et
wick´i-up
wide´—eyed
wid´en
wide´spread
wid´geon
wid´get
wid´ow
wid´ow-er
wid´ow-hood
width
wield
wield´er
wield´y
wie´ner
wie´ner schnit´zel
Wies´ba-den
wife
wife´ly
wigged
wig´gle
wig´gling
wig´gly
wig´wag
wig´wam
wild´cat
Wilde
Wil´der
wil´der-ness
wild´—eyed
wild´fire
wild´fowl
wild´ness
wild´wood
wil´ful
Wil´helm
Wil´helms-ha-ven
wil´i-ly
wil´i-ness
Wilkes—Bar´re
Wil-lam´ette
wil´lem-ite
will´ful
will´ful-ly
will´ful-ness
Wil´liam
Wil´liams-burg

will´ing
will´ing-ness
will´—o'—the—wisp
wil´low
wil´lowy
wil´ly—nil´ly
Wil´ming-ton
Wil´son
Wil´ton
wil´y
wim´ble
wim´ple
wince
Win´ches-ter
winc´ing
wind´age
wind´bag
wind´blown
wind´break
wind´break-er
wind´ed
wind´er
Win´der-mere
wind´fall
wind´flow-er
wind´i-er
wind´i-ness
wind´ing
wind´ing—sheet
wind´jam-mer
wind´lass
win´dle
wind´less
win´dle-straw
wind´mill
win´dow
win´dow-pane
win´dow—shop-ping
win´dow-sill
wind´pipe
wind´row
wind´shield
Wind´sor
wind´storm
wind´up
wind´ward
wind´y
wine cel´lar
wine´glass

wine´grow-er
wine´press
win´ery
Wine´sap
wine´skin
winged
wing´ed
wing´ed-ly
wing´less
wing´spread
wink´ing
win´kle
Win-ne-ba´go
win´ner
win´ning
Win´ni-peg
win´now
win´now-er
Wins´low
win´some
win´some-ness
Win´ston—Sa´lem
win´ter
win´ter-green
win´ter-ize
win´ter-time
win´try
win´y
wip´er
wip´ing
wire´less
wire´pho-to
wir´er
wire´weed
wir´i-ness
wir´ing
wir´y
Wis-con´sin
wis´dom
wise´acre
wise´crack
wise´ly
wis´est
wish´bone
wish´ful
wish´y—washy
wisp´y
wis-tar´ia
Wis-te´ria

wist´ful
wist´ful-ly
wi´tan
witch´craft
witch´ery
witch ha-zel
witch´ing
with-al´
with-draw´
with-draw´al
with-drawn´
with-drew´
with´er
with´ered
with´er-ing
with-held´
with-hold´
with-hold´ing
with-in´
with-out´
with-stand´
with-stand´ing
with´y
wit´less
wit´ness
wit´ti-cism
wit´ti-ly
wit´ting-ly
wit´ty
wiz´ard
wiz´ard-ry
wiz´ened
woad
wob´ble
wob´bly
wob´bu-la-tor
woe´be-gone
woe´ful
woe´ful-ness
wolf
Wolfe
Wolff´ian
wolf´hound
wolf´ish
wolf´ish-ly
Wol´sey
wol´ver-ine´
wolves
wom´an

wom´an-hood
wom´an-ish
wom´an-kind
wom´an-like
wom´an-ly
womb
wom´bat
wom´en
wom´en-folk
won´der
won´dered
won´der-ful
won´der-land
won´der-ment
won´der—work-er
won´drous
won´drous-ly
wont
wood´bine
wood´chuck
wood´cock
wood´craft
wood´cut
wood´cut-ter
wood´ed
wood´en
wood´en-ware
wood´i-er
wood´land
wood´lot
wood´man
wood´peck-er
wood´pile
wood pulp
wood´ruff
wood´shed
woods´man
Wood´stock
woods´y
wood´work
wood´y
woo´er
woof
woof´er
wool´en
wool´gath-er-ing
wool´li-ness
wool´ly
wool´sack
Wool´worth
Worces´ter
word´age
word´i-est
word´i-ly
word´ing
word´less
word´ster
Words´worth
word´y
work-abil´i-ty
work´able
work´a-day
work´bas-ket
work´bench
work´book
work´box
work´day
work´er
work´horse
work´house
work´ing
work´ing-man
work´man
work´man-like
work´man-ship
work´men
work´out
work´room
work´shop
work´ta-ble
work´week
world´li-ness
world´ling
world´ly
world´ly—wise
world´wide´
worm´hole
worm´wood
worm´y
worn—out
wor´ried
wor´ri-ment
wor´ri-some
wor´ry
wor´ry-ing
wors´en
wor´ship
wor´shiped
wor´ship-er
wor´ship-ful
wor´ship-ing
worst´ed
wor´sted
wor´thi-ly
wor´thi-ness
worth´less
worth´while´
wor´thy
would
wound
wound´ed
wo´ven
wrack
wraith
wran´gle
wran´gler
wran´gling
wrap´per
wrap´ping
wrath´ful
wrath´i-ly
wreak
wreath
wreathe
wreath´ing
wreck
wreck´age
wreck´er
wrench
wrest
wres´tle
wres´tler
wres´tling
wretch
wretch´ed
wretch´ed-ness
wrig´gle
wrig´gler
wrig´gly
wright
wring´er
wring´ing
wrin´kle
wrin´kled
wrin´kling
wrin´kly
wrist

wrist´band
wrist´let
wrist´lock
wrist pin
wrist´watch
write´—off
writ´er
write´—up
writhe
writhed
writh´er
writh´ing
writ´ing
writ´ten
wrong
wrong´do-er
wrong´do-ing
wrong´ful
wrong´ly
wroth
wrought
wrought iron
wry´ly
Wurt´tem-berg
Wy´an-dotte
Wyc´liffe
Wy´lie
Wy-o´ming

X

xan´the-nyl
xan´thine
Xan-thip´pe
xan´tho-gen-ate
xan-tho-ma-to´sis
xan´thom´a-tous
xan-thom´e-ter
xan´thous
xan-thox-y-le´tin
xan-thy´drol
Xav´i-er
xe´bec
xe´nia
xe´nial
xe-nog´a-my
xen´o-gen´e-sis
xen´o-ge-net´ic
xen´o-lith
xe´non
xeno-pho´bia
xeno-pho´bic
Xen´o-phon
xe´ric
xer´o-graph´ic
xe-rog´ra-phy
xe´ro-phyte
xe´ro-phyt´ic
xe´ro-sere
xe-ro´sis
Xer´xes
x ray
xy´lem
xy´lene
xy´le-nol
xy´le-nyl
xy´lic
xy´lo-graph´ic
xy-log´ra-phy
xy´loid
xy-lol´o-gy
xy-lom´e-ter
xy-loph´a-gous
xy´lo-phone
xy´lo-phon-ist
xy´lo-side
xy-lot´o-my
xy´lo-yl
xy´lu-lose
xy´lyl-ene
Xy´ris

Y

yacht
yacht´ing
yachts´man
Yah´weh
yak
Yak´i-ma
yam
Yang´tze´
Yan´kee
yap´ping
Ya´qui
yard´age
yard´arm
yard´stick
yar´row
yaw´ing
yawl
yaw´me-ter
yawn
yawn´ing-ly
year´book
year´ling
year´long
year´ly
yearn
yearn´ing
yeast
yeast´i-ness
yeast-y
yel´low
yel´low-bird
yel´low fe´ver
yel´low-fin
yel´low-ish
yel´low jack-et
Yel´low-stone
yelp´er
Yem´en
yeo´man
yeo´man-ry
yes´ter-day
yes´ter-morn
yes´ter-year
yew
Yid´dish
yield
yield´able
yield´ing
yip´ping
yo´del
yo´del-er
yo´del-ing
yo´ga
yo´gi
yo´gurt
yoke
yo´kel
Yo´ko-ha´ma
yolk
Yom Kip´pur
yon´der
Yon´kers
yore

York´shire
Yo-sem´i-te
young
young´ber-ry
young´ish
young´ling
young´ster
Youngs´town
youn´ker
your-self´
youth´ful
youth´ful-ly
Yo´—Yo
yt-ter´bi-um
yt-ter´bous
yt-trif´er-ous
yt´tri-um
Yu´ca-tan´
yuc´ca
Yu-go-slav´ia
Yu´kon
Yule
Yule´tide

Z

Zach-a-ri´ah
Zaire
Zam´bia
za´ny
Zan´zi-bar´
Zea´land
zeal´ot
zeal´ot-ry
zeal´ous
Zeb´e-dee
ze´bra
ze´bu
Zech-a-ri´ah
ze´nith
Ze´no
ze´o-lite
ze-ol´i-tize
zeph´yr
zeph´yr-e´an
Zep´pe-lin
ze´ro
ze´roes
ze´ro-ize
ze´ros
zest
zest´ful
zig´zag
zig´zag-ging
Zim-ba´bwe
zinc
zinc´ate
zinc´ic
zinc´i-fy
Zin´fan-del
zin´nia
Zi´on
Zi´on-ism
Zi´on-ist
zip´per
zip´py
zir´con
zir´con-ate
zir-co´ni-um
zith´er
zo´di-ac
zo-di´a-cal
zom´bi
zon´al
zoned
zon´ing
zo-og´a-my
zo´o-ge´o-graph´ic
zo´o-ge-og´ra-phy
zo-og´ra-pher
zo-og´ra-phy
zo-ol´a-ter
zo-o-log´i-cal
zo-ol´o-gist
zo-ol´o-gy
zo-om´e-ter
zo´o-spo-ran´gi-um
zo´o-spore
Zo´ro-as-ter
Zo´ro-as´tri-an
Zo-ys´ia
zuc-chi´ni
Zu´lu
Zu´ñi
zun´yite
Zu´rich
zwie´back
Zwing´li
Zwing´li-an-ism
zy´go-mat´ic
zy´gote
zy-got´ic
zy-mol´o-gy
zy´mo-plas´tic
zy´mos-then´ic
zy-mot´ic
zy´mur-gy

WEBSTER'S DICTIONARY

WEBSTER'S DICTIONARY

PMC Publishing Company, Inc.

PMC Publishing Company, Inc.
118 East 28 Street
New York, New York 10016

ISBN: 1-881275-00-0

A

ab´a-cus *n.* device for counting
a-ban´don *vt.* give up; desert
a-base´ *vt.* humble; degrade; debase
a-bate´ *vi.* & *vt.* lessen
ab´at-toir *n.* slaughter house
ab´bey *n.* (**ab´beys**) monastery or nunnery
ab´bot *n.* superior of an abbey; **ab´-bess** *n. fem.*
ab-bre´vi-ate *vt.* abridge; shorten; **ab-bre´vi-a´tion** *n.* shortening; part of a word put for a whole
ab´di-cate *vi.* & *vt.* renounce; **ab´di-ca´tion** *n.*
ab-do´men *n.* belly
ab-duct´ *vt.* kidnap; **ab-duc´tion** *n.*; **ab-duc´tor** *n.*
ab´er-ra´tion *n.* mental derangement
a-bey´ance *n.* state of suspension
ab-hor´ *vt.* loathe
a-bide´ *vt.* wait for, endure; *vi.* dwell
a-bil´i-ty *n.* power, faculty
ab´ject *a.* mean; contemptible
ab-jure´ *vt.* renounce solemnly; **ab-ju-ra´tion** *n.*
ab-lu´tion *n.* act of washing
ab´ne-ga´tion *n.* denial; renunciation
ab-nor´mal *a.* not normal or according to rule
a-bode´ *n.* dwelling place
a-bol´ish *vt.* annul; **ab´o-li´tion** *n.*
a-bom´i-na-ble *a.* hateful; **a-bom´-in-a-bly** *adv.*
ab´o-rig´i-nal *a.* primitive
ab´o-rig´i-nes *n. pl.* first inhabitants
a-bor´tion *n.* premature birth, esp. if voluntarily brought about; miscarriage of plans; **a-bor´tive** *a.*
a-bound´ *vi.* be plentiful, in great abundance
a-brade´ *vt.* scrape or wear away; **a-bra´sion** *n.*
a-bridge´ *vt.* shorten; **a-bridg´ment** *n.*
a-broad´ *adv.* at large; in foreign lands
ab´ro-gate´ *vt.* repeal; annul; **ab´ro-ga´tion** *n.*
a-brupt´ *a.* sudden; unexpected; steep
ab-scond´ *vi.* go away secretly to avoid legal action
ab´sence *n.* being away; want, lack
ab-sent´ *vt.* keep oneself away
ab´sent *a.* not present; **ab´sen-tee´** *n.*; **ab´sen-tee´ism** *n.* frequent absence of workers from job
ab´so-lute *a.* complete; perfect; **zero** *n.* 459.6° F. below zero; **ab´so-lute´ly** *adv.*
ab-solve´ *vt.* acquit; remit sin; pardon
ab-sorb´ *vt.* suck in; swallow up; engage wholly; **ab-sorp´tion** *n.*
ab-stain´ *vi.* refrain (from)
ab-ste´mi-ous *a.* temperate
ab´sti-nence *n.* abstaining; **ab´sti-nent** *a.*
ab-stract´ *vt.* take away, separate; epitomize
ab´stract *n.* abridgment; essence; **abstract art** *n.* art making use of non-pictorial designs
ab-struse´ *a.* difficult to understand
ab-surd´ *a.* irrational
a-bun´dance *n.* overflowing, plenty; **a-bun´dant** *a.*
a-buse´ *n.* ill use, misapplication, contumely; **a-bu´sive** *a.*
a-buse´ *vt.* use wrongly
a-bys´mal *a.* bottomless
a-byss´ *n.* bottomless gulf; vast depth
ac´a-dem´ic *a.* scholastic
a-cad´e-my *n.* preparatory school

ac-cede´ *vi.* agree, assent to
ac-cel´er-ate *vt.* increase the speed of; *vi.* move more rapidly; **ac-cel´er-a´tion** *n.*
ac-cel´er-a´tor *n.* pedal which controls speed of car by regulating flow of gasoline
ac´cent *n.* stress; *vt.* emphasize
ac-cen´tu.ate *vt.* give prominence to
ac-cept´ *vt.* receive; agree to
ac-cept´a-ble *a.* agreeable; **ac-cept´a-bil´i-ty** *n.*
ac´cess *n.* admission, admittance; approach to; passage
ac-ces´si-ble *a.* permitting access
ac-ces´so-ry *n.* abettor; *a.* aiding, contributing
ac´ci-dent *n.* unexpected occurrence; **ac´ci-dent´al** *a.*
ac-claim´ *vt.* applaud; shout applause; *n.* applause
ac´cla-ma´tion *n.* applause
ac´cli-mate, ac-cli´ma-tize´ *vt.* grow used to a new climate
ac-cliv´i-ty *n.* upward slope
ac-com´mo-date´ *vt.* supply, furnish; adapt; **ac-com´mo-da´tion** *n.*
ac-com´pa-ny *vt.* go with; play or sing an accompaniment; **ac-com´-pa-ni-ment** *n.*; **ac-com´pa-nist** *n.*
ac-com´plice *n.* associate in crime; confederate
ac-com´plish *vt.* perform; fulfill; *a.* complete in acquirements; polished
ac-cord´ *vt.* grant; *vi.* agree; harmonize; *n.* harmony, agreement; spontaneous action
ac-count´ *vt.* compute; *vi.* assign a reason (for); *n.* computation; statement; value; behalf; **ac-count-a-bil´i-ty** *n.*
ac-count´ing *n.* settlement; statement of accounts
ac-cre´tion *n.* growth; increase
ac-crue´ *vi.* come to; be added to
ac-cu´mu-late *vi.* & *vt.* amass; **ac-cu´mu-la´tion** *n.*; **ac-cu´mu-la-tive** *a.*
ac´cu-ra-cy *n.* correctness; exactness; accurateness
ac´cu-rate *a.* very exact
ac-cuse´ *vt.* bring a charge against; **ac´cu-sa´tion** *n.*
a-cer´bi-ty *n.* sourness; barshness
ac´e-tate´ *n.* a salt or ester of acetic acid, used in making cellulosic fibers and plastics
a-cet´y-lene *n.* gas used in welding
a-chieve´ *vt.* accomplish
acid *a.* sharp; sour; *n.* substance that will unite with a base to form a salt; **a-cid´i-ty** *n.*
ac-knowl´edge *vt.* admit; certify; **ac-knowl´edg-ment** *n.* recognition
acme *n.* highest point; perfection; climax
ac´o-lyte *n.* minor order in R.C. priesthood; an assistant
a-cous´tics *n. sg. & pl.* science of sounds
ac-quaint´ *vt.* cause one to know; inform
ac´qui-esce´ *vi.* assent to; accept; **ac´qui-es´cence** *n.*
ac-quire´ *vt.* get; gain
ac´qui-si´tion *n.* anything gained or acquired
ac-quis´i-tive *a.* eager to acquire
ac-quit´ *n.* pronounce innocent; discharge a trust
acre *n.* tract of land containing 4,840 square yards
ac´rid *a.* biting to the taste; pungent; **a-crid´i-ty** *n.*
ac´ri-mo-ny *n.* bitterness; **ac´ri-mo´ni-ous** *a.*
ac´ro-bat *n.* trapeze performer; **ac´ro-bat´ic** *a.*
a-cryl´ic *a.* pertaining to acrylic acid or one of its uses, as in fibers and

plastics

ACTH *n.* adrenocorticotropic hormone, used in treating arthritis and other diseases

ac´tion *n.* state or process of acting; thing done; law suit

ac´ti-vate *vt.* make active; purify sewage

ac´tive *a.* energetic; operative; **ac-tiv´i-ty** *n.*

ac´tor *n.* one who acts; stage-player; **ac´tress** *n. fem.*

ac´tu-al *a.* real; existing in fact; **ac´-tu-al´i-ty** *n.*

ac´tu-ary *n.* one skilled in insurance computations

ac´tu-ate *vt.* cause to act

a-cu´men *n.* acuteness of mind

a-cute´ *a.* sharp; keen; shrill; penetrating; **acute angle** *n.* angle less than 90º

ad´age *n.* old saying

ad´a-mant *a.* unyielding

a-dapt´ *vt.* adjust; accommodate

ad´dict *n.* one given over to a habit or drug; **ad-dic´tion** *n.*

ad-di´tion *n.* act of adding

ad-dress´ *vt.* speak or write to; discourse; *n.* formal speech; one´s name and place of residence, etc.; bearing

ad-duce´ *vt.* bring forward; cite; **ad-duc´i-ble** *a.*

ad´e-noids *n. pl.* glandular tissues between nose and throat

a-dept´ *a.* proficient; *n.* one fully skilled

ad´e-quate *a.* equal to the task; **ad´-e-qua-cy** *n.*

ad-here´ *vi.* stick (to); **ad-her´ence** *n.*; **ad-her´-ent** *n.*

ad-he´sion *n.* act of adhering; **ad-he´sive** *a.*

a-dieu´ *inter.* (**a-dieus´**, **a-dieux´**) goodbye, farewell; *n.*

ad-ja´cent *a.* close by; contiguous

ad´jec-tive *n.* word (like *fair/fairer/fairest*) used to modify a noun, etc.

ad-join´ *vi. & vt.* be next to

ad-journ´ *vi. & vt.* close a meeting

ad´junct *n.* something united or joined

ad-jure´ *vt.* charge on oath; **ad´ju-ra´tion** *n.*

ad-just´ *vt.* arrange properly

ad´ju-tant *n.* military officer who assists the commanding officer

ad´lib´ *vi. & vt.* speak without a script; improvise

ad-min´is-ter *vt.* manage; dispense; tender (an oath); give, as medicine; *vi.* act as administrator

ad-min´is-tra´tion *n.* act of administering; power or party that administers; **ad-min´is-tra´tive** *a.*; **ad-min´is-tra´tor** *n.*; **ad-min´is-tra´trix** *n. fem.*

ad´mi-ra-ble *a.* worthy of being admired

ad´mi-ral *n.* naval officer of highest rank

ad-mire´ *vt.* regard, esteem; **ad-mir´er** *n.*

ad-mis´si-ble *a.* allowable; **ad-mis´-si-bil´i-ty** *n.*

ad-mis´sion *n.* leave to enter; price paid for entrance; acknowledgement

ad-mit´ *vt.* permit to enter; concede

ad-mon´ish *vt.* warn

ad´mo-ni´tion *n.* reproof; **ad-mon´i-to´ry** *a.*

a-dopt´ *vt.* receive or assume as one's own; **a-dop´tion** *n.*

a-dor´a-ble *a.* worthy of love; delightful

a-dore´ *vt.* worship; love; **ad´o-ra´-tion** *n.*

a-dorn´ *vt.* decorate, embellish

ad-ren´al-ine *n.* hormone secreted

by adrenal glands

a-droit´ *a.* dexterous

ad´u-la´tion *n.* flattery

a-dult´ *a.* mature; *n.* grown person

a-dul´ter-ate´ *vt.* make impure by admixture; **a-dul´ter-a´tion** *n.*

a-dul´ter-y *n.* infidelity in marriage

ad-vance´ *n.* progress; rise; loan; *vi.* progress; rise in rank or value, etc.; *vt.* put or move forward; promote; supply; loan

ad-van´tage *n.* superiority; gain; benefit; **ad´van-ta´geous** *a.*

ad-ven´ture *n.* enterprise of hazard; *vi.* attempt, dare; *vt.* risk, hazard

ad´verb´ *n.* word (like *quickly, slowly*) said to qualify a verb, adjective, or other adverb

ad´ver-sar´y *n.* opponent

ad´verse *a.* opposing; **ad-verse´ly** *adv.*; **ad-ver´si-ty** *n.* misfortune

ad´ver-tise´, ad´ver-tize´ *vi.* publish an advertisement; *vt.* give public notice of

ad-vice´ *n.* counsel; information, intelligence

ad-vis´a-ble *a.* expedient

ad-vise´ *vi.* consult with; *vt.* counsel; communicate notice to

ad´vo-cate *n.* one who pleads the cause of another; *vt.* defend, plead; **ad´vo-ca-cy** *n.*

a-e´re-al *a.* having to do with the air; *n.* antenna used in radio or TV

aer´o-dy-nam´ics *n.* part of physics which treats of air in motion

aer´o-nau´tics *n.* study of aviation

aer´o-sol´ bomb´ *n.* container holding liquid under pressure to be released as spray or foam

aer´o-space´ *a.* pertaining to technology and military uses of atmosphere and near outer space

aes-thet´ic *a.* having a sense of the beautiful; pertaining to the fine arts

af´fa-ble a. courteous, amiable; **af´-fa-bil´i-ty** *n.*

af-fair´ *n.* business; dispute

af-fect´ *vt.* act upon, change; touch the feelings of; make pretense of; be partial to; **af´fec-ta´tion** *n.* pretense

af-fec´tion *n.* feeling; fondness; love

af´fi-da´vit *n.* a sworn written declaration

af-fil´i-ate´ *vi.* join or associate (with); **af-fil´i-a´tion** *n.*

af-fin´i-ty *n.* relationship; chemical attraction

af-firm´ *vt.* assert, declare; **af´fir-ma´tion** *n.*

af-firm´a-tive *a.* ratifying; opposed to *negative*

af-flict´ *vt.* oppress; pain; **af-flic´-tion** *n.* mental or bodily distress

af´flu-ent *a.* wealthy

af-ford´ *vt.* be able to give

af-front´ *n.* contemptuous treatment; *vt.* insult

a-fraid´ *a.* struck with fear

Af´ro *n.* rounded hairdo patterned on an African style

Af´ro-A-mer´i-can *n.* American Negro; *a.*

aft´er-burn´er *n.* device in jet engine to ignite unburned gas

age´ism *n.* belief that one age group is superior to another

a´gen-cy *n.* operation, means; office

a-gen´da *n.* details or programs of business to be carried out

a´gent *n.* person or thing that acts; one who acts for another; accredited official

ag-glom´er-ate´ *vi.* & *vt.* make or grow into a mass; *a.*; *n.*

ag´gran-dize *vt.* make or become great or greater; **ag-gran´dize-ment** *n.*

ag´gra-vate´ *vt.* provoke; make worse; **ag´gra-va´tion** *n.*
ag´gre-gate´ *vi. & vt.* collect, accumulate; *a.* pertaining to any sum formed from parts; *n.* sum total; **ag´gre-ga´tion** *n.*
ag-gres´sion *n.* first act of hostility or injury; **ag-gres´sive** *a.*; **ag-gres´sor** *n.*
a-ghast´ *a.* horrified
ag´ile *a.* nimble; **a-gil´i-ty** *n.*
ag´i-tate´ *vi.* rouse public interest; *vt.* disturb; **ag´i-ta´tion** *n.*; **ag´i-ta´tor** *n.*
ag´o-ny *n.* extreme pain
a-gree´ *vi.* be of one mind; match, correspond; promise
ag´ri-cul´ture *n.* science of cultivating the land
aid *n.* assistance; helper; *vi. & vt.* help
AIDS *n.* Acquired Immune Deficiency Syndrome, viral disease which attacks the body´s immune system, rendering it unable to fight cancer, pneumonia, and a variety of other diseases
ail *vi. & vt.* affect with pain or uneasiness
aim *vi. & vt.* point, as a firearm; strive; *n.* act of aiming; purpose, design
air *n.* atmosphere; tune; manner; *vt.* ventilate
air´borne´ *a.* carried by air; in the air, flying
air´ brake´ *n.* brake controlled by air
air´ con-di´tion-ing *n.* process of controlling temperature of air
air´craft´ *n.* flying machine
air´craft´ car´ri-er *n.* ship for carrying airplanes, which take off from or land on its deck
air´frame´ *n.* structural framework of an aircraft, excluding the engine
air´freight´ *n.* freight shipped by airplane
air´lift´ *n.* movement of supplies by air; *vt.*
air´mail´ *n.* mail sent by airplane; *vt.*; *a.*
air´plane´ *n.* heavier than air flying machine
air´port´ *n.* flying field
air´space´ *n.* space above a nation´s territory and subject to its control
aisle *n.* passageway between seats or counters
al´a-bas´ter *n.* kind of gypsum
à la carte´ *a.* (foods) ordered individually
a-lac´ri-ty *n.* briskness; readiness
à la mode´ *a.* with ice cream
a-larm´ *n.* notice of danger; contrivance to warn; *vt.* give notice of danger; terrify
al´ba-tross´ *n.* sea bird of the petrel family
al-bu´men *n.* white of eggs; **al-bu´mi-nous** *a.*
al´cove *n.* a recess
a-lert´ *a.* watchful
al´gae *n. pl.* seaweed
al´ge-bra *n.* mathematical science which uses a highly systematized notation
a´li-as *n.* assumed name
al´i-bi *n.* plea that the accused was elsewhere at time of crime
al´i-en *a.* foreign; *n.* foreigner
al´i-en-ate´ *vt.* estrange, transfer; **al´i-en-a´tion** n.
a-light´ *a.* lighted; *vi.* dismount, descend
a-lign´ *vi. & vt.* adjust in a line
al´i-ment *n.* nourishment
al´ka-li´ *n.* sustance which neutralizes acids; **al´ka-loid´** n. alkaline substance in plants, etc.

al-lay´ *vt.* calm, soften
al´le-ga´tion *n.* affirmation, assertion
al-lege´ *vt.* affirm; aver
al-le´giance *n.* loyalty
al´le-go´ry *n.*symbolic representation in literature
al´ler-gy *n.* unusual sensitiveness to certain foods, pollens, etc.; **al-ler´gic** *a.*
al-le´vi-ate´ *vt.* ease, lessen; **al-le´vi-a´tion** *n.*
al´ley *n.* narrow passage
al-li´ance *n.* union by treaty or marriage
al´li-ga´tor *n.* American crocodile; *sl.* jazz or swing enthusiast
al-lit´er-a´tion *n.* words beginning with the same letter
al´lo-ca´tion *n.* distribution, apportionment
al-lot´ *vt.* parcel; bestow by lot
all´—out´ a. wholehearted, intense
al-low´ *vi.* & *vt.* permit; admit
al´loy *n.* fusion of metais; *vt.* debase by mixing
all´—time´ *a.* continuing, enduring; record-breaking
al-lude´ *vi.* refer to
al-lure´ *vt.* entice, tempt
al-lu´sion *n.* indirect reference; **al-lu´sive** *a.*
al-lu´vi-um *n.* earth deposited by water; **al-lu´vi-al** *a.*
al´ly *n.* person or state allied with another; *vt.* unite
al´ma-nac *n.* calendar and book of information
al´mond *n.* fruit of the almond tree
alms *n. pl.* gifts to the poor
a-loof´ *adv.* apart, away from
al´pha-bet´ *n.* letters of a written language; **al´pha-bet´ic** *a.*
al´pha ray´ *n.* stream of helium nuclei
al´tar *n.* place for sacred offerings
al´ter *vi.* & *vt.* change, modify
alter-cate´ *vi.* contend in words; **al´ter-ca´tion** *n.*
al´ter-nate *a.* reciprocal; *n.* that which occurs by turns; substitute; *vi* & *vt.* do or happen by turns; **al´ter-na´tion** *n.*
al-ter´na-tive *a.* offering a choice; *n.* choice between two things
al-tim´e-ter *n.* instrument for measuring altitude
al´ti-tude´ *n.* height
al´to´ *n.* part sung by the lowest female voices
al´to-geth´er *adv.* wholly
al´tru-ism *n.* selflessness; **al´tru-ist** *n.*
a-lu´mi-num´ *n.* a light metallic element
a-lum´nus *n. masc.* **(a-lum´ni)** college graduate; **a-lum´na (a-lum´nae)** *n. fem.*
A.M., (amplitude modulation) *n.* a means of radio broadcasting
a-mal´gam *n.* combination of mercury and other metal; mixture
a-man´u-en´sis *n.* **(a-man´u-en´ses)** secretary
am´a-ranth´ *n.* imaginary plant with enduring flowers
am´a-teur´ *n.* a nonprofessional
a-maze´ *vt.* confound with surprise; bewilder
am-bas´sa-dor *n.* diplomat of highest rank
am´ber-gris´ *n.* fragrant substance in the sperm whale
am´bi-dex´trous *a.* using both hands equally well
am-big´u-ous *a.* doubtful, not clear; **am´bi-gu´i-ty** *n.*
am-bi´tion *n.* desire for anything; **am-bi´tious** *a.*
am´bu-lance *n.* vehicle for trans-

porting the sick
am´bu-la-to´ry *a.* walking or moving around
am´bus-cade´ *n.* ambush
am´bush *vt.* lie in wait for; *n.* surprise attack
a-mel´i-o-rate´ *vi.* & *vt.* make or grow better
a-men´a-ble *a.* answerable; obedient
a-mend´ *vi.* & *vt.* correct, change, add to
a-men´i-ty *n.* social pleasantness
am´e-thyst *n.* bluish-violet kind of quartz; bluish-violet color
a´mi-a-ble *a.* kindly, pleasing; **a´mi-a-bil´i-ty** *n.*
am´i-ca-ble *a.* friendly
a-mi´no ac´id *n.* organic acid containing the amino group NH_2 part of the protein molecule
a-miss´ *a.* wrong, in error; *adv.* in faulty manner
am´i-ty *n.* friendship; good will
am´me-ter *n.* instrument fro measuring strength of electric current
am-mo´ni-a *n.* compound of nitrogen and hydrogen
am´mu-ni´tion *n.* military stores (bullets, etc.); material for debate
am-ne´si-a *n.* loss of memory
am´nes-ty *n.* pardon
a-mount´ *n.* whole sum, effect; *vi.* result
am´pere *n.* unit for measuring the strength of electric current.
am-phib´i-ous *a.* living both in water and on land
am´phi-the´a-ter *n.* theater with seats all around
am´ple *a.* abundant
am´pli-fi´er *n.* apparatus for strengthening electrical impulses
am´pli-fy *vi.*expand, dilate; *vt.* add to; **am´pli-fi-ca´tion** *n.*; **am´pli-tude´** *n.* extent, largeness
am´pu-tate´ *vt.* cut off; **am´pu-ta´-tion** *n.*
Am´trak *n.* U.S. public corporation providing railroad service
am´u-let *n.* a charm
a-muse´ *vt.* entertain
a-nach´ro-nis´m *n.* mistake in chronology
an´a-gram´ *n.* word or phrase formed by transposing the letters of another
a-nal´o-gy *n.* illustration by comparison; **a-nal´o-gous** *a.* similar
a-nal´y-sis *n.* separating a thing into parts; **an´a-lyt´ic** *a.*; **an´a-lyze´** *vt.*
an´arch-y *n.* society without government; **an´arch-ist** *n.*
a-nat´o-my *n.* bodily structure
an´ces-tor *n.* forebear, progenitor; **an´ces-try** *n.*
an´chor *n.* hooked iron instrument that holds a ship; anything that gives stability; *vi.* & *vt.* fasten
an´cho-vy *n.* herring-like fish
an´cient *a.* belonging to former times; very old
an-drog´y-nous *a.* having both male and female characteristics; **an-drog´y-ny** *n.*
an´ec-dote´ *n.* jest or short story
a-ne´mi-a *n.* deficiency in red corpuscles or hemoglobin in blood
a-nem´o-ne *n.* plant of the crowfoot family
an´es-the´si-a *n.* loss of feeling
an´es-the´si-ol-o-gy *n.* science related to anesthesia and its effects
an´es-thet´ic *n.* drug producing anesthesia
an´gel *n.* divine messenger; ministering spirit; financial backer
an´ger *n.* rage; *vt.* make angry
an-gi´na pec´to-ris *n.* heart disease characterized by severe pains
an´gle *n.* any figure made by two

lines; ulterior motive; stratagem
an´gry *a.* excited with anger
an´guish *n.* mental or physical agony
an´gu-lar *a.* having angles; awkward
an´i-line *n.* substance used in dyeing
an´i-mal *n.* a living, moving being
an´i-mate *a.* possessing life; *vt.* give life to; **an´i-ma´tion** *n.*
an´i-mos´i-ty *n.* bitter hatred; active enmity
an´ise *n.* plant bearing aromatic seeds
an´kle *n.* joint connecting the foot and the leg
an´nals *n. pl.* historical records
an-nex´ *vt.* add; connect; unite; **an´nex-a´tion** *n.*
an-ni´hi-late *vt.* destroy; **an-ni´hi-la´tion** *n.*
an´ni-ver´sa-ry *n.* day on which an event happened in some previous year
an´no-tate´ *vt.* make notes upon
an-nounce´ *vt.* give notice of
an-noy´ *vt.* trouble, vex, irritate
an´nu-al *a.* yearly
an-nu´i-ty *n.* sum of money payable yearly
an-nul´ *vt.* abolish
an´ode *n.* positive electrode
an´o-dyne´ *n.* medicine that allays pain
a-noint´ *vt.* spread oil or ointment on; consecrate
a-nom´a-ly *n.* irregularity; **a-nom´a-lous** *a.*
a-non´y-mous *a.* without the name of the author
an´swer *n.* reply; solution; *vi.* reply; act in response; *vt.* reply; satisfy, solve; refute
an-tag´o-nism *n.* opposition; **an-tag´o-nize´** *vt.*
ant´arc´tic *a.* relating to the south polar regions; *n.*
an´te-ced´ent *a.* going before, prior; *n.* noun or pronoun to which a relative pronoun refers
an´te-lope´ *n.* graceful quadruped similar to the deer
an´te-me-rid´i-an *a.* before midday
an-ten´na *n.* (**an-ten´na-e**) insect´s feeler; (**an-ten´nas**) wire or wires used in radio or TV for transmitting or receiving
an-te´ri-or *a.* in front; prior
an´ther *n.* top of stamen containing the pollen in a flower
an´thra-cite´ *n.* kind of hard coal
an´thro-pol´o-gy *n.* study of man
an´ti-air´craft´ *n.* artillery used for defense against enemy aircraft
an´ti-bi-ot´ic *n.* substance derived from bacteria or molds which kills other microorganisms
an´ti-bod´y *n.* natural defense against invading bodies in blood, etc.
an´tic *n.* caper
an-tic´i-pate´ *vt.* forestall; foresee; be prepared for; **an-tic´i-pa´tion** *n.*
an´ti-cli´max *n.* a second and ineffective climax
an´ti-dote´ *n.* anything that counteracts a poison
an´ti-his´ta-mine´ *n.* drug used to treat cold syptoms and some allergies
an´ti-knock´ *n.* chemical added to gasoline to reduce noise; *a.*
an´ti-mat´ter *n.* particles composed of negative protons and positive electrons
an´ti-mis´sile *a.* related to defense against missiles; *n.* antimissile weapon
an-tip´a-thy *n.* aversion
an´ti-quat´ed *a.* grown old or out of

fashion
an-tique´ *a.* old-fashioned; *n.* relic
an-tiq´ui-ty *n.* ancient time; relic
an´ti-sep´tic *n.* drug which destroys germs
an-tith´e-sis *n.* words or thoughts set in contrast to each other
an´ti-tox´in *n.* serum for inoculation against disease
an´to-nym´ *n.* word having opposite meaning to another word
a´nus *n.* terminal opening of alimentary canal
anxious *a.* in suspense; desirous; **anx-i´e-ty** *n.*
a-part´heid *n.* doctrine of racial segregation in the Union of South Africa
a-part´ment *n.* suite of rooms
ap´a-thy *n.* indifference; **ap´a-thet´-ic** *a.*
ape *n.* large tailless monkey with human-like teeth; silly imitator; *vt.* imitate servilely; mimic
ap´er-ture´ *n.* opening, hole
a´pex *n.* highest point
aph´o-ris´m *n.* brief pithy saying
a´pi-ar´y *n.* place where bees are kept
a-poc´a-lypse´ *n.*Revelation of St. John; any revelation
a-poc´ry-phal´ *a.* not genuine; dubious
a-pol´o-get´ic *a.* excusing
a-pol´o-gy´ *n.* defense, justification; **a-pol´o-gist´** *n.*; **a-pol´o-gize´** *vi.*
ap´o-plex´y *n.* disease caused by bursting of blood vessel in brain; **ap´o-plec´tic** *a.*
a-pos´ta-sy *n.* abandonment of one´s principles; **a-pos´tate** *n.*
a-pos´tle *n.* one of the twelve sent by Christ to preach the gospel; any devoted advocate
a-pos´tro-phe´ *n.* mark used to show the omission of a letter or to indicate the possessive case
ap´o-thegm´ *n.* short pithy sentence
ap-pall´, ap-pal´ *vt.* dismay, cause apprehension
ap´pa-ra´tus *n.* instrument or equipment
ap-par´el *n.* raiment
ap-par´ent *a.* evident; seeming
ap-pa-ri´tion *n.* specter
ap-peal´ *vi.* call for aid or sympathy; *vt.* remove a case to a higher court; *n.* act of appealing
ap-pear´ *vi.* become visible; be evident
ap-pease´ *vt.* pacify; **ap-pease´ment** *n.*
ap-pel´lant *n.* one who appeals
ap´pel-la´tion *n.* name, title
ap-pend´ *vt.* attach; **ap-pen´dix**
ap-pen´di-ci´tis *n.* inflammation of the vermiform appendix
ap´per-tain´ *vi.* belong, relate to
ap´pe-tite´ *n.* natural desire, esp. for food; **ap´pe-tiz´er** *n.*; **ap´pe-tiz´ing** *a.*
ap-plaud´ *vi.* & *vt.* praise, express approval; **ap-plause´** *n.*
ap-pli´ance *n.* apparatus, esp. electrical
ap´pli-ca-ble *a.* suitable
ap´pli-cant *n.* one who applies; candidate
ap-ply´ *vi.* solicit; *vt.* lay on; employ; devote
ap-point´ *vt.* assign; equip
ap-por´tion *vt.* divide in shares
ap-praise´ *vt.* value; **ap-prais´al** *n.*
ap-pre´ci-a-ble *a.* big enough to be estimated
ap-pre´ci-ate *vt.* value; **ap-pre´ci-a´-tion** *n.*
ap´pre-hend´ *vt.* take hold of; comprehend; expect with fear; **ap´pre-hen´sion** *n.*

ap-pren´tice *n.* learner, beginner; one learning a trade
ap-prise´ *vt.* give notice, inform
ap-proach´ *vi.* draw near to; *vt.* come near; make advances; *n.* act of drawing near; access, avenue
ap´pro-ba´tion *n.* commendation
ap-pro´pri-ate´ *vt.* take to oneself; set apart; *a.* suitable; peculiar; **ap-pro´pri-a´tion** *n.*
ap-prov´al *n.* opinion or decision in favor of something
ap-prove´ *vi.* express or feel approbation; *vt.* commend; sanction; **ap-prov´al** *n.*
ap-prox´i-mate *a.* near; *vt.* come near
ap-pur´te-nance´ *n.* appliance; adjunct; that which appertains to a thing
ap´ro-pos´ *a.* pertinent; *adv.* by the way; appropriately; with regard to
apt *a.* pertinent; able; **ap´ti-tude** *n.*
aq´ua-cade´ *n.* elaborate swimming or diving exhibit
aq´ua-lung´ *n.* small oxygen tank for underwater swimming
a-quar´i-um *n.* placewhere water plants or animals are kept
aq´ue-duct´ *n.* artificial channel for conveying water
a´que-ous *a.* watery
Ar´a-bic *n.* prominent language of the Middle East; **Arabic numerals** the figures 1, 2, 3, 4, 5, 6, 7, 8, 9, 0
ar´bi-ter *n.* judge
ar´bi-trar´y *a.* unreasoned; despotic
ar´bi-trate´ *vi.* & *vt.* settle by arbitration; **ar´bi-tra´tion** *n.* submitting disputes to a disinterested party; **ar´bi-tra´tor** *n.* judge
ar´bor *n.* enclosed space covered with vines
arc *n.* segment of a circle; **arc light** electric light formed by passing current between two carbon points
ar-cade´ *n.* arched gallery, sometimes with shops on both sides
arch *n.* curved structure resting on supports; *vi.* be shaped like a curve; *vt.* form into a curve; *a.* roguish
ar-cha´ic *a.* ancient; **ar´cha-ism** *n.* obsolete expression
ar´che-ol´o-gy *n.* study of antiquities
ar´chi-pel´a-go *n.* sea abounding in small islands
ar´chi-tect´ *n.* one who designs buildings; **ar´chi-tec´ture** *n.*
ar´chives´ *n. pl.* place where public records are kept; records
arc´tic *a.* pertaining to the polar regions
ar´dent *a.* intense, eager
ar´dor *n.* warmth of feeling
ar´du-ous *a.* difficult
a´re-a *n.* plain surface; range; region
a-re´na *n.* place for contest
ar´gue *vi.* dispute; *vt.* prove by argument
ar´gu-ment *n.* discussion; reason offered as proof; topic, theme; **ar´gu-ment´a-tive** *a.*
ar´id *a.* dry
a-rise´ *vi.* rise, ascend
ar´is-toc´ra-cy *n.* government by nobles; the nobility; wealthy class
a-ris´to-crat´ *n.* member of an aristocracy
a-rith´me-tic´ *n.* science of numbers or computation
arm *n.* upper limb from shoulder to hand; weapon; *vt.* furnish with weapons
ar-ma´da *n.* fleet of warships
ar´ma-ged´don *n.* any last cataclysmic battle
ar´mis-tice *n.* truce
ar´mor *n.* defensive arms or dress;

plating of ships, tanks, etc.; *vt.* put on armor; **ar´mor-y** *n.* place where arms are kept

ar´my *n.* body of armed men trained for war; great number

a-ro´ma *n.* fragrance; **ar´o-mat´ic** *a.*

a-rouse´ *vt.* wake; stir

ar-raign´ *vt.* accuse; call to account in court

ar-range´ *vt.* put in order

ar-ray´ *n.* arrangement or order; rich clothing; *vt.* arrange; deck

ar-rest´ *n.* seizure; *vt.* stop, detain; apprehend by legal warrant

ar-rive´ *vi.* reach; **ar-riv´al** *n.*

ar´ro-gant *a.* haughty; **ar´ro-gance** *n.*

ar´ro-gate *vt.* make undue claims to

ar´row *n.* pointed weapon shot from a bow

ar´se-nal *n.* place where arms and munitions are made or stored

ar´se-nic *n.* poisonous metallic element

arson *n.* crime of willfully burning a building

art *n.* skill, occupation requiring skill; productions of the beautiful

ar-ter´i-o-scle-ro´sis *n.* disease characterized by hardening of the arteries

ar´ter-y *n.* vessel which conveys blood from the heart; any channel of communication

ar´ti-choke´ *n.* edible plant resembling the thistle

ar´ti-cle *n.* separate element; one of the words *a, an, the*

ar-tic´u-late *vi.* formed with joints; distinct; *vi.* pronounce distinctly; *vt.* form with joints; **ar-tic´u-la´-tion** *n.*

ar´ti-fact´ *n.* any article made by human beings

ar´ti-fice *n.* crafty scheme

ar´ti-fi´cial *a.* made by art; not natural

ar-til´ler-y *n.* ordnance, cannon; branch of military using ordnance

ar´ti-san *n.* one skilled in a mechanical art

art´ist *n.* one who practices a fine art; **ar-tis´tic** *a.*

Ar´y-an *n.* Caucasian; Caucasian super-race of Nazi doctrine

as-bes´tos *n.* fibrous, noncombustible mineral

as-cend´ *vi. & vt.* climb or go up; **as-cen´sion** *n.*; **as-cent´** *n.*

as´cer-tain´ *vt.* determine

as-cet´ic *a.* austere

as-cribe´ *vt.* attribute

a-sep´sis *n.* condition of being free from disease germs

a-skance´, a-skant´ *adv.* sideways; with suspicion

a-skew´ *adv.*·awry

a-par´a-gus *n.* plant with tender, edible shoots

as´pect *n.* appearance; position; view

as-per´i-ty *n.* roughness, harshness

as-perse´ *vt.* calumniate, accuse falsely; **as-per´sion** *n.*

as´phalt´ *n.* a bitumen used for paving, etc.

as-phyx´i-a *n.* suspended respiration; suffocation; **as-phyx´i-a´tion** *n.*

as´pic *n.* gelatin mold, often using tomato juice

as´pir-ant *a.* aspiring; *n.* candidate

as´pi-ra´tion *n.* ambition

as-pire´ *vi.* aim at; long for

as´pi-rin *n.* salicylic acetate, used for headaches, colds, etc.

as-sail´ *vt.* assault

as-sas´sin *n.* one who kills by secret assault; **as-sas´si-nate** *vt.*

as-sault´ *n.* attack; *vt.* make an attack upon

as-say´ *vt.* determine the amount of metal in an ore; try

as-sem´ble *vi.* meet; *vt.* call together; collect; fit together; **as-sem´bly** *n.*; **assembly line** *n.* mass assembly of products

as-sent´ *n.* consent; compliance; *vi.* concur

as-sert´ *vt.* affirm; maintain; **as-ser´tion** *n.*

as-sess´ *vt.* tax; value for taxation; **as-ses´sor** *n.*

as´sets *n. pl.* property

as-sid´u-ous *a.* diligent

as-sign´ *vt.* allot; fix, appoint; transfer

as-signment *n.* task, job

as-sim´i-late´ *vt.* absorb; convert into a like substance; *vi.* be absorbed; become similar; **as-sim´i-la´tion** *n.*

as-sist´ *vi.* render help; *vt.* attend; help

as-so´ci-ate´ *vi.* keep company with; *vt.* unite, join; *a.* connected; *n.* partner; **as-so´ci-a´tion** *n.*

as-sort´ *vt.* classify

as-suage´ *vt.* mitigate; appease

as-sume´ *vt.* take upon oneself; take for granted

as-sump´tion *n.* act of assuming; supposition

as-sure´ *vt.* make sure; **as-sur´ance** *n.*

as´ter *n.* plant with star-like flowers of many colors

as´ter-isk *n.* star (*) used as reference mark

asth´ma *n.* disease affecting the respiration

a-stig´ma-tis´m *n.* defect causing blurred vision

as-ton´ish *vt.* stun with surprise or wonder

as´tral *a.* pertaining to the stars

as-trol´o-gy *n.* study of the stars for their supposed influence over human destiny

as´tro-naut´ *n.* explorer of space

as-tron´o-my *n.* science of the heavenly bodies; **as-tron´o-mer** *n.*

as´tro-phys´ics *n.* science dealing with physical properties of stars, planets

as-tute´ *a.* keen; shrewd

a-sy´lum *n.* sanctuary; home for the sick

a´the-ism *n.* disbelief in God; **a´the-ist** *n.*

ath´lete *n.* one skilled in physical exercises; **ath´let´ics** *n.*

at´las *n.* volume of maps

at´mos-phere´ *n.* air surrounding the earth

at´om *n.* smallest particle of any element

a-tom´ic bomb, at´om bomb, A-bomb *n.* weapon whose tremendous power comes from sudden liberation of atomic energy

a-tom´ic en´er-gy *n.* energy liberated by fission or fusion of atoms

at´om-ize´ *vt.* to separate into atoms; to make into a fine spray

a-tone´ *vi.* & *vt.* expiate; make reparation

a-tro´cious *a.* cruel; terrible; **a-troc´i-ty** *n.*

at´ro-phy *vi.* & *vt.* waste away

at-tach´ *vi.* adhere; *vt.* fasten on, connect with; win over; take by legal process

at-tack´ *n.* assault; criticism; abuse; *vi.* make an assault; abuse; *vt.* fall upon with violence

at-tain´ *vi.* come, arrive; *vt.* reach; gain; achieve

at-tempt´ *n.* effort; *vt.* try, endeavor

at-tend´ *vi.* listen; be in attendance;

vt. accompany; be present at
at-ten´tion *n.* polite heed; care; concentration; military command
at-ten´tive *a.* heedful
at-ten´u-ate´ *vi.* & *vt.* make or become slender; **at-ten´u-a´tion** *n.*
at-test´ *vt.* certify officially
at-tire´ *vt.* dress; *n.* clothes
at´ti-tude´ *n.* position; bearing
at-tor´ney *n.* one who practices law
at-tract´ *vt.* draw by gravitation, moral influence, etc.; **at-trac´tion**
at´tri-bute´ *n.* that which is inherent in anything; a quality
at-tri´bute *vt.* ascribe, impute
at-tri´tion *n.* wearing away by friction
au´burn *a.* & *n.* reddish-brown
auc´tion *n.* public sale to the highest bidder; *vt.* dispose of at public sale
au-da´cious *a.* daring; impudent; **au-dac´i-ty** *n.*
au´di-ble *a.* loud enough to be heard
au´di-ence *n.* formal interview; assembly of hearers or viewers
au´di-o-phile´ *n.* person interested in high-fidelity sound equipment
au´di-o-vis´u-al *a.* having to do with materials such as pictures and records used in teaching or lecturing
au´dit *n.* examination and verification of accounts; *vt.*; **au´di-tor** *n.*
au´di-to´ri-um *n.* room intended for an audience
aug´ment *vi.* & *vt.* increase; intensify
au´gur *vi.* foretell the future
au-gust´ *a.* inspiring reverence or admiration
au´ral *a.* pertaining to the ear or sense of hearing
au´re-o-my´cin *n.* an antibiotic
aus´pice *n.* omen; patronage
aus-pi´cious *a.* favorable
aus-tere´ *a.* harsh, stern; **aus-ter´i-ty** *n.*
au-then´tic *a.* authorized; genuine; **au-then´ti-cate´** *vt.* prove genuine; **au´then-tic´i-ty** *n.*
au´thor *n.* one who creates or writes
au-thor´i-ta´tive *a.* with authority
au-thor´i-ty *n.* right to command or act; person invested with power
au´thor-ize´ *vt.* empower; permit
au´to-crat´ *n.* absolute ruler; **au-toc´ra-cy** *n.* absolute government
au´to-graph´ *n.* one´s own signature
au´to-mat´ic *a.* self-operating
au´to-ma´tion *n.* self-operating machinery and factories
au´to-mo-bile *n.* self-propelled passenger vehicle, auto
au-ton´o-my *n.* self government
au´to-pi´lot *n.* instrument that flies an aircraft automatically
au´top-sy *n.* medical examination of a corpse
au´tumn *n.* fall season
aux-il´ia-ry *a.* helping; subsidiary; *n.* assistant; verb (like *have, be*) that helps to form verbal phrases
a-vail´ *vi.* be of use; *vt.* be of benefit to; *n.* use
av´a-lanche´ *n.* mass of snow falling from a height
av´a-rice *n.* covetousness; **av-a-ri´-cious** *a.*
a-venge´ *vt.* inflict punishment for an injury
a-ver´ *vt.* affirm
av´er-age *a.* containing a mean value; *n.*; *vi.* & *vt.* find or fix a mean value
a-verse´ *a.* disinclined; **a-ver´sion** *n.* dislike
a-vert´ *vt.* turn from or aside; prevent
a´vi-ar´y *n.* place for keeping birds

a´vi-a´tion *n.* science of operating aircraft
av´o-ca´tion *n.* diversion, hobby
a-void´ *vt.* keep away from
a-vow´ *vt.* declare; confess
a-wake´ **(a-woke´, a-waked´)** *vt.* arouse; *vi.* waken, bestir; *a.* not sleeping
a-ward´ *n.* judgment, decision; prize; *vt.* adjudge; assign
a-ware´ *a.* apprised; conscious
awe *vt.* strike with reverential fear; *n.*; **aw´ful** *a.*
awk´ward *a.* lacking dexterity; embarrassing
awn´ing *n.* artificial shelter from sun's rays
AWOL *a.* & *n.* col. absent without official leave
awry´ *a.* & *adv.* crooked
ax, axe *n.* edged tool for chopping
ax´i-om *n.* self-evident truth; **ax´i-o-mat´ic** *a.*
ax´is *n.* **(ax´es)** line on which a body revolves
ax´le *n.* shaft or spindle on which a wheel revolves
a-zal´ea *n.* flowering plant allied to the rhododendron
az´ure *a.* sky-blue; *n.*

B

bab´ble *vi.* make inarticulate sounds; *vt.* disclose through careless talk; *n.*
ba´bel *n.* confused talk or sounds
ba´boon´ *n.* large monkey
ba-bush´ka *n.* square scarf worn as a head-covering by women
ba´by-sit´ *vi.* & *vt.* care for children, etc., while parents are away
bac´ca-lau´re-ate *n.* degree of Bachelor of Arts
bach´e-lor *n.* unmarried man
ba-cil´lus *n.* **(ba-cil´li)** type of bacteria; **bac´il-lar´y** *a.*
back´bite´ *vt.* speak evil of one in his absence
back´lash´ *n.* sudden hostile reaction
back´log´ *n.* large log at back of fireplace; sustaining reserve of supplies, orders, etc.
ba´con *n.* back or side of a hog, cured
bac-te´ri-a *n. pl.* small plants, usually one-celled, which cause various diseases, fermentation, ete.; **bac´te-ri-ol´o-gy** *n.*
badge *n.* a decoration
badg´er *n.* quadruped with thick body and short legs; *vt.* tease, annoy
bad´i-nage *n.* playful raillery
baf´fle *vt.* elude; defeat
bag´a-telle´ *n.* trifle
bag´gage *n.* trunks, luggage of a traveler
bag´pipe´ *n.* musical instrument of Scotland
bail *vt.* set a person free by giving security; *n.* one who furnishes bail; the security given
bail *vt.* free (a boat) from water by dipping it out
bait *n.* lure for fish, etc.; any lure; *vt.* use food to attract animals; provoke and harass
bal´ance *n.* pair of scales; sum due on account; *vi.* be equal; *vt.* weigh; make equal; poise
bal´co-ny *n.* platform outside the window of a room
bald *a.* without hair on the head; unadorned
bale´ful *a.* woeful
balk *vi.* stop abruptly; *vt.* disappoint; check
ball *n.* spherical body; game played

with a ball; formal dance; **on the ball** alert, receptive
bal´lad *n.* sentimental song; poem or song that tells a story
bal´last *n.* material used to steady anything
ball´ bear´ing *n.* loose metal ball inserted into machine bearing to lessen friction
bal-let´ *n.* theatrical exhibition acted chiefly by dancers
bal-lis´tic mis´sile *n.* a missile, guided during its ascent, that is capable of hitting a distant target
bal-lis´tics *n.* study of the motion of projectiles
bal-loon´ *n.* bag inflated with gas so as to float
bal´lot *n.* written or printed vote; secret vote
ball´point´ pen´ *n.* pen with ball bearing for point
balm *n.* ointment; anything that soothes
bam-boo´ *n.* large hollow-stemmed reed plant
ban *n.* proclamation; curse
ba-nan´a *n.* tropical plant or its fruit
band´age *n.* cloth used to bind up a wound; *vt.* bind with a bandage
ban´dit *n.* outlaw; robber
bane *n.* cause of ruin
bang *n.* sudden noise; hair cut straight across the forehead; *vt.* beat; slam
ban´gle *n.* bracelet, small decoration
ban´ish *vt.* condemn to exile
ban´jo *n.* **(ban´jos, ban´joes)** musical instrument resembling a guitar and tambourine
bank *n.* mound; margin of river, etc.; place where money is deposited, etc.; *vi.* do banking; *vt.* deposit in a bank
bank´rupt´ *a.* insolvent; *vt.* cause to become bankrupt
ban´ner *n.* military flag
bap´tism *n.* initiatory rite of the Christian Church; **bap´tis´mal** *a.*
bar *n.* oblong piece of iron or other solid substance; bolt; bank, as of sand; enclosure where liquors are sold; place in court where criminals stand when arraigned; lawyers collectively; stripe; division in music to mark off time; *vt.* fasten; hinder
barb *n.* one of the teeth or jags of an arrow, fish-hook, etc.
bar-bar´i-an *a.* savage; *n.* uncivilized person, savage; **bar-bar´ic** *a.*; **bar´bar-ism** *n.* rude state, brutality
bar´be-cue´ *vt.* roast and baste an animal over charcoal fire; *n.*
bar´bi-tal´ *n.* drug used as a sleeping potion
bar´bit´u-rate, bar´bi-tu´rate *n.* non-narcotic drug used as a sedative
bare *a.* naked; unfurnished; mere; *vt.* strip
bar´gain *n.* agreement; advantageous offer or purchase; *vi.* barter
barge *n.* flat-bottomed boat
bar´i-tone´ *n.* male voice between bass and tenor
bark *n.* yelp, peculiar noise made by dogs; *vi.*
bark *n.* outer covering of a tree
bar´ley *n.* grain used for making breakfast food, etc., and malt
bar´na-cle *n.* shellfish which adhere to the bottoms of ships, etc.
ba-rom´e-ter *n.* instrument for measuring atmospheric pressure
bar´on *n.* in Great Britain, rank next above a baronet and below a viscount
bar´racks *n. pl.* large building for soldiers

bar-rage´ *n.* curtain of shell-fire
bar´rel *n.* round vessel for storing foods; cylinder
bar´ren *a.* unfruitful
bar´ri-cade´ *n.* fortification to close street, etc., to traffic; *vt.*
bar´ri-er *n.* defense; obstruction
bar´tend´er *n.* mixer of alcoholic drinks in a bar
bar´ter *n.* exchange of goods; *vi.* & *vt.* trade
base *a.* low; humble; *n.* foundation; place of starting; compound with which an acid unites to form a salt; *vt.* place on a foundation
base´ball´ *n.* game played on a diamond-shaped field
base´ment *n.* floor below the main floor
bash´ful *a.* very shy
ba´sin *n.* open vessel; area drained by a stream
ba´sis *n.* **(ba´ses)** foundation; first principle; chief ingredient
bask *vi.* lie in warmth
bas´ket *n.* vessel made of plaited twigs
bas´ket-ball´ *n.* indoor ball game
bass *a.* low; deep; *n.* low part in music; *n.* food fish of several species
bas-soon´ *n.* double-reed wind instrument of bass note range
baste *vt.* sew with long stitches; drip sauce over meat while roasting
batch *n.* quantity of things made at a time
bath *n.* act of bathing; water for bathing
bathe *vi.* & *vt.* wash; take a bath
bathy´scaphe´ *n.* bulbous, manned capsule for deep-sea study
bat-tal´ion *n.* military unit next above company level
bat´ter *vt.* beat with blows; wear with beating or use; *n.* liquid mixture used to make cakes, cookies, etc.
bat´ter-y *n.* unit of artillery; unlawful beating of a person; apparatus for storing electricity
bat´tle *n.* military contest; *vi.* fight
baux´ite *n.* mineral from which aluminum is obtained
bay´o-net´ *n.* long dagger attached to a rifle; *vt.* stab with the bayonet
ba-zaar´ *n.* place for selling goods; a fair
ba-zoo´ka *n.* launcher for small rockets
beach *n.* sandy shore; *vt.* strand a boat on a beach
beach´head´ *n.* coastal territory serving as foothold for an invasion
bea´con *n.* signal fire
beak *n.* bill of a bird; anything pointed
beak´er *n.* large goblet
beam *n.* large straight piece of timber or iron; part of a balance; ray of light, etc.; *vi.* & *vt.* shine, emit
bear *vt.* **(bore, borne, born)** carry; endure; bring forth; give birth to; *vi.* suffer; have reference to
bear *n.* wild quadruped with shaggy hair; one who speculates upon a decline in prices
beard *n.* hair on a man´s face
beast *n.* any quadruped; animal-like person
beat *vi.* **(beat´en)** give strokes repeatedly; dash with force; pulsate; *vt.* strike; vanquish; *n.* stroke, blow; round covered by a reporter, etc.; *a. col.* worn out, tired
be-at´i-tude´ *n.* heavenly happiness; **be-at´i-tudes** *n. pl.* sayings of Christ recorded in Matthew V
beat´nik´ *n.* exotic nonconformist who rejects a conventional society

as false and hollow, who is unconventional in behavior and in dress, emphasizing self-expression and experiences of the moment

beau´ti-fy´ *vt.* make beautiful

beau´ty *n.* pleasing assemblage of physical qualities; lovely specimen or woman; **beau´ti-ful** *a.*

bea´ver *n.* amphibious quadruped valuable for its fur; hat

beck´on *vi.* & *vt.* make a sign by nod or gesture

be-come´ *vi.* **(be-came´; be-come´)** come to be; happen; *vt.* suit, accord with; **be-com´ing** *a.* suitable

bed´lam *n.* madhouse; great uproar

Bed´ou-in *n.* Arab of the nomad type

beef *n.* ox or cow or its flesh

bee´tle *n.* insect with hard, shelly body and wingcases

be-fall´ *vi.* & *vt.* **(be-fell´, be-fal´len)** happen (to)

beg *vi.* ask for alms; *vt.* ask for charity; ask earnestly

beg´gar *n.* one who begs; *vt.* reduce to beggary

be-gin´ *vi.* **(be-gan´, be-gun´)** take rise; start; *vt.* start, commence

be-grudge´ *vt.* envy

be-guile´ *vt.* cheat, deceive; cause to pass pleasingly

be-have´ *vi.* & *vt.* conduct oneself well; **be-hav´ior** *n.*

be-hold´ *vt.* **(be-held´)** look upon

belch *vi.* eject wind from the stomach

bel´fry *n.* bell tower

be-lie´ *vt.* misrepresent; prove untrue

be-lief´ *n.* confidence, faith; creed, platform

be-lieve´ *vi.* have faith; think; *vt.* accept as true

belle *n.* reigning beauty

bel´li-cose´ *a.* warlike

bel-lig´er-ent *a.* hostile; waging war; *n.* party engaged in hostilities

bel´low *vi.* & *vt.* roar in a loud voice; *n.* outcry

bel´lows *n. sg.* & *pl.* contrivance for blowing a fire or supplying wind to an organ

be-long´ *vi.* pertain; be part of

be-lov´ed *a.* loved; *n.* one loved

bench *n.* long seat; work table; judge's seat

bend *vi.* **(bent)** be curved; lean over; bow in submission; *vt.* curve; subdue; *n.* crook

ben´e-dick´, ben´e-dict´ *n.* newly married man

ben´e-dic´tion *n.* blessing

ben´e-fac´tion *n.* act of conferring a benefit; benefit conferred; **ben´e-fac´tor** *n.*

ben´e-fice *n.* ecclesiastical living; **be-nef´i-cence** *n.* active goodness; **be-nef´i-cent** *a.*; **ben´e-fi´cial** *a.* advantageous; **ben´e-fi´ci-ar-y** *n.* one who holds or receives a benefit or inheritance

ben´e-fit *n.* advantage; public performance to a person or cause; *vi.* & *vt.* serve, profit

be-nev´o-lence *n.* disposition to do good; **be-nev´o-lent** *a.*

be-nign´ *a.* gracious, harmless in nature

bent *n.* fixed tendency

ben´zene´ *n.* volatile, flammable hydrocarbon derived from coal tar

ben´zine´ *n.* volatile, flammable petroleum derivative

be-queath´ *vt.* give away by will

be-quest´ *n.* legacy

be-reave´ *vt.* **(be-reft´)** deprive; **be-reave´ment** *n.*grievous loss, esp. through death

ber´i-ber´i *n.* tropical disease result-

ing from eating polished rice
ber´ry *n.* small pulpy fruit
berth *n.* small sleeping place; ship´s station at anchor
be-siege´ *vt.* lay siege to
be-smirch´ *vt.* soil
be-stir´ *vi.* & *vt.* move about; stir up
be-stow´ *vt.* apply; give
bet *vi.* & *vt.* wager; *n.* act of betting; thing pledged
be´ta ray´ *n.* stream of electrons
be´ta-tron´ *n.* atom smasher operated by speeding up electrons to extremely high velocities
be-tray´ *vt.* deliver by treachery; disclose treacherously; be unfaithful to; lead astray
be-troth´ *vt.* engage to marry
bev´a-tron´ *n.* atom smasher operated by speeding up protons to extremely great velocities
bev´er-age *n.* drink
bev´y *n.* flock of birds; small group of anything
be-wail´ *vt.* bemoan
be-ware´ *vi.* & *vt.* take care against
be-wil´der *vt.* confuse
be-witch´ *vt.* enchant; charm
bi-an´nu-al *a.* occurring two times each year
bi´as *n.* slant to one side; prejudice; *vt.* prejudice
Bible *n.* the Scriptures; **bib´li -cal** *a.*
bick´er *vi.* wrangle
bi´cy-cle *n.* two-wheeled vehicle propelled by the rider
bid *vt.* **(bade, bid, bid´den, bid)** command; invite; offer; *n.* offer
bi-en´ni-al *a.* lasting two years; occurring once in two years; *n.* plant that lives two years
bi´fo-cals *n. pl.* spectacles with bifocal lenses, one pair for near vision and the other for distant vision
big´a-my *n.* state of having two spouses at the same time; **big´a-mist** *n.*
big´ot *n.* intolerant person
Bi-ki´ni *n.* island in the Pacific; scanty bathing suit
bile *n.* secretion of the live; ill-humor; **bil´ious** *a.*
bilge *n.* bulging part of a cask; water in the hull of a ship; nonsense, hooey
bill *n.* beak of a bird; draft of a law; account of money due; *vt.* enter in a bill; charge
bil´let *n.* ticket directing soldiers to quarters; quarters, position; *vt.* quarter
bil´liards *n.* game played with cues and balls
bil´lion *n.* one thousand millions
bil´low *n.* great wave; *vi.* surge
bin *n.* box for coal, corn, etc.
bind *vi.* **(bound)** become contracted; hinder; be obligatory; *vt.* tie; sew a binding on; fasten together and cover; cause to become obligatory
bin-oc´u-lars *n. pl.* set of telescopic lenses for both eyes
bi´o-as-tro-nau´tics *n.* medicine of space travel
bi´o-chem´is-try *n.* chemistry of living things
bi´o-de-grad´a-ble *a.* able to decompose through bacterial action
bi-og´ra-phy *n.* written history of a person´s life; **bi-og´ra-pher** *n.*
bi-ol´o-gy *n.* science of life; **bi-ol´o-gist** *n.*
bi-par´ti-san *a.* representing two political parties
bi´ped´ *n.* animal with two feet
birch *n.* tree with smooth white bark
bird *n.* warm-blooded, winged and feathered animal; ballistic missile
birth *n.* act of coming into life; lineage

bis´cuit *n.* small bread cake
bisect´ *vt.* divide into two equal parts
bi-sex´u-al *a.* having chatacteristics of or attracted to both sexes
bish´op *n.* head of a diocese; piece in the game of chess; **bish´op-ric** *n.* office and jurisdiction of a bishop
bi´son *n.* wild animal like the ox; American buffalo
bit *n.* small piece of anything; tool for boring; minor stage business in a play; mouthpiece of bridle
bitch *n.* female dog; *vi. col.* complain, gripe
bite *vi. & vt.* **(bit, bit-ten)** seize or tear with the teeth; take hold of; *n.* a grasp by the teeth; something bitten off; wound made by the teeth
bit´ter *a.* having a disagreeable taste like quinine; mentally painful; hostile
bi-tu´men *n.* asphalt
bi-tu´min-ous coal´ *n.* soft coal
bi´valve´ *n.* mollusk having a shell of two parts
biv´ou-ac´ *n.* night encampment
bi-zarre´ *a.* odd
Black *n. & a.* Afro-American, Negro
black´ball´ *vt.* reject a candidate for membership
black´board´ *n.* board for marking on with chalk
black´mail´ *n.* extortion by threats; *vt.*
black´mar´ket *n.* illegal traffic in a commodity
Black Mus´lim *n.* member of a segregationist Afro-American group which follows the teachings of Islam
black´out´ *n.* extinguishing of lights over a wide area; temporary loss of consciousness
bladder *n.* thin sac in animals serving as a receptacle for fluids
blade *n.* spear of grass; cutting part of knife; flat part of an oar
blanch *vi. & vt.* grow white, whiten
bland *a.* mild
blan´ket *n.* woolen covering
blare *n.* noise; roar; *vi.* sound loudly
blar´ney *n.* wheedling talk
blas´pheme´ *vi. & vt.* speak impiously of; curse and swear; **blas´phe-my** *n.*
blast *n.* explosion; blare of a trumpet; violent gust of wind; *vi. & vt.* blight; injure
blast´—off´ *n.* firing of a missile or rocket
bla´tant *a.* noisy; coarse
blaze *vi.* burn with a flame; *vt.* send forth a flaming light; *n.*
bleach *vi. & vt.* make or grow white or pale
bleak *a.* cheerless; cold
bleed *vi. & vt.* **(bled)** draw blood from; lose blood
blem´ish *n.* that which will tarnish; defect; *vt.* tarnish
blend *n.* mixture; *vi.& vt.* mix
bless *vt.* invoke divine favor; approve; make happy; praise
blight *n.* disease in plants; *vt.* affect with blight; destroy
blind *n.* something to mislead; shutter; *a.* having no outlet; unable to see; *vt.* deprive of sight
blink *vi.* shut the eyes quickly, wink
bliss *n.* highest bappiness
blister *n.* thin watery sac on the skin
blithe *a.* joyous, gay
blitz´krieg´, blitz *n.* lightning war, overwhelming offensive; **blitz** *vt.*
bliz´zard *n.* violent whirling snowstorm

bloat *vi.* & *vt.* swell
block *n.* mass of any substance; section,as a group of houses; pulley or pulleys in a frame; obstruction; *vt.* obstruct; shape into blocks; mark out a rough plan
block´ade´ *n.* military action similar to a siege; obstruction to traffic; *vt.*
block´head´ *n.* dolt
blond, blonde *a.* of fair complexion
blond *n. masc.,* **blonde** *n. fem.* person of fair complexion
blood *n.* vital fluid pumped by the heart; connection by descent
blood´bank´ *n.* depository for liquid or dried human blood
bloom *n.* blossom; glow of health; *vi.* blossom, flourish
blos´som *n.* flower; *vi.* bear flowers; flourish
blot *n.* spot; *vi.* & *vt.* stain; dry with blotting paper
blotch *n.* spot; eruption on the skin; *vt.* disfigure with blotches
blouse *n.* light, loose, shirt-like garment
blow *vt.* **(blew, blown)** sound a wind instrument; put in motion by a stream of air; *i.* produce a current of air; sound; **blow up** *vt.* explode; enlarge a photograph
blow *n.* severe stroke or calamity
blub´ber *n.* fat of whales; *vi.* sob
bludg´eon *n.* heavy stick; *vt.*
blue *n.* azure; *a.* sky-colored; melancholy; *vt.* treat with bluing
blue´ ba´by *n.* child with beart defect affecting skin color
blues *n. pl.* melancholia; kind of sad, mournful song
bluff *n.* steep bank; act of bluffing; *vt.* deceive, hoodwink
blun´der *n.* awkward mistake; *vi.* make an awkward error
blunt *a.* having a dull edge or point; curt; *vt.* dull
blur *n.* indistinct mark; indistinctness; *vi.* & *vt.* make or become indistinct
blurt *vt.* utter suddenly
blush *n.* sudden redness of the face; *vt.*
blus´ter *vi.* act boisterously; **blus´ter-y** *a.*
bo´a *n.* large non-venomous snake; long fur wrap
boar *n.* male of swine
board *n.* long, broad, thin piece of timber; meals; council; *vt.* supply with meals; enter a vessel; *vi.* take meals regularly for a stipulated price
boast *vi.* & *vt.* brag; *n.*
boat *n.* any watercraft
bob *vi.* & *vt.* move in a jerking manner
bob´bin *n.* spool, reel
bob´by pin´ *n.* wire clip for holding the hair
bob´by socks´ *n. pl.* ankle-length hose with rolled tops
bob´by sox´er *n.* formerly, girl in her early teens
bod´y *n.* physical structure; main part; person; number of persons or things; substance
bog *n.* quagmire, marsh
bo´gus *a.* spurious
boil *vi.* & *vt.* bubble or make bubble from heat; cook in a seething liquid
bois´ter-ous *a.* noisy
bold *a.* daring; striking; impudent
bo´lo *n.* Philippine knife
Bol´she-vik *n.* Communist
bolster *vt.* support or prop up; *n.* long pillow
bolt *n.* stout pin of metal; bar for fastening; roll of cloth, etc.; sudden start; *vt.* fasten with a bar; blurt

out; swallow bastily; *vi.* dart about

bomb *n.* metal shell filled with explosive

bom'bard' *vt.* attack with bombs or artillery

bom'bast' *n.* high-sounding, but meaningless language

bomb'er *n.* airplane equipped to deliver bombs

bo-nan'za *n.* very productive mine; any good investment

bond *n.* obligation; formally contracted obligation; *vt.* put under bond; mortgage; place in a bonded warehouse

bone *n.* hard substance composing a skeleton

bon'fire' *n.* open-air fire

bon'net *n.* covering for a woman's head

bo'nus *n.* extra allowance; premium

book *n.* sheets of paper bound together; literary composition; division of a volume

book'mo-bile' *n.* vehicle fitted out as a moving library or store used to bring books to less populated areas

boom *n.* bollow sound; *vi.* make such a sound

boom *n.* period of business activity; *vi.*

boor *n.* coarse or rude person

boost *vt.* push upward; support; *n.*

boot *n.* covering for the foot and lower leg

booth *n.* stall at a fair

boot'leg' *vi.* & *vt.* deal illegally in a commodity, esp. liquor

bor'der *n.* edge; *vi.* & *vt.* adjoin; be adjacent to

bore *n.* hole made by boring; tiresome person; *vt.* pierce; weary

bo'ric ac'id *n.* white crystalline compound used as an antiseptic

bor'ough *n.* incorporated town or its citizens

bor'row *vi.* & *vt.* obtain a loan; appropriate

bos'om *n.* breast

boss *n.* master; *vi.* & *vt.* superintend

bot'a-ny *n.* science of plants; **bot'a-nist** *n.*

botch *vt.* make a poor job of something

bot'tle *n.* vessel with a narrow neck; *vt.* put into bottles

bot'tle-neck' *n.* anything that impedes progress

bot'tom *n.* lowest part; foundation; low land; keel of a ship

bough *n.* branch of a tree

boul'der *n.* large rounded stone

bou'le-vard' *n.* broad, smoothly paved avenue

bounce *vi.* leap; rebound; *vt.* drive against and rebound; eject suddenly; *n.* sudden spring; rebound

bound *n.* limit; *vt.* surround; state the boundaries or limits of

bound *a.* obliged; destined; determined

bound'a-ry *n.* border line

boun'te-ous *a.* abundant; **boun'ti-ful** *a.*

boun'ty *n.* liberality; premium given

bou-quet' *n.* bunch of flowers; fragrance, as of wine

bout *n.* contest

bow *n.* curved piece of wood for shooting arrows

bow *n.* inclination of the head or body; forepart of a ship; *vi.* & *vt.* bend the body in saluting; yield

bowl *n.* cup-like vessel; *vt.* play at ten-pins

boy'cott' *vt.* combine in refusing to have commercial or social dealings with

bra *n.* brassière

brace *n.* support; suspender; pair of marks { } connecting lines together; pair; *vt.* strengthen; furnish with braces

brace´let *n.* ornament for the wrist

brack´et *n.* support fastened to a wall; pair of marks [ ] used to enclose words; *vt.* support or enclose by brackets

brack´ish *a.* slightly salt; disagreeable

brag *vi.* boast; *n.*; **brag´art** *n.* boaster

braid *vt.* plait; sew on trimming; *n.*

brain *n.* contents of the skull; the intellect; *col.* highly intelligent person

brain´wash´ *vt.* forcibly persuade one to change his beliefs

braise *vt.* stew in a covered pan

brake *n.* contrivance for slowing the motion of wheels

branch *n.* limb of a tree; anything like a limb; *vi.* & *vt.* ramify

brand *n.* mark made by burning; trademark; *vt.* mark with a brand; stigmatize

bran´dish *vt.* wave

brass *n.* alloy of copper and zinc; affrontery; insignia; military officers

bra-va´do *n.* boastful or arrogant boldness

brave *a.* courageous; *n.* Indian warrior; *vt.* meet boldly; **brav´er-y** *n.* courage

brawl *vi.* quarrel noisily

brawn *n.* muscle; muscular strength

bra´zen *a.* made of or like brass; impudent

bra´zier *n.* open pan for burning charcoal

breach *n.* opening; breaking, as of a law; quarrel

breadth *n.* broadness, width

break *vt.* **(broke, broken)** part by force; weaken make bankrupt; *vi.* fail, as in health; happen as a sudden storm or dawn; depart from tradition

breakfast *n.* first meal of day; *vi.*

break´—e´ven point´ *n.* number of sales needed to pay for the cost of producing an article

break´through´ *n.* sudden solution to a problem, often the result of intense organized effort

breast *n.* front of the body between neck and abdomen

breath *n.* air drawn into the lungs; power of breathing, life

breathe *vi.* & *vt* take breath; whisper

breeches *n. pl.* trousers

breed *vt.* bring forth; bring up; beget; *vi.* be produced; *n.* class, kind

breeze *n.* gentle wind

brev´i-ty *n.* shortness

brew *vi.* & *vt.* prepare beer; contrive

bribe *n.* anything given to influence unduly; *vi.* influence by a bribe; **brib´er-y** *n.*

bric´—a—brac´ *n.* curiosities

brick *n.* piece of burned clay; anything shaped like a brick; *vt.* lay with brick

brid´al *a.* pertaining to a wedding

bride *n.* woman about to be or newly married

bridge *n.* structure over a river, etc.; card game for four players

bridge´head´ *n.* seized territory serving as a foothold for a military invasion

bri´dle *n.* horse´s headgear; restraint; *vt.* check, restrain; *vi.* become visibly offended

brief *a.* short; *n.* short account

brig *n.* two-masted square-rigged vessel; Navy jail

bri-gade´ *n.* body of troops consisting of two or more regiments

brig´a-dier gen´er-al *n.* officer in command of a brigade

bright *a.* full of light

bril´liant *a.* sparkling; bright; *n.* diamond of fine cut; **bril´liance** *n.*

brim *n.* edge, rim; *vi.* be full

brine *n.* salt water; sea

bring *vt.* **(brought)** fetch, procure

brink *n.* edge

brisk *a.* lively

bris´tle *n.* short, stiff bair; *vi.* stand erect, as bristles; **bris´tly** *a.*

brittle *a.* easily broken

broach *vt.* utter; begin

broad *a.* wide; great in range; *n. col.* a woman

broad´cast´ *vi.* & *vt.* send out by radio; *n.*

broad´cloth´ *n.* fine, smooth cloth

bro-cade´ *n.* figured silk cloth

bro-chure´ *n.* pamphlet

brogue *n.* dialect, esp. Irish English

broil *vi.* & *vt.* grill; cook over hot coal or under a flame

bro´ken *a.* in pieces; infirm; humbled

bro´ker *n.* one who buys and sells for others

bron-chi´tis *n.* inflammation of the bronchia

bron´co *n.* **(bron´cos)** small western horse, often only partly tamed

bronze *n.* mixture of copper and tin

brooch *n.* ornamental pin

brood *vi.* & *vt.* sit on eggs; think anxiously; *n.* number hatched at once

brook *n.* small stream

broom *n.* wild shrub; brush for sweeping

broth *n.* thin meat soup

brow *n.* forehead; edge of a hill

browse *vi.* feed on the shoots or leaves of plants; inspect or sample books

bruise *n.* slight injury to the skin, contusion; *vt.* injure the skin without cutting

brunch *n.* combination breakfast and luncheon

bru-nette´ *n.* woman of dark complexion and hair

brunt *n.* main shock of any onset

brush *n.* implement for removing dust, etc.; brushwood; skirmish; *vi.* move lightly; *vt.* remove dust; touch lightly

brusque *a.* blunt

bru´tal *a.* unfeeling; animal-like in cruelty; **bru´tal´i-ty** *n.*

brute *n.* beast

bub´ble *n.* air or other gas inside a spherical film of water or other liquid; *vi.* rise in bubbles

buck *n.* male of the deer, etc.; *vi.* & *vt.* attempt to throw (a rider) by springing from the ground; **buck up** *vt.* cheer (a person)

buck´et *n.* vessel for holding water, etc.

buck´le *n.* fastening for clothing; *vt.* fasten with a buckle; *vi.* bend

budge *vi.* move; stir

budg´et *n.* financial statement

buf´fa-lo *n.* large kind of wild ox; American bison

buf-fet´ *n.* sideboard; *a.* served informally as from a sideboard

buf-foon´ *n.* clown

bug *n.* any insect; beetle; bedbug; *col.* microorganism; *col.* defect, flaw; *vt. col.* conceal a microphone in a room for eavesdropping

bug´gy *n.* single-seated four-wheeled carriage drawn by a horse

bu´gle *n.* hunting or military horn

build *vt.* **(built)** erect; construct; *vi.* rest or grow (on)

bulb *n.* onion-like root of many

plants; incandescent lightglobe

bulge *n.* widest part of a cask; swelling; *vi.* swell out

bulk *n.* greater part

bull *n.* male of the ox kind; edict of the Pope; speculator who favors higher prices

bull´doz´er *n.* powerful tractor-machine used for building roads, air strips, etc.

bul´let *n.* ball of lead fired from gun

bul´le-tin *n.* brief official report

bull´frog´ *n.* species of large frog

bul´lion *n.* uncoined gold and silver in the mass

bul´ly *n.* ruffian; *vi.* & *vt.* intimidate

bul´wark *n.* rampart; safeguard

bum *n.* tramp, hobo; *vt.* live in tramp fashion; ask or beg for something

bum´ble-bee´ *n.* large buzzing bee

bump *n.* dull, heavy blow; swelling; *vi.* make a heavy noise; *vt.* strike with a dull sound

bump´er *n.* front and rear metal guard on cars

bun *n.* small roll

bunch *n.* number of things together; *vt.* put together in bunches

bun´dle *n.* number of things bound together; *vi.* & *vt.* tie into bundles

bun´ga-low´ *n.* tent-like, single-storied cottage with verandas

bun´gle *vi.* & *vt.* act or make clumsily; *n.*

bun´ion *n.* inflamed swelling on the great toe

bunk *n.* bed fastened to the wall; nonsense, meaningless words intended to sound well; *vi.* sleep in a bunk

buoy *n.* float to indicate shoals; *vi.* & *vt.* keep afloat

bur´den *n.* load; obligation; *vt.* oppress

bu´reau *n.* **(bu´reaus)** chest of drawers; department of a government

bur´glar *n.* one who breaks into a house to steal

bur´i-al *n.* interment

bur´lap´ *n.* a coarse fabric

bur-lesque´ *n.* low parody; type of musical-theatrical entertainment; *vt.* turn into ridicule

bur´ly *a.* bulky, brawny; bluff

burn *vt.* consume or injure by fire; *vi.* be on fire; feel excess of heat; be inflamed with passion; *n.* hurt or mark caused by fire

bur´nish *vt.* shine, polish; *n.* luster

bur´ro *n.* **(bur´ros)** small donkey

bur´row *n.* hole dug by animals; *vi.* make holes under ground

burst *vi.* & *vt.* break into pieces; *n.* sudden outbreak

bur´y *vt.* place in the ground or grave; inter

bush *n.* shrub thick with branches; thicket

bush´el *n.* dry measure containing 32 dry quarts

bust *n.* sculpture representing a person from head to shoulders or chest; the chest

bus´tle *vi.* hustle; *n.* hurried activity

bus´y *a.* diligent; fully employed

butch´er *n.* slaughterer; dealer in meat; one who delights in bloody deeds; *vt.* slaughter animals for food; kill cruelly

but´ler *n.* servant in charge of liquors, plate, etc.

but´ter *n.* substance obtained from cream by churning

but´ter-fly´ *n.* insect with beautiful wings

but´ter-milk´ *n.* sour milk that remains after churning

but´ton *n.* knob for fastening clothing; *vt.* fasten by means of buttons

bux´om *a.* healthy; cheerful
buy *vt.* **(bought)** purchase; bribe
buzz *vi.* make a humming noise like bees; *n.*
buz´zard *n.* a bird of prey
by´pass´ *n.* road or detour around something; *vt.* detour; circumvent
by´—prod´uct *n.* secondary product
by´word´ *n.* common saying; person or thing whose name is used proverbially and with scorn

C

cab *n.* taxicab; part of engine occupied by engineer
ca-bal´ *n.* small party united for some intrigue
ca-ba´na *n.* tent for changing clothes at a beach or swimming pool
cab´in *n.* small hut; room in a ship
cab´i-net *n.* storage cupboard; advisors of a ruler
ca´ble *n.* strong rope or chain; wire rope; *vt.* fasten with a cable; send a submarine message
cack´le *n.* sound made by a hen
cac´tus *n.* **(cac´ti, cac´tus-es)** plant with prickles instead of leaves
ca-dav´er *n.* corpse
cad´die, cad´dy *n.* attendant, esp. at golf
ca´dence *n.* rhythm; accent
ca-det´ *n.* student in a military school
ca-fe´ *n.* restaurant; **caf´e-te´ri-a** *n.* lunch room where patrons serve themselves
cage *n.* place of confinement for animals; *vt.* confine in a cage
ca-jole´ *vi.* & *vt.* coax, wheedle; cheat by flattery
ca-lam´i-ty *n.* disaster
cal´cu-late´ *vi.* & *vt.* count; estimate; compute
cal´dron, caul´dron *n.* large kettle
cal´en-dar *n.* chart showing the months, weeks, and days of the year; list of cases for trial
calf *n.* **(calves)** young of the cow; fleshy part of leg below the knee
cal´i-ber *n.* size of a gun´s bore; intellectual capacity
cal´i-co´ *n.* kind of printed cotton cloth
cal´i-pers *n. pl.* device for measuring thickness of spheres, etc.
cal´is-then´ics *n. pl.* physical development exercises
cal-li´o-pe´ *n.* series of tuned steam whistles
cal´lous *a.* hardened
cal´low *a.* unfledged, inexperienced
calm *a.* still; serene; *n.* absence of wind; serenity; *vt.* quiet
cal´o-rie *n.* unit for stating the energy in foods, etc.
cal´um-ny *n.*slander
ca-lyp´so *n.* rhythmic kind of song, orig. from Trinidad
cam´bric *n.* fine white linen fabric
cam´el *n.* animal of Asia and Africa
cam´e-o´ *n.* precious stone carved in relief
cam´cor-der *n.* device for recording home movies to play back on a video screen
cam´er-a *n.* instrument for making photographs
cam´ou-flage´ *n.* art of protective and deceptive coloring and construction
cam-paign´ *n.* time during which an army keeps the field; political contest
cam´phor *n.* dried juice of the laurel tree
cam´pus *n.* college grounds
ca-nal´ *n.* artificial watercourse;

duct, channel
ca-nard´ *n.* fabricated or sensational story; hoax
ca-nar´y *n.* bird orig. from the Canary islands; light yellow color
ca-nas´ta *n.* card game
can´cel *vt.* annul
can´cer *n.* malignant tumor; any spreading evil
can´did *a.* frank
can´di-date *n.* contestant for an office or honor
can´dle *n.* wax or tallow surrounding a wick
can´dor *n.* frankness
cane *n.* reed; walking stick; *vt.* beat with a cane
ca´nine´ *a.* like a dog; *n.* dog; canine tooth
can´is-ter *n.* case; case containing shot
can´ker *n.* ulcer in the mouth; anything that corrupts; *vi.* & *vt.* corrupt
can´ni-bal *n.* person who eats human flesh
can´non *n.* large gun; artillery piece
ca-noe´ *n.* small boat
can´yon *n.* deep gorge
can´on *n.* law, esp. in ecclesiastical matters; body of accepted writings; church dignitary; list of saints
can´o-py *n.* covering suspended overhead; *vt.*
cant *n.* jargon, the special words of a profession or trade; hypocritical or affected style of speech
can´ta-loupe´ *n.* variety of muskmelon
can-ta´ta *n.* dramatic poem set to music; choral song
can-teen´ *n.* tin vessel holding liquids; post exchange
can´ter *n.* easy gallop; *vi.* move at an easy gallop
can´to *n.* principal division of a long poem
can´vas *n.* cloth used for sails and for painting on
can´vass *vi.* & *vt.* solicit; examine, as votes
can´yon *n.* deep gorge
ca´pa-ble *a.* having skill
ca-pac´i-ty *n.* power of holding; comprehensiveness
cape *n.* covering for the shoulders, cloak; headland
caper *vi.* leap,dance, frolic; *n.* leap; prank
cap´il-lar´y *n.* minute blood vessel; *a.* as fine as a hair
cap´i-tal *a.* chief; excellent; *n.* top of a column; chief city; large letter; money invested
Cap´i-tol *n.* building in which Congress or a state legislature meets
ca-pit´u-late´ *vi.* surrender on conditions
ca-price´ *n.* sudden change of humor; **ca-pri´cious** *a.*
cap´size´ *vt.* overturn
cap´sule´ *n.* seed vessel; small shell, case, or gelatin container for medicine
cap´tain *n.* chief officer; military officer below major in rank
cap´tion *n.* chapter, cartoon, or page heading
cap´tious *a.* ready to find fault
cap´ti-vate´ *vt.* charm; fascinate
cap´tive *n.* prisoner; *a.* taken or kept prisoner; subdued; **cap´tiv´i-ty** *n.*; **cap´tor** *n.*
cap´ture *n.* act of seizing or taking prisoner; thing taken; *vt.* take prisoner
car *n.* automobile; railway coach
car´a-mel *n.* kind of candy; burnt sugar used as flavoring
car´at *n.* unit for weighing gems,

containing 1/24th part of pure gold

car´a-van´ *n.* company of travelers in a desert.

car´bo-hy´drate *n.* organic compound (such as sugar, starch, or cellulose) composed of carbon, hydrogen, and oxygen

car´bon *n.* pure charcoal one of the elements; **car´bon 14** heavy isotope of carbon used to date relics

car´bun-cle *n.* red semiprecious stone; inflammation similar to a boil

car´cass *n.* corpse

car´di-ac´ *a.* pertaining to the heart

car´di-nal *a.* principal, basic; *n.* dignitary in the R. C. Church; vermilion

ca-reen´ *vi.* & *vt.* tip, sway

career´ *n.* profession; course of life

ca-ress´ *vt.* fondle; *n.*

car´et *n.* mark (^) used in writing to show that something has been inserted

car´go *n.* load of a ship

car´i-bou´ *n.* type of American reindeer

car´i-ca-ture *n.* distorted likeness; parody; *vt.* ridicule

carnage *n.* slaughter

car´nal *a.* sensual

car-nation *n.* well-known garden flower

car´ni-val *n.* time before Lent; festival

car-niv´o-rous *a.* flesh-eating

car´ol *n.* song of joy; *vi.*

ca-rouse´ *vi.* drink freely and noisily; **ca-rous´al** *n.*

carp *vi.* catch at small faults.

car´pen-ter *n.* worker in timber; *vi.* do carpenter´s work; **car´pen-try** *n.*

car´riage *n.* vehicle; manner

car´ri-on *n.* dead flesh

car´rot *n.* edible root similar to parsnip

car´ry *vt.* move, transport, or take a thing; bear; **car´ri-er** *n.*

car´tel´ *n.* agreement to fix prices and production

car´ton *n.* thin pasteboard box

car´toon´ *n.* large sketch; caricature

car´tridge´ *n.* shell containing a charge; case containing roll of film, phonograph needle, etc.

carve *vt.* cut into slices or pieces

cas´cade´ *n.* waterfall

case´ment *n.* window that opens on hinges

cash-ier´ *n.* one who handles money in a business

cask *n.* barrel

cas´ket *n.* small case; coffin

cas-sette *n.* small cartridge of film rolls or magnetic tape reels

cast *vi.* & *vt.* throw; *n.* act of casting; thing thrown; distance thrown; mold; form received from a mold; assignment of parts in a play

cas´ta-net´ *n.* small clapper

caste *n.* class of society; one of the divisions of the Hindu classes

cas´ti-gate´ *vt.* chastise, punish; criticize; **cas´ti-ga´ton** *n.*

cas´tle *n.* fortified house, residence of a nobleman; in chess, a rook

cas´u-al *a.* occasional; chance; unconcerned

cas´u-al-ty *n.* accident; person hurt or killed

cat *n.* familiar domestic animal, feline; woman who makes unpleasant insinuations

cat´a-clysm *n.* upheaval

cat´a-comb´ *n.* cavern used as a burial place

cat´a-log´, cat´a-logue´ *n.* list of articles, merchandise, etc.; *vt.*

cat´a-ma-ran´ *n.* a raft of logs tied together; a twin-hulled boat
cat´a-ract´ *n.* waterfall; disease of the eye
ca-tas´tro-phe *n.* calamity
catch´er *n.* playing position in baseball
catch´up, cat´sup, ketch´up *n.* sauce made of tomatoes, etc.
cat´e-go´ry *n.* class; **cat´e-gor´i-cal** *a.* absolute, explicit
ca´ter *vi.* provide entertainment or commodities
cat´er-pil´lar *n.* grub (esp. of butterfly or moth) that lives upon leaves; *tr.* powerful motor truck with belted wheels used to haul heavy guns, move earth, etc.
ca-the´dral *n.* principal church of a diocese
cath´ode *n.* negative electrode
cath´o-lic *a.* universal
Cath´o-lic *a.* pertaining to the Roman Catholic Church; *n.* adherent of the Roman Catholic Church; **ca-thol´i-cism** *n.*
cat´tle *n.* livestock
Cau-ca´sian *n.* member of the Indo-European family white person
cau´cus *n.* party conference
cau´li-flow´er *n.* edible vegetable, a variety of cabbage
cau-sa´tion *n.* act of causing; **caus´-a-tive** *a.*
caus´tic *a.* corrosive, biting
cau´ter-ize *vt.* burn tissues with a hot iron or chemical for medical purposes
cau´tion *n.* heedfulness; wariness; warning; *vt.* warn; **cau´tous** *a.*
cav´al-cade´ *n.* train of persons on horseback; parade
cav´a-lier´ *n.* knight; *a.* gay
cav´al-ry *n.* soldiers on horseback
cav´ern *n.* hollow place in the earth, cave
cav´il *vi.* make trifling objections; *n.* frivolous objection
cav´i-ty *n.* a hollow; hole in tooth
CD *n.* compact disc; a device for storing sounds such as music or data as for a computer.
cease *vi.* & *vt.* stop
ce´dar *n.* cone-bearing evergreen
cede *vt.* give up
ceil´ing *n.* roof of a room; upper limit, as of prices or visibility
cel´e-brate´ *vi.* & *vt.* observe with joy; honor; **cel-e-bra´tion** *n.*
ce-leb´ri-ty *n.* fame; person who is famous
cel´er-y *n.* vegetable of the carrot family
ce-les´tial *a.* heavenly
cel´i-ba-cy *n.* unmarried state; hence, sexual purity; **cel´i-bate** *a.* & *n.* unmarried; pure
cell *n.* room for a prisoner; elementary structure in animal and plant tissues; single element of an electric battery
cel´lar *n.* underground storeroom
cel´lo-phane´ *n.* thin, transparent paper made from cellulose
Cel´lu-loid´ *n.* *tr.* plastic used to make photographic film and as a substitute for ivory, etc.
cel´lu-lose *n.* a white substance found in the cell walls of plants, used in manufacture of paper and rayon
ce-ment´ *n.* mortar; adhesive preparation; *vt.* unite with cement; join firmly
cem´e-ter´y *n.* burying ground
cen´sor *n.* inspector of printed matter, letters, movies,etc.; **cen-so´ri-ous** *a.* censuring
cen´sure *n.* reproof; *vt.* condemn, reprimand

cen´sus *n.* enumeration of inhabitants

cen-ten´ni-al *n.* hundredth anniversary

cen´ter *n.* middle; playing position on football or basketball team; *vi.* be central; *vt.* place on, or collect to, a center

cen´ti-grade´ *a.* divided into a hundred degrees; pertaining to the centigrade thermometer

cen´ti-me´ter *n.* one hundredth part of a meter, about .4 of an inch

cen´ti-pede´ *n.* insect-like creature with many feet

cen´tral *a.* relating to or containing the center; basic

cen´trif´u-gal *a.* tending away from the center

cen´trip´e-tal *a.* tending toward the center

cen´tu-ry *n.* one hundred years

ce-ram´ic *a.* pertaining to pottery, etc.; **ce-ram´ics** *n.* craft of making pottery, etc.; ceramic products

ce´re-al *n.* edible grain; breakfast food, etc., made of grain; *a.*

cer´e-bel´lum *n.* back part of the brain

cer´e-brum *n.* front part of the brain

cere´ment *n.* shroud

cer´e-mo´ny *n.* rite; **cer´e-mo´ni-al** *a.* & *n.*

cer´tain *a.* sure; indefinite quantity

cer-tif´i-cate *n.* written declaration; **cer´ti-fi-ca´tion** *n.*

cer´ti-fy *vt.* make known as certain; declare in writing

chaff *n.* covering of grain; worthless matter

chaf´ing dish´ *n.* vessel for cooking over an alcohol flame

cha-grin´ *n.* vexation; *vt.* vex,annoy

chain *n.* connected series of links; *vt.* bind with a chain

chain´ re-ac´tion *n.* fission which spreads from one atom to another

chaise´ lounge´ *n.* elongated chair for relaxing

chalk *n.* type of limestone, esp. for marking; *vt.* mark with chalk; score, credit

chal´lenge *n.* summons to a contest; exception to a juror; demand of a sentry; *vt.* call on one to settle a matter, as by fighting; call in question

chamber *n.* room; assembly room; assembly; hall of justice

cha-me´le-on *n.* lizard which changes, its color

cham´ois *n.* kind of antelope; leather made from its skin

cham´pi-on *n.* one who fights for a cause; successful athlete; winner; *vt.* defend

chan´cel-lor *n.* president of a university; chief justice of a court of chancery; prime minister

chan´cer-y *n.*court of equity

chan´de-lier´ *n.* elaborate hanging frame for holding lights

change *vi.* & *vt.* make or grow different; exchange; *n.* alteration; small number of coins

chan´nel *n.* bed of a stream; frequency range over which radio and TV signals are sent; *vt.* wear into channels

chant *n.* type of song; *vt.*

chaos *n.* confusion; disorder; **cha´-ot´ic** *a.*

chap´el *n.* small church

chap´er-on´ *n.* lady escort; *vt.* act as chaperon to

chap´lain *n.* clergyman, esp. one in military service

chap´ter *n.* division of a book; branch of an organization

char *vt.* reduce to charcoal

char´ac-ter *n.* letter, sign, figure; individual traits; trait of good quality; reputation; peculiar person; one of the cast in a play or novel
cha-rade´ *n.* acted riddle
char´coal´ *n.* charred wood
charge *vt.* ask a certain price; buy and pay later; accuse; attack; renew the life of a battery; *n.*
char´i-ty *n.* almsgiving; institution for giving aid; **char´i-ta-ble** *a.*
char´la-tan *n.* quack
charm *n.* magic spell; talisman; quality which attracts or fascinates; *vt.* enchant, captivate
char´nel *a.* pertaining to a place of burial; sepulchral
chart *n.* map; outline
char´ter *n.* patent; grant; *vt.* establish by charter; let or hire
char´y *a.* careful; sparing
chase *vt.* pursue; *n.* pursuit; that which is hunted
chasm *n.* abyss
chaste *a.* virtuous, pure; modest; **chas´ti-ty** *n.*
chas´ten *n.* discipline; free from faults
chas´tise´ *vt.* punish; **chas´tise´-ment** *n.*
chat´tel *n.* personal property
chat´ter *vi.* & *vt.* talk idly, jabber
chauf´feur *n.* hired driver of an automobile
chau´vin-ism *n.* exaggerated and aggressive patriotism
cheap *a.* low in price; of small value
cheat *vi.* & *vt.* defraud; be dishonest in games, etc.; *n.* one who cheats
check´ers *n.* game played on a checkered board
cheer *n.* shout of approbation; entertainment; *vt.* applaud by cheers; make glad; comfort
cheese *n.* product of the curd of milk
chef *n.* head cook
chem´i-cal *a.* pertaining to chemistry; *n.* substance used in chemistry
che-mise´ *n.* type of dress or undergarment for women
chem´is-try *n.* science of the properties of elements and their compounds; **chem´ist** *n.*
chem´ur-gy *n.* application of chemistry to industrial use of farm and forest products
cher´ish *vt.* hold dear
cher´ry *n.* small fruit with stone; tree which bears it
cher´ub *n.* **(cher´ubs, cher´ub-im)** celestial spirit; beautiful child
chest *n.* front part of body between neck and waist; strongbox
chew *vt.* masticate
Chi-ca´no *n.* & *a.* Mexican American
chick´en *n.* familiar domestic fowl or its young; *a. col.* afraid, cowardly; pointlessly strict or severe
chide *vt.* **(chid´ed, chid, chid´den)** rebuke, scold
chief *a.* head, principal; *n.* principal person
chif-fon´ *n.* type of cloth, usually made of silk or rayon
chill *a.* slightly cold; *n.* coldness; shivering caused by a disease; *vt.* make cold
chime *n.* tuned bell; harmonious sound of bells; *vi.* sound in harmony; take part in
chi-me´ra *n.* fabulous monster; wild fancy; **chi-mer´i-cal** *a.*
chim´ney *n.* passage for smoke
chim´pan´zee *n.* African ape
chin´chil´la *n.* small rodent or its soft, gray fur
Chi-nese´ *a.* pertaining to China; *n.* language of China; *n. sg.* & *pl.* native of China

chintz *n.* glazed cotton cloth printed in colors

chip´munk´ *n.* small, striped animal of squirrel family

chi´rog´ra-phy *n.* penmanship

chi´rop´o-dist *n.* physician specializing in disorders of the foot

chi´ro-prac´tor *n.* one who treats diseases by manipulating the joints

chis´el *n.* tool to hollow out wood, etc.; *vt.* cut with a chisel; *col.* cheat, bamboozle

chiv´al-ry *n.* system of knighthood; gallantry; **chiv´al-rous** *a.*

chlo´ro-form´ *n.* an anesthetic; *vt.* administer chloroform to

chlo´ro-phyl´, chlo´ro-phyll´ *n.* green matter in plants

choc´o-late *n.* substance or beverage made of cacao beans

choice *n.* act or power of choosing; thing chosen; preference; *a.* select

choir *n.* chorus of singers, esp. in church; part of church occupied by singers

choke *vi.* & *vt.* throttle; obstruct; *n.*

chol´er-a *n.* infectious, often deadly disease of the bowels

cho-les´ter-ol´ *n.* fatty alcohol in animal tissues

choose *vi.* & *vt.* **(chose, cho´sen)** decide; select; elect

chop *vt.* cut with a blow; cut into small pieces; *n.* act of chopping; slice of mutton, etc.

chord *n.* combination of tones in harmony; straight line joining the ends of an arc

chore *n.* small job or duty

cho´re-og´ra-phy *n.* creation and direction of dances

chorus *n.* band of singers; refrain; **cho´ral** *a.*

christen *vt.* baptize; name

chro´mat´ic *a.* relating to colors; in music, proceeding by semitones

chro´mo-some´ *n.* an elongated body occurring in number in the cell nucleus and carrying genes

chron´ic *a.* continuous; stretching over a period

chron´i-cle *n.* record of events in order of time; *vt.* record

chro-nol´o-gy *n.* science of time and dates; record of events in order of time; **chron´o-log´ic** *a.*

chro-nom´e-ter *n.* instrument for measuring time accurately

chrys´a-lis *n.* pupa, or form between larva and winged state, of butterflies etc.

chrys-an´the-mum *n.* garden flower of aster family

chub´by *a.* short, round, and thick

chuck´le *n.* quiet laugh; *vi.* laugh quietly

chunk *n.* short, thick piece of anything

churl *n.* ill-bred fellow

churn *vt.* shake violently; make butter; *n.* vessel in which cream is churned

chute *n.* inclined trough

ci´der *n.* apple juice

ci-gar´ *n.* roll of tobacco for smoking

cig´a-ret´, cig´a-rette´ *n.* finely cut tobacco rolled in paper for smoking

Ci´ne-ma-scope´ *n. tr.* process for filming large curved-screen motion pictures

Ci´ne-ra´ma *n. tr.* large curved-screen motion pictures requiring three simultaneous projectors

cin´na-mon *n.* spicy bark of trees of the laurel family

cir´cle *n.* round figure; set of people; *vi.* & *vt.* hover or move around

cir´cuit *n.* round made in the exercise of a calling; hence, path or route, as of an electric current, etc.

cir´cu-lar *a.* round; *n.* printed advertisement sent to many persons
cir´cu-late´ *vi.* & *vt.* go or cause to go around; **cir´cu-la´tion** *n.*
cir-cum´fer-ence *n.* boundary line of a circle
cir´cum-flex´ *n.* diacritical mark (^)
cir´cum-lo-cu´tion *n.* roundabout language
cir´cum-nav´i-gate´ *vt.* sail around
cir´cum-scribe´ *vt.* limit; encircle
cir´cum-spect´ *a.* cautious
cir´cum-stance´ *n.* related fact; detail; **cir´cum-stan´tial** *a.*
cir´cum-vent´ *vt.* outwit
cir´cus *n.* outdoor entertainment usually performed in a tent
cit´ron *n.* fruit or preserved peel of the citron tree
cit´rus fruit´ *n.* orange, lemon, grapefruit, etc.
civ´ic *a.* pertaining to a citizen or city
civ´il *a.* pertaining to citizens; polite; **ci-vil´ian** *n.*; **ci-vil´i-ty** *n.* good breeding; **civ´il defense** *n.* defense of civilians against air attack or natural disaster
claim *vt.* call for; demand as a right; maintain; *n.* demand; thing claimed
clam *n.* common bivalve mollusc
clam´ber *vi.* climb awkwardly
clam´or *n.* loud or continuous outcry; *vi.* cry aloud
clamp *n.* device used to fasten things together; *vt.* bind with a clamp
clan *n.* tribe; clique
clan-des´tine *a.* done secretly
clang *vi.* make a noisy, ringing sound; *n.*
clar´i-fy *vi.* & *vt.* make or become clear
clar´i-net´ *n.* single-reed woodwind instrument
clash *n.* loud noise; opposition; skirmish, battle; *vi.* & *vt.* dash noisily together; meet in opposition
clasp *n.* hook for fastening; embrace; *vt.* grasp; fasten with a clasp
clas´sic *a.* of the highest class or style; *n.* literary work, etc., of highest rank; **clas´si-cal** *a.*
clas´si-fy *vt.* arrange into classes; **clas´si-fi-ca´tion** *n.*
clat´ter *n.* rattling noise; *vi.* rattle; talk fast or idly
clause *n.* part of a sentence or document
clef *n.* character used in music
cleft *n.* fissure
clem´en-cy *n.* leniency; mildness
cler´gy *n.* body of ministers of religion
cler´i-cal *a.* pertaining to a clerk or to the clergy
clerk *n.* one employed as a salesman or to handle records
clev´er *a.* skillful, smart
cli-ché´ *n.* wornout expression
click *n.* short, sharp sound; *vi.* make such a sound
cli´ent *n.* one who employs a lawyer, etc.
cliff *n.* high, steep rock
cli´mate *n.* the weather of an area
cli´max´ *n.* highest point
climb *vi.* & *vt.* ascend by use of the hands and feet
cling *vi.* **(clung)** adhere; stick close
clip *vt.* cut; *n.* clasp; blow; fast pace
clique *n.* faction
cloak *n.* long cape; *vt.* conceal
clod *n.* lump of earth; stupid person
clog *vt.* obstruct; *n.* obstruction; wooden-soled shoe
clois´ter *n.* covered arcade; place of religious retirement

close *a.* near; hidden, reserved; stuffy
close *vi.* & *vt.* shut; end; stop
clot *n.* concreted mass; *vi.* form clots
cloth *n.* woven material; the clergy
clothe *vt.* **(clothed, clad)** dress, supply with clothing; **clothes** *n. pl.*
clo´ver-leaf´ *a.* pertaining to an elaborate highway crossing of clover shape
clown *n.* professional jester; boor; *vi.*
club´foot´ *n.* deformity of the foot
cluck *n.* call of a hen
clump *n.* mass; cluster; *vi.* tread clumsily; cluster
clum´sy *a.* awkward; shapeless
clus´ter *n.* bunch; *vi.* & *vt.* grow or gather into clusters
clutch *vt.* seize; *n.* grip; that which clutches; part of gear shift in cars, etc.
clut´ter *vi.* & *vt.* disarrange; litter; *n.* disorder; clatter
coach *n.* two-door sedan; railroad passenger car; closed four-wheeled carriage; instructor, esp. one who trains an athletic team; *vt.* teach or train a person or team for an athletic contest or for any examination
co-ag´u-late *vi.* & *vt.* clot; curdle
co´a-lesce´ *vi.* unite, merge, mix
co´a-li´tion *n.* temporary union
coarse *a.* rough; gross
coast *n.* seashore; *vi.* slide downhill on a sled; travel along on a vehicle´s momentum; *vi.* & *vt.* sail near a coast; skirt
co-ax´i-al ca´ble *n.* cable used for transmitting TV signals, etc.
cob´bler *n.* shoe repairman; kind of pie
co´bra *n.* poisonous snake of Asia and Africa
cob´web´ *n.* spider web
co´caine´ *n.* narcotic obtained from the coca plant
cock *n.* male of birds; tap for liquids; striking part of the lock of a gun; small pile of hay; *vt.* set erect
cock´le *n.* shellfish having two wrinkled shells
cock´roach´ *n.* insect infesting kitchens and pantries
cock´tail´ *n.* mixed alcoholic drink
co´coa´ *n.* powder or beverage made from cacao beans
co-coon´ *n.* silk covering spun by many insect larvae
C. O. D. cash on delivery
code *n.* collection of laws, etc.; system of signs or signals
cod´i-fy *vt.* collect into a body or code; **cod´i-fi-ca´tion** *n.*
co´ed´ *n.* female student in college
co-erce´ *vt.* force; compel
cof´fin *n.* casket for a corpse
cog *n.* tooth on a wheel
co´gent *a.* convincing; **co´gen-cy** *n.*
cog´i-tate´ *vi.* think about; **cog´i-ta´tion** *n.*
cog´nate´ *a.* related
cog-ni´tion *n.* knowing; perception, intuition
cog´ni-zance *n.* knowledge gained by observation; state of awareness
cog´no´men *n.* surname; nickname
co´here´ *vi.* hold or stick together; **co´her´ence** *n.*; **co´her´ent** *a.*
coif-fure´ *n.* styling of the hair
coin *n.* metal legally stamped as money; *vt.* convert metal into money; make, invent
co´in-cide´ *vi.* agree, be identical; **co-in´ci-dence** *n.* occurrence of two events at the same time; **co-in´ci-dent** *a.*
co´i-tus *n.* sexual intercourse
cold´ war´ *n.* state ot unfriendly re-

lations between countries without actual fighting

col´i-se´um *n.* amphitheater or other large hall for entertainment

col-lab´o-rate´ *vi.* work together or jointly; **col-lab´o-ra´tor** *n.*

col-lapse´ *vi.* break down; *n.*

col´lar *n.* anything worn about the neck

col-lat´er-al *a.* accompanying; *n.* anything pledged as security

col´la´tion *n.* comparison, as of two texts; light repast

col´league´ *n.* associate in work

col-lect´ *vi.* & *vt.* come or bring together; secure money due; **col-lec´-tion** *n.*; **col-lec´tor** *n.*

col-lec´tiv-ism *n.* socialistic doctrine that land and production should belong to the people as a group

col´lege *n.* school for advanced learning; association; **col-le´gi-an** *n.* member of or student at a college; **col-le´gi-ate** *a.*

col-lide´ *vi.* strike together

col´lie *n.* shepherd dog

col-li´sion *n.* clash; conflict; crash

col´lo-quy *n.* formal conversation; **col-lo´qui-al** *a.* used in conversation; informal; **col-lo´qui-al-ism** *n.* conversational expression

co-logne´ *n.* perfumed preparation

co´lon *n.* mark (:) used in punctuation; part of the intestinal tract

colo´nel *n.* chief of a regiment

col´o-nist *n.* inhabitant of a colony; pioneer; **col´o-nize´** *vt.*; **col´o-ni-za´tion** *n.*

col´o-ny *n.* settlement in a foreign country or distant place; **co-lo´nial** *a.*

co-los´sal *a.* gigantic; huge

col´umn *n.* cylindrical support; body of troops in deep files; perpendicular row of lines or figures; **col-um´nar** *a.*

col´um-nist *n.* writer of a special column in magazine or newspaper

co´ma *n.* morbid sleep; lethargy

com´bat *n.* battle; fight

com-bat´ *vt.* contend

com-bine´ *vi.* & *vt.* unite; **com´bi-na´tion** *n.*

com´bo *n.* small musical group of four to five players

com-bus´ti-ble *a.* liable to burn or capable of burning; *n.*

com-bus´tion *n.* process of burning or oxidation

co-me´di-an *n.* comic actor

com´e-dy *n.* dramatic piece of a light or humorous character

come´ly *a.* pleasing; **come´li-ness** *n.*

com´et *n.* heavenly body with luminous tail

com´fort *vt.* relieve from pain or distress; cheer; *n.* relief, ease

com´ic *a.* humorous; droll

com´ma *n.* mark (,) of punctuation

com-mand´ *vt.* order; govern; *n.* order, authority; thing commanded

com-mem´o-rate´ *vt.* celebrate, as by a memorial service

com-mence´ *vi.* & *vt.* begin

com-mend´ *vt.* praise; recommend

com-men´su-rate *a.* of the same measure; corresponding

com´ment *n.* note; criticism; *vi.* make critical or explanatory observations; **com´men-tar´y** *n.*

com´merce *n.* trade; intercourse; **com-mer´cial** *a.*

com-mis´er-ate *vi.* sympathize with

com-mis´sion *n.* persons appointed to perform certain duties; charge for transacting business; writing conferring powers; *vt.* give a commission to; appoint

com-mit´ *vt.* perform, do; give in trust; consign to prison; pledge
com-mit´tee *n.* persons appointed to perform certain duties
com-mod´i-ty *n.* article which can be bought or sold
Com´mon Mar´ket *n.* economic alliance of Western European nations, aimed at reducing tariff barriers and promoting the free flow of labor, agricultural products, and merchandise among members
com-mo´tion *n.* tumult
com-mune´ *vi.* converse with
com-mu´ni-cate´ *vt.* impart, tell; *vi.* talk with; join; **com-mu´ni-ca´tion** *n.* letter, news; act of communicating
com´mu-nism *n.* system in which property, means of production, etc., are held in common; **com´mu-nist** *n.*
com-mu´ni-ty *n.* the public
com-mute´ *vt.* substitute; *vi.* work away from home and travel back and forth; **com-mut´er** *n.*
com´pact´ *a.* packed close; terse; *n.* agreement; small automobile which is economical in price and maintenance; **compact disk** *n.* device for storing data to create sounds such as music or for computer files.
com-pan´ion *n.* associate
com´pa-ny *n.* assembly or association of persons; subdivision of a battalion
com´pa-ra-ble *a.* capable or worthy of comparison
com-pare´ *vt.* liken; inflect an adjective; **com-par´a-tive** *a.*; **com-par´i-son** *n.*
com-part´ment *n.* division of an enclosed space
com´pass *n.* circuit; space; instrument which indicates the north; instrument for drawing circles
com-pas´sion *n.* pity
com-pat´i-ble *a.* agreeable or consistent with
com-pel´ *vt.* force; oblige
com´pen-sate´ *vt.* make up for; pay back; **com´pen-sa´tion** *n.*
com-pete´ *vi.* contend; rival
com´pe-tence *n.* fitness; modest income; **com´pe-tent** *a.* suitable; sufficient
com´pe-ti´tion *n.* act of competing; rivalry; **com-pet´i-tor** *n.* rival
com-pile´ *vt.* arrange material from other works in new form; **com´pi-la´tion** *n.*
com-pla´cence *n.* self-satisfaction; **com-pla´cent** *a.*
com-plain´ *vi.* express dissatisfaction with
com-plaint´ *n.* expression of dissatisfaction; accusation
com´ple-ment *n.* that which completes; full number; *vt.* make complete
com´plete´ *a.* entire; *vt.* finish; **com-ple´tion** *n.*
com-plex´ *a.* intricate; **com-plex´i-ty** *n.*
com-plex´ion *n.* color of the face and skin; general appearance
com-pli´ance *n.* disposition to yield; acquiescence; **com-pli´ant** *a.*
com´pli-cate´ *vi.* & *vt.*make or grow complex
com-plic´i-ty *n.* guilty participation
com´pli-ment *n.* expression of regard; *vt.* praise; **com´pli-men´ta-ry** *a.*
com-ply´ *vi.* yield; obey
com-po´nent *n.* ingredient
com-port´ *vt.* behave or conduct oneself
com-pose´ *vt.* form by putting together; place in order; set at rest;

place type in order for printing
com-pos´er *n.* one who composes, esp. music
com´po-si´tion *n.* act or art of putting together; thing composed; **com-pos´i-tor** *n.* one who sets type
com-po´sure *n.* calmness
com´pound´ *a.* composed of parts; *n.* mixture
com´pre-hend´ *vt.* understand; include; **com´pre-hen´sion** *n.* understanding; **com´pre-hen´sive** *a.* extensive
com-press´ *vt.* press together, squeeze; **com-pres´sor** *n.*
com-prise´ *vt.* contain, include
com´pro-mise´ *n.* settlement by concessions; *vt.* settle by concession; bring into a questionable situation
comp-trol´ler *n.* person who supervises and controls spending of money
com-pul´sion *n.* force; necessity; **com-pul´so-ry** *a.*
com-punc´tion *n.* remorse
com-pute´ *vt.* calculate; **com´pu-ta´tion** *n.*
com-put´er *n.* electronic "brain" used for high speed calculating and processing of data
com´rade´ *n.* friend, companion; title and term of address used by communists
con´cave´ *a.* curved inward
con-ceal´ *vt.* hide
con-cede´ *vt.* admit
con-ceit´ *n.* vanity
con-ceive´ *vt.* imagine think; understand; **con-ceiv´able** *a.*
con´cen-trate´ *vt.* condense; make more intense; **con´cen-tra´tion** *n.*
con-cen´tric *a.* having a common center
con´cept´ *n.* idea, thought
con-cern´ *vt.* relate to; make uneasy; interest; *n.* interest; anxiety; business
con´cert´ *n.* musical entertainment; harmony
con-cert´ *vt.* arrange; devise together
con-cer´to *n.* **(con-cer´tos)** musical composition for solo instrument and orchestra
con-ces´sion *n.* act of conceding; thing conceded
con-cil´i-ate´ *vt.* win over; pacify; **con-cil´i-a´tion** *n.*; **con-cil´i-a-to-ry** *a.*
con-cise´ *a.* brief
con-clude´ *vi.* & *vt.* end or bring to an end; infer; **con-clu´sion** *n.*; **con-clu´sive** *a.* final; convincing
con-coct´ *vt.* prepare; **con-coc´tion** *n.*
con´cord´ *n.* harmony; agreement; **con-cord´ance** *n.* agreement; index of leading words in a book
con´course´ *n.* assembly; gathering or meeting
con´crete´ *a.* formed into one mass; specific; *n.* mass formed of distinct parts; mixture of cement, sand, etc., used in building
con-cur´ *vi.* agree
con-cus´sion *n.* collision; violent shock from collision
con-demn´ *vt.* pronounce guilty or unfit; sentence; **con´dem-na´tion** *n.*
con-dense´ *vi.* grow dense; *vt.* reduce in volume; **con´den-sa´tion** *n.*
con´de-scend´ *vi.* deign; **con´de-scen´sion** *n.*
con-dign´ *a.* well deserved
con´di-ment *n.* seasoning or relish served at table
con-di´tion *n.* situation; stipulation;

vt. adjust or make respond in a certain way
con´do-min´i-um *n.* building where tenants own their individual apartments
con-done´ *vt.* excuse; overlook
con-du´cive *a.* promoting or contributing to
con´duct *n.* act or method of managing; behavior
con-duct´ *vt.* transmit; guide; lead an orchestra; **con-duc´tor** *n.* leader; guide; person in charge; material which transmits heat or electricity
con´duit *n.* pipe to convey water or protect wires
con´el-rad´ *n.* U.S. nationwide emergency radio network using two frequencies
con-fec´tion *n.* fancy candy
con-fed´er-a-cy *n.* persons or states leagued together; **con-fed´er-a´tion** *n.*
con-fer´ *vi.* consult; *vt.* give; **con´fer-ence** *n.* meeting
con-fess´ *vt.* admit; tell; **con-fes´sion** *n.*
con´fi-dant´ *n. masc.* **con´fi-dante´** *n. fem.* one entrusted with a secret; bosom friend
con-fide´ *vi.* entrust a secret to; *vt.* entrust; commit
con´fi-dence *n.* firm belief in anyone or anything
con´fi-dent *a.* trusting; **con´fi-den´tial** *a.* secret
con-fig´u-ra´tion *n.* outline
con-fine´ *vt.* limit; enclose; imprison
con-firm´ *vt.* establish; assure; admit to Communion; **con´fir-ma´tion** *n.*
con´fis-cate´ *vt.* appropriate to the state
con´fla-gra´tion *n.* great fire
con-flict´ *vi.* be in opposition
con´flict´ *n.* struggle
con-form´ *vi.* act in agreement with; yield
con-found´ *vt.* confuse; associate by mistake
con-front´ *vt.* face; place face to face
con-fuse´ *vt.* bewilder
con-fute´ *vt.* prove false; confound; **con´fu-ta´tion** *n.*
con-geal´ *vi.* & *vt.* thicken; turn solid
con-gen´ial *a.* agreeable
con-gen´i-tal *a.* existing at birth
con-ges´ted *a.* crowded; filled with blood; **con-ges´tion** *n.*
con-grat´u-late´ *vt.* wish joy
con´gre-gate´ *vi.* gather; assemble; **con´gre-ga´tion** *n.*
con´gress *n.* meeting; formal assembly; federal legislature of U.S.; **con´gres´sion-al** *a.*
con-jec´ture *n.* guess; speculation; *vt.* infer
con´ju-gal *a.* pertaining to marriage
con´ju-gate *a.* coupled; *vt.* give the inflections of a verb; **con´ju-ga´tion** *n.*
con-junc´tion *n.* connection; word (like *and, but, so*) which links words, phrases, and clauses
con´jure *vi.* & *vt.* summon, as by magic
con-jure´ *vt.* implore earnestly
con-nect´ *vt.* join together; establish a relation between
con-nec´tion *n.* union; things joined; relationship
con-niv´ance *n.* voluntary oversight of wrongdoing
con-nive´ *vi.* plot or agree in secret
con´nois-seur´ *n.* able judge, as of art
con-note´ *vt.* imply; include; signify
con-nu´bi-al *a.* pertaining to mar-

riage

con´quer *vi.* & *vt.* defeat; **con´quest** *n.*

con´san-guin´i-ty *n.* blood relationship

con´science *n.* moral faculty; feelings of right and wrong

con´sci-en´tious *a.* influenced by conscience; scrupulous

con´scious *a.* aware; having the use of one´s senses

con´se-crate´ *vt.* render holy; **con´se-cra´tion** *n.*

con-sec´u-tive *a.* following in order

con-sen´sus *n.* agreement, esp. of opinion

con-sent´ *n.* agreement; *vt.* agree; yield

con´se-quence *n.* effect; importance; **con´se-quent** *a.* following

con-serv´a-tive *n.* one who is moderate

con-serv´a-to-ry *n.* greenhouse; school of music or art

con-serve´ *vt.* keep entire; retain; preserve

con-sid´er *vt.* deliberate, study

con-sid´er-ate *a.* thoughtful of others; **con-sid´er-a´tion** *n.* deliberation; compensation

con-sign´ *vt.* transfer

con-sist´ *vi.* be composed of; exist; be contained in; **con-sist´en-cy** *n.* degree of density; uniformity, agreement

con-sole´ *vt.* give solace; **con´so-la´tion** *n.*

con-sol´i-date´ *vi.* & *vt.* unite

con´so-nant *a.* consistent; *n.* sound made by obstructing the breath in any of a number of ways

con´sort´ *n.* partner, companion; mate

con-sort´ *vi.* associate with

con-spic´u-ous *a.* prominent

con-spire´ *vi.* plot against; **con-spir´a-cy** *n.* underhand plotting; **con-spir´a-tor** *n.*

con´stant *a.* fixed; continual; faithful; *n.* that which remains unchanged; **con´stan-cy** *n.*

con´stel-la´tion *n.* group of stars

con´ster-na´tion *n.* confusion; dismay; vexation

con´sti-pate´ *vt.* clog, esp. the intestine

con-stit´u-ent *a.* constituting; essential; *n.* essential part; supporter of a public official

con´sti-tute´ *vt.* form, be a part of

con´sti-tu´tion *n.* natural condition; fundamental principles or laws of a government, organization, etc.

con-strain´ *vt.* force; restrain

con-straint´ *n.* compulsion

con-strict´ *vt.* bind; contract; **con-stric´tion** *n.*

con-struct´ *vt.* put together; **con-struc´tion** *n.*

con´sul *n.* government official stationed abroad; **con´su-lar** *a.*; **con´su-late** *n.*

con-sult´ *vi.* & *vt.* consider together; ask advice

con-sume´ *vt.* use up

con´sum-mate *a.* perfect

con´sum-mate´ *vt.* perfect; bring to a conclusion; **con´sum-ma´tion** *n.* perfection; conclusion

con-sump´tion *n.* act of using up; tuberculosis

con´tact´ *n.* touch; **contact print** *n.* photograph made from direct contact with negative

con-ta´gion *n.* transmission of disease by contact; **con-ta´gious** *a.*

con-tain´ *vt.* hold; restrain

con-tam´i-nate´ *vt.* defile; **con-tam´i-na´tion** *n.*

con-temn´ *vt.* despise, scorn

con´tem-plate´ *vt.* consider; meditate; intend; **con´tem-pla´tion** *n.*

con-tem´po-rar´y *a.* living, happening, or being at the same time; *n.* one living at the same time; **con-tem´po-ra´ne-ous** *a.*

con-tempt´ *n.* scorn; disgrace; disobedience to the judgment or rules of a court; **con-temp´tu-ous** *a.* haughty

con-tend´ *vi.* strive

con-tent´ *a.* satisfied

con´tent´ *n.* capacity; that which is contained

con-ten´tion *n.* debate; strife; **con-ten´tious** *a.* quarrelsome

con´test´ *n.* struggle; competitive game

con-test´ *vt.* call in question; strive for or against

con´text´ *n.* parts preceding or following a passage

con-tig´u-ous *a.* touching; adjoining

con´ti-nence *n.* restraint; chastity; **con´ti-nent** *a.*

con´ti-nent *n.* one of the great land masses of the globe

con-tin´gent *a.* dependent; accidental; **con-tin´gen-cy** *n.*

con-tin´ue *vi.* remain; *vt.* prolong; persist in; **con-tin´u-al** *a.*; **con-tin´u-a´tion** *n.*; **con´tin-u´i-ty** *n.*; **con-tin´uous** *a.*

con-tort´ *vt.* twist; writhe; **con-tor´-tion** *n.*

con´tour´ *n.* outline

con´tra-band´ *n.* illegal commerce; prohibited goods

con´trail´ *n.* condensed vapor trail from high-flying airplanes or rockets

con´tract´ *n.* agreement

con-tract´ *vi.* & *vt.* draw together, shorten; bargain; incur; **con-trac´-tion** *n.*; **con-trac´tor** *n.*

con´tra-dict´ *vt.* deny, refute; **con´-tra-dic´tion** *n.*

con-tral´to *n.* lowest range of the female voice

con´tra-ry *a.* opposite; conflicting; intractable; *n.* opposite

con´trast´ *n.* opposition; unlikeness; exhibition of differences

con-trast´ *vi.* & *vt.* stand or set in opposition

con-tri´bute *vi.* & *vt.* give or pay a share; help; **con´tri-bu´tion** *n.*

con-trite´ *a.* penitent; **con-tri´tion** *n.*

con-triv´ance *n.* invention; artifice; **con-trive´** *vt.* plan; plot; bring about

con-trol´ *n.* restraint; authority; *vt.* govern; restrain

con´tro-ver´sy *n.* vigorous argument or discussion

con´tro-vert´ *vt.* refute

con´tu-ma´cious *a.* obstinately disobedient

con-tu´me-ly *n.* abusive language

con-tu´sion *n.* bruise

con´va-lesce´ *vi.* regain health; **con´va-les´cence** *n.*

con-vene´ *vi.* & *vt.* come or call together

con-ven´ient *a.* timely; handy; **con-ven´ience** *n.*

con´vent *n.* nunnery

con-ven´tion *n.* assembly, of delegates; custom; type of treaty

con-verge´ *vi.* tend to or cluster at one point; meet; **con-ver´gence** *n.*

con-ver´sant *a.* familiar

con-verse´ *vi.* talk familiarly

con´verse *a.* reversed or opposite in order or relationship; *n.*

con-ver´sion *n.* change, esp. in religious beliefs

con-vert´ *vt.* change from one condition to another

con-vert´i-ble *a.* capable of being changed; *n.* car with retractable roof; **con-vert´i-bil´i-ty** *n.*
con-vex´ *a.* curved outward
con-vey´ *vt.* transport; transmit
con´vict´ *n.* one condemned to prison
con-vict´ *vt.* adjudge or prove guilty; **con-vic´tion** *n.*
con-viv´i-al *a.* merry
con-voke´ *vt.* call together; **con´vo-ca´tion** *n.*
con´voy´ *n.* escort
con-vulse´ *vt.* shake violently; **con-vul´sion** *n.*
cook´out´ *n.* any meal prepared out-of-doors
co-op´er-ate´ *vi.* work together in harmony; **co-op´er-a´tion** *n.*; **co-op´er-a-tive** *a.*
co-or´di-nate *a.* of the same order, rank, or time; **co-or´di-nate´** *vt.* make coordinate; **co-or´di-na´tion** *n.*
co´pi-ous *a.* plentiful
cop´per *n.* metallic element of reddish color; coin, etc., made of copper
cop´y *n.* reproduction; one of an edition of a book; manuscript; *vt.* imitate; transcribe
copy´right´ *n.* legal right to an author´s work; *vt.* secure a copyright to
co´quet´ *vi.* & *vt.* flirt; **co-quette´** *n.* flirtatious woman
cor´al *n.* stone-like substance formed from skeletons of small sea animals
cor´date´ *a.* heart-shaped
cor´dial *a.* hearty
cor´don *n.* line of police, etc., around a place
cor´du-roy *n.* thick cotton cloth with ribbed surface
core *n.* inner part of a thing; *vt.* take out the inner part, esp. of fruit
co´ri-an´der *n.* plant with aromatic seeds
cork *n.* outer bark of the cork tree; stopper made of cork; *vt.* stop with a cork
cor´mo-rant *n.* voracious seabird; glutton
cor´net´ *n.* brass wind instrument similar to trumpet
cor´nice *n.* ornamental projection on buildings or walls
cor´nu-co´pi-a *n.* horn-like receptacle, a symbol of abundance
cor´o-na´tion *n.* ceremony in which a monarch is crowned
cor´o-ner *n.* medical officer who inquires into accidental or suspicious deaths
cor-o-net´ *n.* crown indicating inferior sovereignty
cor´po-ral *a.* relating to the body; *n.* lowest non-commissioned officer in U.S. army
cor´po-rate *a.* legally incorporated; belonging to a corporation; **cor´po-ra´tion** *n.* society authorized to act as one individual
cor-po´re-al *a.* material
corps *n. sg.* & *pl.* body of soldiers, diplomats, etc.
corpse *n.* dead human body
cor´pu-lence *n.* fleshiness, fatness; **cor´pu-lent** *a.*
cor-ral´ *n.* pen for cattle; *vt.* drive cattle into a pen
cor-rect´ *a.* true; *vt.* make right; punish; **cor-rec´tion** *n.* amendment; punishment
cor´re-late´ *vt.* discover a relationship between; **cor´re-la´tion** *n.*; **cor-rel´a-tive** *a.* mutually or reciprocally related
cor´re-spond´ *vi.* be similar; be

adapted; hold intercourse by letters

cor´ri-dor *n.* passageway

cor-rob´o-rate´ *vt.* confirm; **cor-rob´o-ra´tion** *n.*

cor-rode´ *vt.* wear away, as by rust; **cor-ro´sion** *n.*; **cor-ro´sive** *a.*

cor´ru-gate´ *vi.* & *vt.* wrinkle; fold; **cor´ru-ga´tion** *n.*

cor-rupt´ *a.* depraved; *vi.* lose purity; *vt.* make putrid; debase; bribe

cor-tege´, cor-tège´ *n.* train of attendants

cor´ti-sone´ *n.* hormone used in treating arthritis and other diseases

cor´us-cate´ *vi.* sparkle

cos´mic ray´ *n.* stream of high-energy particles from outer space

cos-mol´o-gy *n.* science that deals with formation and nature of the universe

cos´mo-pol´i-tan *a.* belonging to the entire world

cos´tume *n.* manner of dressing; dress; dress of a particular period

co´te-rie *n.* clique

co-til´lion *n.* an elaborate dance

couch *n.* sofa; *vt.* say, express

cou´gar *n.* mountain lion; puma

cough *n.* effort of the lungs to expel injurious matter; *vi.* & *vt.*

coun´cil *n.* assembly; consultation

coun´sel *n.* advice; *vt.* give advice

count´down´ *n.* final check of a missile´s components before firing; counting off of seconds before firing a missile

coun´te-nance *n.* features; *vt.* favor

count´er *n.* anyone or anything that counts; table on which money is counted or merchandise laid

coun´ter-act´ *vt.* act in opposition to

coun´ter-feit *vt.* forge, make fake copies, as of money; *a.* false; *n.*

coun´ter in-sur´gen-cy *n.* tactics used against guerrilla infiltration

coun´ter-mand´ *vt.* revoke; contradict; forbid

coun´ter-part´ *n.* opposite; match

coun´ter-poise´ *n.* equal weight on other scale; equilibrium

coun´ter-sign´ *n.* word or sign needed to pass a sentry; *vt.* testify to a signature by signing

coun´ty *n.* division of a state

cou-pé´ *n.* closed two-door automobile seating two to five passengers

cou´ple *n.* pair; *vt.* join

cou´pon *n.* interest warrant; slip entitling one to benefits

cour´age *n.* firmness in danger; **cou-ra´geous** *a.*

cour´i-er *n.* messenger

court´ mar´tial *n.* **(courts´ mar´tial, court´ mar´tials)** military court; *vt.* subject to a court-martial

cour´te-ous *a.* polite

cour´te-sy *n.* civility, politeness; favor, consent

court´ly *a.* elegantly mannered

cove *n.* small bay

cov´e-nant *n.* agreement

cov´ert *a.* concealed

cov´et *vt.* desire eagerly

cow´ard *a.* timid; *n.* person without courage

cow´er *vi.* quail

cow´hide´ *n.* hide of a cow; coarse riding whip

cowl *n.* cap; hood

cox´comb´ *n.* fop; Cocks-comb, a flowering plant

coy *a.* excessively modest; coquettish

coy´ote *n.* prairie wolf

coz´en *vi.* & *vt.* deceive, cheat; beguile

crabbed *a.* peevish; morose

crack *a.* excellent, first-rate; *n.*

sharp, splitting sound; chink; *vi.* & *vt.* produce a sharp sound; split

crack´le *vi.* make frequent snapping or cracking noises

cra´dle *n.* bed in which children are rocked

craft *n.* cunning; dexterity; art, trade; ships

crag *n.* rough, steep rock

cramp *n.* spasmodic contraction of muscles; *vt.* confine

crane *n.* large wading bird; machine for raising heavy objects

cra´ni-um *n.* skull; upper part of skull

crank *n.* arm attached to an axis for winding; eccentric person

cran´ny *n.* small fissure

crap *n. col.* excrement; junk, trash

crash *n.* breaking noise; sudden collapse or collision; *vi.*

crate *n.* case made of slats

cra´ter *n.* mouth of a volcano

cra-vat´ *n.* necktie

crave *vi.* & *vt.* long for; **crav´ing** *n.*

cra´ven *a.* spiritless

craw *n.* crop of fowls

craw´fish´, cray´fish´ *n.* fresh-water animal similar to crab

crawl *vi.* move on all fours

cray´on *n.* chalk pencil for drawing, coloring, etc.

cra´zy *a.* insane; **cra´zi-ly** *adv.*

creak *n.* grating sound; *vi.*

crease *n.* mark made by folding; *vt.* make creases in

cre-ate´ *vt.* bring into being

cre-a´tion *n.* act of creating; that which is created; **cre-a´tive** *a.*; **cre-a´tor** *n.*

crea´ture *n.* any animated being

cre´dence *n.* belief; trust

cre-den´tial *n.* letter or paper of identification

cred´i-ble *a.* believable

cred´it *n.* belief; reputation; time allowed for payment; *vt.* believe; trust; set to the credit of; **cred´i-tor** *n.*

cred´it card´ *n.* identification card showing bearer´s right to purchase merchandise or services on credit

cre-du´li-ty *n.* disposition to believe; **cred´u-lous** *a.*

creed *n.* summary of religious beliefs

creep *vi.* **(crept)** move on hands and knees

cre´mate´ *vt.* burn to ashes, esp. a dead body; **cre-ma´tion** *n.*

cres´cent *a.* growing; *n.* moon as it increases towards half-moon; any object of this shape

crest *n.* comb or tuft; figure placed over coat of arms

cre-vasse´ *n.* fissure

crev´ice *n.* crack

crew *n.* company; operating force of a ship, train, etc.

crib *n.* stall; child´s bed; bin for grain; *vt.* pilfer, cheat

crick´et *n.* insect similar to grasshopper; type of ball game

crime *n.* violation of the law; **crim´i-nal** *a.* & *n.*

crim´son *a.* & *n.* deep red

cringe *vi.* crouch; shrink; to wince; to flinch

crin´kle *vi.* & *vt.* form in wrinkles; twist

crip´ple *n.* lame person; *vt.* make lame

cri´sis *n.* **(cri´ses)** decisive moment, as in a disease

crisp *a.* dry and brittle

cri-te´ri-on *n.* standard; test

crit´ic *n.* judge of literature, art, etc.; fault-finder; **crit´i-cal** *a.* fault-finding; decisive

crit´i-cize´, crit´i-cise´ *vt.* censure;

evaluate, judge; **crit´i-cism** *n.*

croak *vi.* utter a low, rough sound; *col.* die; *n.* raucous sound, as by a frog or raven

cro-chet´ *n.* fancy knitting done with one needle; *vi. & vt.*

croc´o-dile´ *n.* amphibious reptile of Asia, Africa, and America

cro´cus *n.* spring flower

cro´ny *n.* bosom friend or companion

crook *n.* bend; shepherd´s staff bent at the end; professional criminal; *vi. & vt.* bend

crop *n.* harvest; craw, the first stomach of fowl

cro-quet´ *n.* lawn game in which balls are driven by mallets

cross-o´ver net´work *n.* filter circuits for multiple loudspeaker system, separating highs and lows and feeding each to a particular speaker

crotch´et *n.* little hook; perverse fancy

crouch *vi.* squat

crow *n.* large,black bird; cry of a cock; *vi.* cry as a cock; boast

crown *n.* head dress of a monarch; regal power; top; *vt.* invest with a crown; adorn; complete

cru´cial *a.* decisive; severe

cru´ci-ble *n.* earthen pot for melting metals

cru´ci-fix´ *n.* figure of Christ on cross; **cru´ci-fix´ion** *n.* death on the cross

cru´ci-fy´ *vt.* put to death by nailing to a cross; torment cruelly

crude *a.* raw; unpolished; **cru´di-ty** *n.*

cru´el *a.* brutal

cruise *vi.* sail to and fro; *n.* voyage of this kind; **cruis´er** *n.* type of warship

crul´ler *n.* cake fried in melted fat

crum´ble *vi. & vt.* break into small pieces

crum´ple *vi. & vt.* wrinkle; collapse

crunch *vt.* crush with the teeth

cru-sade´ *n.* military expedition to recover Christ´s tomb; concerted action or campaign in any cause

crush *vt.* bruise; press; *n.* violent compression; crowd

crust *n.* hard external surface; *vi. & vt.* cover with a hard surface

crus-ta´cean *n.* class of animals (like lobsters) with hard shell

crypt *n.* vault

crys´tal *n.* superior type of glass; geometrically shaped particles of a chemical; glass covering a watch face; *a.* like crystal

cub *n.* young of bears, etc.

cube *n.* solid body having six square faces; third power of any number (as $2^3 = 2 \times 2 \times 2 = 8$); *vt.* raise to the third power; **cu´bic** *a.*

cuck´oo *n.* bird with a distinctive cry; *col.* crazy

cu´cum´ber *n.* creeping plant with edible fruit

cud *n.* food returned from the first stomache of a ruminating animal for chewing

cudg´el *n.* club

cue *n.* stick used in playing billiards; signal, hint, or suggestion

cuff *n.* part of sleeve near the wrist; blow; *vt.* slap or strike

cu´li-nar´y *a.* pertaining to cookery

cull *vt.* select, pick out

cul´mi-nate´ *vi.* reach the highest point

cul´pa-ble *a.* faulty; guilty

cult *n.* system of worship; small group or sect

cul´ti-vate´ *vt.* till; civilize, refine; **cul´ti-va´tion** *n.*

cul´ture *n.* state of civilization; refinement, esp, in the arts; *vt.* raise, grow, improve
cul´vert *n.* archway over a watercourse; conduit
cun´ning *a.* artful; *n.* skill; deceit
cu-pid´i-ty *n.* covetousness, greed
cu´po-la *n.* small dome on a roof
cu´rate *n.* assistant clergyman to a rector or vicar
cu´ra-tor *n.* custodian
curb *n.* check, hindrance; curbstone; *vt.* subdue; check
curd *n.* coagulated milk
cur´dle *vi.* & *vt.* turn into curd; coagulate
cure *n.* act of healing; remedy; *vt.* heal; preserve (as by salting); **cur´-a-ble** *a.*; **cur´a-tive** *a.*
cu´ri-os´i-ty *n.* inquisitiveness; anything rare
cu´ri-ous *a.* inquisitive; rare; peculiar
curl *n.* ringlet; *vi.* & *vt.* form into ringlets
cur´mudg´eon *n.* ill-natured person
cur´rant *n.* small raisin
cur´ren-cy *n.* circulation; money of a country
cur´rent *a.* general; present; *n.* course; movement of a stream; flow of electricity
cur´ry *n.* mixture of spices; dish prepared with this mixture; *vt.* dress leather; clean a horse´s hair
curse *n.* malediction; *vt.* invoke evil upon; *vi.* swear
cur´so-ry *a.* superficial
curt *a.* short; abrupt
cur´tail´ *vt.* cut short
cur´tain *n.* drapery hung as a screen; *vt.*
curve *n.* bent line; *vi.* & *vt.* bend;
cur´va-ture´ *n.* curving; degree of curve
cush´ion *n.* pillow; *vt.* furnish with a cushion; make softer
cus-to´di-an *n.* guardian
cus´to-dy *n.* guardianship; imprisonment
cus´tom *n.* usage, convention
cu-ta´ne-ous *a.* pertaining to the skin
cut´back´ *n.* reduction in production
cute *a.* clever; attractive
cu´ti-cle *n.* outermost layer of skin, epidermis; skin around the nails
cut´lass *n.* short, broad, curving sword
cut´let *n.* slice of mutton, lamb, or veal, from rib or leg
cy´ber-net´ics *n.* study of communication and control in animal and machine
cy´cle *n.* period of time; orbit of heavenly body; literary, or musical sequence built around a single theme; bicycle
cy´clone´ *n.* rotary storm or tornado
cy´clo-tron´ *n.* machine for the study of atomic structure and for producing artificial radioactivity
cyg´net *n.* young swan
cyl´in-der *n.* round body whose ends are equal and parallel circles; **cy-lin´dri-cal** *a.*
cym´bal *n.* disc-shaped percussion instrument
cyn´ic *n.* sneering critic or faultfinder; one of an austere sect of Greek philosophers; **cyn´i-cism** *n.*
cy´press *n.* evergreen tree
cyst *n.* internal sac containing morbid matter
cy-tol´o-gy *n.* study of plant and animal cells
Czar *n.* emperor of Russia

D

dachs´hund´ *n.* dog with long body and short legs

Da´cron *n. tr.* a synthetic fiber

daf´fo-dil´ *n.* bulbous plant with yellow flowers

daft *a.* idiotic; foolish

dag´ger *n.* kind of knife or short sword; mark of reference

dahl´ia *n.* type of garden flower

dain´ty *a.* delicate; *n.* delicacy; **dain´ti-ly** *adv.*

dair´y *n.* place which produces milk, butter, and cheese

dai´sy *n.* common spring flower

dal´ly *vi.* trifle; delay

dam *n.* embankment to restrain water; *vt.* keep back water by a bank

dam´age *n.* injury; compensation; *vt.* injure

damp *a.* moist; *n.* moist air; *vt.* wet slightly; discourge

dan´de-li´on *n.* common plant with yellow flower

dan´dle *vt.* play with (as a child)

dan´druff *n.* scaly scurf on the head

dan´dy *a.* very fine; *n.* dude; *col.* anything very fine

dan´ger *n.* peril

dan´gle *vi.* & *vt.* swing freely

dap´per *a.* neat

dare *vi.* be bold enough; *vt.* challenge

dart *n.* pointed weapon for throwing; *vi.* start forth rapidly

dash *vi.* rush forward; *vt.* throw violently; destroy; *n.* mark (-) of punctuation; slight admixture

da´ta pro´cess´ing *n.* method of analyzing information by electronic computer

date *n.* fruit of the date palm; time of any event; appointment, esp. for social purposes; *vi.* have a social engagement; take origin; reckon; *vt.* affix a date to; make a date, court

daub *vt.* paint coarsely; coat with plaster, etc.

daunt *vt.* discourage

daw´dle *vi.* waste time

dawn *n.* daybreak; beginning; *vi.* begin to grow light; appear

daze *vt.* render dull or insensible

daz´zle *vt.* daze with light; overwhelm by attractiveness

DDT *n.* dischloro-diphenyl-trichloroethane, an insecticide

dea´con *n.* order of clergy below priests; principal lay official

dead *a.* lifeless; useless; without vegetation

deaf *a.* unable to hear

deal *n.* quantity; act of distributing; business transaction; *vt.* **(dealt)** distribute; *vi.* trade with

dean *n.* chief priest in certain churches; one of various officials in a college

dearth *n.* scarcity

death *n.* extinction of life

de-bar´ *vt.* exclude

de-base´ *vt.* lower in worth; adulterate

de-bate´ *n.* formal argument; *vi.* & *vt.* argue, discuss

de-bauch´ *vi.* indulge in revelry to an extreme; *vt.* corrupt; **deb´au-chee´** *n.* libertine

de-bil´i-tate´ *vt.* weaken; **de-bil´i-ty** *n.*

deb´it *n.* debt; debtor side of an account; *vt.* charge with debt

dé-bris´ *n.* rubbish; ruin

debt *n.* that which one owes

debt´or *n.* one who owes

de´but´ *n.* first appearance before the public

dec´ade *n.* period of ten years

dec´a-dence *n.* state of decay or decline; **dec´a-dent** *a.*
de-cal´co-ma´ni-a *n.* process of transferring pictures and designs from paper to glass, wood, etc.
Dec´a-log´, Dec´a-logue´ *n.* the Ten Commandments
de-cant´ *vt.* pour from one vessel into another
de-cap´i-tate´ *vt.* behead; **de-cap´i-ta´tion** *n.*
de-cay´ *vi.* corrupt, rot; *n.* deterioration
de-cease´ *n.* death; *vi.* die
de-ceit´ *n.* fraud
de-ceive´ *vt.* mislead; cheat
de´cen-cy *n.* propriety; **de´cent** *a.*
de-cep´tion *n.* fraud, trickery
dec´i-bel´ *n.* unit for measuring the loudness of sound
de-cide´ *vt.* determine; settle
de-cid´u-ous *a.* falling off, as leaves in autumn
dec´i-mal *n.* decimal fraction
de-ci´pher *vt.* translate code; read or make out what is obscure
de-ci´sion *n.* determination, fixed purpose; judgment
de-ci´sive *a.* final, conclusive
deck *n.* floor of a ship; pack of playing cards; *vt.* adorn
de-claim´ *vi.* & *vt.* recite; speak for effect
de-clare´ *vt.* proclaim, tell; **dec´la-ra´tion** *n.*
de-cline´ *vi.* & *vt.* refuse; fail; *n.* deviation; decay
de-coc´tion *n.* extract made by boiling
de´com-pose´ *vi.* & *vt.* resolve into original elements; decay; **de-com´-po-si´tion** *n.*
dec´o-rate´ *vt.* ornament **dec´o-ra´-tion** *n.*
dec´o-rous *a.* proper, decent; **de-co´rum** *n.*
de´coy *n.* snare, allurement; lure for fowl, etc.; *vt.* allure, entrap
de-crease´ *vi.* & *vt.* grow or make less; *n.*
de-cree´ *n.* order made by one in authority; *vt.* appoint; command, order
de-crep´it *a.* worn by age; **de-crep´i-tude´** *n.*
ded´i-cate´ *vt.* set apart; inscribe; **ded´i-ca´tion** *n.*
de-duce´ *vt.* infer
de-duct´ *vt.* subtract; **de-duc´tion** *n.* that which is subtracted or omitted from taxation; logical inference
deed *n.* act; writing conveying property title
deem *vi.* & *vt.* think, suppose
deep´freeze´ *vt.* to freeze food quickly to very low temperature
deep space *n.* outer space beyond the solar system
de-face´ *vt.* disfigure, mar
de-fame´ *vt.* destroy the reputation of, slander; **def´a-ma´tion** *n.*
de-fault´ *n.* failing; neglect of duty; *vi.* fail in meeting an obligation; *vt.* declare in default; enter judgment against
de-feat´ *vt.* overcome; *n.* overthrow; undoing
de-feat´ist *n.* pessimist; one who admits or foresees his defeat
de-fect´ *n.* imperfection; *vi.* desert to the enemy
de-fend´ *vt.* shield, protect; vindicate, uphold
de-fense´, de-fence´ *n.* protection; plea made by defendant; **de-fen´si-ble** *a.*
de-fer´ *vi.* & *vt.* postpone; yield; **def´er-ence** *n.* respectful yielding; **def´er-en´tial** *a.* respectful

de-fi´ance *n.* resistance; challenge; **de-fi´ant** *a.*
de-fi´cien-cy *n.* defect; amount wanting; **de-fi´cient** *a.*
def´i-cit *n.* deficiency
de-file´ *vt.* pollute
de-fine´ *vt.* determine with precision; explain the meaning of
def´i-nite *a.* having distinct limits; precise; **def´i-ni´tion** *n.* description of a thing by its properties; explanation, of the exact meaning
de-fla´tion *n.* mild depression
de-flect´ *vi. & vt.* turn aside; **de-flec´tion** *n.*
de-fo´li-a´tion *n.* shedding of leaves
de-form´ *vt.* put out of shape, warp
de-fraud´ *vt.* cheat
de-fray´ *vt.* pay or help pay for
de-frost´ *vt.* remove frost or ice, as from refrigerator or windshield
deft *a.* handy, skillful
de-funct´ *a.* dead
de-fy´ *vt.* challenge; resist
de-gen´er-ate *a.* deteriorated; *n.* one who has deteriorated, as in morals; *v.* grow worse
de-grade´ *vt.* debase; **deg´ra-da´tion** *n.*
de-gree´ *n.* grade; extent; 360th part of a circle
de-his´cence *n.* opening of seed pod
de-hy´drate´ *vt.* free from water, as with foods to reduce their weight and bulk
de-ic´er *n.* device for keeping ice off airplanes
de´i-fy´ *vt.* exalt to the rank of a god
deign *vi.* condescend
de´i-ty *n.* a god; divine being
de-ject´ *vt.* dishearten; **de-jec´tion** *n.*
de-lay´ *vi.* pause; *vt.* put off; hinder; *n.* stop; hindrance
de-lec´ta-ble *a.* delightful; **de´lec-ta´tion** *n.*
del´e-gate´ *vt.* send as a representative; entrust; *n.* representative; **del´e-ga´tion** *n.*
del´e-te´ri-ous *a.* harmful; tending to destroy
de-lib´er-ate *a.* well considered; slow in determining; *vi. & vt.* weigh in one´s mind; **de-lib´er-a´tion** *n.*
del´i-ca-cy *n.* refinement; dainty food; **del´i-cate** *a.* refined; dainty
de-li´cious *a.* pleasing, esp. to taste, or smell
de´light *n.* high degree of pleasure; *vi.* have great pleasure; *vt.* please highly
de-lin´e-ate´ *vt.* sketch, picture, describe; **de-lin´e-a´tion** *n.*
de-lin´quen-cy *n.* fault, misdemeanor
de-lin´quent *a.* failing in duty; unpaid; *n.* transgressor, esp. if young
de-lir´i-ous *a.* wandering in mind; **de-lir´i-um** *n.*
de-liv´er *vt.* send out; give; pronounce; liberate
del´ta *n.* triangular tract of soil at the mouth of a river
de-lude´ *vt.* deceive, hoodwink
del´uge *n.* great flood; *vt.* inundate; overwhelm
de-lu´sion *n.* fraud; error; **de-lu´sive** *a.*
delve *vt.* dig
de-mand´ *n.* claim; requirement; *vt.* claim; require, need; call for
de-mean´ *vt.* behave oneself
de-ment´ed *a.* out of one´s mind
de-men´tia prae´cox´ *n.* schizophrenia
de-mer´it *n.* deficiency mark given for bad conduct
de-mil´i-tar-ize´ *vt.* to free an area from armed forces; to neutralize an area

de-mise´ *n.* transfer of property or crown; death, esp. of a sovereign
de-moc´ra-cy *n.* government by the people
Dem´o-crat´ *n.* member of the Democratic Party in the U.S.
de-mog´ra-phy *n.* statistical study of human population
de-mol´ish *vt.* destroy wreck; **dem´-o-li´tion** *n.*
de´mon *n.* evil spirit; **de-mo´ni-ac** *a.*
dem´on-strate´ *vt.* prove; **dem´on-stra´tion** *n.*
de-mor´al-ize´ *vt.* subvert morals, morale, or discipline; **de-mor´al-i-za´tion** *n.*
de-mur´ *vi.* hesitate; object; *n.* objection; hesitation
de-mure´ *a.* modest
de-ni´al *n.* act of denying; contradiction; refusal
den´i-zen *n.* inhabitant, esp. one originally from another place
de-nom´i-na´tion *n.* name; title; sect
de-nounce´ *vt.* accuse, criticize
dense *a.* close, compact; stupid; **den´si-ty** *n.*
den´tal *a.* pertaining to the teeth
den´tist *n.* one who treats the teeth
den´ture *n.* set of teeth, esp. artificial teeth
de-nude´ *vt.* bare, strip bare
de-nun´ci-a´tion *n.* act of denouncing
de-ny´ *vt.* declare not true; refuse
de-o´dor-ant *n.* preparation for counteracting disagreeable odors; **de-o´dor-ize´** *vt.*
de-part´ *vi.* go away; die; **de-par´-ture** *n.*
de-part´ment *n.* a division, as in government or schools
de-pend´ *vi.* be conditional upon; trust
de-pict´ *vt.* picture; describe minutely
de-plete´ *vt.* empty, exhaust
de-plore´ *vt.* lament
de-pop´u-late´ *vt.* deprive of inhabitants
de-port´ *vt.* banish; behave; **de´por-ta´tion** *n.* banishment
de-pose´ *vt.* put down; dethrone; state under oath
de-pos´it *vt.* place; entrust; *n.* that which is deposited; pledge, down payment; **de-pos´i-to´ry** *n.*
de´pot´ *n.* railway station; military storehouse
de-prave´ *vt.* corrupt
dep´re-cate´ *vt.* disapprove of, regret; **dep´re-ca´tion** *n.*; **dep´re-ca-to´ry** *a.*
de-pre´ci-ate´ *vi.* fall in value; *vt.* lower the value of; disparage
dep´re-date´ *vt.* plunder; **dep´re-da´tion** *n.*
de-press´ *vt.* press down, lower; dispirit
de-pres´sion *n.* melancholy; severe state of business inactivity
de-prive´ *vt.* dispossess, rob; **dep´ri-va´tion** *n.*
depth *n.* deepness; deep place; deepest part
dep´u-ta´tion *n.* delegation
dep´u-ty *n.* assistant
de-range´ *vt.* put out of order; make insane
der´e-lict *a.* abandoned; *n.*
de-ride´ *vt.* ridicule
de-ri´sion *n.* mockery; **de-ri´sive** *a.*
de-rive´ *vt.* deduce; trace words, etc., to an origin; proceed from an origin; **der´i-va´tion** *n.*; **de-riv´a-tive** *a.* & *n.*
der´o-ga´tion *n.* detraction; depreciation; **de-rog´a-to´ry** *a.* disparag-

ing

der´rick *n.* large crane; rigging over an oil well

de-scend´ *vi.* & *vt.* go down

de-scent´ *n.* motion downward; slope, declivity; lineage

de-scribe´ *vt.* trace out; give an account of; **de-scrip´tion** *n.*; **de-scrip´tive** *a.*

de-scry´ *vt.* discover by the eye, see

des´e-crate´ *vt.* profane; **des´e-cra´-tion** *n.*

de-seg´re-gate´ *vt.* end separation, esp. of Negroes and whites; **de-seg´re-ga´tion** *n.*

des´ert *n.* wilderness

des-ert´ *vi.* & *vt.* forsake, abandon; **de-ser´tion** *n.*

de-serve´ *vi.* & *vt.* be worthy of

des´ha-bille´ *n.* undress; careless dress

des´ic-cate´ *vi.* & *vt.* dry up; **des´ic-ca´tion** *n.*

de-sid´er-a´tum *n.* **(de-sid´er-a´ta)** anything required

de-sign´ *vt.* draw; plan; *n.*

des´ig-nate´ *vt.* show; name; set apart; **des´ig-na´tion** *n.*

de-sire´ *vt.* wish for, long for; request; *n.*; **de-sir´a-ble** *a.*

de-sist´ *vi.* stop

des´o-late´ *vt.* lay waste; *a.* forsaken; **des´o-la´tion** *n.*

de-spair´ *vi.* abandon hope; *n.*

des-per-a´do *n.* **(des-per-a´dos, des-per-a´does)** dangerous or desperate outlaw

des´per-ate *a.* hopeless; **des´per-a´-tion** *n.*

des-pic´a-ble *a.* contemptible

de-spise´ *vt.* scorn, hate

de-spoil´ *vt.* spoil; rob; **de-spo´li-a´-tion** *n.*

de-spond´ *vi.* despair

des´pot *n.* tyrant

des-sert´ *n.* last course of a meal

des´tine *vt.* plan, design; determine, as by fate; **des´ti-na´tion** *n.* end; fate; place to which one is going

des´ti-ny *n.* fate

des´ti-tute´ *a.* in want; **des´ti-tu´-tion** *n.*

de-stroy´ *vt.* ruin

des´ha-bille´ *n.* undress; careless dress

des´ic-cate´ *vi.* & *vt.* dry up; **des´ic-ca´tion** *n.*

de-sid´er-a´tum *n.* **(de-sid´er-a´ta)** anything required

de-sign´ *vt.* draw; plan; *n.*

des´ig-nate´ *vt.* show; name; set apart; **des´ig-na´tion** *n.*

de-sire´ *vt.* wish for, long for; request; *n.*; **de-sir´a-ble** *a.*

de-sist´ *vi.* stop

des´o-late´ *vt.* lay waste; *a.* forsaken; **des´o-la´tion** *n.*

de-spair´ *vi.* abandon hope; *n.*

des-per-a´do *n.* **(des-per-a´dos, des-per-a´does)** dangerous or desperate outlaw

des´per-ate *a.* hopeless; **des´per-a´-tion** *n.*

des-pic´a-ble *a.* contemptible

de-spise´ *vt.* scorn, hate

de-spoil´ *vt.* spoil; rob; **de-spo´li-a´-tion** *n.*

de-spond´ *vi.* despair

des´pot *n.* tyrant

des-sert´ *n.* last course of a meal

des´tine *vt.* plan, design; determine, as by fate; **des´ti-na´tion** *n.* end; fate; place to which one is going

des´ti-ny *n.* fate

des´ti-tute´ *a.* in want; **des´ti-tu´-tion** *n.*

de-stroy´ *vt.* ruin

de-struc´tion *n.* ruin; death

des´ul-to´ry *a.* rambling; random

de-tach´ *vt.* separate

de-tail´ *vt.* relate minutely; set apart
de´tail, de-tail´ *n.* small part; minute account; detachment of troops
de-tain´ *vt.* hold back
de-tect´ *vt.* discover; **de-tec´tion** *n.*; **de-tec´tive** *n.* one employed to discover criminals
dé-tente´ *n.* easing of tensions (between nations)
de-ten´tion *n.* detaining, delay
de-ter´ *vt.* hinder
de-ter´gent *n.* cleansing agent
de-te´ri-o-rate´ *vi.* & *vt.* become worse; **de-te´ri-o-ra´tion** *n.*
de-ter´mine *vt.* limit; settle, judge; find out; **de-ter´mi-na´tion** *n.*
de-test´ *vt.* dislike intensely
det´o-nate´ *vi.* & *vt.* explode
de´tour´ *n.* roundabout way
de-tract´ *vi.* reduce in merit; disparage; defame; **de-trac´tion** *n.*
det´ri-ment *n.* damage; cause of damage; **det´ri-ment´al** *a.*
de-val´u-a´tion *n.* reducing the value of money with respect to gold
dev´as-tate´ *vt.* lay waste; **dev´as-ta´tion** *n.*
de-vel´op *vi.* & *vt.* change, grow, expand; process photographic film
de´vi-ate *vi.* turn aside from a standard or course; **de´vi-a´tion** *n.*
de-vice´ *n.* contrivance
de´vi-ous *a.* roundabout
de-vise´ *vt.* contrive; bequeath
de-vote´ *vt.* give or donate
dev´o-tee´ *n.* one devoted to some purpose or thing
de-vo´tion *n.* prayer; strong attachment
de-vour´ *vt.* consume, eat
de-vout´ *a.* pious
dex´ter´i-ty *n.* skill; **dex´ter-ous, dex´trous** *a.*
di´a-bol´ic *a.* devilish
di´a-crit´ic *n.* mark (such as ^) which serves to distinguish letters' sounds
di´a-dem´ *n.* type of crown
di´ag-no´sis *n.* determination of a disease
di´ag´o-nal *a.* going from one corner to another
di´a-gram´ *n.* plan, drawing
di´al *n.* face of a watch, clock, or telephone
di´a-lect´ *n.* language or variety of language spoken in an area
di´a-log´, di´a-logue´ *n.* conversation between two or more
di-am´e-ter *n.* line passing through the center of a circle
di´a-mond *n.* precious stone; four-sided figure
di´a-per *n.* baby´s undergarment
di´a-phragm´ *n.* any dividing membrane
di´ar-rhe´a *n.* morbid looseness of the bowels
di´a-ry *n.* daily record
di-as´to-le *n.* rhythmic expansion of heart cavities as they fill with blood
di´a-ther´my *n.* electric apparatus to heat tissues under the skin; deep heat
dick´er *vi.* haggle, bargain
dick´ey *n.* woman´s half-blouse
Dic´ta-phone´ *n.* *tr.* business machine that records speech for later transcription
dic´tate´ *vt.* command, order; speak aloud for transcription by a secretary; *n.* order; **dic´ta´tion** *n.*
dic´ta´tor *n.* despot, tyrannical ruler; **dic´ta-to´ri-al** *a.*
dic´tion *n.* manner of oral expression; choice of words
dic´tion-ar´y *n.* lexicon; list of words with their definitions, etc.
die *vi.* **(died; dying)** lose one´s life
die *n.* **(dice)** small cube used in

gambling; **(dies)** metal stamp

di´et *n.* course of food, fare; special course of food prescribed by physician; *vi.* take food according to rule

dif´fer *vi.* disagree; be unlike

dif´fer-ence *n.* distinguishing mark; excess in quantity; quarrel

dif´fi-cult´ *a.* hard to do; **dif´fi-cul´-ty** *n.*

dif´fi-dent *a.* shy; **dif´fi-dence** *n.* lack of confidence

dif-fuse´ *a.* widely spread

di´gest´ *n.* body of laws; body of information arranged in useful order; magazine which condenses articles of interest

di-gest´ *vt.* prepare for assimilation; assimilate; distribute and arrange; **di-ges´tion** *n.*

dig´it *n.* finger or toe; one of the figures 0 to 9

dig´ni-fy´ *vt.* exalt; give dignity to

dig´ni-tar´y *n.* one who holds a high position

dig´ni-ty *n.* state of being worthy or decorous

di-gress´ *vi.* depart from main subject; ramble; **di-gres´sion** *n.*

di-lap´i-date´ *vi.* & *vt.* ruin, become ruined

di´late´ *vi.* & *vt.* expand; **di´la´tion** *n.*

dil´a-to´ry *a.* causing delay; delaying

di-lem´ma *n.* predicament with only two solutions, both unpleasant

dil´i-gence *n.* industry; **dil´i-gent** *a.*

di-lute´ *vt.* make thinner or weaker in strength; *a.*; **di-lu´tion** *n.*

di-men´sion *n.* extent; measure

di-min´ish *vi.* & *vt.* make or grow less

dim´i-nu´tion *n.* lessening, decrease

di-min´u-tive *a.* small; *n.* suffix, like *-ette (room-ette)* indicating small size

di´o-cese´ *n.* district supervised by a bishop

diph´the´ri-a *n.* inflammatory, contagious disease of the air passages

diph´thong´ *n.* sequence of vowels pronounced as one syllable

di-plo´ma *n.* document testifying to graduation from a school

di-plo´ma-cy *n.* international negotiations; tactfulness; **dip´lo-mat´** *n.*; **dip´lo-mat´ic** *a.*

dip´so-ma´ni-a *n.* alcoholism

di-rect´ *a.* straight; sincere; *vt.* point out; order

di-rec´tion *n.* line in which anything moves; guidance

di-rec´tor *n.* one who directs; one who directs acting in play, movie, or TV

di-rec´to-ry *n.* body of directors; guide; book with names, addresses, etc., of residents or members

dirge *n.* funeral song

dir´i-gi-ble *n.* gas-filled, engine-driven aircraft

dis-a´ble *vt.* make unable; **dis´a-bil´i-ty** *n.*

dis´ad-van´tage *n.* handicap

dis´a-gree´ *vi.* differ in opinion

dis´al-low´ *vt.* refuse to permit, refuse

dis´ap-pear´ *vi.* vanish from sight; cease to be

dis´ap-point´ *vt.* fail to meet expectations

dis´ap-prove´ *vt.* think ill of; reject; **dis´ap-prov´al** *n.*

dis´arm´ *vt.* deprive of weapons; **dis´ar´ma-ment** *n.* reduction of military power

dis´ar-range´ *vt.* disorder

dis-as´ter *n.* misfortune; **dis-as´-**

trous *a.*
dis´a-vow´ *vt.* disclaim
dis-band´ *vi.* & *vt.* break up; disperse
dis´be-lieve´ *vt.* refuse to believe; **dis´be-lief´** *n.*
dis-burse´ *vt.* pay out
disc *n.* variant spelling of *disk*
dis-card´ *vt.* throw away; **dis´card** *n.*
dis-cern´ *vt.* distinguish clearly
dis-charge´ *vt.* unload; fire a gun; fire an employee; fulfill an obligation
dis´charge´ *n.* act of discharging; that which is discharged; separation from military service
dis-ci´ple *n.* learner; follower
dis´ci-pline *n.* training; subjection to control; punishment; *vt.* train; bring under control; punish
disc´ jock´ey *n.* radio announcer who plays recorded music
dis-claim´ *vt.* renounce claim to
dis-close´ *vt.* reveal; **dis-clo´sure** *n.*
dis-com´fort *n.* physical or mental uneasiness; *vt.* make uneasy
dis´com-pose´ *vt.* disturb, upset; **dis´com-po´sure** *n.*
dis´con-cert´ *vt.* confuse, embarrass
dis´con-nect´ *vt.* separate
dis´con´so-late *a.* hopeless
dis´con-tent´ *a.* dissatisfied; *n.* lack of content; *vt.* make unhappy
dis´con-tin´ue *vi.* & *vt.* stop
dis´cord´ *n.* strife; inharmonious sounds; **dis´cord´ant** *a.*
dis´co-thèque´ *n.* night club where customers dance to recorded music
dis´count´ *n.* deduction; **discount house** *n.* store where merchandise is sold at less than usual price
dis-count´ *vt.* allow a discount on; advance money on, deducting interest; reject as untrue
dis-coun´te-nance *vt.* abash; discourage
dis-cour´age *vt.* deter, demoralize
dis´course´ *n.* conversation; treatise; *vi.* converse with
dis-cour´te-ous *a.* uncivil; **dis-cour´te-sy** *n.*
dis-cov´er *vt.* find out
dis-cred´it *n.* disgrace; *vt.* disbelieve in; disgrace
dis-creet´ *a.* prudent
dis-crep´an-cy *n.* disagreement, as in accounts, texts, etc.; **dis-crep´-ant** *a.*
dis-crete´ *a.* made up of distinct parts
dis-cre´tion *n.* prudence; free judgment
dis-crim´i-nate´ *vi.* & *vt.* distinguish; **dis-crim´i-na´tion** *n.*
dis´cus *n.* heavy disk thrown in athletic contests
dis-cuss´ *vt.* debate, talk over; **dis-cus´sion** *n.*
dis-dain´ *vt.* despise, scorn; *n.* aversion
dis-ease´ *n.* sickness
dis´em-bark´ *vi.* & *vt.* land
dis´en-chant´ *vt.* disillusion
dis´en-gage´ *vt.* separate
dis-fa´vor *n.* lack of favor or esteem; disobliging act
dis-fig´ure *vt.* deform
dis-gorge´ *vt.* vomit; give up
dis-grace´ *n.* shame; cause of shame; *vt.*
dis-guise´ *vt.* conceal by false show; *n.* dress or device to conceal the wearer
dis-gust´ *n.* loathing, repugnance; *vt.* excite repugnance in
dis-heart´en *vt.* discourage
di-shev´el *vt.* disorder, as the hair
dis-hon´est *a.* not honest
dis-hon´or *n.* lack of honor; disgrace; *vt.* deprive of honor; dis-

grace
dis´in-cline´ *vi.* be averse to
dis´in-fect´ *vt.* free from contagion
dis´in-gen´u-ous *a.* not frank or open
dis´in-her´it *vt.* deprive of hereditary rights
dis-in´te-grate´ *vi.* & *vt.* decay, break or fall into parts; **dis´in-te-gra´tion** *n.*
dis´in´ter-est-ed *a.* impartial; not interested
disk *n.* round plate
dis-like´ *vt.* have an aversion to; *n.* aversion
dis-lo´cate´ *vt.* put out of joint; **dis´-lo-ca´tion** *n.*
dis-lodge´ *vt.* force out of, as from hiding
dis-loy´al *a.* false; traitorous
dis´mal *a.* gloomy
dis-man´tle *vt.* deprive of dress, furniture, or guns; take apart a machine
dis-may´ *vt.* discourage; worry; *n.*
dis-miss´ *vt.* send away; remove from office or employinent
dis´o-be´di-ent *a.* unruly, refractory, not obedient; **dis´o-be´di-ence** *n.*
dis´o-bey´ *vt.* neglect or refuse to obey
dis-or´der *n.* want of order; disturbance; disease; *vt.* disarrange
dis-own´ *vt.* disinherit; refuse to acknowledge as ones own
dis-par´age *vt.* depreciate, belittle
dis-par´i-ty *n.* inequality, disagreement
dis-pas´sion-ate *a.* free from bias
dis-patch´ *vt.* send away hastily; dispose of speedily; mail; *n.* rapidity; news message, telegram
dis-pel´ *vt.* drive away
dis-pense´ *vt.* deal out in portions; *vi.* exempt; do without; **dis´pen-sa´tion** *n.* distribution; relaxation of a law; divine order of things
dis-perse´ *vi.* & *vt.* scatter; **dis-per´-sal** *n.*; **dis-per´sion** *n.*
dis-place´ *vt.* put out of place; remove; take the place of;
dis-play´ *vt.* exhibit; *n.* exhibition
dis-please´ *vt.* offend; **dis-pleas´ure** *n.*
dis-port´ *vi.* & *vt.* amuse, be gay
dis-pose´ *vt.* arrange; bestow; incline; **dis-pos´al** *n.*; **dis´po-si´tion** *n.* arrangement; temperament, inherent traits
dis´pos-sess´ *vt.* put out of possession
dis´pro-por´tion *n.* lack of proportion or harmony; *vt.* make unsuitable in form
dis-prove´ *vt.* refute
dis-pute´ *vi.* & *vt.* oppose by argument; *n.* verbal contest; **dis´pu´ta-ble** *a.*; **dis´pu-ta´tion** *n.* debate
dis´qual´i-fy *vt.* make unfit; debar
dis´qui´et *n.* uneasiness; *vt.* disturb, make uneasy
dis´qui-si´tion *n.* elaborate essay
dis´re-gard´ *vt.* pay no attention to; *n.* neglect
dis´re-pute´ *n.* discredit; disgrace; **dis´rep´u-ta-ble** *a.*
dis´re-spect´ *n.* incivility
dis´rupt´ *vt.* break up; **dis-rup´tion** *n.*
dis´sat´is-fy *vt.* displease; **dis-sat´-is-fac´tion** *n.*
dis-sect´ *vt.* take apart and examine (as an animal by cutting)
dis-sem´ble *vi.* & *vt.* feign, pretend
dis-sem´i-nate´ *vi.* & *vt.* scatter, spread; **dis-sem´i-na´tion** *n.*
dis-sen´sion *n.* disagreement
dis-sent´ *vi.* think differently, disagree; *n.* difference of opinion

dis´ser-ta´tion *n.* formal essay; doctoral thesis
dis´sim´i-lar *a.* unlike; **dis-sim´i-lar´i-ty** *n.*
dis-sim´u-la´tion *n.* dissembling; pretension
dis´si-pate´ *vi.* lead a dissolute life; *vt.* squander; **dis´si-pa´tion** *n.*
dis´so-lute a, licentious, loose in morals
dis´so-lu´tion *n.* breaking up, disintegration; death
dis-solve´ *vi.* & *vt.* separate, melt
dis´so-nance *n.* discord, inharmonious sounds; disagreement; **dis´so-nant** *a.*
dis-suade´ *vt.* advise against; **dis-sua´sion** *n.*
dis´tance *n.* space or interval between; remoteness; reserve of manner; **dis´tant** *a.*
dis-taste´ *n.* aversion
dis-tend´ *vi.* & *vt.* swell; **dis-ten´-sion** *n.*
dis-till´, dis-til´ *vt.* purify; concentrate; extract or concentrate the alcoholic content from
dis-tinct´ *a.* separate; clear; **dis-tinc´tion** *n.* separation; difference; regard to differences; eminence
dis-tin´guish *vi.* & *vt.* set apart; recognize by characteristic qualities
dis-tort´ *vt.* force out of shape; twist the true meaning of; **dis-tor´tion** *n.*
dis-tract´ *vt.* confuse; divert; **dis-trac´tion** *n.*
dis-tress´ *n.* calamity; pain; *vt.* afflict with calamity or pain
dis-trib´ute *vt.* divide among several; classify; **dis´tri-bu´tion** *n.*
dis´trict *n.* region, area; administrative region
dis-trust´ *n.* lack of trust; *vt.* be suspicious of
dis-turb´ *vt.* disquiet; interrupt
di´u-ret´ic *a.* tending to increase urination; *n.*
di-ur´inal *a.* daily
div´er *n.* one who dives, as in swimming; man equipped with breathing apparatus, etc., for underwater operations
di-verge´ *vi.* tend toward different directions; **di-ver´gence** *n.*; **di-ver´gent** *a.*
di-verse´ *a.* different; **di-ver´si-ty** *n.* variety
di-ver´si-fy´ *vt.* vary; **di-ver´si-fi-ca´tion** *n.*
di-ver´sion *n.* amusement, pastime; act of turning aside
di-vert´ *vt.* turn aside; amuse
di-vest´ *vt.* deprive; strip
di-vide´ *vi.* & *vt.* separate into parts; allot; *n.* watershed
div´i-dend´ *n.* quantity to be divided; share of profits
di-vine´ *a.* holy; belonging to or proceeding from God; *vt.* foretell; **div´-i-na´tion** *n.* prediction
di-vin´i-ty *n.* divine nature; supreme being
di-vi´sion *n.* dividing, partition; that which is divided; rift, dissension; part of a whole; military unit
di-vorce´ *n.* legal dissolution of marriage; *vt.*
di-vulge´ *vt.* make public
DNA *n.* deoxyribonucleic acid, which carries the genetic code within cells
doc´ile *a.* teachable; easily managed; **do-cil´i-ty** *n.*
doc´trine *n.* teaching, as in religion
doc´u-ment *n.* paper containing information or proof; **doc-u-ment´-ary** *n.* movie or TV which studies in detail some newsworthy event or situation
dog´ger-el *n.* poor verse

do´gie *n.* motherless calf
dog´ma *n.* tenet; authoritative doctrine; **dog-mat´ic** *a.* overbearing, doctrinaire
dole *n.* share; alms; *vt.* deal out in small portions
dole´ful *a.* full of grief
do´lor *n.* grief, pain
dol´phin *n.* animal of the whale kind, porpoise
do-main´ *n.* realm, dominion
dome *n.* vaulted roof
do-mes´tic *a.* belonging to one´s family or country; devoted to home life; tame; *n.* servant in the house; **do´mes-tic´i-ty** *n.*
do-mes´ti-cate´ *vt.* make domestic
dom´i-cile *n.* home, abode
dom´i-nate´ *vt.* prevail over; **dom´i-na´tion** *n.*
do-min´ion *n.* power; country governed; self-governing country within the British Commonwealth
do´nate´ *vt.* give; **do´na´tion** *n.*
don´key *n.* **(don´keys)** ass
do´nor *n.* giver
doo´dle *n.* draw idly; make little sketches
doom *n.* destiny, fate; *vt.* sentence, fate
dor´mant *a.* inactive, sleeping
dor´mer, dor´mer win´dow *n.* vertical window set in sloping roof
dor´mi-to´ry *n.* building with living quarters, as for students
dose *n.* quantity of medicine taken at one time; *vt.* give in doses; give anything noxious to
dot *n.* small round mark, stipple; *vt.* mark with dots; diversify
dote *vi.* be foolishly affectionate; be silly from age; **dot´age** *n.* childishness from old age; foolish fondness; **do´tard** *n.* person in his dotage
dou´ble *a.* twice, twofold; in pairs; *vt.* multiply by two; fold; *vi.* increase twofold; run back; *n.* twice as much; duplicate; **double feature** *n.* two movies for the price of one ticket
dou´ble-deck´er *n.* vehicle with seats on two levels
doubt *vt.* hesitate; suspect; *n.* suspicion; uncertainty of mind
dough *n.* preparation of flour, eggs, etc., for baking; *col.* money
douse *vt.* plunge into or soak with water
dove´tail´ *n.* a fitting of pieces (tenons) into corresponding cavities (mortises); *vi.* & *vt.*
dow´el *n.* wooden pin, fitting into a hole
dow´ry *n.* estate of a bride
dox´ol´o-gy *n.* hymn praising God
doze *vi.* sleep lightly, nap; *n.* short, light sleep
doz´en *n.* collection of twelve
drab *n.* dull brown color; *a.* dull
draft, draught *n.* drawing; levy of men; order for payment of money; rough sketch; act of drinking, gulp; current of air; depth of water needed to float a boat; *vt.* draw an outline of; compose, write; **drafts´man** *n.* one who draws
drag *vt.* draw along the ground; draw slowly; *vi.* trail on the ground; move heavily; *n.* net to catch things underwater; type of carriage; obstacle; harrow; *col.* influence
drag´on *n.* fabulous winged serpent
drain *vi.* & *vt.* draw by degrees; exhaust; *n.* ditch; pipe for conveying waste; exhaustion
drake *n.* male of the duck
dra´ma *n.* a play; **dra-mat´ic** *a.*; **dram´a-tist** *n.* writer of plays; **dram´a-tize´** *vt.*

drape *vt.* cover with cloth; arrange in folds

dras´tic *a.* extreme; violent and quick in action

draw *vi.* & *vt.* pull; attract; inhale; sketch; *n.* undecided contest

draw´back´ *n.* loss of advantage; handicap

drawl *vi.* & *vt.* speak in a slow, lengthened tone; *n.* drawn-out manner of speaking

dread *n.* apprehension, fear; *vt.* fear greatly

dream *n.* train of sights, sounds, etc., during sleep; *vi.* & *vt.* see things in sleep; think idly

dredge *n.* instrument for gathering by dragging; *vi.* & *vt.*

dregs *n. pl.* impurities at bottom of a liquid

drench *vt.* wet; soak

dress *vi.* & *vt.* put clothes on; prepare; cleanse and bandage; *n.* covering; woman´s gown; costume, ensemble

drib´ble *vi.* & *vt.* fall or let fall in small drops

drift *n.* heap driven together; tendency; *vi.* & *vt.* drive or form into heaps

drill *n.* instrument for boring, drill press; training, exercise; *vi.* & *vt.* pierce with a bore; train

drink *vi.* & *vt.* **(drank; drunk)** swallow a liquid; *n.* something to be drunk; liquor

drip *vi.* & *vt.* fall or let fall in drops; *n.* falling in drops

drip´—dry´ *n.* clothing which can be hung to dry without wrinkles

drive *vi.* & *vt.* **(drove; driven)** force, hurry on; guide; travel by vehicle; *n.* excursion by automobile; road for driving on; **driv´er** *n.*

drive´—in´ *n.* restaurant or theater where customer stays in his car

droll *a.* oddly amusing, comic

drom´e-dar´y *n.* camel with one hump on its back

drone *n.* male of the bee; idler; *vi.* make a humming sound

droop *vi.* & *vt.* sink or hang down; grow faint

drop *n.* small round mass of liquid; distance of fall; *vi.* & *vt.* fall or let fall

drop´out´ *n.* person who withdraws from school or other established institution

dross *n.* scum, refuse

drought, drouth *n.* lack of rain

drove *n.* herd

drown *vi.* sink and die in water; *vt.* kill by placing under water

drowse *vi.* doze; **drow´sy** *a.*

drub *vt.* beat

drudge *vi.* labor at dull work; *n.* one who labors at dull or tedious work, plodder, hack; **drudg´er-y** *n.*

drug *vt.* to mix drugs with; *n.* any substance used as medicine; a narcotic

drum *n.* musical percussion instrument with heads made of skin; tympanum of the ear; *vi.* & *vt.* beat a drum

drunk´ard *n.* a habitual drinker of liquors; a sot

dry *a.* free from moisture; thirsty; uninteresting; wittily droll; *vi.* & *vt.* **(dried)** become or make dry; **dry ice** *n.* frozen carbon dioxide, a refrigerant

dual *a.* consisting of two

dub *vt.* call; confer a dignity upon; add sound effects, as in movies; make a copy of a recording

du´bi-ous *a.* doubtful

duck *n.* kind of waterfowl; dipping of the head or body; amphibious

motor vehicle used by armed forces; *vi.* & *vt.* dip in water; lower the head or body suddenly
duct *n.* tube; canal
duc´tile *a.* capable of being drawn out into wire; tractable; **duc´til´i-ty** *n.*
duct´less gland´ *n.* gland which secretes directly into the bloodstream or lymphatic system; endocrine gland
dude *n.* dandy, fop
dud *n.* a shell that fails to explode; any complete failure; **duds** *col.* clothes
due *a.* payable; scheduled to arrive; proper, fit; *n.* anything owed; **dues** *n. pl.* membership fee
du´el *n.* formal combat between two persons; *vi.* fight in single combat
du-et´ *n.* piece of music for two singers or performers
duke *n.* highest order of English nobility; sovereign prince
dul´cet *a.* sweetly melodious
dull *a.* slow of action or understanding; blunt; *vi.* & *vt.* make or become dull
duly *adv.* properly; at the proper time
dumb *a.* speechless; silent
dum´found´ *vt.* confuse with astonishment
dump *n.* place where trash is unloaded; *vt.* unload, cast away
dump´y *a.* heavy and short, squat; sullen
dun *a.* & *n.* dull brown in color; *vt.* urge for or demand payment; *n..* urgent demand for payment
dunce *n.* stupid person
dune *n.* sand hill
dun´ga-rees´ *n. pl.* clothes made of a tough, coarse cloth
dun´geon *n.* underground prison
du´o-dec´i-mal *a.* computed by twelves
du´o-de´num *n.* first portion of the small intestine
du´pli-cate *a.* double; *n.* copy; *vt.* double, repeat; make a copy
du-plic´i-ty *n.* deceit
du´ra-ble *a.* lasting; **du´ra-bil´i-ty** *n.*
du-ra´tion *n.* extent in time
du-ress´ *n.* constraint
dusk *n.* twilight
du´te-ous *a.* dutiful, obedient
du´ti-ful *a.* attentive to duty
duty *n.* obligation, what one is bound to do; tax on imports
dwarf *n.* animal or plant of less than usual size; *vt.* make small; stunt
dwell *vi.* abide, live in; continue long
dwin´dle *vi.* grow less
dye *n.* coloring agent;*vt.* stain, color
dy-nam´ic *a.* active; having to do with physical energy; **dy-nam´ics** *n.* study of physical forces
dy´na-mo´ *n.* apparatus for generating electricity
dy´nas-ty *n.* succession of sovereigns belonging to the same family
dys´en-ter´y *n.* an intestinal disease
dys´pep´si-a *n.* indigestion; **dys´-pep´tic** *a.*

E

ea´ger *a.* desirous, anxious to do or perform
ea´gle *n.* large bird of prey; figure of an eagle when used as an emblem
ear *n.* organ of hearing; spike of grain; *vi.* put forth ears
earl *n.* British title of nobility above viscount and below marquis
earn *vt.* gain by labor
ear´nest *a.* serious; *n.* pledge
earth *n.* soil; dry land; planet on which we live

earth´quake´ *n.* violent trembling of a part of the earth
ear´ring´ *n.* ornament worn in the ear
earth´worm´ *n.* angleworm
ease *n.* freedom from restraint; *vt.* relieve
ea´sel *n.* frame to support a picture for display or while being painted
east *n.* part of the heavens where the sun rises; Orient
eat *vi.* & *vt.* chew and swallow; consume
eaves *n. pl.* projecting edges of a roof
ebb *n.* receding of the tide; decline; *vi.* flow back
eb´on-y *n.* a hard, black wood
ec-cen´tric *a.* departing from the center; not having the same center; odd, strange; *n.* odd person; **ec´-cen-tric´i-ty** *n.*
ec-cle´si-as´tic *a.* pertaining to the church; *n.* clergyman
echo *n.* reflection of a sound; *vi.* & *vt.* send back the sound of
ec-lec´tic *a.* choosing from different sources; *n.* one who chooses parts of different systems
e-clipse´ *n.* obscuration of the light of sun or moon by some other body; *vt.* put in the shade
e-clip´tic *n.* apparent path of the sun
e-col´o-gy *n.* science dealing with the relationship between organisms and their environment
e´co-nom´ic *a.* pertaining to economics
e´co-nom´ic-al *a.* thrifty
e´co-nom´ics *n.* political economy; study of production, distribution, and consumption of wealth
e-con´o-mize´ *vi.* be thrifty
e-con´o-my *n.* management, administration
ec´sta-sy *n.* rapture, excessive joy; **ec-stat´ic** *a.*
ec´u-men´i-cal *a.* wide in scope, not parochial
ec-ze´ma *n.* eruptive disease of the skin
eddy *n.* current running contrary to main stream; small whirlpool; *vi.*
ed´i-ble *a.* eatable
e´dict *n.* decree
ed´i-fice *n.* building
ed´i-fy´ *vt.* instruct, improve, benefit morally; **ed´i-fi-ca´tion** *n.*
ed´it *vt.* prepare for publication; **ed´i-tor** *n.*
e-di´tion *n.* number of copies of a book printed at one time
ed´i-to´ri-al *a.* pertaining to an editor; *n.* interpretive article written by an editor
ed´u-cate´ *vt.* teach, cultivate, train; **ed´u-ca´tion** *n.*
ed´u-ca´tion-ist *n.* specialist in the theory of education
ed´u-ca´tor *n.* teacher
e-duce´ *vt.* extract, elicit
ef-face´ *vt.* blot out, erase
ef-fect´ *n.* consequence, result; **ef-fec´tive** *a.*; **ef-fec´tu-al** *a.*
ef-fects´ *n. pl.* goods; *vt.* accomplish
ef-fem´i-nate *a.* womanish; **ef-fem´-i-na-cy** *n.*
ef´fer-vesce´ *vi.* bubble; be lively, be in high spirits; **ef´fer-ves´cent** *a.*
ef-fete´ *a.* worn out
ef´fi-ca-cy *n.* effectiveness; **ef´fi-ca´-cious** *a.*
ef-fi´cient *a.* effective; **ef-fi´cien-cy** *n.*
ef´fi-gy *n.* figure or mock figure of a person
ef´fort *n.* exertion; force
ef-fron´ter-y *n.* impudence
ef-ful´gence *n.* brightness, radiance

ef-ful´gent *a.* shining; radiant.
ef-fuse´ *vt.* pour forth, as words
egg´head´ *n. col.* intellectual; impractical intellectual
egg´nog´ *n.* alcoholic drink made with eggs and cream
e´go *n.* part of the conscious mind asserting the self or individual
e´go-tism *n.* self-exaltation; **e´gotist** *n.*; **e´go-tis´tic** *a.*
e-gre´gious *a.* flagrant, remarkable in an unfortunate way
e-jac´u-late´ *vt.* eject; utter or cry out suddenly
e-ject´ *vt.* expel; dispossess; **e-jec´tion** *n.*
e-lab´o-rate´ *vt.* develop, perfect; *a.* complicated
e-lapse´ *vi.* pass by, slip away
e-las´tic *a.* springy, able to resume original shape; *n.* fabric containing rubber; **e-las´tic´i-ty** *n.*
e-lect´ *vt.* choose, vote for; *a.* chosen; *n.* person chosen; **e-lec´tion** *n.*; **e-lec´tor-al** *a.*
e-lec´tric, e-lec´tri-cal *a.* pertaining to electricity
e-lec´tric eye *n.* electronic beam that starts an automatic process when intercepted
e-lec´tric´i-ty *n.* a type of energy
e-lec´tro-car´di-o-graph´ *n.* instrument used to diagnose heart disease
e-lec´tro-cute´ *vt.* execute by means of electricity
e-lec´trode *n.* one of the two terminals of an electric current
e-lec´tro-en-ceph´a-lo-graph *n.* an instrument for recording brain waves
e-lec´tron *n.* one of the smallest units of matter, carrying a unit charge of negative electricity; **electron microscope** *n.* electronic instrument for magnifying the image of very minute particles
e-lec´tron´ics *n.* branch of physics treating the behavior and uses of electrons
el´e-gant *a.* graceful, refined; **el´egance** *n.*
el´e-gy *n.* poem for someone dead; **el´e-gi´ac** *a.*
el´e-ment *n.* essential part; rudiment; natural force; one of the 102 simplest known constituents of all compound substances; **el´e-men´tal** *a.*; **el´e-men´tary** *a.*
el´e-phant *n.* large quadruped with long snout and tusks; **el´e-phan´tine** *a.* very large
el´e-vate´ *vt.* raise; place higher; **el´e-va´tion** *n.* raising, exaltation; height
el´e-va´tor *n.* contrivance for lifting; kind of grain warehouse
e-lic´it *vt.* draw out, evoke
el´i-gi-ble *a.* fit or worthy to be chosen
e-lim´i-nate´ *vt.* exclude, leave out
e-li´sion *n.* suppression of a vowel or syllable
el-lipse´ *n.* regular oval figure
el-lip´sis *n.* omission of a word or words; **el-lip´tic** *a.*
elo-cu´tion *n.* art of using correctly voice and gestures in public speaking or reading
e-lon´gate´ *vt.* make longer; **e´lon-ga´tion** *n.*
e-lope´ *vi.* ran away, as with a sweetheart
el´o-quence *n.* fine or persuasive speech; **el´o-quent** *a.*
e-lude´ *vt.* avoid by stratagem; **e-lu´sion** *n.*; **e-lu´sive** *a.*
e-ma´ci-ate´ *vt.* make very thin or underweight; **e-ma´ci-a´tion** *n.*
em´a-nate´ *vi.* issue, spring forth

em´a-na´tion *n.* effluence; that which emanates

e-man´ci-pate´ *vt.* set free; **e-man´ci-pa´tion** *n.*; **e-man´ci-pa-tor** *n.*

em-balm´ *vt.* preserve a corpse from decay

em-bar´go *n.* prohibition, commercial restraint; *vt.*

em-bark´ *vi.* & *vt.* go or put on board; engage upon some affair; **em´bar-ka´tion** *n.*

em-bar´rass *vt.* disconcert; involve in difficulty

em´bas-sy *n.* jurisdiction or office of an ambassador; person or persons sent on an embassy; building housing a foreign delegation

em-bel´lish *vt.* decorate, ornament

em-bez´zle *vt.* appropriate fraudulently

em´blem *n.* symbol

em-brace´ *n.* hug, clasp;*vi.* join in an embrace; *vt.* clasp with the arms; take up, adopt, follow; include

em´bry-o *n.* unborn animal; **em´bry-on´ic** *a.* unborn; still forming

em-broi´der *vt.* ornament with needlework

em-broil´ *vt.* involve in strife

em´cee´, M.C. *n.* master of ceremonies

e´men-da´tion *n.* correction, improvement

em´er-ald *n.* precious stone of green color

e-merge´ *vi.* rise out of

e-mer´gen-cy *n.* sudden pressing necessity; crisis

e-mer´i-tus *a.* retired, as a professor emeritus

e-met´ic *n.* substance that causes vomiting

em´i-grate´ *vi.* move from one´s native country to another; **em´i-gra´tion** *n.*; **em´i-grant** *a.* & *n.*

em´i-nent *a.* distinguished, notable; **em´i-nence** *n.*

em´is-sar´y *n.* one sent on a mission

e-mis´sion *n.* an emitting or sending out; radiation

e-mit´ *vt.* send out; radiate

e-mo´tion *n.* feeling; excited state of mind

em´per-or *n.* ruler of an empire

em´pha-sis *n.* vocal stress on certain words or syllables; **em´pha-size´** *vt.*; **em-phat´ic** *a.*

em´pire´ *n.* several states ruled by one sovereign

em-ploy´ *vt.* give work to

em´press *n. fem.* woman ruler of an empire; wife of an emperor

em´u-late´ *vt.* rival, try to equal, copy the example of; **em´u-la´tion** *n.*

e-mul´sion *n.* suspension of one liquid in another, as cream in milk

en-act´ *vt.* establish as law

en-am´el *n.* type of glaze; *vt.* coat with enamel

en-chant´ *vt.* charm

en-cir´cle *vt.* enclose within a circle

en-co´mi-um *n.* very high praise, tribute

en-com´pass *vt.* surround; enclose, contain

en´core´ *n.* call for a repetition or further performance by an artist; extra performance

en-coun´ter *vt.* meet; oppose; *n.* meeting

en-cour´age *vt.* inspire with hope

en-croach´ *vi.* trespass

en-cum´ber *vi.* impede; load with debt; **en-cum´brance** *n.*

en-cy´clo-pe´di-a, en-cy´clo-pae´di-a *n.* work containing comprehensive information on subjects

en-deav´or *n.* attempt; *vi.* & *vt.* try,

attempt
en´do-crine´ *n.* an endocrine gland or ductless gland (as the thyroid);
en-dorse´ *vt.* write one´s signature on a check for cashing; give approval to
en-dow´ *vt.* settle an income on; enrich with a gift
en-dure´ *vi.* & *vt.* last; **en-dur´ance** *n.*
en´e-my *n.* opponent, foe
en´er-gy *n.* power to do work; force of expression; **en´er-get´ic** *a.*
en´er-vate´ *vt.* deprive of strength, weaken
en-gage´ *vi.* & *vt.* pledge one´s word; enter into contest with; put in or be in gear
en-gen´der *vt.* produce, generate
en´gine *n.* device; instrument; mechanism for producing or converting energy
en´gi-neer´ operator of an engine; specialist in engineering; *vt.* manage, guide, plan
en´gi-neer´ing *n.* application of power and materials for practical purposes
en-grave´ *vt.* cut out designs in wood, steel, etc.; **en-grav´er** *n.*; **en-grav´ing** *n.* plate which has been engraved; print made from such a plate
en-gross´ *vt.* occupy wholly
en-hance´ *vt.* increase or make greater in quality or value
e-nig´ma *n.* riddle, something not easily explained; **en´ig-mat´ic** *a.*
en-joy´ *vt.* delight in; use with joy
en-light´en *vt.* impart knowledge or light to
en´mi-ty *n.* hostility
e-nor´mous *a.* huge, extremely large; **e-nor´mi-ty** *n.*
en´sign *n.* flag, emblem; lowest commissioned rank in U. S. Navy
en-sue´ *vi.* result, follow
en-tan´gle *vt.* enmesh, involve
en´ter-prise´ *n.* undertaking; **en´ter-pris´ing** *a.* venturous, energetic
en´ter-tain´ *vt.* amuse; show hospitality to; treat; take into consideration
en-thu´si-asm *n.* great interest, fervor, zeal; **en´thu-si-as´tic** *a.*
en-tice´ *vt.* tempt; lead astray
en-tire´ *a.* whole
en´to-mol´o-gy *n.* study of insects; **en´to-mol´o-gist** *n.*
en´trance *n.* door; act of entering
en-trance´ *vt.* fill with rapture or delight
en-treat´ *vt.* implore, ask earnestly
en-tree´, en-trée´ *n.* main dish; dish served before main course; entry
en´try *n.* passage into; entering; item entered
e-nu´mer-ate´ *vt.* count, number; **e-nu´mer-a´tion** *n.*
e-nun´ci-ate´ *vi.* & *vt.* pronounce clearly; proclaim; **e-nun´ci-a´tion** *n.*
en-vel´op *vt.* roll or fold in; surround
en´ve-lope´ *n.* cover of a letter; that which envelops
en-vi´ron-ment *n.* surroundings; **en-vi´rons** *n. pl.* neighborhood, surroundings; outskirts of a city
en´voy´ *n.* messenger; special diplomat
en´vy *vt.* covet, look upon grudgingly; *n.*; **en´vi-a-ble** *a.*; **en´vi-ous** *a.*
en´zyme´ *n.* chemical substance that can cause chemical changes in animals´ plants, etc., without itself undergoing change
ep´au-let´ *n.* shoulder ornament sometimes worn on military uni-

forms

e-phem´er-al *a.* passing, transient, lasting only a day or a short time

ep´ic *n.* long heroic poem; *a.* lofty, grand

ep´i-cure´ *n.* connoisseur of food, drink, etc.; **ep´i-cu´re-an** *a.* & *n.*

ep´i-dem´ic *a.* affecting a whole people; *n.* disease afflicting great numbers

ep´i-der´mis *n.* outer layer of the skin

ep´i-glot´tis *n.* cartilage that closes the opening to the larynx in swallowing

ep´i-gram´ *n.* short, witty statement or poem

e-pis´co-pal *a.* of or governed by bishops; Anglican; **E-pis´co-pa´li-an** *a.* & *n.* pertaining to or a member of the Episcopal church

ep´i-sode´ *n.* incident, occurrence

e-pis´tle *n.* formal letter; Eucharistic lesson, generally from the Epistles of the New Testament

ep´i-taph´ *n.* inscription on a tombstone or monument

ep´i-thet´ *n.* adjective, noun, or phrase generally used with someone´s name (*Richard the Lion-Hearted*), etc.

e-pit´o-me *n.* short summary, as of a book; anything brief that characterizes a larger whole

ep´och *n.* era, age

ep-ox´y *n.* oxygen containing synthetic resin used in various kinds of coatings and adhesives

e´qual *a.* alike; adequate; just; uniform; *n.* one neither inferior nor superior; *vt.* make or be equal to; **e-qual´i-ty** *n.*

e´qua-nim´i-ty *n.* evenness of mind or temper

e-qua´tion *n.* statement of the equality of two quantities

e-qua´tor *n.* imaginary circle passing around the middle of the Earth; **e´qua-to´ri-al** *a.*

e-ques´tri-an *a.* pertaining to horses; *n.* one who rides horseback

e´qui-lat´er-al *a.* having all sides equal

e´qui-lib´ri-um *n.* equality of weights or forces; balance

e´quine´ *a.* pertaining to a horse or horses

e´qui-nox´ *n.* time of year when day and night are of equal length

e-quip´ *vt.* fit out, furnish

eq´ui-ta-ble *a.* just, fair

eq´ui-ty *n.* fairness; just claim; legal system apart from common and statute law

e-quiv´a-lent *a.* equal; *n.* thing equal in value

e-quiv´o-cate´ *vi.* use ambiguous language; **e-quiv´o-cal** *a.*; **e-quiv´-o-ca´tion** *n.*

e´ra *n.* age, epoch

e-rad´i-cate´ *vt.* destroy, wipe out

e-rase´ *vt.* rub out, efface; **e-ra´sure** *n.*

e-rect´ *a.* upright; *vt.* set upright; build; **e-rec´tion** *n.*

er´mine *n.* animal of the weasel kind valued for its fur

err *vi.* be mistaken; sin

er´rand *n.* small job or chore requiring a trip

er-rat´ic *a.* strange, deviating; wandering from a set course

er-ro´ne-ous *a.* mistaken

error *n.* inaccuracy

er´satz´ *a.* substitute, fake

er´u-dite´ *a.* learned; **er´u-di´tion** *n.*

e-rupt´ *vi.* & *vt.* break out; throw out violently; **e-rup´tion** *n.*

es´ca-late´ *vi.* & *vt.* increase or intensify

es´ca-la´tor *n.* moving stairway; **es´ca-la´tor clause** *n.* agreement whereby interest rate, salary, etc. changes based on a predetermined guideline
es´ca-pade´ *n.* prank
es-cape´ *vi.* & *vt.* flee; remain unharmed; leak out; *n.* flight; preservation from harm
es-chew´ *vt.* shun
es´cort *n.* guard; social companion
es-cort´ *vt.* accompany
Es´ki-mo´ *n.* **(Es´ki-mos)** one of a tribe of Arctic America; the Eskimo language
e-soph´a-gus *n.* gullet
ESP *n.* extrasensory perception: telepathy and other apparent phenomena not depending upon the ordinary senses
es-pouse´ *vt.* betroth; embrace a cause; **es-pous´al** *n.*
es-quire´ *n.* title of respect still used in England
es´say *n.* written composition, often personal in tone
es-say´ *vt.* try, attempt
es´sence *n.* essential characteristics
es-sen´tial *a.* indispensable; *n.* fundamental principle
es-tab´lish *vt.* settle, fix; found
es-tate´ *n.* fixed condition; property, esp. land
es-teem´ *vt.* value; *n.* favorable regard
es´ti-ma-ble *a.* worthy of esteem
es´ti-mate´ *vt.* rate, evaluate; *n.*; **es´ti-ma´tion** *n.*
estrange´ *vt.* alienate
es´tu-ar´y *n.* passage where the tide meets the current of a river
etch *vi.* & *vt.* make designs on glass or metal by means of an acid; **etch´ing** *n.* an engraving; print made from an engraved plate
e-ter´nal *a.* everlasting; *n.* God
e-ter´ni-ty *n.* time without end
e´ther *n.* flammable fluid used as an anesthetic; subtle medium once thought to fill outer space
e-the´re-al *a.* light, airy
eth´ics *n.* principles of morality
eth´nic *n.* member of a racial or national minority; *a.*
eth´nol´o-gy *n.* science of human races
et´i-quette´ *n.* conventions of decorum or ceremony
et´y-mol´o-gy *n.* study of the origin and history of words; **et´y-mo-log´i-cal** *a.*
Eu´cha-rist *n.* the Lord´s supper
eu´gen´ics *n.* science that deals with the improvement of hereditary qualities, esp. in the human race
eu´lo-gy *n.* speech or writing in praise of someone dead, etc.; **eu´lo-gize´** *vt.*
eu´phe-mism *n.* replacement of a harsh expression by a milder one, as *abdomen* for *belly*
eu´pho-ny *n.* agreeable sound; **eu´pho´ni-ous** *a.*
eu´tha-na´sia *n.* ´mercy´ killing
e-vac´u-ate´ *vt.* empty; withdraw from; **e-vac´u-a´tion** *n.*
e-vade´ *vt.* escape, avoid
ev´a-nes´cent *a.* fleeting
e´van-gel´i-cal *a.* contained in or according to the gospel
e-van´ge-list *n.* traveling revivalist; one of the writers of the four gospels
e-vap´o-rate´ *vi.* & *vt.* escape in or convert into vapor; **e-vap´o-ra´tion** *n.*
e-va´sion *n.* attempt to evade; ambiguous answer; **e-va´sive** *a.*
e-vent´ *n.* happening, incident, occurrence

e-ven´tu-al *a.* final, last; contingent
e-vict´ *vt.* dispossess by law; **e-vic´-tion** *n.*
ev´i-dence *n.* proof, testimony; *vt.* prove; **ev´i-dent** *a.* obvious
e-vince´ *vt.* show, display
e-voke´ *vt.* summon or call forth
e-volve´ *vi.* & *vt.* develop, produce; **ev´o-lu´tion** *n.*
ewe *n.* female of the sheep
ewer *n.* large jug or pitcher
ex-ac´er-bate´ *vt.* irritate, make worse
ex-act´ *a.* precise; *vt.* compel payment of
ex-ag´ger-ate´ *vt.* overstate, misrepresent; **ex-ag´ger-a´tion** *n.*
ex-alt´ *vt.* raise high; praise; **ex´al-ta´tion** *n.*
ex-am´ine*vt.* inspect; question; **ex-am´i-na´tion** *n.*
ex-am´ple *n.* specimen, illustration; pattern, warning, precedent
ex-as´per-ate´ *vt.* make angry, irritate; **ex-as´per-a´tion** *n.*
ex´ca-vate´ *vt.* hollow out, dig; **ex´-ca-va´tion** *n.*
ex-ceed´ *vt.* surpass
ex-cel´ *vi.* & *vt.* surpass or be superior to
ex´cel-lence *n.* superiority, virtue, great value or worth; **ex´cel-lent** *a.*
ex-cess´ *n.* overly large amount; remainder; intemperance; *a.*; **ex-ces´sive** *a.*
ex-change´ *vt.* give in return for some equivalent; barter; *n.* barter
ex´cise´ *n.* tax on some commodities; *vt.* subject to excise duties
ex-cise´ *vt.* cut out; wipe out, erase
ex-cite´ *vt.* stir up; irritate; **ex-cit´a-ble** *a.*
ex-claim´ *vi.* & *vt.* cry out
ex´cla-ma´tion *n.* vehement utterance; mark of punctuation (!)
ex-clude´ *vt.* shut out; except; **ex-clu´sion** *n.*; **ex-clu´sive** *a.*
ex´com-mu´ni-cate´ *vt.* expel from church communion; **ex´com-mu´-ni-ca´tion** *n.*
ex-cres´cence *n.* superfluous growth or increase; **ex-cres´cent** *a.* superfluous
ex-crete´ *vt.* discharge or eliminate wastes; **ex-cre´tion** *n.*
ex´cul-pate´ *vt.* absolve, vindicate, clear of guilt
ex-cur´sion *n.* trip, holiday trip; **ex-cur´sive** *a.* rambling
ex-cuse´ *vt.* free from guilt or obligation; ask pardon for
ex-cuse´ *n.* plea, apology; plea offered to explain a fault
ex´e-crate´ *vt.* curse; abhor; **ex´e-cra-ble** *a.*
ex´e-cute´ *vt.* perform; sign and deliver; put to death by law; **ex´e-cu´-tion** *n.*
ex-ec´u-tive *n.* officer charged with the execution of the laws or other high duties; *a.* having the quality or function of executing
ex-em´pla-ry *a.* serving as a model or warning
ex-em´pli-fy *vt.* illustrate by example; **ex-em´pli-fi-ca´tion** *n.*
ex-empt´ *vt.* grant immunity from, free from; *a.* released, not affected; **ex-emp´tion** *n.* freedom from obligation; tax deduction
ex´er-cise´ *n.* practice; exertion; performance; lesson; *vt.* train
ex-ert´ *vt.* bring into operation with vigor; **ex-er´tion** *n.*
ex´hale´ *vt.* breathe forth; emit as vapor
ex-haust´ *vt.* use up, consume; tire; **ex-haus´tion** *n.*; **ex-haus´tive** *a.*
ex-hib´it *vt.* show, display; *n.*; **ex´hi-bi´tion** *n.*

ex-hil´a-rate´ *vt.* make merry; cheer; enliven; **ex-hil´a-ra´tion** *n.*
ex´hort´ *vt.* urge strongly; **ex´hor-ta´tion** *n.*
ex-hume´ *vt.* disinter, dig up
ex´i-gen-cy *n.* situation needing immediate action; pressing situation; requirement, need; **ex´i-gent** *a.*
ex-ig´u-ous *a.* meager, small, scanty
ex´ile *n.* banishment; person banished; *vt.* banish
ex-ist´ *vi.* be, live, continue to be
ex´is-ten´tial-ism *n.* modern, sometimes pessimistic philosophy, stressing free will and responsibility
ex´it *n.* departure; egress, way out
ex´o-dus *n.* departure, leaving; departure of the Israelites from Egypt
ex-on´er-ate´ *vt.* relieve or clear of some charge; **ex-on´er-a´tion** *n.*
ex-or´bi-tant *a.* excessive
ex´or-cise´ *vt.* free from possession by an evil spirit; **ex´or-cism** *n.*
ex-ot´ic *a.* foreign; foreign in origin, hence alluring
ex-pand´ *vt.* spread out; **ex-panse´** *n.* wide extent; **ex-pan´sion** *n.*; **ex-pan´sive** *a.*
ex-pa´ti-ate´ *vi.* talk at length upon a subject
ex-pect´ *vt.* anticipate; **ex´pec-ta´tion** *n.*
ex-pec´to-rate´ *vi.* & *vt.* spit
ex-pe´di-ent *a.* suitable, advisable; *n.* means suitable to an end; **ex-pe´di-en-cy** *n.*
ex´pe-dite´ *vt.* hasten, free of obstacles
ex´pe-di´tion *n.* journey, excursion; journey for purposes of exploration
ex-pel´ *vt.* drive out, force out, eject
ex-pend´ *vt.* spend
ex-pense´ *n.* outlay, cost; **ex-pen´sive** *a.*
ex-pe´ri-ence *n.* personal observation; knowledge from past observation; *vt.* feel, undergo
ex-per´i-ment *n.* trial; practical test; *vi.* try, test
ex-pert´ *a.* skillful, experienced, proficient
ex´pert´ *n.* one proficient in an art
ex´pi-ate´ *vt.* atone for; **ex´pi-a´tion** *n.*
ex-pire´ *vi.* die; terminate, end; **ex´pi-ra´tion** *n.*
ex-plain´ *vt.* make plain; **ex´pla-na´tion** *n.*
ex-plic´it *a.* clear; distinctly stated
ex-plode´ *vi.* & *vt.* burst with a loud noise
ex´ploit, ex-ploit´ *n.* great achievement, feat; adventure
ex-ploit´ *vt.* make use of; take advantage of
ex-plore´ *vi.* & *vt.* search or examine thoroughly; **ex´plo-ra´tion** *n.*
ex-plo´sion *n.* sudden violent bursting
ex-plo´sive *a.* liable to or causing explosion; *n.* substance, such as dynamite, which causes explosion by swift change into gases
ex-po´nent *n.* representative of a principle or party; symbol indicating how many times a number or symbol is multiplied by itself (as $2^3 = 2 X 2 X 2 = 8$)
ex´port´ *n.* exportation; that which is exported
ex-port´ *vt.* ship goods out of a country
ex´po-sé´ *n.* exposure, esp. of something disreputable
ex-pose´ *vt.* lay forth to view; make liable to injury
ex´po-si´tion *n.* public exhibition; an analytic explanation
ex-po´sure *n.* public disclosure, as

of a scandal; state of being exposed, as to the elements; length of time photographic film is exposed to light; **exposure meter** *n.* photographic device for measuring amount of light

ex-pos´tu-late´ *vi.* remonstrate; **ex-pos´tu-la´tion** *n.*

ex-press´ *vt.* declare, represent in words; *a.* explicit; **ex-pres´sion** *n.*; **ex-pres´sive** *a.*

ex-pul´sion *n.* banishment; state of being forced out or expelled; **ex-pul´sive** *a.*

ex-punge´ *vt.* efface, blot out

ex´qui-site *a.* first-rate; choice; beautiful, delicate; refined

ex´tant *a.* still existing

ex-tem´po-ra´ne-ous, extem´po-rar´y *a.* done without preparation, improvised

ex-tend´ *vi.* & *vt.* stretch out; bestow; enlarge; **ex-ten´sion** *n.*; **ex-ten´sive** *a.*

ex-tent´ *n.* space; size; degree

ex-ten´u-ate´ *vt.* diminish the guilt of, partially excuse; **ex-ten´u-a´-tion** *n.*

ex-te´ri-or *a.* outward; *n.* outward part, surface

ex-ter´mi-nate´ *vt.* destroy, eradicate, wipe out

ex-ter´nal *a.* on the outside, exterior

ex-tinct´ *a.* no longer existing or alive; **ex-tinc´tion** *n.*

ex-tin´guish *vt.* put out, quench; destroy, do away with

ex´tir-pate´ *vt.* uproot, destroy totally, exterminate

ex-tol´ *vt.* praise

ex-tort´ *vt.* obtain by threats or force

ex-tract´ *vt.* draw out; select; quote

ex´tract´ *n.* anything extracted by heat, distillation, etc.; passage quoted from a book

ex´tra-cur-ric´u-lar *a.* outside the usual course of studies

ex´tra-dite´ *vt.* deliver a person to another government for trial

ex-tra´ne-ous *a.* foreign, unrelated, not inborn

ex-tra-or´di-nar´y *a.* out of the ordinary, remarkable, unusual

ex-trap´o-late´ *vt.* project or infer conclusions on the basis of availahle data

ex´tra-sen´so-ry *a.* gotten by some means other than normal senses (as *extra-sensory perception)*

ex-trav´a-gance *n.* lavish expenditure; excess of anything; **ex-trav´a-gant** *a.*

ex-treme´ *a.* outermost, utmost; last; *n.* utmost possible limit or degree

ex-trem´i-ty *n.* utmost point, degree, or peril; arm or leg

ex´tri-cate´ *vt.* free from hindrance

ex´tro-vert´, ex´tra-vert´ *n.* one more interested in the things around him than in himself

ex-u´ber-ant *a.* profuse or overflowing in emotions, etc.; **ex-u´ber-ance** *n.*

ex-ult´ *vi.* rejoice, be extremely happy

ex-ur´ban-ite´ *n.* person who has left the city for the country

eye´ bank´ *n.* depository where eye corneas, willed for surgical use, are preserved for later corneal transplants

F

fa´ble *n.* fictitious story intended to instruct

fab´ric *n.* manufactured cloth; structure of a thing

fab´ri-cate´ *vt.* produce, build; devise falsely; **fab´ri-ca´tion** *n.*

fab´u-lous *a.* fictitious; exceeding probability

fac´et *n.* small plane surface of a jewel; aspect of a subject

fa-ce´tious *a.* humorous

fac´ile *a.* yielding; easy; docile, compliant; fluent

fa-cil´i-tate´ *vt.* make easy

fa-cil´i-ty *n.* ease, absence of difficulty; skill; equipment, etc., that makes a job easier

fac-sim´i-le *n.* exact copy; **facsimile, fax** *n.* machine which sends documents over telephone lines; copy of a document so received.

fact *n.* deed; reality

fac´tion *n.* party, clique

fac´tious *a.* turbulent, contentious

fac-ti´tious *a.* artificial, made up

fac´ti-tive *a.* causative

fac´tor *n.* agent; cause; quantity multiplied by another (as 4 and 3 are factors of 12)

fac´to-ry *n.* building used for manufacturing

fac´ul-ty *n.* facility to act; mental or physical ability; body of teachers or of some profession

fade *vi.* lose freshness or color; diminish, vanish

fail *vi.* & *vt.* fall short, be wanting; decay; disappoint; become bankrupt; **fail safe**, name given the safety procedure to prevent accidental bombing by the Strategic Air Command

faint *a.* wanting in strength or distinctness; *vi.* swoon

Fair´ Deal´ *n.* domestic legislation proposed by Pres. Truman in 1949

fair´y *n.* imaginary being with magical powers

faith *n.* trust, belief

fal´con *n.* type of hawk formerly used in hunting

fall *vi.* drop down; decline; *n.* act of falling ; cascade; autumn

fal´la-cy *n.* illogical argument; **falla´cious** *a.*

fal´li-ble *a.* liable to error; **fal´li-bil´-i-ty** *n.*

fall´out´ *n.* radioactive pollution from atomic explosion

false *a.* deceptive; unfaithful

fal´sies *n. pl.* pads to increase apparent size of female breasts

fal´si-fy´ *vt.* misrepresent, lie; forge; **fal´si-fi-ca´tion** *n.*

fa-mil´iar *a.* intimate, well known; **fa-mil´i-ar´i-ty** *n.*; **fa-mil´iar-ize´** *vt.*

fam´i-ly *n.* household; closest relatives; race, tribe; group, as of languages

fam´ine *n.* critical scarcity of food

fam´ish *vi.* & *vt.* starve

fa´mous *a.* well known, renowned

fa-nat´ic *n.* one overzealous in a cause; *a.* wildly enthusiastic

fan´cy *a.* elaborate, ornamental; intricate; over-priced; *n.* whim; imagination; *vt.* imagine; be pleased with

fang *n.* long, pointed tooth

fan-tas´tic *a.* grotesque; unreal; fanciful

farce *n.* unrestrained comedy or satire; ridiculous or empty actions or ceremony; **far´ci-cal** *a.*

fare *vi.* travel, journey; experience; *n.* food; price of passage

far´ther *a.* more distant; *adv.* beyond; moreover

fas´ci-nate´ *vt.* charm, captivate; **fas´ci-na´tion** *n.*

fas´cism *n.* political doctrine favoring centralized authority and opposed to democratic principles; ac-

tive intolerance; **fas´cist** *n.*
fash´ion *n.* prevailing style; pattern; *vt.* mold, make; adapt
fas´ten *vi.* cling; *vt.* make fast
fas-tid´i-ous *a.* difficult to please; squeamish; very particular
fa´tal *a.* causing death; having to do with fate; **fa´tal´i-ty** *n.*
fate *n.* inevitable destiny; ruin; death
fath´om *n.* nautical measure of 6 feet; *vt.* get to the bottom of, penetrate
fa-tigue´ *n.* weariness, exhaustion; *vi.* & *vt.* become or make weary
fat´u-ous *a.* foolish, simple-minded; **fa-tu´i-ty** *n.*
fau´cet *n.* tap on a water pipe, barrel, etc.
fault *n.* defect
faux´ pas´ *n.* social slip or error; false step
fa´vor *n.* kind deed; kindly regard; partiality; gift; *vt.* treat indulgently
fawn *vi.* flatter in a servile way
faze *vt. col.* discourage
fear *n.* great dread, alarm; deep reverence; *vt.* regard with fear; stand in awe of; *vi.* be afraid
fea´si-ble *a.* practicable, possible
feast *n.* day of joy; elaborate meal; *vi.* eat sumptuously; *vt.* entertain
feat *n.* deed of strength, skill, or courage
fea´ther *n.* one of the growths forming the plumage of a bird; *vt.* furnish or adorn with feathers
fea´ture *n.* characteristic, quality; cast of face; main article, movie, etc.
Feb´ru-ar´y *n.* second month of the year
fe´ces´ *n. pl.* excrement, dung
fed´er-al *a.* pertaining to a federation; pertaining to the U. S. government
fed´er-ate´ *vi.* & *vt.* league or become leagued together; **fed´er-a´tion** *n.*
fee *n.* price paid for services, licenses, etc.
fee´ble *a.* weak, faint
feed *vi.* **(fed)** eat; *vt.* give food to; *n.* fodder; **feed´back´** *n.* portion of the output returned to the input; self-regulating mechanism in animals and machines providing sensitive control
feel *vi.* & *vt.* **(felt)** perceive by touch; handle; be conscious of
feign *vi.* & *vt.* pretend dissemble
feint *n.* stratagem, esp. a pretended attack in fencing; *vi.*
fe-lic´i-tate´ *vt.* congratulate; make happy; **fe-lic´i-ta´tion** *n.*
fe-lic´i-ty *n.* happiness; appropriateness
fe´line´ *a.* pertaining to or like a cat
fel´low *n.* associate; equal; member of a society; person, chap; **fellow traveler** *n.* person sympathetic to communist cause
fel´on *n.* person guilty of a major crime; **fe-lo´ni-ous** *a.*; **fel´o-ny** *n.* major crime
felt *n.* woolen cloth made without weaving
fe´male´ *a.* of the sex that produces young; *n.* one of the female sex
fem´i-nine *a.* pertaining to women
fem´i-nism *n.* advocacy of women's rights and interests; **fem´i-nist** *n.*
fe´mur *n.* thighbone; **fem´o-ral** *a.*
fence *n.* wall or hedge used to divide property or as a barrier; criminal who traffics in stolen goods; *vi.* practice fencing or swordfighting; **fenc´ing** *n.* art of fighting with the sword
fend *vt.* ward off

fend´er *n.* guard over the wheels of an automobile

fer-ment´ *vi.* undergo fermentation; be in excited action; *vt.* excite fermentation; **fer´men-ta´tion** *n.* chemical conversion of an organic substance into alcohol or vinegar; agitation

fe-ro´cious *a.* savage, fierce; **fe-roc´i-ty** *n.*

fer´ry *vt.* carry or convey in a boat; *n.* ferryboat

fer´tile *a.* able to produce or bear young; inventive;

fer´vid *a.* glowing with zeal

fer´vor *n.* intense feeling; heat

fes´ter *vi.* suppurate, give off pus

fes´ti-val *n.* joyful celebration

fes´tive *a.* joyful, gay

fes-tiv´i-ty *n.* festival, festive occasion

fes-toon´ *n.* garland; *vt.* adorn with garlands

fête, fete *n.* festival; *vt.* entertain richly

fe´tish, fe´tich *n.* charm; object or image regarded with undue reverence; **fe´tish-ism** *n.*

fet´id *a.* having a strong, offensive odor

fe-tol´o-gy *n.* branch of medicine concerned with fetuses

fet´ter *n.* chain or shackle for the feet; any similar restraint; *vt.* restrain; put shackles on

fe´tus *n.* embryo, unborn animal

feud *n.* deadly quarrel between families or tribes

fe´ver *n.* condition marked by great body heat and quickening of pulse; extreme excitement

fez *n.* red cap formerly worn by Turks

fi´an-cé´ *n. masc.* one who is affianced or betrothed; **fi´an-cee´** *n. fem.*

fi-as´co *n.* **(fi-as´cos, fi-as´coes)** notorious or blundering failure

fiat *n.* command

fi´ber *n.* thread, filament; **fi´brous** *a.*

fi´ber glass *n.* glass fibers used in textiles, plastics

fick´le *a.* inconstant

fic´tion *n.* imaginary tale

fic´ti´tious *a.* imaginary

fi-del´i-ty *n.* faithfulness

fi-du´ci-ar´y *a.* involving confidence or trust; held in trust; *n.* one who holds in trust

field *n.* open country; ground enclosed for tillage or pasture; locality of a battle

fiend *n.* one motivated by extreme wickedness; devil; one habituated to a drug or to some activity

fierce *n.* ferocious, savage

fi´er-y *a.* consisting of or containing fire; impetuous, hot-tempered

fifth´ col´umn *n.* traitors working secretly inside a country to aid its enemies

fight *vi.* & *vt.* **(fought)** engage in conflict with, struggle, battle; *n.*

fig´ur-a-tive *a.* metaphorical; flowery in language

fig´ure *n.* form; design; statue; character denoting a number; *vi.* calculate; appear conspicuous; *vt.* calculate

fil´a-ment *n.* fiber

file *n.* cabinet for storing papers; rasp, instrument for scraping; row, as of soldiers; *vt.* store in a file; submit records to a court; cut or smooth with a rasp

fil´i-al *a.* pertaining to a son or daughter

fil´i-gree´ *n.* ornamental work of gold or silver wire

Fil´i-pi´no *n.* **(Fil´i-pi´nos)** native of the Philippine Islands

fill *vi.* & *vt.* make or become full; *n.* full or satisfactory supply; anything used to fill in a hole, etc.

fil´ly *n.* young mare

film *n.* very thin layer or coating; roll or sheet of sensitized material used in photography; moving picture; *vi.* & *vt.* cover or become covered with a film

film´strip´ *n.* series of individual pictures, cartoons, etc., used for instruction

fil´ter *n.* strainer; *vi.* & *vt.* pass through a filter

filth *n.* foul matter; dirt

filth´y *a.* dirty; corrupt

fil´trate´ *vt.* filter; *n.*

fin *n.* organ by which a fish swims; stabilizing projection on planes and submarines, ornamental projection on automobiles

fi´nal *a.* last; decisive

fi-nance´ *n.* science of public revenue and expenditure; **fi-nances´** *n. pl.* resources, money; *vt.* manage financially; invest in; **fi-nan´cial** *a.*; **fin´an-cier´** *n.* one skilled in finance

find *vt.* **(found)** discover; arrive at, reach; supply; *n.* rich discovery; anything found

fine *a.* excellent; small, thin subtle; *n.* payment of money imposed as a punishment; *vt.* impose a fine upon

fin´ger *n.* one of the five digits of the hand; *vt.* handle with the fingers

fi´nis *n.* end; conclusion

fin´ish *vt.* end, complete; *n.* end, conclusion

fi´nite´ *a.* having a limit in quantity, capacity, degree, etc.

fiord *n.* long, narrow, rock-bound inlet

fir *n.* cone-bearing evergreen

fire *n.* combustion, conflagration; discharge of firearms; ardor; *vt.* set on fire; inflame; animate; discharge an employee; *vi.* take fire; discharge firearms

fire´pow-er *n.* amount of destructive force that can be delivered on a target

fire´proof´ *a.* incombustible

firm *a.* fixed; compact; *n.* commercial house

fir´ma-ment *n.* sky; heavens

fis´cal *a.* pertaining to public revenue

fis´sion *n.* splitting into parts; disintegration of heavy atoms into lighter ones, releasing great energy

fis´sure *n.* cleft

fist *n.* closed or clenched hand; mark used in printing to direct attention

fit *a.* qualified; *vt.* adapt to; qualify;*vi.* be suited to; *n.* adjustment; adaptation; convulsion

fit´ting *adj.* fit or suitable for any purpose; *n.* act of adjusting or connecting properly

fix *vt.* make stable; direct steadily, as the eye; repair; *n.* difficulty

fix-a´tion *n.* halting of part of the psychological development

fix´ture *n.* anything permanently fastened; equipment, permanent belongings of a house, store, etc.

flab´by *a.* soft and yielding; **flab´bi-ness** *n.*

flac´cid *a.* flabby

flag *n.* banner, standard; *vt.* signal with a flag; *vi.* grow languid, slacken

fla-gi´tious *a.* shameful, scandalous

fla´grant *a.* inescapably obvious

flake *n.* scale-like bit; *vi.* & *vt.* break into flakes

flame *n.* blaze of a fire; *vi.* burn as a flame
flame´out *n.* cessation of jet aircraft engine
flange *n.* raised edge, rim
flank *n.* side; thigh; *vt.* stand at, attack, or pass around the side of
flap *n.* anything broad and flexible that hangs loose; motion or sound of such an object; *vt.* beat or move with a flap; make a flapping noise
flare *n.* unsteady light; sudden blaze; signal light; *vi.* burn with a glaring, unsteady light
flash *n.* momentary light; short, transient state; *vi.* break forth, gleam
flash´back´ *n.* break in main action (in stories, films, etc.) during which some earlier action is presented
flask *n.* narrow-necked bottle
flat *a.* having an even and horizontal surface; prostrate; tasteless; *n.* low tract of land; musical note lowered by a semitone; mark to indicate this; apartment
flat´ter *vt.* please with servile praise
flaunt *vt.* display ostentatiously
fla´vor *n.* taste; *vt.* impart flavor to
flaw *n.* defect; *vt.* mar, crack
flay *vt.* strip the skin from
flea *n.* small bloodsucking insect
fleck *n.* spot; *vt.* speckle
flee *vi.* & *vt.* **(fled)** run away from
fleece *n.* coat of wool shorn from a sheep; *vt.* clip wool from; plunder
fleet *a.* swift, transient; *vi.* & *vt.* pass swiftly; *n.* group of ships, planes, etc., involved in an operation
flesh *n.* meat, substance covering the bones of animals; body; animal nature
flex´i-ble *a.* easily bent; **flex´i-bil´i-ty** *n.*
flight *n.* movement through the air; escape; series of steps
flim´sy *a.* thin; weak
flinch *vi.* wince, shrink back
fling *vt.* **(flung)** hurl; sneer; *n.* act of hurling or throwing; gibe; wild escapade
flint *n.* very hard stone used to strike fire
flip´pant *a.* pert, frivolous
flirt *vi.* trifle with someone´s affections; consider in passing; *n.* coquette; **flir´ta´tion** *n.*
float *vi.* & *vt.* rest or move on the surface of a liquid; *n.*
flock *n.* collection of animals; congregation; *vi.* gather in a crowd
flog *vt.* beat, lash
flood *n.* inundation; rise of the tide; *vt.* inundate
floor *n.* part of a building or room on which one walks; story of a building; right to speak in a formal assembly; *vt.* cover with a floor; strike down
flo´ra *n.* plant life of a particular region; **flo´ral** *a.*
flor´id *a.* flowery, as in speech; reddish
flor´ist *n.* cultivator or seller of flowers
floss *n.* silky substance in the husks of corn, etc.; untwisted thread
flo-til´la *n.* fleet, fleet of small ships
floun´der *n.* small, flat sea fish; *vi.* roll about
flour *n.* meal made from grain; *vt.* reduce to or sprinkle with flour
flour´ish *vi.* thrive; *vt.* adorn; brandish; *n.* decoration, adornment; waving, brandishing; sound of trumpets, fanfare
flout *vi.* & *vt.* sneer; disregard contemptuously; *n.* sneering insult
flow *vi.* run, as water; hang loose

and waving; *n.* current, tide; movement of thought

flow´er *n.* blossom; best of anything; *vi.* bloom

fluc´tu-ate´ *vi.* move to and fro or up and down; waver; **fluc´tu-a´-tion** *n.*

flue *n.* passage for smoke

flu´ent *a.* ready in the use of words; **flu´en-cy** *n.*

flu´id *a.* flowing or capable of flowing; *n.* liquid or gas

fluke *n. sl.* a lucky stroke; an unexpected turn

flunk *vi. & vt. col.* fail,esp. in school

flu´o-res´cence *n.* luminosity of certain chemicals under X-ray, etc., phosphorescence; **flu´o-res´cent** *a.*; **fluorescent lamp** *n.* electric lamp whose light is produced by phosphors

fluor´i-date *vt.* add fluorides to drinking water to reduce tooth decay, **fluor´i-da´tion** *n.*

flush *vi.* flow and spread suddenly; blush; *vt.* wash out by flooding; *n.* sudden flow; blush, reddening; sudden short thrill; *adv.* even with

flus´ter *vi. & vt.* make or become disconcerted or confused; *n.* confusion

flute *n.* musical instrument; channel, as on a pillar

flut´ter *vi. & vt.* move the wings rapidly; move about, bustle, agitate; *n.* agitation; motion, as of wings beating

flux *n.* flowing; state of being liquid or in movement

fly *vi.* **(flew; flown)** move through the air; flee; *vt.* avoid, escape from; *n.* pestiferous insect; type of fish-hook

fly´er, fli´er *n.* aviator

F.M. frequency modulation, a means of radio broadcasting

foam *n.* froth; *vi.* gather foam; be enraged

fo´cus *n.* point at which rays of light,etc., meet; central point; *vt.* bring to a focus; **fo´cal** *a.*

foe *n.* enemy

fog *n.* thick mist; *vt.* darken with fog

foi´ble *n.* slight failing or weakness

foil *vt.* defeat; *n.* thin plate of metal, leaf-like ornament; sword for fencing; anything which provides a contrast (as a foil for someone´s wit)

foist *vt.* pass off as genuine

fold *n.* a doubling; enclosure; flock of sheep; *vt.* double; lay one part of (cloth) over another; enclose

fo´li-age *n.* leaves, greenery

fo´li-o *n.* sheet of paper folded once; size of book, 17 x 22 inches; book with sheets of such size; page number

folk *n.* **(folk)** people; **(folks)** *col.* family, kin; **folk´lore´** *n.* ancient customs, superstitions, etc., of the people

fol´li-cle *n.* small cavity

fol´low *vi. & vt.* go or come after; imitate; result from

fol´low-ing *a.* subsequent; *n.* body of adherents; calling

fol´ly *n.* foolishness; foolish act or enterprise

fo-ment´ *vt.* encourage, incite

fo´men-ta´tion *n.* hot applications to the body

fond *a.* loving

fon´dle *vt.* caress

font *n.* assortment of printer´s type all of one style; vessel for baptismal water or holy water; source, fountain

fool *n.* one who acts stupidly; professional jester; *vt.* deceive, trick, esp. in a harmless way; **fool´ish** *a.*

foot *n.* **(feet)** part of body on which an animal stands or walks; base; measure equal to 12 inches; division of a line of poetry; **foot the bill**, pay for expense

foot´ball´ *n.* game played with elliptical ball which is kicked

fop *n.* dandy

for´age *n.* fodder; provisions; act of foraging; *vi. & vt.* carry off fodder for food; plunder

for´ay *n.* raid; *vt.* pillage

for-bear´ *vi. & vt.* **(for-bore´, for-borne´)** abstain, stop

fore´bear´ *n.* ancestor

for-bear´ance *n.* patience, clemency

for-bid´ *vt.* **(for-bade´, for-bid´den)** prohibit, command not to do

force *n.* strength, energy; validity; military or naval power; *vt.* compel; obtain by violence; **for´ci-ble** *a.*

fore´arm´ *n.* arm between elbow and wrist

fore´bode´ *vi. & vt.* apprehend, foretell; **fore´bod´ing** *n.*

fore´cast´ *n.* prediction of future events, as the weather; *vi. & vt.*

fore´close´ *vi. & vt.* take legal possession of mortgaged property; **fore´clo´sure** *n.*

fore´fa´ther *n.* ancestor

fore´fin´ger *n.* index finger, finger next to thumb

fore-go´ *vt.* **(fore´went´, fore´gone´)** give up

fore´head *n.* brow

for´eign *a.* alien, belonging to another country; unrelated

fore´man *n.* **(fore´men)** overseer

fo-ren´sic *a.* pertaining to debate or rhetoric

fore´run´ner *n.* messenger sent before, annunciator; sign, premonitory token

fore-see´ *vt.* **(fore-saw´, fore-seen´)** know beforehand

fore´sight´ *n.* act or power to know beforehand

for´est *n.* tract of land covered with trees

fore-tell´ *vi. & vt.* **(fore-told´)** prophesy

for-ev´er *adv.* always

for´feit *vt.* lose by fault, crime, etc.; *n.* penalty; **for´fei-ture** *n.*

forge *vt.* counterfeit, sign the name of another; form by heating and hammering; *n.* furnace in which iron is heated; **for´ger-y** *n.*

for-get´ *vi. & vt.* **(for-got´, for-got´ten)** lose or put from memory; neglect

for-give´ *vt.* **(for-gave´, for-giv´en)** pardon, overlook

fork *n.* instrument with prongs at one end; prong; *vi. & vt.* branch or divide into branches; pitch with a fork

for-lorn´ *a.* forsaken

form *n.* shape; mode, ceremony; *vt.* give shape to; make; establish; *vi.* assume a form

for´mal *a.* according to the established mode or ceremony; having only the outer form

for-mal´ity *n.* precise observance of forms

for-ma´tion *n.* form, structure; arrangement

for´mer *a.* coming before in time or order; past; first mentioned

For-mica *n. tr.* resistant plastic surface finish

for´mi-da-ble *a.* hard to overcome; giving cause for fear or doubt

for´mu-la *n.* **(for´mu-lae, for´mulas)** formal statement, as of a chemical equation; recipe; prescribed form

for´mu-late´ *vt.* systematize, reduce to formulas

for´ni-ca´tion *n.* illicit sexual intercourse; **for´ni-cate´** *vi.*

for-sake´ *vt.* **(for-sook´, for-sak´en)** desert, abandon

fort *n.* fortress, stronghold

forte *n.* one´s strong point

for´ti-fi-ca´tion *n.* work of defense, stronghold, fort

for´ti-fy´ *vt.* strengthen

for´tis´si-mo´ *a.* & *adv.* very loud

for´ti-tude´ *n.* strength of mind or character, esp. in adversity

fort´night´ *n.* two weeks

for´tress *n.* stronghold, fort

for-tu´i-tous *a.* happening by accident

for´tune *n.* chance, luck; wealth; **for´tu-nate** *a.* lucky, favorable

fo´rum *n.* place for public discussion

fos´sil *n.* petrified organic remains of a plant or animal

fos´ter *vt.* bring up, nurse; encourage

foul *a.* filthy, impure; stormy; offensive

found *vt.* lay the foundation of; institute; cast metal

foun-da´tion *n.* a founding; basis; endowed institution; setting up of any institution

found´ling *n.* deserted child

foun´dry *n.* art of casting metals; place where metals are cast

foun´tain *n.* spring of water, natural or artificial; source;

4-F *n.* person classified as unfit for military service; *a.*

four´score´ *a.* eighty, four times a score (twenty)

fowl *n.* bird

fox *n.* flesh-eating animal of the dog family

fox´hole´ *n.* dugout shelter for combat soldier

fox´y *a.* sly, crafty

fra´cas *n.* uproar

fraction *n.* fragment; quotient of one number divided by another (as ½, 1½ , .75, etc.)

frac´tious *a.* cross, irritable

fracture *n.* breakage, as of bone; *vi.* & *vt.* break, crack

frag´ile *a.* easily broken, frail; **fragil´i-ty** *n.*

frag´ment *n.* piece broken off; **frag´men-tar´y** *a.*

fragrant *a.* sweet-scented; **fra´grance** *n.*

frail *a.* lacking strength; fragile

frame *vt.* form; put a border on; *n.* form; skeleton; case; state

fran´chise´ *n.* right to vote; privilege

fran´gi-ble *a.* easily broken fragile

frank *a.* candid, open

frantic *a.* wildly excited

fra-ter´nal *a.* pertaining to a brother or brethren; **fra-ter´ni-ty** *n.* society; social organization; **frat´er-nize´** *vi.* have friendly relations with; have intimate relations with an enemy

fraud *n.* unlawful deceit; trickster

fraud´u-lence *n.* fraud, deceit; **fraud´u-lent** *a.*

fray *vi.* & *vt.* wear off by rubbing

freak *n.* monstrosity; unusual occurrence, accident, etc.

freckle *n.* small blemish on the skin; *vt.*

free *a.* at liberty, not bound; lavish; exempt; extra, gratuitous; *vt.* set at liberty; rid

freeze *vi.* & *vt.* **(froze; frozen)** become or make into ice; **freez´er** *n.* apparatus for storing food

freeze´dry´ *vt.* to dehydrate food while frozen for storage at room

temperature
freight *n.* cargo or lading; charge for transporting goods; *vt.* load, as a ship; transport, carry
fren´zy *n.* violent excitement
fre´quen-cy *n.* repetition, repeated occurrence; number of cycles per unit of time
fre´quent *a.* often
fre-quent´ *vt.* visit often
fres´co *n.* painting on wet plaster; *vt.*
fresh *a.* new, recently produced; untried
fret *vi.* & *vt.* worry, disturb; irritate
fret *n.* short ridge on the fingerboard of a guitar
fri´a-ble *a.* easily, reduced to powder
fric´as-see´ *n.* dish of stewed meat in gravy
fric´tion *n.* act or effect of rubbing; antagonism
friend *n.* one loving or attached to a person or cause; Quaker
frig´ate *n.* old-time, fast-sailing ship of war
fright *n.* sudden fear; shocking sight
fright´en *vt.* make afraid, terrify
frig´id *a.* frozen, stiffened with cold; forbidding; sexually cold; **fri-gid´i-ty** *n.*
frill *n.* ruffle; unnecessary frivolity or ornamentation; *vi.* & *vt.* ruffle
fringe *n.* kind of trimming; strips forming a border; extremity; *vt.* adorn with a fringe
frisk *vi.* & *vt.* leap playfully, frolic
frit´ter *n.* fried cake made with corn or fruit; *vt.* break into fragments; waste by degrees, fribble away
friv´o-lous *a.* unimportant, slight; trifling; lacking in seriousness
frock *n.* loose outer garment; dress
frog *n.* well-known amphibian which develops from tadpole; crossing plate of a railway track; **frog´man´** *n.* man trained and equipped for underwater naval action
frol´ic *n.* merrymaking; prank
frond *n.* leafy branch; fern leaf
front *n.* forehead, face, anterior; pretended appearance, bearing; combat zone; *a.* of or in the front
fron-tier´ *n.* boundary of a country; unsettled or unexplored area
fron´tis-piece´ *n.* picture fronting the title page of a book
frost *n.* frozen dew; *vt.* cover with frost or anything resembling it (as icing on cake)
froth *n.* foam; empty show or pretense; *vi.* & *vt.* foam
fro´ward *a.* self-willed, obstinate
frown *n.* scowl; *vi.* & *vt.* scowl, wrinkle the brow; indicate displeasure
fruc´ti-fy´ *vi.* bear fruit; *vt.* make fruitful
frugal *a.* thrifty, economical, sparing; **fru´gal´i-ty** *n.*
fruit *n.* anything produced for nourishment, esp. the sweet, seed-bearing product of trees, shrubs, etc.; product
fru-i´tion *n.* fulfillment
frus´trate´ *vt.* defeat, thwart; **frus´-tra´tion** *n.*
fry *vi.* & *vt.* cook with fat in a pan over the fire
fudge *n.* kind of candy; nonsense
fu´el *n.* anything that feeds a fire, excitement, or produces energy
fu´gi-tive *n.* one who flees, as from justice; *a.* fleeing, passing
ful´crum *n.* prop on which a lever moves
ful-fill´ *vt.* complete, bring into effect
full´back´ *n.* player or position on football team

full´ blast´ *n.* operation at maximum capacity
ful´mi-nate´ *vi.* & *vt.* explode suddenly; *n.* explosive compound; **ful´-mi-na´tion** *n.*
ful´some *a.* disgustingly insincere
fum´ble *vi.* & *vt.* grope about; manage awkwardly
fume *n.* smoke, vapor; *vi.* throw off vapor; be in a rage
fu´mi-gate´ *vt.* disinfect with gas; **fu´mi-ga´tion** *n.*
func´tion *n.* duty; power; action peculiar to an organ or thing; formal social event
fund *n.* sum of money, capital
fun´da-men´tal *a.* basic; *n.* basis, essential, primary principle
fu´ner-al *n.* burial ceremony; *a.* pertaining to a burial
fu-ne´re-al *a.* mournful
fun´gus *n.* **(fun´gus-es, fungi)** type of plant including the mushroom; **fun´gous** *a.*
funnel *n.* smokestack; instrument for pouring fluids into bottles
fur´bish *vt.* polish, spruce up, renovate
fu´ri-ous *a.* raging, full of fury
furl *vi.* & *vt.* roll or be rolled up
fur´lough´ *n.* military leave of absence
fur´nace *n.* apparatus for heating, etc.
fur´nish *vt.* supply, equip
fur´ni-ture *n.* household equipment such as chairs, tables, etc.
fur´row *n.* trench made by a plow; wrinkle; *vi.* & *vt.* make or form furrows in
fur´ther *a.* additional; more distant; *adv.* in addition; to a greater distance or degree; *vt.* promote, advance
fur´tive *a.* stealthy
fu´ry *n.* rage, violent anger
fuse *vi.* & *vt.* melt, blend; **fu´si-ble** *a.*
fuse *n.* tube filled with combustible matter for firing mines, shells, etc.; strip of metal which melts when overloaded with electricity, breaking the circuit
fu´se-lage´ *n.* part of an airplane to which wings and tail are attached
fu´sion *n.* act or state of melting; close union; release of great energy from union of hydrogen nuclei into helium nuclei
fuss *n.* slight quarrel; unnecessary stir or bother; *vi.* make a great stir; wrangle
fus´tian *n.* bombast, useless talk; type of cloth
futile *a.* useless; **fu´til´i-ty** *n.*
fu´ture *n.* time to come; *a.* yet to come

G

gab *n.* talk, chatter; *vi.*
gabble *n.* meaningless talk; *vi.* & *vt.* jabber; cackle
ga´ble *n.* triangular exterior wall of a building
gadg´et *n.* any ingenious device or contrivance
gag *n.* joke; something thrust into the mouth to enforce silence; *vt.* forcibly silence; *vi.* retch
gai´e-ty *n.* merriment
gain *vi.* & *vt.* earn; improve; increase; *n.* profit
gala *a.*festive
gal´ax-y *n.* Milky Way; any great cluster of stars; any splendid assemblage
gale *n.* strong wind
gall *n.* bile, fluid secreted by the liver; gall bladder; *col.* impudence,

'nerve'

gal´lant *a.* gay, splendid; noble, brave; courteous to ladies; *n.* man of fashion, spirit, or mettle; **gal´-lan-try** *n.* bravery; attention to ladies

gal´ler-y *n.* long passage or balcony surrounded by rails; upper floor of seats in an assembly room

gal´ley *n.* long ship propelled by oars; kitchen of a ship; frame in which type is placed

gal´lon *n.* measure of capacity equal to four quarts

gal´lop *vi.* leap in running; *n.* a run in leaps

gal´lows *n.* scaffold on which criminals are hanged

gal´va-nize´ *vt.* coat a metal such as iron, with zinc; excite or shock as if by electricity

gam´ble *vi.* & *vt.* play for money in games of chance; take a calculated risk

gam´bol *vi.* leap, play

gam´in *n.* street boy, urchin

gam´ma glob´u-lin *n.* blood extract rich in antibodies

gamma ray´ *n.* stream of very short, high energy particles emitted by radium, etc.

gan´der *n.* male goose

gang *n.* band, group

gan´gli-on *n.* natural enlargement in a nerve

gang´ster *n.* member of a band of criminals

gan´try *n.* scaffold for building and servicing a rocket before launching

gape *vi.* open the mouth in amazement; stare

ga-rage´ *n.* place where automobiles are stored or repaired

garb *n.* dress; external appearance; *vt.* clothe

gar´bage *n.* refuse, trash

gar´den *n.* plot of ground where flowers, vegetables, etc., are grown; *vi.* & *vt.* work in a garden

gar´gle *n.* preparation for washing the throat; *vi.* & *vt.* wash the throat

gar´ish *a.* showy, gaudy

gar´land *n.* wreath; *vt.* deck with a garland

gar´lic *n.* plant whose strong-smelling, bulbous root is used in cooking

gar´ment *n.* article of clothing

gar´ner *vt.* gather and store, esp. grain

gar´net *n.* precious red stone; deep red color

gar´nish *vt.* adorn decoate; *n.* embellishment

gar´ret *n.* attic

gar´ri-son *n.* group of soldiers stationed in a fortress or town; *vt.* furnish a place with troops

gar´ru-lous *a.* talkative; **gar-ru´li-ty** *n.*

gar´ter *n.* band used to hold up stockings

gas *n.* vapor; gasoline; **gas´e-ous** *a.*

gash *n.* deep, open wound; *vt.* make a deep cut

gasket *n.* washer; device for securing or packing a piston, joint, etc.

gas´o-line´ *n.* colorless liquid fuel obtained from petroleum

gasp *vi.* breathe convulsively; *n.* painful catching of the breath

gas´tric *a.* pertaining to the stomach

gath´er *vi.* & *vt.* collect, garner; infer; plait

gaud´y *a.* showy

gauge *n.* measure; standard of measure; *vt.* measure

gaunt *a.* thin, lean, haggard

gauze *n.* light, transparent fabric

gay *a.* lively, showy, merry; **gai´ly** *adv.*

gaze *vi.* look fixedly, stare; *n.* fixed look, stare

ga-zette´ *n.* journal, newspaper

gaz´et-teer´ *n.* geographical dictionary

gear *n.* device to connect parts of a machine by means of toothed wheels; harness; tackle; belongings

Gei´ger count´er *n.* device for measuring radioactivity

gei´sha, gei´sha girl´ *n.* Japanese entertainer

gel´a-tin *n.* animal jelly

gem *n.* precious stone; writing, saying, or anything regarded as precious

gen´der *n.* distinction among parts of speech, supposedly according to sex (*man* - he; *girl* - she; *stone* - it)

gene *n.* component of living cells which determines their characteristics and transmits them from generation to generation

gen´e-al´o-gy *n.* study of the history or descent of families

gen´er-al *a.* broad in scope, not special or restricted; *n.* Army, Air Force, or Marine officer above colonel

gen´er-ate´ *vt.* produce; bring into life or existence; **gen´er-a´tion** *n.* production; people of the same time or period

gen´er-a´tor *n.* apparatus used to produce gas, steam, or electricity

ge-ner´ic *a.* general, belonging to the same group, class, or set

gen´e-sis *n.* generation, creation; first book of the Old Testament

ge-net´ics *n.* study of heredity

gen´ial *a.* merry, cheering

gen´ius *n.* power of creating or originating; unusual talent or mental ability

gen´o-cide´ *n.* organized extermination of a whole national, cultural or racial group

gen´tile´ *n.* one not a Jew

gen´tle *a.* mild, refined

gen´u-flect´ *vi.* bend the knee in worship; **gen´u-flec´tion** *n.*

gen´u-ine *a.* real, pure

genus *n.* **(gen´er-a)** class, group, or set made up of several related subtypes or species

ge´o-de´sic dome *n.* dome supported by framework of polygons

ge-od´e-sy *n.* applied mathematics relating to measurement and shape of the earth; **ge´o-det´ic, ge´o-des´ic** *a.*

ge-og´ra-phy *n.* description of the earth, its physical characteristics and inhabitants; **ge´o-graph´ic, ge´o-graph´ic-al** *a.*

ge-ol´o-gy *n.* science of the structure of the earth; **ge´o-log´ic, ge´o-log´ic-al** *a.*; **ge-ol´o-gist** *n.*

ge-om´e-try *n.* study of figures, such as lines, angles, surfaces, and solids; **ge´o-met´ric, ge´o-met´ric-al** *a.*

ge´o-phys´ics *n.* study of the earth and the forces affecting it; **ge´o-phys´ic-al** *a.*

ge´o-pol´i-tics *n.* political science treating the dependence of a country upon its geographic and economic position

ger´i-at´rics *n.* branch of medicine dealing with the care of aged persons

germ *n.* microbe, bacterium; rudimentary form; origin, first principle

ger´mi-nate´ *vi.* sprout, begin to grow

ges´tic´u-late´ *vi.* gesture, make gestures while talking

ges´ture *n.* movement expressive of sentiment

get *vt.* **(got; got´ten)** obtain; receive; prepare; urge

gey´ser *n.* natural spring which throws out hot water, etc.

ghast´ly *a.* death-like, hideous

ghet´to *n.* part of a city to which members of a minority group are restricted

ghost *n.* spirit, apparition

GI *n. col.* American soldier

gi´ant *n.* person or thing of extraordinary size

gib´bet *n.* gallows

gib´bous *a.* convex, humped, rounded

gibe *vi. & vt.* sneer, mock, taunt; *n.* contempt; mocking insult

gib´lets *n. pl.* edible internal parts of fowl, such as the liver and gizzard

gift *n.* present, anything given; talent

gi-gan´tic *a.* like a giant

gig´gle *vi.* laugh in a silly manner, titter; *n.* silly laugh, titter

gild *vt.* cover with gold

gilt *a.* gilded; *n.*

gim´mick *n.* clever device, plan, or stratagem

gin *n.* juniper-flavored liquor; machine for removing seeds from cotton; snare, trap; *vt.* clear cotton of its seeds; ensnare

gin´ger *n.* hot, spicy herb

ging´ham *n.* kind of cotton cloth

gi-raffe´ *n.* African animal with very long neck

gird *vt.* bind around

gird´er *n.* beam supported at its ends and sustaining a weight

gir´dle *n.* woman´s form-fitting undergarment; belt; *vt.* bind, enclose

gist *n.* main point

give *vi. & vt.* **(gave, giv´en)** bestow, donate; furnish, supply; yield

gla´cier *n.* field of ice slowly moving down a valley; **gla´cial** *a.*

glade *n.* open space in or space through a wood

glad´i-o´lus *n.* type of iris with sword-like flowers and leaves

glance *n.* darting of the eye, momentary view; sudden flash of light; *vi.* dart; fly off obliquely

gland *n.* fleshy organ (like the liver) which produces various secretions

glare *n.* dazzling light; fierce stare; *vi.* shine with a dazzling light; look with piercing eyes

glass *n.* hard, brittle, transparent substance made chiefly of sand or other silicates; water glass or other object made of glass; **glass´es** *n. pl.* spectacles; **glass´y** *a.*

glaze *vt.* give a glassy finish to; *n.* glassy finish on pottery

gleam *vt.* glow; flash; *n.* small ray of light

glean *vt.* gather what has been left behind or overlooked by others

glee *n.* joy, gaiety; **glee club** *n.* group which sings songs for three or more solo voices

glib *a.* overly fluent, pat

glide *vi.* slide smoothly without use of power; flow gently; *n.* act of gliding

glid´er *n.* motorless airplane

glim´mer *vi.* shine faintly; *n.* faint light

glimpse *n.* hurried view; *vt.* catch sight of briefly

glis´ten, glis´ter *vi.* sparkle, glitter

glit´ter *vi.* sparkle, be showy; *n.* luster, brilliancy

gloat *vi.* look upon something with wicked satisfaction

glob´al *a.* world-wide, concerning the earth as a whole

globe *n.* sphere; Earth
glob´ule *n.* little globe, drop, or particle
gloom *n.* partial darkness; cloudiness; sadness
glo´ry *n.* splendor; honor; *vi.* triumph, exult; boast; **glo´ri-ous** *a.*; **glo´ri-fy´** *vt.*
gloss *n.* brightness, sheen
gloss *n.* comment, explanation; *vi.* & *vt.* explain
glos´sa-ry *n.* lexicon, list of words requiring explanation
glot´tis *n.* entrance from pharynx into larynx
glove *n.* cover for the hand; *vt.* cover with a glove
glow *vi.* shine with heat; be flushed; be excited; *n.* shining heat; physical or emotional warmth
glow´er *vi.* stare angrily, scowl
glue *n.* adhesive substance; *vt.* paste, join with glue
glum *a.* sullen, moody
glut *vt.* swallow greedily; oversupply; *n.* overabundance
glut´ton *n.* one who eats to excess
glyc´er-in, glyc´er-ine *n.* sweet, transparent, viscous alcohol obtained from fats
gnash *vi.* & *vt.* grind the teeth together in rage
gnat *n.* small fly
gnaw *vi.* & *vt.* tear with the teeth; corrode, worry away
goal *n.* aim, ambition; winning post
goat *n.* hollow-horned quadruped allied to the sheep; **goat´ee** *n.* small chin beard
gob´ble *vt.* swallow greedily; *vi.* make a noise like a turkey; *n.* noise of a turkey; **gob´bler** *n.* turkey cock
gob´ble-dy-gook´ *n.* wordy, dull, or meaningless language
goi´ter *n.* morbid enlargement of the thyroid
golf *n.* game played with a set of clubs and a ball
gon´or-rhe´a *n.* type of venereal disease, the clap
good´by´, good´bye´ *inter.* & *n.* farewell
goose *n.* **(geese)** type of waterfowl; silly person
goose´ber´ry *n.* sour berry used in pastries
go´pher *n.* type of burrowing rodent
gorge *vi.* & *vt.* eat greedily, glut
gor´geous *a.* magnificently beautiful, dazzling
go-ril´la *n.* largest of the African apes
gos´sa-mer *n.* thin fabric or garment; spider threads floating through the air
gos´sip *n.* idle talk, scandal; talebearer; *vi.* tell tales
gouge *n.* chisel with a hollow blade; *vt.* scoop out
gourd *n.* a large, fleshy fruit; cup made from a gourd
gour´mand *n.* one who delights in food and drink; glutton
gour´met´ *n.* epicure, one expert in good eating
gout *n.* an inflammation of the joints
gov´ern *vi.* & *vt.* rule, control, determine; **gov´er-nor** *n.*
gown *n.* dress, outer garment
grab *vt.* seize; *n.* seizure
grace *n.* charm, attractiveness; favor; mercy, divine mercy; short prayer at meals; *vt.* mark with favor, adorn
gra´cious *a.* courteous
gra-da´tion *n.* degree; arrangement in ranks
grade *n.* degree; step; degree of

slope; *vt.* arrange systematically; give a grade or mark to; reduce to an even slope or level

grad´u-al *a.* advancing by degrees

grad´u-ate´ *vt.* divide into regular intervals; admit to a grade or degree; *vi.* receive a diploma or degree; *n.* one given a degree

graft *n.* twig or flesh used in grafting; dishonest gains; *vt.*

grain *n.* single, small, hard seed; unit of apothecary´s weight; texture

gram *n.* unit of weight in metric system

gram´mar *n.* sounds, forms, and combinations of forms of any language; **gram-mat´i-cal** *a.*

gran´ar-y *n.* place for storing grain

grand *a.* splendid

grandeur *n.* splendor, magnificence

gran´dil´o-quence *n.* pompous language; **gran´dil´o-quent** *a.*

grant *vt.* bestow, admit; *n.* gift

gran´u-lar *a.* consisting of or like grains; **gran´ule** *n.* grain

grape *n.* fruit of the vine

graph´ic *a.* vivid, clearly described

graph´ite´ *n.* type of carbon used in pencils

grap´ple *vt.* lay hold of; *vi.* contend with

grasp *vt.* seize and hold; understand; *n.* grip of the hand; power of intellect

grass *n.* common herbage; **grass´-hop´per** *n.* insect allied to the locust

grate *n.* framework, esp. for holding coals or fire; *vt.* furnish with grates; rub hard; wear away; irritate

grate´ful *a.* thankful

grat´i-fy´ *vt.* please, satisfy; **grat´i-fi-ca´tion** *n.*

grat´i-tude´ *n.* thankfulness

gra-tu´i-tous *a.* free, voluntary, uncalled for; **gra-tu´i-ty** *n.* present, tip

grave *n.* place of hurial; death; **grave´yard´** *n.* burial place, cemetery

grave *a.* weighty; somber

grav´el *n.* small stones

grav´i-tate´ *vi.* tend towards some object or direction; **grav´i-ta´tion** *n.*

grav´i-ty *n.* importance; seriousness; law of gravitition

gra´vy *n.* juices that issue from meat in cooking; sauce

gray, grey *n.* white mixed with black; *a.*

graze *vi.* & *vt.* feed on grass; pass lightly along the surface

grease *n.* fat, esp. soft animal fat; *vt.* smear with grease; **greas´y** *a.*

great *a.* large; superior, of high rank

greed *n.* covetousness; **greed´y** *a.*

greet *vt.* hail, salute; **greet´ing** *n.* salutation

gre-gar´i-ous *a.* associating in groups; hence companionable, friendly

grem´lin *n.* imaginary creature in airplanes, war factories etc.

gre-nade´ *n.* small explosive shell thrown by hand

grey´hound´ *n.* swift hunting dog

grid´dle *n.* shallow iron pan

grid´i´ron *n.* metal frame used for broiling; football field

grief *n.* sorrow, affliction

grieve *vi.* & *vt.* cause or feel grief; **griev´ance** *n.* cause of grief; hardship, injury

grill *n.* gridiron; network; *vt.* broil

grim *a.* of forbidding aspect

gri-mace´ *n.* facial distortion, wry expression; *vi.*

grime *n.* ingrained dirt

grin *vi.* show the teeth in laughing; *n.* toothy smile

grind *vt.* **(ground)** reduce to powder or sharpen by friction; oppress

grip *n.* grasp; appliance for grasping; suitcase; *vt.* grasp

gris´tle *n.* cartilage; **grist´ly** *a.*

grit *n.* pluck, courage; **grits** *n. pl.* grain coarsely ground; *vt.* grind, grate

groan *vi.* moan; *n.* moaning sound

gro´cer *n.* dealer in foods

groin *n.* depression between thigh and abdomen

groom *n.* bridegroom; one who tends horses; *vt.* tend, as a horse

groove *n.* furrow; long rut; *vt.* cut furrows in

grope *vi.* feel or search in the dark with the hands

gross *a.* coarse; whole; shameful; *n.* main bulk; one dozen dozen

gro-tesque´ *a.* ludicrous, odd, bizarre

ground *n.* surface of the earth; land, floor, etc.; foundation; **grounds** *n. pl.* dregs; *vt.* fix on a foundation; place or run on the ground; *vi.* strike bottom

ground´ ze´ro *n.* spot on earth´s surface over, below, or at which an atomic bomb is set off

group *n.* assemblage, cluster; *vt.* assemble

grove *n.* cluster of trees

grov´el *vi.* crawl or creep; hence, wallow in depravity

grow *vi.* **(grew; grown)** develop, increase; *vt.* cause to grow

growl *vi.* snarl, utter a sound like an angry dog; grumble; *n.* snarl

growth *n.* gradual increase; that which has grown

grub *vi.* & *vt.* dig, dig up, root up; *n.* insect larva; *col.* food

grudge *n.* old cause of quarrel; secret enmity; *vt.* envy, give or take unwillingly

grue´some *a.* horrible, bizarre, ghastly

gruff *a.* bluff, churlish

grum´ble *vi.* complain, growl

grunt *vi.* make a noise like a pig; *n.* sound made by a pig

guar´an-tee´ *vt.* assure, make sure; *n.* surety for another´s performance

guard *vt.* protect from danger; *n.* protection; caution; one who watches or protects; two of the positions and players in football and basketball

guard´i-an *n.* one who guards or protects; one who has the care of a minor; *a.* protecting

gu´ber-na-to´ri-al *a.* pertaining to a governor

guer-ril´la *n.* member of an irregular band of soldiers

guess *vi.* & *vt.* make an offhand estimate; *n.* estimate

guest *n.* visitor

guf-faw´ *n.* loud, unrestrained laugh

guid´ance sys´tem *n.* built-in apparatus to control course of a missile

guide *vt.* lead, direct; *n.* anything that leads; **guid´ed mis´sile** *n.* armed rocket able to seek out its target; **guid´ance** *n.*

guild *n.* association

guile *n.* deceit

guilt *n.* responsibility for a crime

guin´ea pig´ *n.* small South American animal often used in experiments

guise *n.* external appearance disguise

gui-tar´ *n.* musical instrument with 6 strings

gulch *n.* deep ravine

gulf *n.* large bay; chasm

gull *n.* web-footed sea fowl with big wings

gull *vt.* deceive, trick, cheat; *n.* one who is cheated

gul´let *n.* food passage leading to stomach, the esophagus

gul´ly *n.* channel worn by running water; *vt.* wear into a gully

gumbo´ *n.* thick soap usually made with okra

gun *n.* weapon from which explosives are discharged; **gun´ner** *n.* one who tends a cannon; **gun´-powder** *n.* explosive mixture of sulphur, saltpeter, and charcoal

gu´ru *n.* revered spiritual leader

gush *n.* violent flow; **gush´er** *n.* oil well which is out of control; *vi.* flow copiously; make a silly display of sentiment

gust *n.* sudden blast of wind; strong feeling, etc.

gus´ta-to´ry *a.* pertaining to the taste

gut *n.* intestine; **guts** *n. col.* courage, fortitude, stamina

gut´ter *n.* channel for carrying off rainwater ditch

gut´tur-al *a.* pertaining to the throat; *n.* throaty sound

guy *n.* man or boy, fellow; rope or chain to guide or steady a suspended weight

gym´na´si-um *n.* **(gym´na´si-ums, gym´na´si-a)** place for athletic exercise

gyn´e-col´o-gy *n.* branch of medicine concerned with women and their diseases

gypsy *n.* one of a wandering group; any wanderer

gy´rate´ *vi.* revolve; move spirally; **gy´ra´tion** *n.*

gy´ro-scope´ *n.* rotating mechanism used as a stabilizer

H

ha-bil´i-ments *n. pl.* dress, garments

hab´it *n.* personal custom, ordinary course of conduct; dress

hab´it-a-ble *a.* livable

hab´i-ta´tion *n.* dwelling

ha-bit´u-al *a.* customery

ha-bit´u-ate´ *vt.* accustom

ha-bit´u-é´ *n.* habitual frequenter of a place

hack´ney *vt.* make commonplace or trite

had´dock *n.* seafish of the cod family

hag´gard *a.* gaunt, worn out, visibly tired

hag´gle *vi.* bargain over prices, wrangle

hail *vi. & vt.* call to, greet, salute; *n.* loud call

hail *n.* frozen lumps of rain; *vi. & vt.*

hair *n.* filament growing from the skin; mass of such filaments; **hair´pin** *n.* wire pin for fastening a woman´s hair

half *n.* **(halves)** one of two equal parts; *a.* consisting of one of two equal parts; **half´back** *n.* position or player on football team

half´-life´ *n.* length of time needed for half the atoms in any radioactive substance to disintegrate

hal´i-to´sis *n.* bad breath

hal´le-lu´jah *n. & inter.* praise the Lord!

Hal´low-een´ *n.* evening before All Saints´ Day

hal-lu´ci-na´tion *n.* delusion, vision caused by alcoholism, etc.

hal-lu´ci-no-gen *n.* drug that causes hallucinations

ha´lo´ *n.* luminous circle used in art around heads of holy figures

halt *vi.* & *vt.* stop; *a.* lame; *n.* stop, cessation; limp; lameness

hal´ter *n.* article of woman´s clothing; headrope for a horse; noose

ham *n.* thigh of a hog, cured; one who overacts; amateur radio operator; **ham´burg´er** *n.* grilled beef patty, usually in bun; chopped beef

ham´mer *n.* tool for driving nails, etc.; *vt.* drive with a hammer

ham´mock *n.* hanging or swinging couch

ham´per *n.* large basket; *vt.* hinder, slow down

hand *n.* extremity below the wrist; pointer, as of a clock; workman; style of handwriting; cards dealt to a player; *vt.* give with the hand

hand´cuff *n.* manacle; *vt.* put manacles on

hand´i-cap´ *n.* disadvantage; artificial advantage in a race or game; *vt.* place at a disadvantage

hand´i-craft´ *n.* skilled work done by hand

hand´i-work´ *n.* work done by the hands

hand´ker-chief *n.* pocket cloth for wiping the nose, etc.

han´dle *n.* part of any tool, machine, etc., guided by or held in the hand; *vt.* touch, hold; use, manage; deal in

hand´some *a.* good-looking

hand´y *a.* convenient, near; dexterous

hang *vi.* & *vt.* **(hung)** suspend or be suspended

hang *vt.* put to death by the rope

han´gar *n.* shelter for housing or storing aircraft

han´ker *vi.* long for, yearn

hap´haz´ard *a.* accidental, chance, random

hap´pen *vi.* take place, occur

hap´py *a.* joyous; fortunate

ha-rangue´ *n.* loud speech to a multitude, tirade; *vi.* & *vt.* deliver a tirade

har´ass *vt.* annoy or weary by troubles or attacks

har´bin-ger *n.* forerunner; *vt.* usher in

har´bor *n.* refuge; port for ships; *vt.* lodge, shelter; *vi.* take shelter

hard´-core´ *a.* at the center of a group; inflexible

hard´ drug´ *n.* addictive drug

hard´top´ con-ver´ti-ble *n.*car with a metal roof which can be moved out of sight under trunk lid

har´le-quin *n.* clown; traditional clown dressed in motley

harm *n.* injury, damage; *vt.* injure

har´mo-ny *n.* concord; agreement; combination of musical tones; **har´mo´ni-ous** *a.*; **har-mon´ic** *a.*

har´ness *n.* equipment of a horse; *vt.* put the harness on; equip

harp *n.* triangular, stringed musical instrument ; *vi.* play on the harp; dwell tediously on a subject

har´ry *vt.* plunder; harass

harsh *a.* rough; severe

har´vest *n.* time of gathering in the crops; crops gathered; *vi.* & *vt.*

hasp *n.* metal strap secured to a staple by a lock

has´sock *n.* upholstered footstool

haste *n.* speed, dispatch; **has´ten** *vi.* & *vt.* hurry; **hast´y** *a.*

hatch *vi.* come out of the egg; *vt.* produce from the egg, originate

hatch´et *n.* small axe

hate *n.* extreme dislike; *vi.* & *vt.* dislike intensely, loathe

ha´tred *n.* intense dislike

haugh´ty *a.* disdainful

haul *vt.* drag, pull; *n.* act of pulling; booty

haunch *n.* hip

haunt *vi.* & *vt.* visit (as a ghost); follow or frequent; *n.* place much resorted to

have *vt.* **(had)** own, possess; be affected by; be obliged to

ha´ven *n.* place of safety, harbor

hav´oc *n.* destruction; confusion

Ha-wai´ian *n.* native of Hawaii; *a.*

hawk *n.* a bird of prey

haz´ard *n.* chance, risk; *vt.* expose to danger; take a chance

haze *n.* light fog; obscurity

ha´zy *a.* not clear, vague

H´-bomb´, hydro-gen bomb´ *n.* bomb releasing tremendous energy from fusion of hydrogen nuclei

head *n.* foremost part of an animal´s body; chief; *vt.* lead; go in front of

heal *vi.* grow sound again; *vt.* cure, make healthy

health *n.* freedom from sickness

heap *n.* pile; *vt.* pile up

hear *vt.* **(heard)** perceive through the ear; try judicially; *vi.* listen to; have the sense of hearing

hearse *n.* carriage for conveying the dead to the grave

heart *n.* organ that circulates the blood; vital part of anything; seat of the affections

hearth *n.* floor of a fireplace; fireside

heat *n.* form of energy; high temperature; *vi.* become hot; *vt.* make hot; agitate

heave *vt.* lift up; throw; *vi.* rise and fall; try to vomit; *n.* effort to raise something

heav´en *n.* arch of the sky; dwelling place of the blessed

heav´y *a.* weighty; oppressive; afflicted; **heavy water** *n.* water made from oxygen and deuterium, a heavy isotope of hydrogen; **heav´y-weight´** *n.* boxer or wrestler weighing over 175 lbs.

hec´a-tomb´ *n.* any great slaughter

hec´tor *vt.* bully, annoy; tease, vex

hedge *n.* thicket or fence of bushes or trees; *vt.* enclose with a hedge; surround, as with restrictions; reduce a risk; *vi.* give evasive answers

heed *vi.* & *vt.* pay attention to; *n.* notice; care

heel *n.* back part of the foot; back part of shoe; *sl.* craven, scum, low person; *vt.* put a heel on; *vi.* & *vt.* tilt

heif´er *n.* young cow

height *n.* distance upwards; altitude

hei´nous *a.* hateful, atrocious, wicked

heir *n.* one who inherits; **heir´ess** *n. fem.*; **heir´loom** *n.* thing handed down for a long time within a family

hel´i-cop´ter *n.* form of aircraft that rises vertically by use of one or more horizontal propellers

hel´i-port *n.* landing area for helicopters

he´li-um *n.* inert, light, gaseous element

hell *n.* place or state of punishment after death; any extraordinarily unpleasant situation

hel´met *n.* head armor

help *vi.* & *vt.* assist; remedy; prevent; *n.* assistance; relief; one who assists

hem *n.* border of a garment doubled and sewn

hem´i-sphere´ *n.* half-sphere; half of the globe

hem´or-rhage *n.* flowing of blood from ruptured blood vessel

hep´ta-gon *n.* plane figure with seven sides and seven angles

her´ald *n.* proclaimer; forerunner;

vt. proclaim

her´ald-ry *n.* recording of genealogies and coats of arms; **he-ral´dic** *a.*

herb *n.* soft pulpy plant, esp. one used as seasoning or as a drug; **her-ba´ceous** *a.*

herb´age *n.* green food; herbs collectively

her-biv´o-rous *a.* plant eating

herd *n.* number of beasts together, flock, group; *vi.* & *vt.* bunch together like cattle

he-red´i-tar´y *a.* descending by inheritance; transmitted from parent to child; **he-red´i-ty** *n.*

her´e-sy *n.* opinion opposed to established faith or ideas; **her´e-tic** *n.* upholder of a heresy; **he-ret´i-cal** *a.*

her´it-age *n.* that which is inherited, legacy; physical, mental, social, or spiritual status into which one is born

her-met´ic *a.* airtight

her´mit *n.* one who lives in solitude

he´ro *n.* **(he´roes)** man of distinguished bravery; principal figure in a story; **he-ro´ic** *a.*; **her´o-ine** *n. fem.*

hes´i-tate´ *vi.* pause, stop; be in doubt; stammer; **hes´i-tan-cy** *n.*; **hes´i-tant** *a.*; **hes´i-ta´tion** *n.*

het´er-o-dox´ *a.* not orthodox, heretical

het´er-o-ge´ne-ous *a.* mixed, diverse, of different kinds

hew *vt.* chop

hex´a-gon *n.* plane figure with six angles and six sides; **hex´ag´o-nal** *a.*

hi´ber-nate´ *vi.* pass the winter in sleep or torpor; **hi´ber-na´tion** *n.*

hic´cup, hic´cough *n.* involuntary sound made by sudden closing of the glottis

hid *p.p.* put out of sight; not known

hide *vi.* & *vt.* **(hid; hid´den)** conceal or lie concealed

hide, *n.* skin of an animal; *vt.* flog

hid´e-ous *a.* frightful; shocking, revolting; hateful

hi´er-arch´y *n.* any group or any thing divided into ranks

hi´er-o-glyph´ic *n.* picture character in writing of Egyptians, etc.; *a.*

hi´fi´, high´ fi-del´i-ty *a.* pertaining to methods of reproducing sound with great faithfulness to the original; *n.*

high´-rise´ *n.* multistory apartment building

high´way´ *n.* main traffic artery

hi´jack´ *vt.* to rob; to steal goods in shipment

hi-lar´i-ous *a.* gay, merry, funny; **hi-lar´i-ty** *n.*

hilt *n.* handle, esp. of a sword

hin´der *vi.* & *vt.* stop, impede, obstruct; **hin´drance** *n.* obstacle

hinge *n.* movable joint; *vi.* hang or turn as on a hinge; depend upon

hint *n.* allusion; slight mention; suggestion; *vi.* & *vt.* intimate

hip *n.* haunch; thigh joint

hip´pie, hip´py *n.* person who rejects the values of conventional society and professes an ethic of love, peace, and personal freedom

hip´po-pot´a-mus *n.* African quadruped of aquatic habits

hire *n.* wages; *vt.* engage or let for compensation; **hire´ling** *n.* mercenary

hir´sute´ *a.* hairy

hiss *vi.* make a fricative or rubbing sound; *vt.* condemn or show disapproval by hissing; *n.* fricative sound; an expression of contempt

his´to-ry *n.* systematic account of

events; **his´to´ri-an,** *n.*; **his´tor´ic-al** *a.*

hit *vi.* & *vt.* strike; find, win; *n.* lucky stroke; **make a hit**, find favor, be successful

hitch *vi.* hook, unite, yoke; jerk; *n.* sudden halt; obstacle, hindrance; military tour of duty

hive *n.* swarm of bees; habitation of bees; *vt.* collect or store in a hive

hives *n.* type of skin disease

hoard *n.* hidden treasure; *vt.* amass in secret

hoarse *a.* having a thick, harsh voice

hoar´y *a.* white with age

hoax *n.* deceptive trick

hob´ble *vi.* walk with a limp; *n.*

hob´by *n.* favorite pursuit, theme, or avocation; **hob´by-horse´** *n.* stick used as a toy horse

hock´ey *n.* type of ball game played with a bent stick

hod *n.* trough for carrying bricks or mortar; coal scuttle

hodge´ podge´ *n.* mixture

hoe *n.* instrument for digging up weeds, loosening earth, etc.; *vt.*

hog *n.* swine, pig; greedy person; **hog´gish** *a.*

hoist *vt.* raise with tackle; *n.* act of lifting; apparatus for lifting

ho´kum *n.* nonsense; trickery, chicanery

hold *vt.* **(held)** keep; contain; accept; celebrate; esteem; *vi.* remain fixed, adhere; n. power of seizing

hole *n.* pit; hollow place

hol´i-day´ *n.* festival day; day of rest

ho´li-ness *n.* state of being holy or sacred

hol´low *a.* containing an empty space; unsound, empty; pretentious; *n.* cavity; *vt.* make hollow, scoop out

hol´o-caust´ *n.* loss of many lives, esp. by fire; wholesale destruction

hol´ster *n.* leather case for a pistol

ho´ly *a.* sacred, hallowed, set apart to a sacred use

hom´age *n.* profession of fealty or loyalty; worship

home *n.* one´s house or native land; *a.* domestic; close at hand; *adv.* to the point; **home´ly** *a.* plain; **home´stead´** *n.* property occupied as a home

hom´i-cide´ *n.* manslaughter; person who kills another; **hom´i-cid´-al** *a.*

hom´i-ly *n.* sermon

hom´i-ny *n.* corn which has been hulled with lye

ho´mo-ge´ne-ous *a.* of the same kind, order, or nature

ho-mog´e-nize´ *vt.* make homogeneous; **homogenized milk** *n.* milk in which the fat globules are broken up and evenly distributed

hom´o-nym´ *n.* word pronounced like another word, but differing in spelling, origin, etc.

ho´mo-sex´u-al *n.* one who is sexually oriented toward his own sex

hon´est *a.* free from fraud; chaste

hon´ey *n.* syrup produced by hees from nectar; sweetheart; *vt.* sweeten

hon´or *n.* esteem; exalted rank; distinction; *vt.* hold in high esteem; treat in a complimentary way; accept and pay when due

hood *n.* covering for the head; hoodlum; *vt.* cover with a hood

hood´lum *n.* rowdy, thug

hoof *n.* horny substance on the feet of animals

hook *n.* piece of metal bent into a curve; fishhook; sickle; *vt.* catch with a hook

hoop *n.* band holding together the staves of casks, etc.; *vt.* bind with hoops

hoot´e-nan´y *n.* program of folk songs

hop *vi.* leap, jump, esp. on one foot; *n.* short jump

hope *vi.* expect, cherish an expectation of good; *n.* expectation

horde *n.* great crowd, swarm

ho-ri´zon *n.* circle where the earth and sky appear to meet; extent of view

hor´i-zon´tal *a.* level, parallel to the horizon

hor´mone´ *n.* internal secretion (usually from a ductless gland) which is carried through the blood and influences the activity of some organ

horn *n.* organ projecting from the heads of animals; tough material of which horns consist; wind instrument like trumpet, French horn etc.

hor´net *n.* large species of wasp

hor´ri-ble *a.* terrible, dreadful

hor´rid *a.* shocking; **hor´ri-fy´** *vt.* strike with terror

hor´ror *n.* great fear or terror

horse *n.* familiar domestic quadruped; frame for sawing wood, etc.; cavalry; *vt.* mount on a horse; provide with a horse; **horse´pow-er** *n.* unit of power equal to 550 foot-pounds per second

hor´ti-cul´ture *n.* art of cultivating gardens and plants; **hor´ti-cul´tur-ist** *n.*

hose *n.* covering for the feet or legs; **hos´es** flexible pipe for conveying fluids

hos´pi-ta-ble *a.* kind to visitors; receptive; **hos´pi-tal´i-ty** *n.*

hos´pi-tal *n.* building where the sick and wounded are cared for

host *n.* one who entertains a guest; innkeeper; army; multitude; creature to which a parasite attaches itself

hos´tage *n.* one held as a pledge for the fulfillment of promises or payment of money

hos´tile *a.* showing enmity, unfriendly; pertaining to an enemy; **hos´til´i-ty** *n.*

hot´dog´ *n.* wiener

hot´-rod´ *n.* old car reworked to attain high speeds

ho-tel´ *n.* public house offering lodging and meals

hot´line´ *n.* communications line always open for possible emergencies

hound *n.* dog used in hunting; cur; *vt.* urge, dun

hour *n.* sixty minutes; occasion

house *n.* dwelling-place; building; family; mercantile establishment; one of the two branches of a legislature; *vt.* shelter

hov´er *vi.* remain aloft, flapping the wings; wait in suspense; hang around

howl *n.* cry of a dog; wail; *vi.* & *vt.* wail like a dog

hoyden *n.* rude, noisy woman or girl

hub *n.* nave of a wheel; **hub´cap´** *n.* metal covering on hub of car wheel

hub´bub´ *n.* uproar, bustle

huck´ster *n.* peddler; derogatory name for one who works in advertising

hud´dle *vi.* & *vt.* crowd together; *n.* small group or crowd; informal conference

hue *n.* color, tint

hug *vt.* embrace fondly; keep close to; hold fast; *n.* close embrace

huge *a.* very large, tremendous

hulk *n.* body of a ship; anything

large or unwieldy

hull *n.* outer covering, husk; body of a ship; *vt.* husk, as. peas

hum *vi.* & *vt.* make a buzzing sound like bees; sing in a low voice; *n.* noise of bees

hu´man *a.* pertaining to mankind; like man; *n.*

hu´mane´ *a.* merciful, kind

hu´man´i-ty *n.* mankind; nature of man; kindliness; **hu-man´i-tar´i-an** *n.* benevolent person

hum´ble *a.* lowly, meek; *vt.* humiliate

hum´bug´ *n.* hoax, fraud; *vt.* deceive, hoax

hu´mid *a.* moist, damp; **hu´mid´i-ty** *n.* moisture; **hu´mid´i-fi-er** *n.* contrivance for keeping the air moist

hu-mil´i-ate´ *vt.* humble, shame; *n.*; **hu-mil-i-a´tion, hu´mil´i-ty** *n.*

hum´ming-bird´ *n.* small very fast bird of brilliant plumage

hu´mor *n.* mirth; state of mind; *vt.* indulge someone´s humor

hun´ger *n.* desire, esp. for food; *vi.* crave food; long for something; **hun´gry** *a.*; **hun´gri-ly** *adv.*

hunt *vi.* & *vt.* chase, search; *n.* chase after wild animals; search

hurl *vt.* throw with violence; utter vehemently

hur´ri-cane´ *n.* furious storm with high winds

hur´ry *vi.* & *vt.* hasten; *n.* haste; bustle; urgency

hurt *vt.* damage; wound; *n.* wound, injury

hus´band *a.* married man; *vt.* manage with economy

husk *n.* thin covering of certain fruits and vegetables; *vt.* remove the husks from

husk´y *a.* hoarse, rough; strong

hus´tle *vi.* & *vt.* bustle, move energetically; jostle

hy´a-cinth *n.* a precious red stone; bulbous plant and its flower

hy´brid *n.* animal or plant produced from two different species; *a.* mongrel

hy´drant *n.* appliance for drawing water, faucet

hy´drau´lic *a.* relating to hydraulics; **hy´drau´lics** *n.* science of water in motion

hy´dro-e-lec´tric *a.* pertaining to electricity produced by water power

hy´dro-foil *n.* strut supporting the hull of a boat over water; boat so equipped

hy´dro-gen *n.* a gaseous element, the lightest substance known

hy´dro-gen bomb´ *n.* atomic bomb whose force is derived from the fusion of hydrogen atoms into helium

hy´dro-pho´bi-a *n.* rabies

hy-e´na *n.* a bristly-maned, flesh-eating quadruped

hy´giene´ *n.* science of health and sanitation; **hy´gi-en´ic** *a.*

hymn *n.* song of praise or worship; **hym´nal** *n.* book of hymns

hy´per´bo-le *n.* figure of speech involving exaggeration

hy´per-son´ic *a.* moving at many times the speed of sound

hy´per-ten´sion *n.* high blood pressure

hy´phen *n.* mark of punctuation (-) separating syllables, etc.

hyp´no-tism *n.* sleep-like condition artificially induced by suggestion; **hyp´no-tize´** *vt.*

hy-poc´ri-sy *n.* pretended virtue or piety; any pretense; **hyp´o-crite´** *n.*

hy´po-der´mic *a.* under the skin; *n.* hypodermic syringe

hy´po-ten´sion *n.* low blood pressure

hy-pot´e-nuse´ *n.* the side of a right-angled triangle opposite the right angle

hy´poth´e-sis *n.* **(hy´poth´e-ses)** temporary theory, supposition; **hy´po-thet´ic** *adj.*

hys-ter´ics, hys-te´ri-a *n.* nervous disorder; wild emotionalism; **hys-ter´ic, hys-ter´ic-al** *a.* relating to hysteria; frantic

I

ICBM *n.* intercontinental ballistics missile, a self-navigating missile with 5,000 mile range

ice *n.* water congealed by freezing; frozen dessert; *vt.* cool with ice; cover with a frosting; **ice´berg´** *n.* mass of floating ice; **i´cy** *a.*

i´ci-cle *n.* hanging cone of ice

ic´ing *n.* covering of concreted sugar used on cake

i´con *n.* image, picture

i´con´o-clast´ *n.* breaker of images; one who attacks sham or institutions which he considers false gods

id *n.* part of the subconscious mind concerned with primitive feelings

i-de´a *n.* mental image, thought

i-de´al *a.* best conceivable; existing in idea; *n.* highest concept of anything; **i-de´al-ism** *n.* love of the best and highest; **i-de´al-ist** *n.*; **i-de´al-ize´** *vt.* raise to the highest conception

i-den´ti-cal *a.* same, alike in all details

i-den´ti-fy *vt.* prove to be the same; ascertain the identity of

i-den´ti-ty *n.* sameness; characteristic traits

id´e-ol´o-gy *n.* ideas, philosophy, etc., of any group; any set of beliefs or doctrines

id´i-o-cy *n.* anything extremely foolish; extreme mental deficiency

id´i-om *n.* expression or usage peculiar to a language; **id´i-o-mat´ic** *a.*

id´i-ot *n.* one extremely deficient in normal intellect; **id´i-ot´ic** *a.*

i´dle *a.* unemployed; trifling; *vt.* waste in idleness; **i´dly** *adv.*

i´dol *n.* image of a god; anything the object of too much love or worship; **i´dol´a-ter** *n.*; **i´dol´a-trous** *a.*; **i´dol´a-try** *n.* worship of idols; excessive love

i´dol-ize´ *vt.* make an idol of; worship excessively

i´dyl, i´dyll *n.* narrative poem usually about pastoral subjects

ig´ne-ous *a.* like, pertaining to, or containing fire; produced by the action of fire

ig´nite´ *vt.* set on fire; *vi.* take fire

ig-ni´tion *n.* act of igniting or state of being ignited; apparatus for igniting the explosive mixture of gases in the cylinders of an internal-combustion engine

ig-no´ble *a.* mean, dishonorable; low of birth

ig´no-min-y *n.* shame, disgrace; **ig´-no-min´i-ous** *a.*

ig´no-ra´mus *n.* ignorant person

ig´no-rant *a.* without knowledge; unacquainted with; **ig´no-rance** *n.*

ig-nore´ *vt.* disregard; reject

ill *a.* sick; unfavorable; *n.* evil; **ill-bred´** *a.* uncivil

il-le´gal *a.* contrary to law; **il´le-gal´i-ty** *n.*

il-leg´i-ble *a.* impossible to read; **il-leg´i-bil´i-ty** *n.*

il-lic´it *a.* unlawful

il-lit´er-a-cy *n.* inability to read and write; general lack of learning, ignorance

il-lit´er-ate *a.* unable to read or write; ignorant; *n.*
ill´ness *n.* sickness
il-log´i-cal *a.* contrary to logic or reason; unreasonable
il-lum´i-nate´, il-lu´mine *vi.* & *vt.* light up; make clear, illustrate; **il-lu´mi-na´tion** *n.*
il-lu´sion *n.* deceptive impression; **il-lu´sive** *a.*; **il-lu´so-ry** *a.* deceiving, unreal
il´lus-trate´ *vt.* explain; adorn with pictures; **il´lus-tra´tion** *n.* explanation, picture; **il-lus´tra-tive** *a.*
ii-lus´tri-ous *a.* distinguished, famous
im´age *n.* likeness; idol; idea
im´age-ry *n.* imaginative or figurative language
im-ag´i-na´tion *n.* faculty of imagining; that which is imagined
im-ag´ine *vi.* & *vt.* conceive in the mind, invent; **im-ag´i-na-ble** *a.*; **im-ag´i-nary** *a.*
im´be-cile *a.* extremely foolish; *n.* fool, person with a very low intellect; **im´be-cil´i-ty** *n.*
im-bue´ *vt.* tinge deeply, cause to absorb
im´i-tate´ *vt.* copy; **im´i-ta´tion** *n.* act of imitating; copy, likeness
im-mac´u-late *a.* pure, unsoiled
im´ma-nent *a.* inherent
im´ma-te´ri-al *a.* unimportant, insignificant; not consisting of matter
im´ma-ture´ *a.* lacking maturity, childish; not ripe
im-me´diate *a.* instant, with nothing intervening
im-mense´ *a.* unlimited, extremely large
im-merse´ *vt.* plunge into, as water; involve deeply; baptize by dipping; **im-mer´sion** *n.*
im´mi-grant *n.* one who comes into another country
im´mi-grate´ *vi.* move into another country; **im´mi-gra´tion** *n.*
im´mi-nent *a.* impending, near at hand
im´mo-bil´i-ty *n.* firm, fixed, motionless state
im-mor´al *a.* lacking in virtue or morality; **im-mo´-ral´i-ty** *n.*
im-mor´tal *a.* exempt from death; *n.*; **im´mor-tal´i-ty** *n.*
im-mune´ *a.* exempt; **im-mu´ni-ty** *n.*
im´mu-nol´o-gy *n.* science dealing with resistance to disease
im-mu´ta-ble *a.* unchangeable
im-pact´ *n.* force of collision
im-pair´ *vt.* diminish in quantity, quality, value, or strength
im-pal´pa-ble *a.* not perceivable by touch
im-part´ *vt.* give; make known, as information
im-par´tial *a.* not favoring either side; **im-par´ti-al´i-ty** *n.* disinterestedness
im-pas´sive *a.* unmoved, without emotion
im-pa´tient *a.* unable to wait; **im-pa´tience** *n.*
im-peach´ *vt.* formally charge with misconduct in office
im-pede´ *vt.* hinder, obstruct; **im-ped´i-ment** *n.*
im-pel´ *vt.* drive forward, force
im-pend´ *vi.* threaten; be about to happen
im-per´a-tive *a.* obligatory, mandatory, necessary
im-pe´ri-al *a.* pertaining to an emperor or empire; **im-pe´ri-al-ism** *n.* spirit of empire, esp. as a doctrine of expansion
im-pe´ri-ous *a.* haughty, arrogant
im-per´son-ate´ *vt.* portray or pre-

tend to be another; **im-per´son-a´-tion** *n.*

im-per´ti-nent *a.* impudent

im-per´vi-ous *a.* impassable, impermeable

im-pet´u-ous *a.* hasty, impulsive

im´pe-tus *n.* force of motion, momentum

im-pinge´ *vi.* touch or strike upon; infringe upon

im-pla´ca-ble *a.* not to be appeased

im-plant´ *vt.* plant, instill

im´ple-ment *n.* tool, instrument, appliance, utensil

im´pli-cate´ *vt.* involve; **im´pli-ca´-tion** *n.*

im-plic´it *a.* tacitly understood, implied

im-plore´ *vt.* beseech

im-ply´ *vt.* include; signify

im-port´ *vt.* bring from abroad; signify

im´port´ *n.* anything brought from abroad; meaning, signification; **im´por-ta´tion** *n.*

im-por´tant *a.* of great consequence; **im-por´tance** *n.*

im´por-tune´ *vt.* urge with annoying persistency; **im-por´tu-nate** *a.*

im-pose´ *vt.* place or lay on; take advantage of someone; palm off

im´po-si´tion *n.* deception; abuse of kindness; burden

im-pos´si-ble *a.* not capable of existing or of being done; **im-pos´si-bil´i-ty** *n.*

im-pos´tor *n.* one who practices fraud or deception

im´po-tent *a.* powerless; **im´po-tence** *n.*

im-prac´ti-cal *a.* not practical

im´pre-cate´ *vi.* & *vt.* pray, esp. for evil; curse; **im´pre-ca´tion** *n.*

im-preg´nate´ *vt.* imbue, infuse, cause to absorb; get with child

im-press´ *vt.* mark, stamp; fix deeply in the mind; force into public service; **im-pres´sive** *a.*

im-pres´sion *n.* mark; effect; edition

im-promp´tu *a.* & *adv.* unrehearsed, without preparation

im-prop´er *a.* not suitable; indecent; incorrect; **im´pro-pri´e-ty** *n.*

im-prove´ *vi.* & *vt.* make or grow better

im´pro-vise´, im´pro-vise´ *vt.* perform, say, or do without preparation; **im-prov´i-sa´tion** *n.*

im´pu-dent *a.* bold; insolent; lacking modesty

im-pugn´ *vt.* deny, attack as false

im´pulse´ *n.* thrust, sudden short force; sudden stimulus to act

im-pul´sive *a.* acting by impulse, impetuous

im-pun´i-ty *n.* freedom from punishment or loss

impute´ *vt.* charge, ascribe; **im´pu-ta´tion** *n.* insinuation

in´a-bil´i-ty *n.* lack of sufficient power or means

in-ac´cu-ra-cy *n.* mistake, lack of exactness; **in-ac´cu-rate** *a.* not correct or exact

in-ac´tion *n.* idleness; **in-ac´tive** *a.* idle; lazy; inefficient; **in´ac-tiv´i-ty** *n.*

in-ad´e-quate *a.* insufficient; **in-ad´e-qua-cy** *n.*

in´ad-vert´ent *a.* unintentional

in-al´ien-a-ble *a.* not capable of being transferred

in-ane´ *a.* senseless, empty; **in-an´i-ty** *n.*

in-an´i-mate *a.* without life or spirit, dull

in-au´gu-rate´ *vt.* induct into office; cause to begin; **in-au´gu-ra´tion** *n.*

in´can-des´cent *a.* shining with heat (as an incandescent light);

in´can-des´cence *n.*
in´can-ta´tion *n.* magical charm sung or spoken
in-ca´pa-ble *a.* unable
in´ca-pac´i-tate´ *vt.* disable; disqualify; **in´ca-pac´i-ty** *n.* disability
in-car´cer-ate´ *vt.* imprison; **in-car´-cer-a´tion** *n.*
in-car´nate *a.* in bodily form, in the flesh; *vt.* embody in flesh; **in´car-na´tion** *n.*
in-cen´di-ar´y *a.* tending to excite sedition; tending to burn or set aflame; *n.* one who maliciously sets fire to a building; fire bomb; one who stirs up or excites sedition
in´cense´ *n.* spices burned in religious rites
in-cense´ *vt.* inflame with anger
in-cen´tive *n.* motive, stimulation, spur
in-cep´tion *n.* beginning; **in-cep´tive** *a.*
in-ces´sant *a.* continual, unceasing
in´ci-dence *n.* range, occurrence, scope of influence
in´ci-dent *n.* occurrence, minor happening
in-cin´er-ate´ *vt.* burn to ashes; **in-cin´er-a´tor** *n.*
in-cip´i-ent *a.* beginning to be; **in-cip´i-ence** *n.*
in-cise´ *vt.* cut into, engrave
in-ci´sion *n.* cut, gash
in-ci´sive *a.* cutting trenchant, sarcastic in language
in-ci´sor *n.* front or cutting tooth
in-cite´ *vt.* rouse to action, stir up
in-clement *a.* stormy, severe
in-cline´ *vi.* lean; be disposed; deviate; *vt.* tilt, cause to lean; **in´cli-na´tion** *n.*
in´clude´ *vt.* shut in, contain; **in-clu´sion** *n.*; **in-clu´sive** *a.* including
in-cog´ni´to *a.* & *adv.* under an assumed name
in´co-her´ent *a.* unconnected, disorganized; **in´co-her´ence** *n.*
in´come´ *n.* money or revenue coming in regularly
in-com´pa-ra-ble *a.* matchless, unequalled
in´com-pat´i-ble *a.* irreconcilable, mutually repelling; incongruous; **in´com-pat´i-bil´i-ty** *n.*
in-com´pe-tent *a.* lacking adequate qualifications or ability; **in-com´pe-tence** *n.*
in´com-plete´ *a.* imperfect
in´com-pre-hen´si-ble *a.* not understandable
in´con-ceiv´a-ble *a.* unthinkable, unbelievable
in-con´gru-ous *a.* inconsistent, unsuited; **in´con-gru´i-ty** *n.* inconsistency
in´con-sid´er-ate *a.* thoughtless, lacking consideration
in´con-sis´tent *a.* not consistent, illogical; **in´con-sist´en-cy** *n.*
in´con-tro-vert´i-ble *a.* unable to be disproved or refuted; **in-con´tro-vert´i-bil´i-ty** *n.*
in´con-ven´ience *n.* lack of convenience; cause of trouble or discomfort; *vt.* trouble; **in´con-ven´-ient** *a.*
in-cor´po-rate´ *vi.* & *vt.* form into a body, mass, or legal corporation; **in-cor´po-ra´tion** *n.*
in´cor-po´re-al *a.* lacking a physical body
in-cor´ri-gi-ble *a.* bad beyond reform or correction; *n.*; **in-cor´ri-gi-bil´i-ty** *n.*
in-crease´ *vi.* & *vt.* make or become greater
in´crease´ *n.* growth, addition; profit
in-cred´i-ble *a.* surpassing belief;

in-cred´i-bil´i-ty *n.*
in-cred´u-lous *a.* not disposed to believe, skeptical
in´cre-ment *n.* growth; addition, increase
in-crim´i-nate´ *vt.* charge with a crime; involve in anything disreputable; **in-crim´i-na´tion** *n.*
in´cu-bate´ *vt.* sit on eggs to hatch them; hatch; *vi.* hatch; undergo incubation; **in´cu-ba´tion** *n.*; **in´-cu-ba´tor** *n.* machine for hatching eggs; machine for keeping premature babies
in-cul´cate *vt.* impress by repeated forcible warnings; teach; **in´cul-ca´tion** *n.*
in-cul´pate *vt.* incriminate; **in´cul-pa´tion** *n.*
in-cum´bent *a.* binding; lying upon; *n.* one who holds an office or benefice
in-cur´ *vt.* become liable to
in-cur´a-ble *a.* incapable of being cured or corrected
in-cur´sion *n.* hostile inroad, invasion
in-dec´ent *a.* offensive to modesty; **in-de´cen-cy** *n.*
in´de-fat´i-ga-ble *a.* incapable of being tired
in-def´i-nite *a.* vague, uncertain, lacking precise limits or measurements
in-del´i-ble *a.* impossible to erase or wipe away; **in-del´i-bly** *adv.*
in-dem´ni-ty *n.* security from or compensation for loss or injury; reimbursement
in-dent´ *vt.* begin further from the margin than the rest of the paragraph; **in´den-ta´tion** *n.*
in´de-pend´ent *a.* not subordinate; free; self-supporting; **in´de-pend´-ence** *n.* freedom
in-depth´ *a.* detailed
in´de-ter´mi-nate *a.* not fixed, indefinite
in´dex´ *n.* **(in´dex-es, in´di-ces)** alphabetic list of subjects, authors, etc., discussed within a book; list or directory; anything that indicates; ratio, proportion; *vt.* provide with an index
in´di-cate´ *vt.* point out; **in´di-ca´-tion** *n.* symptom
in-dic´a-tive *a.* affirmative; pointing out
in´di-ca´tor *n.* anything which indicates or points out
in-dict´ *vt.* charge with a crime or misconduct; **in-dict´ment** *n.* accusation; formal statement of offense as determined by a grand jury
in-dif´fer-ent *a.* unconcerned; mediocre, unimportant; **in-dif´fer-ence** *n.*
in-dig´e-nous *a.* native; inborn
in´di-gent *a.* destitute, poor; **in´di-gence** *n.* poverty
in´di-gest´i-ble *a.* not easily absorbed or digested; **in´di-ges´tion** *n.*
in-dig´nant *a.* righteously angry, affected with anger and disdain; **in´dig-na´tion** *n.*
in-dig´ni-ty *n.* unmerited insult or injury
in´di-go´ *n.* a blue dye; deep reddish-blue color
in´dis-creet´ *a.* injudicious, imprudent, not discreet; **in´dis-cre´tion** *n.*
in´dis-pen´sa-ble *a.* absolutely necessary
in-dis-put´a-ble *a.* not to be argued, incontrovertible
in´dis-tinct´ *a.* not plain; not easily seen or heard
in´di-vid´u-al existing as one; per-

taining to one only; *n.* single person or thing

in´di-vid´u-al´i-ty *n.* separate existence; distinctive character

in-doc´tri-nate´ *vt.* instruct in a doctrine or ideology; **in-doc´tri-na´tion** *n.*

in´do-lent *a.* lazy; **in´do-lence** *n.*

in-dom´i-ta-ble *a.* invincible, unconquerable

in-du´bi-ta-ble *a.* not to be doubted or questioned

in-duce´ *vt.* prevail upon

in-duce´ment *n.* motive, anything that influences

in-duct´ *vt.* bring in; put in possession; swear into office, military service, etc.

in-duc´tion *n.* reasoning from particulars to a generalization; induction into milititry service

in-duc´tive *a.* proceeding by inductive logic; leading

in-dulge´ *vt.* allow; yield to the wishes of; *vi.* gratify an appetite in; **in-dul´gence** *n.*

in-dus´tri-al *a.* relating to manufacture

in-dus´tri-ous *a.* diligent

in´dus-try *n.* manufacture; steady application to work

in-e´bri-ate´ *vt.* make drunk, intoxicate

in-el´i-gi-ble *a.* not capable or qualified to be chosen; **in-el´i-gi-bil´i-ty** *n.*

in-ept´ *a.* unfit; foolish; **in-ept´i-tude´** *n.*

in-ert´ *a.* lacking power of action; sluggish

in-er´tia *n.* inertness; inherent property of matter by which it tends to remain at rest when resting and in motion when moving

in-ev´i-ta-ble *a.* unavoidable, irresistible

in-ex´o-ra-ble *a.* not to be moved by entreaty

in-fal´li-ble a incapable of error; **in-fal´li-bil´i-ty** *n.*

in´fa-mous *a.* notoriously wicked

in´fa-my *n.* ill repute; extreme vileness

in´fan-cy *n.* early childhood; beginning

in´fant *n.* baby; minor; *a.*

in´fan-try *n.* foot soldiers

in-fat´u-ate´ *vt.* affect with folly; **in-fat´u-a´tion** *n.*

in-fect´ *vt.* taint, esp. with disease; **in-fec´tious** *a.*

in-fer´ *vt.* deduce, conclude; **in´ference** *n.*; **in´fer-en´tial** *a.*

in-fe´ri-or *a.* lower, subordinate; less valuable; *n.* one lower in rank or station; **in-fe´ri-or´i-ty** *n.*

in-fer´nal *a.* belonging to the lower regions; hence, fiendish , devilish

in-fest´ *vt.* disturb by frequency of presence or be overwhelming numbers

in´fi-del´i-ty *n.* unfaithfulness; adultery

in´fi-nite *a.* without end, limitless; *n.* anything without end

in´fin-i-tes´i-mal *a.* infinitely small

in-fin´i-ty *n.* boundlessness; countless number

in-firm´ *a.* sickly, weak; **in-fir´mi-ty** *n.* disease; weakness, as from age

in´flam-ma´tion *n.* redness of part of the body

in-flate´ *vt.* swell with air; *vi.* puff up

in-fla´tion *n.* unhealthy expansion of currency or credit, resulting in higher prices

in-flect´ *vt.* modulate, change in pitch or tone; vary a verb, etc., by conjugation; **in-flec´tion** *n.*

in-flex´i-ble *a.* rigid, unyielding; **in-flex´i-bil´i-ty** *n.*
in-flict´ *vt.* impose punishment; **in-flic´tion** *n.*
in´flu-ence *n.* power, authority; *vt.* affect, move; **in´flu-en´tial** *a.*
in´flu-en´za *n.* contagious disease similar to severe cold
in´flux´ *n.* a flowing in
in-form´ *vt.* impart knowledge or information to; tell; *vi.* betray
in-for´mal *a.* without ceremony; **in´-for-mal´ity** *n.*
infra-red´ *a.* pertaining to heat rays from beyond the red end of the spectrum; **infra-red lamp** *n.* heat lamp
in-fringe´ *vi.* & *vt.* encroach upon, trespass; **in-fringe´ment** *n.*
in-fu´ri-ate´ *vt.* enrage
in-fuse´ *vt.* pour into; inspire with, fill with; steep without boiling; **in-fu´sion** *n.*
in-gen´ious *a.* clever, shrewd, cunning in doing anything
in´ge-nu´i-ty *n.* cleverness; power of ready invention
in-gen´u-ous *a.* frank; naively candid
in´grate´ *n.* one who is ungrateful; *a.*
in-gra´ti-ate´ *vt.* worm one´s way into favor
in-gre´di-ent *n.* component part of a mixture
in-hab´it *vt.* occupy, dwell in
in-hale´ *vt.* draw air, etc., into the lungs
in-her´ent *a.* natural, inborn
in-her´it *vt.* acquire or receive anything, as from someone who has died
in-hib´it *vt.* hinder, check, restrain; **in´hi-bi´tion** *n.*
in-im´i-ta-ble *a.* not capable of imitation
in-iq´ui-ty *n.* injustice, crime, sin; **in-iq´ui-tous** *a.*
in-i´tial *a.* beginning, starting; *n.* letter beginning a name
in-i´ti-ate´ *vt.* make a beginning; admit into some group; introduce to some subject or mystery; **in-i´-ti-a´tion** *n.*
in-i´ti-a-tive *n.* first step; power to originate; industry, energy, motivation to work
in-junc´tion *n.* act of enjoining; writ of prohibition
in´jure *vt.* do injury to
in-jur´i-ous *a.* harmful
in´ju-ry *n.* damage, hurt
in´mate´ *n.* occupant, as of an asylum, prison, etc.
in-nate´ *a.* inborn, native
in´ning *n.* turn for one´s side in games, etc.
in´no-cent *a.* pure; harmless; *n.* one free from sin; **in´no-cence** *n.*
in´no-vate´ *vi.* & *vt.* make changes; add something new; **in´no-va´tion** *n.*
in´nu-en´do *n.* **(in´nu-en´does)** hint, insinuation
in-nu´mer-a-ble *a.* countless, without number
in-oc´u-late´ *vt.* guard against a disease by inserting serum, etc., under the skin; **in-oc´u-la´tion** *n.*
in-or´di-nate *a.* immoderate, beyond the usual bonds
in´put´ *n.* energy fed into any machine, device, etc.
in´quest´ *n.* judicial inquiry, as into cause of death
in-quire´ *vi.* & *vt.* ask, investigate
in´quir-y *n.* search; question
in´qui-si´tion *n.* ecclesiastical body for punishing heretics
in-quis´i-tive *a.* curious

in´road´ *n.* invasion
in-sane´ *a.* unsound of mind; **in-san´i-ty** *n.*
in-sa´ti-a-ble *a.* incapable of being satisfied
in-scribe´ *vt.* write, dedicate, address; engrave
in-scrip´tion *n.* dedication; words which are engraved or written in dedication
in´sect´ *n.* small animal with six legs
in-sec´ti-cide´ *n.* chemical preparation for destroying insects
in-sert´ *vt.* introduce, put in or among; **in-ser´tion** *n.*
in-sid´i-ous *a.* treacherous, deceitfully harmful
in-sig´ni-a *n. pl.* badges of office, rank, or honor
in´sig-nif´i-cant *a.* trivial, unimportant
in´sin-cere´ *a.* deceitful; **in´sin-cer´i-ty** *n.*
in-sin´u-ate´ *vt.* hint; introduce artfully; work into favor
in-sin´u-a´tion *n.* sly hint, intimation
in-sip´id *a.* tasteless, dull, flat
in-sist´ *vi.* persist; demand
in´so-lent *a.* haughtily insulting; **in´so-lence** *n.*
in-sol´u-ble *a.* not to be dissolved; not to be solved; **in-sol´u-bil´i-ty** *n.*
in-sol´vent *a.* unable to pay one´s debts; *n.*
in-som´ni-a *n.* sleeplessness
in-spect´ *vt.* examine; **in-spec´tion** *n.*
in-spire´ *vt.* arouse enthusiasm, stimulate; **in´spi-ra´tion** *n.*
in-stall´ *vt.* establish; put in place; ready for operation; swear into office; **in´stal-la´tion** *n.*
in´stance *n.* example, illustration; request
in´stant *a.* momentary, quick; pressing; current; *n.* moment; **in´stan-ta´ne-ous** *a.*
in´sti-gate´ *vt.* spur, incite, urge; **in´sti-ga´tion** *n.*
in-still´ *vt.* infuse into the mind, implant, indoctrinate
in´stinct´ *n.* natural impulse; **in´stinc´tive** *a.*
in´sti-tute´ *n.* anything formally established, esp. an organization; *vt.* establish
in´sti-tu´tion *n.* act of establishing; established custom, order, etc.; public establishment
in-struct´ *vt.* inform, teach; order, direct; **in-struc´tion** *n.*; **in-struc´tor** *n.*
in´stru-ment *n.* utensil, tool; musical device; written contract; **in´stru-men´tal** *a.*; **in´stru-men-tal´i-ty** *n.* agency
in´sub-or´di-nate *a.* disobedient, mutinous; **in´sub-or´di-na´tion** *n.*
in-suf´fer-a-ble *a.* unbearable
in´su-lar *a.* pertaining to an island; narrow, shut off in scope or point of view
in´su-late´ *vt.* place in a detached situation; separate electric wires by a nonconductor; **in´su-la´tion** *n.*
in´su-la´tor *n.* non-conductor of electricity
in´su-lin *n.* hormone secreted by the pancreas and used to treat diabetes
in-sult´ *vt.* treat with open contempt, give an affront to
in´sult´ *n.* contemptuous treatment or speech
in-su´per-a-ble *a.* insurmountable, not to be overcome
in-sup-port´a-ble *a.* unbearable, insufferable

in-sure´ *vt.* make sure; secure against loss; **in-sur´ance** *n.*
in-sur´gent *a.* rebellious; *n.* rebel
in´sur-rec´tion *n.* uprising, rebellion
in-tact´ *a.* entire, whole, uninjured
in´te-ger *n.* whole number
in´te-gral *a.* whole, entire, not fractional; necessary, essential
in´te-grate´ *vt.* make entire or whole; end racial segregation; **in´te-gra´tion** *n.*
in-teg´ri-ty *n.* moral purity, honesty; unimpaired state
in´tel-lect *n.* understanding, intelligence
in´tel-lec´tu-al *a.* pertaining to the intellect; *n.* intelligent person; one who stresses intellectual things,´ a ´highbrow´
in-tel´li-gence *n.* intellect, mental ability; information communicated, as of an enemy; **in-tel´li-gent** *a.*
in-tel´li-gi-ble *a.* understandable, comprehensible
in-tem´per-ance *n.* lack of restraint; excessive indulgence in alcohol or any physical appetite
in-tend´ *vt.* design, plan
in-tense´ *a.* strained; to a great degree or extent
in-ten´si-fy *vi.* & *vt.* make or grow intense
in-ten´si-ty *n.* strain; degree or extent
in-tent´ *a.* having the mind fixed upon something, absorbed; *n.* design, plan, thing intended
in-ten´tion *n.* direction of mind, purpose
in-ter´ *vt.* bury
inter-cede´ *vi.* plead with or for; act as peacemaker
in´ter-cept´ *vt.* stop and seize; obstruct
in´ter-ces´sion *n.* act of interceding
in´ter-course´ *n.* commerce; connection through dealings; the sex act
in´ter-dict´ *n.* prohibition of the sacraments by the pope; *vt.* prohibit, debar; cut off from the sacraments
in´ter-est *n.* advantage; share; premium paid for the use of money; attention, enthusiasm; *vt.* engage the attention or enthusiasm of
in´ter-fere´ *vi.* meddle with; **in´ter-fer´ence** *n.*
in-te´ri-or *n.* inside, inner part; *a.* being within, inside; inland
in´ter-ject´ *vt.* throw out, throw between, insert
in´ter-jec´tion *n.* word suppossed to express strong feeling, like *oh!*, *gee!*, *gosh!*, etc.
in´ter-lope´ *vi.* meddle, intrude; **in´ter-lop´er** *n.*
in´ter-lude´ *n.* lull, intervening time; music between the acts of a play
in´ter-me´di-ar´y, in´ter-me´di-ate *a.* in the middle, intervening
in-ter´ment *n.* burial
in-ter´mi-na-ble *a.* endless
in´ter-mis´sion *n.* pause; interval between acts of a play, opera, etc.
in´ter-mit´tent *a.* ceasing at intervals
in-tern´ *vt.* confine as an enemy alien, etc.
in´tern´ *n.* physician residing in a hospital
in-ter´nal *a.* interior, inner; domestic
in´ter-na´tion-al *a.* pertaining to or affecting two or more nations
in´ter-plan´e-tar´y *a.* moving between planets (as, an *interplanetary rocket*)

in-ter´po-late´ *vt.* make insertions; introduce new material into a text, conversation, etc.
in´ter-pose´ *vi.* & *vt.* place or come between
in-ter´pret *vt.* translate; explain; **in-ter´pre-ta´tion** *n.*; **in-ter´pre-ter** *n.*
in-ter´ro-gate´ *vi.* & *vt.* question; **in-ter´ro-ga´tion** *n.*
in´ter-rupt´ *vt.* break in; stop; **in-ter-rup´tion** *n.*
in´ter-sect´ *vi.* & *vt.* cut across, divide by cutting across
in´ter-sec´tion *n.* crossing
in´ter-sperse´ *vt.* scatter or strew in between
in´ter-state´ *a.* pertaining to two or more states
in´ter-stel´lar *a.* among the stars
in´ter-val *n.* time between two occurrences; difference in pitch
in´ter-vene´ *vi.* interpose, come between; **in´ter-ven´tion** *n.*
in´ter-view´ *n.* meeting, consultation; *vt.* interrogate
in-tes´tate *a.* without having made a valid will
in-tes´tines *n. pl.* guts, bowels; **in-tes´ti-nal** *a.*
in´ti-mate *a.* familiar; *n.* familiar friend; **in´ti-ma-cy** *n.*
in´ti-mate´ *vt.* hint, allude to; **in´ti-ma´tion** *n.*
in-tim´i-date´ *vt.* frighten, as by threats; **in-tim´i-da´tion** *n.*
in-tone´ *vi.* & *vt.* chant; **in-to-na´tion** *n.*
in-tox´i-cate´ *vt.* make drunk; **in-tox´i-ca´tion** *n.*
in-tran´si-tive *a.* pertaining to verbs which do not take a direct object
in´tra-state´ *a.* within a state
in-trep´id *a.* fearless
in´tri-cate *a.* involved, complex; **in´tri-ca-cy** *n.*
in-trigue´ *n.* involved plot; *vi.* form a plot, scheme
in-trin´sic *a.* inherent, essential
in´tro-duce´ *vt.* lead or bring in; make formally known; **in´tro-duc´tion** *n.*; **in´tro-duc´tory** *a.*
in´tro-vert´ *n.* one more interested in himself than in the world around him
in-trude´ *vi.* & *vt.* enter uninvited or unwelcome; **in-tru´sion** *n.*; **in-tru´sive** *a.*
in´tu-i´tion *n.* knowledge based on guess or instinct rather than reason, a ´hunch´; **in-tu´i-tive** *a.*
in´un-date´ *vt.* overflow; **in´un-da´tion** *n.*
in-ure´ *vt.* accustom to anything unpleasant
in-vade´ *vt.* enter as an enemy; **in-va´der** *n.*
in´va-lid *n.* sick or disabled person; *a.* sick, weak
in-va´lid *a.* null, without value or effect
in-val´i-date´ *vt.* render invalid
in-val´u-a-ble *a.* priceless, beyond price
in-va´sion *n.* act of invading
in-vec´tive *n.* railing, abusive accusation or denunciation; *a.* railing, abusive
in-veigh´ *vi.* rail against
in-vei´gle *vt.* entice
in-vent´ *vt.* create, build for the first time; **in-ven´tion** *n.*
in´ven-to´ry *n.* list of goods, belongings, etc.
in-verse´, in´verse´ *a.* in reverse or contrary order
in-ver´sion *n.* change of position
in-vert´ *vt.* reverse, change, turn upside down
in-ver´te-brate *a.* lacking a verte-

bral column; *n.* animal lacking a spine

in-vest´ *vt.* put money into a likely business; confer, endow; dress; lay siege to

in-ves´ti-gate´ *vi.* & *vt.* inquire into; **in-ves´ti-ga´tion** *n.*

in vet´er-ate *a.* firmly addicted or established

in-vid´i-ous *a.* likely to provoke ill will or envy, as by discriminating comparisons

in-vig´or-ate´ *vt.* give vigor or energy to

in-vin´ci-ble *a.* unconquerable; insuperable

in-vite´ *vt.* ask, summon; attract; **in´vi-ta´tion** *n.*

in´vo-ca´tion *n.* introductory prayer or appeal

in´voice´ *n.* notice of the dispatch of goods together with their quantity and price

in-voke´ *vt.* implore, summon

in-vol´un-tar´y *a.* done unwillingly or without the power of the will

in-volve´ *vt.* complicate; implicate; include by necessity

in-vul´ner-a-ble *a.* impossible to injure or wound

i´on *n.* atom or group of atoms bearing an electrical charge

i-on´o-sphere´ *n.* layer of electrically charged particles in outer part of atmosphere

i´o´ta *n.* ninth letter of the Greek alphabet; jot, very small quantity or degree

IOU *n.* informal acknowledgment of debt

i-ras´ci-ble *a.* irritable, easily angered

IRBM *n.* intermediate range ballistic missile with 1,500 mile range

ire *n.* anger; **i´rate´** *a.*

ir´i-des´cent *a.* colored like the rainbow

irk *vt.* weary, vex, annoy

i´ron cur´tain *n.* former state of censorship and severe restriction in Soviet dominated nations

i´ron lung´ *n.* mechanical respirator

i´ro-ny *n.* mocking form of humor intended to convey the opposite of what is said; **i-ron´ic** *a.*

ir-ra´tion-al *a.* void of reason

ir-rec´on-cil´a-ble *a.* implacable

ir-ref´u-ta-ble *a.* indisputable, undeniable

ir-reg´u-lar *a.* not according to rule or custom; not straight; not uniform; **ir-reg´u-lar´i-ty** *n.*

ir-rel´e-vant *a.* not bearing on the matter at hand

ir´re-proach´a-ble *a.* free from blame

ir´re-spec´tive *a.* having no regard to

ir-rev´o-ca-ble *a.* unalterable

ir´ri-gate´ *vt.* water land by artificial means; cause water to flow upon; **ir´ri-ga´tion** *n.*

ir´ri-ta-ble *a.* easily provoked or angered

Is´lam *n.* Moslem religion

is´land *n.* land surrounded by water

isle *n.* small island

i´so-late´ *vt.* detach from surroundings; insulate; **i´so-la´tion** *n.*

i´so-met´rics *n.* toning muscles by exercise against resistance

i-sos´ce-les´ *a.* having two equal legs or sides, as a triangle

i´so-tope´ *n.* variant form of a chemical element differing slightly in atomic weight

is´sue *vi.* go, flow, or come out; terminate; *vt.* send out; *n.* going or sending out; result; question

isth´mus *n.* neck of land connecting

two larger portions of land

i-tal´ics *n.* sloping variety of type used to set off certain words; **i-tal´-i-cize** *vi.* & *vt.*

it´er-ate´ *vi.* repeat; **it´er-a´tion** *n.*

i-tin´er-ant *a.* traveling; *n.* one who wanders

i-tin´er-ar´y *n.* detailed route of a journey

i´vo-ry *n.* substance composing the tusks of the elephant, walrus, etc.

J

jack *n.* device for lifting weights; receptacle for a plug connector to a phonograph, radio, etc.; **jack up** *vt.* increase, raise

jack´ass´ *n.* male of the ass; blockhead, fool

jack´et *n.* short coat

jade *n.* hard green stone used for ornamental carving; tired horse; vicious woman; *vt.* wear out by overwork, inure

jag´uar´ *n.* beast of prey

ja-lop´y *n.* old car in poor condition

jam *vt.* squeeze; *n.* people or things crowded together; preserves; bad situation

jam´bo-ree´ *n.* raucous get-together, frolic

jamb *n.* sidepiece or post of a door, fireplace, etc.

jam´ ses´sion *n.* impromptu playing by a group of musicians

jan´i-tor *n.* one who has care of a building

jar´gon *n.* professional cant; confused speech

jaun´dice *n.* disease characterized by yellowness of eyes, skin, etc.

jaunt *n.* excursion; **jaun´ty** *a.* dashing

jazz *n.* type of syncopated music orig. from New Orleans

jeal´ous *a.* suspicious of or angry over rivalry; exacting

jeans *n. pl.* garments made of jean, a twilled cotton cloth

jeep *n.* army all-purpose car

jeer *vi. vt.* make sport of; *n.* biting taunt

jel´ly *n.* anything gelatinous; juice of fruit boiled with sugar

jeop´ard-ize´ *vt.* put in jeopardy; **jeop´ard-y** *n.* danger, peril, hazard

jerk *vi.* & *vt.* throw or move with a start; *n.* sudden quick movement; mean or unlikable fellow

jet *n.* spouting stream; *vi.* & *vt.* throw or shoot out; **jet plane** *n.* plane propelled by expulsion of gases from jets instead of by propeller; **jet propulsion** *n.* propelling force caused by release of heated gases from a jet

jet stream *n.* high-altitude wind current that blows at high speeds from the west

jew´el *n.* precious stone; anything valued highly; *vt.* dress or adorn with jewels

jilt *vt.* disappoint in love by a sudden rejection

jingle *n.* jangling sound; jangling rhyme or verse; *vi.* tinkle

jinx *n.* anything that brings bad luck

Job´ Corps´ *n.* U.S. government agency for training unemployed youths

jock´ey *n.* one who rides a horse in a race; *vi.* manipulate

jog *vi.* run slowly and steadily; *vt.* nudge

join *vi.* & *vt.* connect; associate with

joint *n.* place where things join; part of a limb cut off at the joint; dive, low tavern, etc.; *a.* joined

joist *n.* timber to which floorboards are nailed

joke *n.* jest; *vi. & vt.*

jolt *n.* sudden jerk; *vi. & vt.* shake with jerks

jon´quil *n.* flower similar to daffodil

jos´tle *vi. & vt.* push, elbow

jot *n.* tiniest bit; *vt.* write down briefly

jour´nal *n.* diary; periodical

jour´nal-ist *n.* newspaperman

jour´ney *n.* trip, tour, excursion; *vi.* travel

jo´vi-al *a.* merry, in good humor

jowl *n.* cheek

ju´bi-lant *a.* shouting for joy; **ju´bi-la´tion** *n.*

ju´bi-lee´ *n.* season of great public joy; fiftieth anniversary

judge *n.* officer who hears and settles disputes, arbitrator; connoisseur; *vi.* hear and decide; form or pass an opinion; *vt.* sentence; be censorious to

judg´ment *n.* act of judging; reason; opinion formed sentence

ju-di´cial *a.* pertaining to judge or court

ju-di´cious *a.* prudent, discreet

jug´gle *vi. & vt.* play tricks by sleight-of-hand; throw and catch a number of objects in a continuous motion

juice *n.* sap of plants; **juic´y** *a.*

ju´jit´su´ *n.* Japanese art of self-defense without weapons

juke´box´ *n.* coin operated phonograph

jum´per *n.* loose jacket

junc´tion *n.* joining; place or point of union

junc´ture *n.* joining, junction; critical point of time

jun´gle *n.* dense sub-tropical tangle of vegetation

jun´ior *a.* younger; lower in rank; *n.* one younger or less advanced; one in the third year of school or college

junk *n.* scrap metal; worthless items of any kind

jun´ket *n.* picnic excursion; trip

ju´ris-dic´tion *n.* scope of judicial or administrative authority

ju´ror *n.* one who serves on a jury

ju´ry *n.* body of men sworn to declare the truth on the evidence before them

jus´ti-fy *vt.* vindicate; exonerate; **jus´ti-fi´a-ble** *a.*; **jus´ti-fi-ca´tion** *n.*

ju´ve-nile *a.* young, pertaining to youth; *n.* young person; book for young person; **juvenile delinquent** *n.* young thug, hoodlum

K

ka-ra´te *n.* science of fighting, developed in Japan, that makes special use of the edge of the hand as a striking weapon.

kan-ga-roo´ *n.* Australian leaping quadruped; **kangaroo court** *n.* sham court designed to give the appearance of justice

keel *n.* part of a ship extending along the bottom from stem to stern; *vi. & vt.* turn keel up, turn over

keen *a.* sharp; eager

ken´nel *n.* house for dogs; pack of hounds

ker´nel *n.* seed, grain; core

ker´o-sene´ *n.* fuel oil derived from petroleum

ket´tle *n.* metal vessel for heating or boiling liquids

ket´tle-drum´ *n.* large drum shaped like a kettle

khak´i *n.* durable cotton cloth of brownish color favored by U. S. Armed Forces

kib´itz *vi.* give unasked-for advice

kid *n.* child; young goat, or leather made of its skin

kid´nap´ *vt.* carry off a person illegally

kid´ney *n.* one of the two glands which secrete urine

kiln *n.* oven in which bricks, etc., are baked

kil´o-cy´cle *n.* in radio, 1,000 cycles per second

kil´o-gram´ *n.* metric weight equal to 1000 grams or 2.2 lbs.

kil´o-me´ter, ki-lom´e-ter*n.* metric measure of length equal to 1,000 meters or 3,281 ft.

ki-mo´no *n.* traditional Japanese dress resembling a dressing gown

kin´der-gar´ten *n.* school for young children

kin´dle *vt.* set fire to; excite; *vi.* take fire; grow warm or animated

kind´ling *n.* material for starting a fire

kin´e-scope´ *n.* cathode-ray picture tube in television set

ki-net´ic *a.* pertaining to or caused by motion

kink *n.* sharp bend in a rope; obstacle, "hitch"; *vi.* & *vt.* twist into kinks

kitch´en *n.* room where food is prepared

kite *n.* light, paper-covered frame for flying in the air; bird of the hawk family

kit´ten *n.* young cat

klep´to-ma´ni-a *n.* irresistible urge to steal; **klep´to-ma´ni-ac** *n.*

knack *n.* dexterity

knap´sack´ *n.* sack or bag for provisions

knead *vt.* work, as dough

knee *n.* joint between the thigh and shin bones

kneel *vi.* **(knelt, kneeled)** fall or rest on the knees

knell *n.* tolling of a bell, as for someone dead

knife *n.* **(knives)** instrument for cutting

knight *n.* piece used in chess; armed warrior of the Middle Ages

knit *vi.* & *vt.* **(knit, knit´ted)** unite into a network by needles; unite closely, join

knob *n.* round handle; hard bulge or protuberance

knock *vi.* & *vt.* rap, strike

knock´out´ *n.* blow that strikes one unconscious

knot *n.* fastening together of two cords; bond or union; difficulty; cluster; hard mass of timber; nautical mile per hour; *vi.* & *vt.* form or tie in knots

know *vt.* **(knew; known)** recognize; be informed of; *vi.* have information about

know´how´ *n.* technical experience, knowledge, or ingenuity

know´ledge *n.* information; learning; clear perception, understanding

knuck´le *n.* joint of the fingers; *vi.* bend

K.´O.´ *n.* knockout; *vt.*

Ko-ran´ *n.* Mohammedan bible

ko´sher *a.* prepared in accordance with the Jewish dietary laws; proper; legitimate;

krypton´ n colorless, heavy gas found in the air in small amounts

L

la´bel *n.* slip of writing or printing to

affix to anything; *vt.* affix a label to or mark with a label

la´bor *n.* work, toil; *vi.* work; **la-bo´ri-ous** *a.*

lab´o-ra-to´ry *n.* place for scientific experiments; workshop clinic

lab´y-rinth´ *n.* place of intricate windings, a maze; internal ear; **lab´y-rin´thine** *a.*

lace *n.* delicate kind of trimming; *vt.* fasten, tie; adorn with lace

lac´er-ate´ *vt.* tear, wound by tearing; **lac´er-a´tion** *n.*

lack *n.* want; *vi.* & *vt.* be without, need, be destitute of

lac´quer *n.* type of varnish; *vt.* cover with laclacquer

lac´tic *a.* pertaining to milk

lad´der *n.* upright frame with steps

la´dle *n.* large spoon; *vt.* dip with a ladle

la´dy *n.* woman of refined manners; mistress of a house

lag *vi.* move slowly, linger

la´ger *n.* light, aged beer

lag´gard *n.* loiterer, idler; *a.* slow

la-goon´ *n.* shallow pond in the middle of an island or near the sea

lair *n.* den of a wild beast

la´i-ty *n.* people or church goers as distinct from the clergy

lamb *n.* young of sheep

lame *a.* disabled in a limb; unsatisfactory, weak

la-ment´ *vi.* & *vt.* utter or feel grief; deplore; *n.* expression of grief; **lam´en-ta-ble** *a.*

lam´poon´ *n.* personal satire; *vt.* satirize, burlesque

lan´cet *n.* surgical instrument

land´mark´ *n.* anything serving to mark a boundary

land´scape´ *n.* picture or painting of land; aspect of countryside

lan´guage *n.* major dialect, tongue, speech; any means of expressing ideas

lan´guid *a.* spiritless, sluggish

lan´guor *n.* listlessness

lan´guish *vi.* lose strength and animation

lank *a.* long and loosely built

lan´tern *n.* case for holding and enclosing a light

lap *vt.* lick up with the tongue as a cat or dog; *vi.* fold or project over

lapse *n.* slipping; passing; gap; falling from duty; *vi.* pass by degrees; fall from duty; become void

lar´ce-ny *n.* theft, esp. of personal property

lard *n.* fat of swine

lard´er *n.* pantry

lar´i-at *n.* lasso

lark *n.* songbird; escapade

lar´va *n.* **(lar´vae)** first, grub-like stage of an insect after issuing from the egg

lar´ynx *n.* upper part of windpipe containing the vocal cords

la´ser *n.* device for amplifying a beam of light by stimulating atoms

lash *n.* whip, or flexible part of a whip; stroke of a whip; eyelash; *vt.* strike with a lash, flog; make fast with a rope; flail with sarcasm

las´so *n.* **(las´sos, las´soes)** rope with a noose for catching livestock; *vt.* catch with a lasso, rope

last *a.* & *adv.* final, latest; *n.* block for molding shoes; *vi.* endure, continue

latch *n.* catch to fasten a door; *vt.* fasten with a latch

la´tent *a.* potential, hidden; **la´ten-cy** *n.*

lat´er-al *a.* pertaining to or lying at the side

la´tex *n.* milky juice from certain plants used to make rubber

lathe *n.* machine for turning and shaping articles of wood, metal, etc.

lath´er *n.* foam made with soap and water; *vi.* become frothy; *vt.* spread over with lather

lat´i-tude´ *n.* distance north or south of the equator; freedom to act

lat´ter *a.* coming after, following; *n.* last of two mentioned

lat´tice *n.* network of crossed bars, rods, etc.

laugh *vi.* express merriment by voice and face; *n.* sound caused by merriment; **laugh´ter** *n.*

launch *v.* throw; cause to slide into the water or sail into the air; *vi.* slide into the water; *n.* type of boat; **launching pad** *n.* platform and its equipment from which rockets and missiles are fired

laun´dro-mat´ *n.* business making its coin-operated, self-service, electric washing machines available to the public

laun´dry *n.* place where clothes are washed

la´va *n.* melted rock discharged from a volcano

lav´a-to´ry *n.* place or basin for washing

lav´ish *a.* bestowing profusely, extravagant

law´suit´ *n.* action at law

law´yer *n.* attorney at law

lax *a.* slack, loose

lax´-i-ty, lax´-ness *n.* slackness, negligence, lack of firmness

lay *vt.* **(laid)** put down, place; wager; produce eggs; *vi.* produce eggs

lay´er *n.* stratum

lay´man *n.* one not a clergyman; non-professional

lay´out´ *n.* anything arranged or displayed (as the format of a book); state of affairs, situation

lead *n.* soft, heavy metallic element; *vt.* cover or fit with lead; **lead´-en** *a.* made of lead; heavy, dull

lead *vi.* & *vt.* **(led)** show the way by going first, guide; *n.* first place; guidance; clue; **lead´-er** *n.*

leaf *n.* **(leaves)** part of the foliage of plants; sheet; *vi.* produce leaves

league *n.* union, alliance; *vi.* form a union

leak *n.* hole in a vessel or the waste issuing from such a hole; *vi.* let a fluid in or out

lean *vi.* & *vt.* incline, bend

lean *a.* skinny, thin, lacking flesh or fat

leap *vi.* & *vt.* **(leaped, lept)** jump, bound, or spring over; *n.* act of leaping; space passed in leaping

learn *vi.* & *vt.* acquire knowledge

lease *n.* letting of land, building, or apartment, etc., for a certain time; *vt.* let for a certain term; take a lease on

leash *n.* line by which a dog is held; *vt.* put on or hold by a leash

leath´er *n.* prepared skin of animals

leave *vi.* & *vt.* **(leaving, left)** allow to remain; depart from; bequeath; *n.* formal parting; permission, liberty; furlough

leav´en *n.* ferment which makes dough rise

lec´ture *n.* formal instructive speech; formal reproof; *vi.* & *vt.* instruct; reprove

ledge *n.* shelf of rocks; small molding

ledg´er *n.* boot of accounts

leer *n.* sidelong look of malice or lust; *vi.*

lees *n. pl.* sediment

left *a.* pertaining to the side on

which the heart is located; *n.*

left´ist *n.* person holding liberal or radical beliefs

leg´a-cy *n.* bequest, inheritance

le´gal *a.* pertaining to or according to law; **legal´i-ty** *n.*

leg´ate *n.* ambassador or envoy, esp. from the pope

le-ga´tion *n.* delegation, embassy

leg´end *n.* story handed down, myth; words on a coin or medal; **leg´end-ar´y** *a.*

leg´er-de-main´ *n.* sleight of hand

leg´i-ble *a.* readable, easily read

le´gion *n.* great number

leg´is-late´ *vi.* make laws; **leg´is-la´-tion** *n.*; **leg´is-la´tive** *a.*

leg´is-la´ture *n.* body having the power to make laws

le-git´i-mate *a.* lawful; real; of honorable birth

lei´sure *n.* spare time; *a.* free

lem´on *n.* citrus tree and its acid fruit; *sl.* very poor or worthless specimen; **lem´on-ade´** *n.*

lend *vt.* **(lent)** grant the use of for a time, loan

lend´-lease´ *n.* aid program proposed in 1941 by Pres. Roosevelt for countries facing Nazi threat

length *n.* longest side of any thing, height; duration, extent

length´en *vt.* make or grow longer

le´ni-ent *a.* mild, merciful; **le´ni-en-cy, le´ni-ence** *n.*

lens *n.* glass ground in order to change the direction of light rays

Lent *n.* fast of forty days from Ash Wednesday to Easter

le´o-nine´ *a.* like a lion

leop´ard *n.* ferocious animal with spotted coat

lep´er *n.* one afflicted with leprosy

lep´ro-sy *n.* contagious disease of the skin; **lep´rous** *a.*

les´bi-an *n.* woman sexually oriented to other women

les´sen *vi.* & *vt.* make or become smaller or less

les´son *n.* niaterial read or learned at one time; precept; rebuke

let *vt.* give leave to, allow, permit; lease

le´thal *a.* deadly

leth´ar-gy *n.* stupor; heavy, unnatural dullness; prolonged sleep or drowsiness; winter sleep, hibernation; **le-thar´gic** *a.*

let´ter *n.* written message; symbol used to represent a sound or sounds; literal meaning; *vt.* inscribe letters upon

let´tuce *n.* green vegetable whose leaves are used for salad

lev´ee *n.* embankment to prevent flooding

lev´el *n.* horizontal line or plane; instrument for showing the horizontal; *a.* even, flat, horizontal; *vt.* make horizontal or even; flatten, destroy; aim, as firearms

lev´er *n.* bar turning on a support, the fulcrum; **lev´er-age** *n.* action of a lever; power afforded by a lever

le-vi´a-than *n.* anything huge or monstrous; great beast

lev´i-ty *n.* flippancy, lack of seriousness

lev´y *n.* act of collecting, as money or troops; legal seizure of property; *vt.* collect by authority

lex´i-cog´ra-pher *n.* editor or compiler of dictionaries, a harmless drudge; **lex´i-cog´ra-phy** *n.*

lex´i-con *n.* dictionary

li´a-ble *a.* answerable; exposed, as to danger

li´ai-son´ *n.* any link, communication, or a person who acts as a link

li´ar *n.* one who tells lies

li´bel *n.* malicious, defamatory publication; *vt.* defame by libel; **li´belous** *a.*
lib´er-al *a.* generous, lavish; not bound by the orthodox or conservative point of view; *n.*; **lib´er-al´i-ty** *n.*
lib´er-al arts´ *n.* studies undertaken to develop general knowledge
lib´er-ate´ *vt.* set free; **lib´er-a´tion** *n.*
lib´er-ty *n.* freedom; privilege
li-bi´do *n.* sexual drive; **li-bid´i-nous** *a.* lewd
li-brar´i-an *n.* keeper of a library
li´brar´y *n.* collection of books; place for keeping such a collection
li´cense *n.* permission; official permission or registration; excess of freedom; *vt.* grant a permit
li-cen´tious *a.* dissolute
lid *n.* cover; eyelid
lie *n.* falsehood; *vi.* **(ly´ing; lied)** utter a falsehood
lie *vi.* **(ly´ing; lay; lain)** rest in a reclining position; be situated; abide or exist
lieu *n.* place, stead
lieu-ten´ant *n.* officer next below a captain; deputy; aide
lift *vt.* elevate, hoist; filch; *n.* act of lifting; elevator; help; stimulation
lift´-off´ *n.* launching of a rocket
lig´a-ment *n.* anything that binds, esp. a band of connective tissue
lig´a-ture *n.* anything that binds, connects, or ties together; two or three characters printed as one (as æ, fl, ff, ffl)
light´ning *n.* electric flash from the sky
light´weight´ *n.* boxer weighing 127-135 lbs.
light´-year´ *n.* distance traveled by light in one year
lig´nite´ *n.* coal retaining the texture of wood
li´lac *n.* flowering shrub; *a.* & *n.* pale purple
lil´y *n.* bulbous plant with showy flowers
lim´ber *a.* flexible, pliant; *vt.* make pliant
lime *n.* calcium carbonate from limestone, etc., used with sand to make mortar; kind of citrus tree and its fruit
lim´it *n.* boundary, utmost extent; *vt.* confine
limp *a.* lacking stiffness; weak; *vi.* walk lamely; *n.* act of limping
lim´pid *a.* clear
line *n.* long, straight mark used to mark off, separate, etc.; slender cord; straight row; verse; job, profession; *vt.* place in line, mark out in lines; cover the inside of a garment
lin´e-age *n.* descent from a common ancestor
lin´e-al *a.* descended in direct line; pertaining to a line
lin´en *n.* cloth made of flax; *a.*
lin´ger *vi.* remain; loiter
lin´guist *n.* student of linguistics; one well versed in languages
lin-guis´tics *n.* science of language
link *n.* loop or ring of a chain; part of a series; connection, clue; *vi.* & *vt.* connect
lint *n.* fluff scraped from a woolly or wool-like substance
lin´tel *n.* wood, stone, etc., forming the top part of a doorway or window
li´on *n.* large, fierce African quadruped; one who is idolilzed
li´on-ize *vt.* idolize, treat as a popular favorite
lip´stick´ *n.* coloring for the lips

sold in soft-solid sticks
liq´ue-fy *vi.* & *vt.* melt, dissolve, make liquid; **liq´ue-fac´tion** *n.*
li-queur´ *n.* alcoholic beverage made with spices, herbs, etc.
liq´uid *n.* flowing substance; *a.* flowing, fluid, not solid
liq´ui-date´ *vt.* settle, as debts; wipe out, destroy, kill; **liq´ui-da´tion** *n.*
liq´uor *n.* alcoholic beverage; anything liquid
lisp *vi.* & *vt.* articulate or speak faultily or as a child; pronounce *th* for *s* or *z*; *n.*
list *n.* catalog; *vt.* write down, enroll, register
lis´ten *vi.* hear, pay attention to
list´less *a.* languid
lit´a-ny *n.* form of worship, ritual
li´ter *n.* metric measure equal to about one quart
lit´er-al *a.* according to the letter, not figurative
lit´er-ar´y *a.* pertaining to literature
lit´er-a-ture´ *n.* written, usually creative, heritage of any culture
lith´o-graph´ *vt.* engrave on and print from stone, zinc, etc.; *n.* print made by this process; **li-thog´ra-phy** *n.*
lit´i-gant *n.* person engaged in a lawsuit
lit´i-gate´ *vi.* & *vt.* contest in law
lit´ter *n.* scattered collection of objects; heap of straw for animals to lie upon; brood of small quadrupeds; *vt.* scatter carelessly about; **lit´ter-bug´** *n.* one who litters public property with trash
lit´ur-gy *n.* established ritual for religious services; **li-tur´gi-cal** *a.*
live *vi.* have life, exist; dwell; feed; last, endure
live´li-hood´ *n.* means of living
liv´id *a.* black and blue; extremely pale
liz´ard *n.* four-footed reptile
lla´ma *n.* South American beast of burden
load *vt.* heap on; charge, as a gun; *n.* cargo; weight
loaf *n.* **(loaves)** rectangular mass, as of bread
loaf *vi.* loiter; **loaf´er** *n.*
loaf´ers *n. pl.* low-cut, informal shoes without laces
loam *n.* a rich soil
loan *n.* act of lending; permission to use; money loaned on interest; *vt.* lend
loathe *vt.* detest, dislike
lob´by *n.* hall or waiting room; pressure group, persons who try to influence legislators; *vi.* seek to influence legislitors
lobe *n.* rounded projection
lo-bot´o-my *n.* brain surgery which cuts nerve fibers to treat discase
lob´ster *n.* type of marine shellfish
lo´cal *a.* confined to a spot or district
lo-cal´i-ty *n.* position; district
lo´cal-ize *vt.* limit to one place
lo´cate´ *vt.* place, determine the position of
lock *n.* fastening for doors, etc.; enclosure in a canal for raising or lowering boats; part of a rifle; *vt.* fasten with a lock; shut up; *vi.* unite closely; fasten together
lock´-er *n.* storage cabinet; place for storing frozen foods
lock´-jaw *n.* disease in which the muscles of the jaw contract morbidly
lock´-out *n.* temporary closing of a shop as a means of coercing employees
lo´co-mo´tion *n.* movement
lo´co-mo´tive *a.* moving from place

to place; *n.* railway engine

lode *n.* vein of metallic ore

lodge *n.* small house; retreat; secret society; *vi. & vt.* place or remain for a time; settle; **lodg´ing** *n.*

loft *n.* gallery

loft´y *a.* high, exalted

log *n.* bulky piece of wood; journal of a ship

log´ic *n.* science of reasoning correctly; **log´i-cal** *a.*

lo-gis´tics *n.* in military science, problems of supply

loin *n.* part of man or beast between haunch bone and the last false rib

loi´ter *vi.* delay, linger

loll *vi.* lie lazily about; permit the tongue to hang from the niouth

lon-gev´i-ty *n.* long life, extent of life

lon´gi-tude´ *n.* distance east or west of a given meridian

look *vi.* turn the eye to see; watch; seem; *n.* act of looking; sight

loom *n.* machine for weaving cloth

loop *n.* noose, curve; *vt.* fasten or ornament with loops

loop´-hole´ *n.* means of escape from some predicament

loose *a.* slack, free; not coherent; not tightly packed; vague; licentious; *vt.* free, relax; **loos´en** *vt.*

loot *n.* plunder; act of plundering; *vi. & vt.* plunder or steal

lop *vt.* cut short

lop´eared *a.* with ears that droop

lop´sid-ed *a.* with sides uneven

lo-qua´cious *a.* talkative; **lo-quac´i-ty** *n.*

lose *vt.* **(los´ing; lost)** misplace, cease to own; waste; fail to obtain

loss *n.* act of losing; injury; waste

lost *a.* misplaced; unable to find the way

lot *n.* fate; chance; porion; plot of land

lo´tion *n.* liquid for cleansing, bathing a wound etc.

lot´ter-y *n.* distribution of prizes by chance or lot

loud *a.* noisy; gaudy

loud´speak-er *n.* apparatus which re-converts electrical impulses into sound

lounge *vi.* recline at ease; *n.* sofa; place where cocktails are served

louse *n.* **(lice)** parasitic insect; *sl.* low, contemptible person

lous´y *a.* covered with lice; *sl.* low, contemptible

lov´a-ble *a.* worthy of love

low´er *vt.* bring low, diminish; *vi.* fall, sink; *a.*

lox *n.* liquid oxygen; smoked salmon

loy´al *a.* faithful

loy´al-ty *n.* fidelity in duty

loz´enge *n.* small, flavored, medicated cake or candy

lu´bri-cate´ *vt.* oil, grease; **lu´bri-ca´tion** *n.*

lu´cid *a.* clear, easily understood; shining; sane

lu´cra-tive *a.* profitable

lu´di-crous *a.* absurdly funny, ridiculous and laughable

lug´gage *n.* baggage

lull *vt.* soothe, quiet; *vi.* become calm; *n.* off-season, period of inactivity

lull´a-by´ *n.* slumber song sung to children

lum´bar *a.* pertaining to or near the loins

lum´ber *n.* timber sawed for use; anything cumbersome; *vi.* move heavily

lump *n.* small, shapeless mass; *vt.* throw into a mass; take or dispose of in the gross

lu´na-cy *n.* insanity

lunar *a.* pertaining to the moon
lu´na-tic´ *n.* insane person; *a.* affected with lunacy; **lunatic fringe** *n.* persons whose ideas border on the irrational
lunch, lunch´eon *n.* light mid-day meal; snack between meals
lung *n.* one of the two organs of respiration
lunge *n.* sudden thrust, as in fencing; *vi.* thrust
lurch *n.* sudden roll; *vi.* roll suddenly to one side
lure *n.* enticement, bait; fishhook which resembles an insect; *vt.* entice
lu´rid *a.* ghastly, sensational
lurk *vi.* lie in wait; exist unknown
lus´cious *a.* gratifyingly sweet
lush *a.* rich in growth
lust *n.* desire, sexual desire
lus´ter *n.* brightness, radiance
lux-u´ri-ant *a.* exuberant in growth; rank, overabundant
lux-u´ri-ate´ *vi.* be luxuriant; live in affluence
lux´u-ry *n.* indulgence in costly things; expensive rarity
lye *n.* strong alkaline solution
ly´ing *a.* given to telling falsehoods
ly´ing-in´ *a.* pertaining to childbirth (as a lying-in hospital); *n.*
lymph *n.* colorless fluid in animal bodies; **lym-phat´ic** *a.* pertaining to lymph; sluggish
lynch *vt.* punish without the due forms of law, esp. by hanging
lyre *n.* musical instrument similar to the harp
lyr´ic *a.* suitable for singing; expression of the emotions, as a lyric poem; *n.* lyric poem

M

mac´a-ro´ni *n.* wheat paste shaped in slender tubes
mac´a-roon´ *n.* small cake made of almonds, egg whites, and sugar
ma-chine´ *n.* artificial contrivance to do work
ma-chin´er-y *n.* machines in general
mach´ num´ber *n.* unit of speed measured as ratio to speed of sound
mac´ra-mé *n.* fringe or lace made of knotted cords, yarn, or thread
mac´ro-bi-ot´ic *a.* tending to lengthen life, especially through special diet
Ma-don´na *n.* Virgin Mary
mael´strom *n.* whirlpool
mag´a-zine´ *n.* periodical; receptacle from which cartridges are fed to a gun; storehouse, esp. for gunpowder
mag´got *n.* small worm
mag´ic *n.* sorcery, enchantment; *a.* pertaining to magic; **ma-gi´cian** *n.*
mag´is-trate´ *n.* public civil officer; **mag´is-te´ri-al** *a.*
mag-nan´i-mous *a.* nobly unselfish
mag´na-nim´i-ty *n.* magnanimous act or deed; generosity
mag´nate´ *n.* person of importance
mag´net *n.* iron or steel bar which attracts iron and points to the magnetic poles of the earth; **mag-net´ic** a
magnetic tape *n.* paper or plastic tape coated with iron oxide for use in tape recorders
mag´net-ism *n.* attractive power, as of the magnet
mag´net-ize *vt.* make magnetic
mag-ne´to *n.* small dynamo which produces electricity for the ignition

in an internal combustion engine
mag´ne-tom´e-ter *n.* device for measuring magnetic force
mag-nif´i-cent *a.* splendid, grand; **mag-nif´i-cence** *n.*
mag´ni-fy *vi.* & *vt.* make or cause to appear greater
mag´ni-tude´ *n.* great size, importance
mag-no´li-a *n.* tree bearing beautiful white flowers
ma-hog´a-ny *n.* tree of tropical America; its wood
maid, maiden *n.* unmarried woman, virgin
mail *n.* letters, etc., conveyed by the postal service; *vt.* deliver to the post office for transmission
maim *vt.* disfigure
main *a.* chief, leading; *n.* principal part; ocean
main´tain´ *vt.* support; affirm; defend
ma-jes´tic *a.* stately, sublime
maj´es-ty *n.* grandeur; title of emperors and kings
ma´jor *a.* greater; *n.* officer next in rank above captain
ma-jor´i-ty *n.* greater number; legal adulthood
make *vt.* **(mak´ing, made)** fashion, form; produce; force; render; obtain; reach; seduce; *n.* form; texture; brand
make´shift´ *n.* temporary expedient
mal´ad-just´ment *n.* poor or bad emotional adjustment
mal´a-dy *n.* disease
ma-lar´i-a *n.* disease characterized by chills and fever
male *a.* masculine; *n.* one of the male sex
mal´e-dic´tion *n.* invocation of evil, curse
mal´e-fac´tor *n.* criminal
ma-lev´o-lent *a.* malicious
mal´fea´sance *n.* official misconduct
mal´ice *n.* ill will, disposition to harm others
ma-li´cious *a.* disposed to malice
malign´ *vt.* vilify, defame; **ma-lig´ni-ty** *n.*
ma-lig´nant *a.* tending to destroy; **ma-lig´nan-cy** *n.*
mal´le-a-ble *a.* shapable by hammering
mal´nu-tri´tion *n.* poor or imperfect diet
mam´mal *n.* one of the class of animals that suckle their young
mam´moth *a.* huge, extremely large; *n.* extinct species of elephant
man *n.* **(men)** human being; adult male; mankind; *vt.* fortify
man´a-cle *n.* handcuff; *vt.* put handcuffs on
man´age *vi.* conduct business; *vt.* control; contrive
man´age-able *a.* governable
man´age-ment *n.* manner of directing, administration
man´da-rin *n.* Chinese official; tangerine
man´date´ *n.* command, charge; **man´da-to´ry** *a.* binding, imperative
man´do-lin´ *n.* stringed musical instrument similar to guitar
mane *n.* hair flowing from the neck of animals, as the horse
ma-neu´ver *vi.* & *vt.* manage with skill; *n.* stratagem; military exercise
man´gle *vt.* mutilate
man´hat´tan *n.* mixed drink made with whiskey and sweet vermouth
man´-hour´ *n.* amount of work done in one hour by one man
ma´ni-a *n.* insanity; excessive interest

ma´ni-ac *n.* madman; *a.* raving
man´i-cure´ *n.* care and treatment of the hands and nails; *vt.*; **man´i-cur´ist** *n.*
man´i-fest´ *vt.* show plainly; *a.* evident; **man´i-fes-ta´tion** *n.*
man´i-fes´to *n.* public declaration, as of policy
man´i-fold´ *a.* various in kind or quality
man´i-kin *n.* little man; model of the different parts of the human body
ma-nip´u-late´ *vt.* manage, as by hand; control; **ma-nip´u-la´tion** *n.*
man´ne-quin *n.* model hired to display new clothes; dummy used in making or displaying clothes
man´ner *n.* mode of action; style; degree; **man´ner-ism** *n.* peculiarity
man´or *n.* estate belonging to a noble
man´sard´ roof *n.* roof having two slopes of different angle on every side
man´sion *n.* large, fine house
man´slaugh´ter *n.* accidental murder
man´tel, man´tel-piece´ *n.* shelf over a fireplace
man´tle *n.* cloak; *vt.* cover, as by a cloak
man´u-al *a.* pertaining to, made by, or used by the hand; *n.* handbook; keyboard of an organ
man´u-fac´ture *vt.* make from raw materials; *n.* process of manufacturing; anything manufactured
ma-nure´ *n.* fertilizer, animal dung; *vt.* enrich land with a fertilizer
man´u-script´ *n.* book or paper written or typewritten, but not printed
mar *vt.* spoil, disfigure
mar´ble *n.* handsome variety of limestone; anything made of marble; glass ball used in children´s game; *a.* made of or resembling marble; hard, insensible
march *vi.* move in order or in a stately manner; *n.* movement of troops; music for marching
mare *n.* female horse
mar´ga-rine *n.* butter substitute made from vegetable oils
mar´gin *n.* edge, border; difference between cost and selling price; **mar´gin-al** *a.*
mar´i-jua´na *n.* narcotic-like drug
ma-ri´na *n.* dock providing moorings and facilities for small boats
ma-rine´ *a.* pertaining to the sea; *n.* member of U. S. Marine Corps
mar´i-o-nette´ *n.* puppet
mar´i-tal *a.* pertaining to marriage
mar´i-time´ *a.* pertaining to the sea or to navigation
mar´jo-ram *n.* aromatic plant used as a seasoning
mar´ket *n.* public place for buying and selling; sale; *vi.* & *vt.* buy and sell, engage in trade; **mar´ket-a-ble** *a.*
mar´ma-lade´ *n.* type of jam
mar´quis *n.* nobleman next above earl
ma-roon´ *n.* brownish crimson color; *a.*
mar´riage *n.* union of husband and wife; **mar´riage-a-ble** *a.*
marrow *n.* soft, fatty matter in bones; pith
mar´ry *vi.* & *vt.* join in marriage
marsh *n.* low, wet land
mar´shal *n.* chief officer in a ceremony; field marshal; civil officer of a judicial district; *vt.* arrange, lead
marsh´mal´low *n.* type of confection
mar-su´pi-al *a.* carrying its young in a pouch; *n.*
mar´tial *a.* pertaining to the military or to war; warlike

mar´ti-net´ *n.* strict disciplinarian
mar-ti´ni *n.* mixed drink made with gin and dry vermouth
mar´tyr *n.* one who suffers death or persecution for his beliefs; *vt.* persecute someone for his beliefs; **mar´tyr-dom** *n.*
mar´vel *n.* anything astonishing; *vi.* wonder; **mar´vel-ous** *a.*
mar´zi-pan´ *n.* candy made with almond paste
mas´cot´ *n.* object, animal, or person supposed to bring luck
mas´cu-line *a.* male, having the qualities of a man; suitable to a man; expressing male gender
ma´ser *n.* device for amplifying or producing electromagnetic waves
mash *vt.* beat into a mixed mass, mix thoroughly; *n.* mixture; mixture prepared for brewing
mask *n.* anything disguising the face; pretense; *vt.*
mas´o-chism *n.* morbid delight in being hurt; **mas´o-chist** *n.*
mason *n.* builder in stone
mas´quer-ade´ *n.* costume party or dance; disguise; *vi. & vt.* disguise
mass *n.* lump of matter; large quantity; celebration of the Lord´s Supper in Roman Catholic churches
mass´es *n. pl.* the people at large; the lower classes; *vt.* form into a lump
mas´sa-cre *n.* slaughter, carnage; *vt.* slaughter, kill
mas-sage´ *n.* remedial kneading and rubbing of the body; *vt.* treat by process of rubbing and kneading
mas´sive *a.* weighty, bulky
mast *n.* upright pole for sustaining the yards in a ship
mas´ter *n.* lord; owner; leader; employer; *vt.* learn, become skillful in; overcome; **master of ceremonies** *n.* person who acts as host on radio, TV, etc., abbreviated M.C.
mas´ter-piece´ *n.* work of superior skill
mas´ter-y *n.* victory, superiority, highest attainment
mas´ti-cate´ *vi. & vt.* chew
mas´tur-ba´tion *n.* sexual self-gratification
match *n.* wooden stick used to strike fire; thing which agrees with another, an equal; contest; marriage; *vi.* be of the same make, size, etc.; *vt.* be equal to; find an equal to; set against as equal
match´book´ *n.* small folder of safety matches
match´mak-er *n.* one who tries to arrange marriages
mate *n.* companion, spouse; second in command on a merchant ship; *vi. & vt.* marry, pair
ma-te´ri-al *a.* consisting of matter; essential; *n.* stuff from which anything is made
ma-te´ri-al-ize´ *vi.* become actual or tangible
ma-ter´nal *a.* pertaining to a mother
ma-ter´ni-ty *n.* state or condition of motherhood; **ma-ter´ni-ty leave** *n.* leave of absence from work for an expectant mother
math´e-ma-ti´cian *n.* one versed in mathematics
math´e-mat´ics *n.* arithmetic, geometry, algebra, etc., and the science of reasoning which builds upon these
mat´i-nee´ *n.* afternoon entertainment at a play, movie, etc.
ma´tri-cide´ *n.* murder of one´s mother; person who kills his mother
ma-tric´u-late´ *vi. & vt.* admit or be

admitted to membership, esp. in a college; **ma-tric´u-la´tion** *n.*

mat´ri-mo´ny *n.* marriage

ma´trix *n.* **(ma´tri-ces)** mold, die; element in which anything originates or develops

ma´tron *n.* married, elderly, or motherly woman; female superintendent

mat´ter *n.* substance; subject; *vi.* be of importance

mat´u-rate´ *vi.* ripen

ma´ture´ *a.* fully developed, ripe; *vi. & vt.* make or become ripe or adult; *vi.* become payable, as a bill; **ma-tu´ri-ty** *n.*

ma-tu´ti-nal *a.* pertaining to the morning

maud´lin *a.* tearfully sentimental

mau´sole´um *n.* magnificent tomb

mauve *n.* delicate purple, lilac, or violet color

mav´er-ick *n.* unbranded calf; political stray; one who follows no group

mawk´ish *a.* foolishly or weakly sentimental

max´i *n.* dress or coat extending to the ankles; *a.*

max´il-lar´y *a.* pertaining to the upper jaw

max´im *n.* saying, proverb

max´i-mum *a.* greatest; *n.* **(max´i-mums, max´i-ma)** greatest quantity or degree

may´hem´ *n.* crime of violently crippling someone

may´or *n.* chief magistrate of a city

maze *n.* place full of intricate windings, labyrinth; confusion

mea´ger *a.* lean, scanty

meal *n.* food taken at a regular time; grain coarsely ground

mean *a.* low, common; base, sordid

mean *a.* middle, moderate; *n.* middle point, quantity, value, or degree; **means** *n. pl.* instrument; income, estate

mean *vt.* **(meant)** have in mind as a purpose; signify; **mean´ing** *n.* signification; purpose

me-an´der *vi.* wander, wind; *n.* winding course

mea´sles *n.* contagious fever accompanied by red spots on the skin

mea´sure *n.* extent, degree; rule for measuring; moderation; means to an end; meter, musical time; *vt.* determine the dimensions or size; *vi.* extend, have an extent

meat *n.* flesh of animals used as food; edible part of fruit, eggs, etc.

me-chan´ic *a.* one who repairs machines; **me-chan´ic-al** *a.*

me-chan´ics *n.* study of the effect of forces on bodies

mech´a-nism *n.* machine, device, or its parts; physical or mental process

mech´a-nize´ *vt.* make mechanical or like a machine; utilize machinery instead of men or animals

med´al *n.* coin bearing some figure or inscription and bestowed as an honor

me-dal´lion *n.* large medal;

med´dle *vi.* interfere; **med´dle-some** *a.*

me´di-al *a.* mean, middle

me´di-ate´ *vi. & vt.* arbitrate, settle by arbitration; *a.* middle, intervening; acting by or as a means; **me´-di-a´tion** *n.*; **me´di-a´tor** *n.*

med´i-cal *a.* relating to the art of healing; **med´i-cate´** *vt.* treat with medicine; **med´i-ca´tion** *n.*

Med´i-care´ *n.* U. S. program providing health care for persons over sixty-five

me-dic´i-nal *a.* healing
med´i-cine *n.* remedy; drug which remedies; science of prevention and cure of disease
me´di-e´val *a.* relating to the middle ages
me´di-o´cre *a.* middling, average, common; **me´di-oc´ri-ty** *n.*
med´i-tate *vi.* & *vt.* think deeply, ponder; **med´i-ta´tion** *n.*
me´di-um *n.* middle place or degree; means, agency
med´ley *n.* mixture; music containing parts from several compositions
meek *a.* submissive
meer´schaum *n.* clay used for making pipes for smoking; pipe made of such material
meet *vi.* & *vt.* **(met)** encounter; receive, as a welcome; satisfy; *n.* meeting
meg´a-lo-ma´ni-a *n.* mental disorder characterized by delusions of greatness
meg´a-lop´o-lis *n.* large urban complex
meg´a-phone´ *n.* large speaking trumpet
meg´a-ton´ *n.* one million tons
mel´an-chol´y *n.* gloom; depression; *a.* gloomy; **mel´an-chol´ic** *a.*
mel-lif´lu-ous *a.* honey smooth
mel´low *a.* soft and ripe; *vi.* & *vt.* ripen, mature, age
mel´o-dra´ma *n.* sensational, romantic drama; **mel´o-dra-mat´ic** *a.*
mel´o-dy *n.* tune; **me-lo´di-ous** *a.*
mel´on *n.* fruit of an annual trailing plant
mem´ber *n.* limb of an animal; one of a community or group; **mem´ber-ship´** *n.*
mem´brane *n.* thin tissue lining a surface
me-men´to *n.* reminder, souvenir
mem´oir *n.* short biographical or autobiographical sketch; transactions of a society
mem´o-ra-ble *a.* deserving to be remembered
mem´o-ran´dum, mem´o´ *n.* **(mem´o-ran´da)** note to aid the memory, reminder
me-mo´ri-al *a.* bringing to memory; *n.* monument
mem´o-ry *n.* faculty of the mind by which it retains information; thing remembered
men´ace *vt.* threaten; *n.* threat
me-nag´er-ie *n.* collection of wild animals for exhibition
men-da´cious *a.* lying; **men-dac´i-ty** *n.*
men´di-cant *n.* beggar; *a.* practicing beggary
me´ni-al *a.* servile; *n.* domestic servant
men´in-gi´tis *n.* serious inflammation of the membranes covering the brain and spinal cord
men´o-pause´ *n.* end of female ability to reproduce
men´su-ra´tion *n.* act, process, or art of measuring. result of measuring
men´tal *a.* pertaining to the mind or intellect
men´tion *n.* brief notice; *vt.* notice briefly, remark upon
men´tor *n.* counselor
mer´can-tile *a.* commercial
mer´ce-nar´y *a.* actuated by greed; hired for money; *n.* one hired; soldier hired into foreign service
mer´chan-dise´ *n.* goods or wares of a merchant
mer´chant *n.* trader; *a.* pertaining to trade

mer-cu´ri-al *a.* changeable, volatile
mer´cy *n.* leniency
mer´e-tri´cious *a.* wanton; deceitfully gaudy
merge *vi.* & *vt.* combine; **mer´ger** *n.*
me-rid´i-an *a.* pertaining to the meridian or midday; *n.* midday; highest point, zenith; imaginary circle on the earth´s surface passing through the poles and any given place
me-ringue´ *n.* pastry made of egg whites and sugar
mer´it *n.* worth; recompense; *vt.* earn; **mer´i-to´ri-ous** *a.* richly deserving
mer´maid *n.* a fabled marine woman with the tail of a fish
mer´ry *a.* mirthful; **mer´ri-ment** *n.* mirth, jollity
mer´ry-go-round´ *n.* circular frame with wooden horses, seats, etc., for riding, made to revolve by machinery
mesh *n.* network; *vt.* catch, as in a net; *vi.* & *vt.* come together or engage, as parts of a machine
mes´mer-ism *n.* hypnotism; **mes´-mer-ize´** *vt.* bring into a hypnotic state
mess *n.* state of disorder or dirty confusion
mes´sage *n.* communication sent
mes´sen-ger *n.* bearer of a message
Mes-si´ah *n.* anointed one; Christ
me-tab´o-lism *n.* process of building up and wearing out of the cells in a body
met´al *n.* opaque, usually solid material (such as gold, iron, silver, etc.); character, temper; **me-tal´lic** *a.*
met´al-lur´gy *n.* art of removing metals from ores
met´a-mor´pho-sis *n.* **(met´a-mor´-pho-ses)** transformation, striking change
met´a-phor *n.* figurative language (as *sail* for *ship*, *bird* for *missile*, etc.); **met´a-phor´ic, met´a-phor´i-cal** *a.* figurative
met´a-phys´ics *n.* branch of philosophy concerned with fundamental causes and the nature of reality; **met´a-phys´i-cal** *a.*
me´te-or *n.* shooting star; **me´te-or´ic** *a.*; **me´te-or-ite´** *n.*
me´te-or-ol´o-gy *n.* science of weather and the atmosphere; **me´-te-or-ol´o-gist** *n.*
me´ter *n.* apparatus for measuring the amount of water, gas, electricity, etc., consumed; measure of length = 39.37 in.; type of rhythm, as in music or poetry
meth´od *n.* systematic procedure; **me-thod´ic, me-thod´i-cal** *a.*
me-tic´u-lous *a.* mindful or unduly mindful of small details; overly cautious
me-ton´y-my *n.* substitution of one word for another related to it (as *heart* for *affection*)
met´ro-nome´ *n.* device for marking time in music
me-trop´o-lis *n.* chief city of a country or state; large city; **met´ro-pol´i-tan** *a.*
met´tle *n.* temperament
mez´za-nine´ *n.* a half story, often forming a balcony
mi-as´ma *n.* infectious vapor; any undesirable influence
mi´crobe´ *n.* microscopic organism
mi´cro-bi-ol´o-gy *n.* science of microscopic life
mi´cro-cosm *n.* man, or any institution as a model of the universe
mi´cro-film´ *n.* film used for making small photographic copies of

printed or written material

mi´cro-graph´ *n.* representation of the view through a microscope

mi´cro-groove´ *n.* close-set grooves in long-playing phonograph records

mi-crom´e-ter *n.* instrument for making minute measurements, as on a microscope

mi´cro-or´gan-ism *n.* an organism visible only with a microscope

mi´cro-phone´ *n.* apparatus for changing sound into electrical impulses

mi´cro-scope´ *n.* optical instrument for viewing minute objects; **mi´cro-scop´ic** *a.*

mi´cro-wave´ *n.* very short electromagnetic impulse

mid´dle *n.* middle part or point; *a.*

mid´dle-aged *a.* midway in life; over 40

mid´dle-man´ *n.* wholesale merchant, jobber

mid´dle-weight´ *n.* in wrestling or boxing, one who weighs 148-160 lbs.

mid´get *n.* very small creature

mid´i *n.* dress or coat extending to between ankle and knee

mid´riff *n.* diaphragm

mien *n.* appearance, esp. of the face

might *n.* power; ability; **might´y** *a.*

mi´graine´ *n.* severe headache

mi´grate´ *vi.* move from one place to another; **mi-gra´tion** *n.*; **mi´gra-to-ry** *a.*

mild *a.* moderate; gentle

mil´dew *n.* fungi on plants; *vi. & vt.* taint with mildew

mile *n.* 5,280 ft.

mile´age *n.* length in miles

mil´i-tant *a.* fighting

mil´i-ta-rism *n.* excess of military spirit

mil´i-ta-rize *vt.* build up military forces; fill with military spirit

mil´i-tar-y *a.* pertaining to soldiers; *n.* soldiery

mil´i-tate´ *vi.* weigh or operate against

mi-li´tia *n.* citizens enrolled and drilled as soldiers

mill *n.* machine for grinding; place for grinding or manufacturing; *vt.* grind; press or stamp in a mill; indent the edges of

mil-len´ni-um *n.* thousand years

mill´er *n.* one who runs a mill

mil´li-gram´ *n.* one thousandth of a metric gram

mil´li-li´ter *n.* one thousandth of a liter

mil´li-me´ter *n.* one thousandth of a meter

mil´li-ner´y *n.* articles sold by milliners, esp. hats and bonnets; business or trade of a milliner

mil´lion *n.* thousand thousands (1,000,000); **mil´lion-aire´** *n.*

Mim´e-o-graph´ *n. tr.* copying machine in which ink prints through pierced film

mim´ic *vt.* imitate or mock; *n.* one who imitates; **mim´ic-ry** *n.* imitation

min´a-ret´ *n.* turret on a Moslem mosque

mince *vt.* chop fine; pronounce only partly; *vi.* walk with affected nicety; speak affectedly

mince´meat´ *n.* mixture of chopped meat, suet, fruit, etc. used for pie

mind *n.* faculty of thought, memory, etc.; choice; belief; disposition; *vi. & vt.* obey; care about or for

mine *vi. & vt.* dig for metal, etc.; excavate; *n.* place from which metals, etc., are dug; explosive device used to destroy vessels, equipment

min´er-al *n.* inorganic substance, neither animal nor vegetable; *a.*
min´er-al´o-gy *n.* science of minerals
min´gle *vi.* & *vt.* mix
min´i-a-ture *n.* painting on a small scale; *a.* on a small scale; **min´i-a-tur´i-za´tion** *n.* construction of very small, compact electronic apparatus
min´i-mize´ *vt.* reduce to the smallest possible size or degree
min´i-mum *n.* **(min´i-ma)** least quantity possible
min´is-ter *n.* servant; clergy-man; one intrusted with the management of state affairs; representative of a government at a foreign court; *vi.* attend; give the things needed; *vt.* furnish
min´is-tra´tion *n.* act of ministering; office or service of a minister
min´is-try *n.* act of ministering; service; office of a minister; clergy; body of persons employed to administer the government
mink *n.* quadruped of the weasel kind valued for its fur
min´now *n.* very small fresh-water fish
mi´nor *a.* less; inferior; *n.* person under legal age
mi-nor´i-ty *n.* state of being under age, legal infancy; smaller number
mint *n.* place for coining money; aromatic plant producing fragrant oil; *vt.* coin
mi´nus *a.* less
mi´nute´ *a.* very small; attentive to small things
min´ute *n.* sixtieth part of an hour or degree; **min´utes** *n. pl.* brief report of proceedings of a meeting
mi-nu´ti-ae *n. pl.* small particulars or details
mir´a-cle *n.* supernatural event or act
mi-rac´u-lous *a.* done by divine interference; wonderful
mi-rage´ *n.* optical illusion produced by hot air
mir´ror *n.* looking glass; *vt.* reflect
mirth *n.* gaiety; laughter
mis´an-thrope´ *n.* hater of mankind
mis´ap-pre-hend´ *vt.* misunderstand; **mis´ap-pre-hen´sion** *n.*
mis´ap-pro´pri-ate´ *vt.* appropriate wrongfully; **mis´ap-pro´pri-a´-tion** *n.*
mis´be-have´ *vi.* act improperly; **mis´be-hav´ior** *n.*
mis-car´ry *vi.* fail of the intended effect
mis´ce-ge-na´tion *n.* racial interbreeding
mis´cel-la´ne-ous *a.* consisting of several kinds
mis´cel-la´ny *n.* collection of writings on different subjects
mis´chief *n.* evil; damage; disposition to do harm; **mis´chie-vous** *a.*
mis´con-strue´ *vt.* interpret wrongly
mis´cre-ant *n.* villain
mis´de-mean´or *n.* bad conduct; crime
mi´ser *n.* extremely covetous person; niggard
mis´er-y *n.* unhappiness; **mis´er-a-ble** *a.* wretched; causing misery; worthless
mis´fit´ *n.* bad fit
mis-for´tune *n.* ill fortune; calamity; mishap
mis-guide´ *vt.* guide wrongly
mis´hap´ *n.* ill luck, accident
mis´in-form´ *vt.* tell incorrectly; **mis´in-for-ma´tion** *n.* wrong information
mis´in-ter´pret *vt.* understand or explain wrongly; **mis´in-ter´pre-**

ta´tion *n.*
mis-lead´ *vt.* **(mis-led´)** lead astray
mis-man´age *vt.* manage poorly or improperly; **mis-man´age-ment** *n.*
mis-no´mer *n.* wrong name
mi-sog´a-mist *n.* hater of marriage; **mi-sog´a-my** *n.*
mi-sog´y-nist *n.* hater of women; **mi-sog´y-ny** *n.*
mis´print´ *n.* mistake in printing
mis´pro-nounce´ *vt.* pronounce incorrectly; **mis´pro-nun´ci-a´tion** *n.*
mis´re-pre-sent´ *vt.* represent incorrectly; **mis´rep-re-sen-ta´tion** *n.*
miss *vt.* fail to hit, reach, find, or keep; omit; discover the absence of; want; *n.* deviation from the mark
mis-shap´en *a.* deformed
mis´sile *n.* weapon thrown, as a dart, bullet, or rocket projectile
mis´sile-ry *n.* science of missiles or rockets
mis´sion *n.* sending; purpose of life; persons sent; station or association of missionaries
mis´sive *n.* circular letter
mis-spell´ *vt.* spell wrongly
mis-state´ *vt.* state wrongly; **mis-state´ment** *n.*
mist *n.* visible, watery vapor; anything which dims; **mist´y** *a.* obscured by vapor
mis-take´ *vt.* understand wrongly; take one for another; *vi.* err in opinion or judgment; *n.* taking wrongly; error
mis´tle-toe´ *n.* parasitic plant on trees
mis´tress *n.* woman having power of ownership; kept woman
mis-trust´ *n.* want of confidence; *vt.* regard with suspicion
mis´un-der-stand´ *vt.* understand wrongly; **mis´un-der-stand´ing** *n.*
mis´use´ *vt.* misapply; *n.* improper use
mite *n.* very small insect; anything small
mit´i-gate´ *vt.* soften in severity; **mit´i-ga´tion** *n.*
mit´ten *n.* fingerless glove with separate cover for the thumb
mix *vi.* & *vt.* unite; mingle
mix´ture *n.* mixing; mass formed by mixing
mne-mon´ics *n.* art of assisting the memory
moan *vi.* make a low, groaning sound; *n.* audible expression of pain
mob *n.* disorderly crowd; *vt.* attack as a crowd
mo´bile *a.* easily moved; **mo-bil´i-ty** *n.*
mo´bil-ize´ *vi.* & *vt.* get ready for active service, as an army; **mo´bil-i-za´tion** *n.*
mob´ster *n.* member of a criminal gang
moc´ca-sin *n.* shoe of deerskin worn by American Indians; poisonous snake of the southern U. S.
mock *vt.* ridicule through mimicry; *a.* imitation, false; **mock´er-y** *n.*
mock´ingbird´ *n.* American songbird which imitates sounds
mock´-up´ *n.* full-scale model of any apparatus, building, etc.
mode *n.* manner; fashion; mood
mod´el *n.* pattern; person who poses for painter or sculptor; imitation on a smaller scale; *vt.* form after a model
mod´er-ate´ *vi.* & *vt.* keep within bounds; abate; *a.* temperate, not extreme
mod´ern *a.* of the present time; **mod´ern-ize** *vt.*
mod´est *a.* reserved; not forward;

moderate; **mod´es-ty** *n.* absence of presumption; natural delicacy

mod´i-fy *vt.* vary; **mod´i-fi-ca´tion** *n.*; **mod´i-fi´er** *n.*

mo-diste´ *n.* lady´s tailoress

mod´u-late´ *vt.* vary, inflect (as the voice); change the key of; **mod´u-la´tion** *n.*

mo´hair´ *n.* fine silken hair of the Angora goat; cloth made of mohair

Mo-ham´med-an *a.* pertaining to Mohammed or to his religion; *n.* follower of Mohammed

moi´e-ty *n.* a half; approximately a half

moist *a.* slightly wet; **mois´ten** *vt.* make moist

mois´ture *n.* wetness

mo´lar *n.* grinding tooth

mo-las´ses *n.* syrup made from sugar or sugar cane

mold *n.* fungus which grows on a body in a damp atmosphere; *vi.* & *vt.* make or become moldy; **mold´y** *a.*

mold *n.* hollow form from which anything is cast; matrix; pattern; thing molded; *vt.* to form in a mold; fashion; knead bread; ornament by molding; form a mold

mole *n.* small dark-colored patch on the human skin; small burrowing animal

mol´e-cule´ *n.* smallest particle into which a chemical compound can be divided; **mo-lec´u-lar** *a.*

mo-lest´ *vt.* disturb; **mo´les-ta´tion** *n.*

mol´li-fy´ *vt.* assuage; pacify

mol´lusk *n.* animal with a soft, inarticulate body, as shellfish

mo´ment *n.* small portion of time; importance; **mo´men-tar´y** *a.*

mo-men´tous *a.* of consequence

mo-men´tum *n.* quantity of motion in a body; impetus

mon´arch *n.* ruler of a monarchy

mon´arch-y *n.* government by a single person; country ruled by a king

mon´as-ter´y *n.* house for monks; **mo-nas´tic** *a.*

mon-au´ral *a.* relating to single-track sound reproduction

mon´e-tar´y *a.* relating to money; pecuniary

mon´ey *n.* coin; currency; wealth

mon´grel *a.* of mixed breed; *n.* animal of mixed breed

monk *n.* one of a religious community of men living apart from the world

mon´key *n.* order of mammalia next to man

mo-nog´a-my *n.* marriage with one person only; **mo-nog´a-mous** *a.*

mon´o-gram´ *n.* several initial letters interwoven

mon´o-graph´ *n.* treatise on one special subject

mon´o-lith´ *n.* column made of a single stone

mon´o-log´, mon´o-logue´ *n.* speech by one person

mo-nop´o-lize´ *vt.* obtain possession or control

mo-nop´o-ly *n.* sole right or power over something

mon´o-rail *n.* train that runs on one track

mon´o-so´di-um glu´ta-mate *n.* a crystalline salt that enhances food flavors

mo-not´o-nous *a.* wearisome; **mo-not´o-ny** *n.* boring sameness

monster *n.* anything horrible from ugliness or wickedness; **mon-stros´i-ty** *n.*; **mon´strous** *a.*

month *n.* one of the twelve parts of the year

month´ly *a.* performed, happening, or published once a month; *n.* monthly publication

mon´u-ment *n.* anything that perpetuates the memory of a person or event

mood *n.* temporary state of the emotions

mood´y *a.* downcast; affected by moods

moon *n.* natural satellite of a planet, esp. of the earth; **moon´light´** *n.*

moon´light´er *n.* person who holds a second job at night or on weekends

moon´-shine´ *n.* illegally-made liquor

moose *n.* large North American mammal of the deer family

moot *a.* disputable, arguable

mor´al *a.* ethical; virtuous; *n.* practical lesson given by a fable, etc.; **mor´al-ist** *n.*; **mo-ral´i-ty** *n.*

mor´al-ize *vt.* make moral reflections

mor´als *n. pl.* ethical conduct

mo-rass´ *n.* marsh, fen

mor´a-tor´i-um *n.* official delay or halt in payments on a debt; suspension of activity

mor´bid *a.* diseased; abnormal, not natural

morgue *n.* place where dead bodies are exposed for identification; file of clippings kept by journalists

mo´ron *n.* person mentally deficient

mo-rose´ *a.* surly; downcast, gloomy

mor-phol´o-gy *n.* study of form and structure, as of animals, plants, rocks, etc.

mor´sel *n.* small piece

mor´tal *a.* liable to die; causing death; pertaining to mortals; *n.* man, one subject to death

mor´tal´i-ty *n.* condition of being mortal; frequency of deaths

mor´tar *n.* vessel in which substances are pounded with a pestle; type of short cannon; cement made of lime, sand, and water

mort´gage *n.* conveyance of property as security; *vt.* pledge as security

mor-ti´cian *n.* undertaker

mor´ti-fy´ *vt.* destroy the vital functions of; humble; **mor´ti-fi-ca´tion** *n.*

mor´tise *n.* cavity cut in a piece of timber to receive the tenon, the piece made to fit it

mo-sa´ic *n.*design formed by small pieces of colored marble, glass, etc.

Mos´lem *a.* & *n.* follower of Mohammed

mosque *n.* Moslem place of worship

mos-qui´to *n.* **(mos-qui´toes)** bloodsucking winged insect

mo-tel´ *n.* motor hotel; individual cabins rented to motorists

moth *n.* family of insects like butterflies

moth´er *n.* female parent; matron; **moth´er-in-law** *n.*; **moth´er-of-pearl** *n.*

mo-tif´ *n.* in literature or art, a recurring theme; in music, a phrase or melody which is repeated with slight changes

mo´tion *n.*act or state of moving; movement; proposal made in an assembly or court; *vi.* & *vt.* indicate by gesture

mo´tion pic´ture *n.* moving image on screen produced by rapid succession of photographs or cartoons; drama presented by this means

mo´ti-vate´ *vt.* provide with a motive or reason; act as a reason for

mo´tive *n.* that which causes a certain action

mot´ley *a.* consisting of different colors or elements

mo´tor *n.* apparatus for converting the energy of steam, electricity, water, etc., into motive power

mo´tor-boat´ *n.* boat propelled by its own motor

mo´tor-car´ *n.* automobile; **mo´tor-ist** *n.*

mo´tor-cy-cle *n.* bicycle propelled by a motor

mo´tor-cade´ *n.* procession of motor vehicles as in a parade

mot´tled *a.* spotted

mot´to *n.* **(mot´tos, mot´toes)** sentence or phrase expressive of some principle

mount *n.* mountain; that upon which anything is fixed; horse; *vi.* project, rise; get on horseback; amount; *vt.* raise, exalt; place oneself upon; climb; reach; set on horseback

moun´tain *n.* high hill; anything very large

moun´te-bank´ *n.* quack, fake

mourn *vi.* & *vt.* grieve; wear mourning

mouse *n.* **(mice)** rodent found in houses and fields

mouth *n.* opening in an animal through which it takes food; opening or entrance

mou´ton´ *n.* fur of sheep as used for coats

mov´a-ble *a.* able to be moved

move *vt.* set in motion; excite to action; touch the feelings of; propose before an assembly; *vt.* change place or posture; begin to perform; make a motion; *n.* movement; turn or play in a game; act of carrying out a plan

mov´ie, mov´ing pic´ture *n.* motion picture, cinema

mow *vt.* **(mowed, mown)** cut down, as grass; **mow´er** *n.* person or machine that cuts grass

mu´ci-lage *n.* solution of gum, used as an adhesive

muck *n.* decayed vegetable matter; anything filthy

mu´cus *n.* secretion of mucous membranes

mud´dle *vt.* render confused; make a mess of; *n.* confused condition

muf´fler *n.* scarf for the throat; any of various devices for deadening noises, as on an automobile

mug´gy *a.* close and damp

mu-lat´to *n.* offspring of one black and one white parent

mulch *n.* loose straw, etc., spread between plants to keep the soil moist, etc.

mulct *n.* fine; *vt.* fine; defraud

mule *n.* offspring of a mare and an ass; obstinate person

mull *vt.* warm, spice, and sweeten (wine, ale, etc.); ponder, consider

mul´ti-form´ *a.* having many forms

mul´ti-lat´er-al *a.* having many sides

mul´ti-par´tite *a.* having many parts

mul´ti-ple *a.* repeated many times; *n.* number which contains another an exact number of times (without a remainder), as 12 is a multiple of 6, 4, 3, 2, and 1

mul´ti-ple scle-ro´sis *n.* hardening of brain and spinal cord

mul´ti-plex´ *a.* pertaining to signals carried over the same channel, as in stereophonic FM; having many parts

mul´ti-ply´ *vt.* make more numerous; repeat (a quantity) as often as another indicates; *vi.* increase;

mul´ti-pli-ca´tion *n.* act of multiplying; operation by which a given number is multiplied; **mul´ti-plic´-i-ty** *n.* great number
mul´ti-tude´ *n.* great number; **mul´-ti-tu´di-nous** *n.*
mum´ble *vi.* & *vt.* speak or mutter with the lips closed
mum´my *n.* preserved or embalmed corpse
mumps *n.* inflammation of the parotid glands
munch *vi.* & *vt.* chew; masticate
mun´dane´ *a.* earthly
mu-nic´i-pal *a.* pertaining to a city
mu-nic´i-pal´i-ty *n.* self-governing community
mu-nif´i-cence *n.* lavishness, bountifulness
mu-nif´i-cent *a.* generous
mu-ni´tion *n.* ammunition; military supplies
mur´der *n.* act of killing a person from malice; *vt.* commit murder; **mur´der-er** *n.*; **mur´der-ous** *a.*
murk´y *a.* gloomy, dark
mur´mur *n.* low, indistinct sound; complaint made in a low, muttering voice; *vi.* & *vt.* utter a murmur
mus´cle *n.* fleshy part of an animal body, the contraction of which produces motion; **mus´cu-lar** *a.*
mus´cu-lar dys´tro-phy *n.* a wasting disease of the muscles
muse *vi.* & *vt.* meditate
Muse *n.* one of the nine classic deities of the liberal arts
mu-se´um *n.* collection of curiosities or works of art
mush *n.* Indian or oat meal boiled in water
mush´room´ *n.* edible fungus; *a.* of rapid growth and short duration; *vi.* grow rapidly, as a mushroom
mu´sic *n.* combination of pleasant sounds; melody; harmony; written notation representing music; **mu´-si-cal** *a.*; **mu´si´cian** *n.*
musk *n.* strong scented matter obtained from the male muskdeer
mus´lin *n.* thin, white cotton cloth or fabric
mus-tache´, mous-tache´ *n.* growth of hair on the upper lip
mus´tang´ *n.* half-wild horse of the Southwest
mus´tard *n.* herb whose pungent seed is used as a condiment
mus´ty *a.* mouldy, sour, or stale with age
mu´ta-ble *a.* subject to change
mu-ta´tion *n.* change; genetic change in a living thing
mute *a.* incapable of speaking; unpronounced; *n.* one who cannot speak
mu´ti-late´ *vt.* maim; remove a necessary part of; **mu´ti-la´tion** *n.*
mu´ti-ny *vi.* revolt against authority, as in military or naval service; *n.*
mut´ter *vi.* & *vt.* murmur; grumble; growl; *n.* low utterance
mut´ton *n.* flesh of sheep
mu´tu-al *a.* reciprocal
mu´tu-al fund *n.* investment company whose shareholders invest in a group of many securities
muz´zle *n.* snout; cage for the mouth; mouth of a gun; *vt.* restrain from biting
my-o´pi-a *n.* nearsightedness; **my-op´ic** *a.*
myr´i-ad *n.* any immense number
myrrh *n.* bitter, aromatic gum
myr´tle *n.* evergreen shrub with fragrant leaves
mys´ter-y *n.* anything beyond human comprehension; secret, religious rite; **mys-te´ri-ous** *a.*
mys´tic *a.* relating to or containing

mystery; **mys´tic-al** *a.*; **mys´ti-cism** *n.*
mys´ti-fy´ *vt.* involve in mystery; puzzle
myth *n.* fabulous legend; **myth´-i-cal** *a.*
my-thol´o-gy *n.* treatise on myths; body of legends of a people; **myth´-o-log´i-cal** *a.*

N

na´bob´ *n.* viceroy under the Mogul empire; man of great wealth or importance
na´dir *n.* point of the heavens opposite the zenith; lowest point
nag *n.* small or bony horse; *vi.* & *vt.* scold
nail *n.* horny covering at the end of fingers and toes; claw; pointed spike of metal for fastening wood, etc.; *vt.* fasten with nails
na´ked *a.* uncovered; unclothed, nude
name *n.* designation; reputation; authority; *vt.* give a name to; speak of by name; nominate
nap *n.* woolly surface of cloth; short sleep; *vi.* doze, sleep for a short time
nape *n.* rear part of neck
naph´tha *n.* flammable liquid distilled from coal tar, etc.
nar-cis´sus *n.* genus of flowering plants including daffodils, jonquils, etc.
nar´co´sis *n.* stupor produced by a narcotic
nar´cot´ic *a.* producing torpor or sleep; *n.* drug that produces sleep or stupor
nar´rate´ *vt.* tell, recite; **nar-ra´tion** *n.*
nar´ra-tive *n.* story, tale
nar´row *a.* of small width; limited; bigoted
na´sal *a.* pertaining to the nose; sounded through the nose
nas´cent *a.* beginning to exist; incipient
na-stur´tium *n.* garden plant with red and yellow flowers
na´ta-to´ri-um *n.* place for swimming
na´tion *n.* people, often of common descent, under the same government
na´tion-al-ism *n.* devotion to the interests and independence of one´s own country without regard to other countries
na´tive *a.* inborn; characterizing a certain place, indigenous; *n.* one born in a given place
na´tiv´i-ty *n.* birth, esp. of Christ
NA´TO´ *n.* North Atlantic Treaty Organization
nat´ty *a.* trim, spruce
nat´u-ral *a.* inborn, native, produced by nature
nat´u-ral´ist *n.* one who studies nature
nat´u-ral-ize´ *vt.* invest with citizenship; **nat´u-ral-i-za´tion** *n.*
na´ture *n.* essential qualities; natural course; the material world, esp. as a creative force
naught *n.* nothing
naugh´ty *a.* bad; mischievous
nau´se-a *n.* sickness of the stomach
nau´se-ate´ *vi.* & *vt.* feel or cause nausea; **nau´seous** *a.*
nau´ti-cal *a.* pertaining to sailors, navigation, etc.
na´val *a.* pertaining to a navy
nave *n.* middle or body of a church
na´vel *n.* depression in the center of the abdomen
nav´i-gate´ *vt.* manage a ship in

sailing or flying; *vi.* sail; **nav´i-ga-ble** *a.*

nav´i-ga´tion *n.* act, science, or art of sailing or flying; **nav´i-ga´tor** *n.*

na´vy *n.* a nation´s ships of war together with their officers, men, etc.

Na´zi *n.* member of the National Socialist party in fascist Germany

neat *a.* tidy; adroit

neb´u-la *n.* **(neb´u-lae, neb´u-las)** mass of stars or luminous gas in space; **neb´u-lar** *a.*

neb´u-lous *a.* vague, cloudy, hazy

nec´es-sar´y *a.* unavoidable; essential

ne-ces´si-tate´ *vt.* make necessary

ne-ces´si-ty *n.* compulsion; need; that which is necessary

ne-crol´o-gy *n.* list of deaths

nec´ro-man´cy *n.* pretended art of revealing future events by communication with the dead; magic; **nec´ro-man´cer** *n.*

ne-crop´o-lis *n.* cemetery

ne-cro´sis *n.* death of part of an animal tissue

nec´tar *n.* fabled drink of the gods

nec´tar-ine´ *n.* type of peach with a smooth rind

need *n.* want, requirement; *vt.* have occasion for, require; **need´ful** *a.*

nee´dle *n.* small, sharp pointed steel instrument, with an eye for a thread, used for sewing

ne-far´i-ous *a.* grossly vile or wicked

ne-ga´tion *n.* denial; statement that something is not

neg´a-tive *a.* denying, negating; *n.* word (such as *no, not*) that denies; photographic film, etc., in which the lights and shades are reversed

neg-lect´ *vt.* disregard; *n.* slight; omission

neg´li-gee´ *n.* informal dress; informal robe for women

neg´li-gent *a.* careless; **neg´li-gence** *n.* habitual neglect

ne-go´ti-a-ble *a.* transferable

ne-go´ti-ate´ *vi.* bargain; *vt.* arrange for by agreement; **ne-go´ti-a´tor** *n.*; **ne-go´ti-a´tion** *n.*

neigh´bor *n.* person who dwells near another

neigh´bor-hood´ *n.* vicinity; neighbors

neither *a., pron. & conj.* not either

ne-ol´o-gism *n.* new word or expression

ne´on´ *n.* gaseous element used in electric signs

ne´o-phyte´ *n.* new convert; novice, apprentice

neph´ew *n.* son of a brother or sister

nep´o-tism *n.* favoritism to one´s relatives

nep-tu´ni-um *n.* one of the artificially-produced radioactive elements

nerve *n.* one of the fibers which convey sensation to the brain; *col.* assurance, impudence

ner´vous *a.* pertaining to the nerves; fidgety, jittery, unduly sensitive; having disordered nerves

nes´tle *vi.* lie snug, as in a nest

net *n.* twine knotted into meshes for catching fish, etc.; *vt.* take, as with a net

net *a.* clear of all charges and deductions; *vt.* produce as clear profit

net´work´ *n.* piece of work or fabric formed like a net; chain of crossed lines (as a telephone or railroad network); chain of radio or TV stations

neu´ras-the´ni-a *n.* nervous condition apparently caused by emotional disturbances

neu-ri´tis *n.* painful inflammation of

a nerve or nerves
neu-ron´ *n.* one-cell nerve center
neu-ro´sis *n.* mild nervous disorder lacking an organic cause
neu-rot´ic *a.* pertaining to neurosis
neu´ter *a.* neither masculine nor feminine
neu´tral *a.* taking no part with either side; belonging to neither side; *n.* one taking no part in a contest; **neu-tral´i-ty** *n.*
neu-tri´no *n.* uncharged subatomic particle
neu´tron *n.* uncharged constituent of atomic nuclei
neu´tron bomb´ *n.* fusion bomb, to be triggered by chemical rather than atomic explosion
new *a.* having happened or originated recently
news´cast´ *n.* radio or TV broadcast of news
news´pa´per *n.* publication for providing news of recent happenings, etc.
ni´a-cin *n.* nicotinic acid, one of the vitamin-B complex group
niche *n.* recess in a wall
nick´el *n.* silvery metallic element; five-cent piece
nick´name´ *n.* familiar name
nic´o-tine´ *n.* poisonous substance in tobacco
niece *n.* daughter of a brother or sister
nig´gard *n.* miser; **nig´gard-ly** *a.*
night *n.* time from sunset to sunrise; darkness
night´in-gale´ *n.* small European songbird of the thrush family
night´mare´ *n.* terrifying dream
ni´hil-ism *n.* belief in nothing; system seeking to overturn all existing institutions; **ni´hil-ist** *n.*
Ni´ke *n.* Greek goddess of victory; type of guided missile
nim´ble *a.* light and quick
nim´bus *n.* rain cloud; circle of light around the heads of saints
ninth *a.* last of nine; *n.* one of nine parts; musical interval of an octave and a second
nit *n.* egg of an insect
ni´trate´ *n.* salt of nitric acid
ni´tro-gen *n.* gaseous element forming nearly four-fifths of the atmospheric air
ni´tro-glyc´er-in *n.* explosive compound used to make dynamite
no-bil´i-ty *n.* superiority of rank, character, etc.; the aristocracy of a country
no´ble *a.* exalted in rank or birth; high in excellence; generous; *n.* person of exalted rank, peer; **no´ble-man** *n.*
noc-tur´nal *a.* happening by night; roaming at night
noc´turne´ *n.* pensive musical composition; serenade
nod *vi.* & *vt.* give a quick forward motion of the head, as from drowsiness; *n.* a bending forward of the head
node *n.* knot; knob; one of the two points at which the orbit of a planet intersects the ecliptic; point where a curve intersects itself; joint of a stem, or place where the leaves grow out; **nod´al** *a.*
nod´ule *n.* little lump
noise *n.* sound; din; rumor; **nois´y** *a.*
noi´some *a.* unhealthy; disgusting
no´mad´ *n.* one of a tribe of wanderers; **no-mad´ic** *a.*
no´men-cla´ture *n.* terminology
nom´i-nal *a.* existing in name only
nom´i-nate´ *vt.* name; appoint; propose by name; **nom´i-na´tion** *n.*;

nom´i-nee´ *n.*
non´a-ge-nar´i-an *n.* one ninety years old
non´cha-lance´ *n.* coolness; indifference; suave, casual composure; **non´cha-lant´** *a.*
non´com-mit´tal *a.* unwilling to express an opinion
non´con-duc´tor *n.* substance which does not transmit heat, electricity, etc.
non´con-form´ist *n.* one who does not conform
non´de-script´ *n.* person or thing not easily described or classed or of no account; *a.*
non-en´ti-ty *n.* thing not existing; person or thing of no importance
non´pa-reil´ *n.* person or thing without an equal
non-par´ti-san *a.* not controlled by or supporting any political party
non´plus´ *vt.* throw into perplexity
non´sec-tar´i-an *a.* not affiliated with any religion
non´sense *n.* absurd talk or actions
noon *n.* midday
noose *n.* loop with a running knot
norm *n.* rule or standard
nor´mal *a.* regular in form, condition, or function
north *n.* one of the four cardinal points of the comass, opposed to *south;* region lying to the north; **north´ern** *a.*
Nor-we´gian *a.* pertaining to Norway; *n.*
nose *n.* organ of smell; *vt.* smell; pry out
nos-tal´gia *n.* longing for some past time or condition; homesickness
nos´tril *n.* one of the apertures of the nose
nos´trum *n.* quack medicine; pet remedy for any problem
no´ta-ble *a.* remarkable; distinguished; **no´ta-bil´i ty** *n.*
no´ta-ry, no´ta-ry pub´lic *n.* officer who attests deeds, etc.
no-ta´tion *n.* system of signs or symbols
note *n.* mark, sign; brief remark; memorandum, short letter; mark representing a musical sound; paper promising payment; notice; fame; *vt.* make a note of; mark; denote
no´tice *n.* act of noting; information; warning; respectful treatment; *vt.* mark; see; attend to; make observations upon; treat with civility; **no´tice-a-ble** *a.*
no´ti-fy´ *vt.* give notice to; **no´ti-fi-ca´tion** *n.*
no´tion *n.* conception; opinion; disposition; small novelty
no-to´ri-ous *a.* infamous; widely known
nought *n.* nothing
noun *n.* substantive, word (such as *foot, foot´s, feet, feet´s*) having possessive and plural forms
nour´ish *vt.* feed; encourage; **nour´ish-ment** *n.*
no´va *n.* **(no´vas, no´vae)** star that flares up for a period and then recedes
nov´el *a.* new; strange; *n.* fictitious tale; **nov´el-ist** *n.*
nov´el-ty *n.* newness; anything new or strange
nov´ice *n.* beginner
nox´ious *a.* injurious, harmful
noz´zle *n.* spout
nu´cle-ar fis´sion *n.* the splitting of heavy atomic nuclei (as of uranium or plutonium) releasing enormous amounts of energy
nu-cle´ic acid *n.* one of the acids found in cell nuclei

nu´cle-us *n.* kernel or core of anything
nude *a.* naked; bare; **nu´di-ty** *n.*
nug´get *n.* lump
nui´sance *n.* that which annoys, harms, or is offensive
null *a.* void; **nul´li-fy** *vt.* render void
numb *a.* deprived of sensation; *vt.* deaden; stupefy; **numb´ness** *n.*
num´ber *n.* that by which things are counted or computed; collection of things; word or sign denoting a number; difference in words expressing singular or plural; *vt.* count; reckon as one of a multitude; mark with a number; amount to
nu´mer-al *n.* figure used to express a number (as 1, 2, or IV)
nu´mer-ous *a.* many
nu´mis-mat´ics *n.* science of coins and medals; **nu´mis-mat´ic** *a.*
nun *n.* female member of a religious order
nup´tial *a.* pertaining to marriage
nup´tials *n. pl.* wedding ceremony; marriage
nurse *n.* one who has the care of infants or the sick; *vt.* tend; nourish; cherish
nurs´er-y *n.* apartment for young children; place where trees and plants are cultivated
nur´ture *n.* act of nourishing; nourishment; *vt.* nourish; bring up
nu´tri-ent *a.* nourishing; *n.* food
nu´tri-ment *n.* food
nu-tri´tion *n.* process of promoting growth; food
nu-tri´tious, nu´tri-tive *a.* nourishing
ny´lon *n.* synthetic material made from coal, air, and water
nymph *n.* one of the goddesses of the trees, waters, and mountains

O

oak *n.* hardwood tree of many species; its timber
oar *n.* pole with a flat end for rowing
o-a´sis *n.* **(o-a´ses)** fertile spot in a desert
oat *n.* grass, the seeds of which are used as food
oath *n.* solemn statement with an appeal to God as witness; profane curse
ob´du-rate *n.* stubborn; hardhearted
o-be´di-ence *n.* state of being obedient; **o-be´di-ent** *a.* willing to obey, dutiful
o-bei´sance *n.* bow
ob´e-lisk *n.* tall, four-sided, tapering pillar
o-bese´ *a.* fat; **o-bes´-i-ty** *n.*
o-bey´ *vt.* yield or conform
o-bit´u-ar´y *n.* account of a deceased person or published notice of his death
ob-ject´ *vi.* disapprove of, find fault with, protest
ob´ject *n.* thing; motive; goal, aim
ob-jec´tion *n.* act of objecting; argument against; **ob-jec´tion-a-ble** *a.*
ob-jec´tive *a.* relating to an object; impartial, impersonal; *n.* goal, aim
ob-la´tion *n.* religious offering
ob´li-gate´ *vt.* bind to a duty; **ob´li-ga´tion** *n.*; **ob-lig´a-tor´y** *a.*
o-blige´ *vt.* constrain; bind by some favor rendered
ob-lique´ *a.* slanted; indirect
ob-lit´er-ate´ *vt.* wipe out, blot out; **ob-lit´er-a´tion** *n.*
ob-liv´i-on *n.* forgetfulness; careless disregard; **ob-liv´i-ous** *a.*
ob´long´ *a.* longer than broad; *n.*
ob´lo-quy´ *n.* reproachful language, abuse

ob-nox´ious *a.* offensive
ob-scene´ *a.* indecent, grossly lewd; **ob-scen´i-ty** *n.*
ob-scure´ *a.* darkened; not distinct; unknown; *vt.* darken; make less plain; **ob-scu´ri-ty** *n.*
ob´se-quies´ *n. pl.* funeral ceremonies
ob-se´qui-ous *a.* meanly servile
ob-serv´ance *n.* act of observing; attention; rite; **ob-ser´vant** *a.*
ob´ser-va´tion *n.* act or habit of observing; remark
ob-serv´a-to´ry *n.* place for making astronomical observations
ob-serve´ *vi.* & *vt.* take notice; remark
ob´so-les´cent *a.* going out of use
ob´so-lete´ *a.* antiquated
ob´sta-cle *n.* anything which stands in the way, hindrance
ob´sti-nate *a.* blindly or exceedingly firm, stubborn; **ob´sti-na-cy** *n.*
ob-strep´er-ous *n.* noisy; unruly
ob-struct´ *vt.* block, retard; **ob-struc´tion** *n.*
ob-tain´ *vt.* get, procure
ob-trude´ *vi.* & *vt.* thrust in, or enter, when not wanted; intrude; **ob-tru´sive** *a.*
ob-tuse´ *a.* blunt; stupid; greater than 90°
ob-verse´ *n.* face of a coin, etc.; counterpart of anything
ob´vi-ate *vt.* dispose of; prevent
ob´vi-ous *a.* manifest, plain, clear
oc-ca´sion *n.* occurrence; opportunity; cause
oc´ci-dent *n.* the west; **oc´ci-den´-tal** *a.*
oc-clude´ *vt.* absorb as a gas; obstruct
oc-cult´ *a.* hidden, mysterious, supernatural
oc´cu-py´ *vt.* seize or hold possession of; fill
oc´cu-pa´tion *n.* act of occupying; employment, vocation
oc-cur´ *vi.* come to mind; be found here and there; **oc-cur´rence** *n.*
o´cean *n.* vast expanse of salt water that covers the greater part of the globe
o´cean-ar´i-um *n.* aquarium exhibiting marine life, usually in a large pool
o´cean-og´ra-phy *n.* study of phenomena of the sea
oc´ta-gon´ *n.* plane figure of eight sides and eight angles
oc-tane´ *n.* colorless liquid hydrocarbon used in gasoline to prevent knocking
oc´tave *n.* eighth tone, or interval of twelve semitones
oc-tet´ *n.* group of eight musicians; musical composition in eight parts
oc´to-ge-nar´i-an *n.* person who is eighty years old
oc´to-pus *n.* **(oc´to-pus-es, oc´to-pi´, oc-top´o-des)** sea creature having eight arms
oc´u-lar *a.* pertaining to the eye
oc´u-list *n.* physician who treats diseases of the eye
odd *a.* not paired with another, single; left over; not exactly divisible by two; strange; **odd´-i-ty** *n.* strangeness; strange person or thing; **odds** *n. pl.* difference in favor of one against another; advantage
ode *n.* noble, dignified poem
o´di-um *n.* hatred; blame; **o´di-ous** *a.* hateful, offensive, repulsive
o´dor *n.* smell, perfume; **o´dor-ous** *a.*
of´fal *n.* refuse, rubbish
off´col´or *a.* mildly indecent or obscene

of-fend´ *vi.* & *vt.* displease or cause displeasure
of-fense´ *n.* act of offending or attacking; crime, sin
of-fen´sive *a.* giving offense; used in attack; making the first attack; *n.* act or attitude of attacking party
of´fer *vi.* & *vt.* propose, present; *n.* proposal
of´fice *n.* settled duty or employment; act of worship; place for business
of´fi-cer *n.* one who holds an office or responsibility
of-fi´cial *a.* done by authority; *n.* one who holds an office
of-fi´ci-ate´ *vi.* perform official duties
of-fi´cious *a.* meddlesome, too forward in offering service
off´set´ *n.* printing done by photolithography
off´set´ *vt.* compensate, make up for
off´spring´ *n.* child, children, progeny
o´gle *vi.* & *vt.* make eyes at; stare at insinuatingly
ohm *n.* unit of electrical resistance
oil *n.* greasy liquid; *vt.* smear or lubricate with oil
oint´ment *n.* salve
O.´K.´, o´kay´ *vt.* approve; *adv.* all right
o´kra *n.* annual plant whose pods are used for soup, gumbo, etc.
o´le-ag´i-nous *a.* oily
o´le-an´der *n.* poisonous evergreen shrub
o´le-o-mar´ *n.* margarine, a substitute for butter
ol-fac´to-ry, *a.* pertaining to the sense of smell
ol´i-garch´y *n.* government by a few
ol´ive *n.* tree cultivated for its oily fruit; its fruit; dull green color of unripe olive
om´buds-man´, om´buds-wo´man *n.* public official who investigates citizens´ complaints
om´e-let *n.* patty made with eggs
o´men *n.* supernatural warning of a future event
om´i-nous *a.* foreboding
o-mis´sion *n.* act or thing left out or not done
o-mit´ *vt.* leave out
om´ni-bus´ *n.* public vehicle, bus; anthology
om-nip´o-tence *n.* unlimited power, as of God
om-nip´o-tent *a.* all-powerful, almighty
om´ni-pres´ent *a.* universally present
om-nis´cience *n.* unlimited knowledge; **om-nis´cient** *a.* all-knowing
om-niv´o-rous *a.* all-devouring; feeding on both animal and vegetable food
on´er-ous *a.* burdensome
on´ion *n.* common garden plant having an edible, bulbous root
on´set´ *n.* beginning, as of an attack
on´slaught´ *n.* violent attack
o´nus *n.* burden
on´yx *n.* type of quartz with layers of different colors
ooze *vi.* leak out slowly
o-pac´i-ty *n.* opaqueness
o´pal *n.* precious stone, commonly of a milky hue
o-paque´ *a.* not transparent; **o-paque´ness** *n.*
op´er-a *n.* musical drama; theater for exhibiting operas; **op´er-at´ic** *a.*
op´er-ate´ *vi.* & *vt.* act; take effect; perform surgery
op´er-a´tion *n.* operating; agency, influence; surgery
op´er-a´tive *a.* exerting force; pro-

ducing effects

o´pi-ate *n.* narcotic made from opium

o-pin´ion *n.* conviction; judgment

o-pin´ion-at´ed *a.* obstinate

o´pi-um *n.* narcotic juice of the opium poppy

o-pos´sum *n.* four-legged American marsupial noted for its ability to play dead

op-po´nent *a.* opposing; *n.* enemy, adversary

op´por-tune´ *a.* timely

op´por-tu´ni-ty *n.* convenient time or occasion

op-pose´ *vt.* resist, compete with

op´po-site *a.* placed against; contrasted with; *n.*

op´po-si´tion *n.* hostility, resistance

op-press´ *vt.* treat unjustly or cruelly; **op-pres´sion** *n.* tyranny; **op-press´ive** *a.*; **op-press´or** *n.*

op-pro´bri-um *n.* disgrace, shame; **op-pro´bri-ous** *a.*

op´tic *a.* relating to sight, or to optics; **op´tic-al** *a.*

op-ti´cian *n.* one who makes or sells optical instruments

op´tics *n.* science of light, vision, etc.

op´ti-mism *n.* tendency to take the most hopeful view of matters; **op´ti-mist** *n.*

op´tion *n.* right of choosing, choice; right to sell or buy at a future time and at a fixed price; **op´tion-al** *a.*

op-tom´e-try *n.* practice of examining the vision and fitting glasses for sight correction

op´u-lence *n.* riches, wealth; **op´u-lent** *a.*

or´a-cle *n.* answer given by the gods; one famed for wisdom; **o-rac´u-lar** *a.* delivering oracles; ambiguous

o´ral *a.* spoken

or´ange *n.* tree bearing a gold-colored fruit; its fruit; color composed of red and yellow; *a.* orange-colored

o-rang´ou-tang´ *n.* type of anthropoid ape

o-ra´tion *n.* formal public speech

or´a-tor *n.* public speaker, man of eloquence; **or´a-tor´i-cal** *a.*

or´a-to´ry *n.* art of speaking in public; eloquence

or´bit *n.* path, as of a celestial body, electron, missile, etc.

or´chard *n.* garden of fruit trees; fruit trees, collectively

or´ches-tra *n.* group of musicians playing together; part of the theater where musicians play; main floor of a theater; **or-ches´tral** *a.*

or´chid *n.* plant with beautiful flowers of various shapes

or-dain´ *vt.* appoint, decree; invest with ministerial functions

or-deal´ *n.* severe trial, test of endurance

or´der *n.* regular arrangement; method; command; class; religious or other fraternity; scientific division of objects; *vt.* arrange; command; **or´der-ly** *a.*

or´di-nal *a.* showing order or succession (as first, second, third, etc.); *n.*

or´di-nance *n.* city law

or´di-nar´y *a.* usual, common, commonplace; **or´di-na´ri-ly** *adv.*

or´di-na´tion *n.* act of investing with ministerial functions

ord´nance *n.* artillery and artillery supplies

ore *n.* metal in its unreduced, natural state

or´gan *n.* instrument of operation in government, communication, etc.;

part of a body (such as heart, brain, etc.) by which a particular natural function is carried on; musical keyboard instrument operating by compressed air; **or´gan´ic** *a.*

or´gan-ism *n.* organic structure; living being

or´gan-ist *n.* one who plays the organ

or´gan-ize´ *vt.* arrange, formulate; **or´gan-i-za´tion** *n.*

or´gy *n.* revelry; over-indulgence in anything

or´i-ent *a.* eastern; *n.* the east, esp. the countries of Asia; **or´i-en´tal** *a.*

or´i-fice *n.* mouth, opening

or´i-gin *n.* beginning, source

o-rig´i-nal *a.* first in order or existence; not copied, not translated; *n.*

o-rig´i-nate´ *vi.* & *vt.* produce for the first time, start, begin; **o-rig´i-na´-tor** *n.*

or´i-son *n.* prayer

Or´lon´ *n. tr.* synthetic fiber made by DuPont

or´na-ment *n.* anything adding grace or beauty; *vt.* adorn; **or-na-ment´al** *a.*; **or´na-men-ta´tion** *n.*

or-nate´ *a.* overdecorated

or´ni-thol´o-gy *n.* study of birds

o´ro-tund *a.* rich and musical in delivery; pompous

or´phan *n.* child bereft of parent or parents; *a.*; **or´phan-age** *n.* home for orphans

or´tho-don´tics *n.* branch of dentistry that deals with correcting irregularities

or´tho-dox´ *a.* comforming to doctrine

or´tho-e´py *n.* pronunciation; study of standard pronunciation

or-thog´ra-phy *n.* correct or standard spelling; **or´tho-graph´ic** *a.*

or´tho-pe´dics *n.* treatment of deformities

os´cil-late´ *vi.* vibrate; **os´cil-la´tion** *n.*

os´cu-late´ *vt.* kiss; touch, as two curves; **os´cu-la´tion** *n.*

os´si-fy´ *vi.* & *vt.* turn into bone; **os´si-fi-ca´tion** *n.*

os-ten´si-ble *a.* professed, apparent

os´ten-ta´ion *n.* pretentious display; **os´ten-ta´tious** *a.*

os´te-ol´o-gy *n.* study of the bones; **os´te-ol´o-gist** *n.*

os´te-o-path´ *n.* one who practices osteopathy

os´te-op´a-thy *n.* treatment of disease by manipulation of bones, muscles, etc.

os´tra-cize´ *vt.* exclude from society; **os´tra-cism** *n.*

os´trich *n.* largest of birds, remarkable for its speed and its plumes

oth´er-di-rect´ed *a.* guided by the attitudes of the group rather than by personal or ethical considerations

ot´ter *n.* weasel-like aquatic animal

ounce *n.* sixteenth part of a pound avoirdupois

oust *vt.* eject, expel

out´cast´ *a.* exiled, rejected; *n.* person exiled from society

out´come *n.* consequence; result

out´er *a.* external

out´fit´ *n.* equipment; costume

out´ing *n.* excursion

out´land´ish *a.* foreign, strange; rude

out´law´ *n.* person deprived of the protection of the law; *vt.*

out´lay´ *n.* expenditure

out´let´ *n.* passage out; market

out´line´ *n.* outer or exterior line; sketch, rough draft; *vt.* delineate, sketch, draft

out´look´ *n.* prospect

out´ly´ing *a.* on the exterior or frontier
out´put´ *n.* energy derived from a machine; yield or product from any device, machine, or industry
out´rage´ *n.* abuse; wanton mischief; *vt.* abuse, maltreat, injure by violence; **out-ra´geous** *a.*
out´stand´ing *a.* remaining unpaid; distinguished
out-strip´ *vt.* outrun
out-weigh´ *vt.* exceed in weight or importance
out-wit´ *vt.* defeat by cunning
o´val *a.* egg-shaped; *n.*
o´va-ry *n.* female organ which produces the egg
o-va´tion *n.* outburst of popular applause
ov´en *n.* apparatus for baking or drying
o´ver-alls´ *n.* loose trousers worn over others for protection
o´ver-bear´ing *a.* domineering, bullying
o´ver-cast´ *vt.* cloud; *a.*; *n.*
o´ver-charge´ *vt.* charge too much
o´ver-coat´ *n.* coat worn over other clothes
o´ver-come´ *vi.* & *vt.* get the better of, conquer
o´ver-do´ *vi.* & *vt.* do too much; exaggerate
o´ver-due´ *a.* beyond the time at which something is payable
o´ver-flow *vi.* & *vt.* flow over, flood; *n.*
o´ver-hang´ *vi.* & *vt.* project over
o´ver-haul´ *vt.* examine and repair; overtake; *n.*
o´ver-head´ *n.* general expenses (such as rent, utilities, etc.) in running a business
o´ver-hear´ *vt.* hear by accident
o´ver-kill´ *vt.* destroy with more force than required; *n.*
o´ver-lap´ *vt.* lap or hang over
o´ver-load´ *vt.* burden down excessively; *n.*
o´ver-look´ *vt.* neglect; ignore or wink at a fault
o´ver-night´ *a.* & *adv.* for the space of a night
o´ver-pass´ *n.* elevated road built to let traffic cross above other traffic
o´ver-rate´ *vt.* rate or value too high
o´ver-rule´ *vt.* reject
o´ver-run´ *vi.* & *vt.* run or spread over
o´ver-see´ *vt.* superintend; **o´ver-seer** *n.*
o´ver-shoot´ *vt.* shoot beyond; pass swiftly over
o´ver-sight´ *n.* failure to notice
o´ver-sleep´ *vi.* sleep too long
o´ver-step´ *vt.* exceed
o-vert´ *a.* apparent, open
o´ver-take´ *vt.* catch up with; catch up with and exceed
o´ver-throw´ *vt.* upset, demolish
o´ver-time´ *n.* extra work, done beyond regular hours
o´ver-ture *n.* proposal; musical composition opening an opera or ballet
o´ver-turn´ *vt.* subvert, ruin, overthrow; turn over
o´ver-view´ *n.* broad or overall picture
o´ver-ween´ing *a.* arrogant
o´ver-whelm´ *vt.* overspread and crush
o´ver-wrought´ *a.* overexcited
owe *vi.* & *vt.* be bound to pay, give, or do
owl *n.* nocturnal bird with large eyes and hooting cry
own *vt.* acknowledge; possess, have a rightful title to; **own´er** *n.*; **own´er-ship´** *n.*

ox *n.* **(ox´en)** male bovine quadruped, used as a beast of burden
ox´y-gen *n.* gaseous element supporting life and combustion
oys´ter *n.* edible, bivalve shellfish
o´zone´ *n.* blue gas that is a form of oxygen
o-zo´no-sphere´ *n.* layer of concentrated ozone in the earth´s atmosphere

P

pace *n.* step, measure of 30 inches; gait; mode of stepping in horses, amble; *vt.* measure by steps
pace´set´ter *n.* someone or something that sets an example followed by others
pach´y-derm´ *n.* mammal with a thick skin, as the elephant
pa-cif´ic *a.* appeasing, tranquil; **pac´i-fi-ca´tion** *n.*
pac´i-fy´ *vt.* make peaceful, calm, soothe
pac´i-fism *n.* refusal to take part in war or war preparations
pack *n.* bundle; complete set of cards; group of hounds hunting together; *vt.* press together and fasten up; place in close order
pack´age *n.* bundle, bale
pack´et *n.* small package
pact *n.* contract
pad *n.* soft cushion; package of paper for writing upon; *vt.* stuff, furnish with pads or padding
pad´ding *n.* material for stuffing
pad´dle *vi.* & *vt.* row; *n.* short oar
pad´lock´ *n.* lock with a link to pass through a staple; *vt.* fasten with a padlock
pae´an *n.* song of triumph or joy
pa´gan *n.* heathen; *a.* heathen, heathenish
page *n.* one side of a sheet of paper; attendant; *vt.* call for someone in a public place
pag´eant *n.* elaborate parade, outdoor theatrical entertainment, or other public exhibition; **pag´eant-ry** *n.*
pa-go´da *n.* graceful Oriental tower, often a temple
pail *n.* open vessel for holding liquids
pain *n.* physical or mental suffering; *vt.* distress, hurt; **pain´ful** *a.*
paint *vt.* color; draw with colors;describe; *vi.* practice painting; *n.* coloring substance
pair *n.* set of things used together (as a pair of gloves); two things used or belonging together; *vt.* join in couples
pa-ja´mas, py-ja´mas *n. pl.* sleeping garments
pal´ace *n.* splendid building
pal´ate *n.* roof of the mouth; taste, relish; **pal´at-a-ble** *a.* tasty. edible
pa-la´tial *a.* magnificent, like a palace
pa-lav´er *n.* idle talk
pale *a.* of faint hue; *vi.* & *vt.* make or grow pale
pal´ette *n.* board on which a painter mixes his colors
pal´i-sade´ *n.* fence of pointed stakes; *vt.* surround or fortify with a palisade
pall *vi.* & *vt.* make or become tasteless; cloy
pall´bear´er *n.* one who helps bear the coffin at a funeral
pal´let *n.* makeshift bed on the floor
pal´li-ate´ *vt.* excuse, ease, make better; **pal´li-a´tion** *n.*; **pal´li-a´-tive** *a.*
pal´lid *a.* pale; **pal´lor** *n.* paleness
palm *n.* inner part of the hand; trop-

ical tree; *vt.* conceal in the palm of the hand; trick, defraud

pal´pa-ble *a.* able to be felt; readily perceived

pal´pi-ta´tion *n.* throbbing, pulsation; **pal´pi-tate´** *vi.*

pal´sy *n.* paralysis, total or partial

pal´try *a.* worthless, of no account

pam´per *vt.* overindulge a person or an appetite

pam´phlet *n.* small book, leaflet

pan *n.* broad, shallow vessel; *vi.* & *vt.* wash, as gold from dirt

pan´a-ce´a *n.* universal cure-all

pan´cre-as *n.* gland which secretes a digestive fluid into the intestines

pan´de-mo´ni-um *n.* place or state of noisy disorder

pan´der *vi.* & *vt.* minister to the base desires of others, pimp; *n.*

pane *n.* plate of glass

pan´el *n.* section of a wall, window, etc., often with raised borders; list of those summoned as jurors, jury; small discussion group; *vt.* furnish with panels

pang *n.* momentary pain

pan´ic *n.* extreme or sudden fright

pan´o-ply *n.* full suit of armor; any imposing array

pan´o-ra´ma *n.* complete or sweeping view of a thing; **pan´o-ram´ic** *a.*

pant *vi.* & *vt.* gasp; desire

pan´to-mime´ *n.* entertainment acted without words; *vi.* & *vt.*

pan´try *n.* room or closet for storing provisions

pants *n. pl.* trousers

pa´pa-cy *n.* office or authority of the pope; **pa´pal** *a.*

pa´per *n.* material made from pulp of wood, rags, etc.; document; newspaper, paper-hangings; *vt.* cover with paper

pa-pier´-mâché *n.* pulped paper molded into various shapes

pap-ri´ka *n.* red seasoning made from dried peppers

par *n.* equality of nominal value and market value

par´a-ble *n.* fable or allegory illustrating a truth

par´a-chute´ *n.* apparatus for emergency descent through the air

pa-rade´ *n.* arrangement of troops for display; public procession; *vi.* & *vt.* show off; march in procession

par´a-dise´ *n.* garden of Eden; heaven

par´a-dox´ *n.* statement which seems to contradict itself, but which may be true; **par´a-dox´i-cal** *a.*

par´af-fin *n.* wax-like substance obtained from petroleum, coal, etc.

par´a-gon´ *n.* model or example

par´a-graph´ *n.* distinct part of a discourse or writing; mark (¶) used to denote the beginning of a paragraph; *vt.* divide into paragraphs

par´al lel´ *a.* extended in the same direction and equidistant in all parts; like, similar; *n.* line always equidistant from another; likeness; comparison; *vt.* place so as to be parallel; correspond to

pa-ral´y-sis *n.* loss of the power of motion

par´a-lyt´ic *a.* afflicted with paralysis; **par´a-lyze´** *vt.*

par´a-med´ic *n.* auxiliary medical worker

par´a-mount´ *a.* chief

par´a-noi´a *n.* form of insanity characterized by delusions, as of persecution

par´a-pher-na´li-a *n. pl.* trappings, equipment

par´a-phrase´ *n.* rendering something in other words; *vt.*

par´a-psy-chol´o-gy *n.* branch of psychology that deals with psychic experience

par´a-site´ *n.* hanger-on, toady; plant or animal living on another; **par´a-sit´ic** *a.*

par´a-sol´ *n.* sunshade

par´a-troops´ *n. pl.* soldiers trained to jump from planes for the purpose of seizing key points; **par´a-troop´er** *n.*

par´cel *n.* package, bundle; *vt.* divide into portions

parch *vi.* & *vt.* scorch; dry and shrivel

parch´ment *n.* animal skin prepared for writing; fine writing paper

par´don *vt.* forgive; *n.* forgiveness, remission of a punishment; **par´don-a-ble** *a.*

pare *vt.* cut the rind, etc., off; diminish by little bits

par´ent *n.* father or mother; **pa-ren´tal** *a.*

par´ent-age *n.* birth, descent; parenthood

pa-ren´the-sis *n.* **(pa-ren´the-ses)** word or words inserted as an explanation; one of the two marks () used to indicate this in writing; **par´en-thet´ic** *a.*

pa-ri´ah *n.*outcast from society

par´ish *n.* ecclesiastical district; in Louisiana, a county; **pa-rish´ion-er** *n.*

par´i-ty *n.* state of being equal; guaranteed support for farm products based on difference between cost of living and income actually received; outmoded theory in physics that any substance and its mirror-image counterpart have same physical properties

par´lance *n.* diction, idiom

par´ley *vi.* speak, confer; *n.* talk; conference with an enemy

par´lia-ment *n.* legislature, as of Great Britain; **par´lia-men´ta-ry** *a.*

pa-ro´chi-al *a.* relating to a parish; limited, restricted, narrow

par´o-dy *n.* caricature, as of a poem; *vt.*

pa-role´ *n.* early release from prison, as for good behavior; *vt.* release on parole; **pa-rol´ee** *n.*

par´ox-ysm *n.* fit; **par´ox-ys´mal** *a.*

par´quet´ *n.* floor space of a theater between the orchestra and dress-circle; floor laid with wood in geometric designs

par´ri-cide´ *n.* murder of one´s parent or parents; person who slays his parents

par´rot *n.* tropical bird with brilliant plumage and hooked bill

par´ry *vt.* ward off

par´si-mo´ni-ous *a.* stingy

par´son *n.* clergyman

part *n.* portion; constituent; *vt.* divide, separate

par´tial *a.* relating to a part only; inclined to favor one party; **par´tial-ly** *adv.*

par-tic´i-pant *a.* sharing; *n.* partaker

par-tic´i-pate´ *vi.* have a share in

par´ti-cle *n.* little part, fragment

par-tic´u-lar *a.* pertaining to a single person or thing; worthy of special attention; exact; nice in taste; *n.* distinct point; **par-tic´u-lars** *n. pl.* details; **par-tic´u-lar´i-ty** *n.*

par´ti-san *n.* adherent of a party; *a.* adhering to a party

par-ti´tion n, division, separation; wall between apartments; *vt.* divide into parts

part´ner *n.* associate, esp. in business

par´ty *n.* organization of persons to promote certain principles; company, assembly; social entertainment

par´ve-nu´ *n.* person newly risen in wealth or position; upstart

pas´chal *a.* pertaining to the Passover or to Easter

pass *vi.* move; circulate, be regarded; decline to play; *vt.* go by, over, through, etc.; enact; *n.* narrow defile; thrust, movement of the hand; free ticket; **pass the buck** shift responsibility

pas´sage *n.* journey, way; small portion, as of a book

pas-sé´ *a.* past, gone out of use

pas´sen-ger *n.* traveler on a public conveyance

pas´sim *adv.* here and there

pas´sion *n.* strong feeling; ardent love; suffering, esp. the death of Christ; **pas´sion-ate** *a.*

pas´sive *a.* unresisting, not acting; complacent, not opposing; patient

pass´port´ *n.* document giving permission to travel in a foreign country

paste *n.* dough; soft-solid glue or adhesive; kind of glass for making artificial gems; *vt.* fasten with paste

paste´board´ *n.* stiff board made of paper

pas´tel´ *n.* colored crayon; picture drawn with pastels

pas´time´ *n.* amusement

pas´tor *n.* clergyman

pas´to-ral *a.* relating to shepherds or to the pastor of a church; *n.* poem describing country life

pas´try *n.* desserts or articles of food made with dough

pas´ture *n.* grass for grazing; ground covered with grass for grazing; *vi.* & *vt.* graze

patch *vt.* mend, as with a piece of cloth; repair clumsily; *n.* small piece, as of cloth; small piece of ground

pat´ent *a.* evident, public; *n.* official document, conferring the sole right, for a term of years, to an invention; *vt.* grant or secure by patent

pa-ter´nal *a.* fatherly; **pa-ter´ni-ty** *n.* fatherhood; male parentage

pa´ter-nos´ter *n.* the Lord´s prayer

pa-thet´ic *a.* affecting the emotions, sad

pa-thol´o-gy *n.* science of diseases; **pa-thol´o-gist** *n.*

pa´thos *n.* that which excites the emotions, as pity, sorrow, grief, etc.

pa´tient *a.* sustaining trouble unflinchingly; persevering; *n.* person under medical treatment; **pa´-tience** *n.* quality of endurance

pa´tri-arch´ *n.* ruler of a family or church

pa-tri´cian *n.* nobleman, aristocrat

pat´ri-cide´ *n.* murder of a father

pat´ri-mo´ny *n.* heritage

pa´tri-ot *n.* one who loves and serves his country; **pa´tri-ot´ic** *a.*; **pa´tri-ot-ism** *n.*

pa-trol´ *vi.* & *vt.* go the rounds; *n.*

pa´tron *n.* protector; sponsor; customer

pa´tron-age *n.* support given by a patron; **pa´tron-ize** *vt.*

pat´ro-nym´ic *n.* surname taken from father´s given name

pat´ter *vi.* strike with a quick succession of sounds, as rain; chatter; *n.*

pat´tern *n.* model

pau´ci-ty *n.* scantiness

pau´per *n.* one supported by charity; **pau´per-ize´** *vt.*

pause *n.* temporary stop; *vi.* make a pause

pave *vt.* lay with stone; prepare; **pave´ment** *n.*

pa-vil´ion *n.* tent; ornamental building open on all sides, as in a park

pawn *n.* something given as security for payment; one of the pieces in chess; *vt.* give in pledge; **pawn´-bro´ker** *n.* person who lends money on pledges

pay *vt.* **(paid)** satisfy, compensate, discharge (a debt); *vi.* recompense; *n.* wages, reward; **pay´a-ble** *a.*; **pay´ment** *n.* act of paying; recompense

pay´load´ *n.* cargo or explosive carried by a rocket; cargo

pay-o´la *n. col.* secret payment made for promotion favors

pea *n.* common vegetable whose seeds grow in pods

peace *n.* state of quiet, rest; international quiet; **peace´a-ble** *a.*; **peace´ful** *a.*

Peace´ Corps´ *n.* U. S. agency providing skilled workers for developing countries

pea´cock´ *n.* large bird, remarkable for the, beauty of its plumage

peak *n.* point, summit

peal *n.* loud sound, as of thunder or bells; *vi.*

pea´nut´ *n.* plant whose nut ripens underground

pearl *n.* gem found in the pearl oyster

peas´ant *n.* one whose occupation is rural labor

pe-can´ *n.* tall tree or its edible, smooth-shelled nut

pe-cul´iar *a.* strange, unusual; **pe-cu´li-ar´i-ty** *n.*

pe-cu´ni-ar´y *a.* pertaining to money

ped´a-gog´ic *a.* relating to teaching; **ped´a-go´gy** *n.* science of teaching

ped´a-gogue´ *n.* teacher

ped´al *n.* treadle; *vi.* & *vt.* work a pedal

ped´ant *n.* one making a vain display of learning; **pe-dan´tic** *a.*; **ped´ant-ry** *n.*

ped´es-tal *n.* base of a pillar, column, etc.

pe-des´tri-an *a.* going on foot; *n.* one who journeys on foot

pe´di-a-tri´cian *n.* physician who specializes in the care of babies and children

ped´i-gree´ *n.* lineage

peek *vi.* peep, look at slyly

peel *vt.* strip off the skin or bark; *vi.* come off, as dead skin; *n.* skin, rind

peep *vi.* chirp or cry; peek, look at through a small crack, etc.; begin to appear; *n.* cry of a chick; glimpse; **peeping Tom** *n.* voyeur

peer *n.* equal; member of the House of Lords; *vi.* look at narrowly or closely; **peer group** *n.* particular social group against which anyone measures himself; **peer´less** *a.* having no equal

peeve *n.* trifling complaint, gripe

pee´vish *a.* fretful

pel´i-can *n.* large waterfowl having an enormous bill

pel-la´gra *n.* disease caused by improper diet

pell´-mell´ *adv.* in headlong hurry or confusion

pelt *n.* hide with the hair or wool on; *vt.* strike with pellets

pel´vis *n.* bony cavity for the support of the abdominal viscera; **pel´vic** *a.*

pe´nal *a.* pertaining to punishment

pen´al-ty *n.* punishment
pen´ance *n.* self-imposed punishment, repentance; R. C. sacrament
pen´chant *n.* inclination, taste, bias
pen´cil *n.* pointed instrument for writing or drawing without ink; *vt.* write, sketch, or mark with a pencil
pend *vi.* await adjustment
pend´ant *n.* anything hanging
pend´ent *a.* hanging; projecting
pen´du-lum *n.* a weight hung so that it swings freely
pen´e-trate´ *vt.* pierce; affect; *vi.* make way, pass inwards; **pen´e-tra´tion** *n.* act of piercing; discernment
pen´guin *n.* short-winged, aquatic bird
pen-i-cil´lin *n.* antibiotic obtained from certain molds
pen-in´su-la *n.* projecting body of land nearly surrounded by water
pen´i-tence *n.* state of being penitent
pen´i-tent *a.* suffering or sorrowing for sin, repentant; *n.* one grieving for sin
pen´i-ten´tia-ry *n.* prison
pen´nant *n.* streamer, small flag
pen´ni-less *a.* without money
pen´ny *n.* U.S. cent
pen´sion *n.* regular payment, as for past services; *vt.* grant a pension to
pen´ta-gon´ *n.* plane figure having five angles and five sides; **pen-tag´-o-nal** *a.*
pent´house´ *n.* rooftop apartment
pe-nu´ri-ous *a.* stingy
pen´u-ry *n.* poverty
peo´ple *n.* nation, race, tribe; inhabitants; *vt.* stock with inhabitants
pep´per *n.* herb whose fruit has a hot, pungent taste; *vt.* sprinkle with pepper; pelt
pep´sin *n.* digestive enzyme in the gastric juice
pep´tic *a.* promoting or pertaining to digestion
per *prep.* by means of, for each, by the
per-ceive´ *vt.* notice; understand; **per-ceiv´a-ble** *a.*
per-cent´age *n.* rate or proportion by the hundred
per-cep´tion *n.* perceiving, discernment
per´co-late´ *vi.* & *vt.* strain through, filter
per-cus´sion *n.* collision, striking, or tapping (as of cymbals)
per-di´tion *n.* utter loss or ruin; eternal death
per-emp´to-ry *a.* decisive, final; imperious, dictatorial
per-en´ni-al *a.* lasting through the year; perpetual; *n.* plant living or reviving from year to year
per´fect *a.* flawless, unblemished; *vt.* finish, make perfect; **per-fect´i-ble** *a.*
per´fi-dy *n.* treachery; **per-fid´i-ous** *a.*
per´fo-rate´ *vt.* bore through, pierce; **per´fo-ra´tion** *n.*
per-form´ *vi.* & *vt.* do; carry out; act, play; **per-form´ance** *n.* performing, carrying out of something; something done; public exhibition
per´fume´ *n.* sweet-smelling substance
per-func´to-ry *a.* mechanically or carelessly performed
per´il *n.* danger, risk; **per´il-ous** *a.*
per-im´e-ter *n.* boundary of any plane figure; the sum of all its sides
pe´ri-od *n.* time in which something is performed; stated and recurring interval of time; mark at the end of a sentence; **pe´ri-od´ic** *a.*

pe´ri-od´i-cal *n.* publication, which appears at regular intervals
pe-riph´er-y *n.* circumference; surface of a body
per´i-scope´ *n.* instrument used in submarines to see around or above an obstacle
per´ish *vi.* die, suffer destruction; **per´ish-a-ble** *a.*
per´jure *vt.* make (oneself) guilty of a false oath; **per´jur-er** *n.*; **per´ju-ry** *n.* false swearing
per´ma-nent *a.* lasting, fixed; **per´-ma-nence** *n.*
per´me-ate´ *vt.* pass through the pores of, penetrate
per-mis´si-ble *a.* allowable; **per-mis´sion** *n.* liberty or leave granted; **per-mis´sive** *a.*
per-mit´ *vt.* give leave to; consent to; afford means
per´mit *n.* permission, warrant; license
per´mu-ta´tion *n.* change; arrangement of things in every possible order
per-ni´cious *a.* destructive, noxious
per´o-ra´tion *n.* conclusion of a speech
per´pen-dic´u-lar *a.* exactly upright; at right angles to any given line or surface; *n.* perpendicular line or plane
per´pe-trate´ *vt.* perform, commit; **per´pe-tra´tion** *n.*; **per´pe-tra´tor** *n.*
per-pet´u-al *a.* never ceasing; **per-pet´u-ate´** *vt.* make perpetual
per´pe-tu´i-ty *n.* endless duration; something perpetual
per-plex´ *vt.* make hard to understand; puzzle; **per-plex´i-ty** *n.*
per´qui-site *n.* allowance beyond a fixed salary
per´se-cute´ *vt.* oppress, harass; **per´se-cu´tion** *n.*
per´se-vere´ *vi.* persist in; **per´se-ver´ance** *n.*
per-sim´mon *n.* hardwood tree bearing plum-like fruit
per-sist´ *vi.* persevere in; **per-sist´-ence**, **per-sist´en-cy** *n.* perseverance; **per-sist´ent** *a.*
per´son *n.* character; individual; outward appearance, body
per´son-age *n.* distinguished person
per´son-al *a.* pertaining to a person, his private concerns, or external appearance; done in person
per´son-al´i-ty *n.* individuality; combination of emotional traits in a person
per-son´i-fy´ *vt.* ascribe the qualities of a person to an inanimate object; impersonate; **per-son´i-fi-ca´tion** *n.*
per´son-nel´ *n.* all the employees of a certain office, store, etc.
per-spec´tive *n.* view, vista; art of portraying objects to suggest depth
per´spi-ca´cious *a.* of acute understanding
per-spire´ *vi.* & *vt.* sweat; **per´spi-ra´tion** *n.*
per-suade´ *vt.* influence by argument, etc., induce; convince; **per-sua´sion** *n.*; **per-sua´sive** *a.*
per-tain´ *vi.* belong or relate to
per´ti-na´cious *a.* clinging obstinately to an opinion or purpose; **per´ti-nac´i-ty** *n.* firmness, tenacity
per´ti-nent *a.* relevant, clearly pertaining to a subject; **per´ti-nence** *n.*
per-turb´ *vt.* disturb, agitate; **per´-tur-ba´tion** *n.*
pe-ruse´ *vt.* read attentively; **pe-rus´al** *n.*
per-vade´ *vt.* penetrate, spread all

over

per-verse´ *a.* deviant, obstinate; **per-ver´si-ty** *n.*

per-vert´ *vt.* turn from the right course, corrupt; **per´vert** *n.*; **per-ver´sion** *n.*

pes´si-mism *n.* doctrine that the world is entirely evil; looking at the dark side of things; **pes´si-mist** *n.*; **pes´si-mis´tic** *a.*

pes´ti-cide´ *n.* chemical for killing insects

pes´ti-lence *n.* contagious, deadly disease

pes´tle *n.* instrument for pounding anything in a mortar

pet *n.* tame animal adopted into the family; favorite child; fit of peevishness; *vt.* treat as a pet; fondle; *a.* favorite

pet´al *n.* leaf-like segment of a flower

pe-ti´tion *n.* request, prayer, supplication; *vt.* present a petition

pet´ri-fy´ *vt.* turn into stone; **pet´ri-fac´tion** *n.*

pe-tro´le-um *n.* crude oil

pet´ti-coat´ *n.* underskirt

pet´ty *a.* small, contemptible

pet´u-lant *a.* peevish, fretful; **pet´u-lance** *n.*

pew *n.* enclosed seat in a church

pew´ter *n.* alloy of tin and lead

phan´tasm *n.* fancied vision; illusion, specter

phan´tom *n.* apparition, ghost

Phar´i-see´ *n.* one of a Jewish sect marked by its strict observance of law and religious ordinances

phar´ma-cy *n.* art of or place for preparing and mixing medicines; **phar´ma-ceu´tic** *a.*

phar´ynx *n.* portion of the throat between mouth and larynx

phase *n.* appearance or state at a given time; stage of growth

pheas´ant *n.* chicken-like game bird

phe-nom´e-non *n.* **(phe-nom´e-na)** anything perceived by the senses; any fact or happening, esp. if unusual; **phe-nom´e-nal** *a.*

phi-lan´thro-py *n.* love of mankind, esp. as shown by good works; **phi-lan´thro-pist** *n.*

phi-lat´e-list *n.* one who collects postage stamps

phi-lol´o-gy *n.* study of language; literature and civilization, esp. of Greece and Rome; **phi-lol´o-gist** *n.*

phi-los´o-pher *n.* one versed in philosophy; one who acts calmly and rationally; **phil´o-soph´ic** *a.*; **phi-los´o-phize´** *vi.*

phi-los´o-phy *n.* study of the principles of any activity (as reality, ethics, ultimate causes, etc.); practical wisdom

phlegm *n.* mucus; sluggishness

phleg´mat´ic *a.* calm; sluggish, indifferent

pho-net´ic *a.* pertaining to the voice, the raw sounds of a language, or the symbols used to represent these sounds; **pho-net´ics** *n.* study of the raw sounds of a language

pho´no-graph´ *n.* instrument by which sounds can be recorded and mechanically reproduced

phos´pho-rus *n.* poisonous element that is slightly luminous

pho´to-cop´y *n.* instantaneous photographic copy of graphic material

pho´to-e-lec´tric cell´ *n.* cell or vacuum tube in which an electric current is generated by light

pho´to fin´ish *n.* close race, in which winner is determined by photograph

pho´to-gen´ic *a.* anything which

photographs well
pho´to-graph´ *n.* picture produced by photography; *vi.* & *vt.*; **pho-tog´rapher** *n.*; **pho´to-graph´ic** *a.*
pho-tog´ra-phy *n.* art of producing pictures by the action of light on chemically prepared surfaces
pho´to-stat´ *n.* *tr.* photographic copying device; anything copied by Photostat; **pho´to-stat´ic** *a.*
phrase *n.* fragment of a sentence; *vt.* put into words
phra´se-ol´o-gy *n.* style of expression; collection of phrases
phys´i-cal *a.* pertaining to nature or natural objects; pertaining to the body
phy-si´cian *n.* one skilled in the art of healing
phys´ics *n.* science of the phenomena of nature; **phys´i-cist** *n.*
phys´i-og´no-my *n.* supposed art of knowing a person´s disposition from his features; expression of countenance
phys´i-ol´o-gy *n.* study of the functions of living organs, etc.; **phys´i-o-log´i-cal** *a.*; **phys´i-ol´o-gist** *n.*
phy-sique´ *n.* physical structure, esp.of the body
pi-an´o, pi-an´o-for´te *n.* musical instrument with wires struck by hammers moved by keys; **pi-an´ist** *n.*
pi-az´za *n.* porch, veranda
pi´ca *n.* size of type
pick *vt.* open with a pointed instrument (as a lock); pluck, gather; select; *n.* sharp-pointed instrument; choice
pick´et *n.* pointed stake; *vt.* protest against an employer, as by carrying placards
pick´le *n.* food preserved in vinegar; *vt.* preserve with vinegar
pick´pock´et *n.* one who steals from other people´s pockets
pick´up´ *n.* acceleration; small truck; device for converting light or sound into electrical impulses; woman picked up for immoral purposes
pic´nic´ *n.* excursion-dinner in the country; *vi.* go on a picnic
pic-to´ri-al *a.* relating to pictures; illustrated
pic´ture *n.* representation; *vt.* paint represent, describe vividly
pic´ture-phone´ *n.* visual telephone system that transmits pictures of speakers
pic´tur-esque´ *a.* resembling a picture, hence charming
piece *n.* part; single article; gun
piece´meal´ *a.* made of pieces; *adv.* in pieces, little by little
pier *n.* stonework supporting an arch, etc.; wharf
pierce *vi.* & *vt.* make a hole through; force a way into
pi´e-ty *n.* dutifulness, devoutness, veneration
pig *n.* young swine; oblong mass of unforged metal
pig´eon *n.* domestic bird
pig´eon-hole´ *n.* division of a case for papers, etc.; *vt.* file away
pig´gy-back´ *a.* shipped by railroad flatcar
pig´ment *n.* coloring material
pile *n.* heap, mass; *vt.* heap up, amass
pil´fer *vi.* & *vt.* steal
pil´grim *n.* one who travels to a sacred place; wanderer
pil´grim-age *n.* journey to a sacred place
pil´lage *n.* act of plundering; *vt.* plunder
pil´lar *n.* column, prop

pil'low *n.* cushion to support the head

pi'lot *n.* one who conducts ships in and out of a harbor, etc.; guide; aviator; *vt.*

pin *n.* sharp-pointed instrument for fastening articles together; peg; *vt.* fasten with a pin

pin'a-fore' *n.* child's apron

pin'cers *n. pl.* instrument for seizing small articles

pinch *vt.* squeeze; *vi.* bear or press hard; *n.* act of squeezing; amount which can be taken up with the compressed fingers

pine *n.* cone-bearing, resinous evergreen tree

pine'ap'ple *n.* tropical plant and its acid, tasty fruit

pin'ion *n.* wing; small wheel with cogs; *vt.* confine the wings or arms of

pink *n.* group of flowering plants which includes the carnation; shade of light red; person with mild socialistic tendencies; *a.* light red

pin'na-cle *n.* high point

pin'point' *vt.* narrow down or deal precisely with a problem; **pinpoint bombing** *n.* precision bombing

pin'—up' *n.* photograph or drawing of scantily clad woman; *a.*

pi'o-neer' *n.* one who goes before to prepare the way, colonist; *vi.*

pi'ous *a.* reverent, devout

pipe *n.* musical instrument consisting of a tube; any tube; contrivance for smoking tobacco; cask containing about 126 gallons; *vi.* & *vt.* play upon a pipe

pipe'line' *n.* carrier tube for oil, gas, etc.; source of information

pi'quant *a.* pungent; charming

pique *n.* wounded pride *vt.* wound the pride of

pi'ra-cy *n.* robbery on the high seas; literary theft

pi'rate *n.* robber on the high seas; **pi-rat'i-cal** *a.*

pis-ta'chi-o *n.* greenish nut used in types of ice cream, etc.

pis'til *n.* seed-forming organ in plants

pis'tol *n.* hand gun

pis'ton *n.* short, solid cylinder, moving within another hollow cylinder (as in steam engines, etc.)

pit *n.* hole, abyss; hole used as a trap; stone, as of a cheery; *vt.* put in a pit; mark with little hollows; set in competition

pitch *n.* substance obtained from tar; *vt.* throw

pitch'er *n.* large-mouthed jug; one who pitches in baseball

pit'e-ous *a.* pitiful

pith *n.* soft substance in the center of stems of plants, etc.; **pith'y** *a.* like pith; cogent

pit'i-a-ble *a.* deserving pity; **pit'i-ful** *a.* compassionate; causing pity; sorry, mean, despicable; **pit'-i-less** *a.*

pit'tance *n.* small income or portion

pit'y *n.* sympathy; cause of commiseration; *vt.* commiserate

piv'ot *n.* pin on which anything turns; *vi.* & *vt.* place or turn on a pivot

piz'za *n.* thin pie-shaped bread dough, with a topping of tomatoes, cheese, meat, etc.

piz'ze-ri'a *n.* restaurant specializing in pizzas

plac'ard *n.* poster

pla'cate' *vt.* conciliate

place *n.* space, locality, spot; position; *vt.* put in place or condition; invest

pla-ce'bo *n.* medicine given to

please a patient; anything given to soothe or satisfy

pla´cid *a.* peaceful, calm; **pla-cid´i-ty, pla´cid-ness** *n.*

pla´gi-a-rize´ *vt.* take from the writings of another without acknowledgment

plague *n.* great natural evil; deadly epidemic; *vt.* afflict with calamity; vex

plaid *n.* checkered woolen cloth; *a.* checkered

plain *a.* without elevation, ornament, difficulty, etc.; *n.* level land

plain´tive *a.* lamenting, mournful, sad

plain´tiff *n.* one who commences a suit in law

plait *n.* fold; braid; *vt.* fold, interweave

plan *n.* drawing of a building, machine, etc.; scheme; method; *vt.* design

plane *n.* level surface; geometrical surface; carpenters tool; airplane; *vt.* make level

plan´et *n.* one of the large bodies revolving around the sun

plan´e-tar´i-um *n.* domeshaped building housing a machine for showing the stars, etc.

plank *n.* long plain piece of timber, thicker than a board; one of the parts of a political platform, or program

plant *n.* herb, vegetable growth; tools, materials, and fixtures of a business; *vt.* put in the ground for growth

plan-ta´tion *n.* large farm, esp. in the South

plaque *n.* decorative plate of metal or other ware

plas´ma *n.* colorless liquid part of the blood; concentration of subatomic particles as in the sun

plas´ter *n.* composition of lime, water, and sand for overlaying walls, etc.

plas´tic *n.* any of various organic materials which may be molded under heat or pressure and used in making a variety of articles; *a.* capable of being molded or shaped; **plastic surgery** *n.* operation to improve injured or deformed external parts of the body

plate *n.* thin piece of metal; wrought gold and silver; gold or silver household utensils; flat dish; engraved plate of metal, electrotype, etc.; sheet of glass with a coating sensitive to light; *vt.* overlay with a coating of metal

pla´teau´ *n.* **(pla´teaus´, pla´teaux´)** tableland; high, flat ground

plat´form´ *n.* scaffolding, etc., for speakers or workmen; statement of principles

plat´i-num *n.* white, precious metallic element used in jewelry

plat´i-tude´ *n.* trite remark

plau´si-ble *a.* superficially convincing; **plau´si-bil´i-ty** *n.*

play *vi.* engage in sport; trifle; act in a theater; perform on a musical instrument; *vt.* put in motion; perform upon; perform; act a sportive part in; *n.* manner of dealing; dramatic composition; room for motion; **play´ful** *a.*; **play possum,** make a pretense (as of sleep)

play´boy´ *n.* man chiefly interested in pursuing pleasure

play´off´ *n.* game or round played to settle a tie

play´wright´ *n.* writer of plays

pla´za *n.* public square

plea *n.* whatever is alleged in support of a cause; excuse, defense

plead *vi.* & *vt.* argue; beg
plea´sant *a.* pleasing, cheerful
please *vt.* delight; satisfy; *vi.* like, choose
plea´sure *n.* joy; amusement
ple-be´ian *a.* vulgar, common; *n.* one of the common people
pledge *n.* security, surety; promise; *vt.* give as security; promise
ple´na-ry *a.* full, entire
plen´i-po-ten´ti-ar´y *a.* with full powers; *n.* diplomat with full power to act
plen´te-ous *a.* fully sufficient; fruitful
plenty *n.* abundance; **plen´ti-ful** *a.*
pli´a-ble *a.* flexible; easily persuaded
pli´ers *n. pl.* pincers
plight *n.* dangerous condition; *vt.* pledge; betroth
plot *n.* small piece of ground; scheme, conspiracy; chain of incidents in a play, novel, etc.; *vi.* conspire against
plow *n.* instrument for turning the soil; *vt.* turn up with the plow
pluck *vt.* snatch, strip; *n.* courage
pluck´y *a.* courageous, spirited
plug *n.* anything to stop a hole; piece of pressed tobacco; unofficial publicity or praise for a product or a company
plum´age *n.* the feathers of a bird
plumb *n.* mass of lead hung on a string; *vt.* adjust by a plumbline; sound
plumb´er *n.* one who supplies or repairs plumbing
plumb´ing *n.* piping for conveying water, gas, etc.
plume *n.* feather worn as an ornament
plun´der *vt.* seize property unlawfully; *n.*
plunge *vi.* & *vt.* cast suddenly into water; rush headlong; *n.* act of plunging
plung´er *n.* cylinder in pumps
plu´ral *a.* expressing more than one
plu-ral´i-ty *n.* excess of votes cast for any candidate over those cast for any other candidate
plus *a.* increased by
plush *n.* cloth woven like velvet
plu-toc´ra-cy *n.* government by the wealthy; **plu´to-crat´** *n.*
plu-to´ni-um *n.* an artificially produced radioactive element
ply *vt.* use steadily; urge
ply´wood´ *n.* thin layers of wood glued together
pneu-mat´ic *a.* relating to, moved by, or consisting of air
pneu-mo´ni-a *n.* inflammation of the lungs
poach *vi.* steal game; *vt.* cook in boiling water (as eggs without the shells)
pock´et *n.* pouch built into a garment; *vt.* put into the pocket; **pock´et-book´** *n.*
pod *n.* covering of the seed of plants
po´em *n.* composition in verse
po´et *n.* one skilled in making poetry; **po-et´ic** *a.*
po´et-ry *n.* verse, use of rhythm, diction, figures of speech, etc., to produce an elevated composition
poign´ant *a.* penetrating; moving, touching; **poign´an-cy** *n.*
point *n.* sharp end; essential part; *vi.* & *vt.* sharpen; direct or single out by the forefinger
poise *vi.* & *vt.* balance; *n.* equilibrium, carriage, bearing; ease or grace of behavior
poi´son *n.* substance injurious or deadly to life; *vt.* infect, injure, or kill with poison; **poi´son-ous** *a.*

pok´er *n.* rod to stir a fire; game at cards

Polaroid *n. tr.* camera using polarized light (light vibrating in one plane) to take and develop photographs on the spot

pole *n.* one of the ends of the axis of a sphere, esp. of the earth; **po´lar** *a.*; **pole´star´** *n.*

pole *n.* long, slender piece of wood

po-lice´ *n.* body of civil officers for preserving order; **po-lice´man** *n.*; **po-lice´wom´an** *n.*

pol´i-cy *n.* principle of management; insurance contract

pol´ish *vt.* make glossy; refine; *n.* smoothness

po-lite´ *a.* polished, well-bred

pol´i-tic *a.* discreet

po-lit´i-cal *a.* pertaining to politics or government

pol´i-ti´cian *n.* one versed in, or devoted to politics

pol´i-tics *n.* art or science of government; management of a political party

poll *vt.* sample or canvass public opinion; *n.*

pol´len *n.* fertilizing powder in flowers

polls *n. pl.* place where votes are cast

poll´ tax´ *n.* tax, esp. tax on voting

pol-lute´ *vt.* soil, defile, dishonor; **pol-lu´tion** *n.*

pol´troon´ *n.* coward

pol´y-an´dry *n.* state of having more than one husband at the same time

pol´y-eth´y-lene´ *n.* lightweight thermoplastic used for packaging, insulation

po-lyg´a-my *n.* state of having more than one wife at the same time; **po-lyg´a-mist** *n.*

pol´y-glot´ *a.* knowing or containing many languages; *n.*

pol´y-gon´ *n.* figure of many angles

pol´y-graph´ *n.* instrument that records involuntary reactions, a lie detector

pol´yp *n.* aquatic animal with many arms; small tumor on a mucous membrane

pol´y-un-sat´u-rat-ed *a.* rich in unsaturated bonds (oils or fatty acids)

pome´gran´ate *n.* variety of Oriental tree or its seed-filled, sour fruit

pomp *n.* pageantry; ostentation

pomp´ous *a.* displaying pomp; boastful; stuffy in manners; **pomp´ous-ness** *n.*

pon´der *vi.* & *vt.* meditate

pon´der-ous *a.* weighty, dull

pon´tiff *n.* Roman priest; the pope

pon-tif´i-cate´ *n.* office or reign of a pope; *vi.* speak pompously

pon-toon´ *n.* one of several boats supporting a bridge

po´ny *n.* small horse

poo´dle *n.* dog with long, curly hair

pool *n.* small body of water; stakes in certain games; variety of billiard game; joint enterprise; central source or location of a commodity as a motor pool); *vi.* & *vt.* enter into a pool

poor *a.* without money or means; deserving pity

pop *vt.* make a sharp, quick sound; thrust suddenly; explode with a sharp report; *n.* sharp, quick sound or sharp report; *a.* popular

pope *n.* Bishop of Rome, head of the Roman Catholic Church; priest in the Greek Orthodox Church

pop´u-lace *n.* common people, multitudes

pop´u-lar *a.* pertaining to the people; pleasing to, or prevailing

among, the people; **pop´u-lar´i-ty** *n.*; **pop´u-lar-ize´** *vt.*
pop´u-la´tion *n.* inhabitants of a place or country
pop´u-lous *a.* numerously inhabited; densely settled
por´ce-lain *n.* hard, thick type of china
porch *n.* raised floor leading to the entrance of a house
por´cu-pine´ *n.* rodent quadruped, covered with quills
pore *n.* minute opening in the skin; *vi.* study closely, peruse
pork *n.* flesh of swine
po´rous *a.* having pores; **po´rous-ness, po-ros´i-ty** *n.*
por´poise *n.* dolphin
port *n.* demeanor; left side of a ship; harbor
port´a-ble *a.* movable
por´tal *n.* entrance; arch over a gate
por´tent *n.* sign, anything which foreshadows
por-ten´tous *a.* serving to portend; ominous
por´ter *n.* doorkeeper; one who carries baggage or has charge of a sleepingcar; dark malt liquor
port-fo´li-o´ *n.* portable case for keeping papers
port´hole´ *n.* opening, as in a ship´s side
por´ti-co´ *n.* **(por´ti-cos, por´ti-coes)** row of columns in the front of a building
por´tion *n.* part; part allotted; *vt.* divide into portions
por´trait *n.* likeness of a person
por-tray´ *vt.* paint or draw the likeness of; describe in words; **por-tray´al** *n.*
Por´tu-guese´ *n. sing. & pl.* native or people of Portugal; language of Portugal; *a.*
pose *n.* position, attitude; *vi. & vt.* put into, or assume, a studied attitude
po-si´tion *n.* place, situation, attitude; ground taken in an argument
pos´i-tive *a.* clearly expressed; decisive; confident; *n.* that which may be affirmed; photographic picture showing the same shades and lights as the original
pos´i-tron´ *n.* positively charged electron
pos-sess´ *vt.* have, hold, own; **pos-ses´sion** *n.* thing possessed; **pos-sess´ive** *a.*; **pos-sess´or** *n.*
pos´si-ble *a.* able to be or happen; **pos´si-bil´i-ty** *n.* that which is possible
post *n.* pillar; fixed place, as a military station; office; established system of conveying letters; *vt.* inform, as by a public notice; transfer to a ledger
post´age *n.* money paid for conveyance by mail
post´al *a.* pertaining to the mail service
pos´ter *n.* advertisement placed in a public place
pos-te´ri-or *a.* coming after, situated behind
pos-ter´i-ty *n.* succeeding generations
post´grad´u-ate *a.* relating to a course of study after graduation
post´hu-mous *a.* born after the father´s death; published after the death of an author
post´mark´ *n.* cancellation stamp on a letter; *vt.*
post´-mor´tem *a.* after death; *n.* autopsy
post´paid´ *a.* having the postage prepaid
post´pone´ *vt.* put off till later;

post´pone´ment *n.*
post´script´ *n.* part added to a letter after the signature (abbreviated P.S.)
pos´tu-late´ *vt.* assume as true; *n.* axiom, self-evident problem; statement assumed as true
pos´ture *n.* attitude, disposition; carriage of the body
po-ta´to *n.* edible tuber, native of America
po´tent *a.* strong; having great influence; **po´ten-cy** *n.*
po´ten-tate´ *n.* sovereign; powerful person
po-ten´tial *a.* existing in possibility
po´tion *n.* drink; dose of liquid medicine
pot´pour-ri´ *n.* mixture, indiscriminate mixture
pouch *n.* pocket, bag
poul´try *n.* domestic fowl
pounce *vi.* fall (upon) and seize
pound *n.* 16 ounces avoirdupois; 20 shillings in British currency; public pen for stray animals
pound *vt.* beat repeatedly, bruise with a pestle
pour *vt.* cause to flow; give vent to; vi . flow, rush
pout *vi.* & *vt.* push out the lips, look sullen
pov´er-ty *n.* state of being poor, indigence
pow´der *n.* fine particles of a dry substance; gunpowder; *vi.* & *vt.* reduce to powder; sprinkle with powder
pow´er *n.* strength, energy, ability; faculty of the mind; moving force; authority; influence; influential nation; **pow´er-ful** *a.*
prac´ti-ca-ble *a.* capable of being done, used, or followed; **prac´ti-ca-bil´i-ty** *n.*
prac´ti-cal *a.* useful; derived from practice
prac´tice *n.* habit, frequent use performance; exercise of a profession; *vi.* & *vt.* put in practice; exercise as a profession
prac-ti´tion-er *n.* one engaged in the exercise of a profession, esp. medicine or law
prai´rie *n.* land covered with coarse grass and lacking trees
praise *n.* commendation, eulogy; *vt.* commend, extol
prance *vi.* strut, caper
prank *n.* mildly mischievous trick
prat´tle *vi.* prate, babble; *n.* empty or childish talk
pray *vi.* & *vt.* ask earnestly; petition God; **pray´er** *n.*
preach *vi.* & *vt.* discourse on sacred subjects
pre´am´ble *n.* preface
pre´am´pli-fi´er *n.* amplifier that raises weak signals from microphone, etc., to a level usable by main amplifier
pre-car´i-ous *a.* uncertain; unsafe, risky
pre-cau´tion *n.* preventive care or measure
pre-cede´ *vt.* go before
pre-ced´ence *n.* superiority, foremost place, right to go first
prec´e-dent *n.* parallel case in the past
pre´cept´ *n.* commandment, advice intended to guide
pre´cinct´ *n.* municipal district
pre´cious *a.* of great worth
prec´i-pice´ *n.* very steep place, cliff
pre-cip´i-tate´ *vt.* throw headlong; cause to happen; *a.* over hasty
pre-cip´i-ta´tion *n.* haste; deposit of moisture (rain, snow) or amount deposited

pre-cise´ *a.* exact
pre-ci´-sion *n.* exactness
pre-co´cious *a.* developed very early (as in intelligence); **pre-co´cious-ness, pre-coc´i-ty** *n.*
pre´con-cep´tion *n.* notion formed beforehand; prejudice
pred´a-to´ry *a.* living by plunder, rapacious
pred´e-ces´sor *n.* one who has preceded another
pre-des´ti-na´tion *n.* fate as decreed by God
pre-dic´a-ment *n.* unfortunate situation
pred´i-cate´ *vt.* affirm one thing of another; *n.* that which is stated of subject
pre-dict´ *vt.* tell before-hand; **pre-dic´tion** *n.*
pre´di-lec´tion *n.* tendency to like something
pre´dis-pose´ *vt.* incline to **pre´dis-po-si´tion** *n.*
pre-dom´i-nant *a.* ruling; **pre-dom´-i-nance** *n.*
pre-dom´i-nate´ *vi.* prevail, surpass in strength or authority
pre-em´i-nence *n.* superiority; **pre-em´i-nent** *a.*
pre-empt´ *vi. & vt.* take up (land) by pre-emption
pre-emp´tion *n.* right or act of purchasing before others
pre-fab´ri-cate´ *vt.* produce the parts of anything (as a house) for later assembly
pref´ace *n.* introduction; *vt.* introduce with a preface; **pref´a-to´ry** *a.*
pre-fer´ *vt.* esteem above another
pref´fer-a-ble *a.* more desirable
pref´er-ence *n.* choice
pre-fer´ment *n.* advancement
pre-fix´ *vt.* put at the beginning
pre´fix´ *n.* letter or syllables put at the beginning of another word
preg´nant *a.* with child; laden with meaning; **preg´nan-cy** *n.*
pre´his-tor´ic *a.* relating to a time before that known to history
prej´u-dice *n.* bias, unreasonable inclination for or against anything; *vt.* bias the mind of; injure; **prej´u-di´cial** *a.*
prel´ate *n.* clergyman of superior rank
pre-lim´i-nar-y *a.* preparatory; *n.* that which precedes
prel´ude *n.* short piece of music coming before a longer piece
pre´ma-ture´ *a.* mature, or done, before the proper time
pre-mi-er´ *n.* prime minister
pre-mière´ *n.* first performance, as of a play, music, etc.
prem´ise *n.* one of the propositions in a syllogism from which the conclusion is drawn
prem´ises *n. pl.* building and its adjuncts
pre´mi-um *n.* reward, prize; payment made for insurance
pre´mo-ni´tion *n.* foreboding, feeling of disaster
pre-oc´cu-pa´tion *n.* absorption in thought
pre´or-dain´ *vt.* appoint, or determine beforehand
pre-paid´ *a.* paid beforehand
pre-pare´ *vi. & vt.* fit for a purpose; make or get ready for use; **prep´a-ra´tion** *n.*
pre-pon´der-ant *a.* superior in weight or influence
prep´o-si´tion *n.* particle (like *to, for, with, by*) usually followed by pronoun, noun, or noun phrase
pre´pos-sess´ing *a.* pleasing, winning
pre-pos´ter-ous *a.* contrary to rea-

son, absurd

pre-req´ui-site *a.* required beforehand; *n.* anything necessary for an end

pre-rog´a-tive *n.* exclusive or peculiar privilege

Pres´by-te´ri-an *a.* pertraining to a form of church government in which all the clergy are equal in importance; *n.* member of the Presbyterian Church

pre-scribe´ *vt.* lay down for direction

pre-scrip´tion *n.* written direction for the preparation of a medicine

pres´ent *a.* being in a certain place; being at this time; *n.* present time; gift; **pres´ence** *n.* state of being present or face to face

pre-sent´ *vt.* set before, introduce; make a gift of

pre-sent´-a-ble *a.* properly dressed

pres´en-ta´tion *n.* formal representation; formal introduction, as in court

pre-sen´ti-ment *n.* foreboding

pre-serve´ *vt.* keep from injury; season for preservation; keep up; *n.* fruit preserved by beating with sugar and water; place for the protection of game; **pres´er-va´tion** *n.*; **pre-serv´a-tive** *n.* agent or material which preserves

pre-side´ *vi.* superintend

pres´i-den-cy *n.* office of a president

pres´i-dent *n.* chief officer of a college, institution, etc.; chief executive of a republic; **pres´i-den´tial** *a.*

press *vt.* squeeze or crush; drive, urge; make smooth; *vi.* exert pressure; crowd forward; *n.* instrument for squeezing; printing machine

pres´sure *n.* act of pressing; that which presses or afflicts; urgency, hurry

pres´ti-dig´i-ta´tion *n.* sleight of hand

pres´tige´ *n.* influence arising from reputation or position

pre-sume´ *vt.* take for granted; *vi.* act forwardly

pre-sump´tion *n.* supposition; strong probability; forward conduct; **pre-sump´tu-ous** *a.*

pre´sup-pose´ *vt.* assume or suppose beforehand; **pre´sup-po-si´-tion** *n.*

pre-tend´ *vt.* claim falsely, simulate; *vi.* make a pretense, feign

pre-tense´ pre-tence´ *n.* simulation, false claim

pre-ten´tious *a.* presumptuous, arrogant

pre´ter-nat´u-ral *a.* beyond what is natural

pre´text´ *n.* ostensible motive

pret´zel *n.* stiff, salty dough baked in the form of a knot

pre-vail´ *vi.* have influence or effect; gain the advantage; **prev´a-lence** *n.*

prev´a-lent *a.* prevailing; most common

pre-var´i-cate´ *vi.* evade the truth, lie; **pre-var´i-ca´tion** *n.*

pre-vent´ *vt.* hinder; obviate; **pre-ven´tion** *n.*

pre-ven´tive *a.* tending to hinder or obviate; *n.*

pre´view´ *n.* advance notice or showing (as of movies)

pre´vi-ous *a.* former

prey *n.* plunder; *vi.* commit robbery; seize and devour an animal as prey

price *n.* that at which anything is valued; *vt.* set a value on

price´less *a.* invaluable

prick *n.* sharp point; sting, remorse; *vt.* pierce, puncture; erect, as the ears of an animal

pride *n.* extreme self-esteem

priest *n.* one who officiates in sacred offices; **priest´ess** *n. fem.*; **priest´hood** *n.*

prim *a.* exact, affectedly nice

prim´a don´na *n.* leading lady in opera; temperamental person

pri´ma´ry *a.* first, original; *n.* party meeting for nominating candidates

pri´mate *n.* high dignitary, as in a church

prime *a.* first in time, rank, or importance; *n.* best part (as of life); *vt.* put in readiness, as a firearm; lay on the first coat of paint

prim´er *n.* first reading book; either of two sizes of type

pri-me´val *a.* primitive of the first ages

prim´i-tive *a.* belonging the beginning, crude

prince *n.* son of a sovereign; **prin´cess** *n. fem.*

prin´ci-pal *a.* chief; *n.* chief person or thing; money on which interest is paid

prin´ci-ple *n.* fundamental truth or doctrine

print *vt.* mark by pressure; publish; *n.* reproduction made by printing or photography

pri´or *a.* coming before in time

pri-or´i-ty *n.* preference, as in issuing limited supplies in a critical situation

prism *n.* solid whose ends are similar, equal, and parallel planes, and whose sides are parallelograms

pri´son *n.* jail, building for the confinement of criminals

pri´son-er *n.* one confined in prison; captive

pris´tine´ *a.* belonging to the earliest time, original; unspoiled

pri´va-cy *n.* seclusion, esp. in personal affairs

pri´vate *a.* personal, not public; *n.* enlisted soldier of lowest rank

pri-va´tion *n.* destitution, want

priv´i-lege *n.* right which is limited to a few; favor, special treatment

prize *n.* that which is gained by competition, war, etc.; *vt.* value

prob´a-bil´i-ty *n.* likelihood, quality of being probable

prob´a-ble *a.* likely, giving ground for belief; **prob´a-bly** *adv.*

pro´bate´ *n.* proof of a will

pro-ba´tion *n.* time during which a person or thing is proved or examined

probe *n.* instrument for examining a wound, etc.; *vt.* examine with a probe; examine thoroughly

prob´i-ty *n.* tried honesty

prob´lem *n.* matter difficult of solution

prob´lem-at´ic, prob´lem-at´i-cal *a.* of the nature of a problem; doubtful

pro´bos´cis *n.* nose, as of the elephant

pro-ce´dure *n.* order in which things are done

pro-ceed´ *vi.* go forward

proc´ess *n.* group of operations

pro-ces´sion *n.* train of persons in a formal march

pro-claim´ *vt.* announce officially

proc´la-ma´tion *n.* official public announcement

pro-cliv´i-ty *n.* tendency

pro-cras´ti-nate´ *vt.* put off, postpone; **pro-cras´ti-na´tion** *n.*

pro-cure´ *vt.*obtain; **proc´u-ra´tor** *n.* agent

pro-cur´er *n.* purchaser, obtainer; pimp

prod´i-gal *a.* wasteful, lavish; *n.* spendthrift; **prod´i-gal´i-ty** *n.*

pro-di´gious *a.* enormous
prod´i-gy *n.* any extraordinary person or thing; wonder
pro-duce´ *vt.* bring forward; yield, make, cause; extend; **pro-duc´i-ble** *a.*
prod´uce *n.* that which is produced, esp. garden vegetables
pro-duc´er *n.* one who manages the performance of a movie, or radio or TV program
prod´uct *n.* that which is produced; result of numbers multiplied together; **pro-duc´tion** *n.*
pro-fane´ *a.* unholy, impious; *vt.* violate anything holy; debase
pro-fan´i-ty *n.* irreverence; profane language; **prof´a-na´tion** *n.* desecration
pro-fess´ *vt.* state freely; announce one´s skill in
pro-fes´sion *n.* open declaration; employment requiring some degree of learning; body of persons engaged in a profession
pro-fes´sion-al *n.* one who makes his living by an art; **pro-fes´sion-al** *a.*
pro-fes´sor *n.* teacher of high rank in a college
prof´fer *vt.* offer; *n.* offer made
pro-fi´cient *a.* adept, expert, well versed
pro´file´ *n.* side view of head and face; summary of test results (as of abilities, tendencies, etc.)
prof´it *n.* excess of value received over expenditure; advantage; *vi.* & *vt.* gain or be of advantage; **prof´it-a-ble** *a.*
prof´li-gate *a.* abandoned to vice, prodigal
pro-found´ *a.* very deep; learned
pro-fuse´ *a.* abundant; liberal to excess
pro-gen´i-tor *n.* forefather
prog´e-ny *n.* off-spring
prog-no´sis *n.* prediction of the outcome of a disease from its symptoms
prog-nos´ti-cate´ *vt.* foretell; **prog-nos´ti-ca´tion** *n.*
pro´gram *n.* outline of forthcoming proceedings
pro´gram-ming *n.* arrangement of offerings for presentation on radio or TV; sequence of operations set up for a computing machine
prog´ress *n.* advance; improvement
pro-gress´ *vi.* improve; move on
pro-gres´sion *n.* motion onward; sequence
pro-gres´sive jazz´ *n.* modern variety of jazz emphasizing breakup of melody line by extreme variations and contrasts
pro-hib´it *vt.* forbid; **pro-hib´i-tive** *a.*
pro´hi-bi´tion *n.* act of forbidding anything; forbidding by law the sale of alcoholic liquors
pro´hi-bi´tion-ist *n.* one who favors prohibition
proj´ect, *n.* plan, scheme
pro-ject´ *vt.* contrive; throw forward; *vi.* shoot forward, jut out
pro-jec´tile *n.* body projected by force
pro-jec´tion *n.* anything which juts out; image projected on a screen
pro-jec´tor *n.* instrument for projecting a picture on a screen
pro´le-tar´i-an *n.* worker with little or no property
pro´le-tar´i-at *n.* lowest, poorest class; the masses
pro-lif´ic *a.* fertile, fruitful
pro´log´, pro´logue´ *n.* introduction, as to a play
pro-long´ *vt.* extend, lengthen; **pro´-**

lon-ga´tion *n.*
prom´e-nade´ *n.* walk for pleasure or exercise
prom´i-nent *a.* projecting, conspicuous, distinguished
pro-mis´cu-ous *a.* mixed, indiscriminate; indiscriminately lewd
prom´ise *n.* pledge; *vi.* & *vt.* make a pledge
prom´is-so´ry *a.* containing a promise or obligation
prom´on-to´ry *n.* high cape, headland
pro-mote´ *vt.* advance, further; **pro-mo´tion** *n.*
prompt *a.* prepared, ready; acting quickly; *vt.* incite; assist a speaker when at a loss for words; **prompt´ness** *n.*
prom´ul-gate´ *vt.* publish, disseminate
prone *a.* lying with the face downward; disposed
pro´noun´ *n.* word (like *I, my, mine, me*) used instead of a noun
pro-nounce´ *vt.* speak, speak distinctly; utter formally; **pro-nun´ci-a´tion** *n.*
proof *n.* demonstration, test, evidence; degree of alcoholic strength; trial impression taken from type, etc.
prop´a-gan´da *n.* propagation of a doctrine, esp. by insinuating or slanted means
prop´a-gan´dist *n.* person who produces and spreads propaganda; person who campaigns for some cause
prop´a-gate´ *vi.* & *vt.* multiply; **prop´a-ga´tion** *n.*
pro-pel´ *vt.* drive forward
pro-pel´ler *n.* screw for propelling a ship or airplane
pro-pen´si-ty *n.* predisposition or inclination towards anything
prop´er *a.* natural; suitable
prop´er-ty *n.* peculiar or essential quality; things owned
proph´e-cy *n.* prediction, forecast
proph´e-sy *vt.* foretell
proph´et *n.* one who proclaims or interprets the will of God; one who predicts the future
pro´phy-lac´tic *a.* protecting against disease
pro´phy-lax´is *n.* anything that tends to prevent disease
pro-pin´qui-ty *n.* nearness
pro-pi´ti-ate´ *vi.* & *vt.* conciliate
pro-pi´tious *a.* favorable
pro-por´tion *n.* relative magnitude; symmetrical arrangement; equality of ratios
pro-pose´ *vt.* offer for consideration; *vi.* make an offer of marriage; **pro-pos´al** *n.* offer
prop´o-si´tion *n.* offer of terms; statement; theorem to be demonstrated
pro-pound´ *vt.* offer for consideration
pro-pri´e-tar´y *a.* pertaining to a proprietor or to property
pro-pri´e-tor *n.* owner
pro-pri´e-ty *n.* fitness
pro-pul´sion *n.* propelling
pro-sa´ic *a.* common place
pro-sce´ni-um *n.* front part of the stage
pro-scribe´ *vt.* outlaw, denounce; forbid; **pro-scrip´tion** *n.*
prose *n.* ordinary speech or writing (as opposed to verse)
pros´e-cute´ *vt.* take legal action against; **pros´e-cu´tion** *n.*
pros´e-lyte´ *n.* person won over to religion or opinion; *vt.* & *vt.* endeavor to convert
pros´pect´ *n.* view, scene; expecta-

tion; *vi.* & *vt.* search for unworked deposits of ore; **pros´pec´tor** *n.*

pro-spec´tus *n.* outline of a proposed undertaking

pros´per *vi.* & *vt.* make or be successful; **pros´per-ous** *a.*

pros´trate´ *a.* lying at length; *vt.* throw on the ground, lay flat

pros-tra´tion *n.* physical collapse

pro-tect´ *vt.* shelter from injury

pro-tec´tion *n.* defense, guard

pro´té-gé´ *n. masc.* one under the protection or training of another; **pro´té-gée´** *n. fem.*

pro´te-in *n.* amino acid compounds occurring in all living matter

pro-test´ *vi.* & *vt.* object formally

pro´test´ *n.* formal declaration of dissent

Prot´es-tant *n.* Christian who does not belong to the Roman Catholic Church

Prot´es-tant eth´ic *n.* set of values stressing hard work and thrift

prot´es-ta´tion *n.* declaration or avowal (as of love)

pro´to-col´ *n.* minutes of a diplomatic conference; diplomatic etiquette

pro´ton´ *n.* part of the nucleus of an atom which carries a charge of positive electricity

pro´to-type´ *n.* model

pro-tract´ *vt.* prolong; **pro-trac´tion** *n.*

pro-trude´ *vi.* & *vt.* project, jut out; **pro-tru´sion** *n.*

pro-tu´ber-ance *n.* projection

proud *a.* haughty, arrogant; having justifiable pride

prove *vi.* & *vt.* subject to experiment or test, or to a standard; demonstrate

prov´erb *n.* short, pithy sentence expressing a truth; **pro-ver´bi-al** *a.* mentioned in, or like a proverb

pro-vide´ *vt.* prepare; supply; *vi.* procure

prov´i-dence *n.* timely preparation; foresight and care of God over all His creatures; God; **prov´i-dent** *a.* prudent; **prov´i-den´tial** *a.*

prov´ince *n.* portion of an empire or state

pro-vin´cial *a.* relating to a province; narrow, backward, crude; *n.* inhabitant of a province

pro-vi´sion *n.* measures taken beforehand; condition; store of food; *vt.* supply with food; **pro-vi´sion-al** *a.*

pro-vi´so *n.* stipulation

pro-voke´ *vt.* excite to action, offend; **prov´o-ca´tion** *n.* anything which provokes; **pro-voc´a-tive** *a.*

prow´ess *n.* bravery. outstanding ability

prowl *vi.* rove in search of prey or plunder

prox-im´i-ty *n.* nearness; **proximity fuse** *n.* fuse which determines proper moment for explosion by radio waves which indicate nearness of bomb to target

prox´y *n.* agent, person who acts for another

prude *n.* person of excessive modesty; **prud´er-y** *n.*; **prud´ish** *a.*

pru´dent *a.* wise in practical matters; **pru´dence** *n.*

prune *vt.* trim, as trees; *n.* dried plum

pru´ri-ence *n.* lewdness of thought; **pru´ri-ent** *a.*

pry *vi.* search with impertinent curiosity; *vt.* force with a lever

psalm *n.* sacred song

psalm´ist *n.* composer of a psalm

pseu´do-nym´ *n.* fictitious name

psy´che´ *n.* human soul or mind

psy´che-del´ic *a.* producing an intensified mental condition
psy-chi´a-try *n.* study and treatment of mental diseases; **psy-chi´-a-trist** *n.*
psychic *a.* mental; being beyond physical knowledge
psy´cho-a-nal´y-sis *n.* examination of a person's mind as a means of discovering the basic causes of a mental conflict; **psy´cho-an´a-lyze´** *vt.*
psy-chol´o-gy *n.* study of the human mind; **psy´cho-log´i cal** *a.*
psy´cho-neu-rot´ic *a.* neurotic; pertaining to fairly mild mental disorders such its fears and obsessions
psy-cho´sis *n.* severe mental disorder; **psy-chot´ic** *a.*
psy´cho-so-mat´ic *a.* pertaining to the adverse physical effects of mental stress
psy´cho-ther´a-py *n.* treatment of mental disorders, as by psychoanalysis
pto-maine´ *n.* putrescent product of animal origin
pub´lic *a.* pertaining to the people; open, common, commonly known
pub-lic´i-ty *n.* advertising
pub´li-ca´tion *n.* act of publishing or making public, as by printing; anything which is published
pub´li-cize´ *n.* give publicity to
pub´lish *vt.* make public; print and offer for sale
pud´dle *n.* small pool of water
pudg´y *a.* short and fat
pu´er-ile *a.* childish, juvenile, foolish
pug-na´cious *a.* quarrelsome
pull *vi.* & *vt.* draw, tear; *n.* act of pulling; *col.* influence
pul´let *n.* young hen
pul´ley *n.* apparatus consisting of one or more wheels, used with ropes, for raising weights
pul´mo-nar´y *n.* pertaining to the lungs
pulp *n.* soft part of plants or fruits; any soft mass; **pulp´y** *a.*
pul´sate´ *vi.* throb, beat; **pul-sa´tion** *n.*
pulse *n.* beating, as of the heart
pul´ver-ize´ *vt.* reduce to fine powder
pum´ice *n.* hard, light, spongy, volcanic material
pump *n.* machine for raising or conveying fluids; low, thin-soled shoe; *vt.* raise with a pump; *col.* draw out by artful questions
pump´kin *n.* plant of the gourd family with edible fruit
pun *vt.* play upon words; *n.*
punch *n.* beverage made with liquor or wine, water, sugar, etc.; tool for perforating; thrust, blow; *vt.* prick or pierce with sharp tool; strike
punc-til´i-ous *a.* very exact in details
punc´tu-al *a.* exact in keeping appointments; **punc´tu-al´i-ty** *n.*
punc´tu-ate´ *vt.* divide sentences by certain marks; **punc´tu-a´tion** *n.*
punc´ture *n.* small hole; *vt.* pierce
pun´gent *a.* pricking, acrid, stimulating; **pun´gen-cy** *n.*
pun´ish *vt.* chastise or discipline for a fault; **pun´ish -ment** *n.*
pu´ni-tive *a.* pertaining to punishment
punt *n.* flat-bottomed boat; *vt.* propel a boat by pushing with a pole against the bottom of a river; kick a dropped football before it reaches the ground
pu´ny *a.* small, feeble
pu´pa *n.* **(pu´pae, pu´pas)** insect in-

closed in a case before its development into an adult

pu´pil *n.* one under the care of a tutor, scholar; circular opening of the colored part of the eye

pup´pet *n.* small figure moved by wires

pup´py *n.* young dog

pup´ tent´ *n.* small canvas shelter for two

pur´chase *vt.* buy; *n.*; **pur´chas-er** *n.*

pure *a.* free from admixture, guilt, or defilement; **pure´ness, pu´ri-ty** *n.*

pur´ga-to´ry *n.* place or state in which souls are purified from venial sins after death

purge *vt.* cleanse, evacuate; eliminate political enemies; *vi.* become pure; take a purge

pu´ri-fy´ *vt.* make pure; **pu´ri-fi-ca´-tion** *n.*

Pu´ri-tan *n.* one of a religious party in the time of Elizabeth I which desired changes of ceremony and worship in the established church; person who demands a rigid code in morals, religion, etc.; **pu´ri-tan´-ic, pu´ri-tan´i-cal** *a.*

pur´lieu´ *n.* borders, environs

pur-loin´ *vt.* steal

pur´ple *n.* color of blended blue and red; royal rank

pur-port´ *vi.* seem or appear to be

pur´port´ *n.* signification

pur´pose *n.* aim, intention

purse *n.* small bag for money; *vt.* contract into folds

pur-su´ance *n.* following or carrying out

pur-su´ant *a.* conformable, in consequence

pur-sue´ *vt.* follow, chase, be engaged in

pur-suit´ *n.* act of pursuing or chasing after; endeavor, occupation

pu´ru-lent *a.* consisting of, full of, or resembling pus; **pu´ru-lence** *n.*

pur-vey´ *vi.* & *vt.* provide

push *vi.* & *vt.* press against, urge; *n.*

push´o´ver *n. col.* anything easy to do; anyone easy to defeat or to sell to

pu´sil-lan´i-mous *a.* cowardly

pus´tule´ *n.* small pimple containing pus

pu´ta-tive *a.* commonly supposed, reputed

pu´tre-fy´ *vi.* & *vt.* make or become rotten; **pu´tre-fac´tion** *n.*

pu-tres´cent *a.* turning rotten; **pu-tres´cence** *n.*

pu´trid *a.* rotten

put´ty *n.* cement of whiting and linseed oil

puz´zle *n.* perplexity; game to try the ingenuity; *vt.* perplex

pyg´my *n.* dwarf, diminutive animal

py´or-rhe´a *n.* a disease of the gums

pyr´a-mid *n.* solid figure with triangular sides meeting in a point

pyre *n.* pile of wood, etc., on which the dead are burned

Py´rex´ *n. tr.* heat-resistant glass

pyr´i-form´ *a.* pear-shaped

py´ro-tech´nic, py´ro-tech´ni-cal *a.* pertaining to fireworks; **py´ro-tech´nics** *n.*

py´thon´ *n.* large snake allied to the boa

Q

quack *vi.* cry like a duck; *n.* cry of a duck; pretender to medical skill

quad´ran´gle *n.* plane figure with four sides and angles; space enclosed by buildings

quad´rant *n.* fourth part of a circle, arc of 90°; instrument for measuring altitudes

quad´ri-lat´er-al *a.* having four sides; *n.* plane figure having four sides

qua-drille´ *n.* dance for four couples

quad-roon´ *n.* offspring of a mulatto and a white

quad´ro-phon´ic *a.* of a recording system in which sound reaches four microphones and is reproduced by four speakers

quad´ru-ped´ *n.* fourfooted animal

quad´ru-ple *a.* fourfold; *n.* four times the quantity; *vt.* increase fourfold

quad-rup´let *n.* one of four born at a single birth

qua-dru´pli-cate *a.* made fourfold

quail *vi.* cower shrink; *n.* migratory bird like the partridge

quaint *a.* odd or strange

quake *vi.* tremble; *n.* vibration; earthquake

Quak´er *n.* one of the Society of Friends

qual´i-fy´ *vi.* & *vt.* make or become suitable or capable; limit, particularize; **qual´i-fi´a-ble** *a.*; **qual´i-fi-ca´tion** *n.*

qual´i-ty *n.* condition; property, attribute; character, rank

qualm *n.* scruple

quan´da-ry *n.* dilemma

quan´ti-ty *n.* amount, bulk, size; large portion

quan´tum *n.* unit of energy; amount, portion

quar´an-tine´ *n.* isolation of persons infected with contagious disease; *vt.*

quar´rel *n.* angry dispute; *vi.* dispute violently; **quar´rel-some** *a.*

quar´ry *n.* place where stone is taken from the earth, for building; object of the chase; *vt.* dig from a quarry

quart *n.* fourth part of a gallon, two pints

quar´ter *n.* fourth part of anything; U. S. coin worth 25¢; mercy granted to an antagonist, etc.; **quar´ters** *n. pl.* lodgings; *vt.* divide into four equal parts; furnish with lodgings

quar´ter-ly *a.* happening or done once in each quarter of a year; *adv.* once a quarter; *n.* periodical published four times a year

quar´tet´ *n.* musical composition for four players; four persons performing together

quar´to´ *a.* having the sheet folded into four leaves; *n.* book of a quarto size

quartz *n.* crystalline form of silicon dioxide

quash *vt.* crush, annul

qua´si´ *a.* in a manner resembling

quat´rain´ *n.* stanza of four lines

qua´ver *vi.* shake; *n.*

quay *n.* wharf

queen *n.* wife of a king; female sovereign

queer *a.* odd, singular

quell *vt.* crush, allay

quench *vt.* put out

quer´u-lous *a.* complaining, discontented

que´ry *n.* question; *vt.* inquire into, question

quest *n.* search

ques´tion *n.* inquiry; subject of a discussion; *vt.* inquire of; regard as doubtful

ques´tion-a-ble *a.* doubtful, uncertain

queue *n.* pigtail; line of people waiting to buy anything

quib´ble *n.* evasion; *vi.* evade a question; argue, haggle about details

quick *a.* living; lively, fast; *adv.* rapidly, soon; *n.* living animal or plant; living flesh, sensitive parts; **quick´fro´zen** *a.* rapidly frozen as a means of preserving freshness

quick´en *vt.* make quick or alive; *vi.* become alive, move with activity

quick´sand´ *n.* sand readily yielding to pressure

quick´sil´ver *n.* mercury

qui-es´cent *a.* without motion, at rest

qui´et *a.* at rest; silent; *n.* repose, peace; *vt.* bring to rest

quill *n.* feather of a bird; spine, as of a porcupine

quilt *n.* bed cover of two cloths sewed together with padding between them

qui´nine´ *n.* alkaloid substance used to treat malaria, etc.

quin-tes´sence *n.* pure essence

quin´tet´ *n.* musical composition for five players; five performers

quin´tu´ple *a.* fivefold; *vt.* make fivefold

quip *n.* quick, witty retort

quit *vt.* stop, cease, depart from

quit´claim´ *n.* deed giving up title to something

quite *adv.* completely; considerably, very much

quit´tance *n.* discharge from a debt or obligation; requital, recompense

quiv´er *n.* case for arrows; *vi.* shake, shiver

quiz *n.* test; *vt.* question; examine

quiz´zi-cal *a.* teasing, sportive

quon´dam *a.* former

Quon´set hut´ *n.* prefabricated building whose roof and sides are a continuous arch

quo´rum *n.* number of members sufficient to transact business

quota *n.* proportional share (as of work)

quote *vt.* repeat the words of; name as authority; give the current price of; **quot´a-ble** *a.*; **quo-ta´tion** *n.*

quo´tient *n.* result of dividing one number by another

R

rab´bi *n.* Jewish teacher and preacher; **rab-bin´i-cal** *a.*

rab´bit *n.* small, burrowing animal of the hare family

rab´ble *n.* noisy crowd

rab´id *a.* furious, mad; affected with hydrophobia or rabies

rac´coon´ *n.* carnivorous animal of North America

race *n.* one of the groups into which human beings are divided on the basis of physical characteristics; contest; *vi.* run swiftly; contend

rac´ism *n.* belief in the inborn superiority of a racial group

rack *n.* framework to hold articles

rack´et *n.* frame with network used in tennis; noise; *col.* scheme

rack´et-eer´ *n.* criminal who extorts money

ra´dar´ *n.* eletronic device which senses the presence of distant objects; **ra´dar-scope´** *n.* radar receiver viewing screen

ra´di-ance *n.* quality of being radiant; bright, shining

ra´di-ant *a.* emitting light or heat

ra´di-ate´ *vi.* & *vt.* emit rays

ra´di-a´tion *n.* heat, light, and other energy; **radiation sickness** *n.* disease caused by overexposure to atomic radiation

ra´di-a´tor *n.* apparatus for heating

or cooling
rad´i-cal *a.* extreme; *n.* root; extreme reformer
ra´di-o *n.* wireless communication; **radio telescope** *n.* apparatus for detecting electromagnetic emanations from outer space
ra´di-o-ac-tiv´i-ty *n.* process of atomic decay in which radiation is given off; **ra´di-o-ac´tive** *a.*
ra´dio-chem´is-try *n.* study of radioactive phenomena
ra´di-ol´o-gy *n.* science of radiant energy and its use in curing disease
ra´di-om´e-ter *n.* instrument that measures intensity of radiant energy
ra´di-um *n.* one of the radioactive elements
ra´di-us *n.* **(ra´di-uses, ra´di-i´)** straight line from the center to the circumference of a circle; exterior bone of the forearm
raf´fle *n.* kind of lottery
raft *n.* pieces of timber fastened together to float
raft´er *n.* inclined beam supporting a roof
rag *n.* fragment of cloth
rage *n.* fury; fashion, fad; *vi.* be furious; prevail
raid *n.* hostile or predatory invasion foray; **raid´er** *n.*
rail *n.* bar of timber or metal; one of the iron bars on which railway cars run
rail´ler-y *n.* good-humored irony, banter
rail´road´, rail´way´ *n.* road with iron rails on which cars are propelled
raiment *n.* clothing
rain *n.* water from the clouds; *vi.* fall from the clouds; *vt.* pour; **rain´y** *a.*
raise *vt.* cause to rise, exalt, elevate; produce
rais´in *n.* dried, ripe grape
rake *n.* instrument with teeth for smoothing earth, collecting hay, etc.; dissolute man; *vt.* scrape with a rake; search diligently
rak´ish *a.* licentious, loose
ral´ly *vt.* collect and arrange (as troops in confusion); recover; *n.* act of rallying; political meeting
ram *n.* male sheep, engine of war for battering; piston, plunger; *vt.*thrust with violence; drive down hard, compact by driving; **ram jet** *n.* type of jet engine
ram´ble *vi.* wander from place to place without object; wander, as in speech or writing
ram´bling *a.* moving about irregularly
ram´i-fy´ *vi.* & *vt.* divide into branches; **ram´i-fi-ca´tion** *n.*
ra´mose´ *a.* branched (as a stem)
ram´page´ *n.* violent activity
ram´pant *a.* over-leaping restraint
ram´part´ *n.* wall surrounding a fortified place
ranch *n.* stock-farm; **ranch´er** *n.*
ran´cid *a.* unpleasant in taste or smell
ran´cor *n.* deep-seated enmity; **ran´cor-ous** *a.*
ran´dom *a.* aimless
range *vi.* & *vt.* set or exist in a row; rove; *n.* row, rank; class; wandering, space occupied by anything moving; target ground; cooking-stove; **range finder** *n.* device on camera or gun for measuring distance to object sighted
rang´er *n.* officer who has charge of a forest
rank *n.* row or line, esp. of soldiers; class, order; social position; *vt.*

place in a line or class; *vi.* be placed in a rank; have a certain distinction; *a.* growing luxuriant

ran´sack´ *vt.* search thoroughly; pillage

ran´som *n.* release from captivity; price paid for such release; *vt.* redeem

rant *vi.* use extravagant language

rape *n.* plant allied to the turnip; violation of a woman by force; *vt.* commit rape

rap´id *a.* very swift; *n.* part of river where the current is very rapid; **rapid´i-ty, rap´id-ness** *n.*

ra´pi-er *n.* light sword with a narrow blade

rap-port´ *n.* a harmonious relationship

rapt *a.* raised to rapture

rap´ture *n.* extreme delight, ecstasy; **rap´tur-ous** *a.*

rare *a.* not thoroughly cooked; not frequent

rar´i-ty *n.* state of being rare; thing valued for its scarcity

ras´cal *n.* tricking, dishonest fellow

rash *a.* hasty, incautious; *n.* eruption on the skin

rasp *vt.* make a grating sound; *n.* file

rasp´ber´ry *n.* kind of bramble or its fruit

rat *n.* animal of the mouse kind; opprobrious term applied to anyone; **rat on** *vi. col.* inform on someone

rate *n.* ratio, proportion, allowance; standard, value

rat´i-fy´ *vt.* approve and sanction; **rat´i-fi-ca´tion** *n.*

ra´ti-o *n.* relation of one thing to another

ra´tion *n.* daily rate of provisions; allowance, allotment, portion; **ra´-tion-ing** *n.*

ra´tion-al *a.* pertaining to reason; sane, intelligent; **ra´tion-al´i-ty** *n.*

rat-tan´ *n.* climbing palm tree or its stems used for wickerwork

rat´tle *vi.* clatter; chatter aimlessly; *n.* sharp noise rapidly repeated; loud empty talk; toy that rattles

rat´tle-snake´ *n.* poisonous American snake which makes a rattling noise with its tail

rau´cous *a.* hoarse , harsh rough

rav´age *vt.* lay waste

rave *vi.* talk irrationally or wildly; praise extravagantly

rav´e-nous *a.* voracious

ra-vine´ *n.* long, deep hollow, worn by water

rav´ish *vt.* seize or carry away by force; fill with ecstasy

raw *a.* not cooked or prepared; not covered with skin; bleak

raze *vt.* tear down; blot out

ray *n.* line of light or heat proceeding from a point; radiating part of anything

ra´zor *n.* shaving-knife

reach *vt.* stretch, extend; arrive at, gain; *vi.* be extended so as to touch; *n.* limit, extent

re-act´ *vi.* & *vt.* return an impulse; respond; behave

re-ac´tion *n.* response; chemical or subatomic change

re-ac´tion-ar´y *n.* in politics, an over-conservative person

re-actor *n.* atomic pile having carefully controlled fission to produce energy or radioactive substances

read *vi.* & *vt.* peruse or study the written or printed word; **read´a-ble** *a.*

read´y *a.* fully prepared; willing; *adv.* in a state of readiness; **read´i-ly** *adv.*

re´al *a.* actually existing, true; in law, pertaining to land or houses; **re´al-ly** *adv.*

re-al´i-ty *n.* actual existence

re´al-ize´ *vt.* make real, accomplish; feel as real; understand; convert into real property or cash; **re´al-i-za´tion** *n.*

realm *n.* kingdom, province

re´al-ty *n.* real estate

reap *vt.* cut down (as grain), harvest

rear *n.* back or hindmost part; *a.*; *vt.* raise; bring to maturity; *vi.* rise on the hind legs

rea´son *n.* that which justifies an act or opinion; faculty of the mind by which man judges; *vi.* exercise the faculty of reason; argue; *vt.* think a problem through; persuade by reasoning; **rea´son-a-ble** *a.*

re´bate´ *n.* deduction by way of discount

reb´el *n.* one who rebels; *a.* rebellious

re-bel´ *vi.* take up arms against authority, revolt; **re-bel´lion** *n.*; **re-bel´lious** *a.*

re-bound´ *vi.* recoil; *n.* act of recoiling (as from disappointment)

re-buff´ *n.* ungracious refusal; *vt.* repel violently; refuse ungraciously

re-buke´ *vt.* chide, reprove; *n.* reproof

re-call´ *vt.* call back, cancel; remember; *n.*

re-cap´ *vt.* process an old tire in order to renew its life

re´cap´ *n.* tire whose life has been renewed; recapitulation; *vt.* recapitulate

re´ca-pit´u-late´ *vi.* & *vt.* repeat the chief points of, summarize

re-cede´ *vi.* & *vt.* go or fall back

re-ceipt´ *n.* act of receiving; written acknowledgment of anything received; anything received

re-ceive´ *vt.* take that which is offered; admit, welcome; **re-ceiv´a-ble** *a.*

re-ceiv´er *n.* one who receives, esp. one who takes charge of the business or assets of an insolvent

re´cent *a.* of late origin or occurrence; fresh, modern; **re´cent-ly** *adv.*

re-cep´ta-cle *n.* that in which anything is contained (as a jar), repository

re-cep´tion *n.* act of receiving, admission; entertainment; **re-cep´-tive** *a.*

re´cess´ *n.* alcove; temporary suspension

re-cession *n.* economic slump

rec´i-pe *n.* prescription for preparing food or medicine

re-cip´i-ent *n.* one who receives

re-cip´ro-cal *a.* acting in return; *n.* that which is mutually given and received

re-cip´ro-cate´ *vt.* give and receive mutually; **re-cip´ro-ca´tion** *n.*

re´ci-proc´i-ty *n.* mutual obligations and benefits

re-cite´ *vt.* repeat from memory; narrate, recapitulate; **re-cit´al** *n.*; **rec´i-ta´tion** *n.*

reck´less *a.* heedless of the consequences; **reck´less-ness** *n.*

reck´on *vt.* count, account, consider; **reck´on-ing** *n.*

re´claim´ *vt.* regain from error or vice; bring into a state of cultivation; **rec´-la-ma´tion** *n.*

re-cline´ *vi.* & *vt.* lean back, repose, lie

rec´luse *n.* one who lives apart from the world

rec´og-nize´ *vt.* know again, recollect; note; acknowledge acquain-

tance with; **rec´og-ni´tion** *n.*
re-coil´ *vi.* bounce or spring back; shrink; *n.* starting or springing back
rec´ol-lect´ *vt.* remember; **rec´ol-lec´tion** *n.*
rec´om-mend´ *vt.* commend to another; bestow praise on; advise; **rec´om-men-da´tion** *n.*
rec´om-pense´ *vt.* return an equivalent to, repay; *n.* compensation, reward
rec´on-cile´ *vt.* restore to friendship or union; make consistent; **rec´on-cil´i-a´tion** *n.*
re-con´nais-sance *n.* examination of a territory, as military purposes
rec´on-noi´ter *vt.* survey, spy out
rec´ord *n.* register; formal writing of a fact or proceeding; book of such writings; phonograph recording
re-cord´ *vt.* preserve the memory of; register
re-cord´-er *n.* device for preserving sounds on discs or tape; simple wooden flute
re-cov´er *vt.* get possession of again; retrieve; bring back to a former state;. *vi.* regain health or former state; obtain judgment; **re-cov´er-a-ble** *a.*; **re-cov´er-y** *n.*
rec´re-ant *a.* cowardly, false; *n.* cowardly wretch; deserter
rec´re-a´tion *n.* pastime, physical or mental refreshment
re-cruit´ *vi.* & *vt.* obtain fresh supplies, soldiers, etc.; *n.* newly enlisted soldier
rec´tan´gle *n.* four-sided figure with right angles; **rec-tan´gu-lar** *a.*
rec´ti-fy´ *vt.* make right, correct; **rec´ti-fi-ca´tion** *n.*
rec´ti-tude´ *n.* integrity
re-cum´bent *a.* reclining
re-cu´per-ate *vi.* & *vt.* recover, convalesce
re-cur´ *vi.* occur again; return to mind; **re-cur´rent** *a.*; **re-cur´rence** *n.*
re-cy´cle *vi.* & *vt.* convert waste materials to useful products
red *n.* one of the primary colors; communist; dangerous radical; **red tape** *n.* unnecessary or time-consuming official procedure
re-deem´ *vt.* ransom, as from sin, bondage, etc.; atone for, compensate for; perform, as a promise; recover, as a pledge; **re-demp´tion** *n.*
re-dound´ *vi.* result or turn to advantage or disadvantage
re-dress´ *vt.* set right or repair an injury, wrong, etc.; make amends for; *n.* reparation
re-duce´ *vt.* bring into a lower state; subdue; bring into a certain condition, as by pulverizing, diluting, etc.; *vi.* lose weight, as by dieting; **re-duc´tion** *n.*
re-dun´dant *a.* superfluous, wordy; **re-dun´dan-cy** *n.*
reef *n.* chain of rocks near the surface of the water
reek *n.* fume; *vi.* give off fumes
reel *n.* lively dance; turning frame for winding yarn, etc.; *vt.* wind on a reel; *vi.* stagger dizzily
re-fer´ *vt.* submit or direct to another; *vi.* have reference to, relate, allude; **ref´er-a-ble, re-fer´ri-ble** *a.*
ref´er-ee´ *n.* arbitrator, umpire
ref´er-ence *n.* act of referring, allusion; anything which is referred to
ref´er-en´dum *n.* decision by the people on a measure already passed by the legislature
re´fill´ *n.* cartridge, etc. to replace commodity in original container such as a pen or lipstick
re-fine´ *vi.* & *vt.* separate from ex-

traneous matter, make or become fine or pure

re-flect´ *vi.* & *vt.* throw or bend back after striking upon a surface (as light, sound, etc.); ponder; cast reproach; **re-flec´tion** *n.*; **re-flec´-tive** *a.*

re´flex´ *n.* involuntary response of an organ to stimulus

re-form´ *vi.* & *vt.* correct or improve; *n.* improvement; **ref´or-ma´tion** *n.* improvement, correction

re-fract´ *vt.* break the natural coarse of, bend from a direct line (as rays of light); **re-frac´tion** *n.*; **re-frac´tive** *a.*

re-frain´ *n.* phrase recurring at the end of each division of a poem; *vi.* keep from, avoid

re-fresh´ *vt.* renew, replenish; re-store vigor or freshness

re-fresh´ment *n.* food or drink which refreshes

re-frig´er-ant *n.* anything that cools; **re-frig´er-a´tion** *n.*

re-frig´er-a´tor *n.* cabinet or room in which foods, etc., are kept at low temperature

ref´uge *n.* shelter, asylum

ref´u-gee´ *n.* person who flees to another country for protection

re-fuse´ *vi.* & *vt.* reject, decline; **re-fus´al** *n.*

ref´use *n.* rubbish

re-fute´ *vt.* disprove; **ref´u-ta´tion** *n.*

re´gal *a.* kingly, royal

re-gale´ *vi.* & *vt.* entertain in a sumptuous manner

re-ga´li-a *n. pl.* emblems of royalty; ornamental or elaborate dress

re-gard´ *vt.* observe, hold in respect or affection; *n.* esteem

re-gat´ta *n.* boat race

re´gen-cy *n.* office or jurisdiction of a regent; person or group governing for another; period under a regent

re-gen´er-ate´ *vt.* produce anew; **re-gen´er-a´tion** *n.*

re´gent *n.* person ruling for a sovereign

re-gime´ *n.* form of government

reg´i-men *n.* rule of diet

reg´i-ment *n.* military body usually composed of a number of battalions; **reg´i-men´tal** *a.*

re´gion *n.* district, territory, country

reg´is-ter *n.* written record; book containing records; range of pipes on the organ; *vt.* enter in a register; **reg´is-trar´** *n.*; **reg´is-tra´tion** *n.*

re-gret´ *vt.* grieve at; *n.* sorrow over something past; **re-gret´ful** *a.*

reg´u-lar *a.* according to rule or custom; **reg´u-lar´i-ty** *n.*

reg´u-late´ *vt.* make regular, subject to rules

reg´u-la´tion *n.* rule, law; **reg´u-la´-tor** *n.*

re´ha-bil´i-tate´ *vt.* restore; reinstate

re-hearse´ *vt.* recite or practice privately; **re-hears´al** *n.*

reign *n.* royal authority; period during which a sovereign rules; *vi.* rule (as a sovereign)

re´im-burse´ *vt.* pay an equivalent to, for loss or cost; **re´im-burse´-ment** *n.*

rein *n.* strap or line of a bridle

rein´deer´ *n.* type of deer in the far north

re´in-force´ *vt.* strengthen, give support to; **re´in-force´-ment** *n.*

re´in-state´ *vt.* place in a former state; **re´in-state´ment** *n.*

re-it´er-ate´ *vt.* repeat again and again; **re-it´er-a´tion** *n.*

re-ject´ *vt.* refuse to grant; refuse as unfit; **re-jec´tion** *n.*

re-joice´ *vi.* feel or express joy; *vt.* make joyful
re-join´der *n.* answer to a reply or refutation
re-ju´ve-nate´ *vt.* make young again
re-late´ *vt.* describe, tell; *vi.* refer
re-lat´ion *n.* narration; mutual connection; connection by birth or marriage
rel´a-tive *a.* having relation; not absolute; *n.* person or thing which has relation to another
rel´a-tiv´i-ty *n.* theory advanced by Albert Einstein concerning matter, energy, space, and time
re-lax´ *vi.* & *vt.* make or become slack, less tense, or less severe; **re´lax-a´tion** *n.*
re-lease´ *vt.* let loose or free; *n.* discharge, acquittance
rel´e-gate´ *vt.* assign, refer, or consign a person or thing to a particular place, station, or class
re-lent´ *vi.* soften, feel compassion
rel´e-vant *a.* pertinent; **rel´e-vance, rel´e-van-cy** *n.*
re-li´a-ble *a.* trusty, dependable; **re-li´a-bil´-i-ty** *n.*
re-li´ance *n.* trust, dependence
rel´ic *n.* anything left after loss or decay of the rest
re-lief´ *n.* removal of a burden, pain, etc.; release from duty
re-lieve´ *vt.* ease, lessen
re-li´gion *n.* system of faith and worship; **re-li´gious** *a.*
re-lin´quish *vt.* abandon, withdraw from
rel´ish *vt.* enjoy; *n.* appetite; condiment
re-luc´tance *n.* unwillingness; **re-luc´tant** *a.* disinclined
re-ly´ *vi.* trust, depend upon
REM *n.* Rapid Eye Movement; period of sleep associated with dreaming
re-main´ *vi.* stay, be left behind; **re-main´der** *n.*
re-mand´ *vt.* send or put back
re-mark´ *vt.* say, state; *n.* statement, observation; **re-mark´a-ble** *a.*
rem´e-dy *n.* anything that cures disease, counteracts evil, or repairs loss; *vt.* counteract, repair, cure; **re-me´di-al** *a.*
re-mem´ber *vt.* call to or keep in mind; attend to
re-mem´brance *n.* memory; reminder
re-mind´ *vt.* arouse a recollection, bring to mind
re-miss´ *a.* negligent
re-mit´ *vi.* & *vt.* transmit (as money)
re-mit´-tance *n.* money or thing sent
rem´nant *n.* remainder
re-mod´el *vt.* fashion or model anew, make over
re-mon´strate´ *vi.* reason or argue against an act; **re-mon´strance** *n.*
re-morse´ *n.* anguish arising from guilt
re-mote´ *a.* far distant
re-move´ *vt.* put or take away, withdraw; **re-mov´al** *n.*
re-mu´ner-ate´ *vt.* recompense; **re-mu´ner-a´tion** *n.*
rend *vi.* & *vt.* tear or burst asunder by force
rend´er *vt.* give, give up, give back; furnish (as assistance); cause to be; translate; perform; try out
ren´dez-vous´ *n.* place of meeting; meeting by appointment
ren-di´tion *n.* interpretation; translation
ren´e-gade´ *n.* traitor, apostate; fugitive from justice
re-new´ *vi.* & *vt.* revive; begin anew; **re-new´al** *n.*

re-nounce´ *vt.* disown
ren´o-vate´ *vt.* make new again; **ren´o-va´tion** *n.*
rent *n.* tear, break; payment for use of property; *vt.* occupy or let for rent; *vi.* be let for rent; **rent´al** *n.*
re-pair´ *vi.* go, resort; *vt.* restore; make amends for; *n.* restoration
rep´a-ra´tion *n.* repair; amends, compensation
rep´ar-tee´ *n.* quick, witty reply
re-past´ *n.* meal
re-peal´ *vt.* revoke, abrogate, or unmake (as a law); *n.* revocation
re-peat´ *vt.* do or speak again
re-pel´ *vt.* drive back, check the advance of; **re-pel´-lent** *a.* & *n.*
re-pent´ *vi.* & *vt.* sorrow for past acts or omissions; **re-pent´-ance** *n.*; **re-pent´-ant** *a.*
rep´er-toire´ *n.* schedule of plays, music, etc., ready for performance
rep´e-ti´tion *n.* act of repeating
re-place´ *vt.* repay, provide a substitute for; take the place of; **re-place´ment** *n.*
re-plen´ish *vt.* refill, restock, renew a supply
re-plete´ *a.* completely filled; **re-ple´tion** *n.*
re-ply´ *vi.* & *vt.* answer; *n.*
re-port´ *vt.* make a statement concerning; write down (as for a newspaper); *vi.* make a statement; present oneself (as for duty); *n.* statement of facts; rumor; sound, noise; **re-port´er** *n.*
re-pose´ *vt.* lay at rest; *vi.* rest; rest in confidence; *n.* sleep; quiet
re-pos´i-to´ry *n.* place for safekeeping of valuables
rep´re-sent´ *vt.* stand for, stand in the place of; act the part of; describe; **rep´re-sen-ta´tion** *n.*
rep´re-sent´a-tive *a.* representing, typical; *n.* one who stands for another; member of lower house of Congress or of a state legislature
re-press´ *vt.* check, restrain; **re-pres´sion** *n.*; **re-pres´sive** *a.*
re-prieve´ *n.* delay, respite; suspension of a criminal sentence
rep´ri-mand´ *n.* severe reproof; *vt.* reprove severely, rebuke, chide
re-pris´al *n.* act of violence done in retaliation
re-proach´ *vt.* censure, upbraid; *n.* reproof; **re-proach´ful** *a.*
rep´ro-bate´ *a.* given over to sin; *n.* profligate person
re´pro-duce´ *vt.* produce again, copy; produce offspring; **re´pro-duc´tion** *n.*; **re´pro-duc´tive** *a.*
re-prove´ *vt.* censure
rep´tile *n.* crawling animal (including snakes, lizards, alligators, etc.)
re-pub´lic *n.* government in which power is vested in representatives elected by the people
Re-pub´li-can *n.* member of the conservative political party in the U. S.; *a.*
re-pu´di-ate´ *vt.* reject; **re-pu´di-a´-tion** *n.*
re-pug´nant *a.* offensive; **re-pug´-nance** *n.*
re-pulse´ *vt.* drive back, repel; **re-pul´sion** *n.*
re-pul´sive *a.* grossly offensive
re-pute´ *n.* estimate of character; **rep´u-ta-ble** *a.*
rep´u-ta´tion *n.* character in the public estimation; fame
re-quest´ *vt.* ask, desire; *n.* petition, demand; anything requested
re´qui-em *n.* hymn or mass sung for the dead
re-quire´ *vt.* demand; need; **re-quire´ment** *n.*
req´ui-site *a.* needful, indispensa-

ble; *n.* anything which is required; **req´ui-si´tion** *n.* written request

re-scind´ *vt.* revoke, annul

res´cue *vt.* free from danger or violence; *n.* deliverance

re-search´ *n.* careful search into the unknown

re-sem´ble *vt.* be similar to; **re-sem´blance** *n.*

re-sent´ *vi.* & *vt.* be indignant at; **re-sent´ful** *a.*; **re-sent´ment** *n.*

res´er-va´tion *n.*reserving or keeping back; anything withheld or kept apart

re-serve´ *vt.* keep back; keep for future or other use; *n.* anything kept for future use (as part of an army or fleet); absence of freedom in words or actions, caution

res´er-voir´ *n.* place where water is stored for use; supply or store of anything

re-side´ *vi.* dwell permanently, live in

res´i-dence *n.* place where one resides; **res´i-dent** *a.* & *n.*

res´i-due´ *n.* remainder; **re-sid´u-al** *a.*

re-sign´ *vt.* yield up, abandon, submit; *vi.* leave a job; **res´ig-na´-tion** *n.* act of giving up; act of leaving a job

res´in *n.* substance given off by trees and plants (used in varnish, etc.; **res´in-ous** *a.*

re-sist´ *vi.* & *vt.* oppose, strive against; **re-sist´ance** *n.*

res´o-lute´ *a.* constant, determined; **res´o-lu´tion** *n.* fixed determination; formal proposal

re-solve´ *vi.* & *vt.* decide, fix by formal declaration; *n.* resolution

res´o-nant *a.* returning sound, echoing; **res´o-nance** *n.*

re-sort´ *vi.* have recourse to; *n.* recourse; place much frequented

re-source´ *n.* source of help; **re-sources´** *n. pl.* means

res-pect´ *vt.* esteem; *n.* regard; relation; **res-pect´a-bil´i-ty** *n.*; **res-pect´a-ble** *a.*

re-spec´tive *a.* relating to a particular person or thing

res´pi-ra´tion *n.* act or process of breathing

res´pi-ra´tor *n.* apparatus for filtering out gases, etc.; apparatus for giving artificial respiration

res´pite *n.* delay, postponement

res-pond´ *vi.* answer

res-pond´ent *n.* defendant

res-ponse´ *n.* reply

re-spon´si-ble *a.* answerable; capable of discharging one´s duties; **re-spon´si-bil´i-ty** *n.*

re-spon´sive *a.* inclined to respond; sympathetic

rest *n.* remainder, others; cessation from motion, labor, etc.; in music, interval of silence or symbol indicating this; *vi.* repose; *vt.* lay at rest; place on a support, lean

res´tau-rant´ *n.* eating place

res´ti-tu´tion *n.* restoration, amends

re-store´ *vt.* repair, replace; **res´to-ra´tion** *n.*

re-strain´ *vt.* check, hinder; limit; **re-straint´** *n.*

re-strict´ *vt.* limit; **re-stric´tion** *n.*

re-sult´ *vi.* issue (as a consequence); *n.* consequence; **re-sult´ant** *a.*

re-sume´ *vt.* begin again; **re-sump´-tion** *n.*

re-sus´ci-tate´ *vi.* & *vt.* revive; **re-sus´ci-ta´tion** *n.*

re´tail´ *n.* sale direct to consumers

re-tain´ *vt.* continue to hold; employ by a fee; **re-tain´er** *n.* person in the service of another; fee paid to engage a lawyer

re-tal'i-ate' *vi. & vt.* repay in kind

re-tard' *vt.* keep back, hinder

re-ten'tion *n.* act of keeping back or retaining; **re-ten'tive** *a.* having power to retain, tenacious

ret'i-cent *a.* reserved in speech; **ret'i-cence** *n.*

ret'i-na *n.* innermost coating of the back part of the eye

ret'i-nue' *n.* body of followers

re-tire' *vi.* retreat, go to bed; leave off gainful employment; *vt.* withdraw; **re-tire'ment** *n.*

re-tort' *vi. & vt.* make a sharp reply; *n.* sharp reply; vessel used in distillation

re-tract' *vi. & vt.* take back (as an accusation); draw back; **re-trac'-tion** *n.*

re'tread' *n.* automobile tire on which wornout treads have been renewed

re-treat' *n.* refuge, place of saftey; withdrawal; *vi.* withdraw

re-trench' *vi. & vt.* cut down, economize

ret'ri-bu'tion *n.* repayment, reward or punishment

re-trieve' *vt.* recover

re-triev'er *n.* dog trained to fetch game that has been shot

ret'ro-ac'tive *a.* acting or going into effect as of an earlier date

ret'ro-gres'sion *n.* act of moving or going backward; **ret'ro-gres'sive** *a.*

ret'ro-rock'et *n.* auxiliary rocket for directional control in a sacecraft

ret'ro-spect' *n.* contemplation of the past; **ret'ro-spec'tion** *n.*

re-turn' *vi.* come back to the same place; *vt.* give or send back; *n.*

re-veal' *vt.* disclose

rev'eil-le *n.* military ceremony at beginning of day's work

rev'el *vi.* carouse, make merry; delight in; *n.* merriment. **rev'el-ry** *n.*

rev'e-la'tion *n.* act of making something known; anything revealed by God to man

re-venge' *vt.* punish or injure in return, avenge; *n.* retaliation

rev'e-nue' *n.* income from any source

re-ver'ber-ate' *vi.* resound

re-vere' *vt.* venerate

rev'er-ence *n.* veneration; *vt.* venerate

rev'er-end *a.* worthy of reverence; title of the clergy

rev'er-ent *a.* showing reverence

rev'er-en'tial *a.* respectful, reverent

rev'er-ie *n.* idle thinking, daydream

re-ver'sal *n.* act of reversing

re-verse' *vt.* change to the opposite; *n.* opposite; change, misfortune; *a.* turned backward, contrary; **re-vers'i-ble** *a.* able to be reversed or worn on both sides

re-vert' *vi.* return

re-view' *vt.* examine critically; *n.* critique; periodical with critiques of books, etc.; inspection of troops

re-vile' *vt.* calumniate, abuse by harsh language

re-vise' *vt.* review and improve; reread and correct; **re-vi'sion** *n.*

re-vive' *vi. & vt.* return to life; recover; **re-viv'al** *n.* recovery; religious awakening

re-voke' *vt.* annul by recalling, reverse

re-volt' *vi.* rebel; be grossly offended, feel nausea; *vt.* shock; *n.* rebellion

rev'o-lu'tion *n.* revolving; complete change; overthrow of the government

re-volve' *vi. & vt.* roll round on an

axis
re-volv´er *n.* small firearm with a revolving cylinder
re-vul´sion *n.* sudden and complete change, esp. of feelings
re-ward´ *n.* recompense; *vt.* compensate
rhap´so-dy *n.* literary or musical composition in free style
rhet´o-ric *n.* art of elegant speaking or composition
rheu´ma-tism *n.* painful inflammation of the joints or muscles
R´h´ fac´tor *n.* substance in blood of most people causing a certain reaction of the blood corpuscles
rhi-noc´er-os *n.* very large animal with one to two horns on the nose
rho´do-den´dron *n.* small tree with evergreen leaves and flowers like the rose
rhu´barb´ *n.* plant much used in cooking and medicine
rhyme, rime *n.* correspondence of sounds at middle and end of words (as *bread: fed*); *vi.* correspond in sound; make rhymes
rhythm *n.* regular recurrence of accents; movement in musical time; **rhyth´mic, rhyth´mi-cal** *a.*
rib *n.* one of the bones which encircle the chest; anything like a rib
rib´ald *a.* vulgar, base, gross (as of humor); **rib´ald-ry** *n.*
rib´bon *n.* strip or band (as of silk); inked band in a typewriter
ri´bo-fla´vin *n.* vitamin B_2
rice *n.* cereal grown in warm climates
rich *a.* abounding in wealth or possessions; fertile; high in calories
rick´ets *n.* disease of the bones among children
rid *vt.* set free of; **rid´dance** *n.* quittance, liberation
rid´dle *n.* enigma, puzzle
ride *vi.* & *vt.* **(rid´ing, rode, rid´den)** sit or rest on, so as to be carried; *n.* excursion by horse, automobile, etc.; **rid´er** *n.* person who rides; addition to a legislative bill before it is passed
ridge *n.* extended protuberance, as the top of a roof, etc.
rid´i-cule´ *n.* wit exposing one to laughter or mockery; *vt.* expose to mockery; **ri-dic´u-lous** *a.* absurd
rife *a.* abundant, abounding
ri´fle *vt.* strip, rob; *n.* firearm with a barrel spirally grooved
rift *n.* opening, split
rig *vt.* fit with sails and tackling; *n.* dress, odd style of clothing; style of masts and sails
right *a.* straight; true, just; on the right hand; containing 90 degrees; *n.* that which is right or correct; right side, opposite to left; *vt.* make right or straight; set upright; do justice to, relieve from wrong
right´eous *a.* doing right
rig´id *a.* not easily bent, firm; severe, strict; **ri-gid´i-ty** *n.*
rig´ma-role´ *n.* repetition of foolish words; long story
rig´or *n.* stiffness, strictness, severity; **rig´or-ous** *a.*
rile *vt. col.* to irritate; to vex
rim *n.* raised margin
rind *n.* external covering (as the skin of fruit)
ring *n.* circle; small metal band worn as an ornament; arena; clique; prize ring; *vt.* encircle; fit with a ring; cut off a strip of bark around a tree
ring *vi.* sound as a bell when struck; continue to sound; *vt.* cause to sound; *n.* sound (esp. of metals), chime of bells

ring´lead´er *n.* head of a riotous mob
ring´worm *n.* a skin disease
rink *n.* enclosed space for races and games
rinse *vt.* cleanse with clear water
ri´ot *n.* uproar, tumult; breach of the peace by any group; *vi.* raise an uproar; run to excess; disturb the peace; **ri´ot-ous** *a.*
rip *vt.* divide by cutting or tearing, cut open; *n.* place torn
ripe *a.* mature (as fruit); **rip´en** *vi.* & *vt.*
rip´ple *n.* little wave; *vi.* & *vt.*
rise *vi.* **(rose, ris´en)** ascend, grow upward; swell in quantity, rank, or value; take an upright position; leave a place of rest; have its source
risk *n.* hazard, chance. of loss or injury; *vt.* expose to hazard; venture
rite *n.* religious or solemn ceremony
rit´u-al *a.* consisting of or prescribing rites; *n.* manner of performing divine service
ri´val *n.* one competing with another; *a.* standing in competition; *vt.* stand in competition with; **ri´-val-ry** *n.*
riv´er *n.* large stream
riv´et *n.* bolt of metal fastened at both ends; *vt.* fasten with a rivet
road *n.* highway; open way for passengers and traffic; place where ships ride at anchor; **road´-block´** *n.* obstruction placed in road
roam *vi.* & *vt.* rove about
roar *vi.* bellow; *n.* cry of a beast; outcry
roast *vt.* cook by dry heat; *n.* meat that is roasted
rob *vt.* take away from by force; deprive wrongfully; **rob´ber** *n.*; **rob´-ber-y** *n.*
robe *n.* gown
rob´in *n.* small European songbird; American thrush
ro´bot´ *n.* device that operates with almost human ability
ro-bust´ *a.* vigorous, husky
rock *n.* mass of stone; *vi.* & *vt.* move backward and forward, totter
rock´-n-roll´, rock *n.* popular music known for its lively, two-beat rhythms; *a.*
rock´er *n.* curved support on which a cradle or chair rocks; rocking chair
rock´et *n.* propelling mechanism in jet engines, fireworks, etc.; **rock´-et-ry** *n.* study of rocket propulsion
ro´dent *n.* gnawing animal (as a rat)
roe *n.* eggs or spawn of fish; small species of deer; female deer
rogue *n.* dishonest person, knave; mischievous person, wag; **ro´guish** *a.* waggish, playful
role *n.* part an actor takes in a play; function
roll *vi.* & *vt.* turn like a wheel; form into a round mass; press with a roller; *n.* anything folded into cylindrical shape; list of names; little loaf of bread; continued sound of a drum
roll´back´ *n.* reduction, especially of prices or wages, to a former level
rol´lick-ing *a.* frolicsome
ro-mance´ *n.* any fictitious or wonderful tale; love, courtship; *a.* pertaining to the languages developed from Latin
romp *vi.* play noisily; skip about in play
roof *n.* top covering of a building
room *n.* unoccupied space; chamber; freedom to act
roost *n.* pole or support on which a

bird rests

rooster *n.* male of the domestic chicken

root *n.* part of a plant which grows in the earth; word from which others are derived (as *fair. fairness*); *vi.* take root, be firmly established; *vt.* grow by planting

rope *n.* thick, twisted cord; *vt.* fasten; draw in with a rope

ro´sa-ry *n.* string of beads used in prayers

rose *n.* plant of many species valued for its beautiful flower; color of the rose

ro-sette´ *n.* imitation of the form of a rose

ros´in *n.* solid matter left after distilling crude turpentine

ros´ter *n.* list of names

rot *vi.* & *vt.* putrefy, decay; *n.* decay; **rot´ten** *a.*

ro´ta-ry en´gine *n.* engine in which parts move in a circle rather than in a straight line

ro´tate´ *vi.* & *vt.* turn like a wheel; **ro´ta-ry** *a.*; **ro-ta´tion** *n.*

ROTC *n.* Reserve Officer´s Training Corps

rote *n.* mechanical repetition

ro-tis´ser-ie *n.* rotating spit for cooking meat over heat or coals

ro´tor *n.* rotating part of a machine; horizontal propeller that supports a helicopter

ro-tund´ *a.* round, spherical

rouge *n.* red coloring applied to cheeks

rough *a.* coarse, not smooth; **rough´en** *vi.* & *vt.*

round *a.* circular; *n.* anything round in shape; series of actions; volley, single cartridge

round´-the-clock´ *a.* continuous

rouse *vi.* & *vt.* stir up

rout *n.* tumultuous crowd; disorderly flight of troops

route *n.* course to be travelled

rou-tine´ *n.* regular course of action

rove *vi.* & *vt.* wander over

row *n.* line, persons or things in a line; *vi.* & *vt.* impel with an oar

row´dy *a.* noisy, turbulent; *n.* ruffian

roy´al *a.* regal, kingly

roy´al-ty *n.* kingship; anyone born of kingly blood; sum paid to the owner of a patent, copyright, etc.

rub *vt.* move something over a surface with pressure or friction; polish; *vi.* move along with pressure, grate; fret

rub´ber *n.* elastic material used in erasers, tires, etc.; decisive game of a series; overshoe made of rubber

rub´bish *n.* waste matter, debris; nonsense

rub´ble *n.* small stones

ru´by *n.* precious stone of a red color

rud´der *n.* appliance by which a boat is steered

rud´dy *a.* of reddish color

rude *a.* uncultivated

ru´di-ment *n.* first principle, element; **ru´di-men´ta-ry** *a.*

rue, *vt.* be sorry for, lament; *n.* regret, bitterness; **rue´ful** *a.*

ruff *n.* ornamental frill

ruf´fi-an *n.* brutal, boisterous fellow

ruf´fle *vt.* wrinkle; disorder, agitate; *n.* frill

rug *n.* soft mat for the floor

rug´ged *a.* uneven, shaggy; stormy; vigorous

ru´in *n.* destruction, overthrow; remains of a building (usually in plural); *vt.* demolish, defeat; impoverish; **ru´in-ous** *a.*

rule *n.* government, control; principle, regulation; instrument used to draw lines; *vt.* govern, manage; settle by decision; mark with straight lines; *vi.* exercise power, decide; **rul´er** *n.*

rum´ba, rhum´ba *n.* rhythmic Cuban dance or the music for it; *vi.*

rum´ble *vi.* make a noise like thunder; *n.* low, heavy vibration

ru´mi-nate´ *vi.* & *vt.* meditate, ponder; **ru´mi-na´tion** *n.*

rum´mage *vi.* & *vt.* search thoroughly by turning things over

ru´mor *n.* unofficial report, gossip; *vt.* circulate by unofficial report

rump *n.* buttocks, hindquarters

rum´ple *vt.* wrinkle

rum´pus *n.* wrangle

run *vi.* & *vt.* **(run´ning, ran)** move swiftly; flow, melt; *n.* course, flow; series; prevalence

rung *n.* step of a ladder

runt *n.* dwarfed or stunted animal or plant

rup´ture *n.* a breaking or bursting (as in hernia); *vt.* break, burst

ru´ral *a.* pertaining to the country; rustic

ruse *n.* trick, stratagem

rush *vi.* move quickly or hastily; *n.* hasty activity

rus´set *a.* reddish-brown

rust *n.* reddish-brown coating on iron exposed to air; brown or orange spots on leaves; *vi.* & *vt.* make or become rusty or dull by inaction

rus´tic *a.* pertaining to the country; awkward; *n.*

rus´tle *vi.* make a soft, whispering sound

rut *n.* track left by a wheel

ruth´less *a.* without pity

rye *n.* cereal grass allied to wheat

S

Sab´bath *n.* seventh day of the week among the Jews, the first among Christians

sa´ber, sa´bre *n.* one-edged sword slightly curved

sa´ble *n.* animal of the weasel kind prized for its fur

sab´o-tage´ *n.* willful destruction of property (as by enemy agents during a war); *vt.*; **sab´o-teur´** *n.*

sac *n.* natural sack for a liquid in animals or plants

sac´cha-rine *a.* overly sweet; *n.* sugar substitute derived from coal tar

sa-chet´ *n.* bag filled with scent

sack *vt.* plunder, ravage; *n.* devastation of a town; large bag

sac´ra-ment *n.* religious rite

sac´red *a.* dedicated to religion or God; inviolable

sac´ri-fice *vt.* offer up, esp. on the altar of a divinity; destroy or give up for something else; *n.* anything offered as a sacrifice; **sac´ri-fi´cial** *a.*

sac´ri-lege *n.* profanation of sacred things; **sac´ri-le´gious** *a.*

sad *a.* downcast, gloomy; **sad´den** *vt.*; **sad sack** *n.* blunderer, misfit

sad´dle *n.* seat for the rider of a horse; *vt.* put a saddle on; load, heap on

sa-fa´ri *n.* hunting trip, esp. for African game

safe *a.* unharmed; free from danger or injury; *n.* locked chest for valuables

safe´guard´ *n.* protection

safe´ty match *n.* match that lights only when struck against a specially treated surface

safe´ty pin´ *n.* pin bent so that

point is fastened in clasp at the head

sag *vi.* & *vt.* sink or settle in the middle

sa-ga´cious *a.* wise

sage *a.* wise; *n.* wise man, philosopher; aromatic herb

sail *n.* sheet of canvas to propel a ship; ship; *vi.* be moved by sails; go by water; glide or float smoothly; *vt.* navigate; **sail´or** *n.*

saint *n.* holy person; one canonized

sake *n.* cause, account

sal´a-ble, sale´a-ble *a.* able to be sold

sal´ad *n.* raw vegetables cut up and seasoned

sal´a-man´der *n.* amphibious reptile allied to the lizard

sal´a-ry *n.* wages, recompense for services

sale *n.* act of selling; selling at a discount; demand; **sales´man** *n.*

sa´li-ent *a.* prominent

sal´ine´ *a.* consisting of, containing, or resembling salt

sa-li´va *n.* digestive fluid formed in mouth cavity

sal´low *a.* of a yellowish color, unhealthy looking

salm´on *n.* northern food-fish; orange-pink color

sa-lon´ *n.* apartment for the reception of company; fashionable assembly

sa-loon´ *n.* bar room

salt *n.* sodium chloride; seasoning, piquancy, flavor, wit; combination of an acid with a base; old sailor; *vt.* preserve or season with salt

sal´u-tar´y *a.* promoting health, beneficial

sal´u-ta´tion *n.* greeting, welcome

sa-lute´ *vt.* greet formally; *n.*

sal´vage *n.* property saved from loss; *vt.*

sal-va´tion *n.* preservation (as from damnation)

salve *n.* paste form of a drug used to treat wounds; words or deeds used to improve a situation

sal´vo´ *n.* simultaneous discharge (as of firearms)

sam´ple *n.* specimen, part showing the quality of the whole; *vt.* try or examine a specimen of

san´a-to´ri-um *n.* hospital (as for the treatment of tuberculosis), health resort

san´a-to´ry *a.* healing

sanc´ti-fy *vt.* make sacred or holy; **sanc´ti-fi-ca´tion** *n.*

sanc´ti-mo´ni-ous *a.* hypocritically devout

sanc´tion *n.* approval, support; *vt.* give approval to

sanc´ti-ty *n.* holiness

sanc´tu-ar´y *n.* sacred place; place of refuge

san´dal *n.* shoe bound to the foot by straps

sand´pa´per *n.* paper, covered with sand; *vt.* rub with sandpaper

sand´stone´ *n.* stone composed of consolidated sand

sand´wich *n.* two slices of bread with meat, etc., between; *vt.* insert between

sane *a.* sound in mind

san´guine *a.* red, ruddy; hopeful, confident

san´i-tar´i-um *n.* sanatorium

san´i-tar´y *a.* pertaining to health, hygienic; **san´i-ta´tion** *n.*

san´i-ty *n.* soundness of mind

sap *n.* vital juice of plants; *vt.* undermine

sap´phire *n.* precious blue stone

sar´casm *n.* cutting remark; **sarcas´tic** *a.*

sar´coph´a-gus *n.* stone receptacle for a corpse
sar-don´ic *a.* bitter, sarcastic
sash *n.* scarf worn as a belt; frame for panes of glass
sate *vt.* satisfy, glut
sat´el-lite´ *n.* servile follower; natural body which revolves around a planet, man-made vehicle that orbits the earth; country dominated by a larger, agressive power
sa´ti-ate´ *vt.* satisfy
sat´in *n.* closely woven, glossy cloth
sat´ire *n.* use of irony, ridicule, sarcasm, etc., to expose vice or folly; **sa-tir´ic, sa-tir´i-cal** *a.*; **sat´i-rize´** *vt.*
sat´is-fac´tion *n.* gratification, comfort; that which satisfies; atonement; **sat´is-fac´to-ry** *a.*
sat´is-fy´ *vt.* give enough to, supply fully; discharge, pay convince
sat´u-rate´ *vt.* soak completely; **sat´-u-ra´tion** *n.*
sat´yr *n.* sylvan deity, part man and part goat
sauce *n.* liquid seasoning for food, gravy; impertinence; **sau´cy** *a.* pert, insolent
sau´cer *n.* shallow dish to hold a cup
sauer´kraut´ *n.* pickled cabbage
saun´ter *vi.* wander about
sau´sage *n.* chopped meat enclosed in a skin
sav´age *a.* uncivilized; *n.* human being in a wild state
sa-vant´ *n.* man of learning, scholar
save *vt.* rescue; reserve; *vi.* be economical
sav´ior *n.* one who saves from evil or harm
Sav´iour *n.* Jesus Christ
sa´vor *n.* flavor, taste; *vi.* have a particular taste or smell, partake of the nature (of); **sa´vor-y** *a.* pleasing to taste and smell
saw *n.* thin blade with a toothed edge; *vi.* & *vt.* **(sawed, sawn)** cut with a saw
say *vi.* & *vt.* **(said)** utter in words, repeat; *n.* turn to speak
say´ing *n.* aphorism, maxim, proverb
scab *n.* crust over a sore; disease of sheep; one who takes up the work abandoned by a striker
scab´bard *n.* case in which the blade of a sword is kept
scaf´fold *n.* temporary elevated platform, esp. for workmen; platform for the execution of a criminal
scal´a-wag´ *n.* worthless fellow, scamp
scald *vt.* burn or clean with steam or hot liquid
scale *n.* graduated measure or series; series of tones in music; proportion; one of the small, thin plates on a fish or reptile; balance for weighing (chiefly *pl.*); *vt.* clear of scales; cut down; mount
scal´lop *n.* a bivalvular shellfish; one of a series of curves in an edge; *vt.* cut the edge into curves
scalp *n.* skin of the head (on which the hair grows); *vt.* cut the scalp from
scal´pel *n.* small surgical knife for cutting
scamp *n.* rogue, rascal
scam´per *vi.* run about
scan *vt.* count the feet or measures in a verse; examine carefully, scrutinize; examine without care; have an image or surface swept over by a beam (as in TV or radar)
scan´dal *n.* disgrace, ill fame; gossip; **scan´dal-ize** *vt.*; **scan´dal-ous** *a.*

scant *a.* not full, deficient
scape´goat´ *n.* one made to suffer for another´s offense
scar *n.* mark left by a wound or sore; *vt.* mark with scars
scarce *a.* not plentiful; **scar´ci-ty** *n.*
scare *vt.* strike with sudden terror; *n.* fright
scarf *n.* light wrap for the neck
scar´let *n.* bright red color; *a.*
scat´ter *vi. & vt.* disperse, strew
scav´en-ger *n.* person who removes filth; animal that lives on leavings or carrion
scene *n.* place of action, occurrence, or exhibition; separate part of a play, smaller than an act; number of objects presented to the view at once, spectacle, view; **sce´ner-y** *n.*; **sce´nic** *a.*
scent *vt.* smell; perfume
scep´ter *n.* staff borne by sovereigns as an emblem of authority
scep´tic *n.* variant of **skeptic**
sched´ule *n.* list, inventory; timetable; *vt.* place in a list or timetable
scheme *n.* project, plan; *vi. & vt.* plan, contrive
schism *n.* separation in a church from difference of opinion
schiz´o-phre´ni-a *n.* severe mental disorder marked by loss of touch with reality; **schiz´o-phren´ic** *a.*
schol´ar *n.* pupil, student; man of learning; **schol´ar-ly** *a.*
scho-las´tic *a.* pertaining to a scholar or to schools; pedantic
school *n.* place for instruction; pupils of a school; those who hold a common doctrine; *vt.* instruct
schoon´er *n.* swift-sailing vessel, generally two masted
sci´ence *n.* systematized knowledge; **science fiction** *n.* imaginative stories based upon scientific possibilities; **sci´en-tif´ic** *a.*; **sci´en-tist** *n.*
sci´on *n.* cutting or twig for grafting; descendant
scis´sors *n. pl.* cutting instrument
scle-ro´sis *n.* hardening, as of an internal body tissue
scoff *vi. & vt.* mock; **scoff´er** *n.*
scold *vi. & vt.* chide
sconce *n.* ornamental candlestick on a wall
scoop *vt.* lift up with something hollow, empty with a ladle; make hollow, dig out; *n.* large ladle
scoot *vi.* run
scope *n.* room for free outlook or action; range
scorch *vi. & vt.* burn slightly
score *n.* account, reckoning; twenty; *vt.* mark; charge; succeed in winning; **scor´er** *n.*
scorn *n.* lofty contempt; *vt.* hold in contempt, refuse; **scorn´-ful** *a.*
scor´pi-on *n.* small, poisonous creature with eight legs
scoun´drel *n.* rascal; worthless fellow
scour *vt.* clean by rubbing
scourge *n.* punishment; *vt.*
scout *n.* one sent out to observe the enemy, etc.; *vi. & vt.* observe, reconnoiter; *vt.* reject contemptuously
scow *n.* large flat-bottomed boat
scowl *vi.* wrinkle the brows; *n.* look of sullenness, wrinkling of the brow
scrab´ble *n.* scribbling; a struggle with hands or feet; *tr.* game similar to anagrams
scram´ble *vi.* struggle to seize something; move on all fours; *vt.* mix; beat and fry eggs; *n.*
scrap *n.* small piece; extract
scrape *vt.* rub with something sharp; *n.* difficulty

scratch *vi.* & *vt.* mark a surface with something pointed; *n.* mark or tear; slight wound

scrawl *vi.* & *vt.* write hastily; *n.* irregular or hasty writing

scrawny *a.* lean

scream *vi.* shriek; *n.* shrill, sudden cry

screech *vi.* shriek; *n.* harsh, shrill cry

screen *n.* anything that shelters from danger or observation; *vt.* shelter, conceal; pass through a sieve; **screen play** *n.* acting play for motion pictures

screw *n.* cylinder with a spiral groove or ridge; kind of nail having such grooves; *vt.* turn as a screw; oppress by extortion; **screw´driv´er** *n.* instrument for turning screws

scrib´ble *vi.* & *vt.* write carelessly or hastily

scrim´mage *n.* skirmish, tussle; a play in football

scrimp *vi.* & *vt.* make too small or short, be sparing or stingy

script *n.* handwriting; play for radio, TV, etc.

scrip´ture *n.* text from the Bible; the Bible

scroll *n.* roll of paper; spiral ornament

scrub *vi.* & *vt.* rub hard; *n.* stunted underbrush

scruff *n.* nape of the neck

scru´ple *n.* reluctance to act, as from motives of conscience; **scru´pu-lous** *a.*

scru´ti-nize´ *vt.* examine minutely; **scru´ti-ny** *n.*

scu´ba *n.* self-contained underwater breathing apparatus

scuf´fle *vi.* fight confusedly; *n.* struggle at close quarters

sculp´tor *n.* one who carves figures

sculp´ture *n.* art of carving figures in wood, stone, etc.; carved work; *vt.* carve

scum *n.* matter rising to the surface of liquids; refuse

scur´ry *vi.* move hastily

scur´vy *n.* disease of the skin caused by vitamin deficiency; *a.* diseased with scurvy; offensive, mean

scut´tle *vi.* run hastily, hurry; *vt.* sink (as a ship)

scythe *n.* blade for mowing grass, etc., by hand

sea *n.* great mass of salt water; swell of the sea, heavy wave

sea´far-ing *a.* following the life of, or belonging to, a seaman or sailor

seal *n.* engraved stamp for impressing wax, wax so impressed; marine animal valuable for its skin, fur, and oil; *vt.* fasten with a seal

seam *n.* line formed by sewing together two pieces of cloth

sea´man *n.* sailor, mariner

seam´stress *n.* dressmaker

sear *vt.* dry up, scorch

search *vi.* & *vt.* seek, examine; *n.* examination, hunt

search´light´ *n.* powerful light fitted with reflectors

sea´shore´ *n.* land adjacent to the sea

sea´sick´ness *n.* nausea prodticed by the motion of a vessel at sea; **sea´sick´** *a.*

sea´son *n.* one of the four periods of the year; usual or proper time; *vt.* mature; give relish to; *vi.* become matured or inured; **sea´son-a-ble** *a.*

seat *n.* surface of a chair, etc., on which one sits; site, station; *vt.* place on a seat, cause to sit

seat´ belt´ *n.* straps for fastening a

passenger to his seat in auto or airplane as a safety device

sea´weed *n.* plant of the sea

se´cede´ *vi.* withdraw from a political or religions organization; **se-ces´sion** *n.*

se-clude´ *vt.* keep apart; **se-clu´sion** *n.*

sec´ond *a.* immediately following the first, next in position; another; inferior; *n.* one that follows; 60th part of a minute of time, or of a degree; **sec´ond-ar´y** *a.*

sec´ond-hand´ *a.* not new; used by another

se´cret *a.* concealed; *n.* anything kept hidden or concealed; **se´cre-cy** *n.*

sec´re-tar´y *n.* person employed to write for another; officer entrusted with certain affairs of a department of government or an association

se-crete´ *vt.* hide, conceal; produce, give off, exude; **se-cre´tion** *n.* anything secreted (as by glands)

sect *n.* group of people with common philosophy, belief, etc.; group of people who dissent from established church

sec´tion *n.* division, portion; **sec´-tion-al** *a.*

sec´u-lar *a.* pertaining to things not spiritual; worldly

se-cure´ *a.* free from fear, care, or danger; *vt.* make safe, certain, or fast; obtain

se-cu´ri-ty *n.* safety, protection; **security risk** *n.* person considered of doubtful reliability in work concerned with national security

se-dan´ *n.* automobile that seats from four to seven occupants; closed portable chair

se-date´ *a.* quiet, serious

sed´i-tive *n.* medicine that calms

sed´en-tar´y *a.* stationary, inactive; sitting much

sedge *n.* kind of coarse grass

sed´i-ment *n.* dregs

se-di´tion *n.* behavior which leads or incites to rebellion; **se-di´tious** *a.*

se-duce´ *vt.* lead astray from duty or purity; corrupt; **se-duc´tion** *n.*; **se-duc´tive** *a.* alluring

sed´u-lous *a.* diligent, assiduous

see *n.* seat or jurisdiction of a bishop or of the pope; *vt.* **(saw, seen)** perceive by the eye; visit

seed *n.* substance from which new plants and animals are generated; *vi.* & *vt.* sow seed; **seed´ling** *n.* plant reared from the seed; small tree; **seed´y** *a.* run to seed; shabby

seek *vi.* & *vt.* **(sought)** go in search of, try to find or gain

seem *vi.* appear, look

seep *vi.* percolate, trickle

seep´age *n.* that which drains out of a container

seer *n.* one who foresees

seethe *vi.* & *vt.* boil

seg´ment *n.* part cut off, portion

seg´re-gate´ *vi.* & *vt.* separate; **seg´-re-ga´tion** *n.* separation, esp. racial

seine *n.* large net for catching fish; *vi.* & *vt.*

seis´mo-graph´ *n.* device that measures earth vibrations

seis-mol´o-gy *n.* study of earthquakes

seize *vt.* take possession of forcibly, apprehend; **sei´zure** *n.*

sel´dom *adv.* rarely

se-lect´ *vt.* pick out by preference; *a.* choice

self *n.* **(selves)** one´s own person

self´ish *a.* without regard for others

sell *vt.* **(sold)** transfer for money or

some equivalent; betray, cheat
se-man´tics *n.* study of meanings
sem´a-phore´ *n.* system of hand signals; apparatus for signaling trains
sem´blance *n.* resemblance; aspect; appearance
se-mes´ter *n.* course of study lasting about 4½ months
sem´i-cir´cle *n.* half a circle
sem´i-co´lon *n.* mark of punctuation (;)
sem´i-con-duc´tor *n.* any of a group of materials having an electrical conductivity between metals and insulators. They are used in transistors, rectifiers, photoelectric cells and as thermometers
sem´i-con-scious *a.* not fully conscious
sem´i-fi´nal *a.* preceding the final contest. *n.*
sem´i-month´ly *n.* a paper, magazine etc. issued twice a month
sen´ate *n.* legislative or deliberative body, esp. the upper house of a national or state legislature; **sen´a-tor** *n.*
send *vt.* **(sent)** cause to go, dispatch, inflict
se´nile´ *a.* pertaining to old age; **se-nil´i-ty** *n.*
sen´ior *a.* older; *n.* one older than another; student in last year of his school course
sen-sa´tion *n.* perception by the senses
sen-sa´tion-al *a.* gratifying a taste for excitement; **sen-sa´tion-al-ism** *n.*
sense *n.* faculty by which impressions are perceived, as sight, hearing, taste, etc.; perception through the intellect; understanding, inborn feeling for a subject; judgment; meaning
sen´si-ble *a.* intelligent, having good judgment
sen´si-tive *a.* susceptible to stimuli, impressions, or sensation; having delicate feelings
sen´su-al *a.* pertaining to the baser instincts; given to the pleasures of sense; **sen´su-al´i-ty** *n.*
sen´su-ous *a.* appealing to the senses
sen´tence *n.* opinion; judgment pronounced by a court; maxim, axiom; group of words said to convey a thought; *vt.* pronounce judgment on
sen-ten´tious *a.* short and pithy
sen´tient *a.* having perception and awareness
sen´ti-ment *n.* thought occasioned by feeling; opinion, judgment; maxim; toast
sen´ti-men´tal *a.* abounding in emotions, affectedly tender; **sen´ti-men-tal´i-ty** n
sen´ti-nel *n.* one who keeps watch
sen´try *n.* sentinel
sep´a-ra-ble *a.* pertaining to anything that may be separated
sep´a-rate´ *vi.* & *vt.* divide, part; *a.* separated, distinct
sep´a-ra´tion *n.* act of separating; state of being separate; disunion; limited divorce
sep´a-ra´tor *n.* machine that separates (as cream from milk, chaff from wheat, etc.)
sep´ul-cher *n.* tomb; **se-pul´chral** *a.*
se´quel *n.* succeeding part, continuation; consequence
se´quence *n.* order of succession, series; result
se-ques´ter *vt.* set apart; seize and confiscate
ser´e-nade´ *n.* evening music in the

open air; *vt.*
se-rene´ *n.* calm; **se-ren´i-ty** *n.*
serf *n.* slave attached to the soil; **serf´dom** *n.*
serge *n.* cloth of twilled worsted or silk
ser´geant *n.* non-commissioned officer next above corporal
ser´geant-at-arms´ *n.* officer of a legislative body who keeps order
se´ri-al *a.* pertaining to or consisting of a series; *n.* composition appearing in successive parts
se´ries *n. sg. & pl.* succession of things, sequence
se´ri-ous *a.* solemn, grave; in earnest; important
ser´mon *n.* discourse on a text of scripture
ser´pent *n.* snake; **ser´pen-tine´** *a.* resembling a serpent, winding
ser´um *n.* watery part (as of blood), lymph
ser´vant *n.* one in the service of another
serve *vi. & vt.* be a servant to, work for and obey; discharge the duties of an office; attend, wait; distribute; be sufficient
ser´vice *n.* performance of work for another; military or naval duty; labor, assistance, benefit; set of dishes at table
ser´vile *a.* meanly submissive; **ser-vil´i-ty** *n.*
ser´vi-tude´ *n.* slavery
ses´sion *n.* sitting of a court or public body
set *vt.* **(set´ting; set)** make to sit, place, fix; compose, as type; adapt music to; *vi.* sink below the horizon; become fixed; *a.* fixed, rigid, firm; *n.* number of things used together; group, clique
set´ter *n.* dog which crouches when it scents game
set´tle *vt.* fix, establish; render quiet, clear, etc.; decide; adjust; colonize; *vi.* become fixed or stationary; fix one´s residence; grow calm or clear; sink; adjust differences or accounts
set´tle-ment *n.* adjustment of accounts; colonization; hamlet, village
set´-to´ *n.* fight, contest
sev´er *vi. & vt.* separate; **sev´er-ance** *n.*
sev´er-al *a.* various, more than two, a few
se-vere´ *a.* serious, grave; hard to bear
sew *vt.* join or fasten together with needle and thread
sew´age, sew´er-age *n.* refuse carried off by sewers
sew´er *n.* underground passage for drainage
sex *n.* distinction between male and female; *col.* the sex act; **sex appeal** *n.* attraction for one of the opposite sex; **sex´y** *a. col.*
sex´a-ge-nar´i-an *n.* person sixty years old
sex´ism *n.* belief that one sex is superior to the other; discrimination against women
sex-ol´o-gy *n.* science of sexual behavior
sex´tant *n.* instrument for measuring angular distances
sex´ton *n.* officer in charge of church property
sex´u-al *a.* pertaining to sex; **sex´u-al´i-ty** *n.*
shab´by *a.* threadbare, worn; mean; low
shack´le *n.* fetter, handcuff; *vt.* fetter
shad *n.* food fish of the herring fam-

ily

shade *n.* darkness, obscurity; shelter from light, screen; degree of color, very minute change; ghost; *vt.* screen from light; mark with graduations of color; darken; **shad´y** *a.*

shad´ow *n.* shade caused by an object; shade, darkness; trace; *vt.* shade, darken; represent faintly; follow unobserved; **shad´ow-y** *a.*

shaft *n.* anything long and straight (as the stem of an arrow); entrance to a mine

shake *vi.* & *vt.* **(shook, shak´en)** move with quick, short motions; tremble, make afraid; *n.* rapid, tremulous motion; **shak´y** *a.*

shal-lot´ *n.* kind of onion

shal´low *n.* place over which the water is not deep; *a.* not deep, not wise; superficial

sham *n.* pretense imposture; *a.* pretended, false; *vi.* & *vt.*

sham´bles *n. pl.* butcher's stalls; slaughterhouse

shame *n.* feeling of guilt or dishonor; *vt.* make ashamed; **shame´ful** *a.*

sham´poo´ *vt.* wash the head with soap and water; *n.*

sham´rock´ *n.* three-leaf clover, emblem of Ireland

shang´hai´ *vt.* drug and take aboard ship

shank *n.* leg below the knee to the foot

shan´ty *n.* rude dwelling

shape *vt.* form, adapt, fashion, regulate; *n.* form, figure; **shape´ly** *a.*

share *n.* part, portion; *vt.* divide into parts; partake of with others

shark *n.* large voracious fish; swindler

sharp *a.* having a thin cutting edge; severe, keen, biting, sarcastic, shrill; *n.* note raised a semi-tone, mark (#) used to indicate this; **sharp´en** *vi.* & *vt.*

shat´ter *vt.* break to pieces

shave *vt.* cut off (as the hair) with a razor

shawl *n.* cloth used as a covering for the shoulders

sheaf *n.* **(sheaves)** bundle of stalks of grain, paper, etc.

shear *vt.* clip with shears; **shears** *n. pl.* instrument for clipping

sheath *n.* scabbard, case for a sword, etc.; any thin defensive covering

sheathe *vt.* put into or cover with a sheath

shed *vt.* **(shed)** throw off, let fall; *n.* light shelter, hut

sheen *n.* brightness, gloss

sheep *n. sg.* & *pl.* cud-chewing animal covered with wool

sheer *a.* clear; transparent; downright; perpendicular; *vi.* & *vt.* leave or cause to leave a course

sheet *n.* large, thin piece of cloth, paper, etc.; sail

sheik *n.* Arab chieftain

shelf *n.* **(shelves)** board fixed on a wall, etc., for storing things; flat layer of rock

shell *n.* hard covering as of an animal, egg, etc.; metallic cartridge case, bomb; *vt.* break or strip off the shell; take out of the shell; throw bombs upon

shel-lac´ *n.* kind of varnish

shel´ter *n.* anything which protects; *vt.* cover, defend

shelve *vt.* furnish with shelves; place on a shelf; put aside; *vi.* slope

shep´herd *n.* man who tends sheep

sher´bet *n.* flavored ice

sher´iff *n.* highest executive officer in a county

shield *n.* broad plate carried for defense; any defense or protection; *vt.* defend

shift *vi.* & *vt.* change, transfer; *n.* change, evasion; chemise

shil´ling *n.* English coin

shim´mer *vi.* gleam with a wavering light; *n.*

shin *n.* large bone of the leg below the knee; *vi.* & *vt.* use the shins in climbing

shine *vi.* **(shined, shone)** beam with steady radiance; be bright, beautiful, or eminent; *vt.* polish; *n.* brightness, splendor; polish; liking

shin´gle *n.* wood used for outer covering of roofs; *vt.* cover with shingles

ship *n.* any large vessel; airplane; *vi.* & *vt.* put on board a ship; transport by any conveyance; engage for service on board

shirk *vt.* avoid

shirt *n.* man´s garment worn over upper part of body

shiv´er *vi.* shake, tremble; *n.* tremor

shoal *n.* school of fish; place where the water is not deep

shoat *n.* young hog

shock *n.* violent shake or onset; pile of sheaves of grain; *vt.* shake violently; offend, disgust; **shock´ing** *a.*

shod´dy *n.* waste thrown off in spinning wool; fabric woven from such waste

shoe *n.* covering for the foot; rim of iron nailed to the hoof of an animal; anything in form or use like a shoe; *vt.* **(shoe´ing, shod)** furnish with shoes; **shoe´mak-er** *n.*

shoot *vi.* & *vt.* **(shot)** discharge (as firearms); let fly with force; sprout, dart; photograph; *n.* young branch

shop *n.* place in which goods are sold at retail; place where mechanics work; *vi.* visit shops in order to inspect and purchase

shore *n.* land adjacent to an ocean, lake, or large river

short *a.* not long in time or space; abrupt

short´age *n.* deficit

short´com-ing *n.* neglect of duty

short´en *vi.* & *vt.* make shorter; deprive

short´hand´ *n.* stenography

short´stop´ *n.* player stationed between second and third base in baseball

shot *n.* missile, small globules of lead

shoul´der *n.* joint connecting arm and body; abrupt projection; *vt.* push with the shoulder; take upon the shoulder, assume the burden of

shout *n.* loud and sudden outcry; *vi.* & *vt.* utter a shout

shove *vi.* & *vt.* push; *n.* act of shoving, push

shov´el *n.* instrument with a large scoop and a handle; *vt.*

show *vt.* **(showed, shown)** display, teach; usher, explain; confer, bestow, afford; *n.* display; sight, parade, movie; appearance, plausibility, pretext

show´y *a.* conspicuous, gay

show´er *n.* brief rainfall; *vt.* rain in showers; bestow liberally

shrap´nel *n.* explosive shell filled with metal balls; its exploded fragments

shred *n.* strip, fragment; *vt.* cut or tear into shreds

shrew *n.* brawling woman, scold; **shrew´ish** *a.*

shrewd *a.* astute, acute, cunning

shriek *vi.* utter a scream; *n.* shrill outcry

shrill *a.* piercing, sharp

shrimp *n.* small, edible type of shellfish

shrine *n.* place in which sacred things are kept

shrink *vi.* & *vt.* **(shrank, shrunk)** contract, shrivel; **shrink´age** *n.* bulk lost by contraction

shriv´el *vi.* & *vt.* wrinkle, draw up in folds

shroud *n.* dress for the dead; *vt.* enclose in a shroud, hide

shrub *n.* woody plant with many stems from the same root; **shrub´ber-y** *n.* collection of shrubs

shrug *vi.* & *vt.* draw up the shoulders

shuck *n.* husk, pod; *vt.* remove the husk from

shud´der *vi.* tremble in horror; *n.* trembling

shuf´fle *vi.* & *vt.* change the order of cards in a pack; drag the feet as in walking

shun *vt.* avoid

shunt *vt.* turn aside, switch; *n.* act of turning aside; switch

shut *vi.* & *vt.* close; bar, exclude

shut´ter *n.* cover for window or aperture; mechanism on camera for exposing the film to light

shut´tle *n.* bus, train, or boat taking passengers short distances between major lines; instrument for shooting the thread of the woof in weaving; moving holder for the thread in a sewing machine; *vi.* & *vt.* move back and forth

shy *a.* timid; *vi.* start aside (as from fear); **shy´ly** *adv.*

sick *a.* ill, diseased; inclined to vomit; disgusted; **sick´en** *vi.* & *vt.*

sick´le *n.* hooked instrument for cutting grain

side *n.* edge, border; surface of a solid; part of an animal between hip and shoulder, party, faction; *vi.* embrace the opinion or cause of one party against another

sid´ing *n.* short side track of railroad line; covering for a frame building

siege *n.* extended attack upon a fortified place

sieve *n.* screen used to separate the fine particles of anything from the coarse; *vt.*

sift *vt.* separate with a sieve; examine closely

sigh *vi.* inhale and exhale audibly (as in grief); *n.*

sight *n.* faculty of seeing; view; spectacle; small opening for looking through (as on a gun); *vt.* catch sight of, take aim

sign *n.* mark, token, symptom; *vt.* attach a signature to; hire by contract

sig´nal *n.* sign giving notice; *vt.* make signals to, signify

sig´na-ture *n.* sign, mark; name of a person written by himself; sign of a musical key at the beginning of a staff

sig-nif´i-cant *a.* expressive, suggestive; important; **sig-nif´i-cance** *n.*

sig´ni-fy´ *vt.* mean, indicate, import

sign´post´ *n.* guide-post

si´lage *n.* fodder made into winter feed for animals by fermentation

si´lence *n.* state of being silent; calmness; *vt.* cause to be silent, hush

si´lent *a.* free from sound; not speaking

sil´hou-ette´ *n.* shadow outline of a person or figure

sil´i-ca *n.* flint; silicon dioxide in flint, quartz, etc.
silk *n.* delicate thread produced by certain caterpillars in forming cocoons; thread or cloth made from it
sill *n.* timber or stone at the foot of door or window; threshold
sil´ly *a.* foolish, witless; imprudent
si´lo´ *n.* pit or tower for green fodder
silt *n.* sediment (as mud left by water)
sil´ver *n.* valuable metallic element; money or table utensils made of it; *a.* made of or resembling silver; **sil´ver-y** *a.*
sim´i-lar *a.* resembling, alike; **sim´i-lar´i-ty** *n.*
sim´i-le´ *n.* illustrative comparison (as *My love is like a red, red rose*)
si-mil´i-tude´ *n.* resemblance; comparison
sim´mer *vi.* boil gently
sim´per *vi.* smile in a silly manner; *n.* silly smile
sim´ple *a.* single; unaffected, credulous; plain; **sim-plic´i-ty** *n.*
sim´pli-fy´ *vt.* make simpler
sim´u-late´ *vt.* counterfeit; **sim´u-la´tion** *n.*
si´mul-ta´ne-ous *a.* happening at the same time
sin *n.* violation of divine law; wickedness; *vi.* do wrong
sin-cere´ *a.* unfeigned, honest in word or deed; **sin-cer´i-ty** *n.*
si´ne-cure´ *n.* office with salary but without work
sin´ew *n.* tendon
sing *vi.* & *vt.* **(sang, sung)** utter melodious sounds
singe *vt.* **(singe´ing, singed)** scorch; *n.* slight burn
sin´gle *a.* one only, separate; unmarried; unmixed; **single out** *vt.* choose
sing´song´ *a.* having a monotonous rhythm
sin´gu-lar *a.* denoting one person or thing; alone, unique; strange; *n.*
sin´is-ter *a.* suggesting evil
sink *vi.* **(sank, sunk)** descend; fall down; fail in strength; *vt.* cause to sink; make by digging (as a well); *n.* drain to carry off dirty water
sip *vt.* drink in small quantities; *n.* small drink
si´phon *n.* bent tube for drawing liquids from one vessel into another
si´ren *n.* fabulous nymph; wicked, enticing woman; foghorn; loud, wailing horn
sir´loin´ *n.* loin of beef
sir´up, syr´up *n.* solution of sugar and water; juice of fruit, etc., boiled with sugar
sis´ter *n.* female born of the same parents as another child; nun
sit *vi.* **(sat)** rest on the haunches; perch; rest, remain; hold a session; *vt.* seat (oneself)
si-tar´ *n.* stringed instrument of India resembling a guitar with long neck
site *n.* situation, location
sit´-in *n.* protest staged by sitting down in a public place
sit´u-a´tion *n.* place, position; condition; employment
sixth *a.* last of six, one of six equal parts; *n.*
size *n.* extent of volume or surface, bulk, magnitude; *vt.* arrange according to size
siz´zle *vi.* make a hissing sound from heat
skate *n.* frame with a steel runner for gliding on ice; frame with metal wheels; *vi.* glide on skates
skein *n.* loop of thread or yarn

skel´e-ton *n.* bones of an animal or human being preserved in their natural position; framework or outline of anything

skeptic *n.* one who doubts; **skep´ti-cal** *a.*

sketch *n.* first draft, outline; *vt.* make a rough draft of

skew´er *n.* pin for holding meat in form; *vt.* fasten with skewers

ski *n.* wooden runner for the feet for traveling over snow

skid *vi.* slip sideways (as an automobile); *n.*

skiff *n.* small rowboat

skill *n.* dexterity or ease in doing anything; trade; **skill´ful** *a.*

skil´let *n.* small stewpan with a long handle

skim *vi.* & *vt.* clear of cream, scum, etc.; lightly brush the surface of; glide along near a surface

skimp *vi.* & *vt.* supply scantily

skin *n.* membranous outer covering of an animal body; hide, pelt; bark or rind of plants, hull of fruits, etc.; *vt.* strip the skin from

skin diving *n.* underwater swimming with small tank of compressed air or a snorkel; **skin diver** *n.*

skin´-flint´ *n.* niggardly person

skin´ny *a.* extremely thin

skip *vi.* & *vt.* leap, bound; pass over, omit; *n.* light or short leap; omission of a part

skir´mish *n.* irregular battle between small forces; *vi.* fight in small parties

skirt *n.* part of woman´s garment below the waist; petticoat; edge, margin; *vt.* cover with a skirt; move along the edge of

skit *n.* little play or scene acted out

skit´tish *a.* easily frightened

skulk *vi.* sneak away

skull *n.* bony case enclosing the brain

skunk *n.* small North American quadruped noted for its unpleasant odor

sky *n.* heavens; **sky rocket** *n.* type of fireworks that burns as it flies; **sky´rock´et** *vt.* shoot up, rise like a rocket; **sky´scrap´er** *n.* very tall building

slab *n.* thin stone; outer piece sawed from a log

slack *a.* lax, loose; not diligent; *n.* part of rope hanging loose; idle period

slack, slack´en *vi.* & *vt.* make or become less tight

slag *n.* impurities, etc., removed from a metal by melting

slake *vt.* quench; disintegrate by rinsing with water (as lime); *vi.* become disintegrated

slam *vi.* & *vt.* shut noisily; *n.*

slan´der *n.* false, malicious report, gossip; *vt.* malign, calumniate; **slan´der-ous** *a.*

slang *n.* low, inelegant, or shortlived words or expressions; jargon

slant *n.* slope; *vi.* & *vt.* turn in a sloping direction; shape an attitude by selecting facts

slap *n.* blow given with the open hand; *vt.*

slash *vi.* & *vt.* cut by striking with violence; make long cuts; *n.*

slat *n.* thin, narrow strip

slate *n.* stone which splits into thin plates; piece of slate for roofing or for writing; list of political candidates; *vt.* cover with slate; destine for a special purpose

slaugh´ter *n.* slaying, killing, great destruction of life; *vt.* slay, destroy; kill for the market

slave *n.* one in bondage; *vi.* drudge
slay *vt.* **(slew, slain)** kill
slea´zy *a.* flimsy; shoddy
sleek *a.* smooth, glossy
sleep *vi.* **(slept)** slumber; live thoughtlessly; be dead; *n.* slumber, rest; death; **sleep´er** *n.*; **sleep´y** *a.* drowsy
sleep´er *n.* person or thing who becomes an unexpected success, as a horse that wins unexpectedly; railroad car providing beds
sleet *n.* rain mingled with snow or hail
sleeve *n.* part of a garment which covers the arm; tube that fits over another
sleigh *n.* vehicle similar to large sled
sleight *n.* cunning; artful trick; **sleight´of-hand´** *n.* legerdemain, tricks
slen´der *a.* thin, slim; feeble, slight
slice *vt.* cut into thin pieces; *n.* thin, broad piece
slick *a.* sleek; oily, slippery; clever, ingenious
slide *vi.* & *vt.* **(sliding, slid)** slip, glide; *n.* smooth movement; fall of a mass of earth or rock; smooth declivity
slide´ rule´ *n.* instrument for making rapid calculations by the use of logarithmic scales
slight *a.* weak, trifling, small; *vt.* disregard; treat with intentional neglect; *n.* neglect, disrespect
slim *a.* slender, slight
slime *n.* sticky, dirty liquid; **slim´y** *a.*
sling *n.* instrument for throwing stones; hanging bandage for a wounded limb; *vt.* **(slung)** throw with a sling, hurl; hang or swing by means of a rope
slink *vi.* **(slunk)** crawl or sneak away
slip *vi.* slide; escape; err; *vt.* escap from; *n.* error; escape; twig
slip´cov´er *n.* removable cover fo protecting furniture
slip´knot´ *n.* knot which slips alon the rope
slip´per *n.* loose shoe
slip´per-y *a.* not affording a firn footing; untrustworthy
slip´shod´ *a.* slovenly
slit *vt.* **(slit)** cut lengthwise; cut in strips; *n.* long, narrow opening
sliv´er *n.* long narrow strip of wood *vi.* & *vt.* cut or tear in narrov pieces
sloe *n.* small, sour plum, the fruit o the blackthorn
slo´gan *n.* war cry among Scottisl highlanders; any motto
slop *n.* water carclessly spilled poor, watery food *vi.* soil by lettin a liquid spatter; **slop´py** *a.* wet, s as to spatter; muddy, messy
slope *n.* incline; direction downward; *vi.* & *vt.* incline
slot *n.* slat; long, narrow opening
sloth *n.* laziness, sluggishness slow-moving South Americar quadruped; **sloth´ful** *a.*
slouch *n.* drooping posture; *vi.* **slouch´y** *a.*
slough *n.* deep mud, bog, swamp
slough *n.* anything cast off, as skin *vi.* & *vt.* throw or cast off
slov´en-ly *a.* messy, careless o dress; **slov´en-li-ness** *n.*
slow *a.* not swift; behind in time
sludge *n.* mire, slush
slug *n.* snail without a shell; ova bullet; *vt.* strike heavily; **slug´gish** *a.* slow, lazy
slug´gard *n.* one who is habitually idle
sluice *n.* sliding gate for regulatin

the flow of water; stream which flows through it

slum *n.* run-down, seamy neighborhood; *vi.* visit the slums of a city

slum´ber *vi.* sleep, sleep lightly; *n.* light sleep

slump *vi.* fall or sink suddenly; *n.* sudden fall; business slowdown

slur *vt.* disparage; pronounce indistinctly; *n.* slight reproach, disparagement; mark showing that notes are to be sung to same syllable

slush *n.* liquid mud, melting snow; **slush´y** *a.*

sly *a.* cunning, wily; **sly´ly, sli´ly** *adv.*; **sly´ness** *n.*

smack *n.* small quantity; loud, kiss, or any similar sound; slap; *vi.* make a loud noise with the lips

small *a.* little in quantity, degree, or importance; narrow-minded, mean

smart *n.* quick, stinging pain; *vi.* feel a stinging pain, suffer; *a.* clever, intelligent; stylish

smash *vt.* break into pieces

smat´ter-ing *n.* superficial knowledge; little bit

smear *vt.* daub; slander; *n.* stain; slander, subtle defamation

smell *vi.* emit an odor; *vt.* perceive by the nose; *n.* odor

smelt *n.* small food fish; *vt.* melt (ore) to separate out the metal

smile *vt.* express pleasure by a grin; be favorable

smirk *vi.* smile affectedly; *n.* affected smile

smith *n.* worker in metals

smock *n.* chemise; garment worn over regular clothes to protect them

smog *n.* smoke and fog; fog thickened by smoke

smoke *n.* sooty vapor from something on fire; *vi.* emit smoke; draw in and puff out the smoke of tobacco; *vt.* apply smoke to, dry or cure by smoke; inhale the smoke of; **smoke stack** *n.* chimney; **smok´y** *a.*

smol´der, smoul´der *vi.* burn slowly

smooth *a.* having an even surface; bland mild; *vt.* make smooth

smoth´er *vt.* suffocate; *vi.* be suffocated

smudge *n.* suffocating smoke; sooty stain; *vt.* smoke; stain

smug *a.* affectedly neat; self-satisfied

smug´gle *vi.* import or export without paying the legal duty; convey secretly

smut *n.* spot of soot; disease of grain; obscenity, moral filth; **smut´ty** *a.*

snag *n.* stump of a tree below water; root or stump of a decayed tooth; unexpected difficulty

snake *n.* serpent, legless reptile

snap *vi.* & *vt.* break short; bite or catch at suddenly; *n.* snapping noise; small catch or lock; period of (cold) weather; pleasant position; easy chore or assignment

snap´shot´ *n.* photograph

snare *n.* noose, trap

snarl *vi.* growl; *vt.* tangle (as traffic); *n.* tangle

snatch *vi.* & *vt.* seize quickly; *n.* small piece

sneak *vi.* & *vt.* move secretly; behave meanly; *n.* underhanded person

sneer *vi.* speak with scorn; *n.* expression of scorn

sneeze *vi.* eject air rapidly, audibly, and involuntarily through the nose; *n.* act of sneezing

snick´er *vi.* giggle

snide *a.* underhanded, sarcastic, catty

sniff *vi.* & *vt.* draw in air sharply through the nose, test by smelling
snip *vt.* nip; *n.* single cut made with scissors; piece cut off
sniv´el *vi.* run at the nose; cry with sniffling; *n.*
snob *n.* person overly proud of his wealth, station, or ability; **snob´-ber-y** *n.*; **snob´bish** *a.*
snore *vi.* breathe noisily in sleep; *n.*; **snor´er** *n.*
snor´kel *n.* tube by which submarines take in fresh air and release waste gases while remaining submerged; a tube for breathing while swimming with the head submerged; fire equipment in which firemen are lifted for several stories
snort *vi.* force the air noisily through the nostrils
snout *n.* projecting nose
snow *n.* frozen moisture which falls in flakes; *vi.*
snow´ball´ *n.* round mass of snow; *vi.* mount up, accumulate
snow´plow´ *n.* machine to clear roads from snow
snow´shoe´ *n.* broad frame which keeps wearer from sinking in the snow
snow´ suit´ *n.* warm, heavy outer garment, often quilted
snub *vt.* slight; *n.*
snuff *n.* powdered tobacco for inhaling through the nose; *vi.* & *vt.* draw in through the nose; trim or put out a candle
snug *a.* lying close and warm; comfortable; **snug´ness** *n.*
snug´gle *vi.* & *vt.* cuddle, nestle
soak *vi.* & *vt.* steep, drench
soap *n.* compound of oils or fat with soda or potash, used in washing; *vt.* rub or wash with soap
soar *vi.* fly aloft, aspire
sob *vt.* cry or sigh convulsively; *n.*
so´ber *a.* not drunk; temperate grave; *vi.* & *vt.*
so-bri´e-ty *n.* state or habit of being sober
soc´cer *n.* variety of football
so´cial *a.* pertaining to companionship; relating to the public
so´cial-ism *n.* doctrine of government ownership of essential industry; **so´cial-ist** *n.*
so´cial work´ *n.* activities concerned with the improvement of social conditions
so-ci´e-ty *n.* fellowship; number of persons associated for some purpose; leisure class
so´ci-ol´o-gy *n.* study of society
sock *n.* half-stocking; *vt.* strike, hit
sock´et *n.* hollow into which something is inserted
sod *n.* turf; soil
so´da *n.* carbonate of sodium; **soda water** *n.* water charged with carbon dioxide
so´fa *n.* long, upholstered seat with back and arms
soft *a.* easily yielding to pressure; not rough
soft´ drug´ *n.* non-addictive drug
sog´gy *a.* saturated, damp
soil *n.* ground; dirt, spot; *vt.* make dirty; *vi.*
so´journ *vi.* stay; *n.*
sol´ace *n.* consolation; *vt.* comfort
so´lar *a.* pertaining to the sun
solar battery *n.* battery that converts sunlight into electric energy
solar system *n.* sun with the planets and other bodies revolving around it
sol´der *vt.* join two metallic surfaces by a fusible metallic cement; *n.* metallic cement
sol´dier *n.* man engaged in military

service; *vi.* serve as a soldier; pretend to work

sole *n.* underside of the foot or shoe; flat kind of fish; *vt.* furnish with a sole; *a.* solitary single

sol´emn *a.* sacred; impressing with seriousness; **so-lem´ni-ty** *n.* solemn or religious ceremony; **sol´emnize´** *vt.*

so-lic´it *vt.* ask earnestly, petition; **so-lic´i-ta´tion** *n.*; **so-lic´i-tor** *n.* one who solicits; attorney

so-lic´i-tous *a.* concerned, anxious; **so-lic´i-tude´** *n.*

sol´id *a.* not hollow; *n.* non-liquid, non-gaseous substance having length, width and thickness; **so-lid´i-fy´** *vi.* & *vt.* make or become solid

sol´i-dar´i-ty *n.* oneness of interests

so-lil´o-quy *n.* speech made to oneself

sol´i-taire´ *n.* card game played by one person; gem (esp. a diamond) set by itself

sol´i-tar´y *a.* alone, single

sol´i-tude´ *n.* isolation; lonely life

so´lo´ *n.* **(so´los, so´li)** anything performed by only one person, voice, or instrument; **so´lo´ist** *n.*

sol´stice *n.* point along the sun´s path reached on June 21 and December 22

sol´u-ble *a.* capable of being dissolved in a fluid; **sol´u-ble-ness, sol´u-bil´i-ty** *n.*

so-lu´tion *n.* preparation made by dissolving a solid in a liquid; explanation

solve *vt.* clear up, explain; **solv´able** *a.*

sol´vent *a.* having power to dissolve; able to pay debts; *n.* anything that dissolves another; **sol´ven-cy** *n.* state of being able to pay debts

som´ber *a.* dull, gloomy

som´er-sault´, sum´mer-sault, som´er-set´ *n.* leap in which a person flips his heels over his head

som´nam´bu-lism *n.* practice of walking while asleep

so´nant *a.* sounding

so´nar´ *n.* electronic device for detecting objects under water

so-na´ta *n.* musical composition in several movements, usually for one or two instruments

song *n.* poem to be sung; trifling sum paid for something valuable; **song´ster** *n.* singer; singing bird

son´ic bar´ri-er *n.* resistance of air to aircraft traveling at the speed of sound

so-no´rous *a.* sounding when struck, resonant

soot *n.* black substance from smoke; **soot´y** *a.*

soothe *vi.* & *vt.* calm

sooth´say´er *n.* prognosticator, one who foretells the future

sop *n.* anything dipped or soaked in gravy, etc., and then eaten; anything given to satisfy; *vt.* steep, soak

soph´ist *n.* captious, deceptive, or fallacious reasoner

so-phis´ti-cat´ed *a.* knowledgeable about the ways of the world

soph´o-more´ *n.* American student in his second year at school

so-pra´no *n.* **(so-pra´nos, so-pra´ni)** highest female voice

sor´cer-y *n.* magic, witchcraft; **sor´cer-er** *n.*; **sor´cer-ess** *n. fem.*

sor´did *a.* avaricious; vile

sore *n.* wound; *a.* tender

so-ror´i-ty *n.* social organization for women, esp. in college

sor´row *n.* grief, affliction; *vi.* be

sad, grieve
sor´ry *a.* grieving for something past, dejected; poor, worthless
sort *n.* class, kind, manner; *vt.* separate into classes
sor´tie *n.* sally of troops
SOS *n.* international distress signal
sot *n.* habitual drunkard
soul *n.* human spirit; human being; energy, fervor
sound *a.* safe, whole, perfect; healthy, strong; correct, orthodox; a strait; *vi.* & *vt.* make a noise; probe; measure the depth of; *n.* noise; note, tone; **sound barrier** *n.* sonic barrier; **sound track** *n.* part of motion picture film carrying the sound
soup *n.* liquid food obtained by boiling meat or vegetables
sour *a.* having a pungent, acid taste; rancid; crabbed, peevish;
source *n.* spring from which a stream flows, origin
south *n.* direction opposite the north
sou´ve-nir´ *n.* keepsake
sov´er-eign *a.* supreme; *n.* supreme ruler, monarch; British gold coin
So´vi-et *n.* in Russia, a council of representatives of various groups of the people
sow *vi.* & *vt.* **(sowed, sown)** scatter
space *n.* distance between objects, points of time, lines, words, etc.; area beyond earth´s atmosphere; *vt.* make intervals
space´ cap´sule *n.* instrumented chamber attached to rockets, used to carry astronauts into space
space´craft *n.* space ship, vehicle for space travel
space´ plat´form *n.* manned satellite to serve as relay station for spacecraft
space´ ship´ *n.* vessel for traveling in outer space
spa´cious *a.* roomy, capacious
spade *n.* tool for digging; playing card having black, pointed spades; *vt.* dig
spa-ghet´ti *n.* macaroni in the form of small sticks
span *n.* nine inches; spread (as of an arch); space of time; pair of horses; *vt.* measure by spans; stretch across
span´gle *n.* small thin plate of shining metal; *vt.* adorn with spangles
span´iel *n.* breed of dog with large, hanging ears
spar *n.* large pole (as a mast, yard, etc.); a crystalline mineral; *vi.* box with the fists; make motions of boxing
spare *vi.* & *vt.* use savingly; withhold; show mercy to; dispense with, give up; *a.* sparing; lean; superfluous
spark *n.* particle of fire or light; gay fellow
spar´kle *n.* little spark; *vi.* emit sparks; glitter
spas´tic *n.* person afflicted with spastic paralysis in which muscles show frequent spasms
sparse *a.* thinly scattered
spasm *n.* violent, involuntary contraction of the muscles; **spasmod´ic** *a.* convulsive; intermittent
spat´ter *vt.* splash
spat´u-la *n.* broad kind of knife for spreading plaster, paint, etc.; **spat´u-late** *a.*
spawn *n.* eggs of fish, etc.; *vi.* & *vt.* deposit eggs, as fish do; produce issue in great plenty
speak *vi.* & *vt.* **(spoke, spo´ken)** utter words, talk; pronounce

speak´er *n.* one who speaks; chairman

spear *n.* weapon made of a pole pointed with iron; spike of grass, wheat, etc.; *vt.* pierce with a spear

spe´cial *a.* confined to a particular subject; unusual, distinguished; **spe´cial-ly** *adv.*

spe´cial-ist *n.* one who devotes himself to a special subject

spe´cial-ty *n.* anything unusual; special pursuit

spe´cie *n.* coin

spe´cies´ *n. sg. & pl.* type, kind; group of animals, plants, etc., with characteristics that distinguish them from other members of the same genus

spe-cif´ic *a.* precise

spec´i-fy´ *vt.* mention precisely

spec´i-fi-ca´tion *n.* act of specifying; statement of particulars, plans; item specified

spec´i-men *n.* sample that shows kind and quality of the whole

spe´cious *a.* plausible, but not really true

speck *n.* small spot, blemish; very small particle

speck´le *n.* little speck; *vt.* mark with speckles

spec´ta-cle *n.* sight, show, demonstration, pageant

spec´ta-cles *n. pl.* eyeglasses

spec-tac´u-lar *n.* elaborate program

spec´ta´tor *n.* onlooker

spec´ter *n.* ghost; **spec´tral** *a.* ghostly

spec-trom´e-ter *n.* instrument for measuring wavelengths of spectra

spec´tro-scope´ *n.* instrument for determining the composition of luminous bodies

spec´trum *n.* **(spec´tra)** light waves, radio waves, etc., in series according to their wavelength; colors seen when light passes through a prism

spec´u-late *vi.* consider, theorize; traffic for profit upon some uncertainty; **spec´u-la´tor** *n.*; **spec´u-la´tion** *n.* mere theory; buying goods, etc., in hope of a raise in price

speech *n.* language; power of speaking; oration

speed *n.* quickness, velocity; *vi. & vt.* hasten; **speed´y** *a.*

speed-om´e-ter *n.* instrument to indicate speed (as on an automobile)

spell *vt.* name, write, or print the letters of; relieve; *vi.* form words with the proper letters; *n.* turn at work; short period

spend *vt.* **(spent)** give, waste; **spend´thrift´** *n.* prodigal

sperm *n.* male reproductive cell or fluid

spew *vi. & vt.* vomit

sphere *n.* ball, globe; province; **spher´i-cal** *a.*

sphinx *n.* monster with the head of a woman and the body of a lion; enigmatic person

spice *n.* aromatic herb used for seasoning food; anything that adds piquancy; *vt.* season with spice; **spic´y** *a.*

spi´der *n.* small, eight-legged creature which spins webs

spike *n.* large nail; ear of grain; cluster of flowers; *vt.* set or plug with spikes; *col.* add alcohol to

spill *vi. & vt.* run over or waste; shed (as blood)

spin *vi. & vt.* **(spun)** draw out and twist into threads; whirl rapidly; *n.* short run

spin´ach *n.* leafy, green herb used as a vegetable

spin´dle *n.* pin from which thread is spun, pin on which anything turns

spine *n.* thorn; backbone; **spi´nal** *a.*
spin´ster *n.* elderly, unmarried woman
spi´ral *a.* winding like the thread of a screw; *n.* curve which continually recedes from a center
spire *n.* tapering body; steeple
spir´it *n.* vital force, soul; ghost; mental disposition, ardor; real meaning; volatile, flammable liquid (as alcohol); *vt.* take away suddenly or secretly
spir´it-u-al *a.* not material, holy, divine
spir´it-u-al´i-ty *n.* state of being spiritual
spit *n.* rod on which meat is roasted; *vt.* pierce with a spit, impale
spit *vt.* **(spat)** eject from the mouth, expectorate; *n.* spittle, saliva
spite *n.* active hatred; *vt.* vex, thwart; **spite´ful** *a.*
splash *vi.* & *vt.* spatter; *n.*
spleen *n.* spongy body near the stomach; ill-humor; malice
splen´did *a.* possessing splendor; rite, grand
splen´dor *n.* glory, brilliance, magnificence
splice *vt.* unite two pieces of rope, timber, etc.; *n.* joint made by splicing
splint *n.* thin piece of wood, etc., for confining a broken or injured limb
splin´ter *n.* sliver; *vi.*& *vt.* cut or break into slivers or thin pieces
split *vi.* & *vt.* cleave lengthwise; divide; *n.* break, division
splurge *vi.* spend thriftlessly
splut´ter *vi.* & *vt.* sputter
spoil *vt.* make unfit for use; *vi.* decay; *n.* plunder, robbery
spoke *n.* one of the bars from the nave to the rim of a wheel; rung of a ladder
spokes´man´ *n.* one who speaks for others
sponge *n.* porous substance used to suck up water; parasite; *vt.* wipe with a sponge; *vi.* live as a parasite
spon´sor *n.* one who takes responsibility for another; firm that backs programs or events in return for advertising; *vt.*
spon-ta´ne-ous *a.* acting without plan
spool *n.* cylinder for winding yarn or thread
spoon *n.* instrument for conveying liquids to the mouth
spo-rad´ic *a.* occurring separately or randomly
spore *n.* minute seed in flowerless plants like the fern
sport *vi.* play, frolic; *vt.* exhibit, wear; *n.* anything that amuses; derision; athletic diversion
spot *n.* blot; particular place; *vt* mark, stain; detect in the act
spouse *n.* husband or wife
spout *vt.* throw out (as from a pipe); *vi.* issue with violence; *n.* projecting mouth of a vessel; jet of liquid
sprain *vt.* overstrain the muscles of a joint; *n.*
sprawl *vi.* & *vt.* stretch the body carelessly when lying
spray *n.* small particles of water scattered by fountains, etc.; *vi.* & *vt.* scatter a liquid in minute drops
spread *vi.* & *vt.* **(spread)** scatter; stretch, extend; *n.* extent, encompass; cloth used as a cover; banquet
sprig *n.* small shoot or twig
spright´ly *a.* lively
spring *vi.* **(sprang, sprung)** bound, leap, issue; *vt.* start; open; *a.* lean; *n.* elastic power; elastic body; ori-

gin, source; outflow of water from the earth

sprin´kle *vi.* & *vt.* scatter in small drops or particles

sprint *vi.* run fast; *n.* fast run; **sprin´er** *n.*

sprite *n.* elf fairy, super-natural being

sprock´et *n.* projection on a wheel for engaging a chain

sprout *n.* young shoot; *vi.* begin to grow, germinate

spruce *a.* neat; *n.* variety of evergreen tree

spry *a.* nimble

spume *n.* scum, foam

spunk *n.* tinder, punk; pluck

spur *n.* device with spikes attached to horseman´s heels for goading the horse; stimulus; range of mountains extending laterally from a larger range; *vt.* urge on

spu´ri-ous *a.* not genuine

spurn *vt.* reject disdainfully

spurt *vi.* & *vt.* spout or gush out in a sudden stream; *n.* sudden or violent gush; short, sudden effort

Sput´nik´ *n.* name given the artificial satellites launched by the U.S.S.R.

sput´ter *vi.* & *vt.* throw out in small noisy drops; speak rapidly and indistinctly; *n.* a sputtering noise

spy *n.* one who watches others secretly; *vi.* & *vt.* see, inspect secretly

spy´glass´ *n.* small telescope

squab *a.* short and stout; unfledged; *n.* young pigeon

squab´ble *vi.* wrangle; *n.* brawl

squad *n.* small unit of men

squad´ron *n.* unit of men, ships, or planes

squal´id *a.* filthy, foul

squall *n.* violent gust of wind

squal´or *n.* filthiness

squan´der *vt.* spend lavishly; waste

square *a.* having four equal sides and four right angles; forming a right angle; fair, just, honest; *n.* square figure; four-sided space inclosed by, or covered with, houses; product of a quantity multiplied by itself; *vt.* form like a square; adjust, settle, balance; multiply a number by itself

squash *vt.* beat or press to a pulp; flatten; *n.* plant of the gourd kind and its edible fruit

squat *vi.* sit upon the heels; settle on public land without title; *a.* short and thick, dumpy

squaw *n.* American Indian woman

squawk *vi.* utter a harsh outcry; *n.*

squeak *vi.* utter a short, shrill cry; *n.*

squeal *vi.* utter a long, shrill sound; turn informer; *n.*

squeam´ish *a.* easily disgusted, offended, or nauseated

squeeze *vi.* & *vt.* crush or press between two bodies; *n.*

squelch *vt.* subdue

squint *a.* looking obliquely, distorted; *vi.* look obliquely; have the vision distorted; *n.* non-coincidence of the optical axes

squirm *vi.* wriggle, writhe; *n.* wriggling motion

squir´rel *a.* nimble rodent with a bushy tail

squirt *vt.* eject a liquid in a small stream; *n.*

stab *vi.* & *vt.* wound with a pointed weapon; *n.*

sta´bi-lize´ *vt.* make stable or steady; **sta´bi-li-za´tion** *n.*

sta´ble *a.* firmly established; **sta´-ble-ness, sta-bil´i-ty** *n.* steadfastness; fixity; *n.* building for horses and cattle

stack *n.* large pile of hay or grain; chimney; *vt.* lay in a pile

sta´di-um *n.* enclosure for athletic contests with banks of seats for spectators

staff *n.* **(staffs, staves)** stick carried for support or defense

staff *n.* **(staffs)** the five lines and spaces on which music is written; general officers aiding a military commander; editors of a newspaper; teachers of a school, etc.

stag *n.* male deer; *a.* not accompanied by a woman; **stag party** *n.* party for men only

stage *n.* elevated platform, esp. in a theater; the theater; period of development; *vt.* exhibit on a stage

stage´coach *n.* coach that runs regularly

stag´ger *vi.* reel from side to side

stag´nant *a.* not flowing, impure; inactive; **stag´nate** *vi.*; **stag-na´tion** *n.*

staid *a.* steady, sober

stain *vt.* tinge, color, dye; discolor, spot; mark with guilt or infamy; *n.* discoloration, spot; taint of guilt

stair *n.* series of steps for ascending to a higher level; **stairs** *n. pl.* flight of steps

stair´case, stair´way *n.* flight of stairs with their framework and balusters

stake *n.* strong stick or post, pointed at one end; pledge in a wager; *vt.* fasten, or pierce, with a stake; mark the bounds of with stakes; wager

sta-lac´tite *n.* hanging cone formed by dripping of water in a cavern

sta-lag´mite *n.* cone formed by water on the floor of a cavern

stale *a.* no longer fresh; trite

stalk *n.* stem of a plant, flower, fruit, or quill; *vi.* walk with long, slow steps; *vt.* approach game secretly

stall *n.* division of a stable for a single animal; booth where articles are exposedfor sale

stal´lion *n.* male horse

stal´wart *a.* stout, sturdy

sta´men *n.* organ of a flower which produces the pollen

stam´i-na *n.* power of endurance, vigor

stam´mer *vi.* & *vt.* sputter; *n.*

stamp *vi.* plant the foot down firmly; *vt.* strike with the sole of the foot; imprint; coin; affix an adhesive stamp to; *n.* mark made by pressing; instrument for cutting or for making impressions; small certificate to show that a duty or charge has been paid

stam-pede´ *n.* flight by panic; *vt.* cause to start off in a panic

stanch, staunch *vt.* stop the flowing of (as blood); *vi.* cease to flow; *a.* constant, sound, firm

stan´chion *n.* post

stand *vi.* **(stood)** be fixed in an upright position; occupy a certain position; remain fixed or firm; *vt.* set upright; endure, resist; *n.* platform for spectators; small table; stop

stan´dard *n.* rule, model; staff with a flag; flag; *a.* according to a rule or model

stan´za *n.* series of lines of verses

sta´ple *n.* principal product of a country; loop of iron for holding a pin, bolt, etc.; small pin used to bind sheets of paper together

stapp *n.* unit of force equal to an acceleration of one gravity per second

star *n.* one of the bright fixed bodies in the heavens; person of brilliant qualities, esp. a leading actor or actress; asterisk (*); **star´ry** *a.*

star´board *n.* right-hand side of a ship, looking toward the bow

starch *n.* white vegetable carbohydrate used for stiffening cloth, etc.; *vt.* stiffen with starch

stare *vi.* look with a fixed gaze; *n.* fixed look

stark *a.* stiff, rigid; absolute, entire

star´ling *n.* European bird easily tamed; California rock trout

start *vi.* & *vt.* move suddenly; begin; *n.* sudden motion; outset

star´tle *vi.* & *vt.* move suddenly, as in alarm

starve *vi.* die of hunger; suffer extreme hunger; *vt.* kill with hunger; **star-va´tion** *n.*

state *n.* condition, situation; pomp; people united into one body politic, commonwealth; power wielded by the government; *a.* public, relating to the body politic

state *vt.* set, settle, recite; **state´ment** *n.* narrative, declaration; bill

state´ly *a.* majestic, dignified, magnificent

state´room *n.* stately room in a palace or mansion; sleeping apartment in a passenger steamer, or sleeping-car

states´man *n.* one skilled in government and public affairs

stat´ic *a.* pertaining to statics; pertaining to bodies at rest or in equilibrium; **s** *n.* science which studies the action of forces in keeping rest or equilibrium

sta´tion *n.* place where a person or thing stands; state, rank, condition in life; place where railway trains come to stand; *vt.* assign a station to, appoint to a post; **station wagon** *n.* automobile built to hold a large number of passengers

sta´tion-ar´y *a.* standing, fixed, settled; acting from or in a fixed position

sta´tion-er´y *n.* paper, envelopes, etc. used for writing

sta-tis´tics *n.* scientific collection and interpretation of facts and figures concerning a subject; **sta-tis´ti-cal** *a.*; **stat´is-ti´cian** *n.*

stat´u-ar-y *n.* art of carving statues; statue or a collection of statues; one who makes, or deals in, statues

stat´ue *n.* image in stone, wood, etc.

stat´ure *n.* height

sta´tus *n.* state, condition

stat´ute *n.* law enacted by a legislature; regulation by any organization; **stat´u-to´ry** *a.*

stave *n.* one of the pieces of which a cask is made; *vt.* **(staved, stove)** keep off

stay *vi.* remain, continue, wait; cease acting; *vt.* delay; prevent from falling, prop, support; *n.* continuance in a place; prop, support

stead´fast´, sted´fast´ *a.* resolute, steady

steady *a.* stable; constant, resolute; regular, uniform; *vi.* & *vt.* make or become firm; **stead´i-ly** *adv.*

steak *n.* slice of meat, esp. beef

steal *vt.* **(stole, sto´len)** take by theft; move or get surreptitiously; *vi.* practice theft; move secretly

stealth *n.* secret actions

steam *n.* vapor from boiling water; *vi.* rise or pass off in vapor; *vt.* expose to steam; **steam engine** *n.* machine which converts the energy of steam into power

steed *n.* spirited horse

steel *n.* iron combined with carbon; *vt.* harden

steep *a.* precipitous, rising almost

straight up; *vt.* soak in a liquid

stee´ple *n.* tower of a church, ending in a point

steer *n.* young bull; ox; castrated bull; *vt.* guide, govern; *vi.* direct a ship in its course

stel´lar *a.* relating to the stars

stem *n.* little branch supporting flower or fruit; part of a word to which the endings, prefixes, etc., are added; *vt.* stop, check, make progress against

stench *n.* offensive odor

sten´cil *n.* plate of metal, etc., with a pattern cut out; *vt.* print by means of a stencil

ste-nog´ra-pher *n.* one who writes in shorthand

ste-nog´ra-phy *n.* system of symbols devised for speedy writing

step *n.* distance crossed by the foot in walking; stair; round of a ladder; footprint; manner of walking; action, measured progress; *vi.* & *vt.*

ster´e-o-phon´ic *a.* pertaining to multi-directional sound recording

ster´e-o-type´ *a.* in printing, a plate cast from an impression of movable type; stock character lacking individuality; mental image of a national, racial, or social type

ster´ile *a.* unfruitful, barren; **ste-ril´i-ty** *n.*; **ster´i-lize´** *vt.* deprive of fertility; render free from bacteria

ster´ling *a.* of standard value (as money); genuine, pure

stern *a.* severe, rigid; *n.* hind part of a vessel or boat

ster´oid *n.* organic alcohol like cholesterol, basically composed of chains of carbon atoms arranged in rings

steth´o-scope´ *n.* instrument for listening to sounds within the body

ste´ve-dore´ *n.* one who loads or unloads vessels

stew *vi.* & *vt.* boil slowly with little moisture; *n.* meat stewed with vegetables; fuss

stew´ard *n.* one who manages domestic concerns or superintends an estate or farm; waiter on a ship

stick *n.* piece of wood, staff; composing-stick; *vt.* stab, thrust in; affix; *vi.* hold to; be hindered, hesitate

stiff *a.* rigid, formal; **stiff´en** *vi.* & *vt.*

sti´fle *vt.* stop the breath of, suffocate; suppress the sound of; *vi.* suffer from bad air

stig´ma *n.* **(stig´ma-ta, stig´mas)** brand, mark of infamy; top of a pistil receiving the pollen; **stig´ma-tize´** *vt.* brand; disgrace

still *a.* silent; motionless; *vt.* quiet, silence; appease, satisfy; *adv.* yet; nevertheless; *n.* apparatus for distilling liquids

stilt *n.* high support of wood with rest for the foot, used for walking; *vt.*; **stilt´ed** *a.* unnaturally elevated in speech, pompous

stim´u-late´ *vt.* rouse to action, excite; **stim´u-la´tion** *n.*

stim´u-lant *n.* anything that stimulates or excites

stim´u-lus *n.* **(stim´u-li)** goad, anything that rouses to action, stimulant

sting *vi.* & *vt.* stick anything sharp into; pain acutely; *n.* sharp-pointed weapon of certain insects, reptiles, etc.; thrust of a sting into flesh

sting´y *a.* niggardly

stink *vi.* **(stank, stunk)** emit an offensive odor; *n.* disagreeable smell

stint *vt.* confine to a scanty allowance; *n.* limit, restraint; task allotted

stip´ple *vt.* make or cover with dots

stip´u-late´ *vt.* contract, insert as a condition; **stip´u-la´tion** *n.*

stir *vi.* & *vt.* agitate, move, rouse; *n.* tumult, bustle

stir´rup *n.* support for the foot attached to the saddle

stitch *n.* single pass of a needle and thread; loop; *vi.* & *vt.* sew in a line of stitches

stock *n.* lineage; shares in corporations; goods; cattle; liquid preparation of meat and vegetables used in cooking; *vt.* store; supply; *a.* constantly used

stock´bro´ker *n.* broker who deals in securities

stock car race *n.* race between two or more cars of standard manufacture

stock com´pa-ny *n.* corporation whose shares are held by individuals; company of actors regularly engaged at a local theater

stock ex-change´ *n.* place where stocks are bought and sold

stock´hold´er *n.* one who holds stock in a company

stock´pile´ *n.* reserve supply of needed raw materials; *vt.* build up such a reserve

stock´y *a.* stumpy, short and heavy

stock´yard´ *n.* place with pens, sheds, etc., for the temporary keeping of livestock

sto´ic *n.* one indifferent to pleasure or pain; **sto´i-cism** *n.*

stoke *vi.* & *vt.* tend a fire (esp. a furnace)

stole *n.* long garment or scarf, reaching to the feet

stol´id *a.* dull, impassive; **sto-lid´i-ty** *n.*

stom´ach *n.* organ which receives food from the esophagus for digestion; appetite; *vt.* endure

stone *n.* hard mineral matter; precious gem; tombstone; concretion formed in the bladder; hard shell containing the seed of some fruits; standard British weight (14 lbs. avoirdupois); *vt.* pelt with stones; free from stones

stooge *n.* toady, one who makes another appear to best advantage (as a comedian's stooge)

stool *n.* low chair without a back; **stool pigeon** *n.* person used as a decoy or informer

stoop *vi.* bend the body forward; descend from rank or dignity; *n.* inclination forward; porch

stop *vt.* close up; hinder, restrain; *vi.* cease from motion or action; stay, put up; *n.* act of stopping or being stopped; hindrance

stop´per *n.* anything that stops; plug; *vt.* close with a stopper

stop´ple *n.* cork, plug

stor´age *n.* safekeeping of goods in a store; fee for keeping goods in a warehouse; **stor´age battery** *n.* battery for accumulating electricity

store *n.* quantity gathered, provisions; place where goods are sold; *vt.* gather in quantities; place in a warebouse; **store´house´** *n.* place for keeping goods

stork *n.* wading bird allied to the heron

storm *n.* tempest, commotion, tumult; assault on a fortified place; *vi.* raise a tempest; blow with violence; be in a violent passion; *vt.* attack by force, assault; **storm´y** *a.*

sto´ry *n.* narrative, anecdote, novel; falsehood; one of the floors of a building

stout *a.* fat, obese; brave; strong

stove *n.* apparatus for warming or cooking

stow *vt.* place compactly; **stow´age** *n.*

strafe *vt.* subject an enemy to intensive fire (as from planes)

strag´gle *vi.* wander off, stray; **strag´gler** *n.*

straight *a.* direct, in a true line, not crooked; upright, honest; **straight´en** *vt.* make straight

strain *vt.* stretch, exert to the utmost; injure by overtasking; make uneasy or unnatural; filter; *n.* violent effort; injury inflicted by straining; race, stock

strait *a.* difficult, rigorous; narrow, tight; *n.* narrow pass; difficulty

strand *n.* shore; one of the strings that compose a rope; necklace (as of pearls); *vi.* & *vt.* run aground; leave alone in a desperate situation

strange *a.* foreign; not formerly known; marvelous, odd

stran´ger *n.* foreigner; one unknown or unacquainted

stran´gle *vi.* & *vt.* choke; **stran´gu-la´tion** *n.*

strap *n.* narrow strip of metal, leather, etc.; razor strop

strat´a-gem *n.* artifice for deceiving an enemy; cunning scheme

strat´e-gy *n.* art of military planning on a large scale; generalship; **stra-te´gic** *a.*; **strat´e-gist** *n.*

strat´i-fy´ *vt.* form in layers

stra´to-sphere´ *n.* outer portion of the atmosphere, beginning about seven miles above the surface of the earth

stra´tum *n.* **(stra´ta)** bed or layer (as of earth)

straw *n.* stalk on which grain grows; quantity of these after threshing

straw´ber´ry *n.* creeping plant and its tart, red fruit

stray *vi.* wander, err; *n.* domestic animal that is lost

streak *n.* line or long mark; trait of character; *vt.* form streaks in

stream *n.* current of water, air, etc.; anything moving or flowing continuously; drift, tendency; *vi.* flow in a stream; *vt.* cause to flow

stream´er *n.* long, narrow flag, pennant

stream´lined´ *a.* having long, smooth lines which offer little resistance to air or water

street *n.* road in a city

strength *n.* quality of being strong; vigor, force; solidity, toughness; intensity, brightness; support, validity; **strength´en** *vi.* & *vt.* make or grow stronger

stren´u-ous *a.* eagerly active, energetic; **stren´u-ous-ness** *n.*

strep´to-my´cin *n.* antibiotic similar to penicillin

stress *n.* force, pressure, urgency, emphasis; *vt.*

stretch *vt.* extend, expand; exaggerate; *vi.* be extended; *n.* act of stretching; extension; state of being stretched; utmost extent; course, turn, shift; **stretch´er** *n.* anything used for stretching; frame for carrying the sick, wounded, or dead

strew *vt.* **(strewed, strewn)** scatter loosely, spread

strict *a.* exact; severe; **strict´ness** *n.*

stric´ture *n.* morbid contraction of a passage in the body; unfavorable criticism

stride *vi.* **(strode; strid´den)** walk with long steps; *vt.* pass over at a step; *n.* long step

stri´dent *a.* grating

strife *n.* contention

strike *vt.* **(struck, strick´en)** hit with force, dash against; stamp, coin; let down (as a sail or flag); find (as gold); *vi.* give a quick blow, dash; sound; touch; leave work in order to gain some advantage from an employer; *n.* refusal to work until certain demands are granted; sudden discovery

string *n.* small cord; series of things; *vt.* **(strung)** supply with strings; put a string on a musical instrument

strin´gent *a.* strict; binding strongly; **strin´gen-cy** *n.*

strip *vt.* pull off in strips, tear off; deprive of a covering, make bare, expose; deprive, plunder; *vi.* & *vt.* undress; *n.* long, narrow piece; **strip´tease´** *n.* musical act in which girl removes her clothing

stripe *n.* mark made by a lash or rod; long, narrow line or division; *vt.* make stripes upon; form with lines of different colors

strip´ling *n.* youth

strive *vi.* **(strove; striv´en)** make efforts, contend

strob´o-scope´ *n.* device for studying rapidly moving objects through flashing lights off and on as object moves by

stroke *n.* blow; sudden attack, calamity; sweep of an oar in rowing; movement of a piston of a steam engine; *vt.* rub gently in one direction, caress

stroll *vi.* amble, wander on foot; *n.* leisurely walk

strong *a.* healthy, vigorous; solid; well fortified; **strong´arm´** *a.* employing brute force

stron´ti-um *n.* one of the heavy metallic elements; **strontium-90** *n.* dangerous and long-lived radioactive isotope of strontium

strop *n.* strip of leather for sharpening razors

struc´ture n, manner of construction; building; arrangement of parts in a substance or body

strug´gle *vi.* contend, labor; *n.* violent effort, fight

strum *vi.* & *vt.* play on a musical instrument in an informal manner

strut *vi.* walk in a pompous way

strych´nine´ *n.* poisonous vegetable alkaloid

stub *n.* stump left after a tree is cut down; anything stumpy; *vt.* strike the toes against an object

stub´born *a.* unreasonably firm; **stub´born-ness** *n.*

stuc´co *n.* plaster used for decoration; *vt.* face with stucco

stud *n.* collection of breeding horses; place where they are kept; male animal used for breeding; nail with a large head

stu´dent *n.* one who studies; learner, scholar

stu´di-o *n.* room of an artist, used by him for production of his work; room or stage used in producing radio or television programs; **studio couch** *n.* couch, usually backless, which when opened provides a bed

stu´di-ous *a.* given to study, thoughtful, diligent

stud´y *vt.* try to learn thoroughly; *n.* absorbed attention; object of attentive consideration, branch of learning; room for studying

stuff *n.* material; textile, cloth; worthless matter; *vt.* fill by crowding; press in; **stuff´y** *a.* ill-ventilated; stodgy, pompous

stum´ble *vi.* trip in walking, err; **stumble upon** find by accident; *n.*

misstep, blunder

stump *n.* part of a tree left in the ground after the trunk is cut down, remnant, stub

stun *vt.* stupefy with a loudnoise or blow; surprise completely, amaze

stunt *vt.* hinder from growth; *n.* any short or stunted thing; any action which gains attention

stu´pe-fac´tion *n.* act of making stupid or senseless; insensibility

stu´pe-fy´ *vt.* deprive of sense or sensibility

stu-pen´dous *a.* of wonderful magnitude, amazing

stu´pid *a.* deficient in understanding; done without reason or judgment; **stu-pid´i-ty, stu´pid-ness** *n.*

stu´por *n.* suspension of feeling

stur´dy *a.* resolute, firm, stout

stur´geon *n.* large food fish, a source of caviar

stut´ter *vt.* hesitate, stammer; *n.* act of stuttering, hesitation in speaking

sty *n.* enclosure for swine; small, inflamed tumor on the eyelid

style *n.* characteristic or peculiar mode of expression and execution in writing or the fine arts; manner, form, fashion; *vt.* entitle, name; **styl´ish** *a.* fashionable

sty´lus *n.* pointed instrument; phonograph needle

suave *a.* polished, tactful

sub-con´scious *a.* pertaining to the activities of the mind that are carried on below consciousness; *n.*

sub´di-vide´ *vi.* & *vt.* divide into smaller sections or parts; **sub´di-vi-sion** *n.*

sub-due´ *vt.* **(sub-du´ing; sub-dued´)** conquer; soften

sub´ject *a.* under the power of another; liable; *n.* one under the power of another, esp. of a sovereign; topic under consideration

sub-ject´ *vt.* make subject or subordinate; expose, make liable; cause to undergo; **sub-jec´tion** *n.*

sub-jec´tive *a.* derived from one´s own feelings; **sub-jec´tive-ness, sub´jec-tiv´i-ty** *n.*

sub-join´ *vt.* append

sub´ju-gate´ *vt.* bring under control; **sub´ju-ga´tion** *n.*

sub-junc´tive *a.* subjoined, added; denoting that form of a verb (mood) which refers to something not as a fact, but as in the mind of somebody; *n.* subjunctive mood

sub´lease´ *vi.* & *vt.* let or lease by one tenant to another

sub´let´ *vt.* sublease

sub´li-mate´ *vi.* & *vt.* change from a solid to a gas without melting (as iodine); refine, exalt; refine a primitive emotion by giving it an acceptable outlet; **sub´li-ma´tion** *n.*

sub-lime´ *a.* high, lofty, majestic; **sub-lim´i-ty** *n.*

sub-lim´i-nal *a.* below the level of consciousness

sub´ma-rine´ *a.* in or under the sea; *n.* vessel that can travel under water

sub-merge´, sub-merse´ *vi.* & *vt.* plunge under water; **sub-mer´gence, sub-mer´sion** *n.*

sub-mis´sion *n.* act of yielding, resignation; humble behavior, obedience

sub-mis´sive *a.* willing to submit; **sub-mis´sive-ness** *n.*

sub-mit´ *vi.* & *vt.* refer or offer to another; surrender

sub-or´di-nate *a.* lower in order, rank, nature. or power; *n.* an inferior

sub-or´di-nate´ *vt.* place in a lower

order or value; make subject to; **sub-or´di-na´tion** *n.*

sub-orn´ *vt.* cause to take a false oath; **sub´or-na´tion** *n.*

sub-poe´na *n.* writ commanding the attendance of a person in court; *vt.* serve with a subpoena

sub-scribe´ *vi.* & *vt.* write underneath (as a name); give consent or attest to something as by writing one´s name; receive a journal or newspaper regularly by paying in advance; **sub-scrib´er** *n.*

sub-scrip´tion *n.* act of subscribing; sum subscribed (as for a journal)

sub´se-quent *a.* following, succeeding

sub-ser´vi-ent *a.* serving to help in a minor way; subject, submissive; **sub-ser´vi-en-cy** *n.*

sub-side´ *vi.* settle, fall to the bottom; become quiet

sub-sid´i-ar´y *a.* furnishing help; secondary; *n.* company owned by another organization

sub´si-dize´ *vt.* assist or help support by money

sub´si-dy *n.* assistance, pecuniary aid, esp. by a government in enterprises of public importance

sub-sist´ *vi.* have existence; have the means of living; **sub-sist´-ence** *n.* existence; livelihood; **sub-sist´-ent** *a.*

sub-son´ic *a.* slower than the speed of sound

sub´stance *n.* essential part, body; property

sub-stan´tial *a.* having substance, real, weighty; having property

sub-stan´ti-ate´ *vt.* make real; prove, verify

sub´stan-tive *a.* existing; of importance; *n.* word denoting the name of anything

sub´sti-tute´ *vt.* put in place of another; *n.* anything put in place of another; **sub´sti-tu´tion** *n.*

sub´struc´ture *n.* understructure, foundation

sub´ter-fuge´ *n.* evasion, scheme for deceiving

sub´ter-ra´ne-an *a.* situated or occurring under the ground

sub´tle *a.* cunning, sly; **sub´tle-ness, sub´tle-ty** *n.*

sub-tract´ *vt.* take away a part from the rest; find the difference between two numbers; **sub-trac´tion** *n.*

sub´urb *n.* district near, but beyond, the limits of a city; **sub-ur´ban** *a.*; **sub-ur´ban-ite´** *n.* person living in a suburb

sub-ven´tion *n.* money given for some purpose, subsidy

sub-ver´sion *n.* complete overthrow, ruin; **sub-ver´sive** *a.*

sub-vert´ *vt.* overthrow or wreck, as social institutions

sub´way´ *n.* tunnel under a street (for traffic, etc.)

suc-ceed´ *vi.* & *vt.* follow, take the place of; obtain one´s goal

suc-cess´ *n.* anyone or anything that succeeds; **suc-cess´ful** *a.*

suc-ces´sion *n.* act of following after; series of persons or things following each other

suc-ces´sive *a.* following in succession or in order

suc-ces´sor *n.* person who takes the place of another

suc-cinct´ *a.* short; concise

suc´cor *vt.* assist, relieve; *n.* aid, relief

suc´co-tash *n.* Indian corn and beans

suc´cu-lent *a.* full of juice

suc-cumb´ *vi.* sink under, yield; die

such *a.* of the kind mentioned

suck *vt.* draw in with the mouth, absorb; *vi.* draw milk from the breast or udder; suckle

suc´tion *n.* act or power of drawing in fluids

sud´den *a.* unexpected, abrupt; **sud´den-ness** *n.*

suds *n. pl.* soapy water

sue *vt.* **(su´ing; sued)** prosecute at law; *vi.* make legal claim; plead; woo

suede *n.* soft, velvet-like leather

su´et *n.* fatty tissue, particularly about the kidneys

suf´fer *vt.* undergo, bear up under; permit; *vi.* feel pain or punishment, be injured

suf-fi´cien-cy *n.* state of being sufficient; competence; ability

suf-fi´cient *a.* enough, equal to the end or purpose; competent

suf´fix *n.* letter or syllable added to the end of a word

suf´fo-cate´ *vt.* choke by stopping the breath, stifle; **suf´fo-ca´tion** *n.*

suf´frage *n.* vote; right to vote

suf-fuse´ *vt.* cover (as with a liquid, color, etc.)

sug´ar *n.* sweet carbohydrate obtained from sugar cane, sugar beet; etc.; *vt.* sweeten or sprinkle with sugar; make pleasant

sug-gest´ *vt.* introduce indirectly, hint

sug-ges´tion *n.* act of suggesting; hint; idea thus suggested

sug-ges´tive *a.* containing a hint; mildly indecent

su´i-cide´ *n.* one who dies by his own hand; **su´i-cid´al** *a.*

suit *n.* set of clothes of the same material; act of suing; action at law; petition; number of things used together; *vt.* befit; please

suit´a-ble *a.* fitting

suite *n.* train of attendants; set (esp. of rooms)

suit´or *n.* one who sues in love or in law, petitioner, wooer

sul´fa drug´ *n.* powerful germ killer derived from sulphanilic acid and used to treat infections

sulf´a-nil´a-mide´ *n.* type of sulfa drug used in treating streptococcus infections

sul´fur, sul´phur *n.* yellow non-metallic element, brimstone; **sul-fu´-ric** *a.*

sulk *vi.* be sullen; **sulk´y** *a.* morose, sullen

sul´len *a.* gloomily angry and silent; dark, dull; **sul´len-ness** *n.*

sul´ly *vi.* & *vt.* soil, stain, spot; *n.* stain, tarnish

sul´tan *n.* sovereign of a Moslem state, esp. of the Turkish empire

sul´try *a.* sweltering, hot and oppressive; **sul´tri-ness** *n.*

sum *n.* aggregate of two or more quantities; problem in arithmetic; total; summary; *vt.* collect into one amount or whole; **sum up** present in brief

su´mac, su´mach´ *n.* shrub used in tanning and dyeing

sum´ma-ry *a.* summed up; swift or prompt without formality; *n.* condensed statement; **sum´ma-rize´** *vt.* present concisely

sum-ma´tion *n.* summing up

sum´mer *n.* warmest season of the year: June, July, and August in North America; *vi.* pass the summer

sum´mit *n.* highest point

sum´mon *vt.* command to appear (esp. in court); rouse; **sum´mons** *n.* authoritative call

sump´tu-ous *a.* costly, luxurious;

sump´tu-ous-ness *n.*

sun *n.* celestial body which is the source of light and heat; sunshine; *vt.* expose to the sun's rays; **sun´-beam´** *n.* ray of sunlight; **sun´-down´** *n.* sunset; **sun´ lamp´** *n.* lamp giving ultraviolet light; **sun´-rise´** *n.* appearance of the sun above the horizon; **sun´set´** *n.* going down of the sun; **sun´shine´** *n.* shining light of the sun; place on which it shines; warmth, cheerfulness; **sun´stroke´** *n.* sudden, sometimes fatal prostration caused by over exposure to the sun

sun´der *vt.* separate, divide

sun´dry *a.* several; **sun´dries** *n. pl.* various small articles

su´per-a-ble *a.* feasible, possible, surmountable

su´per-a-bun´dant *a.* abundant to excess; **su´per-a-bun´dance** *n.*

su´per-an´nu-ate´ *vt.* allow to retire on a pension on account of old age or infirmity

su-perb´ *a.* excellent; magnificent, grand

su´per-car´go *n.* officer on a ship who attends to commercial transactions

su´per-cil´i-ous *a.* disdainful, haughty; **su´per-cil´i-ous-ness** *n.*

su´per-e´go *n.* part of the mind concerned with conscience

su´per-fi´cial *a.* pertaining to the surface; shallow, slight, not learned

su´per-flu´i-ty *n.* larger quantity than required

su´per-gal´ax-y *n.* a large group of galaxies

su´per-high´way´ *n.* modern multilane highway

su´per-in-tend´ *vt.* have the oversight or charge of, control; **su´per-in-tend´ence** *n.*; **su´per-in-tend´-ent** *n.* overseer; person in charge of a plant, school district, etc.

su-pe´ri-or *a.* higher in rank or excellence; *n.* one higher in rank than another; **su-pe´ri-or´i-ty** *n.* quality or state of being superior

su-per´la-tive *a.* superior to all others, most eminent

su´per-mar´ket *n.* large grocery store

su-per´nal *a.* celestial; very fine

su´per-nat´u-ral *a.* outside the powers of nature

su´per-no´va *n.* nova of tremendous brilliance

su´per-nu´mer-ar´y *a.* above the stated or required number; unnecessary; *n.*

su´per pow´er *n.* dominant nation in the world community; worldwide political body with authority over all other powers

su´per-scribe´ *vi. & vt.* write on outside or top

su´per-scrip´tion *n.* anything written or engraved on top or on the outside

su´per-sede´ *vt.* make useless by superior power; replace

su´per-son´ic *a.* faster than the speed of sound (738 mph at 32° F)

su´per-sti´tion *n.* ignorant and irrational belief in supernatural agency; **su´per-sti´tious** *a.*

su´per-vene´ *vi.* occur or follow unexpectedly

su´per-vise´ *vt.* oversee; **su´per-vi´-sion** *n.*; **su´per-vi´sor** *n.*

su-pine´ *a.* lying on the back; indolent

sup´per *n.* evening meal

sup-plant´ *vt.* displace, take the place of; undermine and thereby displace

sup´ple *a.* pliant, lithe; **sup´ple-ness** *n.*
sup´ple-ment *n.* anything which adds or completes (as a literary supplement to a newspaper); *vt.* supply or fill up, add; **sup´ple-men´tal, sup´ple-men´ta-ry** *a.*
sup´pli-ant *a.* entreating; *n.* humble petitioner
sup´pli-cant *a.* supplicating; *n.* one who supplicates; **sup´pli-cate´** *vt.* entreat earnestly, address in prayer; **sup´pli-ca´tion** *n.*
sup-ply´ *vt.* fill up (esp. a deficiency), add, furnish; fill a vacant place; *n.* act of supplying; that which is supplid or fills a want
sup-port´ *vt.* bear up sustain; endure; patronize, defend; supply with means of living; corroborate, make good; *n.* act of supporting or upholding; prop, assistance, maintenance; **sup-port´a-ble** *a.*
sup-posc´ *vt.* assume as true, imagine as existing
sup´po-si´-tion *n.* act of supposing; thing supposed, assumption, hypothosis
sup-pos´i-ti´tious *a.* put by trick in the place of another, spurious; hypothetical
sup-pos´i-tive *a.* supposed; implying supposition
sup-press´ *vt.* crush, subdue; restrain; prevent publication of; **sup-pres´sion** *n.*; **sup-pres´sive** *a.*
supreme´ *a.* highest, greatest
su-prem´a-cy *n.* state of being supreme
sur´charge´ *n.* excessive load or charge
sure *a.* secure; confident beyond doubt
sure´ty *n.* state of being sure, certainty; person legally obligated
surf *n.* waves breaking upon a shore
sur´face *n.* exterior part of a·thing, outward appearance
surf´board *n.* oval board for riding the ocean surf
sur´feit *vt.* fill to satiety, disgust; *n.* excess in eating and drinking, overfullness
surge *n.* rising of a large wave; *vi.* rise high, swell
sur´geon *n.* one who practices surgery
sur´ger-y *n.* treatment of a disease by cutting
sur´ly *a.* morose, uncivil, churlish; **sur´li-ness** *n.*
sur´mise´ *n.* conjecture; *vt.* imagine, conjecture
sur-mount´ *vt.* pass over, overcome; **sur-mount´a-ble** *a.*
sur´name´ *n.* family name
sur-pass´ *vt.* pass beyond, excel; **sur-pass´a-ble** *a.*
sur´plice *n.* white outer garment worn by the clergy
sur´plus *n.* excess
sur-prise´ *n.* act of taking unwares; emotion caused by anything sudden; *vt.* come upon suddenly or unawares; astonish
sur-ren´der *vi.* & *vt.* yield, deliver; *n.* act of yielding possession
sur´rep-ti´tious *a.* done in secret or by stealth
sur´ro-gate´ *n.* substitute; judge who presides over settlement of estates, etc.
sur-round´ *vt.* encompass, encircle
sur´tax´ *n.* special additional tax; special tax on income above a certain amount
sur-veil´lance *n.* supervision; watch or guard kept on someone
sur-vey´ *vt.* look over, measure and estimate (as land); **sur-vey´or** *n.*

measurer of land; public officer who surveys land

sur´vey´ *n.* general view, measuring of land

sur-vive´ *vt.* outlive; *vi.* remain alive; **sur- viv´al** *n.*; **sur-vi´vor** *n.*

sus-cep´ti-ble *a.* capable of receiving sensitive; **sus-cep´ti-bil´i-ty** *n.*

sus-pect´ *vt.* mistrust; imagine to be guilty

sus´pect´ *n.* person imagined to be guilty

sus-pend´ *vt.* hang; cause to stop for a time, delay

sus-pense´ *n.* state of being suspended; act of withholding judgment; emotional tension caused by uncertainty

sus-pen´sion *n.* act of suspending; interruption, delay; conditional withholding; **sus-pen´sion bridge** *n.* bridge supported by chains or wire cables which pass over piers

sus-pi´cion *n.* act of suspecting (esp. on slender evidence), mistrust; **sus-pi´cious** *a.* doubting, questionable

sus-tain´ *vt.* hold up, prolong, maintain; prove, sanction

sus´te-nance *n.* anything which sustains (as food)

sus´ten-ta´tion *n.* anything that sustains or maintains

su´ture *n.* the sewing together of a wound; seam uniting parts of a bone (as in the skull)

su´ze-rain *n.* feudal lord, supreme ruler; **su´ze-rain-ty** *n.* dominion of a suzerain, paramount authority

swab *n.* mop for cleaning floors or decks; cotton used for mopping a wound; *vt.* clean or dry with a swab

swag´ger *vi.* sway or swing the body; bluster; *n.* insolent manner

swal´low *n.* long-winged migratory bird able to catch insects in flight; *vt.* receive through the gullet into the stomach; absorb; tolerate

swamp *n.* ground saturated with water; *vt.* overset or cause to fill with water (as a boat); saturate (as with water)

swan *n.* large, graceful, long-necked bird larger than a goose

swank, swanky *a. col.* elegant; showy, floridly elegant

swans´down´ *n.* small, soft feathers of the swan; thick, fluffy fabric of wool and cotton or silk

swarm *n.* large body or cluster of insects or other small animals, esp. bees; great number, throng; *vi.* gather as bees do, esp. when leaving a hive; throng

swarth´y *a.* dark-skinned; **swarth´i-ness** *n.*

swash´buck´ler *n.* swaggerer

swas´ti-ka *n.* ornament in the form of a Greek cross with the ends bent at right angles, used by the American Indians (particularly the Navahos); symbol of the German Nazi party

swath *n.* line of grass or grain cut by the scythe; sweep of a scythe

swathe *vt.* bind with a bandage

sway *vi.* & *vt.* incline first to one side and then to the other; influence; *n.*

swear *vi.* **(swore, sworn)** declare, calling God to witness; give evidence on oath; utter the name of God profanely; *vt.* affirm, calling on God to witness; administer an oath to

sweat *n.* perspiration; labor; *vi.* give out sweat; toil; *vt.* give out, as sweat

sweep *vt.* **(swept)** wipe or rub over with a brush or broom; carry with pomp; pass rapidly over; *vi.* pass swiftly and forcibly; pass with pomp; move with a long reach; *n.* extent of a stroke; direction of a curve

sweet *a.* having a pleasant taste (like sugar) rather than sour, salty, or bitter; pleasing to any sense or to the mind; *n.* sweet substance, candy

sweet´en *vi. & vt.* make or become sweet or more agreeable

sweet´heart *n.* lover

sweet´ pea *n.* pea cultivated for its blossoms

sweet´ po-ta´to *n.* creeping plant having tubers resembling the potato

swell *vi.* **(swelled, swol´len)** grow larger, expand; *vt.* increase; *n.* increase in size or sound; rise of ground; wave; *a. col.* handsome, showy; fine, splendid

swel´ter *vi.* be oppressed by the heat

swerve *vi.* turn aside, deviate

swift *a.* moving with great speed; ready, prompt

swig *n.* large draught; *vt.* gulp

swill *vi. & vt.* drink greedily; *n.* liquid food for hogs

swim *vi.* **(swam, swum)** move through water; feel dizzy; be drenched; *vt.* pass by swimming

swin´dle *vt.* cheat; *n.* act of cheating or defaulting; **swin´dler** *n.*

swine *n. sg. & pl.* hog

swing *vi.* **(swung)** move back and forth while hanging; *vt.* move to and fro; whirl, brandish; *n.* act of swinging, waving motion; anything suspended for swinging in; sweep or power of a swinging body; type of jazz marked by interpretive variations

swipe *vi. & vt.* strike with a sweeping blow; *col.* steal; *n.* sweeping stroke or blow

swirl *vi. & vt.* eddy, whirl; *n.* whirling motion; eddy

switch *n.* small, flexible twig; movable rail and its appendages, used for transferring cars from one track to another; *vt.* strike with a switch; shunt

switch´board´ *n.* device for controlling electric currents; apparatus for handling telephone calls

swiv´el *n.* ring or link which turns on a pin

swoon *vi.* faint; *n.* temporary insensibility

swoop *vi. & vt.* sweep down and catch; *n.*

swop *vt.* exchange; barter

sword *n.* weapon with a long blade for cutting or thrusting

sword´fish *n.* large sea-fish, with upper jaw elongated so as to resemble a sword

syc´a-more´ *n.* in America, the plane tree, esp. the buttonwood

syc´o-phan-cy *n.* obsequious flattery; **syc´o-phant** *n.* servile flatterer, parasite

syl´la-ble *n.* vowel or vowel with consonants uttered as a unit; **syl-lab´i-fy´** *vt.* divide into syllables

sylph *n.* imaginary being, with graceful form and nimble movements, which inhabits the air

syl´van *a.* pertaining to trees or a forest

sym´bol *n.* representation of an idea by an object; letter representing a mathematical quantity, operation, etc.; **sym-bol´ic, sym-bol´i-cal** *a.* figurative; **sym´bol-ism** *n.* representation by symbols; system of symbols; **sym´bol-ize´** *vt.* represent by symbols

sym´me-try *n.* state when one part is pleasingly proportionate to another; **sym-met´ri-cal** *a.* having due proportion in parts; composed of two parts which correspond harmoniously to each other

sym´pa-thet´ic *a.* having sympathy or compassion for a person or cause

sym´pa-thize´ *vi.* feel sympathy for a person or thing

sym´pa-thy *n.* agreement of inclination or feeling; compassion, pity, commiseration

sym´pho-ny *n.* elaborate composition, usually in four movements or parts, for full orchestra

sym-po´si-um *n.* collection of speeches or essays on one subject

symp´tom *n.* anything that accompanies and points to the existence of something else (esp. a disease); **symp´to-mat´ic** *a.*

syn´a-gogue´ *n.* Jewish place of worship

syn´chro-nize´ *vt.* cause to occur or happen at the same time; make simultaneous

syn´co-pate´ *vt.* contract (as a word) by taking away letters or syllables from the middle; shift the regular musical beat; **syn´co-pa´tion** *n.*

syn´di-cate *n.* group of persons associated for some business enterprise

syn´drome *n.* group of symptoms that occur together, characterizing a disorder

syn´od *n.* ecclesiastical council

syn´o-nym´ *a.* word having exactly or nearly the same meaning as another; **syn-on´y-mous** *a.*

syn-op´sis *n.* **(syn-op´ses)** brief outline of the content of a work

syn´tax *n.* study of the order and arrangement of words in sentences

syn´the-sis *n.* **(syn´the-ses)** combination of separate ideas, parts, or chemical elements or compounds, into a new unit; **syn-thet´ic** *a.*

syph´i-lis *n.* one of the venereal diseases

syr-inge´ *n.* apparatus for injecting liquids

sys´tem *n.* organism; method, plan, order; **sys´tem-at´ic** *a.* pertaining to or showing system; **sys´tem-a-tize´** *vt.* reduce to a system

sys´to-le´ *n.* contraction of the heart (as opposed to diastole)

T

tab´er-nac´le *n.* temporary habitation; tent; place of worship

table *n.* smooth, flat surface with legs used as an article of furniture; food, entertainment; condensed statement; *vt.* make into a table or catalogue; postpone consideration of

tab´leau´ *n.* picture represented by people who pose silently

ta´ble d´hôte´ *n.* complete meal for which a fixed price is charged

tab´let *n.* writing pad

tab´loid´ *n.* newspaper, usually sensational, half the size of an average paper, containing many illustrations

ta-boo´ *n.* any practice, act, word, etc. which is forbidden by custom; *vt.* forbid approach or use of

tab´u-lar *a.* of the form of or pertaining to a table

tab´u-late´ *vt.* arrange in or reduce to tables

tac´it *a.* implied, but not explicitly expressed

tac´i-turn´ *a.* habitually silent; **tac´-i-tur´ni-ty** *n.*

tack *n.* short, sharp nail with a broad head; *vt.* fasten slightly, as by tacks

tack´le *n.* rope rigging of a ship, or for raising heavy weights; angler´s equipment; one of the positions on a football team; *vt.* seize, attack

tact *n.* ability to deal with people thoughtfully and graciously

tac´tics *n.* art of maneuvering (esp. military units in action)

tad´pole *n.* young toad or frog; polliwog

taf´fe-ta *n.* glossy type of silk fabric

taf´fy *n.* candy made of boiled molasses; flattery

tag *n.* any small thing tacked or attached to another; game in which the person gains who touches another; *vt.* tack, fasten; follow closely

tail *n.* appendage at the end of the backbone of an animal; part resembling a tail; **tail´pipe´** *n.* exhaust vent on a car

tai´lor *n.* person who makes clothes; *vi.* & *vt.* make, fit, or alter clothing

taint *vt.* impregnate with anything noxious; infect, corrupt; *vi.* affect with something corrupting; *n.* infection, corruption; spot

take *vt.* **(tak´ing, took, tak´en)** lay hold of, get into one´s possession, catch, choose, convey; receive, allow, become affected with; *vi.* have the intended effect; gain reception; **take´—home´** *a.* net amount (as *take-home pay*); portable (as *take-home carton*)

talc *n.* mineral of a soapy feeling used in cosmetics

tale *n.* narrative, story

tal´ent *n.* natural ability or aptitude

tal´is-man *n.* charm (sometimes engraved on metal or stone)

talk *vi.* & *vt.* speak, chatter; *n.* conversation; rumor; **talk´a-tive** *a.*

tall *a.* high; long

tal´low *n.* animal fat

tal´ly *n.* account; *vi.* correspond, match

tal´on *n.* claw of a bird of prey

tam´bou-rine´ *n.* shallow drum with one skin and bells in the circular frame

tame *a.* domesticated, lacking native wildness and shyness; gentle; dull; *vt.* reduce to a domesticated state, civilize

tamp *vt.* beat down by repeated light strokes

tamp´er *vi.* meddle

tan *n.* light brown color; *vt.* convert skins into leather by steeping in vegetable solutions containing tannin; thrash

tang *n.* strong taste

tan´gent *n.* line which touches a curve at a 90° angle at point of contact

tan´ge-rine´ *n.* variety of Chinese seedless orange

tan´gi-ble *a.* perceptible to the touch; material; **tan´gi-bil´i-ty** *n.*

tan´gle *n.* knot of things united without order; *vt.* interweave, snarl

tank *n.* large receptacle for holding a liquid or gas; armored military vehicle which moves on treads

tank´er *n.* cargo ship fitted with tanks for carrying oil, etc.

tan´nin *n.* astringent vegetable substance used in tanning leather

tan´ta-lize´ *vt.* vex or torment by promising and then withholding something

tan´ta-mount´ *a.* equivalent to

tan´trum *n.* fit of ill-humor

tap *n.* gentle blow or touch; faucet through which a liquid is run; *vt.* strike gently; open a cask and draw off a liquid

tape *n.* narrow band; **tape´line´, tape measure** *n.* piece of tape marked in inches for measuring; **tape recorder** *n.* electronic device which records sound on magnetized tape

tape´ deck´ *n.* component for playing back magnetic tape in a hi-fi set

tap´er *n.* small candle; *a.* narrowed at one end; *vi.* & *vt.* become or make gradually smaller

tap´es-try *n.* woven hangings

tape´worm´ *n.* parasitic worm with many joints found in the intestines of man and beast

tap´i-o´ca *n.* substance obtained from root of the cassava plant and used in cooking

tar *n.* sticky substance obtained from wood, coal, etc.; sailor; *vt.* smear with tar

ta-ran´tu-la *n.* large poisonous spider

tar´dy *a.* slow; dilatory

tar´get *n.* mark to shot at

tar´iff *n.* list of duties or customs to be paid on goods

tar´nish *vi.* & *vt.* spoil or dim (as by exposure to air)

tar-pau´lin *n.* waterproof cover of coarse canvas

tar´ry *vi.* be tardy or slow; loiter, stay, delay

tart *a.* sharp or sour to the taste; *n.* small pie containing fruit or jelly

tar´tar *n.* salt which forms on the inside of casks containing wine; coating which forms on the teeth

task *n.* set amount of work imposed upon someone; *vt.* burden; charge, accuse

task´ force´ *n.* fully equipped fleet engaged on a special mission

tas´sel *n.* ornamental fringe hanging from a knob

taste *vt.* perceive flavor by eating; eat a little of; partake of; *vi.* have a flavor; *n.* act of tasting; sense by which flavor is perceived; quality, flavor; small portion; intellectual relish, good esthetic judgment; choice, predilection

tat´ter *n.* torn piece; *vt.* tear into rags

tat´tle *vi.* prate, chatter; tell tales or secrets; **tat´tler** *n.*

tat-too´ *vt.* paint the skin with colored figures by sticking with needles; *n.* indelible marks pricked into the skin

taunt *vt.* ridicule; reproach with cutting words; *n.* reproach

taut *a.* stretched tight, without slack

tav´ern *n.* bar, saloon; inn

taw´dry *a.* showy without good taste; **taw´dri-ness** *n.*

taw´ny *a.* yellowish brown, the color of anything tanned

tax *n.* rate imposed on articles, income, etc., for the benefit of the state; any thing imposed, burdensome duty; *vt.* lay a tax on; burden; accuse

tax´i, tax´i-cab´ *n.* passenger car operated for profit

tax´i-der´my *n.* art of preparing, stuffing, and mounting the skins of animals; **tax´i-der´mist** *n.*

tea *n.* dried leaves of a shrub native to China, Japan, and Ceylon; infusion of the leaves in boiling water; any vegetable infusion

teach *vt.* **(taught)** impart knowledge to, show, train; **teach´a-ble** *a.*;

teach´er *n.*

team *n.* numbers of animals moving together; number of persons associated for some purpose

tear *n.* drop of fluid secreted in the eyes by the lachrymal glands

tear *vt.* **(tore, torn)** draw asunder with violence, lacerate, rend; *vi.* be rent; *n.* anything torn

tease *vt.* vex, torment

tech´ni-cal *a.* pertaining to the useful arts or a particular art or profession; **tech´ni-cal´i-ty** *n.* state or quality of being technical; any fine point peculiar to a trade, profession, etc.; **tech´ni-cal-ly** *adv.*

tech-nique´ *n.* technical skill in an art

tech-nol´o-gy *n.* application of science to industry. explanation of technical terms; **tech-nol´o-gist** *n.*

te´di-ous *a.* wearisome; **te´di-ous-ness** *n.*

tee *n.* small wooden spike from which a ball is struck off in golf; **tee up** *vt.* in golf, placing a ball on the tee preparatory to striking

teem *vi.* bring forth, be full or prolific

teen´ag´er *n.* anyone 13-19 years old; **teen´-age´** *a.* characteristic of anyone in his teens

tee-to´tal-er *n.* one who abstains from intoxicating drink

tel´e-cast´ *vi.* & *vt.* broadcast by television; *n.*

tel´e-com-mu´ni-ca´tions *n.* communication over great distances, as by radio, TV

tel´e-gram´ *n.* message sent by telegraph

tel´e-graph´ *n.* electric apparatus for sending signals from a distance over a wire; *vt.* inform by telegraph

te-lem´e-try *n.* use of electronic devices to measure distances and transmit data

te-lep´a-thy *n.* transmission of mental impressions without visible agency

tel´e-phone´ *n.* electric instrument which transmits sound over a wire; *vi.* & *vt.* speak by telephone

tel´e-pho´to lens´ *n.* camera lens for close-up pictures of distant objects

tel´e-promp´ter *n.* device by which a TV script, written in very large letters, is shown to performers

tel´e-scope´ *n.* instrument for viewing distant objects; *vi.* & *vt.* drive together like the joints of a telescope

tel´e-thon´ *n.* a TV program without limited time, put on for some worthy cause

tel´e-vi´sion *n.* broadcasting of images over a distance; television receiver

tell *vt.* **(told)** count; narrate; disclose; discern; explain; inform; order; assure; *vi.* talk; produce or take effect

tem´per *vt.* modify by mixture; adjust, fit; moderate, soften; *n.* due balance of different qualities or ingredients; state of metal hardness; state of mind

tem´per-a-ment *n.* physical and mental characteristics of an individual; mood

tem´per-ance *n.* moderation; abstinence from intoxicating liquors

tem´per-ate *a.* moderate, esp. in the appetites and passions; calm, self-contained; neither very cold or hot in climate

tem´per-a-ture´ *n.* degree of heat or cold

tem-pes´tu-ous *a.* turbulent, in the

way of a storm or tempest

tem´ple *n.* edifice erected to a deity, place of worship; region on either side of the head above the cheekbone

tem´po-ral *a.* worldly, secular; pertaining to time

tem´po-rar´y *a.* for a time only; **tem´po-rar´i-ly** *adv.*

tem´po-rize´ *vi.* appear to yield to the circumstances

ten´a-ble *a.* capable of being retained, kept, or defended

te-na´cious *a.* holding fast, apt to stick, stubborn; retentive (as of memory)

ten´ant *n.* one who holds land or property under another occupant; *vt.* hold as a tenant

tend *vt.* wait upon; *vt.* move, be directed; be apt to operate; contribute

tend´en-cy *n.* inclination to move or act in some special way

ten´der *vt.* present for acceptance, offer; *n.* offer or proposal (esp. of some service); thing offered; *a.* soft, delicate; easily moved to pity, love, etc.; apt to cause pain

ten´der-foot *n.* newcomer, novice; greenhorn

ten´der-loin´ *n.* choice cut of meat from the loin of cattle

ten´don *n.* strong band of fibers by which a muscle is attached to a bone; sinew

ten´dril *n.* slender spiral shoot by which a plant attaches itself to a support

ten´e-ment *n.* dwelling, house, apartment building (esp. one in a slum area)

ten´et *n.* opinion, principle, or doctrine which a person or sect maintains as true

ten´nis *n.* game in which a ball is driven with rackets

ten´on *n.* projection at the end of a piece of wood inserted into a corresponding mortise

ten´or *n.* prevailing course; intent; highest male voice

tense *n.* form of a verb said to indicate time (as ride: rode); *a.* strained

ten´sion *n.* act of stretching; state of being stretched or strained; physical or emotional strain

tent *n.* shelter of canvas stretched on poles

ten´ta-cle *n.* threadlike organ of insects for feeling, etc.; feeler; armlike organ (as of the octopus)

ten´ta-tive *a.* provisional, experimental

ten´u-ous *a.* sparse, slight, unsubstantial

ten´ure *n.* manner or right of holding real estate, office, etc.

te´pee *n.* wigwam

tep´id *a.* lukewarm

term *n.* limit; limited period (as a session of a court); word, expression; name for an idea or thing; **terms** *n. pl.* conditions, arrangements; *vt.* apply a term to, name

ter´mi-nal *a.* pertaining to or growing at the end or extremity; ultimate, final

ter´mi-nate´ *vi.* & *vt.* set a limit to, end, finish, be limited, close, complete

ter´mi-na´tion *n.* act of terminating; limit, end

ter´mi-nol´o-gy *n.* special vocabulary used in any art, science, etc.

ter´mi-nus *n.* **(ter´mi-nus-es, ter´-mi-ni)** end or extreme point; end or important station of a railway

ter´race *n.* raised, level bank of earth

ter´ra cot´ta *n.* type of glazed clay used in making statues, pottery, etc.

ter´ra-my´cin *n.* antibiotic obtained from soil

ter´ra-pin *n.* large variety of turtle, highy valued as food

ter-rar´i-um *n.* enclosure containing an indoor system of small plants or animals

ter-res´tri-al *a.* pertaining to or existing on the earth; earthly, worldly

ter´ri-ble *a.* exciting terror or awe; awful, dreadful; **ter´ri-bly** *adv.*

ter´ri-er *n.* dog which pursues burrowing animals

ter-rif´ic *a.* creating terror

ter´ri-fy´ *vt.* frighten greatly, alarm, cause to fear

ter´ri-tor´y *n.* extent of land belonging to a city or state, domain; **ter´ri-to´ri-al** *a.*

ter´ror *n.* extreme fear; object of fear or dread; **ter´ror-ism** *n.* organized system of intimidation; **ter´ror-ize´** *vt.* keep in terror or continual fear

terse *a.* compact, concise, brief

test *n.* any critical trial; quiz, examination; standard, distinction, proof; *vt.* put to proof; examine critically

tes´ta-ment *n.* solemn declaration of one´s will in writing; one of the two great divisions of the Bible

tes´ti-fy´ *vi.* & *vt.* bear witness, give testimony, make a solemn declaration

tes´ti-mo´ni-al *a.* containing testimony; *n.* writing bearing testimony to one´s character or abilities; gift presented as a token of respect

tes´ti-mo´ny *n.* proof, evidence; declaration to prove some fact

tes´ty *a.* irritable; peevish

tet´a-nus *n.* lockjaw

tête´-à-tête´ *a.* face to face; confidential; *n.* private interview

teth´er *n.* rope or chain for tying a beast to a stake; *vt.*

tet´ra-he´dron *n.* solid figure enclosed by four triangles

Teu-ton´ic *a.* pertaining to the people comprising the Germans, English, Scandinavians, etc., as distinguished from the Latin, Slav, or other groups

text *n.* original words of an author; subject of a sermon or discourse; main body of matter in a book, as distinguished from the notes, illustrations, etc.

tex´tile *n.* woven fabric

tex´ture *n.* quality, character, grain, or smoothness of woven cloth, wood, paint, or any product

thank *vt.* express gratitude to; **thanks** *n. pl.* expression of gratitude; **thank´ful** *a.*; **thanks´giv´ing** *n.* public acknowledgment of Divine goodness

thaw *vi.* & *vt.* melt or become liquid (as ice to water); *n.* melting of ice or snow by heat; change of weather which causes this

the´a-ter *n.* place for dramatic representations, etc.; drama, stage; scene of action; **the-at´ric** *a.*

theft *n.* act of stealing

the´ism *n.* belief in a personal God; **the´ist** *n.*

theme *n.* subject, topic of discussion; important melodic phrase; essay in school

thence *adv.* from that time or place; for that reason; **thence´forth** *adv.*

the-oc´ra-cy *n.* government in which the chiefs of state are priests or ministers of God or gods; state thus governed; **the´o-crat´ic** *a.*

the´o-lo´gi-an *n.* one versed in the-

ology
the-ol´o-gy *n.* science which treats of God and of man´s relation to him; religious truths
the´o-rem *n.* established principle; statement of a mathematical principle that can be demonstrated
the´o-ry *n.* hypothesis; exposition of the absbract principles of a science or art; speculation, as opposed to practice; **the´o-ret´ic, the´o-ret´i-cal** *a.*; **the´o-rist** *n.*
the´o-rize´ *vi.* form a theory, form opinion,; solely by theories
the-os´o-phy *n.* philosophy purporting to be based upon knowledge obtained by direct communion with God
ther´a-peu´tics *n.* branch of medicine concerned with remedies and treatment; **ther´a-peu´tic** *a.*
ther´a-py *n.* treatment for disease and ailments, both mental and physical
ther´mal *a.* pertaining to heat
ther-mom´e-ter *n.* instrument for indicating temperature
ther´mo-nu´cle-ar *a.* pertaining to heat and nuclear energy, as in the H-bomb
ther´mo-stat´ *n.* self-acting apparatus for regulating temperature
the-sau´rus *n.* **(the-sau´ri)** treasury of words, lexicon, dictionary
the´sis *n.* **(the´ses)** proposition, statement set down for argument; long essay, dissertation
thi´a-min, thi´a-mine´ *n.* vitamin B_1, one of the vitamin-B complex group
thick *a.* not thin, having depth; dull; dense, crowded; frequent, in quick succession; **thick´en** *vi.* & *vt.*; **thick´ness** *n.*
thief *n.* **(thieves)** one who steals or is guilty of theft; **thieve** *vi.*; **thiev´-er-y** *n.*
thigh *n.* thick, fleshy part of the leg from the knee to the hip
thim´ble *n.* metal protection for a finger used in sewing
thin *a.* slim, lean; fluid, of little viscosity; not dense, close, or crowded; faint and shrill; transparent, easily seen through; *vt.* make thin; **thin´ness** *n.*
thing *n.* object, object of human thought; detail; event; **things** *n. pl.* belongings (as clothes, etc.)
think *vi.* & *vt.* **(thought)** exercise the mind revolve ideas in the mind; judge, form, or hold (as an opinion); consider, recall, design
thirst *n.* need or craving for drink; eager desire for anything; *vi.* feel thirst; **thirst´i-ness** *n.*; **thirst´y** *a.* feeling thirst; deficient in moisture
this´tle *n.* common name of several prickly plants of the aster family
thith´er *adv.* to that place; to that end or result
tho´rax *n.* chest cavity
thong *n.* strap of leather
tho´ri-um *n.* radioactive chemical element
thorn *n.* sharp spine on the stems of many plants
thor´ough a, passing through or to the end; complete; precise
thor´ough-bred´ *a.* bred from the best blood (as a horse); *n.* thoroughbred animal
thor´ough-fare´ *n.* public way or street
though, tho *conj.* admitting, even if, supposing; *adv.* nevertheless, however
thought *n.* act of thinking; deliberation; idea; **thought´ful** *a.* full of thought; considerate

thou´sand *a.* ten hundred; *n.* ten hundreds

thrall *n.* slave; slavery; **thral´dom, thrall´dom** *n.* slavery, bondage

thrash *vt.* beat soundly; thresh; *vi.* move about violently; thresh

thread *n.* very thin line of any substance twisted and drawn out; prominent spiral part of a screw; main idea running through a discourse; *vt.* pass a thread through the eye of a needle; pass or pierce through (as a narrow way); **thread´bare´** *a.*

threat *n.* menace

threat´en *vi.* & *vt.* declare the intention of inflicting harm upon another, intimidate

thresh *vt.* separate grain from straw by beating; *vi.* perform the act of threshing

thresh´er *n.* person or machine that threshes grain

thresh´old *n.* doorsill, entrance

thrice *adv.* three times

thrift *n.* frugality; careful use of money, time, goods, etc.; **thrift´less** *a.* extravagant; **thrift´lessness** *n.*; **thrift´y** *a.* showing thrift or economy

thrill *vi.* & *vt.* affect with or feel a tingling or piercing sensation

thrive *vi.* **(throve, thrived, thriv´en)** prosper, be successful, grow rich, grow vigorous, flourish

throat *n.* fore part of the neck containing the gullet and windpipe; passage from the mouth to the lungs and stomach, pharynx

throb *vi.* palpitate or beat (as the heart); *n.* strong pulsation

throes *n. pl.* suffering, agony

throm-bo´sis *n.* formation of a clot in a blood vessel or in the heart of an animal

throne *n.* elevated and ornamental chair of state, used by a sovereign, sovereign power and dignity

throng *n.* large number of people crowded or moving together; *vi.* & *vt.* press, crowd

throt´tle *vi.* & *vt.* strangle; slow down or stop as by choking or shutting off power

through, thru *prep.* from end to end of; among; by means of; *adv.* from one end or side to the other, from beginning to end; to the end or purpose

throw *vi.* & *vt.* **(threw; thrown)** hurl, fling, propel; wind, twist

throw´a-way´ *n.* container meant to be disposed of after contents are used

thrum *vi.* & *vt.* pluck rudely, monotonously, or idly on an instrument (like the guitar)

thrush *n.* European songbird

thrust *vi.* & *vt.* push, intrude, stab; *n.* forceful push or impulse; force (as of rockets or jets); assault, stab

thud *n.* sound as that of a heavy stone striking the ground; blow causing a dull sound

thug *n.* member of a fraternity of robbers and assassins in India; hence, any ruffian or bandit

thumb *n.* short, thick first finger of the hand

thump *n.* heavy blow; *vt.* beat with something heavy; *vi.* strike with a dull sound

thun´der *n.* noise made by a discharge of atmospheric electricity; any similar noise; *vi.* sound as thunder; make alarming statements; **thun´der-clap´** *n.* burst of thunder; **thun´der-struck´** *a.* greatly astonished

thwack *vt.* strike with something

blunt and heavy, whack

thyme *n.* aromatic herb used in cooking

thy´roid´ *n.* ductless gland at the front of the neck important to metabolism and growth

ti-ar´a *n.* ornamental headdress similar to a crown; pope´s crown

tick *n.* mite infesting sheep; clicking sound; *vi.* make a small quick noise; beat (as a watch)

tick´et *n.* small piece of paper admitting the purchaser to enter, etc.; *vt.* put a ticket on, label

tick´le *vt.* touch lightly (as on the ribs) and cause to laugh; **tick´lish** *a.* easily tickled; critical, dangerous

tid´bit´ *n.* delicate morsel

tide *n.* time, season; regular rising and falling of the sea; course; **tid´al** *a.*

ti´dings *n. pl.* news

ti´dy *a.* neat, in good order; *vt.* make neat; **ti´di-ness** *n.*

tie *vt.* fasten with a cord, knot; unite; *vi.* score equally; *n.* knot; bond; necktie; equality of numbers (as of votes or points in a game)

tier *n.* rank, one of several rows placed one above another

tiff *n.* fit of peevishness, quarrel

ti´ger *n.* fierce striped animal of the cat family

tight *a.* close, compact; not leaky; fitting closely; not loose, taut; stringent, scant (as with money); **tight´en** *vt.*; **tight´ness** *n.*

tile *n.* piece of baked clay used for covering roofs, floors, etc.; *vt.* cover or adorn with tiles

till *n.* money drawer in a counter, desk, etc.; *vt.* cultivate; **till´age** *n.*; *prep.* to the time of

till´er *n.* lever for turning a rudder

tilt *vi.* thrust or fight with a lance; fall into a sloping posture; *vt.* point or thrust with a lance; slant, raise one end of; *n.* tournament; inclination, slope

tim´ber *n.* wood used for building; standing trees, woods; *vt.* furnish with timber

tim´bre *n.* tone or character of a musical sound

time *n.* duration, era, period, age; space of time at one´s disposal; season, proper time; rhythm; *vt.* do at the proper season; regulate as to time; note the time of; **time´li-ness** *n.*; **time´ly** *a.*

time´keep-er *n.* clock, watch or other instrument for marking time; one who keeps the time of workmen

time´ta´ble *n.* list showing the times at which trains, planes, ships, etc., arrive and depart

tim´id *a.* lacking courage, easily frightened; **ti-mid´i-ty, tim´id-ness** *n.*

tim´or-ous *a.* timid; indicating or showing fear

tin *n.* silvery-white metallic element; **tin´foil´** *n.* tin in thin leaves

tinc´ture *n.* solution of any substance in alcohol

tin´der *n.* anything used for kindling fire from a spark

tine *n.* prong of a fork

tinge *vt.* tint, color, or imbue slightly; *n.* small amount of anything infused into another substance

tin´gle *n.* a prickly or tingling sensation; *vi.* to feel a prickly or stinging sensation

tink´er *vi.* mend; work on or mend equipment in an amateur way

tin´kle *vi.* make small, sharp sounds; clink, jingle; *n.* sharp,

clinking sound
tin´sel *n.* glittering strips of metal used as ornamentation; anything showy but of little value
tint *n.* variety of color made by adding white; *vt.* give a slight coloring to; dye, tinge
ti´ny *a.* very small
tip *n.* point, end, endpiece; *vt.* form a point to, cover the end of
tip *vi. & vt.* lower one end of; furnish with private information; give money for small services rendered; *n.* private information; money given for services rendered
tip´ple *vi. & vt.* drink liquor, as from habit; **tip´pler** *n.*
tip´sy *a.* slightly intoxicated
tip´toe *n.* end. of the toe; *vi.* walk on tiptoe
ti´rade´ *n.* long ranting speech
tire *n.* hoop or band around a wheel; hollow rubber hoop inflated with air; *vt.* harass, vex; exhaust the strength of, weary; *vi.* become weary; **tire´some** *a.*
tis´sue *n.* structure of a particular kind of cells and fibers; fine, gauze-like cloth; paper *n.* very thin paper for wrapping
tithe *n.* tenth part; *vt.* tax a tenth of; give a tenth of
ti´tle *n.* inscription; name of a book, essay, etc.; name indicating rank, office, etc.; anything showing a just right to possession; document that proves a right; *vt.* name
tit´ter *vi.* giggle; *n.*
toad *n.* amphibious animal similar to the frog
toad´y *n.* mean hanger-on and flatterer; sycophant; *vt.* fawn as a sycophant
toast *vt.* dry and brown bread by heat; drink to the health of; *n.* bread which has been browned; sentiment spoken over a drink; **toast´mas´ter** *n.* chairman at a banquet who announces the toasts
to-bac´co *n.* plant of the nightshade family, the leaves of which are cultivated for smoking
to-bog´gan *n.* kind of sled used for sliding down inclines; *vi.* slide down on a toboggan
toc´sin *n.* alarm bell
to-day´ *n.* the present day
tod´dle *vi.* walk (as a small child)
toe *n.* one of the small members at the end of the foot
to-geth´er *adv.* in the same place, time, or company; in union or concert
toil *vi.* labor, work hard; *n.* fatiguing labor
toi´let *n.* dressing table; mode or operation of dressing; water closet
to´ken *n.* sign, souvenir
tol´er-able *a.* capable of being endured; moderately good
tol´er-ance *n.* toleration; **tol´er-ant** *a.* indulgent; unprejudiced; **tol´er-ate** *vt.* endure
tol´er-a´tion *n.* liberty given to a minority to hold their own political or religious opinions
toll *n.* tax; *vi. & vt.* sound slowly (as a bell); **toll´gate´** *n.* where toll is taken; **toll´-way** *n.* highway on which tolls are charged
tom´a-hawk´ *n.* war hatchet of North American Indian
to-ma´to *n.* plant of the nightshade family, cultivated for its fleshy fruit
tomb *n.* vault in which a dead body is placed; **tomb´stone´** *n.*
tom´boy *n.* romping girl
tome *n.* volume, book
to-mor´row *n.* the day after this
ton *n.* measure of weight, 2,240 lbs.

(long ton), or 2,000 lbs. (short ton)

tone *n.* quality of a sound; inflection of the voice; healthy state of the body; **arm** *n.* phonograph arm bearing the stylus

tongs *n. pl.* instrument resembling pincers for handling things, esp. heated metals

tongue *n.* fleshy organ in the mouth, used in tasting, swallowing, speech, etc.; manner of speaking, discourse; language; anything like a tongue in shape (as the catch of a buckle)

ton´ic *a.* relating to tones; giving vigor to the system; *n.* medicine which gives strength or muscular tone

to-night´ *n.* this night

ton´nage *n.* weight in tons of goods in a ship; cubical capacity of a ship; duty on ships, estimated per ton; ships considered collectively

ton´sil *n.* one of two oval tissues at the root of the tongue; **ton´sil-lec´to-my** *n.* removal of the tonsils; **ton´sil-li´tis** *n.* inflammation of the tonsils

ton´sure *n.* act of clipping the hair or of shaving the head; bare place on the head worn by monks, etc.

tool *n.* instrument, implement; dupe, hireling; *vt.* shape with a tool

toot *vi.* & *vt.* sound (as a horn)

tooth *n.* **(teeth)** one of the bony prominences in the jaws, used in biting and chewing; prong, cog; **tooth´ache´** *n.*

top *n.* highest part of anything; *vt.* cover; cover on the top; rise above; remove from the top; **top´notch´** *a.* first-rate, best

to´paz´ *n.* semi-precious stone, generally yellowish

top´flight´ *a.* first-rate, best; excellent

top´ic *n.* subject of discourse or argument

top´i-cal *a.* pertaining to a place, local; relating to a topic or subject

top´most *a.* highest

to-pog´ra-phy *n.* detailed account of the surface features of an area

top´ple *vi.* fall, tumble down

torch *n.* portable lamp; device giving off intensively hot flame for welding, etc.

tor´ment *n.* torture, anguish; anything that causes great pain; *vt.* torture, put to extreme pain, physical or mental; afflict, vex

tor-na´do *n.* violent whirling storm; small cyclone

tor-pe´do *n.* exlosive apparatus for destroying ships

tor´pid *a.* having lost the power of motion and feeling; inactive; sluggish; **tor-pid´i-ty** *n.*

tor´por *n.* numbness; inactivity

tor´rent *n.* rushing stream

tor´rid *a.* parching; dried with heat

tor´sion *n.* twisting, turning; force which tends to return a wire when twisted

tor´so´ *n.* trunk of the body or of a statue without head or limbs

tor´toise *n.* type of turtle

tor´tu-ous *a.* twisted, winding; deceitful, ambiguous

tor´ture *n.* act of putting someone to severe pain; extreme pain, anguish of body or mind; *vt.* put to severe pain; pain, vex

toss *vt.* throw upward; cause to raise and fall; *vi.* tumble about; *n.*

tot *n.* small child

to´tal *a.* whole, complete; *n.* entire amount; **to-tal´i-ty** *n.* entire amount

to-tal´i-tar´i-an-ism *n.* political doctrine under which one group rules a state under a highly centralized government, allowing no recognition or representation to other parties

tot´ter *vi.* stagger, falter

touch *vt.* come in contact with; perceive by feeling; reach; relate to; *n.* contact; sense of feeling; small quantity; **touch´y** *a.* irritable

tough *a.* not easily broken; able to endure hardship; severe, difficult; *n.* bully, rowdy

tour *n.* journey, inspection; *vt.* make a journey through

tour´ist *n.* one who makes a holiday tour; **tour´ist court** *n.* motel; cabins rented to motorists

tour´na-ment *n.* series of contests or games of skill

tour´ney *n.* tournament

tour´ni-quet *n.* bandage tightened by turning a stick to check the flow of blood

tou´sle *vt.* put into disorder, ruffle

tout *vt.* give tips on racehorses; seek support for or play up a product, entertainment, etc.; *n.*

tow *vt.* pull a vessel through the water with a rope; *n.* towline; act of towing; vessel towed; coarse part of flax or hemp; **tow´line´** *n.* line used in towing

tow´el *n.* cloth for wiping or drying anything

tow´er *n.* lofty building, usually much higher than wide; *vi.* rise into the air, be lofty

town *n.* place larger than a village; small city; inhabitants of a town

town´ship *n.* territory or district of a town; in American land measure, six miles square

tox´ic *a.* poisonous; pertaining to poisons

tox´in *n.* poison of animal, vegetable, or bacterial origin

toy *n.* child´s plaything; trifle; *vi.* trifle or play with

trace *n.* mark left, footprint; *vt.* follow by tracks or footsteps; sketch

trac´er-y *n.* ornamental work in flowing outline

tra´che-a *n.* windpipe, formed of rings of gristle; **tra´che-al** *a.*

track *vt.* follow by marks or footsteps; follow the path of a plane missile etc., by radar; make tracks upon; *n.* mark left; footprint; beaten path; two parallel lines of rails on railways

tract *n.* region, district; short treatise

trac´ta-ble *a.* docile, teachable; **trac´ta-bil´i-ty** *n.*

trac´tion *n.* act of drawing out or state of being drawn out; act of moving heavy bodies along a path

trac´tor *n.* motor-propelled vehicle used for pulling farm implements, truck trailers, etc.

trade *n.* buying and selling, commerce; occupation; persons engaged in the same occupation; *vi.* & *vt.* buy and sell; barter; **trad´er** *n.*

trade´mark´ *n.* distinctive device identifying goods produced by a certain firm

trades´—un´ion; trade´—un´ion *n.* society of workers formed for collective bargaining with employers

tra-di´tion *n.* belief or custom handed down orally

traf´fic *n.* commerce, trade; business done on a railway, etc.; *vi.* & *vt.* **(traf´fick-ing, traf´ficked)** exchange

tra-ge´di-an *n.* actor of tragedy

trag´e-dy *n.* drama in which the action and language are elevated and the climax sad or fatal; any fatal or dreadful event; **trag´ic** *a.*

trail *vt.* drag along the ground; hunt by tracking; *vi.* follow after; *n.* track followed by the hunter, road

trail´er *n.* movable living quarters or cargo carrier designed to be pulled by automobile or truck; short advertisement or message usually preceeding a full-lenth motion picture

train *vt.* educate, discipline; tame or teach (as animals); cause to grow in a certain shape (as the branches of a tree); prepare for athletic feats; *n.* anything that is drawn along (as the part of a dress which trails on the ground); retinue of attendants; cars drawn by an engine, etc.

trait *n.* distinguishing feature

trai´tor *n.* one who betrays a sacred trust; person guilty of treason

tra-ject´to-ry *n.* curve formed by bullet, missile, or other projectile

tram´mel *n.* net used in fishing; anything that confines or impedes; *vt.* shackle, confine

tramp *vt.* tread, stamp; *n.* foot journey; act of tramping; vagrant, hobo

tram´ple *vt.* tread under foot

trance *n.* stupor resembling sleep (as brought about by hypnosis)

tran´quil *a.* quiet,serene, undisturbed; **tran-quil´i-ty, tran-quil´li-ty** *n.*; **tran´quil-ize´, tran´quil-lize´** *vt.* make tranquil; **tran´quil-iz´er** *n.* drug (such as reserpine) which relieves anxieties

trans-act´ *vt.* perform, carry through; **trans-ac´tion** *n.* act of transacting; management; affair, business, or thing done

tran-scend´ *vt.* rise above, exceed; **tran-scend´ence** *n.*; **tran-scend´ent** *a.* superior in excellence; lying beyond human knowledge; **tran´scen-den´tal** *a.* concerned with what is independent of experience, metaphysical

tran-scribe´ *vt.* write over again; record, as by writing down or by making a sound recording

tran-script´ *n.* written copy; **tran-scrip´tion** *n.* recording, as of sounds

tran´sept´ *n.* cross aisle of a church

trans-fer´ *vt.* convey to another place, carry; sell, assign, give

trans´fer *n.* conveyance; anything which is transferred; ticket giving transportation on connecting line; **trans-fer´a-ble** *a.*; **trans-fer´ence** *n.*

trans-fig´u-ra´tion *n.* change of form; supernatural change in the appearance of Christ; **trans-fig´ure** *vt.* change the form of

trans-fix´ *vt.* pierce

trans-form´ *vt.* change the shape or nature of; **trans´for-ma´tion** *n.*

trans-fuse´ *vt.* pour out into another vessel; transfer blood from one person to another; **trans-fus´i-ble** *a.*; **trans-fu´sion** *n.*

trans-gress´ *n.* pass beyond a limit; break (as a law); **trans-gres´sion** *n.*

tran´sient *a.* passing, of short duration; *n.* temporary roomer, boarder, etc.

tran-sis´tor *n.* compact electronic mechanism using germanium as substitute for vacuum tube; **tran-sis´tor radio** radio, usually portable, whose small size is obtained by transistors and printed circuits

tran´sit *n.* passage over or through; passage of a heavenly body over the meridian of a place or over the sun's disc

tran-si'tion *n.* change from one place or state to another

tran'si-tive *a.* denoting a verb that requires an object

tran'si-to'ry *a.* lasting for a short time, transient

trans'late *vt.* render into another language; **trans-la'tion** *n.*; **trans'-la-tor** *n.*

trans-lu'cent *a.* allowing light to pass through, but not entirely transparent

trans-mit' *vt.* send; send or broadcast (as in radio and TV); allow to pass through

trans-mute' *vt.* change to another form or substance

tran'som *n.* crossbeam; window built above a door

trans-par'en-cy *n.* quality of being transparent; picture on semi-transparent material; color photograph on celluloid

trans-par'ent *a.* capable of being seen through

tran-spire' *vi.* become known; take place, happen

trans-plant' *vt.* remove and plant in another place

trans-port' *vt.* carry from one place to another; carry away by violence of passion or pleasure; **trans'por-ta'tion** *n.*

trans'port' *n.* carriage from one place to another; vessel for conveyance; conveyance of troops and equipment by land, sea, or air; ecstasy, great joy

trans-pose' *vt.* put one thing in the place of another; change the order or key of

trans-sex'u-al *n.* person who wants to be a member of the opposite sex; person whose sex has been changed by medical treatment

trans-verse' *a.* lying across

trans-ves'tite *n.* person who dresses in the clothing of the opposite sex

trap *n.* instrument for snaring animals; ambush, stratagem; contrivance for hindering the escape of foul air, etc., out of a drain; *vt.* ensnare, catch

tra-peze' *n.* swinging bar for gymnastic excrcises

trap'e-zoid' *n.* plane foursided figure having two sides parallel; one of the bones of the wrist

trash *n.* refuse

trau'ma *n.* sudden, serious injury to mind or body; **trau'ma-tic** *a.* sudden, full of shock to mind or body

trav'el *vi.* walk; journey, move; *vt.* journey over; *n.* journey

trav'erse *a.* lying across; *n.* anything laid or built across; *vt.* cross (as in walking)

trav'es-ty *n.* burlesque, parody, caricature

trawl *vi.* fish with a trawl; *n.* baglike net dragged along after a boat; fishing line with many hooks

tray *n.* shallow, troughlike vessel

treach'er-ous *a.* betraying a trust

tread *vi.* **(trod, trod'den)** set the foot; walk, go; *vt.* walk on; trample; *n.* step; one of the horizontal parts of a stair; part of the wheel in contact with the rail or road

trea'dle *n.* part of a machine worked by the foot to impart motion (as on a sewing machine, bicycle, etc.)

trea'son *n.* betrayal of the government

treas'ure *n.* wealth stored up; thing much valued; *vt.* hoard up; value greatly; **treas'ur-er** *n.*; **treas'ur-y**

n. place for depositing wealth; department of government finances

treat *vt.* handle, attend, prescribe, or administer (as a physician); use; discourse on; entertain (as with food and drink); *vi.* argue; negotiate; *n.* special or unusual entertainment; pleasure

trea´tise *n.* exhaustive essay

trea´ty *n.* formal agreement between independent states

tre´ble *a.* triple, threefold; high in pitch, soprano; *n.* soprano

tree *n.* plant havin a large single trunk and woody branches

tre´foil´ *n.* three-leaved plant (as clover); any ornament like a trefoil

trel´lis *n.* lattice work for supporting plants, etc.

trem´ble *vi.* shake as from cold, etc.

tre-men´dous *a.* very large, great, or fine

trem´or *n.* trembling, shaking

trem´u-lous *a.* quivering

trench *vt.* cut, dig ditches; *vi.* encroach; *n.* ditch, fortified ditch

trench´ant *a.* sharp, cutting

trend *vi.* tend, go in a particular direction

tre-pan´ *n.* small cylindrical saw used in perforating the skull; *vt.* remove a circular piece of the skull

trep´i-da´tion *n.* involuntary trembling; fear

tres´pass *vi.* enter unlawfully upon another´s land; intrude; sin; *n.* act of trespassing

tress *n.* curl or braid of hair

tres´tle *n.* scaffolding

tri´ad *n.* union of three

tri´al *n.* judicial examination; examination by a test; state of being tried, state of suffering temptation

tri´an´gle *n.* plane figure with three angles and three sides; steel musical instrument in the form of a triangle; **tri-an´gu-lar** *a.*

tribe *n.* race, family; class, group; **trib´al** *a.*

trib´la´tion *n.* severe affliction

tri-bu´nal *n.* court of justice; any group with power to judge

trib´u-tar´y *a.* paying tribute; contributing supplies; paid in tribute; *n.* one who pays tribute; stream flowing into another

trib´ute *n.* amount paid for peace or protection; contribution, praise, etc., in honor of a person or cause

trick *n.* fraud, stratagem; clever contrivance to puzzle or amuse; cards falling to a winner at one turn; *vt.* deceive

trick´le *vi.* flow in drops

tri´col´or *a.* of three colors; *n.* national flag of France, red, white, and blue

tri´cy-cle *n.* children´s vehicle having three wheels

tri´dent *n.* three-pronged spear

tri-en´ni-al *a.* containing or happening every three years

tri´fle *vi.* & *vt.* indulge in foolish amusements; waste, spend idly; *n.* anything of little value; **tri´fler** *n.*

trig´ger *n.* catch which releases the hammer of a gun in firing

trig´o-nom´e-try *n.* science of the relations between the sides and angles of triangles

trill *vi.* & *vt.* speak or sing trills; *n.* quaver; sound produced by the vibration of the tongue, etc., against another organ; in music, two notes repeated in rapid succession

tril´lion *n.* in U.S., one thousand billions

trim *vt.* put in due order, decorate; clip, reduce to proper form; arrange for sailing; *a.* in good order

Trin´i-ty *n.* the three persons of the Christian Godhead; union of three in one

tri´ni´tro-tol´u-ene´ *n.* very powerful explosive, abbreviated as TNT

trink´et *n.* small ornament

tri´o *n.* set of three; musical composition for three performers

trip *vi.* move with short, light steps; stumble and fall, err; *vt.* cause to stumble; free, release; *n.* short journey

trip´ham´mer *n.* heavy hammer, tilted or lifted by machinery

tri´ple *a.* threefold; three times repeated; *vt.* make threefold

trip´let *n.* three of a kind united; three lines rhyming together; in music, group of three notes occupying the time of two; one of three children born together

trip´li-cate *a.* threefold; *n.* third copy or item of a set

tri´pod´ *n.* frame with three legs for supporting anything (as a camera)

tri-sect´ *vt.* cut into three equal parts

trite *a.* worn out by use, hackneyed, common

trit´i-um *n.* a heavy isotope of hydrogen

tri´umph *n.* joy over success; victory; *vi.* celebrate a victory with pomp; obtain victory, succeed; **tri-um´phal, tri-um´phant** *a.*

triv´i-al *a.* common, paltry

tro-cha´ic *a.* consisting of trochees; *n.* trochaic verse

tro´chee *n.* in poetry, a metrical foot consisting of one long or accented syllable followed by one short or unaccented syllable

troll *vt.* sing parts in succession; fish; *vi.* fish by trailing a line on the surface

trol´ley *n.* pulley running on an overhead wire and serving to transmit an electric current to the motor of a streetcar, etc.; streetcar; **trolley car** *n.* car propelled by an electric current transmitted through an overhead wire

trom´bone´ *n.* brass wind instrument whose pitch is changed by a sliding crook

troop *n.* collection of people; boy scout unit, **troops** *n. pl.* soldiers; small body of cavalry; *vi.* collect in groups; march in a company, or in haste

tro´phy *n.* memorial of a victory

trop´ic *n.* torrid zone extending 23° 27´ to each side of the equator; **trop´i-cal** *a.*

trop´o-sphere´ *n.* part of the atmosphere below the stratosphere

trot *vi.* go faster than a walk and slower than a run; run (as a horse), lifting one forefoot and one hindfoot of the opposite side at the same time

troth *n.* faith, fidelity; betrothal

trou´ble *vt.* put into a confused or worried state; *n.* disturbance, affliction, uneasiness; **trouble shooter** *n.* expediter; person who eliminates bottlenecks; **trou´blesome** *a.*

trough *n.* long, hollow vessel for water, etc.; long, narrow channel

trounce *vt.* beat severely

troupe *n.* company of actors

trou´sers *n. pl.* breeches

trous´seau´ *n.* bride´s outfit

trout *n.* fresh-water food fish of the salmon family

trow´el *n.* tool used in spreading mortar

troy´ weight´ *n.* system of weights (12 ounces to the pound) used for gold, silver, and precious stones

tru´ant *n.* idler; pupil who misses school without excuse; *a.* wandering from duty

truce *n.* agreement for temporary suspension of hostilities

truck *vi. & vt.* haul or transport by truck; exchange, barter; *n.* small commodities, esp. garden produce; vehicle built to carry heavy articles

truck´le *vi.* yield meanly to the demands of another

truc´u-lent *a.* very fierce; **truc´u-lence** *n.*

true *a.* agreeing with fact; faithfully adhering to friends, promises, etc.; genuine

truf´fle *n.* edible fungus growing underground and used in fine cookery

tru´ism *n.* self-evident or undenied truth; platitude

tru´ly *adv.* according to truth, in fact, faithfully

Truman Doctrine *n.* policy of economic and military aid to Greece and Turkey proposed by Pres. Truman in 1947

trump *n.* one of the suit of cards which takes any other; *vi. & vt.* play a trump card; **trump up** *vt.* manufacture (an accusation, etc.), fabricate, invent

trump´er-y *n.* showy, worthless things; rubbish

trum´pet *n.* brass wind instrument with a ringing tone; *vt.* proclaim sound the praises of

trun´cheon *n.* short staff, cudgel

trun´dle *vi. & vt.* roll, as on wheels; **trundle bed** *n.* low bed on wheels which can be hidden under a bed

trunk *n.* main stock of a tree; body of an animal apart from the limbs; main body of anything; nose of an elephant; chest for holding clothes

truss *n.* bundle; timbers, iron-work, etc., fastened together for supporting a roof, bridge, etc.; device to support an injured part of the body; *vt.* bind up, pack close; furnish with a truss

trust *n.* confidence, reliance, credit; something given in confidence; charge, office; combination of several corporations for controlling prices and defeating competition; *vt.* place trust in, believe; commit to one´s care; **trus-tee´** *n.* one to whom anything is intrusted

truth *n.* freedom from falsehood or error; that which is according to facts; practice of speaking or disposition to speak the truth; true statement, established principle

try *vt.* **(tried)** test by use or experiment; examine in court; examine carefully; experience; attempt; put to severe trial; *vi.* make an effort

tryst *n.* appointment to meet; place of meeting

T´ shirt´ *n.* short-sleeved undershirt of knitted cotton

tu´ba *n.* brass wind instrument of very low pitch

tube *n.* long, hollow cylinder; **tu´bu-lar** *a.*

tu´ber *n.* round, fleshy, underground stem (as the potato)

tu-ber´cu-lo´sis, TB *n.* infectious disease (usually of the lungs) of bacterial origin

tuck *vt.* draw or press in or together, fold under; *n.* fold in a garment

Tues´day *n.* third day of the week

tuft *n.* cluster of small, slender plants, etc.

tug *vi. & vt.* pull with effort; *n.* short pull; small, powerful boat for towing ships

tu-i´tion *n.* charge for instruction; teaching

tu´lip *n.* bulbous garden plant with showy flowers

tum´ble *vi.* fall; roll; *vt.* throw down or over; throw about while examining, rumple; *n.* act of tumbling

tu´mid *a.* swollen, enlarged, inflated

tu´mor *n.* abnormal swelling or growth

tu´mult *n.* uproar of a multitude, violent agitation; **tu-mul´tu-ous** *a.*

tune *n.* melody, air; *vt.* cause to produce the proper tones

tung´sten *n.* metallic element used in electric lights and to harden steel

tu´nic *n.* loose undergarment worn by the Romans

tun´nel *n.* passage cut through a hill or under a river; main flue or shaft of a chimney, kiln, etc.; *vt.* make a passage through

tur´ban *n.* headcovering consisting of a cap with a sash wound round it

tur´bid *a.* muddy; confused

tur´bine *n.* engine driven by the force of water, steam, etc., against rotating blades

tur´bo-jet´ *n.* type of jet engine using a turbine to compress air

tur´bu-lent *a.* in violent commotion; disposed to disorder; **tur´bu-lence** *n.*

tu-reen´ *n.* large dish for holding soup, etc.

turf *n.* surface of land matted with the roots of grass, etc.; cake of turf cut off, sod; racecourse, horse racing; *vt.* cover with turf or sod

tur´gid *a.* swollen, distended; bombastic

tur´key *n.* large bird, a native of America

tur´moil´ *n.* confusion

turn *vi.* & *vt.* move round; hinge, result; change; make or become giddy or sour; shape; *n.* change; revolution, winding, bend; manner, purpose; opportunity

turn´buck´le *n.* metallic loop, the turning of which brings two rods closer together endwise, used for tightening

turn´ta´ble *n.* mechanical device for turning or reversing a locomotive or car; revolving disk on a phonograph for holding the record

tur´nip *n.* edible plant of the mustard family and its solid, bulbous root

turn´out´ *n.* turning out; attendance; equipage

turn´o´ver *n.* semicircular pie having the crust doubled over it; rate of business activity or changes in personnel

turn´pike´ *n.* toll road

turn´stile´ *n.* revolving frame which prevents the passage of cattle or of more than one person at a time

tur´pen-tine´ *n.* resinous sap of the pine and other trees

tur´pi-tude´ *n.* vileness, depravity

tur´quoise´ *n.* bluish-green mineral, valued as a gem

tur´ret *n.* small tower; rotating tower (as on a warship)

tur´tle *n.* four-legged reptile whose body is enclosed in a tough shell

tusk *n.* long, pointed tooth on either side of the mouth of certain animals, as elephants and boars

tus´sle *n.* scuffle

tus´sock *n.* tuft of grass or twigs

tu´te-lage *n.* guardianship; instruction; **tu´te-lar, tu´te-lar´y** *a.* protecting; pertaining to a guardian

tu´tor *n.* one who has charge of the education of another, teacher; *vt.* instruct; have the care of

tux-e´do, tux *n.* men´s semi-formal evening wear

twad´dle *n.* silly talk

twain *n.* two; two fathoms, or twelve feet

twang *n.* sharp, quick sound (as of a tight string when pulled and let go); nasal tone of voice; *vi. & vt.* sound (as a tight string pulled and let go)

tweak *vt.* pinch and pull; *n.* sharp pinch

tweed *n.* woven woolen cloth of rough texture

tweet´er *n.* loudspeaker used exclusively for high frequency sounds

tweez´ers *n. pl.* small pincers for pulling out hair, etc.

twelfth *a.* last of twelve; *n.* one of twelve equal parts

twice *adv.* two times

twig *n.* small branch of a tree

twi´light´ *n.* faint light after sunset

twill *n.* appearance of diagonal ribs in cloth; fabric with a twill; *vt.* weave with a twill

twin *n.* one of two born at a birth

twine *n.* cord composed of two or more threads twisted together; *vt.* wind (as two threads together); wind about; *vi.* unite closely; bend; ascend round a support

twinge *n.* twitch; sudden, sharp pain; *vi. & vt.* have or cause to have a sudden, sharp pain

twin´kle *vi.* shine with an intermittent light; sparkle; *n.* quick motion of the eye; time occupied by a wink; instant

twirl *vi. & vt.* turn round rapidly; *n.* rapid circular motion

twist *vi. & vt.* twine, unite or form by winding together; encircle, wreathe, wind spirally; pervert the true form or meaning; *n.* anything twisted; cord; contortion; spiral or rotary motion (as of a billiard ball)

twitch *vt.* pull with a jerk; *vi.* move spasmodically; *n.* sudden, quick pull; spasmodic contraction of a muscle

twit´ter *n.* series of tremulous, broken sounds; giggle; *vi.* make a succession of small, tremulous noises; chirp; giggle

type *n.* mark stamped upon something; style, model; raised letter used in printing

type´set´ter *n.* person or machine that sets type for printing

type´writ´er *n.* machine for writing by the impression of type letters; **type´write´** *vi. & vt.*

ty´phoid fe´ver *n.* contagious disease caused by bacteria introduced in food

ty´phoon´ *n.* violent hurricane in the Chinese seas

ty´phus *n.* contagious fever, accompanied by prostration, delirium, and eruption

typ´i-cal *a.* pertaining to or constituting a type; characteristic

typ´i-fy´ *vt.* represent or be characteristic of

typ´ist *n.* one who operates a typewriter

ty-pog´ra-phy *n.* art of setting type for printing; **ty-pog´ra-pher** *n.* typesetter; **ty´po-graph´ic, ty´po-graph´i-cal** *a.* pertaining to type

ty-ran´nic, ty-ran´ni-cal, tyr´an-nous *a.* pertaining to a tyrant, unjustly severe

tyr´an-nize´ *vi. & vt.* act as a tyrant; rule with oppressive severity

tyr´an-ny *n.* government or authority of a tyrant; oppression, cruelty

ty´rant *n.* absolute ruler; one who uses his power oppressively

ty´ro *n.* one learning an art; novice, beginner

U

u-biq´ui-tous *a.* all-pervasive, everywhere at the same time; **u-biq´ui-ty** *n.*

ud´der *n.* organ (as of a cow) in which milk is secreted

ug´ly *a.* lacking beauty; offensive to the eye; hateful, ill-natured; **ug´li-ness** *n.*

u-kase´ *n.* Russian imperial decree; any administrative decree

u´ku-le´le *n.* small Hawaiian guita

ul´cer *n.* open sore which discharges pus; **ul´cer-ate´** *vi.* form an ulcer

ul-te´ri-or *a.* on the further side; remote; hidden, secret in intent

ul´ti-mate *a.* furthest, final; last, incapable of further division

ul´ti-ma´tum *n.* **(ul´ti-ma´tums, ul-ti-ma´ta)** last or final proposition or terms

ul´tra high´ fre´quen-cy, UHF *a.* pertaining to frequencies between 300 and 3000 megacyles/sec.

ul´tra-ma-rine´ *n.* sky-blue color

ul´tra-son´ic *a.* pertaining to vibrations (usually above 20,000/sec.) too high for the human ear to hear

ul´tra-vi´o-let *a.* pertaining to invisible rays beyond the violet end of the spectrum

um´ber *n.* brown clay pigment; variety of brown containing red and yellow

um´brage *n.* suspicion of injury; offense; **um-bra´geous** *a.* shady, shaded; resentful, suspicious

um-brel´la *n.* covered frame carried in the hand as a protection from rain or sunshine

um´pire´ *n.* person called in to decide a dispute, arbitrator; judge in the game of baseball, cricket, etc.

un´a-bridged´ *a.* not shortened, complete

un´a-dul´ter-a´ted *a.* pure

un´af-fect´ed *a.* not influenced; free from affectation; natural, simple

u-nan´i-mous *a.* consented to by all; being of one mind; **u´na-nim´i-ty** *n.* state of being unanimous, agreement in opinion, unity of mind

un´as-sum´ing *a.* not forward, modest

un-au´thor-ized´ *a.* without authority, not commissioned or authorized

un-bal´anced *a.* not balanced; mentally disordered

un-bear´a-ble *a.* intolerable, not to be endured

un´be-com´ing *a.* not becoming or suitable; improper, indecent

un-bend´ *vt.* free from a bent state, make straight; free from strain, set at ease; *vi.* become relaxed

un-bi´ased *a.* free from prejudice, impartial

un-bound´ed *a.* unlimited, boundless; unrestrained, without restraint

un-bro´ken *a.* entire, not broken; not subdued (as a colt or wild horse); undisturbed, not interrupted

un-can´ny *a.* weird, mysteriously strange

un-ceas´ing *a.* continuous, never-ending, incessant

un-civ´i-lized´ *a.* rude, barbarous

un´cle *n.* brother of one´s father or mother

un-clean´ *a.* filthy, foul, dirty; morally impure
un-coil´ *vi. & vt.* unwind
un-com´mon *a.* not common; rare, infrequent
un-com´pro-mis´ing *a.* making no concessions; exacting
un´con-di´tion-al *a.* without conditions or reservations
un´con-firmed´ *a.* not established, confirmed, or proved; not proved by authoritative testimony
un-con´scion-a-ble *a.* unreasonable; without conscience
un-con´scious *a.* not conscious, devoid of consciousness
un´con-sti-tu´tion-al *a.* contrary to or not author ized by a constitution
un´con-ven´tion-al *a.* not observing convention, usage, or custom
un-couth´ *a.* awkward, rude
un-cov´er *vt.* remove the cover of; *vi.* take off one´s hat
unc´tion *n.* act of anointing; ointment; hypocritical religious ardor; feeling or fervor, esp. in language; **extreme unc´tion** *n.* R.C. sacrament of anointing persons with consecrated oil in their last hours
unc´tu-ous *a.* fervid, insincerely fervid; oily, greasy
un-daunt´ed *a.* not easily daunted, fearless
un´de-cid´ed *a.* not settled or determined, irresolute
un´de-filed´ *a.* unsullied, immaculate, innocent
un´der-bid´ *vt.* ask a lower price than another
un´der-clothes´ *n. pl.* garments worn next to the skin; **un´der-cloth´ing** *n.*
un´der-cur´rent *n.* current running below the surface
un´der-es´ti-mate´ *vt.* undervalue, place too low a value or estimate upon
un´der-ex-posed´ *a.* in photography, relating to a negative that has not been exposed to the light for a sufficient length of time
un´der-gar´ment *n.* garment worn under another garment or next to the skin
un´der-go´ *vt.* **(un´der-went´; un´der-gone´)** endure, be subject to, go through with
un´der-grad´u-ate *n.* student in college who has not taken his, first degree
un´der-ground´ *a. & adv.* under the surface of the ground; in secret; *n.* organized resistance group opposed to those in power
un´der-hand´ed *a.* by secret means, by fraud
un´der-lie´ *vt.* lie beneath
un´der-line´ *vt.* underscore
un´der-ling *n.* subordinate
un´der-mine´ *vt.* form tunnels under in order to destroy; secretly destroy the support of (as a person´s reputation)
un´der-pin´ *vt.* support a foundation, floor, etc., by placing supports under; prop up
un´der-rate´ *vt.* rate at less than true worth
un´der-score´ *vt.* underline; emphasize
un´der-sell´ *vt.* sell cheaper than; *vi.* defeat fair trade by selling for too little
un´der-shirt´ *n.* shirt worn next to the skin
un´der-stand´ *vt.* comprehend, learn, be informed; mean without expressing, imply; *vi.* have the use of the intellectual faculties; know, be informed

un´der-stand´ing *n.* act of comprehending; faculty of the mind by which it understands; exact comprehension, agreement

un´der-stud´y *n.* actor who has studied the art of another in order to substitute when necessary

un´der-take´ *vi. & vt.* **(un´der-took´, un´der-tak´en)** take under one´s management; attempt, promise, contract

un´der-tak´er *n.* one who undertakes

un´der-tak´er *n.* one who manages funerals

un´der-tak´ing *n.* business or project engaged upon; management of funerals

un´der-tone´ *n.* low note or tone; meaning implied, but not expressed

un´der-tow´ *n.* undercurrent in the sea

un´der-val´ue *vt.* value at less than true worth, esteem lightly

un´der-wear´ *n.* undergarments, underclothes

un´der-write´ *vt.* insure, write insurance policies; subscribe one´s name to, becoming responsible for loss; *vi.* practice insuring; **un´der-writ´er** *n.* one who guarantees; insurance writer

un´de-signed´ *a.* unintentional, not premeditated

un´de-ter´mined *a.* not settled or determined

un-do´ *vt.* **(un-did´, un-done´)** reverse what has been done, bring to naught; loosen, open, unravel; impoverish, ruin; **un-do´ing** *n.* reversal of what has been done; ruin, loss, misfortune

un-dress´ *vi. & vt.* take off one´s clothes

un´dress´ *n.* loose dress; off-duty dress

un-due´ *a.* not due (as a note); improper, unlawful; inordinate, excessive

un´du-late´ *vi. & vt.* move like waves

un-du´ly *adv.* not according to duty; improperly

un-dy´ing *a.* immortal; unceasing

un-eas´y *a.* disturbed in mind or body; constrained, awkward; causing discomfort; **un-eas´i-ness** *n.*

un´en-cum´bered *a.* free from encumbrance or hindrance

un-e´qual *a.* not of the same dimensions, age, characteristics, station, strength, or talents; inferior; unjust, unfair, partial; irregular; **un-e´qualed, un-e´qualled** *a.* unmatched, without equal

un´e-quiv´o-cal *a.* unambiguous, not obscure or uncertain

un-err´ing *a.* certain, sure; infallible

un-e´ven *a.* not regular or even; odd, not divisible by two without a remainder; unsuitable, ill-matched

un-failing *a.* not capable of failing or being exhausted; sure,certain

un-fair´ *a.* dishonest; not impartial; not equitable or just

un-fal´ter-ing *a.* not hesitating or stumbling

un-fas´ten *vt.* loosen, untie, detach from, disconnect, unbutton, uncatch; *vi.* become unloosened or untied

un-fath´om-a-ble *a.* not to be investigated, known, or explained

un-feel´ing *a.* insensible, devoid of feeling or sensibility; hard-hearted, cruel; unsympathetic

un-feigned´ *a.* genuine

un-felt´ *a.* not felt or perceived, insensible

un-flag´ging *a.* maintaining strength

or spirit

un-flinch´ing *a.* not flinching or shrinking

un-fold´ *vt.* open the folds of, spread out; tell

un-for´tu-nate *a.* unlucky, not prosperous or fortunate, unsuccessful; *n.* one who is not fortunate

un-found´ed *a.* not established or built; without foundation, idle, vain

un-furl´ *vt.* unfold, spread out

un-gain´ly *a.* awkward; clumsy, uncouth

un-gov´ern-a-ble *a.* unbridled, uncontrollable

un-guard´ed *a.* not defended or watched; negligent, not cautious

un´guent *n.* ointment

un-guid´ed *a.* not led or guided; not governed or controlled, heedless

un-hand´ *vt.* take the hands off, let go

un-heard´ *a.* not perceived by the ear; not admitted to a hearing; not known to fame; **unheard of** *a.* unprecedented

u´ni-corn´ *n.* fabulous horselike animal with one horn

u´ni-form´ *a.* having the same form, manner, or character; agreeing with a group or set; *n.* dress or livery for persons who belong to the same group

u´ni-form´i-ty *n.* agreement with a pattern or rule; sameness, likeness between the parts of a whole; equality; regularity

u´ni-fy´ *vt.* make into one

u´ni-lat´er-al *a.* one-sided, pertaining to one side; performed by one side

un´im-peach´a-ble *a.* blameless

un´in-ten´tion-al *a.* not designed or premeditated; without intention

un´ion *n.* combination; anything united or made one; body formed by the combination of parts, league; concord, harmony

u-nique´ *a.* without like or equal

u´ni-sex´ *a.* not distinguising between sexes, especially a fashion or style

u´ni-son *n.* oneness, agreement

u´nit *n.* single thing or person; anything taken as one or as a standard of measure

U´ni-tar´i-an *n.* one who asserts the unity of the Godhead as opposed to the Trinity

u´nite´ *vt.* make into one, join; make to agree or adhere, harmonize; *vi.* become one; act together

u´ni-ty *n.* oneness; agreement, harmony

u´ni-ver´sal *a.* comprehending or affecting the whole; having no exception; **u´ni-ver-sal´i-ty** *n.* unlimited application

u´ni-verse´ *n.* all created things viewed as one whole; all creation

u´ni-ver´si-ty *n.* institution for teaching the higher branches of learning, usually including graduate studies, medicine, law, etc., and for research

un-just´ *a.* not just or fair

un-kempt´ *a.* uncombed, messy

un-kind´ *a.* not benevolent, affectionate, or kind; harsh, cruel

un-learn´ *vt.* forget; learn the opposite of that which has been learned; **un-learned´** *a.* ignorant, uneducated

un-leav´ened *a.* not leavened or raised by yeast

un-let´tered *a.* illiterate, uneducated, ignorant

un-like´ *a.* different, dissimilar; **un-like´ly** *a.* improbable, not promising

un-lim´it-ed *a.* boundless, without limitation; indefinite, undefined

un-man´ *vt.* deprive-of the powers of a man (such as courage); deprive of men

un-man´age-a-ble *a.* not easily controlled

un-mount´ed *a.* on foot, not mounted on horseback; without setting (as a diamond); not affixed to a mat or mount (as a photograph)

un-moved´ *a.* not moved or changed; unshaken, not effected or impressed

un-nerve´ *vt.* deprive of nerve, courage, or vigor; weaken

un-par´al-leled´ *a.* without parallel or equal

un-prec´e-dent´ed *a.* never before done or heard of

un´pre-pared´ *a.* not ready

un-prin´ci-pled *a.* without moral principles; wicked, unscrupulous

un-qual´i-fied´ *a.* not qualified; unfit; not limited, unconditional, absolute

un-rav´el *vi.* & *vt.* disentangle, explain

un´re-mit´ting *n.* persevering. incessant

un-rest´ *n.* want of rest; disquiet of mind or body

un-roll´ *vt.* open out; roll out; reveal

un-scathed´ *a.* not harmed, uninjured

un-seem´ly *a.* unbecoming

un-set´tle *vt.* displace, put in disorder or confusion, make uncertain

un-sheathe´ *vt.* draw out of the scabbard

un-sight´ly *a.* not pleasing to the eye; ugly

un´so-phis´ti-cat´ed *a.* natural, artless, genuine; not corrupted or perverted; lacking sophistication

un-speak´a-ble *a.* incapable of being properly described; unutterable, unmentionable

un-til´ *prep.* till, as far as; *conj.* till, up to the time that

un-tir´ing *a.* not tiring or becoming tired or weary

un-veil´ *vt.* disclose to view

un-wont´ed *a.* unaccustomed, unusual

up-braid´ *vt.* chide; rcproach

up-heav´al *n.* violent change or displacement (as of the earth, society, etc.)

up-hold´ *vt.* hold up, sustain; countenance, defend

up-hol´ster *vt.* furnish with hangings, coverings for chairs, etc.

up-lift´ *vt.* lift up, raise aloft

up´per-most´ *a.* highest in place, power, or authority

up´right´ *a.* in an erect position; adhering to rectitude, honest, just

up´ris´ing *n.* revolt, insurrection

up´roar´ *n.* noise, tumult, bustle; **up-roar´i-ous** *a.*

up-root´ *vt.* tear up by the roots

up-set´ *vt.* turn upside down, overthrow; disturb, bewilder, make sick

up´set´ *n.* overturn, overthrow; mild illness

up´shot´ *n.* final issue, end

up´stairs´ *a.* pertaining to an upper story or flat; *n.* upper story

up´start´ *n.* one who has suddenly risen to wealth, etc.

up´ward *a.* & *adv.* directed to a higher place

u-ra´ni-um *n.* radioactive metallic element - its isotope U-235 is used in the atomic bomb and as a source of atomic energy

U´ra-nus *n.* planet, discovered by Herschel, next beyond Saturn

ur´ban *a.* pertaining to a city
ur-bane´ *a.* civilized, courteous; **ur-ban´i-ty** *n.*
ur´chin *n.* hedgehog; child; sea urchin
urge *vi.* & *vt.* press, drive
ur´gent *a.* pressing, calling for immediate attention; **ur´gen-cy** *n.*
u´rine *n.* waste fluid produced by the kidneys; **u´ri-nate´** *vi.*
urn *n.* vase, vessel
us´a-ble *a.* capable of being used
us´age *n.* treatment, custom
use *vt.* put to some purpose; *vi.* be accustomed; *n.* application; service; practice; **use´ful** *a.* serviceable
u´su-al *a.* occurring regularly or in ordinary use; common
u-surp´ *vt.* take possession of by force or without right; **u´sur-pa´-tion** *n.*
u´su-ry *n.* act of charging more than legal interest on a loan
u-ten´sil *n.* instrument (esp. vessel used in the home)
u-til´i-ty *n.* usefulness; public service (such as water, electricity, etc.)
u´ti-lize´ *vt.* put to profitable use; **u´ti-li-za´tion** *n.*
ut´most´ *a.* furthest out, highest; *n.* extreme limit
U-to´pi-an *a.* ideal; fanciful
ut´ter *a.* extreme, total, absolute; *vt.* speak, give out
ut´ter-ance *n.* act of uttering; pronouncement; pronunciation
u´vu-la *n.* fleshy body suspended from the soft palate over the back-part of the tongue

V

vacant *a.* empty, not occupied; **va´-can-cy** *n.*
va´cate *vt.* leave empty, quit possession of; annul
va-ca´tion *n.* temporary freedom from duty or work
vac´ci-nate´ *vt.* inoculate with vaccine
vac´cine´ *n.* preparation of cowpox virus, weakened bacteria, etc., used to inoculate against a disease
vac´il-late´ *vi.* sway to and fro, waver
vac´u-um *n.* empty space devoid of air; **vacuum cleaner** *n.* machine that cleans by sucking in dirt; **vacuum tube** *n.* device used to vary electron flow
vag´a-bond´ *a.* wandering, having no settled home; *n.* tramp
va-gar´y *n.* eccentric action or thought; whim
va´grant *a.* wandering without any settled dwelling; erratic; *n.* vagabond, beggar
vague *a.* lacking precision, unsettled, indefinite
vain *a.* unsatisfying, fruitless; conceited; **vain´glo´ry** *n.* glory in one´s own performances
val´ance *n.* hanging drapery, esp. above a window
val´e-dic´tion *n.* farewell; **val´e-dic´to-ry** *a.* saying farewell; *n.* farewell address at commencement
val´en-tine´ *n.* affectionate greeting card sent to a sweetheart on St. Valentine´s day, Feb. 14; sweetheart to whom card is sent
val´et *n.* manservant
val´iant *a.* brave
val´id *a.* having force, true, sound; **va-lid´i-ty** *n.*
va-lise´ *n.* traveling bag
val´ley *n.* low land between hills or mountains
val´or *n.* fearlessness; **val´or-ous** *a.* courageous

val´u-a-ble *a.* having worth, costly; deserving esteem

val´ue *n.* usefulness, worth; market price; importance; *vt.* estimate the worth of

valve *n.* mechanism regulating the flow of a liquid or gas; **val´vu-lar** *a.*

vam´pire´ *n.* supernatural being said to suck the blood of sleeping victims; large blood-sucking bat

van *n.* front (as of an army); large covered wagon for carrying household goods; recreational vehicle

van´dal *n.* barbarian, one who ruthlessly destroys property; **van´dalism** *n.* act of destroying property or great art

vane *n.* weather cock; blade (as of a windmill, etc.)

van´guard´ *n.* part of an army preceding the others

va-nil´la *n.* aromatic pod of a tropical orchid used as flavoring

vanish *vi.* pass away, disappear

van´i-ty *n.* quality of being vain; empty pride, idle show, vain pursuit

van´quish *vt.* defeat

van´tage *n.* advantage

vap´id *a.* insipid, dull

va´por *n.* water or other substance diffused in the atmosphere; fume; *vt.* evaporate; boast, brag

va´por-ize´ *vt.* convert into vapor; *vi.* pass off in vapor

var´i-a-ble *a.* changeable, liable to change; **var´i-a-bil´i-ty** *n.*

var´i-ance *n.* difference, change of condition, discrepancy

va r´i-ant *a.* varying, differing

var´i-a´tion *n.* change, deviation; extent to which a thing varies; changes in the time, rhythm, key, etc., of a melody or composition

var´i-e-gate´ *vt.* vary, as by different colors; **var´i-e-ga´tion** *n.*

va-ri´e-ty *n.* quality of being various; varied collection; one of a number of things similar to one another

var´i-ous *a.* varied, different, several; changeable

var´nish *n.* sticky liquid which forms a hard, lustrous coating when dry; glossy appearance; *vt.* cover with varnish; gloss over

var´y *vi.* & *vt.* make or become different; deviate; disagree

vase *n.* hollow ornamental vessel

vas-ec´to-my *n.* surgery in men which stops sperm flow to cause sterility

vas´e-line´ *n. tr.* viscous substance obtained from petroleum, used as an unguent

vas´sal *n.* one who holds lands from and renders homage to a superior

vast *a.* of great extent

vat *n.* large vessel or tank

vault *n.* arched ceiling, chamber with an arched roof; bound of a horse, jump; *vt.* shape as a vault, roof with an arch

vaunt *vi.* & *vt.* boast, brag of; *n.* vain display

veal *n.* flesh of a calf

veep *n.* vice president

veer *vi.* & *vt.* change directions (as the wind); turn, swerve

veg´e-ta-ble *n.* plant; edible plant; *a.* belonging to, consisting of, or like plants

veg´e-tar´i-an *n.* person who believes that vegetables are the only proper food for humans

veg´e-tate´ *vi.* sprout, grow profusely; lead an idle, unthinking life; **veg´e-ta´tion** *n.* process of growing (as a plant); vegetable growth; plants

ve´he-ment *a.* passionate, furious; violent; **ve´he-mence** *n.*

ve´hi-cle *n.* any kind of carriage or conveyance

veil *n.* anything that hides an object, curtain; ornamental cloth worn by women to shade or hide the face; *vt.* cover with a veil; conceal

vein *n.* one of the vessels which convey the blood back to the heart; branching rib in a leaf or in an insect´s wing; seam of a different mineral through a rock

vel´lum *n.* fine parchment, esp. when made from the skin of young animals

ve-loc´i-pede´ *n.* child´s tricycle

ve-loc´i-ty *n.* speed, rate of speed

vel´vet *n.* type of silk cloth with a short, close pile

ve´nal *a.* mercenary; corrupt; **ve-nal´i-ty** *n.*

vend *vt.* sell; **vend´er, vend´or** *n.*; **vend´i-ble** *a.* salable, marketable

ve-neer´ *vt.* overlay with a thin layer of another wood; *n.* thin leaf of a valuable wood for overlaying an inferior

ven´er-ate´ vt, regard with respect and awe; **ven´er-a-ble** *a.* worthy of veneration; **ven´er-a´tion** *n.*

ve-ne´re-al dis-ease´, V.D. *n.* disease transmitted through the sex act

ve-ne´tian blind´ *n.* kind of window shade made with slats

ven´geance *n.* infliction of harm in return for an injury; **venge´ful** *a.* eager for revenge

ve´ni-al *a.* pardonable, excusable

ven´i-son *n.* flesh of the deer

ven´om *n.* poison secreted by certain animals; spite, malice

ve´nous *a.* pertaining to veins; pertaining to the blood in the veins

vent *n.* small opening to let air, etc., escape; escape, expression; *vt.* let out

ven´ti-late´ *vt.* open to the free passage of air; expose to examination and discussion; **ven´ti-la´tion, ven´ti-la´tor** *n.*

ven´tri-cle *n.* cavity within an organ (as in the heart)

ven-tril´o-quism *n.* art of speaking so that the voice seems to come from a distance; **ven-tril´o-quist** *n.*

ven´ture *n.* hazardous undertaking; *vt.* expose to hazard; risk, dare; **ven´tur-ous, ven´ture-some** *a.*

Ve´nus *n.* most brilliant planet, second from the sun, between Earth and Mercury; Roman goddess of love

ve-ra´cious *a.* truthful

ve-rac´i-ty *n.* truthfulness; truth

ve-ran´da, ve-ran´dah *n.* long, open porch or portico

verb *n.* part of speech (like *ride / rode / ridden / rides / riding*) said to show action or being

ver´bal *a.* relating to or consisting of words; spoken, oral

ver´bi-age *n.* wordiness

ver-bose´ *a.* wordy; **ver-bos´i-ty** *n.*

ver´dant *a.* green with grass or foliage; fresh

ver´dict *n.* finding of a jury; opinion pronounced

ver´di-gris´ *n.* green or blue coating on copper, brass, or bronze

ver´dure *n.* greenness, freshness of plants

verge *vi.* incline; border upon; *n.* edge

ver´i-fy´ *vt.* show to be true; authenticate; **ver´i-fi-ca´tion** *n.*

ver´i-si-mil´i-tude´ *n.* likelihood, state of being probable or true

ver´i-ta-ble *a.* real, genuine
ver´i-ty *n.* truth
ver´mi-cel´li *n.* very thin spaghetti
ver-mic´u-lar *a.* pertaining to or like a worm
ver´mi-fuge´ *n.* remedy that expels intestinal worms
ver-mil´ion *n.* bright red color or pigment
ver´min *n. sg. & pl.* all noxious animals or insect pests, esp. small insects
ver-nac´u-lar *a.* pertaining to one´s native land or tongue; *n.* mother tongue
ver´nal *a.* pertaining to spring
ver´sa-tile *a.* turning easily from one thing to another; **ver´sa-til´i-ty** *n.*
verse *n.* line of poetry; metrical language, poetry; short division, esp. of the chapters of the Bible
versed *a.* thoroughly acquainted, familiar, skilled
ver´si-fy´ *vi. & vt.* put into verses; write poetry; **ver´si-fi-ca´tion** *n.*
ver´sion *n.* translation, account, description
ver´te-bra *n.* one of the bones composing the spine
ver´te-brate *a.* having a backbone
ver´ti-cal *a.* perpendicular to the horizon; *n.* upright line
ver´ti-go´ *n.* sensation of giddiness, dizziness
ves´sel *n.* utensil for holding something; ship; tube containing a fluid (as blood)
ves´ti-bule´ *n.* hall, anteroom, passage
ves´tige *n.* trace
vest´ment *n.* garment
vet´er-an a, experienced; *n.* one long exercised in service; former member of U.S. military
vet´er-i-nar´i-an *n.* person trained in the treatment of domestic animals and their diseases; **vet´er-i-nar´y** *a.*
ve´to´ *n.* authoritative prohibition; executive power to reject a law proposed by the legislative branch; *vt.* reject by a veto, withbold assent to
vex *vt.* irritate, harass
vi´a *prep.* by way of
vi´a-duct´ *n.* kind of bridge over a valley, etc.
vi´al *n.* small bottle
vi´ands *n. pl.* food
vi´brate´ *vi. & vt.* move to and fro rapidly, oscillate; swing; **vi-bra´-tion** *n.* oscillation; **vi´bra-to´ry** *a.*
vi-car´i-ous *a.* filling the place of another; performed in place of another; experiencing the emotions of another
vice *n.* blemish; immoral conduct, depravity
vice´ge-rent *a.* acting in place of another; *n.* one acting in place of a superior
vice´roy´ *n.* one representing royal authority in a dependency or province
vi´ce ver´sa *a.* in reversed order
vi cin´i-ty *n.* neighborhood
vi´cious *a.* full of vice, depraved, bad
vi-cis´si-tude´ *n.* change, esp. an irregular change
vic´tim *n.* living being offered as a sacrifice; person suffering injury; dupe; **vic´tim-ize´** *vt.* make a victim of, cheat
vic´tor *n.* one who conquers or wins
vic´to-ry *n.* overcoming of an antagonist; **vic-to´ri-ous** *a.*
vict´ual *vt.* supply with provisions; **vict´uals** *n. pl.* food

vid´e-o *n.* television; *a.* pertaining to the picture image in TV

vie *vi.* strive for superiority

view *n.* that which is seen; picture, scene; mode of looking at anything; intention; *vt.* see, look at attentively; **view finder** *n.* camera device enabling photographer to see how much of a scene will be photographed

vig´il *n.* watching; keeping awake for religious exercise

vig´i-lance *n.* watchfulness; **vig´i-lant** *a.* on the lookout for danger, alert

vi-gnette´ *n.* small ornamental engraving not inclosed by a definite border; any small illustration or sketch, including one in words

vig´or *n.* active strength

vile *a.* mean, low, wicked

vil´i-fy *vt.* slander, defame; **vil´i-fi-ca´tion** *n.*

vil´la *n.* country residence

vil´lage *n.* very small town

vil´lain *n.* deliberate scoundrel

vim *n.* strength, energy

vin´di-cate´ *vt.* defend, justify; **vin´-di-ca´tion** *n.*; **vin´di-ca´tor** *n.*

vin-dic´tive *a.* revengeful, implacable

vine *n.* any climbing or trailing plant

vin´e-gar *n.* acid seasoning obtained by fermenting cider, etc.

vi´nous *a.* like or relating to wine

vin´tage *n.* yearly produce of grapes or wine; time of grape-gathering

vinyl *a.* pertaining to a group of plastic resins

vi´o-late´ *vt.* injure, abuse; profane; break, do violence to; **vi´o-la´tion** *n.*

vi´o-lent *a.* acting with physical force or strength; moved by strong feeling; produced by force; **vi´o-lence** *n.*

vi´o-let *n.* any of numerous plants with flowers of purplish blue; color of the violet

vi´o-lin´ *n.* treble-range musical instrument of four strings played with a bow

vi´o-lon-cel´lo *n.* large, bass-range musical instrument with four strings bowed by a seated player

VIP *n.* very important person

vi-ra´go *n.* noisy, wrangling woman

vir´gin *n.* chaste maiden; *a.* maidenly, pure; fresh; new; first

vir´ile *a.* masculine, manly, forceful; **vi-ril´i-ty** *n.*

vi-rol´o-gy *n.* study of viruses and diseases they cause

vir´tu-al *a.* being in effect, though not in fact

vir´tue *n.* moral excellence; excellence; force, power; chastity; **vir´-tu-ous** *a.*

vir´u-lent *a.* full of potion, malignant

vi´rus *n.* any of a large group of sub-microscopic agents that cause many infectious diseases

vi´sa *n.* endorsement on a passport indicating that the proper authorities have examined and approved it

vis´age *n.* face, aspect

vis´cer-a *n. pl.* inner parts of the animal body

vis´count´ *n.* title of nobility next below an earl

vis´cous *a.* sticky, viscid; **vis-cos´i-ty** *n.*

vise, vice *n.* device for holding anything tightly while being worked on

vis´i-ble *a.* apparent, obvious; **vis´i-bil´i-ty** *n.*

vi´sion *n.*act or sense of seeing; anything seen; phantom, creation

of the imagination
vis´it *vt.* go or come to see; inspect, attend; *n.* act of going to see; **vis´-it-a´tion** *n.*; **vis´i-tor** *n.*
vi´sor, vi´zor *n.* movable front part of a helmet; part of a cap projecting over the eyes
vis´ta *n.* prospect or view (as between the trees along an avenue)
vis´u-al *a.* pertaining to sight, used in seeing; **visual tape** *n.* magnetic tape which records images as well as sound
vi´tal *a.* pertaining to or necessary to life; important, as life; essential; **vi-tal´i-ty** *n.* quality of being vital; vital force
vi´ta-min *n.* any of various substances found in foods which are necessary for health and growth
vi´ti-ate´ *vt.* render faulty or less pure
vit´re-ous *a.* glassy; pertaining to or obtained from glass; **vit´ri-fy´** *vi.* & *vt.*
vi-tu´per-ate´ *vi.* & *vt.* censure, scold; **vi-tu´per-a´tion** *n.*
vi-va´cious *a.* lively
viv´id *a.* lifelike, animated
viv´i-sec´tion *n.* operation performed on a living animal for scientific purposes
vix´en *n.* she-fox; ill tempered woman
viz. *adv.* namely, that is
vo-cab´u-lar´y *n.* list of words explained in alphabetical order; lexicon, dictionary; stock of words
vo´cal *a.* pertaining to the voice; uttered by the voice
vo-ca´tion *n.* calling, occupation, trade, profession
vo-cif´er-ous *a.* loud, noisy
vogue *n.* temporary fashion, prevalent way or mode
voice *n.* sound produced by vibration of the vocal cords; language, expression; *vt.* utter
void *a.* unoccupied, empty; having no binding force; *n.* empty space; *vt.* make vacant; send out, discharge; render of no effect
vol´a-tile *a.* apt to evaporate; flighty, apt to change; **vol´a-til´i-ty** *n.*
vol-ca´no *n.* mountain emitting smoke, fire, lava, etc.; **vol-can´ic** *a.*
vo-li´tion *n.* will; exercise of the will, free choice
vol´ley *n.* discharge of many rifles, cannons, etc., at same time; *vt.* discharge in a volley
volt *n.* unit of electromotive force
vol´u-ble *a.* fluent in speech; **vol´u-bil´i-ty** *n.*; **vol´u-bly** *adv.*
vol´ume *n.* book; space occupied; loudness of voice; **vo-lu´mi-nous** *a.* full, complete
vol´un-tar´y *a.* willing, acting by free choice
vol´un-teer´ *n.* one who enters a service of his own free choice; *vi.* & *vt.* offer, do, or go voluntarily
vo-lup´tu-ous *a.* full of pleasure; given to excess of pleasure, sensuous; **vo-lup´tu-ar´y** *n.* sensualist
vom´it *vi.* & *vt.* throw up the contents of the stomach
vo-ra´cious *a.* greedy, very hungry; **vo-rac´i-ty** *n.*
vor´tex´ *n.* whirlpool, eddy
vo´ta-ry *n.* one devoted (as by a vow) to some service or manner of life
vote *n.* formal expression of a wish or opinion; decision of a majority; *vi.* & *vt.* express a choice by vote
vouch *vt.* warrant; *vi.* bear witness; **vouch´er** *n.* one who vouches; pa-

per which confirms the truth of anything, as accounts; **vouch´safe´** *vi. & vt.* condescend, condescend to grant

vow *n.* solemn promise to God; formal promise

vow´el *n.* sound produced by vibration of the vocal cords and modified chiefly by height of tongue; one of the etters a, e, i, o, u, sometimes w, and y

voy´age *n.* passage by water, journey; *vi.* journey by water

vo-yeur´ *n.* peeping Tom, one who delights in watching private or indecent acts

vul´can-ize´ *vt.* improve raw rubber by treating with sulfur and heat; **vul´can-i-za´tion** *n.*

vul´gar *a.* offensive to good taste; pertaining to or used by the common people; **vul-gar´i ty** *n.*

vul´ner-a-ble *a.* liable to injury

vul´ture *n.* large, rapacious bird which lives on the flesh of dead animals

W

wad´dle *vi.* take short, awkward steps

wade *vi. & vt.* walk through water, snow, etc.

wa´fer *n.* thin cake; consecrated bread used in the Eucharist

waf´fle *n.* batter cake baked between two iron plates

waft *vi. & vt.* move or float through a fluid (as air or water)

wag *vi. & vt.* shake to and fro; *n.* droll person, wit

wage *vt.* engage in, carry on; *n.* pay for which one works; **wag´es** *n. pl.*

wag´er *n.* bet; *vi. & vt.*

wag´on *n.* four-wheeled, animal-drawn vehicle for carrying heavy goods

waif *n.* anything found astray or without an owner, as a stray child

wail *vi. & vt.* lament aloud; *n.* cry of woe; shrill moan of grief or of the wind

wain´scot´ *n.* paneled boards on walls; *vt.* line with panels

waist *n.* smallest part of the human trunk between ribs and hips

wait *vi.* postpone action, stay in expectation, remain; *vt.* stay for, await; serve at table; **wait on** *vt.* attend, follow; wait for; *n.* waiting, stop, delay

waive *vt.* relinquish a right or claim to; **waiv´er** *n.* act of waiving or relinquishing

wake *vi.* be awake; leave off sleeping; be roused up; *vt.* rouse from sleep; revive; put in action, excite; *n.* streak of smooth water left in the track of a ship; any similar track; vigil kept by a corpse; **wake´ful** *a.*; **wak´en** *vi. & vt.* wake, awake

walk *vi.* move along on foot, pace; *vt.* pass through or upon; cause to walk; *n.* act or manner of walking; distance walked over; place for walking; **walking papers** *n. pl.* dismissal

walk´ie-talk´ie *n.* portable radio for sending and receiving

wall *n.* structure of brick, stone, etc., for a fence or security; side of a building; *vt.* enclose with a wall

wal´let *n.* pocketbook for money, etc.

wal´lop *vt.* flog , beat

wal´low *vi.* roll about, as in mire

wal´nut´ *n.* shady tree valuable for its wood and its nut

wal´rus *n.* large, marine mammal

with long tusks found in the Arctic Ocean

waltz *n.* dance performed to music in triple time by couples; *vi.* dance a waltz

wan *a.* wanting color, pale; sickly; languid; dim

wand *n.* slender rod

wan´der *vi.* ramble, go astray; be delirious

wane *vi.* decrease, decline, fail; *n.* decline, decrease

want *n.* state of lack, deficiency; *vi.* & *vt.* feel or be in need of; fall short of; wish for, require

wan´ton *a.* reckless; licentious; *n.* lewd person; *vi.* ramble without restraint; be lascivious

war *n.* struggle between nations carried on by force of arms; *vi.* make war, contend

war´ble *vi.* & *vt.* sing, as with a trill; *n.* vibrating modulation of the voice

ward *vt.* guard, take care of; fend off; *vi.* act on the defensive; keep guard; *n.* act of warding; one who is under the care of a guardian; division of a city, hospital, etc.; **ward´en** *n.* keeper, esp. a public officer in penal institutions; **ward´robe´** *n.* room or portable closet for clothes; wearing apparel

war´head´ *n.* explosive package carried by rocket or missile

ware´house´ *n.* storehouse

wares *n. pl.* merchandise, commodities, goods

war´i-ness *n.* cautiousness

warm *a.* moderately hot; ardent; *vi.* &. *vt.* make or become warm

warn *vt.* make aware, give notice of danger, caution

warp *vi.* & *vt.* twist out of shape, pervert; *n.* warped condition; threads stretched out lengthwise in a loom to be crossed by the woof

war´rant *vt.* guarantee, make secure; justify, authorize; *n.* writ for arresting a person; security; **war´rant-y** *n.* deed of security

war´ren *n.* ground for breeding animals, esp. rabbits

war´ri-or *n.* soldier

wart *n.* small, hard growth on the skin

war´y *a.* cautious; **war´i-ly** *adv.*

wash *vt.* cleanse with water; overflow; cover with a thin coat (as of metal or paint); *vi.* endure washing without being injured; *n.* washing, clothes to be washed; lotion; thin coating of paint, metal, etc.; **wash´er** *n.* person or machine that washes; flat ring of iron or leather under the head of a screw, etc.; **wash´out´** *n.* washing away of a roadbed by rain; *sl.* failure

wasp *n.* stinging insect allied to the hornet; **wasp´ish** *a.* irascible, easily angered

waste *a.* desolate, stripped; lying unused, unproductive; *vt.* lay waste, make desolate; wear out gradually; squander; *vi.* dwindle, be consumed; *n.* useless expenditure or destruction; refuse

watch *n.* act of looking out;close observation, guard; one who watches, sentry; time of watching, esp. in a ship; small timepiece; *vi.* keep awake; look with attention; *vt.* keep in view; guard; **watch´ful** *a.*; **watch´word´** *n.* password; rallying cry

wa´ter *n.* fluid compound of hydrogen and oxygen which forms the oceans, lakes, and rivers; any collection of it, as a lake; any fluid resembling water; luster of a diamond; *vt.* wet, overflow, supply, or dilute with water; wet and press so as to give a wavy appearance to

wa´ter col´or *n.* pigment diluted with water and gum, instead of oil

wa´ter-fall´ *n.* perpendicular descent of a body of water, cataract, cascade

wa´ter-line´ *n.* line on a ship to which the water rises

wa´ter-logged´ *a.* rendered unmanageable from being filled or soaked with water

wa´ter-mark´ *n.* mark showing the height to which water has risen; mark wrought into paper in manufacturing it

wa´ter-proof´ *a.* impervious to water; *n.* garment made of waterproof cloth

wa´ter-shed´ *n.* ridge which separates two river basins

wa´ter skis *n.* long, slender runners attached to the feet, on which a person can ride on water when pulled by a boat

wa´ter-tight´ *a.* tight enough to hold water or prevent leakage

watt *n.* unit of electrical power

wave *n.* ridge rising on the surface of water; vibration, undulation; *vt.* move like a wave, undulate; *vt.* move backwards or forwards, brandish

wa´ver *vi.* move to and fro, be unsteady or undetermined

wax *n.* yellow, fatty substance produced by bees; any similar substance; *vi.* increase in size (as the moon); become, grow; *vt.* smear or rub with wax

way *n.* road; distance; passage, journey; direction; manner; **way´-far´er** *n.* traveler; **way´ward** *a.* willful, disobedient

way´lay´ *vt.* lie in wait for, ambush

way´side´ *n.* edge of the road or highway

weak *a.* lacking strength or health, easily overcome; **weak´en** *vi.* & *vt.* make or grow weaker

wealth *n.* riches, abundance

wean *vt.* accustom to do without the mother´s milk; accustom to the lack of anything

weap´on *n.* any instrument of offense or defense

wear *vt.* **(wore, worn)** carry on the body, as clothes; consume by use, time, or exposure; *vi.* be wasted or spent; last under use; *n.* act of wearing; lessening or injury from use, friction, etc.

wea´ry *a.* tired; *vi.* & *vt.* wear out or become weary; **wea´ri-ness** *n.*; **wea´ri-some** *a.*

wea´sel *n.* small, carnivorous animal living on birds, rats, mice, etc.; cargo and personnel carrier designed for use by the armed forces in muddy, swampy areas

weath´er *n.* state of the air as to heat, cold, dryness, etc.; *vt.* affect by exposing to the air; hold out stoutly against

weave *vt.* **(weav´ing, wove. wov´en)** unite, as threads in a loom, to form cloth; *n.* particular style of weaving

web *n.* texture, thing woven; net spun by a spider, snare; skin between the toes of waterfowl; **webbed** *a.* having the toes united by a web; **web´—foot´ed, web´—toed´** *a.* having the toes more or less completely connected by membrane

wed *vi.* & *vt.* marry, join in marriage; unite closely; **wed´ding** *n.* marriage, mar-riage ceremony; **wed´lock´** *n.* matrimony

wedge *n.* piece of wood or metal,

thick at one end and sloping to a thin edge at the other, used in splitting, etc.; anything similar in shape; *vt.* cleave with a wedge; force or fasten with a wedge; press closely

Wednes´day *n.* fourth day of the week

weed *n.* useless plant; *vt.* free from weeds

week *n.* space of seven days

week´ly *a.* coming or happening once a week; *adv.*; *n.* publication appearing once a week

weep *vi.* **(wept)** shed tears, lament; *vt.* shed, lament

wee´vil *n.* small beetle, destructive to grain and fruit

weigh *vt.* ascertain the heaviness of; compare, examine; depress, load; *vi.* have weight; be considered of importance, press heavily

weight *n.* heaviness; heavy thing; system of units for determining the heaviness of bodies; burden, pressure; importance, power

weight´less-ness *n.* absence of weight, as in the case of an orbiting satellite or freely falling object

weird *a.* unearthly, uncanny

wel´come *a.* received with gladness; causing gladness; free to enjoy; *n.* kindly reception; *vt.* receive with kindness; entertain hospitably

weld *vt.* unite (as two pieces of metal) by heating and hammering, etc.; *vi.* be capable of being welded; *n.* welded joint

wel´fare´ *n.* state of faring or being well, prosperity

well *n.* spring; pit or drilled hole in the earth from which water, etc., is obtained; *vi.* issue forth from the earth

well *a.* in good condition, proper, fortunate, in health; *adv.* in a proper manner, rightly; considerably; **well´—bred´** *a.* of good descent; well brought up, gentlemanly, polite; **well´—fa´vored** *a.* good-looking; **well´—nigh´** *a.* almost; **well´—off´, well´—to—do´** *a.* easy in circumstances, rich; **well´wish´-er** *n.* one who favors a person or a cause

Welsh *a.* pertaining to Wales or its inhabitants; *n. pl.* inhabitants of Wales; *n.* their language

welt *n.*swollen stripe made by a lash

welt´er *vi.* wallow

wend *vi.* & *vt.* go, travel

west *n.* direction where the sun sets; *a.* situated toward the west

wet *a.* containing moisture, damp; rainy; *n.* water, moisture; *vt.* make wet

wet´back´ *n.* Mexican who comes to the U. S. illegally

whale *n.* largest of sea mammals; **whale´bone´** *n.* elastic substance from the upper jaw of the whale; **whal´er** *n.* ship or person employed in catching whales; **whal´-ing** *n.* business of catching whales

wharf *n.* structure for loading and unloading vessels

what´not´ *n.* piece of furniture with shelves for bric-a-brac

wheal *n.* discolored ridge on the skin, as one caused by the stroke of a whip

wheat *n.* grassy plant or its seed which furnishes flour for bread

whee´dle *vi.* & *vt.* entice; obtain by flattery

wheel *n.* circular frame turning on an axle; *vt.* cause to whirl; convey on wheels; *vi.* roll forward smoothly

wheeze *vi.* breathe with a hissing sound

whelp *n.* young of the dog, wolf, lion, etc.; cub

whence *adv.* from what place or cause

where´a-bouts´ *n.* place in or near which a person or thing may be found; **where-as´** *conj.* since; **where´fore´** *conj.* for which or what reason, why; **wher-ev´er** *adv.* at whatever place; **where´with-al´** *adv.* with which or what; **where´-with-al´** *n.*

whet *vt.* sharpen by rubbing, make keen; excite; **whet´stone´** *n.* any hard, fine-grained stone used for sharpening the edge of cutting instruments

wheth´er *conj.* in the event that

whey *n.* watery part of milk after separation from the curd

which *pron.* who, what, what one; **which-ev´er** *pron.* every one which; one or the other

whiff *n.* sudden puff of air, etc.; sniff of a gas or scent

while *n.* space of time; *conj.* as long as; *vt.* cause to pass, consume

whim *n.* caprice, fancy

whim´per *vi.* cry with a whining voice

whim´sy, whim´sey *n.* whim; **whim´si-cal** *a.* full of whims; odd

whine *vi.* utter a plaintive cry; complain in an unmanly way

whin´ny *vi.* neigh low and gently, as a horse

whip *vi.* & *vt.* move with a quick motion; strike, lash; beat into a froth; *n.* instrument for driving horses, etc.; **whip´hand´** *n.* hand holding the whip; advantage

whip´cord *n.* hempen cord, hard twisted or braided; catgut; cloth with a small twill

whip´poor-will´ *n.* American bird named for its remarkable cry

whir *n.* sound of rapid whirling; *vi.* whirl round with a noise, hum, buzz

whirl *n.* rapid spin; anything that turns rapidly; *vi.* revolve rapidly; **whirl´i-gig´** *n.* child´s toy spun round rapidly; merry-go-round; **whirl´pool´** *n.* eddy with a cavity in the center; **whirl´wind´** *n.* cyclonic wind

whisk *vi.* & *vt.* move with a quick motion; *n.* rapid sweeping motion; small brush

whisk´ers *n. pl.* hair on a man´s cheek and chin

whis´ky, whis´key *n.* strong distilled spirits; **whiskey sour** *n.* mixed drink made with whiskey

whis´per *vi.* & *vt.* speak or utter with a low sound; *n.* low voice or sound; cautious speaking

whis´tle *vi.* & *vt.* make a shrill sound by forcing the breath through the contracted lips; *n.* sound made in whistling; small wind instrument for making such a sound

whit *n.* small particle

white *a.* reflecting sunlight in its natural state; showing no color or tint; pale; pure; *n.* color of snow; anything white, as the white part of an egg, etc.; **white´fish´** *n.* general name for various kinds of fish; **whit´en** *vi.* & *vt.* make or become white, bleach

white´wash´ *n.* mixture used to whiten ceilings, etc.; *vt.* cover with whitewash; give a fair appearance to

whith´er *adv.* to what place

whit´tle *vt.* cut with a knife

whiz *vi.* make a hissing sound; move with a hissing sound (as an

arrow); *n.*hissing sound
whole *a.* sound, hale; containing the total amount, number, etc.; complete; *n.* entire thing; system; combination; **whol´ly** *adv.*
whole´sale´ *n.* sale of goods in bulk or large quantity
whole´some *a.* healthy, sound
whoop *n.* loud, eager cry; *vi.* give a clear, sharp cry; shout; **whoop´ing cough** *n.* contagious children´s disease named for its violent fits of coughing
whop´per *n.* big thing; monstrous lie
whorl *n.* any whirl or circular pattern (as of leaves around a stem)
wick *n.* threads of cotton which burn in a candle or lamp
wick´ed *a.* evil, sinful
wick´er *n.* small, pliant twig; *a.* made of or covered with twigs
wick´et *n.* small gate or window
wide *a.* broad; **wide-angle lens** *n.* camera lens for taking wide pictures; **wid´en** *vi.* & *vt.* make or grow wide or wider
wid´ow *n.* woman bereft of her husband by death; *vt.* bereave of a husband; **wid´ow-er** *n.* man whose wife is dead
width *n.* wideness, breadth
wield *vt.* use or handle with full command
wife *n.* married woman
wig *n.* artificial covering of hair for the head
wig´gle *vi.* wriggle, squirm
wig´wag´ *vi.* & *vt.* move quickly to and fro; send a message by waving flags, etc.
wig´wam´ *n.* Indian tent, tepee
wild *a.* being in a natural state; not tamed or cultivated, uncivilized. violent; wayward; *n.* wilderness
wil´der-ness *n.* uncultivated, uninhabited region
wile *n.* sly trick or stratagem
will *n.* power of choosing; choice made, decision, purpose; disposition of one´s effects at death; *vi.* & *vt.* wish; determine or be determined or ready; bequeath by testament; **will´ful, wil´ful** *a.* governed only by one´s will; done or suffered by design; **will´ful-ness** *n.*
wil´low *n.* tree of several species with slender, pliant branches
wilt *vi.* droop, fade; cause to languish or droop
wily *a.* full of tricks; sly; **wil´i-ness** *n.*
win *vt.* **(won)** get by labor, gain in contest; gain one´s kindness or consent by alluring; *vi.* gain the victory
wince *vi.* shrink, flinch
winch *n.* crank; windlass
wind *n.* air in motion; breath; *vt.* expose to the wind; drive hard so as to put out of breath; **wind´fall´** *n.* unexpected advantage; **wind´pipe´** *n.* passage for the breath to and from the lungs; **wind´row´** *n.* long ridge or pile, as of hay or leaves; **wind´shield´** *n.* front window of an automobile; **windshield wiper** *n.* moving blade for clearing wind shield; **wind´ward** *n.* point from which the wind blows; **wind´y** *a.* consisting of wind, resembling the wind; full of wind, tempestuous; exposed to wind; garrulous, unsubstantial, empty
wind *vi.* & *vt.* **(wound)** turn, twist, coil; blow (as a horn)
wind´lass *n.* machine for raising weights
win´dow *n.* opening in the wall of a building for air and light; frame in the opening

wing *n.* organ of a bird. insect. etc., by which it flies; flight; any side part (as an addition to a building); *vt.* furnish or transport with wings; wound slightly
wink *vi.* & *vt.* move the eyelids quickly; give a hint by winking; connive at; *n.* act of winking, moment; hint given by winking
win´ning *a.* attractive; **win´nings** *n. pl.* money or prizes gained in a contest, etc.
win´now *vi.* & *vt.* separate chaff from the grain by wind; separate bad from good; select
win´some *a.* gay; pleasing
win´ter *n.* cold season of the year; *vi.* pass the winter; **win´ter-y, win´try** *a.*; **win´ter-green´** *n.* aromatic creeping evergreen
win´ter-ize *vt.* to protect a vehicle, or equipment, against winter weather and low temperatures
wipe *vt.* clean or dry with something soft
wire *n.* thread of metal; *vt.* apply wire to; install a wire or wires; send or notify by telegraph; **wire-less telegraphy** *n.* system of sending messages through the air without the aid of a wire; **wire tapping** *n.* secret monitoring of telephone conversation; **wir´y** *a.* made of or like wire; flexible and strong
wire´pho´to *n.* means of converting photographs into electric impulses to send them over the telephone and telegraph wires
wis´dom *n.* knowledge, discretion, judgment; **wis´dom tooth** *n.* backmost tooth on each side of upper and lower jaw
wise *a.* knowing and sagacious
wish *vi.* & *vt.* desire, long for; *n.* longing, desire; thing desired
wisp *n.* small bundle of straw or hay; small bit of anything
wis-te´ri-a *n.* climbing plant with fragrant purplish flowers
wist´ful *a.* thoughtfully sad
wit *n.* mental agility, cleverness; sprightly humor; person noted for his clever remarks
witch *n.* sorceress; ugly, malignant woman; **witch´craft´, witch´er-y** *n.* sorcery
with-draw´ *vi.* & *vt.* draw back, recall, go back, leave
with´er *vi.* & *vt.* fade, dry, shrivel up
with-hold´ *vt.* hold back
with-stand´ *vt.* **(with-stood´)** resist, oppose successfully
wit´ness *n.* testimony, evidence; person who gives evidence; *vi.* & *vt.* see, give testimony
wit´ti-cism *n.* witty remark
wit´ty *a.* quick at repartee; droll
wiz´ard *n.* magician
wiz´ened *a.* shriveled, shrunken and withered
woe, wo *n.* grief, calamity; **woe´be-gone´** *a.* beset with woe; **woe´ful** *a.* sorrowful, wretched, calamitous
wolf *n.* **(wolves)** wild, rapacious animal of the dog kind
wom´an *n.* **(wom´en)** female human being; female attendant; **wom´an-hood´** *n.*; **wom´an-ish** *a.* feminine
wom´an-pow´er *n.* power provided by the work of women
wom´en´s lib-er-a´tion *n.* movement concerned with gaining equality for women
won´der *n.* surprise; strange thing, miracle; *vi.* feel wonder, be amazed; doubt, question; **won´der-ful** *a.*; **won´drous** *a.*
wont *a.* accustomed; *n.* habit; *vi.* & *vt.* make or be accustomed; **wont´-**

ed *a.* commonly used or done; accustomed

won't *vi.* contraction for *will not*

woo *vi. & vt.* court, try to win the affections of; seek earnestly

wood *n.* solid part of trees; trees cut or sawed; forest; **wood´cut´** *n.* engraving on wood; impression from it; **wood´ed** *a.* supplied or covered with wood; **wood´en** *a.* made of wood; clumsy, stupid; **wood´peck´er** *n.* bird that hunts insects by pecking holes in the wood or bark of trees; **wood´y** *a.* abounding with wood

woof *n.* threads of a woven fabric, those carried to and fro by the shuttle; filling; weft; texture of a fabric

woof´er *n.* loudspeaker for reproducing low frequencies

wool *n.* soft, curly hair of sheep, etc.; **wool´en** *a.* made of wool; **wool gath´er-ing** *n.* idle reverie

word *n.* spoken or written signal said to convey an idea; message; command, signal; promise, declaration; *vt.* express in words; **word´ing** *n.* act or style of expressing in words; **word´y** *a.* full of words, verbose

work *n.* effort directed to an end, toil; result of efforts, product, composition, etc.; anything on which one works; trade; *vi.* make efforts, labor, toil; be occupied; produce effects; *vt.* make by labor; bring into any state by action; give labor to; manage, solve; operate (as a machine); **work´er** *n.* one who works; sexless ant or bee

world *n.* universe, creation; the earth and its inhabitants; one´s range of interests, views, etc.; secular affairs of life; human race; great deal; **world´ly** *a.* pertaining to the world, secular; devoted to enjoyment

worm *n.* small creeping animal with vey short legs or with none; abased being; thread of a screw; *vi.* work slowly or secretly *vt.* effect by slow an secret means; extract; wind spirally; **worm´wood´** *n.* plant having a bitter taste; that which embitters

wor´ry *vt.* harass, vex; *vi.*be unduly anxious; *n.* vexation, anxiety

worse *a. & adv.* bad or evil in a greater degree; more sick

wor´ship *n.* religious service, honor paid to God; *vi. & vt.* pray; idolize; perform religious service

worst *a. & adv.* bad in the greatest degree; *n.* most evil state or degree; **at the worst** in the most unfortunate case; **get the worst of** be defeated (as in a fight)

wor´sted *n.* very strong, twisted yarn, spun of long, combed wool; cloth made from it

worth *n.* value; *a.* equal in value to; deserving of; rich to the amount of

wor´thy *a.* valuable; deserving; *n.* person of eminent worth; **wor´thiness** *n.*

wound *n.* cut, bruise, hurt, injury; *vt.* inflict a wound upon, injure

wran´gle *vi.* dispute noisily, squabble, altercate, quarrel; *n.* noisy dispute

wrap *vt.* roll or fold together; envelop; *n.* wrapper, shawl, any covering

wrap´per *n.* cover; loose outer garment worn by a woman

wrath *n.* fierce anger, indignation

wreak *vt.* inflict

wreath *n.* twisted, circular form, esp. of flowers; garland

wreathe *vi. & vt.* twine, encircle

wreck *n.* destruction; anything remaining after destruction; ruined vessel; *vt.* destroy, shipwreck, ruin
wreck´age *n.* remains of a ship or cargo that has been wrecked
wren *n.* small, insect-eating songbird, easily tamed
wrench *vt.* pull with a twist; force; sprain; *n.* violent twist; sprain; instrument for turning bolts, etc.
wrest *vt.* twist or get by force; twist from the truth; *n.* violent twisting, distortion
wres´tle *vi.* & *vt.* contend by grappling and trying to throw the other down; struggle; **wrest´ler** *n.*
wretch *n.* miserable or despicable person; **wretch´ed** *a.* very miserable; worthless
wrig´gle *vi.* & *vt.* twist to and fro, squirm
wring *vt.* **(wrung)** twist, as by the hands; strain, break, or force out, as by twisting
wrin´kle *n.* small ridge, furrow, or crease; notion, small change or improvement; *vi.* & *vt.* contract into wrinkles or furrows; roughen
wrist *n.* joint between the hand and arm
writ *n.* written document by which one is summoned or required to do something; **Holy Writ** *n.* the Bible
write *vi.* & *vt.* put words on paper by means of a system of representation; form letters, etc. with a pen or pencil; do writing as a clerk, author, correspondent, etc.; compose, tell, record; **writ´ing** *n.*
writhe *vi.* & *vt.* twist violently
wrong *a.* & *adv.* not right or according to rule; not according to fact, desire, or purpose; in error; *n.* wrongfulness, error; violation of duty or propriety; injury; *vi.* injure, treat unjustly; **wrong´ful** *a.* wrong, unjust
wry *vi.* & *vt.* twist out of shape; *a.* twisted, contorted; dryly humorous

X

X´mas *n.* Christmas
X´ray *n.* roentgen ray, a very short type of radiation used for medical and scientific purposes
xy-log´ra-phy *n.* art of engraving in wood
xy´lo-phone´ *n.* musical instrument, consisting of a graduated series of wooden bars and sounded by means of small wooden hammers

Y

yacht *n.* light, swift-sailing vessel
yam *n.* tropical edible plant with a large root like the potato; sweet potato
Yan´kee *n.* New Englander; native of northern U.S.; American
yard *n.* measure of 3 feet; enclosed place, esp. near a house or building; **yard´stick´** *n.* measuring stick, 3 feet long
yarn *n.* spun thread; story, tall tale
yawn *vi.* gape; *n.* act of opening of the mouth as from drowsiness
yea *n.* affirmative vote
year *n.* time during which the earth makes one revolution around the sun; time of revolution of any planet; **year´ling** *n.* animal a year old
year´ly *a.* happening every year; lasting a year; *adv.* once a year, annually
yearn *vi.* feel a desire for, long for; **yearn´ing** *n.* earnest desire; tenderness or pity; strong feeling; *a.*

longing

yeast *n.* fungus preparation which raises dough or causes fermentation

yell *vi.* cry out with a sharp noise; scream from pain or terror

yel´low *a.* of a color like that of gold, butter, etc.; *col.* cowardly; *n.* bright color like that of butter; yolk of an egg

yelp *vi.* utter a sharp bark

yen *n.* Japanese monetary unit; longing, craving

yeo´man *n.* freeman, man of common rank; farmer or man of small landed estate; petty officer in the U.S. Navy

yes´ter-day *n.* the day before this; *adv.* on the day preceding this

yew *n.* long-lived evergreen tree, allied to the pine

yield *vt.* give in return (as for labor performed or capital invested); produce, emit, give, surrender; *vi.* submit, give way, assert; *n.* act of yielding; that which is yielded, product

yo´del *vi.* & *vt.* sing with frequent changes from the ordinary voice to falsetto

yoke *n.* frame of wood joining oxen for drawing; pair, couple; *vt.* put a yoke on; join together; confine

yolk *n.* yellow part of an egg

yon, yon´der *a.* & *adv.* at a distance or being at a distance within view

yore *n.* time long past

young *a.* not long born, in early life, in the first part of growth; inexperienced, green; *n.* offspring;

youth *n.* state of being young; early life; young person, esp. a young man; young persons taken together

yule *n.* Christmas; **yule log** *n.* large log burned in the fireplace at Christmas eve

Z

za´ny *n.* clown, buffoon

zeal *n.* passionate ardor, intense interest, eager striving; **zeal´ot** *n.* one carried to excess by his zeal, fanatic; **zeal´ous** *a.* full of zeal, ardent

ze´bra *n.* wild animal of the horse kind with black and white stripes

ze´nith *n.* point of the heavens directly overhead; greatest height, as of one´s success

zeph´yr *n.* west wind; soft, gentle breeze

ze´ro *n.* cipher, nothing; point from which a thermometer is graduated; lowest point

zest *n.* relish, piquancy; keen enjoyment

zig´zag´ *a.* having short, sharp turns; *vi.* & *vt.* form or move with sharp turns

zinc *n.* bluish-white metallic element

zip´ code´ *n.* nine-digit number which designates a mail delivery zone

zith´er *a.* box-shaped musical instrument with numerous strings

zo´di-ac´ *n.* imaginary belt in the heavens containing the twelve constellations called signs of the zodiac

zone *n.* one of the five great belts into which the earth´s surface is divided; any arbitrary section or division (as of a city)

zoo *n.* place for keeping wild animals on exhibition

zo-ol´o-gy *n.* that part of natural history which treats of animals; **zo´o-log´i-cal** *a.*; **zo-ol´o-gist** *n.*

zoom *n.* act of turning an airplane suddenly upward

zuc-chi´ni *n.* a green, cucumber-shaped squash

zy-mol´o-gy *n.* science of fermentation

zy-mot´ic *a.* denoting all contagious disease; pertaining to fermentation

Metrics Glossary

Ampere A unit for measuring the flow of electricity. Symbol: amp.
Area Amount of surface, measured in square units.
Are A metric surface measure, equal to 100 m^2. Symbol: a.
Atto- A prefix indicating one quintillionth of a given unit.

Barrel The amount contained in a barrel; especially the amount (as 31 gallons of fermented beverage or 42 gallons of petroleum) fixed for a certain commodity and used as a unit of measure for that particular commodity. Symbol: bbl.
Boardfoot A unit of quantity for lumber equal to the volume of a board 12 × 12 × 1 inches. Symbol: fbm.
Bushel A unit of dry capacity equal to 4 pecks (2150.42 in^3) or 35.238 liters

Candela A unit for measuring the luminous intensity (amount) of a light produced by a light source.
Capacity See Volume.
Celsius The name of the scale for temperature commonly used in conjunction with the metric system. Also known as the Centigrade scale. In the Celsius scale, water boils at 100° C and freezes at 0° C, as opposed to 212° F and 32° F, respectively, in the Fahrenheit scale. Symbol: ° C.
Centare A metric surface measure equal to 1 m^2. Symbol: ca.
Centi- A prefix indicating one hundredth of a given unit.
Centigram One hundredth of a gram. Symbol: cg.
Centiliter One hundredth of a liter. Symbol: cl.
Centimeter One hundredth of a meter. One centimeter equals .3937 inch. Symbol: cm.
Chain A unit of measure equal to 66 feet (20.1168 meters). Symbol: ch.
Cubic unit symbols Examples: mm^3, cm^3, m^3, etc., used to denote volume.
Customary unit Units of weights and measures currently in use in the United States, known also as English units. These include: inches, feet, yards, and miles for length; ounces, pounds, and tons for weight; pints, quarts, and gallons.

Deci- A prefix indicating one tenth of a given unit.
Decigram One tenth of a gram. Symbol: dg.
Deciliter One tenth of a liter. Roughly equal to .21 pint. Symbol: dl.
Decimeter Ten centimeters or one tenth of a meter. Symbol: dm.
Deka- A prefix indicating ten times a given unit.
Dekagram Ten grams. Symbol: dag.

Metrics Glossary

Dekaliter Ten liters, roughly equivalent to 2.64 gallons. Symbol: dal.

Dekameter Ten meters. One dekameter roughly equals 10.91 yards. Symbol: dam.

Density The weight of any sample of a substance divided by the volume measure of that sample.

Dram A unit of avoirdupois weight equal to 27.343 grains or .0625 ounce (1.771 grams). Symbol: dr.

Fathom A unit of length equal to 6 feet (1.8288 meters) used for measuring the depth of water. Symbol: fath.

Femto- A prefix indicating one quadrillionth of a given unit.

Furlong A unit of distance equal to 220 yards (201.168 meters). No symbol.

Giga- A prefix indicating a billion times a given unit.

Gill A unit of liquid measure equal to .25 pint or 118.291 milliliters.

Grain A unit of weight equal to .002083 ounce (.0648 gram), originally based on the weight of a grain of wheat. Symbol: gr.

Gram A common metric unit of weight equal to one thousandth of a kilogram. Symbol: g.

Hectare The common unit of land measure in the metric system, equal to 100 acres or 10,000 square meters and equivalent to 2.471 acres. Symbol: ha.

Hecto- A prefix indicating one hundred times a given unit.

Hectogram One hundred grams. Symbol: hg.

Hectoliter One hundred liters. Symbol: hl.

Hectometer One hundred meters. Symbol: hm.

Hogshead A U.S. unit of capacity equal to 63 gallons (238.4809 liters). Symbol: hka.

Hundredweight A unit of weight (avoirdupois) commonly equivalent to 100 lbs. (45.359 kilograms) in the United States and 112 lbs (50.803 kilograms) in England. The former is known as the short hundredweight and the latter as the long hundredweight. Symbol: cwt.

Kelvin scale A temperature scale often used with the metric system and developed by the British physicist Lord Kelvin. The starting or zero point on the Kelvin scale is absolute zero (—273.15° C, —459.67° F)—the lowest theoretical temperature that a gas can reach. On this scale, water freezes at 273.15° K and boils at 373.15° K.

Kilo- A prefix indicating one thousand times a given unit.

Kilogram The standard unit of mass in the metric system.

Metrics Glossary

The kilogram is a cylinder of platinum-iridium alloy kept by the International Bureau of Weights and Measures near Paris. A duplicate kilogram is kept by the National Bureau of Standards in Washington and serves as the mass standard for the United States. One kilogram is approximately equal to 2.2 pounds. Symbol: kg.

Kiloliter One thousand liters. Symbol: kl.

Kilometer One thousand meters, equivalent to 3,280.8 feet or .621 mile. Symbol: km.

Link One of the standardized divisions of a surveyor's chain that is 7.92 inches (201.168 millimeters) long and serves as a measure of length. No symbol.

Liter The basic metric unit of liquid measure, equal to the volume of one kilogram of water at 4° C or one cubic decimeter. A liter is equivalent to 1.057 quarts. Symbol: l.

Lumen A unit for measuring the brightness of light when it reaches the surface of an object.

Mass The amount of material in an object, measured in kilograms (q.v.).

Mega- A prefix indicating one million times a given unit.

Meter The basic unit of length in the metric system. It is defined in terms of the wavelength of orange-red light emitted by a krypton-86 atom (1,650,763.73 such wavelengths to the meter). One meter equals 39.37 inches. Symbol: m.

Metric system A decimal system of weights and measures, adopted first in France and now in common use worldwide.

Metric ton One thousand kilograms, roughly equivalent to 2,200 pounds. Symbol: t.

Micron The millionth part of a meter. Symbol: μ.

Mile, International Nautical A unit of distance in sea and air navigation equal to 1.852 kilometers or 6,076.1033 feet.

Mill A unit of money (but not an actual coin) used primarily in accounting.

Milli- A prefix indicating one thousandth of a given unit.

Milligram One thousandth of a gram. Symbol: mg.

Milliliter One thousandth of a liter. Symbol: ml.

Millimeter One tenth of a centimeter or one thousandth of a meter. Symbol: mm.

Minim The smallest unit of liquid measure, the sixtieth part of a fluid dram, roughly equivalent to one drop.

Nano- A prefix indicating one billionth of a given unit.

Ounce, avoirdupois A unit of weight equal to 437.5 grains or .625 pound avoirdupois (28.349 grams). Symbol: oz. avdp.

Ounce, troy A unit of weight equal to 480 grains or .833 pound troy (31.103 grams). Symbol: oz. tr.

Peck A dry measure of 8 quarts or the fourth part of a bushel (8.89 liters).

Perimeter The measure of the distance around a figure.

Pico- A prefix indicating one trillionth of a given unit.

Pound, avoirdupois A unit of weight and mass equal to 7,000 grains (.453 kilogram) divided into 16 ounces, used for ordinary commercial purposes. Symbol: lb. avdp.

Pound, troy A unit of weight equal to 5,760 grains (.373 kilogram) divided into 12 ounces troy, used for gold, silver, and other precious metals. Symbol: lb. tr.

Radian An arc of a circle equal in length to the radius of that circle. An angle emanating from the center of a circle that subtends (cuts off) such an arc is said to measure one radian. Measuring angles in radians is preferred with the metric system.

Rod A unit of linear, 5.5 yards or 16.5 feet (5.0292 meters). A unit of surface measure 30.25 yd^2 (25.2901 m^2). No symbol.

Second The sixtieth part of a minute of a degree, often represented by the sign ″ as in 13 15′ 45″, read as 13 degrees, 15 minutes, 45 seconds.

Specific gravity The ratio of the density of a substance to the density of water at 4° C.

Square unit symbol Example: mm^2, cm^2, m^2, etc.

Stere A cubic measure equivalent to 35.315 cubic feet or 1.3080 cubic yards (1.001 m^3). Used to measure cordwood. No symbol.

Tera- A prefix indicating a trillion times a given unit.

Ton, metric See Metric ton.

Volume The measure in cubic units of the amount of space inside any given container; also the measure of the amount such a container will hold. The latter is known as the *capacity* of the container and can be given in either units of liquid measure (see Liter, also Milliliter) or in cubic units.

Weight The force of the earth's pull on an object. Weight, in the Metric system, is commonly measured in grams.

WEBSTER'S Handbook for Secretaries

WEBSTER'S HANDBOOK FOR SECRETARIES

Betty W. Brinkerhoff

PMC Publishing Company, Inc.

PMC Publishing Company, Inc.
118 East 28 Street
New York, New York 10016

Manufactured in the United States of America.

ISBN: 1-881275-13-2

CONTENTS

CHAPTER I

THE SECRETARY

To be a valued and sought-after secretary requires much more than graduation from a recognized secretarial school. The secretary needs certain innate qualities that can be enhanced by effort and application but cannot be developed if they are not part of the personality to begin with.

Let it be said at the start that the superlative secretary can be either a woman or a man. Many of the most successful secretaries in the business world are men. Nevertheless, the vast majority of practitioners in the field are women, so this manual uses the feminine gender throughout.

Secretarial positions vary widely with the business firm and the secretary's immediate superior. Some executives expect merely a person to handle mail, telephones, and visitors and to take and transcribe dictation efficiently. Others expect a secretary to be close to an assistant, anticipating needs, making suggestions, and otherwise furthering the work of the office.

Nevertheless, all successful secretaries possess certain personal attributes and professional skills.

Personal Traits

First and foremost, perhaps, is personal integrity. A strong code of ethics is a must. The employer is entitled to unswerving loyalty. The good secretary never talks about business matters outside the office or about her superior's affairs to anyone inside or outside the office. The ability to keep secrets is a valuable asset in any sense of humor are valuable traits. Getting along with one's associates cannot help but grease the wheels of progress, and the ability to laugh at the ridiculous—even if it is oneself at times—can disarm most critics.

One's attitude and outlook on life shape all other aspects of personality. A general air of optimism makes all things seem possible and tends to transmit itself to others. Thus is generated an aura of helpfulness and cooperation. Conversely, a pessimistic viewpoint makes the task at hand seem less likely of accomplishment and more likely to infect one's coworkers with a sense of "Why try?"

The successful secretary works consciously to improve her effect on her fellows. A particularly important attribute is her voice and manner of speaking. To some extent the tone of voice is inborn; but it can be improved with attention and practice. An unattractive local or regional accent can be overcome. A harsh or nasal quality of the voice can be minimized by listening to mellifluous speakers on radio or television and emulating their diction.

Poise is another essential attribute. The good secretary needs to be "unflappable" in the face of awkward situations or difficult people. "A soft answer turneth away wrath," *Proverbs* tells us, and that is surely true in the modern world of business. Courtesy, tact, and discretion are indispensable qualities in the secretary.

Attention to matters of health and appearance is a high priority. One cannot look really well without feeling well. Health does bring a glow to the cheeks and a spring to the step. Cleanliness, of course, is preeminent. Shining hair and a faultless manicure improve anyone's appearance. Regular habits-early to bed, early to rise-help to avoid fatigue, which is a drain on good looks.

Style of dress varies with the type of establishment. Some offices stress the tailored look; others allow more latitude. Some even go so far as to permit slacks and sweaters. Nevertheless, in a working situation conservative dress will stand the secretary in good stead. Jingling bracelets and dangling earrings have no place behind an office desk.

Good work habits are essential to any field of endeavor and are not specific to the position. It should go without saying that the secretary should be punctual, accurate in her work, and intent upon the business at hand. Except in emergency, personal telephone calls should be reserved for her own time. She makes a point of remembering names-if necessary inventing mnemonic tricks to attach names to persons.

An excellent command of spoken and written English is indispensable to the successful secretary. The high school or business school graduate should have this proficiency. If you do not feel fully confident in this area, however, it would be to your advantage in moving ahead in your career to improve your skills. Adult courses and community college courses are widely available at nominal cost. Even failing that, however, much can be accomplished by wide reading-with a good dictionary nearby to check on meanings and pronunciations. Spend a little time becoming familiar with the phonetic symbols in the dictionary that enable you to pronounce the most unfamiliar word correctly.

Stenography and typing are, of course, the basic tools of the trade. Dictation at 120 words per minute is adequate for most situations. In this age of the electric typewriter and word processor, there seems almost no limit to the speed of typing that can be achieved by the determined practitioner.

Other basic tasks include processing of incoming

and outgoing mail, filing, and record-keeping. Knowledge of business arithmetic and simple bookkeeping can be helpful in carrying out these duties.

Competence may be required in placing telephone calls, including conference calls; screening callers and visitors according to the executive's wishes; arranging appointments; keeping and filing expense accounts; ordering supplies; arranging meetings; making travel reservations; writing original letters; operating office machines; doing research, and running the office in the absence of the employer. Not all of these duties may be in a particular job description, but they may well be expected of "the complete secretary."

Planning is an integral part of the secretary's day. She organizes her work, anticipates problems, and paces herself to get all accomplished with minimum wear and tear on herself and her disposition.

The modern office has many devices to facilitate the secretary's work. The electric typewriter and word processor have been mentioned. The photocopier has become a machine of many capabilities beyond merely making file copies of correspondence. It can enlarge or reduce in size; copy on both sides of the page; sort and collate; and even bind pages into pamphlets.

Some color copiers can produce reports fit for the chairman of the board or the annual meeting.

Another piece of office equipment that has become almost indispensable in a very brief span of time is the fax-or, more formally, facsimile machine. The fax sends information virtually instantaneously by telephone wire to a similar machine in another location nearby, in a distant city, or halfway around the world. It can transmit printed, typed, handwritten, or drawn material. Some units can operate with standard bond or xerographic paper. Some can be used to tape and replay spoken messages. Some can even double as copiers for internal office use.

The fax can operate manually or automatically. In manual use the operator dials the telephone number of the party wanted and asks to have the start button pressed. She then starts her machine and hangs up the telephone. In automatic operation, a preprogrammed number is pressed, and the equipment does all the rest.

So ubiquitous has the fax become that it has moved into the home even faster than has the personal computer. Faxes are now in use to place orders to mail-order merchants, to communicate with friends, and even to order pizzas at the neighborhood fast-food emporium.

CHAPTER II

THE SECRETARY'S DUTIES

Office Etiquette

In many offices the secretary is the first person a visitor encounters. The impression made at that first meeting can color an entire business relationship. The secretary's own appearance has been touched upon. Equally important is the appearance of her surroundings. It is unlikely that she will be expected to keep her office clean, but it is certainly her responsibility to keep it tidy and functional: Her desk should be shipshape at all times-no used coffee cups or cluttered ashtrays. If she herself has not overcome a smoking habit, she can do her life a favor by undertaking one of the numerous cessation programs.

Courtesy, patience, and tact are the hallmarks of the successful secretary. These attributes are exhibited in her dealings with everyone with whom she comes in contact-coworkers as well as visitors. She carries out all commitments punctually and fully.

Internal office etiquette must be learned by observation. Some offices operate with considerable informality; others maintain strict decorum. Many adopt a first-name basis between executives and employees. Better, however, to err on the side of formality. Calling a vice president "Joe" without specific invitation could lead to an early perusal of the want ads.

Gossip is to be avoided at all costs. The secretary is often privy to information about office matters-hirings, promotions, firings. Such information should remain private with-her until it has become a matter of open knowledge.

The secretary's relationship with the executive for whom she works is central to her success. She must gauge carefully what is expected of her and adhere carefully to those expectations. Some employers consider a secretary an assistant and are open to comments and suggestions. Others are offended at such a thought and want no more than prompt acquiescence to orders. In either situation, however, the employer's decisions are not open to argument.

Increasingly in today's business world the executive is a woman. The secretary should put aside any notions about its being hard to work for a woman boss. Male or female, the executive has achieved that standing by business acumen and hard work, which should be accorded the respect and deference they deserve. Forget the pejorative terms you have heard applied to women bosses: petty, catty, impossible to get along with. All of them are equally applicable to the male of the species.

A situation frequently encountered in large offices

is the necessity of working for two or more persons. It may be difficult to avoid any show of favoritism, but it is nevertheless essential. One boss may be congenial and the other hard to please, but their work should receive equal treatment from the secretary. In most cases a difference of rank will exist between the several executives, and the secretary may take her cue from that. However, the nature of a given assignment-its immediacy or lack thereof-can also be a guide as to the time preference it receives.

Use of the Telephone

The telephone is so much a part of our daily lives that it may seem gratuitous to discuss its use in the office. Handled properly, however, it can be an instrument for creating goodwill and improved business. On the other hand, poor telephone manners can lose friends and alienate people.

We have discussed the value of a pleasant speaking voice. On the phone, that voice is the whole you. The caller judges you (and sometimes your employer) by what you say, but almost as much by the way you say it. Courtesy is essential-even if you know that the caller is going to represent a major nuisance. The call may be interrupting your other work, but the telephone is a vital communication link in business and must be respected as such.

The telephone should be answered promptly. Many companies have established specific telephone greetings, which should, of course, be followed. Absent such, however, an appropriate formula is, "Mr. Doe's office." If desired, you may add, "Miss Roe speaking."

Some executives prefer to answer their own telephone. If not, most have distinct preferences as to how they are notified of calls.

It may be your duty to screen calls to avoid interrupting the executive for matters that could or should be handled by others. If so, considerable exercise of judgment is required. A caller of whom you have never heard may turn out to be an important source of information or new business for your employer or your company.

If it is necessary to transfer a call to another person, be sure not to leave the caller hanging on an unanswered line. If the person to whom you wish to transfer the call is not available, do the caller the courtesy of taking a message to that person-and delivering it!

Protocol for placing calls for the employer varies. Some executives expect the person called to be on the line before they pick up the telephone. Others consider it a matter of courtesy to be on the line first when they have initiated the call. In some situations relative rank is the determinant: The person of lower rank is on the line before the person of higher rank picks up.

Some offices maintain telephone logs of all incoming and outgoing calls. In fact, in some offices the practice is mandatory. Such information can be useful in case of billing problems. It can also be valuable in reconstructing a sequence of events at a later date. Such logs may be retained for several years.

Types of Telephone Service

Beyond the area of local calls is the vast array of telephone services available. They include station-to station and person-to-person calls, international direct dialing, and conference calls.

When making long-distance calls, you have two options. If you are fairly sure that the person wanted will be available at the time of your call, you can place the call station to station. In that case your call will be charged by the telephone company if anyone answers at the called number. This is the most economical long-distance call.

If you wish to speak only to a specific person, you can make a station-to-station call by dialing **O** before the area code. This will alert an operator, who will come on the line and take the name of the person being called. You will not be connected to the number unless that person is available to take the call. The rate for person-to-person calls is somewhat higher than for station-to-station, but money is obviously saved if your call cannot be completed.

Your telephone directory is usually a source of considerable helpful information, such as area codes for major United States cities and a map showing time zones across the country.

More than one hundred countries around the world, from Algeria to Yugoslavia, can now be called by direct dialing. Of course, these calls are the equivalent of station-to-station calls in the United States: You are charged for the call if anyone answers the telephone.

To place an international call, dial 011, followed by the country and city prefixes (which are like our area codes), then the telephone number of the person or firm wanted. A list of these codes and the time difference relative to Eastern Standard Time is given on pages 204-213.

In these days of cost-consciousness in business, the conference call has assumed ever greater importance as companies seek to reduce travel expenses. A conference call can involve as many persons and locations as desired. To place such a call, dial the operator and ask for the conference operator. Give that operator the time at which you want the call placed and the names and telephone numbers of those who are to participate. At the appointed time the operator will get all parties on the line at once. Conference calls are charged as a person-to-person call to each number involved.

Visitors to the Office

Receiving visitors is an important aspect of the secretary's duties. Visitors must be greeted pleasantly and made to feel welcome, whether or not they are expected.

If you know that your employer has an appointment (and you certainly should know), and the person appears at the expected time, you can say, "Good afternoon, Mr. Roe. Mr. Doe is expecting you." People always like being addressed by name. If you are not aware that your employer has an appointment, you may ask politely, "May I ask who is calling?"

Absent an appointment, the secretary must try to ascertain the reason for the visit. She may say, "Mr. Doe is busy at the moment; could I be of help?" If that does not elicit the desired information, it may be necessary to say that you are not permitted to make appointments without knowing the subject matter.

On the other hand, you may know the visitor and therefore be obliged to decide whether your employer will want to see him if time permits. It may be a personal friend or a very important person. In such case you can either use the intercom to inform your employer or take the caller's card into the office to let him decide on his course of action.

Such an unexpected visitor may have to wait a few minutes. Either take his coat or show him where to put it. Seat him comfortably with access to reading matter, and return to your work.

If you are quite sure that the caller is someone your employer will not want to see, it is up to you to do the unpleasant chore of getting rid of him-tactfully, if possible. You can say that the executive will be busy for quite a while and suggest that the visitor write him a letter stating his business and asking for an appointment.

Announcing Visitors

If the visitor has an appointment, merely buzz your employer on the intercom, say, "Mr. Doe, Mr. Roe is here," and ask Mr. Roe to go right in.

Absent an appointment, if you are fairly sure that your employer will see the visitor, go into the office and inform him who is outside. That gives him the option of saying he is too busy, coming out and speaking to the visitor briefly to save time, or telling you to show the visitor in.

Large offices often have a central reception room staffed by a receptionist to notify individual executives that they have visitors. In such a case, if the visitor is to be escorted to the executive's office, the secretary should identify herself to the visitor: "Good afternoon, Mr. Jones, I am Miss Roe, Mr. Doe's secretary. Will you come this way?"

Desk Calendars

Most executives keep an appointment calendar on their desk. This may take one of several forms: a day at a glance, a week, or a month. When outdated, these calendars are often filed for several years as reference.

The secretary should also keep a desk calendar and keep it up-to-date with her employer's engagements as well as reminders to herself of other time commitments.

Incoming Mail

The method of handling mail depends on the size of the office. In a small office the secretary may sort and distribute the mail. A large firm usually has a central mail facility, and a given secretary is responsible only for the correspondence addressed to her immediate superior.

In the latter case, the secretary opens and sorts the mail. Whether she opens envelopes marked *Personal* or *Confidential* depends on her employer's instructions.

Envelopes should be opened carefully with a letter opener to avoid damaging enclosures. Care should be taken to remove all the contents of each. In many offices the date is stamped on each item.

The mail is sorted by type: letters and memos, bills, orders, advertisements, and publications. They are placed in that order on the executive's desk, with publications to one side.

If a letter refers to or answers a previous letter, some employers like to have such material pulled from the files and attached to the new correspondence.

Outgoing Mail

The handling of outgoing mail also depends on whether or not your company has a mail room. If mail is centrally processed, the secretary's responsibility is limited to being sure that addresses are correct and complete, that letters are properly signed and contain pertinent enclosures, and that instructions such as class of mail or special services are attached.

If the secretary stamps and mails correspondence herself, she must check the weight of each item to determine the amount of postage required and affix it carefully. If special services are called for, such as Registered Mail or Certified Mail, it is her responsibility to go to the post office and procure the necessary documentation and postage.

In today's business even many small offices invest in a postage meter. The postage meter seals envelopes and imprints them with the correct amount of postage and a dated postmark. Formerly it was necessary to take the machine to the post office periodically to have the postage replenished. Currently this can actually be done by telephone. According to postal authorities, these machines improve accuracy and save postage.

No matter who has the final responsibility for outgoing mail, the secretary should check every item before sealing the envelope. Make sure the letter is signed. If you signed it in your employer's absence, be sure to place your initials under his name. Be sure that all enclosures are in the envelope. The Postal Service discourages the use of paper clips because of the widespread use of machines in mail handling-including the postage meter. Enclosures may be stapled, if small. Otherwise fold them with or to the same size as the letter they accompany. Very small enclosures, such as business cards or coins, may be taped to the letter, or to a card or separate sheet of paper, using the type of transparent tape that lifts off with relative ease.

Like everything else done in the office, the appearance of outgoing letters is important. A badly folded letter speaks to the carelessness or indifference of the sender. Most business mail is 8 1/2 x 11 inches in size and takes a No. 10 envelope. Such letters are correctly folded in thirds. The bottom of the sheet is folded upward slightly less than one third. The top of the page is then folded down to within an eighth or a quarter of the original fold. The folded letter is then inserted in the envelope with that small margin at the bottom. In that way the letter will be right side up when removed from the envelope.

Dictation

The practice of dictation has undergone significant changes in recent years as the age of technology has progressed. Dictating machines of various types have increasingly displaced the stenographer's pad and pencil. The machines have decided advantages for both the executive and the secretary. They enable the executive to dictate at any time and place. They free the secretary to do other tasks, thus cutting in half the time involved in the dictation process.

The competent secretary is equally comfortable with either process. In the vast majority of small to mid-sized offices, however, the pad and pencil still reign supreme.

The secretary should always be prepared to report to the call of, "Take a letter." Her shorthand pad should be ready, with a rubber band holding together the filled pages, and a supply of sharpened pencils or a ball-point pen at the ready. Date each dictation session at the beginning. If you work for more than one person, put his or her initials at the end.

Be particularly careful about numbers, dates, and names in taking dictation. It is best to spell out names in longhand and to question them if there is any possibility of error.

The secretary is entitled to ask the dictator to speak more slowly. After all, accuracy is of the essence. Also, the flow of thoughts and speech when a person is intent on the subject at hand may easily outpace even the fastest stenographer.

Some secretaries like to use only the left column of the ruled page, leaving the right column blank for any changes the dictator may make or for clarification that she herself may enter when rereading the shorthand notes before transcribing them.

Your shorthand system will have its own symbols for punctuation, but you might well decide how to indicate words to be capitalized or underscored: perhaps three lines under the word for all capitals and a single line for underscoring.

Take advantage of pauses in the dictation to clarify any doubtful characters that you have written and to make mental notes of questions you might want to ask the dictator when the letter or memorandum is finished.

Transcription

It is wise, when possible, to transcribe shorthand notes immediately. Even the best notes tend to go stale if left too long.

Go over your notes before you begin to type. Be sure to verify the spelling of names and the correctness of addresses and dates. The secretary should ascertain early on how her employer feels about contributions from her to his language. Some executives welcome corrections in grammar; others have considerable pride of authorship and consider that she has overstepped herself. Be sure you know how far you may go in editing and polishing his work. Ask about anything that seems questionable.

Reading your notes before transcribing them will also enable you to estimate the length of a letter in order to position it correctly on the letterhead.

When you have finished transcribing an item, draw a vertical line through the shorthand notes.

If your employer uses mechanical dictation, you will of course familiarize yourself with operation of the machine. In other respects, however, the process is similar. Listen to a section of the material to be transcribed and decide on any grammatical corrections or editorial changes that may be indicated. Ask any questions of fact or style that may occur to you.

Many dictation machines have devices that indicate the number of words in a dictated section. This can assist you in judging placement of the material on the page.

Reminder Systems

The basic reminder system for both executive and secretary, as mentioned earlier, are their coordinated desk calendars. The secretary's calendar, however, should record more than the day's appointments and meetings.

Secretaries often start a new year by entering such other particulars of the employer's business as birthdays and anniversaries, payment dates, renewal dates, and tax dates. An even better idea is to add such reminders on a page a few days before the actual date.

Tickler files are another helpful reminder system. Tickler files take several forms. However, the file folder system is probably the most useful, since it is self-contained.

You might set up a folder for each month of the year. Then behind the folder for the current month set up a folder for each day of the month. When a matter needs follow-up, merely drop copies of the pertinent correspondence or other material into the proper folder.

Each day check the appropriate folder and deal with whatever it contains. The empty folder is then moved ahead to its position in the next month.

Filing

Despite the advance of computerization, filing of original correspondence and copies of replies is a basic part of the secretary's routine. It is imperative for her to be able to produce requested material promptly.

The principal filing systems are alphabetical, by subject, numerical, geographic, and decimal. Of these, the alphabetical system is by far the most widely used in the average office. Material is organized by name and filed alphabetically. Even when other systems are used, material within the various categories may still be alphabetized.

A subject file may be used when names are less important than the subject; for example, Insurance or Taxes.

A geographical file might be useful, for instance, to a sales organization with farflung representatives. The file might be organized by state, county, or city.

Numerical and decimal systems are highly specialized and are not likely to concern the secretary in normal business usage.

Alphabetizing

Alphabetizing can be done in one of two modes: the letter-by-letter mode or the word-by-word mode.

Letter-by-letter alphabetizing is carried throughout the entire entry, ignoring all spaces and punctuation.

Word-by-word alphabetization differs in that the principle stops with the first word. Subsequent words are considered only when two or more entries begin with the same word.

Compare the following lists:

Letter-by-Letter	**Word-by-Word**
Newark	New Bedford
New Bedford	New Canaan
Newbridge	New England
New Canaan	New Mexico
New England	New York
Newfoundland	New Zealand
Newmarket	Newark
New Mexico	Newbridge
New York	Newfoundland
New Zealand	Newmarket

Most style authorities insist on the letter-by-letter system. Be warned, however: Some widely used references use the word-by-word system, notably the telephone directory.

Names of people are typed on file folder labels by

surname, first name, and middle name or initial:

Doe, John J.

Companies named for persons are similarly indexed:

Doe, John J. & Co.

Otherwise firm names are alphabetized by the first word in the name:

Bayside Medical Center

Items are alphabetized by the first word, then the second word, and so on. Articles such as *The* are placed at the end, except in foreign words:

House of Arden, The

Le Maison Arden

Several successive letters are treated as single words, as are abbreviations or acronyms:

XYZ Company

ASCAP

UNICEF

The abbreviation *St.* is alphabetized as if spelled out:

Saint Paul's Cathedral, not

St. Paul's Cathedral

In names, prefixes are considered part of the name:

De la Mare

MacGregor

Numbers are alphabetized as if spelled out:

Eighth Street

Titles follow names in parentheses:

Doe, John J. (Dr.)

The following list illustrates most of the foregoing rules:

Andersen, Arthur A.
Andorra, Bank of
Delaware Bay Company
DeWine, Carl
Jones Haberdashery
Jones, John G.
Jones, John Gunderson
JTC Printing
Livingston, Paul (Dr.)
St. John the Divine Cathedral
Sindbad's Restaurant
27 Wall Street

Cross-References

Some material could logically be filed under more than one name or subject. In such cases a cross-reference sheet may be placed in the file under the alternate name. This sheet should contain the name or subject, what it concerns, the date of the material, and the location of the main entry. The label might read:

Smith & Jones, Inc.
see
Barrington Builders

Bank Accounts

Secretaries are sometimes expected to supervise checking accounts maintained by the employer. In a small business, more than one account may be maintained, one for major expenditures such as rent, and perhaps a smaller one for supplies, petty cash, and other miscellany.

The secretary is also likely to be responsible for making deposits to the account at the bank and reconciling the bank statement each month.

When writing checks for your employer's signature, it is important to enter enough information on each check stub so that a bookkeeper or accountant can identify the payment and record it correctly for tax purposes.

When you have entered the information on the stub, do the necessary arithmetic immediately, so that the balance in the account can always be seen at a glance. It is a good idea to use a calculator for checkbook addition and subtraction. It saves problems with errors when reconciling the monthly statement.

Checks must be completely legible; it is good practice to make them out on the typewriter. Be sure that the date on the check agrees with that on the stub.

Use the full name of the payee, but not titles such as Mr., Mrs., or Dr.

The amount of the check is entered twice. First it is given in numerals in the blank to the right of the payee's name; for example, *$100.00*. It is then spelled out on the next line: *One hundred and no/100*.

Start both amounts as close to the left margin as possible. This makes it impossible for anyone to alter the check to increase the amount for which it was drawn; for instance, to change *$100* to *$2100*, or *One hundred* to *Two thousand one hundred*.

If you should make an error in writing a check, destroy it immediately and write *Void* across the stub. Then carry forward the former balance to the next check stub. If it becomes necessary to stop payment on a check that has already been issued, telephone the bank. Provide the name of the payee and the amount, as well as the title and number of the account and the number of the check. This must be followed by written notification to the bank.

Deposit slips also should be filled out clearly and accurately. Most offices have a rubber stamp for endorsement of checks to be deposited. Checks are endorsed on the back across the left end.

Endorsements may be of three kinds: restrictive, blank, or specific.

A *restrictive* endorsement names the bank in which the check is to be deposited.

A *blank* endorsement is merely the owner's signature. It has elements of risk, because anyone else can appropriate the check by signing his name under the first endorsement and then cashing it. The risk is minimized, however, by writing *For deposit only* before the endorsement.

A *specific* endorsement intentionally turns the check over to someone else: *Pay to the order of John Doe*. Your signature below that relinquishes your right to the check.

Each month the bank sends the depositor a statement of account, giving the opening and closing balances, a list of checks that have cleared the bank, and the checks themselves.

Usually the reverse side of the statement contains a printed form for your use in reconciling the bank's record with that of the checkbook.

Put the canceled checks in order of date and compare them with the checkbook stubs. Put a mark beside each stub entry for which you have the original check. If any check written is not included with the statement, circle the amount on the stub and make a note of its number and amount.

Also check the deposits listed in the statement against those you have made. If any do not appear, add them to the balance shown by the bank.

Total the unpaid checks and deduct the amount from the balance in the statement. Also deduct any debit memos or service charges.

When these steps have been completed, your checkbook should agree with the bank statement.

MEETINGS AND TRAVEL

The nature of business is interaction among people, and that interaction frequently involves meetings. Sometimes one person merely visits the office of another to hold a discussion, or he may summon a subordinate to his office.

Often, however, situations require face-to-face conversation among a number of people, some of whom may live and work in other locations.

When that occurs, travel may come into the picture, although the progress of modern communications increasingly makes that unnecessary, and a conference call may suffice.

Preparing for a Meeting

When it has been decided to hold a meeting, the first considerations are who will attend and where they will meet. Your employer will give you the names of the participants. It is then your responsibility to notify each. In all likelihood this will be done by telephone.

A date and time having been chosen by your employer, you will call each person to find out whether the proposed schedule is acceptable. If some participants cannot be present then, your employer will have to propose another time, and the telephone procedure is undertaken anew. When all parties have agreed to a time and place, you can note those details on your employer's desk calendar and your own.

Make a list of the participants and put it in your tickler file to remind them of the date. Depending on how far in advance the meeting is scheduled, follow up with a reminder by letter or telephone call.

Your next task is to reserve a meeting room in the city chosen. If some participants must come by air, a hotel near the airport would be a convenience. If a dinner or luncheon is involved in the plan, choose a hotel that you know can handle such events satisfactorily. Your employer may also want you to reserve rooms for those participants who will stay overnight.

It may be your responsibility to prepare the meeting room on the appointed day. (If special equipment such as a projector or an audio recorder is required, be sure to reserve it well in advance and confirm that it has been delivered.) Be sure that the seating arrangements are as requested and that the lighting and air conditioning or heating are adequate. See that there are pads and pencils, glasses, and a pitcher of water. A space must also be available for the participants to leave their coats and other articles.

If refreshments are to be served, such as coffee and pastry or soft drinks, be sure the caterer has delivered the supplies and that there is a convenient service place.

Your employer will have prepared an agenda for the meeting, which you will have typed. Make copies and send one to all participants, perhaps with the reminder of the meeting, if that is done by mail.

On the meeting day, see that your employer's place at the table is supplied with everything he might need-pad and pencils, of course, and perhaps a calendar, paper clips, and a copy of the list of participants. You may also need to supply him with material from the files concerning topics on the agenda.

During the Meeting

In an all-day meeting there are likely to be telephone calls for your employer and for some of the participants. Inquire beforehand how these should be handled-whether messages should be taken, or whether the person wanted should be called to the telephone. The usual practice is to handle your employer's calls yourself and to take messages for the others. If a call is urgent, however, type the message on a slip of paper and hand it to the person unobtrusively.

Taking and Typing the Minutes

Ascertain in advance whether you are expected to take full notes to serve as the official minutes of the meeting, or simply to summarize the proceedings for your employer and the files. Verbatim notes may be required for motions, resolutions, and any controversial discussion. If so, you might use a tape recorder to back up your shorthand notes.

It is important to record names of speakers and discussions accurately. You might prepare a seating chart in order to identify speakers. Record attendance at the beginning, and note when the meeting is called to order and when it is adjourned.

After the meeting it is advisable to type the minutes as soon as possible. Submit a rough draft to your employer for approval before typing the final copy. If your company has no specific form for minutes, these general rules may be followed:

- Center the heading-the name of the group and the type of meeting-in capitals. Below that center the date in uppercase and lowercase letters.
- In the first paragraph give the day, date, hour, place, name of presiding officer, and type of meeting. Specify if a quorum was present.
- List the names of the participants, present and absent. This may be done in two columns.

- Double-space the text, with a triple space between items of business, but single-space resolutions.
- Indent paragraphs ten spaces and resolutions fifteen spaces.
- Capitalize RESOLVED and WHEREAS, and capitalize BOARD OF DIRECTORS and CORPORATION when those words refer to the group holding the meeting.
- Spell out sums of money and follow with the figures in parentheses: *One hundred dollars ($100).*
- Use the past tense throughout.
- Make signature lines at the end for the secretary and the chairman to sign the minutes.
- Attach appropriate reports and other documents before placing the signed minutes in the minute book.

Making Travel Arrangements

To perform this duty you must first know the company's travel policies. Some companies provide executives with company credit cards on which to charge travel expenses. Some have procedures for obtaining cash advances for the purpose.

Next you need to know your employer's preferences (*and* the company's requirements) as to type of travel and hotel accommodations and whether a rental car is wanted at all stopovers.

In our day of instant communication, travel arrangements are almost universally made by telephone. Large companies usually have a travel department to coordinate the needs of all executives. In any case, you must obtain full information in advance: travel dates, departure and arrival times, car rental needs, hotel accommodations, and preferred class of travel.

If a travel department makes the actual reservations, tickets will be delivered to the executive in ample time. If you choose to use a travel agency, the tickets will also be delivered to you. If you make the reservations yourself, the tickets will be ready for pickup at the airport or train station.

Preparing the Itinerary

Notes for the itinerary should be begun as soon as the travel plans are proposed. They should cover the places to be visited, including dates and times of departure and arrival; hotel accommodations; and proposed air or rail reservations.

Also keep an appointment schedule, showing the name, title, firm, address, and telephone number of each person to be visited; the date and time of each appointment; and notes as to whether it is a lunch or dinner meeting and the topic to be discussed.

The final itinerary should be prepared in triplicate.

The original is for your employer, one copy for your employer's family, and one copy for you.

Type an appropriate heading and then enter the pertinent information in column style. Specify whether the times shown are Eastern, Central, Mountain, or Pacific time and whether standard or daylight saving time.

FROM: (city)
TO: (city)
VIA: (airline or railroad)
DEPARTURE: (date and time)
ACCOMMODATIONS:(flight or train number)
CAR RENTAL: (type and location)
HOTEL:(name, address, and checkout time)

Follow the same form if there are intermediate stops, and then work in reverse for the return trip.

CHAPTER III

USING THE ENGLISH LANGUAGE

A large part of the writing that the secretary deals with is dictated by her employer. However, she herself may be called upon to draft letters and memos, and it is her responsibility to correct any obvious errors in dictated material.

For these reasons, it is essential that the secretary have a secure command of English usage, grammar, punctuation, and spelling. Also important to the production of business letters that do credit to the company is an understanding of the rules of capitalization and word division. The following sections reflect current trends in writing style in the business world.

WORD RELATIONSHIPS

Agreement of Subject and Verb

A singular subject takes a singular verb; a plural subject requires a plural verb. When other sentence elements come between subject and verb, the agreement may not be so easy to see.

> The book in which all the guests signed their names *was* on the table.
>
> The books donated to the library by Mrs. Doe *were* on the table.

The following words are generally considered to be singular and take singular verbs: *either, neither, each, anyone, someone, everyone, anybody, somebody, nobody, everybody.*

The following words are considered plural and take plural verbs: both, few, many, several.

EITHER/OR; NEITHER/NOR

When a subject is compounded with neither / nor or either / or, the verb is singular if the two nouns are singular, and plural if the nouns are plural. If one noun is singular and the other is plural, the verb agrees with the nearest subject.

Either French or Spanish *is* a good elective.

Neither he nor his associates *support* the proposal.

COLLECTIVE NOUNS

Collective nouns such as *class, company, club, crew, jury, committee* take singular verbs when the whole is considered as a unit. They take plural verbs when members of the whole are considered separately.

The class *has* elected a president.

The jury *were* polled individually after the verdict.

AGREEMENT OF PRONOUN AND ANTECEDENT

The pronoun is singular if the antecedent is singular, and plural if the antecedent is plural.

The boy did *his* best on the test.
All the boys in the class did *their* best.
The boys and the girls did *their* best.
Neither one of the boys did *his* best.

WHICH/THAT

In everyday speech *that* and *which* are often used interchangeably, but in formal writing their use should be carefully differentiated. *That* is used to introduce a restrictive or defining clause-one that defines the noun to which it is attached and cannot be omitted without changing the meaning of the sentence.

The lake *that* is the largest of the Great Lakes is Lake Superior.

Which introduces a nonrestrictive or parenthetical clause, one that could be omitted without changing the sense of the sentence.

Lake Superior, *which* is north of Wisconsin and Michigan, is the largest of the Great Lakes.

A simple way to decide is the comma test: If the clause seems to call for commas before and after it, the word is *which.*

CAPITALIZATION

Trends in capitalization tend to change with the times, as do other matters of English usage and spelling. Currently the trend is toward more use of lowercase letters. Certain fields of activity such as publishing and scientific disciplines adopt their own rules. The secretary should follow the rules of the company or organization in which she finds herself. Lacking such rules, however, the following conventions are correct.

The abbreviations for morning and evening are set lowercase with periods but no space:

a.m.; p.m.

Capitals or small capitals (in printing) are used for B.C. and A.D.

The first word after a colon is capitalized if it begins a complete sentence.

The coach emphasized his philosophy of sports: Winning is everything.

The appendix contained several items: glossary, bibliography, and index.

Important words in the titles of books and articles are capitalized:

The Winning of the West

Gone with the Wind

Geographical divisions are capitalized:

Arctic Circle

The Pacific Rim

Geographical features are capitalized when they precede the name but typed lowercase when following the name:

Lakes Erie and Ontario

The Mississippi and Missouri rivers

Directions are capitalized when part of a name but not when they merely specify a direction.

Midwest

the Union North

eastern Long Island

The river flows south

Capitalize the names of specific streets, buildings, and so on.

Mission Street

Municipal Building

street fair

building code

Capitalize the names of organizations and groups such as political parties. Use lowercase letters for nonspecific references and for political ideologies and systems.

Socialist Party

Union Club

socialism

club dues

Capitalize divisions of government.

United States Supreme Court

the Senate

Ways and Means Committee

Department of Defense

Capitalize titles of principal government officials,

especially those of the President.

Commander-in-Chief

Secretary of State

Chancellor of the Exchequer

Prime Minister

Capitalize names of specific historical periods, but type them in lowercase letters in general references.

Middle Ages

Renaissance

twentieth century

antiquity

Capitalize religious and secular holidays. The names of the seasons are typed in lowercase letters except when personified.

Good Friday

Hanukkah

winter solstice

"Come, gentle Spring . . ."

Capitalize full names of courts. Put types of courts in lowercase letters.

Supreme Court of the U.S.

the Court (Supreme)

New York Court of Appeals

juvenile court

family court

state supreme court

Capitalize titles of legislation such as acts, treaties,

and bills. Type in lowercase letters references to pending legislation and amendments and general references to legislative matters.

Bill of Rights
First Amendment
SALT Treaty
the bill
the pending amendment
treaty ratification

Capitalize the formal names of branches and divisions of the military services. Type general references in lowercase letters.

U.S. Army
National Guard
First Battalion
the army
the guard
the battalion

Capitalize numbers when they are part of a title or part of a street address under ten.

First Bank of Boston
Third Precinct
Eighty-second Congress
One Fifth Avenue

Capitalize names of deities, religious groups and organizations, and historic councils.

the Almighty

Vatican Council II
the Gospels
the Creation
Roman Catholic Church
church
high mass
vespers
rosary
chapel

Capitalize terms of kinship only when used before a name or when standing alone in place of a name.

I talked to Uncle George yesterday.
I called Mother on her birthday.
I forgot to call my mother.

PUNCTUATION

The purpose of punctuation is to help the reader follow the writer's thoughts through twists and turns. In speech, intonation does much of that. On the printed or typed page, however, meaning may be lost without devices to separate the phrases and clauses into groups.

Punctuation can do even more: It can lend emphasis, and it can change meanings.

The careful writer uses the various marks of punctuation to lend clarity and accuracy to the interpretation of his meaning.

The principal punctuation marks are the following, alphabetically, not in order of importance: apostrophe, brackets, colon, comma, dash, ellipses, exclamation point, hyphen, leaders, parentheses, period, question mark, quotation marks, semicolon, and virgule (commonly called slash or diagonal).

Apostrophe

With nouns, the apostrophe is used to show possession. Singular nouns form the possessive by adding the apostrophe and s. Plural nouns take only the apostrophe. This rule covers proper nouns as well, including those that end in s, with a few exceptions.

Jane's book
the river's delta
the Joneses' house
Jesus' birthplace
Moses' descendants

The apostrophe is used in contractions and to indicate where numbers are omitted.

it's (it is; but *its* as a pronoun)
two o'clock
the depression of '82

For ease of reading, the apostrophe is sometimes used in making lowercase letters plural. This was formerly the universal style with numbers and capital letters as well, but it is falling into disuse.

p's and q's
the 1990s
the three Rs
YMCAs

Brackets

Brackets are not the same as parentheses. Brackets are used within quoted material to show that the writer has made an insertion in the way of comment or explanation. They are also used frequently in technical and mathematical material.

"'Twas brillig [Carroll loved to invent words], and the slithy toves . . ."

Many typewriters do not have bracket keys. The typist can improvise by using the diagonal and underscore keys: /‾ ‾/

Colon

The colon may be used between two independent clauses the second of which explains the first.

The summer is fading fast: It is almost September.

In current usage, however, the clauses are often made into separate sentences, using the period.

Quotations or lists are often introduced by a colon, especially if long. The colon is also used to indicate time, in biblical references, after the salutation in letters, and in footnotes and bibliographies.

7:30 p.m.
Dear Mr. Roe:
Acts 1:3
Williams, Elsa S. *Bargello.* New York: Van Nostrand Reinhold, 1967.

Comma

The comma is probably the most widely used of the punctuation marks, although the trend is toward lesser usage.

The comma is used to separate words in a series, to separate clauses in a compound sentence, to set off introductory words in a sentence, to set off the introduction of a quotation, and after interjections and numbers having more than four digits. Commas are placed inside of quotation marks.

Apples, oranges, and pears are good eaten raw.
The plane was canceled, so we stayed overnight.
Because the manuscript was too long, the author deleted a chapter.
Hamlet's famous soliloquy begins: "To be or not to be, . . ."
Yes, our plans are virtually complete.
Well, the committee met to discuss that yesterday.
50,792

In modified block format for letters, the comma is used after the complimentary close. In personal letters it is used after the salutation.

Cordially yours,

Dear Dad,

The comma is *not* used in the following cases:

with numbers in an address:

4230 Douglas Street

to separate short clauses in a compound sentence:

He spoke and then he sat down.

to set off a restrictive appositive:

The book *Alice in Wonderland* has a sequel, *Through the Looking Glass.*

Dash

Dashes are sometimes wrongly used in place of commas or colons. Their proper use is to set off modifiers when commas may not seem strong enough.

The effects of exercise-running, jumping, weight lifting-could be seen in his physique.

The dash may be used to indicate hesitations in speech.

Well-uh-I can't remember right now.

The dash should not be used after a colon.

Ellipses

Ellipses are dots or periods used to indicate the omission of words or sentences. Three dots, spaced, are used for words missing at the beginning or in the middle of a sentence. Four dots indicate words or sentences missing at the end of a sentence; the first dot is typed like a period following the last word, and the other three are spaced.

Driving to Canada, we passed through Yonkers, Poughkeepsie . . . and several other cities.

"Let us now praise famous men . . ."

". . . Hallowed be thy name. . . .Give us this day our daily bread."

Exclamation Point

The exclamation point is intended to emphasize or express strong feeling. It is greatly overused.

Be careful!

How can you say that!

In quotations, the exclamation point is placed inside the quotation marks; otherwise it goes outside the point.

"The pot is about to boil over!" she cried.

The cook replied coolly, "I couldn't care less"!

Hyphen

The hyphen has numerous uses in written English:

To break words at the end of a line:

ridic-ulous

To link words in a compound adjective:

well-built houses

one- and two-page entries

To connect certain compound nouns:

self-esteem

Senator-elect

To indicate inclusive numbers:

pages 130-37

To clarify meaning when adding a prefix forms a different word:

re-cover

co-op

Compound adjectives containing an adverb ending in *-ly* do not take the hyphen:

suddenly busy secretary

fully dressed capon

Leaders

Leaders are a row of periods used to link typed items across a space. They are sometimes used in tables, indexes, and other tabular material, although their use is declining.

Preface iv

Accounts Receivable $900,000

Parentheses

Parentheses are used to set off certain elements from the rest of the sentence. Be sure to keep punctuation where it belongs, within or outside the parentheses.

The parts of a sentence are: (1) subject; (2) predicate; and (3) object.

Thirty-nine cents (39¢) .

The use of dictionaries has already been discussed (see Chapter 6).

The Occupational Directory (OD) is a valuable reference tool.

Period

The period is used to end a declarative or imperative sentence.

The player's next move produced checkmate.

Periods are also used in abbreviations, following the numbers in lists, and as decimals.

42nd St.

i.e.

The proctor's instructions were:

1. Don't talk.
2. Don't leave the room.
3. Don't cheat.

Periods are placed inside quotation marks.

"Twopence a week, and jam every other day."

Periods are not used in a vertical list unless one of the items is a complete sentence.

Periods are not used in initials of agencies, short forms of words, or Roman numerals except in lists.

OPEC
memo
George III
Chapter I.
Chapter II.

Question Mark

Sometimes called interrogation point, the question mark denotes a query or expresses doubt.

When is the first meeting?

Frederick Barbarossa (1123?-90) became Holy Roman Emperor in 1152.

A request couched as a question does not take the question mark.

Will you please deal the cards.

The question mark is placed inside parentheses, brackets, or quotation marks only when it is part of the enclosed material.

Why did he say, "I do not choose to run"?

The teacher asked, "How many have finished the test?"

Quotation Marks

Quotation marks enclose someone else's words.

"This week," he said, "we shall take up the fall of Rome."

Quotation marks also are used to enclose the titles

of magazine articles, television programs, radio programs, songs, and nicknames.

"The Discovery of Antarctica"

"The Cosby Show"

"Symphony Hall"

"Oh, Susanna"

Edward V. "Eddie" Rickenbacker

Colons and semicolons are placed outside quotation marks; periods and commas are placed inside.

Single quotation marks are used to enclose a quotation within a quotation.

"It must sometime come to 'jam today', Alice objected.

Semicolon

The semicolon may be used instead of a period between two independent clauses that are closely related.

It's your deal; I dealt the last hand.

Items in a series that has internal punctuation can be separated by semicolons.

The itinerary included stops in Hoboken, New Jersey; Dover, Delaware, and Baltimore, Maryland, before arrival in the capital.

The semicolon is placed *outside* quotations or parentheses.

Virgule

The virgule (also called *slash or diagonal)* is a slanting line used to indicate a choice between two alternatives.

and/or

in/out

It is sometimes used as a dividing line in dates and fractions.

2/22/92

2/10

The virgule may also be used to indicate the end of a line of poetry.

"I doubt it," said the Carpenter. / And shed a bitter tear."

Division of Words

Ideally, words are not divided across lines. If it is necessary, however, it is best to divide between syllables.

Words of two syllables may be divided at the end of the first syllable.

con-vent

gen-der

In words beginning with prefixes, try to divide at the prefix.

mis-construe

dis-engage

trans-fer

In words ending with suffixes, try to divide at the suffix.

agree-able
hop-ing
fin-est

Most words having double consonants may be divided between the consonants unless the stem ends in a double consonant.

forgot-ten
embar-rass
call-ing
pass-able

Compound nouns are usually divided between the two parts.

door-keeper
book-ends
type-writer

In words in which two vowels fall together but are pronounced separately, divide between the vowels.

tri-angle
pre-eminent

The following suffixes are usually good places for word division: *able, ance, ant, ence, ent, ible, ical, tive.*

compar-able
accord-ance
ten-ant
differ-ence

compon-ent
convert-ible
ident-ical
invent-ive

The list of *don'ts* in word division is longer than the *do's.*

Do not divide words of one syllable.

frieze
tripped
launch
skilled

Do not divide four-letter words.

item
lazy
opus

Do not divide a word on a single letter.

able, *not* a-ble
omit, *not* o-mit

Most suffixes should not be divided: *cial, cion, cious, geous, gious, sion, tial, tion, tious.*

gla-cial
suspi-cion
gra-cious
advanta-geous
ambi-tious
reli-gious

ascen-sion
nup-tial
voca-tion

In general, avoid dividing names of persons or other proper nouns.

Do not separate titles from the names to which they belong.

Do not separate abbreviations such as YMCA, UNICEF.

Do not separate initials from names.

Try to avoid dividing a word at the end of a paragraph or a page.

Do not permit more than two consecutive lines to end in hyphens.

As always, when in doubt look it up!

SPELLING

It is often said that some people can spell and others can't. This is a truism that is not true. Spelling correctly requires attention, careful pronunciation, and frequent resort to a good dictionary. The secretary should have within reach a desk-size dictionary, even if an unabridged version is available in the office.

Two excellent volumes are *Webster's New Collegiate Dictionary* and the *Random House Webster's College Dictionary.* Both desk references are based on their respective unabridged editions.

Those who find spelling troublesome can follow a few simple routines to improve their ability:

1. Learn to spell by syllables. Errors in spelling are often the result of mispronunciation.
2. Keep a list of your spelling errors and study them frequently.
3. Learn the most commonly misspelled words in the list on pages 73-74.
4. Learn the basic spelling rules that follow.
5. When in doubt, look it up.

Forming Plurals

Most nouns form the plural by adding *s:* book, books; chair, chairs.

Nouns ending in *s, x, ch,* or *sh* form the plural by adding es:

class, classes
box, boxes
church, churches
dish, dishes

Exception: Some nouns ending in *f* or *fe* change the final letters to *v* and add *es:*

wife, wives
sheaf, sheaves

Words ending in a consonant and *y* form the plural by changing the *y* to *i* and adding *es:*

berry, berries
cooky, cookies

Words ending in a vowel and *o* form the plural by adding *s:*

video, videos
folio, folios

Words ending in a consonant and *o* form the plural by adding *es:*

hero, heroes
tomato, tomatoes

Exception: Musical terms ending in *o* merely add *s:*

piano, pianos
contralto, contraltos

Compound nouns set as one word add *s* at the end:

cupful, cupfuls
pocketful, pocketfuls

Compound nouns set as two words or hyphenated base the plural form on the main word:

sister-in-law; sisters-in-law
trade union, trade unions

When both words in a compound noun are of equal importance, both are made plural:

woman representative; women representatives
head of department, heads of departments.

The plural of some words is formed by a change in the vowel or a complete change of spelling:

man, men

foot, feet
child, children

Proper nouns are made plural by adding s or-if the name ends in *s*-by adding *es:*

Jane, Janes
Jess, Jesses
Jones, Joneses

Prefixes

The principal prefixes are *in, em, im, em, dis, mis, be, re, de, il,* and *over.* The spelling of a word is not changed when one of these prefixed is added:

inexpert
enfold
impartial
employ
unnatural
disenchant
misspell
beribbon
retrace
deemphasize
illicit
overbearing

A few words add a hyphen with a prefix:

anti-American
self-esteem

Since there is no comprehensive rule governing the situation, it is wise to depend on the dictionary for guidance.

Suffixes

In words ending in silent *e*, drop the *e* when a suffix begins with a vowel:

decide, deciding
use, usage

In words ending in silent *e*, retain the *e* when a suffix begins with a consonant: manage, management

care, carefully

When adding *ed* or *ing*, the pronunciation of the base word may serve as a guide. Most words that end in a single consonant (except *f, h, x*) preceded by a vowel double the final consonant if the word is accented on the last syllable:

plan, planned, planning
extol, extolled, extolling

When the word is not accented on the last syllable, the consonant is usually not doubled:

travel, traveled, traveler
exit, exited, exiting

When the suffix *ness* or *ly* is added to words not ending in *y*, the base word is usually unchanged. In most words ending in *y*, the *y* is changed to *i* when *ly* is added:

literal, literally
similar, similarly
genuine, genuineness
happy, happily, happiness
cloudy, cloudiness

When the suffix *ness* is added to a word ending in *n*, the final *n* is doubled:

sudden, suddenness
mean, meanness

Words ending in silent *e* and preceded by *c* or *g* usually retain the *e* before the suffixes *able* and *ous:*

manage, manageable
outrage, outrageous

Only one English word ends in *sede:* supersede. Only three end in *ceed:* exceed, proceed, and succeed. All others take the ending *cede:* precede, concede.

ie/ei

After *c,* when the sound is long *e,* the *e* usually precedes the *i:*

receive
ceiling

After most other letters, the *i* precedes the *e:*

thief
believe
shield

When the sound is not long *e,* or when the sound is long *a,* the *e* precedes the *i:*

sleigh
veil
eight.

Remember the rhyme: Use *i* before *e* except after *c* or when sounded like *a* as in n*ei*ghbor and w*ei*gh.

POSSESSIVES

The possessive is usually formed by adding *'s:*

Jane, Jane's.

Use no apostrophe with possessive or relative pronouns:

his, hers, ours, yours, theirs, whose.

Use the apostrophe with singular or plural nouns ending in *s:*

hostess, hostess'
duchess, duchesses'
princes' (plural).

It is important not to confuse the possessive form with contractions:

it's (it is); its
they're (they are); their

FREQUENTLY MISSPELLED WORDS

In addition to your personal list of spelling bugaboos suggested above, spend a little time with the following words that have turned up most often on lists of frequent errors by students at various levels and by persons taking Civil Service examinations:

absence
accidentally
accommodate
acknowledgment
advantageous
all right
athletic
benefited
calendar
cemetery
changeable
coolly
{council
counsel
{desert
dessert
dilemma
embarrassed
exercise
existence

February
grammar
grievance
height
hypocrisy
indispensable
interested
judgment
knowledgeable
laboratory
latter
maintenance
mischievous
negligible
noticeable
occasion
occurrence
omitted
parallel
practically

{principal
{principle
privilege
promissory
pronunciation
{quiet
{quite
recommend
referred
relieve
rhythm
seize
separate
{stationary
{stationery
supervisor
transferred
relevant
villain
Wednesday
weird
{woman
{women

WORDS FREQUENTLY CONFUSED

Many words are similar in sound but quite different in meaning. Others are different in both sound and spelling but are confused with each other. The following are some of the most troublesome.

accept, except *Accept* means to receive or agree to: to *accept* an invitation. *Except*, as a verb, means to take out or leave out: to *except* no one from the rules.

addition, edition *Addition* means the process of joining together or finding the sum of. *Edition* refers to the form in which a book or other publication is published: first *edition*.

advice, advise *Advice* is the noun: to give *advice*. *Advise* is the verb: to *advise* a person.

affect, effect *Affect*, as a verb, means to influence: Fear *affects* the mind. *Effect*, as a verb, means to bring about or cause: It is time to *effect* some changes; as a noun, it means the result or outcome: The *effect* of the change was gratifying.

all right, alright *All right* means allowable. It is *all right* to do so. *Alright* is not an acceptable spelling.

allude, elude *Allude* means to make indirect reference: He *alluded* to the earlier quotation. *Elude* means to avoid or escape: The suspect *eluded* capture.

already, all ready *Already* means by the time mentioned: The ship has *already* sailed. *All ready* means fully prepared: We are *all ready* to go.

among, between *Among* means in the midst of several things or persons: Settle it *among* you. *Between* refers to only two persons or things: *Between* you and me.

appraise, apprise *Appraise* means to make an evaluation of: The jeweler *appraised* the ring. *Apprise* means to notify or inform: He was *apprised* of the visitor's arrival.

ascent, assent *Ascent* means rising or climbing: The bird's *ascent* was swift. *Assent* means agreement, consent, permission: *assent* to a course of action.

between *See* among.

can, may *Can* expresses ability to do: You *can* do better than that. *May* expresses permission: You *may* attend the dance.

capital, capitol *Capital* means the official seat of government: Washington is the *capital* of the United States. *Capitol* is a building in which a legislature meets: the U.S. *capitol* is in Washington.

censor, censure *Censor* as a noun means an official examiner of literary works; as a verb it means to delete, suppress: The *censor* examined the library and *censored* a number of books. *Censure* as a verb means to express disapproval of; as a noun it means the expression of disapproval: The judge's *censure* of the defendant was stern; he *censured* both his behavior and his language.

census, senses *Census* means an official count of the population: The 1990 *Census* resulted in redistricting of the states. *Senses* (the plural of sense) means awareness or sanity: He has taken leave of his *senses*.

cite, sight, site *Cite* means to mention: to *cite* a fact. *Sight* as a noun means a view, a vision: a beautiful *sight*. *Site* means a place or location: the *site* of the school.

complement, compliment *Complement* as a noun means a part that completes another part: The feather really *complements* her hat. *Compliment* as a noun means praise, commendation: His gaze was an obvious *compliment* to her.

council, counsel, consul *Council* as a noun means an assembly for consultation: The Security *Council* decided the matter. *Counsel* as a noun means guidance, advice, or a lawyer: Her mother's *counsel* guided her well. *Counsel* for the defense opened his case. *Consul* means an official living in a foreign country to protect the interests of his own country.

creditable, credible *Creditable* means worthy of praise or esteem: His performance on the test was quite *creditable*. *Credible* means worthy of being believed, reliable: He offered a *credible* alibi.

decent, descent, dissent *Decent* means proper, respectable: He waited a *decent* interval. *Descent* means going downward: *descent* of the lighted ball at New Year's. *Dissent* as a noun means disagreement; as a verb, to disagree: He registered a strong *dissent* against the ruling.

device, devise A *device* is something invented or thought up: left to my own *devices*. *Devise* means to invent or contrive: *devise* a plan to get free.

dissent *See* decent.

edition *See* addition.

effective, effectual *Effective* means producing the desired result: The inoculation was *effective* in preventing rabies. *Effectual* means having the ability to produce a desired result: *Effectual* legal steps brought about his release.

elicit, illicit *Elicit* means to bring forth: Careful questioning *elicited* the truth. *Illicit* means illegal or unlawful: An *illicit* shipment of drugs was confiscated.

elude *See* allude.

eminent, imminent *Eminent* means high in stature, distinguished: an *eminent* statesman. *Imminent* means about to happen: in *imminent* danger.

except *See* accept.

formally, formerly *Formally* means with formality: to be introduced *formally*. *Formerly* means at an earlier time: He was *formerly* a soldier.

illicit *See* elicit.

lay, lie *Lay* means to put or place: Please *lay* the book on the desk. *Lay* is also the past tense of *lie*: *lie* down after lunch. *Lie* as a verb means to be in or to take a horizontal position: I *lie* down when I am tired.

learn, teach *Learn* means to acquire knowledge: She must *learn* her lessons. *Teach* means to impart or give knowledge: Her mother will *teach* her to read.

lessen, lesson *Lessen* means to make less, to reduce: A joke will *lessen* the tension. *Lesson* means something to be learned: The teacher assigned the third *lesson*.

loose, lose *Loose* means not fastened: The dog was *loose* in the yard. *Lose* means to mislay or be deprived of: to *lose* one's belongings.

may *See* can.

passed, past *Passed* (the past tense of the verb *to pass)* means went beyond: The sprinter *passed* me easily. *Past* as an adjective means ended, finished: The time for tears is *past;* as a noun it refers to time gone by: I keep remembering the *past.*

militate, mitigate *Militate* means to have a heavy effect: A prison record *militates* against him. *Mitigate* means to lessen in force, to make less severe: The breeze *mitigated* the heat of the day.

persecute, prosecute *Persecute* means to mistreat or harass: The Nazis *persecuted* the Jews in Germany. *Prosecute* means to bring legal action against: The district attorney will *prosecute* the case.

personal, personnel *Personal* pertains to a person: She took her *personal* effects with her. *Personnel* refers to a body of employees: The *personnel* worked on staggered shifts.

practicable, practical *Practicable* means possible of doing, usable: He proposed a *practicable* solution to the problem. *Practical* means pertaining to actual use or action: The manual gave *practical* instructions for assembling the model.

prosecute *See* persecute.

senses *See* census.

sight *See* cite.

site *See* cite.

stationary, stationery *Stationary* means remaining in one place: The diner is a *stationary* eating place. *Stationery* means writing supplies.

suite, sweet *Suite* means a set of things meant to be used together: a *suite* of furniture. *Sweet* means having a taste like sugar.

teach *See* learn

TYPING TIPS

Making Special Characters

Typewriters contain a number of special characters, but not all typewriters have all the characters a secretary is called upon to use. Many of these can be improvised by overtyping various standard letters and symbols; that is, by typing a character, backspacing, and typing another on top of the first. These will not be perfect, but they will suffice for most nontechnical purposes.

To make a paragraph mark: Overtype a capital P with a lowercase 1 (P).

To make a division mark, combine a colon and a hyphen: (÷).

To make an exclamation mark, type an apostrophe over a period (!)

To make a degree mark, turn the platen slightly toward you and type a lowercase o: (°).

To make brackets, use the diagonal and underscore keys (/̄ _/).

To make a section sign, type one lowercase s over another, with the second slightly raised (§).

To make an equals mark, type two hyphens, the second slightly above the first: (=).

To make a cedilla, type a lowercase c and a comma underneath it: (ç).

To make a caret, use the underscore and the diagonal (_/).

To make a plus sign, type a hyphen and a diagonal on top of it: (⫽)

To make a pound sterling sign, type a capital L and a hyphen: (Ł).

To make the signs for minutes and seconds (or inches and feet), type an apostrophe (') and quotation marks (").

Typing on Forms and Ruled Lines

Forms seldom seem designed to fit the typewriter on which they are being filled out. To avoid a sloppy appearance, follow these procedures:

Adjust the form in your machine so that the letters strike slightly above the ruled lines, preferably so that the tails of letters *g*, *p*, *q* and *y* just touch the line. It is quite possible that the line spacing will be different from that of your typewriter; if so, adjust for the difference by using the variable line spacer. It will mean forwarding the platen by hand, but it will yield a neatly typed form.

If the form includes boxes to be checked, it may be necessary to shift the paper slightly to the right or left at the beginning of the task, so that the x falls squarely in the boxes.

Typing Numbers and Fractions

The average secretary has relatively little need to type numbers and fractions, but a few simple rules will cover most situations that you might encounter.

Some typewriters have keys for one half and one quarter. These are fine to use if no other fraction occurs in a particular typing job. All fractions in a given document should be typed in the same style, however (1/8, 2/5, 3/10, 1/2, 1/4).

In typing mixed fractions, leave a space between the whole number and the fraction: 2 1/2.

Numbers that occur in textual material may be handled in one of two ways, depending on your employer's preference:

Numbers ten and below are spelled out; all others are in figures.

Or, numbers one hundred and below, and larger round numbers such as two thousand, are spelled out; all others are in figures.

In either case, if you use a large number (such as 125) within a given paragraph, all other numbers in that paragraph should be typed in figures, including ten and below.

When typing numbers in columns, align them by a sign that they have in common, such as decimals, dollar signs, or percent marks. If there are more than a few, you can set tabular stops to make it easier.

If figures have nothing in common, type them either flush left or centered.

5%	5 percent
$70	seventy dollars
200 lb.	200 pounds

Do not divide numbers at the end of a line of text.

Making Corrections

Some copy is required to be perfect. Certain legal documents, for instance, may not have erasures or other corrections.

In practical usage, however, meticulously made deletions and corrections may be acceptable.

If in typing you notice an error while the page is still in the typewriter, it can be carefully erased or covered by correction fluid and retyped correctly.

If the page has been removed from the typewriter,

however, it must be realigned to permit retyping after the error has keen eliminated. This is best done by finding a capital I or T near the correction to line up with. Failing that, the next best is a lowercase i, using the dot as guide.

Modern typewriters have built-in correction devices that lift the incorrect letters off the page and permit almost undetectable correction.

Correction fluid is painted with a tiny brush over the error. When it is dry, a relatively neat correction can be made by typing over it. Correction fluid is available in a wide assortment of colors to match your paper stock.

Spacing and Punctuation Marks

The rules for spacing after punctuation marks are principally a matter of long usage, but they are widely accepted in business and should be observed by the careful secretary.

The basic rule is that punctuation is not separated from the word it follows. For instance, a dash that follows the word at the end of a line must be on that line, not the succeeding line.

Leave *no* space in the following situations:

- Between a word and the punctuation that follows it:

  to the end;

- Before or after a dash:
  Early-at seven p.m.
- Between quotation marks and the quoted matter:
  "Jane Eyre" is a great novel.
- Before or after a hyphen:
  twenty-six
- Before or after an apostrophe:
  Henry's
  where's
- Between items separated by a virgule (diagonal):
  Day/Glo
  and/or
- Between the initials of an abbreviation:
  p.m.
- Between parentheses or brackets and the words they enclose:
  Seventh (and last) is . . .

Leave *one* space:

- After a comma:
  . . . now, and so forth
- After a semicolon:
  (2) keep it short; and (3) . . .
- After a period following an initial or in an abbreviation:
  John R. Doe

Roe Printing, Inc. is our supplier.

- After a suspended hyphen:
  the first- and second-grade classes.
- Before and after x when standing for *by:*
  9 x 12.

Leave *two* spaces:

- After punctuation ending a sentence:
  . . . it was gone! I couldn't find it anywhere.
- After a figure or letter introducing an item in a list:
  1. Long division
     a. Dividend and divisor

CHAPTER IV

BUSINESS LETTERS

The business letter is a representative of the writer and the company that employs him or her. The content of the letter is largely out of the purview of the writer's secretary; so is the quality and design of the letterhead on which it is typed. Just about everything else about it, however, is the responsibility of the secretary.

The format of the business letter may be established by company policy. If so, of course, the secretary follows it. If not, however, the secretary has considerable latitude in establishing that format.

In the days of handwritten letters, paragraph indention was used for purposes of clarity. The advent of the typewriter put an end to that, and current usage almost universally has adopted either the full block form or the modified block form.

Full Block Form

The full block form is popular in many offices because of its simplicity and air of modernity. Everything under the letterhead-date, address, salutation, body of letter, complimentary close, and signature-is aligned at the left margin, or, as is said in printing, flush left.

Full Block Form

February 6, 1992

Mr. John Doe
John Doe Publishers, Inc.
1234 West 23rd Street
New York, NY 10001

Dear Mr. Doe:
It was a pleasure to meet you yesterday . . .
and I hope to see you when I am in the city again.

Sincerely yours,

Richard Roe
Vice President

Modified Block Form

The modified block form is probably the most widely used in current business practice. In this form the principal elements of the letter are typed flush left, but certain parts-the date, the complimentary close, and the signature-are aligned at the right margin to give a sense of balance to the page.

Modified Block Form

February 24, 1992

Mr. John Doe
John Doe Publishers, Inc.
1234 West 23rd Street
New York, NY 10001

Dear Mr. Doe:
It was a pleasure to meet you yesterday . . .
and I hope to see you when I am in the city again.

Sincerely yours,

Richard Roe
Vice President

Some companies utilize the full block form for short letters, in which it has a more pleasing effect, and the modified form for longer letters.

Semiblock Form

This is a more traditional format. It differs from the modified block only in that paragraphs are indented five to ten spaces.

Official Style

This format is used for official communications, as with members of government or the armed forces. It is also used for personal letters written on special, smaller, company stationery.

The dateline and salutation are placed as in the modified block form. The address, however, is typed flush left two to five lines below the signature. Paragraphs are indented two to ten spaces.

PARTS OF LETTER

Placement

Regardless of format chosen, it is essential that the letter be so placed as to create a pleasing appearance. The body of the letter should be centered in the page, with ample margins to left and right.

Punctuation

The modern trend is to eliminate unnecessary punctuation in all writing. This is also true in business letters.

Especially when using the full block format, secretaries usually choose open punctuation. In this style, punctuation is used only in abbreviations. None is used in the salutation or complimentary close.

Mr. John Doe
John Doe Publishers, Inc.
1234 West 23rd Street
New York, NY 10001
Dear Mr. Doe

Sincerely yours

Many secretaries modify the open style by using punctuation for the salutation and complimentary close.

Mr. John Doe

John Doe Publishers, Inc.
1234 West 23rd Street
New York, NY 10001

Dear Mr. Doe:

Sincerely yours,

Dateline

The dateline customarily gives month, day, and year:

February 6, 1992

Some stylists prefer the form used by the military and in Great Britain: day, month, and year:

6 February 1992

In full block format, the dateline is typed flush left, two to four inches below the letterhead. In modified style is it placed flush right at the margin of the letter. Some secretaries like to vary the style by centering the dateline under the letterhead.

In any case, the month is spelled out, not abbreviated, nor are the suffixes *-st, -nd,* *-rd,* or *-th* used in the day of the month:

February 6, not Feb. 6th.

Inside Address

The inside address consists of the name of the person addressed, the name of the firm if applicable, the street address, and the city, state, and zip code. If the person is addressed at a place of business, his or her title is placed after the name or on a separate line. The title is never abbreviated. The full corporate title of the company is always used; this can be found on the company's letterhead or billhead. Carry-over lines of the address are indented about three spaces.

Only courtesy titles and professional titles precede the name of the addressee: Mr., Mrs., Miss, Ms., and Professor or the Reverend. If a professional degree follows the name, the title is omitted before it:

Dr. John Doe, *but*
John Doe, M.D.

Some stress has been laid on the avoidance of abbreviations. There is one exception, however: The official Postal Service abbreviations should be used in all addresses. These are given on pages 146-148.

With the advance of technology, the five-digit zip code-which took so long to be universally accepted-has now been lengthened by four digits. This addition is currently being phased in and is used principally by large mailers. The alert secretary would be well advised, however, to keep an eye out for the nine-digit code on mail that passes through her hands and make a note of it in addresses that are frequently used in her office. As machines are increasingly pressed into use in the Postal Service, it will become as essential a part of the business address as the "old-fashioned" five-digit code.

Salutation

In business correspondence, salutations are usually formal: Dear Mr. Doe; Dear Dr. Doe; Dear Mrs. Roe; Dear Ms. Roe. If there is a relation of friendship between the writer and the addressee, it is permissible to use first names: Dear John; Dear Mary. If the name of the person addressed is not known, one may write Dear Sir or Dear Madam. If no individual is intended, the salutation may be Gentlemen or Ladies.

Special forms of address are used for government officials and members of the armed forces, the church, and the professions. These are given beginning on page 108.

Body of Letter

The body of the letter is, of course, the heart of the letter. Its quality and effectiveness will depend on the skill of the dictator or writer.

The competent secretary can nevertheless make a difference by ensuring that the letter is visually appealing. Many dictators specify paragraphs. If that is not done, however, paragraphs should be of moderate length and, if possible, be confined to a single idea.

The body of the letter is single-spaced unless it

consists of only a few lines. Double-spacing is used between paragraphs.

References to newspapers, periodicals, books, paintings and sculptures, operas, and long musical compositions are underlined to indicate italic type. References to motion pictures, television and radio programs, and articles in periodicals are placed in quotation marks.

Complimentary Close

The complimentary close takes its tone largely from the salutation and the degree of formality or intimacy shown in that part of the letter. A letter that opens with Dear Sir or Dear Madam would appropriately close with Yours truly, Yours very truly, or Very truly yours.

A letter that opens with Dear Mr. Doe or Dear Ms. Roe might close with Yours sincerely, Very sincerely yours, or even Cordially yours, depending on the degree of friendliness evidenced in the body of the letter.

Letters between friends, of course, may close with an expression of that friendship, such as Regards, or Best regards.

Signature

The signature consists of the name of the writer and his or her position in the firm. If the writer is an officer of the company and his or her name appears in the letterhead, it is not necessary to type the name under the signature.

A four-line space is left for the written signature.

If the company name is part of the signature, it is usually capitalized. The name of the person signing is typed below the actual signature, in uppercase and lowercase letters. A title follows the name on the same line or a separate line.

JOHN DOE PUBLISHERS, INC.

Richard Roe
Vice President

The tendency among women in business is to drop the titles Mrs., Miss, or Ms. in title lines. In some cases, however, married women prefer to use the title to make it easier for correspondents to address them correctly. It is usually typed:

(Mrs.) Jane Doe

and signed:

Jane Doe

Certain additional information is provided in some business letters but not in all. This includes the attention line, the identification line, the enclosure line, the carbon copy line, and the postscript.

Attention Line

This line is used when a letter is addressed to a firm but is intended for the attention of a particular person. Its use indicates that the letter may be opened by others if the person identified is not available.

The attention line appears on both the envelope and the letter. On the envelope it is typed either as the second line of the address, or below and to the left of the address.

In the letter it is typed two spaces below the address and two spaces above the salutation. In a full block form letter the attention line is flush left. In modified or semiblock it is centered on the page.

Attention: John Doe

Since such a letter is addressed to a firm, the salutation is impersonal:

Gentlemen:
Dear Sirs:
Ladies:
Mesdames:

Identification Line

This information is placed flush left one or two lines below the signature. It usually consists of the initials or the full name of the writer and the initials of the secretary, separated by a colon.

JD:jr
John Doe: jr

Enclosure Line

This line notifies the recipient (and reminds the secretary) that additional material has been enclosed with the letter. It is typed flush left directly below the identification line. Several styles are employed:

Enclosure
Enc.
Enc (2)
Enclosure: Check $750.75
Return envelope
Policy #9876-5432

Carbon Copy

This term is still commonly used although carbon paper is not, having largely given way to photocopying. When a copy is to be sent to a person other than the addressee, the fact is indicated in the business letter, just below the identification line.

John Doe: jr
cc: Jane Roe

In a situation in which it is not desired for the addressee to know of the copy, the information is placed only on the office copy of the letter. Called a blind copy, it is then indicated thus:

bc: Jane Roe

Postscript

Postscripts are seldom used in business letters, being considered evidence of sloppy thinking and failure to marshal thoughts on the writer's part. At times, however, the postscript is used deliberately as a method of attracting attention or emphasizing a point in the body of the letter. The postscript is placed two or three lines below the identification line, and preceded by the letters P.S. and a colon.

The Envelope

The appearance of the envelope should match the letter it encloses in style and attractiveness of presentation. The address is usually typed single-spaced and in block form. It is placed slightly to the left and just below the center of the envelope.

If the firm name is imprinted in the upper left corner, the writer's name may be typed above it.

It is advisable to use the Postal Service official two-letter abbreviations for the names of states. It is essential to use the zip code, including the new four-digit addition, if available. No characters of any kind should follow the zip code; they may interfere with the automatic scanning machine.

Notations and directions are handled variously. Attention lines are usually typed at the bottom left of the envelope. Notations such as *Personal*, *Confidential*, or *Hold for Arrival* are customarily placed above and to the left of the address.

Instructions regarding type of postal service, such

as Registered, Certified, and Special Delivery, are typed at the upper right, just below the space for postage stamps or postage meter imprint.

THE MEMORANDUM

This format is used principally for internal use, but it is sometimes utilized for external communications. Most firms have special stationery for memorandums. It is usually of less expensive paper stock and printed instead of engraved.

Some memo stationery has preprinted headings such as the following:

Date:
To:
From:
Subject *or* Re:

The body of the memorandum is typed in block form with one line between paragraphs. No salutation or complimentary close is used. The memo may be signed or not, as wished.

Many companies have interoffice envelopes for inhouse communications. External memos are mailed in regularly addressed letterhead envelopes.

WRITING BUSINESS LETTERS

The secretary is often expected to write letters and memorandums for her own signature. The executive may ask her to take care of minor matters on her own initiative. Some employers make a practice of giving a general idea of a response to a correspondent and ask her to write the letter for his signature. Frequently, too, correspondence comes to the office in the absence of the employer that needs to be acknowledged immediately.

For all those situations, it is important for the secretary to develop a clear and correct writing style. Practice is the best teacher of this skill. Following, however, are samples of such communications: acknowledgment, apology, appointment, appreciation, collection, complaint, confirmation, follow-up, introduction, invitation and reply, informal invitation and reply, order, request, reservation, sympathy, and thank you.

Acknowledgment

Dear Mr. Bryan:

Your letter to Mr. Doe in reference to the meeting in Georgia arrived during his absence from the office. I feel sure that he will be pleased at the progress of your arrangements. He is expected back on Monday and will be in touch with you then.

If I can be of any assistance in the meantime, please feel free to call on me.

Sincerely yours,

Apology

Dear Mr. Carter:

Please accept our apology for failing to let you know of the alteration in Mr. Doe's itinerary. The change was quite unexpected, so there was no time for a letter. We tried to reach you by telephone, but you were unavailable.

Mr. Doe plans to be in your area within the next few months and will make a special point of trying to see you then.

Sincerely yours,

Appointment

Dear Mr. Davis:

Mr. Doe will be glad to see you while you are in New York next month. He suggests Wednesday, February 20, at 3 p.m.

Please let me know whether this is convenient for you.

Sincerely yours,

Appreciation

Dear Jean:

I want to thank you in particular and the committee as a whole for your invaluable assistance on Mr. Doe's recent campaign stop in Nebraska. As you know, the program was a huge success, and much of the credit is due to your efforts.

I look forward to working with you again soon.

Sincerely yours,

Collection

Dear Mr. Elton:

Just a friendly reminder that we have not received the March payment on your account.

If your check has already been mailed, please disregard this letter. If not, your early attention to the matter will be appreciated.

Sincerely yours,

Complaint

Gentlemen:

Your statement of April 1 again shows an outstanding charge of $91.50 for an order of calculator tape placed on January 3. This order was canceled on January 10 and thus was never filled.

Enclosed is a copy of our letter of cancellation. Please correct your records accordingly and send us a revised statement.

Very truly yours,

Confirmation

Dear Mr. Frost:

You are right that Mr. Doe will attend the conference in San Francisco on July 20. He expects to arrive in the city about noon and will telephone you then.

Mr. Doe asks me to thank you for including him and to say that he looks forward to meeting with you and your associates.

Sincerely yours,

Follow-up

To: Jane Gray

From: Mary Roe

Re: Expense Report

Mr. Doe asks me to remind you that Mr. Harvard's expense report is due next week. Please be sure that it includes charges for his recent trip to the home office.

Many thanks.

J.G.

Introduction

Dear Jack:

This will introduce my former associate Richard Roe, who is assuming the position of Vice President of Sanford Manufacturing in your city.

I know he would appreciate your introducing him to the business community of Detroit and helping him find his footing in a new city.

Many thanks, Jack, and I hope to see you soon.

Cordially,

Invitation: Formal

Mr. and Mrs. William Lawrence
request the pleasure of the company of
Mr. and Mrs. Philip Montague
at dinner
on Thursday, the tenth of November
at eight o'clock
Fifteen Chestnut Street
Black tie

R.S.V.P.

Reply: Formal

Mr. and Mrs. Philip Montague
accept with pleasure
the kind invitation of
Mr. and Mrs. William Lawrence
to be present at dinner
on Thursday, the tenth of November
at eight o'clock
Fifteen Chestnut Street

Invitation: Informal

Dear Kitty:

Can you get free to have lunch with John Wood and me a week from next Monday, March 5? If so, I'll make reservations at Alfredo's for 1 p.m.

Drop me a note at your convenience. It will be pleasant picking up on our respective doings.

Sincerely yours,

Reply: Informal

Dear Jane:

I'll be delighted to have lunch with you and John on Monday, March 5. I'll see you at 1 p.m. at Alfredo's.

Many thanks. I'll tell you all the gossip then.

Cordially,

Order

To: Supply Specialists

From: Jane Roe, secretary to Mr. Doe

Re: Xstamps

Please enter our order for two check endorsement stamps to be imprinted as follows:

Petroplex Savings Inc.
1234 Denison Street
Dallas, TX 78702
(801) 973-767.

Your catalog shows this item at $54.25 each. Please send the shipment and invoice to my attention. Thank you.

Request

Gentlemen:

Several members of our staff have expressed interest in your company's new lap-style personal computer for traveling businessmen.

Would it be convenient for one of your representatives to demonstrate the instrument in my office one day next week? Tuesday would be best for us. Call me if that is suitable for you and we can set a time.

Very truly yours,

Reservation

Gentlemen:

Please reserve a single room with bath for the nights of August 1 to 5 inclusive in the name of John Doe. Mr. Doe will arrive in Atlanta at 3 p.m. on August 1, on Delta Flight 234 out of New York.

Mr. Doe will also need the use of a meeting room on the afternoon of August 2, and if possible a recording secretary.

I shall appreciate your prompt confirmation of these arrangements.

Very truly yours,

Sympathy

Dear Jean:

All of us in the Advertising Department were saddened at the news of Carol's tragic death. Our association with her over the years was always a bright spot in a workaday world, and we shall miss her sorely.

Sincerely yours,

Thank You

Dear Fred:

I want to thank you for your cordial reception of my friend Jean. Your introduction to your business associates greatly facilitated her trip, and she tells me she made some important contacts.

Thanks again, Fred, and if I can return the favor just call on me.

Cordially,

FORMS OF ADDRESS

Specific forms of address are used for persons holding government, religious, or honorary titles. Although most such positions are now held by both men and women, the following listing gives the correct form for men. For a woman holding the position, merely substitute Madam for Sir, and Mrs., Miss, or Ms. for Mr.

Care should be taken with the terms Honorable and Reverend. These words are adjectives, not titles. For that reason, they may not be followed by the surname alone.

The Honorable John Doe, not The Honorable Doe

The Reverend John Doe, not The Reverend Doe

In conversation, a clergyman is addressed as Dr. or Mr. Doe, never Reverend Doe.

The forms of address listed here include those for the President and Vice President (page 108-109); the Federal Judiciary (pages 109-111); members of Congress (pages 111-114); heads of Congressional agencies (page 114-115); Executive Department officials (pages 115-117); Ambassadors and ministers of the United States and of foreign countries (page 117-119); United Nations officials (pages 119-120); state and local officials (page 120-121); the clergy (pages 121-124); the military (pages 124-125), and Canadian officials (pages 125-127).

THE WHITE HOUSE

The President

Address: The President
The White House
Washington, DC 20500

Salutation:	Formal:	Mr. President:
	Informal:	Dear Mr. President:
Closing:	Formal:	Most respectfully yours,
	Informal:	Sincerely yours,
In conversation:		Mr. President *or* Sir

The Vice President

Address:		The Vice President United States Senate Washington, DC 20510
Salutation:	Formal:	Mr. Vice President:
	Informal:	Dear Mr. Vice President:
Closing:	Formal:	Very truly yours,
	Informal:	Sincerely yours,
In conversation:		Mr. Vice President *or* Sir

THE FEDERAL JUDICIARY

Chief Justice of the United States

Address:		The Chief Justice of the United States The Supreme Court of the United States Washington, DC
Salutation:	Formal:	Sir:
	Informal:	Dear Mr. Chief Justice:
Closing:	Formal:	Very truly yours,

Informal:		Sincerely yours,
In conversation:		Mr. Chief Justice *or* Sir

Associate Justice of the Supreme Court

Address:		Mr. Justice (surname only) The Supreme Court of the United States Washington, DC
Salutation:	Formal:	Sir:
	Informal:	Dear Mr. Justice:
Closing:	Formal:	Very truly yours,
	Informal:	Sincerely yours,
In conversation:		Mr. Justice *or* Mr. Justice (surname) *or* Sir

Retired Justice of the Supreme Court

Address:		The Honorable (full name) (Local address)
Salutation:	Formal:	Sir:
	Informal:	Dear Mr. Justice:
Closing:	Formal:	Very truly yours,
	Informal:	Sincerely yours,

Presiding Justice of Other Federal Courts

Address:		The Honorable (full name)

	Presiding Justice (Name of court) (Local address)
Salutation: Formal:	Sir:
Informal:	Dear Mr. Justice:
Closing: Formal:	Very truly yours,
Informal:	Sincerely yours,
In conversation:	Mr. Justice *or* Mr. Justice (surname) *or* Sir

Judge of a Federal Court

Address:	The Honorable (full name) Judge of the (name of court; if a U.S. district court, give district) (Local address)
Salutation:	Dear Judge (surname):
Closing:	Sincerely yours,
In conversation:	Judge *or* Sir

MEMBERS OF CONGRESS

Senator

Address:	The Honorable (full name) United States Senate Washington, DC

Salutation: Dear Senator (surname):
Closing: Sincerely yours,
In conversation: Senator

Committee Chairman, United States Senate

Address: The Honorable (full name)
Chairman, Committee on (name)
United States Senate
Washington, DC
Salutation: Dear Mr. Chairman:
Closing: Sincerely yours,
In conversation: Mr. Chairman

Subcommittee Chairman, United States Senate

Address: The Honorable (full name)
Chairman, Subcommittee on (name)
(Name of full committee)
United States Senate
Washington, DC
Salutation: Dear Senator (surname):
Closing: Sincerely yours,
In conversation: Mr. Chairman

Speaker of the House of Representatives

Address:		The Honorable (full name) United States House of Representatives Washington, DC
Salutation:	Formal:	Sir:
	Informal:	Dear Mr. (surname):
Closing:	Formal:	Very truly yours,
	Informal:	Sincerely yours,
In conversation:		Mr. (surname) *or* Sir

Committee Chairman, United States House of Representatives

Address:	The Honorable (full name) Chairman, Committee on (name) House of Representatives Washington, DC
Salutation:	Dear Mr. Chairman:
Closing:	Sincerely yours,
In conversation:	Mr. Chairman

Subcommittee Chairman, United States House of Representatives

Address:	The Honorable (full name) Chairman, Subcommittee on (name) (Name of full committee) House of Representatives Washington, DC
Salutation:	Dear Mr. (surname):
Closing:	Sincerely yours,

HEADS OF CONGRESSIONAL AGENCIES

Librarian of Congress

Address:	The Honorable (full name) Librarian of Congress Library of Congress 101 Independence Avenue Washington, DC 20540
Salutation:	Dear Mr. (surname):
Closing:	Sincerely yours,

Comptroller General

Address:	The Honorable (full name) Comptroller General of the United States General Accounting Office 441 G Street NW Washington, DC 20548
Salutation:	Dear Mr. (surname):
Closing:	Sincerely yours,

Public Printer

Address:	The Honorable (full name) Public Printer U.S. Government Printing Office North Capitol and H Streets NW Washington, DC 20401
Salutation:	Dear Mr. (surname):
Closing:	Sincerely yours,

EXECUTIVE DEPARTMENT OFFICIALS

Cabinet Secretaries

Address:	The Honorable (full name)

	Secretary of (name of department)
	Washington, DC
Salutation:	Dear Mr. Secretary:
Closing:	Sincerely yours,

Postmaster General

Address:	The Honorable (full name)
	Postmaster General
	Washington, DC
Salutation:	Dear Mr. Postmaster General:
Closing:	Sincerely yours,

Attorney General

Address:	The Honorable (full name)
	The Attorney General
	Constitution Avenue and 10th Street NW
	Washington, DC 20530
Salutation:	Dear Mr. Attorney General:
Closing:	Sincerely yours,

Under Secretary of a Cabinet-rank Department

Address:	The Honorable (full name)

		Under Secretary of (name of department) Washington, DC
Salutation:	Dear Mr.	(surname):
Closing:		Sincerely yours,

AMBASSADORS AND MINISTERS OF THE UNITED STATES

Ambassador

Address:		The Honorable (full name) Ambassador of the United States (city, country)
Salutation:	Formal:	Dear Mr. Ambassador:
	Informal:	Sir:
Closing:	Formal:	Very truly yours,
	Informal:	Sincerely yours,
In conversation:		Mr. Ambassador *or* Sir

Chargé d'Affaires, Consul General, Consul, or Vice Consul

Address:		(Full name), Esq. (Title) (City, country)
Salutation:	Formal:	Sir:
	Informal:	Dear Mr. (surname):

Closing: Formal: Very truly yours,
Informal: Sincerely yours,

FOREIGN AMBASSADORS AND MINISTERS

Ambassador

Address: His Excellency, (full name)
Ambassador of (country)
(Local address)

Salutation: Formal: Excellency:
Informal: Dear Mr. Ambassador:

Closing: Formal: Very truly yours,
Informal: Sincerely yours,

In conversation: Mr. Ambassador *or* Sir

Minister

Address: The Honorable (full name)
Minister of (country)
(Local address)

Salutation: Formal: Sir:
Informal: Dear Mr . Minister:

Closing: Formal: Very truly yours,
Informal: Sincerely yours,

In conversation: Mr. Minister *or* Sir

Foreign Chargé d'Affaires

Address: Mr. (full name)
Chargé d'Affaires of (country)

		(Local address)
Salutation:	Formal:	Sir:
	Informal:	Dear Mr. (surname):
Closing:	Formal:	Very truly yours,
	Informal:	Sincerely yours,
In conversation:		Sir *or* Mr. (surname)

UNITED NATIONS OFFICIALS

Secretary General

Address:		His Excellency, (full name) Secretary General of the United Nations New York, NY 10017
Salutation:	Formal:	Excellency:
	Informal:	Dear Mr. Secretary General:
Closing:	Formal:	Very truly yours,
	Informal:	Sincerely yours,

U.S. Representative with Rank of Ambassador

Address:		The Honorable (full name) United States Representative to the United Nations New York, NY 10017

Salutation:	Formal:	Sir:
	Informal:	Dear Mr. Ambassador:
Closing:	Formal:	Very truly yours,
	Informal:	Sincerely yours,

Foreign Representative with Rank of Ambassador

Address:		His Excellency, (full name) Representative of (country) to the United Nations New York, NY 10017
Salutation:	Formal:	Dear Mr. Ambassador:
	Informal:	Excellency:
Closing:	Formal:	Very truly yours,
	Informal:	Sincerely yours,

STATE AND LOCAL OFFICIALS

Governor of a State

Address:		The Honorable (full name) Governor of (state) (City, state)
Salutation:	Formal:	Sir:
	Informal:	Dear Governor (surname):

Closing:	Formal:	Respectfully yours,
	Informal:	Very sincerely yours,

Mayor of a City

Address:		The Honorable (full name) Mayor of (city) City Hall (City, state)
Salutation:		Dear Mayor (surname):
Closing:		Sincerely yours,

THE CLERGY

The Pope

Address:		His Holiness (full name) Vatican City
Salutation:		Your Holiness:
Closing:		Respectfully yours,
In conversation:		Your Holiness

Cardinal

Address		His Eminence (Christian name) Cardinal (surname) Archbishop of (city) (City, state)
Salutation:	Formal:	Your Eminence:

	Informal:	Dear Cardinal (surname):
Closing:	Formal:	Respectfully yours,
	Informal:	Sincerely yours,
In conversation:		Your Eminence

Archbishop

Address:		The Most Reverend (full name) Archbishop of (city) (City, state)
Salutation:	Formal:	Your Excellency:
	Informal:	Dear Archbishop (surname):
Closing:	Formal:	Respectfully yours,
	Informal:	Sincerely yours,
In conversation:		Your Excellency

Bishop

Address:		The Most Reverend (full name) Bishop of (diocese) (City, state)
Salutation:	Formal:	Your Excellency:
	Informal:	Dear Bishop (surname):
Closing:	Formal:	Respectfully yours,
	Informal:	Sincerely yours,
In conversation:		Your Excellency

Priest

Address:		The Reverend (full name, followed by initials of his order, if any) (Local address)
Salutation:		Dear Father (surname):
Closing:		Sincerely yours,

Protestant Bishop

Address:		The Right Reverend (full name) Bishop of (bishopric) (Local address)
Salutation:	Formal:	Right Reverend Sir:
	Informal:	Dear Bishop (surname):
Closing:	Formal:	Respectfully yours,
	Informal:	Sincerely yours,

Protestant Minister

Address:		The Reverend (full name) (Address of church) (City, state)
Salutation:	Formal:	Dear Sir:
	Informal:	Dear Dr. *or* Mister (surname):
Closing:		Sincerely yours,

Rabbi

Address:	Rabbi (full name) (Local address)
Salutation:	Dear Dr. *or* Rabbi (surname)
Closing:	Sincerely yours,

MILITARY OFFICERS

ARMY, AIR FORCE, MARINE CORPS

General, Brigadier General, Major General, Lieutenant General

Address:	(Full rank, full name) (Name of service) (Local address)
Salutation:	Dear General (surname):
Closing:	Sincerely yours,

Colonel, Lieutenant Colonel

Address:	(Same as above)
Salutation:	Dear Colonel:
Closing:	Sincerely yours,

Major, Captain, First Lieutenant, Second Lieutenant

Address:	(Same as above)
Salutation:	Dear (rank) (surname):
Closing:	Sincerely yours,

NAVY, COAST GUARD

Admiral, Vice Admiral, Rear Admiral

Address: (Full rank, full name)
(Name of service)
(Local service)
Salutation: Dear Admiral (surname):
Closing: Sincerely yours,

Commodore, Captain, Commander

Address: (Same as above)
Salutation: Dear (rank) (surname):
Closing: Sincerely yours,

All Other Ranks

Address: (Same as above)
Salutation: Dear Mr. (surname):
Closing: Sincerely yours,

CANADA

Prime Minister

Address: The Right Honorable (full name), P.C., M.P.
Prime Minister of Canada
Parliament Building
Ottawa, Ontario

Salutation:	Formal:	Sir *or* Dear Sir:
	Informal:	Dear Mr. Prime Minister: *or* Dear Mr. (surname):
Closing:	Formal:	Your Excellency's obedient servant,
	Informal:	Yours very sincerely,
In conversation:		Your Excellency

Cabinet Officer

Address:		The Honorable (full name), P.C., M.P. Minister of (department) Ottawa, Ontario
Salutation:	Formal:	Sir: *or* Dear Sir:
	Informal:	Dear Mr. (surname):
In conversation:		Sir *or* Mr. Minister

Member of Parliament

Address:		(Full name), Esq., M.P. House of Commons Ottawa, Ontario
Salutation:	Formal:	Dear Sir:
	Informal:	Dear Mr. (surname):
Closing:		Yours very sincerely,
In conversation:		Sir *or* Mr. (surname)

Mayor

Address:		His Worship The Mayor of (city) (Local address)
Salutation:	Formal:	Dear Sir:
	Informal:	Dear Mr. Mayor:
Closing:		Yours very sincerely,
In conversation:		Sir *or* Mr. Mayor

CHAPTER V

USEFUL REFERENCES

Common Abbreviations

a .... acre, ampere
AA .... author's alterations
A and M .... agricultural and mechanical
AAR .... against all risks
ab .... about
AB .... (L *artium baccalaureus*) bachelor of arts
abbr .... abbreviation
abr .... abridged
abs .... abstract
ac .... account
acad .... academy
ack .... acknowledgment
acpt .... acceptance
actg .... acting
AD .... anno Domini (often small capitals)
ad int .... ad interim
adj .... adjective, adjustment
adm .... administration
ADP .... automatic data processing
ad val .... ad valorem
advt .... advertisement

afft .... affidavit
AG .... attorney general
agt .... agent
AI .... ad interim
aka .... also known as
alw .... allowance
AM .... ante meridiem (often lowercase)
amb .... ambassador
amdt .... amendment
amp .... ampere
amt .... amount
anc .... ancient
anon .... anonymous
ans .... answer
ant .... antonym
AP .... additional premium, author's proof
APO .... army post office
app .... appendix
appl .... applied
appt .... appointment
apt .... apartment
AR .... accounts receivable, annual return
arr .... arrival
ASAP .... as soon as possible
asgmt .... assignment
assn .... association
assoc .... associate

asst .... assistant
at no .... atomic number
att .... attached, attention, attorney
attn .... attention
atty .... attorney
atty gen .... attorney general
at wt .... atomic weight
aux .... auxiliary
AV .... ad valorem, audiovisual
avdp .... avoirdupois
ave .... avenue
avg .... average
BA .... bachelor of arts
bal .... balance
bar .... barometric
bbl .... barrel, barrels
BC .... before Christ (often small capitals)
bd ft .... board foot
bet .... between
bf .... boldface
biog .... biography
bk .... bank, book
bkg .... banking, bookkeeping
bldg .... building
blvd .... boulevard
BO .... back order, box office
bor .... borough

BR .... bills receivable
bros .... brothers
BS .... bachelor of science, balance sheet, bill of sale
bu .... bureau, bushel
bus .... business
ca .... circa
CA .... chartered accountant, current account
CAD .... computer-aided design
CAI .... computer-aided instruction
canc .... canceled
cap .... capacity, capital, capitalize
caps .... capitals
cat .... catalog
CBI .... computer-based instruction
cc .... cubic centimeter
CC .... carbon copy
cent .... centigrade, century
CEO .... chief executive officer
cert .... certificate, certified
cf .... compare
CFO .... chief financial officer
chg .... change, charge
chm .... chairman
CI .... certificate of insurance

cld .... called, cleared
clk .... clerk
cml .... commercial
co .... company, county
c/o .... care of
COD .... cash on delivery
coll .... collateral
COLA .... cost of living adjustment
colloq .... colloquial
coml .... commercial
compd .... compound
conf .... conference, confidential
conj .... conjunction
consol .... consolidated
cp .... coupon
CPI .... consumer price index
CPM .... cost per thousand
cpu .... central processing unit
CS .... capital stock
ctf .... certificate
ctn .... carton
cu .... cubic
cum .... cumulative
cwt .... hundredweight
CY .... calendar year
dat .... dative
db .... debenture

DB .... daybook
d/b/a .... doing business as
deg .... degree
dely .... delivery
dept .... department
diam .... diameter
dict .... dictionary
dir .... director
dis .... discount
div .... dividend
do .... ditto
doc .... document
doz .... dozen
dup .... duplicate
DW .... deadweight
ea .... each
EEO .... equal employment opportunity
e.g. .... (L. *exempli gratia*) for example
elev .... elevation
emer .... emeritus
enc or encl ...... enclosure
env .... envelope
esp .... especially
est .... established, estimated
ETA .... estimated time of arrival
etc .... et cetera
ETD .... estimated time of departure

et seq .... (L. *et sequens*) and the following one
evg .... evening
ex .... example
exch .... exchange
exec .... executive
exp .... expense, express
fax .... facsimile
fcp .... foolscap
fed .... federation
FIFO .... first in, first out
fig .... figurative, figure
fin sec .... financial secretary
fn .... footnote
FOB .... free on board
freq .... frequency
front .... frontispiece
frt .... freight
ft .... feet, foot
fwd .... foreword, forward
FX .... foreign exchange
FYI .... for your information
gal .... gallon
GED .... general equivalency diploma
geog .... geographic
GIGO .... garbage in, garbage out
GMT .... Greenwich mean time
govt .... government

GPA .... grade point average
gram .... grammar
gro .... gross
gr wt .... gross weight
gtd .... guaranteed
hdbk .... handbook
hdwe .... hardware
hgt .... height
hon .... honorable, honorary
hor .... horizontal
hwy .... highway
i.e. .... (L. *id est)* that is
IG .... inspector general
illus .... illustrated
in .... inch
inc .... incorporated
incl .... including, inclusive
indef .... indefinite
inf .... infinitive
inq .... inquire
ins .... insurance
intl .... international
irreg .... irregular
ital .... italic
Jr .... junior
k .... karat
lang .... language

lat .... latitude
lb .... (L. *libra)* pound
lc .... lowercase
LCD .... least common denominator
LCL .... less-than-carload lot
ld .... load
lf .... lightface
LIFO .... last in, first out
liq .... liquid
lith .... lithographic
long .... longitude
ltd .... limited
lt gov .... lieutenant governor
let .... letter
lv .... leave
MA .... (L. *magister artium)* master of arts
mag .... magazine, magnitude
man .... manual
masc .... masculine
max .... maximum
mdse .... merchandise
mech .... mechanical
mfd .... manufactured
mfg .... manufacturing
MFN .... most favored nation
mfr .... manufacturer
mgr .... manager

mi .... mile
min .... minute
misc .... miscellaneous
mktg .... marketing
MLS .... master of library science
Mme .... (F) madame
MO .... mail order, money order
mpg .... miles per gallon
mph .... miles per hour
MS .... manuscript
msg .... message
MSW .... master of social work
mtge .... mortgage
NA .... no account, not applicable, not available
natl .... national
naut .... nautical
NC .... no charge, no credit
neg .... negative
neut .... neuter
NMI .... no middle initial
nom .... nominative
non seq .... non sequitur
num .... numeral
obj .... object
off .... office, officer
OJT .... on-the-job training

opp .... opposite
org .... organization
orig .... original
oz .... ounce, ounces
p .... page
pam .... pamphlet
p and g .... postage and handling
P and L .... profit and loss
par .... paragraph
pat .... patent
payt .... payment
PBX .... private branch exchange
PC .... percent, percentage, personal computer
pd .... paid
PD .... per diem
PE .... printer's error
P/E .... price/earnings
perm .... permanent
pert .... pertaining
pfd .... preferred
pg .... page
pkg .... package
pkwy .... parkway
PM .... post meridiem (often lowercase)
pmk .... postmark
PN .... promissory note

PO .... post office, purchase order
pp .... pages
PP .... parcel post, postpaid, prepaid
ppd .... postpaid, prepaid
pr .... pair, price
PR .... payroll
pref .... preface, preferred
prem .... premium
pres .... present, president
prev .... previously
prf .... proof
prin .... principal
prod .... product, production
prop .... property
PS .... postscript
ptg .... printing
PUD .... pickup and delivery
qty .... quantity
qual .... quality
R .... registered trademark
RAM .... random access memory
R & D .... research and development
rd .... road
rec .... receipt, record
recd .... received
ref .... reference, refund
regd .... registered

rept ....report
reqd ....required
resp ....respective
rev ....revenue, revised
ROI ....return on investment
ROM ....read only memory
RSVP ....(F *repondez s'il vous plait)* please reply
rte ....route
rtw ....ready-to-wear
RV ....recreational vehicle
rwy ....railway
SAE ....self-addressed envelope
SASE ....self-addressed stamped envelope
SC ....small capitals
SRD ....special drawing rights
secy ....secretary
ser ....serial, series
sgd ....signed
shpt ....shipment
shtg ....shortage
SOP ....standard operating procedure
ST ....short ton
std ....standard
stk ....stock
supt ....superintendent
svgs ....savings

sym .... symbol
syn .... synonym
syst .... system
TBA .... to be announced (often lowercase)
tech .... technical
temp .... temperature
terr .... territory
tfr .... transfer
tkt .... ticket
TM .... trademark
TO .... table of organization
tpk .... turnpike
treas .... treasurer, treasury
twp .... township
ugt .... urgent
unan .... unanimous
usu .... usual, usually
UW .... underwriter
val .... value
VAT .... value-added tax
VDT .... video display terminal
VDU .... visual display unit
VHF .... very high frequency
VLF .... very low frequency
vocab .... vocabulary
vou .... voucher
vv .... vice versa

WATS .... Wide-Area Telecommunications Service
WB .... waybill
WC .... without charge
whse .... warehouse
whsle .... wholesale
wi .... when issued
w/o .... without
WPM .... words per minute
XC or xcp .... ex coupon
XD or x div .... ex dividend
XR .... ex rights
XW .... ex warrants

POSTAL INFORMATION

The U.S. Postal Service offers many and varied mail services. Rates for these services are subject to change. Rates are proposed by the Postal Service and reviewed and approved by the Postal Rate Commission. The principal classes of mail are as follows:

First Class

This service includes letters and other material that is sealed and may not be inspected. First-class mail that weighs more than 11 ounces may be sent as Priority Mail (see below). In addition to letters, first-class mail covers postal cards, postcards, and all other written matter except book manuscripts, magazine articles, music, and manuscript copy with galley proofs.

Express Mail

This service is available for any mailable article up to 70 pounds. Next-day delivery between major U.S. cities is guaranteed or fee is refunded. Time of delivery depends on distance of destination. Second-day delivery is offered for destinations not on the Next Day Delivery Network. In most cities, special street mailboxes are provided for Express Mail. Pick-up service is also available for a nominal additional charge.

Third Class

This service covers packages up to but not including 16 ounces in weight. Materials include publications, small parcels, printed matter, booklets, and catalogs.

Fourth Class-Parcel Post

This service for material weighing 16 ounces and over covers merchandise and printed matter of all types. Packages may be sealed, subject to inspection. Rates are set according to zone.

Priority Mail

This service provides the most expeditious handling and transportation available. Parcels weighing up to 70 pounds and not exceeding 108 inches in length and girth combined are accepted, including written and other material, sealed or unsealed. Rates vary according to zone. See also First Class, above.

SPECIAL DOMESTIC SERVICES

Special Handling

This service is available for third-class and fourth-class parcels at a fee in addition to the postage. Parcels are transported as expeditiously as possible, but not by special delivery.

Special Delivery

This service is available at an additional fee for all classes of mail. The material is delivered immediately upon receipt at the post office.

Registered Mail

This service is available only for first-class items. It provides evidence of mailing. For a further fee it offers evidence of receipt and delivery only to the addressee. Registered mail is useful for mailing such items as deeds, bonds, or stock certificates; money, and jewelry. The value of the item must be declared at time of mailing.

Certification

This service is available for first-class mail having no intrinsic value. A receipt is furnished on mailing, and evidence of delivery is supplied.

Insurance

Coverage is available on third-class and fourth-class mail. Rates vary according to declared value of the parcel, up to a limit of $500. To quality for insurance, first-class and priority mail must be registered.

Private Mail Services

Private transfer services are currently in wide use. Delivery is available overnight, second day, and third day. Material ranging from letters to large packages is accepted. Among the best known are Federal Express, United Parcel Service (UPS), DHL Worldwide Courier Express, and TNT Skypak. Local outlets for these and other services can be found in the Yellow pages telephone directory. Messenger service of various types is widely available. Services include individual pick-up and delivery within the city and between cities and towns in metropolitan areas. These firms also are listed in the Yellow Pages.

STATE ABBREVIATIONS

The following abbreviations for states of the U.S. are approved by the Postal Service. They are intended for use only in addresses on envelopes or other mailing labels. They should not be used as abbreviations in other contexts. In text, for instance, the abbreviation for California should be Calif., not CA.

Alabama .... AL
Alaska .... AK
American Samoa .... AS
Arizona .... AZ
Arkansas .... AR
California .... CA
Canal Zone .... CZ
Colorado .... CO
Connecticut .... CT

Delaware .... DE
District of Columbia .... DC
Florida .... FL
Georgia .... GA
Guam .... GU
Hawaii .... HI
Idaho .... ID
Illinois IL
Indiana .... IN
Iowa .... IA
Kansas .... KS
Kentucky .... KY
Louisiana .... LA
Maine .... ME
Maryland .... MD
Massachusetts .... MA
Michigan .... MI
Minnesota .... MN
Missouri .... MO
Mississippi .... MS
Montana .... MT
Nebraska .... NE
Nevada .... NV
New Hampshire .... NH
New Jersey .... NJ
New Mexico .... NM
New York .... NY

North Carolina .... NC
North Dakota .... ND
Northern Mariana Islands .... MP
Ohio .... OH
Oklahoma .... OK
Oregon .... OR
Pennsylvania .... PA
Puerto Rico .... PR
Rhode Island .... RI
South Carolina .... SC
South Dakota .... SD
Tennessee .... TN
Texas .... TX
Trust Territories .... TT
Utah .... UT
Vermont .... VT
Virginia .... VA
Virgin Islands VI
Washington .... WA
West Virginia .... WV
Wisconsin .... WI
Wyoming .... WY

PERPETUAL CALENDAR

Choose the year you want in the key. The number opposite the year is the number of the calendar to use for that year:

Year	Calendar	Year	Calendar	Year	Calendar
1776	9	1799	3	1822	3
1777	4	1800	4	1823	4
1778	5	1801	5	1824	12
1779	6	1802	6	1825	7
1780	14	1803	7	1826	1
1781	2	1804	8	1827	2
1782	3	1805	3	1828	10
1783	4	1806	4	1829	5
1784	12	1807	5	1830	6
1785	7	1808	13	1831	7
1786	1	1809	1	1832	8
1787	2	1810	2	1833	3
1788	10	1811	3	1834	4
1789	5	1812	11	1835	5
1790	6	1813	6	1836	13
1791	7	1814	7	1837	1
1792	8	1815	1	1838	2
1793	3	1816	9	1839	3
1794	4	1817	4	1840	11
1795	5	1818	5	1841	6
1796	13	1819	6	1842	7
1797	1	1820	14	1843	1
1798	2	1821	2	1844	9

1845 4
1846 5
1847 6
1848 14
1849 2
1850 3
1851 4
1852 12
1853 7
1854 1
1855 2
1856 10
1857 5
1858 6
1859 7
1860 8
1861 3
1862 4
1863 5
1864 13
1865 1
1866 2
1867 3
1868 11
1869 6
1870 7
1871 1
1872 9
1873 4
1874 5
1875 6
1876 14
1877 2
1878 3
1879 4
1880 12
1881 7
1882 1
1883 2
1884 10
1885 5
1886 6
1887 7
1888 8
1889 3
1890 4
1891 5
1892 13
1893 1
1894 2
1895 3
1896 11
1897 6
1898 7
1899 1
1900 2
1901 3
1902 4
1903 5
1904 13
1905 1
1906 2
1907 3
1908 11
1909 6
1910 7
1911 1
1912 9
1912 9
1913 4
1914 5
1915 6
1916 14
1917 2
1918 3
1919 4
1920 12
1921 7
1922 1
1923 2
1924 10
1925 5
1926 6
1927 7

Year	Number	Year	Number	Year	Number
1928	8	1956	8	1984	8
1929	3	1957	3	1985	3
1930	4	1958	4	1986	4
1931	5	1959	5	1987	5
1932	13	1960	13	1988	13
1933	1	1961	1	1989	1
1934	2	1962	2	1990	2
1935	3	1963	3	1991	3
1936	11	1964	11	1992	11
1937	6	1965	6	1993	6
1938	7	1966	7	1994	7
1939	1	1967	1	1995	1
1940	9	1968	9	1996	9
1941	4	1969	4	1997	4
1942	5	1970	5	1998	5
1943	6	1971	6	1999	6
1944	14	1972	14	2000	14
1945	2	1973	2	2001	2
1946	3	1974	3	2003	4
1947	4	1975	4	2005	7
1948	12	1976	12	2006	1
1949	7	1977	7	2007	2
1950	1	1978	1	2008	10
1951	2	1979	2	2009	5
1952	10	1980	10	2010	6
1953	5	1981	5	2011	7
1954	6	1982	6	2012	8
1955	7	1983	7	2013	3

2014 4
2015 5
2016 13
2017 1
2018 2
2019 3
2020 11
2021 6
2022 7
2023 1
2024 9
2025 4
2026 5
2027 6
2028 14
2029 2
2030 3
2031 4
2032 12
2033 7
2034 1
2035 2
2036 10
2037 5
2038 6
2039 7
2040 8
2041 3
2042 4
2043 5
2044 13
2045 1
2046 2
2047 3
2048 11
2049 6
2050 7
2051 1
2052 9
2053 4
2054 5
2055 6
2057 2
2058 3
2059 4
2060 12
2061 7
2062 1
2063 2
2064 10
2065 5
2066 6
2067 7
2068 8
2069 3
2070 4
2071 5
2072 13
2073 1
2074 2
2075 3
2076 11
2077 6
2078 7
2079 1
2080 9
2081 4
2082 5
2083 6
2084 14
2085 2
2086 3
2087 4
2088 12
2089 7
2090 1
2091 4
2092 10
2093 5
2094 6
2095 7
2096 8
2097 3
2098 4
2099 5
2100 13

1

JANUARY

S	M	T	W	T	F	S
1	2	3	4	5	6	7
8	9	10	11	12	13	14
15	16	17	18	19	20	21
22	23	24	25	26	27	28
29	30	31				

FEBRUARY

S	M	T	W	T	F	S
			1	2	3	4
5	6	7	8	9	10	11
12	13	14	15	16	17	18
19	20	21	22	23	24	25
26	27	28				

MARCH

S	M	T	W	T	F	S
			1	2	3	4
5	6	7	8	9	10	11
12	13	14	15	16	17	18
19	20	21	22	23	24	25
26	27	28	29	30	31	

APRIL

S	M	T	W	T	F	S
						1
2	3	4	5	6	7	8
9	10	11	12	13	14	15
16	17	18	19	20	21	22
23	24	25	26	27	28	29
30						

MAY

S	M	T	W	T	F	S
	1	2	3	4	5	6
7	8	9	10	11	12	13
14	15	16	17	18	19	20
21	22	23	24	25	26	27
28	29	30	31			

JUNE

S	M	T	W	T	F	S
				1	2	3
4	5	6	7	8	9	10
11	12	13	14	15	16	17
18	19	20	21	22	23	24
25	26	27	28	29	30	

JULY

S	M	T	W	T	F	S
						1
2	3	4	5	6	7	8
9	10	11	12	13	14	15
16	17	18	19	20	21	22
23	24	25	26	27	28	29
30	31					

AUGUST

S	M	T	W	T	F	S
		1	2	3	4	5
6	7	8	9	10	11	12
13	14	15	16	17	18	19
20	21	22	23	24	25	26
27	28	29	30	31		

SEPTEMBER

S	M	T	W	T	F	S
					1	2
3	4	5	6	7	8	9
10	11	12	13	14	15	16
17	18	19	20	21	22	23
24	25	26	27	28	29	30

OCTOBER

S	M	T	W	T	F	S
1	2	3	4	5	6	7
8	9	10	11	12	13	14
15	16	17	18	19	20	21
22	23	24	25	26	27	28
29	30	31				

NOVEMBER

S	M	T	W	T	F	S
			1	2	3	4
5	6	7	8	9	10	11
12	13	14	15	16	17	18
19	20	21	22	23	24	25
26	27	28	29	30		

DECEMBER

S	M	T	W	T	F	S
					1	2
3	4	5	6	7	8	9
10	11	12	13	14	15	16
17	18	19	20	21	22	23
24	25	26	27	28	29	30
31						

2

JANUARY

S	M	T	W	T	F	S
	1	2	3	4	5	6
7	8	9	10	11	12	13
14	15	16	17	18	19	20
21	22	23	24	25	26	27
28	29	30	31			

FEBRUARY

S	M	T	W	T	F	S
				1	2	3
4	5	6	7	8	9	10
11	12	13	14	15	16	17
18	19	20	21	22	23	24
25	26	27	28			

MARCH

S	M	T	W	T	F	S
				1	2	3
4	5	6	7	8	9	10
11	12	13	14	15	16	17
18	19	20	21	22	23	24
25	26	27	28	29	30	31

APRIL

S	M	T	W	T	F	S
1	2	3	4	5	6	7
8	9	10	11	12	13	14
15	16	17	18	19	20	21
22	23	24	25	26	27	28
29	30					

MAY

S	M	T	W	T	F	S
		1	2	3	4	5
6	7	8	9	10	11	12
13	14	15	16	17	18	19
20	21	22	23	24	25	26
27	28	29	30	31		

JUNE

S	M	T	W	T	F	S
					1	2
3	4	5	6	7	8	9
10	11	12	13	14	15	16
17	18	19	20	21	22	23
24	25	26	27	28	29	30

JULY

S	M	T	W	T	F	S
1	2	3	4	5	6	7
8	9	10	11	12	13	14
15	16	17	18	19	20	21
22	23	24	25	26	27	28
29	30	31				

AUGUST

S	M	T	W	T	F	S
			1	2	3	4
5	6	7	8	9	10	11
12	13	14	15	16	17	18
19	20	21	22	23	24	25
26	27	28	29	30	31	

SEPTEMBER

S	M	T	W	T	F	S
						1
2	3	4	5	6	7	8
9	10	11	12	13	14	15
16	17	18	19	20	21	22
23	24	25	26	27	28	29
30						

OCTOBER

S	M	T	W	T	F	S
	1	2	3	4	5	6
7	8	9	10	11	12	13
14	15	16	17	18	19	20
21	22	23	24	25	26	27
28	29	30	31			

NOVEMBER

S	M	T	W	T	F	S
				1	2	3
4	5	6	7	8	9	10
11	12	13	14	15	16	17
18	19	20	21	22	23	24
25	26	27	28	29	30	

DECEMBER

S	M	T	W	T	F	S
						1
2	3	4	5	6	7	8
9	10	11	12	13	14	15
16	17	18	19	20	21	22
23	24	25	26	27	28	29
30	31					

3

JANUARY

S	M	T	W	T	F	S
		1	2	3	4	5
6	7	8	9	10	11	12
13	14	15	16	17	18	19
20	21	22	23	24	25	26
27	28	29	30	31		

FEBRUARY

S	M	T	W	T	F	S
					1	2
3	4	5	6	7	8	9
10	11	12	13	14	15	16
17	18	19	20	21	22	23
24	25	26	27	28		

MARCH

S	M	T	W	T	F	S
					1	2
3	4	5	6	7	8	9
10	11	12	13	14	15	16
17	18	19	20	21	22	23
24	25	26	27	28	29	30
31						

APRIL

S	M	T	W	T	F	S
	1	2	3	4	5	6
7	8	9	10	11	12	13
14	15	16	17	18	19	20
21	22	23	24	25	26	27
28	29	30				

MAY

S	M	T	W	T	F	S
			1	2	3	4
5	6	7	8	9	10	11
12	13	14	15	16	17	18
19	20	21	22	23	24	25
26	27	28	29	30	31	

JUNE

S	M	T	W	T	F	S
						1
2	3	4	5	6	7	8
9	10	11	12	12	14	15
16	17	18	19	20	21	22
23	24	25	26	27	28	29
30						

JULY

S	M	T	W	T	F	S
	1	2	3	4	5	6
7	8	9	10	11	12	13
14	15	16	17	18	19	20
21	22	23	24	25	26	27
28	29	30	31			

AUGUST

S	M	T	W	T	F	S
				1	2	3
4	5	6	7	8	9	10
11	12	13	14	15	16	17
18	19	20	21	22	23	24
25	26	27	28	29	30	31

SEPTEMBER

S	M	T	W	T	F	S
1	2	3	4	5	6	7
8	9	10	11	12	13	14
15	16	17	18	19	20	21
22	23	24	25	26	27	28
29	30					

OCTOBER

S	M	T	W	T	F	S
		1	2	3	4	5
6	7	8	9	10	11	12
13	14	15	16	17	18	19
20	21	22	23	24	25	26
27	28	29	30	31		

NOVEMBER

S	M	T	W	T	F	S
					1	2
3	4	5	6	7	8	9
10	11	12	13	14	15	16
17	18	19	20	21	22	23
24	25	26	27	28	29	30

DECEMBER

S	M	T	W	T	F	S
1	2	3	4	5	6	7
8	9	10	11	12	13	14
15	16	17	18	19	20	21
22	23	24	25	26	27	28
29	30	31				

4

JANUARY

S	M	T	W	T	F	S
			1	2	3	4
5	6	7	8	9	10	11
12	13	14	15	16	17	18
19	20	21	22	23	24	25
26	27	28	29	30	31	

FEBRUARY

S	M	T	W	T	F	S
						1
2	3	4	5	6	7	8
9	10	11	12	12	14	15
16	17	18	19	20	21	22
23	24	25	26	27	28	

MARCH

S	M	T	W	T	F	S
						1
2	3	4	5	6	7	8
9	10	11	12	12	14	15
16	17	18	19	20	21	22
23	24	25	26	27	28	29
30	31					

APRIL

S	M	T	W	T	F	S
		1	2	3	4	5
6	7	8	9	10	11	12
13	14	15	16	17	18	19
20	21	22	23	24	25	26
27	28	29	30			

MAY

S	M	T	W	T	F	S
				1	2	3
4	5	6	7	8	9	10
11	12	13	14	15	16	17
18	19	20	21	22	23	24
25	26	27	28	29	30	31

JUNE

S	M	T	W	T	F	S
1	2	3	4	5	6	7
8	9	10	11	12	13	14
15	16	17	18	19	20	21
22	23	24	25	26	27	28
29	30					

JULY

S	M	T	W	T	F	S
		1	2	3	4	5
6	7	8	9	10	11	12
13	14	15	16	17	18	19
20	21	22	23	24	25	26
27	28	29	30	31		

AUGUST

S	M	T	W	T	F	S
					1	2
3	4	5	6	7	8	9
10	11	12	13	14	15	16
17	18	19	20	21	22	23
24	25	26	27	28	29	30
31						

SEPTEMBER

S	M	T	W	T	F	S
	1	2	3	4	5	6
7	8	9	10	11	12	13
14	15	16	17	18	19	20
21	22	23	24	25	26	27
28	29	30				

OCTOBER

S	M	T	W	T	F	S
			1	2	3	4
5	6	7	8	9	10	11
12	13	14	15	16	17	18
19	20	21	22	23	24	25
26	27	28	29	30	31	

NOVEMBER

S	M	T	W	T	F	S
						1
2	3	4	5	6	7	8
9	10	11	12	12	14	15
16	17	18	19	20	21	22
23	24	25	26	27	28	29
30						

DECEMBER

S	M	T	W	T	F	S
	1	2	3	4	5	6
7	8	9	10	11	12	13
14	15	16	17	18	19	20
21	22	23	24	25	26	27
28	29	30	31			

5

JANUARY

S	M	T	W	T	F	S
				1	2	3
4	5	6	7	8	9	10
11	12	13	14	15	16	17
18	19	20	21	22	23	24
25	26	27	28	29	30	31

FEBRUARY

S	M	T	W	T	F	S
1	2	3	4	5	6	7
8	9	10	11	12	13	14
15	16	17	18	19	20	21
16	17	18	19	20	21	22
22	23	24	25	26	27	28

MARCH

S	M	T	W	T	F	S
1	2	3	4	5	6	7
8	9	10	11	12	13	14
15	16	17	18	19	20	21
22	23	24	25	26	27	28
29	30	31				

APRIL

S	M	T	W	T	F	S
			1	2	3	4
5	6	7	8	9	10	11
12	13	14	15	16	17	18
19	20	21	22	23	24	25
26	27	28	29	30		

MAY

S	M	T	W	T	F	S
					1	2
3	4	5	6	7	8	9
10	11	12	13	14	15	16
17	18	19	20	21	22	23
24	25	26	27	28	29	30
31						

JUNE

S	M	T	W	T	F	S
	1	2	3	4	5	6
7	8	9	10	11	12	13
14	15	16	17	18	19	20
21	22	23	24	25	26	27
28	29	30				

JULY

S	M	T	W	T	F	S
			1	2	3	4
5	6	7	8	9	10	11
12	13	14	15	16	17	18
19	20	21	22	23	24	25
26	27	28	29	30	31	

AUGUST

S	M	T	W	T	F	S
						1
2	3	4	5	6	7	8
9	10	11	12	13	14	15
16	17	18	19	20	21	22
23	24	25	26	27	28	29
30	31					

SEPTEMBER

S	M	T	W	T	F	S
		1	2	3	4	5
6	7	8	9	10	11	12
13	14	15	16	17	18	19
20	21	22	23	24	25	26
27	28	29	30			

OCTOBER

S	M	T	W	T	F	S
				1	2	3
4	5	6	7	8	9	10
11	12	13	14	15	16	17
18	19	20	21	22	23	24
25	26	27	28	29	30	31

NOVEMBER

S	M	T	W	T	F	S
1	2	3	4	5	6	7
8	9	10	11	12	13	14
15	16	17	18	19	20	21
22	23	24	25	26	27	28
29	30					

DECEMBER

S	M	T	W	T	F	S
		1	2	3	4	5
6	7	8	9	10	11	12
13	14	15	16	17	18	19
20	21	22	23	24	25	26
27	28	29	30	31		

6

JANUARY

S	M	T	W	T	F	S
					1	2
3	4	5	6	7	8	9
10	11	12	13	14	15	16
17	18	19	20	21	22	23
24	25	26	27	28	29	30
31						

FEBRUARY

S	M	T	W	T	F	S
	1	2	3	4	5	6
7	8	9	10	11	12	13
14	15	16	17	18	19	20
21	22	23	24	25	26	27
28	29	30				

MARCH

S	M	T	W	T	F	S
	1	2	3	4	5	6
7	8	9	10	11	12	13
14	15	16	17	18	19	20
21	22	23	24	25	26	27
28	29	30	31			

APRIL

S	M	T	W	T	F	S
				1	2	3
4	5	6	7	8	9	10
11	12	13	14	15	16	17
18	19	20	21	22	23	24
25	26	27	28	29	30	

MAY

S	M	T	W	T	F	S
						1
2	3	4	5	6	7	8
9	10	11	12	13	14	15
16	17	18	19	20	21	22
23	24	25	26	27	28	29
30	31					

JUNE

S	M	T	W	T	F	S
		1	2	3	4	5
6	7	8	9	10	11	12
13	14	15	16	17	18	19
20	21	22	23	24	25	26
27	28	29	30			

JULY

S	M	T	W	T	F	S
				1	2	3
4	5	6	7	8	9	10
11	12	13	14	15	16	17
18	19	20	21	22	23	24
25	26	27	28	29	30	31

AUGUST

S	M	T	W	T	F	S
1	2	3	4	5	6	7
8	9	10	11	12	13	14
15	16	17	18	19	20	21
22	23	24	25	26	27	28
29	30	31				

SEPTEMBER

S	M	T	W	T	F	S
			1	2	3	4
5	6	7	8	9	10	11
12	13	14	15	16	17	18
19	20	21	22	23	24	25
26	27	28	29	30		

OCTOBER

S	M	T	W	T	F	S
					1	2
3	4	5	6	7	8	9
10	11	12	13	14	15	16
17	18	19	20	21	22	23
24	25	26	27	28	29	30
31						

NOVEMBER

S	M	T	W	T	F	S
	1	2	3	4	5	6
7	8	9	10	11	12	13
14	15	16	17	18	19	20
21	22	23	24	25	26	27
28	29	30				

DECEMBER

S	M	T	W	T	F	S
			1	2	3	4
5	6	7	8	9	10	11
12	13	14	15	16	17	18
19	20	21	22	23	24	25
26	27	28	29	30	31	

7

JANUARY

S	M	T	W	T	F	S
						1
2	3	4	5	6	7	8
9	10	11	12	13	14	15
16	17	18	19	20	21	22
23	24	25	26	27	28	29
30	31					

FEBRUARY

S	M	T	W	T	F	S
		1	2	3	4	5
6	7	8	9	10	11	12
13	14	15	16	17	18	19
20	21	22	23	24	25	26
27	28					

MARCH

S	M	T	W	T	F	S
		1	2	3	4	5
6	7	8	9	10	11	12
13	14	15	16	17	18	19
20	21	22	23	24	25	26
27	28	29	30	31		

APRIL

S	M	T	W	T	F	S
					1	2
3	4	5	6	7	8	9
10	11	12	13	14	15	16
17	18	19	20	21	22	23
24	25	26	27	28	29	30

MAY

S	M	T	W	T	F	S
1	2	3	4	5	6	7
8	9	10	11	12	13	14
15	16	17	18	19	20	21
22	23	24	25	26	27	28
29	30	31				

JUNE

S	M	T	W	T	F	S
			1	2	3	4
5	6	7	8	9	10	11
12	13	14	15	16	17	18
19	20	21	22	23	24	25
26	27	28	29	30		

JULY

S	M	T	W	T	F	S
					1	2
3	4	5	6	7	8	9
10	11	12	13	14	15	16
17	18	19	20	21	22	23
24	25	26	27	28	29	30
31						

AUGUST

S	M	T	W	T	F	S
	1	2	3	4	5	6
7	8	9	10	11	12	13
14	15	16	17	18	19	20
21	22	23	24	25	26	27
28	29	30	31			

SEPTEMBER

S	M	T	W	T	F	S
				1	2	3
4	5	6	7	8	9	10
11	12	13	14	15	16	17
18	19	20	21	22	23	24
25	26	27	28	29	30	

OCTOBER

S	M	T	W	T	F	S
						1
2	3	4	5	6	7	8
9	10	11	12	13	14	15
16	17	18	19	20	21	22
23	24	25	26	27	28	29
30	31					

NOVEMBER

S	M	T	W	T	F	S
		1	2	3	4	5
6	7	8	9	10	11	12
13	14	15	16	17	18	19
20	21	22	23	24	25	26
27	28	29	30			

DECEMBER

S	M	T	W	T	F	S
				1	2	3
4	5	6	7	8	9	10
11	12	13	14	15	16	17
18	19	20	21	22	23	24
25	26	27	28	29	30	31

8

JANUARY

S	M	T	W	T	F	S
1	2	3	4	5	6	7
8	9	10	11	12	13	14
15	16	17	18	19	20	21
22	23	24	25	26	27	28
29	30	31				

FEBRUARY

S	M	T	W	T	F	S
			1	2	3	4
5	6	7	8	9	10	11
12	13	14	15	16	17	18
19	20	21	22	23	24	25
26	27	28	29			

MARCH

S	M	T	W	T	F	S
				1	2	3
4	5	6	7	8	9	10
11	12	13	14	15	16	17
18	19	20	21	22	23	24
25	26	27	28	29	30	31

APRIL

S	M	T	W	T	F	S
1	2	3	4	5	6	7
8	9	10	11	12	13	14
15	16	17	18	19	20	21
22	23	24	25	26	27	28
29	30					

MAY

S	M	T	W	T	F	S
		1	2	3	4	5
6	7	8	9	10	11	12
13	14	15	16	17	18	19
20	21	22	23	24	25	26
27	28	29	30	31		

JUNE

S	M	T	W	T	F	S
					1	2
3	4	5	6	7	8	9
10	11	12	13	14	15	16
17	18	19	20	21	22	23
24	25	26	27	28	29	30

JULY

S	M	T	W	T	F	S
1	2	3	4	5	6	7
8	9	10	11	12	13	14
15	16	17	18	19	20	21
22	23	24	25	26	27	28
29	30	31				

AUGUST

S	M	T	W	T	F	S
			1	2	3	4
5	6	7	8	9	10	11
12	13	14	15	16	17	18
19	20	21	22	23	24	25
26	27	28	29	30	31	

SEPTEMBER

S	M	T	W	T	F	S
						1
2	3	4	5	6	7	8
9	10	11	12	13	14	15
16	17	18	19	20	21	22
23	24	25	26	27	28	29
30						

OCTOBER

S	M	T	W	T	F	S
	1	2	3	4	5	6
7	8	9	10	11	12	13
14	15	16	17	18	19	20
21	22	23	24	25	26	27
28	29	30	31			

NOVEMBER

S	M	T	W	T	F	S
				1	2	3
4	5	6	7	8	9	10
11	12	13	14	15	16	17
18	19	20	21	22	23	24
25	26	27	28	29	30	

DECEMBER

S	M	T	W	T	F	S
						1
2	3	4	5	6	7	8
9	10	11	12	13	14	15
16	17	18	19	20	21	22
23	24	25	26	27	28	29
30	31					

9

JANUARY

S	M	T	W	T	F	S
	1	2	3	4	5	6
7	8	9	10	11	12	13
14	15	16	17	18	19	20
21	22	23	24	25	26	27
28	29	30	31			

MAY

S	M	T	W	T	F	S
			1	2	3	4
5	6	7	8	9	10	11
12	13	14	15	16	17	18
19	20	21	22	23	24	25
26	27	28	29	30	31	

SEPTEMBER

S	M	T	W	T	F	S
1	2	3	4	5	6	7
8	9	10	11	12	13	14
15	16	17	18	19	20	21
22	23	24	25	26	27	28
29	30					

FEBRUARY

S	M	T	W	T	F	S
				1	2	3
4	5	6	7	8	9	10
11	12	13	14	15	16	17
18	19	20	21	22	23	24
25	26	27	28	29		

JUNE

S	M	T	W	T	F	S
						1
2	3	4	5	6	7	8
9	10	11	12	12	14	15
16	17	18	19	20	21	22
23	24	25	26	27	28	29
30						

OCTOBER

S	M	T	W	T	F	S
		1	2	3	4	5
6	7	8	9	10	11	12
13	14	15	16	17	18	19
20	21	22	23	24	25	26
27	28	29	30	31		

MARCH

S	M	T	W	T	F	S
					1	2
3	4	5	6	7	8	9
10	11	12	13	14	15	16
17	18	19	20	21	22	23
24	25	26	27	28	29	30
31						

JULY

S	M	T	W	T	F	S
	1	2	3	4	5	6
7	8	9	10	11	12	13
14	15	16	17	18	19	20
21	22	23	24	25	26	27
28	29	30	31			

NOVEMBER

S	M	T	W	T	F	S
					1	2
3	4	5	6	7	8	9
10	11	12	13	14	15	16
17	18	19	20	21	22	23
24	25	26	27	28	29	30

APRIL

S	M	T	W	T	F	S
	1	2	3	4	5	6
7	8	9	10	11	12	13
14	15	16	17	18	19	20
21	22	23	24	25	26	27
28	29	30				

AUGUST

S	M	T	W	T	F	S
				1	2	3
4	5	6	7	8	9	10
11	12	13	14	15	16	17
18	19	20	21	22	23	24
25	26	27	28	29	30	31

DECEMBER

S	M	T	W	T	F	S
1	2	3	4	5	6	7
8	9	10	11	12	13	14
15	16	17	18	19	20	21
22	23	24	25	26	27	28
29	30	31				

10

JANUARY

S	M	T	W	T	F	S
		1	2	3	4	5
6	7	8	9	10	11	12
13	14	15	16	17	18	19
20	21	22	23	24	25	26
27	28	29	30	31		

FEBRUARY

S	M	T	W	T	F	S
					1	2
3	4	5	6	7	8	9
10	11	12	13	14	15	16
17	18	19	20	21	22	23
24	25	26	27	28	29	

MARCH

S	M	T	W	T	F	S
						1
2	3	4	5	6	7	8
9	10	11	12	12	14	15
16	17	18	19	20	21	22
23	24	25	26	27	28	29
30	31					

APRIL

S	M	T	W	T	F	S
		1	2	3	4	5
6	7	8	9	10	11	12
13	14	15	16	17	18	19
20	21	22	23	24	25	26
27	28	29	30			

MAY

S	M	T	W	T	F	S
				1	2	3
4	5	6	7	8	9	10
11	12	13	14	15	16	17
18	19	20	21	22	23	24
25	26	27	28	29	30	31

JUNE

S	M	T	W	T	F	S
1	2	3	4	5	6	7
8	9	10	11	12	13	14
15	16	17	18	19	20	21
22	23	24	25	26	27	28
29	30					

JULY

S	M	T	W	T	F	S
		1	2	3	4	5
6	7	8	9	10	11	12
13	14	15	16	17	18	19
20	21	22	23	24	25	26
27	28	29	30	31		

AUGUST

S	M	T	W	T	F	S
					1	2
3	4	5	6	7	8	9
10	11	12	13	14	15	16
17	18	19	20	21	22	23
24	25	26	27	28	29	30
31						

SEPTEMBER

S	M	T	W	T	F	S
	1	2	3	4	5	6
7	8	9	10	11	12	13
14	15	16	17	18	19	20
21	22	23	24	25	26	27
28	29	30				

OCTOBER

S	M	T	W	T	F	S
			1	2	3	4
5	6	7	8	9	10	11
12	13	14	15	16	17	18
19	20	21	22	23	24	25
26	27	28	29	30	31	

NOVEMBER

S	M	T	W	T	F	S
						1
2	3	4	5	6	7	8
9	10	11	12	12	14	15
16	17	18	19	20	21	22
23	24	25	26	27	28	29
30						

DECEMBER

S	M	T	W	T	F	S
	1	2	3	4	5	6
7	8	9	10	11	12	13
14	15	16	17	18	19	20
21	22	23	24	25	26	27
28	29	30	31			

11

JANUARY

S	M	T	W	T	F	S
			1	2	3	4
5	6	7	8	9	10	11
12	13	14	15	16	17	18
19	20	21	22	23	24	25
26	27	28	29	30	31	

FEBRUARY

S	M	T	W	T	F	S
						1
2	3	4	5	6	7	8
9	10	11	12	13	14	15
16	17	18	19	20	21	22
23	24	25	26	27	28	29

MARCH

S	M	T	W	T	F	S
1	2	3	4	5	6	7
8	9	10	11	12	13	14
15	16	17	18	19	20	21
22	23	24	25	26	27	28
29	30	31				

APRIL

S	M	T	W	T	F	S
			1	2	3	4
5	6	7	8	9	10	11
12	13	14	15	16	17	18
19	20	21	22	23	24	25
26	27	28	29	30		

MAY

S	M	T	W	T	F	S
					1	2
3	4	5	6	7	8	9
10	11	12	13	14	15	16
17	18	19	20	21	22	23
24	25	26	27	28	29	30
31						

JUNE

S	M	T	W	T	F	S
	1	2	3	4	5	6
7	8	9	10	11	12	13
14	15	16	17	18	19	20
21	22	23	24	25	26	27
28	29	30				

JULY

S	M	T	W	T	F	S
			1	2	3	4
5	6	7	8	9	10	11
12	13	14	15	16	17	18
19	20	21	22	23	24	25
26	27	28	29	30	31	

AUGUST

S	M	T	W	T	F	S
						1
2	3	4	5	6	7	8
9	10	11	12	13	14	15
16	17	18	19	20	21	22
23	24	25	26	27	28	29
30	31					

SEPTEMBER

S	M	T	W	T	F	S
		1	2	3	4	5
6	7	8	9	10	11	12
13	14	15	16	17	18	19
20	21	22	23	24	25	26
27	28	29	30			

OCTOBER

S	M	T	W	T	F	S
				1	2	3
4	5	6	7	8	9	10
11	12	13	14	15	16	17
18	19	20	21	22	23	24
25	26	27	28	29	30	31

NOVEMBER

S	M	T	W	T	F	S
1	2	3	4	5	6	7
8	9	10	11	12	13	14
15	16	17	18	19	20	21
22	23	24	25	26	27	28
29	30					

DECEMBER

S	M	T	W	T	F	S
		1	2	3	4	5
6	7	8	9	10	11	12
13	14	15	16	17	18	19
20	21	22	23	24	25	26
27	28	29	30	31		

12

JANUARY

S	M	T	W	T	F	S
				1	2	3
4	5	6	7	8	9	10
11	12	13	14	15	16	17
18	19	20	21	22	23	24
25	26	27	28	29	30	31

MAY

S	M	T	W	T	F	S
						1
2	3	4	5	6	7	8
9	10	11	12	13	14	15
16	17	18	19	20	21	22
23	24	25	26	27	28	29
30	31					

SEPTEMBER

S	M	T	W	T	F	S
			1	2	3	4
5	6	7	8	9	10	11
12	13	14	15	16	17	18
19	20	21	22	23	24	25
26	27	28	29	30		

FEBRUARY

S	M	T	W	T	F	S
1	2	3	4	5	6	7
8	9	10	11	12	13	14
15	16	17	18	19	20	21
22	23	24	25	26	27	28
29						

JUNE

S	M	T	W	T	F	S
		1	2	3	4	5
6	7	8	9	10	11	12
13	14	15	16	17	18	19
20	21	22	23	24	25	26
27	28	29	30			

OCTOBER

S	M	T	W	T	F	S
					1	2
3	4	5	6	7	8	9
10	11	12	13	14	15	16
17	18	19	20	21	22	23
24	25	26	27	28	29	30
31						

MARCH

S	M	T	W	T	F	S
	1	2	3	4	5	6
7	8	9	10	11	12	13
14	15	16	17	18	19	20
21	22	23	24	25	26	27
28	29	30	31			

JULY

S	M	T	W	T	F	S
				1	2	3
4	5	6	7	8	9	10
11	12	13	14	15	16	17
18	19	20	21	22	23	24
25	26	27	28	29	30	31

NOVEMBER

S	M	T	W	T	F	S
	1	2	3	4	5	6
7	8	9	10	11	12	13
14	15	16	17	18	19	20
21	22	23	24	25	26	27
28	29	30				

APRIL

S	M	T	W	T	F	S
				1	2	3
4	5	6	7	8	9	10
11	12	13	14	15	16	17
18	19	20	21	22	23	24
25	26	27	28	29	30	

AUGUST

S	M	T	W	T	F	S
1	2	3	4	5	6	7
8	9	10	11	12	13	14
15	16	17	18	19	20	21
22	23	24	25	26	27	28
29	30	31				

DECEMBER

S	M	T	W	T	F	S
			1	2	3	4
5	6	7	8	9	10	11
12	13	14	15	16	17	18
19	20	21	22	23	24	25
26	27	28	29	30	31	

13

JANUARY

S	M	T	W	T	F	S
					1	2
3	4	5	6	7	8	9
10	11	12	13	14	15	16
17	18	19	20	21	22	23
24	25	26	27	28	29	30
31						

FEBRUARY

S	M	T	W	T	F	S
	1	2	3	4	5	6
7	8	9	10	11	12	13
14	15	16	17	18	19	20
21	22	23	24	25	26	27
28	29					

MARCH

S	M	T	W	T	F	S
		1	2	3	4	5
6	7	8	9	10	11	12
13	14	15	16	17	18	19
20	21	22	23	24	25	26
27	28	29	30	31		

APRIL

S	M	T	W	T	F	S
					1	2
3	4	5	6	7	8	9
10	11	12	13	14	15	16
17	18	19	20	21	22	23
24	25	26	27	28	29	30

MAY

S	M	T	W	T	F	S
1	2	3	4	5	6	7
8	9	10	11	12	13	14
15	16	17	18	19	20	21
22	23	24	25	26	27	28
29	30	31				

JUNE

S	M	T	W	T	F	S
			1	2	3	4
5	6	7	8	9	10	11
12	13	14	15	16	17	18
19	20	21	22	23	24	25
26	27	28	29	30		

JULY

S	M	T	W	T	F	S
					1	2
3	4	5	6	7	8	9
10	11	12	13	14	15	16
17	18	19	20	21	22	23
24	25	26	27	28	29	30
31						

AUGUST

S	M	T	W	T	F	S
	1	2	3	4	5	6
7	8	9	10	11	12	13
14	15	16	17	18	19	20
21	22	23	24	25	26	27
28	29	30	31			

SEPTEMBER

S	M	T	W	T	F	S
				1	2	3
4	5	6	7	8	9	10
11	12	13	14	15	16	17
18	19	20	21	22	23	24
25	26	27	28	29	30	

OCTOBER

S	M	T	W	T	F	S
						1
2	3	4	5	6	7	8
9	10	11	12	13	14	15
16	17	18	19	20	21	22
23	24	25	26	27	28	29
30	31					

NOVEMBER

S	M	T	W	T	F	S
		1	2	3	4	5
6	7	8	9	10	11	12
13	14	15	16	17	18	19
20	21	22	23	24	25	26
27	28	29	30			

DECEMBER

S	M	T	W	T	F	S
				1	2	3
4	5	6	7	8	9	10
11	12	13	14	15	16	17
18	19	20	21	22	23	24
25	26	27	28	29	30	31

14

JANUARY

S	M	T	W	T	F	S
						1
2	3	4	5	6	7	8
9	10	11	12	13	14	15
16	17	18	19	20	21	22
23	24	25	26	27	28	29
30	31					

FEBRUARY

S	M	T	W	T	F	S
		1	2	3	4	5
6	7	8	9	10	11	12
13	14	15	16	17	18	19
20	21	22	23	24	25	26
27	28	29				

MARCH

S	M	T	W	T	F	S
			1	2	3	4
5	6	7	8	9	10	11
12	13	14	15	16	17	18
19	20	21	22	23	24	25
26	27	28	29	30	31	

APRIL

S	M	T	W	T	F	S
						1
2	3	4	5	6	7	8
9	10	11	12	13	14	15
16	17	18	19	20	21	22
23	24	25	26	27	28	29
30						

MAY

S	M	T	W	T	F	S
	1	2	3	4	5	6
7	8	9	10	11	12	13
14	15	16	17	18	19	20
21	22	23	24	25	26	27
28	29	30	31			
30	31					

JUNE

S	M	T	W	T	F	S
				1	2	3
4	5	6	7	8	9	10
11	12	13	14	15	16	17
18	19	20	21	22	23	24
25	26	27	28	29	30	

JULY

S	M	T	W	T	F	S
						1
2	3	4	5	6	7	8
9	10	11	12	13	14	15
16	17	18	19	20	21	22
23	24	25	26	27	28	29
30	31					

AUGUST

S	M	T	W	T	F	S
		1	2	3	4	5
6	7	8	9	10	11	12
13	14	15	16	17	18	19
20	21	22	23	24	25	26
27	28	29	30	31		

SEPTEMBER

S	M	T	W	T	F	S
					1	2
3	4	5	6	7	8	9
10	11	12	13	14	15	16
17	18	19	20	21	22	23
24	25	26	27	28	29	30

OCTOBER

S	M	T	W	T	F	S
1	2	3	4	5	6	7
8	9	10	11	12	13	14
15	16	17	18	19	20	21
22	23	24	25	26	27	28
29	30	31				

NOVEMBER

S	M	T	W	T	F	S
			1	2	3	4
5	6	7	8	9	10	11
12	13	14	15	16	17	18
19	20	21	22	23	24	25
26	27	28	29	30		

DECEMBER

S	M	T	W	T	F	S
					1	2
3	4	5	6	7	8	9
10	11	12	13	14	15	16
17	18	19	20	21	22	23
24	25	26	27	28	29	30
31						

FOREIGN EXPRESSIONS

à bientôt (F), so long.
ab initio (L), from the beginning.
à bon marché (F), cheap; a bargain.
ab origine (L), from the origin; from the beginning.
ab ovo (L), from the egg; from the beginning.
ad aperturam (libri) (L), at the opening of the book; wherever the book opens.
ad extremum (L), to the last; extremity.
ad finem (L), to the end; at or near the end.
ad hominem (L), to the man; to one's interests.
ad infinitum (L), to infinity.
ad interim (L), in the meantime.
ad libitum (L), at pleasure; as long as you wish.
ad nauseam (L), to disgust.
ad rem (L), to the purpose; to the point.
à droite (F), to the right.
ad valorem (L), according to the value.
à gauche (F), to the left.
à la carte (F), according to the menu.
à la française (F), after the French style.
à la mode (F), according to the custom or fashion.
al fresco (I), in the open air.
alter ego (L), another self.

alter idem (L), another exactly alike.
amour propre (F), self-love; self-esteem.
ancient régime (F), former order of things.
anno Christi (L),in the year of Christ.
anno Domini (L), in the year of our Lord.
ante meridiem (L), before noon.
à peu près (F), nearly.
à pied (F), on foot.
à point (F), to a point; just in time.
arrière pensée (F), mental reservation.
arrivederci (I), so long.
Artium Magister (L), Master of Arts.
à toute force (F), with all one's might.
à tout prix (F), at any price; at all costs.
au contraire (F), on the contrary.
au courant (F), fully informed; up to date.
au fait (F), well acquainted with; expert.
au fond (F), at bottom; in reality.
auf Wiedersehen (G), till we meet again; so long.
au jour de jour (F), from day to day; from hand to mouth.
au naturel (F), in the natural state; nude.
au pis aller (F), at worst.
au revoir (F); till we meet again; so long.

avant-propos (F), preliminary matter; preface.

bête noire (F), black beast; bugaboo.
bêtise (F), stupidity.
bien entendu (F), well understood.
billet d'amour (F), loveletter.
bona fide (L), in good faith.
bona fides (L), good faith.
bon appetit (F), good appetite.
bon jour (F), good day.
bon soir (F), good evening.
bon vivant (F), one who lives well; gourmet.
bon voyage! (F), good journey; good trip.
breveté (F), patented.

cap à pié (F), from head to foot.
carpe diem (L), enjoy, or use, the present day.
carte d'idéntité (F), identity card.
casus belli (L), that which causes or justifies war.
causa sine qua non (L), an indispensable condition.
cause célèbre (F), celebrated case or matter.
caveat emptor (L), let the buyer beware.
cela va sans dire (F), that goes without saying; needless to say.

c'est à dire (F), that is to say.
chacun à son gout (F), everyone to his own taste.
comme ci, comme ca (F), like this, like that; so-so.
comme il faut (F), as it should be.
cordon bleu (F), blue-ribbon.
cordon sanitaire (F), quarantine.
coup de grâce (F), finishing stroke.
coup d'état (F), sudden, decisive blow.
crême de la crême (F), the very best.
cum grano salis (L), with a grain of salt.

de facto (L), actual; actually.
dei gratia (L), by the grace of God.
de jure (L), from the law; by right.
de luxe (F), unusually fine.
de mal en pis (F), from bad to worse.
dénouement (F), outcome; solution.
de novo (L), anew.
Deo volente (L), God willing.
de rigueur (F), indispensable.
de trop (F), too much.
double entendre (F), double meaning; play on words.
dramatis personae (L), characters in the play.

emeritus (L), retired with honor.
en ami (F), as a friend.
en avant (F), forward.
en effet (F), in effect; actually.
en famille (F) with one's family; at home.
enfin (F), in short; at last; finally.
en masse (F), in a mass; in a body.
en passant (F), in passing.
en rapport (F), in harmony; in agreement.
en route (F), on the way.
entourage (F), surroundings; attendants; associates.
entre nous (F), between us.
en vérité (F), in truth.
esprit de corps (F), feeling of unity; morale.
et cetera (L), and the rest.
excerpta (L), extracts.
exempli gratia (L), for example.
ex libris (L), from the books of (used in bookplates).
ex officio (L), by virtue of one's office.
exposé (F), statement; revelation.
ex post facto (L), after the fact; retrospective.

faire suivre (F), please forward.
fait accompli (F), a thing already done.

faux pas (F), false step, misbehavior.

gentilhomme (F), gentleman.
guten Tag (G), good day.

habitué (F), one who is in the habit of frequenting a place.
hasta la vista (S), so long.
hoi polloi (Gr), the many; the common people.
homme d'affaires (F), businessman.
homme de lettres (F), man of letters.
hors de combat (F), unable any longer to fight; defeated.
hors d'oeuvre (F), out of course; appetizer, or relish.

içi on parle Français (F), French is spoken here.
idée fixe (F), fixed idea.
id est (L), it is (used in abbreviation, *i.e.).*
impedimenta (L), baggage; luggage.
in camera (L), in the judge's chamber; in secret.
in esse (L), in actuality.
in extremis (L), at the point of death.
infra dignitatem (L), colloquially, *infra dig,* beneath one's dignity.
in loco parentis (L), in place of parents.

in medias res (L), in the midst of things.
in memoriam (L), in memory of.
in nomine (L), in the name of.
in perpetuum (L), forever.
in re (L), in the matter of.
in situ (L), in its original situation; in place.
inter alia (L), among other things.
inter nos (L), between us.
in toto (L), entirely.
ipse dixit (L), he himself said it; dogmatic statement.
ipso facto (L), by the fact itself.
ipso jure (L), by the law.

je ne sais quoi (F), I know not what; something or other.
je suis prêt (F), I am ready.
jeu de mots (F), play on words; pun.
jeu d'esprit (F), witticism.

lapsus linguae (L), slip of the tongue.
lares et penates (L), household gods.
l'argent (F), money.
lèse majesté (F), high treason.
le tout ensemble (F), the whole thing.

lettre de créance (F), letter of credit.
lex loci (L), the law of the place.
lingua franca, language used among speakers of other languages; universal language.

ma foi (F), indeed.
magnum opus (L), great work.
maître d'hôtel (F), steward.
mal à propos (F), ill-timed.
mal de mer (F), seasickness.
mal de tête (F), headache.
malentendu (F), misunderstanding; mistake.
mano a mano (S), hand to hand.
modus operandi (L), method of working.
mon ami (F), my friend.
mon cher (F, masc.), my dear.
née (F), born; having as maiden name.
ne plus ultra (L), nothing further; perfection.
n'est çe pas? (F), is it not so?
nicht wahr? (G), is it not so?
n'importe (F), it's no matter.
noblesse oblige (F), obligations of rank.
nolens volens (L), willing or unwilling.
nom de guerre (F), war name; assumed name.

nom de plume (F), pen name.
non compos mentis (L), not of sound mind.
non sequitur (L), it does not follow; incorrect conclusion.
nota bene (L), note well.
nuance (F), shade; subtle variation.

obiter dictum (L), a thing said by the way; passing remark.
oeuvres (F), works.

par avion (F), by airplane; used for airmail.
pardonnez-moi (F), pardon me.
par excellence (F), by way of excellence; superior.
par exemple (F), for example.
pari passu (L), equal; together.
parole d'honneur (F), word of honor.
parvenu (F), person of sudden wealth or position.
passé (F), out of date.
passe-partout (F), masterkey, passport.
pâté de fois gras (F), goose-liver paste.
pâtisserie (F), pastry; pastry shop.
patois (F), dialect.
penchant (F), strong liking.

per annum (L), per year.

per capita (L), by the head; for each person.

per centum (L), by the hundred.

per diem (L), by the day; daily.

per se (L), by, or in, itself.

peu-à-peu (F), little by little; by degrees.

pied-à-terre (F), temporary lodging place.

poco a poco (I), little by little.

poste restante (F), to be left at the post office until called for.

prima facie (L), on first sight; self-evident.

pro bono publico (L), for the good of the public.

pro et contra (L), for and against.

pro forma (L), for the sake of form.

pro rata (L), according to rate; proportionate.

protégé (F), one under the protection of another.

quand même (F), even though; nevertheless.

quid pro quo (L), one thing for another; for value received.

quien sabe? (S), who knows?

quod erat demonstrandum (L), which was to be proved; used in abbreviation, *q.e.d.*

quod vide (L), which see; see that reference; used in abbreviation, *q.v.*

raison d'être (F), reason for existence.

rapprochement (F), act of bringing together.

répondez s'il vous plait (F), reply, if you please; used in abbreviation *RSVP.*

résumé (F), summary or abstract; statement of one's experience.

sang-froid (F), coolness; poise.

sans pareil (F), without equal; superior.

savoir faire (F), knowing how to act; poise.

sic passim (L), so here and there throughout; so everywhere.

s'il vous plait (F), please.

sine die (L), without a day being set.

sine qua non (L), without which, not; indispensable.

sotto voce (I), in an undertone.

status quo (L), the state in which; the existing condition.

sub rosa (L), under the rose; secretly.

sui generis (L), of its own kind; unique.

table d'hôte (F), meal at a fixed price.

tant mieux (F), so much the better.

tant pis (F), so much the worse.

tempus fugit (L), time flies.
terra firma (L), solid earth; a secure foothold.
terra incognita (L), unknown or unexplored region.
tour de force (F), feat of strength or skill.
tout-à-fait (F), wholly, completely.
toute de même (F), all the same.
tout de suite (F), immediately.
tout le monde (F), the whole world.

una voce (L), unanimously.
und so weiter (G), and so forth.

via (L), by way of.
vice versa (L), the order being changed; conversely.
vis-à-vis (F), face to face.
viva voce (L), orally.
voilà tout (F), that's all.

ROMAN NUMERALS

Roman numerals are the system of numbering used by the ancient Romans. The system is based on capital letters, as follows: I (=1), V (=5), X (=10), L (=50), C (=100), D (=500), and M (=1,000). If a letter is followed immediately by one of equal or lesser value, the two values are added: XX=20. If a letter is followed by one of greater value, the first is subtracted from the second: IV=4. A bar over a letter multiplies it by 1,000: $\overline{\text{V}}$=5,000; $\overline{\text{M}}$=1,000,000.

Arabic Numeral	*Roman Numeral*	*Arabic Numeral*	*Roman Numeral*
1	I	18	XVIII
2	II	19	XIX
3	III	20	XX
4	IV	21	XXI
5	V	22	XXII
6	VI	23	XXIII
7	VII	24	XXIV
8	VIII	25	XXV
9	IX	26	XXVI
10	X	27	XXVII
11	XI	28	VVXIII
12	XII	29	XXIX
13	XIII	30	XXX
14	XIV	40	XL
15	XV	50	L
16	XVI	60	LX
17	XVII	70	LXX

Arabic Numeral	*Roman Numeral*	*Arabic Numeral*	*Roman Numeral*
80	LXXX	800	DCCC
90	XC	900	CM
100	C	1,000	M
200	CC	2,000	MM
300	CCC	5,000	$\overline{V}$
400	CD	10,000	$\overline{X}$
500	D	100,000	$\overline{C}$
600	DC	1,000,000	$\overline{M}$
700	DCC		

WEIGHTS AND MEASURES

Linear Measure

12 inches	=1 foot
3 feet	=1 yard
5 1/2 yards	=1 rod, pole, or perch=16 1/2 feet
40 rods	=1 furlong=220 yards=660 feet
8 furlongs	=1 statute mile=1,760 yards=5,280 feet
3 miles	=1 league=5,280 yards=15,840 feet
6,076.12 feet	=1 nautical, geographical, or sea mile

Area Measure

144 square inches	=1 square foot
9 square feet	=1 square yard=1,296 square inches
30 1/4 sq. yards	=1 square rod=272 1/4 square feet
160 square rods	=1 acre=4,840 square yards=43,560 square feet
640 acres	=1 square mile
1 mile square	=1 section of land
6 miles square	=1 township=36 sections=36 square miles

Cubic Measure

1,728 cubic inches	=1 cubic foot
27 cubic feet	=1 cubic yard

Gunter's or Surveyors' Chain Measure

7.92 inches	=1 link
100 links	=1 chain=4 rods=66 feet
80 chains	=1 statute mile=320 rods=5,280 feet

Liquid Measure

4 gills	=1 pint
2 pints	=1 quart
4 quarts	=1 gallon=8 pints=32 gills
16 fluid ounces	=1 pint

Apothecaries' Fluid Measure

60 minims	=1 fluid dram
8 fluid drams	=1 fluid ounce
16 fluid ounces	=1 pint=128 fluid drams
2 pints	=1 quart=32 fluid ounces= 256 fluid drams
4 quarts	=1 gallon=128 fluid ounces =1,024 fluid drams

Dry Measure

2 pints	=1 quart
8 quarts	=1 peck=16 pints
4 pecks	=1 bushel=32 quarts

Avoirdupois Weight

16 ounces	=1 pound
100 pounds	=1 hundredweight

20 hundredweights	=1 ton=2,000 pounds
112 pounds	=1 gross or long hundredweight
20 gross or long hundredweights	=1 gross or long ton=2,240 pounds

Troy Weight

The grain is the same in all three tables of weight (avoirdupois, troy, and apothecaries' weights).

24 grains	=1 pennyweight
20 pennyweights	=1 ounce troy=480 grains
12 ounces troy	=1 pound troy=240 pennyweights= 5,760 grains

Apothecaries' Weight

The grain is the same in all three tables of weight (avoirdupois, troy, and apothecaries' weights).

20 grains	=1 scruple
3 scruples	=1 dram apothecaries'=60 grains
8 drams apothecaries'	=1 ounce apothecaries'=24 scruples=480 grains
12 ounces apothecaries'	=1 pound apothecaries'=96 drams apothecaries'=288 scruples=5,760 grains

METRIC AND COMMON EQUIVALENTS

Equivalents involving decimals are, in most cases, rounded off to the third decimal place, except when they are exact.

Lengths

1 centimeter	= 0.3937 inch
1 chain (Gunter's or surveyors')	= 66 feet
1 chain (engineers')	= 100 feet
1 fathom	= 6 feet = 1.829 meters
1 foot	= 0.305 meter
1 furlong	= 660 feet
1 hand	= 4 inches
1 inch	= 2.540 centimeters (exactly)
1 kilometer	= 0.621 mile
1 league (land)	= 3 statute mile = 4.828 kilometers
1 meter	= 39.37 inches = 1.094 yards
1 mile (statute)	= 5,280 feet = 1.609 kilometers
1 mile (nautical)	= 1.852 kilometers (exactly) = 1.151 statute miles = 6,076.115 feet
1 yard	= 0.9144 meter (exactly)

Areas

1 acre	= 43,560 square feet = 0.405 hectare
1 hectare	= 10,000 square meters
1 centimeter	= 0.155 square inch

1 square meter	= 1.196 square yards
1 square mile	= 259.000 hectares

Volume

1 barrel liquid	= 31 to 42 gallons
1 barrel dry	= 3.281 bushels, struck measure
1 bushel U.S (struck measure)	= 2,150.42 cubic inches (exactly)
1 cord (fire wood)	= 128 cubic feet
1 cubic foot	= 7.481 gallons = 28.317 cubic decimeters
1 cubic meter	= 1.308 cubic yards
1 cubic yard	= 0.765 cubic meter
1 board foot	= 1 foot long, 1 foot wide, 1 inch thick
1 cup, measuring	= 8 fluid ounces = 1/2 liquid pint
1 gallon (U.S.)	= 3.785 liters = 0.833 British gallon
1 liter	= 1.07 liquid quarts = 0.908 dry quart
1 quart dry (U.S.)	= 1.101 liters = 0.969 British quart
1 quart liquid (U. S.)	= 0.946 liter = 0.833 British quart
1 tablespoon	= 3 teaspoons
1 teaspoon	= 1/3 tablespoon

Weights or Masses

1 carat	=200 milligrams
1 gram	=15.432 grains=0.035 ounce avoírdupois
1 hundredweight, gross or long	=112 pounds=50.802 kilograms
1 hundredweight, net or short	=100 pounds=45.359 kilograms
1 kilogram	=2.205 pounds
1 pound avoirdupois	=1.215 troy or apothecaries' pounds=453.59237 grams (exactly)
1 pound troy or apothecaries'	=0.823 avoirdupois pound=373.242 grams
1 ton, gross or long	=2,240 pounds=1.12 net tons (exactly)=1.016 metric tons
1 ton, metric	=2,204.622 pounds=0.984 gross ton=1.102 net tons
1 ton, net or short	=2,000 pounds=0.893 gross ton=0.907 metric ton

CONVERSION OF MEASUREMENTS

Boldface figures are exact; the others are given to seven significant figures.

UNITS OF LENGTH

To Convert from Centimeters:

To	*Multiply by*
Inches	0.393 700 8
Feet	0.032 808 40
Yards	0.010 936 13
Meters	**0.01**

To Convert from Meters

To	*Multiply by*
Inches	39.370 08
Feet	3.280 840
Yards	1.093 613
Miles	0.000 621 37
Millimeters	**1,000**
Centimeters	**.100**
Kilometers	**0.001**

To Convert from Inches

To	*Multiply by*
Feet	0.083 333 33
Yards	0.027 777 78
Centimeters	**2.54**
Meters	**0.025 4**

To Convert from Feet

To	*Multiply by*
Inches	**12**
Yards	0.333 333 3
Miles	0.000 189 39
Centimeters	**30.48**
Meters	**0.304 8**
Kilometers	**0.000 304 8**

To Convert from Yards

To	*Multiply by*
Inches	**36**
Feet	**3**
Miles	0.000 568 18
Centimeters	**91.44**
Meters	0.914 4

To Convert from Miles

To	*Multiply by*
Inches	**63,360**
Feet	**5,280**
Yards	**1,760**
Centimeters	**160,934.4**
Meters	**1,609.344**
Kilometers	**1.609 344**

UNITS OF MASS

To Convert from Grams

To	*Multiply by*
Grains	15.432 36
Avoirdupois drams	0.564 383 4
Avoirdupois ounces	0.035 273 96
Troy ounces	0.032 150 75
Troy pounds	0.002 679 23
Avoirdupois pound	0.002 204 62
Milligrams	**1,000**
Kilograms	**0.001**

To Convert from Avoirdupois Pounds

To	*Multiply by*
Grains	**7,000**
Avoirdupois drams	**256**
Avoirdupois ounces	**16**
Troy ounces	14.583 33
Troy pounds	1.215 278
Grams	**453.592 37**
Kilograms	**0.453 592 37**
Short hundredweights	**0.01**
Short tons	**0.000 5**
Long tons	**0.000 446 428 6**
Metric tons	**0.000 453 592 37**

To Convert from Kilograms

To	*Multiply by*
Grains	15,432.86

Avoirdupois grams	564.383 4
Avoirdupois ounces	35.273 96
Troy ounces	32.150 75
Troy pounds	2.679 229
Avoirdupois pounds	2.204 623
Grams	1,000
Short hundredweights	0.022 046 23
Short tons	0.001 102 31
Long tons	0.000 984 2
Metric tons	**0.001**

To Convert from Metric Tons

To	*Multiply by*
Avoirdupois pounds	2,204.623
Short hundredweights	22.046 23
Short tons	1.102 311 3
Long tons	0.984 206 5
Kilograms	**1,000**

To Convert from Grains

To	*Multiply by*
Avoirdupois drams	0.036 571 43
Avoirdupois ounces	0.002 285 71
Troy ounces	0.002 083 33
Troy pounds	0.000 173 61
Avoirdupois pounds	0.000 142 86
Milligrams	**64.798 91**
Grams	**0.064 798 91**
Kilograms	**0.000 064 798 91**

To Convert from Troy Ounces

To	*Multiply by*
Grains	**480**
Avoirdupois drams	17.554 29
Avoirdupois ounces	1.097 143
Troy pounds	0.083 333 3
Avoirdupois pounds	0.068 571 43
Grams	**31.103 476 8**

To Convert from Long Tons

To	*Multiply by*
Avoirdupois ounces	**35,840**
Avoirdupois pounds	**2,240**
Short hundredweights	**22.4**
Short tons	1.12
Kilograms	1,016.046 908 8
Metric tons	1.016 046 908 8

To Convert from Avoirdupois Ounces

To	*Multiply by*
Grains	**437.5**
Avoirdupois drams	**16**
Troy ounces	0.911 458 3
Troy pounds	0.075 954 86
Avoirdupois pounds	**0.062 5**
Grams	**28.349 523 125**
Kilograms	**0.028 349 523 125**

To Convert from Short Hundredweights

To	*Multiply by*
Avoirdupois pounds	**100**
Short tons	**0.05**
Long tons	0.444 642 86
Kilograms	**45.359 237**
Metric tons	**0.045 359 237**

To Convert from Short Tons

To	*Multiply by*
Avoirdupois pounds	**2,000**
Short hundredweights	**20**
Long tons	0.892 857 1
Kilograms	**907.184 74**
Metric tons	**0.907 184 74**

To Convert from Troy Pounds

To	*Multiply by*
Grains	**5,760**
Avoirdupois drams	210.651 4
Avoirdupois ounces	13.165 71
Troy ounces	**12**
Avoirdupois pounds	0.822 857 1
Grams	**373.241 721 6**

UNITS OF VOLUME, LIQUID MEASURE

To Convert from Milliliters

To	*Multiply by*
Minims	16.230 73

Liquid ounces	0.033 814 02
Gills	0.008 453 5
Liquid pints	0.002 113 4
Liquid quarts	0.001 056 7
Gallons	0.000 264 17
Cubic inches	0.061 023 74
Liters	**0.001**

To Convert from Cubic Meters

To	*Multiply by*
Gallons	264.172 05
Cubic inches	61,023.74
Cubic feet	35.314 67
Liters	**1,000**
Cubic yards	1.307 950 6

To Convert from Liters

To	*Multiply by*
Liquid ounces	33.814 02
Gills	8.453 506
Liquid pints	2.113 376
Liquid quarts	1.056 688
Gallons	0.264 172 05
Cubic inches	61.023 74
Cubic feet	0.035 314 67
Milliliters	**1,000**
Cubic meters	**0.001**
Cubic yards	0.001 307 95

To Convert from Minims

To	*Multiply by*
Liquid ounces	0.002 083 33
Gills	0.000 520 83
Milliliters	0.061 611 52
Cubic inches	0.003 759 77

To Convert from Liquid Pints

To	*Multiply by*
Minims	7,680
Liquid ounces	16
Gills	4
Liquid quarts	0.5
Gallons	0.125
Cubic Inches	28.875
Cubic feet	0.016 710 07
Milliliters	473.176 473
Liters	0.473 176 473

To Convert from Gills

To	*Multiply by*
Minims	1,920
Liquid ounces	4
Liquid pints	0.25
Liquid quarts	0.125
Gallons	0.031 25
Cubic inches	7.218 75
Cubic feet	0.004 177 517
Milliliters	118.294 118 25
Liters	0.118 294 118 25

To Convert from Liquid Ounces

To	*Multiply by*
Minims	**480**
Gills	**0.25**
Liquid pints	**0.062 5**
Liquid quarts	**0.031 25**
Gallons	**0.007 812 5**
Cubic inches	1.804 687 5
Cubic feet	0.001 044 38
Milliliters	29.573 53
Liters	0.029 573 53

To Convert from Cubic Inches

To	*Multiply by*
Minims	265.974 0
Liquid ounces	0.554 112 6
Gills	0.138 528 1
Liquid pints	0.034 632 03
Liquid quarts	0.017 316 02
Gallons	0.004 329 0
Cubic feet	0.000 578 7
Milliliters	**16.387 064**
Liters	**0.016 387 064**
Cubic meters	**0.000 016 387 064**
Cubic yards	0.000 021 43

To Convert from Liquid Quarts

To	*Multiply by*
Minims	**15,360**
Liquid ounces	**32**

Gills	**8**
Liquid pints	**2**
Gallons	**0.25**
Cubic inches	**57.75**
Cubic feet	0.033 420 14
Milliliters	**946.352 946**
Liters	**0.946 352 946**

To Convert from Cubic Feet

To	*Multiply by*
Liquid ounces	957.506 5
Gills	239.376 6
Liquid pints	59.844 16
Liquid quarts	29.922 08
Gallons	7.480 519
Cubic inches	**1,728**
Liters	**28.316 846 592**
Cubic meters	**0.028 316 846 592**
Cubic yards	0.037 037 04

To Convert from Cubic Yards

To	*Multiply by*
Gallons	201 972 0
Cubic inches	**46, 656**
Cubic feet	**27**
Liters	**746.554 857 984**
Cubic meters	**0.764 554 857 984**

To Convert from Gallons

To	*Multiply by*
Minims	**61,440**
Liquid ounces	**128**
Gills	**32**
Liquid pints	**8**
Liquid quarts	**4**
Cubic inches	**231**
Cubic feet	0.133 680 6
Milliliters	**3,785.411 784**
Liters	**3.785 411 784**
Cubic meters	**0.003 785 411 784**
Cubic yards	0.004 951 13

UNITS OF VOLUME, DRY MEASURE

To Convert from Liters

To	*Multiply by*
Dry pints	1.816 166
Dry quarts	0.908 082 98
Pecks	0.113 510 4
Bushels	0.028 377 59
Dekaliters	**0.1**

To Convert from Dekaliters

To	*Multiply by*
Dry pints	18.161 66
Dry quarts	9.080 829 8
Pecks	1.135 104
Bushels	0.283 775 9
Cubic inches	610.237 4
Cubic feet	0.353 146 7
Liters	**10**

To Convert from Cubic Meters

To	*Multiply by*
Pecks	113.510 4
Bushels	28.377 59

To Convert from Dry Pints

To	*Multiply by*
Dry quarts	**0.5**
Pecks	**0.062 5**
Bushels	**0.015 625**

Cubic inches	**33.600 312 5**
Cubic feet	0.019 444 63
Liters	0.550 610 47
Dekaliters	0.055 061 05

To Convert from Dry Quarts

To	*Multiply by*
Dry pints	**2**
Pecks	**0.125**
Bushels	**0.031 25**
Cubic inches	**67.200 625**
Cubic feet	0.038 889 25
Liters	1.101 221
Dekaliters	0.110 122 1

To Convert from Pecks

To	*Multiply by*
Dry pints	**16**
Dry quarts	**8**
Bushels	**0.25**
Cubic inches	**537.605**
Cubic feet	0.311 114
Liters	8.809 767 5
Dekaliters	0.880 976 75
Cubic meters	0.008 809 77
Cubic yards	0.011 522 74

To Convert from Bushels

To	*Multiply by*
Dry pints	**64**

Dry quarts	**32**
Pecks	**4**
Cubic inches	**2,150.42**
Cubic feet	1.244 456
Liters	35.239 07
Dekaliters	3.523 907
Cubic meters	0.035 239 07
Cubic yards	0.046 090 96

To Convert from Cubic Inches

To	*Multiply by*
Dry pints	0.029 761 6
Dry quarts	0.014 880 8
Pecks	0.001 860 10
Bushels	0.000 465 025

To Convert from Cubic Feet

To	*Multiply by*
Dry pints	51.428 09
Dry quarts	25.714 05
Pecks	3.214 256
Bushels	0.803 563 95

To Convert from Cubic Yards

To	*Multiply by*
Pecks	86.784 91
Bushels	21.696 227

UNITS OF AREA

To Convert from Square Centimeters

To	*Multiply by*
Square inches	0.155 000 3
Square feet	0.001 076 39
Square yards	0.000 119 599
Square meters	**0.0001**

To Convert from Square Meters

To	*Multiply by*
Square inches	1.550 003
Square feet	10.763 91
Square yards	1.195 990
Acres	0.000 247 105
Square centimeters	**10,000**
Hectares	**0.0001**

To Convert from Hectares

To	*Multiply by*
Square feet	107,639.1
Square yards	11,959.90
Acres	2.471 054
Square miles	0.003 861 02
Square meters	**10,000**

To Convert from Square Inches

To	*Multiply by*
Square feet	0.006 944 44
Square yards	0.000 771 605

Square centimeters	**6.451 6**
Square meters	**0.000 645 16**

To Convert from Square Feet

To	*Multiply by*
Square inches	**144**
Square yards	0.111 111 1
Acres	0.000 022 957
Square centimeters	**929.030 4**
Square meters	**0.092 903 04**

To Convert from Square Yards

To	*Multiply by*
Square inches	**1,296**
Square feet	**9**
Acres	0.000 206 611 6
Square miles	0.000 000 322 830 6
Square centimeters	**8,361.273 6**
Square meters	**0.836 127 36**
Hectares	**0.000 083 612 736**

To Convert from Acres

To	*Multiply by*
Square feet	**43,560**
Square yards	**4,840**
Square miles	**0.001 562 5**
Square meters	**4,046.856 422 4**
Hectares	**0.404 685 642 24**

To Convert from Square Miles

To	*Multiply by*
Square feet	**27,878,400**
Square yards	**3,097,600**
Acres	**640**
Square meters	**2,589,988.110 336**
Hectares	**258.998 811 033 6**

INTERNATIONAL COUNTRY AND CITY TELEPHONE CODES

When direct dialing countries outside the United States, it is necessary to dial 011 and then to use special codes that correspond to our own area codes. The following chart lists those codes for many countries. The boldface number following the country is the country code. The number following the city is the city code. The plus or minus number at the right is the number of hours ahead of or behind Eastern Standard Time. An asterisk indicates that no city code is required in that country.

Algeria* 213	+6
American Samoa* 684	-6
Andorra 33	+6
All points 628	
Argentina 54	+2
Buenos Aires 1	
Australia 61	+15
Melbourne 3	
Sydney 2	
Austria 43	+6
Vienna 1	
Bahrain* 973	+8

Belgium 32	+6
Brussels 2	
Ghent 91	
Belize* 501	-1
Bolivia 591	+1
Santa Cruz 33	
Brazil 55	+2
Brasilia 61	
Rio de Janeiro 21	
Cameroon* 237	+6
Chile 56	+1
Santiago 2	
Colombia 57	0
Bogota 1	
Costa Rica* 506	-1
Cyprus 357	+7
Czechoslovakia 42	+6
Prague 2	
Denmark 45	+6
Allborg 8	
Copenhagen 1 or 2	
Ecuador 593	0
Cuenca 7	
Quito 2	
Egypt 20	+7
Alexandria 3	

Port Said 66	
El Salvador* 503	-1
Ethiopia 251	+8
Addis Ababa 1	
Fiji* 679	+17
Finland* 679	+17
Helsinki 0	
France 33	+6
Marseilles 91	
Nice 93	
Paris 13, 14, or 18	
French	+1
Antilles* 596	
French Antilles*	+1
Guadeloupe 590	
French Polynesia * 689	-5
Gabon* 241	+6
Germany (former E.Germany) 37	+6
Berlin 2	
Germany (former W.Germany) 49	+6
Berlin 30	
Frankfurt 69	
Munich 89	
Greece 30	+7
Athens 1	
Rhodes 241	

Guam* 671	+15
Guatemala 502	-1
Guatemala City 2	
Antigua 9	
Guyana 592	+2
Georgetown 2	
Haiti 509	0
Port au Prince 1	
Honduras* 504	-1
Hong Kong 852	+13
Hong Kong 5	
Kowloon 3	
Hungary 36	+6
Budapest 1	
Iceland 354	+5
Akureyri 6	
Hafnarfjorour 1	
India 91	+10.5
Bombay 22	
New Delhi 11	
Indonesia 62	+12
Jakarta 21	
Iran 98	+8.5
Teheran 21	
Iraq 964	+8
Baghdad 1	

Ireland 353	+5
Dublin 1	
Galway 91	
Israel 972	+7
Haifa 4	
Jerusalem 2	
Tel Aviv 3	
Italy 39	+6
Florence 55	
Rome 6	
Venice 41	
Ivory Coast* 225	+5
Japan 81	+14
Tokyo 3	
Yokohama 45	
Jordan 962	+7
Amman 6	
Kenya 254	+8
Korea, Republic of 82	+14
Pusan 51	
Seoul 2	
Kuwait* 965	+8
Liberia* 231	+5
Libya 218	+7
Tripoli 21	

Country / City code	Time difference
Liechtenstein 41	+6
All points 75	
Luxembourg* 352	+6
Malawi 265	+7
Domasi 531	
Malaysia 60	+13
Kuala Lumpur 3	
Mexico 52	-1
Mexico City 5	
Tijuana 66	
Monaco 33	+6
All points 93	
Morocco 212	+5
Adadir 8	
Casablanca*	
Namibia 264	+7
Olympia 61	
Netherlands 31	+6
Amsterdam 20	
The Hague 70	
Netherlands Antilles 599	+1
Netherlands Antilles Aruba 297	+1
Aruba 8	

New Caledonia* 687	+16
New Zealand 64	+17
Auckland 9	
Wellington 4	
Nicaragua 505	-1
Managua 2	
Nigeria 234	+8
Lagos 1	
Norway 47	+6
Bergen 5	
Oslo 2	
Oman* 968	+9
Pakistan 92	+10
Islamabad 51	
Panama* 507	0
Papua New Guinea* 675	+15
Paraguay 595	+1
Asuncion 21	
Peru 51	0
Arequipa 54	
Lima 14	
Philippines 63	+13
Manila 2	
Poland 48	+6
Warsaw 22	

Portugal 351	+5
Lisbon 1	
Qatar* 974	+9
Romania 40	+7
Bucharest 0	
Saipan* 670	+15
San Marino 39	+6
All points 541	
Saudi Arabia 966	+8
Riyadh 1	
Senegal* 221	+5
Singapore 65	+13
South Africa 27	+7
Cape Town 21	
Pretoria 12	
Spain 34	+6
Barcelona 3	
Las Palmas (Canary Islands) 28	
Madrid 1	
Seville 54	
Sri Lanka 94	+10.5
Kandy 8	
Surinam* 597	+15
Sweden 46	+6
Goteborg 31	

Stockholm 8	
Switzerland 41	+6
Geneva 22	
Lucerne 41	
Zurich 1	
Taiwan 886	+13
Tainan 6	
Taipei 2	
Thailand 66	+12
Bangkok 2	
Tunisia 216	+6
Tunis 1	
Turkey 90	+8
Istanbul 1	
Izmir 51	
United Arab Emirates 971	+9
Abu Dhabi 2	
Dubai 4	
United Kingdom 44	+5
Belfast 232	
Cardiff 222	
Glasgow 41	
London 1	
Uruguay 598	+2
Mercedes 532	
Montevideo 2	

Vatican City 39	+6
All points 6	
Venezuela 58	+1
Caracas 2	
Maracaibo 61	
Yemen Arab Republic 967	+8
Amran 2	
Yugoslavia 38	+6
Belgrade 11	

INDEX

NOTES

NOTES

WEBSTER'S THESAURUS

WEBSTER'S THESAURUS

PMC Publishing Company, Inc.

PMC Publishing Company, Inc.
118 East 28 Street
New York, New York 10016

ISBN: 1-881275-01-9

A

abandon, *v.* SYN.-abdicate, abjure, relinquish, renounce, resign, surrender, vacate, waive; desert, forsake, leave, quit. ANT.-defend, maintain, uphold; stay, support.

abase, *v.* SYN.-debase, degrade, demote, humble, lower.

abate, *v.* SYN.-assuage, decrease, diminish, lessen, lower, moderate, reduce, suppress. ANT.-amplify, enlarge, increase, intensify, revive.

abbey, *n.* SYN.-cloister, convent, hermitage, monastery, nunnery, priory.

abbreviate, *v.* SYN.- abridge, condense, contract, curtail, diminish, lessen, limit, reduce, restrict. ANT.-elongate, extend, lengthen.

abbreviation, *n.* SYN.-abridgement, contraction, reduction, shortening. ANT.-amplification, enlargement, expansion, extension.

abdicate, *v.* SYN.-abandon, abjure, relinquish, renounce, resign, surrender, vacate, waive; desert, forsake, leave, quit. ANT.-defend, maintain, uphold; stay, support.

aberrant, *a.* SYN.-abnormal, capricious, devious, eccentric, irregular, unnatural, unusual, variable. ANT.-fixed, methodical, ordinary, regular, usual.

abet, *v.* SYN.-aid, assist, encourage, help, incite. ANT.-discourage, hinder, oppose, resist.

abhor, *v.* SYN.-abominate, despise, detest, dislike, hate, loathe. ANT.-admire, approve, cherish, like, love.

abhorrence, *n.* SYN.-antipathy, aversion, disgust, disinclination, dislike, distaste, dread, hatred, loathing, repugnance, repulsion, reluctance animosity, detestation, enmity, hostility, ill will, malevolence, rancor. ANT.-affection, attachment, devotion, enthusiasm attraction, friendship, love.

abide, *v.* SYN.-continue, dwell, endure, live, remain, room, wait, withstand.

ability, *n.* SYN.-aptitude, aptness, capability, capacity, dexterity, efficiency, faculty, power, qualification, skill, talent. ANT.-disability, incapacity, incompetence, unreadiness.

abject, *a.* SYN.-contemptible, debased, despicable, disheartening, groveling, ignoble, low, mean, vile, worthless, wretched. ANT.-attractive, decent, laudable; upright.

able, *a.* SYN.-apt, agile, adept, capable, clever, competent, efficient, experienced, fitted, gifted, qualified, skillful, versatile. ANT.-inadequate, incapable, incompetent, unfitted.

ablution, *n.* SYN. bath, cleansing, washing; ceremony, rite.

abnormal, *a.* SYN.-aberrant, capricious, devious, eccentric, irregular, unnatural, unusual, variable. ANT.-fixed, methodical, ordinary, regular, usual.

abode, *n.* SYN.-dwelling, home, house.

abolish, *v.* SYN.-destroy, end, eradicate, obliterate, overthrow; abrogate, annul, cancel, invalidate, revoke. ANT.-continue, establish, promote, restore, sustain.

abominable, *a.* SYN.-detestable, execrable, foul, hateful, loathsome, odious, revolting, vile. ANT.-agreeable, commendable, delightful, pleasant.

aboriginal, *a.* SYN.-ancient, antiquated, early, old, primary, primeval, primitive primordial, pristine. ANT.-civilized, late, modern, modish, sophisticated.

abound, *v.* SYN.-copious, full, overflow, rich, plenty, plentiful, teem.

above, *a.* SYN.-aloft, beyond, higher, over, overhead, raised, superior. ANT.-low, below, beneath, under.

abrade, *v.* SYN.-rub, scrape, wear.

abridge, *v.* SYN.-abbreviate, condense, contract, curtail, diminish, lessen, limit, reduce, restrict shorten. ANT.-elongate, extend, lengthen.

abridgement, *n.* SYN.-abbreviation, contraction, reduction, shortening. ANT.-amplification, enlargement, expansion, extension.

abrogate, *v.* SYN.-cancel, cross out, delete, eliminate, erase, expunge, obliterate; abolish, annul, invalidate.

abrupt, *a.* SYN.-hasty, precipitate, sudden, unannounced, unexpected; blunt, brusque, curt, rude; craggy, harsh, precipitous, rough, rugged, sharp, steep. ANT.-anticipated, expected; courteous, gradual, smooth.

absent, *a.* SYN.-abroad, away, departed; absent-minded, abstracted, distracted, inattentive, preoccupied. ANT.-attending, present; attentive, watchful.

absolute, *a.* SYN.-actual, complete, entire, perfect, pure, ultimate, unconditional, unqualified, unrestricted; arbitrary, authoritative, despotic, tyrannous. ANT.-accountable, conditional, contingent, dependent, qualified.

absolve, *v.* SYN.-acquit, clear, condone, excuse, forgive, overlook, pardon, release, remit. ANT.-accuse, chastise, condemn, convict, punish.

absorb, *v.* SYN.-assimilate, consume, digest, engulf, imbibe, swallow up; engage, engross, occupy. ANT.-discharge, dispense, emit, expel, exude.

abstain, *v.* SYN.-avoid, decline, desist, fast, forbear, forgo, refrain, renounce, shun, withhold. ANT.-continue, indulge, persist.

abstention, *n.* See **abstinence.**

abstinence, *n.* SYN.-abstention, continence, denial, fasting, forbearance, moderation, self-denial, sobriety, temperance. ANT.-excess, gluttony, greed, intoxication, self-indulgence.

abstract, *v.* SYN.-draw from, part, remove, separate, appropriate, purloin, steal; abridge, summarize; ideal, intellectual. ANT.-add, replace, restore, return, unite.

absurd, *a.* SYN.-foolish, inconsistent, irrational, nonsensical, preposterous, ridiculous, self-contradictory, silly, unreasonable. ANT.-consistent, rational, reasonable, sensible, sound.

abundance, *n.* SYN.-affluence, bounty, overflowing, plenty, profusion, wealth. ANT.-lack, need, want.

abundant, *a.* SYN.-ample, bountiful, copious, overflowing, plenteous, plentiful, profuse, rich, teeming. ANT.-deficient, insufficient, scant, scarce.

abuse, *n.* SYN.-aspersion, defamation, desecration, dishonor, disparagement, insult, invective, maltreatment, misuse, outrage, perversion, profanation, reproach, reviling, upbraiding. ANT.-approval, commendation, laudation, plaudit, respect.

abuse, *v.* SYN.-asperse, defame, disparage, ill-use, malign, revile, scandalize, traduce, vilify; misapply, misemploy, misuse. ANT.-cherish, honor, praise, protect, respect.

academic, *a.* SYN.-bookish, erudite, formal, learned, pedantic, scholarly, scholastic, theoretical. ANT.-common-sense, ignorant, practical, simple.

accede, *v.* SYN.-accord, allow, concede, grant, permit; abdicate, acquiesce, capitulate, cede, quit, relent, relinquish, resign, submit, succumb, surrender, waive, yield. ANT.-deny, dissent, oppose, refuse; assert, resist, strive, struggle.

accelerate, *v.* SYN.-dispatch, expedite, facilitate, forward, hasten, hurry, push, quicken, rush, speed. ANT.-block, hinder, impede, retard, slow.

accent, *n.* SYN.-beat, emphasis, inflection, intonation.

accept, *v.* SYN.-acknowledge, admit, agree, allow, assent, concede, confess, get, grant, permit, receive, take, welcome. ANT.-bestow, deny, dismiss, give, impart, reject, discharge, shun, turn away.

acceptable, *a.* SYN.-agreeable, amiable, charming, gratifying, pleasant, pleasing, pleasurable, suitable, welcome. ANT.-disagreeable, obnoxious, offensive, unpleasant.

access *n.* SYN.-accessibility, admission, admittance; approach, entrance, passage, path.

accessible, *a.* SYN.-available handy, obtainable, prepared, ready, usable. ANT.-inaccessible, unavoidable.

accessory, *n.* SYN.-abettor, accomplice, ally, assistant, associate, confederate. ANT.-adversary, enemy, opponent, rival.

accident, *n.* SYN.-calamity, casualty, contingency, disaster, fortuity, misfortune, mishap. ANT.-calculation, design, intention, purpose.

accidental, *a.* SYN.-casual, chance, contingent, fortuitous, incidental, undesigned, unintended. ANT.-calculated, decreed, intended, planned, willed.

acclaim, *v.* SYN.-applaud, approve, cheer, hail.

accommodate, *v.* SYN.-adapt, adjust, aid, assist, benefit, conform, fit, gratify, help, serve, suit. ANT.-disturb, misapply, misfit.

accompany, *v.* SYN.-associate with, attend, chaperone, consort with, convoy, escort, go with. ANT.-abandon, avoid, desert, leave, quit.

accomplice, *n.* SYN.-abettor, accessory, ally, assistant, associate, confederate. ANT.-adversary, enemy, opponent, rival.

accomplish, *v.* SYN.-achieve, attain, complete, consummate, do, effect, execute, finish, fulfill, perfect, perform. ANT.-block, defeat, fail, frustrate, spoil.

accord, *v.* SYN.-agree, grant, harmonize.

accordance, *n.* SYN.-agreement, coincidence, concord, concurrence, harmony, understanding, unison, bargain, compact, contract, covenant, pact, stipulation. ANT.-difference, disagreement, discord, dissension, variance.

account, *n.* SYN.-chronicle, description, detail, history, narration, narrative, recital, relation; computation, reckoning, record. ANT.-caricature, confusion, distortion, misrepresentation.

account, *v.* SYN.-believe, chronicle,

consider, deem, esteem, estimate, hold, judge, rate, reckon, regard, think, view; elucidate, explain, expound.

accountability, *n.* SYN.-amenability, liability, obligation, responsibility, trustworthiness; duty, trust.

accountable, *a.* SYN.-amenable, answerable, exposed to, liable, reliable, responsible, trustworthy, subject to. ANT.-exempt, careless, negligent, free, immune, independent, irresponsible.

accumulate, *v.* SYN.-accrue, amass, collect, gather, heap, hoard, increase, store. ANT.-diminish, disperse, dissipate, scatter, waste.

accuracy, *n.* SYN.-constancy, exactness, fidelity, precision. ANT.-carelessness, imprecision.

accurate, *a.* SYN.-correct, definite, distinct, exact, faultless, impeccable, precise, proper, right, strict. ANT.-careless, erroneous, false, faulty, untrue, wrong.

accusation, *n.* SYN.-arraignment, charge, imputation, incrimination, indictment. ANT.-exculpation, exoneration, pardon.

accuse, *v.* SYN.-arraign, censure, charge, incriminate, indict. ANT.-absolve, acquit, exonerate, release, vindicate.

accustom, *v.* SYN.-acclimate, familiarize, inure, train. ANT.-ignore, neglect, overlook.

accustomed, *a.* SYN.-customary, habitual, usual.

ache, *n.* SYN.-pang, pain, paroxysm, throe, twinge; agony, anguish, distress, grief, suffering. ANT.-comfort, ease, relief, happiness, pleasure. solace.

achieve, *v.* SYN.-accomplish, acquire, do, effect, execute, gain, obtain, realize, win. ANT.-fail, fall short, lose, miss.

achievement, *n.* SYN.-deed, exploit, feat, accomplishment, attainment, completion, performance, realization. ANT.-neglect, omission; defeat, failure.

acid, *a.* SYN.-biting, sharp, sour, tart.

acknowledge, *v.* SYN.-accept, admit, agree, allow, assent, avow, certify, concede, confess, grant, identify, own, permit, recognize, welcome. ANT.-deny, dismiss, reject, shun.

acquaintance, *n.* SYN.-cognizance, companionship, familiarity, fellowship, friendship, intimacy, knowledge. ANT.-ignorance, inexperience, unfamiliarity.

acquiesce, *v.* SYN.-allow, concede, grant, permit; abdicate, accede, acquiesce, capitulate, cede, quit, relent, relinquish, resign, submit, succumb, surrender, waive, yield. ANT.-deny, dissent, oppose, refuse; assert, resist, strive, struggle.

acquire, *v.* SYN.-assimilate, attain, earn, gain, get, obtain, procure, secure, win. ANT.-forego, forfeit, lose, miss, surrender.

acquisition, *n.* SYN.-award, donation, earnings, fortune, gain, gift, income, purchase, proceeds, profit, riches, salary, wages.

acquit, *v.* SYN.-absolve, condone, excuse, forgive, overlook, pardon, repay, release, remit, return. ANT.-accuse, chastise, condemn, convict, punish.

acquittal, *n.* SYN.-absolution, amnesty, pardon, forgiveness, remission. ANT.-conviction, penalty, punishment, sentence.

acrid, *a.* SYN.-biting, bitter, caustic, distasteful, galling, grievous, harsh, painful, poignant, pungent, sardonic, severe, sharp, sour, tart. ANT.-bland, delicious, gentle, mellow, pleasant, sweet.

act, *n.* SYN.-accomplishment, action, deed, doing, execution, feat, operation, performance, transaction; decree, edict, law, statute. ANT.-cessation, deliberation, inactivity, inhibition, intention.

act, *v.* SYN.-affect, assume, bear, behave, carry, comport, conduct, demean, deport, feign, interact, manage, operate, pretend, profess, sham, simulate.

action, *n.* SYN.-achievement, activity, deed, exercise, exploit, feat, motion, movement, performance, play, procedure. ANT.-idleness, inactivity, inertia, repose, rest.

activate, *v.* SYN.-begin, initiate, stimulate.

active, *a.* SYN.-operative, working; busy, industrious; agile, alert, brisk, lively, nimble, quick, sprightly, supple. ANT.-dormant, inactive; indolent, lazy, passive.

activity, *n.* SYN.-action, agility, briskness, energy, enterprise, exercise, intensity, liveliness, motion, movement, quickness, rapidity, vigor. ANT.-dullness, idleness, inactivity, inertia, sloth.

actor, *n.* SYN.-character, entertainer, ham, mime, mimic, performer, player, tragedian.

actual, *a.* SYN.-authentic, certain, genuine, positive, real, substantial, true, veritable. ANT.-apparent, fictitious, imaginary, supposed, unreal.

actuate, *v.* SYN.-agitate, drive, impel, induce, instigate, move, persuade, propel, push, shift, stir. ANT.-deter. halt, rest, stay, stop.

acute, *a.* SYN.-intense, keen, penetrating, poignant, sharp, shrill; crucial, decisive, important, sensitive, vital.

adamant, *a.* SYN.-firm, hard, immovable, insistent, positive, unyielding.

adage, *n.* SYN.-aphorism, apothegm, byword, maxim, motto, proverb, saw, saying.

adapt, *v.* SYN.-accommodate, adjust, conform, fit, suit. ANT.-disturb, misapply, misfit.

add, *v.* SYN.-adjoin, affix, append, attach, augment, increase, sum, total. ANT.-deduct, detach, reduce, remove, subtract.

addiction, *n.* SYN.-fixation, inclination, obsession.

address, *v.* SYN.-accost, approach, greet, hail, speak to. ANT.-avoid, pass by.

adept, *a.* SYN.-able, accomplished, clever, competent, cunning, expert, ingenious, practiced, proficient, skilled, skillful, versed. ANT.-awkward, bungling, clumsy, inexpert, untrained.

adequate, *a.* SYN.-ample, capable, commensurate, enough, fitting, satisfactory, sufficient, suitable. ANT.-deficient, lacking, scant.

adherent, *n.* SYN.-devotee, disciple, follower, supporter, votary; learner, pupil, scholar, student.

adjacent, *a.* SYN.-abutting, adjoining, adjunct, bordering, close, contiguous, immediate, impending, near, nearby, neighboring, tangent, touching. ANT.-afar, distant, faraway, removed.

adjoin, *v.* SYN.-abut, append, border, connect, join, unite. ANT.-divide, separate.

adjourn, *v.* SYN.-defer, delay, move, postpone, suspend. ANT.-continue, expedite, hasten.

adjunct, *n.* SYN.-accessory, assistant, helper, modifier. ANT.-thing. primary, principal.

adjust, *v.* SYN.-accommodate, adapt, arrange, conform, fit, harmonize, modify, refashion, suit. ANT.-disturb, misapply, misfit.

adjutant, *n.* SYN.-aide, assistant.

administer, *v.* SYN.-direct, manage, supervise; apply, dispense, dole, give, minister, tender, treat.

administration, *n.* SYN.-government, management, supervision; directors, executives, officers, supervisors.

admirable, *a.* SYN.-eminent, fair, honest, honorable, noble, respectable, true, trusty, upright, virtuous; creditable, esteemed, proper, reputable. ANT.-disgraceful, ignominious, infamous, shameful.

admire, *v.* SYN.-adore, appreciate, approve, esteem, regard, respect, revere, venerate, wonder. ANT.-abhor, despise, dislike.

admissible, *a.* SYN.-allowable, fair, justifiable, permissible, probable, tolerable, warranted. ANT.-inadmissible, irrelevant, unsuitable.

admit, *v.* SYN.-accept, acknowledge, agree, allow, assent, concede, confess, grant, permit, welcome. ANT.-deny, dismiss, reject, shun.

admonition, *n.* SYN.-advice, caution, counsel, exhortation, instruction, recommendation, suggestion, warning; information, intelligence, notification.

adopt, *v.* SYN.-accept, appropriate, assume, choose, espouse, select, take.

adore, *v.* SYN.-esteem, honor, love, respect, revere, venerate, worship. ANT.-despise, hate, ignore.

adorn, *v.* SYN.-beautify, bedeck, decorate, embellish, garnish, gild, ornament, trim. ANT.-deface, deform, disfigure, mar, spoil.

adroit, *a.* SYN.-apt, clever, dexterous, quick, quick-witted, skillful, talented, witty; bright, ingenious, sharp, smart. ANT.-awkward, bungling, clumsy, slow, unskilled; dull, foolish, stupid.

adult, *a.* SYN.-developed, grown, mature.

adulterate, *v.* SYN.-abase, alloy, corrupt, debase, defile, degrade, deprave, depress, humiliate, impair, lower, pervert, vitiate. ANT.-enhance, improve, raise, restore, vitalize.

advance, *v.* SYN.-aggrandize, elevate, forward, further, promote, adduce, allege, assign, bring forward, offer, propose, propound, improve, proceed, progress, rise, thrive, augment, enlarge, increase. ANT.-hinder, oppose, retard, retreat, withhold.

advantage, *n.* SYN.-edge, mastery, superiority; benefit, good, profit, service, utility. ANT.-detriment, handicap, harm, impediment, obstruction.

advantageous, *a.* SYN.-beneficial, good, helpful, profitable, salutary, serviceable, useful, wholesome. ANT.-deleterious, destructive, detrimental, harmful, injurious.

adventure, *n.* SYN.-experience, happening, story, tale.

adventurous, *a.* SYN.-bold, chivalrous, daring, enterprising, foolhardy, precipitate, rash. ANT.-cautious, hesitating, timid.

adversary, *n.* SYN.-antagonist, competitor, enemy, foe, opponent, rival. ANT.-accomplice, ally, comrade, confederate, friend, teammate.

adverse, *a.* SYN.-antagonistic, contrary, hostile, opposed, opposite; counteractive, disastrous, unfavorable, unlucky. ANT.-benign, favorable, fortunate, lucky, propitious.

adversity, *n.* SYN.-accident, affliction, calamity, catastrophe, disaster, distress, hardship, misfortune, mishap, ruin. ANT.-blessing, comfort, prosperity, success.

advertise, *v.* SYN.-announce, communicate, declare, display, exhibit, proclaim, publicize.

advertisement, *n.* SYN.- announcement, bulletin, declaration, notification, promulgation. ANT.-hush, muteness, silence, speechlessness.

advice, *n.* SYN.-admonition, caution, counsel, exhortation, guidance, instruction, recommendation, suggestion, warning; information, intelligence, notification.

advise, *v.* SYN.-acquaint, apprise, enlighten, impart, inform, instruct, notify, recommend, teach, tell, warn. ANT.-conceal, delude, distract, mislead.

aesthetic, *a.* SYN.-appreciative, creative, inventive, spiritual.

affable, *a.* SYN.-affable, civil, communicative, friendly, gregarious, hospitable, outgoing, sociable, social. ANT.-antisocial, disagreeable, hermitic, inhospitable.

affair, *n.* SYN.-concern, duty, interest, matter, obligation, pursuit, responsibility.

affect, *v.* SYN.-alter, change, influence, modify, transform; concern, interest, regard; impress, melt, move, soften, subdue, touch; adopt, assume, feign, pretend.

affected, *a.* SYN.-artificial, ceremonious, dramatic, histrionic, melodramatic, showy, stagy, theatrical. ANT.-modest, subdued, unaffected, unemotional.

affection, *n.* SYN.-attachment, endearment, fondness, kindness, love, tenderness; disposition, emotion, feeling, inclination. ANT.-aversion, hatred, indifference, repugnance, repulsion.

affidavit, *n.* SYN.-affirmation, testimony, statement.

affiliate, *v.* SYN.-ally, associate, combine, conjoin, connect, join, link, mingle, mix. ANT.-disrupt, divide, estrange, separate.

affinity, *n.* SYN.-attraction, closeness, fondness, liking.

affirm, *v.* SYN.-assert, aver, declare, maintain, protest, state, swear. ANT.-contradict, demur, deny, dispute, oppose.

affix, *v.* SYN.-adjoin, administer, allot, annex, append, apply, appropriate, assign, attach, avail, connect, devote, direct, employ, use; bear, pertain, refer, relate; appeal, petition, request, join, stick, unite; associate, attribute. ANT.-detach, disengage, separate, unfasten, untie.

afflict, *v.* SYN.-burden, encumber, load, oppress, overload, tax, trouble, weigh. ANT.-alleviate, console, ease, lighten, mitigate.

affluence, *n.* SYN.-abundance, fortune, luxury, money, opulence, plenty, possessions, riches, wealth. ANT.-indigence, need, poverty, want.

affluent, *a.* SYN.-abundant, ample, bountiful, copious, costly, luxurious, opulent, plentiful, prosperous, rich, sumptuous, wealthy, well-to-do. ANT.-beggarly, destitute, indigent, needy, poor.

affront, *n.* SYN.-abuse, defiance, indignity, insolence, insult, offense. ANT.-apology, homage, salutation

afraid, *a.* SYN.-apprehensive, fainthearted, fearful, frightened, scared, timid, timorous. ANT.-assured, bold, composed, courageous, sanguine.

afterward, *a.* SYN.-after, eventually, later, subsequently, ultimately.

against, *a.* SYN.-adverse, facing, opposed, toward, versus.

age, *n.* SYN.-adolescence, adulthood, dotage, senescence, senility, seniority, youth; antiquity, date, duration, epoch, era, generation, period, span, time. ANT.-childhood, infancy, youth.

agency, *n.* SYN.-bureau, company, firm, office, representative.

agent, *n.* SYN.-apparatus, channel, device, instrument, means, medium, tool, utensil, vehicle. ANT.-hindrance, impediment, obstruction, preventive.

aggravate, *v.* SYN.-heighten, increase, intensify, magnify; annoy, chafe, embitter, exasperate, inflame, irritate, nettle, provoke, vex. ANT.-appease, mitigate, palliate soften, soothe.

aggregate, *n.* SYN.-amount, collection, conglomeration, entirety, sum, total, whole. ANT.-element, ingredient, part, particular, unit.

aggression, *n.* SYN.-assault, attack, battle, incursion, invasion, offensive, raid, threat, war.

agile, *a.* SYN.-active, alert, brisk, deft, flexible, lively, nimble, quick, spirited, sprightly, spry, supple. ANT.-awkward, clumsy, heavy, inert, slow, sluggish.

agitate, *v.* SYN.-arouse, disconcert, disturb, excite, jar, perturb, rouse, ruffle, shake, trouble. ANT.-calm, ease, placate, quiet.

agitated, *a.* SYN.-disquieted, disturbed, irresolute, restless, sleepless, uneasy, unquiet; active, roving, transient, wandering. ANT.-at ease, peaceable, quiet, tractable.

agony, *n.* SYN.-ache, anguish, distress, misery, pain, suffering, throe, torment, torture, woe. ANT.-comfort, ease, mitigation, relief.

agree, *v.* SYN.-accede, acquiesce, assent, comply, consent; coincide, concur, conform, tally. ANT.-contradict, differ, disagree, dissent, protest.

agreeable, *a.* SYN.-acceptable, amiable, charming, gratifying, pleasant, pleasing, pleasurable, suitable, welcome. ANT.-disagreeable, obnoxious, offensive, unpleasant.

agreement, *n.* SYN.-accordance, coincidence, concord, concurrence, harmony, understanding, unison; bargain, compact, contract, covenant, pact, stipulation. ANT.-difference, disagreement, discord, dissension, variance.

agriculture, *n.* SYN.-agronomy, cultivation, farming, gardening, horticulture, husbandry, tillage.

ahead, *a.* SYN.-before, first, leading, preceding.

aid, *n.* SYN.- alms, assistance, backing, comfort, furtherance, help, patronage, relief, succor, support. ANT.-antagonism, counteraction, defiance, hostility, resistance.

aid, *v.* SYN.-abet, back, further, help, promote, serve, support, sustain, assist, succor, uphold; facilitate, mitigate, relieve, remedy. ANT.-hamper, hinder, impede, prevent resist, thwart; afflict.

ailment, *n.* SYN.-complaint, disease,

disorder, illness, infirmity, malady, sickness. ANT.-health, healthiness, soundness, vigor.

aim, *n.* SYN.-ambition, aspiration, design, emulation, end, goal, incentive, intent, intention, object, objective, purpose. ANT.-accident, contentment, indifference, indolence, resignation, satisfaction.

aim, *v.* SYN.-level, point, train; conduct, direct, govern, guide, manage, regulate, rule; bid, command, instruct, order. ANT. -deceive, distract, misdirect, misguide.

aimless, *a.* SYN.-blind, careless, capricious, drifting, erratic, pointless, purposeless, rambling, unplanned, unpredictable, wandering. ANT.-considered, directed, purposeful, planned.

air, *n.* SYN.-atmosphere, breeze, draft, oxygen, ventilation, wind.

air, *v.* SYN.-cool, freshen, open, ventilate; broadcast, disclose, expose, reveal.

aisle, *n.* SYN.-corridor, course, opening, passage, passageway, path, walk, way.

ajar, *a.* SYN.-agape, unclosed, uncovered, unlocked, unobstructed, available, open, accessible, exposed, public, unrestricted.

alarm, *n.* SYN.-affright, apprehension, consternation, dismay, fear, fright, signal, terror, warning. ANT.-calm, composure, quiet, security, tranquillity.

alarm, *v.* SYN.-affright, appall, astound, daunt, dismay, frighten, horrify, intimidate, scare, startle, terrify, terrorize. ANT.-allay, compose, embolden, reassure, soothe.

alert, *a.* SYN.-alert, anxious, attentive, careful, cautious, circumspect, observant, vigilant, wakeful, wary, watchful. ANT.-careless, inattentive, lax, neglectful, oblivious.

alibi, *n.* SYN.-assertion, defense, excuse, explanation, reply.

alien, *a.* SYN.-adverse, contrasted, exotic, extraneous, foreign, irrelevant, remote, strange, unconnected. ANT.-akin, germane, kindred, relevant.

alienate, *v.* SYN.-divide, estrange, separate, withdraw.

alike, *a.* SYN.-akin, allied, analogous, comparable, correlative, correspondent, corresponding, like, parallel, similar. ANT.-different, dissimilar, divergent, incongruous, opposed.

alive, *a.* SYN.-animate, breathing, conscious, existing, growing, living, mortal. ANT.-dead, inanimate, lifeless.

all, *n.* SYN.-collection, ensemble, entire, everyone, everything, group, total. ANT.-nobody, none, nothing.

allege, *v.* SYN.-advance, affirm, assign, cite, claim, declare, maintain. ANT.-contradict, deny, disprove, gainsay, refute.

allegiance, *n.* SYN.-constancy, devotion, faithfulness, fealty, fidelity. ANT.-disloyalty, falseness, perfidy, treachery.

alleviate, *v.* SYN.-abate, allay, assuage, diminish, extenuate, mitigate, relieve, soften, solace, soothe. ANT.-aggravate, agitate, augment, increase, irritate.

alliance, *n.* SYN.-association, coalition, combination, confederacy, entente, federation, league, partnership, union; compact, covenant, marriage, treaty. ANT.-divorce, schism, separation.

allocate, *v.* See **allot.**

allot, *v.* SYN.-apportion, deal, dispense, distribute, divide, mete; allocate, appropriate, assign, give, grant, measure. ANT.-confiscate, keep, refuse, retain, withhold.

allotment, *n.* SYN.-apportionment, division, fragment, moiety, part, piece, portion, scrap, section, segment, share, ANT.-entirety, whole.

allow, *v.* SYN.-let, permit, sanction, suffer, tolerate; authorize, give, grant, yield; acknowledge, admit, concede. ANT.-forbid, object, protest, refuse, resist.

allowable, *a.* SYN.-admissible, fair, justifiable, permissible, probable, tolerable, warranted. ANT.-inadmissible, irrelevant, unsuitable.

allowance, *n.* SYN.-alimony, annuity, bequest, commission, gift, grant, legacy, pay, stipend, subsidy, wages.

allude, *v.* SYN.-advert, hint, imply, insinuate, intimate, refer, suggest. ANT.-declare, demonstrate, specify, state.

alluring, *a.* SYN.-attractive, bewitching, captivating, charming, enchanting, engaging, fascinating, winning. ANT.-repugnant, repulsive, revolting.

alone, *a.* SYN.-abandoned, deserted, desolate, isolated, lonely, secluded, unaccompanied, unaided; lone, only, single, sole, solitary. ANT.-accompanied, attended, surrounded.

aloof, *a.* SYN.-distant, far, faraway, remote, removed; cold, reserved, stiff, unfriendly. ANT.-close, near, nigh; cordial, friendly.

also, *adv.* SYN.-besides, furthermore, in addition, likewise, moreover, similarly, too.

alter, *v.* SYN.-change, exchange, substitute; convert, modify, shift, transfigure, transform, vary, veer. ANT.-retain; continue, establish, preserve, settle, stabilize.

alteration, *n.* SYN.-change, modification, mutation, substitution, variation, variety, vicissitude. ANT.-monotony, stability, uniformity.

alternate, *n.* SYN.-agent, deputy, lieutenant, proxy, representative, substitute, understudy. ANT.-head, master, principal, sovereign.

alternative, *n.* SYN.-election, option, choice, preference, selection.

altitude, *n.* distance, elevation, height.

always, *adv.* SYN.-constantly, continually, eternally, ever, evermore, forever, incessantly, perpetually, unceasingly. ANT.-fitfully, never, occasionally, rarely, sometimes.

amass, *v.* SYN.-accumulate, assemble, gather, collect, congregate, convene, muster; cull, garner, glean, harvest, pick, reap; conclude, deduce, infer, judge. ANT.-disband, disperse, distribute, scatter, separate.

amateur, *n.* SYN.-apprentice, beginner, dabbler, dilettante, learner, neophyte, novice. ANT.-adept, authority, expert, master, professional.

amazement, *n.* SYN.-astonishment, awe, bewilderment, curiosity, surprise, wonder, wonderment. ANT.-triviality; apathy, expectation, indifference.

ambiguity, *n.* SYN.-distrust, doubt, hesitation, incredulity, scruple, skepticism, suspense, suspicion, unbelief, uncertainty. ANT.-belief, certainty, conviction, determination. faith.

ambiguous, *a.* SYN.-dubious, enigmatical, equivocal, obscure, uncertain, vague. ANT.-clear, explicit, obvious, plain, unequivocal.

ambition, *n.* SYN.-aspiration, eagerness, emulation, goal, incentive, pretension. ANT.-contentment, indifference, indolence, resignation, satisfaction.

ambush, *n.* SYN.-net, pitfall, ruse, snare, stratagem, trap, trick, wile.

amend, *v.* SYN.-correct, mend, rectify, reform, right; admonish, discipline, punish. ANT.-aggravate, ignore, spoil; condone, indulge.

amiable, *a.* SYN.-agreeable, engaging, friendly, good-natured, gracious, pleasing. ANT.-churlish, disagreeable, hateful, ill-natured, surly.

amicable, *a.* SYN.-affable, companionable, friendly, genial, kindly, neighborly, sociable, social. ANT.-antagonistic, cool, distant, hostile, reserved.

amid, *prep.* See **among.**

among, *prep.* SYN.-amid, amidst, between, betwixt, mingled, mixed, within.

amount, *n.* SYN.-aggregate, number, product, quantity, sum, total, whole.

ample, *a.* SYN.-broad, extensive, great, large, spacious, wide; abundant, bountiful, copious, full, generous, liberal, plentiful, profuse, rich. ANT.-constricted, limited, small; insufficient, lacking, meager.

amplify, *v.* SYN.-accrue, augment, enhance, enlarge, expand, extend, grow, heighten, increase, intensify, magnify, multiply, raise, wax. ANT.-atrophy, contract, decrease, diminish, reduce.

amusement, *n.* SYN.-diversion, entertainment, fun, game, pastime, play, recreation, sport. ANT.-boredom, labor, toil, work.

analogous, *a.* SYN.-akin, alike, allied, comparable, correlative, correspondent, corresponding, like, parallel, similar. ANT.-different, dissimilar, divergent, incongruous, opposed.

analyze, *v.* SYN.-assess, audit, check, contemplate, dissect, examine, inquire, interrogate, notice, question, quiz, review, scan, scrutinize, survey, view, watch. ANT.-disregard, neglect, omit, overlook.

anarchy, *n.* SYN.-chaos, disorder, lawlessness, turmoil.

ancestry, *n.* SYN.-clan, folk, lineage, nation, people, race, stock, strain, tribe.

anchor, *n.* SYN.-ballast, mooring, protection, safeguard, security, tie.

ancient, *a.* SYN.-aged, antiquated, antique, archaic, obsolete, old, old-fashioned, venerable. ANT.-modern, new, young, youthful.

anecdote, *n.* SYN.-account, anecdote, chronicle, fable, fabrication, falsehood, fiction, history, narration, narrative, novel, report, story, tale, yarn.

angelic, *a.* SYN.-beautiful, devout, good, heavenly, lovely, pure, radiant, saintly. ANT.-bad, evil, ugly.

anger, *n.* SYN.-animosity, choler, exasperation, fury, indignation, ire, irritation, passion, petulance, rage, resentment, temper, wrath. ANT.-conciliation, forbearance, patience, peace, self-control.

angry, *a.* SYN. enraged, exasperated, furious, incensed, indignant, irate, maddened, provoked, wrathful, wroth. ANT.-calm, happy, pleased, satisfied.

anguish, *n.* SYN.-agony, distress, grief, misery, suffering, torment, torture. ANT.-comfort, joy, relief, solace.

animosity, *n.* SYN.-bitterness, enmity, grudge, hatred, hostility, malevolence, rancor, spite. ANT.-friendliness, good will, love.

angular, *a.* SYN.-bent, crooked, crotched, forked, jagged, rectangular, staggered, triangular, zig-zag.

animated, *a.* SYN.-active, alive, expressive, gay, lively, spirited.

animosity, *n.* SYN.-abhorrence, dislike, hatred,

annihilate, *v.* SYN.-demolish, destroy, devastate, eradicate, exterminate, extinguish, obliterate, ravage, raze, ruin, wreck. ANT.-construct, establish, make, preserve, save.

announce, *v.* SYN.-advertise, declare, give out, herald, make known, notify, proclaim, promulgate, publish, report. ANT.-bury, conceal, stifle, suppress, withhold.

announcement, *n.* SYN.-advertisement, bulletin, declaration, notification, promulgation. ANT.-hush, muteness, silence, speechlessness.

annoy, *v.* SYN.-bother, chafe, disturb, inconvenience, irk, irritate, molest, pester, tease, trouble, vex. ANT.-accommodate, console, gratify, soothe.

annoying, *a.* SYN.-bothersome, distressing, disturbing, irksome, troublesome, trying, vexatious. ANT.-accommodating, amusing, gratifying, pleasant.

annul, *v.* SYN.-destroy, end, eradicate, obliterate, overthrow; abrogate, cancel, invalidate, revoke, cross out, delete, eliminate, erase, expunge, abolish, nullify, quash, repeal, rescind, ANT.-continue, establish, promote, restore, sustain, confirm, enact, enforce, perpetuate

answer, *n.* SYN.-rejoinder, reply, response, restatement, result, retort, retaliation, solution, total; defense, rebuttal. ANT.-inquiry, questioning, summoning; argument.

antagonistic, *a.* SYN.- contrary, hostile, opposed, opposite; counteractive, disastrous, unfavorable, unlucky adverse, inimical, unfriendly, warlike. ANT.-benign, favorable, fortunate, lucky, propitious amicable, cordial.

antic, *n.* SYN.-caper, frolic, trick.

anticipation, *n.* SYN.-contemplation, expectation, foresight, forethought, hope, preconception, prescience, presentiment. ANT.-doubt, dread, fear, worry.

antipathy, *n.* SYN.-animosity, antagonism, enmity, hatred, hostility, ill-will, invidiousness, malignity. ANT.-affection, cordiality, friendliness, good will, love.

antiquated, *a.* SYN.-ancient, archaic, obsolescent, obsolete, old, out-of-date, venerable. ANT.-current, extant, fashionable, modern, recent.

anxiety, *n.* SYN.-apprehension, care, concern, disquiet, fear, solicitude, trouble, worry, ANT.-assurance, confidence, contentment, equanimity, nonchalance.

anxious, *a.* SYN.-ardent, avid, enthusiastic, eager, fervent, hot, impassioned, impatient, keen, yearning. ANT.-apathetic, indifferent, unconcerned, uninterested.

apart, *a.* SYN.-alone, disconnected, distant, far, isolated, separated.

apathy, *n.* SYN.-disinterestedness, impartiality, indifference, insensibility, neutrality, unconcern. ANT.-affection, ardor, fervor, passion.

apex, *n.* SYN.-acme, climax, consummation, culmination, height, peak, summit, zenith. ANT.-anticlimax, base, depth, floor.

apology, *n.* SYN.-alibi, confession, defense, excuse, explanation, justification. ANT.-accusation, complaint, denial, dissimulation.

apparatus, *n.* SYN.-agent, channel, device, instrument, means, medium, tool, utensil, vehicle. ANT.-hindrance, impediment, obstruction, preventive.

apparel, *n.* SYN.-array, attire, clothes, clothing, drapery, dress, garb, garments, raiment, vestments, vesture. ANT.-nakedness, nudity.

apparent, *a.* SYN.-clear, evident, manifest, obvious, palpable, plain, self-evident, transparent, unambiguous, unmistakable, visible; illusory, ostensible, seeming. ANT.-ambiguous, dubious, indistinct, real, uncertain.

appeal, *n.* SYN.-beg, entreaty, petition, plea, prayer, request, supplication.

appear, *v.* SYN.-look, seem; arise, arrive, emanate, emerge, issue. ANT.-be, exist; disappear, vanish, withdraw.

appearance, *n.* SYN.-advent, apparition, arrival, air, aspect, demeanor, look, manner, mien, fashion, guise, pretense, semblance.

appease, *v.* SYN.-allay, alleviate, assuage, calm, compose, lull, pacify, placate, quell, quiet, relieve, satisfy, soothe, still, tranquilize. ANT.-arouse, excite, incense, inflame.

appetite, *n.* SYN.-hunger, relish, stomach, thirst, zest; craving, desire, inclination, liking, longing, passion. ANT.-disgust, distaste, renunciation, repugnance, satiety.

apply, *v.* SYN.-administer, affix, allot, appropriate, assign, attach, avail, devote, direct, employ, use; bear, pertain, refer, relate; appeal, petition, request.

appoint, *v.* SYN.-call, denominate, designate, entitle, mention, name, specify. ANT.-hint, miscall, misname.

apportion, *v.* SYN.-allot, appropriate, assign, dispense, distribute, divide, parcel, partake, partition, portion, share. ANT.-aggregate, amass, combine, condense.

appraise, *v.* SYN.-assign, assess, calculate, compute, estimate, evaluate, fix, levy, reckon, tax.

appreciate, *v.* SYN.-admire, cherish, enjoy, esteem, prize, regard, value, appraise, estimate, evaluate, rate, apprehend, comprehend, understand, go up, improve, rise. ANT.-belittle, degrade, depreciate, misapprehend, misunderstand.

appreciative, *a.* SYN.-beholden, grateful, indebted, obliged, thankful. ANT.-thankless, unappreciative.

apprehend, *v.* SYN.-arrest, capture, catch, clutch, grasp, grip, lay hold of, seize, snare, trap. ANT.-liberate, lose, release, throw.

apprehension, *n.* SYN.-anxiety, concern, disquiet, fear, trouble, uneasiness, worry. ANT.-contentment, equanimity, peace, satisfaction.

apprehensive, *a.* SYN.-afraid, fainthearted, fearful, frightened, scared, timid, timorous. ANT.-assured, bold, composed, courageous, sanguine.

apprentice, *n.* SYN.-amateur, beginner, learner, student.

approach, *v.* SYN.-advance, approximate, come, gain, near, touch. ANT.-

depart, leave, recede.

appropriate, *a.* SYN.-applicable, apt, becoming, fitting, particular, proper, suitable. ANT.-contrary, improper, inappropriate.

appropriation, *n.* SYN.-allowance, benefaction, bequest, boon, bounty, donation, endowment, gift, grant, subsidy.

approval, *n.* SYN.-approbation, assent, commendation, consent, endorsement, praise, sanction, support. ANT.-censure, reprimand, reproach, stricture.

approve, *v.* SYN.-appreciate, commend, like, praise; authorize, confirm, endorse, ratify, sanction. ANT.-criticize, disparage; condemn, nullify.

approximate, *a.* SYN.-about, almost, guess, imprecise, inexact, rough. ANT.-exact, precise, sure.

apropos, *a.* SYN.-applicable, apposite, appropriate, apt, fit, germane, material, pertinent, related, relating, relevant, to the point. ANT.-alien, extraneous, foreign, unrelated.

aptitude, *n.* SYN.-ability, adroitness, aptness, capability, capacity, cleverness, deftness, dexterity, efficiency, facility, faculty, knack, power, qualification, skill, talent. ANT.-disability, inability, incapacity, incompetence, unreadiness.

arbitrary, *a.* SYN.-absolute, despotic, discretionary, inconsistent, irrational, willful.

arbitrate, *v.* SYN.-decide, decree, determine; adjudicate, condemn, judge, try, umpire; appreciate, consider, estimate, evaluate, measure, think.

arbitrator, *n.* SYN.-arbitrator, critic, judge, justice, magistrate, referee, umpire.

archetype, *n.* SYN.-example, illustration, instance. model, pattern, prototype, sample, specimen. ANT.-concept, precept, principle, rule.

archives, *n. pl.* SYN.-file, library, museum, repository, vault.

ardent, *a.* SYN.-eager, enthusiastic, fervent, fervid, fiery, glowing, hot, impassioned, intense, keen, passionate, vehement, zealous. ANT.-apathetic, cool, indifferent, nonchalant.

ardor, *n.* SYN.-devotion, eagerness, enthusiasm, fervor, fire, passion, rapture, spirit, zeal. ANT.-apathy, disinterest, indifference, unconcern.

arduous, *a.* SYN.-complicated, demanding, hard, intricate, involved, laborious, obscure, perplexing, toilsome, trying burdensome, difficult, onerous, tough; cruel, harsh, rigorous, severe. ANT.-easy, effortless, facile, simple, gentle, lenient, tender.

area, *n.* SYN.-locale, locality, location, place, precinct, region, site, situation, spot, station, territory, township, vicinity, ward.

arena, *n.* SYN.-amphitheater, coliseum, field, grounds, gymnasium, park,

argue, *v.* SYN.-debate, discuss, dispute, plead, reason, wrangle; denote, imply, indicate, prove, show. ANT.-ignore, overlook, reject, spurn.

argument, *n.* SYN.-contention, controversy, debate, disagreement, dispute, quarrel, squabble. ANT.-agreement, concord, decision, harmony.

arid, *a.* SYN.-dehydrated, desiccated, drained, dry, parched, thirsty; barren, dull, insipid, plain, tedious, tiresome, uninteresting, vapid. ANT.-damp, moist; fresh, interesting, lively.

aristocracy, *n.* SYN.-elite, gentry, nobility, noblemen, patricians, privileged, rulers. ANT.-commoners, peasants, peons.

armed, *a.* SYN.-equipped, fortified, loaded, outfitted, protected. ANT.-unprotected, vulnerable.

armistice, *n.* SYN.-compromise, concession, reconciliation, settlement, truce.

aroma, *n.* SYN.-fragrance, fume, incense, odor, perfume, redolence, scent, smell, stench, stink.

arouse, *v.* SYN.-awaken, excite, incite, provoke, rouse, spur, stimulate.

arrange, *v.* SYN.-adjust, assort, classify, dispose, organize, place, regulate; devise, plan, prepare. ANT.-confuse, disorder, disturb, jumble, scatter.

arrangement, *n.* SYN.-method, mode, order, organization, plan, process, regularity, rule, scheme, system. ANT.-chance, chaos, confusion, disarrangement, disorder, irregularity.

array, *n.* SYN.-apparel, attire, clothes, clothing, drapery, dress, garb, garments, raiment, vestments, vesture. ANT.-nakedness, nudity.

arrest, *v.* SYN.-apprehend, check, detain, hinder, interrupt, obstruct, restrain, seize, slow, stop, withhold. ANT.-activate, discharge, free, liberate, release.

arrive, *v.* SYN.-appear, attain, come, emerge, land, reach, visit. ANT.-depart, exit, leave.

arrogant, *a.* SYN.-disdainful, haughty, overbearing, proud, stately, supercilious, vain, vainglorious. ANT.-ashamed, humble, lowly, meek.

art, *n.* SYN.-adroitness, aptitude, cunning, knack, skill, tact; artifice, duplicity, guile, shrewdness, subtlety. ANT.-clumsiness, unskillfulness; forthrightness, honesty, innocence.

artery, *n.* SYN.-conduit, highway, thoroughfare, vein.

artful, *a.* SYN.-conniving, cunning, deceitful, deceptive, sly, tricky.

article, *n.* SYN.-object, particular, thing.

articulate, *v.* SYN.-enunciate, lecture, pronounce, speak, talk, verbalize, vocalize.

artifice, *n.* SYN.-craftiness, deception, device, duplicity, ingenuity, intrigue, machination, ruse, stratagem, trickery, wile,

artificial, *a.* SYN.-affected, assumed, bogus, counterfeit, ersatz, fake, feigned, fictitious, phony, sham, spurious, synthetic, unreal. ANT.-genuine, natural, real, true.

artist, *n.* SYN.-actor, composer, creator, dancer, dramatist, impresario, musician, painter, performer, poet, sculptor, writer.

artistic, *a.* SYN.-creative, cultured, imaginative, inventive, sensitive, talented.

ascend, *v.* SYN.-climb, mount, rise, scale, soar, tower. ANT.-descend, fall, sink.

ascertain, *v.* SYN.-detect, devise, discover, expose, find, find out, invent, learn, originate, reveal. ANT.-cover, hide, lose, mask, screen.

ashamed, *a.* SYN.-abashed, debased, embarrassed, mortified, shamefaced.

asinine, *a.* SYN.-absurd, brainless,

crazy, foolish, idiotic, irrational, nonsensical, preposterous, ridiculous, senseless, silly, simple. ANT.-judicious, prudent, sagacious, sane, wise.

ask, *v.* SYN.-beg, claim, demand, entreat, invite, request, solicit; inquire, interrogate, query, question. ANT.-command, dictate, insist, order, reply.

asperse, *v.* SYN.-abuse, defame, disparage, ill-use, malign, revile, scandalize, traduce, vilify; misapply, misemploy, misuse. ANT.-cherish, honor, praise, protect, respect.

aspiration, *n.* SYN.-aim, ambition, craving, desire, goal, hope, longing, objective, passion.

aspire, *v.* SYN.-attempt, endeavor, strive, struggle, undertake, aim, design, intend, mean, try. ANT.-abandon, decline, ignore, neglect, omit.

assail, *v.* SYN.-assault, attack, besiege, charge, encounter, invade, abuse, censure, impugn. ANT.-aid, defend, protect, repel, resist.

assassinate, *v.* SYN.-butcher, execute, kill, massacre, murder, put to death, slaughter, slay. ANT.-animate, protect, resuscitate, save, vivify.

assault, *v.* SYN.-assail, attack, bombard, charge, invade, pound, storm, strike. ANT.-defend, oppose, protect.

assembly, *n.* SYN.-aggregation, band, brood, bunch, class, cluster, collection, crowd, flock, group, herd, horde, lot, mob, pack, party, set, swarm, throng, troupe.

assent, *v.* SYN.-accede, acquiesce, agree, comply, consent; coincide, concur, conform, tally. ANT.-contradict, differ, disagree, dissent, protest.

assert, *v.* SYN.-affirm, allege, aver, claim, declare, express, maintain, state; defend, support, uphold, vindicate. ANT.-contradict, deny, refute.

assess, *v.* SYN.-appraise, assign, calculate, compute, estimate, evaluate, fix, levy, reckon, tax.

assessment, *n.* SYN.-assessment, custom, duty, exaction, excise, impost, levy, rate, tax, toll, tribute. ANT.-gift, remuneration, reward, wages.

assign, *v.* SYN.-allot, apportion, appropriate, ascribe, attribute, cast, designate, distribute, specify. ANT.-discharge, release, relieve, unburden.

assimilate, *v.* SYN.-absorb, consume, engulf, imbibe, swallow up; engage, engross, occupy. ANT.-discharge, dispense, emit, expel, exude.

assist, *v.* SYN.-abet, aid, back, further, help, promote, serve, support, sustain. ANT.-hamper, hinder, impede, prevent.

assistance, *n.* SYN.-aid, alms, backing, furtherance, help, patronage, relief, succor, support. ANT.-antagonism, counteraction, defiance, hostility, resistance.

assistant, *n.* SYN.-aide, auxiliary, bodyguard, colleague, deputy, helper, henchman, lieutenant, secretary.

associate, *n.* SYN.-attendant, colleague, comrade, consort, crony, friend, mate, partner. ANT.-adversary, enemy, stranger.

associate, *v.* SYN.-affiliate, ally, combine, companion, conjoin, connect, join, link, mingle, mix. ANT.-disrupt, divide, estrange, separate.

association, *n.* SYN.-affinity, alliance, bond, conjunction, connection, link, relationship, tie, union. ANT.-disunion, isolation, separation.

assorted, *a.* SYN.-diverse, heterogeneous, indiscriminate, miscellaneous, mixed, motley, sundry, varied. ANT.-alike, classified, homogeneous, ordered, selected.

assortment, *n.* SYN.-change, difference, dissimilarity, diversity, heterogeneity, medley, miscellany, mixture, multifariousness, variety, variousness. ANT.-homogeneity, likeness, monotony, sameness, uniformity.

assuage, *v.* SYN.-abate, decrease, diminish, lessen, lower, moderate, reduce, suppress. ANT.-amplify, enlarge, increase, intensify, revive.

assume, *v.* SYN.-appropriate, arrogate, conjecture, take, usurp, adopt, affect, pretend, simulate, wear, postulate, presume, suppose, theorize. ANT.-concede, grant, surrender, doff, demonstrate, prove.

assurance, *n.* SYN.-assuredness, certainty, confidence, conviction, courage, firmness, security, self-reliance, surety, pledge, promise, word; assertion, declaration, statement. ANT.-bashfulness, humility, modesty, shyness, suspicion.

assure, *v.* SYN.-corroborate, substantiate, verify; acknowledge, establish, settle; approve, fix, ratify, sanction; strengthen.

astonishment, *n.* SYN.-admiration, amazement, astonishment, awe, bewilderment, curiosity, marvel, surprise, wonder, wonderment. ANT.-familiarity, triviality; apathy, expectation, indifference.

astound, *v.* SYN.-amaze, astonish, disconcert, dumbfound, flabbergast, shock, startle, stun, surprise, take aback. ANT.-admonish, caution, forewarn, prepare.

atrocity, *n.* SYN.-barbarity, brutality, cruelty, inhumanity, outrage, wickedness.

attach, *v.* SYN.-adjoin, affix, annex, append, connect, join, stick, unite; assign, associate, attribute. ANT.-detach, disengage, separate, unfasten, untie.

attachment, *n.* SYN.-adherence, affection, affinity, devotion, friendship, liking, regard. ANT.-alienation, aversion, estrangement, opposition, separation.

attack, *n.* SYN.-aggression, assault, criticism, denunciation, invasion, offense, onslaught; convulsion, fit, paroxysm. ANT.-defense, opposition, resistance, surrender, vindication.

attack, *v.* SYN.-assail, assault, besiege, charge, encounter, invade, abuse, censure, impugn. ANT.-aid, defend, protect, repel, resist.

attain, *v.* SYN.-accomplish, achieve, acquire, arrive, effect, gain, get, obtain, procure, reach, secure, win. ANT.-abandon, desert, discard, relinquish.

attempt, *n.* SYN.-effort, endeavor, essay, experiment, trial, undertaking. ANT.-inaction, laziness, neglect.

attend, *v.* SYN.-accompany, escort, follow, guard, lackey, protect, serve, tend, watch; be present, frequent.

attention, *n.* SYN.-alertness, care, circumspection, consideration, heed, mindfulness, notice, observance, watchfulness; application, contemplation, reflection, study.

ANT.-disregard, indifference, negligence, omission, oversight.

attentive, *a.* SYN.-alert, alive, awake, aware, careful, considerate, heedful, mindful, observant, thoughtful, wary, watchful; assiduous, diligent, studious. ANT.-apathetic, indifferent, oblivious, unaware.

attire, *n.* SYN.-apparel, array, clothes, clothing, drapery, dress, garb, garments, raiment, vestments, vesture. ANT.-nakedness, nudity.

attitude, *n.* SYN.-air, demeanor, disposition, emotion, inclination, mood, propensity, reaction, standpoint, temper, temperament, viewpoint; aspect, pose, position, posture, stand.

attract, *v.* SYN.-allure, captivate, charm, enchant, entice, fascinate, lure. ANT.-alienate, deter, repel, repulse.

attractive, *a.* SYN.-alluring, charming, enchanting, engaging, inviting, magnetic, pleasant, pleasing, seductive, winning. ANT.-forbidding, obnoxious, repellent, repulsive.

attribute, *n.* SYN.-characteristic, distinction, feature, peculiarity, property, quality, trait.

audacious, *a.* SYN.-adventurous, bold, brave, courageous, daring, dauntless, fearless, intrepid; brazen, forward, impudent, insolent, pushy, rude; abrupt, conspicuous, prominent, striking. ANT.-cowardly, flinching, timid; bashful, retiring.

audacity, *n.* SYN.-boldness, effrontery, fearlessness, hardihood, temerity. ANT.-circumspection, fearfulness, humility, meekness.

audible, *a.* SYN.-clear, discernible, emphatic, heard, loud, plain, resounding.

audience, *n.* SYN.-assemblage, band, company, crew, group, horde, party, spectators, throng, troop, witnesses.

audit, *n.* SYN.-check, inspection, report, review, scrutiny.

augment, *v.* SYN.-accrue, amplify, enhance, enlarge, expand, extend, grow, heighten, increase, intensify, magnify, multiply, raise, wax. ANT.-atrophy, contract, decrease, diminish, reduce.

august, *a.* SYN.-dignified, grand, grandiose, high, imposing, lofty, magnificent, majestic, noble, pompous, stately, sublime. ANT.-common, humble, lowly, ordinary, undignified.

austere, *a.* SYN.-harsh, rigid, rigorous, severe, stern, strict, stringent, unyielding. ANT.-elastic, flexible, resilient, supple, yielding.

authentic, *a.* SYN.-genuine, pure, real, true, verifiable, accurate, authoritative, correct, reliable, trustworthy. ANT.-counterfeit, erroneous, false, spurious.

author, *n.* SYN.-columnist, composer, creator, father, inventor, journalist, maker, originator, writer.

authoritarian, *a.* SYN.-arrogant, dictatorial, doctrinaire, dogmatic, domineering, magisterial, opinionated, overbearing, positive; authoritative, doctrinal, formal. ANT.-fluctuating, indecisive, open-minded, questioning, skeptical.

authority, *n.* SYN.-control, domination, dominion, force, justification, power, supremacy, authorization, license, permission, sanction, ground, importance, influence, prestige, weight. ANT.-impotence, incapacity, weakness, denial, prohibition.

autobiography, *n.* SYN.-adventures, biography, experiences, history, journal, letters, life, memoirs.

automated, *a.* SYN.-automatic, computerized, electronic, mechanical, mechanized, motorized, programmed. ANT.-manual.

autonomous, *a.* SYN.-emancipated, exempt, free, independent, liberated, unconfined, uncontrolled, unrestricted, unobstructed. ANT.-confined, restrained, restricted; blocked, clogged, contingent, dependent, impeded; subject.

auxiliary, *a.* SYN.-ancillary, assisting, conducive, furthering, helping, instrumental, subsidiary. ANT.-cumbersome, obstructive, opposing, retarding.

available, *a.* SYN.-accessible, convenient, handy, obtainable, prepared, ready, usable. ANT.-inaccessible, unavoidable.

avaricious, *a.* SYN.-covetous, grasping, greedy, rapacious, selfish; devouring, gluttonous, insatiable, ravenous, voracious. ANT.-generous, munificent; full, satisfied.

avenge, *v.* SYN.-requite, retaliate, revenge, vindicate. ANT.-forgive, pardon, pity, reconcile.

aver, *v.* SYN.-affirm, assert, declare, maintain, protest, state, swear. ANT.-contradict, demur, deny, dispute, oppose.

average, *a.* SYN.-fair, intermediate, mean, median, mediocre, medium, middling, moderate, ordinary. ANT.-exceptional, extraordinary, outstanding.

averse, *a.* SYN.-disinclined, hesitant, loath, reluctant, slow, unwilling. ANT.-disposed, eager, inclined, ready, willing.

aversion, *n.* SYN.-abhorrence, antipathy, disgust, disinclination, dislike, distaste, dread, hatred, loathing, repugnance, repulsion, reluctance. ANT.-affection, attachment, devotion, enthusiasm.

avert, *v.* See **avoid.**

avoid, *v.* SYN.-avert, dodge, escape, eschew, elude, forbear, forestall, free, shun, ward. ANT.-confront, encounter, face, meet, oppose.

awake, *a.* SYN.-alert, alive, aware, conscious, stirring, up. ANT.-asleep, dozing, napping, unconscious.

aware, *a.* SYN.-apprised, cognizant, conscious, informed, mindful, observant, perceptive, sensible. ANT.-ignorant, insensible, oblivious, unaware.

away, *a.* SYN.-abroad, absent, departed, inattentive, preoccupied. ANT.-attending, present; attentive, watchful.

awful, *a.* SYN.-appalling, dire, dreadful, frightful, horrible, terrible, awe-inspiring, imposing, majestic, solemn. ANT.-commonplace, humble, lowly, vulgar.

awkward, *a.* SYN.-clumsy, gauche, gawky, inept, rough, unpolished, untoward. ANT.-adroit, graceful, neat, polished, skillful.

axis, *n.* SYN.-axle, divider, pole, shaft, spindle.

axiom, *n.* SYN.-adage, aphorism, apothegm, byword, fundamental, maxim, postulate, principle, proverb, saw, saying, theorem, truism.

B

babble, *v.* SYN.-chatter, gabble, gush, jabber, prattle, rant, rave.

back, *a.* SYN.-aft, after, astern, behind, following, hind, hindmost, rear. ANT.-ahead, fore, forward, front, head, leading.

backed, *a.* SYN.-abetted, aided, assisted, boosted, championed, encouraged, established, furthered, propelled, pushed.

backward, *a.* SYN.-regressive, retrograde, revisionary, dull, sluggish, stupid, disinclined, hesitating, indisposed, loath, reluctant, unwilling, wavering. ANT.-advanced, civilized, progressive.

bad, *a.* SYN.-baleful, base, deleterious, evil, immoral, iniquitous, noxious, pernicious, sinful, unsound, unwholesome, villainous, wicked. ANT.-excellent, good, honorable, moral, reputable.

badger, *v.* SYN.-aggravate, annoy, bother, disturb, harass, harry, irritate, molest, nag, pester, plague, provoke, tantalize, taunt, tease, torment, vex, worry. ANT.-comfort, delight, gratify, please, soothe.

baffle, *v.* SYN.-balk, circumvent, defeat, disappoint, foil, frustrate, hinder, outwit, prevent, thwart. ANT.-accomplish, fulfill, further, promote.

bag, *n.* SYN.-attaché case, backpack, briefcase, pack, pocketbook, purse, satchel, suitcase, tote.

balance, *n.* SYN.-composure, equilibrium, poise, stability, steadiness, proportion, symmetry, excess, remainder, remains, residue, rest. ANT.-fall, imbalance, instability, unsteadiness.

balance, *v.* SYN.-dangle, hang, poise, suspend, swing. ANT.-continue, maintain, persist, proceed, prolong.

bald, *a.* bare, exposed, naked, nude, stripped, unclad, uncovered, barren, plain, simple, defenseless, open, unprotected. ANT.-clothed, covered, dressed; concealed; protected.

ban, *v.* SYN.-debar, forbid, hinder, inhibit, interdict, prevent, prohibit. ANT.-allow, permit, sanction, tolerate.

banal, *a.* SYN.-commonplace, hackneyed, inane, insipid, trite, vapid. ANT.-fresh, novel, original, stimulating, striking.

band, *n.* SYN.-circle, circumference, latitude, meridian, orbit, zone; bandage, belt, obi, ring, sash, scarf.

banish, *v.* SYN.-deport, dismiss, dispel, eject, exclude, exile, expatriate, expel, ostracize, oust. ANT.-accept, admit, harbor, receive, shelter.

banquet, *n.* SYN.-celebration, dinner, entertainment, feast, festival, regalement.

barbaric, *a.* See **barbarous.**

barbarous, *a.* SYN.-barbarian, barbaric, brutal, crude, cruel, inhuman, merciless, remorseless, rude, ruthless, savage, uncivilized, uncultured, unrelenting. ANT.-civilized, humane, kind, polite, refined.

bargain, *n.* SYN.-agreement, compact, contract, covenant, pact, promise, stipulation, treaty.

barren, *a.* SYN.-devoid, empty hollow, unfilled, unfurnished, unoccupied, vacant, vacuous, void, worthless. ANT.-full, inhabited, occupied, replete, supplied.

barrier, *n.* SYN.-barricade, blockade, fence, hindrance, hurdle, impediment, obstacle, obstruction, restriction, wall.

base, *a.* SYN.-abject, contemptible,

despicable, dishonorable, groveling, ignoble, ignominious, low, lowly, mean, menial, servile, sordid, vile, vulgar. ANT.-teemed, exalted, honored, lofty, noble, righteous.

base, *n.* SYN.-basis, bottom, foundation, ground, groundwork, root, substructure, support, underpinning. ANT.-building, cover, superstructure, top.

bashful, *a.* SYN.-abashed, coy, diffident, embarrassed, humble, modest, recoiling, retiring, shamefaced, sheepish, shy, timid, timorous. ANT.-adventurous, daring, fearless, gregarious, outgoing.

basic, *a.* SYN.-elementary, fundamental, primary, rudimentary, simple. ANT.-abstract, abstruse, complex, elaborate, intricate.

basis, *n.* SYN.-base, bottom, foundation, ground, groundwork, support, underpinning, assumption, postulate, premise, presumption, presupposition, principle. ANT.-derivative, implication, superstructure, trimming.

bath, *n.* SYN.-bathroom, lavatory, sauna, shower, toilet, tub, washroom.

bathe, *v.* SYN.-clean, cleanse, launder, rinse, scrub, wash, wet. ANT.-dirty, foul, soil, stain.

battle, *n.* SYN.-combat, conflict, contest, fight, fray, skirmish, strife, struggle. ANT.-agreement, concord, peace, truce.

battle, *v.* SYN.-brawl, combat, conflict, contend, dispute, encounter, fight, quarrel scuffle, skirmish, squabble, struggle, wrangle.

bay, *n.* SYN.-bayou, cove, gulf, harbor, inlet, lagoon, mouth, sound.

beacon, *n.* SYN.-beam, flare, guide, lamp, lantern, radar, signal, sonar.

bear, *v.* SYN.-support, sustain, uphold, allow, brook, endure, permit, stand, suffer, tolerate, undergo; carry, convey, take, transport; produce, spawn, yield. ANT.-avoid, dodge, evade, refuse, shun.

beast, *n.* SYN.-animal, barbarian, brute, creature, fiend, lout, monster, pervert, savage.

beastly, *a.* SYN.-abominable, base, brutal, coarse, degraded, depraved, disgusting, low, obscene, repulsive, savage, vulgar. ANT.-kind, nice, pleasant, refined, suave.

beat, *v.* SYN.-belabor, buffet, dash, hit, knock, pound, pummel, punch, smite, strike, thrash, thump; conquer, defeat, overpower, overthrow, rout, subdue, vanquish, palpitate, pulsate, pulse, throb. ANT.-defend, shield, stroke, fail, surrender.

beautiful, *a.* SYN.-beauteous, charming, comely, elegant, fair, fine, gorgeous, handsome, lovely, pretty. ANT.-foul, hideous, homely, repulsive, unsightly.

beauty, *n.* SYN.-attractiveness, charm, comeliness, elegance, fairness, grace, handsomeness, loveliness, pulchritude. ANT.-deformity, disfigurement, eyesore, homeliness, ugliness.

because, *conj.* SYN.-as, for, inasmuch as, since.

beckon, *v.* SYN.-call, signal, summon, wave.

bed, *n.* SYN.-berth, bunk, cot, couch, cradle, hammock, mattress; accumulation, deposit, layer, stratum, vein.

bedlam, *n.* SYN.-chaos, clamor, commotion, confusion, disorder, tumult, turmoil, uproar. ANT.-order, quiet, serenity.

befoul, *v.* SYN.-corrupt, contaminate, defile, infect, poison, pollute, sully, taint. ANT.-disinfect, purify.

beg, *v.* SYN.-adjure, ask, beseech, crave, entreat, implore, importune, petition, pray, request, solicit, supplicate. ANT.-bestow, cede, favor, give, grant.

beget, *v.* SYN.-breed, create, engender, father, generate, originate, procreate, produce, propagate, sire. ANT.-abort, destroy, extinguish, kill, murder.

beggar, *n.* SYN.-mendicant, pauper, ragamuffin, scrub, starveling, tatterdemalion, vagabond, wretch.

begin, *v.* SYN.-arise, commence, enter, inaugurate, initiate, institute, open, originate, start. ANT.-close, complete, end, finish, terminate.

beginner, *n.* SYN.-apprentice, amateur, dabbler, dilettante, learner, neophyte, novice. ANT.-adept, authority, expert, master, professional.

beginning, *n.* SYN.-commencement, inception, genesis, opening, origin, outset, source, start. ANT.-close, completion, consummation, end, termination.

behalf, *n.* SYN.-account, advantage, avail, benefit, favor, gain, good, interest, profit, service. ANT.-calamity, distress, handicap, trouble.

behave, *v.* SYN.-act, bear, carry, comport, conduct, demean, deport, interact, manage, operate.

behavior, *n.* SYN.-action, bearing, carriage, conduct, deed, demeanor, deportment, disposition, manner.

behind, *a.* SYN.-after, back, delayed, following, trailing; backward, retarded, slow. ANT.-ahead, forward, leading; clever, quick, smart.

behold, *v.* SYN.-contemplate, descry, discern, distinguish, espy, glimpse, inspect, look at, notice, observe, perceive, scan, scrutinize, see, view, watch, witness.

belief, *n.* SYN.-certitude, confidence, conviction, credence, faith, feeling, notion, opinion, persuasion, reliance, trust. ANT.-denial, doubt, heresy, incredulity.

believe, *v.* SYN.-accept, apprehend, conceive, credit, fancy, hold, imagine, support, suppose. ANT.-distrust, doubt, question, reject.

belittle, *v.* SYN.-decry, depreciate, disparage, derogate, discredit, lower, undervalue minimize, underrate. ANT.-admire, appreciate, esteem. aggrandize, commend, exalt, magnify, praise.

belongings, *n.* SYN.-commodities, effects, estate, goods, possessions, property, stock, wealth.

beloved, *a.* SYN.-adored, dear, esteemed, precious, prized, valued; valuable. ANT.-despised, unwanted.

below, *prep.* SYN.-beneath, lower, under, underneath. ANT.-above, aloft, over, overhead.

bend, *v.* SYN.-bow, crook, curve, deflect, incline, lean, stoop, turn, twist, influence, mold, submit, yield. ANT.-break, resist, stiffen, straighten.

beneath, *prep.* SYN.-below, under, underneath. ANT.-above, over.

beneficial, *a.* SYN.-advantageous, good, helpful, profitable, salutary, serviceable, useful, wholesome. ANT.-deleterious, destructive, detrimental, harmful, injurious.

benefit, *n.* SYN.-account, advantage, avail, behalf, favor, gain, good, interest, profit, service. ANT.-calamity, distress, handicap, trouble.

benefit, *v.* SYN.-aid, assist, attend, help, oblige, succor; advance, forward, promote.

benevolence, *n.* SYN.-altruism, beneficence, charity, generosity, humanity, kindness, liberality, magnanimity, philanthropy, tenderness. ANT.-cruelty, inhumanity, malevolence, selfishness, unkindness.

benevolent, *a.* SYN.-altruistic, benign, charitable, friendly, generous, humane, kind, liberal, merciful, obliging, philanthropic, tender, unselfish. ANT.-greedy, harsh, malevolent, wicked.

bent, *n.* SYN.-bending, inclination, leaning, affection, attachment, bent, bias, desire, disposition, penchant, predilection, preference. ANT.-apathy, aversion, distaste, nonchalance, repugnance.

bequeath, *v.* SYN.-donate, endow, give, will.

bequest, *n.* SYN.-appropriation, benefaction, boon, bounty, concession, donation, endowment, gift, grant, subsidy.

berate, *v.* SYN.-admonish, blame, censure, lecture, rebuke, reprehend, reprimand, scold, upbraid, vituperate. ANT.-approve, commend, praise.

besides, *prep.* SYN.-also, furthermore, in addition, likewise, moreover, similarly, too.

best, *a.* SYN.-finest, greatest, incomparable, top, unequaled. ANT.-common, ordinary, worst.

bestial, *a.* SYN.-barbarous, brutal, brutish, carnal, coarse, cruel, ferocious, gross, inhuman, merciless, remorseless, rough, rude, ruthless, savage, sensual. ANT-civilized, courteous, gentle, humane, kind.

bestow, *v.* SYN.-confer, contribute, deliver, donate, furnish, give, grant, impart, present, provide, supply, ANT.-keep, retain, seize, withdraw.

bet, *v.* SYN.-gamble, hazard, risk, speculate, venture, wager.

better, *v.* SYN.-ameliorate, amend, help, improve, rectify, reform. ANT.-corrupt, damage, debase, impair, vitiate.

bevy, *n.* SYN.-crowd, crush, horde, host, masses, mob, multitude, populace, press, rabble, swarm, throng.

bewilder, *v.* SYN.-confound, confuse, dumfound, mystify, nonplus, perplex, puzzle. ANT.-clarify, explain, illumine, instruct, solve.

bewildered, *a.* SYN.-deranged, disconcerted, disordered, disorganized, indistinct, mixed, muddled, perplexed. ANT.-clear, lucid, obvious, organized, plain.

bias, *n.* SYN.-bent, disposition, inclination, leaning, partiality, penchant, predilection, predisposition, prejudice, proclivity, proneness, propensity, slant, tendency, turn. ANT.-equity, fairness, impartiality, justice.

bicker, *v.* SYN.-altercate, argue, contend, contest, debate, discuss, dispute, quarrel, squabble, wrangle. ANT.-agree, allow, assent, concede.

big, *a.* SYN.-august, bulky, colossal, enormous, grand, great,. huge, hulking, immense, large, majestic, massive, monstrous. ANT.-little, petite, small, tiny.

bigoted, *a.* SYN.-dogmatic, fanatical, illiberal, intolerant, narrow-minded, prejudiced. ANT.-liberal, progressive, radical, tolerant.

bind, *v.* SYN.-attach, connect, engage, fasten, fetter, join, link, oblige, restrain, restrict, tie. ANT.-free, loose, unfasten, untie.

binding, *a.* SYN.-cogent, conclusive, convincing, effective, efficacious, legal, logical, powerful, sound, strong, telling, valid, weighty. ANT.-counterfeit, null, spurious, void, weak.

biography, *n.* SYN.-adventures, biography, experiences, history, journal, letters, life, memoirs.

bit, *n.* SYN.-amount, fraction, fragment, morsel, part, piece, portion, scrap. ANT.-all, entirety, sum, total, whole.

bite, *v.* SYN.-champ, chew, crunch, gnash, gnaw, nibble, nip, pierce, rend, tear.

bitter, *a.* SYN.-acrid, biting, distasteful, pungent, sour, tart; galling, grievous, painful, poignant; cruel, fierce, relentless, ruthless; acrimonious, caustic, harsh, sardonic, severe. ANT.-delicious, mellow, pleasant, sweet.

bizarre, *a.* SYN.-abnormal, curious, eccentric, extraordinary, grotesque, irregular, odd, peculiar, quaint, queer, singular, strange, uncommon, unique, unusual. ANT.-common, conventional, familiar, normal, ordinary, regular, typical.

blab, *v.* SYN.-chatter, confess, divulge, squeal, talk, tell.

black, *a.* SYN.-dark, dim, gloomy, murky, obscure, shadowy, unilluminated; dusky, opaque, sable, swarthy; dismal, gloomy, mournful, somber, sorrowful; evil, sinister, sullen, wicked; hidden, mystic, occult, secret. ANT.-light; bright, clear; pleasant; lucid.

blackball, *v.* SYN.-bar, except, exclude, expel, hinder, omit, ostracize, prevent, prohibit, restrain, shut out. ANT.-accept, admit, include, welcome.

blame, *v.* SYN.-accuse, censure, charge, condemn, implicate, involve, prosecute, rebuke, reproach, slander, upbraid. ANT.-absolve, acquit, exonerate.

blameless, *a.* SYN.-faultless, holy, immaculate, perfect, pure, sinless. ANT.-blemished, defective, faulty, imperfect.

bland, *a.* SYN.-boring, dull, flat, insipid, lifeless, tasteless; gentle, mild soothing. ANT.-exciting, interesting, spicy; irritating, stimulating.

blank, *a.* SYN.-clear, empty, new, open, untouched, vacant, white.

blaze, *n.* SYN.-burning, combustion, conflagration, fire, flame, glow, heat, warmth.

bleak, *a.* SYN.-cheerless, dark, dismal, doleful, dreary, dull, funereal, gloomy, lonesome, melancholy, sad, somber. ANT.-cheerful, gay, joyous, lively.

bleakness, *n.* SYN.-blackness, darkness, gloom, obscurity, shadow; dejection, depression, despondency, melancholy, misery, sadness, woe. ANT.-exultation, frivolity, joy, light, mirth.

blemish, *n.* SYN.-blot, speck, stain; defect, disgrace, fault, flaw, imperfection, tarnish. ANT.-adornment, embellishment, perfection, purity.

blend, *v.* SYN.-amalgamate, coalesce, combine, commingle, conjoin, consolidate, fuse, mingle, mix, merge, unify, unite. ANT.-analyze, decompose, disintegrate, separate.

bless, *v.* SYN.-adore, baptize, celebrate, consecrate, delight, exalt, extol, gladden, glorify. ANT.-blaspheme, curse, denounce, slander.

blessing, *n.* SYN.-absolution, consecration, miracle, unction; asset, boon, benefit, help, luck, windfall.

blind, *a.* SYN.-ignorant, oblivious, sightless, undiscerning, unmindful, unseeing; headlong, heedless, rash. ANT.-aware, calculated, discerning, perceiving, sensible.

bliss, *n.* SYN.-blessedness, blissfulness, ecstasy, felicity, happiness, joy, rapture. ANT.-grief, misery, sorrow, woe, wretchedness.

blithe, *a.* SYN.-effervescent, light, resilient; animated, buoyant, cheerful, elated, hopeful, jocund, lively, spirited, sprightly, vivacious. ANT.-dejected, depressed, despondent, hopeless, sullen.

block, *v.* SYN.-bar, barricade, clog, close, obstruct, stop, delay, impede; hinder. ANT.-clear, open; aid, further, promote.

blockade, *v.* SYN.-barricade, besiege, encircle, isolate.

blossom, *v.* SYN.-bloom, burgeon, flourish, succeed

blond, *a.* SYN.-attractive, comely, fair, light, pale.

blot, *n.* SYN.-blemish, speck, stain; defect, disgrace, fault, flaw, imperfection. ANT.-adornment, embellishment, perfection, purity.

blow, *n.* SYN.-bang, box, clout, cuff, hit, jab, punch, slam, slap, strike, swat, whack.

bluff, *v.* SYN.-con, deceive, delude, fool, mislead, threaten, trick.

blunder, *n.* SYN.-error, indiscretion, lapse, mistake, oversight.

blunt, *a.* SYN.-dull, edgeless, obtuse, pointless, stolid, thick-witted, unsharpened; abrupt, bluff, brusque, impolite, outspoken, plain, rough, rude, unceremonious. ANT.-polished, polite, suave, subtle, tactful.

blustery, *a.* SYN.-gusty, inclement, roaring, rough, stormy, tempestuous, turbulent, windy. ANT.-calm, clear, peaceful, quiet, tranquil.

boast, *v.* SYN.-brag, crow, flaunt, glory, vaunt. ANT.-apologize, deprecate, humble, minimize.

bodily, *a.* SYN.-animal, base, carnal, corporeal, fleshly, gross, lustful, sensual, voluptuous, worldly, ANT.-exalted, intellectual, refined, spiritual, temperate.

body, *n.* SYN.-carcass, corpse, remains; form, frame, physique, torso; bulk, corpus, mass; aggregate, association, company, society. ANT.-intellect, mind, soul, spirit.

boisterous, *a.* SYN.-disruptive, loud, noisy, rude, unruly.

bold, *a.* SYN.-adventurous, audacious, brave, courageous, daring, dauntless, fearless, intrepid; brazen, forward, impudent, insolent, pushy, rude; abrupt, conspicuous, prominent, striking. ANT.-cowardly, flinching, timid; bashful, retiring.

boldness, *n.* SYN.-effrontery, audacity, fearlessness, hardihood, temerity. ANT.-circumspection, fearfulness, humility, meekness.

bolt, *v.* SYN.-bar, clasp, fastening, hook, latch, lock, padlock.

bombast, *n.* harangue, lecture, sermon.

bond, *n.* SYN.-connection, connective, coupler, juncture, link, tie, union. ANT.-break, gap, interval, opening, split.

bondage, *n.* SYN.-captivity, confinement, imprisonment, serfdom, servitude, slavery, thralldom, vassalage. ANT.-freedom, liberation.

bonus, *n.* SYN.-award, bounty, compensation, premium, prize, recompense, remuneration, reward. ANT.-assessment, charge, earnings, punishment, wages.

book, *n.* SYN.-booklet, brochure, compendium, edition, handbook, manual, monograph, pamphlet, publication, textbook, tract, treatise, volume, work.

bookkeeper, *n.* SYN.-accountant, auditor, clerk, comptroller, controller; treasurer.

boor, *n.* SYN.-boob, bumpkin, lout, peasant, rustic, yokel.

boost, *v.* SYN.-advance, assist, abet, encourage, help, promote, support.

border, *n.* SYN.-boundary, brim, brink, edge, fringe, frontier, limit, margin, outskirts, rim, termination, verge. ANT.-center, core, interior, mainland.

boredom, *n.* SYN.-apathy, doldrums, dullness, ennui, indifference, monotony, tedium, weariness. ANT.-activity, excitement, motive, stimulus.

boring, *a.* SYN.-dense, slow, stupid; blunt, obtuse; commonplace, dull, dismal, dreary, monotonous, sad, tedious. ANT.-animated, lively, sharp; clear, interesting.

borrowed, *a.* SYN.-acquired, adopted, appropriated, copied, imitated, plagiarized, taken.

botch, *v.* SYN.-blunder, bungle, mishandle, mismanage, muddle, ruin, spoil, wreck.

bother, *v.* SYN.-annoy, disturb, harass, haunt, inconvenience, molest, perplex, pester, plague, tease, trouble, upset, worry. ANT.-gratify, please, relieve, soothe.

bottle, *n.* SYN.-canteen, carafe, cruet, decanter, flagon, flask, jar, vial.

bottom, *n.* SYN.-base, basis, foot, foundation, fundament, groundwork. ANT.-apex, peak, summit, top.

bought, *a.* SYN.-acquired, contracted, ordered, procured, purchased, requisitioned.

boulder, *n.* SYN.-rock, slab, stone.

bounce, *v.* SYN.-bolt, bound, hop, jump, leap, ricochet, spring, vault.

bound, *v.* SYN.-circumscribe, confine, enclose, encompass, envelop, fence, limit, surround. ANT.-develop, distend, enlarge, expand, expose, open.

boundary, *n.* SYN.-brim, brink, edge, fringe, frontier, limit, margin, outskirts, rim, termination, verge, border, extremity, hem, periphery. ANT.-center, core, interior, mainland.

bountiful, *a.* SYN.-ample, abundant, copious, overflowing, plenteous, plentiful, profuse, rich, teeming. ANT.-deficient, insufficient, scant, scarce.

bow, *v.* SYN.-bend, crook, curve, deflect, incline, lean, stoop, turn, twist, influence, mold, submit, yield. ANT.-break, resist, stiffen, straighten.

boycott, *v.* SYN.-disapprove, oppose, picket, protest, quit, resist.

brag, *v.* SYN.-bluster, boast, crow, flaunt, flourish, vaunt. ANT.-debase, degrade, demean, denigrate.

brand, *n.* SYN.-mark, scar, stain, stigma, trace, vestige; badge, label, sign; characteristic, feature, indication, property, trait.

brave, *a.* SYN.-adventurous, audacious, bold, chivalrous, courageous, daring, dauntless, fearless, gallant, heroic, intrepid, magnanimous, valiant, valorous. ANT.-cowardly, cringing, fearful, timid, weak.

bravery, *n.* SYN.-boldness, chivalry, courage, fearlessness, fortitude, intrepidity, mettle, prowess, resolution. ANT.-cowardice, fear, pusillanimity, timidity.

brazen, *a.* SYN.-adventurous, audacious, bold, brave, courageous, daring, dauntless, fearless, intrepid; forward, impudent, insolent, pushy, rude; abrupt, conspicuous, prominent, striking. ANT.-cowardly, flinching, timid; bashful, retiring.

break, *v.* SYN.-burst, crack, crush, demolish, destroy, fracture, infringe, pound, rack, rend, rupture, shatter, smash, squeeze; disobey, transgress, violate. ANT.-join, mend, renovate, repair, restore.

breakthrough, *n.* SYN.-creation, discovery, finding, innovation, invention.

breed, *n.* SYN.-kind, sort, stock, strain, subspecies, variety. ANT.-homogeneity, likeness, monotony, sameness, uniformity.

breed, *v.* SYN.-bear, beget, conceive, engender, generate, procreate, propagate; foster, nurture, raise, rear, train.

breeding, *n.* SYN.-civilization, culture, cultivation, education, enlightenment, refinement. ANT.-boorishness, ignorance, illiteracy, vulgarity.

breeze, *n.* SYN.-draft, gust, wind, zephyr.

bribe, *n.* SYN.-blackmail, compensation, fee, graft, gratuity, present, protection, reward.

bridge, *n.* SYN.-bond, connection, link, span.

brief, *a.* SYN.-compendious, concise, curt, laconic, pithy, short, succinct, terse; fleeting, momentary, passing, transient. ANT.-extended, lengthy, long, prolonged, protracted.

bright, *a.* SYN.-brilliant, clear, gleaming, lucid, luminous, lustrous, radiant, shining, translucent, transparent; clever, intelligent, witty. ANT.-dark, dull, gloomy, murky, sullen.

brightness, *n.* SYN.-brilliance, brilliancy, effulgence, luster, radiance, splendor. ANT.-darkness, dullness, gloom, obscurity.

brilliant, *a.* See **bright.**

brim, *n.* SYN.-border, edge, lip, margin, rim, top.

bring, *v.* SYN.-carry, convey, transmit, transport; bear, support, sustain. ANT.-abandon, drop.

brisk, *a.* SYN.-cool, fresh, refreshing. ANT.-hackneyed, musty, stagnant.

brittle, *a.* SYN.-breakable, crisp, crumbling, delicate, fragile, frail, splintery. ANT.-enduring, thick, tough, unbreakable.

broad, *a.* SYN.-expanded, extensive, immense, large, sweeping, vast, wide; liberal, tolerant. ANT.-confined, narrow, restricted.

broadcast, *v.* SYN.-air, announce, disseminate, notify, scatter, transmit.

broke, *a.* SYN.-bankrupt, indebted, owing, penniless, poverty-stricken, ruined. ANT.-rich, wealthy.

broken, *a.* SYN.-crushed, destroyed, flattened, fractured, interrupted, reduced, rent, ruptured, separated, shattered, smashed, wrecked. ANT.-integral, repaired, united, whole.

brood, *v.* SYN.-care, fret, grieve, mope, muse, ponder, sulk, think, worry.

brook, *n.* SYN.-rill, rivulet, stream.

broth, *n.* SYN.-brew, concoction, consommé, purée, soup, stock.

brotherhood, *n.* SYN.-brotherliness, fellowship, kindness, solidarity; association, clan, fraternity, society. ANT.-acrimony, discord, opposition, strife.

browbeat, *v.* SYN.-berate, bully, frighten, intimidate, scold, threaten.

browse, *v.* SYN.-examine, glance, peruse, scan, skim.

brusque, *a.* SYN.-abrupt, blunt, curt, discourteous, gruff, short.

brutal, *a.* SYN.-barbarous, bestial, brute, brutish, carnal, coarse, cruel, ferocious, gross, inhuman, merciless, remorseless, rough, rude, ruthless, savage, sensual. ANT-civilized, courteous, gentle, humane, kind.

budget, *v.* SYN.-allocate, allow, estimate, forecast, plan, provide.

build, *n.* SYN.-appearance, configuration, contour, cut, figure, form, frame, guise, image, mold, outline, pattern, shape. ANT.-contortion, deformity, distortion, mutilation.

build, *v.* SYN.-construct, erect, establish, found, raise, rear. ANT.-demolish, destroy, overthrow, raze, undermine.

bulletin, *n.* SYN.-advertisement, announcement, declaration, notification, promulgation. ANT.-hush, muteness, silence, speechlessness.

bulge, *n.* SYN.-appendage, excess, lump, projection, prominence, promontory.

bulk, *n.* SYN.-best, biggest, greater, majority, most. ANT.-least, lesser, fraction, remnant.

bulky, *a.* SYN.-big, cumbersome, large, huge, massive, unwieldy.

bum, *n.* SYN.-beggar, hobo, rover, tramp, vagabond, vagrant, wanderer. ANT.-gentleman, laborer, worker.

bump, *n.* SYN.-bang, clash, crash, hit, jar, jolt, knock, pat, push, shove.

bunch, *n.* SYN.-aggregation, assembly, band, brood, class, cluster, collection, crowd, flock, group, herd, horde, lot, mob, pack, party, set, swarm, throng, troupe.

bungle, *v.* SYN.-blunder, botch, mishandle, mismanage, muddle, ruin, spoil, wreck.

buoyant, *a.* SYN.-effervescent, light, resilient; animated, blithe, cheerful, elated, hopeful, jocund, lively, spirited, sprightly, vivacious. ANT.-dejected, depressed, despondent, hopeless, sullen.

burden, *v.* SYN.-afflict, encumber, load, oppress, overload, tax, trouble, weigh. ANT.-alleviate, console, ease, lighten, mitigate.

burdensome, *a.* SYN.-boring, dilatory, dreary, dull, humdrum, irksome, monotonous, slow, sluggish, tardy, tedious, tire-some, uninteresting, wearisome. ANT.-amusing, entertaining, exciting, interesting, quick.

burglarize, *v.* SYN.-loot, pilfer, pillage, plunder, purloin, rob, snatch, steal, swipe. ANT.-buy, refund, repay, restore, return.

burglary, *n.* SYN.-break in, depredation, larceny, pillage, plunder, robbery, theft.

burn, *v.* SYN.-blaze, char, consume, cremate, incinerate, scald, scorch, sear, singe. ANT.-extinguish, put out, quench.

burst, *v.* SYN.-break, crack, erupt,

explode, fracture, rupture, split.

bury, *v.* SYN.-conceal, cover, entomb, hide, immure, inhume, inter, secrete, stash, stow. ANT.-display, expose, open, reveal.

business, *n.* SYN.-art, commerce, employment, engagement, enterprise, job, occupation, profession, trade, trading, vocation, work. ANT.-avocation, hobby, pastime.

bustle, *n.* SYN.-ado, bother, commotion, confusion, flutter, flurry, haste, hurry, rush, speed.

busy, *a.* SYN.-working; industrious, alert, brisk, lively, nimble, quick, sprightly, supple, active, assiduous, hard-working, industrious, diligent, persevering. ANT.-dormant, inactive; indolent, lazy, passive, apathetic, indifferent, lethargic, unconcerned.

butchery, *n.* SYN.-carnage, massacre, pogrom, slaughter.

buy, *v.* SYN.-acquire, bargain, get, market, obtain, procure, purchase, secure. ANT.-dispose of, sell, vend.

by, *prep.* SYN.-beside, near, next to; by means of, through, with; according to; from.

C

cabal, *n.* SYN.-collusion, combination, conspiracy, intrigue, machination, plot, treachery, treason.

cabinet, *n.* SYN.-administrators, advisors, assistants, council, committee, ministry.

calamity, *n.* SYN.-adversity, accident, casualty, catastrophe, disaster, misfortune, mishap, ruin. ANT.-advantage, fortune, welfare calculation, design, intention, purpose.

calculate, *v.* SYN.-compute, consider, count, estimate, figure, reckon. ANT.-conjecture, guess, miscalculate.

caliber, *n.* SYN.-attribute, characteristic, distinction, feature, peculiarity, property, quality, trait, caliber, grade, value. ANT.-being, essence, nature, substance.

call, *v.* SYN.-cry, exclaim, hail, shout, signal, yell; convene, invite, muster, request, summon.

callous, *a.* SYN.-hard, impenitent, indurate, insensible, insensitive, obdurate, tough, unfeeling. ANT.-compassionate, sensitive, soft, tender.

calm, *a.* SYN.-appease, composed, dispassionate, imperturbable, pacific, peaceful, placid, quiet, serene, still, tranquil, undisturbed, unruffled. ANT.-excited, frantic, stormy, turbulent, wild.

calm, *n.* SYN.-calmness, hush, peace, quiescence, quiet, quietude, repose, rest, serenity, silence, stillness, tranquility. ANT.-agitation, disturbance, excitement, noise, tumult.

calm, *v.* SYN.-allay, alleviate, assuage, compose, lull, pacify, placate, quell, quiet, relieve, satisfy, soothe, still, tranquilize. ANT.-arouse, excite, incense, inflame.

calumny, *n.* SYN.-aspersion, backbiting, defamation, libel, scandal, slander, vilification. ANT.-applause, commendation, defense, flattery, praise.

camouflage, *n.* SYN.-cloak, cover, disguise, hide, mask, shroud, veil; deceit, misdirection.

cancel, *v.* SYN.-cross out, delete, eliminate, erase, expunge, obliterate; abolish, abrogate, annul, invalidate, nullify, quash, repeal, rescind, revoke. ANT.-confirm, enact, enforce, perpetuate

candid, *a.* SYN.-frank, free, honest, ingenuous, open, plain, sincere, straightforward, truthful; fair, impartial, just, unbiased. ANT.-contrived, scheming, sly, wily.

candidate, *n.* SYN.-aspirant, competitor, contestant, nominee.

candor, *n.* SYN.-fairness, frankness, honesty, integrity, justice, openness, rectitude, responsibility, sincerity, trustworthiness, uprightness. ANT.-cheating, deceit, dishonesty, fraud, trickery.

canny, *a.* SYN.-careful, cautious, discreet, prudent, shrewd, wary.

capability, *n.* See **capacity.**

capable, *a.* SYN.-able, clever, competent, efficient, fitted, qualified, skillful. ANT.-inadequate, incapable, incompetent, unfitted.

capacity, *n.* SYN.-ability, capability, faculty, power, skill, talent; magnitude, room, size, volume. ANT.-impotence, inability, incapacity, stupidity.

caper, *n.* SYN.-act, activity, escapade, prank, trick.

capital, *n.* SYN.-assets, cash, equipment, property, wealth.

capitulate, *v.* SYN.-abandon, acquiesce, cede, relinquish, renounce, resign, sacrifice, submit, surrender, yield. ANT.-conquer, overcome, resist, rout.

caprice, *n.* SYN.-fancy, humor, inclination, notion, quirk, vagary, whim, whimsy.

capricious, *a.* SYN.-changeable, fickle, fitful, inconstant, restless, unstable, variable. ANT.-constant, reliable, stable, steady, trustworthy.

captivity, *n.* SYN.-bondage, confinement, imprisonment, serfdom, servitude, slavery, thralldom, vassalage. ANT.-freedom, liberation.

capture, *v.* SYN.-apprehend, arrest, catch, clutch, grasp, grip, lay hold of, seize, snare, trap. ANT.-liberate, lose, release, throw.

carcass, *n.* SYN.-body, corpse, remains; form, frame, torso; bulk, corpus, mass. ANT.-intellect, mind, soul, spirit.

care, *n.* SYN.-anxiety, concern, solicitude, worry; attention, caution, circumspection, regard, vigilance, wariness; charge, custody, guardianship, ward. ANT.-disregard, indifference, neglect, negligence.

careen, *a.* SYN.-incline, list, tip.

careful, *a.* SYN.-attentive, exact, finicky, fussy, heedful, meticulous, painstaking, prudent, scrupulous, thorough, thoughtful; cautious, circumspect, discreet, guarded, suspicious, vigilant, wary. ANT.-forgetful, improvident, indifferent, lax.

careless, *a.* SYN.-heedless, imprudent, inattentive, inconsiderate, indiscreet, reckless, thoughtless, unconcerned; desultory, inaccurate, lax, neglectful, negligent, remiss. ANT.-accurate, careful, meticulous, nice.

carelessness, *n.* SYN.-default, disregard, failure, heedlessness, neglect, negligence, omission, oversight, slight, thoughtlessness. ANT.-attention, care, diligence, watchfulness.

caress, *v.* SYN.-coddle, cuddle, embrace, fondle, hug, kiss, pet, stroke. ANT.-annoy, buffet, spurn, tease, vex.

carnal, *a.* SYN.-animal, base, bodily, corporeal, fleshly, gross, lustful, sensual, voluptuous, worldly. ANT.-exalted, intellectual, refined, spirit-

ual, temperate.
carouse, *v.* SYN.- celebrate, frolic, indulge, party, play, revel.
carping, *a.* SYN.-caviling, censorious, critical, faultfinding, hypercritical. ANT.-cursory, shallow, superficial, uncritical; appreciative, approving, commendatory, encouraging.
carriage, *n.* SYN.-air, attitude, bearing, cast, demeanor, look, poise, pose, posture, presence.
carry, *v.* SYN.-bring, convey, fetch, move, take, transmit, transport; bear, support, sustain. ANT.-abandon, drop.
carve, *v.* SYN.-chisel, create, fashion, form, model, mold, pattern, shape.
case, *n.* SYN.-bag, box, carton, container, crate, grip, holder, sheath.
cast, *v.* SYN.-fling, hurl, pitch, sling, throw, toss.
caste, *n.* SYN.-category, class, denomination, genre, kind; grade, order, rank, set.
casual, *a.* SYN.-accidental, chance, fortuitous, unexpected; incidental, informal, nonchalant, offhand, relaxed, unconcerned, unpremeditated. ANT. expected, intended; formal, planned, pretentious.
casualty, *n.* SYN.-accident, calamity, contingency, disaster, fortuity, misfortune, mishap. ANT.-calculation, design, intention, purpose.
catalogue, *n.* SYN.-bulletin, classification, directory, file, listing, record, register.
catastrophe, *n.* SYN.-accident, adversity, affliction, calamity, casualty, devastation, disaster, distress, misfortune, mishap, ruin. ANT.-advantage, blessing, fortune, welfare.
catch, *v.* SYN.-apprehend, arrest, capture, clutch, grasp, grip, lay hold of, seize, snare, trap. ANT.-liberate, lose, release, throw.
catching, *a.* SYN.-communicable, contagious, infectious, pestilential, virulent. ANT.-healthful, hygienic, non-communicable.
categorical, *a.* SYN.-absolute, certain, definite, indubitable, undeniable.
category, *n.* SYN.-caste, class, denomination, genre, kind; grade, order, rank, set.
cause, *n.* SYN.-agent, determinant, incentive, inducement, motive, origin, principle, reason, source. ANT.-consequence, effect, end, result.
cause, *v.* SYN.-create, effect, evoke, incite, induce, make, occasion, originate, prompt.
caustic, *a.* SYN.-acrimonious, biting, cutting, derisive, ironic, sarcastic, sardonic, satirical, sneering, taunting. ANT.-affable, agreeable, amiable, pleasant.
caution, *n.* SYN.-care, heed, prudence, vigilance, wariness, watchfulness; admonition, counsel, injunction, warning. ANT.-abandon, carelessness, recklessness.
cautious, *a.* SYN.-attentive, heedful, prudent, scrupulous, thoughtful; careful, circumspect, discreet, guarded, vigilant, wary. ANT.-forgetful, improvident, indifferent, lax.
cease, *v.* SYN.-abandon, abstain, arrest, check, desist, discontinue, end, halt, quit, stop; give up, relinquish, resign, stop, surrender, terminate; abandon, depart, leave, withdraw. ANT.-continue, endure, occupy, persist, stay.
celebrate, *v.* SYN.-commemorate, keep, observe, solemnize; commend, extol, glorify, honor, laud,

praise. ANT.-disregard, overlook; decry, disgrace, dishonor, profane.

celebration, *n.* SYN.-anniversary, carnival, commemoration, ceremony, feast, festival, festivity, holiday, jubilee, observance, revelry, spree.

celebrity, *n.* SYN.-dignitary, hero, leader, luminary, notable, personage, star.

celestial, *a.* SYN.-divine, godlike, heavenly, holy, superhuman, supernatural, transcendent. ANT.-blasphemous, diabolical, mundane, profane, wicked.

cell, *n.* SYN.-cage, compartment, coop, keep, lockup, pen, vault.

censor, *v.* SYN.-abridge, ban, control, edit, forbid, inspect, restrict, suppress, void.

censure, *v.* SYN.-blame, condemn, denounce, reprehend, reproach, reprobate, reprove, upbraid; convict, sentence. ANT.-approve, commend, condone, forgive, praise; absolve, acquit, exonerate, pardon.

center, *n.* SYN.-core, heart, middle. midpoint, midst, nucleus. ANT.-border, boundary, outskirts, periphery, rim.

ceremonious, *a.* SYN.-affected, correct, decorous, exact, formal, methodical, precise, proper, regular, solemn, stiff. ANT.-easy, natural, unconstrained, unconventional.

ceremony, *n.* SYN.-formality, observance, parade, pomp, protocol, rite, ritual, solemnity.

certain, *a.* SYN.-assured, convinced, definite, fixed, indubitable, inevitable, positive, satisfied, secure, sure, undeniable, unquestionable. ANT.-doubtful, probable, questionable, uncertain.

certainty, *n.* SYN.-assurance, assuredness, confidence, conviction, courage, firmness, security, self-reliance, surety, pledge, promise, word. assertion, declaration, statement. ANT.-bashfulness, humility, modesty, shyness, suspicion.

certificate, *n.* SYN.-credential, declaration, endorsement, guarantee, license, testimonial, ticket, warrantee.

certify, *v.* SYN.-aver, attest, declare, state, swear, testify.

challenge, *v.* SYN.-object to, question; brave, dare, defy; call, invite, summon; demand, require.

chance, *a.* SYN.-accidental, casual, contingent, fortuitous, incidental, undesigned, unintended. ANT.-calculated, decreed, intended, planned, willed.

chance, *n.* SYN.-accident, contingency, fortuity, fortune, happening, misfortune, mishap, occasion, occurrence, opening, opportunity, possibility. ANT.-calculation, design, intention, purpose.

chance, *v.* SYN.-accidentally, bechance, befall, betide, coincidence, happen, occur, unexpectedly, risk, take place, transpire.

change, *n.* SYN.-alteration, alternation, modification, mutation, substitution, variation, variety, vicissitude. ANT.-monotony, stability, uniformity.

change, *v.* SYN.-exchange, substitute; alter, convert, modify, remodel, shift, transfigure, transform, vary, veer. ANT.-retain; continue, establish, preserve, settle, stabilize.

changeable, *a.* SYN.-fickle, fitful, inconstant, shifting, unstable, vacillating, variable, wavering. ANT.-constant, stable, steady, unchanging, uniform.

channel, *n.* SYN.-artery, canal, conduit, course, ditch, duct, furrow, gutter, tube, vein.

chaos, *n.* SYN.-anarchy, confusion, disorder, disorganization, jumble, muddle. ANT.-order, organization, system.

chaperone, *v.* SYN.-accompany, attend, escort, go with. ANT.-abandon, avoid.

character, *n.* SYN.-class, description, disposition, individuality, kind, nature, reputation, repute, temperament, sort, standing, style; figure, mark, sign, symbol, representation.

characteristic, *n* SYN.-attribute, feature, mark, peculiarity, property, quality, trait.

charade, *n.* SYN.-deception, dodge, fake, fraud, hoax, pretense, pretext, sham, swindle, trick

charge, *n.* SYN.-accusation, arraignment, imputation, incrimination, indictment. ANT.-exculpation, exoneration, pardon.

charge, *v.* SYN.-accuse, arraign, censure, incriminate, indict. ANT.-absolve, acquit, exonerate, release, vindicate.

charisma, *n.*SYN.-allure, appeal, attraction, charm, seductiveness.

charitable, *a.* SYN.-altruistic, benevolent, benign, friendly, generous, humane, kind, liberal, merciful, obliging, philanthropic, tender, unselfish. ANT.-greedy, harsh, malevolent, wicked.

charity, *n.* SYN.-altruism, beneficence, benevolence, generosity, humanity, kindness, liberality, magnanimity, philanthropy, tenderness. ANT.-cruelty, inhumanity, malevolence, selfishness, unkindness.

charlatan, *n.* SYN.-cheat, cheater, fraud, imposter, phoney, swindler.

charm, *v.* SYN.-beguile, bewitch, delight, enrapture, entice, entrance, mesmerize, please.

charming, *a.* SYN.-alluring, attractive, bewitching, captivating, enchanting, engaging, fascinating, winning. ANT.-repugnant, repulsive, revolting.

chart, *n.* SYN.-diagram, graph, map, outline, plan, poster, presentation.

chary, *a.* SYN.-careful, cautious, circumspect, shy, timid, wary.

chase, *v.* SYN.-follow, hunt, persist, pursue, trace, track, trail, seek; drive, scatter. ANT.-abandon, elude, escape, evade, flee.

chaste, *a.* SYN.-decent, demure, guiltless, innocent, modest, moral, proper, pure, sincere, strong, uncorrupted, undefiled, virginal. ANT.-brash, corruptible, foul, polluted, sullied, tainted, tarnished, weak.

chasten, *v.* See **chastise.**

chastise, *v.* SYN.-berate, castigate, correct, discipline, pummel, punish, scold, strike, upbraid. ANT.-acquit, exonerate, free, pardon, release.

chat, *n.* SYN.-chatter, colloquy, conference, conspiracy, conversation, dialogue, interview, intrigue, parley, plan, plot, scheme, talk.

chat, *v.* SYN.-converse, gossip, jabber, speak, talk, tattle; confer, consult, deliberate, discuss, reason.

chattel, *n.* SYN.-assets, belongings, goods, property, wealth.

chatter, *n.* SYN.-conversation, dialogue, discussion, gossip, rumor, talk. ANT.-correspondence, meditation, silence, writing.

chatty, *a.* SYN.-amiable, amicable, friendly, spontaneous, talkative, effusive, garrulous,

cheap, *a.* SYN.-budget, inexpensive, low-priccd, moderate, poor, reasonable, thrifty; beggarly, common, inferior, mean, shabby. ANT.-costly, dear, expensive; dignified, honorable, noble.

cheat, *n.* SYN.-chicanery, con, deception, duplicity, fraud, guile, imposture, swindle, trick; charlatan, cheater, chiseler, conniver, crook, fake, fraud, rogue, swindler, trickster. ANT.-fairness, honesty, integrity, sincerity.

cheat, *v.* SYN.-bilk, circumvent, deceive, defraud, dupe, fool, gull, hoax, hoodwink, outwit, swindle, trick, victimize.

check, *v.* SYN.-analyze, assess, audit, contemplate, dissect, examine, inquire, interrogate, notice, question, quiz, review, scan, scrutinize, survey, view, watch; block, hamper, hinder, impede, obstruct, prevent, resist, restrain, retard, stop, thwart. ANT.-disregard, neglect, omit, overlook; assist, expedite, facilitate, further, promote.

cheeky, *a.* SYN.-audacious, bold, brazen, impertinent, impudent.

cheer, *v.* SYN.-comfort, consolation, contentment, ease, enjoyment, relief, solace, succor. ANT.-affliction, discomfort, misery, suffering, torment, torture.

cheerful, *a.* SYN.-gay, glad, happy, jolly, joyful, lighthearted, merry, sprightly. ANT.-depressed, glum, mournful, sad, sullen.

cherish, *v.* SYN.-appreciate, hold dear, prize, treasure, value; foster, nurture, sustain. ANT.-dislike, disregard, neglect; abandon, reject.

chief, *a.* SYN.-cardinal, essential, first, foremost, highest, leading, main, paramount, predominant, suprcme. ANT.-auxiliary, minor, subordinate, subsidiary, supplemental.

chief, *n.* SYN.-captain, chieftain, commander, head, leader, master, principal, ringleader, ruler, sovereign. ANT.-attendant, follower, servant, subordinate.

childish, *a.* SYN.-adolescent, childlike, foolish, immature, infantile, juvenile, youthful.

chilly, *a.* SYN.-arctic, brisk, cold, cool, crisp, freezing, frigid, frozen, icy, wintry; passionless, phlegmatic, stoical, unfeeling. ANT.-burning, fiery, heated, hot, torrid; ardent, passionate.

chivalrous, *a.* SYN.-brave, courteous, dauntless, gallant, generous, heroic, noble, polite, valiant. ANT.-base, crass, cowardly, crass, ignoble.

choice, *n.* SYN.-alternative, election, favorite, option, preference, selection.

choose, *v.* SYN.-adopt, cull, decide, discriminate, elect, embrace, espouse, favor, judge, opt, pick, prefer, select, take. ANT.-deline, discard, dismiss, refuse, reject.

chronic, *a.* SYN.-continual, continuing, lasting, lingering, perennial, persisting, recurring.

chronicle, *n.* SYN.-account, accounting, annals, history, narrative, record, report.

chronicle, *v.* SYN.-account, elucidate, explain, expound, narrate, record, recount, report, tell.

chronological, *a.* SYN.-classified, consecutive, dated, historical, sequential.

cinema, *n.* SYN.-film, movie, picture.

circle, *n.* SYN.-belt, circuit, circumference, cycle, disk, loop, meridian, orbit, ring, sphere, wheel.

circuitous, *a.* SYN.-crooked, devious, distorted, erratic, indirect, roundabout, swerving, tortuous, wandering, winding; crooked, cunning, tricky. ANT.-direct, straight; honest, straightforward.

circular, *a.* SYN.-complete, curved, cylindrical, entire, globular, round, spherical.

circumspection, *n.* SYN.-anxiety, care, concern, solicitude, worry; attention, caution, regard, vigilance, wariness. ANT.-disregard, indifference, neglect, negligence.

circumstance, *n.* SYN.-cause, condition, contingency, event, fact, factor, happening, incident, occurrence, position, situation.

citation, *n.* SYN.-charge, summons, ticket; award, certificate, commendation.

cite, *v.* SYN.-adduce, advance, affirm, allege, assign, claim, declare, extract, maintain, paraphrase, quote, recite, refer, repeat. ANT.-contradict, deny, disprove, gainsay, refute.

citizen, *n.* SYN.-civilian, commoner, householder, inhabitant, national, native, occupant, resident, subject, taxpayer, voter. ANT.-alien, foreigner, outsider.

city, *n.* SYN.-metropolis, municipality, town, township, village. ANT.-country, suburb.

civil, *a.* SYN.-considerate, courteous, cultivated, genteel, polite, refined, urbane, well-bred, well-mannered. ANT.-boorish, impertinent, rude, uncivil, uncouth.

civilization, *n.* SYN.-cultivation, culture, education, enlightenment, refinement. ANT.-boorishness, ignorance, illiteracy, vulgarity.

claim, *n.* SYN.-application, declaration, deed, interest, petition, right, suit, title.

claim, *v.* SYN.-affirm, allege, assert, aver, avow, declare, express, maintain, recite, recount, say, tell, state, utter; defend, support, uphold, vindicate. ANT.-contradict, deny, imply, refute.

clamor, *n.* SYN.-babel, cry, din, noise, outcry, racket, row, sound, tumult, uproar. ANT.-hush, quiet, silence, stillness.

clan, *n.* SYN.-brotherhood, fellowship, solidarity; association, clan, fraternity, society. ANT.-acrimony, discord, individual, opposition, strife.

clandestine, *a.* SYN.-concealed, covert, hidden, latent, private, secret, surreptitious, unknown. ANT.-conspicuous, disclosed, exposed, known, obvious, overt.

clarify, *v.* SYN.-decipher, elucidate, explain, expound, illustrate, interpret, resolve, unfold, unravel. ANT.-baffle, confuse, darken, muddy, obscure.

clarity, *n.* SYN.-clearness, directness, distinctness, exactness, explicitness, precision, prominence, purity, transparency.

clash, *v.* SYN.-argue, collide, conflict, differ, disagree, encounter, oppose.

clasp, *v.* SYN.-cling, clutch, grasp, grip; have, hold, keep, maintain, possess, retain. ANT.-relinquish, vacate.

class, *n.* SYN.-breed, category, degree, denomination, distinction, genre, family, kind; caste, grade, order, rank, standing, set; elegance, excellence.

classify, *v.* SYN.-arrange, catalogue, categorize, correlate, grade, group, index, label, order, organize, rank, rate. ANT.-combine, disorganize, mix.

clean, *v.* SYN.-cleanse, mop, purify, scrub, sweep, wash. ANT.-dirty, pollute, soil, stain, sully.

cleanse, *v.* SYN.-bathe, clean, launder, mop, purify, sanitize, scald, scrub, sterilize, wash. ANT.-dirty, foul, pollute, soil, stain, sully.

clear, *a.* SYN.-cloudless, fair, sunny; limpid, transparent; apparent, distinct, evident, intelligible, lucid, manifest, obvious, plain, unmistakable, visible; open, unobstructed. ANT.-cloudy, foul, overcast; ambiguous, obscure, unclear, vague.

clemency, *n.* SYN.-charity, compassion, forgiveness, grace, leniency, mercy, mildness, pity. ANT.-cruelty, punishment, retribution, vengeance.

clerical, *a.* SYN.-apostolic, cleric, ecclesiastical, holy, monastic, monkish, ministerial, pontifical, priestly, sacred.

clerk, *n.* SYN.-assistant, bookkeeper, cashier, recorder, registrar, salesperson, stenographer, teller, timekeeper.

clever, *a.* SYN.-adroit, apt, dexterous, quick, quick-witted, skillful, talented, witty; bright, ingenious, sharp, smart. ANT.-awkward, bungling, clumsy, slow, unskilled; dull, foolish, stupid.

cleverness, *n.* SYN.-comprehension, intellect, intelligence, mind, perspicacity, reason, sagacity, sense, understanding; banter, cleverness, fun, humor, irony, pleasantry, raillery, sarcasm, satire, wit, witticism. ANT.-commonplace, frivolity, inanity, platitude, silliness, sobriety, solemnity, stupidity.

cliché, *n.* SYN.-platitude, proverb, saw, saying, slogan.

client, *n.* SYN.-buyer, customer, patron, user.

climax, *n.* SYN.-acme, apex, consummation, crown, culmination, end, extremity, height, peak, pinnacle, summit, zenith. ANT.-anticlimax, base, depth, floor.

climb, *v.* SYN.-ascend, clamber, escalate, mount, rise, scale, soar, tower. ANT.-descend, fall, sink.

cling, *v.* SYN.-adhere, clasp, clutch, grab, grasp, grip, hold, keep, maintain, retain. ANT.-abandon, loose, relinquish.

clip, *v.* SYN.-crop, curtail, cut, prune, shorten, snip, trim.

clique, *n.* SYN.-clan, club, faction, group.

cloak, *v.* SYN.-clothe, conceal, cover, disguise, envelop, guard, hide, mask, protect, screen, shield, shroud, veil. ANT.-bare, divulge, expose, reveal, unveil.

cloister, *n.* SYN.-abbey, convent, hermitage, monastery, nunnery, priory.

close, *a.* SYN.-abutting, adjacent, adjoining, immediate, impending, near, nearby, neighboring; confidential, dear, devoted, intimate. ANT.-afar, distant, faraway, removed.

close, *n.* SYN.-completion, conclusion, end, finale, settlement, termination; ANT.-beginning, commencement, inception, prelude, start.

close, *v.* SYN.-occlude, seal, shut; clog, obstruct, stop; cease, complete, conclude, end, finish, terminate. ANT.-open, unbar, unlock; begin, commence, inaugurate, start.

clothes, *n.* SYN.-apparel, array, attire, clothing, drapery, dress, garb, garments, raiment, vestments, vesture. ANT.-nakedness, nudity.

cloudy, *a.* SYN.-dark, dim, indistinct, hazy, murky, mysterious, obscure, overcast, shadowy. ANT.-bright, clear, distinct, limpid, sunny.

clue, *n.* SYN.-evidence, hint, information, mark, sign, spoor, trace, track.

clumsy, *a.* SYN.-awkward, gauche, inept, rough, unpolished, untoward. ANT.-adroit, graceful, neat, polished, skillful.

clutch, *v.* SYN.-clasp, cling, grasp, grip; have, hold, keep, maintain, possess, retain. ANT.-relinquish, vacate.

coach, *n.* SYN.-drill, instill, instruct, prompt, teach, train, tutor.

coalition, *n.* SYN.-alliance, association, combination, confederacy, entente, federation, league, partnership, union; compact, covenant, marriage, treaty. ANT.-divorce, schism, separation.

coarse, *a.* SYN.-crude, impure, rough, rugged, unrefined; gross, gruff, immodest, indelicate, rude, unpolished, vulgar. ANT.-fine, polished, refined, smooth; cultivated, cultured, delicate.

coax, *v.* SYN.-cajole, inveigle, persuade, wheedle.

coerce, *v.* SYN.-coerce, constrain, drive, enforce, force, impel, oblige. ANT.-allure, convince, induce, persuade, prevent.

coercion, *n.* SYN.-compulsion, constraint, force, restraint, violence. ANT.-persuasion.

cognizant, *a.* SYN.-apprised, aware, conscious, informed, mindful, observant, perceptive, sensible. ANT.-ignorant, insensible, oblivious, unaware.

coherent, *a.* SYN.-articulate, comprehensible, consistent, logical, reasonable, sound, understandable.

coincide, *v.* SYN.-accede, acquiesce, agree, assent, comply, consent; agree, concur, conform, harmonize, match, tally. ANT.-contradict, differ, disagree, dissent, protest; casual, random.

cold, *a.* SYN.-arctic, chilly, cool, freezing, frigid, frozen, icy, wintry; apathetic, indifferent, passionless, phlegmatic, reserved, stoical, unconcerned, unfeeling. ANT.-burning, fiery, heated, hot, torrid; ardent, passionate.

collapse, *v.* SYN.-decline, decrease, deflate, diminish, drop, fall, sink, subside; implode, topple, tumble. ANT.-arise, ascend, climb, mount, soar.

colleague, *n.* SYN.-associate, attendant, collaborator, companion, comrade, consort, crony, friend, mate, partner. ANT.-adversary, enemy, stranger.

collect, *v.* SYN.-accumulate, amass, assemble, concentrate, congregate, consolidate, gather, heap, hoard, mass, pile. ANT.-assort, disperse, distribute, divide, dole.

collected, *a.* SYN.-calm, composed, cool, imperturbable, peaceful, placid, quiet, sedate, tranquil, unmoved. ANT.-agitated, aroused, excited, perturbed, violent.

collection, *n.* SYN.-aggregate,

amount, conglomeration, entirety, sum, total, whole. ANT.-element, ingredient, part, particular, unit.

collision, *n.* SYN.-battle, combat, conflict, duel, encounter, fight, struggle; contention, controversy, discord, inconsistency, interference, opposition, variance. ANT.-amity, concord, consonance, harmony.

collusion, *n.* SYN.-cabal, combination, conspiracy, intrigue, machination, plot, treachery, treason.

color, *n.* SYN.-complexion, dye, hue, paint, pigment, shade, stain, taint, tincture, tinge, tint. ANT.-achromatism, paleness, transparency.

colossal, *a.* SYN.-elephantine, enormous, gargantuan, gigantic, huge, immense, large, prodigious, vast. ANT.-diminutive, little, minute, small, tiny.

combat, *n.* SYN.-battle, collision, conflict, duel, encounter, fight, struggle; contention. ANT.-amity, concord, consonance, harmony.

combat, *v.* SYN.-battle, brawl, conflict, contend, dispute, encounter, fight, quarrel skirmish, struggle.

combination, *n.* SYN.-alliance, association, coalition, confederacy, entente, federation, league, partnership, union, unification; compact, covenant, marriage, treaty. ANT.-divorce, schism, separation.

combine, *v.* SYN.-adjoin, amalgamate, associate, attach, blend, conjoin, connect, consolidate, couple, go with, join, link, merge, unite, unify. ANT.-detach, disconnect, disjoin, separate.

comedy, *n.* SYN.-burlesque, farce, humor, mimicry, satire, slapstick.

comfort, *n.* SYN.-cheer, consolation, contentment, ease, enjoyment, luxury, plenty, relaxation, relief, rest, restfulness, solace, succor, warmth. ANT.-affliction, discomfort, misery, suffering, torment, torture.

comfort, *v.* SYN.-aid, alleviate, calm, cheer, console, encourage, gladden, help, solace, soothe, support, sympathize. ANT.-antagonize, aggravate, depress, dishearten.

comfortable, *a.* SYN.-acceptable, agreeable, contented, gratifying, pleasing, pleasurable, relaxed, restful, soothed, untroubled; cozy, luxurious, protected, rich, roomy, satisfying, sheltered, snug, spacious, warm, wealthy. ANT.-distressing, miserable, troubled, uncomfortable, wretched; mean, poor, wanting.

comical, *a.* SYN.-amusing, droll, farcical, funny, humorous, laughable, ludicrous ridiculous, slapstick, witty. ANT.-melancholy, sad, serious, sober, solemn.

coming, *a.* SYN.-advancing, approaching, anticipated, arriving, close, due, expected, foreseen, imminent, impending, near, nearing, predicted. ANT.-departing, going, leaving.

command, *n.* SYN.-bidding, decree, dictate, injunction, instruction, law, mandate, order, proclamation, requirement. ANT.-consent, license, permission.

command, *v.* SYN.-conduct, govern, guide, manage, regulate, rule; bid, charge, direct, instruct, order, tell. ANT.-deceive, distract, misdirect, misguide.

commemorate, *v.* SYN.-celebrate, honor, remember, solemnize.

commence, *v.* SYN.-arise, begin, enter, inaugurate, initiate, institute, open, originate, start. ANT.-

close, complete, end, finish, terminate.

commencement, *n.* SYN.-beginning, birth, inception, opening, origin, origination, outset, source, start. ANT.-close, completion, consummation, end, termination.

commend, *v.* SYN.-acclaim, applaud, appreciate, approve, compliment, extol, flatter, laud, like, praise; authorize, confirm, endorse, ratify, sanction. ANT.-criticize, disparage; condemn, nullify.

commensurate, *a.* SYN.-adequate, alike, equal, equitable, equivalent, even, fair, judicious, like, proportional, same, similar, uniform. ANT-different, disparate, dissimilar, diverse.

comment, *n.* SYN.-annotation, assertion, conversation, criticism, declaration, notation, observation, remark, statement, talk, utterance.

comment, *v.* SYN.-affirm, assert, aver, criticize, interject, mention, note, observe, remark, speak.

commerce, *n.* SYN.-business, employment, engagement, enterprise, job, occupation, profession, trade, trading, vocation, work. ANT.-avocation, hobby, pastime.

commission, *v.* SYN.-appoint, authorize, charge, command, delegate, deputize, employ, empower, engage, entrust, hire, ordain, select.

commit, *v.* SYN.-do, perform, perpetrate; commend, consign, entrust, relegate, trust; bind, obligate, pledge. ANT.-fail, miscarry, neglect; mistrust, release, renounce; free, loose.

commodious, *a.* SYN.-accessible, appropriate, convenient, fitting, handy, suitable. ANT.-awkward, inconvenient, inopportune, troublesome.

common, *a.* SYN.-familiar, frequent, general, ordinary, popular, prevalent, universal, usual; low, mean, vulgar. ANT.-exceptional, extraordinary, odd, scarce; noble, refined.

commotion, *n.* SYN.-agitation, chaos, confusion, disarrangement, disarray, disorder, ferment, jumble, stir, tumult, turmoil. ANT.-certainty, order, peace, tranquility.

communicable, *a.* SYN.-catching, contagious, infectious, pestilential, virulent. ANT.-healthful, hygienic, non-communicable.

communicate, *v.* SYN.-advise, confer, contact, convey, disclose, divulge, impart, inform, notify, relate, reveal, tell, transmit. ANT.-conceal, hide, withhold.

communion, *n.* SYN.-association, fellowship, intercourse, participation, sacrament, union. ANT.-alienation, non participation.

compact, *a.* SYN.-constricted, contracted, firm, small, snug, tight; mash, tamp. ANT.-lax, loose, open, relaxed, slack.

compact, *n.* SYN.-agreement, bargain, compact, contract, covenant, pact, stipulation. ANT.-disagreement, discord, dissension, variance.

companion, *n.* SYN.-associate, attendant, colleague, comrade, consort, crony, friend, guide, mate, partner, protector. ANT.-adversary, enemy, stranger.

company, *n.* SYN.-assemblage, band, crew, group, horde, party, throng, troop; association, fellowship, society; corporation, firm. ANT.-dispersion, individual, seclusion, solitude.

comparable, *a.* SYN.-akin, alike, allied, analogous, correlative, correspondent, corresponding, equivalent, like, parallel, similar. ANT.-different, dissimilar, divergent, incongruous, opposed.

compare, *v.* SYN.-associate, connect, contrast, critique, describe, differentiate, discriminate, distinguish, equate, examine, link, match, measure, oppose, rate, relate, sample.

comparison, *n.* SYN.-analogy, association, contrast, correspondence, example, metaphor, parable, relation, resemblance,

compassion, *n.* SYN.-commiseration, concern, condolence, consideration, empathy, mercy, pity, sensitivity, sympathy, tenderness, warmth. ANT.-brutality, cruelty, hardness, inhumanity, ruthlessness.

compassionate, *a.* SYN.-affable, benevolent, benign, forbearing, forgiving, gentle, good, humane, indulgent, kind, kindly, merciful, sympathetic, tender, thoughtful. ANT.-cruel, inhuman, merciless, severe, unkind.

compatible, *a.* SYN.-accordant, agreeing, conforming, congruous, consistent, consonant, constant, correspondent. ANT.-contradictory, discrepant, incongruous, inconsistent, paradoxical.

compel, *v.* SYN.-coerce, constrain, drive, enforce, force, impel, oblige. ANT.-allure, convince, induce, persuade, prevent.

compensation, *n.* SYN.-allowance, bonus, commission, consideration, earnings, fee, indemnity, pay, payment, recompense, reimbursement, remuneration, repayment, salary, stipend, wages. ANT.-gift, gratuity, present.

compete, *v.* SYN.-battle, clash, contest, encounter, engage, face, oppose, rival, spar, strive, struggle, vie,

competent, *a.* SYN.-able, capable, clever, efficient, fitted, qualified, skillful. ANT.-inadequate, incapable, incompetent, unfitted.

competitor, *n.* SYN.-adversary, antagonist, enemy, foe, opponent, rival. ANT.-accomplice, ally, comrade, confederate, friend, teammate.

compile, *v.* SYN.-accumulate, amass, arrange, assemble, catalogue, collect, correlate, gather, group, index, label, order, organize, rank, rate.

complacent, *a.* SYN.-contented, happy, pleased, self-satisfied, smug; accommodating, complaisant, compliant, yielding.

complain, *v.* SYN.-criticize, denounce, deplore, deprecate, disapprove, fuss, grouch, grumble, lament, murmur, object, oppose, protest, regret, remonstrate, repine, whine. ANT.-applaud, approve, praise, rejoice.

complete, *a.* SYN.-concluded, consummated, detailed, ended, entire, finished, full, perfect, thorough, total, unbroken, undivided. ANT.-imperfect, lacking, unfinished.

complete, *v.* SYN.-accomplish, achieve, close, conclude, consummate, do, end, execute, finish, fulfill, get done, perfect, perform, terminate.

complex, *a.* SYN.-complicated, compound, intricate, involved, manifold, perplexing. ANT.-plain, simple, uncompounded.

complexion, *n.* SYN.-color, coloration, hue, pigment, pigmentation, shade, texture, tone.

complicated, *a.* SYN.-complex, compound, intricate, involved, perplexing. ANT.-plain, simple, uncompounded.

compliment, *n.* SYN.-adulation, appreciation, approval, commendation, endorsement, eulogy, flattery, honor, praise, regards, respects, salute, tribute. ANT.-affront, criticism, insult, taunt.

comply, *v.* SYN.-accede, acquiesce, agree, assent, consent; coincide, concur, conform, tally. ANT.-contradict, differ, disagree, dissent, protest.

component, *n.* SYN.-division, fragment, moiety, piece, portion, scrap, section, segment, share; element, ingredient, member, organ, part. ANT.-entirety, whole.

compose, *v.* SYN.-construct, create, fashion, forge, make, mold, produce, shape; constitute, form, make up; arrange, combine, organize; devise, frame, invent. ANT.-destroy, disfigure, dismantle, misshape, wreck.

composed, *a.* SYN.-calm, collected, cool, imperturbable, peaceful, placid, quiet, sedate, self-controlled, tranquil, unmoved. ANT.-agitated, aroused, excited, perturbed, violent.

composer, *n.* SYN.-author, creator, father, inventor, maker, originator, writer.

composure, *n.* SYN.-balance, calmness, carriage, complacence, contentment, control, equanimity, equilibrium, poise, self-control, serenity, tranquility. ANT.-agitation, anger, excitement, rage, turbulence.

compound, *v.* SYN.-alloy, amalgamate blend, combine, composite, concoct,, fuse, jumble, mingle, mix. ANT.-dissociate, divide, segregate, separate, sort.

comprehend, *v.* SYN.-appreciate, apprehend, conceive, discern, grasp, know, learn, perceive, realize, see, understand. ANT.-ignore, misapprehend, mistake, misunderstand.

comprehension, *n.* SYN.-apprehension, cognizance, conception, discernment, insight, perception, understanding. ANT.-ignorance, insensibility, misapprehension, misconception.

compress, *v.* SYN.-abbreviate, abridge, compact, condense, consolidate, pack, reduce, shorten, shrink.

comprise, *v.* SYN.-contain, embody, embrace, encompass, hold, include. ANT.-discharge, emit, exclude; encourage, yield.

compulsion, *n.* SYN.-dint, energy, force, intensity, might, potency, power, strength, vigor; coercion. ANT.-feebleness, frailty, impotence, weakness; persuasion.

compute, *v.* SYN.-add, ascertain, calculate, consider, count, derive, divide, divine, estimate, figure, multiply, reckon, subtract. ANT.-conjecture, guess, miscalculate.

comrade, *n.* SYN.-associate, attendant, colleague, companion, consort, crony, friend, mate, partner. ANT.-adversary, enemy, stranger.

conceal, *v.* SYN.-cloak, cover, curtain, disguise, envelop, guard, hide, mask, protect, screen, secrete, shield, shroud, suppress, veil, withhold. ANT.-bare, disclose, divulge, expose, reveal, show, uncover, unveil.

concede, *v.* SYN.-let, permit, suffer, tolerate; authorize, give, grant, yield; acknowledge, admit, allow. ANT. forbid, objcct, protest, refuse, resist.

conceit, *n.* SYN.-complacency, egotism, pride, self-esteem, vanity; caprice, conception, fancy, idea, imagination, notion, whim. ANT.-diffidence, humility, meekness, modesty.

conceited, *a.* SYN.-proud, vain, vainglorious. ANT.-effective, potent, profitable; meek, modest.

conceive, *v.* SYN.-begin, comprehend, concoct, contrive, create, design, devise, fabricate, frame, grasp, invent, understand. ANT.-copy, imitate, reproduce.

concentrated, *a.* SYN.-close, compact, compressed, crowded, dense, thick, undiluted. ANT.-dispersed, dissipated, sparse.

concept, *n.* SYN.-abstraction, conception, fancy, idea, image, impression, notion, opinion, sentiment, thought. ANT.-entity, matter, object, substance, thing.

conception, *n.* SYN.-apprehension, cogitation, cognition, comprehension, consideration, fancy, idea, imagination, impression, judgment, memory, notion, opinion, recollection, reflection, sentiment, thought, understanding, view.

concern, *n.* SYN.-affair, business, matter, transaction; anxiety, care, solicitude, worry. ANT.-apathy, indifference, negligence, unconcern.

concise, *a.* SYN.-brief, compact, condensed, compendious, curt, incisive, laconic, neat, pithy, short, succinct, summary, terse. ANT.-extended, lengthy, long, prolonged, protracted, verbose, wordy.

conclude, *v.* SYN.-close, complete, conclusion, consummate, end, finale, finish, fulfill, get done, perfect, settlement, terminate, termination. ANT.-beginning, commencement, inception, prelude, start.

conclusion, *n.* SYN.-close, completion, end, finale, issue, settlement, termination; decision, deduction, inference, judgment. ANT.-beginning, commencement, inception, prelude, start.

conclusive, *a.* SYN.-concluding, decisive, ending, eventual, final, last, latest, terminal, ultimate. ANT.-first, inaugural, incipient, original, rudimentary.

concord, *n.* SYN.-accordance, agreement, coincidence, concurrence, harmony, understanding, unison, bargain, compact, contract, covenant, pact, stipulation. ANT.-difference, disagreement, discord, dissension, variance.

concrete, *a.* SYN.-definite, firm, positive, precise, real, solid, specific.

concur, *v.* SYN.-accede, acquiesce, agree, assent, comply, consent; coincide, conform, tally. ANT.-contradict, differ, disagree, dissent, protest.

condemn, *v.* SYN.-blame, censure, denounce, reprehend, reproach, reprobate, reprove, upbraid; convict, sentence. ANT.-approve, commend, condone, forgive, praise; absolve, acquit, exonerate, pardon.

condense, *v.* SYN.-abbreviate, abridge, compress, consolidate, compact, dehydrate, reduce, shorten, summarize.

condescend, *v.* SYN.-accommodate,

comply, concede, deign, oblige, patronize.

condition, *n.* SYN.-case, circumstance, plight, predicament, situation, state; prohibition, provision, requirement, restraint, restriction, stipulation, term.

condition, *v.* SYN.-adapt, equip, fit, furnish, get ready, make ready, modify, predispose, prepare, provide, qualify, ready.

conditional, *a.* SYN.-contingent, dependent, depending, relying, subject, subordinate. ANT.-absolute, autonomous, casual, independent, original.

condolence, *n.* SYN.-commiseration, compassion, empathy, pity, sympathy, tenderness, warmth. ANT.-antipathy, harshness, indifference, malevolence, unconcern.

condone, *v.* SYN.-accept, allow, excuse, overlook, pardon.

conduct, *n.* SYN.-action, bearing, behavior, carriage, deed, demeanor, deportment, disposition, manner.

conduct, *v.* SYN.-direct, escort, guide, lead, steer; control, manage, regulate, supervise.

confederate, *n.* SYN.-abettor, accessory, accomplice, ally, assistant, associate. ANT.-adversary, enemy, opponent, rival.

confederation, *n.* SYN.-alliance, association, coalition, combination, confederacy, entente, federation, league, partnership, union; compact, covenant, marriage, treaty. ANT.-schism, separation.

confer, *v.* SYN.-chat, converse, speak; consult, counsel, deliberate, discuss, negotiate, reason, talk.

conference, *n.* SYN.-conversation, discussion, gathering, interchange, meeting.

confess, *v.* SYN.-acknowledge, admit, allow, avow, concede, divulge, grant, own, reveal. ANT.-conceal, deny, disclaim, disown, renounce.

confession, *n.* SYN.-apology, defense, excuse, explanation, justification. ANT.-accusation, complaint, denial, dissimulation.

confidence, *n.* SYN.-assurance, assuredness, certainty, conviction, courage, firmness, security, self-reliance, surety, pledge, promise, word, assertion, declaration, statement. ANT.-bashfulness, humility, modesty, shyness, suspicion.

confine, *v.* SYN.-bound, circumscribe, enclose, encompass, envelop, fence, limit, surround. ANT.-develop, distend, enlarge, expand, expose, open.

confirm, *v.* SYN.-authenticate, corroborate, substantiate, validate, verify; acknowledge, assure, establish, settle; approve, fix, ratify, sanction; strengthen.

confirmation, *n.* SYN.-corroboration, demonstration, evidence, proof, test, testimony, trial, validation, verification. ANT.-failure, fallacy, invalidity.

confiscate, *v.* SYN.-appropriate, capture, catch, purloin, remove, steal, take; grasp, grip, seize; get, obtain; claim, demand; adopt, choose, espouse, select.

conflagration, *n.* SYN.-blaze, burning, combustion, fire, flame, heat.

conflict, *n.* SYN.-battle, collision, combat, duel, encounter, fight, struggle; contention, controversy, discord, inconsistency, interference, opposition, variance. ANT.-amity, concord, consonance, harmony.

conform, *v.* SYN.-acclimate, accommodate, adjust, comply, follow, obey, reconcile, suit.

confounded, *a.* SYN.-abashed, amazed, bewildered, confused, disconcerted, perplexed, puzzled.

confront, *v.* SYN.-contradict, counteract, defy, face, hinder, obstruct, oppose, resist, thwart, withstand. ANT.-agree, cooperate, submit, succumb, support.

confuse, *v.* SYN.-bewilder, confound, disorient, disconcert, dumfound, fluster, mislead, misinform, muddle, mystify, nonplus, obscure, perplex, puzzle. ANT.-clarify, explain, illumine, instruct, solve.

confused, *a.* SYN.-bewildered, chaotic, confounded, deranged, disconcerted, disordered, disorganized, indistinct, jumbled, mistaken, misunderstood, mixed, muddled, perplexed. ANT.-clear, lucid, obvious, organized, plain.

confusion, *n.* SYN.-agitation, chaos, commotion, disarrangement, disarray, disorder, ferment, jumble, stir, tumult, turmoil. ANT.-certainty, order, peace, tranquility.

congratulate, *v.* SYN.-commend, compliment, praise, salute, toast.

congruous, *a.* SYN.-accordant, agreeing, compatible, conforming, consistent, consonant, constant, correspondent. ANT.-contradictory, discrepant, incongruous, inconsistent, paradoxical.

conjecture, *n.* SYN.-hypothesis, supposition, theory. ANT.-certainty, fact, proof.

conjecture, *v.* SYN.-chance, guess, hazard, infer. ANT.-determine, guard, insure, know.

connect, *v.* SYN.-adjoin, affix, annex, append, associate, attach, couple, join, link, stick, unite; assign, associate. ANT.-detach, disengage, separate, unfasten, untie.

connection, *n.* SYN.-affinity, alliance, association, bond, conjunction, link, relationship, tie, union. ANT.-disunion, isolation, separation.

conquer, *v.* SYN.-beat, crush, defeat, humble, master, overcome, quell, rout, subdue, subjugate, surmount, vanquish. ANT.-capitulate, cede, lose, retreat, surrender.

conquest, *n.* achievement, triumph, victory. ANT.-defeat, failure.

conscientious, *a.* SYN.-attentive, careful, exact, fastidious, heedful, meticulous, painstaking, prudent, scrupulous, thorough, thoughtful. ANT.-forgetful, improvident, indifferent, lax.

conscious, *a.* SYN.-alert, alive, apprised, aware, cognizant, discerning, informed, keen, knowing, mindful, observant, perceptive, sensible, understanding, wary. ANT.-ignorant, impassive, indifferent, insensible, oblivious, unaware, unconscious, unfeeling.

consecrate, *v.* SYN.-adore, dignify, enshrine, enthrone, exalt, extol, glorify, hallow, honor, revere, sanctify, venerate. ANT.-abuse, debase, degrade, dishonor, mock.

consecrated, *a.* SYN.-blessed, devout, divine, hallowed, holy, pious, religious, sacred, saintly, spiritual. ANT.-evil, profane, sacrilegious, secular, worldly.

consecutive, *a.* SYN.-chronological, connected, continuous, progressive, sequential, successive.

consensus, *n.* SYN.-accord, agreement, opinion.

consent, *n.* SYN.-approval, authority, authorization, leave, liberty, license, permission, permit. ANT.-denial, opposition, prohibition, refusal.

consent, *v.* SYN.-accede, acquiesce, agree, assent, comply, coincide, concur, conform, tally. ANT.-contradict, differ, disagree, dissent, protest.

consequence, *n.* SYN.-conclusion, effect, importance, outcome, result.

consequently, adv. SYN.-accordingly, hence, so, then, thence, therefore.

conservation, *n.* SYN.-conserving, guarding, keeping, maintenance, preservation, preserving, protecting, protection, safekeeping, saving.

conservative, *a.* SYN.-careful, constant, conventional, cautious, guarded, inflexible, prudent, sober, steady, traditional, unchanging, unimaginative, wary.

consider, *v.* SYN.-contemplate, deliberate, examine, heed, meditate, ponder, reflect, study, weigh; esteem, regard, respect. ANT.-ignore, neglect, overlook.

considerate, *a.* SYN.-attentive, careful, cautious, charitable, concerned, heedful, kind, provident, prudent, thoughtful; contemplative, introspective, meditative, pensive, reflective. ANT.-heedless, inconsiderate, precipitous, rash, thoughtless.

consideration, *n.* SYN.-alertness, attention, care, circumspection, heed, kindliness, mindfulness, notice, observance, watchfulness; application, contemplation, reflection, study. ANT.-disregard, indifference, negligence, omission, oversight.

considered, *a.* SYN.-careful, contemplated, examined, investigated, thoughtful, weighed.

consistent, *a.* SYN.-accordant, agreeing, compatible, conforming, congruous, consonant, constant, correspondent. ANT.-contradictory, discrepant, incongruous, inconsistent, paradoxical.

consolation, *n.* SYN.-comfort, contentment, ease, enjoyment, relief, solace, succor. ANT.-affliction, discomfort, misery, suffering, torment, torture.

console, *v.* SYN.-allay, assuage, cheer, comfort, encourage, solace, soothe. ANT.-annoy, distress, worry.

consolidate, *v.* SYN.-blend, join, merge, mix, solidify, strengthen, unify, unite.

consort, *n.* SYN.-associate, colleague, companion, comrade, friend, mate, partner. ANT.-adversary, enemy, stranger.

conspicuous, *a.* SYN.-clear, distinguished, eminent, illustrious, manifest, noted, noticeable, obvious, outstanding, prominent, salient, striking, visible. ANT.-common, hidden, inconspicuous, obscure.

conspiracy, *n.* SYN.-cabal, collusion, combination, intrigue, machination, plot, treachery, treason.

constant, *a.* SYN.-abiding, ceaseless, continual, enduring, faithful, fixed, immutable, invariant, permanent, perpetual, persistent, unalterable, unchanging, uninterrupted, unwavering. ANT.-fickle, mutable, vacillating, wavering.

constantly, *adv.* SYN.-always, continually, eternally, ever, evermore, forever, invariably, incessantly, perpetually, unceasingly. ANT.-fitfully, never, occasionally, rarely, sometimes.

constituent, *n.* SYN.-component, element, ingredient, part.

constrain, *v.* coerce, compel, confine, force, restrain.

constraint, *n.* SYN.-coercion, compulsion, constriction, destiny, fate, forced, requirement, requisite; awkwardness, embarrassment, shyness. ANT.-choice, freedom, option, uncertainty; confidence.

constrict, *v.* SYN.-block, check, choke, clog, contract, hamper, restrict, retard, slow, tighten.

construct, *v.* SYN.-build, erect, fabricate, form, frame, make, raise. ANT.-demolish, destroy, raze.

construe, *v.* SYN.-analyze, decipher, decode, deduce, elucidate, explain, explicate, interpret, render, solve, translate, unravel. ANT.-confuse, distort, falsify, misconstrue, misinterpret.

consult, *v.* SYN.-chat, converse, speak; comment, discourse; argue, confer, conspire, deliberate, discuss, reason, talk.

consummate, *a.* SYN.-achieve, complete, concluded, ended, entire, finished, full, perfect, thorough, total, unbroken, undivided. ANT.-imperfect, lacking, unfinished.

consummation, *n.* SYN.-acme, apex, climax, culmination, height, peak, summit, zenith. ANT.-anticlimax, base, depth, floor.

contagious, *a.* SYN.-catching, communicable, infectious, pestilential, virulent. ANT.-healthful, hygienic, non-communicable.

contain, *v.* SYN.-accommodate, comprise, embody, embrace, hold, include; repress, restrain. ANT.-discharge, emit, exclude; encourage, yield.

contaminate, *v.* SYN.-befoul, corrupt, defile, infect, poison, pollute, sully, taint. ANT.-disinfect, purify.

contaminated, *a.* SYN.-corrupted, crooked, debased, depraved, impure, profligate, putrid, spoiled, tainted, venal, vitiated.

contamination, *n.* SYN.-ailment, contamination, disease, infection, poison, pollution, taint.

contemplate, *v.* SYN.-conceive, imagine, picture, recall, recollect, remember; cogitate, deliberate, meditate, muse, ponder, reason, reflect, speculate, think; consider, deem, esteem, judge, opine, reckon, regard, suppose. ANT.-conjecture, forget, guess.

contemplative, *a.* SYN.-dreamy, introspective, meditative, pensive, reflective, thoughtful. ANT.-heedless, inconsiderate, precipitous, rash, thoughtless.

contemporary, *a.* SYN.-current, modern, new, novel, present, recent. ANT.-ancient, antiquated, bygone, old, past.

contempt, *n.* SYN.-contumely, derision, detestation, disdain, hatred, scorn. ANT.-awe, esteem, regard, respect, reverence.

contemptible, *a.* SYN.-base, despicable, low, mean, sordid, vile, vulgar; malicious, nasty, offensive, selfish. ANT.-admirable, dignified, exalted, generous, noble.

contend, *v.* SYN.-argue, battle, compete, contest, debate, dispute, fight, rival, struggle, vie; accuse, affirm, assert, aver, claim, testify.

contented, a, SYN.-blessed, cheerful, delighted, fortunate, happy, gay, glad, joyful, joyous, lucky, merry, opportune, pleased, propitious, satisfied. ANT.-blue, depressed, gloomy, morose.

contention, *n.* SYN.-battle, collision, conflict, duel, encounter, fight, struggle; controversy, discord, inconsistency, opposition, variance. ANT.-amity, concord, consonance, harmony.

contentment, *n.* SYN.-beatitude, blessedness, bliss, delight, felicity, gladness, happiness, pleasure, satisfaction, well-being. ANT.-despair, grief, misery, sadness, sorrow.

contents, *n.* SYN.-essence, gist, meaning, significance, substance.

contest, *v.* SYN.-battle, challenge, contention, debate, dispute, duel, encounter, quarrel, squabble, test, trial. ANT.-agreement, concord, decision, harmony.

contestant, *n.* SYN.-adversary, challenger, combatant, competitor, opponent, player, rival.

continence, *n.* SYN.-abstention, abstinence, fasting, forbearance, moderation, self-denial, sobriety, temperance. ANT.-excess, gluttony, greed, intoxication, self-indulgence.

contingent, *a.* SYN.-conditional, dependent, depending, relying, subject, subordinate. ANT.-absolute, autonomous, casual, independent, original.

continual, *a.* SYN.-ceaseless, constant, continuous, endless, everlasting, incessant, perennial, perpetual, unceasing, uninterrupted, unremitting. ANT.-interrupted, occasional, periodic, rare.

continue, *n.* SYN.-advance, extend, proceed; endure, last, remain; persevere, persist, prolong, pursue. ANT.-arrest, check, interrupt; cease, defer, halt, stop, suspend.

contract, *n.* SYN.-agreement, bargain, compact, covenant, pact, pledge, promise, stipulation, treaty.

contract, *v.* SYN.-abbreviate, abridge, condense, curtail, diminish, lessen, limit, reduce, recede, restrict, shorten, shrink, shrivel. ANT.-elongate, extend, lengthen.

contradict, *v.* SYN.-confront, confute, controvert, counter, dispute, gainsay, oppose. ANT.-agree, confirm, support, verify.

contradictory, *a.* SYN.-contrary, discrepant, illogical, incompatible, incongruous, inconsistent, irreconcilable, paradoxical, unsteady, vacillating, wavering. ANT.-compatible, congruous, consistent, correspondent.

contrary, *a.* SYN.-adverse, antagonistic, hostile, opposed, opposite; counteractive, disastrous, unfavorable, unlucky. ANT.-benign, favorable, fortunate, lucky, propitious.

contrast, *n.* SYN.-difference, distinction, divergence, diversity, incompatibility, opposition, variance, variation. ANT.-likeness, similarity, uniformity.

contrast, *v.* SYN.-compare, differentiate, discriminate, distinguish, oppose.

contribute, *v.* SYN.-bequeath, bestow, confer, dispense, donate, endow, give, grant, present, proffer, share.

contrite, *a.* SYN.-penitent, regretful, remorseful, repentant, sorrowful, sorry. ANT.-obdurate, remorseless.

contrition, *n.* SYN.-compunction, grief, penitence, qualm, regret, remorse, repentance, self-reproach, sorrow. ANT.-complacency, impenitence, obduracy, self-satisfaction.

contrive, *v.* SYN.-delineate, design, devise, intend, manipulate, outline, plan, plot, prepare, project, scheme.

control, *n.* SYN.-discipline, order, regulation, restraint, supervision. ANT.-chaos, confusion, turbulence.

control, *v.* SYN.-administer, check, command, direct, dominate, drive, influence, govern, manage, master, regulate, rule, superintend, supervise; bridle, check, curb, repress, restrain. ANT.-abandon, follow, forsake, ignore, submit.

controversy, *n.* SYN.-argument, contention, debate, disagreement, discord, dispute, dissonance, quarrel, squabble. ANT.-agreement, concord, decision, harmony.

convene, *v.* SYN.-assemble, congregate, convoke, gather, meet, sit.

convenient, *a.* SYN.-accessible, accommodating, adapted, advantageous, appropriate, comfortable, commodious, favorable, fitting, handy, helpful, suitable, timely. ANT.-awkward, inconvenient, inopportune, troublesome.

conventional, *a.* SYN.-accepted, accustomed, common, customary, established, familiar, normal, ordinary, prevailing, regular, standard, typical, usual. ANT.-alien, strange, unusual.

conversation, *n.* SYN.-chat, colloquy, conference, dialogue, discussion, gossip, interview, parley, talk.

converse, *v.* SYN.-blab, chat, discuss, gossip, jabber, mutter, prattle, speak, talk, tattle; confer, consult, deliberate, discuss, reason.

convert, *v.* SYN.-exchange, substitute; alter, change, modify, shift, transfigure, transform, vary. ANT.-retain; continue, establish, preserve, settle, stabilize.

convey, *v.* SYN.-bring, carry, transmit, transport; bear. ANT.-abandon, drop.

convict, *n.* SYN.-criminal, delinquent, felon, malefactor, offender, transgressor.

convict, *v.* SYN.-blame, censure, condemn, denounce, reprehend, reproach, reprobate, reprove, upbraid; condemn, sentence. ANT.-approve, commend, condone, forgive, praise; absolve, acquit, exonerate, pardon.

conviction, *n.* SYN.-belief, certitude, confidence, credence, faith, feeling, opinion, persuasion, reliance, trust. ANT.-denial, doubt, heresy, incredulity.

convince, *v.* SYN.-allure, coax, entice, exhort, incite, induce, influence, persuade, prevail upon, satisfy, urge, win over. ANT.-coerce, compel, deter, dissuade, restrain.

cool, *a.* SYN.-brisk, chilly, cold, frigid, frosty, nippy, wintry; apathetic, composed, indifferent, passionless, phlegmatic, reserved, stoical, unconcerned, unfeeling. ANT.-burning, fiery, heated, hot, torrid; ardent, passionate.

cooperation, *n.* SYN.-alliance, coalition, collaboration, concert, confederation, federation, participation.

copious, *a.* SYN.-abundant, ample, bountiful, overflowing, plenteous, plentiful, profuse, rich, teeming. ANT. deficient, insufficient, scant, scarce.

copy, *n.* SYN.-duplicate, exemplar, facsimile, imitation, replica, reproduction, transcript. ANT.-original, prototype.

copy, *v.* SYN.-ape, counterfeit, duplicate, imitate, impersonate, mimic, mock, simulate. ANT.-alter, distort, diverge, invent.

cordial, *a.* SYN.-ardent, earnest, friendly, gracious, hearty, sincere, sociable, warm. ANT.-aloof cool, reserved, taciturn.

core, *n.* SYN.-center, heart, middle. midpoint, midst, nucleus. ANT.-border, boundary, outskirts, periphery, rim.

corporal, *a.* SYN.-bodily, carnal, corporeal, somatic; material, natural, physical. ANT.-mental, spiritual.

corporation, *n.* SYN.-company, firm. ANT.-individual.

corpse, *n.* SYN.-body, carcass, remains; form, frame, torso; corpus. ANT.-intellect, mind, soul, spirit.

correct, *a.* SYN.-accurate, exact, faultless, impeccable, precise, proper, right, strict. ANT.-erroneous, false, faulty, untrue, wrong.

correct, *v.* SYN.-aid, amend, help, improve, mend, rectify, reform, remedy, right; admonish, discipline, punish, reprimand. ANT.-aggravate, ignore, ruin, spoil; condone, indulge.

correction, *n.* SYN.-adjustment, alteration, amendment, improvement, instruction, discipline, punishment.

correlative, *a.* SYN.-akin, alike, allied, analogous, comparable, correspondent, corresponding, like, parallel, similar. ANT.-different, dissimilar, divergent, incongruous, opposed.

correlate, *v.* SYN.-associate, compare, connect, correspond, interact, relate.

correspondent, *a.* SYN.-akin, alike, allied, analogous, comparable, correlative, corresponding, like, parallel, similar. ANT.-different, dissimilar, divergent, incongruous, opposed.

corroborate, *v.* SYN.-attest, authenticate, confirm, prove, substantiate, validate, verify.

corrupt, *a.* SYN.-contaminated, corrupted, crooked, debased, depraved, dishonest, fraudulent, impure, profligate, putrid, spoiled, tainted, unsound, venal, vitiated.

corrupt, *v.* SYN.-abase, adulterate, alloy, contaminate, debase, defile, degrade, deprave, disgrace, dishonor, impair, infect, lower, pervert, spoil, taint, undermine, vitiate. ANT.-enhance, improve, raise, restore, vitalize.

cosmopolitan, *a.* SYN.-cultured, polished, refined, sophisticated, suave, urbane.

cost, *n.* SYN.-charge, expense, payment, price, value, worth.

council, *n.* SYN.-admonition, advice, caution, counsel, exhortation, instruction, recommendation, suggestion, warning; information, intelligence, notification.

counsel, *n.* SYN.-advice, consultation, elucidation, guidance, information, instruction, opinion; lawyer.

counsel, *v.* SYN.-advise, allude, offer, propose, recommend, refer, suggest. ANT.-declare, demand, dictate, insist.

count, *v.* SYN.-calculate, compute, consider, enumerate, estimate, figure, inventory, reckon. ANT.-conjecture, guess, miscalculate.

countenance, *n.* SYN.-appearance, aspect, bearing, demeanor, expression, look.

counterfeit, *a.* SYN.-artificial, assumed, bogus, ersatz, fake, feigned, fictitious, phony, sham, spurious, synthetic, unreal. ANT.-

genuine, natural, real, true.

courage, *n.* SYN.-audacity, boldness, bravery, chivalry, daring, fearlessness, fortitude, intrepidity, mettle, prowess, resolution. ANT.-cowardice, fear, pusillanimity, timidity.

courageous, *a.* SYN.-adventurous, audacious, bold, brave, chivalrous, daring, dauntless, fearless, gallant, heroic, intrepid, valiant, valorous. ANT.-cowardly, cringing, fearful, timid, weak.

course, *n.* SYN.-avenue, channel, passage, path, road, route, street, thoroughfare, track, trail, walk, way; fashion, form, habit, manner, method, mode, plan, practice, procedure, process, style, system.

courteous, *a.* SYN.-civil, considerate, courtly, cultivated, genteel, polite, refined, urbane, well-bred, well-mannered. ANT.-boorish, impertinent, rude, uncivil, uncouth.

courtesy, *n.* SYN.-affability, consideration, cordiality, courteousness, deference, friendliness, gallantry, geniality, graciousness, kindness, manners, polish, politeness, refinement, respect, tact.

covenant, *n.* SYN.-accordance, understanding, agreement, bargain, compact, contract, pact, stipulation. ANT.-difference, disagreement, discord, dissension, variance.

cover, *v.* SYN.-cloak, clothe, conceal, curtain, disguise, envelop, guard, hide, mask, protect, screen, shield. shroud, veil, wrap. ANT.-bare, divulge, expose, reveal, unveil.

covert, *a.* SYN.-clandestine, concealed, hidden, latent, private, secret, surreptitious, unknown. ANT.-conspicuous, disclosed, exposed, known, obvious.

covetousness, *n.* SYN.-avarice, desire, envy, greed, jealousy. ANT.-generosity, geniality, indifference.

cowardice, *n.* SYN.-alarm, apprehension, consternation, dismay, dread, fear, fright, horror, panic, scare, terror, timidity, trepidation. ANT.-assurance, boldness, bravery, courage, fearlessness.

cower, *v.* SYN.-cringe, crouch, fear, hide, quake, run, shake, shiver, shrink, snivel, tremble.

coy, *a.* SYN.-bashful, demure, diffident, humble, modest, recoiling, retiring, shy, timid. ANT.-daring, gregarious, outgoing.

cozy, *a.* SYN.-luxurious, protected, satisfying, secure, sheltered, snug, warm.

craft, *n.* SYN.-ability, aptitude, competence, dexterity, faculty, skill, talent; avocation, business, career, occupation, vocation, work; airplane, boat, jet, ship.

crafty, *a.* SYN.-artful, astute, clandestine, covert, cunning, foxy, furtive, guileful, insidious,. shrewd, sly, stealthy, subtle, surreptitious, tricky, underhanded, wily. ANT.-candid, frank, ingenuous, open, sincere.

cranky, *a.* SYN.-critical, cross, disagreeable, disapproving, fault-finding, fussy, grouchy, hostile, hypercritical, peevish, surly, whiny.

crass, *a.* SYN.-coarse, crude, harsh, rough, uncouth, unpolished, unrefined. ANT.-finished, well-prepared; cultivated, refined.

craving, *n.* SYN.-hunger, relish, stomach, thirst, zest; appetite, desire, inclination, liking, longing, need, passion. ANT.-disgust, distaste, renunciation, repugnance, satiety.

crazy, *a.* SYN.-delirious, demented, deranged, foolish, idiotic, imbecilic, insane, mad, maniacal. ANT.-rational, reasonable, sane, sensible, sound.

create, *v.* SYN.-cause, engender, fashion, form, formulate, generate, invent, make, originate, produce; appoint, constitute, ordain. ANT.-annihilate, demolish, destroy; disband, terminate.

creation, *n.* SYN.-beginning, birth, conception, origin.

creative, *a.* SYN.-clever, fanciful, fresh, imaginative, inventive, mystical, new, novel, original, poetical, visionary. ANT.-dull, literal, prosaic, unromantic.

creature, *n.* SYN.-animal, mammal, organism, reptile.

credence, *n.* SYN.-acceptance, belief, confidence, trust.

credentials, *n.* SYN.-certification, confirmation, evidence, proof.

credibility, *n.* SYN.-belief, confidence, credence, faith, persuasion, reliance, trust

credible, *a.* SYN.-creditable, honest, honorable, noble, reliable, reputable, trusty, virtuous.

credulity, *n.* SYN.-acceptance, belief, confidence, trust.

creed, *n.* SYN.-belief, doctrine, dogma, precept, teaching, tenet. ANT.-conduct, deed, performance, practice.

creeping, *a.* SYN.-crawling, inching, faltering, hobbling, limping, skulking, slinking, sneaking.

crest, *n.* SYN.-acme, apex, head, pinnacle, summit, top. ANT.-base, bottom, foot.

crew, *n.* SYN.-assistants, cast, company, gang, group, hands, helpers, seamen, squad, team, troupe, workers.

crime, *n.* SYN.-atrocity, outrage; aggression, crime, injustice, misdeed, misdemeanor, offense, sin, transgression, trespass, vice, wrong. ANT.-gentleness, innocence, morality, right.

criminal, *n.* SYN.-bandit, convict, crook, culprit, delinquent, felon, lawbreaker, malefactor, offender, transgressor.

crippled, *a.* SYN.-defective, deformed, disabled, feeble, halt, hobbling, lame, limping, maimed, weak. ANT.-agile, athletic, robust, sound, vigorous.

crisis, *n.* SYN.-acme, conjuncture, contingency, emergency, exigency, juncture, pass, pinch, predicament, strait. ANT.-calm, equilibrium, normality, stability.

crisp, *a.* SYN.-bracing; brittle, crumbling, delicate, fragile, frail, fresh, splintery. ANT.-enduring, thick, tough, unbreakable.

criterion, *n.* SYN.-gauge, law, measure, principle, proof, rule, standard, test, touchstone. ANT.-chance, fancy, guess, supposition.

critical, *a.* SYN.-accurate, discerning, discriminating, exact, fastidious, particular; captious, carping, caviling, censorious, faultfinding, hypercritical; acute, crucial, decisive, hazardous, important, momentous. ANT.-cursory, shallow, superficial, uncritical; appreciative, approving, commendatory, encouraging; insignificant, unimportant.

criticize, *v.* SYN.-analyze, appraise, evaluate, examine, inspect, scrutinize; blame, censure, reprehend. ANT.-approve, neglect, overlook.

critique, *n.* SYN.-commentary, criticism, critique, examination, inspection, reconsideration, retrospect, retrospection, review, revision, survey, synopsis.

crony, *n.* SYN.-associate, attendant, colleague, companion, comrade, consort, friend, mate, partner. ANT.-adversary, enemy, stranger.

crooked, *a.* SYN.-corrupt, corrupted, debased, depraved, dishonest, illegal, immoral, impure, profligate, unlawful.

crop, *n.* SYN.-fruit, harvest, proceeds, produce, product, reaping, result, store, yield.

crop, *v.* SYN.-clip, cut, prune, shorten, top, trim.

cross, *a.* SYN.-angry, annoyed, cantankerous, churlish, complaining, critical, exasperated, fault-finding, incensed, indignant, irate, irritable, maddened, provoked. ANT.-calm, happy, pleased, satisfied.

crowd, *n.* SYN.-bevy, crush, horde, host, masses, mob, multitude, populace, press, rabble, swarm, throng.

crown, *n.* SYN.-apex, chief, crest, head, pinnacle, summit, top, zenith; coronet, diadem, tiara. ANT.-base, bottom, foot, foundation.

crucial, *a.* SYN.-acute, critical, decisive, hazardous, imperative, important, momentous, threatening. ANT.-insignificant, unimportant.

crude, *a.* SYN.-coarse, green, harsh, ill-prepared, raw, rough, unfinished, unpolished, unrefined; crass, uncouth. ANT.-finished, well-prepared; cultivated, refined.

cruel, *a.* SYN.-barbaric, bloodthirsty, brutal, callous, debased, degenerate, depraved, evil, ferocious, heartless, inhuman, malevolent, malignant, merciless, monstrous, remorseless, ruthless, sadistic, savage, sinful, spiteful, tyrannical, unfeeling, unmerciful, vengeful, viscious, wicked. ANT.-benevolent, compassionate, forbearing, gentle, humane, kind, merciful.

cruelty, *n.* SYN.-barbarity, brutality, coercion, domination, ferocity, harshness, indifference, inhumanity, injustice, malice, oppression, persecution, rancor, ruthlessness, sadism, severity, venom, wickedness.

crumb, *n.* SYN.-bit, grain, iota, jot, mite, ort, particle, scrap, shred, smidgen, speck, spot. ANT.-aggregate, bulk, mass, quantity.

crumble, *v.* SYN.-corrode, decay, degenerate, disintegrate, rot, rust.

cry, *n.* SYN.-bellow, call, cheer, clamor, exclamation, holler, hullabaloo, outcry, scream, shout, shriek, whoop, yell.

cry, *v.* SYN.-bawl, bemoan, bewail, blubber, grieve, lament, sob, sorrow, wail, weep, whimper, whine.

cuddle, *v.* SYN.-caress, coddle, embrace, fondle, hug, pet, snuggle. ANT.-annoy, buffet, spurn, tease, vex.

cue, *n.* SYN.-alert, hint, prompt, ready, sign, signal, warning.

cull, *v.* SYN.-choose, elect, opt, pick, select. ANT.-refuse, reject.

culmination, *n.* SYN.-acme, apex, climax, completion, consummation, end, finale, finish, height, peak, summit, zenith. ANT.-anticlimax, base, depth, floor.

culprit, *n.* SYN.-criminal, delinquent, felon, malefactor, offender, transgressor.

cultivation, *n.* SYN.-agriculture, agronomy, farming, gardening, horticulture, husbandry, tillage; breeding, education, enhancement, learning, nurturing, refinement.

culture, *n.* SYN.-breeding, civilization, clan, cultivation, education, enlightenment, family, folklore, folkways, instruction, knowledge, refinement, society. ANT.-boorishness, ignorance, illiteracy, vulgarity.

cultured, *a.* SYN.-accomplished, appreciative, blasé, civilized, cultivated, cultured, educated, enlightened, erudite, experienced, informed, lettered, polished, sophisticated, understanding, urbane, worldly, worldly-wise. ANT.-crude, ingenuous, naive, simple, uncouth.

cunning, *a.* SYN.-clever, crooked, distorted, erratic, indirect, ingenious, roundabout, skillful, swerving, tortuous, wandering, winding; circuitous, crooked, devious, tricky. ANT.-direct, straight; honest, straightforward.

cunning, *n.* SYN.-aptitude, cleverness, faculty, ingeniousness, ingenuity, inventiveness, resourcefulness, skill ANT.-clumsiness, dullness, inaptitude, stupidity.

curb, *v.* SYN.-block, bridle, check, constrain, delay, halt, hinder, hold back, impede, inhibit, limit, repress, restrain, retard, stay, stem, stop, suppress. ANT.-aid, encourage, incite, loosen.

cure, *n.* SYN.-antidote, help, medicant, prescription, remedy, restorative; relief, solution.

curiosity, *n.* SYN.-marvel, miracle, phenomenon, oddity, peculiarity, prodigy, rarity, spectacle, wonder; concern, inquisitiveness, interest, meddling, prying, regard. ANT.-familiarity, triviality.

curious, *a.* SYN.-inquiring, inquisitive, interrogative, meddling, nosy, peeping, peering, prying, questioning, searching, snoopy; odd, peculiar, queer, strange, rare, unique, unusual. ANT.-incurious, indifferent, unconcerned, uninterested; common, ordinary.

current, *a.* SYN.-contemporary, fashionable, latest, modern, new, newest, novel, present, recent. ANT.-ancient, antiquated, bygone, old, past.

curse, *n.* SYN.-anathema, ban, blasphemy, cursing, cuss, damning, denunciation, expletive, fulmination, imprecation, irreverence, oath, profanity, vulgarism; affliction, annoyance, bane, calamity, evil, misfortune, plague.

curse, *v.* SYN.-abuse, blaspheme, damn, denounce, fulminate, imprecate, insult, profane, revile; afflict, annoy, doom, plague, scourge, trouble, vex.

cursory, *a.* SYN.-abbreviated, brief, external, flimsy, frivolous, imperfect, offhand, quick, shallow, short, slight, superficial. ANT.-abstruse, complete, deep, profound, thorough.

curt, *a.* SYN.-abrupt, blunt, brief, brusque, concise, impatient, quick, rude, terse. ANT.-anticipated, courteous, expected.

curtail, *v.* SYN.-abbreviate, abridge, condense, contract, curtail, diminish, lessen, limit, reduce, restrict, shorten. ANT.-elongate, extend, lengthen.

curve, *v.* SYN.-bend, bow, crook, turn, twist, ANT.-straighten.

custodian, *n.* SYN.-attendant, caretaker, cleaner, keeper, porter, superintendent, watchman.

custody, *n.* SYN.-care, charge, guardianship, keeping, supervision, ward. ANT.-neglect, negligence.

custom, *n.* SYN.-characteristic, convention, fashion, formality, habit, manner, mores, observance, practice, precedent, procedure, ritual, routine, rule, style, usage, use, way, wont.

customary, *a.* SYN.-accustomed, characteristic, common, conventional, every-day, familiar, general, habitual, normal, ordinary, procedural, usual. ANT.-abnormal, exceptional, extraordinary, irregular, rare.

customer, *n.* SYN.-buyer, client, consumer, patron, user.

cut, *n.* SYN.-divide, furrow, gash, gouge, groove, hole, incision, mark, nick, notch, opening, separation, slash, slice, slit, wound.

cut, *v.* SYN.-amputate, chop, cleave, dice, dissect, gash, gouge, lop, nick, notch, prune, score, separate, shear, slash, slice, slit, snip, split, trim, wound.

cute, *a.* SYN.-alluring, attractive, captivating, charming, dainty, delicate, elegant, engaging, fascinating, fetching, petite, pleasing, sensitive, slender, slight, winsome.

cylindrical, *a.* SYN.-circular, barrel-shaped, curved, round.

cynic, *n.* SYN.-detractor, doubter, egoist, egotist, misanthrope, mocker, pessimist, satirist, scoffer, sneerer, unbeliever.

cynical, a. SYN.-antisocial, acerbic, caustic, derisive, hostile, misanthropic, sardonic, unbelieving, unfriendly, unsociable.

D

dainty, *a.* SYN.-airy, beautiful, delicate, elegant, exquisite, fastidious, feeble, fragile, frail, lacy, lovely, petite, precious, pretty, sensitive, slender, slight, weak; pleasant, pleasing, savory ANT.-brutal, coarse, rude, tough, vulgar.

dam, *n.* SYN.-bank, barrier, dike, ditch, embankment, gate, levee, wall.

dam, *v.* SYN.-bar, barricade, check, choke, clog, close, confine, impede, obstruct, restrict, retard, slow, stop.

damage, *n.* SYN.-adversity, affliction, blemish, breakage, corruption, defacement, deterioration, detriment, erosion, evil, hardship, harm, hurt, illness, infliction, injury, mischief, misfortune, mishap, reverse, suffering, wound, wrong. ANT.-benefit, boon, favor, kindness.

damage, *v.* SYN.-abuse, batter, break, crack, deface, disfigure, harm, hurt, impair, injure, mar, mutilate, ruin, scratch, spoil, tarnish, wreck. ANT.-ameliorate, benefit, enhance, mend, repair.

damaging, *a.* SYN.-deleterious, detrimental, harmful, hurtful, injurious, mischievous. ANT.-advantageous, beneficial, helpful, profitable, salutary.

damages, *n.* SYN.-compensation, cost, indemnification, indemnity, payment, recompense, reimbursement, reparations, repayment, restitution, SYN.-settlement.

danger, *n.* SYN.-hazard, jeopardy, menace, peril, risk, threat, uncertainty. ANT.-defense, immunity, protection, safety.

dangerous, *a.* SYN.-alarming, critical, hazardous, insecure, menacing, perilous, precarious, risky, serious, threatening, unsafe. ANT.-

firm, protected, safe, secure.

dare, *v.* SYN.-attempt, brave, challenge, defy, endeavor, hazard. risk, try, undertake, venture; challenge, confront, denounce, mock, oppose, resist, scorn, threaten.

daring, *a.* SYN.-adventurous, bold, brave, chivalrous, courageous, enterprising, fearless, foolhardy, precipitate, rash, risqué, unconventional. ANT.-cautious, hesitating, timid.

dark, *a.* SYN.-black, dim, dull, indistinct, gloomy, murky, obscure, overcast, shadowy, unilluminated, vague; dusky, opaque, sable, swarthy; dismal, gloomy, mournful, somber, sorrowful; evil, sinister, sullen, wicked; hidden, mystic, occult, secret. ANT.-light; bright, clear; pleasant; lucid.

dart, *v.* SYN.-bolt, dash, fling, flit, fly, heave, hurtle, plunge, rush, shoot, speed, spring, spurt, thrust.

dead, *a.* SYN.-deceased, defunct, departed, dull, gone, inanimate, insensible, lifeless, spiritless, unconscious. ANT.-alive, animate, living, stirring.

dash, *n.* SYN.-alacrity, charge, dispatch, hurry, hustle, plunge, run, rush, spurt; hint, little, sprinkling, scattering, touch, trace.

dash, *v.* SYN.-chill, dampen, dismay, discourage; bolt, dart, fly, hurry, race, speed.

data, *n.* SYN.-abstracts, details, evidence, facts, figures, information, reports, results, statistics.

date, *n.* SYN.-day, duration, epoch, era, generation, period, spell, term, year; appointment, assignation, call, engagement, rendezvous, tryst, visit.

daze, *n.* SYN.-astonishment, bewilderment, confusion, distraction, muddle, stupor.

daze, *v.* SYN.-amaze, confound, confuse, dazzle, perplex, puzzle, stun, stupefy.

deafening, *a.* SYN.-loud, noisy, resounding, sonorous, stentorian, vociferous ANT.-dulcet, inaudible, quiet, soft, subdued.

dead, *a.* SYN.-anesthetized, deadened, deceased, defunct, departed, gone, inanimate, inert, lifeless, numb, perished, spent, still, tired, unconscious, wearied, worn.

deaden, *v.* SYN.-anesthetize, benumb, desensitize, dull, impair, numb, paralyze, repress, slow.

deadly, *a.* SYN.-bloodthirsty, dangerous, deathly, destructive, fatal, harmful, injurious, lethal, mortal, violent. ANT.-invigorating, stimulating, vital, wholesome.

deal, *n.* SYN.-affair, agreement, business, compromise, contract, negotiation, pact, pledge, proceeding, transaction, understanding.

dear, *a.* SYN.-beloved, cherished, esteemed, precious, valued; costly, expensive, valuable. ANT.-despised, unwanted; cheap.

death, *n.* SYN.-decease, demise, departure, doom, expiration, extinction, mortality, passing, rest, end. ANT.-beginning, birth, life.

debase, *v.* SYN.-abase, adulterate, alloy, corrupt, defile, degrade, deprave, depress, humiliate, impair, lower, pervert, vitiate. ANT.-enhance, improve, raise, restore, vitalize.

debate, *v.* SYN.-altercate, argue, bicker, contend, contest, differ, discuss, dispute, quarrel, oppose, question, reason, squabble, wrangle; denote, imply, indicate, prove, refute, show. ANT.-agree, allow, assent, concede, ignore, overlook, reject, spurn.

debris, *n.* SYN.-fragments, garbage, litter, pieces, refuse, rubbish, ruins, trash, waste, wreckage.

debt, *n.* SYN.-arrears, bill, deficit, indebtedness, liability, obligation, mortgage, note. ANT.-asset, capital, credit, excess, grace, trust.

decadent, *a.* SYN.-brutal, callous, debased, degenerate, depraved, evil, heartless, immoral, inhuman, malignant, merciless, monstrous, remorseless, ruthless, sadistic, savage, sinful, spiteful, unfeeling, unmerciful, vengeful, viscious, wicked.

decay, *n.* SYN.-blight, collapse, consumption, corrosion, corruption, decadence, decline, decomposition, degeneration, deterioration, disintegration, downfall, failure, putrefaction, ruin, ruination.

decay, *v.* SYN.-blight, decline, decompose, decrease, disintegrate, dwindle, ebb, putrefy, rot, spoil, wane, waste, wither. ANT.-flourish, grow, increase, luxuriate, rise.

deceased, a, SYN.-dead, defunct, departed, gone, lifeless. ANT.-alive, animate, living, stirring.

deceit, *n.* SYN.-beguilement, cheat, chicanery, cunning, deceitfulness, deception, duplicity, fraud, guile, sham, trick, wiliness. ANT.-candor, honesty, openness, sincerity, truthfulness.

deceitful, *a.* SYN.-deceptive, delusive, delusory, dishonest, fallacious, false, illusive, misleading, specious. ANT.-authentic, genuine, honest, real, truthful.

deceive, *v.* SYN.-betray, defraud, delude, dupe, ensnare, entrap, fleece, fool, hoodwink, mislead, outwit, rob, swindle, victimize.

decent, *a.* SYN.-adequate, becoming, befitting, comely, decorous, ethical, fit, nice, proper, respectable, seemly, suitable, tolerable, trustworthy, upright, virtuous. ANT.-coarse, gross, indecent, reprehensible, vulgar.

deception, *n.* SYN.-beguilement, betrayal, cheat, chicanery, craftiness, cunning, deceit, deceitfulness, dishonesty, duplicity, fraud, guile, sham, treachery, treason, trickery, wiliness. ANT.-candor, honesty, openness, sincerity, truthfulness

deceptive, *a.* SYN.-deceitful, delusive, delusory, fallacious, false, illusive, misleading, specious. ANT.-authentic, genuine, honest, real, truthful.

decide, *v.* SYN.-adjudicate, choose, close, conclude, determine, end, judge, pick, resolve, select, settle, terminate. ANT.-doubt, hesitate, suspend, vacillate, waver.

decipher, *v.* SYN.-clarify, construe, decode, elucidate, explain, explicate, interpret, render, solve, translate, unravel. ANT.-confuse, distort, falsify, misconstrue, misinterpret.

declaration, *n.* SYN.-acknowledgment, affidavit, affirmation, allegation, announcement, assertion, avowal, communication, disclosure, manifesto, notice, notification, presentation, proclamation, profession, proposition, report, resolution, statement, thesis, utterance.

declare, *v.* SYN.-affirm, allege, announce, assert, aver, broadcast, certify, claim, contend, disclose, express, impart, indicate, maintain, make known, notify, proclaim, profess, promulgate, pronounce, protest, state, swear, tell. ANT.-conceal, hide, repress, suppress, withhold.

decline, *v.* SYN.-incline, slant, slope; descend, sink, wane; decay, decrease, degenerate, depreciate, deteriorate, diminish, dwindle, weaken; refuse, reject. ANT.-ameliorate, appreciate, ascend, increase; accept.

decorate, *v.* SYN.-adorn, beautify, brighten, deck, embellish, enhance, enrich, garnish, ornament, renovate, trim. ANT.-debase, defame, expose, strip, uncover.

decoration, *n.* SYN.-adornment, design, embellishment, garnish, improvement, ornament, ornamentation.

decorous, *a.* SYN.-becoming, chaste, decent, modest, proper, respectable, seemly.

decrease, *v.* SYN.-abate, abbreviate, abridge, check, compress, condense, crumble, curb, curtail, cut, decay, decline, deduct, deflate, degenerate, deteriorate, diminish, dwindle, fade, lessen, lower, melt, pare, prune, reduce, remove, shorten, shrink, shrivel, sink, slacken, subside, subtract, trim, wane. ANT.-amplify, augment, enlarge, expand, grow, increase, multiply.

decree, *n.* SYN.-declaration, edict, mandate, order, proclamation, pronouncement, ruling.

dedicated, *a.* SYN.-addicted, affectionate, ardent, attached, devoted, disposed, earnest, faithful, fond, given up to, inclined, loyal, prone, true, wedded. ANT.-detached, disinclined, indisposed, untrammeled.

dedication, *n.* SYN.-affection, ardor, attachment, celebration, consecration, devotion, devoutness, fidelity, love, loyalty, piety, religiousness, zeal. ANT.-alienation, apathy, aversion, indifference, unfaithfulness.

deduct, *v.* SYN.-decrease, diminish, lessen, reduce, remove, shorten, subtract. ANT.-amplify, enlarge, expand, grow, increase.

deduction, *n.* SYN.-answer, conclusion, inference, judgment, opinion, reasoning.

deed, *n.* SYN.-accomplishment, act, action, doing, execution, feat, operation, performance, transaction; agreement, certificate, charter, document, lease, record, voucher, warranty. ANT.-cessation, deliberation, inactivity, inhibition, intention.

deep, *a.* SYN.-below, beneath, bottomless, immersed, impenetrable, submerged, subterranean; absorbing, abstract, abstruse, acute, buried, difficult, incisive, grave, penetrating, rich.

deepen, *v.* SYN.-augment, develop, expand, exacerbate, extend, grow, increase, intensify.

deface, *v.* SYN.-abuse, batter, crack, disfigure, harm, hurt, mar, mutilate, ruin, scratch, spoil, tarnish, wreck. ANT.-ameliorate, benefit, enhance, mend, repair.

defame, *v.* SYN.-abuse, asperse, disparage, ill-use, libel, malign, revile, scandalize, slander, traduce, vilify. ANT.-cherish, honor, praise, protect, respect.

default, *n.* SYN.-dereliction, failure, lapse, neglect, omission, oversight, transgression; deficiency, lack, loss, want. ANT.-achievement, success, victory; sufficiency.

defeat, *n.* SYN.-annihilation, conquest, collapse, destruction, extermination, fall, loss, overthrow, rebuff, reverse, setback, subjugation. ANT.-conquest, triumph, victory.

defeat, *v.* SYN.-annihilate, beat, conquer, crush, decimate, demolish, humble, master, overcome, overrun, overwhelm, quell, repulse, rout, smash, subdue, subjugate, surmount, thrash, trounce, vanquish. ANT.-capitulate, cede, lose, retreat, surrender.

defect, *n.* SYN.-blemish, crack, error, failure, fault, flaw, imperfection, mark, mistake, omission, scratch, shortcoming, vice. ANT.-completeness, correctness, perfection.

defend, *v.* SYN.-fortify, guard, protect, safeguard, screen, shelter, shield; assert, back, espouse, justify, plead, maintain, rationalize, uphold, vindicate. ANT.-assault, attack, deny, oppose, submit.

defense, *n.* SYN.-barricade, bastille, bastion, bulwark, citadel, dike, fence, fort, fortification, fortress, rampart, refuge, shelter, shield, stockade, stronghold, trench, wall; backing, explanation, guard, justification, precaution, preservation, protection, resistance, safeguard, security, stand.

defer, *v.* SYN.-adjourn, delay, postpone, shelve, slacken, suspend, waive; accede, comply, concede, obey, submit, yield. ANT.-advance, dispatch, expedite, further, hasten, press, stimulate, urge.

deference, *n.* SYN.-acclaim, adoration, courtesy, esteem, fame, homage, renown, respect, reverence, veneration, worship.

defiant, *a.* SYN.-audacious, bold, brazen, cheeky, forward, impudent, insolent.

deficient, *a.* SYN.-defective, inadequate, incomplete, insufficient, lacking, scanty, short. ANT.-adequate, ample, enough, satisfactory, sufficient.

define, *v.* SYN.-bound, circumscribe, delimit, establish, fix, limit, mark, outline, set; ascertain, characterize, designate, elucidate, explain, illustrate, interpret, specify. ANT.-confuse, distort; misinform, mislead.

definite, *a.* SYN.-absolute, categorical, certain, correct, decisive, determined, exact, explicit, fixed, positive, precise, prescribed, specific, unequivocal; bold, clear, crisp, distinct, obvious, plain, sharp, unmistakable, vivid. ANT.-ambiguous, confused, dubious, equivocal, indefinite, obscure; indistinct, hazy, unclear.

deformed, *a.* SYN.-askew, contorted, crooked, crushed, damaged, disfigured, distorted, irregular, malformed, mangled, warped. ANT.-regular, shapely, well-formed.

defy, *v.* SYN.-confront, face, hinder, impede, insult, obstruct, oppose, resist, thwart, withstand. ANT.-accede, allow, cooperate, relent, yield.

degenerate, *v.* SYN.-atrophy, descend, sink, wane; decay, decline, decrease, depreciate, deteriorate, diminish, dwindle, weaken; corrupt, debase, depraved, immoral. ANT.-ameliorate, appreciate, ascend, increase; accept.

degrade, *v.* SYN.-abase, abash, adulterate, alloy, corrupt, debase, defile, deprave, depress, humble, humiliate, impair, lower, mortify, pervert, shame, vitiate. ANT.-enhance, improve, raise, restore, vitalize.

degree, *n.* SYN.-caliber, extent, grade, intensity, order, proportion, quality, quantity, range, scope, stage, standing, station, status, step, strength.

deign, *v.* SYN.-condescend, patronize, stoop, submit.

delay, *v.* SYN.-defer, postpone, procrastinate; arrest, detain, hinder, impede, retard, stay; dawdle, linger, loiter, tarry. ANT.-expedite, hasten, precipitate, quicken.

delectable, *a.* SYN.-delicious, delightful, luscious, palatable, savory, sweet, tasty. ANT.-acrid, distasteful, nauseous, unpalatable, unsavory.

delegate, *n.* SYN.-agent, alternate, appointee, deputy, emissary, legate, minister, proxy, representative.

delegate, *v.* SYN.-appoint, assign, authorize, choose, commission, deputize, elect, empower, name, nominate, ordain, select.

deliberate, *a.* SYN.-calculated, conscious, considered, contemplated, designed, intended, intentional, meant, planned, premeditated, purposeful, studied, voluntary, willful. ANT.-accidental, fortuitous.

deliberate, *v.* SYN.-consider, contemplate, examine, heed, meditate, ponder, reflect, study, weigh. ANT.-ignore, neglect, overlook.

delicacy, *n.* SYN.-airiness, daintiness, flimsiness, lightness, smoothness, subtlety, tenderness, transparency; luxury, rarity, tidbit.

delicate, *a.* SYN.-dainty, elegant, exquisite, fastidious, feeble, frail, sensitive, slender, slight, weak; pleasant, pleasing, savory ANT.-brutal, coarse, rude, tough, vulgar.

delicious, *a.* SYN.-appetizing, dainty, delectable, delightful, luscious, palatable, rich, savory, sweet, tasty, tempting. ANT.-acrid, distasteful, nauseous, unpalatable, unsavory

delight, *n.* SYN.-bliss, ecstasy, enjoyment, gladness, happiness, joy, pleasure, rapture, transport. ANT.-annoyance, dejection, melancholy, misery, sorrow.

delighted, *a.* SYN.-amused, blessed, cheerful, contented, fascinated, fortunate, happy, gay, glad, joyful, joyous, merry, pleased, satisfied. ANT.-blue, depressed, gloomy, morose.

delineate, *v.* SYN.-circumscribe, define, demarcate, depict, draw, outline, restrict.

deliver, *v.* SYN.-commit, give, impart, transfer, yield; announce, communicate, impart, proclaim,. publish; emancipate, free, liberate, release, rescue, save. ANT.-confine, withhold; capture, imprison, restrict.

delusion, *n.* SYN.-deception, dream, fallacy, fancy, fantasy, hallucination, illusion, mirage, phantom, vision. ANT.-actuality, reality, substance.

demand, *v.* SYN.-charge, command, direct, order; ask, ask for, challenge, claim, exact, require; inquire, necessitate. ANT.-give, offer, present, tender.

demented, *a.* SYN.-bemused, crazy, deranged, distracted, insane, mad, maniacal, psychotic, troubled, unbalanced, unsound.

demolish, *v.* SYN.-annihilate, destroy, devastate, eradicate, exterminate, extinguish, obliterate, ravage, raze, ruin, wreck. ANT.-construct, establish, make, preserve, save.

demonstrate, *v.* SYN.-confirm, display, establish, evince, exhibit, explain, illustrate, manifest, present, prove, show, teach; march, parade, picket, protest. ANT.-conceal, hide.

denial, *n.* SYN.-disapproval, disavowal, disclaimer, dismissal, dissent, negation, rejection, repudiation.

denounce, *v.* SYN.-accuse, blame, castigate, censure, charge, condemn, implicate, incriminate, indict, prosecute, rebuke, reprehend, reprimand, reproach, reprobate, reprove, revile, scold, upbraid. ANT.-approve, commend, condone, forgive, praise.

dense, *a.* SYN.-close, compact, compressed, concentrated, crowded, solid, thick; dull, obtuse, slow, stupid. ANT.-dispersed, dissipated, sparse; clever, quick.

deny, *v.* SYN.-contradict, contravene, controvert, disagree, gainsay, refute; abjure, disallow, disavow, disown, forbid, refuse, repudiate, withhold. ANT.-affirm, assert, concede, confirm.

depart, *v.* SYN.-abandon, desert, exit, flee, forsake, give up, go, leave, quit, retire, withdraw. ANT.-abide, arrive, enter, remain, stay, tarry.

departure, *n.* SYN.-departing, embarkation, evacuation, exit, exodus, getaway, going, leaving, parting, starting. ANT.-arrival, landing.

dependable, *a.* SYN.-certain, reliable, safe, secure, sure, tried, trustworthy, trusty. ANT.-dubious, fallible, questionable, uncertain, unreliable.

dependent, *a.* SYN.-conditional, contingent, depending, relying, subject, subordinate. ANT.-absolute, autonomous, casual, independent, original.

depict, *v.* SYN.-characterize, describe, draw, explain, narrate, paint, picture, portray, recount, relate, represent, sketch. ANT.-caricature, misrepresent, suggest.

depleted, *a.* SYN.-consumed, destroyed, dissipated, emptied, exhausted, spent, squandered, wasted.

deposit, *v.* SYN.-accumulate, bank, entrust, hoard, invest, keep, save, secure, store. ANT.-pay, spend, withdraw.

depraved, *a.* SYN.-base, corrupted, crooked, debased, dishonest, fraudulent, impure, low, mean, profligate, putrid, spoiled, tainted, unsound, venal.

depreciate, *v.* SYN.-cheapen, decay, decline, decrease, degenerate, denigrate, descend, deteriorate, devalue, diminish, discredit, disparage, downgrade, dwindle, lessen, sink, wane; weaken, refuse, reject. ANT.-accept, ameliorate, appreciate, approve, ascend, exalt, extol, increase, magnify, praise, raise, recommend.

depress, *v.* SYN.-dampen, darken, degrade, discourage, dishearten, dismay, dull, mock, mortify, sadden; lower, reduce, squash.

depression, *n.* SYN.-blues, dejection, despair, desperation, despondency, discouragement, doldrums, gloom, hopelessness, melancholy, misery, oppression, pessimism, sorrow, trouble, unhappiness, worry. ANT.-confidence, elation, hope, optimism.

deputy, *n.* SYN.-aide, agent, alternate, appointee, assistant, delegate, emissary, legate, lieutenant, minister, proxy, representative.

derision, *n.* SYN.-banter, disdain, gibe, irony, jeering, mockery, raillery, ridicule, sarcasm, satire, scorn, sneering.

derivation, *n.* SYN.-beginning, birth, commencement, cradle, foundation, inception, origin, root, source, spring, start. ANT.-end, harvest, issue, outcome, product.

descend, *v.* SYN.-decline, degenerate, dip, drop, plunge, settle, sink, slip, tumble, wane. ANT.-ascend, increase.

describe, *v.* SYN.-characterize, depict, explain, narrate, portray, recount, relate.

describe, *v.* SYN.-characterize, depict, elucidate, illuminate, illustrate, narrate, picture, portray, relate, summarize.

description, *n.* SYN.-account, characterization, chronicle, depiction, detail, history, narration, narrative, portrayal, recital, relation, report. ANT.-caricature, confusion, distortion, misrepresentation.

desert, *v.* SYN.-abandon, defect, forsake, leave, quit. ANT.-defend, maintain, uphold; stay, support.

deserter, *n.* SYN.-betrayer, defector, delinquent, fugitive, runaway, traitor, truant.

desertion, *n.* SYN.-abandonment, defection, departure, escape, flight, renunciation, treason.

design, *n.* SYN.-blueprint, concept, delineation, diagram, draft, drawing, outline, pattern, plan, sketch, treatment; artfulness, contrivance, cunning, plotting, scheming; intent, intention, objective, purpose. ANT.-result; candor, sincerity; accident, chance.

design, *v.* SYN.-contrive, create, devise, invent, plan, scheme; intend, mean, purpose; draw, outline, sketch.

designate, *v.* SYN.-appoint, choose, denote, disclose, indicate, intimate, manifest, reveal, select, show, signify, specify, verify. ANT.-conceal, distract, divert, falsify, mislead.

desire, *n.* SYN.-ambition, appetite, aspiration, attraction, craving, hungering, inclination, longing, lust, propensity, urge, wish, yearning, yen. ANT.-abomination, aversion, distaste, hate, loathing.

desire, *v.* SYN.-choose, covet, crave, long for, want, wish; ask, seek, solicit.

desist, *v.* SYN.-abstain, arrest, bar, cease, check, close, cork, discontinue, end, halt, hinder, impede, interrupt, obstruct, plug, seal, stop, terminate. ANT.-begin, proceed, promote, speed, start.

desolate, *a.* SYN.-abandoned, bare, bleak, deserted, forlorn, forsaken, lonely, solitary, uninhabited, waste, wild. ANT.-attended, cultivated, fertile.

despair, *n.* SYN.-depression, desperation, despondency, discouragement, gloom, hopelessness, pessimism ANT.-confidence, elation, hope, optimism.

desperate, *a.* SYN.-audacious, daring, despairing, despondent, determined, hopeless, reckless, wild. ANT.-assured, composed, confident, hopeful, optimistic.

desperation, *n.* SYN.-anxiety, depression, despair, despondency, discouragement, distress, gloom, hopelessness, pessimism. ANT.-

confidence, elation, hope, optimism.

despicable, *a.* SYN.-base, contemptible, low, malicious, mean, miserable, nasty, offensive, selfish, sordid, vile, vulgar, worthless, wretched. ANT.-admirable, dignified, exalted, generous, noble.

despise, *v.* SYN.-abhor, abominate, detest, dislike, hate, loathe. ANT.-admire, approve, cherish, like, love.

despondent, *a.* SYN.-dejected, depressed, disconsolate, dismal, dispirited, doleful, gloomy, glum, grave, melancholy, moody, pensive, sad, somber, sorrowful. ANT.-buOyant, cheerful, happy, joyous, lively, merry, mirthful, sparkling, spirited.

despotic, *a.* SYN.-absolute, arbitrary, authoritative, brutal, cruel, odious, oppressive, repressive, severe, tyrannical. ANT.-accountable, conditional, contingent, dependent, qualified.

destined, *a.* SYN.-compelled, fated, foreordained, forthcoming, inevitable, inexorable, predetermined,

destiny, *n.* SYN.-consequence, doom, fortune, lot, portion; fate, issue, necessity, outcome, result.

destitute, *a.* SYN.-impecunious, indigent, needy, penniless, poor, poverty-stricken; scanty, shabby. ANT.-affluent, opulent, rich, wealthy.

destroy, *v.* SYN.-annihilate, demolish, devastate, eradicate, exterminate, extinguish, liquidate, obliterate, ravage, raze, ruin, wreck. ANT.-construct, establish, make, preserve, save.

destroyed, *a.* SYN.-broken, crushed, eradicated, flattened, fractured, reduced, rent, ruptured, shattered, smashed, wrecked. ANT.-integral, repaired, united, whole.

destructive, *a.* SYN.-baneful, deadly, deleterious, detrimental, devastating, fatal, injurious, noxious, pernicious, ruinous. ANT.-beneficial, constructive, creative, profitable, salutary.

detail, *n.* SYN.-article, aspect, circumstance, item, minutia, part, particular, trait; detachment, force, party, squad, team, unit. ANT.-generality, haziness, vagueness.

detail, *v.* SYN.-analyze, catalogue, enumerate, itemize, narrate, recapitulate, recite, recount, relate, report, summarize.

detain, *v.* SYN.-arrest, delay, hinder, hold, impede, inhibit, keep, restrain, retard, stay. ANT.-expedite, hasten, precipitate, quicken.

detect, *v* SYN.-ascertain, devise, discover, expose, find, find out, invent, learn, originate, reveal. ANT.-cover, hide, lose, mask, screen.

detention, *n.* SYN.-apprehension, arrest, bonds, custody, confinement, constraint, imprisonment, incarceration, restraint, seizure.

determinant, *n.* SYN.-agent, cause, incentive, inducement, motive, origin, principle, reason, source. ANT.-consequence, effect, end, result.

determination, *n.* SYN.-conviction, courage, decision, firmness, fortitude, obstinacy, perseverance, persistence, resolution, resolve, steadfastness, tenacity, will. ANT.-inconstancy, indecision, vacillation.

determine, *v* SYN.-conclude, decide, end, fix, resolve, settle; ascertain, learn, verify; incline, induce, influence; condition, define, limit; compel, necessitate.

detest, *v.* SYN.-abhor, abominate, despise, dislike, hate, loathe. ANT.-admire, approve, cherish, like, love.

detestable, *a.* SYN.-abominable, disgusting, execrable, foul, hateful, loathsome, odious, revolting, vile. ANT.-agreeable, commendable, delightful, pleasant.

detriment, *n.* SYN.-damage, evil, harm, hurt, ill, infliction, injury, mischief, misfortune, mishap, wrong. ANT.-benefit, boon, favor, kindness.

detrimental, *a.* SYN.-damaging, deleterious, harmful, hurtful, injurious, mischievous. ANT.-advantageous, beneficial, helpful, profitable, salutary.

develop, *v* SYN.-advance, amplify, create, cultivate, elaborate, enlarge, evolve, expand, extend, mature, perfect, promote, unfold. ANT.-compress, contract, restrict, stunt, wither.

development, *n.* SYN.-elaboration, expansion, unfolding, unraveling; evolution, growth, maturing, progress. ANT.-abbreviation, compression, curtailment.

deviate, *v.* SYN.-bend, crook, deflect, digress, diverge, divert, sidetrack, stray, wander. ANT.-continue, follow, persist, preserve. remain.

device, *n.* SYN.-apparatus, appliance, channel, contraption, contrivance, instrument, means, medium, tool, utensil, vehicle; artifice, craft, design, plan, plot, scheme, trick, wile. ANT.-hindrance, impediment, obstruction, preventive.

devious, *a.* SYN.-circuitous, crooked, distorted, erratic, indirect, roundabout, swerving, tortuous, wandering, winding; crooked, cunning, foxy, insidious, shrewd, tricky. ANT.-direct, straight; honest, straightforward.

devoted, *a.* SYN.-addicted, affectionate, ardent, attached, constant, dedicated, disposed, dutiful, earnest, faithful, fond, given up to, inclined, loyal, prone, true, wedded. ANT.-detached, disinclined, indisposed, untrammeled.

devotion, *n.* SYN.-affection, ardor, attachment, consecration, dedication, devoutness, fidelity, love, loyalty, piety, religiousness, zeal. ANT.-alienation, apathy, aversion, indifference, unfaithfulness.

devout, *a.* SYN.-devoted, godly, holy, pietistic, pious, religious, reverent, sanctimonious, spiritual, theological. ANT.-atheistic, impious, profane, secular, skeptical.

dexterity, *n.* SYN.-ability, adroitness, aptitude, aptness, capability, capacity, cleverness, deftness, facility, efficiency, faculty, power, qualification, skill, skillfulness, talent. ANT.-awkwardness, clumsiness, disability, inability, incapacity, incompetence, ineptitude, unreadiness.

dialect, *n.* SYN.-cant, diction, idiom, jargon, lingo, language, phraseology, slang, speech, tongue, vernacular. ANT.-babble, drivel, gibberish, nonsense.

dialogue, *n.* SYN.-chat, colloquy, conference, conversation, exchange, interview, meeting, negotiation, parley, remarks, talk, tête-à-tête.

dictator, *n.* SYN.-autocrat, despot, leader, lord, master, mogul, oppressor, overlord, persecutor, taskmaster, totalitarian, tyrant.

diction, *n.* SYN.-articulation, eloquence, enunciation, fluency, language, locution, style, vocabulary.

die, *v.* SYN.-cease, decay, decease, decline, depart, expire, fade, languish, perish, sink, succumb, wane, wither. ANT.-begin, flourish, grow, live, survive.

differ, *v.* SYN.-alter, change, conflict, contrast, deviate, diverge, diversify, modify, qualify, vary; argue, contradict, disagree, dispute, dissent, object, oppose, quarrel.

difference, *n.* SYN.-disparity, dissimilarity, distinction, divergence, separation, variety, variance; disagreement, discord, dissension, estrangement. ANT.-identity, resemblance, similarity; agreement, harmony.

different, *a.* SYN.-contrary, dissimilar, distinct, divergent, diverse, incongruous, opposite, unlike, variant; divers, miscellaneous, sundry, various. ANT.-alike, congruous, identical, same, similar.

differentiate, *v.* SYN.-descry, detect, discern, discriminate, distinguish, observe, perceive, recognize, see, separate. ANT.-confound, confuse, mingle, omit, overlook.

difficult, *a.* SYN.-arduous, challenging, complicated, demanding, formidable, hard, intricate, involved, laborious, obscure, perplexing, strenuous, thorny, toilsome, troublesome, trying. ANT.-easy, effortless, facile, simple.

difficulty, *n.* SYN.-adversity, annoyance, complication, crisis, distress, embarrassment, frustration, hardship, hindrance, impasse, impediment, irritation, knot, misfortune, obstacle, obstruction, predicament, scrape, setback, snag, struggle, trouble.

dig, *v.* SYN.-burrow, delve, dredge, excavate, exhume, mine, scoop, shovel, uncover, undermine, unearth.

dignified, *a.* SYN.-aristocratic, august, courtly, distinguished, elegant, formal, noble, proud, regal, reserved, solemn, somber, stately, sublime. ANT.-base, crass, rude, undignified.

dignity, *n.* SYN.-air, bearing, culture, elegance, nobility, pride, quality, refinement, restraint, stateliness, style.

digress, *v.* SYN.-deviate, diverge, divert, shift, sidetrack, stray, wander. ANT.-continue, follow, persist, preserve. remain.

dilate, *v.* SYN.-amplify, augment, broaden, distend, enlarge, expand, increase, magnify, widen. ANT.-abridge, contract, diminish, restrict, shrink.

dilemma, *n.* SYN.-complication, difficulty, fix, impasse, predicament, plight, scrape, situation, strait. ANT.-calmness, comfort, ease, satisfaction.

diligent, *a.* SYN.-active, alert, assiduous, busy, careful, earnest, hard-working, industrious, patient, persevering, quick. ANT.-apathetic, careless, indifferent, lethargic, unconcerned.

dim, *a.* SYN.-faded, faint, indistinct, pale, shadowy; feeble, languid, wearied; irresolute, weak. ANT.-conspicuous, glaring; strong, vigorous; forceful.

diminish, *v.* SYN.-abate, assuage, curtail, decline, decrease, dwindle, lessen, lower, moderate, reduce, shorten, suppress, wane. ANT.-amplify, enlarge, expand, grow, increase, intensify, revive.

din, *n.* SYN.-babel, clamor, cry, noise, outcry, racket, row, sound, tumult, uproar. ANT.-hush, quiet, silence, stillness.

dip, *v.* SYN.-bathe, baptize, douse, duck, dunk, lower, plunge, steep, submerge; ladle, scoop, spoon; decline, incline, recede, sink, slant, slide, slope, tilt.

diplomacy, *n.* SYN.-adroitness, dexterity, discretion, finesse, knack, poise, polish, refinement, savoir faire, skill, subtlety, tact. ANT.-awkwardness, blunder, incompetence, rancor, rudeness, sarcasm, vulgarity.

diplomatic, *a.* SYN.-adroit, discreet, discriminating, judicious, politic, tactful. ANT.-boorish, churlish, coarse, gruff, rude.

dire, *a.* SYN.-appalling, calamitous, catastrophic, deadly, dreadful, frightful, ghastly, grim, grisly, gruesome, hideous, horrible, terrible, threatening.

direct, *a.* SYN.-straight, undeviating, unswerving; erect, unbent, upright; fair, honest, honorable, just, square. ANT.-circuitous, winding; bent, crooked; dishonest.

direct, *v* SYN.-aim, level, point, train; advise, conduct, govern, guide, influence, manage, oversee, regulate, rule, show; bid, command, inform, instruct, order. ANT.-deceive, distract, misdirect, misguide.

direction, *n.* SYN.-bearing, course, inclination, tendency, trend, way; administration, management, superintendence; guidance, instruction, order.

dirty, *a.* SYN.-filthy, foul, grimy, muddy, soiled, squalid; indecent, nasty, obscene; base, contemptible, despicable, low, mean, pitiful, shabby. ANT.-clean, neat, presentable; pure, wholesome.

disabled, *a.* SYN.-crippled, defective, deformed, feeble, halt, hobbling, lame, limping, maimed, unconvincing, unsatisfactory, weak. ANT.-agile, athletic, robust, sound, vigorous.

disagreement, *n.* SYN.-altercation, argument, bickering, challenge, conflict, contention, controversy, difference, discord, dispute, dissent, dissentience, feud, objection, protest, quarrel, spat, squabble, variance, wrangle. ANT.-acceptance, agreement, assent, compliance, harmony, peace, reconciliation.

disappear, *v.* SYN.-depart, desert, disintegrate, dissipate, dissolve, escape, evaporate, fade, flee, vanish.

disappoint, *v.* SYN.-anger, annoy, disillusion, dismay, displease, dissatisfy, fail, frustrate, mislead, nettle, offend, vex.

disappointed, *a.* SYN.-annoyed, despondent, discontented, disillusioned, dissatisfied, disturbed, irritated, unsatisfied.

disappointing, *a.* SYN.-discouraging, inadequate, ineffective, inferior, insufficient, failing, lame, mediocre, ordinary, second-rate, uninteresting, unsatisfactory.

disapprove, *v.* SYN.-condemn, criticize, denounce, disparage, object, oppose, resist.

disaster, *n.* SYN.-accident, adversity, calamity, casualty, catastrophe, defeat, emergency, failure, misadventure, mishap, ruin, setback, tragedy. ANT.-advantage, fortune, welfare.

disavow, *v.* SYN.-abandon, forego,

forsake, quit, relinquish, resign; deny, disclaim, disown, reject, renounce, retract, revoke. ANT.-defend, maintain, uphold; acknowledge, assert, recognize.

discard, *v.* SYN.-abandon, discharge, dismiss, eject, expel, reject, renounce, repudiate.

discern, *v.* SYN.-descry, detect, determine, differentiate, discriminate, distinguish, observe, perceive, recognize, see, separate. ANT.-confound, confuse, mingle, omit, overlook.

discerning, *a.* SYN.-accurate, critical, discriminating, exact, fastidious, particular, perceptive. ANT.-cursory, shallow, superficial, uncritical.

discernment, *n.* SYN.-acumen, cultivation, discrimination, insight, intuition, judgment, penetration, perception, perspicuity, refinement, taste. ANT.-obtuseness.

discharge, *v.* SYN.-banish, belch, discard, dismiss, eject, emanate, emit, exile, expel, fire, liberate, oust, release, remove, send off, shed, shoot, spurt, terminate, vent. ANT.-accept, detain, recall, retain.

disciple, *n.* SYN.-adherent, believer, devotee, follower, supporter, votary; learner, pupil, scholar, student.

discipline, *n.* SYN.-control, limitation, order, regulation, restraint, self-control; cultivation, exercise, instruction, practice, training; correction, chastisement, punishment. ANT.-chaos, confusion, turbulence.

disclaim, *v.* SYN.-abandon, forego, forsake, quit, relinquish, resign; deny, disavow, disown, reject, renounce, retract, revoke. ANT.-defend, maintain, uphold; acknowledge, assert, recognize.

disclose, *v.* SYN.-betray, communicate, confess, divulge, expose, identify, impart, mention, reveal, show, testify, uncover, unveil. ANT.-cloak, conceal, cover, disguise, hide, mask, obscure, secrete, withhold.

disconsolate, *a.* SYN.-cheerless, dejected, depressed, despondent, dismal, distressed, doleful, downcast, forlorn, gloomy, heartbroken, lugubrious, melancholy, mournful, sad, somber, sorrowful. ANT.-cheerful, content, ecstatic, glad, happy, joyous, merry, spirited.

discontinue, *v.* SYN.-adjourn, interrupt, postpone, stay, suspend. ANT.-continue, maintain, persist, proceed, prolong.

discourage, *v.* SYN.-abash, appall, chill, dampen, daunt, demoralize, deter, dishearten, dissuade, dull, forbid, hinder, inhibit, prevent, repress, warn. ANT.-advance, advocate, bolster, embolden, encourage, nourish.

discourteous, *a.* SYN.-blunt, boorish, gruff, impolite, impudent, insolent, rough, rude, saucy, surly, uncivil, vulgar; coarse, crude, ignorant, rough, savage, unpolished, fierce, harsh, inclement, tumultuous, violent. ANT.-civil, genteel, polished; courtly, dignified, noble, stately; calm, mild, peaceful.

discover, *v.* SYN.-ascertain, catch, create, detect, determine, devise, discern, expose, find, find out, glimpse, identify, invent, learn, observe, originate, perceive, recognize, reveal, uncover, unearth. ANT.-cover, hide, lose, mask, screen.

discreet, *a.* SYN.-cautious, circumspect, considerate, diplomatic, discerning, discriminating, guarded, judicious, politic, prudent, reserved, sensible, strategic, tactful, wary, watchful. ANT.-boorish, churlish, coarse, gruff, rude.

discrepant, *a.* SYN.-contradictory, contrary, illogical, incompatible, incongruous, inconsistent, irreconcilable, paradoxical. ANT.-compatible, congruous, consistent, correspondent.

discretion, *n.* SYN.-calculation, care, caution, concern, consideration, deliberation, diplomacy, discrimination, foresight, forethought, heed, prudence, responsibility, tact.

discriminate, *v.* SYN.-differentiate, distinguish, favor, incline, know, notice, segregate, separate. ANT.-group, mingle, overlook, unite.

discriminating, a, SYN.-accurate, aesthetic, artistic, critical, cultered, discerning, exact, fastidious, particular, polished, refined. ANT.-cursory, indiscriminate, shallow, superficial, uncritical, uninformed, unselective.

discrimination, *n.* SYN.-discernment, intelligence, judgment, perception, perspicacity, sagacity, taste, understanding, wisdom; bigotry, isolation, persecution. ANT.-arbitrariness, senselessness, stupidity, thoughtlessness.

discuss, *v.* SYN.-chat, converse, speak, tattle; argue, comment, contest, declaim, debate, discourse, dispute; confer, consult, deliberate, explain, reason, talk.

discussion, *n.* SYN.-chat, conference, consultation, conversation, debate, dialogue, discourse, exchange, gossip, lecture, report, symposium, talk. ANT.-correspondence, meditation, silence, writing.

disdain, *n.* SYN.-contempt, contumely, derision, detestation, hatred, scorn. ANT.-awe, esteem, regard, respect, reverence.

disease, *n.* SYN.-ailment, complaint, disorder, illness, infirmity, malady, sickness. ANT.-health, healthiness, soundness, vigor.

diseased, *a.* SYN.-ill, indisposed, infirm, morbid, sick, unhealthy, unwell. ANT.-healthy, robust, sound, strong, well.

disgrace, *n.* SYN.-abashment, chagrin, humiliation, mortification; dishonor, disrepute, ignominy, odium, opprobrium, scandal, shame. ANT.-dignity, glory, honor, praise, renown.

disgraceful, *a.* SYN.-discreditable, dishonorable, disreputable, ignominious, scandalous, shameful. ANT. teemed, honorable, renowned, respectable.

disguise, *n.* SYN.-affectation, cloak, deception, garb, mask, pretense, pretension, pretext, semblance, simulation, subterfuge. ANT.-actuality, fact, reality, sincerity, truth.

disguise, *v.* SYN.-cloak, conceal, cover, hide, mask, screen, secrete, suppress, veil, withhold. ANT.-disclose, divulge, expose, reveal, show, uncover.

dishonest, *a.* SYN.-corrupt, corrupted, crooked, crafty, cunning, debased, deceitful, deceiving, deceptive, depraved, fraudulent, immoral, lying, profligate, treacherous, underhanded.

dishonor, *n.* SYN.-humiliation, mortification; disgrace, disrepute, ignominy, odium, opprobrium, scandal, shame. ANT.-dignity, glory, honor, praise, renown.

disintegrate, *v.* SYN.-decay, decompose, decrease, diffuse, dispell, disseminate, dissipate, dwindle, putrefy, rot, spoil, waste. ANT.-flourish, grow, increase, luxuriate.

dislike, *n.* SYN.-abhorrence, animosity, antipathy, aversion, detestation, disgust, dislike, disinclination, distaste, dread, enmity, hatred, hostility, loathing, malevolence, rancor, repugnance, repulsion, reluctance. ANT.-affection, attachment, attraction, devotion, enthusiasm, friendship, love.

dislike, *v.* SYN.-abhor, abominate, deplore, despise, detest, disapprove, hate, loathe, revulse. ANT.-admire, approve, cherish, like, love.

disloyal, *a.* SYN.-apostate, faithless, false, inconstant, perfidious, recreant, traitorous, treacherous, treasonable. ANT.-constant, devoted, loyal, true.

dismal, *a.* SYN.-bleak, cheerless, dark, depressing, discouraging, doleful, dreary, dull, funereal, gloomy, lonesome, melancholy, sad, somber. ANT.-cheerful, gay, joyous, lively.

dismiss, *v.* SYN.-banish, discard, discharge, eject, exile, expel, fire, oust, reject, release, remove, send off, terminate. ANT.-accept, detain, recall, retain.

disobedient, *a.* SYN. defiant, forward, insubordinate, rebellious, refractory, undutiful, unruly. ANT.-compliant, dutiful, obedient, submissive.

disobey, *v.* SYN.-balk, decline, defy, differ, disagree, disregard, ignore, rebel, refuse, resist, revolt, transgress, violate. ANT.-follow, fulfill, obey.

disorder, *n.* SYN.-agitation, anarchy, chaos, commotion, confusion, disarrangement, disarray, disorganization, ferment, jumble, muddle, stir, tumult, turmoil. ANT.-certainty, order, organization, peace, system, tranquility.

disorganization, *n.* SYN.-anarchy, chaos, confusion, disorder, jumble, muddle. ANT.-order, organization, system.

disorganized, *a.* SYN.-bewildered, confused, deranged, disconcerted, disordered, indistinct, mixed, muddled, perplexed. ANT.-clear, lucid, obvious, organized, plain.

disparage, *v.* SYN.-belittle, decry, defame, depreciate, derogate, discredit, disparage, libel, lower, malign, minimize, slander, undervalue, vility. ANT.-aggrandize, commend, exalt, magnify, praise.

dispatch, *v.* SYN.-cast, discharge, dispatch, emit, impel, propel, send, throw, transmit. ANT.-bring, get, hold, receive, retain.

dispel, *v.* SYN.-diffuse, disperse, disseminate, dissipate, scatter, separate. ANT.-accumulate, amass, assemble, collect, gather.

dispense, *v.* SYN.-allot, apportion, deal, distribute, divide, mete; allocate, appropriate, assign, give, grant, measure. ANT.-confiscate, keep, refuse, rctain, withhold.

disperse, *v.* SYN.-diffuse, dispel, disseminate, dissipate, scatter, separate. ANT.-accumulate, amass, assemble, collect, gather.

displace, *v.* SYN.-dislodge, move, remove, shift, transfer, transport; discharge, dismiss, eject, oust, vacate. ANT.-leave, remain, stay; retain.

display, *v.* SYN.-arrange, demonstrate, disclose, exhibit, expose, flaunt, open, parade, present, reveal, show, spread out, uncover, unveil. ANT.-cloak, conceal, cover, disguise, hide, secrete, withhold.

disposition, *n.* SYN.-action, bearing, behavior, bent, bias, carriage, conduct, demeanor, deportment, inclination, leaning, manner, partiality, penchant, predilection, predisposition, prejudice, proclivity, proneness, propensity, slant, tendency, turn. ANT.-equity, fairness, impartiality, justice.

dispute, *n.* SYN.-altercation, argument, conflict, contention, controversy, debate, disagreement, discussion, misunderstanding, quarrel, squabble. ANT.-agreement, concord, decision, harmony.

dispute, *v.* SYN.-altercate, argue, bicker, contend, contest, debate, disagree, discuss, quarrel, squabble, wrangle. ANT.-agree, allow, assent, concede.

disregard, *v.* SYN.-disdain, disobey, ignore, neglect, omit, overlook, scorn, skip, slight, snub. ANT.-include, notice, regard.

disreputable, *a.* SYN.-discreditable, disgraceful, dishonorable, ignominious, scandalous, shameful. ANT. teemed, honorable, renowned, respectable.

dissent, *n.* SYN.-challenge, difference, disagreement, dissentience, noncompliance, nonconformity, objection, protest, rejection, remonstrance, variance. ANT.-acceptance, agreement, assent, compliance.

dissimilar, *a.* SYN.-different, distinct, divergent, diverse, incongruous, opposite, unlike, variant; divers, miscellaneous, sundry, various. ANT.-alike, congruous, identical, same, similar.

dissipate, *v.* SYN.-despoil, destroy, devastate, strip; consume, corrode, dispel, lavish, misuse, scatter, spend, squander, waste, wear out; decay, diminish, dwindle, pine, conserve, wither. ANT.-accumulate, concentrte, conserve, economize, integrate, preserve, save, unite.

distant, *a.* SYN.-far, faraway, remote, removed; aloof, cold, reserved, stiff, unfriendly. ANT.-close, near, nigh; cordial, friendly.

distinct, *a.* SYN.-apparent, clear, evident, intelligible, lucid, manifest, obvious, plain, unmistakable, visible; open, unobstructed. ANT.-ambiguous, obscure, unclear, vague.

distinction, *n.* SYN.-attribute, characteristic, feature, peculiarity, property, quality, trait; eminence, fame, honor, luster, notability, reputation. ANT.-being, essence, nature, substance; disgrace, disrepute, obscurity.

distinctive, *v.* SYN. eccentric, exceptional, extraordinary, odd, rare, singular, strange, striking, unusual; characteristic, individual, particular, peculiar, special, unique. ANT.-common, general, normal, ordinary.

distinguish, *v.* SYN.-descry, detect, differentiate, discern, discriminate, observe, perceive, recognize, see, separate. ANT.-confound, confuse, mingle, omit, overlook.

distinguished, *a.* SYN.-branded, characterized, conspicuous, differentiated, distinct, identified, marked, separate, unique; elevated, eminent, famed, famous, glorious, illustrious, noted, notorious, outstanding, prominent, renowned, singular. ANT.-common, obscure, ordinary, unimportant, unknown.

distort, *v.* SYN.-alter, deceive, embellish, falsify, fib, lie, misconstrue, misinterpret, mislead, pervert, prevaricate, rig; bend, buckle, contort, crush, deform, twist, warp, wrench.

distress, *n.* SYN.-adversity, affliction, agony, anguish, anxiety, deprivation, destitution, discomfort. grief, indigence, misery, pain, poverty, sorrow, suffering, torment, torture, tribulation, worry. ANT.-comfort, joy, relief, solace.

distribute, *v.* SYN.-allot, apportion, bestow, deal, dispense, disperse, divide, dole, issue, mete, scatter, share, spread; arrange, catalogue, categorize, classify, group, sort. ANT.-accmmulate, amass, conserve, hoard, keep, safeguard, save; blend, combine, consolidate, unify, unite.

district, *n.* SYN.-area, community, division, domain, neighborhood, place, province, quarter, region, section, territory.

distrust, *n.* SYN.-ambiguity, doubt, hesitation, incredulity, scruple, skepticism, suspense, suspicion, unbelief, uncertainty. ANT.-belief, certainty, conviction, determination. faith.

disturb, *v.* SYN.-agitate, alarm, annoy, confuse, decompose, derange, interrupt, perplex, perturb, rattle, rouse, trouble, unsettle, vex, worry. ANT.-order, pacify, quiet, settle, soothe.

disturbance, *n.* SYN.-agitation, bother, clamor, disruption, eruption, racket, riot, stir, turbulence, turmoil, uproar.

disturbing, *a.* SYN.-alarming, annoying, bothersome, disquieting, distressing, foreboding, frightening, ominous, perturbing, startling, threatening, troublesome, trying, upsetting.

diverse, *a.* SYN.-different, dissimilar, divergent, incongruous, opposite, unlike, variant; assorted, divers, miscellaneous, sundry, various. ANT.-alike, congruous, identical, same, similar.

diversity, *n.* SYN.-assortment, change, difference, dissimilarity, heterogeneity, medley, miscellany, mixture, multifariousness, variety, variousness. ANT.-homogeneity, likeness, monotony, sameness, uniformity.

divert, *v.* SYN.-avert, deflect, deviate, swerve, turn; alter, change, redirect, transmute. ANT.-arrest, fix, stand, stop; continue, proceed; endure, perpetuate.

divide, *v.* SYN.-carve, chop, cleave, cut, detach, part, rend, separate, sever, splinter, split, sunder, tear; allocate, allot, apportion, deal out, dispense, distribute, share. ANT.-combine, convene, gather, join unite.

divine, *a.* SYN.-celestial, godlike, hallowed, heavenly, holy, sacred, superhuman, supernatural, transcendent. ANT.-blasphemous, diabolical, mundane, profane, wicked.

divulge, *v.* SYN.-betray, disclose, expose, impart, inform, reveal, show, uncover. ANT.-cloak, conceal, cover, hide, obscure.

do, *v.* SYN.-accomplish, achieve, act, create, complete, conclude, consummate, effect, execute, finish, fulfill, perform, settle, terminate;

carry on, conduct, discharge, labor, transact, work; observe, perform, practice; make, produce, work; answer, serve, suffice.

docile, *a.* SYN.-adaptable, compliant, obedient, pliant, submissive, tame, teachable, tractable, yielding. ANT.-mulish, obstinate, stubborn, ungovernable, unruly.

doctrinaire, *a.* SYN.-opinionated, overbearing, positive; authoritative, theoretical, visionary. ANT.-fluctuating, indecisive, open-minded, questioning, skeptical.

doctrine, *n.* SYN.-belief, concept, convention, creed, dogma, precept, principle, teaching, tenet, tradition. ANT.-conduct, deed, performance, practice.

document, *n.* SYN.-account, archive, chronicle, letter, memorandum, minutes, note, paper, permit, record, report, register; testimonial, trace, verification, vestige.

dogma, *n.* SYN.-creed, doctrine, precept, tenet. ANT.-conduct, deed, performance, practice.

dogmatic, *a.* SYN.-arbitrary, arrogant, authoritarian, bigoted, confident, determined, dictatorial, doctrinaire, domineering, emphatic, fanatical, intolerant, magisterial, narrow-minded, obstinate, opinionated, overbearing, positive; authoritative, doctrinal, formal. ANT.-fluctuating, indecisive, open-minded, questioning, skeptical.

dole, *v.* SYN.-allot, apportion, deal, dispense, distribute, divide, measure, mete, parcel, scatter, share, spread.

doleful, *a.* SYN.-bleak, cheerless, dark, dismal, dreary, dull, funereal, gloomy, lonesome, melancholy, sad, somber. ANT.-cheerful, gay, joyous, lively.

domain, *n.* SYN.-country, district, division, dominion, land, place, province, quarter, region, section, territory.

dominate, *v.* SYN.-command, control, dictate, direct, domineer, govern, influence, manage, regulate, rule, subjugate, superintend, tyrannize. ANT.-abandon, follow, forsake, ignore, submit.

domination, *n.* SYN.-ascendancy, control, mastery, predominance, rule, sovereignty, supremacy, sway, transcendence. ANT.-inferiority.

donation, *n.* SYN.-appropriation, benefaction, bequest, boon, charity, endowment, favor, gift, grant, gratuity, largess, offering, present, subsidy. ANT.-deprivation, earnings, loss, purchase.

done, *a.* SYN.-accomplished, completed, executed, over, perfected, performed, realized, through, settled. ANT.-failed, incomplete, unfinished.

donor, *n.* SYN.-benefactor, contributor, giver, patron, sponsor, subscriber.

doomed, *a.* SYN.-condemned, cursed, fated, foreordained, predestined, sentenced.

dormant, *a.* SYN.-idle, inactive indolent, inert, lazy, quiescent, quiet, slothful, still, unemployed, unoccupied. ANT.-active, employed, industrious, occupied, working.

doubt, *n.* SYN.-ambiguity, apprehension, disbelief, distrust, hesitation, incredulity, misgiving, mistrust, scruple, skepticism, suspense, suspicion, unbelief, uncertainty. ANT.-belief, certainty, conviction, determination. faith.

doubt, *v.* SYN.-hesitate, question, uncertain, waver; distrust, mistrust, puzzled, suspect, wonder. ANT.-believe, confide, decide, rely on, trust.

dour, *a.* SYN.-crabby, fretful, gloomy, glum, moody, morose, sulky, surly. ANT.-amiable, gay, joyous, merry, pleasant.

drab, *a.* SYN.-colorless, dingy, dreary, dull, homely, monotonous, plain.

draw, *v.* SYN.-drag, haul, pull, tow, tug; extract, remove, take out, unsheathe; allure, attract, entice, induce, lure, persuade; delineate, depict, sketch, trace; compose, draft, formulate, write; deduce, derive, get, infer, obtain; extend, lengthen, prolong, protract, stretch. ANT.-alienate, contract, drive, propel, shorten.

drawing, *n.* SYN.-cartoon, engraving, etching, illustration, image, likeness, picture, portrait, portrayal, rendering, representation, resemblance, scene, schematic, sketch, view.

dread, *n.* SYN.-alarm, apprehension, awe, fear, foreboding, horror, reverence, terror. ANT.-assurance, boldness, confidence, courage.

dreadful, *a.* SYN.-appalling, awful, dire, fearful, frightening, frightful, ghastly, hideous, horrible, horrid, repulsive, terrible. ANT.-beautiful, enchanting, enjoyable, fascinating, lovely.

dream, *n.* SYN.-apparition, hallucination, idea, image, nightmare, trance.

dream, *v.* SYN.-conceive, conjure, fancy, hallucinate, idealize, imagine, picture, visualize.

dreary, *a.* SYN.-bleak, cheerless, dark, dismal, doleful, dull, funereal, gloomy, lonesome, melancholy, sad, somber. ANT.-cheerful, gay, joyous, lively.

dress, *n.* SYN.-apparel, array, attire, clothes, clothing, drapery, ensemble, garb, garments, habit, raiment, trappings, vestments, vesture. ANT.-nakedness, nudity.

drift, *n.* SYN.-bent, bias, digression, inclination, leaning, tendency, tenor, trend,

drill, *n.* SYN.-activity, application, conditioning, employment, exercise, exertion, lesson, operation, performance, practice, preparation, repetition, task, training, use. ANT.-idleness, indolence, relaxation, repose, rest.

drive, *v.* SYN.-coerce, compel, constrain, encourage, enforce, force, hasten, impel, incite, induce, instigate, oblige, press, stimulate, urge. ANT.-allure, convince, persuade, prevent.

droll, *a.* SYN.-amusing, comical, farcical, funny, humorous, laughable, ludicrous ridiculous, witty; curious, odd, queer. ANT.-melancholy, sad, serious, sober, solemn.

drop, *v.* SYN.-collapse, decline, decrease, descend, diminish, fall, sink, subside; stumble, topple, tumble; droop, extend downward, hang. ANT.-arise, ascend, climb, mount, soar; steady.

drunk, *a.* SYN.-drunken, high, inebriated, intoxicated, tight, tipsy. ANT.-clearheaded, sober, temperate.

dry, *a.* SYN.-arid, dehydrated, desiccated, drained, parched, thirsty; barren, dull, insipid, plain, tedious, tiresome, uninteresting, vapid. ANT.-damp, moist; fresh, interesting, lively.

dull, *a.* SYN.-dense, obtuse, retarded, slow, stupid; blunt, blunted, toothless, unsharpened; commonplace, dingy, dismal, drab, dreary, gloomy, insipid, plain, sad, sober, somber; banal, boring, common, dry, flat, hackneyed, heavy, monotonous, ordinary, pointless, prosaic, repetitious, routine, senseless, tedious, tiresome, trite, uninspiring, uninteresting, vapid. ANT.-animated, lively, sharp; clear, interesting.

dumb, *a.* SYN.-brainless, crass, dense, dull, foolish, inarticulate, obtuse, senseless, stupid, witless. ANT.-alert, bright, clever, discerning, intelligent.

dunk, *v..* SYN.-dip, douse, immerse, plunge, sink, submerge.

duplicate, *n.* SYN.-carbon, copy, exemplar, facsimile, imitation, likeness, replica, reproduction, transcript. ANT.-original, prototype.

duplicate, *v.* SYN.-copy, counterfeit, iterate, recapitulate, reiterate, repeat, replicate, reproduce.

durability, *n.* SYN.-endurance, fortitude, intensity, might, potency, power, stamina, stoutness, strength, sturdiness, toughness. ANT.-feebleness, frailty, infirmity, weakness.

durable, *a.* SYN.-abiding, changeless, constant, enduring, fixed, indestructible, lasting, permanent, stable, strong, unchangeable. ANT.-ephemeral, temporary, transient, transitory, unstable.

duration, *n.* SYN.-continuance, interval, length, limit, period, season, span, term, time.

duty, *n.* SYN.-accountability, burden, charge, compulsion, contract, obligation, responsibility; assessment, custom, exaction, excise, impost, levy, rate, revenue, tax, toll, tribute. ANT.-choice, exemption, freedom; gift, remuneration, reward, wages.

dwelling, *n.* SYN.-abode, apartment, domicile, flat, habitat, hearth, home, house, hovel, manor, mansion, quarters, residence, seat.

dying, *a.* SYN.-expiring, fading, failing, going, perishing, sinking.

dynamic, *a.* SYN.-active, changing, charismatic, compelling, effective, energetic, forceful, influential, live, potent, productive, progressive, vigorous, vital, vivid.

E

each, *a.* SYN.-all, any, individual, particular, specific; apiece, every, individually, proportionately, respectively, singly.

eager, *a.* SYN.-anxious, ardent, avid, enthusiastic, fervent, hot, impassioned, impatient, keen, yearning. ANT.-apathetic, indifferent, unconcerned, uninterested.

eagerly, *a.* SYN.-actively, anxiously, earnestly, fervently, gladly, heartily, intently, willingly, zealously.

early, *a.* SYN.-ahead, beforehand, preceding, premature, prompt, punctual, quick, speedy, unexpected. ANT.-belated, late, over-due, tardy.

earn, *v.* SYN.-achieve, acquire, attain, derive, deserve, gain, get, merit, obtain, realize, win. ANT.-consume, forfeit, lose, spend, waste.

earned, *a.* SYN.-deserved, merited, proper, suitable. ANT.-improper, undeserved, unmerited.

earnest, *a.* SYN.-candid, frank,

genuine, heartfelt, honest, open, sincere, straightforward, true, truthful, unfeigned, upright. ANT.-affected, dishonest, hypocritical, insincere, untruthful.

earth, *n.* SYN.-continent, country, domain, field, island, land, plain, region, tract; earth, orb, planet, sphere; dirt, ground, humus, loam, soil.

ease, *v.* SYN.-allay, alleviate, assuage, calm, comfort, facilitate, lighten, mitigate, pacify, peace, rest, relieve, soften, soothe, unburden. ANT.-confound, distress, disturb, trouble, worry.

easily, *a.* SYN.-efficiently, effortlessly, freely, readily, simply, smoothly; doubtless, unquestionably.

easy, *a.* SYN.-facile, light, manageable, paltry, pleasant, relaxed, simple, slight, uncomplicated. ANT.-arduous, demanding, difficult, hard.

eat, *v.* SYN.-bite, chew, consume, devour, dine, gorge, nibble, swallow; corrode, decay, rust, squander, waste.

ebb, *n.* SYN.-abatement, decline, decrease, lessening, reduction, regression, shrinkage, wane.

ebb, *v.* SYN.-abate, decline, decrease, recede, retreat, subside, wane.

eccentric, *a.* SYN.-bizarre, curious, distinctive, odd, peculiar, quaint, queer, singular, strange, unique, unusual. ANT.-common, familiar, normal, regular, typical.

economical, *a.* SYN.-careful, close, frugal, mean, miserly, niggardly, provident, prudent, saving, sparing, thrifty; cheap, inexpensive, moderate, reasonable. ANT.-extravagant, improvident, lavish, prodigal, wasteful; expensive, overpriced.

economize, *v.* SYN.-conserve, husband, manage, pinch, save, scrimp, skimp, stint.

ecstasy, *n.* SYN.-delight, exaltation, gladness, rapture, transport; frenzy, madness, trance. ANT.-depression, melancholy.

edge, *n.* SYN.-border, boundary, brim, brink, extremity, hem, margin, periphery, rim, verge; intensity, keenness, sharpness, sting. ANT.-center, interior; bluntness, dullness.

edgy, *a.* SYN.-cross, grouchy, irritable, nervous, peevish, touchy. ANT.-calm, serene.

edict, *n.* SYN.-act, decree, demand, law, ordinance, statute.

edit, *v.* SYN.-alter, arrange, compile, correct, polish, rearrange, revise, rewrite, select; condense, cut, delete, trim; distribute, issue, publish, regulate.

editorial, *n.* SYN.-article, column, essay, feature; opinion, viewpoint.

educate, *v.* SYN.-discipline, inculcate, inform, instill, instruct, school, train, teach, tutor. ANT.-misguide, misinform.

educated, *a.* SYN.-accomplished, civilized, cultured, enlightened, informed, instructed, intelligent, lettered, literate, polished, prepared, scholarly, taught, trained.

education, *n.* SYN.-cultivation, development, instruction, knowledge, learning, schooling, study, training, tutoring.

effect, *n.* SYN.-aftermath, consequence, outcome, results.

effect, *v.* SYN.-accomplish, achieve, attain, cause, complete, consummate, do, execute, finish, fulfill, perfect, perform. ANT.-block, defeat, fail, frustrate, spoil.

effective, *a.* SYN.-capable, competent, efficient, potent, practical, productive, serviceable, telling, useful.

effects, *n.* SYN.-assets, belongings, estate, holdings, possessions, property.

efficiency, *n.* SYN.-ability, capability, competency, effectiveness, efficacy, potency, skillfulness, ANT.-inability, ineptitude, wastefulness.

efficient, *a.* SYN.-adept, capable, competent, dynamic, effective, effectual, efficacious, expedient, practiced, productive, proficient, skillful, streamlined. ANT.-incompetent, ineffectual, inefficient, unskilled.

effort, *n.* SYN.-attempt, endeavor, essay, exertion, trial; labor, pains, strain, strife, struggle, toil, trouble, undertaking.

effortless, *a.* SYN.-easy, offhand, simple, smooth, unconstrained.

effrontery, *n.* SYN.-assurance, audacity, boldness, impertinence, impudence, insolence, presumption, rudeness, sauciness. ANT.-diffidence, politeness, subserviency, truckling.

egotism, *n.* SYN.-arrogance, conceit, overconfidence, pride, self-confidence, self-esteem, vanity. ANT.-diffidence, humility, meekness, modesty.

egotistic, *a.* SYN.-arrogant, boastful, conceited, overbearing, pretentious, proud, self-centered, selfish, self-satisfied, vain.

elaborate, *a.* SYN.-decorated, elegant, embellished, flashy, gaudy, luxurious, showy; complex, complicated, extensive, intricate.

elaborate, *n.* SYN.-comment, develop, embellish, explain, expound, particularize.

elastic, *a.* SYN.-compliant, flexible, lithe, pliable, pliant, resilient, supple, tractable. ANT.-brittle, hard, rigid, stiff, unbending.

elder, *n.* SYN.-ancestor, counselor, dignitary, patriarch, senior, superior, veteran.

elderly, *a.* SYN.-aged, declining, old, patriarchal, venerable

elect, *v.* SYN.-choose, name, opt, pick, select. ANT.-refuse, reject.

elegance, *n.* SYN.-beauty, charm, comeliness, courtliness, culture, fairness, grace, handsomeness, loveliness, polish, politeness, pulchritude, splendor, sophistication. ANT.-deformity, disfigurement, eyesore, homeliness, ugliness.

elegant, *a.* SYN.-beauteous, beautiful, charming, comely, fair, fine, handsome, lovely, ornate, pretty. ANT.-foul, hideous, homely, repulsive, unsightly.

elementary, *a.* SYN.-basic, fundamental, introductory, primary, rudimentary, simple. ANT.-abstract, abstruse, complex, elaborate, intricate.

elevate, *v.* SYN.-exalt, heighten, hoist, lift, raise, uplift; promote. ANT.-abase, depreciate, depress, destroy, lower.

elevated, *a.* SYN.-high, lofty, tall, towering; eminent, exalted, proud. ANT.-small, stunted, tiny; base, low, mean.

eligible, *a.* SYN.-acceptable, authorized, available, fit, qualified, satisfactory, suitable, suited. ANT.-ineligible, unfit, unsuitable.

eliminate, *v.* SYN.-abolish, discard, dislodge, disqualify, eject, eradicate, erase, exclude, expel, exterminate, extirpate, oust, remove. ANT.-accept, admit, include, involve.

elongate, *v.* SYN.-distend, distort, expand, extend, lengthen, protract, spread, strain, stretch. ANT.-contract, loosen, shrink, slacken, tighten.

elite, *n.* SYN.-aristocracy, chosen, nobility, privileged, royalty, selected, society, wealthy.

eloquence, *n.* SYN.-appeal, articulation, delivery, diction, expressiveness, fluency, poise, power, wit.

elude, *v.* SYN.-abscond, avert, avoid, dodge, escape, eschew, evade, flee, forbear, forestall, free, shun, ward. ANT.-confront, encounter, face, meet, oppose.

emanate, *v.* SYN.-belch, breathe, discharge, eject, emit, expel, exude, hurl, radiate, shed, shoot, spurt, vent.

emancipate, *v.* SYN.-deliver, discharge, free, let go, liberate, release, set free. ANT.-confine, imprison, oppress, restrict, subjugate.

embargo, *n.* SYN.-ban, injunction, penalty, prohibition, punishment, restriction, sanction.

embarrass, *v.* SYN.-abash, chagrin, discomfit, distress, entangle, fluster, hamper, hinder, mortify, perplex, rattle, shame, trouble. ANT.-cheer, encourage, help, relieve.

embarrassing, *a.* SYN.-annoying, awkward, delicate, distressing, flustering, inauspicious, mortifying, shameful, touchy, uncomfortable, unpleasant.

embarrassment, *n.* SYN.-abashment, chagrin, clumsiness, confusion, discomfiture, distress, humiliation, mortification, unease; indebtedness, poverty. ANT.-composure, self-confidence.

embellish, *v.* SYN.-adorn, beautify, deck, decorate, enhance, enrich, garnish, ornament, trim. ANT.-debase, defame, expose, strip, uncover.

embezzle, *v.* SYN.-forge, misappropriate, pilfer, steal.

emblem, *n.* SYN.-badge, crest, design, flag, image, insignia, mark, seal, sign, symbol.

embody, *v.* SYN.-accommodate, combine, comprise, contain, embrace, hold, include, incorporate, integrate, unitize. ANT.-discharge, emit, exclude.

embrace, *v.* SYN.-clasp, hug; accept, adopt, espouse, receive, welcome; comprehend, comprise, contain, embody, include, incorporate, subsume. ANT.-reject, renounce, repudiate, scorn, spurn.

emerge, *v.* SYN.-appear, arise, arrive, emanate, issue. ANT.-be, exist; disappear, vanish, withdraw.

emergency, *n.* SYN.-contingency, crisis, exigency, jam, juncture, pass, pinch, predicament, scrape, strait, urgency.

emigrant, *n.* SYN.-alien, colonist, émigré, exile, expatriot, foreigner, migrant, refugee.

emigration, *n.* SYN.-crossing, departure, displacement, exodus, expatriation, flight, journey, migration, shift, trek, voyage, wandering.

eminent, *a.* SYN.-celebrated, conspicuous, distinguished, elevated, famous, glorious, illustrious, noted, prominent, renowned. ANT.-common, obscure, ordinary, unimportant, unknown.

emissary, *n.* SYN.-agent, ambassador, consul, delegate, deputy, envoy, intermediary, proxy, representative.

emit, *v.* SYN.-belch, breathe, discharge, eject, emanate, erupt, expel, hurl, ooze, shed, shoot, spew, spurt, squirt, vent.

emotion, *n.* SYN.-affection, agitation, feeling, passion, perturbation, sentiment, trepidation, turmoil. ANT.-calm, dispassion, indifference, restraint, tranquility.

emotional, *a.* SYN.-demonstrative, excitable, fervent, hysterical, highstrung, impetuous, irrational, maudlin, neurotic, overwrought, passionate, sensitive, sentimental, temperamental. ANT.- calm, rational, tranquil, unruffled.

empathy, *n.* SYN.-feeling, insight, pity, understanding.

emphasize, *v.* SYN.-accent, accentuate, articulate, dramatize, highlight, stress, underscore.

emphatic, *a.* SYN.-definitive, dogmatic, earnest, energetic, forceful, pointed, positive, powerful, stressed, strong.

employ, *v.* SYN.-adopt, apply, avail, busy, devote, engage, manipulate, occupy, operate, use, utilize. ANT.-banish, discard, discharge, reject.

employed, *a.* SYN.-active, busy, engaged, hired, laboring, occupied, operating, performing, used, utilized, working.

employee, *n.* SYN.-agent, assistant, flunky, hireling, laborer, lackey, servant, worker.

employer, *n.* SYN.-boss, business, company, corporation, executive, manager, owner, proprietor; operator, user.

employment, *n.* SYN.-business, engagement, function, occupation, service, vocation, work. ANT.-idleness, leisure, slothfulness.

empty, *a.* SYN.-bare, barren, devoid, hollow, senseless, unfilled, unfurnished, unoccupied, vacant, vacuous, vain, void, worthless. ANT.-full, inhabited, occupied, replete, supplied.

empty, *v.* SYN.-deplete, drain, dump, evacuate, exhaust, leak, pour, spill.

enact, *v.* SYN.-constitute, decree, institute, legislate, ordain, order, pass, ratify.

enchant, *v.* SYN.-allure, bewitch, captivate, charm, enrapture, enthrall, entice, entrance, fascinate,

enclose, *v.* SYN.-bound, circumscribe, confine, encompass, envelop, fence, limit, surround. ANT.-develop, distend, enlarge, expand, expose, open.

encounter, *n.* SYN.-battle, collision, combat, conflict, duel, fight, meeting, struggle. ANT.-amity, concord, consonance, harmony.

encounter, *v.* SYN.-collide, confront, engage, greet, intersect, meet. ANT.-cleave, disperse, part, scatter, separate.

encourage, *v.* SYN.-animate, cheer, countenance, embolden, exhilarate, favor, foster, hearten, impel, incite, promote, sanction, stimulate, support, urge. ANT.-reject, deter, discourage, dispirit, dissuade.

encouraged, *a.* SYN.-cheered, confident, enlivened, enthusiastic, heartened, inspired, revived, roused.

encouragement, *n.* SYN.-assistance, backing, comfort, help, reassurance, support.

encroach, *v.* SYN.-infringe, intrude, invade, penetrate, trespass, violate.

ANT.-abandon, evacuate, relinquish, vacate.

end, *n.* SYN.-aim, cessation, close, completion, conclusion, culmination, expiration, extremity, finish, fulfillment, intention, object, purpose, realization, result, termination, terminus, tip. ANT.-beginning, commencement, inception, introduction.

end, *v.* SYN.-close, complete, conclude, consummate, execute, finish, fulfill, get done, perfect, terminate.

endanger, *v.* SYN.-expose, hazard, imperil, jeopardize, peril; risk. ANT.-insure, protect, secure.

endeavor, *n.* SYN.-attempt, effort, enterprise, exertion, trial; labor, strain, strife, struggle, toil.

endless, *a.* SYN.-boundless, eternal, illimitable, immeasurable, immense, incalculable, infinite, interminable, unbounded, unlimited, vast. ANT.-bounded, circumscribed, confined, finite, limited.

endorse, *v.* SYN.-affirm, approve, praise, recommend, sanction, sign, support, underwrite.

endorsement, *n.* SYN.-approbation, approval, assent, commendation, consent, praise, sanction, support. ANT.-censure, reprimand, reproach, stricture.

endow, *v.* SYN.-bequeath, bestow, contribute, donate, give, grant, subsidize.

endurance, *n.* SYN.-forbearance, fortitude, long-suffering, patience, perseverance, resignation, tolerance. ANT.-impatience, nervousness, restlessness, unquiet.

endure, *v.* SYN.-bear, brook, experience, suffer, sustain, tolerate, undergo; abide, continue, last, persist, remain, survive. ANT.-fail, falter, succumb; disperse, wane.

enduring, *a.* SYN.-abiding, ceaseless, constant, continual, durable, eternal, faithful, firm, fixed, immutable, invariant, lasting, permanent, perpetual, persistent, stable, steadfast, unalterable, unchanging, unwavering. ANT.-changeable, fickle, irresolute, mutable, vacillating, wavering.

enemy, *n.* SYN.-adversary, antagonist, competitor, foe, opponent, rival. ANT.-accomplice, ally, comrade, confederate, friend.

energetic, *a.* SYN.-active, animated, blithe, brisk, frolicsome, lively, spirited, sprightly, supple, vigorous, vivacious. ANT.-dull, insipid, listless, stale, vapid.

enforce, *v.* SYN.-administer, compel, demand, dictate, impel, oblige, require.

energy, *n.* SYN.-dint, force, might, potency, power, strength, vigor. ANT.-feebleness, frailty, impotence, weakness; persuasion.

engage, *v.* SYN.-commission, contract, employ, hire, retain, secure; absorb, bewitch, captivate, charm, engross, fascinate.

engaged, *a.* SYN.-absorbed, busy, employed, occupied, working.

engender, *n.* SYN.-cause, create, fashion, form, formulate, generate, invent, make, originate, produce. ANT.-annihilate, demolish, destroy; disband, terminate.

engross, *v.* SYN.-assimilate, consume, engulf, swallow up; absorb, engage, occupy. ANT.-discharge, dispense, emit, expel, exude.

enhance, *v.* SYN.-amplify, embellish, heighten, improve, increase, inflate, magnify.

enigma, *n.* SYN.-ambiguity, conundrum, mystery, problem, puzzle, riddle. ANT.-answer, clue, key, resolution, solution.

enjoyment, *n.* SYN.-amusement, comfort, delight, ecstasy, entertainment, gladness, gratification, happiness, joy, pleasure, rapture, satisfaction. ANT.-affliction, annoyance, dejection, melancholy, misery, pain, sorrow, suffering, trouble, vexation.

enlarge, *v.* SYN.-amplify, augment, broaden, dilate, distend, expand, increase, magnify, spread, swell, widen. ANT.-abridge, contract, diminish, restrict, shrink.

enlighten, *v.* SYN.-brighten, clarify, educate, elucidate, illuminate, illumine, illustrate, inform, irradiate, show, teach. ANT.-complicate, confuse, darken, obfuscate, obscure.

enlist, *v.* SYN.-enroll, induce, join, obtain, procure, volunteer; employ, engage, hire, recruit, retain.

enmity, *n.* SYN.-animosity, antagonism, antipathy, hatred, hostility, ill-will, invidiousness, malice, malignity. ANT.-affection, cordiality, friendliness, good will, love.

ennoble, *v.* SYN.-aggrandize, consecrate, dignify, elevate, exalt, extol, glorify, hallow, raise. ANT.-debase, degrade, dishonor, humble, humiliate.

enormous, *a.* SYN.-colossal, elephantine, gargantuan, gigantic, huge, immense, large, prodigious, vast. ANT.-diminutive, little, minute, small, tiny.

enough, *a.* SYN.-abundant, adequate, ample, commensurate, fitting, plenty, satisfactory, sufficient, suitable. ANT.-deficient, lacking, scant.

enrage, *v.* SYN.-affront, agitate, anger, annoy, arouse, bait, chafe, goad, inflame, incense, infuriate, madden, provoke, vex.

enrich, *v.* SYN.-adorn, embellish, improve.

ensue, *v.* SYN.-succeed, come next; trail; follow, result. ANT.-precede; guide, lead; avoid, elude, flee; cause.

entangle, *v.* SYN. embroil, entwine, envelop, implicate, include, incriminate, involve, ravel, snare. ANT.-disconnect, disengage, extricate, separate.

entente, *n.* SYN.-alliance, association, coalition, combination, confederacy, federation, league, partnership, union; compact, covenant, marriage, treaty. ANT.-divorce, schism, separation.

enterprise, *n.* SYN.-art, business, commerce, employment, engagement, job, occupation, profession, trade, trading, vocation, work. ANT.-avocation, hobby, pastime.

enterprising, *a.* SYN.-adventurous, bold, chivalrous, clever, daring, precipitate, rash. ANT.-cautious, hesitating, timid.

entertain, *v.* SYN.-consider, contemplate, harbor, hold; amuse, beguile, cheer, delight, divert, gladden, please, regale. ANT. -annoy, bore, disgust, disturb, repulse.

entertainment, *n.* SYN.-amusement, diversion, fun, game, pastime, play, recreation, sport. ANT.-boredom, labor, toil, work.

enthusiasm, *n.* SYN.-ardor, devotion, earnestness, excitement, fanaticism, fervency, fervor, inspiration, intensity, vehemence, warmth, zeal. ANT.-apathy, detachment, ennui, indifference, unconcern.

enthusiastic, *a.* SYN.-absorbed, anxious, ardent, avid, delighted, eager, ecstatic, enraptured, excited, exhilarated, fascinated, fervent, fevered, hot, impassioned, impatient, keen, thrilled, yearning. ANT.-apathetic, indifferent, unconcerned, uninterested.

entice, *v.* SYN.-allure, attract, captivate, charm, enchant, fascinate, lure. ANT.-alienate, deter, repel, repulse.

entire, *a.* SYN.-all, complete, intact, integral, perfect, total, undivided, unimpaired, whole. ANT.-deficient, imperfect, in complete, partial.

entrance, *n.* SYN.-access, doorway, entry, inlet, opening, portal; admission, arrival, debut, entry, induction, penetration. ANT.-departure, exit.

entreaty, *n.* SYN.-appeal, invocation, petition, plea, prayer, request, suit, supplication.

entrust, *v.* SYN.-commend, commit, consign, relegate, trust; bind, obligate, pledge. ANT.-fail, miscarry, neglect; mistrust, release, renounce; free, loose.

envious, *a.* SYN.-begrudging, covetous, desirous, greedy, jealous, resentful.

environment, *n.* SYN.-background, conditions, habitat, scene, setting, surroundings.

envoy, *n.* SYN.-agent, ambassador, consul, delegate, deputy, emissary, intermediary, proxy, representative.

envy, *n.* SYN.-covetousness, jealousy, malevolence, malice, rivalry, spitefulness. ANT.-generosity, geniality, indifference.

episode, *n.* SYN.-circumstance, event, happening, incident, issue; occurrence, outcome.

epoch, *n.* SYN.-age, antiquity, date, epoch, era, generation, period, time.

equal, *a.* SYN.-alike, commensurate, equitable, equivalent, even, identical, impartial, like, proportionate, regular, same, uniform, unvarying. ANT-different, disparate, dissimilar, diverse.

equal, *n.* SYN.-complement, counterpart, double, likeness, match, parallel, peer, twin.

equality, *n.* SYN.-balance, equilibrium, evenness, fairness, impartiality, parity, symmetry, uniformity.

equalize, *v.* SYN.-balance, even, level, match.

equilibrium, *n.* SYN.-balance, composure, poise, stability, steadiness, proportion, symmetry. ANT.-fall, imbalance, instability, unsteadiness.

equip, *v.* SYN.-fit out, furnish, provide, supply; afford, give. ANT.-denude, despoil, divest, strip.

equipment, *n.* SYN.-apparatus, gear, implements, machinery, material, paraphernalia, supplies, tools, trappings, utensils.

equitable, *a.* SYN.-fair, honest, impartial, just, reasonable, unbiased. ANT.-dishonorable, fraudulent, partial.

equity, *n.* SYN.-fairness, impartiality, justice, justness, law, rectitude, right; investment, money, property. ANT.-inequity, partiality, unfairness, wrong.

equivalent, *a.* SYN.-coincident, equal, identical, indistinguishable, like, same. ANT.-contrary, disparate, dissimilar, distinct, opposed.

equivocal, *a.* SYN.-ambiguous, dubious, enigmatical, obscure, uncertain, vague. ANT.-clear, explicit, obvious, plain, unequivocal.

equivocate, *v.* SYN.-conceal, dissemble, dodge, evade, prevaricate, sidestep.

era, *n.* SYN.-age, antiquity, date, epoch, generation, period, time.

eradicate, *v.* SYN.-abolish, delete, demolish, destroy, erase, eliminate, expel, expunge, exterminate, extirpate, level, obliterate, oust, raze, remove, terminate. ANT.-accept, admit, include, involve.

erase, *v.* SYN.-cancel, cross out, delete, eliminate, expunge, obliterate; abolish, abrogate, annul, invalidate, nullify, quash, repeal, rescind, revoke. ANT.-confirm, enact, enforce, perpetuate

erect, *a.* SYN.-straight, unbent, upright, vertical. ANT.-bent, crooked.

erect, *v.* SYN.-build, construct, establish, fabricate, found, raise. ANT.-demolish, destroy, overthrow, raze, undermine.

err, *v.* SYN.-blunder, bungle, confound, mistake, overlook, slip, stumble, trip

erratic, *a.* SYN.-eccentric, inconsistent, irregular, random, unpredictable.

erroneous, *a.* SYN.-amiss, askew, awry, fallacious, false, faulty, inaccurate, incorrect, mistaken, unprecise, untrue; improper, inappropriate, unsuitable, wrong. ANT.-correct, right, true; suitable; proper.

error, *n.* SYN.-blunder, erratum, fallacy, fault, inaccuracy, misconception, misinterpretation, misprint, mistake, oversight, slip. ANT.-accuracy, precision, truth.

erudite, *a.* SYN.-academic, bookish, educated, enlightened, knowledgeable, learned, pedantic, scholarly, scholastic, theoretical. ANT.-common-sense, ignorant, practical, simple.

erudition, *n.* SYN.-discretion, education, enlightenment, foresight, information, insight, intelligence, judgment, knowledge, learning, prudence, reason, refinement, sagacity, sageness, sense, wisdom. ANT.-foolishness, ignorance, imprudence, nonsense, stupidity.

escalate, *v.* SYN.-complicate, compound, enlarge, extend, increase, intensify, grow, heighten, multiply. ANT.-lessen, reduce.

escape, *n.* SYN.-avoidance, breakout, departure, evasion, flight, release.

escape, *v.* SYN.-abscond, decamp, flee, fly; avert, avoid, elude, evade, shun. ANT.-catch, confront, face, invite, meet.

eschew, *v.* SYN.-abstain, avert, avoid, dodge, escape, elude, forbear, forestall, free, shun, ward. ANT.-confront, encounter, meet, oppose.

escort, *v.* SYN.-accompany, associate with, attend, chaperone, conduct, consort with, convoy, go with, guard, guide, protect, squire. ANT.-abandon, avoid, desert, leave, quit.

especially, *a.* SYN.-abnormally, extraordinarily, notably, particularly, remarkably, unusually; chiefly, mainly, primarily.

essay, *n.* SYN.-composition, subject, text, theme, thesis, topic.

essence, *n.* SYN.-basis, core, fundamentals, gist, heart, pith, root, substance.

essential, *a.* SYN.-basic, fundamental, imperative, important, indispensable, intrinsic, necessary, requisite, vital. ANT.-expendable, extrinsic, optional, peripheral.

establish, *v.* SYN.-form, found, institute, organize, raise; confirm, fix, ordain, sanction, settle, strengthen; prove, substantiate, verify. ANT.-abolish, demolish, overthrow, unsettle, upset; disprove, refute.

estate, *n.* SYN.-belongings, bequest, commodities, effects, goods, lands, manor, merchandise, possessions, property, stock, wealth; inheritance. ANT.-deprivation, destitution, poverty, privation, want.

esteem, *v.* SYN.-admire, appreciate, honor, prize, regard, respect, revere, reverence, value, venerate; consider, deem, hold, regard, think. ANT.-abhor, depreciate, dislike, scorn.

esteemed, *a.* SYN.-dear, distinguished, honored, precious, respectable, respected, valued, venerable. ANT.-despised, unwanted; cheap.

esthetic, *a.* SYN.-artistic, beautiful, creative, emotional, natural, pleasant.

estimate, *v.* SYN.-appraise, assess, calculate, compute, consider, count, evaluate, figure, fix, guess, levy, reckon.

eternal, *a.* SYN.-ceaseless, deathless, endless, everlasting, immortal, infinite, perpetual, timeless, undying. ANT. ephemeral, finite, mortal, temporal, transient.

eternally, adv. SYN.-always, constantly, continually, eternally, ever, evermore, forever, incessantly, perpetually, unceasingly. ANT.-fitfully, never, occasionally, rarely, sometimes.

ethereal, *a.* SYN.-celestial, divine, ghostly, holy, immaterial, incorporeal, religious, sacred, spiritual, supernatural, unearthly, unworldly. ANT.-carnal, corporeal, material, mundane, physical.

ethical, *a.* SYN.-decent, good, honorable, just, moral, pure, right, righteous, scrupulous, virtuous. ANT.-amoral, libertine, licentious, sinful, unethical.

evacuate, *v.* SYN.-abandon, desert, empty, leave, vacate.

evade, *v.* SYN.-avert, avoid, deceive, dodge, elude, escape, lie, shun. ANT.-catch, confront, face, invite, meet.

evaluate, *v.* SYN.-analyze, appraise, assess, assign, calculate, compute, criticize, estimate, evaluate, examine, inspect, rate, scrutinize.

evaporate, *v.* SYN.-disappear, dissipate, dissolve, fade, vanish.

even, *a.* SYN.-balance, flat, level, smooth, uniform.

evenly, *a.* SYN.-equally, equitably, fairly, impartially, justly, proportionately, symmetrically.

event, *n.* SYN.-circumstance, episode, happening, incident, issue, occasion, occurrence, phenomenon; consequence, end, outcome, result.

ever, adv. SYN.-always, constantly, continually, eternally, evermore, forever, incessantly, perpetually, unceasingly. ANT.-fitfully, never, occasionally, rarely, sometimes.

everlasting, *a.* SYN.-ceaseless, deathless, endless, eternal, immortal, infinite, perpetual, timeless, undying. ANT. ephemeral, finite, mortal, temporal, transient.

every, *a.* SYN.-all, each.

evidence, *n.* SYN.-confirmation, corroboration, demonstration, proof, testimony, verification. ANT.-fallacy, invalidity.

evident, *a.* SYN.-apparent, clear, conspicuous, indubitable, manifest, obvious, open, overt, patent, unmistakable. ANT.-concealed, covert, hidden, obscure.

evil, *a.* SYN.-bad, baleful, base, deleterious, immoral, iniquitous, noxious, pernicious, sinful, unsound, unwholesome, villainous, wicked. ANT.-excellent, good, honorable, moral, reputable.

evil, *n.* SYN.-crime, iniquity, offense, sin, transgression, ungodliness, vice, wickedness, wrong. ANT.-goodness, innocence, purity, righteousness, virtue.

evolve, *v.* SYN.-create, develop, elaborate, enlarge, expand, mature, unfold. ANT.-compress, contract, restrict, stunt, wither.

exact, *a.* SYN.-accurate, correct, definite, distinct, precise, strict, unequivocal; ceremonious, formal, prim, rigid, stiff. ANT. erroneous, loose, rough, vague; careless, easy, informal.

exaggerate, *v.* SYN.-amplify, caricature, embroider, enlarge, expand, heighten, magnify, misrepresent, overstate, stretch. ANT.-belittle, depreciate, minimize, understate.

exalt, *v.* SYN.-aggrandize, consecrate, dignify, elevate, ennoble, erect, extol, glorify, hallow, raise. ANT.-debase, degrade, dishonor, humble, humiliate.

exalted, *a.* SYN.-dignified, elevated, eminent, grand, illustrious, lofty, majestic, noble, stately. ANT.-base, low, mean, plebeian, vile.

examination, *n.* SYN.-audit, exploration, inquiry, interrogation, investigation, observation, query, quest, question, research, scrutiny, test, trial. ANT.-disregard, inactivity, inattention, negligence.

examine, *v.* SYN.-analyze, assess, audit, check, contemplate, dissect, inquire, interrogate, notice, probe, question, quiz, review, scan, scrutinize, survey, view, watch. ANT.-disregard, neglect, omit, overlook.

example, *n.* SYN.-archetype, illustration, instance. model, pattern, prototype, sample, specimen. ANT.-concept, precept, principle, rule.

exasperate, *v.* SYN.-aggravate, annoy, chafe, embitter, inflame, irritate, nettle, provoke, vex. ANT.-appease, mitigate, palliate soften, soothe.

exasperation, *n.* SYN.-annoyance, chagrin, irritation, mortification, pique, vexation. ANT.-appeasement, comfort, gratification, pleasure.

exceed, *v.* SYN.-beat, excel, outdo, pass, surpass, transcend.

excellent, *a.* SYN.-conscientious, exemplary, honest, moral, pure, reliable, virtuous, worthy; admirable, commendable, genuine, good, precious, safe, sound, valid; benevolent, gracious, humane, kind; agreeable, cheerful, friendly, genial, pleasant; fair, honorable, immaculate; auspicious, beneficial, favorable, profitable, useful; able, capable, efficient, expert, proficient, skillful.

exception, *n.* SYN.-exclusion, omission, preclusion; anomaly, deviation, unusual case; affront, objection, offense. ANT.-inclusion, rule, standard.

exceptional, *a.* SYN.-choice, incomparable, precious, rare, scarce, singular, uncommon, unique. ANT.-customary, ordinary, usual; abundant, commonplace, numerous, worthless.

excess, *n.* SYN.-abundance, extravagance, immoderation, intemperance, profusion, superabundance, superfluity, surplus. ANT.-dearth, deficiency, lack, paucity, want.

excessive, *a.* SYN.-abundant, copious, extravagant, exuberant, immoderate, improvident, lavish, luxuriant, overflowing, plentiful, prodigal, profuse, wasteful. ANT.-economical, meager, poor, skimpy, sparse.

exchange, *v.* SYN.-barter, change, substitute, swap, trade, transpose; alter, convert, transfigure, transform. ANT.-retain; continue, establish, preserve, settle, stabilize.

excite, *v.* SYN.-agitate, arouse, awaken, disquiet, disturb, incite, irritate, provoke, rouse, stimulate, stir up. ANT.-allay, calm, pacify, quell, quiet.

exclaim, *v.* SYN.-call out, cry, cry out, ejaculate, shout, vociferate. ANT.-intimate, whisper, write.

exclude, *v.* SYN.-bar, blackball, except, expel, hinder, omit, ostracize, prevent, prohibit, reject, restrain, shut out. ANT.-accept, admit, include, welcome.

exclusive, *a.* SYN.-aristocratic, choice, clannish, excluding, fashionable, only, particular, private, privileged, prohibitive, restricted, segregated, select, sole, special.

excusable, *a.* SYN.-allowable, defensible, forgivable, justifiable, pardonable, permissible, plausible, reasonable, trivial, understandable.

excuse, *n.* SYN.-alibi, apology, defense, explanation, justification, reason. ANT.-accusation, complaint, denial, dissimulation.

excuse, *v.* SYN.-absolve, acquit, condone, exculpate, exempt, forgive, free, justify, overlook, pardon, remit. ANT.-convict, prosecute, punish, retaliate, revenge.

execrable, *a.* SYN.-abominable, detestable, foul, hateful, loathsome, odious, revolting, vile. ANT.-agreeable, commendable, delightful, pleasant.

execution, *n.* SYN.-accomplishment, act, action, deed, doing, feat, operation, performance, transaction. ANT.-cessation, deliberation, inactivity, inhibition, intention.

exemplar, *n.* SYN.-copy, duplicate, example, facsimile, imitation, model, replica, reproduction, specimen. ANT.-original, prototype.

exemplary, *a.* SYN.-faultless, excellent, honest, honorable, ideal, immaculate, moral, perfect, pure, reliable, supreme, virtuous. ANT.-faulty, imperfect.

exercise, *n.* SYN.-activity, application, drill, employment, exertion, lesson, operation, performance, practice, task, training, use. ANT.-idleness, indolence, relaxation, repose, rest.

exhaust, *v.* SYN.-bore, fatigue, jade, tire, tucker, wear out, weary. ANT.-amuse, invigorate, refresh, restore, revive.

exhausted, *a.* SYN.-fatigued, spent, tired, wearied, weary, worn; consumed, depleted, expended, used. ANT.-fresh, hearty, invigorated, rested.

exhaustion, *n.* SYN.-enervation, fatigue, languor, lassitude, tiredness, weariness. ANT.-freshness, rejuvenation, restoration, vigor, vivacity.

exhibit, *v.* SYN.-display, expose, flaunt, parade, present, reveal, show, spread out; demonstrate, evidence, prove, verify. ANT.-conceal, cover, disguise, hide.

exhibition, *n.* SYN. array, display, exposition; demonstration, flourish, ostentation, parade, show, spectacle, splurge.

exile, *n.* SYN.-banishment, deportation, expatriation, expulsion, extradition, ostracism, proscription. ANT.-admittance, recall, reinstatement, retrieval, welcome.

existence, *n.* SYN.-being, life, liveliness, spirit, vitality, vivacity. ANT.-death, demise.

exorbitant, *a.* SYN.-excessive, extravagant, immoderate, unreasonable.

exotic, *a.* SYN.-alien, different, extrinsic, foreign, outstanding, strange, unusual.

expand, *v.* SYN.-augment, develop, distend, enlarge, extend, grow, increase, swell. ANT.-contract, diminish, shrink, wane.

expanse, *n.* SYN.-area, extent, magnitude, measure, range, reach, scope, size.

expansion, *n.* SYN.-development, elaboration, unfolding, unraveling; evolution, growth, maturing, progress. ANT.-abbreviation, compression, curtailment.

expatriation, *n.* SYN.-banishment, deportation, exile, expulsion, extradition, ostracism, proscription. ANT.-admittance, recall, reinstatement, retrieval, welcome.

expect, *v.* SYN.-anticipate, await, contemplate, demand, hope for, suppose; demand, exact, require. ANT.-get, obtain, realize, receive.

expectation, *n.* SYN.-anticipation, contemplation, expectancy, foresight, forethought, hope, optimism, preconception, prescience, presentiment. ANT.-doubt, dread, fear, worry.

expedient, *a.* SYN.-advantageous, appropriate, convenient, desirable, discreet, fit, judicious, opportune, practical, proper, prudent, suitable, useful.

expedite, *v.* SYN.-accelerate, dispatch, facilitate, forward, hasten, hurry, push, quicken, rush, speed. ANT.-block, hinder, impede, retard, slow.

expedition, *n.* SYN.-cruise, incursion, jaunt, journey, passage, pilgrimage, safari, tour, travel, trip, voyage.

expel, *v.* SYN.-banish, discharge, dismiss, disown, excommunicate, exile, expatriate, ostracize, oust, proscribe; dislodge, eject, eliminate, void. ANT.-admit, favor, include, recall.

expend, *v.* SYN.-consume, disburse, employ, exhaust, pay, spend, use.

expense, *n.* SYN.-budget, charge, cost, debt, expenditure, liability, price.

expensive, *a.* SYN.-costly, high-priced, precious; dear, prized, valuable. ANT.-cheap, mean, poor; trashy, worthless.

experience, *n.* SYN.-background, judgment, knowledge, maturity, practice, seasoning, training, wisdom.

experiment, *v.* SYN.-analyze, assay, examine, explore, inspect, investigate, probe, research, sample, test, try.

expert, *a.* SYN.-able, accomplished, adept, clever, competent, cunning, ingenious, practiced, proficient, skilled, skillful, versed. ANT.-awkward, bungling, clumsy, inexpert, untrained.

expire, *v.* SYN.-cease, conclude, decease, die, end, finish, perish, stop, terminate. ANT.-begin, live, survive.

explain, *v.* SYN.-clarify, decipher, elucidate, expound, illustrate, interpret, resolve, unfold, unravel. ANT.-baffle, confuse, darken, obscure.

explanation, *n.* SYN.-alibi, apology, clarification, confession, defense, elucidation, excuse, justification, recapitulation, report. ANT.-accusation, complaint, denial, dissimulation.

explicit, *a.* SYN.-categorical, clear, definite, definitive, express, lucid, manifest, outspoken, plain, specific. ANT.-ambiguous, diplomatic, equivocal, implicit, obscure, vague.

exploit, *n.* SYN.-accomplishment, achievement, attainment, deed, escapade, feat, performance, realization, venture. ANT.-neglect, omission; defeat, failure.

exploit, *v.* SYN.-apply, avail, employ, manipulate, operate, use, utilize; consume, exhaust, expend; handle, manage, treat. ANT.-ignore, neglect, overlook, waste.

explore, *v.* SYN.-examine, hunt, inspect, seek, test.

explorer, *n.* SYN.-adventurer, forerunner, searcher, trailblazer, pioneer, voyager.

explosive, *a,* SYN.-fiery, forceful, frenzied, hysterical, raging, savage, uncontrollable, violent.

expose, *v.* SYN.-air, bare, betray, debunk, disclose, display, open, reveal, show, unmask.

exposed, *a.* SYN.-disclosed, discovered, revealed, unclosed, uncovered; accessible, open, public, unrestricted; candid, frank, honest, overt, plain.

expound, *v.* SYN.-clarify, comment, decipher, elucidate, explain, explicate, illustrate, interpret, resolve, unfold, unravel. ANT.-baffle, confuse, darken, obscure.

express, *a.* SYN.-clear, definitive, explicit, lucid, manifest, specific. ANT.-ambiguous, equivocal, implicit, obscure, vague.

express, *v.* SYN.-affirm, assert, avow, claim, declare, explain, propound, recite, recount, say, specify, state, tell, utter. ANT.-conceal, deny, imply, retract.

expressive, *a.* SYN.-bright, brilliant, dramatic, intense, spirited, stirring, striking; animated, clear, demonstrative, eloquent, fresh, graphic, lively, lucid, vivid. ANT.-dull, vague; dim, dreary, dusky.

extend, *v.* SYN.-distend, distort, elongate, expand, lengthen, protract, spread, stretch. ANT.-contract, loosen, shrink, slacken, tighten.

extended, *a.* SYN.-drawn out, elongated, lasting, lengthy, lingering, long, prolix, prolonged, protracted, tedious, wordy. ANT.-abridged, brief, concise, short, terse.

extensive, *a.* SYN.-broad, expanded, large, sweeping, vast, wide; liberal. ANT.-confined, narrow, restricted.

extending, *a.* SYN.-continuing, perpetual, ranging, reaching, spreading, stretching.

extent, *n.* SYN.-amount, area, compass, degree, expanse, limit, length, magnitude, measure, range, reach, scope, size, stretch.

exterior, *n.* SYN.-cover, facade, face, front, outer, surface, veneer. ANT.-back, interior, rear.

extol, *v.* SYN.-aggrandize, celebrate,

elevate, ennoble, observe; commend, exalt, glorify, hallow, honor, laud, praise, raise. ANT.-disregard, overlook; decry, disgrace, dishonor, profane.

extra, *a.* SYN.-added, additional, another, auxiliary, other, reserve, spare, supplementary.

extract, *v.* SYN.-dislodge, eject, extricate, oust, remove, vacate; derive, distill, withdraw. ANT.-leave, remain, stay; retain.

extradition, *n.* SYN.-banishment, deportation, exile, expatriation, expulsion, ostracism, proscription. ANT.-admittance, recall, reinstatement, retrieval, welcome.

extraneous, *a.* SYN.-alien, contrasted, extraneous, foreign, irrelevant, remote, strange, unconnected. ANT.-akin, germane, kindred, relevant.

extraordinary, *a.* SYN.-exceptional, marvelous, peculiar, rare, remarkable, singular, uncommon, unusual, wonderful. ANT.-common, frequent, ordinary, usual.

extravagance, *n.* SYN.-excess, immoderation, intemperance, profusion, superabundance, superfluity, surplus. ANT.-dearth, deficiency, lack, paucity, want.

extravagant, *a.* SYN.-abundant, copious, excessive, exuberant, immoderate, improvident, lavish, luxuriant, overflowing, plentiful, prodigal, profuse, wasteful. ANT.-economical, meager, poor, skimpy, sparse.

extreme, *a.* SYN.-acute, exacting, excessive, harsh, inordinate, intense, radical, relentless, rigorous, severe, unmitigated, unreasonable, unyielding. ANT.-genial, indulgent, yielding.

F

fable, *n.* SYN.-allegory, chronicle, fiction, legend, myth, parable, saga, tale. ANT.-fad, history.

fabricate, *v.* SYN.-build, construct, erect, form, frame, make, manufacture, raise; contrive, devise, fake, lie, prevaricate. ANT.-demolish, destroy, raze.

facade, *n.* SYN.-appearance, deceit, face, front, look, mask.

face, *n.* SYN.-countenance, mug, visage; assurance, audacity; cover, exterior, front, surface. ANT.-timidity; back, interior, rear.

facilitate, *v.* SYN.-aid, allay, alleviate, assuage, calm, comfort, ease, lighten, mitigate, pacify, relieve, soothe. ANT.-confound, distress, disturb, trouble, worry.

facility, *n.* SYN.-ability, adroitness, cleverness, cunning, deftness, dexterity, ingenuity, knack, readiness, skill, skillfullness; building, company, plant, tools. ANT.-awkwardness, clumsiness, inability, ineptitude.

facsimile, *n.* SYN.-copy, duplicate, facsimile, imitation, replica, reproduction, transcript. ANT.-original, prototype.

fact, *n.* SYN.-actuality, certainty, reality, truth; act, circumstance, deed. event, incident, occurrence. ANT.-fiction, supposition, theory; delusion, falsehood.

faction, *n.* SYN.-division, fragment, moiety, piece, portion, section, segment; component, element, ingredient, member, organ; concern, interest, part, party, side. ANT.-entirety, whole.

factual, *a.* SYN.-accurate, authentic, exact, genuine, specific, true.

faculty, *n.* SYN.-ability, aptitude, aptness, capability, capacity, dexterity, efficiency, power, qualification, skill, talent. ANT.-disability, incapacity, incompetence, unreadiness.

fad, *n.* SYN.-craze, curiosity, fashion, gimmick, innovation, novel, oddity, style, vogue.

faded, *a.* SYN.-dim, faint, indistinct, pale; feeble, languid, wearied; irresolute, timid, weak. ANT.-conspicuous, glaring; strong, vigorous; brave, forceful.

fail, *v.* SYN.-blunder, cease, crash, decline, default, deteriorate, disappoint, falter, fizzle, flag, flop, founder, miss.

failure, *n.* SYN.-fiasco, miscarriage; default, dereliction, omission; decay, decline; deficiency, lack, loss, want. ANT.-achievement, success, victory; sufficiency.

faint, *a.* SYN.-dim, faded, indistinct, pale; feeble, languid, wearied; irresolute, timid, weak. ANT.-conspicuous, glaring; strong, vigorous; brave, forceful.

fair, *a.* SYN.-bright, clear, light; attractive, blond, comely, lovely; equitable, honest, impartial, just, reasonable, unbiased; average, mediocre, passable. ANT.-foul, ugly; dishonorable, fraudulent, partial; excellent, first-rate, worst.

fairness, *n.* SYN.-decency, equity, honesty, impartiality, integrity, justice, justness, law, truth, rectitude, right. ANT.-inequity, partiality, unfairness, wrong.

faith, *n.* SYN.-confidence, credence, dependence, reliance, trust; belief, creed, doctrine, dogma, persuasion, religion, tenet; constancy, fidelity, loyalty. ANT.-doubt, incredulity, mistrust, skepticism; infidelity.

faithful, *a.* SYN.-conscientious, constant, dependable, devoted, honest, incorruptible, loyal, staunch, steadfast, true; accurate, genuine, reliable, trusty. ANT.-disloyal, false, fickle, treacherous, untrustworthy.

faithless, *a.* SYN.-apostate, disloyal, false, perfidious, recreant, traitorous, treacherous, treasonable. ANT.-constant, devoted, loyal, true.

fake, *a.* SYN.-affected, artificial, assumed, bogus, counterfeit, ersatz, fabrication, feigned, fictitious, imitation, phony, sham, spurious, synthetic, unreal. ANT.-genuine, natural, real, true.

fall, *v.* SYN.-collapse, decline, decrease, descend, diminish, drop, sink, subside; stumble, topple, tumble; droop, extend downward, hang. ANT.-arise, ascend, climb, mount, soar; steady.

fallacy, *n.* SYN.-ambiguity, error, fault, inaccuracy, inconsistency, mistake, paradox, slip. ANT.-accuracy, precision, truth.

falling, *a.* SYN.-declining, decreasing, descending, diminishing, dropping, ebbing, plunging, sinking, tumbling.

false, *a.* SYN.-amiss, deceitful, dishonest, disloyal, erroneous, fallacious, faulty, inaccurate, incorrect, lying, mistaken, treacherous, underhanded, untrue, wrong; bogus, copied, counterfeit, fabricated, faked, forged, pseudo, spurious, synthetic. ANT.-authentic, correct, factual, genuine, right, true.

falsehood, *n.* SYN.-deception, delusion, equivocation, exaggeration, fib, fiction, illusion, lie, prevarication, untruth. ANT.-axiom, canon, fact, truism.

falsify, *v.* SYN.-alter, counterfeit, deceive, equivocate, fib, lie, misrepresent, prevaricate. ANT.-confirm, establish, prove.

falter. *v.* SYN.-delay, demur, doubt, hesitate, pause, scruple, stammer, stutter, vacillate, waver. ANT.-continue, decide, persevere, proceed, resolve.

fame, *n.* SYN.-acclaim, credit, distinction, eminence, glory, honor, notoriety, renown, reputation. ANT.-disrepute, ignominy, infamy, obscurity.

familiar, *a.* SYN.-acquainted, aware, cognizant, conversant, intimate, knowing, versed; affable, amicable, close, courteous, friendly, informal, sociable, unreserved; accustomed, common, commonplace, customary, everyday, homespun, prosaic, simple, unsophisticated, well-known. ANT.-affected, cold, distant, reserved, unfamiliar.

familiarity, *n.* SYN.-acquaintance, fellowship, friendship, sociability; frankness, informality, intimacy, liberty, unreserve. ANT.-constraint, distance, haughtiness, presumption, reserve.

family, *n.* SYN.-ancestry, clan, descendants, extraction, forbears, genealogy, genre, group, heirs, house, kin, kindred, kinsfolk, lineage, pedigree, progeny, relations, relationship, relatives, tribe, type. ANT.-disconnection, foreigners, strangers.

famished, *a.* SYN.-craving, hungry, ravenous, starved, thirsting, voracious. ANT.-full, gorged, sated, satiated; satisfied.

famous, *a.* SYN.-acclaimed, celebrated, distinguished, eminent, glorious, illustrious, influential, noted, notorious, prominent, recognized, renowned, well-known. ANT.-hidden, ignominious, infamous, obscure, unknown.

fanatical, *a.* SYN.-arbitrary, dogmatic, excessive, extravagant, extreme, fanatic, frenzied, intemperate, intolerant, narrow-minded, obsessed, obstinate, passionate, stubborn, zealous.

fanciful, *a.* SYN.-dreamy, fantastic, fictitious, ideal, idealistic, imaginative, maudlin, mawkish, picturesque, poetic, romantic, sentimental. ANT.-factual, literal, matter-of-fact, practical, prosaic.

fancy, *a.* SYN.-adorned, capricious, distinctive, elaborate, elegant, embellished, fanciful, gaudy, lavish, ornate, ostentatious, resplendent, showy, whimsical.

fancy, *n.* SYN.-caprice, conception, creation, dream, fantasy, hallucination, idea, imagination, impression, invention, notion, thought, whimsy; fondness, inclination, liking, preference, taste, whim.

fantastic, *a.* SYN.-capricious, extravagant, farfetched, freakish, outlandish, preposterous, ridiculous, whimsical, wonderful. ANT.-conventional, ordinary, routine.

fantasy, *n.* SYN.-caprice, dream, fancy, hallucination, illusion, imagination, vision, whim.

far, *a.* SYN.-away, distant, faraway, remote, removed. ANT.-close, near, nigh; cordial, friendly.

farewell, *n.* SYN.-departure, good-by, leave-taking, valediction. ANT.-greeting, salutation, welcome.

farming, *n.* SYN.-agriculture, agronomy, cultivation, gardening, horticulture, husbandry, tillage.

fascinate, *v.* SYN.-attract, beguile,

bewitch, captivate, charm, delight, enamor, enchant, enrapture, enthrall, entice, intoxicate, lure, overpower, overwhelm, stimulate, titillate. ANT.-alienate, deter, disgust, displease, repel, repulse, tire.

fascinating, *a.* SYN.-alluring, appealing, attractive, bewitching, captivating, charming, delightful, enchanting, engaging, seductive, winning. ANT.-repugnant, repulsive, revolting.

fashion, *n.* SYN.-approach, conformity, convention, custom, formality, manner, method, mode, practice, tendency, usage, way; craze, fad, rage, style, vogue.

fashion, *v.* SYN.-construct, create, forge, form, make, mold, produce, shape; compose, constitute, make up; arrange, combine, organize; devise, frame, invent. ANT.-destroy, disfigure, dismantle, misshape, wreck.

fast, *a.* SYN.-expeditious, fleet, quick, rapid, speedy, swift; constant, firm, inflexible, secure, solid, stable, steadfast, steady, unswerving, unyielding. ANT.-slow, sluggish; insecure, loose, unstable, unsteady.

fasten, *v.* SYN.-affix, anchor, attach, bind, fix, link, place, secure, set, stick, tie. ANT.-displace, remove, unfasten.

fastidious, *a.* SYN.-accurate, choosy. critical, delicate, discerning, discriminating, exact, finicky, fussy, particular, precise. ANT.-cursory, shallow, superficial, uncritical.

fat, *a.* SYN.-chubby, corpulent, heavy, husky, obese, paunchy, plump, portly, pudgy, rotund, stocky, stout, thickset. ANT.-gaunt, lean, slender, slim, thin.

fatal, *a.* SYN.-deadly, destructive, disastrous, final, lethal, mortal, predestined. ANT.-life-giving; divine, immortal.

fate, *n.* SYN.-consequence, doom, fortune, lot, portion; circumstance, destiny, issue, karma, necessity, outcome, result.

father, *v.* SYN.-beget, create, engender, father, generate, originate, procreate, produce, propagate, sire. ANT.-abort, destroy, extinguish, kill, murder.

fatigue, *n.* SYN.-enervation, exhaustion, languor, lassitude, tiredness, weariness. ANT.-freshness, rejuvenation, restoration, vigor, vivacity.

fatigued, *a.* SYN.-bored, exhausted, faint, jaded, spent, tired, wearied, weary, worn. ANT.-fresh, hearty, invigorated, rested.

fault, *n.* SYN.-blemish, defect, error, failure, flaw, imperfection, mistake, omission, shortcoming, vice, weakness. ANT.-completeness, correctness, perfection.

faultless, *a.* SYN.-complete, entire, finished, full, utter, whole; blameless, holy, immaculate, perfect, pure, sinless; consummate, excellent, ideal, superlative, supreme; absolute, downright, unqualified, utter. ANT.-deficient, incomplete, lacking; blemished, defective, faulty, imperfect.

faulty, *a.* SYN.-blemished, damaged, defective, deficient, flawed, imperfect, tainted, unsound; inadequate, incomplete, insufficient, substandard, unfit, unsatisfactory. ANT.-complete, perfect, whole.

favor, *n.* SYN.-advantage, bias, exemption, immunity, liberty, license, partiality, preference, prerogative, privilege, right, sanction; accommodation, boon, courtesy, kindness. ANT.-disallowance, inhibition, prohibition, restriction.

favor, *v.* SYN.-animate, cheer, countenance, embolden, encourage, exhilarate, hearten, impel, incite, inspirit, urge; esteem, foster, like, prefer, prize, promote, sanction, stimulate, support ANT.-reject, deter, discourage, dispirit, dissuade.

favorite, *a.* SYN.-adored, beloved, cherished, pet, popular, precious, preferred, prevailing, prevalent. ANT.-ignored, unimportant, unpopular.

fealty, *n.* SYN.-allegiance, constancy, devotion, faithfulness, fidelity, homage, loyalty. ANT.-disloyalty, faithlessness, perfidy, treachery.

fear, *n.* SYN.-alarm, apprehension, consternation, cowardice, dismay, dread, fright, horror, panic, scare, terror, timidity, trepidation. ANT.-assurance, boldness, bravery, courage, fearlessness.

fearful, *a.* SYN.-afraid, apprehensive, fainthearted, frightened, scared, timid, timorous. ANT.-assured, bold, composed, courageous, sanguine.

fearless, *a.* SYN.-adventurous, audacious, bold, brave, courageous, daring, dauntless, intrepid; brazen, forward. ANT.-cowardly, flinching, timid; bashful, retiring.

feasible, *a.* SYN.-achievable, attainable, credible, expedient, likely, plausible, possible, practicable, practical, probable, usable, workable, worthwhile. ANT.-impossible, impracticable, visionary.

feast, *n.* SYN.-banquet, celebration, dinner, entertainment, festival, regalement.

feature, *n.* SYN.-attribute, characteristic, mark, peculiarity, property, quality, trait; highlight, innovation, specialty.

fecund, *a.* SYN.-bountiful, fertile, fruitful, luxuriant, plenteous, productive, prolific, rich, teeming. ANT.-barren, impotent, sterile, unproductive.

feeble, *a.* SYN.-decrepit, delicate, enervated, exhausted, faint, forceless, impaired, infirm, languid, powerless, puny, weak. ANT.-forceful, lusty, stout, strong, vigorous.

feed, *v.* SYN.-cater, cram, dine, encourage, fatten, feast, nourish, nurture, provide, stock, stuff, supply, support, sustain.

feel, *v.* SYN.-accept, acknowledge, believe, consider, deem, observe, perceive, savor, sense, think; caress, clutch, fondle, grip, grope, handle, paw, press, squeeze.

feeling, *n.* SYN.-awareness, consciousness, perception, reaction, sensation, sensibility; affection, emotion, intuition, judgment, passion, sensibility, sentiment, sympathy, tenderness; impression, opinion. ANT.-anesthesia; coldness, imperturbability, insensibility; fact.

feign, *v.* SYN.-act, affect, assume, fabricate, pretend, profess, sham, simulate. ANT.-display, exhibit, expose, reveal.

felicity, *n.* SYN.-beatitude, blessedness, bliss, contentment, delight, gladness, happiness, pleasure, satisfaction, well-being. ANT.-despair, grief, misery, sadness, sorrow.

fellowship, *n.* SYN.-amity, brotherhood, brotherliness, camaraderie, communion, friendliness, intimacy, solidarity, togetherness; alliance, association, brotherhood, clan, club, fraternity, society. ANT.-acrimony, discord, opposition, strife.

felon, *n.* SYN.-convict, criminal, culprit, delinquent, malefactor, offender, transgressor.

feminine, *a.* SYN.-delicate, fair, female, gentle, girlish, ladylike, maidenly, sensitive, tender, womanish, womanly. ANT.-male, manly, mannish, masculine, virile.

ferment, *n.* SYN.-agitation, chaos, commotion, confusion, disorder, disturbance, excitement, hubbub, insurrection, stir, revolt, tempest, tumult, turbulence, turmoil, uprising. ANT.-certainty, order, peace, tranquility.

ferocious, *a.* SYN.-barbarous, bestial, brutal, brute, brutish, carnal, coarse, cruel, fierce, gross, inhuman, merciless, remorseless, rough, rude, ruthless, savage, sensual. ANT-civilized, courteous, gentle, humane, kind.

fertile, *a.* SYN.-bountiful, fecund, fruitful, luxuriant, plenteous, productive, prolific, rich, teeming. ANT.-barren, impotent, sterile, unproductive.

fervent, *a.* SYN.-ardent, eager, enthusiastic, fervid, fiery, glowing, hot, impassioned, intense, keen, passionate, vehement, zealous. ANT.-apathetic, cool, indifferent, nonchalant.

fervor, *n.* SYN.-ardor, devotion, earnestness, enthusiasm, excitement, fanaticism, fervency, inspiration, intensity, vehemence, warmth, zeal. ANT.-apathy, detachment, ennui, indifference, unconcern.

festive, *a.* SYN.-blithe, cheerful, gay, gleeful, hilarious, jolly, jovial, joyous, lively, merry, mirthful, sprightly. ANT.-gloomy, melancholy, morose, sad, sorrowful.

fetish, *n.* SYN.-compulsion, craze, fixation, mania, obsession, passion; amulet, charm, talisman.

fetter, *v.* SYN.-attach, bind, connect, fasten, join, link, restrain, restrict, tie. ANT.-free, loose, unfasten, untie.

feud, *n.* SYN.-affray, altercation, argument, bickering, contention, disagreement, dispute, quarrel, spat, squabble, wrangle. ANT.-agreement, friendliness, harmony, peace, reconciliation.

few, *a.* SYN.-any, inconsiderable, meager, negligible, rare, scant, scanty, scattering, some, sparse, thin, trifling.

fickle, *a.* SYN.-capricious, changeable, erratic, fitful, flighty, frivolous, inconstant, restless, unstable, variable. ANT.-constant, reliable, stable, steady, trustworthy.

fiction, *n.* SYN.-allegory, fable, fabrication, falsehood, invention, narrative, novel, romance, story, tale. ANT.-fact, history, reality, truth, verity.

fictitious, *a.* SYN.-affected, artificial, assumed, bogus, counterfeit, ersatz, fake, feigned, phony, sham, spurious, synthetic, unreal, untrue. ANT.-genuine, natural, real, true.

fidelity, *n.* SYN.-allegiance, constancy, devotion, faithfulness, fealty, loyalty; accuracy, exactness, precision. ANT.-disloyalty, faithlessness, perfidy, treachery

field, *n.* SYN.-acreage, ground, land, meadow, pasture, patch, plain, plot, range, region, soil, tract; domain, estate, farm, realm.

fiend, *n.* SYN.-barbarian, beast, brute, demon, devil, maniac, monster; addict, aficionado, fan, fanatic, junkie.

fierce, *a.* SYN.-angry, boisterous, enraged, forceful, frenzied, frightening, furious, impetuous, monstrous, passionate, powerful, raging, raving, savage, turbulent, untamed, vehement, violent, wild; acute, awful, extreme, intense, severe, violent. ANT.-calm, feeble, gentle, quiet, soft.

fiery, *a.* SYN.-burning, hot, scalding, scorching, torrid, warm; ardent, fervent, fiery, hot-blooded, impetuous, intense, passionate; peppery, pungent. ANT.-cold, cool, freezing, frigid; apathetic, impassive, indifferent, passionless, phlegmatic; bland.

fight, *n.* SYN.-altercation, battle, brawl, clash, combat, conflict, confrontation, contention, dispute, encounter, feud, fracas, quarrel, scuffle, skirmish, strife,

fight, *v.* SYN.-argue, attack, battle, brawl, combat, conflict, contend, debate, dispute, encounter, grapple, oppose, quarrel, scuffle, skirmish, squabble, struggle, tussle, wrangle.

fighter, *n.* SYN.-aggressor, antagonist, assailant, bully, competitor, contender, opponent, rival.

figurative, *a.* SYN.-allegorical, emblematic, illustrative, metaphorical, symbolic.

figure, *n.* SYN.-appearance, build, cast, configuration, contour, cut, form, frame, guise, image, mold, outline, pattern, shape. ANT.-contortion, deformity, distortion, mutilation.

figure, *v.* SYN.-calculate, compute, consider, count, estimate, number, reckon. ANT.-conjecture, guess, miscalculate.

fill, *v.* SYN.-fill up, occupy, pervade; furnish, replenish, stock, store, supply; content, glut, gorge, pack, sate, .satiate, satisfy, stuff. ANT.-deplete, drain, empty, exhaust, void.

filling, *n.* SYN.-contents, dressing, filler, insides, lining, padding, stuffing, wadding.

film, *n.* SYN.-celluloid, cinema, filmstrip, image, movie, negative, photograph, picture, portrayal, print, representation, slide, transparency; coating, covering, fabric, gauze, membrane, skin.

filter, *v.* SYN.-clarify, clean, distill, filtrate, purify, refine, separate, sift, strain; seep, trickle.

filth, *n.* SYN.-contamination, dirt, garbage, grime, impurity, muck, pollution, sewage, slop, trash.

filthy, *a.* SYN.-dirty, foul, grimy, muddy, soiled, squalid. ANT.-clean, neat, presentable.

final, *a.* SYN.-concluding, conclusive, decisive, ending, eventual, last, latest, terminal, ultimate. ANT.-embryonic, first, inaugural, incipient, original, rudimentary.

finally, *a.* SYN.-at last, conclusively, decisively, definitely, irrevocably, permanently, ultimately.

find, *v.* SYN.-ascertain, detect, devise, discern, discover, encounter, expose, find out, learn, locate, notice, reveal, uncover. ANT.-cover, hide, lose, mask, screen.

fine, *a.* SYN.-choice, dainty, delicate, elegant, exquisite, nice, pure, refined, splendid, subtle; beautiful, handsome, pretty; minute, powdered, pulverized, sharp, slender, small, thin. ANT.-blunt, coarse, large, rough, thick.

finish, *v.* SYN.-accomplish, achieve, close, complete, conclude, consummate, do, end, execute, fulfill, get done, perfect, perform, terminate.

finished, *a.* SYN.-accomplished, ceased, complete, concluded, consummated, done, ended, executed, finalized, full, perfect, settled, stopped, thorough, total, unbroken, undivided. ANT.-imperfect, lacking, unfinished.

fire, *n.* SYN.-blaze, burning, combustion, conflagration, embers, flame, glow, heat, sparks, warmth. ANT.-cold; apathy, quiescence.

firm, *a.* SYN.-constant, durable, enduring, established, fixed, hardy, immovable, immutable, lasting, permanent, secure, stable, staunch, steadfast, steady, strong, sturdy, tough, unwavering; callous, incorruptible, obdurate, stubborn. ANT.-changeable, erratic, irresolute, vacillating, variable.

firm, *n.* SYN.-association, business, company, concern, corporation, partnership. ANT.-dispersion, individual.

first, *a.* SYN.-beginning, earliest, initial, original, primary, prime, primeval, primitive, pristine; chief, foremost. ANT.-hindmost, last, latest; least, subordinate.

fit, *a.* SYN.-applicable, appropriate, becoming, befitting, beneficial, comely, competent, decent, decorous, desirable, equitable, fitting, likely, proper, qualified, respectable, rightful, seemly, suitable, suited, tolerable; healthy, robust, trim. ANT.-awkward, brash, gross, ill-timed, improper, inappropriate, unqualified.

fit, *v.* SYN.-accommodate, adapt, adjust, agree, belong, conform, harmonize, match, relate, suit. ANT.-clash, disturb, misapply, misfit.

fitting, *a.* SYN.-applicable, appropriate, apt, becoming, particular, proper, suitable. ANT.-contrary, improper, inappropriate.

fix, *v.* SYN.-affix, attach, bind, fasten, link, place, plant, secure, set, stick, tie; define, determine, establish, limit, set, settle; adjust, correct, mend, patch, rectify, regulate, rejuvenate, repair. ANT.-displace, remove, unfasten; alter, change, disturb, modify; damage, mistreat.

fixed, *a.* SYN.-abiding, ceaseless, constant, continual, enduring, faithful, immutable, invariant, permanent, perpetual, persistent, unalterable, unchanging, unwavering; adjusted, corrected, improved, mended, restored. ANT.-fickle, mutable, vacillating, wavering.

flagrant, *a.* SYN.-conspicuous, disgraceful, glaring, gross, heinous, obvious, outrageous, overt, prominent, shameful.

flamboyant, *a.* SYN.-adorned, bombastic, decorated, elaborate, flashy, lavish, ornate, ostentatious, resplendent, showy, superficial

flame, *n.* SYN.-brightness, fire, flare, illumination, light, radiance. ANT.-darkness, gloom, obscurity, shadow.

flash, *n.* SYN.-burst, flicker, glimmer, glitter, illumination, impulse, moment, reflection, spark, sparkle, vision, wink.

flashy, *a.* SYN.-adorned, decorated, elaborate, embellished, flamboyant, garnished, gaudy, lavish, ornate, ostentatious, pretentious, showy, superficial, tawdry.

flat, *a.* SYN.-even, horizontal, level, low, plane, smooth; boring, pointless, prosaic, tedious, unanimated; dull, flavorless, insipid, stale, tasteless, unsavory, vapid; absolute, downright, positive, unqualified. ANT.-broken, hilly, irregular, oloping; exciting, racy; savory, tasty.

flattery, *n.* SYN.-acclamation, adulation, applause, approval, commendation, compliment, eulogy, fawning, homage, praise, tribute. ANT.-affront, criticism, insult, taunt.

flaunt, *v.* SYN.-boast, brag, crow, display, glory, flourish, parade, show, vaunt. ANT.-apologize, deprecate, humble, minimize.

flavor, *n.* SYN.-characteristic, essence, quality, relish, savor, seasoning, style, tang, taste.

flaw, *n.* SYN.-blemish, blot, scar, speck, stain; defect, error, fault, imperfection, mistake, omission, shortcoming, vice. ANT.-adornment, embellishment, perfection, purity.

flee, *n.* SYN.-abscond, decamp, escape, fly, hasten, run away. ANT.-appear, arrive, remain, stay.

fleet, *a.* SYN.-expeditious, fast, quick, rapid, speedy, swift. ANT.-slow, sluggish.

fleeting, *a.* SYN.-brief, ephemeral, evanescent, momentary, short-lived, temporary, transient. ANT.-abiding, immortal, lasting, permanent, timeless.

flexible, *a.* SYN.-compliant, ductile, elastic, formative, impressionable, limber, lithe, pliable, pliant, resilient, supple, tractable, yielding. ANT.-brittle, hard, rigid, stiff, unbending.

flighty, *a.* SYN.-capricious, erratic, fickle, frivolous, inconstant, unstable, volatile, whimsical. ANT.-disciplined, reliable, restrained.

flimsy, *a.* SYN.-decrepit, fragile, frail, inadequate, weak; ineffectual, poor, superficial.

flippant, *a.* SYN.-disrespectful, facetious, frivolent, impertinent, impudent, offhand, rude, saucy, smart.

flop, *v.* SYN.-blunder, bomb, fail, falter, flunk, founder, miscarry; flap, flounder, flounce, jerk, quiver, squirm, wiggle, wriggle.

flourish, *v.* SYN.-burgeon, flower, grow, increase, luxuriate, prosper, thrive; brandish, display, flaunt, gesture, parade, vaunt, wave; adorn, decorate, embellish.

flow, *v.* SYN.-gush, run, spout, spurt, stream; come, emanate, issue, originate, proceed, result; abound, be copious.

flowing, a, SYN.-ample, complete, copious, extensive, plentiful, sweeping; full, loose, voluminous. ANT.-depleted, devoid, empty, vacant; insufficient, lacking, partial.

fluctuate, *v.* SYN.-change, hesitate, oscillate, undulate, vacillate, vary, waver. ANT.-adhere, decide, persist, resolve, stick.

fluent, *a.* SYN.-articulate, eloquent, garrulous, glib, mellifluent, persuasive, smooth, talkative, vocal, wordy; copious, flowing.

fluid, *a.* SYN.-flowing, fluent, juicy, liquid, running, watery. ANT.-congealed, frozen, solid, stiff.

fluster, *v.* SYN.-abash, chagrin, discomfit, distress, embarrass, entangle, hamper, hinder, mortify, perplex, rattle, trouble. ANT.-cheer, encourage, help, relieve

fly, *v.* SYN.-flit, float, flutter, glide, hover, mount, sail, soar; dart, rush, shoot, spring; abscond, decamp, escape, flee, run away. ANT.-descend, fall, plummet, sink.

foil, *v.* SYN.-baffle, balk, circumvent, defeat, disappoint, frustrate, hinder, outwit, prevent, thwart. ANT.-accomplish, fulfill, further, promote.

folk, *n.* SYN.-clan, community, culture, family, kindred, lineage, nation, relations, society, tribe.

follow, *v.* SYN.-succeed, come next; comply, heed, obey, observe; adopt, copy, imitate; accompany, attend; chase, pursue, trail; ensue, result. ANT.-precede; guide, lead; avoid, elude, flee; cause.

follower, *n.* SYN.-adherent, admirer, advocate, attendant, backer, believer, companion, devotee, disciple, helper, henchman, member, partisan, participant, pupil, successor, supporter, votary, witness. ANT.-chief, head, leader, master.

folly, *n.* SYN.-foolishness, imbecility, silliness; absurdity, extravagance, imprudence, indiscretion. ANT.-sense, wisdom; judgment, prudence, reasonableness.

fond, *a.* SYN.-affectionate, attached, dedicated, devoted, disposed, given up to, inclined, prone, wedded. ANT.-detached, disinclined, indisposed, untrammeled.

fondle, *v.* SYN.-caress, coddle, cuddle, embrace, hug, kiss, pet. ANT.-annoy, buffet, spurn, tease, vex.

fondness, *n.* SYN.-affection, attachment, endearment, kindness, love, tenderness; disposition, emotion, feeling, inclination. ANT.-aversion, hatred, indifference, repugnance, repulsion.

food, *n.* SYN.-diet, edibles, fare, feed, meal, nutriment, provisions, rations, repast, sustenance, viands, victuals. ANT.-drink, hunger, starvation, want.

fool, *n.* SYN.-buffoon, clown, harlequin, jester; blockhead, dolt, dunce, idiot, imbecile, nincompoop, numbskull, oaf, simpleton. ANT.-genius, philosopher, sage, scholar.

foolish, *a.* SYN.-absurd, asinine, brainless, crazy, idiotic, irrational, nonsensical, preposterous, ridiculous, senseless, silly, simple. ANT.-judicious, prudent, sagacious, sane, wise.

forbear, *v.* SYN.-abstain, cease, desist, omit, refrain, spare, stop, withhold. ANT.-continue, indulge, persist.

forbid, *v.* SYN.-ban, bar, block, deny, debar, disallow, embargo, hinder, inhibit, interdict, prevent, prohibit, restrain. ANT.-allow, authorize, permit, recommend, sanction, tolerate.

force, *n.* SYN.-dint, emphasis, energy, intensity, might, potency, power, strength, vigor; coercion, compulsion, constraint, dominance, violence. ANT.-feebleness, frailty, impotence, weakness; persuasion.

force, *v.* SYN.-coerce, command, compel, constrain, demand, drive, enforce, impel, impose, insist, make, oblige, order, require. ANT.-allure, convince, induce, persuade, prevent.

forceful, *a.* SYN.-cogent, commending, dominant, firm, forcible, fortified, hale, hardy, impregnable, mighty, potent, powerful, robust, sinewy, strong, sturdy, tough. ANT.-brittle, delicate, feeble, fragile, insipid.

foreboding, *n.* SYN.-anticipation, apprehension, dread, expectation, fear, feeling, premonition, prescience, presentiment.

forecast, *n.* SYN.-anticipation,

augury, conjecture, divination, estimate, guess, prediction, prognosis, prognostication, projection, prophecy.

foreign, *a.* SYN.-alien, contrasted, exotic, extraneous, imported, irrelevant, outlandish, remote, strange, unconnected, unknown. ANT.-akin, germane, kindred, relevant.

foreigner, *n.* SYN.-alien, immigrant, newcomer, outsider, stranger. ANT.-acquaintance, associate, countryman, friend, neighbor.

foresight, *n.* SYN.-anticipation, carefulness, contemplation, expectation, forethought, hope, preconception, prescience, presentiment, prudence. ANT.-doubt, dread, fear, worry.

foretell, *v.* SYN.-augur, divine, forecast, foresee, portend, predict, prophesy.

forever, adv. SYN.-always, constantly, continually, eternally, ever, evermore, forever, incessantly, perpetually, unceasingly. ANT.-fitfully, never, occasionally, rarely, sometimes.

forge, *v.* SYN.-coin, copy, counterfeit, duplicate, fabricate, falsify, imitate, reproduce; create, fabricate, fashion, make, produce.

forgery, *n.* SYN.-bogus, copy, counterfeit, fabrication, fake, hoax, phony.

forgive, *v.* SYN.-absolve, acquit, condone, excuse, exonerate, forget, overlook, pardon, release, remit. ANT.-accuse, chastise, condemn, convict, punish.

forgiveness, *n.* SYN.-absolution, acquittal, amnesty, clemency, leniency, mercy, pardon, remission. ANT.-conviction, penalty, punishment, sentence.

forlorn, *a.* SYN.-abandoned, alone, comfortless, deserted, desolate, disconsolate, destitute, distressed, forgotten, forsaken, heartbroken, miserable, pitiable, sad, wretched. ANT.-contented, fortunate, happy.

form, *n.* SYN.-approach, ceremony, conformity, custom, formality, manner, method, practice, procedure, ritual, system; appearance, arrangement, configuration, design, fashion, formation, structure,

form, *v.* SYN.-construct, create, fashion, forge, make, mold, produce, shape; compose, constitute, make up; arrange, combine, organize; devise, frame, invent. ANT.-destroy, disfigure, dismantle, misshape, wreck.

formal, *a.* SYN.-affected, ceremonious, correct, decorous, exact, methodical, precise, proper, regular, solemn, stiff; external, outward, perfunctory. ANT.-easy, natural, unconstrained, unconventional; heartfelt.

formed, *a.* SYN.-built, carved, created, cultivated, developed, established, modeled, molded, patterned, shaped.

former, *a.* SYN.-aforesaid, antecedent, earlier, erstwhile, late, once, onetime, preceding, previous, prior. ANT.-consequent, following, later, subsequent, succeeding.

formulate, *v.* SYN.-compose, create, draw, engender, fashion, form, frame, generate, invent, make, originate, prepare, produce. ANT.-annihilate, demolish, destroy; disband, terminate.

fornication, *n.* SYN.-adultery, carnality, debauchery, lechery, lewdness, licentiousness, promiscuity.

forsake, *v.* SYN.-abandon, abdicate, abjure, abstain, relinquish, renounce, resign, surrender, vacate, waive; desert, leave, quit. ANT.-defend, maintain, uphold; stay, support.

forthcoming, *a.* SYN.-anticipated, approaching, coming, destined, expected, fated, imminent, impending, inevitable, near, prospective.

fortified, *a.* SYN.-armed, armored, defended, enclosed, guarded, protected, secured, walled; heartened, invigorated, reinforced, strengthened.

fortitude, *n.* SYN.-boldness, bravery, chivalry, courage, durability, fearlessness, intrepidity, mettle, might, potency, power, prowess, stamina, stoutness, strength, sturdiness, resolution, toughness. ANT.-cowardice, fear, pusillanimity, timidity.

fortuity, *n.* SYN.-accident, chance, contingency, exigency, incidence, luck, mishap, predicament. ANT.-calculation, design, intention, purpose.

fortunate, *a.* SYN.-advantageous, auspicious, benign, blessed, favored, felicitous, flourishing, fortuitous, happy, lucky, propitious, prosperous, successful. ANT.-cheerless, condemned, ill-fated, persecuted, unlucky.

fortune, *n.* SYN.-accident, break, chance, fate, fluke, lot, luck, windfall; assets, bundle, estate, inheritance, mint, money, possessions, property, riches, treasure, wealth.

forward, *n.* SYN.-beginning, introduction, overture, preamble, preface, prelude, prologue, start. ANT.-completion, conclusion, end, epilogue, finale.

forward, *v.* SYN.-advance, further, promote; improve, proceed, progress, rise, thrive. ANT.-hinder, oppose, retard, retreat, withhold.

fossil, *a.* SYN.-ancient, antique, archaic, out-of-date, prehistoric, venerable.

foster, *v.* SYN.-advance, cherish, cultivate, encourage, favor, further, help, nourish, nurture, raise, retain, support, sustain. ANT.-abandon, dislike, disregard, neglect, reject.

foul, *a.* SYN.-dirty, filthy, grimy, muddy, soiled, squalid; indecent, nasty, obscene; base, contemptible, despicable, low, mean, pitiful, shabby. ANT.-clean, neat, presentable; pure, wholesome.

found, *v.* SYN.-begin, create, endow, erect, establish, form, institute, organize, raise. ANT.-abolish, demolish, overthrow, unsettle, upset.

foundation, *n.* SYN.-base, basis, bedrock, bottom, footing, ground, groundwork, root, substructure, support, underpinning; authority, data, facts, justification, observation, reason; association, charity, company, endowment, establishment, institute, institution, organization, society. ANT.-building, cover, superstructure, top.

fracture, *v.* SYN.-break, burst, cleave, crack, crush, demolish, destroy, rend, rupture, separate, sever, shatter, shear, smash, split. ANT.-join, mend, renovate, repair, restore.

fragile, *a.* SYN.-breakable, brittle, delicate, exquisite, feeble, fine, frail, infirm, weak. ANT.-durable, hardy, strong, sturdy, tough.

fragment, *n.* SYN.-division, moiety, part, piece, portion, remnant, scrap, section, segment, share; component, element, faction, fraction, ingredient. ANT.-entirety, whole.

fragrance, *n.* SYN.-aroma, bouquet, essence, incense, odor, perfume, scent, smell.

frail, *a.* SYN.-breakable, brittle, dainty, delicate, feeble, fragile, infirm, weak. ANT.-durable, hardy, strong, sturdy, tough.

frame, *v.* SYN.-build, conceive, construct, contrive, devise, erect, fabricate, form, make, outline, sketch. ANT.-demolish, destroy, raze.

frank, *a.* SYN.-artless, blunt, bold, candid, direct, familiar, free, forthright, honest, ingenious, open, outspoken, plain, sincere, straightforward, truthful, undisguised; fair, impartial, just, unbiased, uninhibited. ANT.-contrived, scheming, sly, wily.

frantic, *a.* SYN.-crazy, delirious, deranged, desperate, distracted, excited, frenzied, mad, raging, rash, reckless, raving, wild. SYN.-calm, composed, serene.

fraternity, *n.* SYN.-brotherliness, fellowship, kindness, solidarity; association, brotherhood, clan, society. ANT.-acrimony, discord, opposition, strife.

fraternize, *v.* SYN.-associate, consort, hobnob, join, mingle, mix, socialize. ANT.-dissociate, divide, segregate, separate, sort.

fraud, *n.* SYN.-artifice, cheat, chicanery, deceit, deception, duplicity, guile, imposition, imposture, misrepresentation, racket, sham, swindle, trick, trickery; charlatan, cheat, fake, impostor, pretender, quack. ANT.-fairness, honesty, integrity, sincerity.

freak, *n.* SYN.-aberration, curiosity, malformation, monstrosity, mutation, oddity, rarity; abnormal, bizarre, capricious, erratic odd, peculiar, strange, unusual.

free, *a.* SYN.-autonomous, emancipated, exempt, freed, independent, liberated, unconfined, unrestricted; clear, loose, open, unfastened, unobstructed; immune, uninfected; artless, careless, easy, familiar, frank; bounteous, bountiful, complimentary, generous, gratis, liberal, munificent. ANT.-confined, restrained, restricted; blocked, clogged, impeded; subject; illiberal, parsimonious, stingy.

free, *v.* SYN.-absolve, acquit, deliver, discharge, disentangle, dismiss, emancipate, let go, liberate, loosen, pardon, release, rid, set free, untie. ANT.-confine, imprison, oppress, restrict, subjugate.

freedom, *n.* SYN.-exemption, familiarity, immunity, impunity, independence, latitude, leeway, liberation, liberty, license, privilege, unrestraint. ANT.-bondage, compulsion, constraint, necessity, servitude.

freely, *a.* SYN.-abundantly, deliberately, easily, extravagantly, frankly, intentionally, loosely, openly, profusely, spontaneously, unhindered, voluntarily, willingly.

freezing, *a.* SYN.-arctic, chilly, cold, cool, frigid, frosty, frozen, icy, polar, wintry. ANT.-burning, fiery, heated, hot, torrid.

freight, *n.* SYN.-burden, cargo, encumbrance, goods, load, packages, shipment.

frenzied, *a.* SYN.-frantic, impetuous, irregular, mad, turbulent, wanton, wayward, wild; boisterous, stormy, tempestuous; extravagant, foolish, giddy, rash, reckless. ANT.-civilized, gentle; calm, placid, quiet.

frequent, *a.* SYN.-common, continual, general, habitual, incessant, often, periodic, persistent, repeated, usual. ANT.-exceptional, rare, recurrent, regular, scanty, solitary, unique.

frequent, *v.* SYN.-attend, hang out, haunt, visit.

frequently, *adv.* SYN.-commonly, generally, often, recurrently, regularly, repeatedly. ANT.-infrequently, occasionally, rarely, seldom, sporadically.

fresh, *a.* SYN.-modern, new, novel, original, recent; additional, further; bracing brisk, cool, invigorating, refreshing, stimulating; artless, green, inexperienced, natural, raw, unskilled, untrained. ANT.-decayed, faded, hackneyed, musty, stagnant.

fretful, *a.* SYN.-fractious, ill-natured, ill-tempered, irritable, peevish, petulant, snappish, testy, touchy, waspish. ANT.-affable, genial, good-natured, good-tempered, pleasant.

friend, *n.* SYN.-acquaintance, ally, associate, chum, colleague, companion, compatriot, comrade, confidant, crony, intimate; accomplice, advocate, backer, defender, patron, supporter, well-wisher. ANT.-adversary, enemy, stranger.

friendly, *a.* SYN.-affablc, affectionate, amiable, amicable, attentive, civil, close, companionable, congenial, cordial, devoted, familiar, gracious, helpful, intimate, kind, kindly, neighborly, pleasant, sociable, social, sympathetic, warmhearted. ANT.-aloof, antagonistic, cool, distant, hostile, reserved.

friendship, *n.* SYN.-acquaintance, affection, association, brotherhood, camaraderie, cognizance, companionship, congeniality, devotion, esteem, familiarity, fellowship, friendship, harmony, intimacy, kindliness, kindness, sympathy. ANT.-ignorance, inexperience, unfamiliarity.

fright, *n.* SYN.-affright, alarm, apprehension, consternation, dread, fear, horror, panic, scare, terror, trepidation. ANT.-assurance, boldness, calm, composure, bravery, courage, fearlessness, quiet, security, tranquillity.

frighten, *v.* SYN.-affright, alarm, appall, astound, badger, daunt, dismay, disturb, horrify, intimidate, panic, petrify, scare, startle, terrify, terrorize, threaten. ANT.-allay, compose, embolden, reassure, soothe.

frightened, *a.* SYN.-afraid, apprehensive, disturbed, fainthearted, fearful, horrified, intimidated, scared, terrified, timorous. ANT.-assured, bold, composed, courageous, sanguine.

frigid, *a.* SYN.-arctic, chilly, cold, cool, freezing, frosty, frozen, icy, wintry; indifferent, passionless, phlegmatic, stoical, unfeeling. ANT.-burning, fiery, heated, hot, torrid; ardent, passionate.

frisky, *a.* SYN.-active, alive, animated, boisterous, dapper, dashing, gleeful, jaunty, lively, playful, spirited.

frivolous, *a.* SYN.-childish, cursory, dizzy, exterior, flighty, flimsy, foolish, imperfect, paltry, petty, shallow, slight, superficial, trifling, trivial, unimportant. ANT.-abstruse, complete, deep, profound, thorough.

frolic, *n.* SYN.-fun, lark, merriment, play, prank, sport.

frolic, *v.* SYN.-caper, cavort, gamble, gambol, play, revel, rollick, romp, sport.

front, *n.* SYN.-anterior, bow, exterior, facade, face, foreground, frontage, nose, prow, vanguard; appearance, aspect, carriage, countenance, demeanor, expression, mask, mien, presence. ANT.-back, posterior, rear.

frontier, *n.* SYN.-border, boundary, brim, brink, edge, fringe, hinterland, limit, outskirts, rim, termination, verge. ANT.-center, core, interior, mainland.

frozen, *a.* SYN.-arctic, chilled, cold, freezing, frigid, frosted, frosty, iced, icy, wintry. ANT.-burning, fiery, heated, hot, torrid.

frugal, *a.* SYN.-careful, economical, niggardly, parsimonious, provident, prudent, saving, spare, sparing, stingy, temperate, thrifty. ANT.-extravagant, intemperate, self-indulgent, wasteful.

frustrate, *v.* SYN.-baffle, balk, bewilder, circumvent, confuse, defeat, disappoint, foil, hinder, mystify, nonplus, outwit, perplex, prevent, thwart. ANT.-accomplish, fulfill, further, promote.

fulfill, *v.* SYN.-accomplish, achieve, complete, comply, conclude, consummate, discharge, effect, execute, finish, perform, terminate.

full, *a.* SYN.-abundant, ample, complete, copious, crammed, entire, extensive, filled, gorged, lavish, packed, perfect, plentiful, replete, satiated, satisfied, saturated, soaked, sufficient; baggy, flowing, loose, voluminous; broad, detailed, exhaustive, ranging, unlimited. ANT.-depleted, devoid, empty, vacant; insufficient, lacking, partial.

fully, *a.* SYN.-abundantly, adequately, amply, completely, entirely, perfectly, sufficiently, thoroughly, well, wholly.

fun, *n.* SYN.-amusement, antic, caper, comedy, diversion, enjoyment, entertainment, festivity, foolery, frolic, game, glee, jest, lark, laughter, mirth, pastime, play, pleasure, prank, recreation, relaxation, romp, sport, trifling.

function, *n.* SYN.-business, capacity, duty, employment, faculty, office, province, purpose, service, utility; banquet, celebration, meeting, party, reception, social.

function, *n.* SYN.-business, capacity, duty, office, purpose, service.

function, *v.* SYN.-act, do, go, move, officiate, operate, perform, run, work.

fund, *n.* SYN.-accumulation, donation, endowment, hoard, provision, reserve, stock, store, supply.

fundamental, *a.* SYN.-absolute, basic, cardinal, central, crucial, elemental, elementary, essential, first, important, intrinsic, key, precise, primary, rudimentary, simple, specific. ANT.-abstract, abstruse, auxiliary, common, complex, dispensable, elaborate, intricate, secondary, subordinate, unimportant.

funds, *n.* SYN.-assets, capital, cash, collateral, currency, money, reserves, resources, revenue, savings, wealth, wherewithal

funny, *a.* SYN.-amusing, comic, comical, droll, entertaining, facetious, farcical, hilarious, humorous, jocular, laughable, ludicrous ridiculous, whimsical, witty; curious, odd, peculiar, queer, strange, suspicious, unusual. ANT.-melancholy, sad, serious, sober, solemn.

furious, *a.* SYN.-agitated, angry, enraged, exasperated, incensed, indignant, irate, maddened, provoked, raging, tumultuous, wrathful, wroth; extreme, frantic, frenetic, frenzied, intense. ANT.-calm, happy, pleased, satisfied.

furnish, *v.* SYN.-appoint, endow, equip, fit, fit out provide, purvey, stock, supply; afford, cater, give, produce, yield. ANT.-denude, despoil, divest, strip.

further, *v.* SYN.-advance, aggrandize, elevate, forward, promote, bring forward, offer, propose, propound, proceed, progress, rise, thrive, augment, enlarge, increase. ANT.-hinder, oppose, retard, retreat, withhold.

furor, *n.* SYN.-agitation, bedlam, clamor, commotion, disturbance, excitement, rumpus, shouting, stir, tumult.

fury, *n.* SYN.-anger, choler, fierceness, indignation, ire, irritation, passion, petulance, rage, resentment, temper, turbulence, vehemence, violence, wrath. ANT.-conciliation, forbearance, patience, peace, self-control.

fusion, *n.* SYN.-combination, concurrence, incorporation, joining, solidarity, unification, union; alliance, amalgamation, coalition, concert, confederacy, league, marriage. ANT.-division, schism, separation; disagreement, discord.

fussy, *a.* SYN.-careful, conscientious, demanding, exact, exacting, fastidious, meticulous, particular, precise.

futile, *a.* SYN.-abortive, bootless, empty, fruitless, idle, ineffective, ineffectual, pointless, unavailing, unproductive, unsatisfactory, useless, valueless, vain, vapid, worthless. ANT.-effective, potent, profitable.

G

gab, *v.* SYN.-babble, chatter, discuss, gossip, jabber, prate, prattle, ramble, speak, talk.

gaily, *a.* SYN.-brightly, brilliantly, colorfully, extravagantly, jovially, joyfully, joyously, gaudily, showily, spiritedly.

gain, *n.* SYN.-accrual, accumulation, addition, advantage, benefit, favor, goods, increase, interest, profit, profits. ANT.-calamity, distress, handicap, trouble.

gain, *v.* SYN.-achieve, acquire, advance, approach, attain, augment, benefit, earn, get, improve, net, obtain, procure, profit, progress, reach, secure, win. ANT.-forfeit, lose, surrender.

gale, *n.* SYN.-blow, gust, hurricane, squall, storm, typhoon, wind.

gallant, *a.* SYN.-bold, brave, chivalrous, courageous, courtly, daring, dauntless, fine, intrepid, magnificent, noble, polite, splendid, valiant.

gallery, *n.* SYN.-arcade, balcony, grandstand, mezzanine, veranda; audience, onlookers, public, spectators; exhibit, hall, museum, salon, showroom, wing.

game, *n.* SYN.-amusement, contest, diversion, fun, match, merriment, pastime, play, recreation, sport. ANT.-business drudgery, hardship, labor, work.

gap, *n.* SYN.-aperture, breach, break, cavity, fissure, gulf, hole, opening, orifice, pore, rift, void; arroyo, canyon, chasm, gulch, gully, hollow, ravine; hiatus, interim, intermission, lag, lull, pause, recess.

garb, *n.* SYN.-appearance, fashion, form, guise, mode, style, uniform; attire, clothes, garments, vestments.

garish, *a.* SYN.-colorful, flashy, gaudy, loud, ornate, ostentatious, showy, spirited, tawdry.

garment, garments, *n.* SYN.-apparel, array, attire, clothes, clothing, drapery, dress, garb, raiment, vestments, vesture. ANT.-nakedness, nudity.

garnish, *v.* SYN.-adorn, beautify, bedeck, decorate, embellish, enhance, enrich, ornament, trim. ANT.-debase, defame, expose, strip, uncover.

garrulous, *a.* SYN.-articulate, chattering, chatty, communicative, effusive, glib, loquacious, talkative, verbose, voluble. ANT.-laconic, reticent, silent, taciturn, uncommunicative.

gash, *n.* SYN.-cut, slash, slit, wound.

gate, *n.* SYN.-barrier, entrance, entry, inlet, opening, passage, portal.

gather, *v.* SYN.-accumulate, amass, associate, assemble, collect, congregate, convene, hoard, muster, rally, reunite, swarm; cull, garner, glean, harvest, pick, pluck, reap, select, sort; assume, conclude, deduce, infer, judge, learn. ANT.-disband, disperse, distribute, scatter, separate.

gathered, *a.* SYN.-assembled, collected, congregated, convened, convoked, grouped, joined, massed, met, rallied, thronged, united.

gathering, *n.* SYN.-assembly, association, caucus, committee, company, conclave, conference, congregation, convention, convocation, council, crowd, flock, herd, legislature, meet, reunion, society, throng, turnout.

gaudy, *a.* SYN.-colorful, decorated, elaborate, embellished, flamboyant, flashy, garish, loud, meretricious, ornamented, ornate, ostentatious, showy, spirited, superficial, tasteless, tawdry, vulgar.

gaunt, *a.* SYN.-emaciated, haggard, lank, lean, scrawny, skinny, slender, slight, slim, spare, tenuous, thin. ANT.-broad, bulky, fat, thick, wide.

gay, *a.* SYN.-cheerful, frolicsome, glad, happy, jolly, jovial, joyful, joyous, lighthearted, merry, sprightly, vivacious. ANT.-depressed, glum, mournful, sad, sullen.

gear, *n.* SYN.-accouterments, equipment, material, outfit, rigging, tackle, things.

gem, *n.* SYN.-bauble, jewel, ornament, stone; cherished, prized, treasured.

general, *n.* SYN.-broad, common, comprehensive, customary, ecumenical, extensive, inclusive, ordinary, popular, prevalent, regular, ubiquitous, universal, usual, widespread; imprecise, indefinite, inexact, vague. ANT.-exceptional, rare, singular; definite, particular, specific.

generate, *v.* SYN.-afford, bear, bestow, breed, cause, create, engender, form, impart, induce, make, originate, pay, produce, provoke, sire, spawn, supply, yield.

generation, *n.* SYN.-age, antiquity, date, epoch, era, period, span, time; creation, formation, invention, procreation, production. ANT.-childhood, infancy, youth; breeding, creation, procreation, reproduction.

generous, *a.* SYN. altruistic, beneficent, charitable, giving, lavish, liberal, magnanimous, munificent, noble, openhanded, philanthropic, unselfish; abundant, ample, bountiful, copious, flowing, overflowing, plentiful. ANT.-covetous, greedy, miserly, selfish, stingy.

genial, *a.* SYN.-affable, agreeable, amicable, companionable, cordial, friendly, hearty, kindly, neighborly, pleasant, sociable, social. ANT.-antagonistic, cool, distant, hostile, reserved.

genius, *n.* SYN.-ability, aptitude, brains, capability, creativity, faculty, gift, inspiration, intellect, intelligence, originality, sagacity, talent, wisdom; adept, gifted, intellectual, prodigy, proficient. ANT.-ineptitude, obtuseness, shallowness, stupidity; dolt, dullard, moron.

genre, *n.* SYN.-category, class, grade, kind, order, rank, set. sort. variety.

gentle, *a.* SYN.-amiable, benign, calm, considerate, cultivated, disciplined, docile, kind, mild, peaceful, placid, pliant, polite, refined, relaxed, respectable, sensitive, serene, soft, soothing, tame, temperate, tender, tractable, well-bred. ANT.-fierce, harsh, rough, savage, violent.

gently, *a.* SYN.-benevolently, carefully, cautiously, considerately, delicately, kindly, mildly, sensitively, tenderly.

genuine, *a.* SYN.-accurate, actual, authentic, bona fide, certain, certified, legitimate, natural, original, precise, positive, proven, real, sincere, tested, true, unadulterated, unaffected, valid, veritable. ANT.-artificial, bogus, counterfeit, false, sham.

germ, *n.* SYN.-antibody, bacteria, contagion, infection, microbe, pest, virus; ailment, contamination, disease, poison, pollution, taint; beginning, genesis, inception, origin, seed, source.

gesture, *n.* SYN. indication, motion, portent, sign, signal, symbol, token; appearance, attitude, concession, display, formality, posture.

get, *v.* SYN.-achieve, acquire, attain, earn, gain, get, obtain, procure, purchase, reach, realize, receive, secure, seize, take, win; apprehend, comprehend, grasp, learn, perceive, understand. ANT.-forfeit, leave, lose, renounce, surrender.

ghastly, *a.* SYN.-abhorrent, cadaverous, deathlike, disgusting, dreadful, frightful, grisly, gruesome, hideous, horrible, repulsive, shocking.

ghost, *n.* SYN.-apparition, demon, phantom, shade, specter, spirit, spook, vision; hint, shadow, suggestion.

giant, *a.* SYN.-colossal, enormous, gigantic, huge, immense, large, monstrous, tremendous.

gift, *n.* SYN.-award, benefaction, bequest, boon, bounty, charity, donation, endowment, favor, grant, gratuity, handout, largess, legacy, offering, present, token; ability, aptitude, capability, capacity, faculty, forte, genius, power, talent. ANT.-deprivation, earnings, loss, purchase; incapacity, ineptitude, stupidity.

gigantic, *a.* SYN.-broad, colossal, elephantine, enormous, gargantuan, huge, immense, large, prodigious, tremendous, vast. ANT.-diminutive, little, minute, small, tiny.

giggle, *n.* SYN.-cackle, chortle, chuckle, laugh, snicker, snigger, titter.

gimmick, *n.* SYN.-apparatus, artifice, contraption, contrivance, device, gadget, mechanism, ruse, scheme, trick, trickery.

gingerly, SYN.-carefully, cautiously, daintily, easily, fastidiously, gently. ANT.-boisterous, brusk, roughly.

girl, *n.* SYN.-child, coed, damsel, lassie, maid, maiden, miss, young lady, young woman.

gist, *n.* SYN.-basis, connotation, core, drift, essence, explanation, heart, implication, import, intent, interpretation, meaning, meat, point, purport, purpose, sense, significance, signification, substance.

give, *v.* SYN.-assign, award, bequeath, bestow, confer, contribute, deliver, donate, endow, furnish, grant, impart, issue, offer, present, provide, render, supply. ANT.-keep, retain, seize, withdraw.

glad, *a.* SYN.-cheerful, contented, delighted, exhilarated, exulting, gratified, happy, jovial, joyous, lighthearted, merry, pleased. ANT.-dejected, depressed, despondent, melancholy, sad.

gladly, *a.* SYN.-blissfully, cheerfully, cordially, delightfully, enthusiastically, gaily, gleefully, happily, heartily, joyfully, joyously, lovingly, passionately, readily, sweetly, warmly, willingly.

gladness, *n.* SYN.-beatitude, blessedness, bliss, contentment, cheer, delight, felicity, gaiety, glee, happiness, merriment, pleasure, satisfaction, well-being. ANT.-despair, grief, misery, sadness, sorrow.

glance, *n.* SYN.-behold, eye, gaze, glimpse, look, observe, regard, scan, see, survey, view. ANT.-avert, miss, overlook, stare.

glare, *v.* SYN.-blind, dazzle, gleam, radiate, shine; frown, glower, scowl, stare.

gleam, *v.* SYN.-beam, flash, flicker, glare, glimmer, glisten, glitter, glow, shimmer, shine, sparkle, twinkle.

glib, *a.* SYN.-artful, articulate, diplomatic, facile, fluent, polished, sleek, slick, smooth, suave, superficial, urbane. ANT.-bluff, blunt, harsh, rough, rugged.

glide, *v.* SYN.-coast, descend, drift, float, flow, fly, slide, slip, slither, soar, waft,

gloom, *n.* SYN.-blackness, bleakness, darkness, dimness, obscurity, shadow; apprehension, dejection, depression, despair, despondency, foreboding, grief, malaise, melancholy, misery, misgiving, mourning, pessimism, sadness, sorrow, woe. ANT.-exultation, frivolity, joy, light, mirth.

gloomy, *a.* SYN.-bleak, cheerless, dark, dejected, depressed, despondent, disconsolate, dismal, dispirited, doleful, dreary, dull, funereal, glum, lonesome, melancholy, moody, sad, somber, sorrowful. ANT.-cheerful, gay, happy, joyous, lively, merry.

glorify, *v.* SYN.-acclaim, adore, aggrandize, bless, commend, consecrate, dignify, enshrine, enthrone, exalt, extol, hallow, honor, laud, revere, venerate. ANT.-abuse, debase, degrade, dishonor, mock.

glorious, *a.* SYN.-admirable, celebrated, distinguished, elevated, esteemed, exalted, excellent, grand, gratifying, high, honorable, honored, illustrious, lofty, magnificent, majestic, memorable, noble, notable, praiseworthy, raised, splendid, sublime, supreme. ANT.-base, ignoble, low, ordinary, ridiculous.

glory, *n.* SYN.-admiration, adoration, deference, dignity, esteem, fame, homage, honor, praise, renown, respect, reverence, worship; beauty, brilliance, grandeur, magnificence, majesty, pomp, radiance, resplendence, richness; exult, rejoice, triumph. ANT.-contempt, derision, disgrace, dishonor, reproach.

glow, *v.* SYN.-blaze, flicker, glare, gleam, glimmer, glisten, glitter, radiate, scintillate, shimmer, shine, sparkle, twinkle.

glum, *a.* SYN.-dejected, depressed, despondent, disconsolate, dismal, dispirited, doleful, dour, fretful, gloomy, melancholy, moody, morose, plaintive, sad, somber, sorrowful, sulky, sullen, surly. ANT.-amiable, cheerful, happy, joyous, merry, pleasant.

glut, *v.* SYN.-clog, congest, fill up, inundate, occupy, overstock, pervade; cram, devour, feast, fill, gorge, overeat, sate, satiate, satisfy, stuff. ANT.-deplete, drain, empty, exhaust, void.

go, *v.* SYN.-depart, exit, fade, flee, leave, move, proceed, quit, retire, run, vacate, vanish, walk, withdraw; advance, continue, endeavor, journey, operate, perform, persevere, persist, proceed, progress, travel ANT.-arrive, come, enter, stand, stay.

goad, *v.* SYN.-coerce, drive, encourage, force, impel, induce, press, prod, prompt, push, stimulate, spur, urge, whip; bully, instigate, needle, provoke, tease.

goal, *n.* SYN.-aim, ambition, aspiration. craving, design, desire, hope, intent, intention, longing, object, objective, plan, passion.

godlike, *a.* SYN.-almighty, boundless, celestial, divine, eternal, excellent, heavenly, holy, invincible, omnipotent, spiritual, superhuman, supernatural, transcendent, universal. ANT.-blasphemous, diabolical, mundane, profane, wicked.

godly, *a.* SYN.-angelic, divine, devout, holy, pious, righteous, spiritual.

going, *v.* SYN.-auspicious, flourishing, growing, operating, profitable, running, successful, thriving; bound, destined, directed.

gone, *a.* SYN.-abandoned, departed, disappeared, disintegrated, dissipated, dissolved, extinct, left, moved, removed, retired, vanished, withdrawn.

good, *a.* SYN.-able, admirable, agreeable, benevolent, capable, cheerful, commendable, conscientious, efficient, exemplary, expert, fair, friendly, genial, gracious, honest, honorable, humane, kind, moral, pleasant, proficient, pure, reliable, skillful, virtuous, worthy; excellent, genuine, immaculate, precious, safe, sound, valid; auspicious, beneficial, favorable, profitable, useful; adequate, ample, sufficient.

gossip, *n.* SYN.-babble, chatter, hearsay, meddling, news, rumor, scandal, slander; backbiter, blabbermouth, chatterbox, meddler, muckraker, snoop, tattler.

gouge, *v.* SYN.-channel, chisel, cut, dig, scoop; cheat, defraud, extort, overcharge.

govern, *v.* SYN.-administer, command, conduct, control, dictate, direct, handle, legislate, manage, oversee, regulate, reign, rule, superintend, supervise, sway, tyrannize. ANT.-acquiesce, assent, obey, submit, yield.

graceful, *a.* SYN.-adroit, agile, controlled, dexterous, elegant, flowing, fluid, lithe, natural, nimble, pliant, poised, skilled, smooth, sprightly, supple, willowy; artistic, balanced, beautiful, comely, dainty, delicate, elegant, exquisite, harmonious, neat, pretty, slender, trim. ANT.-awkward, clumsy, deformed, gawky, ungainly.

gracious, *a.* SYN.-agreeable, amiable, condescending, cordial, courteous, courtly, earnest, engaging, elegant, friendly, good-natured, hearty, hospitable, kind, patronizing, pleasing, polite, sincere, warm. ANT.-churlish, disagreeable, hateful, ill-natured, surly.

grade, *n.* SYN.-caliber, category, class, denomination, genre, kind, order, rank, set; attribute, characteristic, distinction, feature, peculiarity, property, quality, trait, value. ANT.-being, essence, nature, substance.

gradual, *a.* SYN.-continuous, creeping, dawdling, delaying, deliberate, leisurely, slow, sluggish, unhurried. ANT.-fast, quick, rapid, speedy, swift.

grandeur, *n.* SYN.-amplitude, beauty, brilliance, ceremony, dignity, greatness, immensity, impressiveness, luxury, magnificence, pomp, resplendence, richness, splendor, stateliness, vastness.

grandiose, *a.* SYN.-august, dignified, grand, high, imposing, lofty, magnificent, majestic, noble, ostentatious, pretentious, pompous, showy, stately, sublime. ANT.-common, humble, lowly, ordinary, undignified.

grant, *n.* SYN.-allowance, appropriation, benefaction, bequest, boon, bounty, concession, donation, endowment, gift, gratuity, present, reward, subsidy.

grant, *v.* SYN.-allocate, allot, apportion, appropriate, assign, award, bestow, bequeath, confer, dispense, distribute, divide, give, measure, mete; accord, allow, concede, grant, permit, yield. ANT.-confiscate, keep, refuse, retain, withhold.

graph, *n.* SYN.-chart, design, diagram, picture, plan, plot, sketch.

graphic, *a.* SYN.-clear, colorful, comprehensive, depicted, descriptive, detailed, distinct, drawn, eloquent, explicit, forcible, illustrated, moving, outlined, pictured, picturesque, portrayed, sketched, striking, strong, telling, visual.

grasp, *v.* SYN.-capture, catch, clutch, grip, lay hold of, seize; assimilate, comprehend, conceive, follow, perceive, realize, understand. ANT.-liberate, lose, release.

grateful, *a.* SYN.-appreciative, beholden, gracious, indebted, obliged, pleased, thankful. ANT.-heedless, rude, thankless, unappreciative, unmindful.

gratifying, *a.* SYN.-acceptable, agreeable, amusing, comfortable, convenient, cozy, delightful, enjoyable, pleasant, pleasing, pleasurable, relaxed, restful, welcome.

ANT.-distressing, miserable, troubling, uncomfortable, wretched.

grave, *a.* SYN.-consequential, critical, dangerous, important, momentous, ominous, serious, weighty; dignified, sedate, serious, sober, solemn, staid, thoughtful. ANT.-insignificant, trifling, trivial; flighty, frivolous, light, merry.

grave, *n.* SYN.-barrow, catacomb, crypt, mausoleum, mound, pit, sepulcher, tomb, vault.

great, *a.* SYN.-big, enormous, gigantic, huge, immense, large, vast; countless, numerous; celebrated, eminent, famed, illustrious, prominent, renowned; critical, important, momentous, serious, vital, weighty; august, dignified, elevated, grand, majestic, noble; excellent, fine, magnificent. ANT.-diminutive, little, minute, small; common, obscure, ordinary, unknown; menial, paltry.

greedy, *a.* SYN.-avaricious, covetous, grasping, mercenary, miserly, niggardly, parsimonious, rapacious, selfish, stingy, tight; devouring, gluttonous, insatiable, intemperate, ravenous, voracious. ANT.-generous, munificent; full, satisfied.

green, *a.* SYN.-artless, callow, fresh, immature, ignorant, inexperienced, innocent, naive, natural, new, novice, raw, unsophisticated, untrained, young, youthful. ANT.-decayed, faded, hackneyed, musty, stagnant.

greet, *v.* SYN.-accost, acknowledge, address, approach, bow, hail, nod, receive, recognize, salute, speak to, welcome. ANT.-avoid, pass by.

gregarious, *a.* SYN.-affable, civil, communicative, congenial, convivial, friendly, gay, genial, hospitable, jovial, merry, outgoing, sociable, social. ANT.-antisocial, disagreeable, hermitic, inhospitable.

grief, *n.* SYN.-affliction, anguish, desolation, distress, gloom, heartache, lamentation, malaise, melancholy, misery, mourning, pain, regret, remorse, sadness, sorrow, trial, tribulation, unhappiness, woe. ANT.-comfort, consolation, happiness, joy, solace.

grievance, *n.* SYN.-affliction, burden, complaint, damage, detriment, encumbrance, hardship, harm, injury, mischief, injustice, ordeal, prejudice, trial, wrong. ANT.-benefit, improvement, repair.

grieve, *v.* SYN.-agonize, bemoan, bewail, deplore, depress, distress, lament, mourn, sadden, sorrow, suffer, weep. ANT.-carouse, celebrate, rejoice, revel.

grieved, *a.* SYN.-afflicted, aggrieved, depressed, distressed, hurt, pained, sad, sorrowful, sorry, vexed. ANT.-cheerful, delighted, splendid.

grim, *a.* SYN.-appalling, austere, bleak, crusty, dire, forbidding, frightful, gloomy, glowering, glum, grouchy, grumpy, harsh, morose, scowling, severe, sour, stern, sullen, sulky,

grip, *v.* SYN.-capture, catch, clasp, clench, clutch, embrace, grab, grasp, hold, seize, snare, squeeze, trap. ANT.-liberate, loose, release, throw.

groceries, *n.* SYN.-comestibles, edibles, food, foodstuffs, perishables, produce, staples.

gross, *a.* SYN.-aggregate, entire, total, whole; brutal, enormous, glaring, grievous, manifest, plain; coarse, crass, earthy, indelicate, lewd, obscene; rough, rude, vulgar;

big, bulky, corpulent, fat, great, large, obese. ANT.-proper, refined; appealing, comely, delicate.

grotesque, *a.* SYN.-abnormal, deformed, distorted, hideous, malformed, repulsive, ugly; absurd, fantastic, ludicrous, outrageous, ridiculous, scary.

grouch, *n.* SYN.-bear, complainer, crank, growler, grumbler, sourpuss.

grouch, *v.* SYN.-complain, grouse, grumble, lament, murmur, mutter, protest, remonstrate, repine, whine. ANT.-applaud, approve, praise, rejoice.

group, *n.* SYN.-aggregation, assembly, band, brood, bunch, class, cluster, collection, crowd, flock, herd, horde, lot, mob, pack, party, set, swarm, throng, troupe.

grovel, *v.* SYN.-abase, beg, cower, crawl, flatter, kneel, kowtow, obey, prostrate, snivel, stoop, surrender, wheedle, yield.

grow, *v.* SYN.-advance, alter, build, develop, distend, enlarge, evolve, expand, extend, flourish, gain, germinate, increase, mature, mount, multiply, progress, spread, sprout, swell, thrive. ANT.-atrophy, contract, decay, diminish, shrink, wane.

growth, *n.* SYN.-augmentation, development, elaboration, evolution, expansion, increase, maturing, progress, unfolding, unraveling. ANT.-abbreviation, compression, curtailment.

gruff, *a.* SYN.-abrupt, blunt, brusque, churlish, coarse, crude, curt, discourteous, harsh, rough, rude, severe, short, uncivil, unpolished. ANT.-calm, placid, tranquil, unruffled; civil, courteous, gentle, mild.

guarantee, *n.* SYN.-assurance, bail, bond, earnest, guaranty, pawn, pledge, promise, security, surety, token, warrant, warrantee.

guarantee, *v.* SYN.-affirm, assure, attest, confirm, endorse, insure, pledge, reassure, secure, stake, support, vouch, wager, warrant.

guard, *n.* SYN.-bulwark, defense, protection, safeguard, safety, security, shelter, shield; defender, guardian, protector, sentinel, sentry, watchman..

guard, *v.* SYN.-cloak, conceal, cover, curtain, defend, envelop, hide, protect, safeguard, screen, shelter, shield, shroud, veil; attend, check, observe, oversee, patrol, picket, superintend, supervise, tend, watch. ANT.-bare, divulge, expose, reveal, unveil; desert, disregard, forsake, ignore, leave, neglect.

guardian, *n.* SYN.-baby-sitter, curator, custodian, defender, guard, keeper, nursemaid, overseer, parent, preserver, protector, regent, sentinel, sentry, trustee.

guess, *n.* SYN.-assumption, conjecture, estimate, hypothesis, notion, opinion, presumption, speculation, supposition, suspicion, theory.

guess, *v.* SYN.-assume, believe, conjecture, estimate, hypothesize, imagine, predicate, presume, reckon, speculate, suppose, surmise, suspect, theorize, think.

guidance, *n.* SYN.-administration, care, conduct, control, direction, execution, instruction, leadership, management, supervision.

guide, *n.* SYN.-conductor, director, escort, guru, helmsman, lead, leader, pathfinder, pilot, scout; beacon, mark, sign, signal.

guide, *v.* SYN.-conduct, direct, escort, instruct, lead, manage, pilot, point, teach, train, steer.

guile, *n.* SYN.-beguilement, chicanery, cunning, deceit, deceitfulness, deception, duplicity, fraud, trick, wiliness. ANT.-candor, honesty, openness, sincerity, truthfulness.

guilt, *n.* SYN.-blame, culpability, fault, liability; compunction, contrition, remorse, shame.

guilty, *a.* SYN.-censured, charged, condemned, damned, derelict, impeached, incriminated, indicted, judged, liable, sentenced; ashamed, contrite, sorrowful, remorseful.

gullible, *a.* SYN.-artless, believing, credulous, guileless, innocent, naive, simple, trustful, trusting, unsophisticated.

gypsy, *n.* SYN.-bohemian, itinerant, maverick, nomad, nonconformist, outcast, rover, traveler, vagabond, wanderer.

H

habit, *n.* SYN.-addiction, bent, characteristic, convention, custom, disposition, fashion, fixation, manner, mode, observance, penchant, practice, routine, tradition, turn, usage, use, way, wont; clothes, costume, dress, garb.

habitual, *a.* SYN.-accustomed, automatic, common, continual, established, fixed, frequent, general, ingrained, often, periodic, perpetual, persistent, recurrent, regular, repeated, repetitious, routine, usual. ANT.-exceptional, rare, scanty, solitary, unique.

hackneyed, *a.* SYN.-banal, common, ordinary, overused, pedestrian, prosaic, stale, stereotyped, trite. ANT.-fresh, modern, momentous, novel, stimulating.

hag, *n.* SYN.-crone, fishwife, harridan, shrew, virago, witch.

hairy, *a.* SYN.-bearded, bewhiskered, bristly, downy, fluffy, furry, fuzzy, hirsute, shaggy, unshorn, whiskered.

hall, *n.* SYN.-anteroom, armory, assembly, auditorium, ballroom, chamber, church, clubroom, corridor, dormitory, entry, foyer, gallery, gym, gymnasium, hallway, lobby, lounge, room, salon, theater.

hallow, *v.* SYN.-aggrandize, bless, consecrate, dedicate, dignify, elevate, ennoble, erect, exalt, extol, glorify, worship, raise. ANT.-debase, degrade, dishonor, humble, humiliate.

hallowed, *a.* SYN.-blessed, consecrated, devotional, divine, holy, religious, reverential, sacred, sacrosanct.

hallucination, *n.* SYN.-aberration, allusion, apparition, chimera, fantasy, ghost, illusion, phantasm, specter, vision.

halt, *v.* SYN.-abstain, arrest, bar, block, cease, check, contravene, curb, desist, discontinue, end, hinder, impede, interrupt, obstruct, quell, stall, stem, stop, suspend, terminate. ANT.-begin, proceed, promote, speed, start.

hamlet, *n.* SYN.-community, settlement, village.

hamper, *v.* SYN.-block, check, constrain, delay, encumber, fetter, hinder, impede, obstruct, restrain, restrict, retard. ANT.-encourage, facilitate, promote.

handicap, *n.* SYN.-affliction, block, disability, disadvantage, hindrance, impairment, impediment, inability, incapacity, limitation, obstacle, penalty, weakness. ANT.-ability, capability, power, strength.

handle, *v.* SYN.-advise, check, control, examine, feel, finger, manage, manipulate, operate, supervise, touch, wield, work.

handsome, *a.* SYN.-aristocratic, athletic, attractive, beautiful, charming, clean-cut, comely, dapper, elegant, fair, fine, gracious, jaunty, noble, personable, princely, robust, stately, well-dressed; ample, considerable, generous, magnanimous. ANT.-foul, hideous, homely, repulsive, unsightly.

handy, *a.* SYN.-accessible, advantageous, appropriate, convenient, fitting, helpful, near, suitable, timely, usable, valuable; able, adept, dexterous, ingenious, resourceful, skillful. ANT.-awkward, inconvenient, inopportune, troublesome; clumsy, inept, unskilled.

hanging, *a.* SYN.-attached, dangling, drooping, flapping, hovering, projecting, swaying, swinging, waving; deadlocked, iffy, pending, tentative, uncertain, unresolved.

haphazard, *a.* SYN.-capricious, careless, casual, erratic, infrequent, incidental, irregular, loose, offhand, random, slipshod. uncoordinated, unplanned.

happen, *v.* SYN.-bechance, befall, betide, chance, ensue, occur, take place, transpire.

happening, *n.* SYN.-accident, affair, circumstance, event, incident, instance, moment, occasion.

happily, *a.* SYN.-agreeably, brightly, cheerfully, contentedly, delightedly, freely, gaily, gladly, graciously, joyfully, pleasantly,

happiness, *n.* SYN.-beatitude, blessedness, bliss, contentment, delight, felicity, gaiety, gladness, glee, joy, pleasure, satisfaction, well-being. ANT.-despair, grief, misery, sadness, sorrow.

happy, *a.* SYN.-blissful, carefree, cheerful, congenial, contented, delighted, ecstatic, elated, exuberant, gay, glad, intoxicated, jesting, joyful, joyous, jubilant, laughing, merry, smiling, sparkling; apt, befitting, blessed, favored, fortunate, lucky, opportune, propitious, prosperous. ANT.-blue, depressed, gloomy, morose.

harass, *v.* SYN.-aggravate, annoy, badger, bother, disturb, harry, irritate, molest, nag, pester, plague, provoke, tantalize, taunt, tease, torment, vex, worry. ANT.-comfort, delight, gratify, please, soothe.

hard, *a.* SYN.-compact, firm, impenetrable, rigid, solid, strong, tempered, unyielding; arduous, burdensome, complex, difficult, formidable, intricate, laborious, onerous, perplexing, puzzling, strenuous, tough, trying; callous, cruel, exacting, harsh, oppressive, rigorous, severe, stern, strict, unfeeling, unmerciful. ANT.-brittle, elastic, flabby, fluid, plastic, soft; easy, effortless, facile; simple; gentle, lenient, tender.

harden, *v.* SYN.-clot, coagulate, compact, crystallize, fossilize, freeze, petrify, solidify, stiffen; acclimate, accustom, discipline, fortify, toughen.

hardship, *n.* SYN.-affliction, burden, calamity, difficulty, distress, grief, misery, misfortune, ordeal, pain, problem, sorrow, suffering, test, trial, tribulation, trouble, woe.

ANT.-alleviation, consolation, ease, pleasure.

harm, *n.* SYN.-damage, detriment, evil, hurt, ill, infliction, injury, mischief, misfortune, mishap, wrong. ANT.-benefit, boon, favor, kindness.

hardy, *a.* SYN.-acclimatized, bold, conditioned, courageous, dauntless, firm, fit, hale, hardened, healthy, hearty, robust, rugged, solid, sound, sturdy, tough. ANT.-delicate, feeble, fragile, weak.

harm, *v.* SYN.-damage, disfigure, hurt, impair, injure, maltreat, mar, spoil, wound; abuse, affront, dishonor, insult, wrong. ANT.-ameliorate, benefit, help, preserve; compliment, praise.

harmful, *a.* SYN.-corrupting, damaging, deleterious, detrimental, destructive, evil, hurtful, injurious, malignant, menacing, painful, ruinous, sinister, subversive, toxic, unhealthy, virulent. ANT.-advantageous, beneficial, helpful, profitable, salutary.

harmless, *a.* SYN.-disarmed, docile, friendly, impotent, innocent, innocuous, passive, powerless, pure, reliable, safe, secure, sterile, trustworthy. ANT.-dangerous, hazardous, insecure, perilous, unsafe.

harmony, *n.* SYN.-accordance, agreement, coincidence, compatibility, concord, concurrence, congruence, congruity, equanimity, peace, rapport, understanding, unison. ANT.-difference, disagreement, discord, dissension, strife, variance.

harsh, *a.* SYN.-cacophonous, clashing, discordant, dissonant, grating, jangling, jarring, rasping, shrill; austere, acrimonious, blunt, brusque, coarse, gruff, rigorous, rough, rugged, severe, strict, stringent. ANT.-melodious, tuneful; gentle, mild, smooth, soft.

harvest, *n.* SYN.-crop, fruit, gathering, proceeds, produce, product, reaping, result, store, yield.

harvest, *v.* SYN.-acquire, amass, collect, cull, gain, garner, gather, glean, pick, reap. ANT.-lose, plant, sow, squander.

haste, *n.* SYN.-abruptness, alacrity, bustle, carelessness, dispatch, excitement, flurry, hurry, hustle, impatience, impetuosity, rashness, recklessness.

hasten, *v.* SYN.-accelerate, expedite, goad, hurry, hustle, precipitate, press, push, quicken, rush, scoot, scramble, scurry, speed, stimulate, urge. ANT.-delay, detain, hinder, retard, tarry.

hasty, *a.* SYN.-abrupt, brisk, careless, fast, fleet, foolhardy, hurried, impetuous, indiscreet, lively, precipitate, quick, rapid, rash, reckless, speedy, sudden, swift, thoughtless, unannounced, unexpected. ANT.-anticipated, expected; courteous, gradual, smooth.

hate, *v.* SYN.-abhor, abominate, despise, detest, dislike, loathe, resent, scorn, spurn. ANT.-admire, approve, cherish, like, love.

hateful, *a.* SYN.-abominable, abusive, detestable, execrable, foul, insulting, loathsome, nasty, odious, offensive, repugnant, revolting, vile. ANT.-agreeable, commendable, delightful, pleasant.

hatred, *n.* SYN.-abhorrence, abomination, alienation, animosity, antagonism, antipathy, bitterness, contempt, detestation, disgust, dislike, enmity, grudge, hostility, ill will, loathing, malevolence, prejudice, rancor, repugnance, venom. ANT.-affection, attraction, friendship, love.

haughty, *a.* SYN.-arrogant, disdainful, egotistical, lofty, overbearing, proud, stately, supercilious, vain, vainglorious. ANT.-ashamed, humble, lowly, meek.

haunt, *v.* SYN.-annoy, bedevil, beset, bother, frighten, harass, hound, obsess, pester, plague, possess, terrify, terrorize, trouble, worry, vex,

have, *v.* SYN.-contain, control, hold, occupy, own, possess, retain. ANT.-abandon, lose, renounce, surrender.

haven, *n.* SYN.-asylum, harbor, hermitage, hideaway, port, refuge, retreat, sanctuary, shelter.

hazard, *n.* SYN.-chance, danger, jeopardy, peril, risk, uncertainty, venture. ANT.-defense, immunity, protection, safety.

hazard, *v.* SYN.-chance, conjecture, dare, endanger, gamble, imperil, jeopardize, peril, risk, speculate, try, venture. ANT.-determine, guard, insure, know.

hazardous, *a.* SYN.-chancy, dangerous, menacing, perilous, precarious, risky, speculative, threatening, uncertain, unsafe. ANT.-firm, protected, safe, secure.

hazy, *a.* SYN.-ambiguous, blurred, cloudy, dim, dull, foggy, indefinite, indistinct, misty, murky, obscure, smoky, uncertain, unclear, undetermined, unsettled, vague, veiled. ANT.-clear, explicit, lucid, precise, specific.

head, *n.* SYN.-authority, chief, commander, director, leader, master, principal, ruler; acme, crest, peak, pinnacle, summit, top; climax, crisis, conclusion, culmination, ending, finale. ANT.-follower, subordinate, underling; base, bottom, foot.

head, *v.* SYN.-command, direct, govern, lead, manage, oversee, precede, supervise.

heading, *n.* SYN.-banner, caption, headline, legend, preface, streamer, title.

heal, *v.* SYN.-attend, cure, medicate, purify, regenerate, rehabilitate, remedy, renew, restore, salve, soothe, treat. ANT.-damage, harm, infect, injure.

healthful, *a.* SYN.-beneficial, bracing, clean, fresh, healing, hygienic, invigorating, nourishing, nutritious, preventive, pure, regenerative, salubrious, sanitary, stimulating, sustaining, unpolluted, untainted, wholesome.

healthy, *a.* SYN.-able-bodied, blooming, fit, hale, hardy, hearty, hygienic, invigorating, normal, nourishing, robust, salubrious, salutary, sound, strong, vigorous, virile, well, wholesome. ANT.-delicate, diseased, frail, infirm; injurious, noxious.

hear, *v.* SYN.-apprehend, attend, detect, eavesdrop, hearken, heed, listen, overhear, perceive, regard.

hearing, *n.* SYN.-audience, audit, audition, conference, consultation, interview, meeting, review, test, trial, tryout,

heart, *n.* SYN.-center, core, crux, essence, middle. midpoint, midst, nucleus; bravery, courage, fortitude, gallantry, mettle, nerve, valor. ANT.-border, boundary, outskirts, periphery, rim.

heartache, *n.* SYN.-affliction, anguish, despair, distress, grief, lamentation, misery, mourning, sadness, sorrow, trial, tribulation, woe. ANT.-comfort, consolation, happiness, joy, solace.

heartbroken, *a.* SYN.-comfortless, disconsolate, distressed, doleful, forlorn, melancholy, miserable, pitiable, sorrowful, wretched. ANT.-contented, fortunate, happy.

hearten, *v.* SYN.-assure, cheer, embolden, encourage, enthuse, exhilarate, favor, foster, impel, incite, inspire, promote, reassure, stimulate, support, urge. ANT.-deter, discourage, dispirit, dissuade, reject.

hearty, *a.* SYN.-ardent, authentic, cheery, cordial, eager, earnest, enthusiastic, genial, gracious, hale, healthy, jovial, profuse, robust, sincere, sociable, sound, strong, unrestrained, warm, well, wholehearted, wholesome, zealous. ANT.-aloof cool, reserved, taciturn.

heat, *v.* SYN.-boil, char, cook, fry, roast, scald, scorch, sear, singe, warm.

heathen, *a.* SYN.-amoral, barbarous, uncivilized.

heathen, *n.* SYN.-atheist, barbarian, infidel, nonbeliever, pagan.

heavenly, *a.* SYN.-celestial, divine, godlike, holy, superhuman, supernatural, transcendent. ANT.-blasphemous, diabolical, mundane, profane, wicked.

heavy, *a.* SYN.-bulky, hefty, huge, massive, ponderous, portly, stout, weighty; burdensome, cumbersome, depressing, distressing, gloomy, grave, grievous, harsh, oppressive, serious, troublesome, trying; boring, clumsy, dull, listless, ponderous, slow, sluggish, tedious, tiresome; complicated, complex, concentrated, difficult, important, intense, momentous, obscure, pithy, serious, trying. ANT.-animated, brisk, light.

heckle, *v.* SYN.-badger, bait, bother, harass, pester, ridicule, tease, torment.

heed, *n.* SYN.-alertness, attention, care, consideration, mindfulness, notice, observance, watchfulness. ANT.-disregard, indifference, negligence, omission, oversight.

heed, *v.* SYN.-attend, consider, contemplate, deliberate, examine, listen, mark, mind, notice, obey, ponder, reflect, study, weigh. ANT.-ignore, neglect, overlook.

heedless, *a.* SYN.-blind, careless, hasty, headlong, ignorant, impetuous, impulsive, oblivious, rash, unaware, undiscerning, unmindful, unseeing. ANT.-aware, calculated, discerning, perceiving, sensible.

height, *n.* SYN.-apex, climax, culmination, elevation, extent, peak, prominence, stature, summit, zenith. ANT.-anticlimax, base, depth, floor.

heighten, *v.* SYN.-aggravate, amplify, augment, elevate, emphasize, enhance, exalt, increase, intensify, lift, magnify, raise, uplift. ANT.-appease, lessen, lower, mitigate, palliate soften, soothe.

help, *n.* SYN.-advice, aid, assistance, backing, comfort, encouragement, furtherance, guidance, patronage, relief, succor, support. ANT.-antagonism, counteraction, defiance, hostility, resistance.

help, *v.* SYN.-abet, accommodate, advise, advocate, aid, assist, back, bolster, encouragement, facilitate, foster, further, mitigate, promote, relieve, remedy, succor, support, uphold. ANT.-afflict, hinder, impede, oppose, resist, thwart.

helpful, *a.* SYN.-accommodating, advantageous, beneficial, essential, good, invaluable, kind, obliging, practical, profitable, salutary, serviceable, useful, valuable, wholesome. ANT.-deleterious, destructive, detrimental, harmful, ineffective, injurious, useless.

hence, adv. SYN.-accordingly, consequently, so, then, thence, therefore.

heretic, *n.* SYN.-apostate, cynic, dissenter, dissident, nonconformist, schismatic, sectarian, sectary, skeptic, unbeliever.

heritage, *n.* SYN.-ancestry, birthright, estate, inheritance, legacy, lot; convention, culture, custom, endowment, fashion, tradition.

hero, *n.* SYN.-champion, conqueror, master, model, protagonist, protector, star.

heroic, *a.* SYN.-adventurous, audacious, bold, brave, chivalrous, courageous, daring, dauntless, desperate, drastic, excessive, extreme, fearless, gallant, great, intrepid, magnanimous, noble, valiant, valorous. ANT.-cowardly, cringing, fearful, timid, weak.

hesitant, *a.* SYN.-averse, diffident, disinclined, doubtful, irresolute, loath, reluctant, skeptical, slow, uncertain, unwilling. ANT.-disposed, eager, inclined, ready, willing.

hesitate, *v.* SYN.-consider, defer, delay, deliberate, demur, doubt, falter, pause, ponder, scruple, stammer, stop, stutter, vacillate, wait, waver, weigh. ANT.-continue, decide, persevere, proceed, resolve.

hesitation, *n.* SYN.-ambiguity, dawdling, delaying, distrust, doubt, faltering, halting, incredulity, indecision, irresolution, pause, procrastination, scruple, skepticism, stammering, suspicion, unbelief, uncertainty. ANT.-belief, certainty, conviction, determination. faith.

hidden, *a.* SYN.-clandestine, clouded, concealed, covert, disguised, eclipsed, latent, obscured, potential, private, quiescent, secluded, secret, shadow, shrouded, suppressed, surreptitious, undeveloped, unseen. ANT.-conspicuous, evident, explicit, manifest, visible.

hide, *v.* SYN.-cloak, conceal, cover, curtain, disguise, mask, screen, secrete, shelter, shroud, suppress, veil, withhold. ANT.-disclose, divulge, expose, reveal, show, uncover.

high, *a.* SYN.-elevated, lofty, tall, towering; distinguished, eminent, exalted, important, preeminent, prominent, proud. ANT.-small, stunted, tiny; base, low, mean.

hinder, *v.* SYN.-arrest, bar, block, bottleneck, burden, check, delay, encumber, foil, frustrate, hamper, handicap, impede, inhibit, interrupt, neutralize, obstruct, prevent, resist, restrain, retard, stall, stop, thwart. ANT.-assist, expedite, facilitate, further, promote.

hint, *n.* SYN.-allusion, clue, cue, implication, inference, inkling, innuendo, insinuation, intimation, reference, reminder, taste, tip, trace. ANT.-affirmation, declaration, statement.

hint, *v.* SYN.-advert, allude, foreshadow, imply, infer, insinuate, intimate, mention, prompt, refer, suggest. ANT.-declare, demonstrate, specify, state.

hire, *v.* SYN.-appoint, charter, commission, delegate, employ, engage, enlist, lease, retain, use, utilize. ANT.-banish, discard, discharge, reject.

history, *n.* SYN.-account, annals, antiquity, archives, chronicle, evidence, memoir, records, writings.

hit, *v.* SYN.-bash, beat, buffet, bump, collide, cuff, hurt, jab, knock, pelt, pound, pummel, punch, rap, slap, smack, smite, sock, strike, thump, whack.

hoard, *n.* SYN.-accumulation, cache, riches, stockpile, store, treasure, wealth.

hoard, *v.* SYN.-accumulate, acquire, keep, save, stash, store, stow.

hoarse, *a.* SYN.-harsh, husky, grating, gruff, guttural, rasping, raucous, rough, scratchy. thick, throaty.

hoax, *n.* SYN.-antic, artifice, deceit, deception, fabrication, fraud, joke, ploy, prank, ruse, stratagem, stunt, swindle, subterfuge, trick, wile. ANT.-candor, exposure, honesty, openness, sincerity.

hobby, *n.* SYN.-activity, amusement, avocation, craft, diversion, fancy, pastime, relaxation, sideline, whimsy.

hold, *v.* SYN.-adhere, attach, clasp, cling, clutch, continue, endure, fasten, grasp, grip, have, keep, last, maintain, occupy, own, persist, possess, remain, retain, stick, support, sustain; check, confine, contain, curb, detain, hinder, restrain; believe, consider, deem, embrace, entertain, espouse, esteem, think. ANT.-abandon, relinquish, surrender, vacate.

hole, *n.* SYN.-abyss, aperture, breach, break, burrow, cavity, chasm, cleft, crack, cranny, crater, fissure, fracture, gap, gash, gorge, gulf, incision, opening, orifice, perforation, pit, pore, puncture, ravine, rent, rupture, shaft, slit, split, tear, tunnel, void.

hollow, *a.* SYN.-depressed, empty, unfilled, vacant, vacuous, void; false, hypocritical, insincere, vain. ANT.-full, solid, sound; genuine, sincere.

holy, *a.* SYN.-angelic, blessed, consecrated, dedicated, devout, divine, godly, good, hallowed, humble, just, moral, pious, religious, reverent, righteous, sacred, saintly, sanctified, spiritual, venerable. ANT.-evil, profane, sacrilegious, secular, worldly.

home, *n.* SYN.-abode, apartment, base, chalet, domicile, dwelling, flat, habitat, hearth, homestead, house, household, hovel, lodging, mansion, quarters, residence, seat, shelter.

homely, *a.* SYN.-coarse, ill-favored, inelegant, plain, repellent, simple, ugly, unattractive, uncomely, unrefined; cozy, crude, modest, simple, snug, unpretentious. ANT.-attractive, beautiful, fair, handsome, pretty.

honest, *a.* SYN.-above-board, candid, conscientious, decent, factual, fair, genuine, honorable, just, legitimate, moral, open, realistic, scrupulous, sincere, sound, straightforward, true, trustworthy, truthful, unreserved, upright, virtuous. ANT.-deceitful, dishonest, fraudulent, lying, tricky.

honesty, *n.* SYN.-candor, character, conscience, fairness, fidelity, frankness, goodness, integrity, justice, morality, openness, rectitude, reliability, responsibility, sincerity, trustworthiness, uprightness, virtue. ANT.-cheating, deceit, dishonesty, fraud, trickery.

honor, *n.* SYN.-admiration, adoration, deference, dignity, distinction, esteem, faith, fame, glory, homage, praise, renown, recognition, reference, reputation, repute, respect, reverence, trust, veneration, worship. ANT.-contempt, derision, disgrace, dishonor, reproach.

honor, *v.* SYN.-admire, adore, celebrate, commemorate, esteem, extol, glorify, keep, laud, observe, praise, regard, respect, revere, solemnize, value, venerate, worship. ANT.-decry, disgrace, dishonor, disregard, overlook, profane.

honorable, *a.* SYN.-admirable, creditable, dignified, distinguished, eminent, equitable, esteemed, estimable, ethical, fair, honest, illustrious, just, noble, proper, reputable, respectable, true, trusty, upright, virtuous. ANT.-disgraceful, ignominious, infamous, shameful.

hope, *n.* SYN.-anticipation, assurance, belief, confidence, desire, dream, expectancy, expectation, faith, goal, longing, optimism, reliance, trust, wish. ANT.-despair, despondency, pessimism.

hopeless, *a.* SYN.-desperate, disastrous, fatal, foreboding, impossible, incurable, irreversible, lost, pointless, tragic, vain, worthless.

hopelessness, *n.* SYN.-depression, despair, desperation, despondency, discouragement, gloom, grief, heartache, pessimism, sorrow, torture. ANT.-confidence, elation, hope, optimism.

horde, *n.* SYN.-band, bevy, crowd, crush, gathering, group, host, masses, mob, multitude, pack, populace, press, rabble, swarm, throng.

horrible, *a.* SYN.-abominable, appalling, awful, deplorable, dire, disgusting, dreadful, fearful, frightful, ghastly, hideous, horrid, odious, offensive, repulsive, shameful, shocking, terrible. ANT.-beautiful, enchanting, enjoyable, fascinating, lovely.

horror, *n.* SYN.-abomination, alarm, antipathy, apprehension, aversion, awe, dread, fear, foreboding, fright, hatred, loathing, panic, repugnance, terror. ANT.-assurance, boldness, confidence, courage.

hostile, *a.* SYN.-adverse, antagonistic, conflicting, hateful, inimical, opposed, repugnant, unfriendly, warlike. ANT.-amicable, cordial, favorable.

hostility, *n.* SYN.-abhorrence, animosity, aversion, bitterness, dislike, enmity, grudge, hatred, ill will, malevolence, rancor, spite. ANT.-friendliness, good will, love.

hot, *a.* SYN.-baking, blazing, blistering, burning, flaming, parching, scalding, scorching, sizzling; ardent, fervent, fiery, hot-blooded, impetuous, intense, passionate, torrid; acrid, biting, peppery, piquant, pungent, spicy. ANT.-cold, cool, freezing, frigid; apathetic, impassive, indifferent, passionless, phlegmatic; bland.

however, *adv.* SYN.-but, nevertheless, notwithstanding, still, yet.

hue, *n.* SYN.-color, complexion, pigment, shade, stain, tincture, tinge, tint. ANT.-achromatism, paleness, transparency.

hug, *v.* SYN.-caress, clinch, coddle, cuddle, embrace, squeeze. ANT.-buffet, spurn.

huge, *a.* SYN.-ample, big, capacious, colossal, enormous, extensive, giant, great, immense, large, mammoth, tremendous, vast, wide. ANT.-little, mean, short, small, tiny.

humane, *a.* SYN.-benevolent, charitable, clement, compassionate, forbearing, forgiving, humanitarian, kind, kindhearted, kindly, lenient, merciful, softhearted, sympathetic, tender, tenderhearted, tolerant, understanding, warmhearted. ANT.-brutal, cruel, pitiless, remorseless, unfeeling.

humanity, *n.* SYN.-altruism, beneficence, benevolence, charity, compassion, generosity, kindness, liberality, love, magnanimity, philanthropy, sympathy, tenderness, understanding. ANT.-cruelty, inhumanity, malevolence, selfishness.

humble, *a.* SYN.-compliant, deferential, diffident, lowly, meek, mild, modest, ordinary, passive, plain, quiet, simple, submissive, unassuming, unpretentious. ANT.-arrogant, boastful, haughty, proud, vain.

humble, *v.* SYN.-abase, abash, break, chasten, crush, debase, degrade, demean, humiliate, mortify, shame, subdue. ANT.-elevate, exalt, honor, praise.

humiliate, *v.* See **humble**

humiliation, *n.* SYN.-abasement, chagrin, mortification, shame; disgrace, dishonor, disrepute, embarrassment, ignominy, mortification, scandal, shame. ANT.-dignity, glory, honor, praise, renown.

humor, *n.* SYN.-amusement, comedy, facetiousness, fun, irony, jocularity, joke, pleasantry, sarcasm, satire, waggery, wit; disposition, mood, temper, tendency, temperament, vagary, whim. ANT.-gravity, seriousness, sorrow.

humor, *v.* SYN.-comfort, coddle, gratify, indulge, pamper, placate, please, spoil.

humorous, *a.* SYN.-amusing, comic, comical, droll, entertaining, farcical, funny, laughable, ludicrous ridiculous, whimsical, witty. ANT.-melancholy, serious, sober, solemn.

hunch, *n.* SYN.-clue, feeling, foreboding, idea, intuition, notion, portent, premonition, prescience; bulge, bump, hump, protuberance.

hunger, *n.* SYN.-appetite, craving, desire, inclination, liking, longing, passion, relish, thirst, yearning, zest. ANT.-disgust, distaste, renunciation, repugnance, satiety.

hungry, *a.* SYN.-craving, famished, ravenous, starved, thirsting, voracious; avid, greedy, longing. ANT.-full, gorged, sated, satiated; satisfied.

hunt, *v.* SYN.-chase, explore, follow, hound, inquire, investigate, pursue, probe, ransack, rummage, scour, scrutinize, search, seek, stalk, trail, trace, track.

hurl, *v.* SYN.-cast, fling, heave, pitch, propel, throw, thrust, toss. ANT.-draw, haul, hold, pull, retain.

hurry, *v.* SYN.-accelerate, dash, expedite, hasten, precipitate, quicken, race, rush, scoot, speed. ANT.-delay, detain, hinder, retard, tarry.

hurt, *n.* SYN.-damage, detriment, disservice, harm, injury, mischief, grievance, injustice, prejudice, wound, wrong. ANT.-benefit, improvement, repair.

hurt, *v.* SYN.-abuse, affront, damage, disfigure, dishonor, distress, harm, impair, injure, insult, lash, mar, smite, spoil, wound, wrong. ANT.-ameliorate, benefit, compliment, help, praise, preserve.

hush, *n.* SYN.-calm, lull, peace, quiet, serenity, silence, stillness.

hustle, *v.* SYN.-hasten, hurry, race, rush, scramble; beg, con, panhandle, swindle.

hygienic, *a.* SYN.-clean, decontaminated, disinfected, healthy, pure, sanitary, wholesome. ANT.-contaminated, diseased, infected, injurious, noxious, unsanitary.

hypocrisy, *n.* SYN.-bigotry, cant, deceit, dissimulation, pretense, sanctimony. ANT.-candor, frankness, honesty, openness, truth.

hypothesis, *n.* SYN.-assumption, conjecture, law, notion, postulate, supposition, theory. ANT.-certainty, fact, proof.

hysterical, *a.* SYN.-delirious, demonstrative, distraught, emotional, excitable, fervent, frenzied, overwrought, possessed, raging, raving, uncontrolled.

I

idea, *n.* SYN.-abstraction, belief, concept, conception, fancy, image, impression, notion, opinion, sentiment, theory, thought. ANT.-entity, matter, object, substance, thing.

ideal, *a.* SYN.-exemplary, fancied, faultless, imaginary, perfect, supreme, unreal, utopian, visionary. ANT.-actual, faulty, imperfect, material, real.

idealistic, *a.* SYN.-dreamy, extravagant, fanciful, fantastic, fictitious, ideal, imaginative, impractical, maudlin, mawkish, picturesque, poetic, quixotic, romantic, sentimental, utopian, visionary. ANT.-factual, literal, matter-of-fact, practical, prosaic.

identical, *a.* SYN.-coincident, equal, equivalent, indistinguishable, like, same, twin. ANT.-contrary, disparate, dissimilar, distinct, opposed.

identify, *v.* SYN.-acknowledge, apprehend, avow, concede, confess, own, perceive, recognize, recollect, remember. ANT.-disown, renounce, repudiate.

ideology, *n.* SYN.-belief, convictions, culture, dogma, ethics, ideas, philosophy, tenets.

idiot, *n.* SYN.-buffoon, clown, harlequin, jester; blockhead, dolt, dunce, fool, imbecile, nincompoop, numbskull, oaf, simpleton. ANT.-genius, philosopher, sage, scholar.

idiotic, *a.* SYN.-absurd, asinine, brainless, crazy, foolish, irrational, nonsensical, preposterous, ridiculous, senseless, silly, simple. ANT.-judicious, prudent, sagacious, sane, wise.

idle, *a.* SYN.-dormant, inactive, indolent, inert, fallow, lazy, slothful, unemployed, unoccupied; insignificant, trifling, trivial, unimportANT. ANT.-active, employed, engaged, industrious, occupied, working.

idol, *n.* SYN.-deity, figurine, icon, image, statue, symbol, totem; beloved, favorite, hero, model.

ignominious, *a.* SYN.-abject, base, contemptible, despicable, dishonorable, groveling, ignoble, ignominious, low, lowly, mean, menial, shameful, sordid, vile, vulgar. ANT.-teemed, exalted, honored, lofty, noble, righteous.

ignorant, *a.* SYN.-coarse, crude, dense, dumb, illiterate, oblivious, shallow, superficial, uncultured, uneducated, uninformed, unlearned, unlettered, untaught, vulgar. ANT.-cultured, educated, erudite, informed, literate.

ignore, *v.* SYN.-disdain, disregard, neglect, omit, overlook, skip, slight. ANT.-include, notice, regard.

ill, *a.* SYN.-afflicted, ailing, diseased, indisposed, infirm, morbid, sick, unhealthy, unwell; bad, evil, naughty, wicked. ANT.-healthy, robust, sound, strong, well; good.

illegal, *a.* SYN.-criminal, dishonest, illegitimate, illicit, outlawed, prohibited, unlawful, wrongful. ANT.-honest, lawful, legal, permitted.

illicit, *a.* SYN.-banned, illegal, illegitimate, outlawed, prohibited, unauthorized, unlawful. ANT.-allowed, authorized, lawful, legal, permitted.

illness, *n.* SYN.-ailment, complaint, disease, disorder, infirmity, malady, sickness. ANT.-health, healthiness, soundness, vigor.

illogical, *a.* SYN.-absurd, contradictory, fallacious, groundless, implausible, inconsistent, incongruous, irrational, untenable.

illuminate, *v.* SYN.-brighten, clarify, edify, elucidate, enlighten, explain, illumine, illustrate, inform, irradiate. ANT.-complicate, confuse, darken, obfuscate, obscure.

illusion, *n.* SYN.-apparition, delusion, dream, fantasy, hallucination, mirage, phantom, vision. ANT.-actuality, reality, substance.

illusive, *a.* SYN.-apparent, deceptive, delusive, delusory, fallacious, false, misleading, ostensible, presumable, seeming, specious. ANT.-authentic, genuine, real, truthful.

illustration, *n.* SYN.-drawing, effigy, engraving, etching, image, landscape, likeness, painting, panorama, picture, portrayal, print, rendering, representation, resemblance, scene, sketch, view.

illustrious, *a.* SYN.-august, celebrated, dignified, distinguished, elevated, eminent, excellent, famed, famous, fine, grand, great, magnificent, majestic, noble, prominent, renowned. ANT.-common, menial, obscure, ordinary, paltry, unknown.

image, *n.* SYN.-concept, conception, idea, notion, perception; copy, effigy, figure, form, icon, idol, likeness, picture, representation, semblance, statue.

imagination, *n.* SYN.-awareness, conception, creation, daydream, fancy, fantasy, idea, insight, invention, inventiveness, notion, wit.

imaginative, *a.* SYN.-artistic, clever, creative, fanciful, inventive, mystical, poetical, sublime, talented, visionary. ANT.-dull, literal, prosaic, unromantic.

imagine, *v.* SYN.-assume, believe, conceive, conjecture, dream, envision, fancy, guess, opine, perceive, picture, pretend, suppose, surmise, think.

imbecile, *n.* SYN.-blockhead, dolt, dunce, fool, idiot, jerk, moron, nincompoop, numbskull, oaf, simpleton. ANT.-genius, philosopher, sage, scholar.

imbibe, *v.* SYN.-absorb, assimilate, consume, drink, ingest, guzzle, partake, receive, swallow. ANT.-discharge, dispense, emit, expel, exude.

imitate, *v.* SYN.-ape, copy, counterfeit, duplicate, echo, impersonate, mimic, mirror, mock, parallel, reflect, reproduce, simulate. ANT.-alter, distort, diverge, invent.

imitation, *n.* SYN.-copy, duplicate, exemplar, facsimile, fake, forgery, replica, reproduction, simulation, transcript. ANT.-original, novelty, prototype.

immaculate, *a.* SYN.-bright, clean, impeccable, spotless, unsullied; innocent, sinless, virginal.

immaterial, *a.* SYN.-extraneous, inapplicable, insubstantial, irrelevant.

immature, *a.* SYN.-callow, childish, childlike, green, innocent, juvenile, naive, provincial, puerile, raw, silly, unseasoned, unsophisticated, young, youthful. ANT.-aged, elderly, mature, old, senile.

immeasurable, *a.* SYN.-boundless, endless, eternal, immense, indefinite, infinite, interminable, limitless, unbounded, unlimited, vast. ANT.-bounded, circumscribed, confined, finite, limited.

immediately, adv. SYN.-directly, forthwith, instantaneously, instantly, now, presently, promptly, straight-away. ANT.-distantly, hereafter, later, shortly, sometime.

immense, *a,* SYN.-colossal, elephantine, enormous, gargantuan, gigantic, huge, large, prodigious, tremendous, vast. ANT.-diminutive, little, minute, small, tiny.

immerse, *v.* SYN.-dip, douse, dunk, plunge, sink, submerge; absorb, bury, engage, engross, involve. ANT.-elevate, recover, uplift.

immigration, *n.* SYN.-arrival, colonization, journey, migration, relocation, settlement. ANT.-displacement, emigration, exodus.

imminent, *a.* SYN.-approaching, close, coming, impending, menacing, near, nigh, overhanging, threatening. ANT.-afar, distant, improbable, remote, retreating.

immodest, *a.* SYN.-bold, candid, forthright, frank, indelicate, indiscreet, open, outspoken, unblushing.

immoderation, *n.* SYN.-dissipation, excess, extravagance, glut, intemperance, luxuriance, overindulgence, profusion, superabundance, superfluity, surplus. ANT.-dearth, deficiency, lack, paucity, wANT.

immoral, *a.* SYN.-anti-social, bad, corrupt, debased, debauched, dissolute, indecent, libertine, licentious, profligate, shameless, sinful, unprincipled, vicious, wicked. ANT.-chaste, high-minded, noble, pure, virtuous.

immortal, *a.* SYN.-ageless, deathless, endless, eternal, everlasting, imperishable, indestructible, infinite, permanent, perpetual, timeless, undying. ANT. ephemeral, finite, mortal, temporal, transient.

immune, *a.* SYN.-excused, exempt, free, freed, independent, liberated, unaffected, unconfined, unrestricted.

immunity, *n.* SYN.-exemption, freedom, immunization, impunity, liberty, license, prerogative, privilege, resistance, right.

immutable, *a.* SYN.-abiding, ceaseless, consistent, constant, continual, enduring, even, faithful, fixed, invariable, permanent, perpetual, persistent, steady, unalterable, unchanging, uniform, unwavering. ANT.-fickle, mutable, vacillating, wavering.

impact, *n.* SYN.-collision, crash, effect, influence.

impair, *v.* SYN.-damage, deface, diminish, harm, hurt, injure, lessen, mar, spoil. ANT.-ameliorate, benefit, enhance, mend, repair, vitiate.

impart, *v.* SYN.-bestow, cede, communicate, confer, convey, disclose, divulge, give, grant, inform, notify, relate, relinquish, reveal, tell, transmit. ANT.-conceal, hide, withhold.

impartial, *a.* SYN.-detached, dispassionate, equitable, fair, honest, just, reasonable, unbiased. ANT.-dishonorable, fraudulent, partial.

impartiality, *n.* SYN.-candor, disinterestedness, equality, fairness, indifference, insensibility, justice, neutrality, objectivity. ANT.-bias, favoritism, prejudice.

impasse, *n.* SYN.-deadlock, delay, draw, halt, stalemate, standoff, standstill; circumstance, condition, plight, predicament.

impeach, *v.* SYN.-accuse, arraign, challenge, charge, cite, criticize, denounce, discredit, incriminate, question. ANT.-absolve, acquit, clear, exonerate.

impeccable, *a.* SYN.-excellent, exquisite, faultless, flawless.

impede, *v.* SYN.-arrest, bar, block, check, clog, delay, deter, encumber, frustrate, hamper, hinder, interrupt, obstruct, restrain, retard, stop, thwart. ANT.-advance, assist, further, help, promote.

impediment, *n.* SYN.-bar, barrier, block, check, difficulty, handicap, hindrance, limitation, obstacle, obstruction, setback, snag. ANT.-aid, assistance, backing, encouragement, guidance, help, relief, support.

impel, *v.* SYN.-coerce, compel, drive, enforce, force, incite, motivate, oblige, prod, push, spur, urge. ANT.-allure, convince, induce, persuade, prevent.

impending, *a.* SYN.-approaching, close, immediate, imminent, menacing, nigh, overhanging, threatening. ANT.-distant, improbable, remote, retreating.

impertinent, *a.* SYN.-arrogant, discourteous, impolite, impudent, insolent, rude. ANT.-civil, courteous, humble, refined.

impenetrable, *a.* SYN.-compact, firm, hard, impervious, inscrutable, inviolable, rigid, solid, tough; incomprehensible, inexplicable, inscrutable, obscure, unintelligible. ANT.-flabby, plastic, soft; clear, understandable.

imperative, *a.* SYN.-cogent, compelling, critical, crucial, exigent, immediate, impelling, important, importunate, insistent, instant, necessary, pressing, serious, urgent; aggressive, autocratic, bossy commanding, domineering, imperial, masterful, powerful. ANT.-insignificant, petty, trifling, trivial, unimportant; feeble, impotent, powerless, weak, yielding.

imperceptible, *a.* SYN.-ambiguous, blurred, cryptic, dim, esoteric, inaudible, indistinct, indistinguishable, invisible, obscure, shadowy, indiscernible, unseen. ANT.-evident, perceptible, seen, visible.

imperfection, *n.* SYN.-blemish, defect, deformity, error, failure, fault, flaw, mistake, omission, shortcoming, vice. ANT.-completeness, correctness, perfection.

imperial, *a.* SYN.-majestic, princely, monarchical, regal, royal.

imperil, *v.* SYN.-hazard, jeopardize, risk, venture.

imperious, *a.* SYN.-arrogant, despotic, dictatorial, domineering, lordly, tyrannical.

impersonal, *a.* SYN.-detached, fair, impartial, objective, unbiased.

impersonate, *v.* SYN.-ape, copy, counterfeit, duplicate, imitate, mimic, mock, portray, pose, pretend, represent, simulate. ANT.-alter, distort, diverge, invent.

impertinence, *n.* SYN.-affront, audacity, boldness, disrespectfulness, effrontery, impudence, inappropriateness, injury, insolence, insult, offense, rudeness, sauciness, slight, slur. ANT.-diffidence, politeness, subserviency.

impertinent, *a.* SYN.-abusive, arrogant, brazen, contemptuous, discourteous, impolite, impudent, insolent, insulting, offensive, rude, saucy. ANT.-considerate, courteous, polite, respectful.

impetus, *n.* SYN.-cause, force, impulse, incentive, pressure, push, stimulus, thrust.

impetuous, *a.* SYN.-blind, careless, hasty, headlong, heedless, impulsive, irrational, passionate, quick, rash, uncontrolled, unreasonable. ANT.-calculating, cautious, reasoning.

implicate, *v.* SYN.-accuse, associate, blame, charge, cite, concern, condemn, hint, imply, include, involve, link, relate, suggest. ANT.-absolve, acquit, exonerate, ignore.

implicit, *a.* SYN.-absolute, accurate, assured, certain, confident, definite, doubtless, positive, satisfied, unequivocal, unquestionable; alluded, indicated, inferred, insinuated, intended, meant, suggested, tacit, understood.

implore, *v.* SYN.-adjure, appeal, ask, beg, beseech, crave, entreat, importune, petition, plead, pray, request, solicit, supplicate. ANT.-bestow, cede, favor, give, grANT.

imply, *v.* SYN.-connote, infer, insinuate, involve, mean, signify, suggest. ANT.-assert, express, state.

impolite, *a.* SYN.-arrogant, blunt, boorish, brazen, coarse, crude, discourteous, gruff, impudent, insolent, insulting, moody, primitive, rough, rude, saucy, surly, uncivil, unpolished, vulgar. ANT.-civil, genteel, polished; courtly, dignified, noble, stately.

importance, *n.* SYN.-emphasis, gravity, heaviness, import, influence, pressure, significance, stress, value, weight. ANT.-buoyancy, levity, lightness; insignificance, triviality.

important, *a.* SYN.-consequential, critical, decisive, grave, influential, material, meaningful, momentous, paramount, pressing, primary, prominent, relevant, significant, substantial, valuable, weighty. ANT.-commonplace, foolish, insignificant, irrelevant, little, mean, paltry, petty, trivial.

imposing, *a.* SYN.-august, dignified, exciting, grand, grandiose, high, impressive, lofty, magnificent, majestic, noble, overwhelming, pompous, stately, stirring, sublime, substantial. ANT.-common, humble, lowly, ordinary, undignified.

impossible, *a.* SYN.-fruitless, futile, hopeless, impractical, inaccessible, inconceivable, unattainable, unworkable, useless, vain.

impression, *n.* SYN.-concept, conjecture, feeling, image, notion, opinion, perception, sensation, sense, supposition, understanding; dent, indentation, mark, scar. ANT.-fact, insensibility, reality.

impressive, *a.* SYN.-absorbing, affecting, arresting, august, beautiful, commanding, dazzling, dramatic, eloquent, exciting, extraordinary, forceful, gorgeous, grand, grandiose, imposing, inspiring, magnificent, majestic, moving, notable, overpowering, profound, remarkable, splendid, stirring, striking, sumptuous, superb, thrilling, touching. ANT.-commonplace, ordinary, regular, unimpressive.

improve, *v.* SYN.-ameliorate, amend, augment, better, correct, enhance, enrich, help, modernize, progress, rectify, refine, reform, update. ANT.-corrupt, damage, debase, impair, vitiate.

improvement, *n.* SYN.-advance, advancement, alteration, amendment, betterment, development, enhancement, enrichment, growth, modernization, progress, progression, reformation, renovation, reorganization. ANT.-decline, delay, regression, relapse, retrogression.

imprudent, *a.* SYN.-careless, excessive, heedless, immoderate, improvident, inattentive, indiscreet, inordinate, lavish, lax, neglectful, negligent, prodigal, reckless, remiss, thoughtless. ANT.-accurate, careful, meticulous, nice.

impudence, *n.* SYN.-assurance, audacity, boldness, brass, cheek, discourtesy, effrontery, impertinence, insolence, nerve, presumption, rudeness, sauciness, temerity. ANT.-diffidence, politeness, subserviency, truckling.

impudent, *a.* SYN.-bold, brazen, discourteous, forward, fresh, impertinent, insolent, pushy, rude. ANT.-cowardly, flinching, timid; bashful, retiring.

impulsive, *a.* SYN.-careless, hasty, heedless, impetuous, offhand, passionate, quick, rash, spontaneous, unconstrained. ANT.-calculating, cautious, reasoning.

impure, *a.* SYN.-adulterated, contaminated, corrupt, corrupted, crooked, debased, depraved, diluted, dirty, immoral, profligate, putrid, spoiled, tainted, unclean, unsound, venal, vitiated.

inability, *n.* SYN.-disability, failure, handicap, impotence, incapacity, incompetence, weakness. ANT.-ability, capability, power, strength.

inaccurate, *a.* SYN.-amiss, askew, awry, distorted, erroneous, fallacious, false, faulty, imprecise, inexact, incorrect, mistaken, unprecise, untrue, wrong. ANT.-correct, right, true.

inactive, *a.* SYN.-dead, dormant, idle, indolent, inert, lazy, sluggish, slothful, stagnant, still, torpid, unemployed, unoccupied. ANT.-active, employed, industrious, occupied, working.

inadequate, *a.* SYN.-bare, defective, deficient, imperfect, incomplete, ineffective, insufficient, lacking, little, meager, scanty, scarce, short, spare, sparse, sufficient, wanting, weak. ANT.-adequate, ample, enough, satisfactory, sufficient.

inadvisable, *a.* SYN.-improper, imprudent, inappropriate, injudicious, unsuitable, unwise, wrong. ANT.-appropriate, correct, recommended, suitable.

inane, *a.* SYN.-absurd, dumb, foolish, pointless, ridiculous, silly, stupid.

inanimate, *a.* SYN.-dead, deceased, defunct, inert, insensible, lifeless, senseless, spiritless, unconscious, unfeeling. ANT.-alive, animate, living, spirited, stirring.

inattentive, *a.* SYN.-away, absent, absent-minded, abstracted, careless, distracted, forgetful, heedless, indifferent, indiscreet, neglectful, preoccupied, slack. ANT.-attending, present; attentive, watchful.

inaudible, *a.* SYN.-faint, indistinct, soft.

inaugurate, *v.* SYN.-begin, commence, induct, initiate, install, launch, originate, start.

inauspicious, *a.* SYN.-adverse, detrimental, negative, unfavorable.

incalculable, *a.* SYN.-bounless, immense, indefinite, infinite, limitless, uncertain, unpredictable, vast.

incantation, *n.* SYN.-charm, hex, spell.

incapacity, *n.* SYN.-disability, handicap, impotence; inability, incompetence, weakness. ANT.-ability, capability, power, strength.

incentive, *n.* SYN.-aim, bait, consideration, enticement, impetus, inducement, instigation, motive, rationale, reason, stimulation.

inception, *n.* SYN.-beginning, cause, commencement, derivation, opening, origin, outset, root, source, start. ANT.-close, completion, consummation, end, termination.

incessant, *a.* SYN.-ceaseless, constant, continual, continuous, endless, everlasting, nonstop, perennial, perpetual, persistent, unceasing, uninterrupted, unremitting. ANT.-interrupted, occasional, periodic, rare.

incident, *n.* SYN.-circumstance, condition, episode, event, fact, happening, occurrence, situation.

incidental, *a,* SYN.-accidental, ancillary, casual, chance, fortuitous, lucky, random, secondary, subordinate, supplemental, unplanned.

incinerate, *v.* SYN.-burn, char, consume, cremate, incinerate, scorch, sear, singe. ANT.-extinguish, put out, quench.

incisive, *a.* SYN.-acute, biting, brief, concise, condensed, crisp, cutting, neat, penetrating, pithy, succinct, summary, terse. ANT.-casual, lengthy, prolix, verbose, wordy.

incite, *v.* SYN.-arouse, cause, encourage, excite, foment, galvanize, goad, induce, inspire, instigate, prompt, provoke, rouse, spur, stimulate, urge. ANT.-bore, pacify, quiet, soothe.

inclination, *n.* SYN.-angle, bending, incline, lean, pitch, slope, tilt; affection, attachment, bent, bias, desire, disposition, leaning, liking, penchant, predilection, preference, propensity. ANT.-antipathy, apathy, aversion, coldness, dislike, distaste, indifference, nonchalance, repugnance, unconcern.

include, *v.* SYN.-accommodate, admit, combine, comprise, contain, cover, embody, embrace, entail, hold, incorporate, involve. ANT.-bar, discharge, emit, exclude, omit.

included, *a.* SYN.-admitted, combined, counted, entered, incorporated, inserted, merged, noted, numbered

incongruous, *a.* SYN.-absurd, alien, bizarre, contradictory, contrary, discrepant, inappropriate, incompatible, inharmonious, paradoxical, strange, unfitting, unsuitable. ANT.-consistent, harmonious, logical, proper, sensible.

inconsistency, *n.* SYN.-conflict, contention, controversy, deviation, difference, disagreement, discord, discrepancy, disparity, paradox, variance. ANT.-amity, concord, consonance, harmony.

inconsistent, *a.* SYN.-contradictory, changeable, contrary, discrepant, erratic, fickle, illogical, incompatible, incongruous, irreconcilable, paradoxical, unstable, unsteady, vacillating, wavering. ANT.-compatible, congruous, consistent, correspondent, harmonious, suitable.

inconspicuous, *a.* SYN.-blurred, cloudy, dim, faded, faint, indistinct, murky, obscure, quiet, sly, subtle.

inconstant, *a.* SYN.-capricious, changeable, fickle, fitful, shifting, uncertain, unreliable, unstable, vacillating, variable, wavering. ANT.-constant, stable, steady, unchanging, uniform.

inconvenient, *a.* SYN.-annoying, awkward, bothersome, difficult, disturbing, troublesome, untimely. ANT.-convenient, opportune, welcome.

incorporate, *v.* SYN.-add, blend, combine, consolidate, embody, fuse, include, join, merge, unite.

increase, *v.* SYN.-accrue, aggrandize, amplify, augment, boost, broaden, build, deepen, develop, dilate, enhance, enlarge, expand, extend, grow, heighten, intensify, lengthen, magnify, multiply, raise, supplement, thicken, wax, widen. ANT.-atrophy, contract, decrease, diminish, lessen, reduce.

incredible, *a.* SYN.-extraordinary, implausible, improbable, inconceivable, suspect, unbelievable, unimaginable, unthinkable. ANT.-believable, convincing, probable, rational.

indebted, *a.* SYN.-accountable, appreciative, beholden, grateful, gratified, obligated, obliged, responsible, thankful. ANT.-thankless, unappreciative.

indecent, *a.* SYN.-coarse, dirty, disgusting, filthy, gross, immodest, immoral, impure, indelicate, lascivious, lewd, nasty, obscene, offensive, pornographic, shameless, smutty, sordid. ANT.-decent, modest, pure, refined.

indefinite, *a.* SYN.-ambiguous, dim, equivocal, hazy, indecisive, indistinct, inexact, obscure, uncertain, unclear, vague; boundless, endless, eternal, infinite, unlimited.

indelible, *a.* SYN.-abiding, enduring, impressive, lasting, memorable, permanent, unforgettable.

independence, *n.* SYN.-autonomy, exemption, freedom, immunity, liberation, liberty, license, privilege, unrestraint. ANT.-bondage, captivity, compulsion, constraint, necessity, servitude, submission.

independent, *a.* SYN.-alone, autonomous, free, self-reliant, separate, unconstrained, uncontrolled, unrestrained, unrestricted, voluntary. ANT.-contingent, dependent, enslaved, restricted.

indestructible, *a.* SYN.-abiding, changeless, constant, durable, enduring, fixed, lasting, imperishable, permanent, stable, unchangeable. ANT.-ephemeral, temporary, transient, transitory, unstable.

indicate, *v.* SYN.-announce, attest, betoken, connote, denote, designate, disclose, hint, imply, insinuate, intimate, manifest, mark, point, reveal, say, show, signify, specify, suggest, symbolize, verify. ANT.-conceal, contradict, distract, divert, falsify, misdirect, mislead.

indication, *n.* SYN. clue, evidence, gesture, hint, implication, mark, omen, portent, proof, sign, signal, symbol, symptom, token.

indictment, *n.* SYN.-accusation, allegation, arraignment, censure, charge, complaint, imputation, incrimination, reproach. ANT.-exculpation, exoneration, pardon.

indifference, *n.* SYN.-aloofness, apathy, callousness, coldness, coolness, detachment, disdain, disinterestedness, heedlessness, impartiality, insensibility, insensitivity, neutrality, nonchalance, unconcern. ANT.-affection, ardor, attention, compassion, concern, enthusiasm, feeling, fervor, heed, importance, inclination, passion.

indifferent, *a.* SYN.-aloof, apathy, callous, cold, cool, detached, distant, heartless, impassive, mediocre, nonchalant, reserved, unemotional, unfeeling, unmoved, unsympathetic; average, common, conventional, fair, mediocre, ordinary, passable, undistinguished. ANT.-aroused, concerned, warm; exceptional, outstanding.

indigence, *n.* SYN.-destitution, distress, insolvency, necessity, need, penury, poverty, privation, WANT. ANT.-abundance, affluence, plenty, riches, wealth.

indigenous, *a.* SYN.-congenital, domestic, endemic, inborn, inherent, innate, local, native, natural.

indigent, *a.* SYN.-broke, destitute, distressed, impoverished, insolvent, needy, poor, poverty-stricken.

indignation, *n.* SYN.-anger, exasperation, ire, irritation, outrage, passion, resentment, temper, umbrage, wrath. ANT.-conciliation, forbearance, patience, peace, self-control.

indignity, *n.* SYN.-abuse, affront, betrayal, defilement, insolence, insult, mistreatment, offense, violation. ANT.-apology, homage, salutation

indirect, *a.* SYN.-circuitous, crooked, cunning, devious, distorted, erratic, implied, meandering, oblique, obscure, rambling, roundabout, sinister, swerving, tricky, tortuous, wandering, winding. ANT.-direct, honest, straight, straightforward.

indiscreet, *a.* SYN.-extravagant, foolish, hasty, naive, precipitate, rash, reckless, silly, tactless.

indiscretion, *a.* SYN.-absurdity, extravagance, folly, foolishness, imprudence, silliness. ANT.-judgment, prudence, reasonableness, sense, wisdom.

indispensable, *a.* SYN.-basic, essential, fundamental, imperative, important, intrinsic, necessary, needed, required, requisite, vital. ANT.-expendable, extrinsic, optional, peripheral.

indistinct, *a.* SYN.-abstruse, ambiguous, blurred, cloudy, cryptic, dark, dim, dusky, enigmatic, mysterious, obscure, unintelligible, unknown, vague. ANT.-bright, clear, distinct, lucid.

individual, *a.* SYN.-definite, distinct, distinctive, exclusive, marked, particular, personal, private, select, separate, singular, special, specific, unique. ANT.-common, general, ordinary, universal.

individuality, *n.* SYN.-character, description, disposition, distinctiveness, habit, identity, idiosyncrasy, kind, manner, nature, peculiarity, personality, reputation, repute, singularity.

indoctrinate, *v.* SYN.-convince, edify, enlighten, influence, initiate, instruct, orient, teach, train, tutor.

indomitable, *a.* SYN.-dauntless, impregnable, insurmountable, invincible, invulnerable, unassailable, unconquerable. ANT.-powerless, puny, vulnerable, weak.

induce, *v.* SYN.-begin, cause, create, effect, engender, evoke, generate, incite, influence, instigate, make, muster, occasion, originate, persuade, produce, prompt, spur, start, urge.

inducement, *n.* SYN.-cause, incentive, incitement, motive, principle, purpose, reason, spur, stimulus. ANT.-action, attempt, deed, effort, result.

indulge, *v.* SYN.-allow, cater, coddle, entertain, gratify, humor, pamper, permit, placate, please, suffer, tolerate,

indurate, *a.* SYN.-callous, cold, hard, hardened, heartless, impenitent, inured, insensible, insensitive, obdurate, tough, unfeeling. ANT.-compassionate, sensitive, soft, tender.

industrious, *a.* SYN.-active, assiduous, busy, diligent, hard-working, intent, patient, persevering. ANT.-apathetic, careless, indifferent, lethargic, unconcerned.

inebriated, *a.* SYN.-drunk, drunken, high, intoxicated, tight, tipsy. ANT.-clearheaded, sober, temperate.

ineffective, *a.* SYN.-debilitated, decrepit, delicate, feeble, impotent, infirm, illogical, inadequate, lame, poor, vague; irresolute, pliable, vacillating, wavering, weak; assailable, defenseless, exposed, vulnerable. ANT.-potent, powerful, robust, strong, sturdy.

inept, *a.* SYN.-awkward, clumsy, dumb, foolish, graceless, inappropriate, ridiculous, unfitting, unsuited. ANT.-adroit, appropriate, apt, competent, fit, skillful, suitable.

inertia, *n.* SYN.-idleness, inactivity, indolence, laziness, listlessness, passivity, sluggishness.

inequity, *n.* SYN.-bias, favoritism, grievance, inclination, iniquity, injury, injustice, partiality, unfairness, wrong. ANT.-equity, justice, lawfulness, righteousness.

inevitable, *a.* SYN.-assured, certain, definite, destined, fated, fixed, impending, indubitable, ordained, positive, predestined, secure, sure, unavoidable, undeniable, unquestionable. ANT.-doubtful, indeterminate, possible, probable, questionable, uncertain.

inexpensive, *a.* SYN.-cheap, common, economical, fair, inferior, low-priced, mean, moderate, modest, poor, reasonable, shabby, thrifty. ANT.-costly, dear, expensive.

inexperienced, *a.* SYN.-amateur, artless, fresh, green, innocent, naive, new, raw, uncultivated, unskilled, untrained, untried, youthful.

inexplicable, *a.* SYN.-abnormal, bizarre, cryptic, dark, dim, enigmatical, extraordinary, hidden, incomprehensible, inscrutable, mysterious, mystical, obscure, occult, peculiar, recondite, secret, strange, unusual. ANT.-clear, explained, obvious, plain, simple.

infect, *v.* SYN.-adulterate, befoul, contaminate, corrupt, defile, pervert, poison, pollute, sully, taint.

ANT.-disinfect, purify.

infection, *n.* SYN.-ailment, contagion, contamination, disease, germ, pest, poison, pollution, taint, virus.

infectious, *a.* SYN.-catching, communicable, contagious, pestilential, virulent. ANT.-healthful, hygienic, non-communicable.

infer, *v.* SYN.-hint, imply, insinuate, suggest; conclude, deduce, gather,

inference, *n.* SYN.-conclusion, consequence, corollary, deduction, judgment, reason, result, supposition. ANT.-assumption, foreknowledge, preconception, presupposition.

inferior, *a.* SYN.-common, lesser, lower, mediocre, minor, poor, poorer, secondary, subordinate, substandard. ANT.-better, greater, higher, superior.

infest, *v.* SYN.-defile, fill, flood, infect, invade, jam, overrun, pack, plague, press, pollute, ravage, spread, swarm, teem.

infidel, *n.* SYN.-agnostic, atheist, heathen, unbeliever.

infidelity, *n.* SYN.-betrayal, denial, disavowal, disloyalty, faithlessness, renunciation, unfaithfulness. ANT.-fealty, loyalty.

infiltrate, *n.* SYN.-join, penetrate, permeate, pervade, saturate.

infinite, *a.* SYN.-boundless, countless, endless, eternal, illimitable, immeasurable, immense, incalculable, inexhaustible, interminable, limitless, unbounded, unlimited, vast. ANT.-bounded, circumscribed, confined, finite, limited, restricted.

infirm, *a.* SYN.-decrepit, delicate, enervated, exhausted, faint, feeble, forceless, impaired, languid, powerless, puny, weak. ANT.-forceful, lusty, stout, strong, vigorous.

infirmity, *n.* SYN.-ailment, complaint, debility, disease, disorder, frailty, illness, malady, malaise, sickness, weakness. ANT.-health, healthiness, soundness, vigor.

inflame, *v.* SYN.-aggravate, arouse, chafe, disturb, enrage, excite, gall, grate, incense, incite, provoke, rile, stimulate. ANT.-alleviate, appease, calm, mollify, pacify.

inflate, *v.* SYN.-balloon, bloat, boost, enlarge, exaggerate, exalt, expand, fill, magnify, overestimate, stretch, swell.

inflection, *n.* SYN.-accent, articulation, emphasis, enunciation, intonation, pronunciation, tone.

inflexibility, *n.* SYN.-firmness, obstinacy, rigidity, stability, stiffness, stubbornness, tenacity, toughness.

inflexible, *a.* SYN.-determined, dogged, firm, headstrong, immovable, implacable, intractable, obdurate, obstinate, pertinacious, resolute, rigid, steadfast, stubborn, taut, unbending, uncompromising, unyielding. ANT.-amenable, compliant, docile, submissive, yielding.

inflict, *v.* SYN.-coerce, compel, demand, force, require.

influence, *n.* SYN.-authority, command, control, domination, effect, esteem, importance, prestige, power, prominence, weight. ANT.-impotence, inferiority, subjection, timidity.

influence, *v.* SYN.-activate, actuate, affect, bias, control, convince, direct, impel, impress, incite, induce, influence, inspire, mold, persuade, shape, stir, sway, train.

influential, *a.* SYN.-consequential, convincing, critical, decisive, effective, forceful, grave, important, material, momentous, powerful, prominent, relevant, significant, substantial. ANT.-insignificant, irrelevant, mean, petty, trivial.

inform, *v.* SYN.-acquaint, advise, apprise, enlighten, familiarize, impart, instruct, notify, relate, squeal, tattle, teach, tell, testify, warn. ANT.-conceal, delude, distract, mislead.

informal, *a.* SYN.-congenial, easy, familiar, intimate, natural, offhand, ordinary, relaxed, simple, spontaneous, unceremonious, unofficial. ANT.-ceremonious, conventional, distant, formal, precise, proper, reserved, restrained.

informality, *n.* SYN.-closeness, familiarity, frankness, friendliness, intimacy, liberty, unconstrained, unreserved. ANT.-constraint, distance, haughtiness.

information, *n.* SYN.-data, evidence, facts, figures, knowledge, learning, material, statistics.

infraction, *n.* SYN.-breach, indiscretion, infringement, transgression, violation.

infrequent, *a.* SYN.-exceptional, limited, occasional, rare, scarce, seldom, singular, uncommon, unique, unusual. ANT.-abundant, commonplace, frequent, numerous, often, ordinary, usual.

infringe, *v.* SYN.-encroach, intrude, invade, offend, poach, transgress, violate.

infuriate, *v.* SYN.-affront, aggravate, anger, enrage, madden, provoke.

infuse, *v.* SYN.-fill, imbue, impregnate, indoctrinate, ingrain, permeate, saturate.

ingenious, *a.* SYN.-acute, adroit, apt, astute, bright, clever, dexterous, keen, original, quick, quick-witted, sharp, skillful, smart, talented, witty. ANT.-awkward, bungling, clumsy, dull, foolish, slow, stupid, unskilled.

ingenuity, *n.* SYN.-ability, aptitude, artifice, cleverness, cunning, faculty, imagination, ingeniousness, inventiveness, resourcefulness, skill ANT.-clumsiness, dullness, inaptitude, stupidity.

ingenuous, *a.* SYN.-artless, candid, frank, free, guileless, honest, innocent, instinctive, naive, open, plain, simple, sincere, spontaneous, straightforward, truthful. ANT.-contrived, scheming, sly, wily.

ingest, *v.* SYN.-consume, devour, eat, swallow.

ingredient, *n.* SYN.-additive, component, constituent, element, part.

inhabit, *v.* SYN.-abide, dwell, fill, live, occupy, permeate, possess, reside, stay. ANT.-abandon, release, relinquish.

inhabitant, *n.* SYN.-dweller, native, occupant, resident.

inherent, *a.* SYN.-congenital, inborn, inbred, innate, instinctive, intrinsic, native, natural, real. ANT.-acquired, external, extraneous, extrinsic, superficial.

inherit, *v.* SYN.-acquire, gain, get, obtain, receive, secure.

inhibit, *v.* SYN.-arrest, ban, bridle, check, constrain, curb, discourage, forbid, frustrate, hinder, limit, obstruct, prohibit, repress, restrain, stop, suppress. ANT.-adopt, aid, allow, authorize, consent, encourage, grant, incite, loosen.

inhuman, *a.* SYN.-barbarous, brutal, callous, cruel, ferocious, heartless, malignant, merciless, monstrous, pitiless, ruthless, satanic, savage. ANT.-benevolent, compassionate, forbearing, gentle, humane, kind, merciful.

inimical, *a.* SYN.-antagonistic, averse, contrary, harmful, hurtful, noxious, repugnant.

inimitable, *a.* SYN.-incomparable, matchless, peerless, rare, singular, uncommon, unequaled, unique, unsurpassed.

iniquitous, *a.* SYN.-bad, baleful, base, corrupt, deleterious, depraved, evil, immoral, noxious, pernicious, sinful, unjust, unsound, unwholesome, villainous, wicked. ANT.-excellent, good, honorable, moral, reputable.

iniquity, *n.* SYN.-corruption, depravity, evil, inequity, injury, injustice, sin, unfairness, wrong. ANT.-equity, justice, lawfulness, righteousness.

initial, *a.* SYN.-beginning, earliest, elementary, first, inaugural, introductory, original, primary, prime, primeval, primitive, pristine; chief, foremost, leading, primary. ANT.-hindmost, last, latest; least, subordinate.

initiate, *v.* SYN.-arise, begin, commence, inaugurate, induct, install, instate, institute, introduce, launch, open, originate, propose, sponsor, start. ANT.-close, complete, end, finish, terminate.

injudicious, *a.* SYN.-foolish, impolitic, imprudent, indiscreet, senseless, silly.

injure, *v.* SYN.-abuse, affront, batter, damage, disfigure, dishonor, harm, hurt, impair, insult, maltreat, mar, spoil, wound, wrong. ANT.-ameliorate, benefit, compliment, help, praise, preserve.

injurious, *a.* SYN.-abusive, damaging, defamatory, deleterious, derogatory, detrimental, destructive, harmful, hurtful, inequitable, insulting, libelous, offensive, slanderous, unfair, unjust. ANT.-advantageous, beneficial, good, helpful, profitable, salutary, useful.

injury, *n.* SYN.-abrasion, affliction, blemish, damage, detriment, grievance, harm, hurt, impairment, injustice, laceration, mischief, outrage, prejudice, slight, wound, wrong. ANT.-aid, assistance, benefit, improvement, relief, repair, service.

injustice, *n.* SYN.-abuse, breach, crime, grievance, inequity, iniquity, injury, transgression, unfairness, villainy, wrong. ANT.-equity, fairness, honest, impartiality, integrity, just, justice, lawfulness, right, righteousness.

inkling, *n.* SYN.-clue, hint, hunch, inference, insinuation, notion, suggestion.

innate, *a.* SYN.-ancestral, congenital, hereditary, inborn, inbred, inherent, inherited, innate, intrinsic, intuitive, native, natural, real. ANT.-acquired, external, extraneous, extrinsic.

innocent, *a.* SYN.-artless, blameless, faultless, forthright, guileless, harmless, honest, innocuous, lawful, legitimate, naive, pure, simple, sinless, unblemished, undefiled, virtuous ANT.-corrupt, culpable, guilty, sinful, unrighteous.

innocuous, *a.* SYN.-harmless, innocent, safe.

innovation, *n.* SYN.-alteration, change, difference, diversity, feature, highlight, modification, specialty, variation.

innovate, *v.* SYN.-alter, change, conceive, create, ideate, modify, renew, switch, transform, vary.

innuendo, *n.* SYN.-affront, blot, defamation, insult, slander, slight, slur, smear, vilification.

innumerable, *a.* SYN.-countless, incalculable, immeasurable, indefinite, infinite, many, numerous, unlimited.

inoffensive, *a.* SYN.-harmless, innocent, innocuous.

inopportune, *a.* SYN.-awkward, embarrassing, improper, inappropriate, uncomfortable, unpleasant, untimely.

inordinate, *a.* SYN.-excessive, exorbitant, extravagant, imprudent, lavish, prodigal.

inquire, *v.* SYN.-ask, interrogate, investigate, probe, pry, query, question, search. ANT.-command, dictate, insist, order, reply.

inquiring, *a.* SYN.-curious, inquisitive, interrogative, meddling, nosy, peeping, peering, prying, searching, snoopy. ANT.-incurious, indifferent, unconcerned, uninterested.

inquiry, *n.* SYN.-examination, exploration, inquest, interrogation, investigation, probe, query, quest, question, research, scrutiny. ANT.-assumption, conjecture, disregard, guess, inactivity, inattention, intuition, negligence, supposition.

inquisitive, *a.* SYN.-curious, inquiring, interested, interrogative, nosy, peeping, peering, prying, questioning, searching, snoopy. ANT.-incurious, indifferent, unconcerned, uninterested.

insane, *a.* SYN.-crazy, daft, delirious, demented, deranged, frenzied, lunatic, mad, maniacal, psychotic, touched. ANT.-rational, reasonable, sane, sensible, sound.

insanity, *n.* SYN.-aberration, compulsion, craziness, delirium, dementia, derangement, frenzy, hysteria, lunacy, madness, mania, obsession, psychosis. ANT.-rationality, sanity, stability.

insatiable, *a.* SYN.-avaricious, gluttonous, grasping, greedy, ravenous, starved, voracious.

inscribe, *v.* SYN.-catalog, engrave, enter, inventory, list, record, register.

inscrutable, *a.* SYN.-impenetrable, incomprehensible, inexplicable, mysterious, strange.

insecurity, *n.* SYN.-anxiety, doubt, indecision, uncertainty, vulnerability; danger, exposure, hazard, jeopardy, liability, peril, pitfall, vulnerability.

insensitive, *a.* SYN.-callous, hard, impenitent, indurate, insensible, obdurate, obstinate, remorseless, tough, unfeeling. ANT.-compassionate, sensitive, soft, tender.

inseparable, *a.* SYN.-attached, connected, indivisible, integrated, integral, joined, united.

insert, *v.* SYN.-add, append, enclose, include, inject, introduce.

insidious, *a.* SYN.-artful, beguiling, corrupting, crafty, cunning, deceitful, evil, treacherous.

insight, *n.* SYN.-acumen, awareness, discernment, discretion, intuition, penetration, perception, perspicuity, recognition, sense, understanding. ANT.-obtuseness.

insignificant, *a.* SYN.-frivolous, irrelevant, paltry, petty, small, trifling, trivial, unimportant, worthless. ANT.-important, momentous, serious, weighty.

insincere, *a.* SYN.-deceitful, dishonest, hypocritical, pretentious, shifty, superficial.

insinuate, *v.* SYN.-allude, connote,

hint, imply, intimate, involve, mean, signify, suggest. ANT.-assert, express, state.

insipid, *a.* SYN.-banal, bland, dull, flat, prosaic, stale, tasteless, uninteresting, vapid. ANT.-exciting, racy, savory, tasty.

insist, *v.* SYN.-allege, ask, assert, charge, claim, contend, demand, expect, maintain.

insistent, *a.* SYN.-determined, obstinate, persistent, relentless, resolute, tenacious, unrelenting.

insolence, *n.* SYN.-arrogance, audacity, boldness, defiance, disdain, effrontery, haughtiness, impertinence, impudence, loftiness, presumption, pride, rudeness, sauciness. ANT.-diffidence, politeness, subserviency, truckling.

insolent, *a.* SYN.-abusive, arrogant, bold, brazen, contemptuous, defiant, disrespectful, haughty, impertinent, impudent, insulting, offensive, overbearing, proud, rude. ANT.-considerate, courteous, polite, respectful.

inspect, *v.* SYN.-ascertain, determine, examine, eye, fathom, gaze, investigate, look, observe, probe, regard, scan, see, stare, survey, view, watch, witness. ANT.-avert, hide, miss, overlook.

inspection, *n.* SYN.-critique, examination, retrospect, retrospection, review, survey, synopsis, test.

inspiration, *n.* SYN.-ability, aptitude, bent, creativity, faculty, genius, gift, hunch, impulse, inclination, intellect, motivation, notion, originality, sagacity, stimulus, talent, whim. ANT.-ineptitude, obtuseness, shallowness, stupidity.

inspire, *v.* SYN.-animate, encourage, enliven, hearten, invigorate, motivate, spark, spur, stimulate.

instability, *n.* SYN.-changeability, fickleness, fluctuation, imbalance, immaturity, inconsistency, transience, vacillation.

install, *v.* SYN.-build, establish, inaugurate, induct, initiate, introduce.

instance, *n.* SYN.-case, example, illustration, occurrence, representation, sample, situation, specimen.

instantaneous, *a.* SYN.-abrupt, hasty, immediate, rapid, sudden, unexpected. ANT.-anticipated, gradual, slowly.

instantly, adv. SYN.-directly, forthwith, immediately, instantaneously, now, presently, promptly, straight-away. ANT.-distantly, hereafter, later, shortly, sometime.

instigate, *v.* SYN.-encouage, foment, foster, incite, induce, influence, persuade.

instill, *v.* SYN.-educate, imbue, impute, indoctrinate, inform, infuse, instruct.

instinctive, *a.* SYN.-automatic, extemporaneous, impulsive, inborn, inherent, innate, intuitive, offhand, spontaneous, subconscious, voluntary, willing. ANT.-compulsory, forced, planned, prepared, rehearsed.

institute, *v.* SYN.-establish, form, found, organize, raise. ANT.-abolish, demolish, overthrow, unsettle, upset.

instruct, *v.* SYN.-brief, command, direct, educate, guide, help, inculcate, inform, instill, order, school, teach, train, tutor. ANT.-misguide, misinform.

instruction, *n.* SYN.-admonition, advice, caution, counsel, exhortation, recommendation, suggestion;

information, intelligence, notification.

instrument, *n.* SYN.-agent, apparatus, device, means, medium, tool, utensil, vehicle. ANT.-hindrance, impediment, obstruction, preventive.

instrumental, *a.* SYN.-contributory, effective, helpful, useful.

insubordinate, *a.* SYN.- defiant, disobedient, mutinous, rebellious, refractory, seditious, undutiful, unruly. ANT.-compliant, dutiful, obedient, submissive.

insubstantial, *a.* SYN.-ephemeral, ethereal, flimsy, immaterial, inconsequential, insignificant, insubstantial, intangible, negligible, tenuous, trifling, trivial, unimportant.

insufferable, *a.* SYN.-disagreeable, intolerable, obnoxious, odious, offensive, onerous, painful, repulsive, taxing.

insufficient, *a.* SYN.-low, undersized; deficient, inadequate, lacking, limited, meager, short, skimpy, thin, wanting, weak. ANT.-abundant, ample, enough, extended, protracted.

insulation, *n.* SYN.-alienation, covering, isolation, loneliness, protector, quarantine, retirement, seclusion, segregation, separation, solitude, withdrawal. ANT.-association, communion, connection, fellowship, union.

insult, *n.* SYN.-abuse, affront, derision, discourtesy, indignity, insolence, invective, libel, offense, ridicule, scorn, slander, slap, slur. ANT.-apology, homage, praise, salutation

insult, *v.* SYN.-abuse, affront, belittle, dishonor, hurt, injure, libel, mock, offend, revile, ridicule, slander, slur, taunt, wound, wrong. ANT.-compliment, praise.

insulting, *a.* SYN.-abusive, contemptuous, degrading, humiliating, impertinent, nasty, offensive, outrageous.

intact, *a.* SYN.-complete, entire, perfect, sound, unbroken, undamaged, undivided, whole

intangible, *a.* SYN.-ethereal, hypothetical, immaterial, incorporeal, vague, vaporous.

integrated, *a.* SYN.-blended, combined, mixed, synthesized, united.

integrity, *n.* SYN.-candor, fairness, frankness, goodness, honesty, honor, justice, morality, openness, perfection, principle, rectitude, responsibility, sincerity, trustworthiness, uprightness, virtue. ANT.-cheating, corruption, deceit, disgrace, dishonesty, duplicity, fraud, meanness, trickery.

intellect, *n.* SYN.-ability, acumen, brain, intelligence, mentality, mind, propensity, reason, sense, talent, understanding. ANT.-emotion, feeling, passion.

intelligence, *n.* SYN.-comprehension, discernment, information, knowledge, perspicacity, reason, sense, understanding

intelligent, *a.* SYN.-alert, astute, bright, clever, contemplative, discerning, discriminating, enlightened, intellectual, keen, knowledgeable, perceptive, profound, quick, reasonable, reasoning, smart, well-informed. ANT.-dull, foolish, insipid, obtuse, slow, stupid.

intend, *v.* SYN.-aim, aspire, contrive, delineate, design, determine, devise, expect, mean, outline, plan, plot, prepare, project, propose, resolve, scheme.

intense, *a.* SYN.-acute, animated, bright, brilliant, clear, concentrated, deep, earnest, expressive, fervent, fresh, graphic, heightened, impassioned, intensive, keen, lively, lucid, piercing, powerful, profound, severe, stinging, striking, strong, vivid. ANT.-dim, dreary, dull, dusky, vague.

intensify, *v.* SYN.-amplify, augment, compound, confound, emphasize, enhance, enlarge, exacerbate, expand, extend, grow, heighten, increase, magnify, multiply, raise, sharpen, strengthen, wax. ANT.-atrophy, contract, decrease, diminish, reduce.

intensity, *n.* SYN.-ardor, concentration, depth, emphasis, fervor, force, magnitude, passion, power, severity, stress, vehemence, vigor.

intent, *a.* SYN.-engrossed, firm, rapt, resolute, steadfast.

intent, *n.* SYN.-aim, delineation, design, focus, import, intention, meaning, objective, outline, plan, purpose, significance. ANT.-accident, chance.

intention, *n.* SYN.-aim, contrivance, delineation, design, draft, end, intention, objective, outline, plan, plotting, purpose, scheming. ANT.-accident, candor, chance, result.

intentional, *a.* SYN.-conscious, considered, contemplated, deliberate, designed, intended, premeditated, studied, voluntary, wanton, willful. ANT.-accidental, fortuitous.

intercept, *v.* SYN.-ambush, block, catch, interfere, overtake, reach.

interest, *n.* SYN.-attention, concern, curiosity, regard; advantage, benefit, claim, gain, percentage, profit, share, stake.

interested, *a.* SYN.-absorbed, affected, attentive, attracted, biased, curious, drawn, engrossed, impressed, inquiring, inquisitive, inspired, involved, moved, prying, nosy, responsive, stimulated, stirred, touched.

interesting, *a.* SYN.-absorbing, amusing, arresting, captivating, enchanting, engaging, enticing, exciting, fascinating, impressive, pleasing, satisfying

interfere, *v.* SYN.-compete, conflict, contend, interpose, interrupt, intervene, meddle, mix in, monkey, pry, question, tamper, vie.

interior, *a.* SYN.-center, central, inmost, inner, internal, intrinsic, inward. ANT.-adjacent, exterior, external, outer.

interject, *v.* SYN.-include, inject, insert, interpose, introduce.

interjection, *n.* SYN.-cry, exclamation, utterance.

interminable, *a.* SYN.-boundless, ceaseless, dull, endless, eternal, illimitable, immeasurable, immense, infinite, monotonous, unbounded, unlimited, vast. ANT.-bounded, circumscribed, confined, finite, limited.

intermittent, *a.* SYN.-broken, disconnected, erratic, irregular, periodic, recurrent, spasmodic.

internal, *a.* SYN.-constitutional, domestic, indigenous, inherent, innate, inside, inward, organic, private.

interpose, *v.* SYN.-arbitrate, inject, insert, intercede, interfere, interject, intervene, introduce, intrude, meddle, mediate. ANT.-avoid, disregard, overlook.

interpret, *v.* SYN.-clarify, construe,

decipher, decode, define, diagnose, elucidate, explain, explicate, portray, render, solve, translate, unravel. ANT.-confuse, distort, falsify, misconstrue, misinterpret.

interpretation, *n.* SYN.-account, analysis, commentary, definition, description, diagnosis, explanation, portrayal, rendering, representation, translation, version.

interrogate, *v.* SYN.-ask, audit, check, examine, inquire, pump, query, question, quiz. ANT.-disregard, omit, overlook.

interrupt, *v.* SYN.-adjourn, break, check, defer, delay, discontinue, interfere, interject, intervene, intrude, postpone, stay, suspend. ANT.-continue, maintain, persist, proceed, prolong.

intervene, *v.* SYN.-arbitrate, intercede, interfere, interpose, meddle, mediate, negotiate. ANT.-avoid, disregard, overlook.

intimacy, *n.* SYN.-affection, closeness, familiarity, fellowship, frankness, friendship, informality, liberty, love, sociability, warmth. ANT.-constraint, distance, haughtiness, reserve.

intimate, *a.* SYN.-affectionate, chummy, close, confidential, familiar, friendly, loving, near, personal, private. ANT.-ceremonious, conventional, distant, formal.

intimation, *n.* SYN.-allusion, connotation, hint, implication, indication, inference, innuendo, insinuation, reminder, suggestion. ANT.-affirmation, declaration, statement.

intolerant, *a.* SYN.-biased, bigoted, dogmatic, fanatical, narrow, narrow-minded, opinionated, parochial, prejudiced. ANT.-liberal, progressive, radical, tolerant.

intoxicate, *v.* SYN.-befuddle, confuse, elate, excite, exhilarate, inebriate, invigorate, muddle, stimulate, thrill.

intoxicated, *a.* SYN.-drunk, drunken, high, inebriated, tight, tipsy; elated, euphoric, excited, exhilarated, infatuated, stimulated. ANT.-clearheaded, sober, temperate; calm, cool, unconcerned.

intricate, *a.* SYN.-abstract, abstruse, complex, complicated, compound, involved, perplexing, puzzling. ANT.-plain, simple, uncomplicated.

intrigue, *n.* SYN.-artifice, cabal, conspiracy, design, machination, plan, plot, scheme, stratagem.

intriguing, *a.* SYN.-appealing, attractive, charming, engaging, entertaining, fascinating, interesting, pleasing.

intrinsic, *a.* SYN.-congenital, inborn, inbred, ingrained, inherent, innate, native, natural, real. ANT.-acquired, external, extraneous, extrinsic.

introduce, *v.* SYN.-add, advance, begin, inaugurate, initiate, insert, insinuate, institute, interject, offer, present, propose,

introduction, *n.* SYN.-admittance, baptism, beginning, debut, forward, initiation, overture, preamble, preface, prelude, presentation, prologue, start. ANT.-completion, conclusion, end, epilogue, finale.

introductory, *a.* SYN.-basic, beginning, early, initial, opening, original, preparatory, primary, starting.

intrude, *v.* SYN.-encroach, impose, infringe, intervene, invade, penetrate, trespass, violate. ANT.-abandon, evacuate, relinquish, vacate.

intuition, *n.* SYN.-acumen, clue, discernment, feeling, hunch, insight, penetration, perspicuity, premonition, prescience, presentiment. ANT.-obtuseness.

intuitive, *a.* SYN.-automatic, natural, spontaneous; clairvoyant, discerning, insightful, perceptive.

invade, *v.* SYN.-assault, attack, encroach, infringe, intrude, penetrate, raid, storm, transgress, trespass, violate. ANT.-abandon, evacuate, relinquish, vacate.

invalid, *a.* SYN.-defective, erroneous, fallacious, groundless, illogical, irrational, null, void.

invalidate, *v.* SYN.-annul, belie, cancel, contradict, deny, discredit, negate, nullify, refute, reject, repeal, revoke, void.

invaluable, *a.* SYN.-expensive, inestimable, precious, priceless, valuable. ANT.-cheap, useless, worthless.

invariable, *a.* SYN.-changeless, consistent, constant, static, unchanging, uniform.

invasion, *n.* SYN.-aggression, assault, attack, incursion, offensive, onslaught, raid. ANT.-defense, opposition, resistance, surrender.

invective, *n.* SYN.-abuse, aspersion, censure, defamation, denunciation. desecration, dishonor, disparagement, insult, outrage, perversion, profanation, reproach, reviling, scorn, upbraiding, vituperation. ANT.-approval, commendation, laudation, plaudit, respect.

invent, *v.* SYN.-conceive, concoct, contrive, create, design, devise, discover, fabricate, fashion, forge, frame, originate, plan. ANT.-copy, imitate, reproduce.

inventive, *a.* SYN.-bright, clever, creative, fanciful, imaginative, resourceful, visionary. ANT.-dull, literal, prosaic, unromantic.

inventiveness, *n.* SYN.-ability, adroitness, cleverness, cunning, dexterity, expertise, faculty, imagination, ingeniousness, ingenuity, resourcefulness, skill. ANT.-clumsiness, dullness, inaptitude, stupidity.

invert, *v.* SYN.-change, overthrow, overturn, reverse, subvert, transpose, unmake, upset. ANT.-maintain, stabilize.

investigate, *v.* SYN.-analyze, examine, explore, ferret, inquire, interrogate, look, probe, question, research, scour, scrutinize, search, seek, study, test.

investigation, *n.* SYN.-examination, exploration, inquiry, interrogation, query, quest, question, research, scrutiny. ANT.-disregard, inactivity, inattention, negligence.

invincible, *a.* SYN.-impregnable, indomitable, insurmountable, invulnerable, unassailable, unconquerable. ANT.-powerless, puny, vulnerable, weak.

invigorate, *v.* SYN.-animate, energize, enliven, excite, exhilarate, rejuvenate, revive, stimulate.

invigorating, *a.* SYN.-bracing, cool, exhilarating, fresh, quickening, refreshing, stimulating.

invisible, *a.* SYN.-ethereal, imperceptible, indistinguishable, intangible, obscure, undiscernible, unseen. ANT.-evident, perceptible, seen, visible.

invitation, *n.* SYN.-attraction, encouragement, lure, offer, overture, request, summons, temptation.

invite, *v.* SYN.-ask, attract, beg, bid, draw, entice, implore, lure, persuade, petition, request, solicit, summon, tempt.

inviting, *a.* SYN.-alluring, appealing,

attractive, bewitching, captivating, encouraging, fascinating, magnetic, tempting.

involve, *v.* SYN.-comprise, embrace, embroil, entangle, envelop, implicate, include, incriminate. ANT.-disconnect, disengage, extricate, separate.

involved, *a.* SYN.-absorbed, complex, complicated, compound, elaborate, implicated, intricate, mesmerized, perplexing. ANT.-plain, simple, uncompounded.

invulnerable, *a.* SYN.-impenetrable, impervious, impregnable, indomitable, insurmountable, invincible, steadfast, unassailable, unconquerable. ANT.-powerless, puny, vulnerable, weak.

irate, *a.* SYN.-angry, enraged, furious, incensed, mad, raging.

ire, *n.* SYN.-anger, animosity, choler, frenzy, fury, indignation, irritation, passion, petulance, rage, raving, resentment, temper, vehemence, wrath. ANT.-conciliation, forbearance, patience, peace, self-control.

irk, *v.* SYN.-annoy, beset, bother, chafe, disturb, inconvenience, irritate, molest, pester, tease, torment, trouble, vex, worry. ANT.-accommodate, console, gratify, soothe.

ironic, *a.* SYN.-caustic, contradictory, contrary, cynical, derisive, incongruous, mocking, paradoxical, sardonic, scathing.

irrational, *a.* SYN.-absurd, contradictory, fallacious, foolish, illogical, inconsistent, nonsensical, preposterous, ridiculous, silly, specious, unreasonable, untenable. ANT.-consistent, rational, reasonable, sensible, sound.

irregular, *a.* SYN.-aberrant, abnormal, capricious, devious, divergent, eccentric, fitful, inconstant, intermittent, random, sporadic, unequal, uneven, unnatural, unusual, variable. ANT.-fixed, methodical, ordinary, regular, usual.

irrelevant, *a.* SYN.-alien, contrasted, extraneous, foreign, inapplicable, pointless, remote, strange, unconnected. ANT.-akin, germane, kindred, relevant.

irresistible, *a.* SYN.-alluring, charming compelling, enchanting, enticing, fascinating, invincible, overwhelming, tantalizing, tempting.

irresolute, *a.* SYN.-assailable, bending, inadequate, ineffective, insecure, pliable, pliant, undecided, unstable, unsteady, vacillating, vulnerable, wavering, weak, yielding. ANT.-potent, powerful, robust, strong, sturdy.

irresponsible, *a.* SYN.-capricious, fickle, flighty, immoral, loose, rash, shiftless, thoughtless, unreliable, unstable.

irritable, *a.* SYN.-choleric, excitable, fiery, hasty, hot, irascible, peevish, petulant, sensitive, snappish, tense, testy, touchy. ANT.-agreeable, calm, composed, tranquil.

irritant, *n.* SYN.-aggravation, annoyance, bother, inconvenience, nuisance, pest.

irritate, *v.* SYN.-annoy, bother, chafe, disturb, gall, harass, harry, haze, irk, molest, pester, provoke, tease, torment, trouble, vex. ANT.-accommodate, console, gratify, soothe.

irritation, *n.* SYN.-annoyance, bother, displeasure, exasperation, pique, stress, vexation. ANT.-appeasement, comfort, gratification, pleasure.

isolated, *a.* SYN.-alone, apart, deserted, desolate, lone, lonely, only, remote, secluded, segregated, separate, single, sole, solitary, withdrawn. ANT.-accompanied, attended, surrounded.

isolation, *n.* SYN.-alienation, detachment, insulation, loneliness, privacy, quarantine, retirement, seclusion, segregation, separation, solitude, withdrawal. ANT.-association, communion, connection, fellowship, union.

issue, *v.* SYN.-abound, come, discharge, emanate, emerge, emit, flow, gush, originate, release, run, spout, spurt, stream, vent.

itinerant, *a.* SYN.-drifting, nomadic, roaming, roving, wandering.

itinerant, *n.* SYN.-nomad, tramp, vagabond, vagrant, wanderer.

J

jabber, *n.* SYN.-babble, chatter, drivel, gibberish, nonsense, patter, twaddle.

jaded, *a.* SYN.-cold, impassive, indifferent, nonchalant, numbed, weary.

jam, *n.* SYN.-difficulty, predicament, problem, trouble.

jam, *v.* SYN.-compress, crowd, crush, jostle, mob, pack, press, ram, squeeze.

jammed, *a.* SYN.-blocked, caught, congested, crowded, frozen, obstructed, overflowing, swarming, wedged.

jargon, *n.* SYN.-cant, colloquialism, dialect, idiom, language, lingo, patter, phraseology, slang, speech, tongue, vernacular. ANT.-babble, drivel, gibberish, nonsense.

jaunt, *n.* SYN.-excursion, journey, junket, pilgrimage, tour, trip, voyage, walk.

jealous, *a.* SYN.-apprehensive, demanding, doubting, envious, mistrustful, possessive, resentful, suspicious, vigilant, watchful.

jealousy, *n.* SYN.-covetousness, distrust, envy, invidiousness, mistrust, possessiveness, resentfulness, resentment, suspicion. ANT.-geniality, indifference, liberality, tolerance.

jeer, *v.* SYN.-boo, deride, flout, gibe, insult, mock, ridicule, scoff, sneer, taunt. ANT.-compliment, flatter, laud, praise.

jeering, *n.* SYN.-banter, derision, gibe, insult, irony, mockery, raillery, ridicule, sarcasm, satire, sneering.

jeopardize, *v.* SYN.-endanger, expose, hazard, imperil, peril, risk, venture. ANT.-guard, insure.

jerk, *n.* SYN.-convulsion, flick, jiggle, quiver, tic, twitch; ass, fool, nincompoop, rascal, scamp, scoundrel, simpleton.

jester, *n.* SYN.-buffoon, clown, fool, harlequin. ANT.-philosopher, sage, scholar.

jewel, *n.* SYN.-adornment, bangle, bauble, gem, ornament, trinket.

job, *n.* SYN.-assignment, business, career, chore, employment, errand, function, labor, mission, obligation, occupation, pursuit, position, post, profession, situation, stint, task, toil, work, undertaking, vocation.

join, *v.* SYN.-accompany, adjoin, assemble, associate, attach, cement, clamp, combine, conjoin, connect, consolidate, contact, couple, fuse, link, marry, touch, unite, weld. ANT.-detach, disconnect, disjoin, separate.

joined, *a.* SYN.-allied, affiliated, associated, attached, banded, blended, cemented, combined, connected, coupled, fused, involved, linked, melded, mingled, unified, united, wed.

joke, *v.* SYN.-banter, fool, frolic, jest, josh, kid, laughter, play, pun, quip, tease, trick.

jolly, *a.* SYN.-cheerful, gay, glad, happy, jovial, joyful, joyous, lighthearted, merry, mirthful, sprightly. ANT.-depressed, glum, mournful, sad, sullen.

jolt, *v.* SYN.-bounce, jar, quake, rock, shake, shudder, tremble, vibrate, waver.

journey, *n.* SYN.-cruise, expedition, jaunt, passage, pilgrimage, safari, tour, travel, trip, venture, voyage.

journey, *v.* SYN.-drive, go, jaunt, ramble, ride, roam, rove, tour, travel, trek. ANT.-stay, stop.

jovial, *a.* SYN.-affable, amiable, congenial, convivial, cordial, friendly, happy, jocular, jolly, merry.

joy, *n.* SYN.-bliss, delight, ecstasy, elation, exultation, festivity, gaiety, glee, felicity, happiness, jubilation, levity, merriment, mirth, pleasure, rapture, rejoicing, transport. ANT.-affliction, depression, despair, grief, sorrow.

joyful, *a.* SYN.-blessed, cheerful, contented, delighted, fortunate, gay, glad, happy, joyous, lucky, merry, opportune, propitious. ANT.-blue, depressed, gloomy, morose.

joyous, *a.* SYN.-blithe, cheerful, festive, gay, gleeful, hilarious, jolly, jovial, lively, merry, mirthful, sprightly. ANT.-gloomy, melancholy, morose, sad, sorrowful.

judge, *n.* SYN.-adjudicator, arbitrator, critic, justice, magistrate, referee, umpire.

judge, *v.* SYN.-; adjudicate, arbitrate, condemn, try, umpire; appreciate, consider, decide, decree, deem, determine, estimate, evaluate, measure, think.

judgment, *n.* SYN.-acuity, appraisal, assessment, awareness, belief, comprehension, consideration, conviction, discernment, discrimination, finding, grasp, intelligence, knowledge, mentality, opinion, perspicacity, profundity, prudence, rationality, sagacity, taste, understanding, view, wisdom. ANT.-arbitrariness, senselessness, stupidity, thoughtlessness.

judicious, *a.* SYN.-discreet, expedient, intelligent, politic, practical, prudent, rational, sensible, sober, sound, wise. ANT.-blind, foolish, ill-advised, hasty, rash.

jumble, *n.* SYN.-agitation, chaos, clutter, commotion, confusion, disarrangement, disarray, disorder, ferment, medley, mixture, stir, tumult, turmoil. ANT.-certainty, order, peace, system, tranquility.

jumble, *v.* SYN.-amalgamate blend, combine, commingle, concoct, confound, confuse, mess, mingle, mix, muddle. ANT.-classify, dissociate, divide, file, isolate, segregate, separate, sort, straighten.

jump, *v.* SYN.-bolt, bound, caper, hop, jerk, leap, skip, spring, start, vault.

just, *a.* SYN.-appropriate, apt, fair, good, honest, honorable, equitable, honorable, impartial, legal, legitimate, proper, righteous, rightful, scrupulous, sincere, trustworthy, truthful, upright, virtuous. ANT.-deceitful, dishonest, fraudulent, lying, tricky.

justice, *n.* SYN. equity, fairness, impartiality, integrity, justness, law, rectitude, right, virtue. ANT.-inequity, partiality, unfairness, wrong.

justifiable, *a.* SYN.-admissible, allowable, defensible, fair, fit logical, permissible, probable, proper, tolerable, warranted. ANT.-inadmissible, irrelevant, unsuitable.

justify, *v.* SYN.-absolve, acquit, assert, clear, defend, excuse, exonerate, support, uphold, vindicate. ANT.-abandon, accuse, blame, convict.

K

keen, *a.* SYN.-acute, anxious, ardent, bright, clever, cunning, cutting, discerning, eager, excited, incisive, intent, interested, quick, piercing, sensitive, shrewd, wily, witty, zealous. ANT.-slow, sluggish; dull, inattentive, unaware.

keep, *v.* SYN.-celebrate, commemorate, conserve, continue, guard, honor, maintain, observe, own, possess, preserve, protect, reserve, retain, save, support, sustain, tend; confine, detain, hold, restrain, store. ANT.-abandon, discard, dismiss, forsake, ignore, neglect, reject, relinquish.

kidnap, *v.* SYN.-abduct, capture, grab, pirate, shanghai, snatch, steal, waylay.

kill, *v.* SYN.-assassinate, butcher, dispatch, execute, exterminate, liquidate, massacre, murder, sacrifice, slaughter, slay; cancel, halt, forbid, negate, nullify, prohibit, stop, veto. ANT.-animate, protect, resuscitate, save, vivify.

kin, *n.* SYN.-connection, family, kinsman, relation, relative, sibling.

kind, *a.* SYN.-accommodating, affable, benevolent, benign, charitable, compassionate, considerate, forbearing, gentle, good, helpful, humane, indulgent, kindly, loving, merciful, obliging, solicitous, sympathetic, tender, thoughtful, understanding. ANT.-cruel, inhuman, merciless, severe, unkind.

kind, *n.* SYN.-breed, character, class, classification, denomination, designation, family, genus, race, sort, species, stock, strain, type, variety.

kindness, *n.* SYN.-altruism, benevolence, charity, compassion, consideration, courtesy, friendliness, generosity, goodness, helpfulness, humanity, mercy, philanthropy, sympathy, tact, tenderness, thoughtfulness, understanding. ANT.-cruelty, harshness, injury, malevolence, selfishness.

kindred, *a.* SYN.-alike, allied, assimilated, associated, family, germane, kin, like, related, similar

kindred, *n.* SYN.-affinity, clan, consanguinity, family, folks, house, kin, kinsfolk, relations, relationship, relatives, tribe. ANT.-disconnection, foreigners, strangers.

kingdom, *n.* SYN.-country, domain, dominion, empire, lands, nation, possessions, principality, realm, state, territory.

kinship, *n.* affiliation, affinity, alliance, cohesion, connection, familiarity, family, intimacy, kin, kindred, relationship, unity.

kiss, *v.* SYN.-caress, coddle, cuddle, embrace, greet, fondle, hug, pet. ANT.-annoy, buffet, spurn, tease, vex.

knack, *n.* SYN.-ability, adroitness, aptitude, capability, cleverness, cunning, deftness, dexterity, endowment, facility, genius, gift, ingenuity, readiness, skill, skillfulness, talent. ANT.-awkwardness, clumsiness, inability, ineptitude.

knife, *n.* SYN.-bayonet, blade, broadsword, cutter, dagger, dirk, edge, lance, machete, point, poniard, razor, saber, scalpel, scimitar, scythe, sickle, stiletto, sword.

knit, *v.* SYN.-affiliate, braid, cable, connect, crochet, intertwine, net, ossify, web

knot, *n.* SYN.-bond, bunch, clinch, cluster, conundrum, crowd, difficulty, entanglement, group, perplexity, snarl, tangle, tie, twist.

know, *v.* SYN.-acquaint, appreciate, apprehend, ascertain, befriend, cognize, comprehend, differentiate, discern, distinguish, experience, familiarize, fathom, perceive, recognize, see, understand. ANT.-dispute, doubt, ignore, suspect.

knowing, *a.* SYN.-acute, awake, aware, clever, cognizant, conscious, intelligent, sharp.

knowingly, *a.* SYN.-consciously, deliberately, intentionally, willfully.

knowledge, *n.* SYN.-apprehension, awareness, cognizance, education, enlightenment, erudition, expertise, information, intelligence, learning, lore, scholarship, science, understanding, wisdom. ANT.-ignorance, illiteracy, misunderstanding, stupidity.

known, *a.* SYN.-accepted, acknowledged, admitted, certified, disclosed, established, familiar, learned, noted, prominent, proverbial, public, recognized, revealed.

L

label, *n.* SYN.-classification, description, identification, mark, marker, name, stamp, sticker, tag.

labor, *n.* SYN.-diligence, drudgery, effort, employment, endeavor, exertion, industry, striving, task, toil, travail, undertaking, work; childbirth, parturition. ANT.-idleness, indolence, leisure, recreation.

lacking, *a.* SYN.-deficient, destitute, inadequate, incomplete, insufficient, needed, scant, scanty, short. ANT.-adequate, ample, enough, satisfactory, sufficient.

lag, *n.* SYN.-cessation, retardation, slowdown, slowing, slowness.

lame, *a.* SYN.-crippled, defective, deformed, disabled, feeble, halt, hobbling, limping, maimed, unconvincing, unsatisfactory, weak. ANT.-agile, athletic, robust, sound, vigorous.

lament, *v.* SYN.-bemoan, bewail, deplore, grieve, mourn, repine, wail, weep.

land, *n.* SYN.-acreage, area, continent, country, domain, earth, estate, expanse, farm, field, ground, island, nation, plain, property, province, realm, region, soil, terrain, tract, turf.

land, *v.* SYN.-alight, arrive, berth, disembark, dock,

language, *n.* SYN.-cant, dialect, diction, idiom, jargon, lingo, phraseology, slang, speech, tongue, vernacular. ANT.-babble, drivel, gibberish, nonsense.

languish, *v.* SYN.-decline, deteriorate, droop, dwindle, fade, fail, flag, pine, shrink, shrivel, sink, waste, weaken, wilt, wither. ANT.-refresh, rejuvenate, renew, revive.

lapse, *n.* SYN.-backsliding, blunder boner, degeneration, error, mistake, slip.

larceny, *n.* SYN.-burglary, crime, depredation, embezzlement, fraud, pillage, plunder, robbery, theft, thievery.

large, *a.* SYN.-ample, big, capacious, colossal, considerable, cumbersome, enormous, extensive, extravagant, grand, great, huge, immense, lavish, massive, substantial, vast, wide. ANT.-little, mean, short, small, tiny.

largely, *a.* SYN.-chiefly, essentially, mainly, mostly, predominantly, primarily, principally.

last, *a.* SYN.-climactic, closing, concluding, crowning, decisive, ending, extreme, final, hindmost, latest, terminal, ultimate, utmost. ANT.-beginning, first, foremost, initial, opening.

lasting, *a.* SYN.-abiding, enduring permanent

late, *a.* SYN.-behind, belated, delayed, overdue, slow, tardy; advanced, contemporary, modern, new, recent. ANT.-early, timely.

latent, *a.* SYN.-concealed, dormant, hidden, inactive, potential, quiescent, secret, undeveloped, unseen. ANT.-conspicuous, evident, explicit, manifest, visible.

laugh, *n.* SYN.-amusement, cackle, chortle, chuckle, giggle, guffaw, jeer, merriment, mirth, mock, roar, scoff, snicker, titter.

laughable, *a.* SYN.-amusing, comic, comical, droll, funny, humorous, ludicrous.

launch, *v.* SYN.-begin, drive, inaugurate, introduce, originate, propel, start.

launched, *a.* SYN.-begun, driven, sent, started.

lavish, *a.* SYN.-excessive, extravagant, generous, improvident, plentiful, unstinting, wasteful.

lavish, *v.* SYN.-consume, dissipate, expend, misuse, profligate, scatter, spend, squander, waste. ANT.-accumulate, economize, preserve, save.

law, *n.* SYN.-act, code, constitution, decree, edict, enactment, injunction, order, ordinance, rule, ruling, statute.

lawful, *a.* SYN.-allowable, authorized, constitutional, enacted, legal, legalized, legitimate, permissible, permitted, rightful. ANT.-criminal, illegal, illegitimate, illicit, prohibited.

lawless, *a.* SYN.-barbarous, fierce, savage, tempestuous, uncivilized, violent, uncontrolled, untamed, wild.

lax, *a.* SYN.-careless, desultory, inaccurate, indifferent, neglectful, negligent, remiss, slack. ANT.-accurate, careful, meticulous.

lay, *a.* SYN.-earthly, laic, secular, temporal, worldly; amateur, beginner, novice, neophyte. ANT.-ecclesiastical; experienced, trained.

lay, *v.* SYN.-arrange, deposit, dispose, place, put, set. ANT.-disarrange, disturb, mislay, misplace, remove.

layman, *n.* SYN.-amateur, dilettante, nonprofessional, novice.

layout, *n.* SYN.-arrangement, blueprint, design, draft, organization, plan, scheme, strategy.

lazy, *a.* SYN.-idle, inactive, indifferent, indolent, inert, remiss, slothful, sluggish, supine, torpid. ANT.-active, alert, assiduous, diligent.

lead, *v.* SYN.-allure, beat, conduct,

control, convince, direct, entice, escort, excel, guide, induce, influence, manage, outstrip, persuade, pilot, precede, regulate, steer, supervise, surpass.

leader, *n.* SYN.-captain, chief, chieftain, commander, conductor, director, guide, head, manager, master, principal, ruler. ANT.-attendant, follower, servant, subordinate, underling.

leadership, *n.* SYN.-administration, authority, control, direction, guidance, influence, management, power, superiority

league, *n.* SYN.-alliance, association, brotherhood, club, coalition, combination, confederacy, entente, federation, fellowship, fraternity, partnership, union.

league, *v.* SYN.-band, combine, confederate, cooperate, unite.

lean, *v.* SYN.-bend, incline, list, sag, slant, slope, tend; depend, rely, trust. ANT.-erect, raise, rise, straighten.

leaning, *n.* SYN.-bent, bias, drift, inclination, partiality, penchant, predisposition, proclivity, proneness, propensity, tendency, trend. ANT.-aversion, deviation, disinclination.

leap, *v.* SYN.-bound, caper, clear, hop, hurdle, jump, spring, start, surmount, vault.

learn, *v.* SYN.-acquire, ascertain, determine, discover, get, master, memorize, understand, unearth.

learned, *a.* SYN.-able, academic, accomplished, adept, cultured, educated, enlightened, erudite, experience, expert, informed, intelligent, knowing, lettered, pedantic, professional, professorial, proficient, profound, sagacious, scholarly, skilled, trained, wise. ANT.-foolish, illiterate, shallow, simple.

learning, *n.* SYN.-cognizance, education, erudition, information, knowledge, lore, scholarship, science, understanding, wisdom. ANT.-ignorance, illiteracy, misunderstanding, stupidity.

least, *a.* SYN.-infinitesimal, microscopic, minimal, minute, slightest, smallest, tiniest, trivial, unimportant.

leave, *v.* SYN.-abandon, abscond, depart, desert, embark, emigrate, flee, forsake, go, move, quit, relinquish, renounce, retire, vacate, withdraw. ANT.-abide, remain, stay, tarry.

lecture, *v.* SYN.-address, admonish, declaim, discourse, expound, harangue, preach, reason, reprimand, scold, speak, spout, talk, teach, upbraid.

led, *a.* SYN.-accompanied, escorted, guided, taken, taught.

legal, *a.* SYN.-allowable, authorized, constitutional, decreed, fair, forensic, just, lawful, legalized, legitimate, licit, permissible, right, rightful, sanctioned, sound, statutory, warranted. ANT.-criminal, illegal, illegitimate, illicit, prohibited.

legend, *n.* SYN.-allegory, chronicle, fable, fiction, myth, parable, saga, story, tradition. ANT.-fad, history.

legendary, *a.* SYN.-allegorical, apocryphal, celebrated, created, fabulous, famous, fanciful, historical, imaginary, immortal, invented, mythical, mythological, romantic, storied, traditional.

legible, *a.* SYN.-clear, comprehensible, conspicuous, distinct, intelligible, lucid, perceptible, plain, sharp, visible.

legitimate, *a.* SYN.-authentic, authorized, bona fide, correct, genuine, justifiable, lawful, legal, licit, logical, official, proper, proven, real, reasonable, regular, rightful, sanctioned, sensible, sincere, statutory, true, unadulterated, unaffected, valuable, veritable, warranted. ANT.-artificial, bogus, counterfeit, false, sham.

leisure, *n.* SYN.-calm, ease, freedom, intermission, pause, peace, quiet, recess, recreation, relaxation, repose, respite, rest, tranquility. ANT.-agitation, commotion, disturbance, motion, tumult.

leisurely, *a.* SYN.-dawdling, delaying, deliberate, dull, gradual, laggard, lethargic, premeditated, slow, slowly, sluggish. ANT.-fast, quick, rapid, speedy, swift.

lend, *v.* SYN.-accommodate, adjust, advance, allow, comply, confer, conform, contribute, entrust, furnish, give, grant, impart, loan, oblige, present, supply.

length, *n.* SYN.-dimension, distance, duration, expanse, interval, measure, period, range, reach, season, span, stretch.

lengthen, *v.* SYN.-attenuate, draw, elongate, extend, prolong, protract, stretch. ANT.-contract, shorten.

leniency, *n.* SYN.-charity, clemency, compassion, forgiveness, grace, indulgence, mercy, mildness, patience, pity, understanding. ANT.-cruelty, punishment, retribution, vengeance.

lenient, *a.* SYN.-clement, compassionate, forbearing, forgiving, humane, indulgent, kind, merciful, tender, tolerant. ANT.-brutal, cruel, pitiless, remorseless, unfeeling.

lessen, *v.* SYN.-abate, curtail, decline, decrease, deduct, degrade, diminish, dwindle, ease, fade, lighten, lower, reduce, shorten, shrink, subtract, truncate, wane. ANT.-amplify, enlarge, expand, grow, increase.

lessening, *a.* SYN.-abating, declining, decreasing, dwindling, ebbing, falling, reducing, shrinking, waning, weakening.

lesser, *a.* SYN.-diminutive, inferior, insignificant, minor, negligible, petty, secondary, trivial.

lesson, *n.* SYN.-assignment, drill, education, example, explanation, guide, instruction, lecture, model, schooling, study, teaching, tutoring.

let, *v.* SYN.-allow, approve, authorize, condone, consent, permit, tolerate.

lethargy, *n.* SYN.-apathy, daze, inactivity, indolence, languor, numbness, passivity, sloth, stupefaction, stupor, torpor. ANT.-activity, alertness, liveliness, readiness, wakefulness.

letter, *n.* SYN.-character, mark, sign, symbol, type; communication, dispatch, epistle, memorandum, message, missive, note, report, writ.

level, *a.* SYN.-aligned, balanced, equal, equivalent, even, flat, flush, horizontal, plane, smooth, stable, steady, uniform. ANT.-broken, hilly, irregular, sloping.

levy, *n.* SYN.-assessment, custom, duty, exaction, excise, impost, rate, tax, toll, tribute. ANT.-gift, remuneration, reward, wages.

lewd, *a.* SYN.-carnal, coarse, debauched, dirty, disgusting, dissolute, filthy, gross, impure, indecent, obscene, offensive, pornographic, prurient, ribald, smutty.

ANT.-decent, modest, pure, refined.

liability, *n.* SYN.-accountability, burden, debt, disadvantage, encumbrance, obligation, pledge, responsibility.

liable, *a.* SYN.-accountable, amenable, answerable, bound, exposed, likely, obliged, prone, responsible, sensitive, subject. ANT.-exempt, free, immune, independent, protected.

libel, *n.* SYN.-aspersion, backbiting, calumny, defamation, denigration, lie, scandal, slander, vilification. ANT.-applause, commendation, defense, flattery, praise.

liberal, *a.* SYN.-abundant, ample, bountiful, broad-minded, expanded, extensive, impartial, indulgent, large, left, progressive, radical, reform, sweeping, tolerant, unconventional, understanding, vast, wide. ANT.-confined, narrow, restricted.

liberate, *v.* SYN.-deliver, discharge, emancipate, free, loose, release, set free. ANT.-confine, imprison, oppress, restrict, subjugate.

liberated, *a.* SYN.-autonomous, discharged, dismissed, emancipated, exempt, free, freed, independent, loose, open, unconfined, unobstructed, unrestricted. ANT.-confined, restrained, restricted; blocked, impeded.

liberty, *n.* SYN.-autonomy, deliverance, freedom, holiday, immunity, independence, leave, license, leisure, permission, privilege, self-government, vacation. ANT.-captivity, imprisonment, submission; constraint.

library, *n.* SYN.-archives, books, collection, den, manuscripts, museum, studio, study.

license, *n.* SYN.-consent, excess, exemption, freedom, grant, immoderation, immunity, independence, latitude, liberation, liberty, permit, prerogative, privilege, right, sanction, unrestraint, warrant. ANT.-bondage, compulsion, constraint, necessity, servitude.

lie, *n.* SYN.-delusion, equivocation, fabrication, falsehood, fib, fiction, illusion, invention, prevarication, untruth. ANT.-axiom, canon, fact, truism.

lie, *v.* SYN.-deceive, distort, equivocate, exaggerate, falsify, fib, mislead, misrepresent, prevaricate.

life, *n.* SYN.-activity, animation, being, buoyancy, energy, entity, existence, growth, liveliness, mortality, spirit, vigor, vitality, vivacity. ANT.-death, demise, dullness, languor, lethargy.

lifeless, *a.* SYN.-dead, deceased, defunct, departed, dull, expired, extinct, gone, inactive, inanimate, inert, insensible, insipid, listless, passive, sluggish, spiritless, torpid, unconscious. ANT.-alive, animate, living, stirring.

lift, *v.* SYN.-elevate, exalt, heave, heighten, hoist, raise, uplift; recall, repeal, rescind, revoke. ANT.-depreciate, depress, lower.

light, *a.* SYN.-animated, blithe, buoyant, cheerful, elated, effervescent, lively, resilient, spirited, sprightly, vivacious. ANT.-dejected, depressed, despondent, hopeless, sullen.

light, *n.* SYN.-beam, brightness, dawn, flame, gleam, illumination, incandescence, lamp, luminosity, radiance, shine; enlightenment, insight, knowledge, understanding. ANT.-darkness, gloom, obscurity, shadow.

lighten, *v.* SYN.-allay, alleviate, cheer, console, ease, lessen, mitigate, reduce, unburden

like, *a.* SYN.-analogous, coincident, comparable, equal, equivalent, identical, indistinguishable, resembling, same, similar, uniform. ANT.-contrary, disparate, dissimilar, distinct, opposed.

like, *v.* SYN.-admire, approve, esteem, love; enjoy, fancy, relish, savor.

likely, *a.* SYN.-anticipated, apparent, appropriate, credible, encouraging, expected, feasible, hopeful, possible, promising, reasonable.

likeness, *n.* SYN.-affinity, analogy, congruence, correspondence, facsimile, image, parity, representation, resemblance, semblance, similarity, similitude. ANT.-difference, distinction, variance.

limit, *n.* SYN.-border, bound, boundary, confine, edge, end, extent, limitation, restraint, restriction, terminus. ANT.-boundlessness, endlessness, extension, infinity, vastness.

limitation, *n.* SYN.-barrier, check, condition, control, defect. deficiency, failing, fault, flaw, frailty, hindrance, inadequacy, obstruction, restriction, stipulation, stricture.

limp, *a.* SYN.-bending, feeble, flaccid, flimsy, frail, limber, pliable, pliant, relaxed, supple, yielding.

limpid, *a.* SYN.-clear, cloudless, crystalline, lucid, pure, transparent, unclouded. ANT.-cloudy; ambiguous, obscure, unclear, vague.

line, *n.* SYN.-arrangement, band, border, course, file, groove, limit, mark, path, queue, road, route rank, row, seam, stripe, streak, string, succession.

lineage, *n.* SYN.-ancestry, blood, breed, clan, descent, folk, line, nation, parentage, pedigree, people, race, species, stock, strain, tribe.

linger, *v.* SYN.-abide, amble, bide, dawdle, delay, drift, hesitate, lag, loiter, procrastinate, remain, rest, saunter, stay, stroll, tarry, wait. ANT.-act, expedite, hasten, leave.

link, *n.* SYN.-bond, connection, connective, coupler, juncture, loop, ring, splice, tie, union. ANT.-break, gap, interval, opening, split.

link, *v.* SYN.-adjoin, attach, combine, conjoin, connect, couple, join, loop, splice, tie, unite. ANT.-detach, disconnect, disjoin, separate.

lip, *n.* SYN.-brim, edge, flange, margin, portal, rim.

liquid, *a.* SYN.-flowing, fluent, fluid, juicy, liquor, molten, viscous, watery, wet. ANT.-congealed, gaseous, solid.

liquidate, *v.* SYN.-abolish, annihilate, assassinate, cancel, destroy, eliminate, eradicate, execute, obliterate, purge, reimburse, remove, repay.

list, *n.* SYN.-agenda, catalogue, directory, docket, index, muster, register, roll, roster, slate, tally.

list, *v.* SYN.-arrange, catalogue, enumerate, index, record, tabulate, tally; careen, incline, lean, tilt.

listen, *v.* SYN.-attend, hear, hearken, heed, learn, list, mark, mind, note, notice, obey, overhear. ANT.-disregard, ignore, reject, scorn.

listless, *a.* SYN.-apathetic, indifferent, indolent, languid, lethargic, passive, slow, sluggish, torpid.

literal, *a.* SYN.-accurate, complete, correct, exact, precise, true, verbatim, veritable.

literate, *a.* SYN.-educated, erudite, intelligent, learned, lettered, scholarly,

little, *a.* SYN.-diminutive, insignificant, miniature, minor, minute, paltry, petite, petty, puny, slight, small, tiny, trivial, wee; bigoted, mean, selfish, stingy. ANT.-big, enormous, huge, immense, large.

livelihood, *n.* SYN.-business, career, living, means, support, sustenance, vocation, work.

lively, *a.* SYN.-active, alive, animated, blithe, brisk, energetic, frolicsome, spirited, sprightly, spry, supple, vigorous, vivacious; bright, brilliant, clear, fresh, glowing, sparkling, vivid. ANT.-dull, insipid, listless, stale, vapid.

load, *n.* SYN.-burden, cargo, charge, encumbrance, obligation, onus, responsibility, trust, weight.

load, *v.* SYN.-burden, encumber, oppress, overload, recharge, resupply, stack, supply, tax, trouble, weigh. ANT.-alleviate, console, ease, lighten, mitigate.

loaf, *v.* SYN.-dawdle, idle, loiter, loll, lounge, relax

loathe, *v.* SYN.-abhor, abominate, despise, detest, dislike, hate. ANT.-admire, approve, cherish, like, love.

loathsome, *a.* SYN.-abominable, detestable, execrable, foul, hateful, odious, revolting, vile. ANT.-agreeable, commendable, delightful, pleasant.

locale, *n.* area, district, locality, place, region, site, spot, territory, vicinity.

locality, *n.* SYN.-area, district, environs, neighborhood, place, position, province, range, region, section, sector, sphere, zone. ANT.-distance, remoteness.

locate, *v.* SYN.-discover, find, pinpoint, position, recover; dwell, inhabit, reside, settle.

location, *n.* SYN.-area, discovering, finding, locale, locality, place, point, position, region, site, situation, spot, station, vicinity, whereabouts.

lock, *n.* SYN.-bar, bolt, catch, clasp, closure, fastening, hook, latch, padlock; curl, plait, ringlet, tress, tuft.

lodge, *n.* SYN.-cabin, chalet, cottage, hostel, house, inn, resort, shelter; association, brotherhood, club, society.

lofty, *a.* SYN.-august, dignified, grand, grandiose, high, imposing, magnificent, majestic, noble, pompous, stately, sublime. ANT.-common, humble, lowly, ordinary, undignified.

logic, *n.* SYN.-deduction, discernment, induction, intellect, judgment, rationalism, reason, understanding.

logical, *a.* SYN.-cogent, coherent, conclusive, convincing, effective, efficacious, powerful, probable, rational, sound, strong, telling, valid, weighty. ANT.-counterfeit, null, spurious, void, weak.

loiter, *v.* SYN.-dally, dawdle, lag, linger, pause, remain, shuffle, tarry, trail, wait.

lone, *a.* SYN.-alone, apart, deserted, desolate, isolated, lonely, only, secluded, single, sole, solitary, unaided. ANT.-accompanied, attended, surrounded.

loneliness, *n.* SYN.-alienation, detachment, isolation, privacy, refuge, retirement, retreat, seclusion, solitude. ANT.-exposure, notoriety, publicity.

lonely, *a.* SYN.-abandoned, alone, deserted, desolate, forsaken, friendless, isolated, secluded. ANT.-accompanied, attended, surrounded.

long, *a.* SYN.-elongated, extended, extensive, lasting, lengthy, lingering, prolix, prolonged, protracted, tedious, wordy. ANT.-abridged, brief, concise, short, terse.

look, *v.* SYN.-anticipate, behold, discern, examine, eye, gaze, glance, hunt, inspect, observe, regard, scan, scrutinize, see, seek, stare, survey, view, watch, witness. ANT.-avert, hide, miss, overlook.

looks, *n.* SYN.-appearance, aspect, bearing, countenance, demeanor, features, manner.

loose, *a.* SYN.-careless, corrupt, detached, disengaged, dissolute, free, heedless, imprecise, indefinite, lax, limp, promiscuous, slack, unbound, unfastened, unrestrained, untied, vague, wanton. ANT.-fast, inhibited, restrained, tight.

lose, *v.* SYN.-drop, fail, forfeit, mislay, misplace, succumb, surrender, yield.

loser, *n.* SYN.-defeated, dispossessed, dud, failure, flop, prey, ruined, victim, washout.

lost, *a.* SYN.-adrift, astray, bewildered, condemned, confused, consumed, dazed, defeated, destroyed, distracted, doomed, forfeited, gone, missing, misspent, perplexed, preoccupied, squandered, used, vanquished, wasted. ANT.-anchored, found, located.

lot, *n.* SYN.-circumstance, consequence, destiny, fate, fortune, issue, outcome, portion, result; acreage, parcel, plat, plot, tract.

loud, *a.* SYN.-blaring, booming, brash, clamorous, deafening, noisy, offensive, resonant, resounding, sonorous, stentorian, vociferous ANT.-dulcet, inaudible, quiet, soft, subdued.

lounge, *v.* SYN.-languish, loaf, loll, relax, rest, sprawl.

lousy, *a.* SYN.-bad, disliked, horrible, offensive, pedicular, undesirable, unwanted.

love, *n.* SYN.-adoration, affection, ardor, attachment, beloved, darling, devotion, endearment, fondness, passion, rapture. ANT.-aversion, dislike, enmity, hatred, indifference.

love, *v.* SYN.-adore, caress, cherish, embrace, fancy, hug, idolize, prize, treasure. ANT.-detest, loathe, spurn.

loveliness, *n.* SYN.-appeal, attractiveness, beauty, charm, comeliness, elegance, fairness, grace, handsomeness, pulchritude. ANT.-deformity, disfigurement, eyesore, homeliness, ugliness.

lovely, *a.* SYN.-beauteous, beautiful, charming, comely, elegant, fair, fine, handsome, pretty. ANT.-foul, hideous, homely, repulsive, unsightly.

loving, *a.* SYN.-affectionate, amorous, attentive, caring, close, concerned, considerate, devoted, familiar, generous, intimate, near, passionate, solicitous, tender, thoughtful. ANT.-ceremonious, conventional, distant, formal.

low, *a.* SYN.-abject, base, coarse, contemptible, crude, dejected, depressed, despicable, dishonorable, dispirited, groveling, ignoble, ignominious, inferior, lowly, mean, menial, plebeian, rude, servile, sordid, vile, vulgar. ANT.-teemed, exalted, honored, lofty, noble, righteous.

lower, *a.* SYN.-inferior, minor, poorer, secondary, subordinate. ANT.-better, greater, higher, superior.

lower, *v.* SYN.-abase, corrupt, debase, degrade, deprave, depress, impair, pervert, vitiate. ANT.-enhance, improve, raise, restore, vitalize.

lowly, *a.* SYN.-humble, ignoble, meek, menial, servile, unpretentious.

loyal, *a.* SYN.-ardent, attached, constant, dedicated, devoted, disposed, earnest, faithful, fond, inclined, prone, staunch, true, trustworthy, wedded. ANT.-detached, disinclined, indisposed, untrammeled.

loyalty, *n.* SYN.-allegiance, constancy, dependability, devotion, faith, faithfulness, fealty, fidelity, obedience, support. ANT.-disloyalty, falseness, perfidy, treachery.

lucid, *a.* SYN.-apparent, bright, brilliant, clear, cloudless, distinct, evident, intelligible, limpid, luminous, manifest, obvious, open, plain, radiant, rational, sane, shining, transparent; unmistakable, unobstructed, visible. ANT.-cloudy; ambiguous, obscure, unclear, vague.

lucky, *a.* SYN.-advantageous, auspicious, benign, favored, felicitous, fortuitous, happy, lucky, propitious, successful. ANT.-cheerless, condemned, ill-fated, persecuted, unlucky.

luminous, *a.* SYN.-bright, brilliant, clear, gleaming, lucid, lustrous, radiant, shining. ANT.-dark, dull, gloomy, murky, sullen.

lunacy, *n.* SYN.-craziness, delirium, dementia, derangement, frenzy, insanity, madness, mania, psychosis. ANT.-rationality, sanity, stability.

lure, *v.* SYN.-allure, attract, charm, draw, enchant, entrap, entice, fascinate, induce, lure, persuade, seduce, tempt. ANT.-alienate, contract, drive, propel.

lurk, *v.* SYN.-creep, crouch, hide, prowl, skulk, slink, sneak, steal.

luscious, *a.* SYN.-delectable, delicious, delightful, palatable, savory, sweet, tasty. ANT.-acrid, distasteful, nauseous, unpalatable, unsavory

lush, *a.* SYN.-dense, extensive, lavish, luxurious, opulent, ornate, profuse, rich.

lust, *n.* SYN.-appetite, aspiration, craving, desire, hungering, longing, passion, sensuality, urge, wish, yearning. ANT.-abomination, aversion, distaste, hate, loathing.

luster, *n.* SYN.-brightness, brilliance, brilliancy, effulgence, glory, gloss, polish, radiance, sheen, splendor. ANT.-darkness, dullness, gloom, obscurity.

lustful, *a.* SYN.-animal, base, carnal, corporeal, fleshly, gross, sensual, voluptuous, worldly, ANT.-exalted, intellectual, refined, spiritual, temperate.

lusty, *a.* SYN.-bold, energetic, hardy, healthy, hearty, robust, stout, strong, sturdy, vigorous, virile. ANT.-effeminate, emasculated, weak.

luxuriant, *a.* SYN.-abundant, ample, bountiful, copious, exuberant, fecund, fertile, fruitful, luxurious, opulent, ornate, plentiful, profuse, prolific, rich. ANT.-barren, sterile, unfruitful, unproductive.

luxurious, *a.* SYN.-affluent, bounteous, bountiful, lavish, opulent, ornate, plenteous plentiful, replete, rich, sumptuous. ANT.-deficient, insufficient, rare, scanty, scarce.

luxury, *n.* SYN.-abundance, affluence, fortune, money, opulence, plenty, possessions, riches, wealth. ANT.-indigence, need, poverty, want.

M

machine, *n.* SYN.-appliance, automaton, contrivance, device, implement, instrument, movement, organization, robot.

mad, *a.* SYN.-angry, crazy, delirious, demented, enraged, exasperated, furious, incensed, insane, lunatic, maniacal, provoked, wrathful. ANT.-calm, happy, healthy, pleased, sane, sensible.

made, *a.* SYN.-built, created, fashioned, formed, manufactured, shaped.

madly, *a.* SYN.-crazily, hastily, hurriedly, rashly, wildly.

madness, *n.* SYN.-craziness, delirium, dementia, derangement, frenzy, insanity, lunacy, mania, psychosis. ANT.-rationality, sanity, stability.

magic, *n.* SYN.-charm, conjuring, enchantment, hex, legerdemain, necromancy, occultism, sorcery, voodoo, witchcraft, wizardry.

magical, *a.* SYN.-astral, charmed, cryptic, enchanted, enchanting, entrancing, fascinating, miraculous, mysterious, mystical, mythical, spellbinding, spiritualistic, supernatural, uncanny.

magnanimous, *a.* SYN.-beneficent, charitable, exalted, forgiving, generous, giving, honorable, liberal, lofty, munificent, noble, openhanded, unselfish. ANT.-covetous, greedy, miserly, selfish, stingy.

magnetic, *a.* SYN.-alluring, appealing, attractive, captivating, charming, fascinating, inviting, irresistible.

magnificent, *a.* SYN.-brilliant, dazzling, dignified, exalted, extraordinary, grand, imposing, lavish, luxurious, majestic, noble, splendid, stately

magnify, *v.* SYN.-amplify, augment, enhance, enlarge, exaggerate, expand, extend, grow, heighten, increase, intensify, overstate, stretch, wax. ANT.-belittle, depreciate, minimize, understate.

magnitude, *n.* SYN.-amplitude, bigness, bulk, consequence, dimensions, eminence, enormity, expanse, extent, greatness, importance, largeness, mass, quantity, significance, size, volume.

maim, *v.* SYN.-cripple, disable, disfigure, hurt, lame, mutilate, scar.

main, *a.* SYN.-cardinal, chief, dominant, essential, first, foremost, highest, leading, paramount, predominant, principal, significant. ANT.-auxiliary, minor, subordinate, subsidiary, supplemental.

mainly, *a.* SYN.-chiefly, essentially, largely, mostly, predominantly, primarily, principally.

maintain, *v.* SYN.-affirm, allege, assert, claim, contend, continue, declare; defend, hold, justify, keep, preserve, support, sustain, uphold, vindicate. ANT.-deny, discontinue, neglect, oppose, resist.

majestic, *a.* SYN.-august, dignified, exalted, grand, grandiose, high, imposing, lofty, magnificent, noble, pompous, regal, stately, sublime. ANT.-common, humble, lowly, ordinary, undignified.

make, *v.* SYN.-assemble, build, cause, compel, construct, create, establish, execute, fashion, form, gain, generate, manufacture, mold, plan, produce, shape. ANT.-break, demolish, destroy, undo, unmake.

makeshift, *n.* SYN.-alternative, equivalent, expedient, replacement, stopgap, substitute. ANT.-master, original, prime, principal.

malady, *n.* SYN.-ailment, complaint, disease, disorder, illness, infirmity, sickness. ANT.-health, healthiness, soundness, vigor.

malevolence, *n.* See **malice.**

malice, *n.* SYN.-animosity, enmity, grudge, hatred, ill will, malevolence, malignity, rancor, spite. ANT.-affection, kindness, love, toleration.

malicious, *a.* SYN.-bitter, evil-minded, hostile, malevolent, malignant, rancorous, spiteful, virulent, wicked. ANT.-affectionate, benevolent, benign, kind.

malign, *v.* SYN.-abuse, accuse, asperse, defame, disparage, ill-use, insult, libel, revile, scandalize, slander, traduce, vilify. ANT.-cherish, honor, praise, protect, respect.

malignant, *a.* SYN.-dangerous, destructive, growing, harmful, lethal, malicious, rancorous, vicious, virulent.

malleable, *a.* SYN.-flexible, impressionable, pliant, soft, supple, yielding. ANT.-hard, rigid, rough, tough, unyielding.

manage, *v.* SYN.-administer, arrange, command, conduct, contrive, control, direct, dominate, educate, engineer, govern, guide, influence, lead, manipulate, officiate, oversee, pilot, regulate, rule, superintend, train. ANT.-abandon, follow, forsake, ignore, misdirect, misguide, submit.

manageable, *a.* SYN.-adaptable, compliant, controllable, docile, flexible, gentle, governable, humble, obedient, orderly, teachable, tractable.

manager, *n.* SYN.-administrator, coach, director, executive, handler, mentor, supervisor, trainer.

mandate, *n.* SYN.-command, decree, dictate, order, ordinance, regulation.

mandatory, *a.* SYN.-compulsory, imperative, obligatory, required, requisite.

maneuver, *n.* SYN.-action, design, execution, movement, operation, performance, plan, plot, proceeding, ruse, scheme, stratagem, tactics, trick. ANT.-cessation, inaction, inactivity, rest.

maneuver, *v.* SYN.-conspire, contrive, design, devise, intrigue, manage, manipulate, plan, plot, scheme, trick.

mania, *n.* SYN.-craze, enthusiasm, excitement, fad, frenzy, lunacy, madness, obsession.

manifest, *a.* SYN.-apparent, clear, distinct, evident, intelligible, lucid, obvious, open, plain, unmistakable, unobstructed, visible. ANT.-ambiguous, obscure, unclear, vague.

manifest, *v.* SYN.-confirm, declare, demonstrate, denote, designate, disclose, display, exhibit, indicate, prove, reveal, show, signify, specify. ANT.-conceal, distract, divert, falsify, mislead.

manipulate, *v.* SYN.-command, control, direct, govern, guide, handle, lead, manage, mold, shape.

manner, *n.* SYN.-custom, fashion, habit, method, mode, practice, style, way.

manners, *n.* SYN.-air, appearance, aspect, behavior, carriage, conduct, demeanor, deportment, look.

mansion, *n.* SYN.-castle, chateau, estate, manor, palace, residence, villa.

manufacture, *v.* SYN.-assemble, build, construct, fabricate, fashion, form, make, produce.

manuscript, *n.* SYN.-article, book, composition, document, essay, original, script, text, writing.

many, *a.* SYN.-divers, manifold, multifarious, multitudinous, numerous, several, sundry, various. ANT.-few, infrequent, meager, scanty, scarce.

map, *n.* SYN.-blueprint, chart, diagram, graph, outline, plan, plat, projection, sketch.

mar, *v.* SYN.-blemish, bruise, damage, deface, harm, hurt, injure, maim, ruin, scratch, spoil. ANT.-ameliorate, benefit, enhance, mend, repair.

marine, *a.* SYN.-maritime, nautical, naval, ocean, oceanic.

mark, *n.* SYN.-badge, brand, characteristic, distinction, emblem, feature, imprint, indication, label, property, scar, sign stain, stigma, symptoms, trace, trademark, trait, vestige.

mark, *v.* SYN.-brand, characterize, imprint, inscribe, label, tag; behold, descry, discover, distinguish, heed, notice, note, observe, perceive, recognize, regard, remark, see. ANT.-disregard, ignore, overlook, skip.

marriage, *n.* SYN.-espousal, matrimony, nuptials, union, wedding, wedlock. ANT.-celibacy, divorce, virginity.

marvelous, *a.* SYN.-astonishing, exceptional, extraordinary, peculiar, rare, remarkable, singular, uncommon, unusual, wonderful. ANT.-common, frequent, ordinary, usual.

masculine, *a.* SYN.-bold, hardy, lusty, male, manly, mannish, robust, strong, vigorous, virile. ANT.-effeminate, emasculated, feminine, unmanly, weak, womanish.

mask, *v.* SYN.-cloak, conceal, cover, disguise, hide, screen, secrete, suppress, veil, withhold. ANT.-disclose, display, divulge, expose, reveal, show, uncover.

mass, *n.* SYN.-accumulation, aggregate, body, bulk, chunk, collection, company, conglomerate, crowd, heap, hunk, mob, piece, pile, portion, rabble, section, stack. ANT.-intellect, mind, soul, spirit.

massacre, *n.* SYN.-atrocity, butchery, carnage, holocaust, killing, murder, pogrom, slaughter.

massacre, *v.* SYN.-annihilate, butcher, execute, exterminate, kill, liquidate, murder, slaughter, slay. ANT.-animate, protect, resuscitate, save, vivify.

masses, *n.* SYN.-crowd, mob, multitude, people, populace, proletariat, rabble.

massive, *a.* SYN.-bulky, burdensome, cumbersome, enormous, gigantic, heavy, huge, immense, imposing, impressive, monumental, ponderous, tremendous, weighty. ANT.-light, small.

master, *n.* SYN.-adept, authority, boss, chief, commander, employer, expert, head, leader, lord, maestro, manager, overseer, owner, proprietor, ruler, sage, teacher. ANT.-servant, slave.

mastery, *n.* SYN.-authority, command, control, domination, expertise, influence, jurisdiction, predominance, proficiency, skill, sovereignty, supremacy, sway, transcendence. ANT.-inferiority.

match, *v.* SYN.-balance, coordinate, equalize, equate, harmonize, liken, mate, pair, unite.

mate, *n.* SYN.-associate, buddy, colleague, companion, complement, comrade, consort, crony, counterpart, friend, partner, spouse. ANT.-adversary, enemy, stranger.

material, *a.* SYN.-bodily, corporeal, palpable, physical, real, sensible, solid, tangible; consequential, considerable, essential, germane, important, momentous, relevant, significant, substantial, weighty. ANT.-mental, metaphysical, spiritual; immaterial, insignificant.

material, *n.* SYN.-component, data, element, facts, figures, information, matter, stuff, substance; cloth, fabric, textile.

matrimony, *n.* SYN.-espousal, marriage, nuptials, union, wedding, wedlock. ANT.-celibacy, divorce, virginity.

matter, *n.* SYN.-element, material, stuff, substance, thing; affair, business, cause, concern, essence, focus, interest, occasion, situation, subject, theme, thing, topic, undertaking; consequence, difficulty, distress, importance, moment, perplexity, trouble. ANT.-immateriality, phantom, spirit.

mature, *a.* SYN.-adult, aged, complete, consummate, cultivated, developed, finished, full-grown, matured, mellow, old, ready, ripe, sophisticated. ANT.-crude, green, immature, raw, undeveloped.

mature, *v.* SYN.-age, culminate, develop, evolve, grow, mellow, perfect, ripen, season.

maxim, *n.* SYN.-adage, axiom, epithet, foundation, precept, principle, proverb, saying.

meager, *a.* SYN.-lacking, lean, scant, slight, stinted, wanting.

mean, *a.* SYN.-base, coarse, common, contemptible, despicable, low, malicious, mercenary, nasty, offensive, plebeian, selfish, shabby, sordid, stingy, treacherous, undignified, vile, vulgar. ANT.-admirable, dignified, exalted, generous, noble.

mean, *n.* SYN.-average, center, medium, middle, midpoint.

meander, *v.* SYN.-ramble, stroll, turn, twist, wander, wind.

meaning, *n.* SYN.-acceptation, connotation, drift, explanation, gist, implication, import, intent, interpretation, purport, purpose, sense, significance, signification.

meaningful, *a.* SYN.-consequential, explicit, important, material, pithy, profound, significant, substantial, useful.

meaningless, *a.* SYN.-insignificant, nonsensical, senseless, trivial, unimportant.

means, *n.* SYN.-agent, apparatus, approach, backing, channel, device, instrument, medium, method, mode, property, resources, substance, support, tool, utensil, vehicle, way, wealth. ANT.-hindrance, impediment, obstruction, preventive.

measure, *n.* SYN.-action, maneuver, move, procedure, proceeding; capacity, criterion, dimension, gauge, law, magnitude, mass, quantity, principle, proof, rule, size, standard, test, volume. ANT.-chance, fancy, guess, supposition.

meddle, *v.* SYN.-encroach, interfere, intervene, interpose, interrupt, intrude, monkey, pry, snoop, tamper.

mediocre, *a.* SYN.-average, common, fair, intermediate, mean, median, medium, middling, moderate, ordinary. ANT.-exceptional, extraordinary, outstanding.

meditate, *v.* SYN.-cogitate, consider, contemplate, deem, deliberate, muse, imagine, picture, plot, ponder, reason, recall, recollect, reflect, remember, speculate, study, think, weigh. ANT.-disregard, ignore, neglect, overlook.

meditation, *n.* SYN.-contemplation, examination, reflection, thought.

meek, *a.* SYN.-compliant, demur, docile, gentle; mild, passive, reserved, resigned, serene, shy, subdued, submissive, tame, timid, unassuming. ANT.-fierce, savage, spirited, wild; animated, exciting, lively, spirited.

meet, *v.* SYN.-assemble, collect, collide, confront, congregate, convene, converge, encounter, engage, face, find, greet, intersect. ANT.-cleave, disperse, part, scatter, separate.

melancholy, *a.* SYN.-dejected, depressed, despondent, disconsolate, dismal, dispirited, doleful, gloomy, glum, grave, moody, pensive, sad, somber, sorrowful, unhappy, wistful. ANT.-cheerful, happy, joyous, merry.

melodramatic, *a.* SYN.-affected, artificial, ceremonious, dramatic, emotive, histrionic, showy, stagy, theatrical. ANT.-modest, subdued, unaffected, unemotional.

mellow, *a.* SYN.-aged, cultured, genial, gentle, good-natured, jovial, mature, quiet, peaceful, perfected, ripe, soft, sweet. ANT.-crude, green, immature, raw, undeveloped.

melodramatic, *a.* SYN.-artificial, exaggerated, overdone, overemotional, sensational, theatrical.

melody, *n.* SYN.-air, aria, ballad, composition, lyric, music, song, strain, tune.

melt, *v.* SYN.-decrease, disintegrate, dissolve, dwindle, fade, liquefy, soften, thaw, vanish.

member, *n.* SYN.-affiliate, component, constituent, element, ingredient, organ, part; faction, party, side. ANT.-entirety, whole.

memorable, *a.* SYN.-decisive, distinguished, eventful, exceptional, great, impressive, lasting, momentous, monumental, notable, noteworthy, outstanding, remarkable, significant, singular, unforgettable, unusual.

memorandum, *n.* SYN.-directive, letter, message, memo, missive, note, summary.

memorial, *n.* SYN.-commemoration, memento, monument, remembrance, souvenir.

memory, *n.* SYN.-consciousness, image, recall, recollection, remembrance, reminiscence, retrospection, vision. ANT.-forgetfulness, oblivion.

menace, *n.* SYN.-caution, danger, hazard, intimidation, peril, threat.

menace, *v.* SYN.-impend, intimidate, loom, portend, threaten.

mend, *v.* SYN.-ameliorate, amend, better, correct, improve, fix, patch, reconstruct, rectify, refit, reform, remedy, renew, repair, restore, sew. ANT.-deface, destroy, hurt, injure, rend.

menial, *a.* SYN.-abject, base, common, humble, low, mean, servile.

menial, *n.* SYN.-attendant, domestic, flunky, footman, hireling, lackey, minion, serf, servant.

mentality, *n.* SYN.-brain, comprehension, disposition, faculties, inclination, intellect, intelligence, intention, judgment, liking, mind, psyche, purpose, reason, understanding, will, wish, wit. ANT.-body, corporeality, materiality, matter.

mention, *v.* SYN.-cite, declare, disclose, discuss, divulge, impart, infer, intimate, introduce, notice, quote, remark, specify, state, suggest.

mercenary, *a.* SYN.-avaricious, corrupt, greedy, miserly, niggardly, parsimonious, penurious, selfish, sordid, stingy, tight, venal. ANT.-generous, honorable, liberal.

merchant, *n.* SYN.-businessman, dealer, exporter, importer, retailer, shopkeeper, storekeeper, trader, tradesman, wholesaler.

merciful, *a.* SYN.-clement, compassionate, forbearing, forgiving, gentle, gracious, humane, indulgent, kind, lenient, mild, tender, tolerant. ANT.-brutal, cruel, pitiless, remorseless, unfeeling.

merciless, *a.* SYN.-barbarous, bestial, brutal, brute, brutish, carnal, coarse, cruel, ferocious, gross, inhuman, pitiless, remorseless, rough, rude, ruthless, savage, sensual. ANT-civilized, courteous, gentle, humane, kind.

mercy, *n.* SYN.-charity, clemency, compassion, forgiveness, grace, leniency, mildness, pity. ANT.-cruelty, intolerance, punishment, retribution, selfishness, vengeance.

mere, *a.* SYN.-bare, insignificant, minor, scant, small.

merely, *a.* SYN.-but, exactly, hardly, just, only, solely.

merge, *v.* SYN.-amalgamate, blend, coalesce, combine, commingle, conjoin, consolidate, fuse, join, mingle, mix, unify, unite. ANT.-decompose, divide, disintegrate, separate.

merit, *n.* SYN.-credit desert, due, effectiveness, efficacy, entitlement, excellence, goodness, integrity, morality, probity, rectitude, value, virtue, worth. ANT.-corruption, fault, lewdness, sin, vice.

merit, *v.* SYN.-achieve, acquire, attain, deserve, earn, gain, get, justify, obtain, rate, warrant, win. ANT.-consume, forfeit, lose, spend, waste.

merited, *a.* SYN.-adequate, appropriate, condign, deserved, earned, fitting, proper, suitable. ANT.-improper, undeserved, unmerited.

merry, *a.* SYN.-blithe, cheerful, festive, gay, gleeful, hilarious, jolly, jovial, joyous, lively, mirthful, sprightly. ANT.-gloomy, melancholy, morose, sad, sorrowful.

mess, *n.* SYN.-chaos, clutter, confusion, congestion, difficulty, disorder, hodgepodge, jumble, melange, muddle, predicament, snag, unpleasantness, untidiness.

message, *n.* SYN.-annotation, comment, directive, information, letter, memorandum, missive, note, observation, remark, tidings.

messenger, *n.* SYN.-angel, bearer, courier, crier, emissary, envoy, herald, minister, prophet, runner.

messy, *a.* SYN.-dirty, disorderly, rumpled, sloppy, slovenly, untidy.

metaphor, *n.* SYN.-allegory, comparison, correlation, likening, resemblance, similarity, substitution. symbolism.

metaphorical, *a.* SYN.-allegorical, figurative, symbolic.

metaphysical, *a.* SYN.-abstract, mystical, spiritual, supernatural, transcendent.

mete, *v.* SYN.-allocate, allot, apportion, assign, deal, dispense, distribute, divide, dole, give, grant, measure, parcel. ANT.-confiscate, keep, refuse, retain, withhold.

method, *n.* SYN.-arrangement, design, fashion, manner, mode, order, plan, procedure, process, routine, style, system, technique, way. ANT.-confusion, disorder.

methodical, *a.* SYN.-accurate, careful, correct, definite, distinct, exact, orderly, regulated, strict, systematic, unequivocal; ceremonious, formal, precise, prim, rigid, stiff. ANT.erroneous, loose, rough, vague; careless, easy, informal.

mettle, *n.* SYN.-ardor, boldness, bravery, character, chivalry, courage, disposition, fearlessness, fortitude, intrepidity, nerve, pluck, prowess, resolution, spirit, temperament. ANT.-cowardice, fear, pusillanimity, timidity.

microscopic, *a.* SYN.-detailed, exact, infinitesimal, little, miniature, minute, particular, precise, small, tiny. ANT.-enormous, huge, large.

middle, *n.* SYN.-center, central, core, heart, intermediate, mean, median, midpoint, nucleus. ANT.-border, boundary, outskirts, periphery, rim.

midst, *n.* SYN.-center, core, heart, middle. midpoint, nucleus. ANT.-border, boundary, outskirts, periphery, rim.

might, *n.* SYN.-ability, dynamism, energy, force, intensity, potency, power, strength, vigor. ANT.-inability, weakness.

mighty, *a.* SYN.-firm, forceful, forcible, fortified, hale, hardy, impregnable, potent, powerful, robust, sinewy, strong, sturdy, tough. ANT.-brittle, delicate, feeble, fragile, insipid.

migrate, *v.* SYN.-emigrate, immigrate, leave, move.

mild, *a.* SYN.-bland, gentle, kind, meek, moderate, peaceful, soft, soothing, tender. ANT.-bitter, fierce, harsh, rough, severe.

militant, *a.* SYN.-aggressive, bellicose, belligerent, combative, contentious, firm, forceful, inflexible, obstinate, offensive, positive, quarrelsome, resolute, rigid, unbending.

militant, *n.* SYN.-activist, demonstrator, protester, radical.

mimic, *v.* SYN.-ape, copy, exaggerate, imitate, impersonate, mock, pantomime, parody, simulate. ANT.-alter, distort, diverge, invent.

mind, *n.* SYN.-brain, faculties, intellect, intelligence, judgment, memory, mentality, psyche, reason, recall, sense, soul, spirit, understanding, wit; belief, bias, disposition, inclination, intention, judgment, liking, proclivity, purpose, temper, will, wish, wont. ANT.-body, corporeality, materiality, matter.

mind, *v.* SYN.-attend, behave, heed, listen, mark, note, notice, obey, regard.

mindless, *a.* SYN.-asinine, brainless, careless, foolish, heedless, idiotic, inattentive, indifferent, oblivious, senseless, simple, stupid.

mingle, *v.* SYN.-amalgamate, blend, coalesce, combine, commingle, conjoin, consolidate, mix, merge, unify, unite. ANT.-analyze, decompose, disintegrate, separate.

miniature, *a.* SYN.-baby, diminutive, little, petite, small, tiny.

minimize, *v.* SYN.-contract, decrease, diminish, lessen, reduce.

minister, *n.* SYN.-chaplain, clergyman, cleric, curate, deacon, parson, pastor, preacher, prelate, priest, rector, vicar; ambassador, consul, diplomat, statesman.

minister, *v.* SYN.-aid, attend, comfort, heal, help, sustain, tend.

minor, *a.* SYN.-inconsequential, inferior, insignificant, lesser, lower, poorer, secondary, subordinate. ANT.-better, greater, higher, superior.

minute, *a.* SYN.-detailed, exact, fine, microscopic, miniature, particular, precise, tiny. ANT.-enormous, huge, large; general.

miraculous, *a.* SYN.-awesome, extraordinary, incredible, marvelous, metaphysical, phenomenal, preternatural, prodigious, spiritual, stupefying, superhuman, supernatural, unearthly, wondrous. ANT.-common, human, natural, physical, plain.

mirage, *n.* SYN.-apparition, delusion, dream, fantasy, hallucination, illusion, phantom, vision. ANT.-actuality, reality, substance.

mirror, *v.* SYN.-embody, epitomize, exemplify, illustrate, reflect, represent, symbolize, typify.

misbehave, *v.* SYN.-blunder, defy, disobey, fail, offend, rebel, sin, trespass.

miscarriage, *n.* SYN.-default, dereliction, failure, fiasco, malfunction, mistake, omission. ANT.-achievement, success, victory; sufficiency.

miscellaneous, *a.* SYN.-assorted, different, dissimilar, diverse, heterogeneous, indiscriminate, mixed, motley, odd, sundry, varied. ANT.-alike, classified, homogeneous, ordered, selected.

mischief, *n.* SYN.-damage, detriment, evil, fault, harm, hurt, ill, infliction, injury, malice, misconduct, misfortune, mishap, naughtiness, transgression, vandalism, wrong. ANT.-benefit, boon, favor, kindness.

misconception, *n.* SYN.-delusion, error, misapprehension, misinterpretation, mistake, misunderstanding.

miser, *n.* SYN.-cheapskate, skinflint, tightwad.

miserable, *a.* SYN.-afflicted, comfortless, disconsolate, distressed, forlorn, heartbroken, pitiable, sickly, suffering, tormented, troubled, wretched; abject, contemptible, despicable, low, mean, paltry, worthless. ANT.-contented, fortunate, happy; noble, significant.

miserly, *a.* SYN.-acquisitive, avaricious, greedy, niggardly, parsimonious, penurious, stingy, tight. ANT.-altruistic, bountiful, extravagant, generous, munificent.

misery, *n.* SYN.-agony, anguish, desolation, distress, grief, sadness, sorrow, suffering, torment, trial, tribulation, trouble, unhappiness, woe. ANT.-delight, elation, fun, joy, pleasure.

misfortune, *n.* SYN.-accident, adversity, affliction, calamity, catastrophe, disaster, distress, hardship, mishap, ruin, unpleasantness. ANT.-blessing, comfort, prosperity, success.

misgiving, *n.* SYN.-cynicism, distrust, doubt, mistrust, skepticism, suspicion.

misguided, *a.* SYN.-confused, deceived, delinquent, misled, mistaken, wayward.

mislead, *v.* SYN.-beguile, betray, cheat, deceive, defraud, delude, dupe, fool, misrepresent, outwit, trick, victimize.

misleading, *a.* SYN.-ambiguous, deceitful, deceptive, delusive, delusory, dubious, equivocal, fallacious, false, illusive, specious, unclear, vague. ANT.-authentic, genuine, honest, real, truthful.

misplace, *v.* SYN.-confuse, displace, disturb, lose, mislay, remove.

miss, *n.* SYN.-blunder, error, failure, fumble, mishap, mistake, slip.

missed, *a.* SYN.-desired, craved, gone, hidden, needed, neglected, strayed, mislaid, misplaced, unseen, wanted.

mistake, *n.* SYN.-blunder, error, fallacy, fault, inaccuracy, inadvertence, inattention, misapprehension, misconception, misprint, mistake, misunderstanding, neglect, omission, oversight, slip. ANT.-accuracy, precision, truth.

mistaken, *a.* SYN.-confounded, confused, deceived, deluded, duped, erroneous, faulty, fooled, imprecise, inaccurate, incorrect, misguided, misinformed, misled, untrue, wrong. ANT.-correct, right, true.

mistreat, *v.* SYN.-abuse, bully, harm, injure, maltreat, wrong.

mistress, *n.* SYN.-caretaker, concubine, courtesan, housekeeper, lover, manager, mother, paramour, wife.

misty, *a.* SYN.-dim, drizzly, foggy, hazy, murky, obscure, rainy, shrouded.

misuse, *v.* SYN.-abuse, asperse, defame, disparage, malign, misapply, misemploy, revile, scandalize, traduce, vilify. ANT.-cherish, honor, praise, protect, respect.

mitigate, *v.* SYN.-abate, allay, alleviate, assuage, diminish, extenuate, relieve, soften, solace, soothe. ANT.-aggravate, agitate, augment, increase, irritate.

mix, *v.* SYN.-alloy, amalgamate blend, combine, commingle, compound, concoct, confound, fuse, jumble, mingle; associate, consort, fraternize, join. ANT.-dissociate, divide, segregate, separate, sort.

mixture, *n.* SYN.-assortment, blend, combination, diversity, heterogeneity, medley, miscellany, multifariousness, variety, variousness. ANT.-homogeneity, likeness, monotony, sameness, uniformity.

mob, *n.* SYN.-bevy, crowd, crush, horde, host, masses, multitude, populace, press, rabble, swarm, throng.

mock, *a.* SYN.-counterfeit, fake, false, feigned, forged, fraudulent, pretended, sham.

mock, *v.* SYN.-caricature, challenge, dare, defy, deride, flout, gibe, imitate, jeer, mimic, ridicule, scoff, sneer, taunt. ANT.-compliment, flatter, laud, praise.

mockery, *n.* SYN.-banter, derision, gibe, irony, jeering, raillery, ridicule, sarcasm, satire, sneering.

model, *n.* SYN.-archetype, copy, example, ideal, guide, mold, pattern, prototype, specimen, standard, type. ANT.-imitation, production, reproduction.

moderate, *a.* SYN.-average, balanced, calm, careful, considered, cool, deliberate, disciplined, frugal, gentle, judicious, modest, reserved, restrained, tepid, tranquil.

moderate, *v.* SYN.-abate, appease, assuage, calm, decline, decrease, diminish, modulate, restrain; arbitrate, chair, preside, referee, regulate.

moderation, *n.* SYN.-balance, caution, constraint, continence, discretion, forbearance, restraint, temperance.

modern, *a.* SYN.-chic, contemporary, current, late, latest, new, novel, present, recent, stylish. ANT.-ancient, antiquated, bygone, old, past.

modest, *a.* SYN.-bashful, demure, diffident, humble, meek, moderate, proper, reasonable, reserved, restrained, retiring, shy, simple, unassuming, unpretentious, virtuous. ANT.-arrogant, bold, conceited, forward, immodest, ostentatious, proud.

modesty, *n.* SYN.-constraint, control, decency, diffidence, dignity, humility, inhibition, innocence, meekness, reserve, restraint, temperance.

modification, *n.* SYN.-adjustment, alteration, alternation, change, substitution, transformation, variation, variety. ANT.-monotony, stability, uniformity.

modify, *v.* SYN.-adjust, alter, change, convert, curb, exchange, limit, mitigate, qualify, shift, substitute, temper, transfigure, transform, vary. ANT.-retain; continue, establish, preserve, settle, stabilize.

mold, *v.* SYN.-arrange, cast, combine, compose, constitute, construct, convert, create, devise, fashion, forge, form, frame, influence, invent, make, organize, pattern, produce, shape, transfigure, transform. ANT.-destroy, disfigure, dismantle, misshape, wreck.

molest, *v.* SYN.-annoy, attack, bother, chafe, disturb, frighten, inconvenience, intrude, irk, irritate, meddle, pester, scare, tease, terrify, trouble, vex. ANT.-accommodate, console, gratify, soothe.

momentary, *a.* SYN.-brief, concise, curt, ephemeral, fleeting, laconic, meteoric, passing, pithy, quick, short, succinct, terse, transient. ANT.-extended, lengthy, long, prolonged, protracted.

momentous, *a.* SYN.-consequential, critical, decisive, grave, important, influential, material, pressing, prominent, relevant, significant, weighty. ANT.-insignificant, irrelevant, mean, petty, trivial.

monarch, *n.* SYN.-autocrat, despot, governor, king, lord, master, prince, ruler, sovereign.

monastery, *n.* SYN.-abbey, cloister, convent, hermitage, nunnery, priory, refuge, retreat. monopolize

monotonous, *a.* SYN.-boring, burdensome, dilatory, dreary, dull, humdrum, irksome, slow, sluggish, tardy, tedious, tiresome, uninteresting, wearisome. ANT.-amusing, entertaining, exciting, interesting, quick.

monster, *n.* SYN.-beast, brute, chimera, demon, fiend, freak, miscreant, monstrosity, villain, wretch.

monstrous, *a.* SYN.-abnormal, atrocious, colossal, dreadful, enormous, fantastic, frightful, gigantic, great, grotesque, hideous, horrible, large, massive, prodigious, repulsive, stupendous, unusual.

monument, *n.* SYN.-commemoration, landmark, masterpiece, memorial, remembrance, souvenir.

monumental, *a.* SYN.-classic, enormous, grand, great, immense, impressive, lofty, majestic, massive, memorable.

mood, *n.* SYN.-attitude, bent, caprice, disposition, humor, propensity, temper, temperament, tendency, whim.

mope, *v.* SYN.-brood, despair, fret, grieve, pine, sorrow, sulk.

moral, *a.* SYN.-chaste, courteous, decent, ethical, good, honorable, just, kindly, principled, proper, pure, respectable, right, righteous, scrupulous, trustworthy, truthful, virtuous. ANT.-amoral, libertine, licentious, sinful, unethical.

morale, *n.* SYN.-assurance, confidence, resolve, spirit.

morality, *n.* SYN.-chastity, decency, ethics, goodness, honesty, integrity, morals, probity, purity, rectitude, righteousness, virtue. ANT.-corruption, fault, lewdness, sin, vice.

morals, *n.* SYN.-belief, custom, dogma, mores, standards.

morbid, *a.* SYN.-aberrant, depressed, gloomy, gruesome, melancholic, morose, sullen; ailing, diseased, sickly, unhealthy.

morose, *a.* SYN.-crabbed, dejected, dour, downhearted, fretful, gloomy, glum, melancholy, moody, sad, sorrowful, sulky, surly, unhappy. ANT.-amiable, gay, joyous, merry, pleasant.

mortal, *a.* SYN.-deadly, destructive, fatal, final, killing, lethal, malignant, poisonous; ephemeral, frail, human, momentary, perishable, temporal. ANT.-life-giving; divine, immortal.

mostly, *a.* SYN.-chiefly, customarily, especially, frequently, generally, often, particularly, regularly.

motherly, *a.* SYN.-devoted, gentle, kind, loving, maternal, protective, supporting, sympathetic, tender, watchful.

motion, *n.* SYN.-action, activity, change, gesture, move, movement, sign, stirring; plan, proposal, proposition, suggestion. ANT.-equilibrium, immobility, stability, stillness.

motivate, *v.* SYN.-arouse, begin, cause, encourage, goad, ignite, induce, instigate, prompt, start, whet.

motive, *n.* SYN.-cause, grounds, impulse, incentive, incitement, inducement, principle, purpose, reason, spur, stimulus.

motley, *a.* SYN.-assorted, diverse, heterogeneous, indiscriminate, miscellaneous, mixed, mottled, multicolored, sundry, varied, variegated. ANT.-alike, classified, homogeneous, ordered, selected.

motto, *n.* SYN.-adage, aphorism, axiom, credo, maxim, principle, rule, saying, sentiment, slogan, tenet, truism.

mount, *v.* SYN.-ascend, climb, grow, increase, rise, scale, tower; frame, secure, set. ANT.-descend, fall, sink.

mourn, *v.* SYN.-bemoan, bewail, deplore, grieve, lament, suffer, weep. ANT.-carouse, celebrate, rejoice, revel.

move, *v.* SYN.-actuate, advance, agitate, arouse, drive, excite, impel, impress, induce, influence, instigate, persuade, proceed, propel, propose, push, recommend, shift, stimulate, stir, suggest, sway, transfer. ANT.-deter. halt, rest, stay, stop.

moved, *a.* SYN.-carried, conveyed, departed, disturbed, excited, recommended, shifted, stimulated, taken, transferred.

movement, *n.* SYN.-action, activity, change, gesture, inclination, motion, move, progress, rhythm, tempo, tendency. ANT.-equilibrium, immobility, stability, stillness.

much, *a.* SYN.-abundant, ample, considerable, plentiful, profuse, substantial.

muddled, *a.* SYN.-addled, bewildered, confused, disconcerted, disordered, disorganized, indistinct, mixed, perplexed. ANT.-clear, lucid, obvious, organized, plain.

muddy, *a.* SYN.-blurred, cloudy, confused, dark, indistinct, indistinguishable, murky, obscure, unclear.

multitude, *n.* SYN.-army, crowd, host, legion, mob, throng. ANT.-few, handful, paucity, scarcity.

mundane, *a.* SYN.-earthly, laic, lay, normal, ordinary, practical, routine, secular, temporal, worldly. ANT.-ecclesiastical, religious, spiritual, unworldly.

municipality, *n.* SYN.-borough, city, community, district, town, village.

murder, *v.* SYN.-assassinate, butcher, destroy, execute, kill, mar, massacre, ruin, slaughter, slay, spoil. ANT.-animate, protect, resuscitate, save, vivify.

murky, *a.* SYN.-ambiguous, cloudy, dark, devious, dim, dusky, esoteric, gloomy, hazy, obscure, shadowy.

murmur, *n.* SYN.-complaint, grumble, mumble, mutter, plaint, rumor, whimper.

murmur, *v.* SYN.-babble, complain, grouse, growl, grumble, moan, mumble, rumble, trickle, whisper.

museum, *n.* SYN.-archive, depository, gallery, library, treasury.

music, *n.* SYN.-air, consonance, harmonics, harmony, melody, song, symphony, tune.

muss, *n.* SYN.-chaos, clutter, confusion, disarry, disorder, disorganization, jumble, mess, muddle, turmoil.

muss, *v.* SYN.-crumple, disarrange, dishevel, disturb, jumble, ruffle, rumple, tousle.

must, *n.* SYN.-condition, contingency, demand, obligation, necessity, prerequisite, provision, requisite, requirement.

muster, *v.* SYN.-accumulate, amass, assemble, collect, congregate, convene, gather, marshal, summon. ANT.-disband, disperse, distribute, scatter, separate.

mute, *a.* SYN.-inarticulate, dumb, hushed, noiseless, peaceful, quiet, silent, still, taciturn, tranquil. ANT.-clamorous, loud, noisy, raucous.

mutiny, *n.* SYN.-agitation, commotion, coup, insurrection, overthrow, rebellion, revolt, revolution, sedition, uprising.

mutual, *a.* SYN.-collective, communal, common, correlative, interchangeable, joint, public, reciprocal, shared. ANT.-dissociated, separate, unrequited, unshared.

myriad, *a.* SYN.-endless, indefinite, innumerable, multiple, variable.

mysterious, *a.* SYN.-cabalistic, cryptic, dark, dim, enigmatic, esoteric, hidden, incomprehensible, inexplicable, inscrutable, mystical, obscure, occult, recondite, secret, strange. ANT.-clear, explained, obvious, plain, simple.

mystery, *n.* SYN.-cabal, conundrum, enigma, problem, puzzle, riddle, secret. ANT.-answer, clue, key, resolution, solution.

mystical, *a.* SYN.-abstruse, cabalistic, enigmatic, incomprehensible, mysterious.

mystique, *n.* SYN.-appearance, attitude, character, characteristics, demeanor, deportment, manner, nature, style.

myth, *n.* SYN.-allegory, chronicle, fable, fiction, legend, parable, saga. ANT.-fad, history.

N

nag, *v.* SYN.-aggravate, annoy, badger, bother, disturb, harass, harry, irritate, pester, plague, provoke, tantalize, taunt, tease, torment, vex, worry. ANT.-comfort, delight, gratify, please, soothe.

naive, *a.* SYN.-artless, callow, candid, fanciful, frank, guileless, ingenuous, innocent, instinctive, natural, open, provincial, romantic, simple, spontaneous, unaffected, unsophisticated. ANT.-crafty, cunning, sophisticated, worldly.

naked, *a.* SYN.-bare, defenseless, exposed, mere, nude, open, plain, simple, stripped, unclad, uncovered, unprotected; bald, barren, unfurnished. ANT.-clothed, covered, dressed; concealed; protected.

name, *n.* SYN.-appellation, denomination, designation, epithet, style, surname, title; acclaim, character, distinction, eminence, fame, honor, note, renown, reputation, repute. ANT.-misnomer, namelessness; anonymity.

name, *v.* SYN.-address, appoint, baptize, call, characterize, christen, classify, denominate, entitle, enumerate, identify, indicate, label, mention, specify. ANT.-hint, miscall, misname.

named, *a.* SYN.-appointed, commissioned, delegated, designated, nominated, ordained, picked, selected.

nap, *n.* SYN.-catnap, doze, drowse, nod, repose, rest, sleep, slumber, snooze.

narrate, *v.* SYN.-declaim, deliver, describe, detail, enumerate, mention, recapitulate, recite, recount, rehearse, relate, repeat, tell.

narrative, *n.* SYN.-account, chronicle, description, detail, history, narration, recital, relation, story, yarn. ANT.-caricature, confusion, distortion, misrepresentation.

narrow, *a.* SYN.-close, confined, cramped, meager, slender, slim, spare, tight; bigoted, dogmatic, fanatical, illiberal, intolerant, narrow-minded, opinionated, parochial, prejudiced. ANT.-liberal, progressive, radical, tolerant.

nasty, *a.* SYN.-base, contemptible, defiled, despicable, disagreeable, disgusting, foul, gross, horrid, low, malicious, mean, nauseous, offensive, repellent, revolting, sordid, unpleasant, vile, vulgar. ANT.-admirable, amiable, attractive, decent, delightful, dignified, exalted, generous, nice, noble, pleasant.

nation, *n.* SYN.-commonwealth, community, country, domain, dominion, kingdom, nationality, people, populace, principality, realm, republic, state.

nationalism, *n.* SYN.-allegiance,

chauvinism, loyalty, provincialism, patriotism.

native, *a.* SYN.-aboriginal, congenital, domestic, endemic, fundamental, hereditary, inborn, indigenous, inherent, innate, natural, original.

natural, *a.* SYN.-actual, characteristic, common, congenital, crude, fundamental, general, genetic, genuine, ingenuous, inherent, innate, intrinsic, involuntary, native, normal, original, real, regular, simple, spontaneous, tangible, typical, unaffected, unconstrained, unfeigned, usual. ANT.-affected, artificial, embellished, forced, formal.

nature, *n.* SYN.-character, class, description, disposition, essence, individuality, kind, qualifications, reputation, repute, sort, standing, temperament.

nautical, *a.* SYN.-marine, maritime, naval, ocean, oceanic.

near, *a.* SYN.-adjacent, approaching, beside, bordering, close, coming, contiguous, expected, imminent, impending, neighboring, nigh, proximate; dear, familiar, intimate. ANT.-distant, far, removed.

neat, *a.* SYN.-clear, dapper, deft, exact, nice, orderly, precise, prim, smart, spruce, systematic, taut, tidy, trim, unadulterated, undiluted. ANT.-dirty, disheveled, sloppy, slovenly, unkempt.

necessary, *a.* SYN.-compulsory, essential, expedient, fundamental, indispensable, inevitable, needed, obligatory, requisite, unavoidable. ANT.-accidental, casual; contingent, nonessential, optional.

necessity, *n.* SYN.-compulsion. demand, exigency, fundamental, need, qualification, requirement, requisite, want. ANT.-choice, freedom, luxury, option, uncertainty.

need, *v.* SYN.-claim, covet, crave, demand, desire, lack, require, want, wish.

needless, *a.* SYN.-groundless, pointless, superfluous, unnecessary, useless.

negate, *v.* SYN.-annul, belie, cancel, contradict, impugn, repeal, retract.

neglect, *n.* SYN.-carelessness, default, dereliction, disregard, failure, heedlessness, indifference, negligence, omission, oversight, slight, thoughtlessness. ANT.-attention, care, diligence, watchfulness.

neglect, *v.* SYN.-affront, disregard, ignore, insult, omit, overlook, procrastinate, slight. ANT.-do, guard, perform, protect, satisfy.

negligence, *n.* SYN.-carelessness, default, dereliction, disregard, failure, heedlessness, neglect, nonchalance, omission, oversight, slight, thoughtlessness. ANT.-attention, care, diligence, watchfulness.

negligent, *a.* SYN.-careless, delinquent, derelict, desultory, heedless, imprudent, inaccurate, inattentive, lax, neglectful, remiss, thoughtless, unconcerned. ANT.-accurate, careful, meticulous, precise.

negotiate, *v.* SYN.-arbitrate, bargain, barter, conciliate, confer, consult, intercede, mediate, parley, referee.

neighbor, *n.* SYN.-acquaintance, associate, friend.

neighbor, *v.* SYN.-abut, adjoin, border, touch, verge.

neighborhood, *n.* SYN.-adjacency, block, district, environs, locality, nearness, vicinity. ANT.-distance, remoteness.

neighborly, *a.* SYN.-affable, amicable, companionable, congenial, friendly, genial, helpful, hospitable, kindly, sociable, social. ANT.-antagonistic, cool, distant, hostile, reserved.

nerve, *n.* SYN.-audacity, courage, fortitude, impudence, intrepidity, mettle, presumption, resolution, spirit, temerity.

nerves, *n.* SYN.-anxiety, apprehension, emotion, misgivings, strain, stress, tension.

nervous, *a.* SYN.-excitable, impatient, irritable, moody, restless, sensitive, tense, touchy, uneasy, unstable.

network, *n.* SYN.-arrangement, channels, complex, labyrinth, mesh, net, structure, system, tangle, web.

neurotic, *a.* SYN.-deranged, disturbed, erratic, irrational, troubled, unstable.

neutral, *a.* SYN.-detached, disinterested, impartial, inactive, indifferent, nonpartisan, unbiased.

new, *a.* SYN.-contemporary, current, fashionable, fresh, late, modern, newfangled, novel, original, recent, unique. ANT.-ancient, antiquated, archaic, obsolete, old.

news, *n.* SYN.-account, advice, copy, description, discovery, enlightenment, information, intelligence, message, narration, publication, report, tidings.

nice, *a.* SYN.-agreeable, amiable, considerate, courteous, cultured, genial, good, gracious, obliging, pleasant, pleasing, refined.

niche, *n.* SYN.-alcove, corner, cranny, cubbyhole, nook, recess.

nick, *n.* SYN.-dent, gouge, indentation, mar, notch, score, scrape, scratch.

niggardly, *a.* SYN.-avaricious, cheap, greedy, miserly, parsimonious, penurious, stingy, tight. ANT.-altruistic, bountiful, extravagant, generous, munificent.

nimble, *a.* SYN.-active, agile, alert, bright, brisk, clever, flexible, lively, quick, spry, supple. ANT.-clumsy, heavy, inert, slow, sluggish.

noble, *a.* SYN.-courtly, cultivated, dignified, distinguished, elevated, eminent, exalted, grand, illustrious, imposing, impressive, lofty, lordly, majestic, refined, stately, virtuous. ANT.-base, low, mean, plebeian, vile.

nod, *v.* SYN.-acknowledge, assent, concur, consent, greet.

noise, *n.* SYN.-babel, clamor, cry, din, outcry, racket, row, sound, tumult, uproar. ANT.-hush, quiet, silence, stillness.

noisy, *a.* SYN.-cacophonous, clamorous, deafening, loud, resounding, sonorous, stentorian, vociferous ANT.-dulcet, inaudible, quiet, soft, subdued.

nonchalant, *a.* SYN.-aloof, apathetic, calm, casual, composed, detached, impassive, unconcerned. ANT.-active, attentive, emotional, enthusiastic.

nonconformist, *n.* dissenter, eccentric, maverick, radical, rebel.

nonexistent, *a.* SYN.-fictitious, imaginary, unreal.

nonsensical, *a.* SYN.-absurd, foolish, inconsistent, irrational, ludicrous, meaningless, preposterous, ridiculous, self-contradictory, silly, unreasonable. ANT.-consistent, rational, reasonable, sensible, sound.

normal, *a.* SYN.-common, conventional, customary, natural, ordinary, regular, steady, systematic, typical, uniform, unvaried, usual. ANT.-abnormal, erratic, exceptional, rare, unusual.

nosy, *a.* SYN.-curious, inquiring, inquisitive, interrogative, meddling, peeping, peering, prying, searching, snoopy. ANT.-incurious, indifferent, unconcerned, uninterested.

notable, *a.* SYN.-celebrated, conspicuous, distinguished, eminent, famous, notable, remarkable, striking, unusual.

note, *n.* SYN.-indication, mark, sign, symbol, token; annotation, comment, letter, memorandum, message, observation, remark.

noted, *a.* SYN.-celebrated, distinguished, eminent, famous, glorious, illustrious, renowned, well-known. ANT.-hidden, ignominious, infamous, obscure, unknown.

notice, *n.* SYN.-alertness, attention, cognizance, heed, mindfulness, observance, watchfulness; advertisement, announcement, circular, declaration, notification, proclamation, sign, warning. ANT.-disregard, indifference, negligence, omission, oversight.

notice, *v.* SYN.-attend, behold, descry, distinguish, heed, mark, note, observe, perceive, recognize, regard, remark, see. ANT.-disregard, ignore, overlook, skip.

notify, *v.* SYN.-advise, announce, apprise, caution, communicate, convey, disclose, enlighten, inform, herald, mention, proclaim, reveal, telephone, tell, warn, write. ANT.-conceal, delude, distract, mislead.

notion, *n.* SYN.-assumption, belief, fancy, idea, impression, inkling, opinion, sentiment, thought, whim.

novel, *n.* SYN.-allegory, fiction, narrative, romance, story, tale. ANT.-fact, history, reality, truth, verity.

novice, *n.* SYN.-amateur, apprentice, beginner, learner, neophyte. ANT.-adept, authority, expert, master, professional.

now, *n.* SYN.-immediate, present, promptly, soon, today.

nuance, *n.* SYN.-difference, gradation, shade, subtly, variation.

nude, *a.* SYN.-bare, exposed, naked, stripped, unclad, uncovered. ANT.-clothed, covered, dressed.

nudge, *v.* SYN.-bump, dig, jab, poke, tap, touch.

nuisance, *n.* SYN.-aggravation, annoyance, bother, irritation, pest, vexation.

nullify, *v.* SYN.-abolish, abrogate, annul, cancel, cross out, delete, eliminate, erase, expunge, invalidate, obliterate, quash, repeal, rescind, revoke. ANT.-confirm, enact, enforce, perpetuate

numb, *a.* SYN.-anesthetized, apathetic, callous, deadened, disinterested, lethargic, unfeeling.

number, *n.* SYN.-aggregate, amount, count, extent, enumeration, estimate, measure, portion, quantity, sum, total, volume. ANT.-nothing, nothingness, zero.

numerous, *a.* SYN.-divers, manifold, many. multifarious, multitudinous, several, sundry, various. ANT.-few, infrequent, meager, scanty, scarce.

nuptials, *n.* SYN.-espousal, marriage, matrimony, union, wedding, wedlock. ANT.-celibacy, divorce, virginity.

nurture, *v.* SYN.-cherish, feed, nourish, nurse, prize, sustain, treasure, value. ANT.-abandon, disregard, neglect, reject.

nutriment, *n.* SYN.-diet, edibles, feed, food, meal, provisions, rations, repast, sustenance, viands, victuals. ANT.-drink, hunger, starvation, want.

nymph, *n.* SYN.-dryad, fairy, goddess, mermaid, sprite.

O

oath, *n.* SYN.-affidavit, declaration, deposition, pledge, promise, testimony, vow.

obdurate, *a.* SYN.-callous, hard, impenitent, indurate, insensible, insensitive, tough, unfeeling. ANT.-compassionate, sensitive, soft, tender.

obedient, *a.* SYN.-compliant, deferential, dutiful, loyal, submissive, tractable, yielding. ANT.-insubordinate, intractable, obstinate, rebellious.

obese, *a.* SYN.-chubby, corpulent, fat, paunchy, plump, portly, pudgy, rotund, stocky, stout, thickset. ANT.-gaunt, lean, slender, slim, thin.

object, *n.* SYN.-article, particular, thing; aim, design, end, goal, intention, mark, objective, purpose. ANT.-shadow, spirit, vision; consequence, result.

object, *v.* SYN.-abominate, disagree, disapprove, oppose, protest, reject, remonstrate. ANT.-acquiesce, approve, assent, comply, concur.

objection, *n.* SYN.-challenge, difference, disagreement, dissent, dissentience, protest, remonstrance. ANT.-acceptance, agreement, assent, compliance.

objective, *n.* SYN.-aim, ambition, aspiration. craving, design, desire, end, goal, hope, intent, intention, object, passion, purpose.

obligate, *v.* SYN.-bind, commit, consign, entrust, force, oblige, pledge, relegate, trust. ANT.-free, loose, neglect, release, renounce.

obligation, *n.* SYN.-accountability, bond, compulsion, contract, debt, duty, engagement, responsibility. ANT.-choice, exemption, freedom.

oblige, *v.* SYN.-coerce, compel, constrain, drive, enforce, force, impel; accommodate, aid, assist, favor, help, please. ANT.-allure, convince, exempt, induce, persuade; annoy, forsake.

obliterate, *v.* SYN.-annihilate, demolish, destroy, devastate, eradicate, exterminate, extinguish, ravage, raze, ruin, wreck. ANT.-construct, establish, make, preserve, save.

oblivious, *a.* SYN.-blind, ignorant, preoccupied, undiscerning, unmindful, unseeing. ANT.-aware, calculated, discerning, perceiving, sensible.

obnoxious, *a.* SYN.-annoying, disagreeable, displeasing, impertinent, insulting, nasty, odious, offensive

obscene, *a.* SYN.-coarse, dirty, disgusting, filthy, gross, impure, indecent, lewd, offensive, pornographic, smutty. ANT.-decent, modest, pure, refined.

obscure, *a.* SYN.-abstruse, ambiguous, cloudy, cryptic, dark, dim, dusky, enigmatic, indistinct, mysterious, unintelligible, vague. ANT.-bright, clear, distinct, lucid.

observance, *n.* SYN.-ceremony, formality, parade, pomp, protocol, rite, ritual, solemnity; awareness, cognizance, heed, notice, observation.

observant, *a.* SYN.-alert, assiduous, attentive, aware, careful, considerate, diligent, discerning, heedful, mindful, perceptive, sensitive, thoughtful, wakeful, wary, watchful. ANT.-apathetic, careless, inattentive, indifferent, oblivious, unaware.

observe, *v.* SYN.-behold, detect, discover, examine, eye, inspect, mark, note, notice, perceive, recognize, see, view, watch; celebrate, commemorate, honor, keep, solemnize; express, mention, remark, utter. ANT.-disregard, ignore, neglect, overlook.

obsession, *n.* SYN.-compulsion, craze, fascination, fixation, mania, passion.

obsolete, *a.* SYN.-ancient, antiquated, archaic, obsolescent, old, out-of-date, venerable. ANT.-current, extant, fashionable, modern, recent.

obstacle, *n.* SYN.-bar, barrier, block, check, difficulty, hindrance, impediment, obstruction, snag. ANT.-aid, assistance, encouragement, help.

obstinate, *a.* SYN.-contumacious, determined, dogged, firm, headstrong, immovable, inflexible, intractable, obdurate, pertinacious, stubborn, uncompromising, unyielding. ANT.-amenable, compliant, docile, submissive, yielding.

obstruct, *v.* SYN.-bar, barricade, block, clog, close, delay, impede, hinder, stop. ANT.-aid, clear, further, open, promote.

obtain, *v.* SYN.-acquire, assimilate, attain, collect, earn, get, glean, gather, procure, reap, recover, secure, win. ANT.-forego, forfeit, lose, miss, surrender.

obtuse, *a.* SYN.-blunt, boring, commonplace, dense, dull, slow, stupid, tedious. ANT.-animated, lively, sharp; clear, interesting.

obvious, *a.* SYN.-apparent, clear, conspicuous, distinct, evident, manifest, palpable, patent, plain, prominent, self-evident, unmistakable, visible. ANT.-abstruse, concealed, hidden, obscure.

occupation, *n.* SYN.-business, commerce, employment, engagement, enterprise, job, profession, trade, vocation, work. ANT.-avocation, hobby, pastime.

occupy, *v.* SYN.-absorb, busy, dwell, fill, have, hold, inhabit, keep, possess, remain. ANT.-abandon, release, relinquish.

occur, *v.* SYN.-appear, arise, bechance, befall, betide, chance, happen, transpire.

occurrence, *n.* SYN.-circumstance, episode, event, happening, incident, issue.

odd, *a.* SYN.-bizarre, curious, eccentric, peculiar, quaint, queer, singular, strange, unique, unusual. ANT.-common, familiar, normal, regular, typical.

odious, *a.* SYN.-abject, base, debased, depraved, despicable, foul, ignoble, loathsome, low, mean, obscene, revolting, sordid, vicious, vile, vulgar, wicked, worthless, wretched. ANT.-attractive, decent, honorable, laudable, upright.

odor, *n.* SYN.-aroma, fetidness, fragrance, fume, incense, perfume, redolence, scent, smell, stench, stink.

offend, *v.* SYN.-annoy, antagonize, bother, insult, slight.

offense, *n.* SYN.-aggression, affront, atrocity, crime, indignity, injustice, insult, outrage, misdeed, sin, transgression, trespass, vice, wrong. ANT.-gentleness, innocence, morality, right.

offensive, *a.* SYN.-disagreeable, disgusting, distressing, dreadful, foul, horrid, invidious, nauseous, nasty, repugnant, unpleasant.

offer, *n.* SYN.-bid, overture, proposal, proposition, suggestion, tender. ANT.-acceptance, denial, rejection, withdrawal.

offer, *v.* SYN.-advance, exhibit, extend, present, proffer, propose, sacrifice, tender, volunteer. ANT.-accept, receive, reject, retain, spurn.

offering, *n.* SYN.-alms, charity, contribution, donation, gift, present, sacrifice.

office, *n.* SYN.-building, cubicle, facility, site, station, suite; berth, incumbency, job, place, position, post, rank, situation, standing, status.

often, *adv.* SYN.-commonly, frequently, generally, recurrent, repeatedly. ANT.-infrequently, occasionally, rarely, seldom, sporadically.

old, *a.* SYN.-aged, ancient, antiquated, antique, archaic, elderly, obsolete, old-fashioned, senile, superannuated, venerable. ANT.-modern, new, young, youthful.

omen, *n.* SYN. augury, foretoken, gesture, indication, mark, portent, presage, sign, symbol, token, warning.

ominous, *a.* SYN.-dire, forbidding, foreboding, gloomy, grim, menacing, portentous, threatening.

omission, *n.* SYN.-default, deletion, failure, neglect, oversight. ANT.-attention, inclusion, insertion, notice.

omit, *v.* SYN.-cancel, delete, disregard, drop, eliminate, exclude, ignore, miss, neglect, overlook, skip. ANT.-enter, include, insert, introduce, notice.

onslaught, *n.* SYN.-aggression, assault, attack, criticism, denunciation, invasion, offense. ANT.-defense, opposition, resistance, surrender, vindication.

open, *a.* SYN.-accessible, agape, ajar, available, candid, clear, disengaged, exposed, frank, free, honest, overt, passable, plain, public, unclosed, uncovered, unlocked, unobstructed, unoccupied, unrestricted.

open, *v.* SYN.-exhibit, expand, spread, unbar, unfasten, unfold, unlock, unseal. ANT.-close, conceal, hide, shut.

opening, *n.* SYN.-abyss, aperture, cavern, cavity, chasm, gap, gulf, hole, pore, slit, slot, void.

operate, *v.* SYN.-act, function, employ, interact, manage, manipulate, proceed, run, use, utilize.

operation, *n.* SYN.-action, agency, control, effort, enterprise, execution, handling, instrumentality, maneuver, manipulation, performance, proceeding, running, surgery, working. ANT.-cessation, inaction, inactivity, rest.

operative, *a.* SYN.-active, effective, serviceable, working. ANT.-dormant, inactive.

opinion, *n.* SYN.-belief, conviction, decision, feeling, idea, impression, judgment, notion, persuasion, sentiment, view. ANT.-fact, skepticism, misgiving, knowledge.

opinionated, *a.* SYN.-arrogant, authoritarian, bigoted, doctrinaire, dogmatic, domineering, magisterial, obstinate, overbearing, positive, stubborn. ANT.-fluctuating, indecisive, open-minded, questioning, skeptical.

opponent, *n.* SYN.-adversary, antagonist, challenger, competitor, contestant, enemy, foe, rival. ANT.-ally, comrade, confederate, teammate.

opportunity, *n.* SYN.-chance, contingency, freedom, fortune, happening, occasion, opening, possibility, probability. ANT.-disadvantage, hindrance, obstacle.

oppose, *v.* SYN.-argue, bar, combat, confront, contradict, counteract, debate, defy, deny, disapprove, hinder, mutiny, obstruct, protest, rebel, resist, thwart, withstand. ANT.-agree, cooperate, submit, succumb, support.

opposed, *a.* SYN.-adverse, antagonistic, contrary, hostile, opposite. ANT.-benign, favorable.

opposition, *n.* SYN.-conflict, contention, controversy, discord, encounter, fight, interference, struggle. ANT.-amity, concord, consonance, harmony.

oppress, *v.* SYN.-afflict, harass, harry, hound, persecute, plague, torment, torture, vex, worry. ANT.-aid, assist, comfort, encourage, support.

optimism, *n.* SYN.-anticipation, confidence, expectancy, expectation, faith, hope, trust. ANT.-despair, despondency, pessimism.

option, *n.* SYN.-alternative, choice, election, preference, selection.

opulence, *n.* SYN.-abundance, affluence, fortune, luxury, money, plenty, possessions, riches, wealth. ANT.-indigence, need, poverty, want.

oral, *a.* SYN.-literal, spoken, verbal, vocal. ANT.-documentary, recorded, written.

ordain, *v.* SYN.-appoint, cause, constitute, create, engender, fashion, form, formulate, generate, invent, make, originate, produce. ANT.-annihilate, demolish, destroy, disband, terminate.

ordeal, *n.* SYN.-affliction, examination, experiment, hardship, misery, misfortune, suffering, test, trial, tribulation, trouble. ANT.-alleviation, consolation.

order, *n.* SYN.-arrangement, class, method, plan, rank, regularity, sequence, series, succession, system; bidding, command, decree, dictate, injunction, instruction, mandate, requirement. ANT.-confusion, disarray, disorder, irregularity; consent, license, permission.

order, *v.* SYN.-bid, command, conduct, direct, govern, guide, instruct, manage, regulate, rule. ANT.-misdirect, misguide.

orderly, *a.* SYN.-arranged, methodical, neat, organized, systematic, tidy.

ordinary, *a.* SYN.-accustomed, common, conventional, customary, familiar, habitual, normal, plain, regular, typical, usual, vulgar. ANT.-extraordinary, marvelous, remarkable, strange, uncommon.

organization, *n.* SYN.-arrangement, method, mode, order, plan, process, regularity, rule, scheme, system. ANT.-chance, chaos, confusion, disarrangement, disorder, irregularity.

organize, *v.* SYN.-arrange, assort, classify, devise, place, plan, prepare, regulate, sort. ANT.-confuse, disorder, disturb, jumble, scatter.

origin, *n.* SYN.-beginning, birth, commencement, cradle, derivation, foundation, inception, source, spring, start. ANT.-end, harvest, issue, outcome, product.

original, *a.* SYN.-first, initial, primary, primeval, primordial, pristine; creative, fresh, inventive, new, novel. ANT.-derivative, later, modern., subsequent, terminal; banal, plagiarized, trite.

originate, *v.* SYN.-arise, begin, cause, commence, create, engender, establish, fashion, form, formulate, found, generate, inaugurate, initiate, institute, invent, make, organize, originate, produce, start; appoint, constitute, ordain. ANT.-annihilate, complete, demolish, destroy, disband, end, finish, terminate.

ornament, *n.* SYN.-adornment, decoration, embellishment, garnish, ornamentation.

ornate, *a.* SYN.-adorned, embellished, flashy, gaudy, lavish, showy, stylish, tawdry, trimmed

oscillate, *v.* SYN.-change, fluctuate, undulate, swing, vary, waver. ANT.-adhere, persist, resolve, stick.

ostentation, *n.* SYN.-boasting, display, flourish, pageantry, parade, pomp, show, vaunting. ANT.-humility, modesty, reserve, unobtrusiveness.

ostracize, *v.* SYN.-bar, blackball, except, exclude, expel, prevent, prohibit, restrain, shut out. ANT.-accept, admit, include, welcome.

oust, *v.* SYN.-banish, depose, discharge, dismiss, eject, evict, expel, overthrow, remove.

outline, *n.* SYN.-brief, contour, delineation, draft, figure, form, plan, profile, silhouette, sketch.

outrageous, *a.* SYN.-abominable, atrocious, disgraceful, exorbitant, heinous, infamous, notorious, scandalous, shameless, shocking.

outsider, *n.* SYN.-alien, foreigner, immigrant, newcomer, stranger. ANT.-acquaintance, associate, countryman, friend, neighbor.

outspoken, *a.* SYN.-abrupt, bluff, blunt, brusque, candid, direct, frank, impertinent, impolite, insulting. plain, rough, rude, unceremonious. ANT.-polished, polite, suave, subtle, tactful.

overcast, *a.* SYN.-cloudy, dark, dim, murky, shadowy. ANT.-bright, clear, distinct, limpid, sunny.

overcome, *v.* SYN.-beat, conquer, crush, defeat, humble, master, quell, rout, subdue, subjugate, surmount, vanquish. ANT.-capitulate, cede, lose, retreat, surrender.

overload, *v.* SYN.-afflict, burden, encumber, load, oppress, tax, trouble, weigh. ANT.-alleviate, console, ease, lighten, mitigate.

overlook, *v.* SYN.-disregard, exclude, ignore, miss, neglect, omit, pass, pass over, skip. ANT.-enter, include, insert, introduce, notice.

overseer, *n.* SYN.-employer, foreman, head, leader, manager, master, owner, proprietor, superintendent, supervisor. ANT.-servant, slave; amateur.

oversight, *n.* SYN.-error, inadvertence, inattention, mistake, neglect, omission; charge, control, inspection, management, superintendence, supervision, surveillance. ANT.-attention, care, observation, scrutiny.

overturn, *v.* SYN.-destroy, overcome, replace, rout, ruin, supplant, upset. ANT.-conserve, maintain, preserve, uphold.

overthrow, *v.* SYN.-demolish, destroy, overcome, overturn, rout, ruin, supplant, upset, vanquish. ANT.-build, conserve, construct, preserve, uphold.

overwhelmed, *a.* SYN.-beaten crushed, extinguished, obliterated, ravaged, swamped; affected, impressed, moved, touched.

P

pacific, *a.* SYN.-calm, composed, dispassionate, imperturbable, peaceful, placid, quiet, serene, still, tranquil, undisturbed, unruffled. ANT.-excited, frantic, stormy, turbulent, wild.

pacify, *v.* SYN.-allay, alleviate, appease, assuage, calm, compose, lull, placate, quell, quiet, relieve, satisfy, soothe, still, tranquilize. ANT.-arouse, excite, incense, inflame.

packed, *a.* SYN.-crammed, filled, full, gorged, replete, satiated, soaked, stuffed, tamped. ANT.-depleted, devoid, empty, vacant; insufficient, lacking, partial.

pact, *n.* SYN.-accordance, agreement, bargain, compact, concord, concurrence, contract, covenant, stipulation, understanding, ANT.-difference, disagreement, discord, dissension, variance.

pageant, *n.* SYN.-array, celebration, display, exhibition, exposition, parade.

pain, *n.* SYN.-ache, agony, anguish, distress, grief, pang, paroxysm, suffering, throe, twinge. ANT.-comfort, ease, relief, happiness, pleasure. solace.

painful, *a.* SYN.-acrimonious, biting, bitter, caustic, distasteful, galling, grievous, harsh, poignant, sardonic, severe. ANT.-delicious, mellow, pleasant, sweet.

painting, *n.* SYN.-illustration, landscape, likeness, panorama, picture, portrait, portrayal, rendering, representation, scene, view.

pale, *a.* SYN.-anemic, ashen, blanched, haggard, pallid, sickly, wan.

pamper, *v.* SYN.-coddle, humor, indulge, spoil.

panic, *n.* SYN.-alarm, apprehension, dread, fear, fright, horror, terror, trembling. ANT.-calmness, composure, serenity, tranquility.

parable, *n.* SYN.-allegory, anecdote, fable, legend, narrative, story, tale, yarn.

parade, *n.* SYN.-cavalcade, ceremony, cortege, file, pageant, procession, review, train.

paradox, *n.* SYN.-ambiguity, contradiction, enigma, mystery, puzzle.

paradoxical, *a.* SYN.-ambiguous, contradictory, curious, discrepant, illogical, incompatible, incongruous, inconsistent, ironic, irreconcilable, obscure, puzzling, strange. ANT.-compatible, congruous, consistent, correspondent.

parallel, *a.* SYN.-akin, alike, allied, analogous, comparable, correlative, correspondent, corresponding, equal, like, similar. ANT.-different, dissimilar, divergent, incongruous, opposed.

parched, *a.* SYN.-arid, burned, dehydrated, desiccated, dry, thirsty, withered. ANT.-damp, moist.

pardon, *n.* SYN.-absolution, acquittal, amnesty, exoneration, forgiveness, remission. ANT.-conviction, penalty, punishment, sentence.

pardon, *v.* SYN.-absolve, acquit, condone, excuse, forgive, overlook, release, remit. ANT.-accuse, chastise, condemn, convict, punish.

park, *n.* SYN.-boulevard, common, esplanade, green, lawn, plaza, preserve, promenade, reservation, square, tract.

parley, *n.* SYN.-chat, colloquy, conference, conversation, dialogue, discourse, discussion, encounter, interview, meeting, negotiation, talk.

part, *n.* SYN.-allotment, apportionment, component, division, element, fragment, ingredient, member, moiety, piece, portion, scrap, section, segment, share; character, lines, role. ANT.-entirety, whole.

part, *v.* SYN.-break, cleave, detach, divide, separate, sever, sunder; allot, apportion, distribute, mete, parcel, share. ANT.-combine, convene, gather, join unite.

partake, *v.* SYN.-appropriate, cooperate, experience, participate, receive, share.

partiality, *n.* SYN.-affection, bent, bias, favoritism, fondness, inclination, leaning, predisposition, preference, prejudice, taste, tendency. ANT.-dislike, equality, fairness, impartiality, justice, proof, reason.

participation, *n.* SYN.-allotment, dividend, interest, quota, part, proportion; association, communion, encouragement, fellowship, intercourse, sacrament, sharing, union. ANT.-alienation, non participation.

particle, *n.* SYN.-atom, bit, corpuscle, crumb, grain, iota, jot, mite, scrap, shred, smidgen, speck. ANT.-aggregate, bulk, mass, quantity.

particular, *a.* SYN.-characteristic, distinctive, individual, peculiar, specific; singular, unusual; circumstantial, detailed, exact, minute, specific; careful, choosy, fastidious, finicky, squeamish. ANT.-comprehensive, general, universal; ordinary; general, rough; undiscriminating.

particular, *n.* SYN.-circumstance, detail, feature, item, minutia, point, specification. ANT.-generality.

partisan, *n.* SYN.-adherent, attendant, devotee, disciple, follower, henchman, successor, supporter, votary. ANT.-chief, head, leader, master.

partner, *n.* SYN.-accomplice, ally, associate, attendant, cohort, colleague, companion, comrade, consort, crony, friend, mate, spouse. ANT.-adversary, enemy, stranger.

passable, *a.* SYN.-acceptable, admissible, average, fair, mediocre, marginal. ANT.-excellent, first-rate, worst.

passion, *n.* SYN.-affection, craving, desire, emotion, feeling, lust, sentiment, trepidation, turmoil. ANT.-calm, dispassion, indifference, restraint, tranquility.

passionate, *a.* SYN.-ardent, burning, excitable, fervent, fervid, fiery, glowing, hot, impetuous, impassioned, intense, irascible, moving, tempestuous, vehement. ANT.-apathetic, calm, cool, deliberate, quiet.

passive, *a.* SYN.-acquiescent, enduring, idle, inactive, inert, patient, quiet, relaxed, resigned, stoical, submissive. ANT.-active, aggressive, alert, dynamic, energetic, hostile, impatient.

pastime, *n.* SYN.-amusement, avocation, contest, diversion, fun, game, hobby match, merriment, play, recreation, sport. ANT.-business drudgery, hardship, labor, work.

patent, *a.* SYN.-apparent, clear, conspicuous, evident, indubitable, manifest, obvious, open, overt, unmistakable. ANT.-concealed, covert, hidden, obscure.

path, *n.* SYN.-avenue, channel, course, passage, road, route, street, thoroughfare, track, trail, walk, way.

pathetic, *a.* SYN.-affecting, moving, piteous, pitiable, poignant, sad, touching. ANT.-comical, funny, ludicrous.

patience, *n.* SYN.-composure, endurance, forbearance, fortitude, long-suffering, perseverance, resignation. ANT.-impatience, nervousness, restlessness.

patient, *a.* SYN.-composed, forbearing, indulgent, long-suffering, passive, resigned, stoical, uncomplaining. ANT.-chafing, clamorous, high-strung, hysterical, turbulent.

patron, *n.* SYN.-advocate, ally, backer, benefactor, champion, friend, helper, protector.

patronizing, *a.* SYN.-condescending, contemptuous, disdainful, disparaging, egotistic, overbearing, scornful.

pause, *v.* SYN.-delay, deliberate, demur, doubt, falter, hesitate, interrupt, reflect, rest, suspend, vacillate, waver. ANT.-continue, decide, persevere, proceed.

pay, *n.* SYN.-allowance, compensation, consideration, earnings, fee, payment, proceeds, recompense, return, salary, stipend, wages. ANT.-gift, gratuity, present.

peace, *n.* SYN.-calm, calmness, hush, quiescence, quiet, quietude, repose, serenity, silence, stillness, tranquility; cease fire, disarmament, treaty, truce. ANT.-agitation, disturbance, excitement, noise, tumult; hostility, war.

peaceful, *a.* SYN.-calm, gentle, mild, pacific, placid, quiet, serene, still, tranquil, undisturbed. ANT.-agitated, disturbed, noisy, turbulent, violent.

peak, *n.* SYN.-acme, apex, climax, consummation, crown, culmination, height, summit, top, zenith. ANT.-anticlimax, base, depth, floor.

peculiar, *a.* SYN.-characteristic, distinctive, eccentric, exceptional, extraordinary, individual, odd, particular, rare, singular, special, strange, striking, unusual. ANT.-common, general, normal, ordinary.

peculiarity, *n.* SYN.-attribute, characteristic, feature, mark, property, quality, trait.

pedantic, *a.* SYN.-academic, bookish, erudite, formal, learned, scholarly, scholastic, theoretical. ANT.-common-sense, ignorant, practical, simple.

peevish, *a.* SYN.-fractious, fretful, ill-natured, ill-tempered, irritable, petulant, snappish, testy, touchy, waspish. ANT.-affable, genial, good-natured, good-tempered, pleasant.

penalty, *n.* SYN.-chastisement, fine, forfeiture, punishment, retribution; disadvantage, handicap. ANT.-compensation, pardon, remuneration, reward.

penance, *n.* SYN.-amends, atonement, compensation, expiation, mortification, purgation, reparation, repentance, restitution, suffering.

penetrating, *a.* SYN.-abstruse, deep, discerning, perspicacious, profound, recondite, solemn. ANT.-shallow, slight, superficial, trivial.

penitent, *a.* SYN.-apologetic, contrite, regretful, remorseful, repentant, sorrowful, sorry. ANT.-obdurate, remorseless.

pensive, *a.* SYN.-contemplative, dreamy, introspective, meditative, reflective, thoughtful. ANT.-heedless, inconsiderate, precipitous, rash, thoughtless.

people, *n.* SYN.-clan, community, folk, humanity, humankind, mankind, masses, multitude, nation, populace, proletariat, public, rabble, race, tribe.

perceive, *v.* SYN.-apprehend, comprehend, conceive, discern, note, notice, observe, recognize, see, understand. ANT.-ignore, miss, overlook.

perceptible, *a.* SYN.-appreciable, apprehensible, discernible, measurable, practical, reasonable, sensible, understandable. ANT.-absurd, impalpable, imperceptible, stupid.

perception, *n.* SYN.-apprehension, cognizance, comprehension, conception, discernment, insight, understanding. ANT.-ignorance, insensibility, misapprehension, misconception.

perceptive, *a.* SYN.-alert, astute, aware, cognizant, conscious, discerning, keen, mindful, observant, sensitive, shrewd, wise. ANT.-oblivious, unaware.

perfect, *a.* SYN.-absolute, blameless, complete, consummate, downright, entire, excellent, faultless, finished, full, holy, ideal, immaculate, pure, sinless, superlative, supreme, unqualified, utter, whole. ANT.-blemished, defective, deficient, faulty, imperfect, incomplete, lacking.

perfection, *n.* SYN.-accuracy, completion, consummation, fulfillment, ideal, paragon, precision, realization, standard, ultimate.

perform, *v.* SYN.-accomplish, achieve, act, complete, discharge, do, entertain, execute, finish, fulfill, impersonate, play, pretend, render, transact.

performance, *n.* SYN.-accomplishment, act, demonstration, entertainment, exhibition, play, production, show, spectacle.

perfunctory, *a.* SYN.-artificial, careless, cursory, dull, mechanical, stiff. ANT.-easy, heartfelt, natural, unrestrained.

peril, *n.* SYN.-danger, hazard, jeopardy, risk. ANT.-defense, immunity, protection, safety.

perilous, *a.* SYN.-critical, dangerous, hazardous, insecure, menacing, precarious, risky, threatening, unsafe. ANT.-firm, protected, safe, secure.

period, *n.* SYN.-age, date, duration, epoch, era, interim, season, span, spell, term, time.

periphery, *n.* SYN.-border, boundary, extremity, frontier, limit, outpost, perimeter.

perish, *v.* SYN.-cease, decay, decease, depart, die, expire. ANT.-begin, flourish, grow, live, survive.

permanent, *a.* SYN.-abiding, changeless, constant, durable, enduring, fixed, indestructible, lasting, stable, unchangeable. ANT.-ephemeral, temporary, transient, transitory, unstable.

permeate, *v.* SYN.-fill, infiltrate, penetrate, pervade, run through, saturate.

permissible, *a.* SYN.-admissible, allowable, fair, probable, tolerable, warranted. ANT.-inadmissible, irrelevant, unsuitable.

permission, *n.* SYN.-approval, authority, authorization, consent, grace, grant, leave, liberty, license, permit, sanction. ANT.-denial, opposition, prohibition, refusal.

permit, *v.* SYN.-allow, authorize, give, grant, indulge, let, sanction, suffer, tolerate, yield. ANT.-forbid, object, protest, refuse, resist.

permitted, *a.* SYN.-allowed, authorized, granted, legalized, licensed, sanctioned.

perpetrate, *v.* SYN.-commit, do, execute, perform. ANT.-fail, miscarry, neglect.

perpetual, *a.* SYN.-ceaseless, continual, endless, eternal, everlasting, infinite, timeless, undying. ANT. ephemeral, finite, mortal, temporal, transient.

perpetually, *adv.* SYN.-always, constantly, continually, eternally, ever, evermore, forever, incessantly, unceasingly. ANT.-fitfully, never, occasionally, rarely, sometimes.

perplex, *v.* SYN.-bewilder, confound, confuse, dumfound, mystify, nonplus, puzzle. ANT.-clarify, explain, illumine, instruct, solve.

perplexed, *a.* SYN.-bewildered, confused, deranged, disconcerted, disordered, disorganized, indistinct, mixed, muddled. ANT.-clear, lucid, obvious, organized, plain.

perplexing, *a.* SYN.-complex, complicated, intricate, involved. ANT.-plain, simple, uncompounded.

persecute, *v.* SYN.-afflict, annoy, badger, harass, harry, hound, oppress, pester, plague, torment, torture, vex, worry. ANT.-aid, assist, comfort, encourage, support.

persevere, *v.* SYN.-abide, continue, endure, last, press, persist, strive. ANT.-desist, discontinue, vacillate, waver.

perseverance, *n.* SYN.-constancy, determination, fortitude, industry, persistence, persistency, pertinacity, resolution, steadfastness, tenacity. ANT.-cessation, idleness, laziness, rest, sloth.

persist, *v.* SYN.-abide, continue, endure, last, persevere, remain. ANT.-cease, desist, discontinue, vacillate, waver.

persistence, *n.* SYN.-constancy, endurance, grit, perseverance, pluck, resolve, tenacity,

persistent, a, SYN.-constant, dogged, enduring, fixed, immovable, indefatigable, lasting, obstinate, persevering, perverse, steady, stubborn. ANT.-hesitant, unsure, vacillating, wavering.

persuade, *v.* SYN.-allure, coax, convince, entice, exhort, incite, induce, influence, prevail upon, urge, win over. ANT.-coerce, compel, deter, dissuade, restrain.

persuasion, *n.* SYN.-belief, conviction, decision, feeling, idea, impression, judgment, notion, opinion, sentiment, view. ANT.-fact, skepticism, misgiving, knowledge.

pertain, *v.* SYN.-apply, bear, concern, include, involve, refer, relate.

pertinent, *a.* SYN.-applicable, apposite, appropriate, apropos, apt, fit, germane, material, related, relating, relevant. ANT.-alien, extraneous, foreign, unrelated.

perturb, *v.* SYN.-annoy, agitate, bewilder, bother, confound, disturb, irritate, perplex, pester, worry.

pervade, *v.* SYN.-diffuse, fill, infiltrate, penetrate, permeate, run through, saturate.

perverse, *a.* SYN.-contrary, disobedient, forward, fractious, intractable, obstinate, peevish, perverted, petulant, sinful, stubborn, ungovernable, untoward, wicked. ANT.-agreeable, docile, obliging, tractable.

perverted, *a.* SYN.-corrupt, degenerate, depraved, deviated, distorted, kinky, lascivious, sick, twisted, unnatural, warped.

pesky, *a.* SYN.-annoying, disturbing, irritating, irksome, nagging, provoking, troublesome, unpleasant, vexing.

pessimistic, *a.* SYN.-cynical, despairing, fatalistic, foreboding, gloomy, hopeless, morbid, morose, sullen, troubled.

pester, *v.* SYN.-annoy. bother, chafe, disturb, irk, irritate, tease, trouble, vex. ANT.-accommodate, console, gratify, soothe.

petite, *a.* SYN.-baby, diminutive, inconsequential, little, tiny, small, trifling, trivial, unimportant.

petition, *n.* SYN.-appeal, entreaty, invocation, plea, prayer, request, suit, supplication.

petrify, *v.* SYN.-fossilize, harden, ossify, solidify; benumb, frighten, paralyze, scare, startle, terrify,

petty, *a.* SYN.-frivolous, insignificant, paltry, small, trifling, trivial, unimportant. ANT.-important, momentous, serious, weighty.

petulant, *a.* SYN.-fretful, irritable, peevish, testy, touchy. ANT.-affable, genial, good-natured, good-tempered, pleasant.

phase, *n.* SYN.-level, procedure, stage, step.

phenomenon, *n.* SYN.-happening, incident, marvel, miracle, occurrence, wonder.

philanthropy, *n.* SYN.-altruism, beneficence, benevolence, charity, generosity, humanity, kindness, liberality, magnanimity. ANT.-malevolence, selfishness, unkindness.

philosophic, *a.* SYN.-pensive, profound, rational, reflective, thoughtful.

phlegmatic, *a.* SYN.-cold, cool, frigid, passionless, stoical, unfeeling. ANT.-hot, torrid; ardent, passionate.

phobia, *n.* SYN.-apprehension, anxiety, aversion, avoidance, concern, dread, fear, trepidation.

phony, *a.* SYN.-affected, artificial, assumed, bogus, counterfeit, ersatz, fake, feigned, fictitious, sham, spurious, synthetic, unreal. ANT.-genuine, natural, real, true.

phrase, *n.* SYN.-clause, excerpt, expression, idiom, maxim, slogan, term, word.

physical, *a.* SYN.-bodily, carnal, corporal, corporeal, material, natural, somatic, tangible, visible. ANT.-mental, spiritual.

pick, *v.* SYN.-accumulate, acquire, choose, collect, criticize, cull, get, elect, opt, pluck, reap, select. ANT.-refuse, reject.

picky, *a.* SYN.-aesthetic, choosy, cultivated, discerning, discriminating, fastidious, particular, selective

picture, *n.* SYN.-appearance, cinema, drawing, effigy, engraving, etching, film, illustration, image, landscape, likeness, painting, panorama, photograph, portrait, portrayal, print, rendering, representation, resemblance, scene, sketch, view.

picturesque, *a.* SYN.-charming, colorful, impressive, interesting, pictorial, striking

piece, *n.* SYN.-amount, bit, fraction, fragment, morsel, part, portion, scrap, section, share. ANT.-all, entirety, sum, total, whole.

piety, *n.* SYN.-devotion, devoutness, faith. grace, godliness, homage, sanctity.

pigment, *n.* SYN.-color, dye, hue, paint, shade, stain, tincture, tinge, tint. ANT.-achromatism, paleness, transparency.

piker, *n.* SYN.-cheapskate, miser, skinflint, tightwad.

pilfer, *v.* SYN.-appropriate, cop, embezzle, filch, rob, steal, swindle, swipe.

pillage, *n.* SYN.-booty, destruction, plunder, spoils,

pillage, *v.* SYN.-despoil, loot, plunder, ravage, rob, sack.

pinnacle, *n.* SYN.-apex, crest, crown, head, summit, top, zenith; ornament, steeple, turret. ANT.-base, bottom, foot, foundation.

pious, *a.* SYN.-blessed, consecrated, devout, divine, hallowed, holy, religious, sacred, saintly, spiritual. ANT.-evil, profane, sacrilegious, secular, worldly.

pirate, *n.* SYN.-criminal, marauder, robber, swindler, thief.

pirate, *v.* SYN.-adopt, appropriate, confiscate, overcharge, plagiarize, steal, usurp

pitch, *v.* SYN.-cast, fling, hurl, propel, throw, thrust, toss. ANT.-draw, haul, hold, pull, retain.

pitfall, *n.* SYN.-ambush, scam, snare, scheme, stratagem, trap, trick, wile.

pitiable, *a.* SYN.-contemptible, insignificant, pathetic, piteous, poignant, sad. ANT.-comical, funny, ludicrous.

pitiful, *a.* SYN.-afflicted, depressing, dismal, distressed, miserable, mournful, pathetic, sorrowful, suffering, tearful, touching.

pity, *n.* SYN.-charity, commiseration, compassion, condolence, mercy, understanding, sympathy. ANT.-brutality, cruelty, hardness, inhumanity, ruthlessness.

placate, *v.* SYN.- appease, assuage, calm, mollify, pacify, satisfy, soothe.

place, *v.* SYN.-arrange, deposit, dispose, lay, locate, put, set. ANT.-disarrange, disturb, mislay, misplace, remove.

placid, *a.* SYN.-calm, composed, dispassionate, imperturbable, pacific, peaceful, quiet, serene, still, tranquil, undisturbed, unruffled. ANT.-excited, frantic, stormy, turbulent, wild.

plagiarize, *v.* SYN.-adopt, appropriate, copy, duplicate, filch, pilfer, steal.

plague, *v.* SYN.-aggravate, annoy, badger, bother, chafe, disturb, gall, harass, harry, irritate, nag, pester, vex.

plain, *a.* SYN.-even, flat, level, smooth; apparent, clear, distinct, evident, manifest, obvious, palpable, visible; candid, frank, modest, open, simple, sincere, unpretentious; absolute, unqualified. ANT.-abrupt, broken, rough, undulatory, uneven; abstruse, ambiguous, enigmatical, obscure; adorned, embellished, feigned, insincere.

plan, *n.* SYN.-delineation, design, draft, drawing, method, outline, plat, plot, scheme, sketch; intent, intention, objective, purpose, system. ANT.-result; accident, chance, confusion, disorder.

plan, *v.* SYN.-contrive, delineate, design, devise, intend, outline, plot, prepare, project, scheme, sketch.

platitude, *n.* SYN.-banality, bromide,

cliché, inanity, motto, saying, truism

plausible, *a.* SYN.-believable, credible, feasible, possible, practicable, probable, reasonable. ANT.-impossible, impracticable, visionary.

play, *n.* SYN.-amusement, diversion, entertainment, fun, game, pastime, recreation, romp, sport. ANT.-boredom, labor, toil, work.

play, *v.* SYN.-caper, frolic, gamble, gambol, revel, romp, sport, stake, toy, wager; execute, perform; act, impersonate, pretend.

plea, *n.* SYN.-appeal, entreaty, invocation, overture, petition, prayer, request, suit, supplication.

plead, *v.* SYN.-appeal, ask, beg, beseech, entreat, implore, petition, supplicate; argue, defend, discuss, rejoin. ANT.-deny, deprecate, refuse.

pleasant, *a.* SYN.-acceptable, agreeable, amiable, charming, gratifying, pleasing, pleasurable, suitable, welcome. ANT.-disagreeable, obnoxious, offensive, unpleasant.

please, *v.* SYN.-appease, beguile, captivate, charm, delight, enchant, enrapture, gratify, satisfy, suffice. ANT.-annoy, displease, dissatisfy.

pleasing, *a.* SYN.-agreeable, delightful, engaging, gentle, honeyed, luscious, mellifluous, melodious, saccharine, sugary, sweet, winning, ANT.-acrid, bitter, offensive, repulsive, sour.

pleasure, *n.* SYN.-amusement, comfort, delight, enjoyment, felicity, gladness, gratification, happiness, joy. ANT.-affliction, pain, suffering, trouble, vexation.

pledge, *n.* SYN.-agreement, assurance, assuredness, certainty, contract. conviction, guarantee, oath, pact, security, surety, promise, word, vow; assertion, declaration, statement.

pledge, *v.* SYN.-consign, entrust, relegate, trust; bind, commit, guarantee, obligate, promise, swear, vouch, vow. ANT.-fail, miscarry, neglect; mistrust, release, renounce; free, loose.

plentiful, *a.* SYN.-abundant, ample, bounteous, bountiful, copious, luxurious, plenteous profuse, replete. ANT.-deficient, insufficient, rare, scanty, scarce.

pliable, *a.* SYN.-compliant, ductile, elastic, flexible, limber, lithe, pliant, resilient, supple, tractable. ANT.-brittle, hard, rigid, stiff, unbending.

plight, *n.* SYN.-danger, difficulty, dilemma, fix, peril, predicament, scrape, situation, strait. ANT.-calmness, comfort, ease, satisfaction.

plot, *n.* SYN.-cabal, conspiracy, design, intrigue, machination, plan, scheme, stratagem; chart, diagram, graph, sketch.

plotting, *n.* SYN.-artfulness, contrivance, cunning, design, planning, scheming. ANT.-candor, sincerity.

ploy, *n.* SYN.-antic, artifice, deception, device, fraud, guile, hoax, imposture, ruse, stratagem, stunt, subterfuge, trick, wile. ANT.-candor, exposure, honesty, openness, sincerity.

plump, *a.* SYN.-chubby, corpulent, fat, obese, paunchy, portly, pudgy, rotund, stocky, stout, thickset. ANT.-gaunt, lean, slender, slim, thin.

plunge, *v.* SYN.-bound, dash, descend, dive, fall, immerse, jump, leap, lunge, plummet, submerge, surge. ANT.-extricate, raise, rescue.

poignant, *a.* SYN.-affecting, heart-rending, impressive, moving, pitiable, sad, tender, touching. ANT.-animated, enlivening, exhilarating, removed.

point, *v.* SYN.-aim, direct, indicate, level, train. ANT.-deceive, distract, misdirect, misguide.

pointed, *a.* SYN.-acute, cutting, keen, sharp; acrid, biting, bitter, pungent; penetrating, piercing, severe, shrill. ANT.-bland, blunt, gentle.

poise, *n.* SYN.-balance, calmness, carriage, composure, equanimity, equilibrium, self-possession. ANT.-agitation, anger, excitement, rage, turbulence.

poise, *v.* SYN.-balance, dangle, hang, hover, ready, suspend.

poison, *v.* SYN.-contaminate, corrupt, infect, pollute, taint. ANT.-disinfect, purify.

polished, *a.* SYN.-courtly, cultivated, cultured, diplomatic, genteel, glib, polite, refined, suave, urbane, well-bred; glossy, shiny, sleek, slick, smooth. ANT.-boorish, bluff, coarse, crude, rude, vulgar; harsh, rough, rugged.

polite, *a.* SYN.-accomplished, civil, considerate, courteous, cultivated, genteel, refined, urbane, well-bred, well-mannered. ANT.-boorish, impertinent, rude, uncivil, uncouth.

pollute, *v.* SYN.-befoul, contaminate, corrupt, defile, infect, poison, sully, taint. ANT.-disinfect, purify.

pomp, *n.* SYN.-affectation, display, flourish, ostentation, pageantry, parade, show, splendor, vaunting, vanity. ANT.-humility, modesty, reserve, unobtrusiveness.

pompous, *a.* SYN.-arrogant, condescending, contemptuous, haughty, proud, superior.

ponder, *v.* SYN.-cogitate, contemplate, deliberate, meditate, muse, reflect, study, think, weigh.

poor, *a.* SYN.-destitute, impecunious, indigent, needy, penniless, poverty-stricken; bad, deficient, inferior, scanty, shabby, unfavorable, wrong. ANT.-affluent, opulent, rich, wealthy; ample, good, right, sufficient.

popular, *a.* SYN.-common, familiar, favorite, general, prevailing, prevalent. ANT.-esoteric, exclusive, restricted, unpopular.

portal, *n.* SYN.-doorway, entrance, entry, gate, inlet, opening. ANT.-departure, exit.

portion, *n.* SYN.-bit, division, fragment, parcel, part, piece, section, segment, share. ANT.-bulk, whole.

portray, *v.* SYN.-delineate, depict, describe, draw, paint, picture, represent, sketch. ANT.-caricature, misrepresent, suggest.

position, *n.* SYN.-locality, place, site, situation, station; caste, condition, place, rank, standing, status; berth, incumbency, job, office, post, situation; attitude, bearing, pose, posture.

positive, *a.* SYN.-assured, certain, definite, fixed, indubitable, inevitable, secure, sure, undeniable, unquestionable. ANT.-doubtful, probable, questionable, uncertain.

possess, *v.* SYN.-control, have, hold, occupy, own; affect, obtain, seize. ANT.-abandon, lose, renounce, surrender.

possessions, *n.* SYN.-belongings, effects, estate, goods, property, stock, wares, wealth. ANT.-deprivation, destitution, poverty, privation, want.

possible, *a.* SYN.-credible, feasible, likely, plausible, practicable, practical, probable. ANT.-impossible, impracticable, visionary.

possibility, *n.* SYN.-chance, contingency, opening, opportunity. ANT.-disadvantage, hindrance, obstacle.

post, *n.* SYN.-locality, place, site, situation, station; berth, incumbency, job, office, position, situation.

postpone, *v.* SYN.-defer, delay, interrupt, pause, stay, suspend. ANT.-continue, maintain, persist, proceed.

postulate, *n.* SYN.-adage, aphorism, apothegm, axiom, byword, fundamental, maxim, principle, proverb, saw, saying, theorem, truism.

posture, *n.* SYN.-attitude, carriage, demeanor, presence, pose, stance.

potency, *n.* SYN.-ability, capability, competency, effectiveness, efficacy, efficiency, power, strength. ANT.-inability, ineptitude, wastefulness.

pound, *v.* SYN.-beat, belabor, buffet, conquer, dash, defeat, hit, knock, overpower, overthrow, pummel, punch, rout, smite, strike, subdue, thrash, thump, vanquish; palpitate, pulsate, pulse, throb. ANT.-defend, shield, stroke, fail, surrender.

poverty, *n.* SYN.-destitution, indigence, necessity, need, penury, privation, want. ANT.-abundance, affluence, plenty, riches, wealth.

power, *n.* SYN.-ability, authority, capability, cogency, command, competency, control, dominion, energy, faculty, force, influence, might, predominance, potency, sovereignty, strength, sway, talent, validity, vigor. ANT.-debility, disablement, fatigue, impotence, incapacity, inaptitude, weakness.

powerful, *a.* SYN.-athletic, cogent, concentrated, firm, forceful, forcible, fortified, hale, hardy, impregnable, mighty, potent, robust, sinewy, strong, sturdy, tough. ANT.-brittle, delicate, feeble, fragile, insipid.

practical, *a.* SYN.-aware, cognizant, discreet, intelligent, judicious, prudent, reasonable, sagacious, sage, sensible, sober, sound, wise. ANT.-absurd, impalpable, imperceptible, stupid, unaware.

practice, *n.* SYN.-custom, drill, exercise, habit, manner, training, usage, use, wont. ANT.-disuse, idleness, inexperience, speculation, theory.

pragmatic, *a,* SYN.-intelligent, logical, practical, rational, realistic, sensible, utilitarian.

praise, *n.* SYN.-acclaim, adulation, applause, approval, commendation, compliment, eulogy, flattery, laudation. ANT.-abuse, censure, condemnation, disapproval.

praise, *v.* SYN.-acclaim, applaud, commend, compliment, eulogize, extol, flatter, glorify, laud. ANT.-censure, condemn, criticize, disparage, reprove.

prayer, *n.* SYN.-appeal, entreaty, invocation, petition, plea, request, suit, supplication.

preach, *v.* SYN.-discourse, exhort, harangue, lecture, moralize, sermonize, teach.

preamble, *n.* SYN.-beginning, forward, introduction, preface, prelude, prologue, start. ANT.-completion, conclusion, end, epilogue, finale.

precarious, *a.* SYN.-critical, dangerous, hazardous, insecure, menacing, perilous, risky, threatening, unsafe. ANT.-firm, protected, safe, secure.

precept, *n.* SYN.-belief, creed, doctrine, dogma, teaching, tenet. ANT.-conduct, deed, performance, practice.

precious, *a.* SYN.-costly, expensive, valuable; dear, esteemed; profitable. ANT.-cheap, mean, poor; trashy, worthless.

precise, *a.* SYN.-accurate, ceremonious, correct, definite, distinct, exact, formal, prim, rigid, stiff, strict, unequivocal. ANT. careless, easy, erroneous, informal, loose, rough, vague.

preclude, *v.* SYN.-bar, ban eliminate, forestall, hinder, impede, obstruct, obviate, omit, prevent, thwart. ANT.-aid, encourage, expedite, permit, promote.

preclusion, *n.* SYN.-exception, exclusion, omission. ANT.-inclusion.

predicament, *n.* SYN.-condition, difficulty, dilemma, fix, impasse, plight, scrape, situation, strait. ANT.-calmness, comfort, ease, satisfaction.

predilection, *n.* SYN.- affection, attachment, bent, bias, desire, disposition, inclination, leaning, penchant, preference. ANT.-apathy, aversion, distaste, nonchalance, repugnance.

predominant, *a.* SYN.-cardinal, chief, foremost, highest, leading, main, overwhelming, paramount, principal, supreme. ANT.-auxiliary, minor, subordinate, subsidiary, supplemental.

preference, *n.* SYN.-alternative, choice, disposition, election, favorite, fondness, liking, option, partiality, predisposition, predilection, selection.

prejudice, *n.* SYN.-bias, bigotry, disposition, partiality, preconception, predisposition, slant. ANT.-fairness, impartiality, proof, reason.

prejudiced, *a.* SYN.-bigoted, disposed, dogmatic, fanatical, illiberal, intolerant, narrow-minded. ANT.-liberal, progressive, radical, tolerant.

premeditated, *a.* SYN.-contemplated, deliberate, designed, intended, intentional, studied. ANT.-accidental, fortuitous.

premeditation, *n.* SYN.-deliberation, forecast, forethought, intention. ANT.-accident, extemporization, hazard, impromptu.

premise, *n.* SYN.-assumption, base, basis, foundation, ground, groundwork, postulate, presumption, presupposition, principle, support, underpinning. ANT.-conclusion, derivative, implication, superstructure, trimming.

preoccupied, *a.* SYN.-abroad, absent, absent-minded, abstracted, away, departed, distracted, inattentive. ANT.-attending, present; attentive, watchful.

prepare, *v.* SYN.-concoct, condition, contrive, equip, fit, furnish, get ready, make ready, predispose, provide, qualify, ready.

preposterous, *a.* SYN.-absurd, foolish, inconsistent, irrational, nonsensical, ridiculous, self-contradictory, silly, unreasonable. ANT.-consistent, rational, reasonable, sensible, sound.

prerogative, *n.* SYN.-authority, grant, liberty, license, privilege, right. ANT.-encroachment, injustice, violation, wrong.

present, *n.* SYN.-boon, donation, gift, grant, gratuity, largess; instant, moment, now, today.

present, *v.* SYN.-advance, exhibit, extend, introduce, offer, proffer, propose, sacrifice, submit, tender, volunteer. ANT.-accept, receive, reject, retain, spurn.

presentation, *n.* SYN.-award. contribution, donation, gift, grant, present, remembrance; demonstration, display, exhibition, exposition, performance, show, unveiling.

presented, *a.* SYN.-bestowed, conferred, given.

preserve, *v.* SYN.-conserve, defend, guard, keep, maintain, protect, rescue, safeguard, save, secure, spare, uphold. ANT.-abandon, abolish, destroy, impair, injure.

preside, *v.* SYN.-arbitrate, chair, control, direct, lead, moderate, referee, regulate, umpire.

press, *v.* SYN.-crowd, drive, force, impel, propel, push, shove; hasten, pressure, promote, urge. ANT.-drag, falter, halt, pull, retreat; ignore, oppose.

pressing, *a.* SYN.-cogent, compelling, critical, crucial, exigent, impelling, imperative, important, importunate, insistent, instant, necessary, serious, urgent. ANT.-insignificant, petty, trifling, trivial, unimportant.

pressure, *n.* SYN.-compression, force; constraint, influence; compulsion, exigency, hurry, press, stress, urgency. ANT. ease, lenience, recreation, relaxation.

prestige, *n.* SYN.-fame, name, renown, reputation, standing, status.

presume, *v.* SYN.-apprehend, assume, believe, conjecture, deduce, guess, imagine, speculate, suppose, surmise, think. ANT.-ascertain, conclude, demonstrate, know, prove.

presumption, *n.* SYN.-audacity, boldness, effrontery, impertinence, impudence, insolence, rudeness, sauciness. ANT.-diffidence, politeness, subserviency, truckling.

pretend, *v.* SYN.-act, affect, assume, feign, imitate, profess, sham, simulate. ANT.-display, exhibit, expose, reveal.

pretense, *n.* SYN.-affectation, cloak, disguise, excuse, garb, mask, pretension, pretext, semblance, show, simulation, subterfuge. ANT.-actuality, fact, reality, sincerity, truth.

pretty, *a.* SYN.-attractive, beauteous, beautiful, charming, comely, elegant, fair, fine, handsome, lovely. ANT.-foul, hideous, homely, repulsive, unsightly.

prevalent, *a.* SYN.-common, customary, efficacious, familiar, frequent, general, ordinary, popular, regular, superior, universal, usual. ANT.-exceptional, extraordinary, odd, rare, scarce, singular.

prevent, *v.* SYN.-arrest, block, forestall, frustrate, hinder, impede, obstruct, obviate, preclude, stop, thwart. ANT.-aid, encourage, expedite, permit, promote.

previous, *a.* SYN.-aforesaid, antecedent, anterior, foregoing, former, preceding, prior. ANT.-consequent, following, later, subsequent, succeeding.

price, *n.* SYN.-charge, cost, expenditure, expense, payment, value, worth.

pride, *n.* SYN.-arrogance, conceit, haughtiness, self-esteem, self-respect, superciliousness, vainglory, vanity. ANT.-humility, lowliness, meekness, modesty, shame.

prim, *a.* SYN.-decorous, demur, formal, orderly, precise, stiff, tidy, trim.

primary, *a.* SYN.-beginning, earliest, first, initial, original, prime, primeval, primitive, pristine; chief, foremost. ANT.-hindmost, last, latest; least, subordinate.

prime, *a.* SYN.-beginning, best, chief, choice, earliest, first, fundamental, original, primary, principal, top.

primitive, *a.* SYN.-aboriginal, ancient, antiquated, crude, early, old, primary, primeval, primordial, pristine, raw, rough, simple, undeveloped. ANT.-civilized, late, modern, modish, sophisticated.

princely, *a.* SYN.-abundant, ample, generous, grand, lavish, liberal, luxurious, noble, profuse, regal, stately, sumptuous.

principal, *a.* SYN.-cardinal, chief, essential, first, foremost, highest, leading, main, paramount, predominant, supreme. ANT.-auxiliary, minor, subordinate, subsidiary, supplemental.

principal, *n.* SYN.-chief, commander, dean, director, head, leader, master; asset, capital, equipment, property. ANT.-follower, subordinate, underling; base, bottom, foot.

principle, *n.* SYN.-axiom, canon, formula, guide, law, maxim, method, order, precept, regulation, rule, standard, statute, system. ANT.-chance, deviation, exception, hazard, irregularity.

prior, *a.* SYN.-aforesaid, foregoing, former, past, preceding, previous. ANT.-consequent, following, later, subsequent, succeeding.

privacy, *n.* SYN.-isolation, retreat, seclusion, solitude, withdrawal.

private, *a.* SYN.-clandestine, concealed, confidential, covert, exclusive, hidden, isolated, latent, masked, personal, remote, secret, separate, special, surreptitious, unknown. ANT.-conspicuous, disclosed, exposed, known, obvious.

privilege, *n.* SYN.-advantage, exemption, favor, immunity, liberty, license, prerogative, right, sanction. ANT.-disallowance, inhibition, prohibition, restriction.

prize, *n.* SYN.-accolade, award, bonus, booty, bounty, compensation, honor, plunder, premium, recompense, remuneration, reward. ANT.-assessment, charge, earnings, punishment, wages.

prize, *v.* SYN.-appreciate, cherish, esteem, treasure, value.

probable, *a.* SYN.-conceivable, feasible, inclined, liable, likely, possible, prone.

probe, *v.* SYN-ask, explore, extend, inquire, investigate, penetrate, query, question, reach, search, seek, stretch.

problem, *n.* SYN.-difficulty, dilemma, enigma, issue, obstacle, predicament, puzzle, riddle.

procedure, *n.* SYN.-course, deed, fashion, form, habit, maneuver, manner, method, mode, operation, plan, practice, process, style, system, way.

proceed, *v.* SYN.-advance, arise, continue, emanate, further, improve, issue, progress, rise, thrive. ANT.-hinder, oppose, retard, retreat, withhold.

proceeding, *n.* SYN.-affair, business, deal, deed, gathering, meeting, negotiation, occurrence, transaction.

procession, *n.* SYN.-cavalcade, cortege, file, parade, retinue, sequence, succession, train.

proclaim, *v.* SYN.-affirm, announce,

assert, aver, broadcast, declare, express, make known, profess, promulgate, protest, state, tell. ANT.-conceal, repress, suppress, withhold.

procure, *v.* SYN.-acquire, attain, buy, earn, gain, get, obtain, purchase, secure. ANT.-dispose of, sell, vend.

prodigal, *a.* SYN.-abundant, bountiful, copious, extravagant, lavish, plentiful, profligate, profuse, reckless, wasteful.

prodigal, *n.* SYN.-carouser, playboy, spendthrift, wastrel

prodigious, *a.* SYN.-amazing, astonishing, astounding, enormous, huge, immense, marvelous, monstrous, monumental, remarkable, stupendous, vast. ANT.-commonplace, insignificant, small.

prodigy, *n.* SYN.-curiosity, marvel, spectacle, wonder.

produce, *n.* SYN.-crop, fruit, harvest, proceeds, product, reaping, result, store, vegetables, yield.

produce, *v.* SYN.-bear, breed, conceive, exhibit, fabricate, fashion, generate, hatch, make, manufacture, procreate, show, supply, yield; accomplish, cause, effect, occasion, originate. ANT.-consume, destroy, reduce, waste; conceal, hide.

productive, *a.* SYN.-bountiful, fecund, fertile, fruitful, luxuriant, plenteous, prolific, rich, teeming. ANT.-barren, impotent, sterile, unproductive.

profane, *v.* SYN.-debauch, defile, deflower, desecrate, dishonor, infringe, invade, pollute, ravish, transgress, violate,

profess, *v.* SYN.-affirm, announce, assert, aver, broadcast, declare, express, make known, proclaim, promulgate, protest, state, tell. ANT.-conceal, repress, suppress, withhold.

profession, *n.* SYN.-avocation, business, calling, career, employment, occupation, vocation, work; allegation, assertion, claim, contention, declaration, statement, vow.

professional, *a.* SYN.-adept, competent, efficient, expert, learned, licensed, proficient, skilled, trained.

proficient, *a.* SYN.-able, accomplished, adept, clever, competent, cunning, expert, ingenious, practiced, skilled, skillful, versed. ANT.-awkward, bungling, clumsy, inexpert, untrained.

profit, *n.* SYN.-advantage, avail, benefit, emolument, gain, improvement, service, use. ANT.-damage, detriment, loss, ruin, waste.

profitable, *a.* SYN.-advantageous, beneficial, favorable, lucrative, productive, remunerative, valuable.

profligate, *a.* SYN.-contaminated, corrupt, corrupted, crooked, debased, depraved, dishonest, impure, putrid, spoiled, tainted, unsound, venal, vitiated.

profound, *a.* SYN.-abstruse, deep, intellectual, intense, penetrating, recondite, solemn, wise. ANT.-shallow, slight, superficial, trivial.

profuse, *a.* SYN.-abundant, copious, excessive, extravagant, exuberant, immoderate, improvident, lavish, luxuriant, overflowing, plentiful, prodigal, wasteful. ANT.-economical, meager, poor, skimpy, sparse.

profusion, *n.* SYN.-abundance, excess, extravagance, immoderation, intemperance, superabundance, superfluity, surplus. ANT.-dearth, deficiency, lack, paucity, want.

program, *n.* SYN.-agenda, bulletin, calendar, curriculum, plan, presentation, schedule.

progress, *n.* SYN.-advance, advancement, betterment, course, development, growth, improvement, proceeding, progression. ANT.-decline, delay, regression, relapse, retrogression.

progress, *v.* SYN.-advance, augment, elevate, enlarge, further, improve, increase, proceed, promote, rise, thrive. ANT.-hinder, oppose, retard, retreat, withhold.

progression, *n.* SYN.-arrangement, chain, following, gradation, order, sequence, series, string, succession.

prohibit, *v.* SYN.-ban, debar, enjoin, forbid, halt, hinder, impede, inhibit, interdict, obstruct, prevent, restrain. ANT.-allow, permit, sanction, tolerate.

project, *n.* SYN.-aim, contrivance, design, device, intention, plan, proposal, proposition, scheme. ANT.-accomplishment, performance, production.

project, *v.* SYN.-brew, concoct, contemplate, contrive, devise, forecast, frame, plan.

prolific, *a.* SYN.-bountiful, fecund, fertile, fruitful, luxuriant, plenteous, productive, rich, teeming. ANT.-barren, impotent, sterile, unproductive.

prolong, *v.* SYN.-drag, draw, extend, lengthen, protract, stretch. ANT.-abbreviate, contract, curtail, shorten.

prominent, *a.* SYN.-celebrated, conspicuous, distinguished, eminent, famous, illustrious, influential, noteworthy, outstanding, remarkable, renowned. ANT.-common, humble, low, ordinary, vulgar.

promiscuous, *a.* SYN.-careless, confused, garbled, immoral, indiscriminate, licentious, loose, mixed.

promise, *n.* SYN.-agreement, assurance, bestowal, contract, covenant, engagement, fulfillment, guarantee, oath, pledge, undertaking, vow.

promote, *v.* SYN.-advance, advocate, aid, assist, back, champion, encourage, facilitate, forward, foster, patronize, support, urge. ANT.-demote, discourage, hinder, impede, obstruct.

prompt, *a.* SYN.-exact, precise, punctual, timely. ANT.-dilatory, late, slow, tardy.

prompt, *v.* SYN.-arouse, cause, coach, create, cue, effect, evoke, help, incite, induce, inspire, instigate, make, occasion, originate, provoke, remind, suggest.

promptly, *adv.* SYN.-directly, forthwith, immediately, instantaneously, instantly, now, quickly, presently, rapidly, straight-away. ANT.-distantly, hereafter, later, shortly, sometime.

promulgate, *v.* SYN.-affirm, announce, assert, aver, broadcast, declare, express, make known, proclaim, profess, state, tell. ANT.-conceal, repress, suppress, withhold.

proof, *n.* SYN.-confirmation, corroboration, demonstration, evidence, experiment, test, testimony, trial, verification. ANT.-failure, fallacy, invalidity.

propaganda, *n.* SYN.-advertising, broadcasting, inducement, influence, notice, persuasion, promotion, publicity.

propagate, *v.* SYN.-bear, beget, breed, conceive, engender, generate, procreate.

propel, *v.* SYN.-actuate, agitate, drive, impel, induce, instigate, move, persuade, push, shift, stir, transfer. ANT.-deter, halt, rest, stay, stop.

propensity, *n.* SYN.-bent, bias, capacity, drift, inclination, leaning, predisposition, proclivity, proneness, talent, tendency, trend. ANT.-aversion, deviation, disinclination.

proper, *a.* SYN.-appropriate, befitting, conventional, correct, decent, fit, formal, legitimate, meet, respectable, right, seemly, suitable.

property, *n.* SYN.-belongings, commodities, effects, estate, goods, merchandise, possessions, stock, wares, wealth; attribute, characteristic, peculiarity, quality, trait. ANT.-deprivation, destitution, poverty, privation, want.

prophesy, *v.* SYN.-anticipate, augur, divine, envision, forecast, foresee, predict.

prophet, *n.* SYN.-astrologer, clairvoyant, economist, forecaster, fortuneteller, medium, meteorologist, oracle, palmist, seer, soothsayer, sorcerer, wizard.

proponent, *n.* SYN.-advocate, champion, defender, patron, promoter, supporter.

proportion, *n.* SYN.-balance, dimensions, distribution, equilibrium, extent, part, percentage, piece, portion, ratio, share, size, symmetry.

proposal, *n.* SYN.-bid, motion, offer, overture, plan, proposition, suggestion, tender. ANT.-acceptance, denial, rejection, withdrawal.

propose, *v.* SYN.-design, intend, move, offer, present, proffer, propound, purpose, suggest, tender. ANT.-effect, fulfill, perform.

propound, *v.* SYN.-adduce, advance, advise, allege, elevate, forward, further, offer, promote, propose, submit, suggest. ANT. hinder, oppose, retard, retreat, withhold.

proprietor, *n.* SYN.-employer, head, leader, master, manager, overseer, owner. ANT.-employee. helper, laborer, servant, slave, worker.

propriety, *n.* SYN.-aptness, congruity, decency, decorum, dignity, etiquette, fitness, modesty, protocol, seemliness.

prosper, *v.* SYN.-achieve, burgeon, flourish, flower, gain, grow, increase, prevail, succeed, thrive, win. ANT.-fail, miscarry, miss.

prosperous, *a.* SYN.-affluent, ample, bountiful, copious, exorbitant, luxurious, opulent, plentiful, rich, sumptuous, wealthy, well-to-do. ANT.-beggarly, destitute, indigent, needy, poor.

protect, *v.* SYN.-defend, guard, keep, maintain, preserve, safeguard, save, secure, uphold. ANT.-abandon, abolish, destroy, impair, injure.

protection, *n.* SYN.-bulwark, defense, fence, guard, refuge, safeguard, security, shelter, shield.

protest, *n.* SYN.-challenge, demonstration, disagreement, dissent, dissentience, objection, remonstrance, revolt, riot. ANT.-acceptance, agreement, assent, compliance.

protest, *v.* SYN.-complain, demonstrate, demur, disagree, disapprove, object, oppose, rebel, reject, remonstrate, riot. ANT.-acquiesce, approve, assent, comply, concur.

prototype, *n.* SYN.-archetype, example, illustration, instance, model, pattern, sample, specimen. ANT.-concept, precept, principle, rule.

protract, *v.* SYN.-distend, distort, elongate, expand, extend, lengthen, spread, strain, stretch. ANT.-contract, loosen, shrink, slacken, tighten.

proud, *a.* SYN.-arrogant, conceited, disdainful, egotistical, haughty, imposing, lofty, magnificent, majestic, overbearing, stately, supercilious, vain, vainglorious. ANT.-ashamed, humble, lowly, meek.

prove, *v.* SYN.-affirm, confirm, corroborate, demonstrate, document, establish, justify, manifest, substantiate, test, try, validate, verify. ANT.-contradict, disprove, refute.

proverb, *n.* SYN.-adage, aphorism, apothegm, axiom, byword, maxim, motto, platitude, saw, saying.

provide, *v.* SYN.-accommodate, afford, assist, endow, equip, fit, furnish, give, help, oblige, outfit, produce, supply, yield. ANT.-denude, despoil, divest, strip.

provident, *a.* SYN.-careful, economical, frugal, niggardly, saving, sparing, thrifty. ANT.-extravagant, improvident, lavish, prodigal, wasteful.

provincial, *a.* SYN.-awkward, boorish, bucolic, callow, coarse, crude, ignorant, rough, rustic, simple, unpolished, unrefined, unsophisticated

provision, *n.* SYN.-accumulation, arrangement, fund, hoard, plan, preparation, reserve, stock, store, supply; condition, requirement, stipulation.

provoke, *v.* SYN.-agitate, arouse, awaken, cause, disquiet, disturb, encourage, excite, foment, goad, incite, induce, instigate, irritate, rouse, stimulate, stir up, urge. ANT.-allay, calm, pacify, quell, quiet.

prowess, *n.* SYN.-boldness, bravery, chivalry, courage, fearlessness, fortitude, intrepidity, mettle, resolution. ANT.-cowardice, fear, pusillanimity, timidity.

proxy, *n.* SYN.-agent, alternate, deputy, lieutenant, representative, substitute, understudy. ANT.-head, master, principal, sovereign.

prudence, *n.* SYN.-care, caution, heed, vigilance, wariness, watchfulness. ANT.-abandon, carelessness, recklessness.

prudent, *a.* SYN.-aware, cognizant, comprehending, conscious, discreet, intelligent, judicious, perceiving, practical, reasonable, sagacious, sage, sensible, sentient, sober, sound, wise. ANT.-absurd, impalpable, imperceptible, stupid, unaware.

prying, *a.* SYN.-curious, inquiring, inquisitive, interrogative, meddling, nosy, peeping, peering, searching, snoopy. ANT.-incurious, indifferent, unconcerned, uninterested.

psychic, *a.* SYN.-extrasensory, mental, mystic, telepathic, supernatural.

psychosis, *n.* SYN.-delirium, dementia, derangement, frenzy, insanity, lunacy, madness, mania. ANT.-rationality, sanity, stability.

publication, *n.* SYN.-advertisement, airing, announcement, broadcast, disclosure, dissemination, notification, statement.

publish, *v.* SYN.-advertise, air, announce, broadcast, declare, disclose, disseminate, divulge, issue, proclaim.

pull, *v.* SYN.-allure, attract, drag, draw, entice, haul, induce, lure, persuade, tow, tug. ANT.-drive, propel, push, repel.

pulsate, *v.* SYN.-beat, buffet, palpitate, pound, pulse, throb, thump, vibrate.

punctual, *a.* SYN.-exact, nice, precise, prompt, ready, timely. ANT.-dilatory, late, slow, tardy.

punish, *v.* SYN.-castigate, chastise, correct, discipline, pummel, reprove, strike. ANT.-acquit, exonerate, free, pardon, release.

punishment, *n.* SYN.-chastisement, correction, discipline, fine, forfeiture, penalty, retribution. ANT.-chaos, confusion, turbulence.

puny, *a.* SYN.-decrepit, delicate, enervated, exhausted, faint, feeble, forceless, impaired, infirm, languid, powerless, weak. ANT.-forceful, lusty, stout, strong, vigorous.

purchase, *v.* SYN.-acquire, buy. get, obtain, procure. ANT.-dispose of, sell, vend.

pure, *a.* SYN.-chaste, clean, clear, genuine, guiltless, immaculate, innocent, modest, sincere, spotless, unadulterated, undefiled, untainted; virginal; absolute, bare, sheer, utter. ANT.-foul, polluted, sullied, tainted, tarnished; corrupt, defiled.

purified, *a.* SYN.-clarified, clean, cleansed, distilled, pure, purged, refined, sweet. ANT.-boorish, coarse, crude, rude, vulgar.

purify, *v.* SYN.-clean, cleanse, disinfect, filter, mop, refine, rinse, scrub, sweep, wash. ANT.-dirty, pollute, soil, stain, sully.

purpose, *n.* SYN.-aim, aspiration, design, drift, end, expectation, goal, intent, intention, object, objective. ANT.-accident, fate, hazard.

pursue, *v.* SYN.-chase, endeavor, follow, hunt, maintain, persist, proceed, seek, track, trail. ANT.-abandon, disregard, elude, escape, evade, flee, ignore.

push, *v.* SYN.-crowd, drive, force, impel, jostle, press, propel, shove; hasten, promote, urge. ANT.-drag, falter, halt, pull, retreat; ignore, oppose.

put, *v.* SYN.-deposit, establish, install, lay, plant, set, situate.

puzzle, *n.* SYN.-conundrum, enigma, mystery, problem, riddle. ANT.-answer, clue, key, resolution, solution.

puzzle, *v.* SYN.-bewilder, confound, confuse, dumfound, mystify, nonplus, perplex. ANT.-clarify, explain, illumine, instruct, solve.

Q

quack, *n.* SYN.-charlatan, fake, impostor, phony, pretender, rogue, swindler.

quaint, *a.* SYN.-curious, cute, eccentric, odd, peculiar, queer, strange, unusual, whimsical. ANT.-common, familiar, normal, ordinary, usual.

qualified, *a.* SYN.-able, capable, clever, competent, efficient, fitted, skillful. ANT.-inadequate, incapable, incompetent, unfitted.

quality, *n.* SYN.-attribute, characteristic, distinction, feature, peculiarity, property, trait; caliber, grade, value. ANT.-being, essence, nature, substance.

quantity, *n.* SYN.-aggregate, amount, content, extent, measure, number, portion, sum, volume. ANT.-nothing, nothingness, zero.

quarrel, *n.* SYN.-affray, altercation,

argument, bickering, contention, disagreement, dispute, feud, spat, squabble, wrangle. ANT.-agreement, friendliness, harmony, peace, reconciliation.

queer, *a.* SYN.-curious, droll, eccentric, odd, peculiar, quaint, singular, strange, unusual, whimsical. ANT.-common, familiar, normal, ordinary, usual.

quest, *n.* SYN.-examination, exploration, inquiry, interrogation, investigation, query, question, research, scrutiny, search. ANT.-disregard, inactivity, inattention, negligence.

question, *v.* SYN.-ask, challenge, dispute, doubt, examine, inquire, interrogate, pump, query, quiz. ANT.-accept, answer, reply, respond, state.

quick, *a.* SYN.-active, brisk, excitable, fast, hasty, impatient, irascible, lively, nimble, precipitate, rapid, sharp, speedy, swift, testy, touchy; acute, clever, discerning, keen, sensitive, shrewd. ANT.-slow, sluggish; dull, inattentive, unaware.

quicken, *v.* SYN.-accelerate, dispatch, expedite, facilitate, forward, hasten, hurry, push, rush, speed. ANT.-block, hinder, impede, retard, slow.

quiet, *a.* SYN.-calm, gentle, hushed, meek, mild, modest, motionless, passive, patient, peaceful, placid, quiescent, silent, still, tranquil, undisturbed. ANT.-agitated, disturbed, loud, perturbed, strident.

quiet, *n.* SYN.-calm, calmness, hush, peace, quiescence, quietude, repose, rest, serenity, silence, stillness, tranquility. ANT.-agitation, commotion, disturbance, excitement, noise, tumult.

quiet, *v.* SYN.-allay, alleviate, appease, assuage, calm, compose, lull, pacify, placate, quell, relieve, satisfy, soothe, still, tranquilize. ANT.-arouse, excite, incense, inflame.

quirk, *n.* SYN.-caprice, characteristic, flavor, idiosyncrasy, irregularity, oddity, peculiarity, style, temperament, whim.

quit, *v.* SYN.-abandon, cease, depart, desist, discontinue, leave, relinquish, resign, stop, surrender, withdraw. ANT.-continue, endure, occupy, persist, stay.

quiver, *v.* SYN.-quake, shake, shiver, shudder, tremble, tremor.

quiz, *v.* SYN.-ask, examine, inquire, interrogate, pump, query, question. ANT.-answer, reply, respond, state.

quote, *v.* SYN.-adduce, cite, extract, paraphrase, plagiarize, recite, repeat. ANT.-contradict, misquote, refute, retort.

R

rabble, *n.* SYN.-crowd, masses, mob, people, populace, proletariat.

race, *n.* SYN.-ancestry, clan, culture, family, folk, lineage, nation, people, stock, strain, tribe.

racket, *n.* SYN.-cacophony, clamor, clatter, din, noise, pandemonium, row, rumpus, sound, tumult, uproar. ANT.-hush, quiet, silence, stillness.

racy, *a.* SYN.-erotic, indecent, lewd, risqué, suggestive.

radiance, *n.* SYN.-brightness, brilliance, brilliancy, effulgence, luster, splendor. ANT.-darkness, dullness, gloom, obscurity.

radiant, *a.* SYN.-brilliant, bright, dazzling, effulgent, glorious, gorgeous, grand, illustrious, magnificent, resplendent, shining, showy, splendid, sumptuous, superb. ANT.-dull, mediocre, modest, ordinary, unimpressive.

radical, *a.* SYN.-basic, complete, constitutional, extreme, fundamental, inherent, innate, insurgent, intrinsic, natural, organic, original, total, thorough, ultra, uncompromising. ANT.-conservative, moderate, superficial; extraneous.

rage, *n.* SYN.-anger, animosity, choler, fury, indignation, ire, passion, resentment, temper, wrath. ANT.-conciliation, forbearance, patience, peace, self-control.

raging, *a.* SYN.-acute, boisterous, extreme, fierce, forceful, furious, impetuous; intense, passionate, powerful, raving, severe. turbulent, vehement, violent, wild. ANT.-calm, feeble, gentle, quiet, soft.

raid, *n.* SYN.-assault, attack, foray, incursion, invasion.

rain, *v.* SYN.-deluge, drench, drizzle, drop, fall, mist, patter, pour, shower, storm.

raise, *v.* SYN.-elevate, erect, exalt, heave, heighten, hoist, lift, uplift; breed, cultivate, grow, produce; gather, levy, muster. ANT.-abase, depreciate, depress, destroy, lower.

ram, *v.* SYN.-bump, butt, collide, crash, cram, hit, jam, pound, stuff.

ramble, *v.* SYN.-deviate, digress, err, range, roam, rove, saunter, stray, stroll, traipse, wander. ANT.-halt, linger, settle, stay, stop.

rampant, *a.* SYN.-frantic, furious, raging, tumultuous, turbulent, uncontrolled, violent, widespread, wild.

rancor, *n.* SYN.-animosity, enmity, grudge, ill-will, malevolence, malice, malignity, spite. ANT.-affection, kindness, love, toleration.

random, *a.* SYN.-accidental, aimless, casual, chance, haphazard, indiscriminate, unplanned, unpredictable,

rank, *n.* SYN.-blood, class, degree, dignity, distinction, eminence, estate, grade, quality, standing, station, status; fetid, foul, gamy, malodorous, nasty, putrid, rancid, reeking, smelly, stinking. ANT.-disrepute, shame, stigma; clean, pleasant, sweet.

rapid, *a.* SYN.-expeditious, fast, fleet, hasty, lively, precipitate, quick, speedy, swift. ANT.-slow, sluggish.

rapture, *n.* SYN.-blessedness, bliss, blissfulness, delight, ecstasy, exaltation, felicity, happiness, joy, pleasure, satisfaction, transport, trance. ANT.-grief, misery, sorrow, woe, wretchedness.

rare, *a.* SYN.-choice, exceptional, incomparable, infrequent, occasional, precious, scarce, singular, strange, uncommon, unique, unusual. ANT.-abundant, commonplace, customary, frequent, numerous, ordinary, usual, worthless.

rascal, *n.* SYN.-beggar, bum, cad, charlatan, knave, rake, reprobate, rogue, scalawag, scamp, sneak, scoundrel, tramp, villain, wastrel, wretch,

rash, *a.* SYN.-blind, careless, hasty, headlong, heedless, impetuous, impulsive, oblivious, passionate, quick, undiscerning, unmindful, unseeing. ANT.-aware, calculated, cautious, discerning, perceiving, reasoning, sensible.

rate, *v.* SYN.-appraise, assess, classify, evaluate, grade, judge, rank, value.

ratify, *v.* SYN.-approve, authorize, confirm, endorse, sanction.

rational, *a.* SYN.-calm, circumspect, cool, discerning, intelligent, judicious, logical, prudent, reasonable, sane, sensible, sober, sound, wise. ANT.-absurd, foolish; irrational, insane.

rationale, *n.* SYN.-aim, argument, basis, design, excuse, explanation, ground, intelligence, justification, motive, purpose, reason, rationalization, sake.

ravage, *v.* SYN.-annihilate, demolish, despoil, destroy, devastate, exterminate, extinguish, pillage, plunder, ransack, ruin, sack, strip, waste. ANT.-accumulate, economize, preserve, save.

ravish, *v.* SYN.-debauch, defile, desecrate, dishonor, pollute, profane, violate.

raw, *a.* SYN.-coarse, crass, crude, green, harsh, ill-prepared, rough, uncouth, unfinished, unpolished, unrefined. ANT.-finished, well-prepared; cultivated, refined.

raze, *v.* SYN.-annihilate, demolish, destroy, devastate, eradicate, exterminate, extinguish, obliterate, ravage, ruin, wreck. ANT.-construct, establish, make, preserve, save.

reach, *v.* SYN.-approach, arrive, attain, extend, overtake, stretch, touch. ANT.-fail, fall short, miss.

react, *v.* SYN.-answer, counter, counteract, experience, feel, rejoin, reply, respond, retort. ANT.-disregard, ignore, overlook.

reaction, *n.* SYN.-answer, backlash, feedback, rejoinder, reply, response, retort.

ready, *a.* SYN.-aged, available, complete, consummate, convenient, finished, full-grown, handy, mature, matured, mellow, prepared, ripe, seasonable, steeled. ANT.-crude, green, immature, raw, undeveloped.

ready, *v.* SYN.-condition, equip, fit, furnish, get ready, make ready, predispose, prepare, provide, qualify.

real, *a.* SYN.-actual, authentic, certain, genuine, positive, substantial, true, veritable. ANT.-apparent, fictitious, imaginary, supposed, unreal.

realize, *v.* SYN.-appreciate, apprehend, comprehend, conceive, discern, grasp, know, learn, perceive, see, understand. ANT.-ignore, misapprehend, mistake, misunderstand.

realm, *n.* SYN.-area, circle, domain, kingdom, orbit, province, sphere

reap, *v.* SYN.-acquire, gain, garner, gather, get, glean, harvest, obtain, pick, receive. ANT.-lose, plant, sow, squander.

reaping, *n.* SYN.-crop, harvest, proceeds, produce, product, result, yield.

rear, *v.* SYN.-bear, beget, breed, conceive, engender, foster, generate, nurture, procreate, propagate, raise, train.

reason, *n.* SYN.-aim, argument, basis, cause, design, ground, motive, purpose, sake; intelligence, mind, rationality, sense, understanding.

reason, *v.* SYN.-argue, conclude, deduce, deliberate, discuss, infer, judge, reflect. ANT.-bewilder, confuse, guess.

reasonable, *a.* SYN.-appreciable, apprehensible, perceptible; alive, awake, aware, cognizant, comprehending, conscious, discreet, intelligent, judicious, perceiving, practical, prudent, sagacious, sage, sensible, sentient, sober, sound, wise. ANT.-absurd, impalpable, imperceptible, stupid, unaware.

rebel, *v.* SYN.-defy, mutiny, oppose, resist, revolt, strike.

rebellion, *v.* SYN.-coup, insurrection, mutiny, overthrow, revolt, revolution, uprising.

rebellious, *a.* SYN. defiant, disobedient, insubordinate, undutiful, unruly. ANT.-compliant, dutiful, unruly. ANT.-compliant, dutiful, obedient, submissive.

rebuild, *v.* SYN.-reconstruct, reestablish, rehabilitate, renew, renovate, repair, restore.

rebuke, *v.* SYN.-censure, chide, reprimand, reprove, scold, upbraid.

rebuttal, *n.* SYN.-answer, defense, rejoinder, reply, response, retort; ANT.-argument, inquiry, questioning, summoning;

recall, *v.* SYN.-recollect, remember, remind, reminisce. ANT.-disregard, forget, ignore, overlook.

recede, *v.* SYN.-abate, decline, decrease, drop, ebb, lessen, retreat, subside.

receive, *v.* SYN.-accept, admit, entertain, gain, get, inherit, shelter, take, welcome. ANT.-bestow, discharge, give, impart, reject, turn away.

recent, *a.* SYN.-fresh, late, modern, new, newfangled, novel, original. ANT.-ancient, antiquated, archaic, obsolete, old.

recitation, *n.* SYN.-address, discourse, interpretation, lecture, monologue, narration, reading, soliloquy, speech, recital.

recite, *v.* SYN.-declaim, deliver, describe, detail, enumerate, mention, narrate, recapitulate, recount, rehearse, relate, repeat, tell.

reckless, *a.* SYN.-careless, heedless, imprudent, inattentive, inconsiderate, indiscreet, neglectful, negligent, remiss, thoughtless, unconcerned, ANT.-accurate, careful, meticulous, nice.

reckon, *v.* SYN.-assess, consider, estimate, evaluate, judge, weigh.

recognize, *v.* SYN.-acknowledge, apprehend, avow, concede, confess, identify, own, perceive, recollect, remember. ANT.-disown, forget, ignore, overlook, renounce, repudiate.

recollection, *n.* SYN.-memory, remembrance, reminiscence, retrospection. ANT.-forgetfulness, oblivion.

recommend, *v.* SYN.-advise, allude, counsel, hint, imply, insinuate, intimate, offer, propose, refer, suggest. ANT.-declare, demand, dictate, insist.

recommendation, *n.* SYN.-advice, caution, counsel, exhortation, instruction, suggestion, warning.

reconsider, *v.* SYN.-analyze, consider, ponder, review, revise. ANT.-ignore, reject.

record, *n.* SYN.-account, achievement, archive, career, chronicle, document, history, mark, memorandum, memorial, minute, note, report, register, trace, vestige,

recount, *v.* SYN.-describe, narrate, recite, relate, report, tell.

recover, *v.* SYN.-cure, rally, recuperate, restore, revive; recapture, recoup, redeem, regain, repossess, retrieve. ANT.-regress, relapse, revert, weaken; forfeit, lose.

recreation, *n.* SYN.-amusement, diversion, entertainment, fun, game, pastime, play, sport. ANT.-boredom, labor, toil, work.

rectify, *v.* SYN.-amend, correct, mend, reform, right. ANT.-aggravate, ignore, spoil.

recuperate, *v.* SYN.-heal, rally, recover, restore, revive; recapture, recoup, redeem, regain, repossess, retrieve. ANT.-regress, relapse, revert, weaken; forfeit, lose.

redeemer, *n.* SYN.-deliverer, liberator, protector, rescuer.

reduce, *v.* SYN.-abate, assuage, curtail, decline, decrease, deduct, diminish, lessen, lower, moderate, shorten, subtract, suppress. ANT.-amplify, enlarge, increase, intensify, revive.

refined, *a.* SYN.-courtly, cultivated, cultured, genteel, polished, polite, well-bred; clarified, purified. ANT.-boorish, coarse, crude, rude, vulgar.

refinement, *n.* SYN.-breeding, civilization, cultivation, culture, education, enlightenment. ANT.-boorishness, ignorance, illiteracy, vulgarity.

reflect, *v.* SYN.-apprehend, cogitate, consider, contemplate, deliberate, imagine, meditate, muse, opine, picture, ponder, reason, recall, recollect, reckon, regard, remember, speculate, suppose, think. ANT.-conjecture, forget, guess.

reflection, *n.* SYN.-cogitation, conception, consideration, contemplation, delibcration, fancy, idea, imagination, impression, judgment, meditation, memory, notion, opinion, recollection, regard, retrospection, sentiment, thought, view.

reform, *v.* SYN.-ameliorate, amend, better, change, correct, help, improve, mend, rectify, renew, right. ANT.-aggravate, corrupt, damage, debase, ignore, impair, spoil.

refrain, *v.* SYN.-abstain, desist, forbear, withhold. ANT.-continue, indulge, persist.

refreshing, *a.* SYN.-modern, new, novel, recent; artless, brisk, cool, fresh, green, inexperienced, natural, raw. ANT.-decayed, faded, hackneyed, musty, stagnant.

refuge, *n.* SYN.-asylum, harbor, haven, retreat, sanctuary, shelter. ANT.-danger, exposure, hazard, jeopardy, peril.

refuse, *v.* SYN.-decline, deny, rebuff, reject, repudiate, spurn, withhold. ANT.-accept, grant, welcome.

refute, *v* SYN.-confute, controvert, disprove, rebut. ANT.-accept, affirm, confirm, establish, prove.

regain, *v.* SYN.-recapture, recoup, recover, redeem, repossess, retrieve. ANT.-forfeit, lose.

regal, *a.* SYN.-courtly, dignified, grand, imperial, kingly, lordly, majestic, monarchal, noble, princely, royal, ruling, sovereign, stately, supreme. ANT.-common, humble, low, plebeian, proletarian, servile, vulgar.

regard, *n.* SYN.-affection, attention, care, concern, consideration, esteem, liking, notice, observation. ANT.-antipathy, disgust, disaffection, neglect.

regard, *v* SYN.-esteem, honor, respect, value; behold, contemplate, look, mark, notice, observe, see, view, watch; account, believe, deem, hold, imagine, reckon, suppose, think. ANT.-insult, mock; ignore, neglect, overlook.

region, *n.* SYN.-area, belt, locale, locality, location, place, sector, site, situation, spot, station, vicinity, zone.

regret, *n.* SYN.-compunction, contrition, grief, penitence, qualm, remorse, repentance, self-reproach, sorrow. ANT.-complacency, impenitence, obduracy, self-satisfaction.

regular, *a.* SYN.-customary, methodical, natural, normal, orderly, ordinary, periodical, steady, systematic, uniform, unvaried. ANT.-abnormal, erratic, exceptional, rare, unusual.

regulation, *n.* SYN.-canon, control, correction, discipline, guide, law, order, principle, punishment, regulation, restraint, rule, self-control, standard, statute. ANT.-chaos, confusion, turbulence.

rehabilitate, *v.* SYN.-cure, heal, rebuild, reconstruct, recover, reestablish, refresh, rejuvenate, renew, reinstate, renovate, repair, replace, restore, return, revive

reiterate, *v.* SYN.-cite, copy, duplicate, iterate, quote, recapitulate, recite, relate, repeat, reproduce.

reject, *v.* SYN.-decline, deny, discard, eliminate, exclude, rebuff, refuse, repudiate, spurn. ANT.-accept, grant, welcome.

rejection, *n.* SYN.-challenge, disagreement, dissent, dissentience, noncompliance, nonconformity, objection, protest, remonstrance, variance. ANT.-acceptance, agreement, assent, compliance.

relate, *v* SYN.-describe, narrate, recite, recount, rehearse, repeat, report, tell; ally, associate, connect, correlate, link, pertain, refer.

relation, *n.* SYN.-alliance, association, coalition, combination, compact, confederacy, connection, covenant, dependence, entente, federation, league, marriage, partnership, treaty, union. ANT.-divorce, schism, separation.

relationship, *n.* SYN.-affinity, alliance, association, bond, conjunction, connection, link, tie, union. ANT.-disunion, isolation, separation.

relatives, *n.* SYN.-clan, blood, family, kin, kindred, kinsfolk, people, race, relations, tribe. ANT.-disconnection, foreigners, strangers.

relaxed, *a.* SYN.-casual, cozy, gratifying, informal, nonchalant, offhand, pleasing, restful, unconcerned, unpremeditated. ANT. formal, planned, pretentious.

release, *v.* SYN.-deliver, discharge, emancipate, fire, free, lay off, let go, liberate, loose, set free, terminate, unloose, unfetter, untie. ANT.-confine, imprison, oppress, restrict, subjugate.

relent, *v.* SYN.-abdicate, accede, acquiesce, capitulate, cede, quit, relinquish, resign, submit, succumb, surrender, waive, yield. ANT.-assert, resist, strive, struggle.

relevant, *a.* SYN.-applicable, apposite, appropriate, apropos, apt, fit, germane, material, pertinent, related, relating, to the point. ANT.-alien, extraneous, foreign, unrelated.

reliable, *a.* SYN.-certain, dependable, safe, secure, sure, tried, trustworthy, trusty. ANT.-dubious, fallible, questionable, uncertain, unreliable.

reliance, *n.* SYN.-belief, confidence, constancy, conviction, credence, dependence, faith, fidelity, hope, loyalty, trust. ANT.-doubt, incredulity, mistrust, skepticism; infidelity.

relief, *n.* SYN.-aid, assistance, back

ing, furtherance, help, succor, support. ANT.-antagonism, counteraction, defiance, hostility, resistance.

relieve, *v.* SYN.-abate, allay, alleviate, assuage, comfort, diminish, ease, extenuate, lighten, mitigate, soften, solace, soothe. ANT.-aggravate, agitate, augment, increase, irritate.

religion, *n.* SYN.-belief, creed, doctrine, dogma, faith, persuasion, tenet; constancy, fidelity, loyalty. ANT.-doubt, incredulity, mistrust, skepticism; infidelity.

religious, *a.* SYN.-devout, divine, godly, holy, pietistic, pious, reverent, sacred, sanctimonious, spiritual, theological. ANT.-atheistic, impious, profane, secular, skeptical.

religiousness, *n.* SYN.-ardor, consecration, dedication, devotion, devoutness, fidelity, loyalty, piety, zeal. ANT.-alienation, apathy, aversion, indifference, unfaithfulness.

relinquish, *v.* SYN.-abandon, acquiesce, capitulate, cede, renounce, resign, sacrifice, submit, surrender, yield. ANT.-conquer, overcome, resist, rout.

relish, *v.* SYN.-anticipate, appreciate, enjoy, fancy, like, prefer.

reluctance, *n.* SYN.-abhorrence, antipathy, aversion, disinclination, distaste, dread, hatred, loathing, repugnance, repulsion. ANT.-affection, attachment, devotion, enthusiasm.

reluctant, *a.* SYN.-averse, disinclined, hesitant, loath, slow, unwilling. ANT.-disposed, eager, inclined, ready, willing.

remain, *v* SYN.-abide, continue, dwell, endure, halt, last, rest, stay, survive, tarry, wait. ANT.-depart, go, leave; dissipate, finish, terminate.

remains, *n.* SYN.-balance, relics, remainder, residue, rest, surplus.

remark, *n.* SYN.-annotation, assertion, comment, declaration, observation, statement, utterance.

remark, *v.* SYN.-aver, comment, express, mention, note, observe, state, utter. ANT.-disregard, ignore.

remarkable, *a.* SYN.-arresting, commanding, exciting, imposing, impressive, majestic, moving, overpowering, splendid, stirring, striking, thrilling, touching. ANT.-commonplace, ordinary, regular, unimpressive.

remedy, *n.* SYN.-antidote, cure, help, medicant, restorative; redress, relief, reparation.

remedy, *v.* SYN.-ameliorate, better, correct, cure, fix, heal, improve, mend, patch, rectify, refit, reform, repair, restore. ANT.-deface, destroy, hurt, injure, rend.

remember, *v* SYN.-mind, recall, recollect, remind, reminisce. ANT.-disregard, forget, ignore, overlook.

remembrance, *n.* SYN.-commemoration, memento, memorial, monument, recollection, reminiscence, souvenir, token.

remonstrate, *v.* SYN.-complain, grouch, grumble, lament, murmur, protest, regret, repine, whine. ANT.-applaud, approve, praise, rejoice.

remorse, *n.* SYN.-contrition, grief, penitence, regret, repentance, self-reproach, sorrow. ANT.-impenitence, obduracy, self-satisfaction.

remote, *a.* SYN.-distant, far, faraway, removed; aloof, cold, reserved, stiff, unfriendly. ANT.-close, near, nigh; cordial, friendly.

remove, *v.* SYN.-dislodge, displace,

move, shift, transfer, transport; discharge, dismiss, eject, oust, vacate; extract, withdraw. ANT.-leave, remain, stay; retain.

renounce, *v.* SYN.-abandon, deny, disavow, disclaim, disown, forego, forsake, quit, reject, relinquish, resign, retract, revoke, sacrifice. ANT.-acknowledge, assert, defend, maintain, recognize, uphold.

renovate, *v.* SYN.-rebuild, reconstruct, reestablish, refresh, rehabilitate, renew, repair, restore.

renown, *n.* SYN.-acclaim, distinction, eminence, fame, honor, luster, notability, reputation. ANT.-disgrace, disrepute, obscurity.

renowned, *a.* SYN.-celebrated, distinguished, eminent, famous, glorious, illustrious, noted, well-known. ANT.-hidden, ignominious, infamous, obscure, unknown.

repair, *v.* SYN.-amend, correct, darn, fix, mend, patch, refit, redress, remedy, renew, renovate, restore, retrieve, tinker. ANT.-break, destroy, harm.

repay, *v.* SYN.-avenge, compensate, indemnify, pay, recompense, refund, reimburse, retaliate, settle.

repeal, *v.* SYN.-abolish, abrogate, annul, cancel, eliminate, expunge, invalidate, nullify, obliterate, quash, rescind, revoke. ANT.-confirm, enact, enforce, perpetuate

repeat, *v* SYN.-cite, copy, duplicate, iterate, quote, recapitulate, recite, rehearse, reiterate, relate, reproduce.

repentance, *n.* SYN.-contrition, grief, penitence, regret, remorse, self-reproach, sorrow. ANT.-impenitence, obduracy, self-satisfaction.

repentant, *a.* SYN.-contrite, penitent, regretful, remorseful, sorrowful, sorry. ANT.-obdurate, remorseless.

repine, *v.* SYN.-complain, grouch, grumble, lament, murmur, protest, regret, remonstrate, whine. ANT.-applaud, approve, praise, rejoice.

replace, *v.* SYN.-displace, reinstate, restore, return, substitute, supplant.

replica, *n.* SYN.-copy, duplicate, exemplar, facsimile, imitation, Photostat, reproduction, transcript. ANT.-original, prototype.

reply, *n.* SYN.-answer, defense, rebuttal, rejoinder, response, retort. ANT.-inquiry, questioning, summoning; argument.

reply, *v.* SYN.-answer, react, rebut, rejoin, respond. ANT.-disregard, ignore, overlook.

report, *v.* SYN.-advertise, announce, declare, give out, herald, make known, notify, proclaim, promulgate, publish. ANT.-bury, conceal, stifle, suppress, withhold.

repose, *n.* SYN.-calm, calmness, hush, peace, quiescence, quiet, quietude, rest, serenity, silence, stillness, tranquility. ANT.-agitation, disturbance, excitement, noise, tumult.

represent, *v.* SYN.-depict, describe, draw, paint, picture, portray, sketch. ANT.-caricature, misrepresent, suggest.

representation, *n.* SYN.-drawing, effigy, engraving, etching, illustration, image, landscape, likeness, painting, panorama, photograph, picture, portrait, portrayal, print, rendering, resemblance, scene, sketch, view.

representative, *n.* SYN.-agent, ambassador, delegate, deputy, emissary, envoy, legislator, proxy.

repress, *v.* SYN.-bridle, check, constrain, curb, hinder, hold back, inhibit, limit, restrain, stop, suppress. ANT.-aid, encourage, incite, loosen.

reprimand, *v.* SYN.-admonish, berate, blame, censure, lecture, rate, rebuke, reprehend, scold, upbraid, vituperate. ANT.-approve, commend, praise.

reproduction, *n.* SYN.-copy, duplicate, exemplar, facsimile, imitation, Photostat, replica, transcript. ANT.-original, prototype.

repugnance, *n.* SYN.-abhorrence, antipathy, aversion, disgust, disinclination, dislike, distaste, dread, hatred, loathing, repulsion, reluctance. ANT.-affection, attachment, devotion, enthusiasm.

repulsive, *a.* SYN.-deformed, despicable, disgusting, hideous, homely, horrid, nauseating, offensive, plain, repellent, repugnant, revolting, ugly, uncomely, vile. ANT.-attractive, beautiful, fair, handsome, pretty.

reputation, *n.* SYN.-character, description, estimation, individuality, kind, nature, repute, sort, standing.

repute, *n.* SYN.-character, class, disposition, esteem, estimation, fame, honor, name, nature, reputation, sort, standing.

request, *v* SYN.-appeal, ask, beg, beseech, desire, entreat, implore, importune, petition, pray, seek, sue, supplicate. ANT.-demand, require.

require, *v* SYN.-ask, claim, command, demand, exact, lack, necessitate, need, order, prescribe, want.

requisite, *a.* SYN.-basic, essential, fundamental, important, indispensable, intrinsic, necessary, needed, vital. ANT.-expendable, extrinsic, optional, peripheral.

rescind, *v.* SYN.-abolish, abrogate, annul, cancel, delete, eliminate, expunge, invalidate, nullify, quash, repeal, revoke. ANT.-confirm, enact, enforce, perpetuate

rescue, *v.* SYN.-deliver, free, liberate, recover, retrieve, save,

research, *n.* SYN.-exploration, interrogation, inquiry, investigation, query, quest, question, scrutiny. ANT.-disregard, inactivity, inattention, negligence.

resemblance, *n.* SYN.-analogy, correspondence, likeness, parity, similarity, similitude. ANT.-difference, distinction, variance.

reserve, *n.* SYN.-accumulation, fund, hoard, provision, stock, store, supply.

reserved, *a.* SYN.-aloof, cautious, cold, demure, diffident, distant, modest, remote, reserved, retiring, stiff, unfriendly. ANT.-audacious, close, cordial, friendly.

residence, *n.* SYN.-abode, base, castle, domicile, dwelling, estate, habitat, hearth, home, house, hovel, manor, palace, quarters, seat, shack.

resign, *v.* SYN.-abandon, depart, discontinue, give up, leave, quit, relinquish, stop, surrender, withdraw. ANT.-continue, endure, occupy, persist, stay.

resignation, *n.* SYN.-composure, endurance, forbearance, fortitude, long-suffering, patience, perseverance. ANT.-impatience, nervousness, restlessness, unquiet.

resigned, *a.* SYN.-composed, forbearing, indulgent, long-suffering, passive, patient, stoical, uncomplaining. ANT.-chafing, clamorous, high-strung, hysterical, turbulent.

resist, *v.* SYN.-attack, confront, defy, hinder, impede, obstruct, oppose, repel, repulse, thwart, withstand. ANT.-accede, allow, cooperate, relent, yield.

resolution, *n.* SYN.-courage, decision, determination, firmness, fortitude, persistence, resolve, steadfastness. ANT.-inconstancy, indecision, vacillation.

resolve, *n.* See **resolution.**

resolve, *v.* SYN.-adjudicate, conclude, decide, determine, end, fix, settle, terminate. ANT.-doubt, hesitate, suspend, vacillate, waver.

respect, *v.* SYN.-admire, consider, heed, honor, regard, revere, reverence, value, venerate. ANT.-abuse, despise, disdain, neglect, scorn.

respectable, *a.* SYN.-adequate, befitting, decent, decorous, fit, fitting, proper, seemly, suitable, tolerable. ANT.-coarse, gross, indecent, reprehensible, vulgar.

respond, *v.* SYN.-answer, react, rejoin, reply. ANT.-disregard, ignore, overlook.

response, *n.* SYN.-answer, defense, rebuttal, rejoinder, reply, retort. ANT.-inquiry, questioning, summoning; argument.

responsibility, *n.* SYN.-accountability, amenability, burden, capability, duty, liability, obligation, reliability, trust, trustworthiness.

responsible, *a.* SYN.-accountable, amenable, answerable, bound, capable, dependable, liable, obligated, reliable, stable, trusty, trustworthy. ANT.-exempt, free, immune; careless, negligent.

rest, *n.* SYN.-calm, ease, leisure, peace, quiet, relaxation, repose, sleep, slumber, tranquility; cessation, intermission, pause, respite; balance, remainder, remains, residue, surplus. ANT.-agitation, commotion, disturbance, motion, tumult.

restless, a SYN.-active, agitated, disquieted, disturbed, irresolute, roving, sleepless, transient, uneasy, unquiet, wandering. ANT.-at ease, peaceable, quiet, tractable.

restore, *v.* SYN.-cure, heal, rebuild, reconstruct, recover, reestablish, refresh, rehabilitate, reinstate, rejuvenate, renew, renovate, repair, replace, return, revive.

restrain, *v.* SYN.-bridle, check, constrain, curb, hinder, hold back, inhibit, limit, repress, stop, suppress. ANT.-aid, encourage, incite, loosen.

restraint, *n.* SYN.-control, discipline, order, regulation, self-control; correction, punishment. ANT.-chaos, confusion, turbulence.

restrict, *v.* SYN.-circumscribe, confine, contain, control, hamper, impede, inhibit, limit, regulate, restrain, suppress, tether.

result, *n.* SYN.-conclusion, consequence, determination, effect, end, eventuality, issue, resolution, resolve.

retain, *v.* SYN.-hold, keep, maintain, preserve, save.

retaliation, *n.* SYN.-reprisal, requital, retribution, revenge, vengeance, vindictiveness. ANT.-mercy, pardon, reconciliation, remission, forgiveness.

retard, *v.* SYN.-arrest, delay, detain, hamper, hinder, impede, slow, stay. ANT.-expedite, hasten, precipitate, quicken.

retort, *n.* SYN.-answer, defense, rebuttal, rejoinder, reply, response. ANT.-inquiry, questioning, summoning; argument.

retribution, *n.* SYN.-punishment, reparation, reprisal, retaliation, reward, revenge. ANT.-mercy, pardon, forgiveness.

return, *v.* SYN.-go back, recur, retreat, revert; repay, replace, requite, restore. ANT.-appropriate, keep, retain, take.

reveal, *v.* SYN.-betray, disclose, discover, divulge, expose, impart, show, uncover. ANT.-cloak, conceal, cover, hide, obscure.

revelation, *n.* SYN.-apparition, dream, ghost, hallucination, mirage, phantasm, phantom, prophecy, specter, vision. ANT.-reality, substance, verity.

revenge, *n.* SYN.-reparation, reprisal, requital, retaliation, retribution, vengeance, vindictiveness. ANT.-mercy, pardon, reconciliation, remission, forgiveness.

revenge, *v.* SYN.-avenge, requite, retaliate, vindicate. ANT.-forgive, pardon, pity, reconcile.

revere, *v.* SYN.-adore, esteem, honor, venerate, worship. ANT.-despise, hate, ignore.

reverence, *n.* SYN.-adoration, deference, dignity, esteem, homage, honor, praise, respect, worship. ANT.-contempt, derision, disgrace, dishonor, reproach.

reverse, *v.* SYN.-annul, countermand, invert, overthrow, overturn, repeal, rescind, revoke, subvert, transpose, turn about, unmake, upset. ANT.-affirm, confirm, endorse, maintain, stabilize, vouch.

revert, *v.* SYN.-go back, repay, replace, restore, retreat, return. ANT.-keep, retain.

review, *n.* SYN.-commentary, criticism, critique, examination, inspection, reconsideration, retrospect, retrospection, revision, survey, synopsis; digest, journal, periodical.

review, *v.* SYN.-analyze, consider, criticize, discuss, edit, examine, inspect, reconsider, revise, survey. ANT.-ignore, reject.

revision, *n.* SYN.-amendment, change, correction, remedy.

revoke, *v.* SYN.-abolish, abrogate, annul, cancel, delete, eliminate, erase, expunge, invalidate, nullify, obliterate, quash, repeal, rescind. ANT.-confirm, enact, enforce, perpetuate

revolting, *a.* SYN.-abominable, detestable, execrable, foul, hateful, loathsome, odious, vile. ANT.-agreeable, commendable, delightful, pleasant.

revolution, *n.* SYN.-coup, insurrection, mutiny, overthrow, rebellion, revolt, uprising.

revolve, *v.* SYN.-circle, gyrate, rotate, spin, turn, twirl, wheel, whirl. ANT.-proceed, stop, stray, travel, wander.

reward, *n.* SYN.-award, bonus, bounty, compensation, premium, prize, recompense, remuneration, requital. ANT,-assessment, charge, earnings, punishment, wages.

rich, *a.* SYN.-abundant, affluent, ample, bountiful, copious, costly, exorbitant, luxurious, opulent, plentiful, prosperous, sumptuous, wealthy, well-to-do; fecund, fertile, fruitful, luxuriant, prolific. ANT.-beggarly, destitute, indigent, needy, poor; barren, sterile, unfruitful, unproductive.

riddle, *n.* SYN.-conundrum, enigma, mystery, problem, puzzle. ANT.-answer, clue, key, resolution, solution.

ridicule, *n.* SYN.-banter, derision, gibe, irony, jeering, mockery, raillery, sarcasm, satire, sneering.

right, *a.* SYN.-accurate, appropriate, correct, direct, erect, ethical, fair, fit, just, lawful, legitimate, proper, real, seemly, straight, suitable, true, upright. ANT.-bad, false, improper, wrong.

right, *n.* SYN.-authority, grant, liberty, license, prerogative, privilege; equity, honor, justice, propriety, virtue. ANT.-encroachment, injustice, violation, wrong.

righteous, *a.* SYN.-chaste, decent, ethical, good, honorable, just, moral, pure, right, scrupulous, virtuous. ANT.-amoral, libertine, licentious, sinful, unethical.

rigid, *a.* SYN.-austere, harsh, inflexible, rigorous, severe, stern, stiff, strict, stringent, unbending, unyielding. ANT.-compassionate, lax, lenient, mild, yielding; elastic, flexible, resilient, supple.

rigorous, *a.* SYN.-arduous, burdensome, cruel, difficult, hard, harsh, jarring, onerous, rough, rugged, severe, stern, strict, stringent, tough, unfeeling. ANT.-easy, effortless, facile; simple; gentle, lenient, tender.

rim, *n.* SYN.-border, boundary, brim, brink, edge, fringe, frontier, limit, margin, outskirts, termination, verge. ANT.-center, core, interior, mainland.

ring, *v.* SYN.-circle, confine, encircle, encompass, loop, surround; chime, clap, clang, peal, resound, strike, toll.

rinse, *v.* SYN.-bathe, clean, dip, soak, wash.

rip, *v.* SYN.-disunite, lacerate, rend, rive, sever, split, sunder, tear. ANT.-join, mend, repair, sew, unite.

ripe, *a.* SYN.-aged, complete, consummate, finished, full-grown, mature, matured, mellow, ready, seasonable. ANT.-crude, green, immature, raw, undeveloped.

rise, *v.* SYN.-adduce, advance, climb, elevate, further, improve, mount, proceed, progress, promote, scale, soar, thrive. ANT.-descend, fall, hinder, retard, retreat, sink.

risk, *n.* SYN.-danger, hazard, jeopardy, peril. ANT.-defense, immunity, protection, safety.

risk, *v.* SYN.-endanger, expose, hazard, jeopardize, peril; speculate, venture. ANT.-insure, protect, secure.

risky, *a.* SYN.-critical, dangerous, hazardous, insecure, menacing, ominous, perilous, precarious, threatening, unsafe. ANT.-firm, protected, safe, secure.

rite, *n.* SYN.-act, ceremony, custom, formality, liturgy, practice, protocol, ritual, system.

ritual, *n.* SYN.-ceremony, form, formality, observance, parade, pomp, protocol, rite, solemnity.

rival, *n.* SYN.-adversary, antagonist, competitor, contestant, enemy, foe, opponent. ANT.-ally, comrade, confederate, teammate.

rivalry, *n.* SYN.-adversary, antagonist, competition, contention, dispute, opposition, struggle.

road, *n.* SYN.-boulevard, drive, highway, parkway, roadway, street, thoroughfare, turnpike.

roam, *v.* SYN.-drift, meander, ramble, range, rove, stray, wander.

ANT.-halt, linger, settle, stay, stop.

rob, *v.* SYN.-burglarize, cheat, defraud, despoil, fleece, loot, pilfer, pillage, plunder, sack, steal, strip.

robber, *n.* SYN.-burglar, cheat, pirate, plunderer, raider, swindler, thief, thug.

robbery, *n.* SYN.-burglary, depredation, larceny, pillage, plunder, theft.

robust, *a.* SYN.-hale, healthy, hearty, sound, strong, well. ANT.-delicate, diseased, frail, infirm.

rock, *n.* SYN.-boulder, gravel, jewel, pebble, stone.

rogue, *n.* SYN.-cheat, criminal, knave, outlaw, rascal, scamp, scoundrel.

role, *n.* SYN.-character, function, lines, impersonation, part, performance.

romantic, *a.* SYN.-dreamy, extravagant, fanciful, fantastic, fictitious, ideal, idealistic, imaginative, maudlin, mawkish, picturesque, poetic, sentimental. ANT.-factual, literal, matter-of-fact, practical, prosaic.

room, *n.* SYN.-abode, apartment, chamber, cubicle, dormitory, flat, garret, hotel, inn, motel, niche, office; latitude, leeway, scope, space, vastness.

roomy, *a.* SYN.-ample, broad, capacious, extensive, large, spacious, vast, wide. ANT.-confined, cramped, limited, narrow.

root, *n.* SYN.-ancestor, base, basis, bottom, foundation, ground, groundwork, substructure, support, underpinning.

roster, *n.* SYN.-catalogue, document, index, list, register, roll, scroll.

rot, *v.* SYN.-decay, decompose, disintegrate, putrefy, spoil, waste. ANT.-flourish, grow, increase, luxuriate, rise.

rotten, *a.* SYN.-bad, decayed, defective, depraved, disgusting, filthy, offensive, putrid, putrefied, rancid, rank, spoiled,

rotate, *v.* SYN.-circle, circulate, invert, revolve, spin, turn, twirl, twist, wheel, whirl. ANT.-arrest, fix, stand, stop.

rotund, *a.* SYN.-bulbous, chubby, plump, round.

rough, *a.* SYN.-blunt, brusque, churlish, coarse, craggy, crude, cursory, gruff, harsh, imperfect, incomplete, irregular, jagged, rude, rugged, scabrous, scratchy, severe, stormy, tempestuous, turbulent, uncivil, uneven, unfinished, unpolished, violent; approximate, imprecise, inexact. ANT.-calm, civil, courteous, even, fine, finished, gentle, level, mild, placid, polished, refined sleek, slippery, smooth, tranquil, unruffled.

round, a, SYN.-bulbous, chubby, circular, complete, curved, cylindrical, entire, globular, plump, rotund, spherical.

roundabout, *a.* SYN.-circuitous, crooked, cunning, devious, distorted, indirect, tortuous, tricky, wandering, winding. ANT.-direct, honest, straight, straightforward.

rouse, *v.* SYN.-anger, aggravate, annoy, animate, awaken, excite, incitc, irk, provoke, startle, stimulate, urge.

rout, *v.* SYN.-beat, conquer, crush, defeat, humble, master, overcome, quell, subdue, subjugate, surmount, vanquish. ANT.-capitulate, cede, lose, retreat, surrender.

route, *n.* SYN.-avenue, channel, course, passage, path, road, street, thoroughfare, track, trail, walk, way.

routine, *n.* SYN.-act, custom, fashion, habit, norm, practice, procedure, system, usage, use, wont.

rove, *v.* SYN.-explore, meander, range, roam, wander.

rowdy, *n.* SYN.-bully, rascal, ruffian, thug.

royal, *a.* SYN.-courtly, dignified, grand, imperial, kingly, lordly, majestic, monarchal, noble, princely, regal, ruling, sovereign, stately, supreme. ANT.-common, humble, low, plebeian, proletarian, servile, vulgar.

rub, *v.* SYN.-brush, burnish, chafe, clean, massage, polish, scour, scrub, shine.

rude, *a.* SYN.-blunt, boorish, coarse, crude, discourteous, fierce, gruff, harsh, ignorant, illiterate, impolite, impudent, inclement, insolent, primitive, raw, rough, saucy, savage, surly, tumultuous, uncivil, unpolished, untaught, violent, vulgar. ANT.-calm, civil, courtly, dignified, genteel, mild, noble, peaceful, polished, stately.

ruffle, *v.* SYN.-agitate, anger, annoy, bother, disturb, fret, harass, irritate, rumple, torment, tousle, upset.

rugged, *a.* SYN.-craggy, harsh, irregular, jagged, rough, scabrous, severe, stormy, tempestuous, turbulent, uneven, violent. ANT.-even, fine, finished, level, polished, refined, sleek, slippery, smooth.

ruin, *v.* SYN.-annihilate, bankrupt, demolish, destroy. devastate, drain, fleece, obliterate, ravage, raze, sabotage, vandalize, wreck. ANT.-construct, establish, make, preserve, save.

ruinous, *a.* SYN.-baneful, deadly, deleterious, destructive, detrimental, devastating, fatal, injurious, noxious, pernicious. ANT.-beneficial, constructive, creative, profit able, salutary.

rule, *n.* SYN.-axiom, canon, formula, guide, law, maxim, method, order, precept, principle, propriety, regulation, standard, statute, system; authority, control, direction, dominion, government, jurisdiction, mastery, reign, sovereignty, sway. ANT.-chance, deviation, exception, hazard, irregularity; anarchy, chaos, misrule.

rule, *v.* SYN.-command, control, direct, dominate, govern, manage, regulate, superintend. ANT.-abandon, follow, forsake, ignore, submit.

rumor, *n.* SYN.-chatter, fabrication, gossip, hearsay, news, scandal, slander.

run, *v.* SYN.-bound, dart, dash, escape, go, hurry, jog, move, race, rush, scramble, scurry, sprint, trot,

rupture, *v.* SYN.-break, burst, crack, crush, demolish, destroy, fracture, rack, rend, shatter, smash. ANT.-join, mend, renovate, repair, restore.

rural, *a.* SYN.-agrarian, agricultural, bucolic, pastoral, rustic, suburban.

ruse, *n.* SYN.-artifice, deception, device, fraud, guile, hoax, imposture, ploy, stratagem, stunt, subterfuge, trick, wile. ANT.-candor, exposure, honesty, openness, sincerity.

rush, *v.* SYN.-accelerate, expedite, hasten, hurry, precipitate, quicken, speed. ANT.-delay, detain, hinder, retard, tarry.

rustic, *a.* SYN.-boorish, bucolic, coarse, country, homely, pastoral, plain, rural, simple, uncouth, unsophisticated. ANT.-cultured, elegant, polished, refined, urbane.

ruthless, *a.* SYN.-barbarous, bestial, brutal, brute, brutish, carnal, coarse, cruel, ferocious, fierce, gross, inhuman, merciless, remorseless, rough, rude, savage, sensual. ANT-civilized, courteous, gentle, humane, kind.

S

sabotage, *v.* SYN.-attack, damage, destroy, subvert, undermine, vandalize.

sacrament, *n.* SYN.-association, ceremony, communion, covenant, fellowship, intercourse, observance, participation, pledge, rite, union. ANT.-alienation, non participation.

sacred, *a.* SYN.-blessed, consecrated, devout, divine, hallowed, holy, pious, religious, saintly, scriptural, spiritual. ANT.-evil, profane, sacrilegious, secular, worldly.

sacrifice, *n.* SYN.-atonement, forfeiture, offering, penance, reparation, tribute.

sacrifice, *v.* SYN.-forfeit, forgo, relinquish, renounce, surrender.

sad, *a.* SYN.-cheerless, dejected, depressed, despondent, disconsolate, dismal, doleful, downcast, gloomy, lugubrious, melancholy, mournful, somber, sorrowful. ANT.-cheerful, glad, happy, joyous, merry.

sadness, *n.* SYN.-blues, dejection, depression, despondency, gloom, grief, melancholy, sorrow,

safe, *a.* SYN.-certain, dependable, harmless, protected, reliable, secure, snug, trustworthy. ANT.-dangerous, hazardous, insecure, perilous, unsafe.

safeguard, *n.* SYN.-bulwark, defense, guard, protection, refuge, security, shelter, shield.

safety, *n.* SYN.-asylum, protection, refuge, sanctuary, security, shelter.

sagacity, *n.* SYN.-discretion, erudition, foresight, information, insight, intelligence, judgment, knowledge, learning, prudence, reason, sageness, sense, wisdom. ANT.-foolishness, ignorance, imprudence, nonsense, stupidity.

sage, *n.* SYN.-disciple, intellectual, learner, philosopher, pupil, savant, scholar, student. ANT. dolt, dunce, fool, idiot, ignoramus.

saint, *n.* SYN.-altruist, believer, example, ideal, martyr, paragon.

salary, *n.* SYN.-compensation, earnings, fee, pay, payment, recompense, stipend, wages. ANT.-gift, gratuity, present.

sale, *n.* SYN.-barter, commerce, deal, marketing, selling, trade, transaction,

salient, *a.* SYN.-clear, conspicuous, distinguished, manifest, noticeable, obvious, projecting, prominent, protruding, striking, visible. ANT.-common, hidden, inconspicuous, obscure.

salutary, *a.* SYN.-advantageous, beneficial, good, helpful, profitable, serviceable, useful, wholesome. ANT.-deleterious, destructive, detrimental, harmful, injurious.

salve, *n.* SYN.-balm, cream, emollient, lubricant, ointment, unguent.

same, *a.* SYN.-coincident, equal, equivalent, identical, indistinguishable, like, similar. ANT.-contrary, disparate, dissimilar, distinct, opposed.

sample, *n.* SYN.-case, example, illustration, instance, model, pattern, prototype, specimen.

sanction, *n.* SYN.-approbation, approval, assent, commendation, consent, endorsement, praise, support. ANT.-censure, reprimand, reproach, stricture.

sanction, *v.* SYN.-allow, authorize, give, grant, let, permit, suffer, tolerate, yield. ANT.-forbid, object, protest, refuse, resist.

sanctuary, *n.* SYN.-asylum, church, cover, harbor, haven, protection, refuge, retreat, safety, security, shelter, shrine, temple. ANT.-danger, exposure, hazard, jeopardy, peril.

sane, *a.* SYN.-intelligent, logical, lucid, normal, rational, reasonable, sensible, sound.

sarcasm, *n.* SYN.-asperity, banter, bitterness, contempt, derision, irony, lampooning, mockery, ridicule, satire,

sarcastic, *a.* SYN.-acrimonious, biting, caustic, cutting, derisive, ironic, sardonic, satirical, sneering, taunting. ANT.-affable, agreeable, amiable, pleasant.

sardonic, *a.* SYN.-acrimonious, bitter, caustic, cruel, fierce, harsh, relentless, ruthless, severe. ANT.-delicious, mellow, pleasant, sweet.

satiate, *v.* SYN.-accomplish, cloy, deluge, fulfill, glut, gratify, inundate, meet, oversupply, satisfy.

satire, *n.* SYN.-banter, cleverness, fun, humor, irony, mockery, ridicule, sarcasm, wit, witticism. ANT.-commonplace, platitude, sobriety, solemnity, stupidity.

satirical, *a.* SYN.-acrimonious, biting, caustic, cutting, derisive, ironic, sarcastic, sardonic, sneering, taunting. ANT.-affable, agreeable, amiable, pleasant.

satisfactory, *a.* SYN.-adequate, ample, commensurate, enough, fitting, sufficient, suitable. ANT.-deficient, lacking, scant.

satisfy, *v.* SYN.-appease, compensate, content, fulfill, gratify, please, remunerate, satiate, suffice. ANT.-annoy, displease, dissatisfy, frustrate, tantalize.

saturate, *v.* SYN.-fill, impregnate, overfill, penetrate, permeate, pervade, soak.

sauciness, *n.* SYN.-audacity, boldness, effrontery, impertinence, impudence, insolence, presumption, rudeness. ANT.-diffidence, politeness, subserviency, truckling.

savage, *a.* SYN.-barbarous, bestial, brutal, brute, brutish, carnal, coarse, cruel, ferocious, gross, inhuman, merciless, remorseless, rough, rude, ruthless, sensual. ANT-civilized, courteous, gentle, humane, kind.

save, *v.* SYN.-conserve, defend, guard, keep, maintain, preserve, protect, rescue, safeguard, secure, spare, uphold. ANT.-abandon, abolish, destroy, impair, injure.

savings, *n.* SYN.-accumulation, assets, cache, hoard, investment, property, reserve, resources, security.

savor, *v.* SYN.-appreciate, enjoy, like, relish, sample, sip, taste.

savory, *a.* SYN.-appetizing, aromatic, agreeable, delectable, delicious, delightful, luscious, hearty, palatable, tasty. ANT.-acrid, distasteful, nauseous, unpalatable, unsavory

say, *v.* SYN.-articulate, converse, declare, discourse, express, harangue, speak, talk, tell, utter. ANT.-be silent, hush, refrain.

saying, *n.* SYN.-adage, aphorism, apothegm, byword, maxim, motto, proverb, saw.

scamper, *v.* SYN.-dash, hasten, hurry, run, speed, sprint.

scan, *v.* SYN.-browse, consider, examine, inspect, peruse, scrutinize, skim, study, survey.

scandal, *n.* SYN.-abasement, chagrin, disgrace, dishonor, disrepute, humiliation, ignominy, mortification, odium, opprobrium, shame. ANT.-dignity, glory, honor, praise, renown.

scandalize, *v.* SYN.-abuse, asperse, defame, disparage, ill-use, malign, revile, traduce, vilify. ANT.-cherish, honor, praise, protect, respect.

scandalous, *a.* SYN.-abusive, damning, discreditable, disgraceful, dishonorable, disreputable, false, ignominious, infamous, gossiping, libelous, malicious, outrageous, shameful, slanderous, sordid. ANT. teemed, honorable, renowned, respectable.

scanty, *a.* SYN.-inadequate, insufficient, lean, little, meager, paltry, scarce, sparse.

scar, *n.* SYN.-blemish, defect, disfigurement, flaw, mark.

scarce, *a.* SYN.-choice, exceptional, incomparable, infrequent, occasional, precious, rare, singular, uncommon, unique, unusual. ANT.-abundant, commonplace, customary, frequent, numerous, ordinary, usual, worthless.

scare, *v.* SYN.-affright, alarm, appall, daunt, dismay, frighten, horrify, intimidate, startle, terrify, terrorize. ANT.-allay, compose, embolden, reassure, soothe.

scared, *a.* SYN.-afraid, apprehensive, fainthearted, fearful, frightened, terrified, timid, timorous. ANT.-assured, bold, composed, courageous, sanguine.

scatter, *v.* SYN.-broadcast, diffuse, dispel, disperse, disseminate, dissipate, separate, sprinkle, strew, throw. ANT.-accumulate, amass, assemble, collect, gather.

scenery, *n.* SYN.-countryside, landscape, panorama, spectacle, view, vista.

scenic, *a.* SYN.-beautiful, breathtaking, dramatic, picturesque, pretty, spectacular, unspoiled.

scent, n, SYN.-aroma, fetidness, fragrance, fume, incense, odor, perfume, redolence, smell, stench, stink.

schedule, *n.* SYN.-agenda, calendar, catalogue, inventory, plan, program, record, register, roll, timetable.

scheme, *v.* SYN.-contrive, design, devise, outline, plan, plot, prepare, project, sketch.

scheme, *n.* SYN.-arrangement, artfulness, cabal, conspiracy, contrivance, cunning, design, diagram, intrigue, machination, outline, pattern, plan, planning, plotting, program, project, sketch, stratagem, system. ANT.-candor, result, sincerity.

scheming, *a.* SYN.-crafty, crooked, deceitful, devious, dishonest, foxy, perverse, planning, plotting, sly, treacherous, underhanded, unfaithful.

scholar, *n.* SYN.-disciple, intellectual, learner, pupil, sage, savant, student. ANT. dolt, dunce, fool, idiot, ignoramus.

scholarly, *a.* SYN.-academic, bookish, erudite, formal, learned, pedantic, scholastic, theoretical. ANT.-

common-sense, ignorant, practical, simple.

scholarship, *n.* SYN.-cognizance, comprehension, erudition, information, knowledge, learning, lore, understanding, wisdom. ANT.-ignorance, illiteracy, misunderstanding, stupidity.

school, *n.* SYN.-academy, conservatory, institution.

science, *n.* SYN.-discipline, enlightenment, knowledge, learning, scholarship. ANT.-ignorance, nascence, superstition.

scold, *v.* SYN.-admonish, berate, blame, censure, chide, lecture, rate, rebuke, reprehend, reprimand, upbraid, vituperate. ANT.-approve, commend, praise.

scoot, *v.* SYN.-bustle, dart, hasten, hurry, rush, speed.

scope, *n.* SYN.-amount, area, compass, degree, expanse, extent, length, magnitude, measure, range, reach, size, stretch.

scorch, *v.* SYN.-blister, burn, char, scald, sear, singe. ANT.-extinguish, put out, quench.

scorn, *n.* SYN.-contempt, contumely, derision, detestation, disdain, hatred, loathing. ANT.-awe, esteem, regard, respect, reverence.

scoundrel, *n.* SYN.-blackguard, cad, knave, rascal, rogue, scamp, villain.

scrap, *v.* SYN.-discard, dismiss, eliminate, exclude, reject; bicker, clash, conflict, fight, feud, quarrel, squabble.

scream, *v.* SYN.-cry, howl, shout, shriek, yell.

screen, *v.* SYN.-cloak, conceal, cover, hide, protect, shelter, shield, shroud, veil; choose, eliminate, select, sift.

scrimp, *v.* SYN.- conserve, curtail, economize, limit, pinch, save, skimp, squeeze, tighten.

scrub, *v.* SYN.-brush, clean, cleanse, mop, rub, scour, wash. ANT.-dirty, pollute, soil, stain, sully.

scruple, *n.* SYN.-compunction, doubt, hesitation, misgiving, reluctance, uncertainty, uneasiness.

scrupulous, *a.* SYN.-accurate, careful, cautious, conscientious, exact, particular, precise, strict.

scrutinize, *v.* SYN.-analyze, appraise, assess, audit check, contemplate, criticize, dissect, evaluate, examine, inspect, notice, question, review, scan, survey, view, watch. ANT.-approve, disregard, neglect, overlook.

search, *n.* SYN.-examination, exploration, inquiry, investigation, pursuit, quest. ANT.-abandonment, cession, resignation.

search, *v.* SYN. examine, explore, ferret, hunt, investigate, look, probe, ransack, rummage, scour, scrutinize, seek.

searching, *a.* SYN.-curious, inquiring, inquisitive, nosy, peeping, peering, prying, seeking, snoopy. ANT.-incurious, indifferent, unconcerned, uninterested.

seasoned, *a.* SYN.-experienced, established, mature, practiced, settled, skilled, versed.

secede, *v.* SYN.-depart, leave, retire, retreat, withdraw.

secluded, *a.* SYN.-alone, deserted, desolate, isolated, lone, lonely, only, single, sole, solitary, unaided. ANT.-accompanied, attended, surrounded.

seclusion, *n.* SYN.-isolation, insulation, loneliness, quarantine, retirement, segregation, separation, solitude, withdrawal. ANT.-association, communion, connection, fellowship, union.

secondary, *a.* SYN.-dependent, derived, indirect, inferior, lesser, lower, poorer, subordinate, subsequent, subsidiary. ANT.-better, greater, higher, superior.

secrecy, *n.* SYN.-concealment, confidence, hiding, mystery, privacy, seclusion, stealth, solitude.

secret, *a.* SYN.-clandestine, concealed, covert, hidden, latent, mystical, private, secluded, secretive, shrouded, surreptitious, unknown, veiled. ANT.-conspicuous, disclosed, exposed, known, obvious.

secrete, *v.* SYN.-cloak, conceal, cover, curtain, disguise, envelop, hide, mask, protect, screen, shield, shroud, veil. ANT.-bare, divulge, expose, reveal, unveil.

section, *n.* SYN.-district, division, domain, dominion, land, place, province, quarter, region, territory.

secular, *a.* SYN.-earthly, laic, lay, mundane, profane, temporal, worldly. ANT.-ecclesiastical, religious, spiritual, unworldly.

secure, *a.* SYN.-assured, certain, definite, fixed, indubitable, inevitable, positive, sure, undeniable, unquestionable. ANT.-doubtful, probable, questionable, uncertain.

secure, *v.* SYN.-achieve, acquire, attain, earn, gain, get, obtain, procure, receive. ANT. -forfeit, leave, lose, renounce, surrender.

security, *n.* SYN.-assurance, bail, bond, earnest, guarantee, guaranty, pawn, pledge, surety, token, warrant.

seduce, *v.* SYN.-allure, attract, bait, beguile, deceive, delude, dupe, entice, induce, lure, pervert, stimulate, tempt, trick, violate.

see, *v.* SYN.-behold, contemplate, descry, discern, distinguish, espy, glimpse, inspect, look at, notice, observe, perceive, scan, scrutinize, view, watch, witness.

seek, *v.* SYN.-ask, attempt, endeavor, ferret, hunt, investigate, look, probe, pursue, rummage, scour, scrutinize, search, try.

seem, *v.* SYN.- appear, look, resemble, suggest. ANT.-be, exist.

segment, *n.* SYN.-allotment, apportionment, division, fragment, moiety, part, piece, portion, scrap, section, share. ANT.-entirety, whole.

segregate, *v.* SYN.-detach, divide, insulate, isolate, separate, sever, split.

seize, *v.* SYN.-apprehend, arrest, capture, catch, check, clutch, confiscate, detain, grab, grasp, grip, hinder, hold, interrupt, obstruct, restrain, retain snatch, stop, take, withhold. ANT.-activate, discharge, free, liberate, release.

seldom, *a.* SYN.-hardly, infrequently, occasionally, rarely.

select, *a.* SYN.-best, choice, chosen, cream, elite, exceptional, pick, picked, preferred.

select, *v.* SYN.-choose, cull, elect, opt, pick, prefer, winnow. ANT.-refuse, reject.

selection, *n.* SYN.-alternative, choice, decision, election, option, preference.

selfish, *a.* SYN. egoistic, illiberal, mercenary, narrow, parsimonious, self-centered, self-seeking, stingy, ungenerous. ANT.-altruistic, charitable, liberal, magnanimous.

sell, *v.* SYN.-barter, liquidate, market, merchandise, peddle, trade, vend.

send, *v.* SYN.-cast, discharge, dispatch, emit, impel, propel, ship, throw, transmit. ANT.-bring, get, hold, receive, retain.

senior, *n.* SYN.-ancestor, elder, master, older, patiarch, superior.

seniority, *n.* SYN.-age, dotage, precedence, priority, senescence, senility, senior, rank. ANT.-childhood, infancy, junior, youth.

sensation, *n.* SYN.-apprehension, feeling, image, impression, perception, sense, sensibility. ANT.-apathy, insensibility, stupor, torpor.

sensational, *a.* SYN.-astonishing, breathtaking, dramatic, incredible, moving, spectacular, startling, thrilling.

sense, *n.* SYN.-connotation, drift, explanation, gist, implication, import, intent, interpretation, meaning, purport, purpose, significance, signification.

senseless, *a.* SYN.-brainless, crass, dense, dull, dumb, foolish, obtuse, stupid, witless. ANT.-alert, bright, clever, discerning, intelligent.

sensibility, *n.* SYN.-appreciation, awareness, judgment, perceptiveness, rapport, sensitivity, understanding.

sensible, *v.* SYN.-alive, appreciable, apprehensible, awake, aware, cognizant, comprehending, conscious, perceiving, perceptible, sentient; discreet, intelligent, judicious, practical, prudent, reasonable, sagacious, sage, sober, sound, wise. ANT.-absurd, impalpable, imperceptible, stupid, unaware.

sensitive, *a.* SYN.-delicate, impressionable, nervous, perceptive, prone, responsive, sentient, susceptible, sympathetic, tender, tense, touchy. ANT.-callous, dull, hard, indifferent, insensitive.

sensitivity, *n.* SYN.-awareness, consciousness, sensibility, sympathy.

sensual, *a.* SYN.-carnal, earthy, lascivious, lecherous, lewd, licentious, moving, pleasing, sensory, sensuous, sexual, stimulating, stirring, voluptuous, wanton. ANT.-abstemious, ascetic, chaste, continent, virtuous.

sentence, *n.* SYN.-decree, decision, dictum, edict, judgment, order, pronouncement.

sentence, *v.* SYN.-blame, censure, confine, convict, condemn, damn, denounce, incarcerate, imprison, judge, punish. ANT.-absolve, acquit, exonerate, pardon.

sentient, *a.* SYN.-aware cognizant, conscious, feeling, rational, reasoning, sensitive.

sentiment, *n.* SYN.-affection, emotion, feeling, impression, opinion, passion, sensibility, tenderness. ANT.-coldness, imperturbability, insensibility.

sentimental, *a.* SYN.-dreamy, extravagant, fanciful, ideal, idealistic, imaginative, maudlin, mawkish, picturesque, poetic, romantic. ANT.-factual, literal, matter-of-fact, practical, prosaic.

sentinel, *n.* SYN.-guard, lookout, sentry, scout, watch.

separate, *v.* SYN.-disconnect, divide, isolate, part, sever, split, sunder. ANT.-combine, gather, join unite.

separation, *n.* SYN.-alienation, insulation, isolation, quarantine, seclusion, segregation, solitude, withdrawal. ANT.-association, communion, connection, fellowship, union.

sequel, *n.* SYN.-continuation, epilogue, installment, postscript, supplement.

sequence, *n.* SYN.-arrangement, chain, classification, continuity, distribution, flow, following, gradation, order, placement, progression, series, string, succession, train.

serene, *a.* SYN.-calm, composed, dispassionate, imperturbable, pacific, peaceful, placid, quiet, still, tranquil, undisturbed, unruffled. ANT.-excited, frantic, stormy, turbulent, wild.

serenity, *n.* SYN.-calm, calmness, hush, peace, quiescence, quiet, quietude, repose, rest, silence, stillness, tranquility. ANT.-agitation, disturbance, excitement, noise, tumult.

series, *n.* SYN.-arrangement, chain, following, gradation, order, progression, sequence, string, succession, train.

serious, *a.* SYN.-alarming, critical, dangerous, earnest, grave, great, important, momentous, risky, sedate, sober, solemn, staid, weighty. ANT.-informal, relaxed, small, trifling, trivial.

sermon, *n.* SYN.-discourse, guide, homily, lesson, lecture, message, oration, speech, talk.

servant, *n.* SYN.-aid, aide, attendant, domestic, helper, hireling, menial, orderly, retainer,

serve, *v.* SYN.-administer, aid, assist, attend, benefit, cater, contribute, distribute, enlist, follow, forward, help, obey, oblige, promote, purvey, succor, work; provide, satisfy, suffice, supply. ANT.-command, dictate, direct, rule.

service, *n.* SYN.-aid, assistance, attendance, co-operation, duty, help, ministration, use, value; ceremony, rite, sermon, worship.

servile, *a.* SYN.-abject, base, contemptible, despicable, dishonorable, groveling, ignoble, ignominious, low, lowly, mean, menial, sordid, vile, vulgar. ANT.-teemed, exalted, honored, lofty, noble, righteous.

servitude, *n.* SYN.-apprenticeship, bondage, captivity, confinement, imprisonment, serfdom, slavery, subjugation, thralldom, vassalage. ANT.-freedom, liberation.

session, *n.* SYN.-assembly, conference, confrontation, congress, council, encounter, gathering, meeting, parley, rally.

set, *v.* SYN.-arrange, deposit, lay, place, put. ANT.-disarrange, disturb, mislay, misplace, remove.

setback, *n.* SYN.-blow, calamity, check, delay, difficulty, hindrance, misfortune, mishap, reversal, shock.

setting, *n.* SYN.-arena, atmosphere, backdrop, circumstances, context, environment, milieu, perspective, position, scene, stage, surroundings, viewpoint.

settle, *v.* SYN.-adjudicate, conclude, confirm, decide, determine, end, judge, resolve, terminate. ANT.-doubt, hesitate, suspend, vacillate, waver.

settlement, *n.* SYN.-agreement, close, completion, conclusion, decision, deduction, end, finale, issue, judgment, termination. ANT.-beginning, commencement, inception, prelude, start.

sever, *v.* SYN.-chop, cut, divide, part, separate, split, sunder. ANT.-combine, convene, gather, join unite.

severe, *a.* SYN.-acute, arduous, distressing, exacting, extreme, hard, harsh, intense, relentless, rigid, rigorous, sharp, stern, stringent, unmitigated, unyielding, violent. ANT.-considerate, genial, indulgent, merciful, yielding.

shabby, *a.* SYN.-deficient, inferior, mean, paltry, poor, ragged, scanty, seedy, threadbare, worn. ANT.-ample, good, new, opulent.

shack, *n.* SYN.-hovel, hut, shanty, shed.

shade, *n.* SYN.-amount, cast, color, complexion, hint, hue, obscurity, pigment, shadow, stain, tinge, tint, trace, variation. ANT.-achromatism, paleness, transparency.

shadowy, *a.* SYN.-dark, dim, dismal, gloomy, mournful, murky, obscure, somber, sorrowful, unilluminated; evil, sinister, sullen, wicked; hidden, mystic, occult, secret. ANT.-bright, clear, light, lucid, pleasant.

shake, *v.* SYN.-agitate, flutter, jar, jolt, quake, quaver, quiver, rock, shiver, shudder, sway, totter, tremble, vibrate, waver.

shaky, *a.* SYN.-dubious, faltering, insecure, loose, precarious, questionable, rickety, tentative, tenuous, uncertain, unreliable, unsteady, unsound, unstable, vacillating.

shallow, *a.* SYN.-cursory, exterior, flimsy, frivolous, imperfect, inconsequential, slight, superficial, trite. ANT.-abstruse, complete, deep, profound, thorough.

sham, *n.* SYN.-counterfeit, cover, fabrication, fake, forgery, fraud, imitation, pretense.

shame, *n.* SYN.-abasement, chagrin, disgrace, dishonor, disrepute, humiliation, ignominy, mortification, odium, opprobrium, scandal. ANT.-dignity, glory, honor, praise, renown.

shameful, *a.* SYN.-discreditable, disgraceful, dishonorable, disreputable, humiliating, immoral, ignominious, indecent, lewd, mortifying, obscene, odious, outrageous, scandalous, vulgar. ANT. teemed, honorable, renowned, respectable.

shameless, *a.* SYN.-audacious, blatant, bold, brazen, corrupt, depraved, forward, immodest, incorrigible, insolent, unabashed, unashamed. ANT.-modest, principled, proper.

shape, *n.* SYN.-appearance, build, cast, configuration, contour, cut, figure, form, frame, guise, image, mold, outline, pattern. ANT.-contortion, deformity, distortion, mutilation.

shape, *v.* SYN.-arrange, combine, compose, constitute, construct, create, devise, fashion, forge, form, frame, invent, make, mold, organize, produce. ANT.-destroy, disfigure, dismantle, misshape, wreck.

share, *n.* SYN.-allotment, allowance, bit, division, fragment, parcel, part, piece, portion, section, segment. ANT.-bulk, whole.

share, *v.* SYN.-accord, allot, apportion, appropriate, assign, bestow, cooperate, dispense, distribute, divide, give, parcel, partake, participate, partition, portion. ANT.-aggregate, amass, combine, condense.

shared, *a.* SYN.-common, communal, correlative, interchangeable, joint, mutual, reciprocal. ANT.-dissociated, separate, unrequited, unshared.

sharp, *a.* SYN.-acrid, acute, biting,

bitter, cutting, keen, penetrating, piercing, pointed, pungent, severe, shrill; astute, clever, cunning, quick, shrewd, wily, witty. ANT.-bland, blunt, gentle, shallow, stupid.

shatter, *v.* SYN.-break, burst, crack, demolish, destroy, fracture, pound, rack, rend, rupture, smash. ANT.-join, mend, renovate, repair, restore.

shattered, *a.* SYN.-broken, crushed, destroyed, flattened, fractured, reduced, rent, ruptured, smashed, wrecked. ANT.-integral, repaired, united, whole.

shed, *v.* SYN.-cast, discard, drop, emit, molt, radiate, scatter, spread.

sheer, *a.* SYN.-delicate, fine, flimsy, gossamer, thin, transparent; absolute, downright, pure, simple, utter; abrupt, precipitous, steep.

shelter, *n.* SYN.-asylum, cover, harbor, haven, protection, refuge, retreat, safety, sanctuary, security. ANT.-danger, exposure, hazard, jeopardy, peril.

shelter, *v.* SYN.-clothe, cover, defend, envelop, fortify, guard, protect, safeguard, shield. ANT.-bare, expose, reveal.

shelve, *v.* SYN.-delay, postpone, scrap, suspend.

shield, *v.* SYN.-cloak, clothe, conceal, cover, curtain, disguise, envelop, guard, hide, mask, protect, screen, shroud, veil. ANT.-bare, divulge, expose, reveal, unveil.

shift, *v.* SYN.-alter, change, convert, modify, transfigure, transform, vary, veer. ANT.-continue, establish, preserve, settle, stabilize.

shiftless, *a.* SYN.-idle, indolent, lazy, sluggish, useless, worthless.

shifting, *a.* SYN.-changeable, fickle, fitful, inconstant, unstable, vacillating, variable, wavering. ANT.-constant, stable, steady, unchanging, uniform.

shifty, *a.* SYN.-artful, capricious, conniving, deceitful, deceptive, guileful, questionable, sly, treacherous, tricky, undependable, unreliable.

shine, *v.* SYN.-beam, blaze, flash, flicker, glare, gleam, glimmer, glisten, glitter, glow, radiate, scintillate, shimmer, sparkle, twinkle; brush, buff, burnish, clean, polish, wax.

shining, *a.* SYN.-brilliant, bright, dazzling, effulgent, glorious, gorgeous, grand, illustrious, magnificent, radiant, resplendent, showy, splendid, sumptuous, superb. ANT.-dull, mediocre, modest, ordinary, unimpressive.

ship, *v.* SYN.-consign, dispatch, forward, remit, send, transport

shirk, *v.* SYN.-avoid, disdain, disregard, dodge, duck, evade, ignore, malinger, neglect, shun, sidestep, slack.

shock, *v.* SYN.-alarm, amaze, astonish, astound, disconcert, dumbfound, flabbergast, startle, stun, surprise, take aback. ANT.-admonish, caution, forewarn, prepare.

shocked, *a.* SYN.-aghast, appalled, astonished, astounded, awed, bewildered, dumbfounded, offended, overwhelmed, startled, stunned, upset.

shocking, *a.* SYN.-appalling, dreadful, fearful, frightful, gruesome, hideous, horrible, horrid, severe, terrible. ANT.-happy, joyous, pleasing, safe, secure.

shoddy, *a.* SYN.-defective, deficient, inferior, faulty, flawed, imperfect, mediocre, poor, second-rate, substandard.

short, *a.* SYN.-dumpy, dwarfed, little, low, pudgy, small, squat, undersized; abrupt, brief, compendious, concise, curt, laconic, succinct, summary, terse; deficient, inadequate, insufficient, lacking, limited. ANT.-abundant, ample, big, extended, protracted.

shorten, *v.* SYN.-abbreviate, abridge, condense, contract, curtail, diminish, lessen, limit, reduce, restrict. ANT.-elongate, extend, lengthen.

shortsighted, *a.* SYN.- expedient, improvident, impulsive, incautious, heedless, mindless, rash, reckless, thoughtless, unmindful, unthinking.

shout, *v.* SYN.-bellow, call, call out, cry, cry out, holler, scream, vociferate, yell. ANT.-intimate, whisper, write.

show, *n.* SYN.-array, display, exhibition, exposition; demonstration, flourish, ostentation, parade, spectacle, splurge; entertainment, movie, performance, production.

show, *v.* SYN.-demonstrate, disclose, display, evidence, exhibit, expose, indicate, manifest, parade, present, prove, reveal, unfold, verify; conduct, direct, guide, inform, instruct, teach, usher. ANT. conceal, confuse, hide.

showy, *a.* SYN.-affected, artificial, ceremonious, dramatic, flashy, gaudy, histrionic, melodramatic, ostentatious, pretentious, stagy, superficial, tawdry, theatrical. ANT.-modest, subdued, unaffected, unemotional.

shred, *n.* SYN.-bit, crumb, fragment, ort, particle, piece, scrap, snip, tatter.

shred, *v.* SYN.-lacerate, rend, rip, rive, sever, slit, split, sunder, tear. ANT.-join, mend, repair, sew, unite.

shrewd, *a.* SYN.-artful, astute, calculating, clever, crafty, cunning, foxy, furtive, guileful, insidious, intelligent, keen, perceptive, quick, sharp, sly, stealthy, subtle, surreptitious, tricky, underhanded, wily. ANT.-candid, frank, ingenuous, open, sincere.

shriek, *n.* SYN.-cry, howl, scream, screech, squawk.

shrill, *a.* SYN.-acute, cutting; biting, penetrating, piercing, sharp. ANT.-bland, blunt, gentle.

shrine, *n.* SYN.-column, crypt, mausoleum, memorial, monolith, monument, obelisk, statue.

shrink, *v.* SYN.-cringe, flinch, recoil, wince, withdraw; decrease, diminish, dwindle, lessen, reduce, shrivel.

shrivel, *v.* SYN.-abate, contract, decline, dry, parch, shrink, wilt, wither, wizen. ANT.-refresh, rejuvenate, renew.

shun, *v.* SYN.-avert, avoid, disregard, dodge, eschew, elude, evade, forbear, forestall, ignore, reject, scorn, slight, snub, spurn. ANT.-confront, encounter, face, meet, oppose.

shut, *v.* SYN.-close, conclude, fasten, lock, secure, seal. ANT.-open.

shy, *a.* SYN.-bashful, cautious, chary, demure, diffident, fearful, modest, reserved, retiring, sheepish, shrinking, timorous, wary. ANT.-audacious, bold, brazen, forward, immodest.

sick, *a.* SYN.-ailing, diseased, ill, indisposed, infirm, morbid, unhealthy, unwell. ANT.-healthy, robust, sound, strong, well.

sicken, *v.* SYN.-appall, disgust, displease, horrify, nauseate, offend, outrage, repel, repulse, revolt, shock. ANT.-approve, charm, delight, like, please.

sickly, *a.* SYN.-debilitated, delicate, feeble, frail, fragile, infirm, puny, unhealthy, weak.

sickness, *n.* SYN.-ailment, complaint, disease, disorder, illness, infirmity, malady. ANT.-health, healthiness, soundness, vigor.

sidestep, *v.* SYN.-avoid, bypass, circumvent, dodge, elude, evade, skirt.

siege, *n.* SYN.-assault, attack, blockade, invasion, offensive, onslaught, raid, strike.

sight, *n.* SYN.-display, scene, spectacle, view, vision.

sign, *n.* SYN.-beacon, clue, emblem, foreboding, gesture, hint, indication, mark, note, omen, premonition, portent, proof, signal, suggestion, symbol, symptom, token.

signal, *n.* SYN.-alarm, beacon, call, flag, impulse, warning, wave. ANT.-calm, inactivity, quiet, security, tranquillity.

significance, *n.* SYN.-connotation, drift, explanation, gist, implication, import, intent, interpretation, meaning, purport, purpose, sense, signification.

significant, *a.* SYN.-critical, grave, important, indicative, material, momentous, telling, weighty. ANT.-insignificant, irrelevant, meaningless, negligible, unimportant.

signify, *v.* SYN.-denote, designate, disclose, imply, indicate, intimate, manifest, reveal, show, specify. ANT.-conceal, distract, divert, falsify, mislead.

silence, *n.* SYN.-hush, quiet, quietude, serenity, stillness, tranquility. ANT.-noise, tumult.

silent, *a.* SYN.-calm, dumb, hushed, mute, noiseless, peaceful, quiet, still, taciturn, tranquil. ANT.-clamorous, loud, noisy, raucous.

silly, *a.* SYN.-absurd, asinine, brainless, crazy, foolish, idiotic, irrational, nonsensical, preposterous, ridiculous, senseless, simple, witless. ANT.-judicious, prudent, sagacious, sane, wise.

similar, *a.* SYN.-akin, alike, allied, analogous, comparable, correlative, correspondent, corresponding, like, parallel. ANT.-different, dissimilar, divergent, incongruous, opposed.

similarity, *n.* SYN.-analogy, correspondence, likeness, parity, resemblance, similitude. ANT.-difference, distinction, variance.

simile, *n.* SYN.-association, comparison, connection, kinship, parity, relationship, similarity.

simmer, *v.* SYN.-boil, bubble, fret, fume, rage, seeth, stew, worry.

simper, *v.* SYN.-grimace, smile, smirk.

simple, *a.* SYN. easy, effortless, elementary, facile, mere, pure, single, uncompounded, unmixed; artless, frank, homely, humble, naive, natural, open, plain, unsophisticated; asinine, credulous, foolish, silly. ANT.-adorned, artful, complex, intricate, wise.

simpleton, *n.* SYN.-clod, dolt, dope, dunce, fool, idiot.

simplify, *v.* SYN.-aid, ease, encourage, facilitate, promote

simply, *a.* SYN.-absolutely, directly, easily, frankly, honestly, merely, openly, plainly, purely, sincerely, utterly.

simulate, *v.* SYN.-ape, copy, counterfeit, duplicate, feign, imitate, impersonate, mimic, mock. ANT.-alter, distort, diverge, invent.

sin, *n.* SYN.-crime, evil, guilt, iniquity, offense, transgression, ungodliness, vice, wickedness, wrong. ANT.-goodness, innocence, purity, righteousness, virtue.

sincere, *a.* SYN.-candid, earnest, frank, genuine, heartfelt, honest, open, straightforward, true, truthful, unfeigned, upright. ANT.-affected, dishonest, hypocritical, insincere, untruthful.

sincerity, *n.* SYN.-candor, fairness, frankness, honesty, integrity, justice, openness, rectitude, responsibility, trustworthiness, uprightness. ANT.-cheating, deceit, dishonesty, fraud, trickery.

sinful, *a.* SYN.-bad, corrupt, dissolute, immoral, indecent, licentious, profligate, unprincipled, vicious, wicked. ANT.-chaste, high-minded, noble, pure, virtuous.

sing, *v.* SYN.-carol, chant, croon, hum, intone, lilt, warble.

singe, *v.* SYN.-burn, char, scorch, sear. ANT.-extinguish, put out, quench.

single, *a.* SYN.-alone, distinct, distinctive, exclusive, individual, lone, only, particular, separate, singular, sole, solitary, special, specific, unattached, unwed, unique. ANT.-common, general, ordinary, universal.

singly, *a.* SYN.-apart, independently, individually, separately.

singular, *a.* SYN.-choice, curious, distinctive, exceptional, extraordinary, individual, matchless, odd, particular, peculiar, rare, remarkable, special, strange, striking, uncommon, unequaled, unique, unusual. ANT.-common, general, normal, ordinary.

sinister, *a.* SYN.-bad, base, dire, evil, foreboding, malevolent, menacing, ominous, perverse, threatening, unlucky, wicked. ANT. beneficent, desirable, encouraging, favorable, fortunate, good, lucky.

sinless, *a.* SYN.-blameless, clean, faultless, innocent, pure, spotless, untainted, virtuous.

sip, *v.* SYN.-drink, imbibe, partake, sample, savor, taste.

sire, *v.* SYN.-beget, breed, create, engender, father, generate, originate, procreate, produce, propagate. ANT.-abort, destroy, extinguish, kill, murder.

site, *n.* SYN.-locale, locality, location, place, plat, plot, position, section, spot, station.

situated, *a.* SYN.-entrenched, established, fixed, located, placed, placement, positioned.

situation, *n.* SYN.-case, circumstance, condition, employment, job, plight, predicament, post, rank, standing, state, station, status.

size, *n.* SYN.-amount, amplitude, area, bigness, bulk, dimensions, expanse, extent, greatness, largeness, magnitude, mass, proportions, scope, stature, volume.

skeptic, *n.* SYN.-agnostic, cynic, deist, doubter, freethinker, infidel, non-believer, questioner, unbeliever. ANT.-adorer, believer, follower, worshiper.

skepticism, *n.* SYN.-ambiguity, distrust, doubt, incredulity, scruple, suspicion, unbelief, uncertainty. ANT.-belief, certainty, conviction, determination. faith.

sketch, *n.* SYN.-blueprint, chart, contour, delineation, description, draft, drawing, illustration, image, likeness, outline, plan, portrayal, profile, rendering, representation, scene, silhouette, view.

sketch, *v.* SYN.-chart, compose, delineate, depict, draft, draw, formulate, outline, picture, portray, represent, trace, write.

skill, *n.* SYN.-ability, adroitness, cleverness, cunning, deftness, dexterity, facility, ingenuity, knack, readiness, skillfulness. ANT.-awkwardness, clumsiness, inability, ineptitude.

skilled, *a.* See **skillful.**

skillful, *a.* SYN.-able, accomplished, adept, clever, competent, cunning, expert, ingenious, practiced, proficient, skilled, versed. ANT.-awkward, bungling, clumsy, inexpert, untrained.

skimpy, *a.* SYN.-deficient, lacking, inadequate, insufficient, scant, scarce, short.

skinflint, *n.* SYN.-cheapskate, hoarder, miser, piker, tightwad.

skirmish, *n.* SYN.-assault, attack, battle, clash, conflict, encounter, engagement, fight, offensive.

skittish, *a.* SYN.-excitable, high-strung, jittery, jumpy, nervous, restless

slack, *a.* SYN.-baggy, disorderly, limp, loose, negligent, relaxed, remiss, slovenly, unbound, unfastened, unkempt, untied. ANT.-tight, restrained.

slacken, *v.* SYN.-abate, decrease, diminish, lessen, mitigate, weaken.

slake, *v.* SYN.-allay, appease, gratify, mollify, placate, please, sate, satiate, satisfy.

slander, *n.* SYN.-aspersion, backbiting, calumny, defamation, libel, scandal, vilification. ANT.-applause, commendation, defense, flattery, praise.

slang, *n.* SYN.-argot, cant, jargon, lingo, patter.

slant, *n.* SYN.-grade, incline, pitch, slope; bent, bias, inclination, judgment, leaning, opinion, prejudice.

slant, *v.* SYN.-incline, lean, skew, tilt; color, distort, misconstrue, misinterpret, misrepresent, prejudice.

slap, *v.* SYN.-buffet, hit, pat, punch, smack, spank, strike, whack.

slash, *v.* SYN.-cut, gash, sever, slice; abridge, curtail, decrease, diminish, lessen, lower, reduce.

slate, *n.* SYN.-ballot, line-up, list, roll, roster, ticket.

slattern, *n.* SYN.-harlot, hooker, hussy, prostitue, strumpet, tramp, trollop, whore.

slaughter, *n.* SYN.-bloodshed, butchery, carnage, massacre, murder, pogrom, slaying.

slaughter, *v.* SYN.-assassinate, butcher, devastate, execute, kill, massacre, murder, slay. ANT.-animate, protect, resuscitate, save, vivify.

slavery, *n.* SYN.-bondage, captivity, confinement, imprisonment, serfdom, servitude, thralldom, vassalage. ANT.-freedom, liberation.

sleazy, *a.* SYN.-base, cheap, flimsy, shoddy, tacky, trashy.

sleek, *a.* SYN.-glossy, polished, silky, slick, smooth. ANT.-harsh, rough, rugged.

sleep, *n.* SYN.-catnap, doze, drowse, nap, nod, repose, rest, slumber, snooze, trance.

slender, *a.* SYN.-lean, skinny, slight, slim, spare, thin. ANT.-broad, bulky, fat, thick, wide.

slight, *a.* SYN.-delicate, emaciated,

flimsy, frail, insignificant, lean, paltry, petty, scrawny, skinny, slender, slim, spare, superficial, thin, trifling, unimportant. ANT.-broad, bulky, fat, thick, wide.

slight, *n.* SYN.-affront, disdain, contempt, disregard, insult, neglect, scorn.

slightly, *a.* SYN.-barely, hardly, inconsiderably, lightly, little, scarcely.

slink, *v.* SYN.-cower, lurk, prowl, skulk, sneak, steal.

slip, *n.* SYN.-blunder, error, fallacy, fault, inaccuracy, indiscretion, lapse, mistake, misstatement. ANT.-accuracy, precision, truth.

slogan, *n.* SYN.-axiom, device, legend, motto, trademark.

slope, *n.* SYN.-bank, bending, grade, inclination. incline, leaning, ramp

slothful, *a.* SYN.-idle, inactive, indolent, inert, lazy, slow, sluggish, supine, torpid. ANT.-active, alert, assiduous, diligent.

slow, *a.* SYN.-dawdling, delaying, deliberate, dull, gradual, laggard, leisurely, sluggish, tired. ANT.-fast, quick, rapid, speedy, swift.

sluggish, *a.* See **slow, slothful.**

slumber, *n.* SYN.-inactivity, quiescence, repose, rest, sleep.

slumber, *v.* SYN.-catnap, doze, drowse, nap, nod, repose, rest, sleep, snooze.

sly, *a.* SYN.-artful, astute, clandestine, covert, crafty, cunning, foxy, furtive, guileful, insidious, shrewd, stealthy, subtle, surreptitious, tricky, underhanded, wily. ANT.-candid, frank, ingenuous, open, sincere.

small, *a.* SYN.-diminutive, insignificant, little, miniature, minute, petty, puny, slight, tiny, trivial, wee. ANT.-big, enormous, huge, immense, large.

smart, *a.* SYN.-adroit, adept, alert, astute, bright, clever, discerning, enlightened, ingenious, intellectual, intelligent, knowledgeable, quick, quick-witted, sharp, talented, well-informed, witty. ANT.-awkward, bungling, clumsy, dull, foolish, slow, stupid.

smart, *n.* SYN.-affront, bite, burn, hurt, insult, prick, sting, wound.

smash, *v.* SYN.-break, burst, crack, crush, demolish, destroy, fracture, pound, rack, rend, rupture, shatter. ANT.-join, mend, renovate, repair, restore.

smell, *n.* SYN.-aroma, fetidness, fragrance, fume, incense, odor, perfume, redolence, scent, stench, stink.

smolder, *v.* SYN.-burn, fester, fret, fume, stew, seethe, smoke.

smooth, *a.* SYN.-diplomatic, even, flat, glib, level, plain, polished, sleek, slick, suave, urbane. ANT.-bluff, blunt, harsh, rough, rugged.

smother, *v.* SYN.-choke, drench, gag, quench, stifle, throttle.

smug, *a.* SYN.-complacent, conceited, egotistical, satisfied, self-righteous, snobbish.

snag, *n.* SYN.-adversity, complication, barrier, difficulty, hindrance, obstacle, pitfall, problem.

snare, *v.* SYN.-capture, catch, enmesh, entangle, grasp, grip, seize, trap. ANT.-liberate, lose, release.

snatch, *v.* SYN.-grab, grasp, nab, pluck, seize, steal, swipe.

sneak, *v.* SYN.-creep, lurk, prowl, skulk, slink.

sneer, *v.* SYN.-deride, flout, gibe, jeer, mock, scoff, scorn, taunt. ANT.-compliment, flatter, laud, praise.

sneering, *n.* SYN.-derision, gibe, jeering, mockery, raillery, ridicule, sarcasm.

snob, *n.* SYN.- elitist, egotist, pretender, showoff, upstart

snoopy, *a.* SYN.-curious, inquiring, inquisitive, interrogative, meddling, nosy, peeping, peering, prying, searching. ANT.-incurious, indifferent, unconcerned, uninterested.

snub, *v.* SYN.-disdain, disregard, humiliate, ignore, neglect, slight.

snug, *a.* SYN.-close, comfortable, compact, cozy, constricted, homey, intimate, secure, tight. ANT.-lax, loose, open.

soar, *v.* SYN.-flit, float, flutter, fly, glide, hover, mount, sail. ANT.-descend, fall, plummet, sink.

sober, *a.* SYN.-calm, composed, controlled, earnest, grave, rational, restrained, sedate, serious, solemn, somber, sound, staid, steady, subdued, temperate. ANT.-boisterous, informal, joyful.

sobriety, *n.* SYN.-abstention, abstinence, continence, forbearance, moderation, self-denial, temperance. ANT.-excess, gluttony, greed, intoxication, self-indulgence.

social, *a.* SYN.-affable, civil, communicative, congenial, friendly, gregarious, hospitable, outgoing, pleasant, sociable. ANT.-antisocial, disagreeable, hermitic, inhospitable.

soft, *a.* SYN.-compassionate, flexible, gentle, lenient, malleable, meek, mellow, mild, subdued, supple, tender, yielding. ANT.-hard, rigid, rough, tough, unyielding.

soil, *n.* SYN.-dirt, earth, ground, land, loam.

soil, *v.* SYN.-befoul, blemish, spot, stain, sully, tarnish. ANT.-clean, cleanse.

solace, *n.* SYN.-alleviate, comfort, consolation, contentment, ease, relief, soothe, succor. ANT.-affliction, discomfort, misery, suffering, torment, torture.

sole, *a.* SYN.-alone, deserted, desolate, isolated, lonely, secluded, unaided, lone, only, single, solitary. ANT.-accompanied, attended, surrounded.

solemn, *a.* SYN.-august, awe-inspiring, ceremonious, earnest, formal, grave, imposing, impressive, majestic, reverential, ritualistic, sedate, serious, sober, staid. ANT.-boisterous, informal, joyful, ordinary.

solicitude, *n.* SYN.-anxiety, care, caution, circumspection, compassion, concern, consideration, thoughtfulness, regard, wariness, worry. ANT.-disregard, indifference, neglect.

solid, *a.* SYN.-compact, dependable, firm, fixed, genuine, hard, reliable, sound, stable, substantial, unbroken, whole. ANT.-counterfeit, divided, elastic, flimsy, frail.

solitary, *a.* SYN.-alone, deserted, desolate, isolated, lone, lonely, only, secluded, single, sole, unaided. ANT.-accompanied, attended, surrounded.

solitude, *n.* SYN.-alienation, asylum, concealment, isolation, loneliness, privacy, refuge, retirement, retreat, seclusion. ANT.-exposure, notoriety, publicity.

somber, *a.* SYN.-bleak, cheerless, dark, dismal, doleful, dreary, dull, funereal, gloomy, melancholy, morose, sad, sullen. ANT.-cheerful, gay, joyous, lively.

song, *n.* SYN.-air, aria, lyric, melody, music, strain, tune.

soon, adv. SYN.-beforehand, betimes, early, easily, readily, shortly, speedily. ANT.-belated, late, over-due, tardy.

soothe, *v.* SYN.-cheer, comfort, console, encourage, gladden, mitigate, relieve, soften, solace, sympathize. ANT.-antagonize, aggravate, depress, dishearten.

soothing, *a.* SYN.-benign, calm, comforting, docile, gentle, mild, peaceful, placid, relaxed, serene, soft, tame, tractable. ANT.-fierce, harsh, rough, savage, violent.

sophisticated, *a.* SYN.-artificial, blasé, complex, cultivated, cultured, mature, practical, precious, refined, worldly, worldly-wise. ANT.-crude, ingenuous, naive, simple, uncouth.

sorcery, *n.* SYN.-alchemy, black art, conjuring, enchantment, legerdemain, magic, necromancy, voodoo, witchcraft, wizardry.

sordid, *a.* SYN.-abject, base, debased, depraved, despicable, foul, ignoble, loathsome, low, mean, obscene, odious, revolting, vicious, vile, vulgar, wicked, worthless, wretched. ANT.-attractive, decent, honorable, laudable, upright.

sorrow, *n.* SYN.-affliction, anguish, distress, grief, heartache, lamentation, misery, mourning, sadness, tribulation, woe. ANT.-comfort, consolation, happiness, joy, solace.

sorry, *a.* SYN.-afflicted, beggarly, contemptible, grieved, hurt, mean, pained, paltry, pitiable, pitiful, poor, sad, shabby, sorrowful, vexed, vile, worthless, wretched; contrite, penitent, remorseful, repentant. ANT.-cheerful, delighted, impenitent, splendid; unrepentant.

sort, *n.* SYN.-category, character, class, description, kind, nature, type. ANT.-deviation, eccentricity, monstrosity, peculiarity.

sound, *a.* SYN.-binding, dependable, healthy, hearty, legal, orthodox, powerful, proper, prudent, rational, reasonable, reliable, robust, sane, stable, strong, valid, vigorous, weighty. ANT.-counterfeit, null, spurious, void, weak.

sound, *n.* SYN.-din, intonation, noise, note, resonance, timbre, tone, vibration. ANT.-hush, quiet, silence, stillness.

sound, *v.* SYN.-articulate, echo, enunciate, pronounce, reverberate, say, shout, utter,

sour, *a.* SYN.-acid, acrimonious, bitter, glum, morose, peevish, rancid, sharp, sullen, tart. ANT.-genial, kindly, sweet, wholesome.

source, *n.* SYN.-agent, beginning, cause, determinant, incentive, inducement, motive, origin, principle, reason. ANT.-consequence, effect, end, result.

sovereignty, *n.* SYN.-authority, command, control, dominion, influence, power, predominance, sway.

spacious, *a.* SYN.-ample, broad, capacious, extensive, large, roomy, vast, wide. ANT.-confined, cramped, limited, narrow.

sparkle, *v.* SYN.-flicker, gleam, glimmer, glisten, glitter, glow, radiate, shimmer, shine, twinkle.

sparse, *a.* SYN.-barren, deficient, lean, meager, scanty.

speak, *v.* SYN.-articulate, converse, declare, discourse, express, harangue, lecture, say, talk, tell, utter. ANT.-be silent, hush, refrain.

special, *a.* SYN.-distinctive, exceptional, extraordinary, individual, particular, peculiar, uncommon, unusual. ANT.-broad, comprehensive, general, prevailing, widespread.

specific, *a.* SYN.-definite, explicit, limited, precise; categorical, characteristic, especial, peculiar. ANT.-general, generic, vague.

species, *n.* SYN.-class, division, family, genus, kind, order, variety, sort.

specify, *v.* SYN.-appoint, call, categorize, choose, classify, denominate, differentiate, distinguish, entitle, identify, mention, name, stipulate. ANT.-hint, miscall, misname.

specimen, *n.* SYN.-example, illustration, model, pattern, prototype, sample.

spectacle, *n.* SYN.-array, display, exhibition, exposition; demonstration, flourish, ostentation, parade, show, splurge.

speculate, *v.* SYN.-apprehend, assume, believe, conjecture, deduce, guess, imagine, presume, suppose, surmise, think. ANT.-ascertain, conclude, demonstrate, know, prove.

speech, *n.* SYN.-conversation, dialogue, discourse, discussion, lecture, report, talk. ANT.-correspondence, meditation, silence, writing.

speed, *v.* SYN.-accelerate, dispatch, expedite, facilitate, forward, hasten, hurry, push, quicken, rush. ANT.-block, hinder, impede, retard, slow.

spend, *v.* SYN.-circulate, consume, deplete, disburse, dispense, pass, pay, squander

spherical, *a.* SYN.-bulbous, circular, curved, cylindrical, globular, plump, rotund, round.

spirit, *n.* SYN.-apparition, ghost, phantom, soul, specter; courage, enthusiasm, fortitude, liveliness, temper, verve, vigor, vitality, zeal. ANT.-body, flesh, substance; languor, listlessness.

spirited, *a.* SYN.-active, alive, animated, blithe, lively, sprightly, vivacious.

spiritual, *a.* SYN.-divine, ethereal, ghostly, holy, immaterial, incorporeal, religious, sacred, supernatural, unearthly, unworldly. ANT.-carnal, corporeal, material, mundane, physical.

spiteful, *a.* SYN.-disagreeable, ill-natured, malicious, surly, vengeful, vicious. ANT.-peaceful, placid.

splendid, *a.* SYN.-brilliant, bright, dazzling, effulgent, glorious, gorgeous, grand, illustrious, magnificent, radiant, resplendent, shining, showy, sumptuous, superb. ANT.-dull, mediocre, modest, ordinary, unimpressive.

splendor, *n.* SYN.-brightness, brilliance, brilliancy, effulgence, grandeur, luster, magnificence, radiance. ANT.-darkness, dullness, gloom, obscurity.

split, *v.* SYN.-cleave, rend, rip, rive, sever, shred, slit, sunder, tear. ANT.-join, mend, repair, sew, unite.

spoil, *v.* SYN.-decay, decompose, disintegrate, putrefy, rot, ruin, waste. ANT.-flourish, grow, rise.

spoken, *a.* SYN.-literal, oral, phonetic, told, uttered, verbal, vocal. ANT.-documentary, recorded, written.

spontaneous, *a.* SYN.-automatic, extemporaneous, impulsive, instinctive, offhand, voluntary, willing. ANT.-compulsory, forced, planned, prepared, rehearsed.

sport, *n.* SYN.-amusement, contest, diversion, fun, game, match, merriment, pastime, play, recreation. ANT.-business drudgery, hardship, labor, work.

sport, *v.* SYN.-caper, frolic, gamble, gambol, play, revel, romp, stake, wager

spread, *v.* SYN.-air, broadcast, distribute, exhibit, expand, extend, open, scatter, smear, unfold, unfurl. ANT.-close, conceal, shut.

sprightly, *a.* SYN.-animated, blithe, buoyant, cheerful, effervescent, elated, gay, light, lively, resilient, spirited, vivacious. ANT.-dejected, depressed, despondent, hopeless, sullen.

spur, *n.* SYN.-cause, impulse, incentive, incitement, inducement, motive, principle, purpose, reason, stimulus. ANT.-action, attempt, deed, effort, result.

squabble, *v.* SYN.-altercate, argue, bicker, contend, contest, debate, disagree, discuss, dispute, quarrel, wrangle. ANT.-agree, allow, assent, concede.

squalid, *a.* SYN.-dirty, filthy, foul, grimy, mean, muddy, nasty, pitiful, shabby, soiled, wretched. ANT.-clean, neat, presentable; pure, wholesome.

squander, *v.* SYN.-dissipate, lavish, misuse, waste, wear out. ANT.-accumulate, economize, preserve, save.

stable, *a.* SYN.-constant, durable, enduring, established, firm, fixed, immovable, immutable, lasting, permanent, secure, staunch, steadfast, steady, unwavering. ANT.-changeable, erratic, irresolute, vacillating, variable.

staff, *n.* SYN.-assistants, cadre, crew, employees, force, help, helpers, organization, personnel.

staid, *a.* SYN.-demure, grave, modest, sedate, serious, sober, solemn. ANT.-boisterous, informal, joyful, ordinary.

stain, *v.* SYN.-befoul, blemish, blight, defile, discolor, disgrace, soil, spot, sully, tarnish; color, dye, tinge, tint. ANT.-bleach, cleanse, decorate, honor, purify.

stale, *a.* SYN.-banal, common, dry, dull, flat, insipid, musty, old, trite.

stand, *v.* SYN.-abide, bear, continue, endure, suffer, sustain, tolerate; halt, pause, remain, rest, stay, stop. ANT.-advance, progress, run, submit, yield.

standard, *n.* SYN.-criterion, gauge, law, measure, norm, rule, test, touchstone. ANT.-chance, fancy, guess, supposition.

start, *n.* SYN.-beginning, commencement, genesis, inception, opening, origin, outset, source. ANT.-close, completion, consummation, end, termination.

start, *v.* SYN.-arise, begin, commence, establish, found, inaugurate, initiate, institute, organize, originate. ANT.-complete, end, finish, terminate.

startle, *v.* SYN.-alarm, amaze, astonish, astound, disconcert, dumbfound, flabbergast, frighten, panic, scare, shock, stun, surprise, terrify. ANT.-admonish, caution, forewarn, prepare.

starved, *a.* SYN.-craving, famished, hungry, ravenous, voracious. ANT.-full, gorged, sated, satiated, satisfied.

state, *n.* SYN.-case, circumstance,

condition, plight, predicament, situation; commonwealth, community, kingdom, nationality, people, realm.

state, *v.* SYN.-affirm, assert, avow, claim, declare, explain, express, propound, recite, recount, say, specify, tell, utter. ANT.-conceal, deny, imply, retract.

stately, *a.* SYN.-courtly, dignified, grand, imperial, kingly, lordly, majestic, monarchal, noble, princely, regal, royal, ruling, sovereign, supreme. ANT.-common, humble, low, plebeian, proletarian, servile, vulgar.

statement, *n.* SYN.-allegation, announcement, assertion, communication, declaration, mention, proposition, report, thesis.

station, *n.* SYN.-level, location, occupation, office, order, place, position, post, rank, spot, standing.

statuesque, *a.* SYN.-august, beautiful, dazzling, divine, elegant, exquisite, gorgeous, graceful, grand, impressive, radiant, stately, venerable.

status, *n.* SYN.-caste, class, condition, estate, grade, incumbency, job, office, place, position, post, quality, rank, situation, standing, station.

statute, *n.* SYN.-act, decree, edict, law, ordinance.

stay, *v.* SYN.-abide, arrest, check, delay, halt, hinder, linger, obstruct, remain, sojourn, stand, tarry, wait. ANT.-advance, expedite, hasten, leave, progress.

steadfast, *a.* SYN.-authoritative, constant, dependable, dogmatic, fast, firm, fixed, inflexible, reliable, secure, solid, stable, steady, unswerving, unyielding. ANT.-insecure, loose, unstable, unsteady.

steal, *v.* SYN.-burglarize, embezzle, loot, pilfer, pillage, plagiarize, plunder, purloin, rob, snatch, swipe. ANT.-buy, refund, repay, restore, return.

steep, *a.* SYN.-abrupt, hilly, precipitous, sharp, sheer, sudden. ANT.-flat, gradual, level.

steer, *v.* SYN.-direct, conduct, control, escort, guide, lead, manage, regulate.

stench, *n.* SYN.-aroma, fetidness, fragrance, fume, incense, odor, perfume, redolence, scent, smell, stink.

stern, *a.* SYN.-absolute, austere, dogmatic, exacting, hard, harsh, intense, relentless, rigid, rigorous, severe, sharp, stringent, unmitigated, unyielding. ANT.-considerate, genial, indulgent, merciful, yielding.

stiff, *a.* SYN.-constrained, formal, inflexible, obstinate, prim, resolved, rigid, severe, stern, stilted, strict, stringent, unbending, unyielding; abrupt, awkward, clumsy, crude. ANT.-compassionate, lax, lenient, mild, yielding; elastic, flexible, resilient, supple.

stigma, n, SYN.-brand, mark, scar, stain, stigmata, trace, vestige.

still, *a.* SYN.-hushed, motionless, noiseless, peaceful, placid, quiescent, quiet, silent, tranquil, undisturbed; calm, silent. ANT.-loud, strident.

stimulate, *v.* SYN.-agitate, arouse, disquiet, excite, incite, irritate, provoke, rouse, stir up. ANT.-allay, calm, pacify, quell, quiet.

stimulus, *n.* SYN.-arousal, encouragement, goad, incentive, instigation, motive, provocation, spur, stimulant. ANT.-depressant, discouragement, dissuasion, response.

stingy, *a.* SYN.-acquisitive, avaricious, greedy, miserly, niggardly, parsimonious, penurious, tight. ANT.-altruistic, bountiful, extravagant, generous, munificent.

stock, *n.* SYN.-accumulation, fund, goods, hoard, inventory, merchandise, provision, reserve, store, supplies, supply.

stock, *v.* SYN.-equip, fill, furnish, have, replenish, retain, save, store, supply. ANT.-deplete, drain, empty, exhaust.

stoical, *a.* SYN.-calm, composed, forbearing, impassive, passive, patient, resigned, serene, uncomplaining. ANT.-chafing, clamorous, hysterical, turbulent.

stone, *n.* SYN.-boulder, gravel, jewel, pebble, rock.

stop, *v.* SYN.-abstain, arrest, bar, cease, check, close, cork, desist, discontinue, end, halt, hinder, impede, interrupt, obstruct, plug, seal, terminate. ANT.-begin, proceed, promote, speed, start.

storm, *n.* SYN.-blizzard, cloudburst, cyclone, downpour, hurricane, squall, tempest, tornado.

stormy, *a.* SYN.-blustery, gusty, inclement, roaring, rough, tempestuous, turbulent, windy. ANT.-calm, clear, peaceful, quiet, tranquil.

story, *n.* SYN.-account, anecdote, chronicle, fable, fabrication, falsehood, fiction, history, narration, narrative, novel, report, tale, yarn.

stout, *a.* SYN.-chubby, corpulent, fat, obese, paunchy, plump, portly, pudgy, rotund, stocky, thickset. ANT.-gaunt, lean, slender, slim, thin.

straight, *a.* SYN.-direct, erect, fair, honest, honorable, just, right, square, unbent, undeviating, unswerving, upright, vertical. ANT.-bent, circuitous, crooked; dishonest, winding.

strain, *n.* SYN.-ancestry, breed, extraction, kind, sort, species, stock, subspecies, variety; effort, exertion, force, pressure; bruise, injury, sprain, twist, wrench; anxiety, pressure, stress, tension.

strange, *a.* SYN.-abnormal, bizarre, curious, eccentric, extraordinary, foreign, grotesque, irregular, odd, mysterious, peculiar, queer, singular, surprising, uncommon, unusual. ANT.-common, conventional, familiar, ordinary, regular.

stranger, *n.* SYN.-alien, foreigner, immigrant, interloper, intruder, newcomer, outsider. ANT.-acquaintance, associate, countryman, friend, neighbor.

strategy, *n.* SYN.-approach, method, plan, procedure, scheme, system, tactics.

stray, *v.* SYN.-deviate, digress, err, ramble, range, roam, rove, saunter, stroll, traipse, wander. ANT.-halt, linger, settle, stay, stop.

stream, *v.* SYN.-abound, come, emanate, flow, gush, issue, run, spout, spurt; abound.

street, *n.* SYN.-avenue, boulevard, court, lane, passage, path.

strength, *n.* SYN.-durability, force, fortitude, intensity, lustiness, might, potency, power, stamina, stoutness, sturdiness, toughness, vigor. ANT.-feebleness, frailty, infirmity, weakness.

strengthen, *v.* SYN.-approve, confirm, encourage, fix, fortify, hearten, intensify, ratify, reinforce, sanction, temper, toughen.

stress, *n.* SYN.-accent, compulsion, constraint, distress, exigency, force, hurry, importance, influence, press, pressure, significance, strain, tension, urgency. ANT. ease, lenience, recreation, relaxation.

stretch, *v.* SYN.-distend, distort, elongate, expand, extend, lengthen, protract, spread, strain. ANT.-contract, loosen, shrink, slacken, tighten.

strict, *a.* SYN.-austere, critical, demanding, exacting, harsh, rigorous, rough, rugged, severe, stringent. ANT.-gentle, melodious, mild, smooth, soft.

strife, *n.* SYN.-battle, clash, combat, conflict, fight, struggle.

strike, *v.* SYN.-beat, clout, cuff, hit, knock, pound, pummel, punch, slap, smite; boycott, picket, quit, stop.

striking, *a.* SYN.-affecting, arresting, august, commanding, exciting, forceful, grandiose, imposing, impressive, majestic, moving, overpowering, remarkable, splendid, stirring, thrilling, touching. ANT.-commonplace, ordinary, regular, unimpressive.

stringent, *a.* SYN.-forcible, harsh, rigorous, rough, rugged, severe, strict. ANT.-gentle, melodious, mild, smooth, soft.

strive, *v.* SYN.-aim, attempt, endeavor, try, struggle, undertake. ANT.-abandon, neglect.

stroll, *v.* SYN.-amble, meander, ramble, roam, saunter, walk.

strong, *a.* SYN.-athletic, cogent, concentrated, enduring, firm, forceful, forcible, fortified, hale, hardy, impregnable, mighty, potent, powerful, robust, sinewy, sturdy, tough. ANT.-brittle, delicate, feeble, fragile, insipid.

struggle, *n.* SYN.-battle, combat, conflict, contest, encounter, fight, fray, skirmish, strife. ANT.-agreement, concord, peace, truce.

struggle, *v.* SYN.-battle, brawl, combat, conflict, contend, dispute, encounter, fight, scuffle, skirmish.

stubborn, *a.* SYN.-contumacious, determined, dogged, firm, headstrong, immovable, inflexible, intractable, obdurate, obstinate, pertinacious, uncompromising, unyielding. ANT.-amenable, compliant, docile, submissive, yielding.

student, *n.* SYN.-disciple, learner, observer, pupil, scholar.

study, *v.* SYN.-cogitate, contemplate, examine, investigate, learn, master, meditate, muse, ponder, reflect, scrutinize, weigh.

stuff, *n.* SYN.-items, material, matter, substance, thing. ANT.-immateriality, phantom, spirit.

stuff, *v.* SYN.-cram, fill, glut, gorge, occupy, pervade, sate, satiate, satisfy. ANT.-deplete, drain, empty, exhaust, void.

stumble, *v.* SYN.-blunder, drop, fall, falter, hesitate, sink, topple, trip, tumble. ANT.-arise, ascend, climb, mount, soar.

stun, *v.* SYN.-amaze, astound, dumbfound, flabbergast, shock, startle, surprise, take aback. ANT.-admonish, caution, forewarn, prepare.

stunning, *a.* SYN.-astonishing, astounding, beautiful, charming, dazzling, exquisite, gorgeous, marvelous, remarkable, shocking, staggering, striking.

stupid, *a.* SYN.-addled, brainless, crass, dense, dull, dumb, foolish, obtuse, senseless, witless. ANT.-alert, bright, clever, discerning, intelligent.

stupor, *n.* SYN.-daze, drowsiness, insensibility, languor, lethargy, numbness, stupefaction, torpor. ANT.-activity, alertness, liveliness, readiness, wakefulness.

sturdy, *a.* SYN.-enduring, firm, formidable, fortified, hard, hardy, impregnable, mighty, potent, powerful, robust, sinewy, stout, strong, tough. ANT.-brittle, delicate, feeble, fragile, insipid.

suave, *a.* SYN.-courtly, cultured, elegant, genteel, glib, polished, refined, smooth, sophisticated, urbane.

subdue, *v.* SYN.-beat, conquer, crush, defeat, humble, master, overcome, quell, rout, subjugate, surmount, vanquish. ANT.-capitulate, cede, lose, retreat, surrender.

subject, *n.* SYN.-citizen, dependent, inferior, liegeman, subordinate, vassal; argument, case, matter, object, patient, point, theme, thesis, topic.

sublime, *a.* SYN.-elevated, exalted, glorious, grand, high, lofty, majestic, noble, raised, splendid, supreme. ANT.-base, ignoble, low, ordinary, ridiculous.

submerge, *v.* SYN.-absorb, bury, dip, dunk, engage, engross, immerse, plunge, sink. ANT.-elevate, recover, uplift.

submissive, *a.* SYN.-compliant, deferential, dutiful, obedient, tractable, yielding. ANT.-insubordinate, intractable, obstinate, rebellious.

submit, *v.* SYN.-abdicate, accede, acquiesce, capitulate, cede, quit, relent, relinquish, resign, succumb, surrender, waive, yield. ANT.-assert, resist, strive, struggle.

subordinate, *a.* SYN.-following, inferior, lesser, lower, minor, poorer, secondary. ANT.-better, greater, higher, superior.

subordinate, *n.* SYN.-aide, assistant, citizen, dependent, helper, inferior, liegeman, subject, underling, vassal.

substantial, *a.* SYN.-abundant, ample, considerable, plentiful; actual, concrete, corporeal, material, physical, tangible, visible; firm, large, sound, strong; affluent, important, influential, rich, wealthy.

substantiate, *v.* SYN.-attest, authenticate, confirm, corroborate, validate, verify.

substitute, *n.* SYN.-agent, alternate, deputy, double, lieutenant, proxy, representative, stand-in, surrogate, understudy; equivalent, expedient, makeshift. ANT.-head, master, principal, sovereign.

substitution, *n.* SYN.-alteration, alternation, change, modification, variation, variety, vicissitude. ANT.-monotony, stability, uniformity.

subterfuge, *n.* SYN.-alibi, disguise, evasion, excuse, pretense, pretext. ANT.-actuality, fact, reality, sincerity, truth.

subtract, *v.* SYN.-decline, decrease, deduct, diminish, lessen, reduce, remove, shorten, wane. ANT.-amplify, enlarge, expand, grow, increase.

succeed, *v.* SYN.-achieve, flourish, gain, prevail, prosper, thrive, win; ensue, follow, inherit, supersede, supplant. ANT.-fail, miscarry, miss; anticipate, precede.

successful, *a.* SYN.-auspicious, flourishing, fortunate, lucky, prosperous, triumphant.

succession, *n.* SYN.-arrangement, chain, following, gradation, order, progression, sequence, series, string, train.

succinct, *a.* SYN.-brief, compendious, concise, curt, fleeting, laconic, momentary, passing, pithy, short, terse, transient. ANT.-extended, lengthy, long, prolonged, protracted.

succor, *n.* SYN.-aid, assistance, comfort, consolation, relief, solace, support. ANT.-affliction, discomfort, misery, suffering, torment, torture.

sudden, *a.* SYN.-abrupt, hasty, immediate, instantaneous, rapid, unexpected. ANT.-anticipated, gradual, slowly.

sue, *v.* SYN.-appeal, beg, claim, demand, entreat, indict, litigate, petition, plead, pray, prosecute, solicit,

suffer, *v.* SYN.-bear, endure, feel, stand, sustain, tolerate, undergo; allow, indulge, let, permit, tolerate. ANT.-banish, discard, exclude, overcome.

suffering, *n.* SYN.-ache, agony, anguish, distress, misery, pain, throe, torment, torture, woe. ANT.-comfort, ease, mitigation, relief.

sufficient, *a.* SYN.-adequate, ample, commensurate, enough, fitting, satisfactory, suitable. ANT.-deficient, lacking, scant.

suggest, *v.* SYN.-advise, allude, counsel, hint, imply, insinuate, intimate, offer, propose, recommend, refer. ANT. declare, demand, dictate, insist.

suggestion, *n.* SYN.-admonition, advice, caution, counsel, exhortation, hint, information, instruction, intelligence, notification, recommendation, warning.

suitable, *a.* SYN.-acceptable, agreeable, amiable, gratifying, pleasant, pleasing, pleasurable, welcome. ANT.-disagreeable, obnoxious, offensive, unpleasant.

sullen, *a.* SYN.-dour, fretful, gloomy, glum, moody, morose, sulky, surly. ANT.-amiable, gay, joyous, merry, pleasant.

sum, *n.* SYN.-aggregate, entirety, total, whole. ANT.-fraction, ingredient, part, sample.

sum, *v.* SYN.-add, affix, append, attach, augment, increase, total. ANT.-deduct, detach, reduce, remove, subtract.

summarize, *v.* SYN.-abridge. abstract, outline, part, recap. ANT.-add, replace, restore, return, unite.

summit, *n.* apex, crest, crown, head, pinnacle, top, zenith. ANT.-base, bottom, foot, foundation.

sundry, *a.* SYN.-different, divers, few, miscellaneous, several, unlike, various. ANT.-alike, congruous, identical, same, similar.

sunny, *a.* SYN.-bright, clear, cloudless, fair. ANT.-cloudy, foul, overcast.

superb, *a.* SYN.-beautiful, elegant, excellent, impressive, grand, magnificent, marvelous, splendid.

superficial, *a.* SYN.-cursory, exterior, flimsy, frivolous, imperfect, shallow, slight. ANT.-abstruse, complete, deep, profound, thorough.

superintend, *v.* SYN.-command, control, direct, dominate, govern, manage, regulate, rule. ANT.-abandon, follow, forsake, ignore.

superiority, *n.* SYN.-advantage, edge, lead, mastery, supremacy. ANT.-handicap, weakness.

supernatural, *a.* SYN.-marvelous, metaphysical, miraculous, other-worldly, preternatural, spiritual, superhuman, unearthly. ANT.-common, human, natural, physical, plain.

supervise, *v.* SYN.-boss, command, control, direct, dominate, govern, manage, oversee, regulate, rule, superintend. ANT.-abandon, forsake, ignore.

supervision, *n.* SYN.-charge, control, direction, inspection, instruction, management, oversight, superintendence, surveillance. ANT.-attention, care, observation, scrutiny .

supplant, *v.* SYN.-overcome, overthrow, overturn, remove, replace, rout, ruin, uproot, upset, vanquish. ANT.-build, conserve, construct, preserve, uphold.

supple, *a.* SYN.-compliant, ductile, elastic, flexible, lithe, pliable, pliant, resilient, tractable. ANT.-brittle, hard, rigid, stiff, unbending.

supply, *n.* SYN.-accumulation, fund, hoard, provision, reserve, stock, store.

supply, *v.* SYN.-endow, equip, fit, fit out furnish, provide. ANT.-denude, despoil, divest, strip.

support, *n.* SYN.-base, basis, brace, buttress, foundation, groundwork, prop, stay; aid, assistance, backing, comfort, encouragement, favor, help, patronage, succor; livelihood, living, maintenance, subsistence; confirmation, evidence. ANT.-attack, enmity, opposition.

support, *v.* SYN.-advocate, assist, back, bear, brace, encourage, foster, further, help, keep, maintain, preserve, prop, sustain, uphold, ANT.-abandon, betray, destroy, discourage, oppose.

supporter, *n.* SYN.-adherent, apologist, apostle, attendant, devotee, disciple, follower, henchman, partisan, successor, votary. ANT.-chief, head, leader, master.

suppose, *v.* SYN.-apprehend, assume, believe, conjecture, deduce, guess, imagine, presume, speculate, surmise, think. ANT.-ascertain, conclude, demonstrate, know, prove.

supremacy, *n.* SYN.-ascendancy, domination, mastery, predominance, sovereignty, sway, transcendence. ANT.-inferiority.

supreme, *a.* SYN.-cardinal, chief, foremost, highest, leading, main, paramount, predominant, principal. ANT.-auxiliary, minor, subordinate, subsidiary, supplemental.

sure, *a.* SYN.-assured, certain, definite, fixed, indubitable, inevitable, positive, secure, undeniable, unquestionable. ANT.-doubtful, probable, questionable, uncertain.

surly, *a.* SYN.-disagreeable, dour, ill-natured, quarrelsome, rude, spiteful, sullen, vicious. ANT.-friendly, pleasant.

surplus, *n.* SYN. abundance, excess, extra, extravagance, overs, profusion, remains, superabundance, superfluity, . ANT.-dearth, deficiency, lack, paucity, want.

surprise, *n.* SYN.-amazement, astonishment, awe, bewilderment, wonder, wonderment. ANT.-apathy, expectation, indifference.

surprise, *v.* SYN.-alarm, amaze, astonish, astound, disconcert, dumbfound, flabbergast, shock, startle, stun, take aback. ANT.-admonish, caution, forewarn, prepare.

surrender, *v.* SYN.-abandon, acquiesce, capitulate, cede, relinquish, renounce, resign, sacrifice, submit, yield. ANT.-conquer, overcome, resist, rout.

surround, *v.* SYN.-bound, circumscribe, confine, enclose, encompass, envelop, fence, limit. ANT.-develop, distend, enlarge, expand, expose, open.

survey, *n.* SYN.-critique, examination, inspection, outline, poll, review, study.

survey, *v.* SYN.-examine, inspect, observe, scan, scrutinize, view, watch.

survive, *v.* SYN.-endure, last, persevere, persist, outlast, outlive, remain, weather.

suspect, *v.* SYN.-distrust, doubt, hesitate, mistrust, question, waver, wonder. ANT.-believe, confide, decide, rely on, trust.

suspend, *v.* SYN.-adjourn, defer, delay, discontinue, interrupt, postpone, stay; balance, dangle, hang, poise, swing. ANT.-continue, maintain, persist, proceed, prolong.

suspense, *n.* SYN.-apprehension, doubt, hesitation, indecision, irresolution, uncertainty, vacillation, wavering.

suspicion, *n.* SYN.-distrust, doubt, hesitation, incredulity, misgiving, mistrust, skepticism, unbelief, uncertainty. ANT.-belief, certainty, conviction, determination. faith.

suspicious, *a.* SYN.-distrustful, doubtful, dubious, peculiar, questionable, shady, skeptical, strange, suspect, untrustworthy, unusual, wary.

sustain, *v.* SYN.-advocate, back, encourage, foster, further, help, keep, maintain, preserve, prop, support, uphold, ANT.-abandon, betray, destroy, discourage, oppose.

sustenance, *n.* SYN.-diet, edibles, fare, feed, food, meal, nutriment, provisions, rations, repast, subsistence, viands, victuals. ANT.-drink, hunger, starvation, want.

swap, *v.* SYN.-barter, exchange, interchange, switch, trade.

swarm, *n.* SYN.-bevy, crowd, flock, horde, host, mass, multitude, pack, throng.

sway, *n.* SYN.-authority, control, dominion, influence, mastery, power.

sway, *v.* SYN.-actuate, affect, bias, control, direct, dominate, govern, impel, incite, influence, prevail, rule; fluctuate, oscillate, swing, wave.

swear, *v.* SYN.-affirm, assert, aver, declare, maintain, promise, protest, state, testify. ANT.-contradict, demur, deny, dispute, oppose.

sweeping, *a.* SYN.-broad, exaggerated, extravagant, expanded, extensive, large, vast, wide; liberal, tolerant. ANT.-confined, narrow, restricted.

sweet, *a.* SYN.-agreeable, delightful, engaging, gentle, honeyed, luscious, mellifluous, melodious, pleasing, saccharine, sugary, winning, ANT.-acrid, bitter, offensive, repulsive, sour.

swell, *v.* SYN.-balloon, bloat, bulge, dilate, enlarge, expand, grow, increase, inflate.

swift, *a.* SYN.-abrupt, expeditious, fast, fleet, quick, rapid, speedy, sudden, unexpected. ANT.-slow, sluggish.

swindle, *n.* SYN.-cheat, chicanery, deceit, deception, duplicity, fraud, guile, imposition, imposture, trick. ANT.-fairness, honesty, integrity, sincerity.

swindle, *v.* SYN.-bilk, cheat, circumvent, deceive, defraud, dupe, fool, gull, hoax, hoodwink, outwit, trick, victimize.

switch, *v.* SYN.-alter, exchange, rearrange, replace, shift, substitute.

syllabus, *n.* SYN.-abridgement, brief, condensation, digest, outline, summary, synopsis.

symbol, *n.* SYN.-character, emblem, mark, representation, sign, token.

symbolic, *a.* SYN.-characteristic, illustrative, indicative, representative, typical.

sympathetic, *a.* SYN.-affable, benevolent, benign, compassionate, forbearing, gentle, good, humane, indulgent, kind, kindly, merciful, tender, thoughtful. ANT.-cruel, inhuman, merciless, severe, unkind.

sympathize, *v.* SYN.-cheer, comfort, commiserate, console, empathize, encourage, gladden, solace, soothe. ANT.-antagonize, aggravate, depress, dishearten.

sympathy, *n.* SYN.-affinity, agreement, commiseration, compassion, concord, condolence, congeniality, empathy, harmony, pity, tenderness, warmth. ANT.-antipathy, harshness, indifference, malevolence, unconcern.

synonymous, *a.* SYN.-corresponding, equivalent, identical, like, same.

synopsis, *n.* SYN.-See **syllabus.**

synthetic, *a.* SYN.-artificial, bogus, counterfeit, ersatz, fake, feigned, fictitious, phony, sham, spurious, unreal. ANT.-genuine, natural, real, true.

system, *n.* SYN.-arrangement, method, mode, order, organization, plan, process, regularity, rule, scheme. ANT.-chance, chaos, confusion, disarrangement, disorder, irregularity.

T

tact, *n.* SYN.-acumen, address, adroitness, dexterity, diplomacy, discrimination, finesse, knack, perception, poise, prudence, refinement, savoir faire, skill. ANT.-awkwardness, blunder, incompetence, rudeness, vulgarity.

tactful, *a.* SYN.-adroit, attentive, careful, concerned, delicate, diplomatic, discreet, discriminating, gentle, judicious, politic. ANT.-boorish, churlish, coarse, gruff, rude.

tactless, *a.* SYN.-clumsy, crude, discourteous, gruff, hasty, impolite, imprudent, rough, stupid.

tainted, *a.* SYN.-contaminated, corrupt, corrupted, debased, depraved, impure, poisoned, profligate, putrid, spoiled, unsound, venal, vitiated.

take, *v.* SYN.-accept, adopt, appropriate, assume, capture, catch, choose, claim, clasp, clutch, confiscate, demand, ensnare, espouse, gain, get, grasp, grip, obtain, purloin, receive, remove, require, seize, select steal; bear, endure, stand, tolerate; bring, carry, convey, escort; attract, captivate, charm, delight, interest.

tale, *n.* SYN.-account, anecdote, chronicle, exaggeration, fable, fabrication, fiction, narration, narrative, novel, story, yarn.

talent, *n.* SYN.-ability, aptitude, capability, cleverness, endowment, faculty, genius, gift, knack, skill. ANT.-incompetence, ineptitude, stupidity.

talented, *a.* SYN.-able, adroit, apt, bright, clever, dexterous, ingenious, quick, quick-witted, sharp, skillful, smart, witty. ANT.-awkward, bungling, clumsy, dull, foolish, slow, stupid, unskilled.

talk, *n.* SYN.-chatter, conference, conversation, dialogue, discourse, discussion, gossip, lecture, report, rumor, speech. ANT.-correspondence, meditation, silence, writing.

talk, *v.* SYN.-argue, blab, chat, comment, confer, consult, converse, declaim, deliberate, discourse, discuss, gossip, harangue, jabber, lecture, mutter, plead, prattle, preach, rant, reason. speak, spout, tattle.

talkative, *a.* SYN.-chattering, chatty, communicative, garrulous, glib, loquacious, verbose, voluble. ANT.-laconic, reticent, silent, taciturn, uncommunicative.

tall, *a.* SYN.-elevated, high, lofty, towering; exaggerated, outlandish, unbelievable. ANT.-small, stunted, tiny; actual, honest, true.

tame, *a.* SYN.-docile, domestic, domesticated, gentle, meek, subdued, submissive; dull, flat, insipid, tedious. ANT.-fierce, savage, spirited, wild; animated, exciting, lively, spirited.

tangible, *a.* SYN.-corporeal, manifest, material, palpable, perceptible, physical, real, sensible, substantial. ANT.-mental, metaphysical, spiritual.

tarnish, *v.* SYN.-blemish, blight, defile, discolor, disgrace, soil, spot, sully, stain. ANT.-cleanse, honor, purify.

tart, *a.* SYN.-acrid, acrimonious, biting, bitter, caustic, distasteful, galling, grievous, harsh, painful, poignant, pungent, sardonic, severe, sour. ANT.-delicious, mellow, pleasant, sweet.

taste, *n.* SYN.-flavor, relish, savor, tang; discernment, disposition, inclination, judgment, liking, predilection, sensibility, zest. ANT.-antipathy, disinclination, indelicacy, insipidity.

taught, *a.* SYN.-directed, educated, instructed, trained.

taunt, *v.* SYN.-badger, deride, flout, gibe, harass, harry, jeer, mock, sneer, torment, worry. ANT.-compliment, flatter, laud, praise.

taunting, *a.* SYN.-biting, caustic, contemptuous, cutting, derisive, insulting, rude, sarcastic, scornful, sneering. ANT.-affable, agreeable, amiable, pleasant.

taut, *a.* SYN.-contracted, firm, stretched, tense, tight. ANT.-lax, loose, open, relaxed, slack.

tax, *n.* SYN.-assessment, custom, duty, exaction, excise, impost, levy, rate, toll, tribute; burden, encumber, strain. ANT.-gift, remuneration, reward, wages.

tax, *v.* SYN.-appraise, assess, calculate, compute, evaluate, levy, reckon; burden, demand, encumber.

teach, *v.* SYN.-educate, inculcate, inform, instill, instruct, school, train, tutor. ANT.-misguide, misinform.

tear, *v.* SYN.-cleave, disunite, lacerate, rend, rip, rive, sever, shred, slit, split, sunder, wound. ANT.-join, mend, repair, sew, unite.

tease, *v.* SYN.-aggravate, annoy, badger, bother, disturb, harass, harry, irritate, molest, nag, pester, plague, provoke, tantalize, taunt, torment, vex, worry. ANT.-comfort, delight, gratify, please, soothe.

tedious, *a.* SYN.-boring, burdensome, dilatory, dreary, dull, humdrum, irksome, monotonous, slow, sluggish, tardy, tiresome, uninteresting, wearisome. ANT.-amusing, entertaining, exciting, interesting, quick.

tedium, *n.* SYN.-boredom, doldrums, dullness, ennui, monotony, weariness. ANT.-activity, excitement, motive, stimulus.

telepathy, *n.* SYN.- insight, premonition, prescience.

tell, *v.* SYN.-acquaint, announce, apprise, betray, communicate, confess, describe, direct, disclose, divulge, express, inform, instruct, mention, narrate, notify, order, publish, recount, rehearse, relate, report, request, reveal, speak, state, utter; discern, discover, distinguish, recognize.

temerity, *n.* SYN.-audacity, boldness, foolhardiness, precipitance, rashness, recklessness. ANT.-caution, hesitation, prudence, timidity, wariness.

temper, *n.* SYN.-anger, choler, fury, ire, irritation, passion, petulance, rage, resentment, wrath. ANT.-conciliation, forbearance, patience, peace, self-control.

temperament, *n.* SYN.-character, constitution, disposition, humor, mood, nature, temper.

temperance, *n.* SYN.-abstention, abstinence, continence, fasting, forbearance, moderation, self-denial, sobriety. ANT.-excess, gluttony, greed, intoxication, self-indulgence.

tempest, *n.* SYN.-blast, gale, gust, hurricane, squall, storm, wind.

temporal, *a.* SYN.-earthly, laic, lay, mundane, profane, secular, worldly. ANT.-ecclesiastical, religious, spiritual, unworldly.

temporary, *a.* SYN.-brief, ephemeral, evanescent, fleeting, momentary, short-lived, transient. ANT.-abiding, immortal, lasting, permanent, timeless.

temptation, *n.* SYN.-appeal, enticement, fascination, inducement, lure, stimulus.

tenacity, *n.* SYN.-cohesion, obstinance, perseverance, persistence, persistency, pertinacity, steadfastness. ANT.-cessation, idleness, laziness, rest, sloth.

tend, *v.* SYN.-accompany, attend, escort, follow, guard, protect, serve, watch.

tendency, *n.* SYN.-aim, bent, bias, drift, inclination, leaning, predisposition, proclivity, proneness, propensity, trend. ANT.-aversion, deviation, disinclination.

tender, *a.* SYN.-affectionate, compassionate, considerate, delicate, gentle, kind, mild, moderate, soft, soothing, sympathetic, sweet. ANT.-bitter, fierce, harsh, rough, severe.

tenderness, *n.* SYN.-commiseration. compassion, condolence, empathy, endearment, fondness, kindness, love, pity, sweetness, sympathy, warmth. ANT.-hatred, indifference, repugnance.

tenet, *n.* SYN.-belief, concept, creed, doctrine, dogma, opinion, precept, principle, teaching. ANT.-conduct, deed, performance, practice.

tense, *a.* SYN.-agitated, excited, nervous, strained. ANT.- calm, composed, relaxed.

term, *n.* SYN.-boundary, duration, interval, limit, period, time; condition, expression, name, phrase, word.

terminal, *a.* SYN.-concluding, conclusive, decisive, ending, eventual, extremity, final, last, latest, limit, terminus, ultimate. ANT.-first, inaugural, incipient, original, rudimentary.

terminate, *v.* SYN.-abolish, cease, close, complete, conclude, end, expire, finish, stop. ANT.-begin, commence, establish, initiate, start.

terms, *n.* SYN.-agreement, conditions, details, particulars, settlement, understanding.

terrible, *a.* SYN.-appalling, awful, dire, dreadful, fearful, frightful, gruesome, hideous, horrible, horrid, severe, shocking. ANT.-happy, joyous, pleasing, safe, secure.

terrify, *v.* SYN.-affright, alarm, daunt, frighten, horrify, intimidate, scare, startle, terrorize. ANT.-allay, compose, embolden, reassure, soothe.

territory, *n.* SYN.-country, district, division, domain, dominion, land, place, province, quarter, region, section.

terror, *n.* SYN.-alarm, consternation, dismay, dread, fear, fright, horror, panic. ANT.-assurance, calm, peace, security.

terse, *a.* SYN.-brief, compact, concise, condensed, incisive, neat, pithy, succinct, summary. ANT.-lengthy, prolix, verbose, wordy.

test, *v.* SYN.-analyze, assay, examine, experiment, inspect, prove, try, verify.

testimony, *n.* SYN.-attestation, confirmation, declaration, evidence, proof, witness. ANT.-argument, contradiction, disproof, refutation.

testy, *a.* SYN.-choleric, churlish, fractious, ill-natured, ill-tempered, irritable, peevish, petulant, snappish, touchy, waspish. ANT.-affable, genial, good-natured, good-tempered, pleasant.

theatrical, *a.* SYN.-affected, artificial, ceremonious, dramatic, histrionic, melodramatic, showy, stagy. ANT.-modest, subdued, unaffected, unemotional.

theft, *n.* SYN.-burglary, depredation, larceny, pillage, plunder, robbery.

theme, *n.* SYN.-composition, essay, motive, subject, text, thesis, topic.

theory, *n.* SYN.-conjecture, doctrine, hypothesis, opinion, postulate, presupposition, speculation. ANT.-fact, practice, proof, verity.

therefore, *adv.* SYN.-accordingly, consequently, hence, so, then, thence.

thick, *a.* SYN.-abundant, close, compact, compressed, concentrated, crowded, heavy; dull, dense, obtuse, slow, stupid; guttural, husky, indistinct, muffled. ANT.-dispersed, dissipated, sparse, thin; clever, quick; clear, distinct.

thin, *a.* SYN.-attenuated, diaphanous, diluted, emaciated, fine, flimsy, gaunt, gauzy, gossamer, lank, lean, meager, narrow, rare, scanty, scrawny, skinny, slender, slight, slim, spare, tenuous. ANT.-broad, bulky, fat, thick, wide.

think, *v.* SYN.-apprehend, believe, cogitate, conceive, consider, contemplate, deem, deliberate, esteem, imagine, judge, meditate, muse, opine, picture, ponder, reason, recall, reckon, recollect, reflect, regard, remember, speculate, suppose; devise, intend, mean, plan, purpose. ANT.-conjecture, forget, guess.

thorough, *a.* SYN.-accurate, attentive, complete, careful, detailed, painstaking, perfect, persevering, thoroughgoing, total, unbroken, uncompromising, undivided. ANT.-imperfect, lacking, superficial, unfinished.

thought, *n.* SYN.-cogitation, conception, consideration, contemplation, deliberation, fancy, idea, imagination, impression, judgment, meditation, memory, notion, opinion, recollection, reflection, regard, retrospection, sentiment, view.

thoughtful *a.* SYN.-attentive, careful, cautious, concerned, considerate, heedful, provident, prudent: contemplative, dreamy, introspective, meditative, pensive, reflective. ANT.-heedless, inconsiderate, precipitous, rash, thoughtless.

thoughtless, *a.* SYN.-careless, desultory, heedless, imprudent, inaccurate, inattentive, inconsiderate, indiscreet, lax, neglectful, negligent, reckless, remiss, unconcerned. ANT.-accurate, careful, meticulous, nice.

threatening, *a.* SYN.-approaching, dangerous, grave, imminent, impending, menacing, nigh, ominous, serious, troublesome. ANT.-afar, distant, improbable, remote, retreating.

thrifty, *a.* SYN.-economical, frugal, parsimonious, provident, saving, sparing, stingy, temperate. ANT.-extravagant, intemperate, self-indulgent, wasteful.

throb, *v.* SYN.-beat, palpitate, pound, pulsate, pulse, thump, vibrate. ANT.-defend, shield, stroke, fail, surrender.

throng, *n.* SYN.-bevy, crowd, crush, horde, host, masses, mob, multitude, populace, press, rabble, swarm.

throw, *v.* SYN.-cast, fling, hurl, pitch, propel, thrust, toss. ANT.-draw, haul, hold, pull, retain.

thrust, *v.* SYN.-drive, force, impel, propel. ANT.-drag, falter, halt, pull, retreat.

thwart, *v.* SYN.-baffle, block, check, circumvent, defeat, disappoint, foil, frustrate, hinder, impede, obstruct, outwit, prevent, restrain, stop. ANT.-accomplish, fulfill, further, promote.

tidings, *n.* SYN.-greetings, information, intelligence, message, news, report.

tidy, *a.* SYN.-neat, orderly, precise, spruce, trim. ANT.-dirty, disheveled, sloppy, slovenly, unkempt.

tie, *n.* SYN.-accord, agreement, alliance, association, bond, conjunction, connection, connective, juncture, link, pact, relationship, union. ANT.-disunion, isolation, separation.

tie, *v.* SYN.-attach, bind, connect, engage, fasten, fetter, join, link, oblige, restrain, restrict. ANT.-free, loose, unfasten, untie.

tight, *a.* SYN.-close, compact, constricted, contracted, firm, narrow, snug, stretched, taut, tense; close-fisted, niggardly, parsimonious, penny-pinching, stingy. ANT.-lax, loose, open, relaxed, slack.

time, *n.* SYN.-age, date, duration, epoch, era, interim, period, season, span, spell, tempo, term.

timid, *a.* SYN.-afraid, apprehensive, bashful, coy, diffident, faint-hearted, fearful, frightened, humble, recoiling, scared, sheepish, shy, timorous. ANT.-adventurous, assured, bold, composed, courageous, daring, fearless, gregarious, outgoing, sanguine.

tiny, *a.* SYN.-diminutive, insignificant, little, miniature, minute, petty, puny, slight, small, trivial, wee. ANT.-big, enormous, huge, immense, large.

tire, *v.* SYN.-bore, exhaust, fatigue, jade, tucker, wear out, weary. ANT.-amuse, invigorate, refresh, restore, revive.

tired, *a.* SYN.-exhausted, fatigued, spent, wearied, weary, worn. ANT.-fresh, hearty, invigorated, rested.

title, *n.* SYN.-appellation, denomination, designation, epithet, name; claim, due, privilege, right.

toil, *n.* SYN.-drudgery, effort, labor, slave, travail, work. ANT.-ease, leisure, play, recreation, vacation.

tolerant, *a.* SYN.-broad, compassionate, forbearing, forgiving, humane, kind, lenient, liberal, long-suffering, merciful, patient, understanding. ANT.-confined, narrow, restricted.

tolerate, *v.* SYN.-abide, allow, bear, brook, endure, permit, stand. ANT.-forbid, prohibit; protest.

toll, *n.* SYN.-assessment, exaction, excise, impost, levy, tax, tribute; burden, damage, destruction, losses, sacrifice, strain. ANT.-gift, remuneration, reward, wages.

too, *adv.* SYN.-also, besides, furthermore, in addition, likewise, moreover, similarly.

tool, *n.* SYN.-agent, apparatus, device, instrument, means, medium, utensil. ANT.-hindrance, impediment, obstruction, preventive.

top, *n.* SYN.-apex, chief, crest, crown, head, pinnacle, summit, zenith. ANT.-base, bottom, foot, foundation.

topic, *n.* SYN.-discourse, issue, matter, point, subject, theme, thesis.

torment, *n.* SYN.-ache, agony, anguish, distress, misery, pain, suffering, throe, torture, woe. ANT.-comfort, ease, mitigation, relief.

torment, *v.* SYN.-aggravate, annoy, badger, bother, disturb, harass, harry, haze, irritate, molest, nag, pain, persecute, pester, plague, provoke, tantalize, taunt, tease, trouble, vex, worry. ANT.-comfort, delight, gratify, please, soothe.

torpor, *n.* SYN.-apathy, daze, insensibility, languor, lethargy, numbness, stupefaction, stupor. ANT.-activity, alertness, liveliness, readiness, wakefulness.

torrid, *a.* SYN.-burning, hot, scalding, scorching, steaming, sweltering, tropical,; ardent, fervent, fiery, hot-blooded, impetuous, intense, passionate. ANT.-cold, cool, freezing, frigid; apathetic, impassive, indifferent, passionless, phlegmatic.

torture, *n.* SYN.-ache, anguish, agony, distress, misery, pain, suffering, throe, torment, woe. ANT.-comfort, ease, mitigation, relief.

torture, *v.* SYN.-badger, harass, harry, hound, oppress, persecute, plague, torment. ANT.-aid, assist, comfort, encourage, support.

toss, *v.* SYN.-cast, fling, hurl, pitch, propel, throw, thrust. ANT.-draw, haul, hold, pull, retain.

total, *a.* SYN.-all, complete, concluded, consummated, detailed, ended, entire, finished, full, perfect, thorough, unbroken, undivided, whole. ANT.-imperfect, lacking, unfinished.

total, *n.* SYN.-aggregate, amount, collection, conglomeration, entirety, sum, whole. ANT.-element, ingredient, part, particular, unit.

total, *v.* SYN.-add, calculate, count,

figure, sum.

touching, *a.* SYN.-affecting, heart-rending, impressive, moving, pitiable, poignant, sad, tender; adjacent, adjunct, bordering, tangent. ANT.-animated, enlivening, exhilarating, removed.

touchy, *a.* SYN.-choleric, excitable, fiery, hasty, hot, irascible, irritable, peevish, petulant, snappish, testy. ANT.-agreeable, calm, composed, tranquil.

tough, *a.* SYN.-cohesive, firm, hardy, stout, strong, sturdy, tenacious; difficult, formidable, hard, laborious, troublesome, trying; callous, incorrigible, obdurate, stubborn, vicious. ANT.-brittle, fragile, frail; easy, facile; compliant, forbearing, submissive.

toughness, n, SYN.-durability, fortitude, might, potency, power, stamina, stoutness, strength, sturdiness. ANT.-feebleness, frailty, infirmity, weakness.

tour, *v.* SYN.-go, journey, ramble, roam, rove, travel, trek, visit. ANT.-stay, stop.

tow, *v.* SYN.-drag, draw, haul, pull, tow, tug.

train, *v.* SYN.-direct, educate, inform, instill, instruct, school, teach, tutor; aim, level, point. ANT.-misdirect, misguide.

training, *n.* SYN.-cultivation, development, drill, education, exercise, instruction, knowledge, learning, lesson, operation, schooling, study, tutoring.

trait, *n.* SYN.-attribute, characteristic, feature, mark, peculiarity, property, quality.

traitorous, *a.* SYN.-apostate, disloyal, faithless, false, perfidious, recreant, treacherous, treasonable. ANT.-constant, devoted, loyal, true.

tramp, *n.* SYN.-beggar, bum, hobo, rover, vagabond, vagrant, wanderer. ANT.-gentleman, laborer, worker.

tranquil, *a.* SYN.-appease, calm, collected, composed, dispassionate, imperturbable, pacific, peaceful, placid, quiet, sedate, serene, still, undisturbed, unmoved, unruffled. ANT.-excited, frantic, stormy, turbulent, wild.

tranquility, *n.* SYN.-calm, calmness, hush, peace, quiescence, quiet, quietude, repose, rest, serenity, silence, stillness. ANT.-agitation, disturbance, excitement, noise, tumult.

transact, *v.* SYN.-carry on, conduct, execute, manage, negotiate, perform, treat.

transaction, *n.* SYN.-affair, business, deal, deed, negotiation, occurrence, proceeding.

transfer, *v.* SYN.-assign, consign, convey, dispatch, relegate, remove, send, transmit, transplant, transport.

transform, *v.* SYN.-alter, change, convert, modify, remodel, shift, transfigure, vary, veer. ANT.-retain; continue, establish, preserve, settle, stabilize.

transient, *a.* SYN.-brief, ephemeral, evanescent, fleeting, momentary, short-lived, temporary. ANT.-abiding, immortal, lasting, permanent, timeless.

translate, *v.* SYN.-decipher, decode, elucidate, explain, explicate, interpret, render. ANT.-confuse, distort, falsify, misconstrue, misinterpret.

transmit, *v.* SYN.-convey, disclose, divulge, impart, inform, notify, relate, reveal, send, tell. ANT.-conceal, hide, withhold.

transparent, *a.* SYN.-clear, crystalline, limpid, lucid, thin, translucent; evident, explicit, manifest, obvious, open. ANT.-muddy, opaque, thick, turbid; ambiguous, questionable.

transpire, *v.* SYN.-bechance, befall, betide, chance, happen, occur, take place.

transport, *v.* SYN.-bear, carry, convey, move, remove, shift, transfer; enrapture, entrance, lift, ravish, stimulate.

trap, *n.* SYN.-ambush, artifice, bait, intrigue, lure, net, pitfall, ruse, snare, stratagem, trick, wile.

travel, *v.* SYN.-go, journey, ramble, roam, rove, tour. ANT.-stay, stop.

treachery, *n.* SYN.-collusion, conspiracy, deception, dishonesty, disloyalty, intrigue, machination, perfidy, plot, subversion, treason, violation.

treason, *n.* SYN.-betrayal, cabal, collusion, combination, conspiracy, intrigue, machination, plot, subversion, treachery.

treasure, *v.* SYN.-adore, appreciate, cherish, hold dear, prize, protect, value. ANT.-dislike, disregard, neglect.

treat, *v.* SYN.-apply, conduct, employ, handle, manage, manipulate, use. ANT.-ignore, neglect.

treaty, *n.* SYN.-alliance, association, coalition, compact, confederacy, covenant, entente, federation, league, marriage, partnership, union. ANT.-divorce, schism, separation.

tremble, *v.* SYN.-agitate, flutter, quake, quaver, quiver, shake, shiver, shudder, vibrate, waver.

trespass, *v.* SYN.-encroach, infringe, intrude, invade, penetrate, violate. ANT.-abandon, evacuate, relinquish, vacate.

trial, *n.* SYN.-examination, experiment, proof, test; attempt, effort, endeavor, essay; affliction, hardship, misery, misfortune, ordeal, suffering, tribulation, trouble. ANT.-alleviation, consolation.

trick, *n.* SYN.-antic, artifice, cheat, deception, device, fraud, guile, hoax, imposture, ploy, ruse, stratagem, stunt, subterfuge, wile. ANT.-candor, exposure, honesty, openness, sincerity.

tricky, *a.* SYN.-artful, covert, crafty, cunning, foxy, furtive, guileful, shrewd, sly, stealthy, subtle, surreptitious, underhanded, wily. ANT.-candid, frank, ingenuous, open, sincere.

trifling, *a.* SYN.-frivolous, immaterial, insignificant, paltry, petty, slight, small, trivial, unimportant, worthless. ANT.-important, momentous, serious, weighty.

trim, *v.* SYN.-adorn, beautify, bedeck, decorate, embellish, garnish, gild, ornament. ANT.-deface, deform, disfigure, mar, spoil.

trip, *n.* SYN.-cruise, expedition, jaunt, journey, passage, pilgrimage, safari, tour, travel, vacation, voyage.

trite, *a.* SYN.-banal, common, hackneyed, ordinary, stale, stereotyped. ANT.-fresh, modern, momentous, novel, stimulating.

triumph, *n.* SYN.-achievement, conquest, jubilation, ovation, victory. ANT.-defeat, failure.

trivial, *a.* SYN.-frivolous, insignificant, paltry, petty, small, trifling, unimportant. ANT.-important, momentous, serious, weighty.

trouble, *n.* SYN.-affliction, annoyance, anxiety, bother, calamity, care, disorder, distress, disturbance, embarrassment, grief, hardship, irritation, misery, pain, problem, sorrow, torment, woe, worry; effort, exertion, labor, toil.

trouble, *v.* SYN.-agitate, annoy, bother, chafe, disturb, inconvenience, interrupt, irk, irritate, molest, pester, tease, vex, worry. ANT.-accommodate, console, gratify, pacify, settle, soothe.

troublesome, *a.* SYN.-annoying, arduous, bothersome, burdensome, difficult, distressing, disturbing, irksome, laborious, tedious, trying, vexatious. ANT.-accommodating, amusing, easy, gratifying, pleasant.

true, *a.* SYN.-accurate, actual, authentic, correct, exact, genuine, real, veracious, veritable; constant, faithful, honest, loyal, reliable, sincere, steadfast, trustworthy. ANT.-counterfeit, erroneous, false, fictitious, spurious; faithless, false, fickle, inconstant.

trust, *n.* SYN.-confidence, constancy, credence, dependence, faith, fidelity, loyalty, reliance. ANT.-doubt, incredulity, infidelity, mistrust, skepticism.

trust, *v.* SYN.-believe, commit, confide, credit, depend on, entrust, esteem, hope, reckon on, rely on. ANT.-doubt, impugn, question, suspect.

trustworthy, *a.* SYN.-dependable, honest, honorable, reliable, safe, secure, sure, tried, trusty. ANT.-dubious, fallible, questionable, uncertain, unreliable.

truth, *n.* SYN.-accuracy, actuality, authenticity, correctness, exactness, fact, honesty, rightness, truthfulness, veracity, verisimilitude, verity. ANT.-falsehood, falsity, fiction, lie, untruth.

truthful, *a.* SYN.-accurate, candid, correct, exact, frank, honest, open, reliable, sincere, true, veracious. ANT.-deceitful, misleading, sly.

try, *v.* SYN.-aim, aspire, attempt, design, endeavor, intend, mean, strive, struggle, undertake; afflict, prove, test, torment, trouble. ANT.-abandon, decline, ignore, neglect, omit; comfort, console.

trying, *a.* SYN.-annoying, bothersome, distressing, disturbing, irksome, troublesome, vexatious. ANT.-accommodating, amusing, easy, gratifying, pleasant.

tumult, *n.* SYN.-chaos, clamor, commotion, confusion, din, disarray, disorder, jumble, noise, racket, row, stir, turmoil, uproar. ANT.-certainty, order, peace, tranquility.

tune, *n.* SYN.-air, harmony, melody, strain.

turbulent, *a.* SYN.-blustery, gusty, roaring, rough, stormy. tempestuous, windy. ANT.-calm, clear, peaceful, quiet, tranquil.

turmoil, *n.* SYN.-agitation, chaos, commotion, confusion, disarrangement, disarray, disorder, ferment, jumble, stir, tumult. ANT.-certainty, order, peace, tranquility.

turn, *v.* SYN.-circle, circulate. invert, revolve, rotate, spin, twirl, twist, wheel, whirl; avert, deflect, deviate, divert, swerve; alter, change, transmute. ANT.-arrest, fix, stand, stop; continue, proceed; endure, perpetuate.

twist, *v.* SYN.-bend, bow, crook, curve, deflect, lean, revolve, rotate, spin, turn, twirl, whirl; influence, mold. ANT.-break, resist, stiffen, straighten.

type, *n.* SYN.-emblem, mark, sign, symbol; category, character, class, description, exemplar, kind, model, nature, pattern, sort, stamp. ANT.-deviation, eccentricity, monstrosity, peculiarity.

typical, *a.* SYN.-common, customary, familiar, habitual, normal, ordinary, plain, regular, usual. ANT.-extraordinary, marvelous, remarkable, strange, uncommon.

tyrant, *n.* SYN.-autocrat, despot, dictator, oppressor, persecutor.

U

ugly, *a.* SYN.-deformed, hideous, homely, plain, repellent, repulsive, uncomely; disagreeable, ill-natured, spiteful, surly, vicious. ANT.-attractive, beautiful, fair, handsome, pretty.

ultimate, *a.* SYN.-extreme, final, last, latest, terminal, utmost. ANT.-beginning, first, foremost, initial, opening.

unadulterated, *a.* SYN.-clean, clear, genuine, immaculate, pure, spotless, undefiled, untainted. ANT.-foul, polluted, sullied, tainted, tarnished.

unassuming, *a.* SYN.-compliant, humble, lowly, meek, modest, plain, simple, submissive, unostentatious, unpretentious. ANT.-arrogant, boastful, haughty, proud, vain.

uncertain, *a.* SYN.-ambiguous, dim, hazy, indefinite, indistinct, obscure, unclear, undetermined, unsettled, vague. ANT.-clear, explicit, lucid, precise, specific.

uncertainty, *n.* SYN.-ambiguity, distrust, doubt, hesitation, incredulity, scruple, skepticism, suspense, suspicion, unbelief, uncertainty. ANT.-belief, certainty, conviction, determination. faith.

uncompromising, *a.* SYN.-dogged, firm, headstrong, immovable, inflexible, intractable, obdurate, obstinate, pertinacious, stubborn, unyielding. ANT.-amenable, compliant, docile, submissive, yielding.

unconcern, *n.* SYN.-apathy, disinterestedness, impartiality, indifference, insensibility, neutrality. ANT.-affection, ardor, fervor, passion.

unconditional, *a.* SYN.-absolute, actual, complete, entire, perfect, pure, ultimate, unqualified, unrestricted. ANT.-accountable, conditional, contingent, dependent, qualified.

uncouth, *a.* SYN.-awkward, clumsy, coarse, crass, crude, discourteous, harsh, ill-mannered, rough, rude, unfinished, unpolished, unrefined, vulgar. ANT.-cultivated, refined.

uncover, *v.* SYN.-disclose, discover, divulge, expose, impart, reveal, show. ANT.-cloak, conceal, cover, hide, obscure.

under, *prep.* SYN.-below, beneath, under, underneath. ANT.-above, over.

undergo, *v.* SYN.-bear, brave, encounter, endure, experience, stand, suffer, sustain, tolerate. ANT.-banish, discard, exclude, overcome.

understand, *v.* SYN.-appreciate, apprehend, comprehend, conceive, discern, grasp, know, learn, perceive, realize, see. ANT.-ignore, misapprehend, mistake, misunderstand.

understanding, *n.* SYN.-accordance, agreement, bargain, coincidence, compact, concord, concurrence, contract, covenant, harmony, pact, stipulation, unison. ANT.-difference, disagreement, discord, dissension, variance.

understudy, *n.* SYN.-alternate, proxy, representative, substitute. ANT.-principal.

undertaking, *n.* SYN.-attempt, effort, endeavor, essay, experiment, trial. ANT.-inaction, laziness, neglect.

undivided, *a.* SYN.-all, complete, entire, intact, integral, perfect, total, whole. ANT.-deficient, incomplete, partial.

undying, *a.* SYN.-ceaseless, deathless, endless, eternal, everlasting, immortal, infinite, perpetual, timeless. ANT. ephemeral, finite, mortal, temporal, transient.

unearthly, *a.* SYN.-metaphysical, other-worldly, preternatural, spiritual, supernatural. ANT.-common, human, natural, physical, plain.

uneducated, *a.* SYN.-ignorant, illiterate, uncultured, uninformed, unlearned, unlettered, untaught. ANT.-cultured, educated, erudite, informed, literate.

unemployed, *a.* SYN.-dormant, idle, inactive, indolent, inert, lazy, slothful, unoccupied. ANT.-active, employed, industrious, occupied, working.

unexpected, *a.* SYN.-abrupt, sudden, unforeseen. ANT.-anticipated, gradual, slowly.

unfasten, *v.* SYN.-free, loosen, open, unbar, unlock, untie. ANT.-bar, close, fasten, lock, shut.

unfavorable, *a.* SYN.-adverse, antagonistic, contrary, counteractive, disastrous, hostile, opposed, opposite, unlucky. ANT.-benign, favorable, fortunate, lucky, propitious.

unfold, *v.* SYN.-amplify, develop, elaborate, enlarge, evolve, expand, open. ANT.-compress, contract, restrict.

uniform, *a.* SYN.-methodical, orderly, periodical, regular, steady, systematic, unvaried. ANT.-abnormal, erratic.

uninteresting, *a.* SYN.-boring, burdensome, dreary, dull, humdrum, monotonous, tedious, tiresome. ANT.-amusing, entertaining, exciting, interesting, quick.

union, *n.* SYN.-agreement, alliance, amalgamation, coalition, combination, concert, concord, concurrence, confederacy, fusion, harmony, incorporation, joining, league, marriage, solidarity, unanimity, unification. ANT.-disagreement, discord, division, schism, separation.

unique, *a.* SYN.-choice, distinctive, exceptional, matchless, peculiar, rare, singular, sole, solitary, uncommon, unequaled. ANT.-common, commonplace, frequent, ordinary, typical.

unison, *n.* SYN.-accordance, agreement, coincidence, concord, concurrence, harmony, understanding. ANT.-difference, disagreement, discord, dissension, variance.

unite, *v.* SYN.-amalgamate, associate, attach, blend, combine, conjoin, connect, consolidate, embody, fuse, join, link, merge, unify. ANT.-disconnect, disrupt, divide, separate, sever.

universal, *a.* SYN.-broad, common, familiar, frequent, general, omnipotent, omnipresent, ordinary, popular, prevalent, ubiquitous, usual, vast. ANT.-exceptional, extraordinary, odd, scarce.

unlawful, *a.* SYN.-criminal, illegal, illegitimate, illicit, outlawed, prohibited. ANT.-honest, lawful, legal, permitted.

unlike, *a.* SYN.-different, dissimilar, distinct, divergent, diverse, incongruous, opposite, variant; divers, miscellaneous, sundry, various. ANT.-alike, congruous, identical, same, similar.

unlimited, *a.* SYN.-boundless, endless, eternal, illimitable, immeasurable, immense, infinite, interminable, unbounded, vast. ANT.-bounded, circumscribed, confined, finite, limited.

unobstructed, *a.* SYN.-clear, free, immune loose, open, unconfined, unfastened, unrestricted. ANT.-blocked, clogged, confined, impeded, restrained, restricted.

unsafe, *a.* SYN.-chancy, critical, dangerous, hazardous, insecure, menacing, perilous, precarious, risky, threatening. ANT.-firm, protected, safe, secure.

unselfish, *a.* SYN.-beneficent, bountiful, generous, giving, liberal, magnanimous, munificent, openhanded. ANT.-covetous, greedy, miserly, selfish, stingy.

unsophisticated, *a.* SYN.-artless, candid, frank, ingenuous, innocent, naive, natural, open, simple. unlearned, untutored. ANT.-crafty, cunning, sophisticated, worldly.

unstable, *a.* SYN.-capricious, changeable, fickle, fitful, inconstant, restless, unreliable, variable. ANT.-constant, reliable, stable, steady, trustworthy.

untainted, *a.* SYN.-clean, clear, genuine, immaculate, spotless, pure, unadulterated. ANT.-foul, polluted, sullied, tainted, tarnished.

untamed, *a.* SYN.-barbarous, boisterous, extravagant, fierce, foolish, frenzied, giddy, impetuous, irregular, mad, outlandish, rash, reckless, rough, rude, savage, stormy, tempestuous, turbulent, uncivilized, uncultivated, undomesticated, wanton, wayward, wild. ANT.-calm, civilized, gentle, placid, quiet.

unusual, *a.* SYN.-aberrant, abnormal, capricious, devious, eccentric, irregular, unnatural, variable. ANT.-fixed, methodical, ordinary, regular, usual.

unyielding, *a.* SYN.-constant, fast, firm, inflexible, secure, solid, stable, steadfast, steady, unswerving. ANT.-slow, sluggish; insecure, loose, unstable, unsteady.

upbraid, *v.* SYN.-admonish, berate, blame, censure, lecture, rebuke, reprehend, reprimand, scold, vituperate. ANT.-approve, commend, praise.

uphold, *v.* SYN.-advocate, bolster, defend, endorse, help, maintain, protect, safeguard, screen, shield, support, sustain. ANT.-assault, attack, deny, submit.

upright, *a.* SYN.-erect, straight, unbent, vertical; direct, fair, honest, honorable, just, right, square, undeviating, unswerving. ANT.-bent, crooked; circuitous, devious, dishonest, fraudulent, winding.

upset, *v.* SYN.-annoy, bother, disturb, harass, haunt, inconvenience, molest, perplex, pester, plague, tease, trouble, worry. ANT.-gratify, please, relieve, soothe.

urge, *n.* SYN.-appetite, aspiration, craving, desire, hunger, hungering, longing, lust, wish, yearning. ANT.-abomination, aversion, distaste, hate, loathing.

urge, *v.* SYN.-allure, coax, entice, exhort, incite, induce, influence, persuade, prevail upon. ANT.-coerce, compel, deter, dissuade, restrain.

urgency, *n.* SYN.-compulsion, crisis, emergency, exigency, press, pressure, stress.

urgent, *a.* SYN.-cogent, compelling, critical, crucial, exigent, impelling, imperative, important, importunate, insistent, instant, necessary, pressing, serious. ANT.-insignificant, petty, trifling, trivial, unimportant.

use, *n.* SYN.-custom, habit, manner, practice, training, usage, wont. ANT.-disuse, idleness, inexperience, speculation, theory.

use, *v.* SYN.-apply, avail, consume, employ, exercise, exert, exhaust, expend, exploit, handle, manage, manipulate, operate, practice, treat, utilize; accustom, familiarize, inure, train. ANT.-ignore, neglect, overlook, waste.

useful, *a.* SYN.-advantageous, beneficial, funcional, good, handy, helpful, serviceable, utilitarian, workable. ANT.-deleterious, destructive, detrimental, harmful, injurious.

usefulness, *n.* SYN.-advantage, application, edge, gain, merit, utility, value, worthiness. ANT.-cheapness, uselessness, valueless.

useless, *a.* SYN.-abortive, empty, fruitless, futile, idle, ineffectual, obsolete, pointless, unavailing, unusable, valueless, vain, vapid, worthless. ANT.-effective, potent, profitable.

usual, *a.* SYN.-accustomed, common, customary, every-day, familiar, general, habitual, normal, ordinary. ANT.-abnormal, exceptional, extraordinary, irregular, rare.

usurp, *v.* SYN.-adopt, appropriate, assume, confiscate, expropriate, occupy, take. ANT.-reject, repel, surrender.

utensil, *n.* SYN.-apparatus, appliance, device, gadget, instrument, tool.

utilize, *v.* SYN.-apply, avail, employ, occupy, use. ANT.-banish, discard, discharge, reject.

utter, *a.* SYN.-absolute, complete, entire, total, unconditional. ANT.-incomplete, inconsiderable, meager, paltry.

utter, *v.* SYN.-announce, orate, proclaim, say, speak, state, talk, verbalize, vocalize

V

vacant, *a.* SYN.-bare, barren, blank, empty, unoccupied, vacuous, void. ANT.-busy, employed, engaged, full, replete.

vacate, *v.* SYN.-abandon, abdicate, abjure, desert, forsake, leave, quit, relinquish, renounce, resign, surrender, waive. ANT.-defend, maintain, uphold; stay, support.

vacillate, *v.* SYN.-change, fluctuate, hesitate, oscillate, totter, undulate, vary, waver. ANT.-adhere, decide, persist, resolve, stick.

vacillating, *a.* SYN.-fluctuating, inconsistent, irreconcilable, irresolute, unsteady, wavering. ANT.-consistent, sure.

vacuity, *n.* SYN.-blank, emptiness, idleness, insignificance, nothingness, stupidity, unimportance, vacuum, void.

vacuous, *a.* SYN.-barren, blank, empty, vacant.

vagabond, *n.* SYN.-beggar, mendicant, nomad, pauper, ragamuffin, rascal, scrub, starveling, tatterdemalion, tramp, wanderer, wretch.

vagrant, *n.* SYN.-beggar, bum, hobo, rover, tramp, vagabond, wanderer. ANT.-gentleman, laborer, worker.

vague, *a.* SYN.-ambiguous, dim, hazy, indefinite, indistinct, obscure, uncertain, unclear, undetermined, unsettled. ANT.-clear, explicit, lucid, precise, specific.

vain, *a.* SYN.-abortive, bootless, empty, fruitless, futile, idle, ineffectual, pointless, unavailing, useless, valueless, vapid, worthless; conceited, proud, vainglorious. ANT.-effective, potent, profitable; meek, modest.

vainglory, *n.* SYN.-boastfulness, conceit, haughtiness, pomp, pride, self-esteem, self-respect, vainglory, vanity. ANT.-humility, lowliness, meekness, modesty, shame.

valiant, *a.* SYN.-adventurous, audacious, brave, bold, chivalrous, courageous, daring, dauntless, fearless, gallant, heroic, intrepid, valorous. ANT.-cowardly, cringing, fearful, timid, weak.

valid, *a.* SYN.-binding, cogent, conclusive, convincing, effective, efficacious, legal, logical, powerful, sound, strong, telling, weighty. ANT.-counterfeit, null, spurious, void, weak.

validate, *v.* SYN.-authenticate, certify, confirm, document, endorse, notarize, prove, sanction, substantiate, verify

valuable, *a.* SYN.-costly, dear, esteemed, expensive, precious, profitable, use. ANT.-cheap, mean, poor, trashy, worthless.

valuation, *n.* SYN.-appraisal, assessment, consideration, estimate, estimation, guess, judgment, opinion, theory.

value, *n.* SYN.-excellence, merit, price, usefulness, utility, worth, worthiness. ANT.-cheapness, uselessness, valueless.

value, *v.* SYN.-appraise, appreciate, cherish, esteem, hold dear, prize, treasure. ANT.-dislike, disregard, neglect.

vandalism, *n.* SYN.-damage, destruction, ruin, waste, wreckage.

vanish, *v.* SYN.-disappear, disintegrate, disperse, dissipate, dissolve, evaporate, fade, scatter, vaporize.

vanity, *n.* SYN.-conceit, egotism, haughtiness, pride, self-esteem, vainglory, vanity. ANT.-diffidence, humility, meekness, modesty.

vanquish, *v.* SYN.-beat, conquer, crush, defeat, humble, master, overcome, quell, rout, subdue, subjugate, surmount. ANT.-capitulate, cede, lose, retreat, surrender.

variable, *a.* SYN.-changeable, fickle, fitful, inconstant, shifting, unstable, vacillating, wavering. ANT.-constant, stable, steady, unchanging, uniform.

variant, *a.* SYN.-changing, contrary, different, differing, dissimilar, divergent, diverse, fickle, incongruous, inconstant, restless, unlike. ANT.-alike, congruous, identical, same, similar; constant.

variation, *n.* SYN.-alteration, alternation, change, modification, mutation, substitution, variety, vicissitude. ANT.-monotony, stability, uniformity.

variety, *n.* SYN.-assortment, change, difference, dissimilarity, diversity, heterogeneity, medley, miscellany, mixture, multifariousness, variety; breed, kind, sort, stock, strain, subspecies. ANT.-homogeneity, likeness, monotony, sameness, uniformity.

various, *a.* SYN.-divers, miscellaneous, several, sundry. ANT.-same, singular.

vary, *v.* SYN.-alter, change, convert, modify, remodel, shift, transfigure, transform. ANT.-retain; continue, establish, preserve, settle, stabilize.

vassalage, *n.* SYN.-bondage, serfdom, servitude, slavery, thralldom. ANT.-freedom, liberation.

vast, *a.* SYN.-big, capacious, colossal, extensive, great, huge, immense, large, wide. ANT.-little, mean, short, small, tiny.

vehement, *a.* SYN.-ardent, burning, fervent, fervid, fiery, impetuous, passionate. ANT.-apathetic, calm, cool, deliberate, quiet.

veil, *v.* SYN.-cloak, conceal, cover, curtain, disguise, envelop, guard, hide, mask, protect, screen, shield, shroud. ANT.-bare, divulge, expose, reveal, unveil.

venerate, *v.* SYN.-admire, adore, appreciate, approve, esteem, respect, revere, worship. ANT.-abhor, despise, dislike.

vengeance, *n.* SYN.-reprisal, requital, retaliation, retribution, revenge, vindictiveness. ANT.-mercy, pardon, reconciliation, remission, forgiveness.

vent, *v.* SYN.-breathe, discharge, eject, emanate, emit, expel, express, hurl, shed, shoot, spurt, utter, verbalize.

venture, *v.* SYN.-brave, dare, hazard, jeopardy, peril, risk. ANT.-defense, immunity, protection, safety.

verbal, *a.* SYN.-literal, oral, spoken, vocal. ANT.-documentary, recorded, written.

verbose, *a.* SYN.-chattering, chatty, garrulous, glib, loquacious, talkative, voluble. ANT.-laconic, reticent, silent, taciturn, uncommunicative.

verbosity, *n.* SYN.-long-windiness, redundancy, talkativeness, verboseness, wordiness. ANT.-conciseness, laconism, terseness.

verification, *n.* SYN.-confirmation, corroboration, demonstration, proof, testimony. ANT.-failure, fallacy, invalidity.

verify, *v.* SYN.-ascertain, conclude, confirm, corroborate, define, determine, substantiate; acknowledge, assure, establish, settle.

veritable, *a.* SYN.-accurate, actual, authentic, correct, exact, genuine, real, true, veracious. ANT.-counterfeit, erroneous, false, fictitious, spurious.

vertical, *a.* SYN.-erect, perpendicular, plumb, straight, upright. ANT.-horizontal, inclined, level, oblique, prone.

vex, *v.* SYN.-aggravate, anger, annoy, bother, chafe, disturb, embitter, exasperate, harass, inflame, irritate, nettle, pester, plague, provoke. ANT.-appease, palliate soften, soothe.

vexation, *n.* SYN.-annoyance, chagrin, exasperation, irritation, mortification, pique. ANT.-appeasement, comfort, gratification, pleasure.

vibrate, *v.* SYN.-agitate, flutter, quake, quaver, quiver, shake, shiver, shudder, sway, tremble, waver.

vice, *n.* SYN.-corruption, crime, depravity, evil, immorality, iniquity, offense, sin, transgression, ungodliness, wickedness, wrong. ANT.-goodness, innocence, purity, righteousness, virtue.

vicinity, *n.* SYN.-area, district, environs, locality, neighborhood; adjacency, closeness, nearness, propinquity, proximity. ANT.-distance, remoteness.

victory, *n.* SYN.-accomplishment, achievement, attainment, conquest, mastery, overthrow, success, triumph. ANT.-defeat, failure.

view, *n.* SYN.-observation, outlook, panorama, perspective, prospect, range, scene, regard, review, sight, survey, vista; belief, conception, impression, judgment, opinion, sentiment.

view, *v.* SYN.-behold, discern, examine, eye, gaze, glance, inspect, look, observe, regard, scan, see, stare, survey, watch, witness. ANT.-avert, hide, miss, overlook.

viewpoint, *n.* SYN.-angle, aspect, attitude, outlook, perspective, pose, position, posture, slant, stand, standpoint.

vigilant, *a.* SYN.-alert, anxious, attentive, careful, cautious, circumspect, observant, wakeful, wary, watchful. ANT.-careless, inattentive, lax, neglectful, oblivious.

vigor, *n.* SYN.-endurance, energy, enthusiasm, health, liveliness, potency, power, spirit, stamina, strength, temper, verve, vitality, zeal. ANT.-languor, listlessness.

vigorous, *a.* SYN.-active, alert, animated, blithe, bright, brisk, clear, effective, energetic, forceful, fresh, frolicsome, glowing, lively, spirited, sprightly, striking, strong, supple, vivacious, vivid. ANT.-dull, insipid, listless, stale, vapid.

vile, *a.* SYN.-abject, base, debased, depraved, despicable, foul, ignoble, loathsome, low, mean, obscene, odious, revolting, sordid, vicious, vulgar, wicked, worthless, wretched. ANT.-attractive, decent, laudable; honorable, upright.

vilify, *v.* SYN.-abuse, asperse, assail, criticize, defame, denounce, disparage, ill-use, impugn, malign, revile, scandalize, traduce. ANT.-cherish, honor, praise, protect, respect.

villainous, *a.* SYN.-bad, baleful, base, deleterious, evil, immoral, iniquitous, noxious, pernicious, sinful, unsound, unwholesome, wicked. ANT.-excellent, good, honorable, moral, reputable.

vindicate, *v.* SYN.-absolve, acquit, assert, clear, defend, excuse, exonerate, justify, support, uphold. ANT.-abandon, accuse, blame, convict.

violate, *v.* SYN.-break, defile, debauch, deflower, desecrate, dishonor, disobey, infringe, invade, pollute, profane, ravish, transgress.

violence, *n.* SYN.-brutality, clash, coercion, compulsion, commotion, disorder, disturbance, energy, force, fury, injury, intensity, might, outrage, passion, potency, power, severity, strength, vehemence, vigor. ANT.-feebleness, frailty, gentleness, impotence, mildness, persuasion, respect, weakness.

violent, *a.* SYN.-boisterous, fierce, forceful, furious, impetuous, passionate, powerful, raging, raving, turbulent, vehement, wild; acute, extreme, intense, severe. ANT.-calm, feeble, gentle, quiet, soft.

virgin, *a.* SYN.-chaste, guiltless, innocent, pure, undefiled. ANT.-defiled, sullied, tainted.

virtue, *n.* SYN.-chastity, goodness, integrity, morality, probity, purity, rectitude, virginity; effectiveness, efficacy, excellence, force, merit, power, strength, worth. ANT.-corruption, lewdness, sin, vice; fault.

virtuous, *a.* SYN.-chaste, decent, ethical, good, honorable, just, moral, pure, right, righteous, scrupulous. ANT.-amoral, libertine, licentious, sinful, unethical.

visible, *a.* SYN.-apparent, clear, distinct, evident, intelligible, lucid, manifest, obvious, open, plain, unobstructed. ANT.-ambiguous, obscure, unclear, vague.

vision, *n.* SYN.-apparition, daydream, dream, ghost, hallucination, mirage, phantasm, phantom, prophecy, revelation, specter. ANT.-reality, substance, verity.

visionary, *a.* SYN.-exemplary, fancied, faultless, ideal, imaginary, perfect, supreme, unreal, utopian. ANT.-actual, faulty, imperfect, material, real.

vital, *a.* SYN.-active, alive, animate, animated, energetic, lively, living, spirited, sprightly, vigorous, vivacious; basic, cardinal, critical, essential, fundamental, imperative, indispensable, necessary, paramount, urgent. ANT.-inanimate, inert, lifeless; nonessential, unimportant.

vitality, *n.* SYN.-animation, ardor, buoyancy, enthusiasm, life, liveliness, spirit, vigor, vivacity, zeal. ANT.-death, demise, dullness, languor, lethargy.

vitiate, *v.* SYN.-abase, adulterate, alloy, corrupt, debase, defile, degrade, deprave, depress, pervert. ANT.-enhance, improve, raise, restore, vitalize.

vitiated, *a.* SYN.-contaminated, corrupted, crooked, debased, depraved, dishonest, impure, profligate, putrid, spoiled, tainted, venal, vitiated.

vivid, *a.* SYN.-animated, bright, brilliant, clear, expressive, fresh, graphic, intense, lively, lucid, striking. ANT.-dull, dim, dreary, dusky, vague.

vocation, *n.* SYN.-business, employment, engagement, enterprise, job, occupation, profession, trade, work. ANT.-avocation, hobby, pastime.

void, *a.* SYN.-bare, barren, blank, empty, unoccupied, vacant, vacuous. ANT.-busy, employed, engaged, full, replete.

volatile, *a.* SYN.-animated, blithe, cheerful, effervescent, elated, hopeful, jocund, light, lively, resilient, spirited, sprightly, vivacious; changeable, ephemeral, transient. ANT.-dejected, depressed, despondent, hopeless, sullen; constant, sure, unchanging.

volition, *n.* SYN.-choice, decision, desire, determination, intention, preference, resolution, taste, testament, will, wish. ANT.-coercion, compulsion, disinterest, indifference.

volume, *n.* SYN.-amount, bulk, capacity, cube, extent, magnitude, mass, measure, quantity, size; book, edition, encyclopedia, manuscript, tome; amplification, loudness, intensity.

voluntary, *a.* SYN.-automatic, extemporaneous, impulsive, instinctive, offhand, spontaneous, willing. ANT.-compulsory, forced, planned, prepared, rehearsed.

volunteer, *v.* SYN.-contribute, donate, enlist, offer, proffer, propose, propound, render, submit, suggest, tender. ANT.-rejection, withdrawal.

vulgar, *a.* SYN.-common, familiar, general, ordinary, plebeian, popular; base, coarse, gross, impolite, indecent, low, nasty, obscene, odious, ribald, rude, tasteless, unrefined. ANT.-esoteric, select; aristocratic, polite, refined.

W

wages, *n.* SYN.-compensation, earnings, pay, payment, recompense, salary, stipend. ANT.-gift, gratuity, present.

wait, *v.* SYN.-abide, bide, delay, linger, remain, rest, stay, tarry; await, expect, watch; attend, minister, serve. ANT.-act, expedite, hasten, leave.

wander, *v.* SYN.-deviate, digress, err, ramble, range, roam, rove, saunter, stray, stroll, traipse. ANT.-halt, linger, settle, stay, stop.

want, *v.* SYN.-covet, crave, desire, lack, long for, need, require, wish.

wariness, *n.* SYN.-care, caution, heed, prudence, vigilance, watchfulness. ANT.-abandon, carelessness, recklessness.

warm, *a.* SYN.-amiable, amicable, ardent, cordial, eager, earnest, enthusiastic, friendly, gracious, hearty, sincere, sociable. ANT.-aloof cool, reserved, taciturn.

warn, *v.* SYN.-admonish, advise, alert, apprise, caution, counsel, inform, notify.

warning, *n.* SYN.-admonition, advice, caution, indication, information, notice, portent, sign.

wary, *a.* SYN.-alert, alive, awake, aware, careful, heedful, mindful, observant, thoughtful, vigilant, watchful. ANT.-apathetic, indifferent, oblivious, unaware.

wash, *v.* SYN.-bathe, clean, cleanse, launder, rinse, scrub, wet. ANT.-dirty, foul, soil, stain.

waste, *a.* SYN.-abandoned, bare, barren, bleak, deserted, desolate, devastated, extra, forlorn, forsaken, lonely, ravaged, ruined, solitary, uninhabited, useless, wild. ANT.-attended, cultivated, fertile.

waste, *v.* SYN.-consume, corrode, decay, despoil, destroy, devastate, diminish, dissipate, dwindle, lavish, misuse, pillage, plunder, ravage, ruin, sack, scatter, spend, squander, strip, wear out, wither. ANT.-accumulate, economize, preserve, save.

watch, *v.* SYN.-behold, discern, distinguish, espy, inspect, look at, observe, perceive, scan, scrutinize, view, witness.

waver, *v.* SYN.-distrust, doubt, falter, flicker, hesitate, mistrust, quiver, question, suspect, sway, tremble, vacillate. ANT.-believe, confide, decide, rely on, trust.

wavering, *a.* SYN.-changeable, fickle, fitful, inconstant, shifting, unstable, vacillating, variable. ANT.-constant, stable, steady, unchanging, uniform.

wax, *v.* SYN.-accrue, amplify, augment, enhance, enlarge, expand, extend, grow, heighten, increase, intensify, magnify, multiply, raise. ANT.-atrophy, contract, decrease, diminish, reduce.

way, *n.* SYN.-avenue, channel, course, passage, path, road, route, street, thoroughfare, track, trail, walk; fashion, form, habit, manner, method, mode, plan, practice, procedure, process, style, system.

weak, *a.* SYN.-bending, debilitated, decrepit, delicate, feeble, fragile, frail, impotent, infirm, illogical , inadequate, ineffective, irresolute, lame, pliable, pliant, poor, tender, vacillating, vague, wavering, yielding; assailable, defenseless, exposed, vulnerable. ANT.-potent, powerful, robust, strong, sturdy.

weakness, *n.* SYN.-disability, handicap, impotence; inability, incapacity. ANT.-ability, capability, power, strength.

wealth, *n.* SYN.-abundance, affluence, fortune, luxury, money, opulence, plenty, possessions, riches. ANT.-indigence, need, poverty, want.

wealthy, *a.* SYN.-affluent, luxurious, opulent, plentiful, prosperous, rich, sumptuous, well-to-do. ANT.-beggarly, destitute, indigent, needy, poor.

wearied, *a.* SYN.-bored, dim, drained, faded, faint, feeble, languid, pale. ANT.-conspicuous, glaring; strong, vigorous; brave, forceful.

weary, *a.* SYN.-bored, exhausted, faint, fatigued, jaded, spent, tired, wearied, worn. ANT.-fresh, hearty, invigorated, rested.

weary, *v.* SYN.-annoy, distress, exhaust, fatigue, harass, irk, jade, tire, tucker, vex, wear out. ANT.-amuse, invigorate, refresh, restore, revive.

wedlock, *n.* SYN.-espousal, marriage, matrimony, nuptials, union. ANT.-celibacy, divorce, virginity.

weigh, *v.* SYN.-consider, contemplate, deliberate, examine, meditate, ponder, reflect, study. ANT.-ignore, neglect, overlook.

weight, *n.* SYN.-burden, gravity, heaviness, load, pressure; emphasis, import, importance, influence, significance, stress, value. ANT.-buoyancy, levity, lightness; insignificance, triviality.

well, *a.* SYN.-hale, happy, healthy, hearty, sound; beneficial, convenient, expedient, good, profitable. ANT.-depressed, feeble, infirm, weak.

whim, *n.* SYN.-caprice, fancy, humor, impulse, inclination, notion, quirk, thought, urge, vagary, whimsy.

whole, *a.* SYN.-all, complete, entire, intact, integral, perfect, total, undivided, unimpaired; hale, healed, healthy, sound, well. ANT.-defective, deficient, imperfect, incomplete, partial.

wholesome, *a.* SYN.-hale, healthy, hearty, robust, sound, strong, well; hygienic, salubrious, salutary. ANT.-delicate, diseased, frail, infirm; injurious, noxious.

wicked, *a.* SYN.-bad, baleful, base, deleterious, evil, immoral, iniquitous, malevolent, malicious, noxious, pernicious, sinful, unsound, unwholesome, villainous, virulent. ANT.-benevolent, excellent, good, honorable, kind, moral, reputable.

wide, a, SYN.-broad, expanded, extensive, large, sweeping, vast. ANT.-confined, narrow, restricted.

wild, *a.* SYN.-barbarous, boisterous, fierce, outlandish, rude, savage, stormy, tempestuous, uncivilized, undomesticated, untamed; deserted, desolate, rough, uncultivated, waste; extravagant, foolish, frantic, frenzied, giddy, impetuous, irregular, mad, rash, reckless, turbulent, wanton, wayward. ANT.-civilized, gentle; calm, placid, quiet.

willful, *a.* SYN.-contemplated, deliberate, designed, intended, intentional, premeditated, studied, voluntary. ANT.-accidental, fortuitous.

will, *n.* SYN.-choice, decision, desire, determination, intention, pleasure, preference, resolution, testament, volition, wish. ANT.-coercion, compulsion, disinterest, indifference.

win, *v.* SYN.-achieve, gain, prevail, prosper, succeed, thrive. ANT.-fail, miscarry, miss.

wind, *n.* SYN.-blast, breeze, draft, gale, gust, hurricane, squall, storm, tempest, zephyr.

wisdom, *n.* SYN.-discretion, erudition,. foresight, information, insight, intelligence, judgment, knowledge, learning, prudence, reason, sagacity, saneness, sense. ANT.-foolishness, ignorance, imprudence, nonsense, stupidity.

wise, a, SYN.-deep, discerning, enlightened, erudite, informed, intelligent, knowing, learned, penetrating, profound, sagacious, scholarly, sound; advisable, expedient, prudent. ANT.-foolish, shallow, simple.

wish, *n.* SYN.-aspiration, craving, desire, hungering, longing, yearning. ANT.-abomination, aversion, distaste, hate, loathing.

wish, *v.* SYN.-covet, crave, desire, hanker, hunger, long, thirst, want, yearn. ANT.-decline, despise, reject, repudiate, scorn.

wit, *n.* SYN.-comprehension, intellect, intelligence, mind, perspicacity, reason, sagacity, sense, understanding; banter, cleverness, fun, humor, irony, pleasantry, raillery, sarcasm, satire, witticism. ANT.-commonplace, platitude, sobriety, solemnity, stupidity.

witchcraft, *n.* SYN.-black art, conjuring, enchantment, legerdemain, magic, necromancy, sorcery, voodoo, wizardry.

withdraw, *v.* SYN.-depart, give up, go, leave, quit, relinquish, renounce, retire, vacate. ANT.-abide, remain, stay, tarry.

wither, *v.* SYN.-decline, droop, dry, fail, languish, sear, shrink, shrivel, sink, waste, weaken, wilt, wizen. ANT.-refresh, rejuvenate, renew, revive.

withhold, *v.* SYN.-abstain, desist, forbear, refrain, restrain. ANT.-continue, indulge, persist.

witness, *n.* SYN.-attestation, confirmation, declaration, evidence, proof, testimony. ANT.-argument, contradiction, disproof, refutation.

witty, *a.* SYN.-amusing, bright, clever, comical, droll, funny, humorous, ingenious, quick, quick-witted, sharp, smart. ANT.-dull, foolish, melancholy, sad, serious, sober, solemn, stupid.

wonder, *n.* SYN.-curiosity, marvel, miracle, phenomenon, prodigy, rarity, spectacle; admiration, amazement, astonishment, awe, bewilderment, curiosity, surprise, wonderment. ANT.-familiarity, triviality; apathy, expectation, indifference.

word, *n.* SYN.-account, assertion, assurance, commitment, declaration, expression, guarantee, name, news, phrase, pledge, promise, report, statement, tidings, utterance.

work, *n.* SYN.-achievement, business, drudgery, effort, employment, labor, occupation, opus, performance, production; task, toil, travail. ANT.-ease, leisure, play, recreation, vacation.

worldly, *a.* SYN.-base, carnal, corporeal, fleshly, gross, lustful, sensual; cultured, discriminating, sophisticated, urbane. ANT.-exalted, spiritual, temperate.

worn, *a.* SYN.-exhausted, fatigued, jaded, spent, tired, wearied; frayed, tattered, threadbare, shabby. ANT.-fresh, hearty, invigorated, rested; new, unused.

worry, *n.* SYN.-anxiety, apprehension, concern, disquiet, fear, misgiving, trouble, uneasiness. ANT.-contentment, equanimity, peace, satisfaction.

worry, *v.* SYN.-annoy, bother, disturb, gall, harass, harry, haze, irritate, pain, persecute, tease, torment, trouble, vex; care, chafe, fidget, fret, fume, fuss. ANT.-comfort, console, solace.

worship, *v.* SYN.-adore, deify, honor, idolize, respect, revere, reverence, venerate. ANT.-blaspheme, curse, despise, loathe, scorn.

worth, *n.* SYN.-excellence, merit, price, usefulness, utility, value, virtue, worthiness. ANT.-cheapness, uselessness, valueless.

worthless, *a.* SYN.-abortive, empty, fruitless, futile, ineffectual, irrelevant, pointless, unavailing, unnecessary, useless, vain, valueless, vapid. ANT.-effective, potent, profitable.

wound, *v.* SYN.-abuse, cut, damage, disfigure, harm, hurt, injure, maim; affront, dishonor, insult, wrong. ANT.-benefit, help, preserve; compliment, praise.

wrap, *v.* SYN.-cloak, clothe, cover, envelop, shield, shroud, veil. ANT.-bare, expose, reveal.

wrath, *n.* SYN.-anger, choler, fury, indignation, ire, passion, rage, resentment, temper. ANT.-conciliation, forbearance, patience, peace, self-control.

wreck, *v.* SYN.-annihilate, demolish, destroy, devastate, eradicate, exterminate, extinguish, obliterate, ravage, raze, ruin. ANT.-construct, establish, make, preserve, save.

wretched, *a.* SYN.-comfortless, disconsolate, distressed, forlorn, heartbroken, miserable, pitiable; abject, beggarly, contemptible, despicable, low, mean, paltry, pitiful, poor, shabby, sorry, vile, worthless. ANT.-contented, fortunate, happy; noble, significant.

writer, *n.* SYN.-author, artist, composer, essayist, reporter.

wrong, *a.* SYN.-amiss, askew, awry, erroneous, fallacious, false, faulty, inaccurate, incorrect, mistaken, imprecise, untrue; improper, inappropriate, unsuitable; aberrant, bad, criminal, evil, immoral, iniquitous, reprehensible. ANT.-correct, right, true; suitable; proper.

Y

yearning, *n.* SYN.-appetite, aspiration, craving, desire, hungering, longing, lust, urge. ANT.-abomination, aversion, distaste, hate, loathing.

yield, *n.* SYN.-crop, fruit, harvest, proceeds, produce, product, profit, reaping, result.

yield, *v.* SYN.-afford, bear, bestow, breed, generate, impart, pay, produce, supply; accord, allow, concede, grant, permit; abdicate, accede, acquiesce, capitulate, cede, quit, relent, relinquish, resign, submit, succumb, surrender, waive. ANT.-deny, dissent, oppose, refuse; assert, resist, strive, struggle.

yielding, *a.* SYN.-compliant, deferential, dutiful, obedient, submissive, tractable. ANT.-insubordinate, intractable, obstinate, rebellious.

yokel, *n.* SYN.-boor, bumpkin, hayseed, hick, klutz.

young, *a.* See **youthful.**

youthful, *a.* SYN.-adolescent, boyish, callow, childish, childlike, girlish, immature, inexperienced, juvenile, puerile, young. ANT.-aged, elderly, mature, old, senile.

Z

zeal, *n.* SYN.-ardor, devotion, earnestness, enthusiasm, excitement, fanaticism, fervency, fervor, intensity, vehemence. ANT.-apathy, detachment, ennui, indifference, unconcern.

zealous, *a.* SYN.-ardent, eager, enthusiastic, fervent, fervid, fiery, impassioned, intense, keen, passionate, vehement. ANT.-apathetic, cool, indifferent, nonchalant.

zenith, *n.* SYN.-acme, apex, climax, consummation, culmination, height, peak, summit. ANT.-anticlimax, base, depth, floor.

zone, *n.* SYN.-belt, climate, locality, region, sector, tract.